ARGUING CONSERVATISM

ARGUING CONSERVATISM

Four Decades of the Intercollegiate Review

EDITED BY
MARK C. HENRIE

Wilmington, Delaware

Copyright © 2008 ISI Books

All rights reserved. No part of this publication may be reproduced or transmitted in any form or by any means, electronic or mechanical, including photocopy, or any information storage and retrieval system now known or to be invented, without permission in writing from the publisher, except by a reviewer who wishes to quote brief passages in connection with a review written for inclusion in a magazine, newspaper, or broadcast.

Arguing conservatism : four decades of the Intercollegiate review / edited by Mark C. Henrie. – 1st ed. – Wilmington, DE : ISI Books, c2008.

    p. ; cm.

    ISBN: 978-1-933859-51-4
    Includes index.
    Partial contents: Interrogating modernity, rethinking tradition – Scholarship & opinion – America's constitutional identity – Education and its enemies – Free markets and civil society – The long, twilight struggle – Crises, controversies, and curiosities – People, poetry, and prose – Arguing conservatism – Books in review.

    1. United States–Politics and government–1945-1989. 2. United States–Politics and government–1989- 3. United States–Intellectual life–20th century. 4. United States–Intellectual life–21st century. 5. Conservatism–United States. I. Henrie, Mark C. II. Four decades of the Intercollegiate review. III. Intercollegiate review.

E743 .A74 2008   2008932977
320.520973—dc22   0808

ISI Books
Intercollegiate Studies Institute
Post Office Box 4431
Wilmington, DE 19807-0431
www.isibooks.org

Manufactured in the United States of America

to T. Kenneth Cribb, Jr.,
in memory of E. Victor Milione and John F. Lulves, Jr.,
and, always, for Claudia

Contents

II. Scholarship & Opinion

III. America's Constitutional Identity

VI. The Long, Twilight Struggle

VII. Crises, Controversies & Curiosities

VIII. People, Poetry & Prose

IX. Arguing Conservatism

X. Books in Review

XI. SUMMARY JUDGMENTS

Mark C. Henrie

EDITOR'S INTRODUCTION

The conservatives are the stupid party—or so many on the left like to think, turning a comment by John Stuart Mill into a familiar trope. We have grown used to media characterizations of conservative politicians as dim bulbs—George W. Bush, Ronald Reagan, Gerald Ford—while liberal political figures are hailed for their sophistication and brilliance—John F. Kennedy, both Clintons, John Kerry, Barack Obama, even Al Gore. This relative deprecation of conservatives and conservative thought is not a new development in America life; on the contrary, it has a long history. Famously, the Columbia literary critic Lionel Trilling in *The Liberal Imagination* (1950) argued that

> [i]n the United States at this time liberalism is not only the dominant but even the sole intellectual tradition. For it is the plain fact that nowadays there are no conservative or reactionary ideas in general circulation. This does not mean, of course, that there is no impulse to conservatism or to reaction. . . . But the conservative impulse and the reactionary impulse do not, with some isolated and some ecclesi-

astical exceptions, express themselves in ideas but only in action or in irritable mental gestures which seek to resemble ideas.

Nor has this self-flattering liberal perspective shown any sign of waning. In 2004, the chairman of the philosophy department at Duke University turned Mill's *bon mot* into a cockeyed syllogism that "explained" the very low proportion of conservatives on the Duke faculty: "We try to hire the best, smartest people available. . . . If, as John Stuart Mill said, stupid people are generally conservative, then there are lots of conservatives we will never hire." Q.E.D.

For conservative views to be associated with stupidity is probably less offensive than an alternative approach on the left, which discovers their source instead in psychological abnormality. Such an approach was pioneered, as was so much else, by members of the Frankfurt School. Theodor Adorno and colleagues at Berkeley produced in 1950 *The Authoritarian Personality*, a study with an elaborately technical theoretical apparatus that endeavored to demonstrate "scientifically" that, among other things, traditional family life generated personality disorders leading straight to fascism. The appeal of this resort to mental illness to explain the persistence of conservatism in our enlightened age has also not diminished. In 2003, a team of researchers, again based at Berkeley, "discovered" that conservative values stem from a personality steeped in "fear and aggression, dogmatism and the intolerance of ambiguity." Q.E.D.

That the Left would prefer to explain away, rather than to engage, the arguments of its adversaries is understandable. It is in the nature of political partisanship to seek advantages, and not always justly. What is more perplexing is to find that the equation of traditional conservative views with intellectual backwardness is also sometimes evident in certain precincts of the Right. In particular, many essays and books recounting the rise of the "neoconservatives" in the 1970s are oriented around such a presumption. What passed for American conservatism before the advent of these sophisticated latecomers, it is said, was characterized by philistinism at best. Only with the arrival of the neoconservative neophytes could everything that was right and true in conservatism receive its proper intellectual defense, while all that was false and distasteful could be cast aside. In such a retrospective account, those who became neoconservatives were right to be on the left or center-left before the rise of the New Left in the late 1960s, and they were right to be on the center-right thereafter. Indeed, as some neoconservatives sometimes assert: they did not change, the political spectrum did.

This now standard account of the genesis and meaning of neoconservatism raises complicated questions that have yet to be resolved. What exactly was false in American conservatism before neoconservatism? What was distasteful? Were the neoconservatives really "converts" at all, or was the conservative label, with whatever qualifier, a misnomer? What was lacking or "improper" about the intellectual defense of conservative ideas before the arrival of the neoconservatives? Above all, for our purposes, is it true that the older elements of the American conservative movement were fundamentally philistine?

In a certain way, this volume is a sustained rejoinder to the charge of an older conservative philistinism. The shimmering intellectuality of those "New York Intellectuals" who became the neoconservatives is by now evident to all. And certainly neoconservatism enhanced American conservatism significantly by bringing in its wake large numbers of respected social scientists, policy experts, and journalists—some of the most prominent public intellectuals of the last three decades of the twentieth century. But while the young men in the cafeteria of City College, New York, in the late 1930s—those, such as Irving Kristol and Nathan Glazer, who would later become neoconservatives—may rightly be celebrated for "arguing the world," it is also the case that many other men and women, young and old, were undertaking no less intense an engagement with the great questions of our time elsewhere in the country.

Unlike the City College luminaries, these others were not originally Trotskyites: they were conservatives, simply, hostile to Marxism in both theory and practice, appreciative of the freedom and decency of America's constitutional order and Judeo-Christian values, intent on defending the "free society" of the West, but also keenly aware that the revolutionary turmoil and totalitarian temptations of the twentieth century required a sustained and in some ways unprecedented inquiry. What could it mean to be a conservative in modern America? Amidst galloping technological change, social revolution, and the rise of mass culture, what could be conserved, and how?

Paradoxically, while often rooted in the values of the American heartland, these older or aboriginal American conservative thinkers produced a body of thought that is the furthest thing from provincial. On the contrary, it is notably speculative, explorative, cosmopolitan— willing to engage minds across the globe and across the ages, and to ask questions at the deepest levels. What is more, this older body of reflection was not superseded by the growth of neoconservatism. Rather, it has continued through the years, inspiring new generations to take up the task of "arguing conservatism." If the history of this older conservative intellectual movement is not as well known as its quality, originality, and practical importance would warrant, it is perhaps owing to the peculiar nature of the central institution through which these thinkers mediated their ideas from the mid-1950s until the present day.

THE INTERCOLLEGIATE Society of Individualists (ISI) was founded in 1953 by the libertarian journalist Frank Chodorov. Chodorov had written a series of articles in the newspaper *Human Events* observing that the growth of the welfare state in America had been aided by a prior advance of socialist ideas among university students, future members of what we now call the "knowledge class." In particular, the Intercollegiate Society of *Socialists* had cultivated in the early years of the twentieth century a cadre of intellectuals and activists who would later play key roles in Franklin Roosevelt's New Deal. Chodorov argued that if free-market policies were ever to succeed again in America, minds and hearts must first be changed; conservatives must undertake a concerted effort to reach college students, to expose them to the arguments for liberty that were scorned within the academy.

Chodorov's notional plan for such a "fifty-year project" became a reality with an unexpected check for one thousand dollars from the Philadelphia industrialist J. Howard Pew. Overcoming hesitations about whether to proceed with the project at all, Chodorov named the young William F. Buckley Jr.—a celebrity since the publication of *God and Man at Yale* (1951), and a personal friend of Chodorov's—as ISI's first president, though Buckley's role was largely titular. More significantly, he soon hired a young Philadelphian, E. Victor Milione, to serve as ISI's executive director. It was Milione who would fundamentally stamp the character of ISI, which quickly became and today remains by far the largest conservative organization in America working with university students and faculty.

At first ISI was little more than a speaker's bureau, making available lecturers for student clubs. Later, off-prints of the best lectures were distributed to a growing student membership, and summer schools were added. Later still there would be graduate fellowships, support for student publications and newspapers, colloquia, debates, conferences, journals, a book-publishing operation, and more.

Milione also broadened ISI's intellectual agenda. In particular, he believed that the events of the age demonstrated that Western civilization was undergoing a "total" crisis. Any adequate response must therefore address the total range of culture. So, to classical liberal political economy—the central intellectual discipline for most American conservatives, in part because it was so immediately relevant to public policy, especially under the challenge of collectivism—Milione added a sustained engagement with history, political philosophy, literature, sociology, and religion. He also hoped for, but never finally achieved, an equally extensive engagement with the fine arts. ISI would constitute within itself an entire intellectual world, a veritable para-university. And while that world would be mediated through a conservative lens, broadly conceived, Milione for his part eschewed partisan labels, finding them more hindrance than help: in 1966, he would even change ISI's name from the Intercollegiate Society of Individualists to the Intercollegiate Studies Institute.

As student membership burgeoned beyond 10,000 and then beyond 20,000, ISI struggled with the problem of making *membership* in the organization a reality. There were simply not enough resources to provide every student group with a lecturer, nor could every student attend an ISI summer school. What, then, was the meaning of ISI membership for those thousands of often isolated students who could not be reached through ISI's programs? Milione's solution to this problem, in 1965, was the *Intercollegiate Review* (the *IR*), "a journal of scholarship and opinion" that would be received free of charge by every member of the organization. Through the journal, *all* ISI students would be exposed to the intellectual ferment among conservative intellectuals on subjects ranging from foreign policy to literary criticism, from fiscal policy to political philosophy, from the critique of mass culture to the critique of the modern university. Even today, after four decades and growth to more than 50,000 members—now including thousands of

university faculty as well as students—receiving the *Intercollegiate Review* remains the defining feature of ISI membership.

A perusal of the masthead of the first issue of the *IR* illustrates immediately the significance of the journal. Below founding editor Robert Ritchie and associate editor F. R. Wilson was a young business manager, Edwin J. Feulner Jr.—now the long-serving president of the Heritage Foundation and a leading architect of the American conservative movement as a whole. The editorial advisory board included names that would loom large in any history of American conservatism: Richard Allen, later to serve as National Security Advisor under President Reagan; Philip Crane of Bradley University, later a U.S. congressman with national conservative appeal; Gerhart Niemeyer and Stanley Parry of Notre Dame; the legendary Willmoore Kendall at the University of Dallas; Leo Strauss of Chicago; Thomas Molnar and Stephen J. Tonsor; Donald Davidson of the Vanderbilt Agrarians; a young M. Stanton Evans of the *Indianapolis News*. Others were notable in their time, but are no longer. Here were assembled many of the finest academic minds in America: they were conservatives, and not in the least philistine. As the years have passed, the journal has continued to attract thinkers of no less intellectual power.

Something elementary about the *Intercollegiate Review* must be noted. It was, and is, an interdisciplinary scholarly journal—for students. In many ways, in fact, the *IR* was modeled on the *New Individualist Review*, a student-run scholarly journal founded in 1961 by the ISI group at the University of Chicago. ISI could have chosen to reach its members through a newsletter: indeed, that would have been the more typical choice for a large national organization. ISI could also have attempted something grander, something on the order of a magazine that commented on the issues of the day: such a choice would have been natural after the defeat of Barry Goldwater in 1964. Instead, ISI chose to devote a very significant portion of its limited resources to a scholarly journal. This choice reflected the organization's vision: its project has been, above all, an educational one. This choice also shaped the organization's future: throughout its history, but perhaps especially after the launch of the *IR*, ISI has appealed most strongly to students who were genuinely attracted to the life of the mind. Over the years, therefore, an uncommonly high proportion of ISI students would pursue graduate studies and become university professors themselves.

To gauge the sophistication and amplitude of American conservative intellectual life, then, whether before the rise of neoconservatism or after, there are few better places to look than the pages of the *Intercollegiate Review*. However, because the *IR* has been a membership publication, and never promoted for general subscription, the journal is not well known beyond ISI's own (admittedly quite large) membership. Very few academic libraries, for example, acquire the *Intercollegiate Review* for their collections. Hence the paradox of a historically influential publication whose influence is not widely recognized.

THIS COLLECTION aims to convey in broad outline the contents of this "hidden" conservative discourse over the past four decades. The essays are grouped thematically, but within each section the order is simply chronological. An effort has been made to include across the volume roughly equal numbers of essays from each of the four decades. From the era of Lyndon Johnson to the era of George W. Bush, the substance of American politics and public policy has undergone numerous revolutions, and these revolutions leave their traces in the essays included here. From the foreign policy crises of the Cold War to the "multiculturalism" of the 1990s, and from the student upheavals of the 1960s to the current War on Terror, there is scarcely a major public controversy which the *IR* has not addressed. To read these more topical essays is to relive our recent history through conservative eyes. And it is well to consider, first, to what extent the views expressed conform to what is usually taken to be "the conservative view" of a given issue—might it be the case that conservative ideas are often dismissed because, if known at all, they are caricatured?—and second, how insightful (or not) the judgments reached now look in retrospect.

More striking than these necessarily changeable reactions to the passing scene is the marked continuity that is evident. This is not to say that the essays repeat themselves or merely burnish an ideological line. Rather, the continuity in question concerns the subjects of inquiry.

For example, the *IR* has returned again and again to the problematic nature of modernity. On modernity's own self-understanding, nothing truly of value is lost in the new dispensation that begins at about the time of the Renaissance—and a great deal is gained. While conservatives can agree that a great deal has been gained, they also notice real losses: the loosening of the ties that bind one human being to another in authentic community, the loss of the "sacred canopy" of public religion, the ironic deprecation of aspirations to personal virtue, the disorienting disempowerment brought on by technologies that seem to master men rather than serving them. Is the conservative vocation, then, to attempt to "turn back the clock"? Or to search the horizon for a kind of postmodernity? Or to consciously reject nostalgia and hold fast to that which is good in the present age?

Again and again, the *IR* has also inquired into the nature of America's constitutional order, the American "regime." Clearly, the United States of America is the most successful nation state in modern times. But what accounts for the singular success of the *novus ordo seclorum*? Has America prospered because it was founded on Lockean principles, which in fact are the principles of the best political order for all times and places? Or must America's virtue be understood to rest on exceptional features of the American nation, such as its commitment to low-church Protestantism or its unique division of sovereignty between the federal and state governments? Is America a "modern" nation? A "universal" nation? A "proposition" nation? Or did our Founding Fathers rather look to the past to undertake a retrieval of older political models?

As would be expected, again and again the *IR* considers the virtues of a free-market economy in comparison with available alternatives. But this advocacy is tempered surprisingly often with caveats and concerns. How does the "creative destruction" of a free economy relate to the foundations of political order? To personal virtue? To the informal authorities of civil society? To human values that are higher than mere prosperity?

Concerning higher education, on the other hand, there is little disagreement. The academics writing in the *Intercollegiate Review* are united in their appreciation for liberal learning, and in their sense that the modern university largely fails in this most central task. They differ only as to the tactics by which

a genuinely liberal education might be recovered in our country.

Rounding out this collection, a set of belletristic essays, a miscellany, and the book reviews convey something of the broad range of interests that the *IR* has presumed in its readership. And there is a final group of essays which directly engage the meaning—and the dilemmas—of conservatism in America. As will be seen, on even the most basic questions, strong controversy has been a permanent feature of the conservative conversation. But the project of "arguing conservatism" has also borne real fruit. Over the span of four decades, the thinkers writing for the *Intercollegiate Review* have cultivated a secluded intellectual landscape with great originality and depth. This collection is but a taste of the harvest.

FOR SOME years, I had advocated within ISI the project of an *Intercollegiate Review* anthology, and I had even taken initial steps to review the hundreds of articles in the journal's run. But the daily press of other responsibilities made progress on the project desultory—until my colleague Jeremy Beer, ISI's vice president for publications and the editor-in-chief of ISI Books, intervened. With characteristic imagination and expedition, Jeremy proposed that he and I retreat for a week to assemble the table of contents. With only a handful of changes, therefore, the contents of this volume were selected over six days spent in a cottage in Mount Gretna, Pennsylvania, in the fall of 2006. The work was difficult, the long hours exhausting, but our conversations most rewarding. This anthology was greatly strengthened by Jeremy's keen insights.

Of course, selecting a table of contents is only the first step in such a large project. Scanning the texts left thousands of errors. Erica Ford labored to proof the results, which in turn were reproofed by a number of other colleagues: Douglas Minson, Darryl Hart, John Joseph Shanley, Miriam Keim, and Meghan Duke. A final review was undertaken by Jennifer Connolly and Adam Koontz. For all their hard work, and for Kara Beer and Kelly Cole's work on the book's design, I am most grateful.

Will Herberg

Prologue:
What Is the Moral
Crisis of Our Time?

VOL. 4, NO. 2–3, 1968

Every age has its own challenge to morality, and the character of this challenge may well come to serve as a significant indication of the spirit of the times. What is the character of the challenge to morality that our age offers? Everyone seems to agree that we find ourselves in a moral crisis of an aggravated kind. But what is the nature of this crisis? What shall we make of it? What is its meaning and portent? And how deep is it, how far does it go? These are some of the questions I should like to raise and discuss.

I

The moral crisis of our time cannot, it seems to me, be identified merely with the widespread violation of accepted moral standards, for which our time is held to be notorious. There has never been any lack of that at any time; and comparisons often prove quite misleading. No—the moral crisis of our time goes deeper, and is much more difficult to define and account for. Briefly, I should say that the moral crisis of our time consists primarily not in the widespread violation of accepted moral standards—again I ask, when has any age been free of that?—but in the repudiation of those very moral standards themselves. And this, indeed, is our time's challenge to morality; not so much the all-too-frequent breakdown of a moral code, but the fact that today there seems to be no moral code to break down.

Sexual "irregularity" among young people has always been common enough, though it was only in recent years that a combination of sociological factors has extended it as a possibility to young women of the middle classes. There is, no doubt, a marked increase in premarital sexual activity to be found among the younger generation, especially among the younger generation on the college campuses; but however disturbing this may be, it is not the real moral problem involved. The real moral problem, the real challenge to morality, is provided not by the girl who goes along, but by the girl who shrugs her shoulders and says: "Well, so what? What's so bad about sleeping around? It's natural, and it's lots of fun, too."

Cheating may or may not be more widespread on the college campuses of this country today; it is certainly not new. The student who cheats and knows that he is doing wrong is a moral problem, of course; but much more profound is the challenge to morality flung out by the student who cheats and says: "What's so bad about cheating? It gets you ahead, doesn't it?"

Fraud or near-fraud in the mass media of communication is something we have learned to expect and protect ourselves against. But what can we do with the attitude that shrugged off the deceptions practiced with official connivance over TV some years ago by a young professor of honored name, with an indifferent, "Well, so what if it was all fixed in advance? It was a good show, wasn't it?"

I could multiply illustrations to the same effect from every sphere of contemporary life; but the point, I think, has been made. It is my belief that the really serious threat to morality in our time consists not in the multiplying violations of an accepted moral code, but in the fact that the very notion of morality or moral code seems to be itself losing its meaning for increasing numbers of men and women in our society. It is here that we find a breakdown of morality in a radical sense, in a sense almost without precedent in our Western history. To violate moral standards while at the same time acknowledging their authority is one thing; to lose all sense of the moral claim, to repudiate all moral authority and every moral standard as such, is something far more serious. It is this loss of the moral sense, I would suggest to you, that constitutes the real challenge to morality in our time.

II

It is difficult to discover the sources of this kind of moral anarchy that is coming to pervade our culture; it is difficult even to distinguish between cause and effect. But one thing we may notice: in every one of the typical cases I have mentioned, there appears to be not merely a repudiation of morality as such, but a repudiation of morality in favor of a way of life governed by a self-indulgent quest for pleasure and fun. Everything is justified by the "kicks" you get out of it. "Have fun" has become our parting injunction, replacing the long-obsolete "God be with you." In fact, if our time has retained from times past some sense of binding obligation in the conduct of life, it is just this obligation to "have fun." If we have a morality at all, it is a "fun-morality": to "have a good time" is, with many of our modern-minded people, as stern an obligation as serving God was to an old-time Calvinist. Not to be interested in having a "good time" condemns you as a neurotic with a "puritan conscience"—and what could be worse in the eyes of the moderns?

Don't think that this pursuit of "fun," of a "good time," is an easy matter. It often demands a single-minded pursuit of status, adjustment, and sociability so strenuous as to shame many an ascetic saint. Children are shown no mercy; whatever their own gifts or predilections, they are dragooned very early into the "have fun" and "be a good fellow" competition of their elders. In fact, teenagers have become the favorite vehicles of status display for their parents: they are lavishly provided with money and other facilities for having a "good time," and they are earnestly enjoined not to falter in this pursuit. It has become not uncommon for parents to supply their minor children with hard liquor and contraceptive devices when they go out to parties and other "fun" gatherings. In this kind of euphoric culture—where "feeling good" and "being sociable" are the pressing requirements—morality and moral codes in the older sense are obviously irrelevant.

Our emerging euphoric culture is closely connected with the affluence of our "affluent society." Until very recently, our country, and the rest of the Western world very largely, operated as dynamic, production-minded societies driven on by need and scarcity. An ethic of duty, character, hard work, and achievement dominated the culture—that celebrated "Protestant ethic" that is in such bad repute today. Within the past generation, however, a profound change has been taking place in this country and in the more Americanized parts of Western Europe; the older "inner-directed" culture (to use David Riesman's terminology) is being rapidly replaced by a new "other-directed" culture under an economy of plenty, preoccupied with consumption, leisure, and enjoyment. Our current "fun" morality is obviously an expression of this emerging "other-directed" culture. Affluence brings with it moral problems more perplexing than those that poverty breeds.

The "fun" morality of our time is also closely connected with the new stress on sociability and adjustment so characteristic of our society, for nothing can so spoil "having a good time" as a taste for solitude and a dislike of being adjusted. But the sociability and adjustment so prized by our euphoric society are of a very curious kind. It is a "non-involved sociability," and an adjustment that swallows up both the so-called conformist and the so-called nonconformist—the junior executive in his "gray flannel suit" and the beatnik in his leather jacket. It is with this kind of "non-involved sociability" that we are particularly concerned at this point.

I am sure you all remember those horrifying stories coming from New York and other big cities, of women being at-tacked, raped, and sometimes throttled to death, while dozens of people looked on, none of them feeling sufficiently "involved" to phone the police from the security of their apartments. These were all respectable middle-class folk, friendly and sociable, all sharing the "liberal" outlook for which New York is so celebrated. One of the cases reported in the press is particularly interesting. A young woman was being attacked at the foot of the stairs in the hallway of a building in the Bronx. A number of men came out at the first landing to see what was going on. They saw, and they returned to their own business—which was, believe it or not, passing resolutions on world peace and racial justice! You see, they were the executive committee of one of the best known "liberal" organizations in the city. They were all deeply interested in the welfare of their fellow-men—in the abstract, at a distance, by way of passing a resolution or making a speech. The more humanitarianism in the abstract, apparently, the less humanity in the concrete. . . . This kind of "non-involved sociability" is as much part of our euphoric mass culture as the "fun" we are always enjoined to be having. The euphoric way of life requires sociability, but it views with embarrassment and distaste any kind of serious personal involvement; that would spoil everything.

III

But the moral crisis of our time has even deeper roots than these comparatively recent developments I have been describing. The moral crisis of our time, let me remind you, consists not so much in the violation of standards generally accepted as in the attrition, to the point of irrelevance, of these very standards themselves. Violation of moral standards there has always been aplenty in every age, but until modern times the standards themselves were not questioned; or more accurately, it was never questioned that there were such standards: this was taken for granted by the very ones who violated them, who, therefore, even in their violation, paid tribute to their authority. In the modern world, for the first time, at least on a mass scale, the very possibility of such standards has been thrown into question, and with it all essential distinctions between right and wrong. Today's culture comes very close to becoming a non-moral, normless culture.

What has been happening? Something that runs deep in our history and gives our culture its characteristically "modernistic" tone. It is the transformation of the very concept of truth, upon which the whole spiritual structure of a society may be said to depend. Until the dawn of modernity, truth was conceived of as something anchored in objective and transcendental reality, and the whole of man's intellectual and moral life was built upon this foundation. In very early times, truth had been seen as embodied in ancestral tradition and ancestral wisdom, the "wisdom of the fathers." But when this was challenged, as it was by the sophists during the breakdown of the older Greek culture, it was re-established on an even firmer foundation by the philosophers. Such, I imagine, was the essential task that Plato set for himself, and with Plato, all of subsequent Greek philosophy of whatever school. The philosophers sought to ground the truth, in its objectivity and transcendence, on the rational nature of things. The Hebrew prophets sought the truth in the revealed word of God. But despite the difference between the two approaches, basic and irreconcilable as they are at some points,

Greek philosopher and Hebrew prophet were at one at least on this, that the truth by which man lived was something ultimately independent of him, beyond and above him, expressing itself in norms and standards to which he must conform if he was to live a truly human life.

It was precisely this conviction about truth that was the first to be challenged with the emergence of modernity. It was challenged on one level by the rise of relativism. What sense did it make to speak of truth in the old way when truth was so relative, so obviously man-made and culture-made, varying (as Pascal had put it) with the degree of latitude, or (in the later vocabulary) with the psychological conditioning and cultural pattern? This kind of relativism was full of contradictions, to be sure, and flew in the face of the best evidence, but it appealed to the modern mind, which was rapidly losing all sense of transcendence. Relativism, of a kind more radical and pervasive than the Greeks had ever dreamed of, soon came to dominate the advanced thought of the West, and increasingly also the convictions and the feelings of the common man. In this kind of cultural climate, the dissolution of moral standards, in the sense in which Greek philosophy and Hebraic religion had understood them, was only a matter of time.

But if relativism began the process, it was the triumph of technology that carried it to its disastrous completion. We are not yet in a position to grasp fully what the accelerated and unfettered expansion of technology has done to human life in the past three hundred years. But we can at least begin to assess its major impact upon the consciousness of the West, and that is the *exaltation of power over truth as the object of man's intellectual and moral quest*. From the earliest times, the object of the knowledge-seeking enterprise had been truth—the truth of reason for the philosopher, the truth of revelation for the man of biblical faith—but truth as something to apprehend *intellectually* and live by *morally*. Now, however, some time in the sixteenth or seventeenth century, perhaps, a new conviction arose, constituting a radical subversion of the older view. The whole tradition of the West—that "knowledge is *truth*"—was overturned, and replaced by the new, militantly proclaimed creed, "Knowledge is *power*!"—first, power of man over nature; then power of man over man. This shift from truth to power marks the full scope of the revolution effected by the technological spirit at the very dawn of modernity.

The evacuation of moral standards soon came to aggravate the effects of technology. Nearly a hundred years ago, Jacob Burckhardt, the great historian who so well discerned the ominous outlines of the twentieth century, pointed out with great penetration:

> When men lose their sense of established standards, they inevitably fall victim to the urge for pleasure or power.

This "urge for pleasure or power" defines as nothing else can the pseudo-ethic of our time.

The technological spirit exalting power, and the ideological relativism that destroys the authority of all moral norms, have cooperated to undermine the older foundations of morality, in fact, the very meaning of morality itself. Human problems are increasingly seen as technological problems, to be dealt with by adjustment and manipulation; the test is always how it satisfies desires or enlarges power, not conformity to a truth beyond man's control. In fact, the belief seems

to have emerged that there is nothing beyond man's desires, nothing beyond man's power. His "values" are his to make or unmake, the only criterion being satisfaction and power. Pleasure and power have taken over, and the bitch-goddess Success, which William James so scornfully denounced, has come into her own. This is the moral crisis of our time in all its amplitude.

IV

Some twenty years ago, in a happier day, Bertrand Russell raised a question that we are still far from being able to answer:

> There are certain old conceptions [he said] which represent man's belief in the limits of human power: of these, the two chief are God and truth. . . . Such conceptions tend to melt away; even if not specifically negated, they lose importance and are retained only superficially. . . . What then?

Traditionally, through centuries and millenia, the limits upon pleasure and power had been set by the "higher law," a law beyond all human manipulation and control. And this "higher law" was understood to emanate from that which was ultimate in the universe, God for the Hebrews, Reason for the Greeks. The entire spiritual structure of the Western world was built upon these convictions. With these convictions so rapidly losing their appeal to the modern mind, nothing has been left but the indulgence of pleasure, the anarchy of power, and the chaos of "self-created values." The moral crisis of our time is, at bottom, a metaphysical and religious crisis.

It is hardly surprising, though it is painfully ironical, that man's success in his frantic search for pleasure and power has brought with it the gravest threat to his humanity. Without grounding his being in something beyond, man cannot preserve his humanness. At the very moment when Algernon Charles Swinburne, echoing the new modernity, was singing "Glory to Man in the highest, the Maker and Master of All," forces were coming to a head that were to drive Western man, through unimaginable disasters, to a point where his very survival would come into question. But even more than physical survival, it is the survival of man in his humanness that is becoming problematic.

I wish I had a more cheerful report to present to you. I wish I could offer a word of reassurance, and tell you that the moral crisis of our time is merely a surface phenomenon, an interim thing, transitional between the old and the new. I wish I could report that I have discovered, as some observers claim to have done, the fundamentals of a "new" morality already emerging out of the shattered ruins of the old. I wish I could announce these things; but I can't since I am simply not able to see things that way. The contextualism and situationalism so eagerly espoused by exponents of the "new morality" have their point, of course, but allow them to be carried away by their own logic, and you end up in either moral platitudes or moral anarchy. They do not offer a way out.

Situationalism, especially, seems to offer a strong appeal to the philosophical and theological champions of the "new morality," and therefore deserves closer attention. Its fundamental insight, shared by the contextualist in a weaker form, is that one must make his moral decisions not in the abstract, or in obedience to some eternal code of law forced upon him from the outside. I must respond

here and now, not then and there; in this my situation, not in terms of some other—and if *my* response is to be genuine and authentic, it must be made with true inwardness, as my response, not in imitation of someone else's. The one "rule" of situational ethics would appear to be: "Respond from *within* your situation, and respond authentically, with the wholeness of being." After all, has not St. Augustine counseled us: "Love [God], and do what you will"?

But while this situationalist principle, rooted in a profound existentialist insight, is, in itself, quite valid, it is hardly enough to rescue the man who acts on it from moral chaos and ethical arbitrariness. For there is not the slightest hint in the situationalist principle as to content, positive or negative. The worst abominations of a Hitler or a Stalin may meet the demand of authenticity as well as the finest act of heroism or charity. Sartre himself tells the story of the young man in Paris under the Nazi occupation who came to consult him about a dilemma in which he found himself. The young man, it appears, did not know what to do—to join the Nazis in collaboration, and thus gain a secure position for himself and his family; or to go into the underground Resistance, and thus bring himself and his family into the direst peril. And what did Sartre, who was himself at the time in the Resistance, say to him? By his own account, Sartre told the young man that the important thing was not which of the two ways he chose; the important thing was that he choose his way with inwardness and authenticity. A philosophy that can say this, but cannot and will not say anything more, may be able to create something new, but not a new morality!

Or take another case. The barbarous vandals, many of them teenagers, who invaded the magnificent Spanish Stairs in

Rome some time ago, and gleefully fouled up the world-famous work of art in a nihilistic protest against beauty and culture, may well have been acting out of their inner authenticity as much as the anonymous builders who, four centuries ago, created that magnificent structure. In fact, that's exactly what they claimed. Yet is there anyone bold enough to maintain that the two courses—creating and defiling—are morally on the same level if only one acts in either case with true inwardness?

No, authenticity may be a primary quality of a moral response, but it cannot be all there is to it. Unless *some* principle, some standard, *transcending* the particular context or situation, is somehow operative *in* the context or situation, nothing but moral chaos and capriciousness can result. No human ethic is possible that is not itself grounded in a higher law and a higher reality beyond human manipulation or control. In the depths of our tradition, we find this higher reality to be, for the Hebrews, God, for the Greeks, Reason; and the higher law derived therefrom, the divine or the natural law. But, as Russell notes, in our time these foundation-conceptions "tend to melt away," and we are left with no grounding or anchorage. A contextual or situational ethic will not save us; rather, in accentuated form, it points to that which we are to be saved *from*.

For it is the humanity of man that is at stake. The humanity of man—our wisdom and our suffering ought to have taught us—is ultimately grounded in that which is *above* and *beyond* man, or the pride and power of man. To realize this profound truth is to realize the full depth and measure of the moral crisis of our time. How to revalidate the moral life in a culture in which the very idea of a moral law binding on man because it is grounded in what is beyond man, has been eroded almost to nullity: this, rather than any particular problem of personal or social morality, no matter how acute or how urgent, seems to me to be the moral dilemma of our time and culture—a dilemma in which we are caught, and from which we, as yet, see no way of escape. Real standards come in and through tradition. "Only he who has the tradition has the standards," the old Greek poet Theognis was wont to say. We have lost, we are losing, the tradition—the tradition of the higher law and the higher reality—and are therefore also losing our standards. Is it ever really possible simply to regain what has once been lost? We do not know. That is our problem, our plight, and our task.

I.

INTERROGATING MODERNITY, RETHINKING TRADITION

Will Herberg

What Keeps Modern
Man from Religion?

VOL. 6, NO. 1–2, 1969–70

What keeps modern man from religion? Of course, it may be contended that this question is quite misleading, no real question at all. It may be contended that modern man, in this country at least, is not in any special sense alienated from religion. Never, certainly not in the past century and a half, have church membership, religious belonging, or attendance at religious services been so high in the United States as in recent decades. That is well established and beyond controversy. Yet, acknowledging all this, we nevertheless cannot escape the feeling—and it is a feeling considerably buttressed by facts—that however impressive the high religiosity of the American people may be, modern man, even in America, seems to have become peculiarly insensitive to religion and its historic appeal; in a way, it might be said that, although the churches are full, the man of today, even in America, has become virtually religion-blind and religion-deaf. And so the question still remains: what keeps modern man from religion?

Through the past two hundred years, explanations or quasi-explanations of this phenomenon have accumulated in the West. It would not be very profitable to examine these attempted explanations in detail, and to point out their manifest inadequacies. I will merely mention three, perhaps the best known of the lot.

At the moment, the most popular of the three, at least in some intellectual circles, is the one derived as a sort of by-product from the speculations of Rudolf Bultmann, the distinguished Protestant New Testament scholar and theologian, on the theme of "demythologization." It traces modern man's defection from religion to the discrepancy between the "primitive world-picture" of the Bible and the so-called "modern scientific world-view." That the world-picture of the Bible is "primitive," that is, pre-scientific (flat earth, three-story universe, etc.), is obvious enough; but that it is this discrepancy that has played any part in discrediting religion is more than doubtful. After all, this discrepancy was as real and as obvious in the thirteenth century, or even earlier, as it is today: recall the planetary orbs, the crystalline spheres, and the round earth of the Ptolemaic system as against the flat earth of the Bible. Yet religion did not suffer in the least on that account, nor does it today. The reader of the Bible either ignores the discrepancy or "demythologizes," automatically and unconsciously, as he goes along. There is no point in this kind of explanation.

Perhaps equally popular, this time among what are called "socially conscious" intellectuals, is an explanation that stems from a kind of Marxist attitude, though Marx himself did not employ it. The church has so flagrantly sided with the ruling classes, it is alleged, that it has alienated the masses from religion. Whatever grain of truth there may be in this account so far as French anti-clericalism is concerned, it has no relevance whatever to this country or to Great Britain. In these countries there never has been any significant anti-clericalism. In the United States, moreover, the Catholic Church has always stood with the working people, while in Great Britain, the labor movement was virtually born in the dissenting chapel. And yet it is in these countries precisely that the problem is most perplexing today.

Finally, there are explanations stemming from the notion traceable to Dietrich Bonhoeffer, another distinguished Protestant theologian, that now, in our time, the world has at long last "come of age" (*die mündige Welt*). It is a world in which "modern man" can "stand on his own feet." His alienation from religion is seen quite simply as a consequence of his spiritual and intellectual maturity. But this is, perhaps, the most futile explanation of all. Every age, from Homer's to Bonhoeffer's, a quick glance at our cultural history will tell us, has always tended to regard itself as having at last achieved "maturity"—a pretension that the succeeding age could only regard with amused contempt, knowing full well that "maturity" was really being achieved in its own, the succeeding time,

and not before. This notion of finally achieving "maturity" in our time, and therefore no longer needing the "props" of religion, is one of the most pathetic illusions of Western mankind, and flies in the face of everything we know about man, phenomenologically and historically. No explanation here.

It appears to me that we ought to look in a rather different direction. There are a number of aspects of modern Western culture, there are a number of aspects of massive social and cultural forces that have been operative since the eighteenth century at least, that seem to have affected modern attitudes to religion deeply. These are, I should say: (1) the triumph of the technological spirit in our time; (2) the triumph of the omnicompetent, all-engulfing modern Welfare State; (3) the triumph of mass society and the Mass-Man.

In other words, what keeps modern man from religion, it seems to me, is the pervasive dehumanization that comes of the technologized mass society which characterizes our world.

Let us examine each of these factors in some detail.

I. The Triumph of the Technological Spirit

It should be clear from the very beginning that I am not engaged in an indictment of technology, which is man's way of coping with the harshness and recalcitrance of nature and, as such, is in the ordinary providence of God. It is not technology as such that is the problem; that has accompanied man through his history from the earliest times. It is the incredibly rapid, high-pressure elaboration of technology in the West in the past two centuries, and its consequences for the social and spiritual life of Western man, that constitute the problem. Sand-hogs, who work deep underground, descend into the bowels of the earth gradually and by stages, to acclimate themselves, so to speak; failure to do so would result in the "bends," agonizing cramps that sometimes prove fatal. Well, we are suffering from the social, cultural, and spiritual "bends" induced by an intense, high pressure, technological progress, that has compressed the work of many centuries, perhaps a millennium, in the brief period of hardly two hundred years. That is our problem.

The tremendous advance of science and technology, under high pressure, through the nineteenth and twentieth centuries, has engendered in modern Western man a monstrous sense of technological arrogance. Man, collective man, has come to see himself replacing God as "Maker and Master of all"; and, most ironically, he has come to see himself not only as Creator and Maker, but also as his own destroyer! The same technological spirit has promoted in Western culture a pervasive technological climate, with a mechanistic bias toward depersonalization and "thingification." Everything about man—body, mind, and spirit—tends to be mechanized. One of the most telling indications of this way of thinking is the way modern Western man dreams of the World of Tomorrow. Beginning, with the Crystal Palace exhibition in London in 1851, or perhaps even earlier, the dream World of Tomorrow has been regularly projected as a prefabricated technological paradise—machines, mechanisms, technological wonders, gadgets.

Perhaps the most deep-going effect of the technological spirit engendered by the incredibly rapid development of technology under high pressure has been our tendency to convert all human problems into technological problems, to be dealt with by some kind of machinery, mechanical or organizational. We have lost all sense of what a human problem really is, and therefore all sense of the profound distinction between knowledge and wisdom, which Gabriel Marcel has examined in such an illuminating way.

Technological problems are, in principle, always solvable; and the movement from problem to solution is negotiated by way of increasing technical knowledge and know-how. Human or social problems, on the other hand, however simple they may appear at first sight, are of an entirely different kind. The more we deal with a human problem, the more deeply we think ourselves and "live" ourselves into it, the more the difficulties and dimensions multiply. The more we pursue solutions to human problems, the more, like the horizon, they recede into the distance—until, finally, we come to see that human problems, utterly unlike technological problems, which are always solvable in principle, really have no solution; the best we can hope for is a kind of makeshift arrangement to get us over the immediate agony that has brought forth the problem. What is needed in human problems is wisdom, which goes deeper and deeper, rather than scientific-technical knowledge, which extends more and more widely.

THIS WHOLE attitude runs so contrary to our technological prepossessions that it may, perhaps, be worth-while to buttress it with some documentation. I am taking this documentation from what may appear the most unlikely sources, two of the acknowledged and certified liberals of our time. Wrote Arthur M. Schlesinger Jr., the American liberal historian, some twenty years ago: "Man generally is entangled in unsolvable problems; history is consequently a tragedy in which we are all involved, whose keynote is anxiety and frustration, not progress and fulfillment."[1]

And Gunnar Myrdal, the Swedish liberal sociologist, commenting on his book, An American Dilemma, published in 1944, makes a like distinction between technical problems, which can in principle be solved, and human or social problems, which are, in their very nature, incapable of solution in the proper sense of the term, (see the interview with Dr. Myrdal in U.S. News & World Report, November 18, 1963).

To see this is wisdom, even when it comes from a liberal; to overlook it is the great intellectual and spiritual pitfall of our technologized culture.

It should now be clear what is meant by the technological spirit which so dominates our culture. But it is precisely this technological spirit that is so fundamentally hostile to the sense of personal being and personal relation, which is at the heart of living religion. It is fundamentally hostile to the sense of transcendence, the sense of beyondness, that is the proper dimension of living religion. It is fundamentally hostile to the sense of human insufficiency and limitation, without which there can be no living religion. In all these respects—in its depersonalizing effect, in the erosion of the sense of transcendence, in its thoroughgoing mechanization of life—the technological spirit, so pervasive in our culture, tends to dry up the very sources of religion in modern life.

Perhaps the most revealing example of how our incredible preoccupation with technology at the expense of everything else has tended to relegate religion to the margin of life is President Nixon's spontaneous exclamation that the landing of the astronauts on the moon was the "great event in the history of mankind since the Creation." Mr. Nixon, who is so concerned—and, I think, sincerely—with his religious services in the White House, Mr. Nixon, the Christian, apparently forgot all about the "event" known as Jesus Christ! Mr. Nixon was only responding in a way reflecting the general trend of our culture.

II. The Triumph of the Omnicompetent Welfare State

Along with this overwhelming impact of the technological spirit on our culture, and therefore on our religion, we must take account of the effects of the Welfare State, of our Welfare Society, on religious attitudes in this country. Through the past century, the welfare services that ordinarily support human life in society have more and more passed over to the modern state, operating as a huge, centralized, bureaucratic, omnicompetent welfare agency. This has come as the culmination of the relentless secularization of life in the past four hundred years. In earlier days, through antiquity and the middle ages, into the sixteenth century, most of the welfare services that sustain life—taking care of orphans, jobless, old people, sick and incapacitated—were regularly rendered by family and friends within the scope and function of the church, which was thus bound to the people by a thousand threads of everyday welfare interest. For the Amish people, this is still a reality today. In April 1965, wind and flood did wide damage in the Midwest and destroyed many an Amish community. Groups of Amish people from the outside came to help their brothers rebuild their communities and their lives. On a TV news broadcast, a commentator noted: These days, when people are in trouble, there is one direction in which they look—to the federal government in Washington. But the Amish people don't look to the federal government in Washington for help. They look to each other in their church.

That's how it still is with the Amish people, but that's how it was once all over in Christendom. I bring this forward not to encourage us to try to restore conditions long gone—that is a human impossibility—but to illustrate the profound changes that have taken place in recent centuries in our relation to religion and the church.

With the deep and thoroughgoing secularization of Western society, the hopes and expectations of the masses of people have steadily been turning from church to state, from religion to politics. This is a fact that no one, whatever his opinion or ideology, can deny, or has, in fact, denied. Consider how far this has gone in our own mass society, and our American society is only beginning to take its first steps in the direction of the Welfare State; if you want to see a Welfare State in its full development, look at Sweden. But already in our own society people have been so stripped of their human bonds in church and community that they are driven to look to the state for the most ordinary human associations and services. The state has not only become Big Father and Big Brother. It is actually brought to the point of having to supply to the forlorn members of the "lonely crowd" a state-appointed Good Friend. For, what is the modern social worker but a state-appointed Good Friend to the friendless denizens of mass society?

The modern state, in fact, becomes a divinized Welfare-Bringer. In the ancient world, the Hellenistic monarchs, and later the Roman emperors, prided themselves on being Welfare-Bringers (*Euergetes,*

Benefactor), passing on the gifts of the gods to their subjects. They depicted themselves on their coins—the primary vehicle of state propaganda in those days which were without journalistic mass media, radio, or TV—as divinized figures holding a cornucopia, a horn of plenty, from which everything good is shown flowing to the grateful people. This is the modern Welfare State; even some of the ancient symbols are being revived in cartoons and pictures. The omnicompetent Welfare State thus becomes the modern substitute for God and the church, "from whom all blessings flow."

Seen in this perspective, it is not difficult to understand why the church as a religious institution has become more and more marginal in the everyday life of the people. The broad scope of its interests has become drastically narrowed by the galloping secularization of life. What does the church do, what can it do, when the state takes over everything and comes to engage our deepest loyalties and emotions? Our religious feelings and religious interests have been more and more diverted from the attenuating church to the expanding state. Is it any wonder that people are losing their interest in religion? They identify themselves religiously, belong to churches, and attend religious services, but for very different reasons (I have discussed this elsewhere) than once bound them to religion and the church.[2]

III. The Triumph of Mass Society

All of these tendencies converge in the triumph of mass society. Mass society is not merely large-scale society. Mass society is a society of vast anonymous masses in which the individual person is increasingly atomized and homogenized, stripped bare of whatever particularities of background, tradition, and social position he may have possessed, and converted into a homogenized featureless unit in a vast impersonal machine. In our homogenizing mass society, we have a horror of distinctions and differences, which are felt to be "discriminatory"; we want everybody to be like everybody else, only more so! This tendency toward homogenization, which John Stuart Mill saw and denounced a century ago as destructive of all real freedom (*On Liberty*, 1859; Mill called it "assimilation"), is now welcomed by liberal writers. "The ideal human society," one recent writer promulgates as a self-evident truth, "is one in which distinctions of race, nationality, and religion, are totally disregarded. . . ."

Mass society is ruthless. Person-to-person relationships are systematically eroded in mass society, and replaced by the remote impersonal connections of ever-proliferating state agencies and institutions. In this way, there is engendered that very curious phenomenon in mass society—"non-involved sociability" (the term is Riesman's), a spurious sociability without personality, community, or responsibility.

What is this "non-involved sociability" of mass society? An illustration or two will help make it clear. Over five years ago, in March 1964, New Yorkers were startled to hear of a girl, Kitty Genovese, who was attacked and stabbed to death by an aggressor who had pursued her into the courtyard of a big apartment house in Kew Gardens, a respectable middle-class neighborhood in Queens. Awakened by the noise, thirty-four tenants showed enough curiosity to open their windows to see what was going on. They saw, and their curiosity satisfied, they shut their windows and went back to sleep! Kitty Genovese was then done to death. Subsequent inquiry elicited the explana-

tion: "We didn't want to get involved . . ." (all they had to do was to phone the police, without leaving their names, if that's how they wanted it).

I have before me twenty-three such newspaper reports from eleven large cities across the United States in the past five years. I will merely mention one more, later the same year, in May 1964, also in New York, but this time in the Bronx. Here, too, a girl was attacked; she ran into an old four-story building, where her assailant caught up with her. (Fortunately, two policemen, some blocks away, heard her cries, and came to her assistance.) Here, too, the girl's screams brought out people from the upper floors, who came out to see what was going on, saw, and went back to their business. And what was the business of the three men who came out from the first floor apartment, looked, and went back? Believe it or not, they were members of a committee of one of the most liberal organizations in a city full of liberal organizations; they were engaged in drawing up resolutions on "racial justice," and obviously couldn't be bothered about the girl's plight! As always, abstract humanitarianism, passing resolutions, making speeches, and the like, reflected the erosion of concrete humanity.

BUT WHY did these people, from New York to California, act this way? They were probably no worse morally and culturally than the inhabitants of Paris or London in the Middle Ages; if anything, were you to take them at their word, they were considerably better. And yet, in London or Paris in the Middle Ages, which had no police departments, a "hue and cry" would arouse neighbors to come to the aid of anyone beset in the neighborhood. Why not in New York or San Francisco?

Because in a modern urban metropolis, unlike London or Paris in earlier days, there are no neighbors. In a mass society, people live in close propinquity, but there are no neighbors in the proper sense, no people bound by genuine community bonds. Therefore, while there are all kinds of sociability in a mass society, often factitious and contrived, it is a sociability false and spurious, a "non-involved sociability." That is what mass society is like. Everything is big—Big Business, Big Labor, Big Government, Big Communications, Big Education, Big Entertainment, and . . . Big Religion. But in all this bigness, there is no room for the individual, the person, who is often reduced to nothing, and to less than nothing.

By atomizing, depersonalizing, and homogenizing the very substance of human life, mass society withers the roots of humanness, and thus, as Martin Buber has so well shown, it withers the roots of community and religion. It in fact leaves no room for religion and the church except as another Big Enterprise in mass society.

The technological spirit, the Welfare State, mass society: is it any wonder that in this cultural ambience religion tends to lose its proper and vital appeal? What keeps modern man from religion? The answer is here plain to see.

The criticism of the religious situation is a criticism of society and culture; this is true in a sense rather different from what Marx intended. The drying up of the living sources of religious response and religious consciousness in modern man means the dessication of the vital spirit of the culture itself, for the vital spirit of any culture, ours perhaps more than most others, is its religion. In religion, this development means that the religious task has become not primarily the saving of souls; before that even, it has become how to have human beings at all, how to have persons, not things; how to have persons, not personnel. That, it seems to me, has become the primary religious problem of our time.

Notes

1. "The Causes of the Civil War," by Arthur M. Schlesinger Jr., *Partisan Review*, October 1949.
2. Will Herberg, *Protestant, Catholic, Jew: An Essay in American Religious Sociology* (Doubleday-Anchor, 1955).

Thomas Molnar

Tradition and Social Change

VOL. 7, NO. 4, 1971

Tradition is one of those fundamental concepts which today is overused, with the result that its futurist opponents ignorantly despise it, while its faithful defenders often do not really understand it. The first believe that tradition is the opposite of change, the latter are unsure about the manner of distinguishing between tradition and the merely old; both tend to think of tradition as the bottom of the time-ocean, covered by layers upon heavy layers of time, hardly lit by anything but arbitrarily focusing memory.

In a recent series of lectures on tradition and social change, I attempted to describe tradition as a more dynamic concept than what is today consecrated as a cliché. I spoke of the "sacred model" in archaic societies, serving as an archetype in foundation myths, to which the community periodically returned for self-renewal. From this regular "immersion in the origins" (in *illo tempore,* as Mircea Eliade calls it), archaic man derived the energy to continue societal existence; without the sacred model, the community was incapable of "repairing" (reforming) itself; with its help, natural degeneracy

was arrested, or rather abolished, so that life might begin again.

This static concept of tradition, hostile to innovation and change (which was considered decay, as a falling-away from the original model), was challenged by the Greek philosophers. Plato, for one, was also preoccupied with the concept of society's degeneracy, but no longer saw it as a *mechanical* necessity; he saw it as the soul's disorder spreading from the older to the younger generation, from the few to the many, but still within the soul's capacity to resist and cure. Greek philosophy and political history prove for the first time that continuity and change are compatible.

With Judaism, and particularly with Christianity, the norm is no longer the past, and it is no longer situated in the cosmic order either (as interpreted through the cosmogonic myth—the myth of creation). The norm is in the eternal order which, however, unfolds in time and includes the future. Thus God himself participates in history, pulling man and nations toward His design. The God of Christians and Jews is neither immobile as are the archaic deities, nor

Big Brown
& Pay Lakes

ere the fish are
lways biting.

0 acre facility.
nic tables, Park
ches & Pavilion.

e Rental, Bait &
Tackle Shop.

mobile as taught by the existen-
heologians (Bultmann, Gogarten,
ner) in whose view history begins
t every moment and with every
ual decision, (Every moment is es-
gical—writes Rudolf Bultmann.)
at then is a good formulation of
on and change"? Perhaps John
Newman provided it: "A true de-
ent," he wrote in *An Essay on the
oment of Christian Doctrine,* "may
ribed as one which is conservative
ourse of antecedent developments,
eally those antecedents and some-
esides them; it is an addition which
tes, not obscures, corroborates, not
s, the body of thought from which
eds; and this is its characteristic as
ted with a corruption."

e reflect on this rich formulation
ust substitute, of course, "com-
" for "body of thought"), we find
dition is not *the past* (the bottom
ocean), but the lived past, insepa-
om the present and the future. For
ividual (let us take the optimum
he educated individual) myriad
es represent this coexistence, the
um of which is the shared expe-
nd the common vision of reality
ed through historical events, politi-
sions, and the guideposts they left,
ary works, or simply the traces of
dividuals with which he now con-
The conversation is two-sided, the
reaches us as regularly as we care
he question. In the past the very
man being lived, suffered, hoped
d, so that our present is inseparable
echoes, our quest meets intelligi-
vers. In fact, there is a permanent
nge between past and present, the
onsults the former while reshap-
f in the light of new experience.
ise how could we read the works
st? If, as we are now told, there are

unbridgeable gaps between generations, and biopsychological mutations between epochs, how could I, child of the twentieth century, reflect not just on Plato or Pascal but reflect *with* them on identical subjects, on the ills of our different yet same societies, on the existential anguish caused by silent spaces and mute objects? At a certain level of penetration even the diversity of circumstances is of little import, so shared are the experiences and the wounded reflection on them: could we tell, even after a second glance, whether Plato or Voegelin wrote this, facing their respective societies: "All of a sudden it appears that the older generation has neglected to build the substance of order in the younger men, and an amiable lukewarmness and confusion shifts within a few years into the horrors of social catastrophe." (In Eric Voegelin's *Plato.*)

This much for the (educated) individual; for a community, a nation, the reality and the presentness of tradition finds adequate expression in the symbols of order which survive the ages. By "order" I do not mean that which is secured by law, namely orderly procedures. Rather, order as the given community has interpreted its own passage from chaos to cosmos, from nonexistence to intelligible existence, from dispersion to unity. This sentence is not as abstract as it seems: we may concretely understand it when facing those for whom historical-social existence is literally meaningless, who see in communal experience a mystification perpetrated by the power elite, or the resultant exclusively of socioeconomic components. One does not have to be an anarchist or a cynic to hold that society is meaningless; no less a personage than a U.S. ambassador to a South American country—Mr. John Cabot Lodge—said in a recent ceremonial public speech that "society is an abstraction, only individuals are real." This latter-day nominalism is destructive and silly: society is "man writ large," and the proof is that no two communities are interchangeable—precisely because they embody experiences which make increasing sense within a given framework, which translates the reality of the world into the language of specific shared relationships.

The "real individualists" of whom the ambassador spoke, like Rousseau's "natural man"—do not exist. It is no adherence to collectivist ideology which prompts me to say that every man—with the possible exception of Tarzan—is born surrounded with the community's signs, symbols and guideposts, so that by the time he begins to feel, act, and reason, he has been shaped by them. Even his sense of freedom is shaped by the communal experiences of freedom and its absence.

ALL THIS by no means denies innovation and change. In the spirit of Newman's definition of "development," it even suggests them since well-understood tradition invites the addition which illustrates the conserved order while bringing to it a kind of plus sign. The difficulty is, of course, to judge the magnitude and the direction of this plus sign: usually, this too can only be negatively experienced: we seem to know what is *not* in our tradition, in our interpretation of the structure of reality. Americans know, for example, that monarchy is not only unsuitable for the United States, it is also unimaginable, although a few miles away, in Canada, this was the regime until recently. Time and collective experience do give directives as to what can be passed on, what discarded or adopted, but they must also be protected against attempts at compression (radical impatience) and the arbitrariness of interpretation.

Yet, this statement needs to be at once qualified. Many of history's great decision-makers chose to act *against* tradition, only to end up creating new situations which, in retrospect, proved to be shapers of that tradition. Alexander the Great, King of Macedon and leader of the Greeks, broke in ten brief years Hellas's traditional repugnance for the Asian barbarians, arranged the marriage of ten thousand of his soldiers with Persian girls, and adopted the oriental-imperial ceremonies (for example, prostration before the King's person) at his court. The Macedonians and Greeks grumbled—yet Alexander had enlarged hellenic vision and given depth to the Mediterranean world.

Another illustration is the Apostle Paul who broke with the tradition of the Law and turned the face of the new religion towards the Gentiles. Or take Emperor Constantine who abolished almost at one stroke the immemorial pagan state, adopted Christianity, then proceeded to pass on to the latter the former's sacred objects and ceremonies: incense, candles, votive offerings, holy water, processions, tonsure, the marriage ring. Nearer to us we may reflect upon the break between the Founding Fathers and the English throne, yet a break leaving so much of tradition and so many institutions intact.

In each of these instances the decisive acts were clearly outside the sphere of tradition, they were even in opposition to it. Yet, we are aware that something positive, and positively good, passed from the old onto the new, in Newman's words, a corroboration of the tradition, not a corruption of it. And on a larger canvas, the same thing happened when the cosmogonic myths, as intelligible renderings of the structure of reality, yielded to Philosophy and Revelation.

The reader has noticed the apparent contradiction: I argued earlier that, as

ers of a community, we know when
ion, an act, a choice goes against
in of the tradition. Yet, I just now
ted that this knowledge may at
be superseded by great and com-
oves like Alexander's, St. Paul's, or
nders' of this country. The contra-
is solved when we admit—with
odesty—that we have short lives
orter perspectives; it follows that
y hardly know which decisions
main part of the tradition; nor do
sess sufficient genius to become
—otherwise than in retrospect,
through history—of the points
adition becomes enlarged.
by no means suggested that there-
are condemned to move blindly
th extreme caution within our
n. As we shall see in a moment,
ofile" of a tradition can he clearly
ed, so that it is no exaggeration
hat people move almost inerra-
in their tradition. The "plusses"
d to the past are, in the immense
y of cases, not individual idio-
es but approaches engendered by
ng the tradition in new circum-
The "great moves" are weighty

there is no such thing as auto-
radition-building. Archaic man
e wise observation that societies
d to decay in time; modern man,
uses to recognize a regenerating
model," bears a heavy burden: he
he model with him, so to speak,
serts its sacredness by studying
nilating the tradition. Time cor-
society too unless he repairs and
it with wisdom and care. With
and care because, as Voegelin
n a letter), "truth in history re-
elf not on a single line, but in
ted patterns, parallels, conver-
nd fusions."

All this may create the impression that *tradition* is something rather vague; particularly the term "Western tradition" tends to fade today in the penumbra of ideological battles. Against this view we might find that, as so often, "otherness" is the mediator of self-knowledge: a juxtaposition with other traditions will clarify the nature of our own.

Islam, G. Von Grunebaum writes, "is eminently human in that it takes man for what he is, but it is not humanist in that it is not interested in the richest possible unfolding and evolving of man's potentialities, in that it never conceived of the forming of man as civilization's principal and most noble task." The Muslim's quality of repose, he adds, could develop only as the result of a static conception of the ideal world and the ideal society (*Medieval Islam*). All this is inscribed in Islamic history which knew no such thing as the doctrine of the two swords; which, although it was repeatedly the scene of power struggle between ecclesiastic and military leaders, nonetheless did not interpret it as the articulation of the soul itself. The result is *(was* until recently, until Western penetration) submission to the inevitably secular, since the Messenger of God had nothing more to say to the faithful than what the Koran contained from the beginning. "You shall find no change in God's way," taught Hayy b. Yaqzan, "of dealing with those which were gone before" and those living now.

Muslim authorities, secular and ecclesiastic, preserved the tradition, and did little else. Religion and education were endless repetitions of sacred texts and rites; social institutions were practically stagnant, social change shunned, relationships among social classes static. The great Arab philosophers' ideas never influenced Islam's statecraft—although they revolutionized the medieval West. Only Christian missionaries brought to the Arabic world opportunities for mobility and charitable institutions, vocational schools, homes for the aged, for orphans, for unwed mothers.

TURNING TO African tribal society, we find it selfless. This is the price the individual pays for cradle-to-grave security. Improvement of his crop invites the tribe's suspicion that he has commerce with evil spirits; personal ambition is thwarted by obligations to the whole of the extended family; outstanding qualities call forth the Chief's jealousy. Even today, in decolonized Africa, the individual as official of the Government prefers foreign posts to domestic ones because at home the family lays claim on all his possessions, on his person.

In the Orient, with the clear exception of the Chinese and Japanese, the basic attitudes are not very different: the collective prevails by far over the self. "Harmony with tribal life and with the surrounding natural order was viewed as coinciding with the harmony of the holy cosmic order. Life was static and conservative, since the decisive moment lay in the past, when the holy cosmic order had made itself manifest at a holy moment and at a holy place through holy persons." So writes the Indonesian writer-philosopher, S. Takdir Alisjabana. No wonder then that in semi-modern Indonesia "authority depends on charisma, on an irrational image based on emotional response; criticism in general appears as a manifestation of basic hostility, a threat to collective life itself. To criticize any facet of a leader's program or attitude is to weaken his charisma. This is why administrators in Indonesia generally react negatively to criticism" (Arief Budiman).

These are only a few, but the dominant character traits of some *other* traditions. In one way or another they are archaic societies so attached to their model in the past that eventual removal causes deep and perhaps irreparable crises. In one sentence we may say that they are unable (or are able only with enormous difficulty) to integrate change with their historical continuity. In spite of this—or because of it—Western man may find them esthetically or ethically appealing, but only because visiting them or even living in their midst, he lives in them, not of them. In conclusion, therefore, let us briefly examine the character traits of Western tradition.

We may begin with the recognition of the person as bearer of a conscience. But note that in the West conscience historically articulated itself as a divided entity, held together in tension: divided between tribal law and moral law, the Jewish king and the Jewish prophet, "Antigone" and "Kreon," state and church. Out of this tension was then born the supreme recognition that man is able to "turn around" (*periagoge*—as in Plato's cave), to become converted to another vision through a movement of his soul and intellect. True, the Gnostics, this alien yet brotherly body in Western tradition, also teach that the spirit turns around and rejoins the One; but from the start this spirit was an exile down here, "alienated" in this world because made of a different substance than the rest of mankind; he merely returns to the One out of which he had been torn. The world of men, men made of matter (*hyle*) and soul (*psyche*), does not concern him since he is pure spirit (*pneuma*).

Periagoge, on the other hand, translates the movement of conversion which does not presuppose the soul's change of essence, only a new understanding. It does not have to be a mystic experience, only a philosophical one; but even when it is a mystic experience, the mystic (the *Western* mystic, in opposition to the Buddhist) is eager to "turn around" again towards other men in order to share with them the overflow of his vision, of his spiritual wealth. And this is, of course, love, expressed in the Western tradition as the recognition also of our right, indeed our duty to exert influence, to teach, to build channels, for example, institutional channels, with a view toward "converting," influencing, changing. In imperial China, the public official—mandarin—memorized the Confucian texts; in Islam, as we saw, the Koran was the source of authority and of teaching authority as well.

Of conversion (teaching) and of institutions for conveying influence other than the consecrated governmental, there was very little in either tradition.

These Western philosophical underpinnings are, in turn, the source of personal right, rights to initiate, rights to public action, rights to property. Conscience is not locked up in meditation; on the contrary, it is extended toward the sphere of objects (science), toward the past (heritage), toward the future (initiative)—things unknown in most other traditions, or known, as it were, through a veil. If they are known to us, so must be their roots, their presuppositions, their unfolding, their history. And the reasons for defending them.

Donald Atwell Zoll

ON TRADITION

VOL. 9, NO. 1, 1973–74

One of the curiosities of the history of conservative social thought has been its persistent invocation of *tradition* without rigorously specifying what is being alluded to. It would be possible on this basis for the critic unsympathetic to conservatism to accuse it of a palpable irrationalism: appealing to a justification for its social preferences that is merely a nebulous, pseudo-honorific piece of terminology. Conservative language about "tradition" does not appear to allay misgivings about such an accusation. Such writing, since Burke, has been singularly vague.

But merely because it is vague does not necessarily mean that the appeal to "tradition" is either nonsensical or a bald rhetorical fallacy. It is possible to fault conservatively oriented writers, even the great Burke, for a lack of philosophical rigor, and it is certainly fair to criticize some contemporary conservative writers for flabby imprecision in the matter of "tradition," but such reservations do not, per se, demolish what I take to be a crucial cornerstone in the conservative position.

But what is the "tradition" to which post-Burkean writers refer? Indeed, are they talking about "tradition" qua "tradition"—a general conception of cultural inheritance—or are they referring to an explicit "tradition,"—a particular national experience, as with the "British tradition"—or the "American tradition"? Surely it must be either the former or both, for it is difficult to invoke a specific national tradition without having some idea of what tradition in general terms is all about. While that would seem to be obvious, I should point out that certain twentieth-century conservatives have tried to do expressly that, the late Willmoore Kendall, for illustration. What results is the claim that a given national tradition (political, constitutional, intellectual, etc.) is superior without advancing any philosophical explanation for why that is so. As a matter of fact, the arguments of Kendall and others are really not a traditionalist argument at all (at least not in the philosophical sense). Kendall would contend, in sum, that the products of the Founding Fathers were the result of extraordinary political wisdom, that this wisdom has proven uniquely efficacious and that subsequent departures from these original concepts were the result of distinctly inferior political judgment. What is being appealed to is not a "tradition," but an explicit historical-political outlook deemed to be qualitatively superior; it is a "tradition" only in the sense that it belongs to a reasonably remote past, despite the frequent employment of phraseology such as the "American political tradition."

In like fashion, Daniel Boorstin does not offer a philosophically grounded concept of tradition in his reflections on American history. Boorstin believes that he can detect certain singular features in the American historical experience and, no doubt, he is quite correct about that. These perennial motifs are the result of distinctive characteristics (demographic and, in, a wide sense, cultural) that affected the American outlook. But this is not really an appeal to tradition, either, because as the external variables are modified, so are the cultural attitudes: the source of the American "mind" is not some continuous, cross-generational accumulation, but habitual responses to environmental factors. Tradition, for Boorstin, is simply a handy word to use to refer to past patterns of social behavior.

I am not asserting that either Mr. Kendall or Mr. Boorstin are wrong, only that their arguments do not constitute a defense of tradition as I believe historical conservatives conceived it, despite the ambiguities of their language. We confront in an effort to make distinctions regarding the meaning of tradition some semantic problems, the principal one being a common inclination to use the word "tradition" as an omnibus reference to the historical past; thus, a "traditionalist" is thought of as one being fond of retaining or reviving the practices of the past. But this is an awkward usage if any philosophical clarity is sought. The mere fact that I, for the sake of argument, might seek to encourage the return of the

bustle for feminine fashion hardly places me in the position of being an advocate of tradition. An affection for the past, particularized or even generalized, does not, ipso facto, make one a defender of tradition.

This is true for a fairly obvious reason: "tradition," whatever it is, is a paradigmatic term, it refers to some pattern or cognizable order that presumably surfaces in historical experience. This must be the case, for the opposite assumption is clearly to contend that history cannot be evaluated or interpreted save on the basis of immediate preferences. This latter viewpoint, I take it, is the fundamental anti-traditionalist outlook. On what basis can we judge the merits of historical experience? We can either refer to some paradigmatic interpretation of history or we can espouse an essentially pragmatic one. How can we evaluate a specific historical practice—like slavery, for instance, certainly a "tradition" in numerous cultures? We do so in one of two ways: the practice is either compatible or not with some paradigmatic theory of human experience or we judge it in terms of a prevailing moral (and I use the word in its strict generic sense) outlook. "Tradition" is, thus, not the "past," but a segment of the past differentiated from the totality of previous events by one of two assumptions: a) that "tradition" refers to a pattern of some sort that is actualized in the historical process, or b) that it refers to some historical practices retrospectively *and* contemporaneously deemed to be, for one reason or another, desirable or praiseworthy.

Are both interpretations of "tradition" equally valid, granting the necessity to endow the word "tradition" with some cogent meaning? I don't think so, because the second conception contains a fatal defect: it "begs the question." Let us return to the example of slavery. If I apply the second conception of tradition I may well condemn slavery on the following grounds: slavery is immoral, but it is immoral because it violates concepts of morality I currently espouse. What I have done is not to appeal to tradition at all, but rather to identify tradition with prevailing ideas, good or bad, that I presently hold. I have said nothing at all about history other than to discriminate among historical events on the basis of my immediate prejudices. The validity of those prejudices or preferences turn upon criteria totally unrelated to the historical process, per se. Put another way: the "traditionalist" seeks to *learn* from history, the "anti-traditionalist" seeks to employ his present insights as a means of making judgments about history.

It is not my intention to suggest here that one viewpoint is finally superior to the other, but only to introduce some useful clarity to the discussion by limiting the meaning of tradition to the first interpretation for the reasons set forth. But to accept, initially, a paradigmatic view of tradition is not to disclose much about it or to give reasons why the inferences drawn from tradition ought to be highly regarded in contemporary social decision-making. In fact, this preliminary orientation is qualitatively neutral—it does not tell us what paradigms are to be preferred to other ones. It does not imply that an ethical mandate necessarily follows from the discovery of tradition.

Of course, some arguments have been made on behalf of tradition on the grounds of sheer endurance. It is often assumed, wrongly I think, that Burke's doctrine of "prescription" (which I shall return to later) falls into this category—as, indeed, he defended the English Constitution on the basis that it had "existed time out of mind." It may well be

that certain human proclivities appear to have a trans-temporal character; certain characteristics appear to persist in the face of cultural modification. I am inclined to believe that this is true, but I am equally of the view that these enduring factors do not in themselves offer direct recommendation or justification for social action. They may well constitute the objective data within which social options must be exercised, but they are not simply "binding" upon human choice. Conservatives are wont to allude to reverence or aesthetic awareness as immemorial human motifs—and I have no doubt that they are constant factors, so to speak. But savage predation and carnality are equally "immemorial" and hardly would seem to posit ethical imperatives, except to the extent that such human predilections are factors in the ethical predicament not to be lightly dismissed.

Endurance is, in itself, no qualitative justification for the mandate of tradition, except as it is indicative of what I might call "ohtic strength," the relative potency of objective elements that form the ontological skeleton, as it were, of cognate nature. Such an observation, of course, brings us full tilt toward some discursive definition of the nature of tradition.

Tradition vs. Dialectical History

If tradition is thought to refer to paradigmatic themes in the historical process, one must, I think, attempt to differentiate "tradition" from other "dialectical" or even deterministic theories of history. Tradition is distinct from various dialectical accounts of the historical process in two principal ways: 1) tradition is not simply the surfacing of biological imperatives (at least not as construed in reductionistic varieties of naturalism, such as that of Marx); 2) tradition is not the configuration of the historical process by a superior, supernatural stratum of reality, especially as that configuration is presumed to be conveyed in pan-logistic terms, as with Hegel. These distinctions require comment.

1) The first account of the undeniably paradigmatic character of the historical process must be rejected on grounds of adequacy stemming, principally, from the vulnerabilities of reductionistic theories of human nature. It is dubious to assume that the elements that conform to the historical process could emerge from a concept of human nature so radically constricted. Man certainly is more than "what he eats" and to suppose that the subtle complexities of historical patterns are wholly attributable to animalistic appetition (as suggested by the dialectical materialists) is unacceptable.

2) The metaphysical ambiguities aside (the primary being the basic Idealist premise), it is questionable that the historical process can be described as the peregrinations of ideas (with either an upper or a lower case "i"). While it is likely true that the human act of discovery is itself predicated upon pre-experiential capacities and even predispositions, it is difficult to suppose that the underlying fabric of historical phenomena consists of categories that appear to be less elemental than those which are involved with man's awareness of his universe. We do not, in fact, confront that universe in ideational terms, at least not initially and fundamentally. Our cognitive apprehensions are the products, not the causes, of our being able to confront the universe and render it intelligible—and, indeed, the genius of tradition may well be involved with this elemental confrontation. It seems altogether questionable to suppose that our rudimentary knowledges are essentially conscious and rational and the historical phenomena that are the reflections of the underlying universal processes seem, as well, to be essentially apprehended not by conscious dialectic, but by the similar means by which we possess elemental natural knowledge.

Tradition vs. a "Code" Theory

Approaching from a somewhat different angle, tradition (the emergence of continuities of historical patterns) is projected by an essentially monistic worldview. Those patterns which are recognized and labeled as "tradition" are neither the cultural manifestations of a strictly physical nature nor are they symbolic constructs of an active and immanent supernatural being or Idea. Some conservatives have leaned heavily on this latter interpretation (recalling, perhaps, Burke's "divine tactic" reference). Such a position is fraught with philosophical perils, not the least of which is a full-blown historical determinism, ultimately reminiscent of St. Augustine's. This argument, theological disputes aside, reduces to a "code" theory of history in which it must be assumed that buried in the welter of historical intransigence is a rational plan open to "decoding" by human reason. Apart from speculation regarding why God would choose, thus, to be so secret or perverse in disclosing his inexorable intentions, this conjecture features all those disabilities of historical "positivism" rightly castigated by R. G. Collingwood. Its prime defect is a confusion between a *teleological* concept of history and a finally *deterministic* one, or at least one predicated upon the manipulation of a divine codex, the nature of which presumes a notion of an original deception.

I have referred to a concept of tradition as being "monistic" simply because one cannot, I assert, take tradition very seriously if one is an ontological dualist. If one is the latter, one is obliged to know (whatever the means) what is the ultimate meaning of history *before* one confronts it and interprets it. For the true traditionalist, therefore, with his monistic perspective, history must be self-interpreting. He may require self-knowledge as a prerequisite for observation, but he assumes that tradition will *tell him something,* as against one who assumes that tradition will confirm something he already knows.

Four Prior Types of Knowledge

Of course, the traditionalist does not come to reflect on tradition tabula rasa. He confronts tradition with four types of prior knowledge: a) he operates (as I will argue momentarily) with an *intentional* predisposition toward traditional insight; b) he functions with a subrational continuity of knowledge; c) he possesses an instinctual base of behavior; and d) he has conscious knowledge, extensive or limited, of the explicit cultural continuities of which he is a part.

a) Tradition (and, perhaps, to avoid a holistic impression, "traditions" might be a more useful term) must enjoy, in a generative sense, an ontological status. That is to say that the patterns or paradigms designated as "tradition" (as apart from conventions) are not accidental confluences or theoretically originated "systems" imposed on phenomena by the observer. To suppose that tradition is the latter is to deny, quite obviously, tradition altogether. This is not, of course, a disreputable position and the existence of tradition (as we have so far defined it)

is, I submit, an empirical question—are there or are there not indisputable enduring paradigms in historical phenomena? I am not trying to avoid this empirical question, but only to limit this essay to a clarification of tradition on the admittedly contentious grounds that it exists.

If, then, to return to the main argument, tradition is not accident or a priori systematization (or some version of a historical dialectic), what is it? It is the manifestation within the historical process of partial actualizations of the objective order of nature—or, to use the language of Whitehead to whom I am invariably indebted, tradition is the nexus of "eternal objects" as they actualize in patterns of historical "durations" or "events." In this sense, the cognizable paradigms are recurring ontological motifs, clothed in the historical and symbolic dress of human cultural experience. As such, these patterns, these traditions, are "lures for feeling," they exert a "requiredness" to which human nature is attuned for the altogether cogent reason that the human being is himself an actualization of the very same class of "eternal objects" that participate in the on-going patterns which he recognizes. It is in this sense that the observer of traditions has an "intentional" vector toward recognition of tradition and, by implication, a response to the directives of that tradition. This is what, I believe, Burke meant by his concept of "prescription," the communication of ontological data via tradition, a transmission made possible by the compatibility of human receptivity to these directives. I would wish to define, by the way, a "traditionalist" as one with a particularly high level of intensity of feeling in regard to the "lure" of tradition.

b) We cannot view tradition and the observer in a subject-object relationship (except for explanatory metaphor).

Tradition is not only as we have partially defined it in (a). It is an "enduring occasion"—a continuity, a transmission of subrational knowledge. Tradition is not the perpetuation of a fixed code, conveyed in necessarily random human experience. Only in part is it the manifestation of the natural ontology. The very act of actualization in the historical flow renders tradition in part novel, dynamic, reflective of cultural variations. To the degree that it is cognitively specific, it is expressive of unique cultural experience. It is also cumulative in the sense that its vehicle is human culture, the aggregate experiences of cognate human societies and communities. Its paradigmatic aspect is reflective of the accumulations that are made specific in the evolutionary processes of given societies. This social accumulation is transferable on two levels; first, a cognitive communal history that participates in the "enculturation" of the individual and, second, a subrational transmission of the social accumulations, the general and particularized aspects of tradition. I do not pretend to be able to explain the nature of this "social imprinting" which is vastly more resistant to empirical inquiry than is that artifactual culture well-described by anthropology. But I do contend that it is observable as a phenomenon and no account of culture seems complete without its addition.

Thus, the observer of tradition is at once observer and participant—and in a process never static and always in change. Further, (c) his relationship with tradition is founded upon his own instinctual composition which represents an ontological compatibility between the basis of his self-knowledge and behavior and the tradition to which he responds. His internal "wiring" is teleological, not only in the semi-mechanistic sense advanced by cybernetics, but also in a meta-psychological sense. Thus, tradition and instinctual motivation are both teleological in nature (as I will argue presently), harmonious, and mutually reinforcing. It is likely that tradition restrains human behavior, as virtually all conservatives have contended, but not in the fashion advanced by numerous contemporary conservatives who rather view tradition as some culturally generated set of social habits that happily restrain the "natural man" with his anti-social proclivities. If the base of tradition is naturalistic, as I am content that it is, tradition cannot war with the self as correspondingly defined; they are, rather, parallel manifestations of natural directive.

d) Finally, of course, the observer of tradition comes to his task armed with a conscious awareness of his social continuity, its immediate cognitive protocols. It is here that he must distinguish between *tradition* and *convention*. He may be far more aware, initially, of the latter than the former. There are two or more principal means of differentiating between a tradition and a convention. The first method involves, by implication, a definition of a "convention" as being a social practice with two distinguishable features: a) it is a fairly explicit and limited social or institutional practice or arrangement, and b) it is not directly concerned with the survival potentiality of the society. Put another way: conventions are non-imperative social options, perhaps of long standing, relating to reasonably specific aspects of human activity. It is not a convention, for example, that murder is socially prohibited, but it is a convention to be required to rise when hearing the national anthem. The family is very likely not merely a conventional human institution, but having the male as head of the family may very well be only conventional.

There is another difference. Human responses to conventions (as being more or less the result of free choices) are only intense when it is assumed that they are, in fact, traditions; otherwise conventions can come and go like the lengths of skirts. But traditions are never so specific in nature that they can be postulated as limited aspects of human activity. And to say this clearly implies that not all that we deem necessary or desirable can be justified by tradition. We do not prohibit murder on traditional grounds, but on directly ethical ones. Our knowledge of the ethical character of the natural order is only in part traditional; it is in large measure directly observable or cognizable. Further, many of our social arrangements are justifiable because they are beneficial, efficient, pleasant and so on, not because they are traditional. But to say that tradition is not the sole basis for social life is not to deny its mandate where applicable. Genuine tradition *deserves* conservation. Practices in direct violation of the insight of tradition ought to be avoided, as being suggestive of the aberrational. Moreover, it is necessary in order to preserve bona fide tradition to extricate it from narrow and more ephemeral conventions. To insist zealously upon the ultimately transient and superficial may obscure the permanent and real in the sense that conventions are free choices as against the natural mandates and are, in a social context, expendable.

Tradition and Purpose

These observations still leave much to be said on the nature of tradition. The salient assumption, if one concedes the existence of tradition, is that the natural order from which tradition emerges is teleological. Tradition presupposes purpose. This conclusion is not a very radical one if one has already acquiesced to the general definition of tradition offered. At a very fundamental level, one must ask oneself if one thinks the natural order to be teleologically structured or not? I do not deny that this is a sweeping question and one cannot be categorical in answering it. It is a matter of weighing and interpreting the evidence, but I conclude that anyone who is willing to think about tradition seriously must have made some type of assent, however tentative, to the proposition that, on balance, the probabilities are that the universe is not merely an accidental, chaotic, fortuitous, or inscrutable entity.

But when one concedes to the rudimentary premise that the universe is a teleological entity, what then? What kind of purpose? To what extent? To what end? Here the imponderables multiply disturbingly. I cannot trace down all the inferences in this brief essay, but I wish to disengage the concept of tradition from a more or less explicit teleological concept, especially one with marked eschatological overtones. I am struck, for example, by the peculiar tension in Burke's teleological viewpoint in which an orthodox religious eschatology is wedded with an implicitly vitalistic view of nature—almost as if Burke were some sort of latter-day Averroist. I think the issue, pro and con, regarding the inseparability of theism and traditionalism (so beloved by conservative writers) is largely irrelevant, except for the truly Augustinian Christians for whom no doctrine of tradition could make any sense, save some trivial regard for accustomed pieties. The nature of the teleologically conceived natural order has, I think, very little to do with theistic propositions. If one accounts for the genesis of the teleologically structured natural order in terms of God, the *prima mobile,* the logos, the Absolute, so be it. The matter is of intense personal significance on theological grounds, perhaps, but it does not affect the foundation of tradition. Burke's apparent tension is really reflective of a healthy philosophical outlook (despite an effort, now and again, to enlist his authority on behalf of various religious preferences; a recent ludicrous example being an attempt to describe Burke as a "Christian activist"!). I am tempted to say that far too many conservative writers who invoke "tradition" do so under the regrettably parochial assumption that "tradition" really means the "Christian tradition." What they fail to perceive is that the ultimate effect of that contention would be to destroy the philosophical credibility of tradition.

Another conservative penchant, which is another form of the "code" theory, is the notion that tradition is "something" conveyed by the "great books" of the wise men of the past or some such allegation. Of course, if one read all the serious philosophical and literary works of history (not just the "pet" lists), one could come to no other conclusion except that every tradition, every worldview, under the sun was at one time or another advocated. The philosophical Tower of Babel, indeed. The argument, of course, really consists of asserting that there were "correct" and "incorrect" thinkers of the past and that "tradition" is carried forth by the "correct thinking" variety. Such a conclusion may appeal to the "ultramontanes," but it rests, willy-nilly, not on the wisdom of tradition, but on the literary tastes and philosophical preferences of living commentators. Indeed, it is finally extremely awkward, I think, to be a *traditionalist* (as earlier defined) and a *transcendentalist*. Traditional wisdom is the antithesis of mysticism. The wisdom of tradition is, actually, an "earthy" wisdom, at least it

is a naturalistic one; it rests upon a universality of knowledge and a regard for historical and empirical analysis over revelation. To conclude that the universe is a purposive system is not to contend that its processes necessarily imply the realization of some dominant and discrete end, the fruition of an exhaustively elaborate plan. Such a viewpoint is too extravagant a concept, going far beyond the intimations of either traditional or empirical knowledge. Tradition itself is not the unfolding of an explicit code for human existence; it is, rather, a continuity constructed both of the actualizations of the natural order and the superorganic accumulations of culture. It is a supportive but not a dominant factor in social life. It provides both a general criterion and a guide to human discretion. It is purposive in that the natural order from which it, in part, springs is purposive and the human faculties that respond to it are purposive, and it participates in the perpetuation of forms of life that transcend the transient character of individual life.

The counsel provided by the "wisdom experts" of previous eras is hardly to be slighted. No one would deny that we are the descendents, in a manner of speaking, of Plato, Aristotle, Plotinus, Lucretius, and so on. Their writings do reveal common concerns. Perhaps central to all is a preoccupation with the question of value. However their express viewpoints may differ, this virtually universal attention to the activity of valuation suggests certain discriminations between the human tradition and other teleological natural processes. Regardless of other potential differences between men and beasts, man alone is a "valuing animal" in the sense that he consciously makes value choices and endows objects or activities with valuational significance. He is a complex valuing animal because there are, at base, three sources of his valuing process: 1) Instinctual response, 2) Tradition, 3) Conscious discriminatory capability.

The first source he shares with other natural species (although the clarity and vigor of these responses may be progressively obscured due to the fact that man's instinctual responses can be "short-circuited" by independent acts of will). The second source—tradition—is, in fact, a *via media* between instinctual response and conscious deliberative value discrimination, because it contains elements of both the elemental, subrational communication characteristic of instinctual awareness ("feeling") and cognitive apprehension. Tradition relates man as a conscious valuing animal (as a moral philosopher, indeed) to his primordial natural status. It renders possible a compatibility between man's intellectual grasp of values and his instinctual responses. In this sense, tradition is a monitor of our conscious acts of valuation, it provides a unique insight into more rudimentary and non-cognitive foundations of value.

Tradition and Specific Values

But tradition is not, I think, a repository of specific values, at least in the sense that it is not a progressive unveiling of those articulated "values" or "moral principles" or "ethical verities" that we associate with consciously constructed value systems. That tradition may comprehensively project the "Good" in the precise sense employed by G. E. Moore is an interesting possibility and, in any event, our awareness of tradition as a form of transmission of knowledge may certainly be non-cognitive. Again, we both feel *and* perceive tradition; it links the particularities of the two other modes of value apprehension. Tradition invokes the rudimentary moral

order that is at once the natural order and relates these consciously indeterminate ethical commands with the value-actualizations that emerge from a specific cultural experience. Such a synthesis is not, I believe, morally imperative—by that I mean that tradition is more ethically suggestive than it is mandatory. Viewed from another perspective, the defense of a moral axiom on grounds of tradition is "second-best evidence"—the best evidence is the noetic justification. Indeed, there is a hierarchical relationship between "instinct," "tradition," and noetic judgment. The first is the most universal, undifferentiated, and behaviorally obligatory; the second represents the impact of the particularities and novelties of human culture upon the first; the third represents man's discrete ethical potentiality, less universal and less mechanistically compelling, but revealing the creative possibilities inherent in human reason and being more expressly pertinent to human value resolution. Man's ethical life involves all three elements, but his immediate life is dominated by the quality of his reason, the ethical choices he consciously makes, hopefully the creative extension of the intimations of instinct and tradition. Tradition is synthetic, historically and ontologically; we add to it by the wisdom of our present decisions and acts. We can also obscure and depress it by temporary aberrations and hubristic insensitivities. But we are never totally free of its influences, if only for the reason that we are never wholly liberated from those natural configurations that, in part, comprise it.

The immediate effect of tradition is "conservative." Its influence tends to both conserve the social continuities that it itself projects and to restrain the range of social options thought to be acceptable by offering an implicit definition of cultural tolerability. Tradition makes the sense of community possible because it invests a form of significant knowledge in those members of the community who might not be equipped to make ethical judgments on a purely noetic basis. Tradition alone makes the idea of popular government intellectually respectable—without it there is no really rational defense against the claim of the intellectually superior to rule by fiat. Of course, traditional wisdom by itself is likely an inadequate basis for social leadership, as it is not, by itself, an adequate basis for moral judgment. But traditional knowledge makes participation in the ethical and political life of the community at once possible and desirable. It provides a brake—far better than the paper checks of constitutions—on the despotic exercise of power. It provides, as well, the firmest available base for law, superior to either the declaration of transcendentally delivered statutes or to some shifting "consensus."

It is popular in our times to deride tradition. We like to think that we are emancipated from it. This really means that we are convinced that the recognition of tradition, the entertainment of its knowledge, will inhibit our desires, will constrict the free play of our egos. This is correct in a sense, since tradition reinforces the primacy of community over individual self-interest, but the anti-traditionalist thesis is founded on an erroneous psychology: the assumption that the sublimation of the self occurs in defiance of the social paradigms implied by tradition. The reverse is true. The attainment of self-realization involves *participation*, participation in the natural order, participation in the cultural-social paradigms. Traditional knowledge offers a means of relating self to existence beyond the requirements of physical appetition; it provides a guide to vital participation.

Tradition, I repeat, is not the only knowledge, but it is an immensely formidable variety.

The significance of tradition is also denigrated because of the frequently spurious modes of its defense by self-announced "traditionalists" who are, in fact, special pleaders of one type or another who wish to use the venerable word "tradition" to lend authority to their conventional preferences. Put another way, these pseudo-traditionalists are guilty of "over-selling" tradition by giving it a particularity, an express social mandate, that it does not possess. For example: it is highly doubtful that the cultural traditions of Western man reveal any explicit recommendations regarding the conformation of political institutions. I see, historically, no valid "traditional" defense of legislative supremacy, separation of powers, majority rule, separation of church and state, proportional representation, and so on, ad infinitum. The desirability of these and other political arrangements may well involve some appeal to traditional knowledge as a basis for judgment, but the "Western" or even "American" experience does not vouchsafe so precise a disclosure of traditional wisdom so as to allow us to insist, prima facie, on one or another form of political institution. Institutions and practices of a political nature are rarely creatures of "prescription." To defend them, not on the grounds of social efficacy, but by an appeal to tradition is not only rationally discreditable, but also does a disservice to the real importance of tradition. An appeal to tradition does not, per se, really settle immediate social issues. Consider private property as an illustration. A very persuasive case can be made for the retention of private property on the grounds that it represents a traditional mandate. It may conceivably even be a natural paradigm that it would be aberrational to tamper with. Traditional wisdom would seem to support strongly private property as a persistent historical pattern. But the argument is not conclusive, only highly suggestive. Some cultures have not featured this institution and yet have not disintegrated thereby nor lost their regard for more elemental human values. It may be that private property is best defended, within our cultural framework, on broadly utilitarian grounds, denying it a "prescriptive" justification. I am not attempting to resolve the question; on the contrary, I am trying to show the difficulty in transposing traditional wisdom into specific recommendations on immediate social questions.

It may well be that tradition is not only fundamentally subrational, but that its phenomenal articulations in a culture are almost wholly symbolic or mythic, in contrast to being discursive, Perhaps tradition is essentially conveyed, transtemporally, by art and ritual, in contrast to philosophy and social theory. Perhaps we can see in art and in the central cultural myths those patterns and motifs that configure history and convince us that there is intelligibility in the human experience, that there is a "great chain of being" after all.

The traditionalist is thus open not only to the instruction of history, but to an expansive range of transmissions wherein the wisdom of accumulated experience might lie. He dare not have an insular outlook or one predicated on some neo-gnostic exclusiveness. He is open to experience, because he believes experience to reflect more than the spontaneous interaction of forces; in experience he sees order and purpose and an explanation for the peculiarities of his private existence. Regardless of his ultimate metaphysical convictions, the traditionalist sees in tradition a sort of eschatology after all: that there is a significance to human life beyond immediate sensation, an on-going natural economy to which he belongs, contributes, and shares.

Gerhart Niemeyer

Beyond "Democratic Disorder"

VOL. 16, NO. 2, 1981

The title of this essay suggests that a political form, democracy, might be to blame for our current crisis. I submit that no political form is that important. Forms are secondary in politics, capable of helping or hindering, but they are not at the core of political destiny. If we feel like blaming our present decline on democracy as such, let us remember the Swiss, a living historical example assuring us that democracy is fully compatible with a strong sense of purpose and vigorous action when needed. What we now call "democratic disorder" is precisely an absence of purpose, a faltering sense of reality, a shrinking from vigorous action, a failure of nerve. One should look deeper than mere form to discover the sources of such ailments.

Let me suggest that we are observing an advanced state of dissolution of our cultural patrimony, which is Christian. We are a Christian society, a fact that has little to do with the number of faithful and active Christians in our midst, but rather with the foundation of our culture. Western civilization came into existence through the unifying impulse of Latin Christianity. No other religion has ever wielded a similarly powerful influence in the centuries of our existence. The historical metamorphoses of our culture can be understood only in their relations to the Christian origins, even though not all these mutations have worked in favor of Christianity. Modernity, indeed, has been a great movement disparaging and attacking both the Christian Church and its faith. In the course of this movement much of Western life was profanized, meaning that God and the sacred were driven out to the point of disappearance. To a larger extent, though, modernity brought about processes of secularization which, in the act of perverting, maintained Christian modes of thinking and living.[1] Marxism, whose vision of a socialist future is an "immanentization of the Christian eschaton," could not have been spawned in a non-Christian culture. Indeed, all modern ideologies are perverted, secularized varieties of the Christian message of salvation, and the vision of man's transfiguration. Well they may assert the certainties of science in their analysis and prediction, but they require faith all the same, in their case, faith in history, in the Revolution, in psychoanalysis, in collective economics, in the Party: faith grievously misplaced but faith nevertheless.

No need to dwell on the pseudo-religious quality of modern ideologies, which has been sufficiently belabored and is now accepted as correct analysis. Not all of our modern culture consists of ideologies. The ideologies have come to overshadow everything else because, and in so far as, they are organized, armed, and wield a huge club of terroristic power. Still, much of contemporary life, particularly outside of the metropolis, goes on under the peaceful ordering of Christian consciousness. Even when one visits a country in plain political turmoil and economic disarray, like Italy, one is astonished to find the family largely intact. That kind of discovery is by no means confined to Italy. In many parts the tradition of our culture continues, and not merely as a sectarian backwater.

Now, between the ideologies and the tradition no peace is possible. A deep hostility stems not merely from the ideologist's disparagement of piety, Christian dogma, and the transcendence. This is not a contemporary version of the religious conflicts of the sixteenth and seventeenth centuries. Irreconcilable hostility rather is caused by the ideologists' total subversion of the practical order of politics, rooting in their false image of man, their presumption of certainty about future destiny, their quest for total power, their principled polarization of all humans. Thus, wherever ideologies organize and arm themselves for action, the gulf of latent warfare opens between them and the tradition, and ideologists have not been able to close that gulf when they established themselves in the place of a people's government. In Russia, Spain, Yugoslavia, open war did erupt, and that remains a possibility in almost all other Western countries, in the presence of armed ideologies.

If other countries have managed to escape civil war until now, it is because of the existence of a third element, an urbanized middle class committed to neither the Christian tradition nor the ideologies, and occupying most leading positions in society. One may describe them as a class of profanized people. They have rejected the Christian assumption of man's fallen nature and thus have little or no sense of the reality of evil. Conversely they feel no need for God's salvation and manage to put their whole trust in efforts of human enlightenment, which must be called their ultimate hope. For about two hundred years these people have lived on the leftovers of Christian moral capital. They kept the concept of the human soul, using it without visible embarrassment. They spoke easily of human dignity, without being very clear about what it is that dignifies even the lowest and least intelligent man. The equality of men as creatures made in God's image, as well as all alike being sinners, became in their minds a postulate of equality *tout court*. Human freedom, the outreach of consciousness as it overflowed any intended object and also marveled at its own thinking, as well as the freedom of faith-formed-by-love, assured by the evidence of "God's humility," was turned into a limitless ambition for human power. For a while love was still seen as "the greatest" of the excellences, even though it took the disguise of "altruism." Men continued to call each other brothers even while having little use for a common father. Victorian civilization managed to instill considerable residual moral strength into a largely profanized Christian milieu.

Today the leading elements of our culture have come to the end of their tether. This is what we mean when speaking of "democratic disorder." The Christian capital has been used up in the hearts and minds of those who have discarded its regenerating faith. The Enlightenment's vision of a brave new world is known to have been a Fata Morgana. When once there seemed to be something of great promise, there now is nothing. And thus the deepest convictions, long held over as souvenirs of an erstwhile Christian faith, go limp and drop to the ground, like so many worn-through rags. Our judges, even when imposing punishment, often are unsure of its meaning and justification, and frequently doubt whether what is called evil is not merely an effect of circumstances. Professor Walter Berns reports how, at a meeting of the Advisory Council of the National Institute of Law Enforcement and Criminal Justice, he asked this gathering of eminent men of the law: "Why *not* commit crimes?", a question which no one answered, amidst great embarassment.[2]

We are materially living by an economic system of free enterprise which has generated unprecedented wealth, but our politicians feel a call to play an adversary role toward that system, and dedicate themselves to an expanding system of freely handed-out incomes. Educators, while steadily enlarging their apparatus, lack a vision of purpose. They are largely hostile to the cultural tradition it is their business to transmit, and to the standards of excellence that form the quintessence of education. One can multiply these examples *ad libitum.* In the multiple, they may give an impression of so many unfortunate derailments, each of which may well be "fixed." The full scope of the crisis comes into view only as we look at countless and typical middle-aged men and women engaged in desperate quests for "their identity," "their lifestyles," and "values they will create," "the new person"

they will make out of themselves as they go from one programmed panacea to another: "I'm OK, you're OK," Transcendental Meditation, "est," "touch therapy," "Hare Rama, Hare Krishna," and a multitude of other similar ones. For a day or a week they believe they have been saved from the inner void, only to fall back into it with an ever greater sense of helplessness. Here is the urban educated middle class, in the final stage of profanization which attends the crumbling of the last vestiges of Christian legacy so that no beliefs are left any more.

Western humanity thus falls into three distinct elements: 1) the nihilistic ideologists who, under the sway of History deified, believe in nothing; 2) the urbanized and educated middle class of cultural leaders who know not in what to believe; and 3) those who believe in the God of Christianity. The first element is "the specter haunting Europe" (Marx, *Communist Manifesto),* the last element abide on quiet islands of order, as it were, but the profanized-second element furnishes the leaders of education, the media, the bureaucracy, and the government. In other words, the power of making policies and setting our direction is in the hands of people who are spiritually, intellectually, and morally adrift. This includes many leaders of the younger generation, the thirty- to fifty-year-olds who were still impressionable in the 1960s and came out with their world in ruins.

The lack of conviction of this element does not mean that they are lacking in motives. The motives, however, have shallow roots. Or, to put it in different words, there are motives but no principles. We see an abundance of feelings which are alleged to be capable of serving as reliable guides. Even these feelings still bear the stamp of their Christian origins. Politicians vaunt their "compassion." One need not doubt their sincerity, but the emotion is no longer controlled by understandings of ultimate reality, of human nature, and even of the causal relations between things in this world. Freedom likewise has become a mere emotional aspiration without shape or relevance to order.

Something similar happened to the concept of virtue in ancient Rome: At first it was not any virtuous deed that won the award of glory but only that deed of excellence which served the *salus publica,* the wellbeing and endurance of Rome. Later, after the Punic Wars, there developed that "excessive lust of glory" which craved sensational fame in the eyes of the masses, by deeds that were remarkable without in any way serving Rome, and in some cases even directed against Rome. "Glory" was taken to be identical with "being a celebrity." As virtue in ancient Rome separated itself gradually from the public good, so now freedom has cast loose from order, community, and the Creation. It has become void of any content of value except itself, so that it is experienced in a process of denying, one after another, obligations, limitations, bonds, values, and distinctions. Other motives there are, for instance: perfection (also an adopted child of erstwhile Christian parentage) but now become a brat throwing tantrums in its desire to get, instantly, flawless human institutions, and yelling for a club to go after the parents who are responsible for the flawed ones. And equality is still around, once a humble assumption about the human condition ("we all are in the same boat," "we all alike are sinners," "Christ died to save us all") but now bloated into a domineering, uncompromising imperative, served emotionally rather than rationally, an *ideé fixe* perniciously feeding a more and more universalized discontent.

That discontent, in turn, has none of the dignity of genuine rebellion, in Camus' sense. It manifests itself in a whimpering withholding of affirmation and loyalty, in a bleating "nay" towards everything that can be called existing structure. The unsatisfiable emotional drive for equality, the frustrated demand for perfect human performance, the peacelessness of pursuing unshaped freedom, all induce people to withhold allegiance and respect on the grounds that imperfect institutions of order have no right to exist. "There ought to be something better than our penal system." "Our economy consists of sinful institutions." "Nothing but the absolutely safe car cap satisfy us." With such attitudes we criticize not merely this or that action or practice, but the entire set of institutions, and ultimately deny piety and loyalty to the nation whose history has nourished us. As we feel that the state no longer deserves our prayers, national security appears as a guilty use of power, compulsory service for its defense a public abomination, and any vigorous foreign policy a part of "imperialism." Thus, while we still have the technology, the money, the weapons, the manpower, we are lacking the mind that can relate these means to the nation's purpose among other nations. Our absence of will, our "failure of nerve," are symptoms of the void at the heart of human beings, who, having lost their beliefs, have no firm grasp on reality. In an editorial, "Ronald Reagan?", the *Wall Street Journal* drew this sketch of the situation: "Four years ago, the political system . . . reached outside the mainstream, for a fresh new face. . . . This time the system is reaching for an old face . . . because it then can have some confidence in where he stands. . . . If Mr. Reagan fails, the failure will not be his alone. This week the political news is dominated by an old face speaking an old message. That is an indictment not of Ronald Reagan, but of an entire generation of American political leadership" (July 14, 1980).

II

If the "democratic disorder," then, is properly assessed as stemming from spiritual roots, as a crisis of profanized man and the power he wields in our society, no merely political remedy can avail. New policies, new programs, fewer programs, new parties, even the return of "old men," all these would be tantamount to mere bandaid treatment of a disease of a spiritual core. Our minds are attuned, not to spiritual problems and evaluations, but to political analysis and political recommendations. Our crisis had been rightly diagnosed in terms of the failures of "profanized man" even before 1950. It has been said, that early, that this malady of a spiritual "dead end" requires the cure of a total collapse—not merely what one calls a historical catastrophe, but the kind of collapse that extends into the particular souls of men.

Profanization of life can be transcended only in and through suffering: not any kind of suffering, but the extreme suffering in which even the last possibility of life seems to be lost. The human being who undergoes this kind of suffering may then experience that, as he is falling straight down, apparently into a bottomless abyss, he actually is not dropping into nothingness but rather finds himself being carried.[3] Wilhelm Kamlah, who made this statement, arrived at this insight in the World War II situation. Since then, a philosopher's idea expressed in an academic book has been borne out by the great event of the spiritually regenerative experiences of *zeks* in Soviet

Labor camps. In the extremity of personal and collective annihilation, men like Solzhenitsyn discovered the divine reality, without help from dogma or *kerygma*. The community of this experience—or rather, of experiences in forms of a variety of religions—shines forth in the title of a witnessing book: *From Under the Rubble.* A number of different individuals, with varying backgrounds, describe the movement of healing from the disorder of a profanized existence, and the resulting emergence "into history." So far, the Soviet Union seems to be the only place where that movement has occurred on a significantly large scale, even though its testimony has stirred the souls of Czechs, Poles, and Hungarians with great power.

It is a fact which we must duly note that Western publics have had great difficulty with Solzhenitsyn's report and, even more, with the inferences he has drawn from this event (the "event" not being confined to the one Solzhenitsyn but to a great number of Russian *zeks*). His conclusion, in his *Letter to the Soviet Leaders,* that "Christianity is the sole alternative," is a statement of clinical precision. Western leaders, even those of the profanized type, seemed willing to accept that much, even though they immediately placed Solzhenitsyn in the pigeonhole of a "romantic reactionary." What they could not forgive him, however, was his criticism of the West, particularly as expressed in his Harvard Commencement Speech. Yet, Solzhenitsyn neither rejects the West as an ally nor turns against it in hostility. His criticism is confined to manifestations of disorder which diminish the West's effectiveness in the common fight. Western leading countries, after all, have not undergone an experience of healing suffering comparable to that of the Gulag *zeks*. Solzhenitsyn is far from recommending that we seek such suffering. The early church discovered and taught the truth that suffering must not be sought but merely patiently endured when it comes. All the same, the United States has not been defeated, occupied, subjected to starvation and to systematic public falsehood. Its citizens have not lived together in situations where both physical and moral existence trembled on the edge of the abyss.

I believe that Solzhenitsyn's critique of the West is correct, that his is a friendly criticism 180 degrees different from his criticism of the Soviet regime. What is more, his complaint about our shortcomings does apply to the entire West. Some experience comparable to that of the *zeks* might have been had in Germany, where in fact it did occur, but only in desperately few and isolated cases which did not give rise to a movement, as in Russia. Rather the broader healing effect of these experiences was blocked by the desperate endeavor of most people for personal justification in the face of the collective odium of Nazi guilt falling on Germany.

All this really constitutes an excursus about a question that must concern all who reflect on the problem "Beyond Democratic Disorder." There is, indeed, such a "beyond," but accessible only by a strait gate and narrow way. The wide gate and broad way of conventional politics allows of no hope except that of temporary palliatives. Actually, this is not a new insight. Ever since Augustine's *City of God* Western man has been aware that government, public policy, and administration cannot offer human salvation. That, however, does not mean that the differences between better and worse government deserve to be slighted or despised. They are important, albeit within the limits of politics in the wider range of human existence. It is not only fitting, then, but

necessary that we turn to the practical possibilities available to a government consisting not of profanized men, but of persons living in the Christian tradition, even though their hold on it may be tenuous. What can they do? What criteria of order are available to them?

III

One first thinks of *principles,* chiefly because the profanized man is unable to muster any consistency of principle, as he is largely swayed by emotions. Our judicial system, above all its penal code, are badly in need of some restoration of principles. We need a renewal of the principle of punishment, and a new will to discover principles in the face of abortion, sexual libertinism, and drugs. Our foreign policy requires an acknowledgement of principle with regard to communism, and the Soviet Union in particular. The particular problem we face here is that of a selective moralism which singles out the Soviet Union, from all other countries, for special condemnation, and thus poses the question of morality in foreign policy in a new way.[4] Principle in foreign policy serves as a criterion to distinguish between impermissible compromises which would destroy moral substance, and permissible negotiations which leave the moral code intact. On the other hand, a universal fusion of moral principle with foreign policy in the Carter style of "support for human rights" must be avoided because of its utopianism, tendency to imperialism, and the likelihood of resulting Quixotic policies.[5] On the other hand the policies of ideological and millenarian parties claim to be principled, and are indeed principled in their own way, but the principles themselves are fallacious and irrational. More about this later.

Secondly, a government of persons rooted in the Christian tradition should be capable of more *realism* than profanized men can attain. An editorial in the *Washington Star* on the death of William J. Baroody characterized him as a "profoundly religious man," but continued: "At the same time, this man of values a good many people find old-fashioned if not downright anachronistic, had an extraordinarily cool and discerning eye for trends. . . . Mr. Baroody maneuvered AEI front and center to a position where it is financed by leading foundations and respected by old opponents as well as by a widening—and bipartisan—circle of new friends." (July 31, 1980) The "realism" of tradition-anchored people may manifest itself in a concern for a preservation of structures, political, economic, and cultural. In that perspective, contemporary politics falls into the dichotomy between doctrinaire activism, basically rebellious, and the politics of structure, governed not merely by "piety" in the ancient Roman sense but also by a clear assessment of "real possibilities."

The contrasting concern of doctrinaire activists is rather with "possible realities." As one looks at the politics of structure from the point of view of principle, one may find it frequently unprincipled, because it does what is expedient for the structures rather than what is required by doctrine. All the same the concern for structure is essentially a "long view" toward principle. A masterly analysis of a politician of structure is contained in Eugene Davidson's *The Making of Adolf Hitler* (New York, 1977). General von Seeckt, the commanding officer of the Reichswehr in the first decade of the Weimar Republic, was a man of monarchical principle. He made up his mind, however, to serve with utmost loyalty any viable government that would be produced by the leftist policies of the postwar years and to disregard his own principles, so that his support might serve to preserve the existence of Germany as a political entity. One might call this a case of principled abandonment of principle.

In today's world a politics of structure finds itself beset with enemies who have exclusive use of slogans of utopian perfection. A traditionalist government must not remain silent under this kind of attack. It must counter with steady and principled *praise for the structures* it protects, as well as for the principle of piecemeal reform as distinct from wholesale destruction. In doing so, there is some danger of confusion regarding that which is to be defended. At least four different structures need to be distinguished:

a) a system of capitalist production and distribution, with its attendant legal framework of private property rights, a system which also produces the power of corporations and financiers;

b) A system of rapidly advancing technology which entails the increasing dependence of all persons on complex networks of technical operations, and requires much subordination of the personal element to impersonal functions; this system is as characteristic of socialism as it is of capitalism;

c) An individualist culture prone to insist on "my thing," "my values," "my lifestyle"—all anarchistic notions denying not merely authority but also larger community;

d) A system of democratic diffusion of power, with its attendant need to make a success of complex procedures designed to produce decisions out of a multiplicity of wills and interests.

Each of these structural systems tends toward its own kind of evil. Contemporary politics inclines to seize on these evils, universalizing them into a "total critique," or global condemnation, under the formula that evil is "systemic." The truth is that evil, in this as in every other situation, roots in the human heart, and that each system tends to magnify and manifest human evil in its own way. A government committed to the protection of structures must not on account of that commitment excuse itself from counteracting those by-products of the system that have come to threaten both community and individual lives. The cultivation of power is surely a legitimate function of government, but in practicing it one must not turn one's back on goodness.

Thirdly, in Western countries the cause of freedom ranks high, possibly highest, among priorities. To this extent, an ideological element is mixed into all Western politics. For freedom, as we have just seen, can be an instrument of anarchical dissolution of society into millions of atoms. On the other hand, it can also nourish a vision of man as a conqueror of nature, or of his own past, and as an omnipotent builder of a blissful future. The latter is the vision of revolutionary humanism and the source of energy for doctrinaire politics. Freedom, as Burke already observed, can be a heady brew. A government of tradition-rooted people must aim to discern ordered freedom from its demonically destructive perversion. There is no getting around the fact that the human quest for freedom involves always man's relation with his Creator, a relation capable of taking the path of faith formed by love, as well as the path of metaphysical revolution resulting in demonic nothingness. Thus beyond all political solutions there is always the need of man for attaining freedom in his own heart, as he wrestles with the forces of corruption within him and looks for the redemption available to him.

On the other hand, freedom today is no longer seen, as it once was, merely as freedom of "society" from the "state." That kind of freedom is still not forgotten where the regime is totalitarian. "What's happening in Poland can be best described as a renaissance of civil society. All the main social and professional groups are following the workers who won a right to organize independent unions."[6] In the industrialized countries of the West, however, the issue frequently is seen as freedom within society, i.e., within non-governmental economic and social structures. The slogans in vogue are quite individualistic, but one may surmise that underneath there is a desire for the protection of, and respect for, patterns of habits, traditional relationships, i.e., values which each person, effortlessly sharing with others, tends to regard peculiarly his own. From the Enlightenment we derived the contempt for what Burke called "prejudices," the order of habitual judgments constituting man's "second nature." Thomas Aquinas insisted that laws should be "just, possible to nature, according to the customs of the country, adapted to time and place." He added that laws should be changed only with great care, for "when a law is changed, the binding power of law is diminished, as far as custom is concerned." The individualistic rhetoric of the Right might therefore benefit by a period of benevolent neglect, as government focuses its concern on the way in which people habitually live in groups and secondary structures.

Thus freedom to move within the easy yoke of habits must be defended today against two threats: a) the armed violence of doctrinaire politics which destroys all habits in favor of the Party's total organization, and b) the overbearing disposition of compassionate governments to overlay habits with ubiquitous regulations and thus to narrow freedom by a multitude of irritating small reins. As one seeks to stop this tendency one need not defend prevailing habits as morally flawless. Their good consists to a large extent in that they are the people's own. One is reminded that after the fall of Napoleon's brother Joseph, who as king of Spain had set up a very enlightened and modern government, the people welcomed their own king at the border. Ferdinand VII, a monster on the throne if ever there was one, was pulled across the border by the people who had put themselves into the horses' harness, welcoming their own bad man as "*El Deseado*," the "desired one." We should allow ourselves to be taught by this and other historical examples that freedom is not always identical with letter-perfect procedures of election, legislation, and administration. If a society is felt by its members to "fit like a glove," it means that its people move in it with a sense of freedom, no matter what the conditions may be in our eyes.

Finally, a government that is returned to power as the hope for a radically new course of events should aim above all for *sobriety*. It is true that the two alternatives, liberalism/socialism on the one side, and traditionalist conservatism on the other, are political currents pointing in opposite directions, like rivers at a watershed. In the long run they will result in types of social order utterly incompatible with each other. Precisely for this reason,

both sides have somewhat the air of a crusade, with fanfares of a "final battle" being heard in the background. Peregrine Worsthorne showed us, ten years ago, that no Labour Party will ever be able to muster the power required to bring about the changes it projects, given the politics of a modern democratic state. He spoke of the 1968 Wilson government in England, but what he said also applies to an American or German conservative administration. The crusading spirit remains confined to words: it has no ability to translate itself into a spirit of sacrifice and unquestioning loyalty sufficient to brave the heavy storms of systemic change. One can therefore say with some confidence that the return to power of a conservative government will be no earthshaking event, just as little as will be the return of a social-democratic party. In our days, the only earth-shaking event that is an ever-present possibility is a Communist takeover.

Conservatives aspiring to power thus should avoid the rhetoric of ultimates. Ronald Reagan made a great mistake in repeatedly using Tom Paine's phrase about the power we have "to make the world anew." A similar mistake is to recall John Winthrop's myth of "the city shining on a hill." The mention of "enduring peace" reflects a millennarian mentality, and the word "aggression" belongs to the same group of concepts, all hatched in the heady days of League of Nations enthusiasm. These are manifestations of utopian enthusiasm, which entails a refusal of sobriety, and that in an age that needs sobriety as much as its daily bread. All the same, it is true that Western civilization stands at a political watershed and must choose whether it wants to go in one or the other of opposite directions. Since it can have no power, thought to wheel on its heels in a sudden resolve, it must content itself with gradual, piecemeal, and hardly noticeable change. Meanwhile, a government must appeal to its citizens in terms of competence, realism, sobriety, and personal character. Rather than whipping up enthusiasm, it must seek to bring calm to agitated souls. In the language of Camus, it must restore a sense of limits. Its rhetoric must endeavor to make the limits plausible. The most terrifying limit, of course, is a government's inability to bring about a resolution of the spiritual crisis, which also dictates the modest amount of political power it can mobilize apart from war, and maybe even in the presence of war. And we, the intellectuals among citizens, must learn to control our own yearnings for a "new world," as we learn to live in the one we inhabit, affirming our own history and the "real possibilities" it offers.

Notes

1. On the distinction of profanization and secularization cf. Wilhelm Kamlah, *Christentum und Geschichtlichkeit* (Stuttgart, 1951), 19.
2. *Modern Age,* vol. 24, no. 1, Winter 1980, 20.
3. *Der Mensch in der Profanität* (Stuttgart, 1949), n. 18.
4. Cf. my "Foreign Policy and Morality," *Intercollegiate Review*, Spring 1980, 77–84.
5. Cf. my "Freedom and Rights: What Is To Be Done," *Review of Politics*, vol. 40, no. 2, April 1978, 183–95.
6. "Poland's Right to Life," *Wall Street Journal*, Dec. 17, 1980.

Frederick D. Wilhelmsen

Technology and Its Consequences

VOL. 28, NO. 1, 1992

For the pagan Martin Heidegger it is at least arguable that modern technology, itself the product of Western genius, presages the end of Western civilization. For the Catholic Gabriel Marcel, the pathos of modern man consists in his standing against and being powerless before the juggernaut of contemporary technics. *Man Against Mass Society* is the title of one of his most powerful works. The French peasant philosopher Gustaf Thibon raised the banner of the France of five hundred cheeses against the homogenization of culture, the flattening out of all differences that is seemingly intrinsic to the monolithic mechanization of life produced by a mindless technology respecting neither cultural differences nor the richness and density of a life lived close to the rhythms of a nature increasingly obliterated by the machine.

Yet to a philosopher the subject of technics must be approached, at least initially, with neither pessimism nor optimism, without any apocalyptic foreboding or futuristic adulation, but rather as a dimension of human existence without which we would be reduced to living in caves or huddled in the ruts left along the roadside by men who had forgotten the use of the wheel.

In this as in so many fundamental issues, Aristotle can be our guide, at least for a time. Man is a *homo faber,* a "making" man, and this definition follows from his nature as a rational animal. His technological vocation is attested to by his very body—arms and hands, legs and feet pertaining to a being who walks upright and not on all fours. These extensions of the human body are themselves not only an invitation to a technological destiny but without them men would perish. Physically, man was built by God to master his world, hands and arms to the pottery he fashions and legs to the plow he pushes.

The elucidation of the nature of technology is complicated by an ambiguity inscribed in human life. Art or technics is "the exact determination of things to be made," *recta ratio factabilium* in St. Thomas's translation. The ethical order, governed by the virtue of prudence, is the proper application of the moral law to the concrete circumstances in which a man finds himself. From these basic truths we can draw two very general and overarching conclusions. The end of prudential activity is the good of man while the end of artistic activity is the good of the thing to be made. I cannot build a bridge with my moral probity nor can my ability to build that bridge help me in any moral decision as to the wrongness or rightness of some moral act proposed for my consideration. The moral order points to man's goodness and the artistic order points to the perfection of things that are made or produced. We perforce must ask ourselves: what hierarchy ought to be established in the relationships between technics, art, and prudence, intelligent morality?

Aristotle's solution, followed and expanded upon with delicacy by St. Thomas Aquinas, runs somewhat as follows. The good of art within the exercise of an artistic habit or skill is the good of the thing to be produced. The artistic habit runs clean from the artist's intention or "idea" of what he wants to make, to the thing crafted by him into being. But moral habits, especially as orchestrated by the virtue of prudence, move toward man's own goodness, toward *his* perfection and not the perfection of the thing he makes. We all know the proverbial tale about the romantic sculptor, always tubercular and ensconced in a Paris attic, who ruins his health for the sake of his art. We sense, even without Aristotle, that there is something basically wrong about such a waste of human life. The statue of a man is not worth the man.

From this there emerges a tension explored by Jacques Maritain early in his career in *Art and Scholasticism.* Morality cannot dictate to art from within art itself. When morality tries to do so art is botched: you cannot write a good poem or build a house with good intentions. Intrinsically considered, looked at formally, art has nothing to do with

morality. Nonetheless, moral activity concerns man's proper good as a moral agent in the world. It follows that we must establish here a hierarchy nuanced in its applications. Morals cannot dictate to art from within art itself, but art is externally subordinate to morals. Ethics, morals— in a word, politics (which is an extension of ethics)—ought to dominate art for the good of man. Let man the moral agent say to man the artist and technician: make or do not make; produce or do not produce. But once the green light has been given, art comes into its own and from that point on everything the artist does is subordinated to the good of what he makes.

THESE FUNDAMENTAL principles were enunciated in the West by Aristotle and were commented on extensively by Aquinas and others. By a curious historical irony these judgments, often granted theoretical truth, were ignored in practice. The West had all the theoretical principles it needed in order to control the growth of technology but simply chose to ignore its own teachings. Interestingly enough, medieval China, after discovering gun powder some centuries before the West, banned its use on the highly moral grounds that extensive use of gun powder would destroy Chinese culture. Their rulers opted for the good of the culture over its potential technological progress.

In the West, the control of art by morality tended to narrow to issues concerning the fine arts: i.e., the prohibition of pornographic literature, the depiction of nudity, and issues of this nature. But this was only a pimple on the face of the body politic. The larger issues concerning technology and culture were left untouched. There were some exceptions, however. In sixteenth-century England,

King Charles I forbade the introduction of a number of technological innovations on the grounds that they threw men out of jobs; they "worked to the detriment of the poorest of our subjects." This admirable effort to limit technology in the name of the common good soon ended on the block where Cromwell and the other "godded men" beheaded the King. Charles has been symbolically beheaded ever since by Whiggery and the dreary world it ushered into existence. Only as a consequence of the advent of nuclear power, and with it the possibility of finishing off the human race (or at least civilization itself) and thereby reducing mankind to grubbing off roots in a soil already ruined by radioactivity, has Western man turned to the very possibility of realizing Aristotle's project of controlling technology for the good of its maker, man.

The advent of machine technology in Western Europe and subsequently in the rest of the world points to two kinds of technics governed each by its respective internal principles. Karl Marx called them "unrationalized" and "rationalized" work. The description is not altogether bad. By non-rationalized work we mean the technics man develops in such fashion that his artistry and craftsmanship works *with* rhythms, tendencies, and structures already found in nature. As a very simple example, I might evidence the skill of pipemakers in Denmark and Calabria, who work with the grain of the woods to sculpt into existence splendid pipes for the pleasure of the men who heft and smoke them. The wood is altered and put to man's service, but it is altered following the grain of materials already present in the trees and roots from which pipemakers extract natural being soon to be fashioned into artefacted being. To take another, more significant example, we might think of how a sailing vessel uses the winds to move over a body of water and how, when these winds are contrary, the ship tacks or zigzags against them in order to bend the wind to the will of man. A steam or motor vessel, both admirable instances of "rationalized" technology, simply pushes against the wind when it blows from forward and comes into port not working with, but against, nature.

IS THERE anything particularly good or evil about this? The obvious answer is no. The difference here is ontological, not moral. Non-rationalized technics works with the finalities of nature whereas rationalized machine production works against these finalities. The former is a kind of marriage, often a seduction by man of nature. The latter is an act of violence. Yet, it would be absurd romanticism to consider this violence necessarily evil.

After all, what is violence? Romano Guardini in his remarkable little book *The End of the Modern World,* which was followed by an even smaller volume *Power and Responsibility,* developed an ontology of power. Power, according to Guardini, always implies personhood, and hence, responsibility. Mere force or violence, on the contrary, involves some one thing's frustrating the natural end of something else. If a tree falls on my head and I sustain a concussion, the natural tendency of my brain is violated. If I chop down a tree, its natural tendency to continue to grow is violated. Force and violence are interchangeable terms. Violence can be a good in the service of man or violence can be an impersonal force without any moral connotations; or violence can be evil when exercised by human power against man's dignity. The policeman's billy club and pistol are crafted out of nature which is thus "violated," but they are aimed specifically at preventing wrongdoing, social violence, on the body politic. We need the cop on the block, and he had better have the force necessary to preserve public order and peace.

When Genesis says that God willed man to be master over the world, He willed man to exercise the violence needed in order to bend nature to his will.

But the introduction of mechanization to the West added a new dimension to these somewhat elementary principles. Until the Renaissance, Western Christendom was dominated by an ideal of science that went back to Aristotle and the Greek world in which he lived. *Episteme*, science in the Greek philosophical sense of the term, was thought to be fulfilled at its highest in man's contemplative understanding of the world and of its order. Speculative or disinterested contemplation marked the development of intellect at its best. Practical or useful knowledge was indispensable for the maintenance of life, but it was understood to be in the service of philosophical contemplation. Something of a shift occurred within medieval Christendom when the primacy of charity everywhere was insisted on by Christian doctors. But contemplation still remained the ideal: principally, the contemplation of God, and secondarily, the contemplation of His creation. Practical knowledge was praised for what it was, more so than in pagan antiquity (had not the Son of God been a carpenter?), but it played second fiddle.

SOMETHING, THOUGH, happened in the Renaissance. Man's scientific ideal shifted from an understanding of being, to power over it. Even today, scholars are puzzled over the origins of this shift. I sensed it powerfully some years ago in the main *piazza* of Florence, where a new world was born late in the fourteenth century, but I am hard put to express that sentiment of mine in rational terms. Some say that the new ideal was Eastern and was prefigured by the Persian tale of Aladdin and his lamp: rub the lamp and your heart's desires will be magically materialized into existence. Certainly, this epochal change had something to do with the recrudescence of magic during the Renaissance. All magic aims at power over reality, achieved by reading the future in the stars or the cards or by the evocation of signs that bewitch into being what they signify. We need only think of the voodoo doll representing the enemy, pierced by a pin through its heart that results in the death of the hated person; or, more innocently, of a Navajo rain dance that, when performed, produces the rain it signifies. Magic was suppressed during the Middle Ages by both the spiritual and the temporal powers but it surged back with a vengeance during the Renaissance. Even great pioneers in science such as Copernicus drew astrological charts for their aristocratic masters, and the famous General Wallenstein would not engage his Protestant enemies in battle unless the signs of his chart were favorable. The desire, the *eros*, of Western man shifted from a passion to understand to a passion to control. Knowledge is Power, wrote Francis Bacon.

Bacon also fingered the weakness in the new hermetical magical tradition. Magic cannot deliver the goods it promises. I do not oppose magic because of what it aims at achieving, but I oppose it because it usually fails! But the New Science is able to deliver the goods promised by magic. It yields power over the real.

WHAT WAS this New Science? Basically, it consisted in the application of mathematical methods of abstracting and reasoning to physical nature—thus was born Mathematical Physics. Mathematics deals with reality as quantified, quantities are repeatable, the repeatable is predictable, the predictable is controllable. Mathematize nature and you will master it, was the motto, and René Descartes, the founder of modern philosophy, was a preeminent exponent and practitioner of this New Science that would soon dominate Western man. All modern science—to the degree to which it is genuinely modern—advances by mathematizing the physical world for the purpose of mastering it. First, the new science was applied to physics and its child, mechanics; later, to chemistry; now, to biochemistry. In modern physics, Albert Einstein summed up material reality in one concise mathematical formula about matter and energy. The application of mathematical principles to the world around us very soon opened up dizzying possibilities as Western man, in effect, turned himself into a demiurge. This science is often called "demiurgical science" after that quasi-god spoken of by Plato who descended to a world of chaos in order to fashion it anew.

Technical mastery over the real follows on a dialectic of estrangement from things as they are. This dialectic exacts its price: alienation from reality, the suppression of nature, the removal of man from the springs of piety, the destruction of reverence. Nature in our larger cities is fenced off in parks and preserved against the ravages of a technology that everywhere else threatens the countryside, leveling it with bulldozers, spreading it over with concrete, pulling down fruit orchards, setting up antennae, destroying settled communities and bringing in the restlessness of the factory, the anonymity of the suburbs, the drab uniformity of housing projects, the cheapness and arrogance of a way of life that leaves in its wake junkyards full of last year's machinery, now twisted, rusting under an empty sky, discarded in favor of this year's special model for raping existence. Venerable trades passed on from father to son through generations simply cease to be, and, in the United States at least, the family farm—praised from Cicero to Pius XII as the seedplot of virtue—is no longer beleaguered: it no longer is.

The mechanization and standardization of civilization has undoubtedly brought with it many benefits: better medicine and a longer life for the majority; cheaper prices; a more comfortable life for a greater number of people. These benefits cannot be denied, but they have been bought by a flattening of society, a continuing destruction of diversity, a withering away of the freedom of the man who once lived on his own, free. Today not five percent of our American population lives and makes its living on land owned by themselves. (What this has done to man's religious sensibility is an issue I will not dwell upon in this essay. But the effects have been enormous.)

Mechanization and industrialization were the products of the mathematizing of nature, as suggested. Machine technology, in turn, lives on violence. There is nothing more violent than the workings of an internal combustion engine. Ask any mechanic.

But the history of modern technics today reveals something new, the advent of an electronic technology that has little in common with the older machine order. Perhaps I can illustrate this by pointing out that most histories of science are duped by analogies drawn from the theory of evolution, which is basically a biological explanation. Given that men do develop from embryos to fully mature specimens of the race, given that comparable developments are observable in the whole animal order, Darwin and others insisted that all life and indeed all reality is evolutionary. But these scientists tended to restrict life to organic life. They overlooked spiritual or rational life. Their biological model simply does not work when we study the history of Western technology, a work of the human spirit. Happenstance discoveries burst into new worlds. Almost absent-minded observations turn the world upside down. The history of science and technology is *not* evolutionary. If by evolution we mean the actualization of potencies pre-existent in the past, then we can discover only internal and partial evolutions, for example, the Ford Model-T into the Model-A and the Model-A into the V-8 and beyond. This is an analytic differentiation by the genius of man into what is already given him, already there before his hands and mind. He spots new possibilities in potencies latent in the machinery known to him and he develops, "evolves" them into better models of the same.

GOOD ENOUGH: but what, let us say, about the leap from sail power to motor power in maritime transportation? You can contemplate the essence of sails from now to eternity and you will never discover implicitly therein the principle of the internal combustion engine. Fulton's discovery (if it was indeed his) was not a discovery but an invention, an *in-venire*. There was no "movement" or "progress" or "evolution" from sail power to motor power. Rather, there was a leap in being achieved by human reason. Aristotle teaches us that movement involves a common potentiality between the two terms of the movement. Here there is none—

simply a brand-new breakthrough due to the genius of the man who hit upon the principle of the piston-driven engine. The history of technology is not evolutionary. Expressing myself more modestly, we can discover progress or evolution *within* one given technology, as suggested, but the movement from one technology to another is not really a movement at all. It is the appearance of something brand new thanks to man's genius.

The telegraph in the mid-nineteenth century did not mark an advance in the dominant machine technology. It was rather an invasion of a brand new technological principle that was to feed upon—and it still does—the older mechanized order, but which effectively cuts through it and renders it obsolete in many ways. Permit me to posit a rather elementary example. In all older technologies, mechanical or not, I go from one place to another; I traverse a "space." I do so whether I walk, whether I ride a horse or mount a buggy, sit in an automobile, whether I get on a train or an airplane. Space is traversed—slowly or rapidly. But when I make a phone call from Dallas to New York, space is totally bypassed. Space is not annihilated or destroyed, but rendered obsolete, unimportant. My example is significant because it indicates that the new electronic technology does not violate nature, does not feed off nature, except in the obvious sense that the "hardware" comes from nature. The new technics, understood formally, simply ignores nature. Old Marshall McLuhan used to say that man today approaches—but never achieves—the status of the angels. According to Dr. McLuhan, the most important intellectual work to be studied today is St. Thomas's *De Spiritualibus Creaturis*. He expressed this opinion to the Canadian bishops and they did not have the faintest idea what he was talking about. He shared with me personally his conviction that the gravest problem facing Christianity in our time is the following: how do you preach an incarnational religion to a discarnate man? And man today is discarnate, divorced from his body. We do indeed enter into a new technological world, wherein man's very capacity to understand reality as it is has been deeply altered by his new media of communication.

The older mechanical order destroys nature. The newer electronic technology destroys nothing, although its base at the moment remains mechanical. Let us take television as typical of the new order of things. Statistics estimate that the average household in the United States has the TV running seven-and-a-half hours a day. (This includes, of course, time in which the television is on but not looked at.) Two-thirds of Americans no longer read a daily newspaper. Almost all afternoon papers have gone out of business. Americans read only in the morning. In the evening they become "couch potatoes." Today, the attention span for a television watcher is only about a minute to a minute-and-a-half at most. This has nothing to do with intelligence, education, or the lack thereof, but is built into the very nature of the technology. Very soon television technology, synthesized with other electronic technologies, will so perfectly mimic human action that the viewer will be tricked into believing he is actually *there*. This "virtual reality," as it is called, will be a substitute for the "real thing." Instead of taking a vacation in Florida a man will be programmed electronically to be in Florida, never moving from his front room. How many will decide to make love electronically with some Hollywood glamour star? Everything solid that a man can seize with his hands dissolves into holograms and holograms, in turn, become being. Image does duty for existence. Indeed, from an epistemological point of reference, every single sense with the exception of touch can be duped, as Father Robert Henle pointed out a few years ago. The possibilities here are morally frightening, but the technology currently exists to pull off this immense fakery of nature.

Today, the political image of the candidate for office wins or loses at the polls. The better the image, the more swiftly it is conveyed, the less reflection demanded of the viewer, the more it gains the day. A vast industry of public relations has mushroomed into history in the past half-century. Its magicians program candidates for the quick TV ad or "bite." So-called "issues" have little to do with victory or defeat. Indeed, the candidate who constantly emphasizes that he is going to talk about the "issues" rarely ever does so. "Issues" become another myth. The message, if not obliterated, is profoundly altered by television and its satellite media. Often cheapened by the nature of the medium in which it is eviscerated, the truth needed for sound political action is often bruised, but more usually silenced.

IN CONCLUSION, I return to my point of departure. The West had all the philosophical principles needed to control the development of technology but ultimately surrendered to the internal dynamics of its own technics. One astronaut, when asked by a journalist why he was going into outer space, answered: "Because we can go there." His moral innocence was compounded by the fact that he died in one of the two space catastrophes we have known. But his answer summed up five hundred years of Western technology. Prometheus Unbound. The Demiurge

Triumphant. The ecological crisis confronting the planet today certainly will—indeed, is—calling back to public consciousness the primacy of man's good over the good and perfection of his artifacts. But, in my judgment, I gravely doubt whether modern technology will be rolled back to manageable limits by society. We have forgotten a hierarchy built by sanity itself: Religion ought to dominate Politics; Politics ought to dominate Economics; and Economics ought to dominate Science and Technology. Since early in the modern experience the hierarchy has been reversed. Science and Technology today dominate Economics; Economics dominates Politics; and Politics dominates Religion. It is to this inversion of the natural order that we owe our winter of discontent.

Gabriel Marcel once warned the world that it is easy to take up a technology but very difficult to lay it down. We cannot undo the new world of electronic wizardry surrounding us. We can, however, set up a few roadblocks from within the human spirit rendering it less difficult for these media to trick us. A serious philosophical study of the effects of technology gives us a kind of first-aid kit, enabling us to recognize what is happening and not to be taken in by it. There are signs that the American public is beginning to do this. This self-reflection on the world we have created is an irony exercised upon ourselves, a shrugging of the shoulders in which we admit to ourselves that we not only kid others with technics but fool ourselves as well. This is the deck of cards we have dealt in the declining years of this century, but let us remember that we dealt the deck ourselves.

Paul C. Vitz

Back to Human Dignity: From Modern to Postmodern Psychology

VOL. 31, NO. 2, 1996

The hallmarks of modern psychology have been reductionism, determinism, and autonomous individualism, all undergirded by a stringent materialism. These tenets reflect the impact of nineteenth-century natural science, which supplied the basis for modern psychology. New developments in contemporary natural science, however, are helping to move modern psychology into a postmodern phase, one which promises to be more hospitable both to human dignity and to personal responsibility.

This essay explores some of the implications of this postmodern psychology, using the psychology of Viktor Frankl as a framework. Frankl is useful here because his position, first published some forty years ago, anticipated important postmodern ideas that are just now coming into prominence.

A MAJOR postmodern characteristic of Frankl's psychology—and it is perhaps what is most widely known about his work—is his emphasis on the human search for meaning. The very name of Frankl's kind of psychotherapy, "Logo-therapy," incorporates this central theme. For Frankl (1963), a major part of human motivation consists in the search for a higher meaning, and Frankl assumed that the finding of this meaning was of central importance for psychological health.

Frankl's deep appreciation of the need for meaning came to a significant extent from his personal experience in a Nazi concentration camp during World War II. There he observed that those who had a strong sense of the meaning of their life tended reliably to survive, as compared with those who had no such overriding purpose.

Modern psychological thought has, however, ignored higher meaning and has emphasized lower levels as accounting for or explaining the presumed higher levels of human significance. For example, it is often physiology or neurology which is seen as accounting for the life of the human mind. Another common interpretation of the higher mental life of ideals, aspirations, and meaningfulness has been to see such things as epiphenomenal expressions of the lower drives of sex and self-interest. In the same spirit, reason and truth were often interpreted as rationalizations of lower needs and desires. In marked distinction to the modern tendency to materialist reductionism has been Logotherapy's focus (e.g., Frankl, 1959) on higher meaning and even the human spirit—an emphasis that can be called *constructionist*.

A second postmodern characteristic of Frankl's thought is his concern with a person's free will. This basic assumption is, of course, commonly found in existential positions, of which Frankl's is one example. Nevertheless, the opposite assumption—that of determinism, especially materialistic determinism—has reliably characterized modern thought. The free will position has been a minority view in psychology, as well as in most other modern disciplines.

One of the most powerful expressions of determinism in psychology has been the behaviorist approach, as expressed in the Russian school of Pavlov and his associates and in the United States by Watson, Skinner, and others. And of course Sigmund Freud was well known for his claim that psychoanalysis was scientific, and ultimately based on some kind of physiological determinism. Both Freud and the behaviorists were strongly influenced by materialism and the general positivist character of science in the nineteenth century. Academic psychologists with their keen ambition to be accepted as scientists championed this kind of materialist determinism and found those few psychologists who argued for free will to be embarrassments.

Determinism of a materialist nature has also characterized social theories of human life, as expressed in Marxism and in much of sociology. Here again positivistic science was the controlling model.

Along with determinism and reductionism, modernism also has very reliably emphasized the isolated individual, or the autonomous self. This emphasis is found dramatically in the so-called "humanistic" psychologies of Carl Rogers and Abraham Maslow (for critiques, see Vitz, 1977/1994; Lasch, 1978; Bellah, et al., 1985). An extreme emphasis on autonomy, independence from others, separation, and freedom has infused modern psychology. The meaning of this freedom has been above all antisocial, or anti-other, in nature. (One is reminded of Jean-Paul Sartre's statement: "Hell is other people.")

Here, let me introduce an anecdote about Dr. Frankl told to me recently by a colleague. (This anecdote has been verified by the Viktor Frankl Institute in Vienna; 1995, personal communication.) When Frankl first arrived in the United States, he was much impressed by the Statue of Liberty in New York Harbor, and with the love of and concern for freedom so prevalent in the United States. Certainly Frankl's own rejection of totalitarianism and concern for free will is consistent with this emphasis. But the modern focus—most especially in America—has been on freedom from other people: freedom from social restraints, from tradition, and from moral systems. To return to my story: as Frankl became more familiar with the American understanding of freedom, particularly as his visits took him to the West Coast, he began to have serious misgivings about the American veneration of liberty, and he said that the United States should also have a Statue of Responsibility, preferably located in California, perhaps in San Francisco Harbor.

This story identifies another major postmodern emphasis found in Frankl's thought: his concern with human meaning as it derives from relationships with others. Thus, for Frankl, the kind of understanding also expressed by Buber in

I and Thou (1958) is a major part of his psychological system.

To summarize, then, modern thought has emphasized scientific reductionism, materialist determinism, and autonomous individualism, while Frankl has emphasized the search for higher meaning, freedom of will, and interpersonal commitment. It is for these reasons that Frankl can be thought of as anticipating several concepts understood today as "postmodern."

WE NOW turn to examples of contemporary theorists who share these basic assumptions. It is unlikely that any of these theorists have been directly influenced by Frankl; many of them have not been influenced by psychology at all. These contributions are coming mostly from the physical and biological sciences and are having their primary impact in those fields. But we should keep in mind that it is these sciences that developed the original determinist and reductionist paradigms that psychologists, and other thinkers, imported into their respective disciplines. What has impact in the natural sciences may well move on to other domains and disciplines.

First, consider the new cognitive science, especially cognitive psychology, a field which has emerged with increasing power in the last thirty years. I will summarize the understanding of this field as found in the work of Roger W. Sperry, a biologist and brain scientist who received the Nobel Prize a few years ago for his research on the functional differences between the two hemispheres of the human cortex. Most of the characterization of his position is taken from a recent paper (Sperry, 1993) in which he presented in short form his understanding of the theoretical implications of cognitive science:

[T]he cognitive revolution represents a diametric turnaround in the centuries-old treatment of mind and consciousness in science. The contents of conscious experience, with their subjective qualities, long banned as being mere acausal epiphenomena or as just identical to brain activity . . . have now made a dramatic comeback. Reconceived in the new outlook, subjective mental states become functionally interactive and essential for a full explanation of conscious behavior. . . . The cognitive consciousness revolution thus also represents a revolt against the longtime worship of the atomistic in science. Reductive micro-deterministic views of personhood and the physical world are replaced in favor of a more holistic, top-down view in which the higher, more evolved entities throughout nature, including the mental, vital, social, and other high-order forces, gain their due recognition along with physics and chemistry. (879)

The cognitive position, as Sperry went on to describe it, means that behavior is mentally and subjectively driven, not merely physiologically or neurologically determined. In the new synthesis of the mental and physical realms, consciousness is understood as inextricably connected to the functioning brain, but consciousness is also seen as a qualitatively new and emergent property. Furthermore, it is an emergent property which can affect levels *lower* than that of the emergent property itself. The new cognitive understanding of mind is one that accepts two directions of causality: both the traditional bottom-up model of materialistic causality, and the new top-down model elaborated by cognitive science.

This new approach is certainly deterministic in a general sense, but not in the older, now-dated, modern sense of materialist determinism. After all, the newly understood higher mental levels do "determine" things. And, as Sperry noted: "We would not want it otherwise; we would not want to live in an indeterminate non-causal . . . universe, totally unpredictable and with no reliability or rational higher meaning" (879).

Sperry also pointed out that large numbers of scientists, especially cognitive psychologists, shifted, in the 1965–75 period, from the older bottom-up model of determinism to the new mixed model of bottom-up plus top-down causality.

Particularly in attempts to build computer models of mental activities, it has become clear, in a practical day-to-day scientific sense, that the emergent organization of something is a causal factor not found in the elements from which the pattern or Gestalt is made. A very simple example is the fact that elementary computer program instructions can be combined in many configurations in order to do many different tasks. Programs typically do not differ in their constitutive elements but only in their configurations. Sperry made this same point when he rejected microdeterministic models such as those that might be based upon particle physics. He wrote: "subatomic features are the same for any macro-entity, be it a great cathedral or a sewage outlet" (880).

Apparently the study of mental functions, using computer programs and particularly different levels of programs, has driven home to the scientific community that patterns, at different levels, have their own causative logic which are unpredictable from the laws of the individual components, or even from knowledge of the lower level program. That is, computer models gave clear examples of nested levels of causality in which higher levels can affect the lower levels.

ONE OF the new theoretical positions that has lent support to the position articulated by Sperry is known as "Chaos Theory." This theory is not really so much about chaos as about order, and about determinism without predictability in non-linear systems. It is not easy precisely to describe Chaos Theory without a more mathematical discussion than is possible here—nor would this author's expertise prove up to the task. Nevertheless, the general significance of Chaos Theory is not hard to summarize and to grasp, thanks to several very competent treatments, on which this discussion will draw. (Prigogine and Stengers, 1984; Gleick, 1987; Wieland-Burston, 1992; Kellert, 1993.)

One of the phenomena that Chaos Theory addresses is the emergence of new levels of organization unpredictable from knowledge of the prior, lower-level states. For example, a typical "chaos" situation goes something like this: A system, only describable with non-linear equations, is in a "relatively" stable situation. However the values of the different variables describing the system are increasing. At some point, the system suddenly becomes very unstable or "chaotic." After a period of chaotic turbulence, the system suddenly restabilizes in a new form—a more complex form, of a higher order than that of the lower pre-chaotic period. Of course, not all systems that go into chaos restabilize, much less do they restabilize at a more organized level, but some definitely do. As an example, consider what are known as Bénard convection cells, as described by the physicist Ernst Brun (1985). (This description is based on Wieland-Burston, 1992.) A pan containing aluminum powder and silicone oil is heated. When the temperature reaches a certain point, an apparently disordered activity starts to take place. Totally irregular cells form—this is the result of convection. These cells move about in a random manner, changing in size and shape. At a still higher temperature, the cells become more uniform in size and shape. They finally come together in a clear pattern—a kind of honeycomb shape. (See Wieland-Burston, 75). The scientist who has done the most in observing and understanding such processes is Ilya Prigogine (Nobel Prize, 1977), a theoretical physicist who studied thermodynamic systems in far from equilibrium states. It was Prigogine who first noted how component molecules can move from chaos to order. In short, Chaos Theory supports the notion of emergent higher levels of organization within some natural systems.

LET US now turn to the assumption of determinism, particularly in its cruder materialist understanding, as found in psychology. Again, we will look at Chaos Theory and some of its additional important characteristics.

Large numbers of physical and biological systems, especially those that are even moderately complex, cannot be described with linear equations—that is, with equations that assume simple additivity. Instead, many, perhaps most, complex natural systems can only be described with non-linear equations. (Even some simple systems, especially if they contain feedback mechanisms, require non-linear equations.) In psychology, it has already become clear that predictions of many elementary human responses to a variety of sensory stimuli are commonly non-linear in nature. The interesting discovery, which is central to Chaos Theory, is that

often in non-linear systems, it is impossible to predict the system's behavior. This unpredictability occurs because it is typical for infinitely small differences in the starting conditions to lead to very large and qualitatively different outcomes.

Let's take an example that was important in the development of Chaos Theory itself. (For discussion of this, see Gleick, 1987; Kellert, 1993.) In the 1960s, a meteorologist and physicist named Edward Lorenz was developing equations for the prediction of the weather. The equations were non-linear, since weather was known to require such. Lorenz had developed a model for forecasting the weather in which the variables were specified to six decimal places, and he had plotted out the predictions that the equations gave for some weeks in the future. At one point, because he was in a hurry, he used the same equations and the same input data, but the variables were specified only to three decimal places. He expected—as did everyone else—that the weather forecast for the weeks to come would be almost the same as when predicted using six decimal places. Instead, what he discovered was that, after a few days, the two predictions completely diverged. That such tiny differences in initial conditions could lead to such large differences in outcome some time later has been called "the Butterfly Effect": that is, the presence, or the absence, of one butterfly—and of the impact of its wings on wind velocity—can make for totally different weather in a particular place some days hence.

Another common kind of chaos situation goes something like this: a dynamic system goes into a time of turbulence or chaos and then moves to one of two or sometimes more new stable states. Which of these new stable states will take place is unpredictable because of the system's sensitivity to initial conditions. Of course, the process is deterministic but, as already mentioned, not predictable. In such situations, scientists can study and describe the qualitatively different states of a non-linear system, but they cannot predict which of them will occur.

In the psychological and social sciences, where the relevant starting conditions are often unknown—and if known are rarely measurable to even one decimal point—Chaos Theory solidly undermines the long-assumed goal of being able to predict human behavior. After all, if tiny initial differences can make for very divergent, even qualitatively different outcomes, then predicting human behavior becomes impossible.

Chaos Theory therefore makes a fundamental distinction between determinism and predictability: systems (for example, the weather) can be deterministic, but nonetheless dramatically unpredictable. While the principle of determinism remains theoretically intact, it has lost much of its force. In psychology, such dramatically different states as elation, anxiety, depression, and the like—even if known to be determined by prior emotional conditions (i.e., certain interpersonal experiences or certain brain states) and even if the variables which caused these states were measurable with some precision—still *which* of these states would actually occur could not be accurately predicted.

The basic idea that small differences in starting conditions can make a big difference in outcome is an important support for the notion of free will. The idea behind free will is *not* that human beings are indeterminate, or in some sense random, but that the human will, however small a force it is—sometimes hardly larger than a butterfly wing—can be a deciding factor in our behavior. It is

the phenomenological experience that the force of our will could be applied to either side of a particular choice that gives rise to the psychological or intuitive evidence that free will exists. Chaos Theory very clearly allows for this possibility.

In summary, the will itself can now be understood as receiving support from contemporary postmodern science in three distinct ways: 1) The will can be conceptualized as a mental force which, however small, exists as an initial condition prior to our decisions. Although the will, like the wind and other aspects of non-linear systems, is part of a deterministic system, its subsequent effects on behavior can be quite substantial yet *not* predictable (the butterfly effect). 2) The will can be understood as an emergent factor: a factor that could "emerge," as a qualitative new state, after a period of prior mental turbulence. This emergent phenomenon also follows from the new possibilities inherent in Chaos Theory. 3) The will can be interpreted in a cognitive science framework as a higher level mental factor which can causally affect lower levels. That is, the will can be interpreted as a factor in the new top-down model of causality.

FINALLY, WE will look at some new interpretations of the self which are also postmodernist. To begin, it should be pointed out that a number of recent theorists of the self have argued that the very notion of the autonomous self is incoherent in important respects. These theorists are deconstructing the self, and their critiques signal the beginning of the end of the modern self.

Kenneth Gergen (1985, 1991) has provided an influential description of the crisis of the contemporary self by interpreting today's self as "saturated." That is, the variety and complexity of today's styles of living make for a self that is complex, overburdened, and saturated to the point of incoherence. The contemporary American self often lives in two or three different places each year, relates to people in different cities, jobs, and cultures on a regular basis. Meanwhile the media flood each person with still more lifestyles, historical periods, different values, philosophies and religions, hobbies, types and places of travel. Many of these late-modern selves have had two or three marriages, and have extraordinarily complex and unstable family situations. Many of these selves have had two, three, or four different careers. Just keeping up with all this leaves no time for reflection or integration, no time to develop a coherent core to the self. The result is a self that is so busy responding to immediate, dramatically different situations that no strong, independent self develops. This is what Gergen means by "saturated."

Philip Cushman (1990) has gone still further than Gergen in claiming that the modern self is basically empty. Cushman is especially interested in showing that the concept of self is always a reflection of the historical and cultural context—something most psychological theories of the self ignore. (For a related position, see Baumeister, 1987.) In his critique, Cushman expresses a clear postmodernist logic, arguing that the modern, so-called autonomous self has always been a kind of an illusion. He defines the modern self as a "bounded masterful self that has specific psychological boundaries, an internal locus of control, and a wish to manipulate the external world for its personal ends" (1990, 600).

His critique develops along the following lines: Cushman accepts the notion of the traditional self—what is often called the premodern self: one that is rooted in family, religious faith, tradition, and community. He accepts these relationships as legitimate and as central to the traditional self. However, with the rise of modern industrial and technological society, the individual was rapidly, or slowly, torn away from these relationships.

Cushman, in stimulating and convincing ways, has proposed that the empty self created by the loss of the traditional structures has been filled by two major modern social forces. The first and perhaps most important force is the consumer society, especially its advertising. Thus, today's self is constructed from the meaning of our purchased products, and from the commercial meaning of our lifestyles. The self is now defined by its automobiles and vacations, by its button-down shirts and barn jackets, even by its brands of beer and perfume. Since we now define the self increasingly through consumption rather than traditional relationships, it is not surprising that the pathologies of our time are narcissism and borderline personality disorder, and the inability to maintain long-term commitments to others. Additional media-influenced problems of our day include low self-esteem, values confusion, eating disorders, drug abuse, and chronic consumerism.

According to Cushman, the other force which has filled the void at the center of the modern self has been psychology. Psychotherapy, with its search for the origins of personality, with its emphasis on past traumas, on expressing archetypes, and on self-actualization, has constructed the other half of the modern self. Vitz (1977/1994) has made similar criticisms and has pointed out, for example, that the Jungian theory of the self with its array of unconscious archetypes such as the persona, animus/anima, wise old man, earth mother, the shadow, etc., has provided a new structure for the self—a new set of characters. Once the relationships provided by traditional family and community are removed, psychology fills the void by introducing a new internal "psychological village" made up of new characters, to take their place. Of course, the basically narcissistic character of the psychological "solution" is obvious. A person's relationship with his anima or her animus is not the same as a relationship with another person of the opposite sex.

In the late twentieth century, developing this kind of "Personality"—whether Jungian or Rogerian or whatever—has taken precedence over building a religious and traditional character. And of course most individuals have turned to popularized forms of psychology to get advice on how to impress others, to become popular, and to achieve monetary success and peace of mind. Advertising strategies have capitalized on this need to glamorize the personality by identifying a particular product with an ideal state of being. Successful ads give the impression that buying the product will free the consumer of personal fears and feelings of inadequacy. Thus both psychotherapy and advertising are attempting to relieve the individual's sense of emptiness.

Ultimately, of course, Cushman thinks that these modern forces are fundamentally phony, and the self they create is an illusion. He believes that they profoundly fail to satisfy the needs of the self in the way that the older relationships once did. As a consequence, Cushman has concluded that the modern self is like a package covered with beautiful wrapping but empty inside.

Perhaps the most extreme position on the contemporary self is proposed by Robert Landy (1993), who has written that there is no autonomous self at

all. Landy writes out of a background in theatre, and has claimed that the contemporary self consists only of roles, as in theatrical roles, which the person chooses. Just as an actor chooses roles, Landy has proposed that the self consists only of these roles, and since they have no coherent focus, there is in fact no integrated autonomous self at all. There are many selves instead—a kind of polyvalent or multi-centered self. Thus we must let go of what has been thought of as the modern self. Landy admits that letting go of this self goes against scores of philosophers, poets and theologians who have advocated a core entity that contains the essence of one's being and can be known (1993, 19). The concept of a core self implies that certain behaviors are authentic (true self) and other behaviors are not (social masks). Inherent in this view is a moral framework wherein rages a battle "between the authentic and God-given forces of light and the inauthentic, demonic forces of darkness" (1993, 19). But this notion of self, however familiar, is—Landy argues—mistaken and must be abandoned. For Landy, the very notion of an authentic self is inauthentic.

THE PRECEDING postmodern theories of the self are primarily critical or negative, in that they deconstruct the modern autonomous self, but offer no positive alternative. Frankl's emphasis on committed interpersonal relationships is thus neither modern nor postmodern, but is similar to that of certain other recent theorists, who propose interpersonal commitment as central to the construction and therefore to the basic idea of the self. These contributions include the writings of de Rivera (1989) and some of myself (e.g., 1977, 1987, 1995 in press). In both instances, these theories of the self can be thought of in part as mutualist, or as a fleshed-out understanding of the position of Frankl and others. Because these writers have opposed modernist assumptions, and also because they provide a positive response to the culturally relativistic, nihilist logic of postmodernism, they can be called "transmodern." By this term I mean that they transcend both modernism and postmodernism in the interest of reaching a new synthesis.

Let us look at de Rivera's contributions in a way that can make this transmodern idea clearer. De Rivera has postulated two basic models of the self that describe the world situation today. The first model he calls "individualist," and this model is what has been described here as the Western autonomous self. The second model is described as "collectivist" and it is based on family and community relationships. This kind of self de Rivera identifies with many Eastern societies (e.g., China and Japan), and with Europe prior to recent centuries. A name already introduced for this kind of self would be "premodern," since it corresponds to the self created through traditional interpersonal relationships given by one's status in the family and society into which one is born. After describing the serious limitations of each of these models, de Rivera proposed a third model of self, called "mutualist." In this model, which is implicitly transmodern, the core of mutuality consists of loving relationships with others. His emphasis on relationship is important, and it resonates with Frankl's similar emphasis. I have also written (1987) in this vein, and in the process quoted from the Protestant theologian Thomas Torrance (1983), who has argued that in significant respects, a person or self is constructed from or through relationships. That is, in a sense we are our relationships. Torrance has noted that

certain theoretical concepts from physics provide useful analogies. Specifically, in certain ways subatomic particles are no longer thought of as separate elements but "we have come to think of particles as continuously connected in dynamic fields of force where the interrelations between particles are part of what particles actually are" (58).

The notion of relationship is thus central to a postmodern, or better still transmodern model of the self or person. One crucial new ingredient in this concept of relationship is that of free choice. We can summarize: the premodern self is based on relationships without true freedom; the modern self is based on freedom without true relationships; the transmodern self is based on relationships with freedom. It is such freely chosen relationships which constitute the basis of a mature love of others. So it is finally the case that love, understood as higher than sex or self-interest, is beginning to be taken seriously as central to the formation of the self or person.

There is a great deal more to this kind of "transmodern" solution to the crisis of the contemporary self. However, its dependence on relationship, freedom and love shows that the contributions of Viktor Frankl's psychology are still alive and well. In addition, it is equally clear that the "modern" materialistic psychology, with its reductionistic spirit is now rightly understood as inadequate and out-of-date.

References

Baumeister, R. (1987). "How the Self became a Problem: A Psychological Review of Historical Research." *Journal of Personality and Social Psychology*, 52, 163–76.

Bellah, R., Madsen, R., Sullivan, W., Swidler, A. & Tipton, S. (1985). *Habits of the Heart: Individualism and Commitment in American Life*. Berkeley, CA: Univ. of California Press.

Brun, E. (1985). *Von Ordnung und chaos in der Synergetik. Physik und Didaktik*, 4, 289–305.

Buber, M. (1958). *I and Thou*. (Trans. R. G. Smith) New York: Scribner.

Cushman, P. (1990). "Why the Self Is Empty: Toward a Historically Situated Psychology." *American Psychologist*, 45, 599–611.

de Rivera, J. (1989). "Love, Fear and Justice: Transforming Selves for the New World." *Social Justice Research*, 3, 387–426.

Frankl, V. (1959). "The Spiritual Dimension in Existential Analysis and Logotherapy." *Journal of Individual Psychology*, 157–65.

Frankl, V. (1963). *Man's Search for Meaning*. New York: Simon & Schuster.

Gergen, K. (1985). "The Social Constructionist Movement in Modern Psychology." *American Psychologist*, 40, 266–75.

Gergen, K. (1991). *The Saturated Self: Dilemmas of Identity in Contemporary Life*. New York: Basic Books.

Gleick, J. (1987). *Chaos: Making a New Science*. New York: Viking.

Kaye, B. (1993). *Chaos and Complexity*. VCH: Weinheim.

Kellert, S. (1993). *In the Wake of Chaos: Unpredictable Order in Dynamical Systems*. Chicago and London: Univ. of Chicago Press.

Landy, R. (1993). *Persona and Performance: The Meaning of Role in Drama, Therapy and Everyday Life*. New York: Guilford Press.

Lasch, C. (1978). *The Culture of Narcissism*. New York: Norton.

Prigogine, I. and Stengers, I. (1984) *Order Out of Chaos*. Toronto and New York: Bantam.

Sperry, R. (1993). "The Impact and Promise of the Cognitive Revolution." *American Psychologist*, 48, 878–85.

Torrance, T. (1983). *The Mediation of Christ*. Grand Rapids, MI: Eerdmans.

Vitz, P. C. (1977/1994). *Psychology as Religion: The Cult of Self-Worship*. Grand Rapids, MI: Eerdmans. (2nd edition, 1994).

Vitz, P. C. (1987). "A Christian Theory of Personality: Covenant Theory." In T. Burke (Ed.) *Man and Mind: A Christian Theory of Personality*. Hillsdale, MI: Hillsdale College Press.

Vitz, P. C. *From the Theology of the Trinity to the Psychology of the Person: A Christian Theory of Personality*.

Wieland-Burston, J. (1992). *Chaos and Order in the World of the Psyche*. London and New York: Routledge.

Robert P. Kraynak

CONSERVATIVE CRITICS OF MODERNITY: CAN THEY TURN BACK THE CLOCK?

VOL. 37, NO. 1, 2001

It is not easy to be a conservative in the modern world. In fact, it takes a high degree of moral courage, for conservatives are almost always on the defensive, fighting for causes that seem hopeless or lost because they go against the most powerful currents of the modern age.

In praising the courage of conservatives, I am referring primarily to cultural rather than to economic or political conservatives. The proponents of free-market capitalism and limited government that are today called conservatives (in the economic and political sense) actually enjoy a certain momentum in their favor so they need not think of themselves as defenders of lost causes. But cultural conservatives are different. They are die-hard adherents of religious, philosophical, and artistic traditions that are out of place in the modern world. They are like dinosaurs who inexplicably missed the mass extinction sixty-five million years ago. As creatures from another era, cultural conservatives were not made for modern civilization and do not fit into the universe of respectable opinion. This gives them the distinction of being the last genuine radicals, and usually makes them the most interesting figures in today's intellectual circles. To these wonderful pre-historic creatures, I would like to offer some words of encouragement by sketching a broad picture of modern culture that indicates why History is not as overpowering as it sometimes seems to be and why, in the long run, traditional patterns of culture are favored by the natural order of things and even by divine providence.

LET ME begin with a simple definition: Cultural conservatives are those daring thinkers who are willing to question the basic assumption of historical progress—the assumption that the modern world as it has developed over the last four hundred years in the West (and now around the globe) is superior in decisive respects to all the civilizations of the past. This question has been raised by many great cultural conservatives and answered in a variety of provocative ways.

One striking example is the Russian writer and former dissident, Aleksandr Solzhenitsyn; he is a cultural conservative who shocked his audience during the

Harvard Commencement Address of 1978 by asking if Western civilization took a wrong turn at the time of the Renaissance when it replaced God-centered societies with Man-centered societies, producing a world of secular humanism that now appears to be spiritually exhausted. Another great thinker who could be classified as a cultural conservative is Leo Strauss whose scholarly writings are dedicated to reviving classical Greek philosophy as a genuine alternative to modern philosophy—a proposal that implies no real progress in philosophy has occurred since its peak 2,400 years ago.

Other cultural conservatives look to the Middle Ages as the high point of Western civilization: For example, Henry Adams, who preferred Gothic cathedrals dedicated to the Virgin Mary to the dynamo of the industrial revolution; or traditional Catholics, who think that Latin Scholasticism is the peak of Christendom; or Eastern Orthodox believers, who believe that monasticism and the centuries-old liturgy are the authentic sources of Christian spirituality. Orthodox Jews are also cultural conservatives because they believe that traditional Judaism, faithful to the divinely revealed Mosaic Law, is superior to Reform Judaism. And one should not forget America's Southern Agrarians, including Richard Weaver, who held fast to the conviction that the Old South, despite the evil of slavery, represented a higher civilization than the more "progressive" industrial and commercial society of the North.

Reflecting on these examples, one may infer that cultural conservatives are driven by a profound dissatisfaction with the modern world and look to the premodern world for sources of inspiration, especially for models of lost greatness. The root of their dissatisfaction is the belief that modernity does not constitute

unmixed "progress" over the past because the advances in freedom, material prosperity, and technology that we presently enjoy are offset by a decline in the highest aspirations of the human soul—the aspirations for heroic virtue, spiritual perfection, philosophical truth, and artistic beauty. Seen in this light, modernity is not superior to past civilizations because it has ushered in an un-heroic age. It has sacrificed the highest achievements of culture for a more equitable and secure but more prosaic existence that, in the last analysis, is not justified because it has lowered the overall aim of life and debased the human spirit.

THE OBVIOUS objection to this kind of thinking is that cultural conservatives are, at best, hopeless romantics with an incurable nostalgia for the past or, at worst, dangerous reactionaries who want to "turn back the clock" and repeal the modern age. Both sentiments are usually met with derision or with the advice that cultural conservatives should learn to accept defeat graciously because historical progress (articulated in various forms by Kant, Hegel, Marx, Mill, Dewey, and most recently by Francis Fukuyama) is not only desirable; it is also inevitable and irreversible. In response, those who share the intuitions of cultural conservatives that something is wrong with modernity—but who feel trapped by theories of the inescapable nature of "progress"—need to see that modern civilization is not as mighty as it claims. Let me offer a few proposals for freeing our minds from the grip of modernist thinking.

The first step is to devise a philosophical equivalent of long-range planning. The "future," after all, is not simply the next decade or even the next generation. We need to think about civilization after the next century or after the next millennium or (I add somewhat facetiously) after the next ice age. To gain an idea of what civilization might look like in the distant future, we must wait for all the forces of modernity to play themselves out and then see what kind of reaction will occur. Who knows, for example, what Western Europe will look like in a hundred years? Will it still be European and social democratic? One strange and alarming statistic that foreshadows major changes is the "population implosion" or "birth dearth"—the declining birth rate of advanced industrial societies resulting from the sexual revolution and modern technology. Nations like Italy now have negative replacement rates that are so low that there may be no more Italians in 150 years. Will there be a reaction that repeals modern trends? Or will European races simply die out and be replaced by African and Arab races shaped by Islamic culture? All that one can say at this point is that the modern trends will likely continue for some time (perhaps a generation or two), following the present pattern which combines permissive freedom, materialism, half-baked nihilism, and strange New Age cults on the fringes. This situation will remain until modern Western civilization subverts its existing foundations and collapses or is transformed by reactions that resemble more traditional structures of authority.

In addition to proposing the long view, I would urge people to stop thinking in terms of historical progress in a rational and linear direction and to think instead in terms of cycles of civilization in which narrow trends play themselves out over finite periods while the full range of human possibilities remains permanently viable. The underlying assumption is that civilization has ups and downs, but beneath it is an order of Nature—a set of laws, patterns, and forms that give human nature and the natural universe an enduring structure. Though not truly eternal like God, the natural patterns will endure as long as created being endures. The implication is that human nature may be temporarily distorted (sometimes for centuries) by the rise and fall of historical civilizations; but certain natural patterns that God has imprinted on created beings will persist and re-assert themselves. What looks inevitable today—democracy, industrial and technological society, even modern science—can be seen more realistically as a transient phase in the rise and fall of civilization. The present order of things is therefore not an inevitable culmination of history but a diluted version of something better that is livable until older patterns, including older patterns of greatness, are able to re-emerge. How and when this will occur is impossible to predict. But let us not confuse the last few centuries with a necessary or best order, and let us remain open to the permanent possibilities of the human soul.

TO ILLUSTRATE the way cultural conservatives might challenge the present order and recover enduring patterns of human nature, I would like to speculate about four idols of the modern age—democracy, women's "liberation," modern art, and modern science. Contrary to conventional wisdom, I doubt that these phenomena are as inevitable or as desirable as most people have been led to believe by the dogma of historical progress.

Consider the status of democracy. Is it really the best form of government or the one toward which all nations are converging? Every serious conservative must wrestle with these questions because the deepest prejudice of our age is the belief that democracy based on human rights (liberal democracy) is the best, indeed the *only* legitimate form of government. Thomas Jefferson said the idea was "self-evident" to all enlightened minds and therewith shut down discussion of the issue. He made it seem un-patriotic to question this view, although patriots like Alexander Hamilton did entertain the possibility that monarchy was better. One should also remember that most of the great political thinkers of the classical and Christian tradition were at odds with present thinking. Despite the differences among Plato, Aristotle, St. Augustine, St. Thomas Aquinas, Martin Luther, John Calvin, and the early American Puritans, all agreed that democracy is not the best form of government and that monarchy, aristocracy, or some kind of mixed constitution is the best regime in most cases. It would be a major step in liberating our minds if we could recover their reasoning and take it seriously once again.

Their argument, in a nutshell, is that democracy is not the best regime because it tends to level distinctions between high and low in society and in the souls of citizens; and this leveling tendency undermines the quest for virtue or human excellence. Instead of judging life by the peaks of humanity—the philosophers, saints, and heroes—democracy glorifies the tastes and opinions of the average man, producing a popular culture or mass society that weakens the highest impulses of the soul. In extreme forms of mass democracy, the people as well as the educated elites become ashamed of the moral superiority implied in true virtue and tear it down by treating it with indifference or contempt. This leads to "democratic tyranny," something we have witnessed in violent forms under socialism or communism and in softer forms in the debased mass culture of America and the social democracies of Europe.

Because democracy tends to level distinctions between high and low, the classical and early Christian thinkers favored more hierarchical regimes than democracy. Following Plato's maxim that the "regime in the city shapes the regime in the soul," they favored monarchy or aristocracy in order to perfect the minds and characters of citizens; or they defended mixed regimes that combined wisdom and virtue in rulers with the demands of the people for consent. Of the various models proposed, the one that makes the most sense to me is St. Thomas Aquinas's idea of mixed or constitutional monarchy—a regime that combines elements of kingship, aristocracy, and democracy in a balanced order. This was the order of the English Constitution for centuries, a balance of King, Lords, and Commons. It was also the order of the Spartan regime, which combined kingship (actually two kings) with an aristocratic body of venerable elders (the *gerousia*) and the elected representatives of the people (the *ephors*). The mixed constitution was also the political order endorsed by the great conservative, Edmund Burke, and by Plato in his *Laws* and Cicero in his *Republic*. It is the basis of the Catholic Church, which I would describe as an elective constitutional monarchy in which the supreme Pontiff is elected by the College of Cardinals and governs in communion with the bishops, the ordained priesthood, and the people. It is the regime underlying most corporate hierarchies in business, the military, and tribal life where one boss or chief governs by consensus in partnership with qualified elites and the broad mass of people.

Is it possible today to believe that those favoring constitutionally mixed monarchies are right and that advocates of pure republicanism or democracy are wrong about the best form of government? I believe that it is possible to hold this view, even if it cannot be implemented in the present age. The decisive issue that favors the traditional view is the connection between a hierarchical political regime and the need to maintain a high or heroic culture over a popular or mass culture. Without high culture, the human soul is degraded to the point where it becomes indistinguishable from animal or plant life and human existence rarely rises above comfortable self-preservation. For anyone concerned with human nobility, it is crucial to establish a regime that promotes high culture over popular culture—that promotes Mozart over the Beatles, as it were, or Michelangelo over Hollywood, or opera over rap music, or the classical liberal arts over professional training. Since all high culture is aristocratic culture—taking aristocratic in its broad sense to mean rule by the best souls rather than mere hereditary privilege but not excluding hereditary privilege in some areas—it follows that hierarchical regimes would be better at promoting high culture than purely democratic or republican regimes.

While we can appreciate the freedom, prosperity, and dynamism of modern liberal democracies, we cannot forgive the "cultural wasteland" they have produced through the leveling of high culture by the masses and its even more devastating deconstruction by the educated elites in the democratic age. What is unnatural about the present arrangement is precisely the contempt shown by elites for true and meritorious elitism—for the natural inequalities of mind and spirit which cannot be eliminated from human nature and which elites in healthier ages channeled into noble and spiritual cultures that actually spoke to all classes of society. Under present conditions, the mission of cultural conservatives should be the de-

fense of high culture over popular culture and the reassertion of traditional hierarchies wherever possible while waiting for modernity to spend its last energies on nihilistic self-destruction.

A SECOND way to resist mass democracy is to reexamine women's liberation or feminism. Such a re-assessment should begin by recognizing the familiar trade-offs of so-called "progress." The gains in freedom and equality by modern women are offset by declines in the higher, intangible realms—in romantic love (including decline in the grace of women as they are coarsened by efforts to imitate men), in the seriousness of marriage as a permanent commitment, in the responsibilities of motherhood and child rearing, in respect for authority as a result of feminizing authority, and in manly honor as men conform to the new code of androgyny. Driving the whole feminist movement is a notion of personal autonomy that equates moral worth with nothing higher than having a salaried career or a middle class profession. How durable and satisfying is this new social experiment?

It may sound shocking to hear, but it is possible that the new experiment will not last more than two generations because it goes against the practices of all pre-existing cultures and against Nature "herself." The present trend assumes that men and women are interchangeable—that no distinct roles should be assigned by custom or by law to the two sexes and that both men and women find their fulfillment in bourgeois careerism. Yet all previous cultures have established different roles for males and females, usually assigning political, military, and religious authority to men while giving social and moral power to women in varying degrees. This pattern is often overlooked by academic proponents of multiculturalism, who seem to forget that non-Western societies have always distinguished the roles of men and women and nearly all have been patriarchal. How long can modern society defy the wisdom of the ages? It cannot do so indefinitely if the universal experience of peoples and cultures is rooted in Nature—and plenty of evidence suggests that it is.

One bit of evidence is that modern Western societies preserve natural differences without admitting it. While officially requiring men and women to be treated not merely equally but identically—as in the training of women for hard-hat construction jobs, military combat, weight-lifting, and professional boxing—the double standard quite reasonably persists beneath the surface. "Men are from Mars, women are from Venus," proclaims a best-selling book on male-female relations. Moreover, new studies in sociobiology and genetic research support the claims of natural differences between the sexes. Feminists themselves refer to feminizing authority and the work place, by which they mean making them less hierarchical and competitive. The new school of "difference" feminism recasts old stereotypes by describing female reasoning as intuitive and personalized compared to male reasoning, which is abstract and impersonal. In addition, everyone knows that males are much more aggressive and violent than females—as evidenced by violent crime statistics, male addiction to violent video games, the macho swagger of computer hackers, and the rowdy behavior of boys. From all of this evidence, one may reasonably infer that traditional cultures were more natural in thinking that men are better suited for military and political life and women for domestic, aesthetic, and moral life and that efforts to transform

roles distorts both spheres by unduly homogenizing them.

The reason why the facts of life are so readily denied today is that several powerful forces are at work—ideology, technology, and prosperity—and these forces have created a temporary artificial world in which sexual differences seem obsolete. On one level, ideology causes people to deceive themselves in order to uphold the myth that gender is a social construction and the sexes are the same. This is akin to socialism's "big lie" that private property and religion are merely social constructs—an anti-natural ideology that kept tyrannical systems operating for seventy years, until human nature reasserted itself. On another level, technology and material prosperity conspire to make natural differences seem unimportant because all tasks have become easier and life is less heroic, creating the illusion of interchangeable sex roles. In addition, the higher authority of traditional religions, all of which are patriarchal, seems irrelevant in a modern secular culture dominated by materialism and technology. As long as there are no great wars and emergencies, as long as no harsh demands are placed on people in advanced industrial societies, as long as sex is detached from procreation and parenting is detached from serious moral authority, then all people will seem like interchangeable parts in a consumer-worker society. But this is an artificial state of things that cannot last indefinitely.

Where will dissatisfaction and reactions begin to appear? Certainly, great events like wars and social breakdowns will cause some re-evaluations. But even without such crises, in middle-class society one can already see reactions caused by the "eternal feminine" in women rebelling against pressures to be little more than imperfect imitations of men. I refer to mundane troubles like eating disorders in women who have been taught by a unisex society to hate every ounce of extra flesh on their female bodies. I think also about educated and professional women who admit that careers are not as satisfying as they first appear and that deeper meaning can be found in traditional religion than in bourgeois careerism—a recognition that there is higher dignity in devoting oneself to family, church, and local community than in slaving away as, say, a lawyer for material success and power.

Admittedly, the novelty of careers among first generation feminists is still a significant force, and the second generation naively takes for granted an artificial unisex world without seeing the special conditions on which it rests. But there are also underground trends in the opposite direction that have been ignored by the popular media. One recent book, for example, records the stories of young career women who have rejected the sexual revolution and returned to the divine wisdom about men and women found in the Orthodox Jewish tradition. Such women are the vanguard of a "resistance" movement that will eventually change modern norms, just as human nature eventually defeated socialist ideology in countries where it seemed firmly established for two generations.

A THIRD trend that needs to be challenged is "modernism" in the fine arts and architecture. Here we face the most bizarre contradiction of all between an imposed modernist ideology and the true feelings of people. While the general public recognizes that modern art has reached a dead end, the art establishment of museums and schools of fine arts still uphold modernism. Most people see clearly that the rejection of beauty and the contempt

for visible reality by modern artists is absurd; and most are offended by art that has been reduced to gimmickry or shock value or the nihilism of abstract chaos. Beneath the quiet surface, nearly everyone thinks about modern art like the little boy in *The Emperor's New Clothes*: There is nothing there! Unfortunately, the inner voices of people are still stifled by fears of sounding philistine.

As with other modern ideologies, however, modernism in art will eventually give way to the natural demands of the body and the soul—in this case, to the demand for depictions of visible realities and beautiful forms which earlier art celebrated. We will then see a titanic clash between the earlier classical and medieval styles and the modern style. By the classical style, I mean art which imitates Nature or idealizes Nature following canons of perfect proportion and symmetry. By the medieval style, I mean the Gothic style and iconography, in which art is intended to glorify God by depicting visible realities as images of invisible beauties. These earlier styles should be revived in order to defeat the modernist style, which equates art with subjective self-expression and substitutes the energy of the artistic process for the beauty of Nature and the glories of Creation. Modern architecture, too, fits this pattern by rejecting higher beauty for the cold and lifeless utility of abstract functionalism. Here, the seeds of a reaction are already evident within the architectural establishment. To Mies van der Rohe's lapidary dictum of modernist dogma that "Less is more," Philadelphia architect Robert Venturi famously responded, "Less is a bore."

To see what returning to earlier styles of art and architecture might look like, I would point to two examples. The first is the crusade of Prince Charles in England to tear down ugly modern buildings in certain sectors of London and to restore the more humane styles of beauty from earlier periods. A more serious case is the struggle that took place recently at the University of Notre Dame School of Architecture. There, the dean of the school, Thomas Gordon Smith, fought a successful battle against the reigning "modernism" and hired a new team of faculty to teach the next generation of architects the classical and medieval styles of church architecture—Romanesque, Byzantine, Gothic, and Renaissance. His point is not to slavishly imitate everything done in the past but to develop variations on the older styles based on the recognition that a church should offer a glimpse of otherworldly beauties and give physical embodiment to the transcendent truths of the Christian faith. The underlying assumption is that certain styles are eternally viable—they never go out of style—because they constitute the perfection of the thing in question; and it is only the false belief in historical progress and the restless desire for novelty that cause modern people to look upon older perfections as boring or outmoded.

FINALLY, I would like to encourage cultural conservatives to question the premises of modern science. This is the most difficult challenge because modern science is true in some sense; and a return to many claims of premodern science would be false and dishonest. Obviously, much of modern cosmology is true. The earth is not at rest at the center of the universe, and the universe is not simply a finite sphere. The general picture of an expanding and evolving natural universe put forward in Big Bang cosmology and Darwinian evolution has more evidence to support it than a static Aristotelian model. Yet the modern scientific model is

far from being conclusively proven. One must take seriously the objections raised, for example, to Darwinian theory by those who argue that the chances of life emerging from non-life are nearly zero and that the fossil record for transitional forms between stable species is almost nonexistent. Such criticisms, cogently stated by Phillip E. Johnson in *Darwin on Trial,* are necessary for every serious conservative to ponder.

But the main ground for challenging the modern scientific view of the universe is not the insufficiency of evidence; it is the incompleteness of modern science's theoretical claims. Modern natural science has nothing to say about the ultimate purpose of the universe beyond the orderly movement of natural bodies in accordance with mathematical laws. The reason for omitting the most important question (that of purpose) is that modern science deliberately lowers the goals of science in order to make progress in lesser realms of knowledge—a trade-off that follows the logic of the entire modern project. In its version of modernism, science restricts itself to explaining "how" Nature works rather than "why" Nature works as she does. It postpones indefinitely the question of Nature's ultimate purposes or designs (the question of natural teleology). Stated in more precise Aristotelian language, modern science focuses on material and efficient causes and dispenses with formal and final causes. But how long can modern science ignore formal and final causes? Once again, I believe that such issues cannot be ignored indefinitely because the highest kind of knowledge is required to understand the natural world and to satisfy the human soul. One should not be surprised, then, to see an underground movement of thinkers who have revived formal and final causes in the concept of "intelligent design."

According to the school of intelligent design, Nature is not a product of blind mechanical forces because her complex structures cannot be reduced to numerous small parts that accidentally came together over time. As Michael Behe argues, many of the critical parts of animals, such as eyes or wings, exhibit "irreducible complexity": they cannot function as anything but complete units and therefore could not have evolved through incremental changes. The whole animal also functions as a complete unit that could not have gradually evolved, just as twenty or even eighty per cent of an airplane is not capable of flying. The implication is that formal causality of some kind, not excluding special creation by intelligent design, is needed to explain organic functionalism. On a cosmic scale, Paul Davies suggests that the entire natural universe exhibits design and direction. He acknowledges that Nature is evolving (as modern science says), but it does so by producing "self-organizing wholes" of ever-greater complexity—beginning with simple structures like stars and galaxies and moving toward more complex forms such as living cells and human minds. Since the chance appearance of complex forms is extremely low, Davies infers that living and intelligent beings must result from Nature's self-organizing tendencies. Nature is therefore alive and directed toward intelligent life and could be said to aim at conscious understanding as its natural end. While the school of intelligent design is still speculative, it challenges the narrow thinking of much of modern science because it is simply more plausible than the theory of a purposeless universe driven by blind mechanical causes.

IF THESE arguments are correct, then we conservatives have reason to be encouraged. They show that we can resist the degradations of modern culture and can hope to reverse the tide of history with positive results. They show that we are freer than we have been taught to believe. There is no historical determinism to trap us because the forces of Nature and of Nature's God are stronger than the forces of progress. Not only can we imagine alternatives to modern civilization, we can also recover some of the greatness of the past.

And time is on our side. Modernity is not a permanent stage but a transient period in historical civilization, temporarily supported by the distortions of modernist ideologies and modern technology. Against those pressures, we can push back. And we can take heart at the words of William F. Buckley, who once said that the job of the conservative intellectual is "to stand athwart history and shout, 'Slow down! Stop! Return to ancient wisdom'." To this courageous call, I would add the observation that ancient wisdom is worth recovering not merely because it is ancient but because it testifies to the permanent possibilities of the human soul as well as the natural order of things. These possibilities will eventually triumph over modern illusions.

II.

SCHOLARSHIP & OPINION

Frederick D. Wilhelmsen

Donoso Cortés and the Meaning of Political Power

VOL. 3, NO. 3, 1967

The study of politics demands a mind which is eminently practical. Intuiting the crisis in our own civilization, sensing—often obscurely—that something comparable to a second fall of man must be responsible for the moral decay which rots the hull of our own culture, the student of politics seeks the causes of this decline because he knows that the medicine of restoration depends upon a true diagnosis of the disease affecting the body politic. If the student of politics is wise, he will not reduce these causes to the purely philosophical order. He will be aware that factors both superior and inferior to the philosophical have contributed to the illness of the West, but he will never surrender to the materialist temptation to mesmerize away the role that ideas have played within history, even materialist ideas. What follows here is an exercise in both philosophical detection and political restoration. We address ourselves to the following questions: What happened to political Power in the past four centuries, enabling it to expand so enormously that it threatens to engulf every dimension of human existence? How can we come to know the true meaning of Power so that we may domesticate it to work for the good of man?

WERE WE to illustrate the history of modern political theory and practice, we might well follow the example of Aristotle and use the analogy of the domestic household. The master of the modern political house is the creation of the genius of Machiavelli. Hobbes fashioned the servant. Jean Bodin supplied the roof, which we have known ever since as the "state."

Neither Machiavelli nor Hobbes conceived of political existence as though it were an entity, a Thing. Even Hobbes's *Leviathan* is an aggregate and not a being in itself. The concept of the state as something sovereign unto itself and hence constituting a fusion of both authority and power was the invention of Bodin. Although there are analogies to the modern state in both the Greek polis and the late Roman Empire, it is not correct to refer to "the state" as having existed in any strict sense before Bodin and the centralized absolute French monarchy whose theoretician he came to be.

Jurisprudence in the early centuries of the Roman Republic rested authority in the wisdom and prudence of the judges. But the judges themselves remained silent until society itself asked them to render an opinion on some concrete case. It follows that Roman Law, before its transformation and corruption at the hands of the Hellenic mind, was constituted by an act of judging which was always an act of answering, a *respondere*.[1] This response was simply the answer given to the questions put to wise men by the community. Thus it was that Roman law clearly distinguished between the concepts of Authority and Power. Public Power, whose concrete expression is government, waited upon the voice of the repositories of the law. It followed that the Authority of the judges was sharply differentiated from the Power of the magistrates. We can even assert that not only was the Roman judiciary independent of the power of the executive but that Power itself was subordinate to an Authority that was respected so highly it could stand without any buttressing it might have received from the executive. We have trouble today even articulating the distinction because we live within a political order that has accepted Bodin's state as though it were as natural as the rise and fall of the tides, a political order in which Authority is identified with public Power and in which Power is Sovereign.

Classical thought recognized very early in the game that there was a link between the authoritative and the personal, between judgments and judges, but it did so only in an obscure way. We refer, of course, to Plato's elaboration of the doctrine about the Philosopher-King. Although tyranny is government in defiance of the Laws, the rule of the Philosopher-King is government which transcends the Laws. Because his intervention in time is a quasi-providential event whose mystery is heightened by the rareness of the occurrence and by the impossibility of even preparing for its advent, government by law is superior to rule by men in the normal course of history.[2] The *absolute* superiority of the politics of the Philosopher-King is located within the Laws' necessity to legislate in the universal and in their occasional failure to reach complexities which are consubstantial with individuality. It follows, according to Plato, that the very universality of the Law frequently misses the particular and thus does violence to the justice due particular men. Nonetheless, the marginality of this possibility justifies government by the impersonal majesty of the Law.

Historically, the theory of the natural law grew out of and perfected the previously elaborated philosophy of natural justice. Natural justice, conceived by Plato and Aristotle, was expanded into the natural law philosophy of the Stoics and Cicero. According to Stoic theory, "law" is an intelligible or rational measure or standard because it would indeed be insane to postulate the existence of reason within a supposedly irrational cosmos. It would be even more irrational, continues Stoic theory, to deny to man's own nature that measured harmony already found within the physical cosmos. Because man's nature is self-consciously rational, human nature is not led blindly by the law but is developed accordingly to both deliberation and freedom. Insofar as man can know the law proper to himself, man can embrace it and thus will his own perfection, and affirm the excellence inscribed in his nature as a promise and a hope. Far from involving a kind of ethical totalitarianism that would bind man to a set of imperatives understood as though they were *dei ex machina*, the natural law—as understood first in the classical and later within the Christian tradition—is a liberating force which leads men towards their own end, a force involving a discipline at times harsh in its commands but nonetheless an always civilizing and humane force. Natural law theory, as expanded by Thomas Aquinas,[3] involves: a) a moment of reflection in which a man meditates upon the exigencies of his own nature, be they prohibitions or commands, be these exigencies indemonstrable first principles consubstantial with the ontological nature of humanity itself or "secondary" precepts deduced from these first principles; b) a moment of decision in which he embraces or rejects, in the fullness of his freedom, the demands he has discovered within himself.

Although, according to natural law theory, natural law is nothing other than nature itself, man's articulation of the law—a slow and laborious business which depends upon both ethical maturity and intellectual sophistication—is an attempt to fuse within consciousness that which is (already fused) in reality. Given that law must legislate in broad and very often properly universal terms; given that law as understood within the human mind can never totally reach the concrete complexities of existence, it follows that the law as theory can never identify itself completely with reality. Law as known and formulated must remain a mere map of reality and is never a perfect one with the road it charts. Aristotle's virtue of prudence was a bridge between universal law and its concrete application.[4] The prudent man, according to Aristotle, knows how to read the map. Something similar happened in the early flowering of Roman Law under the Republic. Authority belonged to the Law but only to the Law as interpreted and rendered concrete in cases by the judges. Thus the relation between Authority and the personal, reserved by

Plato to the mythological reign of the Philosopher-King, inserted itself more modestly if more effectively in the theory underlying Roman jurisprudence.

The medieval experience made its own the teaching of the early Roman jurists but it did so according to a radically new political situation introduced by the new configuration given society by Christianity. The break-up of the Roman Empire in the West gave birth to a new civilization which was highly decentralized in government, which rested upon a feudal basis, which abandoned any attempt to identify ultimate authority and sovereignty within itself because it located both within a transcendent God; a civilization which was marked by the autonomy of religious orders, by the virtual independence of towns and cities from royal or imperial power, and by "parliaments" in France and "Cortés" in Spain which held the power to grant or to withhold subsidies from the national government. Authority in medieval Christendom was broadened beyond the authority proper to the judges until it was diffused throughout a whole host of institutions that marked the medieval world and made it the unique political thing that it was. Authority was as pluralistic as life itself. Public Power, government in the plain sense of the term, grew out of a society whose complexity exceeded the experience of classical politics. Sovereignty was reserved to God.

THE MEDIEVAL checking of political power by authority—more exactly, by a host of authorities—resident within the very tissue of the community, is crucially pertinent to any theory of power. Suffice it to say here that the theoretical problem posed by Plato in this connection found its solution within what might be called, with some reservations, the Christian politics of transcendence. Plato's complaint that the wise and the good are without Power and that Power is more often the perquisite of the evil or the stupid, his insistence that an absolutely good political order depends upon the identification of Power and Wisdom, and his pessimism about the possibility of this union being found in history were theoretically solved by the Christian identification of Power and Authority in God. The subsequent scholastic teaching concerning the Power of God as ordained by His Goodness and His Wisdom simply pointed to the Divine Government of creation by the Lord of History. But the Christian dispensation heightened rather than diminished the distinction between Authority and Power written into early Roman jurisprudence. If Sovereignty pertains to the fullness of Authority, then only God is sovereign because only He speaks with an underived Authority. The political order for medieval man was even less "sovereign" than it was for classical antiquity. Authority, wheresoever it might be found, was thought to be a participation in a Divine Attribute and in no sense a property belonging essentially and restrictively to the public power of the political order, the medieval kingdom or *regnum*. Expressing the issue more exactly, we must say that if Power or its representatives did possess Authority in medieval times their Authority did not accrue to Power simply because of Power itself. The Two Swords, although symbolically valuable, inadequately expressed the relations between church and empire. What theologians were wont to call Peter's indirect "Power" in things secular was not Power at all but simply Authority.[5] Medieval man saw clearly, as did the Roman jurists, that *all authority is moral!* A breakdown of Authority is always a breakdown in the moral order. A

papal interdict, for instance, *worked* just as long as men respected Rome's Authority. As soon as men and nations ceased to respect that authority, it became ridiculous for Rome to hurl its thunderbolts. In a word, Authority can do nothing other than speak. The execution of its commands depends upon a Power humble enough to listen. Moralists will find here a deep paradox which strikes at the heart of hierarchy and which suggests, to this author at least, the parable of the humble being exalted and the lords of this world being laid low. In any event, medieval man neither respected nor obeyed any authority that could not trace its origins to, and legitimize them in, the Authority of God. This no doubt irritated kings, for they proclaimed their sovereignty all the more because they really had so little of it.

The same cannot be said of the national French monarchy at the time Jean Bodin. France by then was already a highly centralized political unit and all Europe was following in its footsteps. The old medieval order was in full decay. Sovereignty was made immanent by Bodin, who located it within terrestrial existence, within politics as such. The *res publica* came to be the thing that we understand today under the rubric of the state. According to Bodin, that grouping of families which forms the basis of society is governed by a highest political power, a *summum potestas*. This power is both absolute and perpetual: "power— One, Absolute, and Perpetual."[6] This Power is also Sovereign.[7] Should Power lose Sovereignty, the republic would cease to exist.[8]

THE POLITICS of Absolute Power and the politics of the modern state depend, as do all politics, upon metaphysical presuppositions. Medieval man never had to face the problem of an absolute power in politics because he could never have conceived of its possibility. The arbitrary use of power was discussed only within the classical context of tyranny. But tyranny as such has nothing to do with the absoluteness of power but with its unlawful use. (It can even be argued that the classical Platonic and Aristotelian tyrant can never exercise absolute power because such an exercise would involve satisfying the tyrant's passions which are assumed to be necessarily incapable of being gratified. It is for this reason that the classical tyrant is always unhappy.) The unlawful use of power might be good accidentally because occasionally the Law might violate the concrete good in the existential order. A tyrant can at times get good things done that the Laws prohibit. In any event, the term "absolute" as applied to Power means, within medieval presuppositions, the following: Power is totally unconditioned either from within itself or from any extraneous factors upon which Power might exercise itself; in this sense only God's Power is Absolute because only He can make things be altogether without fashioning anew some pre-existent subject.[9] Medieval thought tended, therefore, to locate the treatise on Power within the context of the treatise on creation, as did Thomas Aquinas in his *De Potentia Dei*. Absolute as applied to Power could also mean a Power absolved or divorced from any other dimension of the real. This is suggested by the very term, *absolvere*. Medieval speculation tended to talk about a naked and lonely Power stripped of every other consideration in terms of the possibility or impossibility of God's annihilating the human soul once He had created it.[10]

Some theologians settled the problem by distinguishing between God's Absolute Power and that same Power as ordained by His Wisdom and Goodness. Absolutely speaking, according to this theory, God could annihilate the human soul because it depends totally on Him for being. Given, however, the truth that God's Power always harmonizes with His Wisdom and Goodness, God *would not* do so. Probably the distinction between *could* and *would* breaks down in this case because of the Unity of Power, Wisdom, and Goodness in the Being of God. In any case we have grasped the point at issue when we see that medieval Christian thought was so suspicious of any absolute Power that it felt constrained even to hedge that Power when found within God Himself, hedge it around with these attributes which precisely make God sovereign: His Wisdom and His Goodness. The issue has enormous political consequences, as we hope to demonstrate, but it suffices to note here that Bodin's elevation of the political order to the status of an *absolute* of Perpetual Power was another step along the road in the divinization of political existence.

Although Bodin's understanding of his own religion was defective, he was a Christian and he did hope that the sovereign would exercise his power in harmony with the moral and divine law.[11] But this hope could only have been, and in fact was, little more than a pious exhortation. If political Power is absolute—it behooves us to take Bodin's use of language as seriously as he took it himself—it cannot be conditioned by extraneous considerations drawn from the moral order. Such a conditioning would limit Power and strip it of its supposed absoluteness. Any harmonizing of Power and the Wisdom from which comes Authority is possible only under two conditions: 1) either Power is identically Wisdom (and, *a fortiori*, Goodness) as the theologians had taught;

or 2) Power is limited from outside itself. Power can remain absolute and good only when it is Divine. If Power is to act other than in a merely powerful way, if Power is to act wisely and prudently in harmony with justice and truth, then Power must be specified or limited by dimensions of being that are not formally identified with Power as such. Medieval political experience found these dimensions of reality within the community, which was regarded as the repository of an analogical incarnation of authorities themselves derived from God.[12] But Bodin's public Power is really absolute. No matter how much he might speak of the sweet reasonableness of a sovereign Power as exercised by a Christian prince he cannot square this reasonableness with his insistence upon the absolute character of the sovereign. That Bodin is serious in what he says, we know, because he not only revindicates for the *res publica* the imperium of the Hellenized Empire; he not only preaches a sovereignty which is one and indivisible and hence superior to any other Authority either religious or social; but he also teaches that the state is the substantial form of civil society, its animating principle.

WE HERE witness the birth of the modern state. The comparison of political sovereignty with the Aristotelian substantial form is decisive, so decisive that modern men often find it difficult to understand what the politics of Christendom were all about because Bodin is a wall separating that age from our own. Medieval Christendom was so firmly structured through a series of self-governing institutions, each of which claimed an analogous participation in Authority, that Public Power—the Power of the Crown—was usually restricted to

leading the political community that it crowned or to fighting with it in an effort to reduce its pretensions. The king could put his sword at the service of his kingdom or turn it against the kingdom, but he could not absorb that kingdom within himself by his own power. No one phrase better sums up the limitations placed on royal power by the medieval political community than the warning read Spanish kings in Castille upon the occasion of their coronation: "Thou shalt be King if thou workest justice and if Thou dost not do so, thou shalt not be King."[13] The medieval public Power, incarnated in the person of the king (more accurately, in his family), did not constitute the *res publica christiana* but crowned it in the temporal order so that the society in question might act corporately within history.[14] The legitimate power of the king was the fruit of a hundred pacts solemnly entered upon by princes and subjects, themselves represented by a thicket of institutions which were the work of generations and even centuries of common experience.

When Bodin published his *Six Books of the Commonwealth* in 1576 the medieval kingdom was just about dead in France and in plain agony in most of Europe. A new Thing had come into being: the state. Most of the old medieval institutions still gave an appearance of life, but the heart had gone out of them. Townships and guilds, provincial parliaments, regional charters, and the rest were being reduced to so many quaint relics from a past age, preserved as facades because they were still dear to men who had grown up among them and who looked upon them as the flesh of corporate life.

Bodin's use of the symbol of substantial form to define the role of the state within civil society is not without interest. Aristotle's substantial form was understood by the intellectual community of Bodin's time to mean more or less what Aristotle himself intended it to mean: i.e., the substantial form is that interior principle of growth and specification (*dynamis*) which quickens a reality from within and makes it to be what it is. It follows that hylomorphism could never have been used in any properly symbolic sense to describe medieval politics. The articulation of public power into government in the older Christendom grew out of the community in the sense of crowning that community, as indicated, or of serving as the community's representative for secular ends. Public Power or government, conceived as an active harmonizing of an already heavily differentiated and institutionalized society; understood as being enjoined by the community with the specific function of seeing that justice was done or the law fulfilled as well as repelling Invaders and securing the peace of the realm; public Power, limited to these crucial but still moderate roles, would not be spoken of by serious men in terms of an Aristotelian substantial form. Medieval man preferred to draw analogies from human anatomy. Thus Sir John Fortescue—as Voegelin reminds us—in articulating the meaning of political representation, compared the *res publica* to a body which could not function without a head.[15] Public Power became absolute only when it truly did become the substantial form of the republic. The community, reduced to an amorphous dough without any institutions with significant political representative functions, was shaped this way and that by Power which absorbed all Authority within itself and proclaimed itself Sovereign. In this fashion the modern state—conceived in France, suckled in Germany, and matured in Russia—replaced the *res publicum christianum.*

THE THEORETICAL problem of Power from Montesquieu to our day has been that of the possibility and desirability of setting limits to its tendency toward absolutism. Montesquieu deduced the desirability of limiting Power from man's imperative to be free.[16] He tried to find freedom within the context of the state he knew: i.e., Bodin's. His dilemma was: how can we avoid tyranny within a political situation in which the republic has become sovereign and the sovereign has been identified with perpetual and absolute power? Unless we understand the factors which went into the drama of freedom as seen by Montesquieu, by Sieyés, by the Encyclopedists, and by the European Liberal tradition that grew from them we cannot understand either Montesquieu's solution or the theoretical weaknesses found therein by European Traditionalism in the person of its most eloquent and profound spokesman, Donoso Cortés.

We can provisionally define European Liberalism as the continental system of political thought and practice which grew out of the French Revolution and dominated the entire nineteenth century excepting the time of the short White Reaction in France (1814–30) and in Germany (1814–48). Dedicated to the doctrine of national sovereignty, buttressed by the religion of progress, and bent upon the secularization of society, European Liberalism's preferred form of government was a highly centralized parliamentary democracy based upon the "party system" and tempered by an allegiance to commercial and industrial interests. While linked to the Jacobin tradition of the previous century, nineteenth-century liberalism was more comfortable than crusading, more oligarchic than egalitarian. In all cases, however, European Liberals firmly opposed any restoration of the authority of either church or crown,

Montesquieu and the liberalism that looked to him for guidance never questioned the presuppositions of the sovereign state endowed with absolute Power, even though liberalism wished to use that Power sparingly in the service of a wider distribution of liberty. If we assume that Power is sovereign; if we assume further that Authority has lost its independence and has been absorbed within Power; if we postulate the national state as the substantial form of the republic, it follows that any limitation of Power must come from within Power itself. Society could not limit Power because society, on the assumptions in question, would not possess the independent institutions with the requisite Authority to speak in the name of Wisdom and Truth and thus demand that they be heard. Montesquieu wanted the sovereign to listen carefully to the people and to govern in accordance with prevailing customs. But custom in Montesquieu and liberalism had already lost the force of law that it possessed in the medieval world.[17]

Neither custom nor what Willmoore Kendall and this writer like to call "the public orthodoxy" exercised any *political* role within the liberal commonwealth. They are not authoritative voices in the liberal republic. Although the liberal commonwealth must listen to society, it is under no obligation to heed an Authority society may claim to enflesh within itself. It follows that public Power, be it democratic, aristocratic, or monarchical, can offend the liberty of the subject and most probably will do so unless we can discover *within* Power some possible principle of limitation.

Montesquieu's solution is so famous and has influenced both politics and history so profoundly that it suffices here merely to state again in capsule form a teaching that can be found in any manual of politics published in the Western world in modern times, a teaching which history has honored by permitting it to pass into folklore. Liberty is assured a permanent role within the commonwealth when Power is limited through its "separation" into legislature, executive, and judiciary. A built-in system of "checks and balances" assures the citizenry that any tendency towards tyranny will be curbed. But let us permit Montesquieu to speak for himself:

> The political liberty of the subject is a tranquility of mind arising from the opinion each person has of his safety. In order to have this liberty, it is requisite the government be so constituted as one man need not be afraid of another.
>
> When the legislative and executive powers are united in the same person, or in the same body of magistrates, there can be no liberty; because apprehensions may arise, lest the same monarch or senate should enact tyrannical laws, to execute them in a tyrannical manner.
>
> Again, there is no liberty, if the judiciary power be not separated from the legislative and executive. Were it joined with the legislative, the life and liberty of the subject would be exposed to arbitrary control; for the judge would be then the legislator. Were it joined to the executive power, the judge might behave with violence and oppression.
>
> There would be an end of everything, were the same man or the same body, whether of the nobles or of the people, to exercise those three powers, that of enacting laws, that of executing the public resolutions, and of trying the causes of individuals.[18]

The theory has its antecedents in Polybius's analysis of the constitution of the Roman Republic, but Polybius was less concerned with the problem of the liberty of the subject than with the impossibility of fitting the Roman constitution into the Greek *tripartite* division of governments.[19] Montesquieu, however, found in *his* ideal constitution, the English, an explanation for the freedom of the English subject. The English Crown, according to the French Anglophile, functions as executor of the law and as commander in chief of the armed forces; parliament legislates; and the judiciary is in the hands of the people because juries are drawn from the populace at large and at random. Most historians of politics agree that Montesquieu would not have approved of some of the subsequent developments within English constitutional law because the executive today has virtually lost its independence except in moments of crisis. Nor can we imagine Montesquieu's approving of a ceremonial monarch whose functions are reduced to opening Parliament and presiding over Derby Day. But notwithstanding these vicissitudes of history Montesquieu would recognize in contemporary England substantially the same division of Power he praised when he wrote *The Spirit of the Laws* in 1748.

The doctrine of the separation of powers was more descriptive in Montesquieu than prescriptive, but European Liberalism seized upon "checks and balances" and "separation of powers" as a theoretical justification of the majoritarian parliamentarianism that ever since has been looked upon as the *conditio sine qua non* of democratic liberty.[20] This conviction was substantial with the dominant mood of the liberalism that occupied the continent in 1848. The identification of free government with the "separation of powers" had by then become a settled conviction within the galaxy of judgments forming the liberalism of the times. This conviction was written into the French Constitution of 1830, which gave the throne to Louis-Philippe (who agreed to be the policeman of the Revolution, thus proving himself a true heir to the traditions of his house). The separation of powers was behind that apeing of British institutions indulged in by the heirs of Napoleon and it is among the ironies of modern history that continental liberalism found a model for its political institutions in the very country and tradition that brought to heel the first soldier of the Revolution.

It was in opposition to this spirit that Don Juan Donoso Cortés wrote his famous letter to the editor of the *Revue des Deux Mondes,* November 15, 1852, in answer to an attack made upon him by the liberal (Orleanist) royalist, M. Albert de Broglie.[21] His answer contains a theory of Power which is the most serious challenge to the presuppositions of liberalism as we have inherited them from the nineteenth century. That this theory has hitherto not been studied dispassionately and with philosophical detachment is due largely to the calumny heaped upon the head of its author by the entire liberal tradition.

The student of political philosophy, upon approaching the text of Donoso Cortés, must keep in mind that he is about to be instructed by the finest intelligence that placed itself at the service of what we tend to call today "The Counter-Revolution" in contradistinction to English conservatism. Donoso belongs, therefore, to what continental political thought simply calls "Traditionalism."[22] The student ought to make an effort to locate Donoso Cortés within the context of his times: Donoso, an architect of the Spanish Pragmatic Succession; an early pillar of the liberal monarchy of Isabel II; an opponent of the claims of Don Carlos Isidro of the principal of legitimacy and of a nation at arms against the imposition of the centralizing radicalism of Madrid; in short, a man who owed everything, his title of Marqués de Valdegamas as well as his own career in diplomacy, to the liberalism he came to loathe in the last brilliant years of his short life. The reader newly come to Donoso will also want to know that he is about to meet the man most hated by the European Left and most especially by the Catholic Left, hated with a venom that so puzzled Carl Schmitt that he concluded that its intensity was "not normal and proper to political opposition," that it must spring from "motives which are deeper, metaphysical"[23] and which cause his contemporary Spanish biographer, Don Federico Suarez, to wonder why it was that the enemies of Donoso—they are legion—would have preferred him to have been a "romantic or a primitive"[24] rather than an elegant diplomat who graced with equal ease the salons of Europe from Madrid to St. Petersburg. The reader must also set aside any propensities he might entertain about academic and scientific departmentalism. To the theologian, Donoso looks like a political theorist; to the political philosopher, he seems a theologian; to the man of action, a theoretician; to the academician, a politician. In truth he was all of these things and yet were we to seek a formula capable of defining the man we could do worse than call him the absolute negation of the Revolution in all its forms.

Broglie had accused Donoso of worshipping the Middle Ages and of urging upon the church "an absolute and universal domination" in European affairs, of "inculcating in the minds of men the need for a restoration of the Middle Ages." It was this last accusation that Donoso considered to have been the most significant of them all and it was the spur moving him to write *The Letter* of 1852. Donoso begins by candidly pleading guilty to the charges as far as political principle and not historical form is concerned. The Middle Ages, he begins, were set in motion by a tendency which sought to "constitute Power in accord with the principles making up the public law of Christian nations."[25] Modern Europe, however, is engaged presently upon the task of shaping Power according to "certain theories and conceptions . . . foreign to Catholic norms,"[26] As a consequence we in Europe will soon come to know, in a future not distant, a "Power infallibly . . . demagogic, pagan in its structure and satanic in its grandeur."[27] So that this prophecy may be intelligible to his readers, Donoso proposes to develop rapidly in his reply to Broglie a theory about the nature of Power itself.

He advises us that "God has imposed upon the world a sovereign law in virtue of which it is necessary that the very unity and variety found in God Himself be found in all things."[28] Although not articulated in *The Letter*, it is clear that Donoso here refers to the orthodox Christian doctrine of the Trinity of Persons and Unity of Nature of the Christian God. In his famous *Essay on Catholicism, Liberalism, and Socialism*, published one year earlier in 1851, Donoso had explored a paradox that recalls the mind of the Patristic Age and that would not be emphasized again in modem times until Chesterton wrote his *Orthodoxy*:

> The same God who is author and governor of political society is author and governor of all domestic society. In the most hidden depths and in the highest places, in the most serene and

luminous of the heavens there resides a Tabernacle inaccessible even to the choir of the angels: in that inaccessible Tabernacle there is worked perpetually the prodigy of all prodigies and the Mystery of all Mysteries. There is the Catholic God, One and Triune: unity expanding itself, engendering an eternal variety as well as variety condensing itself and resolving itself into an eternal unity . . . because He is One, He is God; because He is God, He is perfect; because He is perfect, He is most fecund; because He is most fecund, He is Variety and because He is Variety, He is family. In His Essence are contained, in an unerring and incomprehensible way, the laws of creation. . . . All has been made in His Image and because of this, creation is one and varied.[29]

This law of unity found in variety and variety in unity, the metaphysical character of which Donoso does not leave in doubt, works within the heart of the family where the unity of the child is born of the variety of the parents in a circularity which prohibits our affirming that variety is prior to unity or unity to variety.[30] This last clearly cuts Donoso away from that kind of individualism which at bottom denies all reality to social relations and separates him from Hegelian "organicism," which sees the individual as growing out of, and as constituted by, society considered as a pre-existent whole. We might be tempted to seek Donoso's Law of Variety and Unity in the Thomistic analogy of Being were it not that a reading of the Donosian texts fails to reveal any systematic dependence upon St. Thomas.[31] Furthermore, we must remember that the intellectual climate of the early nineteenth century, even when Catholic, was not dominated by Thomism. Thomistic

studies were revived some four decades after Donoso's death. Donoso's conviction represents, perhaps, an obscure awareness that if Being is not ultimately pluralistic in structure the West would have to embrace the lonely God of Islam.

"Who does not see in this law," insists Donoso in *The Essay*, "a high and hidden mystery: unity engendering variety perpetually and variety perpetually constituting unity?"[32] Not content with stating his law, Donoso is constrained to explore it further: this is "the hidden law presiding over the generation of the One and the Many which ought to be considered the most high, the most excellent and the most mysterious of all laws since God has subjected all things to it, human as well as divine, created as well as uncreated, visible as well as invisible."[33] Nor must this law be thought of as though it were a univocal formula which applied to all things in the same way as do mathematical proportions. The Law of Variety and Unity is, paradoxically enough, subjected to itself:

> being one in its essence, it is infinite in its manifestations; all things that exist would seem not to be at all except to manifest the same law; and each and all of the things that are manifest this law in a different fashion: in one way it is in God, in another way it is in God made Man; now in a new way it is in His Church, in the family, and then in another way the law is in the universe; but it is in all things and in every part of the whole; here in one place it is invisible and an incomprehensible mystery and there in another place it is a visible phenomenon, and a palpable fact.[34]

The "sovereign law" of Unity and Variety appealed to in *The Letter*, therefore, is understood by Donoso to be a philosophical principle in the most rigorous sense of the term, a law he had explored with exquisite care in the early chapter of *The Essay*. This law must, however, remain unintelligible to any reader who approaches it with the prejudices modernity has inherited from the rationalist tradition. We are not concerned here with a law either intuited by the intelligence or deduced from undemonstrable first principles. Donoso's Law of Variety and Unity is a consequence of his own acceptance of the Christian doctrine concerning the Trinitarian God. It depends formally upon an act of faith. On this point at least Donoso is closer to the Augustinian than to the Thomistic tradition because his *episteme* or political "knowledge" is the fruit of his meditation upon a Truth which transcends the naked capacity of the human mind. Once the Christian teaching on God is accepted, however, it becomes capable of illuminating a whole area of experience far more intelligibly than would a purely immanentist political philosophy.[35] All things partake of unity and variety but man is able to see this truth clearly only in the light of a doctrine, a dogma, which he does not "see" but believes. Donoso is clearly in the *credo ut intelligam* tradition of St. Augustine.

With so much said we can proceed to affirm that whereas uniformity and univocity govern the rationalist and liberal universe, variety and unity rule the Christian traditionalist world of Donoso Cortés. Donoso finds his supreme principle of being working within political existence in the following fashion: "in society unity manifests itself through Power, and Variety manifests itself through hierarchies."[36] Both are inviolable and sacred. "Their co-existence is simultaneously the fulfillment of the will of God and the assurance of the liberty of the people."[37] The burden of the argument of *The Letter* is Donoso's demonstration that political sanity involves an essential unity of Power on the one hand and the essential variety of "hierarchies" on the other hand. The marriage between Power and Hierarchy (our principle of "Authority," as shall be seen) is the *conditio sine qua non* for a Christian political and social order.

The careful reader will note that Donoso insists that unity is found within Power. Although of itself this does not constitute an anti-liberal and anti-Montesquian position it does suggest the tack Donoso actually will take. The suggestion is heightened by Donoso's distinction between the medieval and the absolute monarchy. The former reflected proper relations that ought to exist between Power and "the hierarchies." "Power was one, perpetual, and limited: it was one in the person of the king; it was perpetual in his family; it was limited because it was forever checked by a material resistance encountered in an organized hierarchy."[38] Donoso denies flatly that medieval assemblies such as the Spanish Cortés or the English Parliament formed part of the public Power. When monarchy was strong without being absolute, representative assemblies were a dike to the tendency of Power to expand itself indefinitely; when monarchy was weak, these assemblies were a "field of battle" which reflected a society in chaos. He insists that those historians who see in medieval representative institutions the source of modern parliamentarianism are "ignorant of what a parliamentary government is and they know nothing of its origin."[39] Donoso thus denies any strict continuity in the experience of Western man between the autonomous political institutions of the Middle Ages and the liberal parliamentary system of nineteenth-century Europe. Historically it seems difficult to gainsay the Spanish thinker despite the fact that the revolt against absolutism was often mounted by men who used medieval limited-government rhetoric as a cloak for their own revolutionary goals. Modern civilization—returning to our analysis of the text—owes its decadence in the moral, political, and religious orders to its failure to obey the tensions that ought to exist between Power and Hierarchy, between—reverting to our earlier discussion—Power and Authority.

THE ABSOLUTE monarchy had the good fortune, according to Donoso, of having conserved the unity and perpetuity of Power in the person of the king and the dynastic family. Absolute monarchy, however, sinned in that "it despised and suppressed all resistances" to Power by destroying those corporate hierarchies in which these resistances had grown up and which incarnated them. Absolutism thus "violated the law of God". In so doing it violated the Law of Variety and Unity. What follows in the text is an eloquent defense of freedom foreign to the rhetoric of liberalism:

> A Power without limits is an essentially Anti-Christian Power and it is simultaneously an outrage done the majesty of God and the dignity of man. A Power without limits can never be a ministry or a service and political Power under the imperatives of Christian civilization can never be anything less. Unlimited Power is also an idolatry lodged within both subject and king: idolatry in the subject because he adores the king; idolatry in the king because he worships himself.[40]

But if Donoso finds much to condemn in the absolutism that culminated in the Enlightenment, he finds even more to attack in the political system that grew out of the French Revolution. The absolute monarchy, "although negating the Christian monarchy" in one fundamental aspect, did affirm it in two other fundamentals: Power remained one and perpetual and thus obeyed the metaphysics of political power as understood by our author. Parliamentarianism, however, violated the structure of Power in all of its essential notes and hence in their consequences. Liberalism, writes Donoso:

> denies power's unity because it converts into three through the division of powers that which really is one; liberalism denies this principle in its perpetuity because it grounds the principle itself in a contract and no power is inviolable if its foundation is variable; Liberalism denies Power's limitation; this is so because this political trinity in which Power resides either cannot function due to is impotency, an organic sickness itself the result of Power's division or Power acts tyranically not recognizing outside of itself, or discovering around itself, any legitimate resistance. It thus follows that the parliamentary system which denies the Christian monarchy in all of the conditions of its unity also denies that institution in its variety and in all the conditions producing variety because the parliamentary system suppresses the 'social hierarchies.'[41]

Wherever the liberal system has taken root all "corporations" tend to disappear, along with the hierarchical order within society that they establish. By "corporations" Donoso does not mean any specific kind of institution but that analogous whole which includes an aristocracy; free guilds (themselves heavily attacked and ultimately destroyed by liberalism); self-governing townships; regional assemblies representing regional interests (what we in this country call the principle of "states' rights"); free universities belonging to ecclesiastical or other private interests and not extensions of the state (the state university was the creation of the Continental European system of liberalism); a strong free peasantry whose concrete rights rest upon customary law; in a word—that whole complex of autonomous institutions that disappeared upon the continent due to both Absolutism and liberalism and that has survived, if only in a truncated way, within the Anglo-Saxon world. Free institutions naturally group themselves within a hierarchy and their destruction involves a leveling of the whole community and the disappearance of the very principle of hierarchy from the political order. The theory of parliamentary supremacy, involving as it does the concentration of political power within a body which claims to be sovereign, admits of no dialogue between the executive and deliberative assemblies except one carried out through cabinet ministers who are themselves nothing other than ambassadors of parliament and extensions of its will. Donoso insists that no discussion can be found between the Liberal parliament and the people that is continuous. The lone exception admitted is of course the "dialogue" expressed by free elections, but these elections are exercised at limited concrete moments of time. The brief corporate cohesion which society finds at election time falls back—Donoso believes—into either the indifference of men who have lost their role within the political order or into that chaos which follows upon the refusal of the defeated to accept the decision of the polls.

Donoso is thinking concretely and historically when he attacks the Revolution; the drying up of the last vestiges of medieval liberties at the hands of the centralizers: i.e., the abolition of what little still remained, especially in France, of regional liberties; the division of France into administrative units dependent totally upon Paris; the abolition of the last of the guilds in both Spain and France and the subsequent reduction of artisans and laborers to a *Lumpenproletariat* without any political or economic voice in the land; the confiscation and forced sale of municipal and church properties under the government of Mendizábol in Spain which saw a quarter of Spain's land under the auctioneer's block in less than a year, thus creating a new liberal middle class "which was less a political party," in the words of Menendez y Pelayo, "than a bad conscience"; the steady war of attrition against religious orders; the flattening of Latin Europe into a grey field administered as though it were occupied territory by ever-increasingly centralized governments dominated by party ideologues. Donoso adds that those who see any significant difference between liberalism and socialism err. Whereas the former violates the nature of Power in the political order, the latter does so in the social.

LET US be very careful that we understand what Donoso is saying. He is not denying the existence or value of political contracts. He could hardly have done so in the light of the history of his own country. The supremacy of the Crown of Castile gained legitimacy in the eyes of Spain because it was the product of an intricate network of pacts contracted by Castile and the other Spanish kingdoms, counties, and lordships. This legitimacy was written into the very law of the land

and it lingers even today in the Province of Navarre which enjoys a number of "state rights" (*fueros*) that are a thousand years old and that have been respected by the centralist Madrid government to some extent at least, because Navarre's contract with Castile involved the sanctity of these ancient laws and customs, of a juridical corpus as venerable and as complex as any in the civilized world.[42] Donoso's contention is not, therefore, a denial of the juridical validity and existentiality of contracts but rather a denial that political Power can be understood philosophically to be constituted by a contract.

Power can always be seized from the "ins" by the "outs," but political Power itself—understood as a dimension of human existence—persists in being, perpetual except in moments of total breakdown within a society. The absence of Power is anarchy. In a word: wherever there exists a political society we find there a Power that is just as perpetual as is that society itself. Donoso's note of perpetuity as belonging to Power does not mean eternity nor does it exclude an ethic of revolution. The issue really is self-evident. There can be many public Powers successively in time, many governments, the one following the other due to the disappearance and appearance of new political societies produced by invasion, revolution, decay of the old public orthodoxy, or any other cause capable of altering the fabric of an existent community. Power itself, however, must be conceived as being co-terminal with any given political society. Behind Donoso's contention lies his own reiterated conviction that Power is simply a necessary expression and representation of a living historical community. An admission that Power is non-perpetual *within* some existent community involves a denial that political society is a temporal and psychic continuum. Nineteenth-century liberalism did just this, however. In its excessive reaction against that Absolutism whose ape it was, liberalism so shattered the unity of Power that it reduced society to a battleground or a boxing ring. It follows that liberal theory not only denies the limitation of Power which is the fruit of hierarchical variety but it shatters society from within, fragmenting it, denying it the coherence which is the product of what I have called here and elsewhere a "public orthodoxy."[43]

Let it be noted clearly that Donoso is elaborating here a metaphysics of Power in total opposition to that prevalent in the rhetoric which fills the literature of liberalism, a rhetoric which drew—as indicated earlier—on its own understanding of what Montesquieu had written about the British Constitution. We have already seen that the liberal insistence that the subject or citizen finds freedom only when Power is divided into three was deeply ingrained in the European mentality at the time Donoso composed *The Letter*. We have noted that the political model buttressing the theory was thought to be England. It followed, therefore, that Donoso had to face the imposing fact of the English Constitution, come to terms with it theoretically in the light of his own teaching on Power, or abandon the field.

Donoso was keenly aware of the fact that his political theory on the issue at hand stood or fell with his own analysis of the British experience. He begins his attack by pointing out that these men who "attend only to appearance and to forms" will conclude that parliamentarianism has existed "in all times and places."[44] These forms can be found "in England where the nation is governed by the Crown and the two Houses of Parliament; and they can be found in past times in all the nations of Europe where clergy, nobility, and cities were called together to deliberate over affairs of a public nature."[45] But, he insists, if we suppress appearances and attend to "the spirit" animating them, we must conclude that the medieval parliaments as well as the modern British Constitution *have nothing to do with European Liberal parliamentarianism.*[46] His words are better than any gloss:

> If, beginning with the British Constitution, we set ourselves the task of examining not only its external organization but also and principally its internal organism before the late reforms, we shall discover that the division of Power was altogether lacking in reality, being nothing other than a vain appearance. The Crown was not a Power nor did it even form part of Power: it was a symbol and the image of the nation; to be a king there in England was neither to rule nor to govern: it was, purely and simply, to be adored. This passive attitude of the Crown excludes by its very nature the meaning itself of Power and the idea of government which is incompatible with the idea of a perpetual inaction and an eternal repose. The House of Commons in both its composition and its spirit was a younger brother of the House of Lords. Its voice was not a voice but an echo. The House of Lords under this modest title was the only true Power in the State. England was not a monarchy but an aristocracy and this aristocracy was a Power which was one, perpetual and limited: one, because it resided in a moral person, quickened by a single spirit; perpetual, because this moral person was a class endowed by legislation with the necessary means to endure perpetually; unlimited, because the Constitution and the traditions and the customs

obliged the House of Lords to behave in accordance with the modesty of its title.[47]

THE BRITISH Constitution that emerged from the Protestant Succession and the defeat of the Stuart cause in no sense broke with the essential structure of Power found within medieval Christendom: if medieval political Power was one in the king, perpetual in his family, and limited by a hierarchical variety of institutions, modern Great Britain possessed a similar structure, the unity of Power reposing in the aristocracy, perpetuity belonging to the hereditary nature of that aristocracy, and limitation to the traditions, customs, and laws guaranteeing Englishmen their rights. These rights had—we must admit—decayed considerably since the High Middle Ages under the pressure of Tudor centralization and the loss of independence by the church. Guild principles were in full decay by the time Donoso commented upon England. Nonetheless the rights of Englishmen, as the Burkeans quite properly insist, were largely guaranteed and respected. So far as the Crown is concerned, we need only note that its illusions of Power were unmasked as hollow when the Stuarts tried to take them seriously. What Hilaire Belloc was fond of calling "the popular monarchy" was dead before Charles I raised the royal standard at Nottingham.[48] The Restoration politics of Charles II were a series of brilliant delaying tactics by a Crown already fighting a hopeless battle against a new aristocracy that was the repository of the Reformation Settlement, that was the "representative" (in the Voegelinian sense of the term) of a new public orthodoxy, that was the Power in the land.

The apparent division of Power in the English Constitution was simply a division of labor in the business of government, a division called for by the complexity of the tasks at hand and by the highly desirable need for the *agents* of Power to debate among themselves and with society at large before exercising their mandate as corporate representatives—as a *moral person* in the words of Donoso—of a regime or a public orthodoxy. Donoso's nervous fingering of the essential Unity of political Power made him contemptuous of the forms of debate and of dialogue. In this he may have erred but he can he forgiven his error for having struck at the heart of the affair: i.e., the British Constitution was the representative of a nation led by an aristocracy whose rule was accepted as proper and just by the people at large. This Power, unlimited from within itself, was limited or checked from without by the Common Law, by custom, and by a thicket of traditional rights and duties which were inherited by the American colonies and thus incorporated into the American tradition. Donoso's contribution here was strikingly original: i.e., there simply is no organic link whatsoever between the Anglo-Saxon tradition and the Revolution. If the Anglo-American tradition has any link whatsoever with the political thought of modern Europe, that link has to be with the Counter-Revolutionary philosophy of the nineteenth and early twentieth century.

The French experience illustrates Donoso's insights by contrast, The Bourbons of the eighteenth century had attempted to limit their own power *from within* by appealing to *Parlements* for an impartial reading of the legality of royal actions. This attempt was frustrated at its inception because the supposed limitation was either false, in no sense serious due to its having come out of a royal sov-

ereignty which itself accepted no source of law beyond itself except a vague appeal to the Christian conscience of the king; or because, when serious, the "limitation" tended to identify itself with the class interests and doctrinal predilections of the lawyers who interpreted the law, thus creating a special-interest lobby, so to speak, within the total machinery of government which was bent on securing its own advancement to the detriment of the impartial majesty of the law. Had the French Crown been led consistently by the lawyers instead of only by fits and starts, Power in France would have shifted to the new bourgeoisie before the Revolution instead of afterwards. The Crown would thus have become the agent of a new liberalism some one century or more before it actually did so in the reign of Louis Philippe from 1830 to 1848.

Donoso's metaphysics of Power is thus buttressed by an historical phenomenology which brushes away any illusions about Power's effective limitation from within its own structure. If we link Donoso's insight with Voegelin's insistence that representation cannot be understood on the superficial level of institutional forms but only in the light of Sir John Fortescue's "articulation" of a "head" to serve and govern a society in its action within history, we shall be well on the road in political philosophy to a theory of Power which does justice to both the internal metaphysics of Power and to historical phenomena themselves.[49]

We have already mentioned that, according to *The Letter*, medieval assemblies must not be understood as though they were political Powers. They represented the principle of Authority and not Power and hence kings had to dialogue with them and had to listen to their desires and complaints. These assemblies crystalized the natural resistance to

Power found out in the community itself and hence they chastened kings and humbled crowns. When the purse strings depended on society itself, Power was given an additional motive for heeding the Authority incarnated in society and Power was forced to come to terms with that Authority. Medieval parliaments were, says Donoso, a "social force . . . an organic resistance and a natural limit to the indefinite expansion of Power."[50] Liberal parliamentarianism, on the contrary, developed according to the theory that Power must be perpetually divided, thus placing it—according to Donoso— at the mercy "of a hundred parties." The resultant chaos turned the parliaments of the last century and of this one into battlefields which:

> by suppressing the hierarchies which are the natural and hence divine form of variety and denying to Power its indivisibility which is the divine, natural, and necessary condition of its unity, produced an open insurrection against God as far as He is the creator, the legislator, and the conserver of human societies.[51]

In the grim, steely world of political and social unrest produced by liberalism, God permits the combat but He "denies the victory."[52] Donoso here pushes his philosophy of Power to its final consequences. If the *Law of Unity and Variety* is true to the ultimate order of Being it follows that any attempt at violating its structure must be self-defeating. We would miss the significance of Donoso's critique were we to reduce his study to an analysis of political institutions, some of which he approved of and some of which he disliked. Donoso's preference for the traditional Catholic monarchy of the Middle Ages can be read this way and

political philosophers ought not to deny to their fellow practitioners existential and historical preferences.[53] Nonetheless, behind Donoso's institutional predilections there lies a philosophy which transcends it as well because it purports to teach us something about Power itself, no matter where or in what historical moment in time, or under whatever form it might exist, including—of course—under the form of democracy. The division of Power and the centralization of society are twin ontological monstrosities for Donoso. The decentralized political community that diffuses Authority through it variety of autonomous institutions is a dictate of the law of political existence itself. In our time, Professor Alvaro D'Ors has found this law at work in the early Roman distinction between Power and Authority as indicated earlier in this essay. "In general terms, authority is the truth recognized by society and it is set off against *potestas* which is force or power recognized by society."[54] Both grew out of and represent the same political order or "regime" but they ought "to remain permanently separated because if authority resides in the same organ that possesses *potestas* it follows that authority could never serve as a limit or brake."[55]

THE ALARMING collapse of Christianity today in a society bent upon secularizing itself so profoundly that it even makes of Christianity itself a tool in the desacralizing of political existence,[56] has left the West without an effective representative of the Authority of God and of the Moral Law. Institutional tinkering with the instruments of Power in some vain attempt to play them off one against another is no effective scalpel for ridding the body politic of the diseases of tyranny and chaos.

Politics which sin against the laws of Being do so at their own peril. They fall into either a tyrannical Power which violates the body politic or into a chaos within whose vortex every faction within the community vies with all comers for the palm of a Power possessed by none. Donoso's phenomenology of Power today works out its tragic destiny in the new African and Asiatic countries where the disintegration of tribal loyalties follows the centralizing of Power and its identification with Sovereign Authority. Authority, no longer centrifugal, diffused throughout the community by way of a plurality of institutions that repose ultimately upon some final Representative of Divine Truth, some last Voice which speaks with the Wisdom and even the Thunder of God, loses itself in the insane pretensions of the Tyrannical Soul or gives itself over to gnostic or totalitarian dreams in the name of a supposed fiat written into the flow of history itself. The Revolution was ushered into the West by its outriders and its visionaries from Machiavelli through Bodin and beyond. Don Juan Donoso Cortés, unlike Montesquieu, refused to tinker with the body of the West. It was too far gone in disease. He called for the surgery of The Counter-Revolution.

Notes

1. Cf. Alvaro D'Ors, *Una introducción al estudio del derecho* (Madrid: Ediciónes Rialp, S.A., 1963), 78–84.

2. The classic statements are found in *The Statesman* and *The Republic*; the irony of the Philosopher-King against Society is explored in the Socratic dialogues. Cf. Willmoore Kendall, *El Hombre Ante La Asamblea* (Madrid: O Crece o Muere, 1962); Eric Voegelin, *Order and History: Plato and Aristotle* (Baton Rouge: Louisiana State Univ. Press, 1957), 135–69.

3. The Thomistic treatise on law forms part of his basic theological work: *Summa Theologica*, I–II, Q. 91–95. After locating the natural law within the Divine Law, St. Thomas discusses its structure and meaning.

4. Aristotle, *The Nicomachean Ethics*, VI, esp. Chapters 12–13; Thomas Aquinas, *Exppositio in decem libros Ethicorum Arisiotelis ad Nichomachum, VI; Summa Theologica*, I–II, 57; II–III, 47–56.

5. Relevant medieval testimony is marshalled in Ewart Lewis, *Medieval Political Ideas* (New York: Alfred A. Knopf, 1954), esp. chaps. 2, 3, and 8.

6. Jean Bodin, *Six Books of the Commonwealth*, M. J. Tooley, abgd. trans. (New York: Macmillan, 1955), 25–38.

7. Ibid., 40–47.

8. Ibid., 47–48.

9. As typical of the medieval treatment of power, we might consult Thomas Aquinas. First he treats of the meaning of power; then he demonstrates that power belongs to God; finally, he removes any limits to that power: i.e., *Summa Theologica*, I, Q.25, a. 1–6.

10. E.g., *Summa Theologica*, I.Q. 75, a, 6, ad. 2.

11. "All the princes of the earth are subject to them [i.e., divine and natural laws], and cannot contravene them without treason and rebellion against God. The absolute power of princes and sovereign lords does not extend to the laws of God and of nature." (Bodin, 28.) But let us note that the subject has no legal recourse should the sovereign prince act against the divine and natural law. The prince himself is not even bound by the laws of his predecessors nor is he bound to oaths he takes freely.

12. From this conviction there was deduced what medieval theologians called "The Royal Sovereignty of Christ": i.e., only Christ was King of creation by virtue of His Divine Nature: all earthly kings held their kingdoms from Him by participation, Cf., George de Lagarde, *La Naissance de l'esprit laïque au déclin moyen age* (Louvain: Editions E. Nauwelaerts, 1982), IV, esp. Chap. VIII.

13. "Rey serás si hicieses derecho y si no lo hicieres, no serás Rey." The formula read to the King of Aragon was even more blunt:

"Each one of us is as good as you are and all of us are greater than you are."

14. Eric Voegelin, *The New Science of Politics* (Chicago: Univ. of Chicago Press, 1952), 42–46.

15. Sir John Fortescue, *De laudibus legum Angliae*, S. B. Chrimes, ed. (Cambridge: Cambridge Univ. Press, 1942), ch. 13. Fortescue (1385–1479), chief justice of the king's bench under Henry VI, constitutional lawyer and diplomat, is perhaps most famous for political theory because of his teaching on the difference between English kingship, that *dominium politicum et regale* cherished before him by Thomas Aquinas, the monarchy typical in both England and the Spanish kingdoms, and the French *dominium regale* which bore within itself the seeds of what later was to become absolutism.

16. Baron de Montesquieu, *The Spirit of the Laws,* Thomas Nugent, trans. (New York: Hafner Publishing Co., 1959), bk. IX, 151–62.

17. "Whereas early medieval law had been the declaration of custom, discovered perhaps by itinerant justices or settled by consultation with the magnates, and the purpose of legislation had been to expand and reinforce what had been implicitly present from of old, after the thirteenth century a sovereign body began to emerge slowly as the master, not the creature of law. New law was made, the force of which did not lie in its moral cogency or conformity with ancient usage, but in fact and threat of enactment and enforcement. Here law came to mean statute, and custom sank to an inferior condition. [It] existed on sufferance according to the goodwill of the prince." Thomas Gilby, *The Political Thought of Thomas* Aquinas (Chicago: Univ. of Chicago Press, 1958), 173.

18. Montesquieu, op. cit., 151–52.

19. Polybius, *The Histories,* W. R. Paton, trans. (Cambridge, Mass.: Harvard Univ. Press, 1927), VI, 11–12,

20. The fact that the theory in question had become the common doctrine of European Liberalism by the time Donoso Cortés began to write is evidenced by his *never* (to our knowledge) referring the teaching to its source in Montesquieu. For Donoso, the doctrine of the "three powers" and their "separation" is simply a common liberal position of his times, easily identifiable as a stock in trade of liberal rhetoric and theory.

21. The complete works of Donoso Cortés are found in the very rare *Biblioteca de Autores Cristianos:* "*Obras completas de Donoso Cortés, recopiladas y anotadas, con la aportacion de nuevos escritos, por el Dr. D. Juan Juretschke*" (Madrid: BAC, 1946). Unless otherwise specified, quotations are taken from the more readily available *Textos políticos,* (Madrid: Ediciones Rialp, S.A., 1954). Also helpful is the edition of the *Ensayo sabre el catolicisma, el liberalismo, y el socialismo,* (Argentina: Colección Austral, 1949). Translations are my own.

22. We must distinguish political Traditionalism, itself largely Catholic, from theological Traditionalism. This last doctrine, denying any value to the individual reason, insisted that all truth was reducible to a primitive revelation. Maintained by Bonald (although not, as often claimed, by de Maistre), this position was condemned formally by the Catholic Church. *Tradicionalismo* in Spanish political language means simply Carlism.

23. Carl Schmitt, *Interpetación europea de Donoso Cortés* (Madrid: Rialp, S.P., 1950), 8.

24. Federico Suarez, *Introducción a Donoso Cortés* (Madrid: Rialp, S.A., 1964), 266.

25. Donoso, *Textos politicos,* 461.

26. Ibid.

27. Ibid., 462.

28. Ibid

29. Ibid., 220.

30. I have already pointed to a pervasive tradition in Spanish thought, as old as Ramon Lull, which seeks to find within the specifically Christian doctrine of the Trinity a clue to the metaphysical structure of being. Frederick D. Wilhelmsen, *Metaphysics of Love* (New York: Sheed and Ward, 1962), 93–95. There is some possibility that Donoso's fascination with the trinitarian structure of the real may have been influenced by Hegel. In one place at least Donoso refers to God as "thesis, antithesis, synthesis" but he does not develop the idea. The decisive difference between Donoso's *paradoxical* law and Hegel's *dialectical* law consists in Donoso's refusal to dissolve the

tensions found within existential oppositions, whereas Hegel, in common with all
gnostics, is constrained to dissolve every
existential tension.

31. This is not an argument against their ultimate identity in the metaphysical order.

32. Donoso, op. cit., 210

33. Ibid., 238.

34. Ibid., 239.

35. *Cf.* Charles Norris Cochrane, *Christianity
and Classical Culture* (New York: Oxford
Univ. Press Galaxy Books, 1957), 234–249.

36. Donoso, op. cit., 482.

37. Ibid.

38. Ibid.

39. Ibid.

40. Ibid., 462.

41. Ibid.

42. Raimondo Aldea Eguilaz, *Los Derechos de
Navarra* (Pamplona, Spain: Prontuario de
Divulgación Foral, 1957); *cf* "New 'States
Rights' Challenge to Franco," *Triumph,* I
(September, 1966), 36.

43. Frederick D. Wilhelmsen, *La ortodoxia
pública y les poderes de la irracionalidad*
(Madrid: O Crece o Muere. Rialp, 1964).

44. Donoso, *op. cit.,* 266.

45. Ibid.

46. Donoso wrote immediately after the new
electoral laws and he insisted that his remarks referred principally to England
before the radical reforms which had, in
his opinion, altered profoundly the British
Constitution by shifting the center of
Power.

47. Donoso, op. cit., 267.

48. Hilaire, Belloc, *The Nature of Contemporary
England* (New York: Scribners, 1937),
passim.

49. Fortescue, Op. cit., 31–33; Voegelin, *New
Science of Politics,* 41–95.

50. Donoso, op. cit., 472.

51. Ibid., 474.

52. Ibid.

53. An instance of a contemporary failure
to understand the medieval monarchy
is McIlwain's inability to distinguish
between Thomas Aquinas's *dominium
politicum et regale* (the "traditional monarchy" of Donoso, of Spanish Carlism, and
of European Traditionalism in general)
and the *dominium regale* ("absolute" monarchy). McIlwain's inability to find any
internal division of the three powers forced
him to identify the two [*The Growth of
Political Thought in the West* (New York:
Macmillan, 1932), 331–332, and n. 1, 332].
The error is due, of course, to the author's
tendency to think within terms of the
modern state. Although the medieval *dominium regale* is not limited from within, it
is limited by the *politicum*: i.e., by a highly
structured and autonomous society. What
most authors of political handbooks and
histories call "limited Monarchy," finding—as they do—their best examples in
England and other parliamentary "monarchies," is not even monarchy at all in the
classical Christian understanding of political forms.

54. Alvaro D'Ors, *Una introducción al estudio
del derecho* (Madrid: Rioıp, 1963), 19.

55. Ibid., 63.

56. E.g., Harvey Cox, *The Secular City* (New
York: Macmillan, 1965).

Eric Voegelin

ON DEBATE AND EXISTENCE

VOL. 3, NO. 4–5, 1967

In our capacity as political scientists, historians, or philosophers we all have had occasion at one time or another to engage in debate with ideologists— whether communists or intellectuals of a persuasion closer to home. And we all have discovered on such occasions that no agreement, or even an honest disagreement, could be reached, because the exchange of argument was disturbed by a profound difference of attitude with regard to all fundamental questions of human existence—with regard to the nature of man, to his place in the world, to his place in society and history, to his relation to God. Rational argument could not prevail because the partner to the discussion did not accept as binding for himself the matrix of reality in which all specific questions concerning our existence as human beings are ultimately rooted; he has overlaid the reality of existence with another mode of existence that Robert Musil has called the Second Reality. The argument could not achieve results, it had to falter and peter out, as it became increasingly clear that not argument was pitched against argument, but that behind the appearance of a rational debate there lurked the difference of two modes of existence, of existence in truth and existence in untruth. The universe of rational discourse collapses, we may say, when the common ground of existence in reality has disappeared.

Corollary: The difficulties of debate concern the fundamentals of existence. Debate with ideologists is quite possible in the areas of the natural sciences and of logic. The possibility of debate in these areas, which are peripheral to the sphere of the person, however, must not be taken as presaging the possibility in the future that areas central to the person (Max Scheler's distinction of *personperiphere* and *personzentrale* areas) will also move into the zone of debate. Among students of the Soviet Union there is a tendency to assume that the universe of discourse, at present restricted to peripheral subject-matters, will, by the irresistible power of reason, expand so as to include the fundamentals of existence. While such a possibility should not be flatly denied, it also should be realized that there is no empirical evidence on which such an expectation could be based. The matter is of some interest, because philosophers of the rank of Jaspers indulge in the assumption that there is a community of mankind in existence on the level of the natural sciences, and that scientists form a community. That raises the philosophical question whether community is something that can be established on the level of a common interest in science at all, a question which at present is far from being thought through.

The phenomenon of the breakdown as such is well known. Moreover, the various Second Realities, the so-called ideologies, have been the object of extensive studies. But the nature of the breakdown itself, its implications for the advancement of science, and above all the methods of coping with the fantastic situation, are by far not yet sufficiently explored. The time at our disposition will obviously not allow an exhaustive inquiry concerning so vast a topic; still, I propose in the present paper at least to circumscribe some of the relevant points of such an inquiry. And as a step toward establishing the relevant points, I shall place the phenomenon of the breakdown in historical perspective.

I

The Second Realities which cause the breakdown of rational discourse are a comparatively recent phenomenon. They have grown during the modern centuries, roughly since 1500, until they have reached, in our own time, the proportions of a social and political force which in more gloomy moments may look strong enough to extinguish our civilization—unless, of course, you are an ideologist yourself and identify civilization with the victory of Second Reality. In order to distinguish the nature of the new growth, as well as to understand its consequences, we must go a little further back in time,

to a period in which the universe of rational discourse was still intact because the first reality of existence was yet unquestioned. Only if we know, for the purpose of comparison, what the conditions of rational discourse are, shall we find our bearings in the contemporary clash with Second Realities. The best point of departure for the comparative analysis of the problem will be St. Thomas's *Summa Contra Gentiles.* The work was written as an exposition and defense of the truth of Christianity against the Pagans, in particular against the Mohammedans. It was written in a period of intellectual turmoil through the contacts with Islam and Aristotelian philosophy, comparable in many respects to our own, with the important difference however that a rational debate with the opponent was still possible or—we should say more cautiously—seemed still possible to Aquinas. I shall reflect, therefore, on the opening chapters of the *Summa* in which Aquinas sets forth the problem of debate, not simple even in his time.

Aquinas assumes the philosopher, as we have done, in the situation of debate with an opponent; he considers this the philosopher's situation of necessity. For "as it is incumbent on the *sapiens* to meditate on the truth of the first principle, and to communicate it to others, so it is incumbent on him to refute the opposing falsehood." Truth about the constitution of being, of which human existence is a part, is not achieved in an intellectual vacuum, but in the permanent struggle with pre-analytical notions of existence, as well as with erroneous analytical conceptions. The situation of debate thus is understood as an essential dimension of the existence that we recognize as ours; to one part, the quest for truth is the perpetual task of disengaging it from error, of refining its expression in contest with the inexhaustible ingenuity of error. Philosophy, as a consequence, is not a solitary but a social enterprise. Its results concern everyman; it is undertaken by the *sapiens* representatively for everyman. More specifically the represented have a right to receive answers not only to their own questions but also to hear answers to brilliant and well propagated errors which threaten to disintegrate the order of society by disintegrating the order of existence in everyman personally. It is a situation and an obligation that must be faced in our twentieth century as much as Thomas had to face it in his thirteenth. Hence, if the *sapiens* shuns the situation of debate, especially if he avoids the crucial intellectual issues threatening the beleaguered city, he becomes derelict in his duties to God and man, his attitude is spiritually, morally and politically indefensible.

The philosopher's office thus is twofold: He must set forth the truth by elaborating it analytically, and he must guard the truth against error. But what is this truth the philosopher has to meditate and to set forth? I have called it the truth of existence, and by using this language I have terminologically modernized the problem that lies at the core of St. Thomas's endeavor, as well as of the earlier one of Aristotle to which Aquinas refers in the passages under consideration. The modernization is legitimate, as you will see presently, because it does not modify the problem but only its symbolic expression; and at the same time it is necessary, because without it we cannot understand that the scholastic and classic problem is indeed identical with our own. The source of the difficulties we moderns have with understanding Aristotle and Aquinas is the fact that the truth of existence, of the first reality as we called it, in their time was not yet questioned;

hence there was no need to distinguish it from an untrue existence; and consequently no concepts were developed for a problem that had not yet become topical. The truth of existence was taken so much for granted that, without further preparation, the analysis could proceed to develop the problems of metaphysics as they presented themselves to men who lived in the truth of existence. But let us now have a look at the manner in which Aquinas and Aristotle expressed their problem of truth.

II

While the supporting argument is voluminous, the crucial formulations are succinct. Aquinas, following Aristotle, considers it the task of the philosopher to consider the highest causes of all being.

> The end of each thing is that which is intended by its first author or mover. But the first author and mover of the universe is an intellect. The ultimate end of the universe must, therefore, be the good of an intellect. This good is truth. Truth must consequently be the ultimate end of the whole universe, and the consideration of the wise man aims principally at truth.

Aquinas then refers to the authority of Aristotle himself who established

> that first philosophy is the science of truth, but of that truth which is the origin of all truth, namely, which belongs to the first principle whereby all things are. The truth belonging to such a principle is, clearly, the source of all truth; for things have the same disposition in truth as in being.

So far the text (SCG I, 1. *Met.* alpha el-laton, 1,993b20–30).

At first hearing, I presume, these formulations will sound as strange to you as they did to me. There is talk about a first mover of the universe—who must be assumed to be an intellect—from whom emanates somehow an order of being that is at the same time an order of truth. Why should we be concerned with a prime mover and his properties?—you will ask. And does the matter really improve when Aquinas identifies the prime mover with the God of revelation and uses the Aristotelian argument for the prime mover as a demonstration of the existence of God? At the risk of arousing the indignation of convinced Aristotelians and Thomists I must say that I consider such questions quite pertinent. The questions must be raised, for we no longer live, as did Aristotle and even Aquinas, at the center of a cosmos, surrounding us from all sides spherically, itself surrounded by the outer sphere of the fixed stars. We can no longer express the truth of existence in the language of men who believed in such a cosmos, moved with all its content by a prime mover, with a chain of *aitia,* of causes, extending from existent to existent down to the most lowly ones. The symbolism of the closed cosmos, which informs the fundamental concepts of classic and scholastic metaphysics, has been superseded by the universe of modern physics and astronomy.

Nevertheless, if we admit all this, does it follow that Aristotelian and Thomist metaphysics must be thrown on the scrap heap of symbolisms that once had their moment of truth but now have become useless?

You will have anticipated that the answer will be negative. To be sure, a large part of the symbolism has become obsolete, but there is a solid core of truth in it that can be, and must be, salvaged by means of some surgery. Two stages of such surgery seem to be indicated:

(1) The first operation must extend to the demonstrations which depend for their validity on the imagery of a cosmos that is no longer ours. If however we survey the body of demonstrations in support of the formulations I have presented, and if we remove from it everything that smacks of cosmological symbolism, there remains as a *piece de resistance* the argument that a universe which contains intelligent beings cannot originate with a *prima causa* that is less than intelligent. Though the context of the argument is still the cosmos, at least the argument itself draws specifically on an experience of human existence which as such is independent of the experience of the cosmos.

(2) The second operation must extend to the prime mover itself. We must distinguish between the symbolic construction and the reality to which it refers; and we must be aware of the curious relations between the firmness of conviction that such a reality exists and the credibility of the construct. If the motivating experiences are known to the reader and shared by him, the construct will appear satisfactory and credible; if the experiences are not shared, or not even too clearly known, the construct will become incredible and acquire the character of an hypostasis. Aristotle could indulge in his construction with assurance because the experiences which motivate the symbolism were taken for granted by everybody without close scrutiny; and Aquinas, in addition to living in the same uncritical safety of experience, could as a Christian theologian blend the truth of the prime mover into the truth of revelation. Today the validity of the symbol, and with its validity the reality to which it refers, is in doubt, because the experiences which

motivated its creation for their adequate expression have slipped from public consciousness; and they could slip from public consciousness with comparative ease, because neither were they set forth with sufficient explicitness, nor did the problem of experience and symbolization come into clear focus at all, in classic and scholastic metaphysics. Hence, in order to reach the truth contained in the apparently hypostatic construct, we must make explicit the motivating experiences.

The immediate experiences presupposed in Aristotelian metaphysics are not difficult to find in the classic sources, if one looks for them; but after all this preparation, I am afraid, they will come as an anticlimax because of their apparent simplicity. For we find ourselves referred back to nothing more formidable than the experiences of finiteness and creatureliness in our existence, of being creatures of a day as the poets call man, of being born and bound to die, of dissatisfaction with a state experienced as imperfect, of apprehension of a perfection that is not of this world but is the privilege of the gods, of possible fulfillment in a state beyond this world, the Platonic *epekeina,* and so forth. I have just mentioned Plato; if we survey this list of experiences, we shall better understand why for Plato (who had a sharper sensitiveness for the problems of existence than either Aristotle or Thomas) philosophy could be, under one of its aspects, the practice of dying; under another aspect, the Eros of the transcendent Agathon; under still another aspect (that leads us back to the formulations of Aristotle and Aquinas) the love of the Wisdom that in its fullness is only God's. In these Platonic conceptions (the catalogue is not complete) we can see philosophy emerging from the immediate experiences as an attempt to illuminate existence, Moreover, we can understand how philosophy, once

it had, thanks to Plato, developed its symbolism and become a going concern, could gain something like an autonomous life of construction and demonstration, apparently independent of the originally motivating experiences, how it could grow into an enterprise that would have to become unconvincing when, due to historical circumstances, the reader did no longer share the philosopher's understanding of existence.

III

We have assembled the data of the problem of experience and symbolization as far as they were immediately connected with the formulations of Aquinas and Aristotle. We can now attempt the exegesis of existence that is implied, though not explicitly given, in classic and scholastic metaphysics. In the course of this attempt, however, further data of the problem will emerge that will compel us to revise the initial propositions. The reader should be warned, therefore, that after the first we have to make a second start.

Human existence, it appears, is not opaque to itself, but illuminated by intellect (Aquinas) or *nous* (Aristotle). This intellect is as much part of human existence as it is the instrument of its interpretation. In the exegesis of existence intellect discovers itself in the structure of existence; ontologically speaking, human existence has noetic structure. The intellect discovers itself, furthermore, as a force transcending its own existence; by virtue of the intellect, existence not only is not opaque, but actually reaches out beyond itself in various directions in search of knowledge. Aristotle opens his *Metaphysics* with the sentence: "All men by nature desire to know." I shall not bother you with the detail of Aristotle's argument on the point, because I suspect that in his etiology of being, i.e., in the doctrine of the four causes and the organization of the demonstrations according to the four causes, we touch again one of the areas of symbols that is incompatible with the present state of science and, therefore, will have to be abandoned to a large part, if not entirely, in order to reach the core of truth. I shall rather use a shortcut and divide the objects to which the desire to know reaches out into the two classes of (1) things of the external world and (2) human actions.

With regard to things the desire to know raises the questions of their origin, both with regard to their existence (I include under this title both the hyletic and kinetic arguments) and their essence (the eidetic argument). In both respects, Aristotle's etiological demonstration arrives ultimately at the eternal, immaterial *prima cause* as the origin of existent things. If now we shift the accent back from the construct of doubtful validity to the experiences that motivate its construction, and search for a modern terminology of greater adequacy, we find it offering itself in the two great metaphysical questions formulated by Leibniz in his *Principes de la Nature et de la Grâce,* in the questions: (1) Why is there something, why not nothing? and (2) Why is something as it is, and not different? These two questions are, in my opinion, the core of true experience which motivates metaphysical constructions of the Aristotelian and Thomist type. However, since obviously no answer to these questions will be capable of verification or falsification, the philosopher will be less interested in this or that symbolism pretending to furnish the "true" answer than in the questions themselves. For the questions arise authentically when reason

is applied to the experiential confrontation of man with existent things in this world; and it is the questions that the philosopher must keep alive in order to guard the truth of his own existence as well as that of his fellow-men against the construction of a Second Reality which disregards this fundamental structure of existence and pretends that the questions are illegitimate or illusionary.

Corollary I: Heidegger stresses very strongly the first of Leibniz's questions, but neglects the second one. Nor does he pay any attention to the Aristotelian argument of the final cause (to be treated presently). His fundamental ontology is based on an incomplete analysis of existence. Even at this initial stage our analysis of existence shows already its importance as an instrument for classifying Second Realities and their various techniques of construction, one of them being the omission of parts of the experience of existence.

Corollary II: The symbolism providing an answer to the questions is of secondary importance to the philosopher. That, however, is not to say that it does not have an important function in protecting the order of existence both in man and society. For the development of an answering construct, even if it should have to be revised in the light of a later, more penetrating analysis of existence, will at least guard for a time against error concerning the truth of existence. But only for a time. For the structure of existence is complicated; it is not known once for all. If it be forgotten that the answer of the construct depends for its truth on the understanding of existence that has motivated it; if it be erected into an idol valid for all time; its effect will be the very opposite of protection. For the sensed, if not clearly known, invalidity of the symbol at a later point in history will be extended by the critics of the symbol to the truth nevertheless contained in it. An obsolete symbol may have the effect of destroying the order of existence it was created to protect.

The second class of objects considered by Aristotle, more immediately our concern as political scientists, is human actions. With regard to this class the demonstration of Aristotle is more easily understood. To be sure, the analysis is cast in the form of an etiological demonstration like the others, this time concerning the final cause, but the etiological skeleton of the analysis can be more easily discounted because the generically human experience cast in the dubious form is immediately intelligible. Moreover, on occasion of the final cause the style of Aristotle changes noticeably; all of a sudden it becomes warm and incisive as if now we had reached the heart of the problem; and it becomes discursive enough to make it clear that here indeed we touch human existence at its center. The demonstration concerning the final cause, we may say, is the model demonstration; the three arguments concerning the *aitia* of things are derivative in the sense that their persuasiveness ultimately derives from the validity of the demonstration concerning the final cause. Hence, I shall quote the decisive passage:

> The final cause is an end which is not for the sake of anything else, but for the sake of which everything else is. So if there is to be a last term of this kind, the process will not he infinite *(apeiron)*; and if there is no such term there will be no final cause. Those who maintain an infinite series do not realize that they are destroying the very nature of the Good, although no one would try to do anything if he were not likely to reach some limit *(peras)*;

nor would there be reason *(nous)* in the world, for the reasonable man always acts for the sake of an end—which is a limit *(peras)*.

We must discount, as I said, the etiological language. If that is done, Aristotle insists that human action is rational, but that rationality hinges on the condition of an ultimate end. The indefinite regress from means to ends, which in their turn are means to further ends, must be cut short at some point by an ultimate end, by a *summum bonum*. The limit to the chain of means and ends is the condition of rationality in action. This in itself is true; to be sure, there would be pragmatic rationality, if a project of action adequately coordinates means toward an end, but there would be no substantive rationality in any action, if the whole network of a man's action could not be oriented toward a highest good from which such rationality radiates down to the single actions. Aristotle, however, goes farther on this occasion. Not only would the nature of the Good be destroyed without a limiting good that is no means to a further end, but there would be no reason *(nous)* in the world at large, because a man who has reason *(noun echon)* will only act for the sake of a limit-end. The limit seems to be something inherent in reason; and this qualification appears in the context of the analysis of action, betraying that here we have reached the experiential origin from which derives the argument concerning a limit also in the demonstrations concerning the knowledge of things. For the demonstrations culminating in the assumption of a prime mover do not rely ultimately on the proof that a thinker who denies the existence of a *prima causa* and assumes an infinite chain of causation will involve himself in contradictions (for there is no reason why the universe should not be unintelligible and on closer analysis should not involve the thinker in unsolvable contradictions), but on an experience that reason is indeed embedded in the order of being and it is the property of reason to have a limit. We have returned to the initial proposition concerning human existence (common to Aristotle and Aquinas) that intellect discovers itself as part of human existence. Here, in the exegesis of existence, seems to lie the critical area in which originate the propositions, advanced as self-evident, on the level of metaphysical doctrine. We must examine this problem of reason in existence once more.

Corollary: The modern reader, unless he is an expert in metaphysics, will have difficulties in understanding the Aristotelian etiology, as well as our present analysis, because the term *aition,* rendered in modern languages as *cause,* does not have the meaning of cause which the modern reader associates with it. The *aitia* have nothing to do with cause and effect in the natural sciences; they refer to a relation in the hierarchy of being that we can neutrally term "derivation." Aristotle can say for instance *(Met.* 994a311): "The hyletic generation of one thing from another cannot go on ad infinitum (e.g., flesh from earth, earth from air, air from fire, and so forth without end): nor can the kinetic causes form an endless series—man, for example, being moved by air, air by the sun, the sun by strife, and so on without limit." Obviously Aristotle's etiology is still deeply embedded in the Ionian speculation on the cosmos, which in his turn is still close to the realm of mythical symbolization. The etiology, therefore, must not be understood as having anything to do with the chain of cause and effect in time, in the modern sense. The problem of the limit belongs strictly to the analysis of existence; it has noth-ing to do with the infinity or createdness of the world. Aristotle himself held firmly that the world exists from infinity; his rejection of the infinite regress pertains exclusively to the hierarchy of being culminating in the prime mover. Moreover Aquinas follows him in this issue: no philosopher, he concedes, has ever given a valid reason why the world should have a beginning in time; his conviction that the world is not infinite in time but created does not rest on philosophical argument but on faith in revelation. It should be noted that Aristotle was not emotionally upset, as far as we know, by the infinity of time; and we may wonder whether he would have been upset by the infinity of space that became acutely apparent with the development of physics and astronomy since the sixteenth century A.D. The question is of interest, because ever since Pascal it has become a fashion in the interpretation of modernity to acknowledge in the loss of man's position at the center of a closed cosmos one of the causes of psychic disturbance and unbalance. The interpretation of modernity would result in a quite different picture, if the infinity of time and space were experienced as disturbing because existence has lost its truth, and with its truth its balance.

IN THE light of the preceding analysis, which has introduced new factors into the problem of existence, we shall now make our second start, repeating first the propositions that will have to stand:

Man discovers his existence as illuminated from within by Intellect or *Nous.* Intellect is the instrument of self-interpretation as much as it is part of the structure interpreted. Existence, we said, has noetic structure. It furthermore turned out that Intellect can transcend existence in various directions in search of knowledge. These tentative formulations can now be given more precision. By virtue of the noetic structure of his existence, we may say, man discovers himself as being not a world unto himself, but an existent among others; he experiences a field of existents of which he is a part. Moreover, in discovering himself in his limitation as part in a field of existents, he discovers himself as not being the maker of this field of existents or of any part of it. Existence acquires its poignant meaning through the experience of not being self-generated but having its origin outside itself. Through illumination and transcendence, understood as properties of the Intellect or *Nous*, human existence thus finds itself in the situation train which the questions concerning origin and end of existence will arise.

Corollary: The preceding description seems to me more exact than Heidegger's descriptive term *Geworfenheit*. The passive *geworfen* requires a subject that does the throwing. Either the state of *Geworfenheit* must be made explicit by naming the subject, perhaps a daemonic creator in the gnostic sense; or the term must be considered methodologically defective inasmuch as it introduces an element of construction into the strictly noetic description of existence.

But where is the origin and end of existence to be found? As a preliminary to the answer we must interpret the phenomenon of questioning itself; and for this purpose we must add to illumination and transcendence two further properties of the Intellect, the properties of ideation and reasoning. Through illumination and transcendence existence has come into view as an existent thing, in a field of existent things. Through the ideational property of the Intellect it is possible to generalize the discovered characteristics of existence into a nature of existence, to create an idea

of existence, and to arrive at the proposition that origin and end of existence are to be found in one existent thing no more than in another. To be not the origin and end of itself is generically the nature of existent things. With this proposition we have reached the experiential basis for extensive demonstrations of both Aristotle and Aquinas that the infinite regress in search of origin can have no valid result; the postulate of the *peras*, of the limit, is the symbolism by which both thinkers acknowledge the truth that the origin and end of existence is not to be found by ranging indefinitely over the field of existent things. But if it is not to be found in the field of existent things, where is it to be found? To this question, Intellect, by virtue of its reasoning power, will answer that it is to be found in something beyond the field of existent things, in something to which the predicate of "existence" is applied by courtesy of analogy.

Corollary: The analysis of existence has to proceed step by step; and it has to use verbal expressions such as "illuminate," "become aware," "transcend," and so forth. The appearance of a process in time thus created, however, must not be taken for reality. The process is inherent to the analysis, not the existence. In reality all the moments of the structure, distended into analytical steps, are present at once and "known" at once in pre-analytical experience. Pre-philosophical wisdom has its compact expressions—such as "What comes into being must perish"—which at an intuitive glance size up the nature of existence. The analysis of existence can do no more than make explicit what everyman knows without it. That situation raises the question: to what purpose is the analysis undertaken at all—a question that will be dealt with presently in the text. And beyond this question arises the further one: to what purpose should an understanding of existence be expanded into the symbolic forms of metaphysics of the Aristotelian or Thomist type; what purpose could be served by the demonstrations of the prime mover, converted by Aquinas into proofs for the existence of God, especially since they prove nothing that is not known before the proof is undertaken? I have tried to show that the knowledge of the something that "exists" beyond existence is inherent to the noetic structure of existence. And this result is confirmed by Aristotelian and Thomist demonstrations in which the postulate of the *peras*, whenever it is formulated, is richly studded with the suspicious adverbial expressions of "evidently," "obviously," "clearly" which indicate that the premise of the argument is not derived from any demonstration, but that the prime mover which emerges from the demonstration has in fact been smuggled in with the unproven premise. In search of the meaning of such demonstrations (setting aside the previously mentioned usefulness of symbols for protective and defensive functions) there seems to suggest itself the possibility that demonstrations of this type are a Myth of the Logos offered by the Intellect as a gift of veneration to the constitution of being.

At this point the analysis must stop. Any further elaboration would only obfuscate the basic structure just outlined. Hence, I shall not enter in such problems as the *via negative*, or *via remotiva*, or *analogia entis,* which are rational instruments for arriving at clarity about the something; for all reasoning in such forms makes sense only if there is agreement on the structure of existence which requires the pursuit of its problems by such means. As in the case of the questions formulated by Leibniz, the philosopher is more interested today in the experiential structure which motivates speculation than in the answers themselves. The analysis has tried to show that the problems of transcendence, the questions of origin and end, and the postulate of the limit, are inherent to the noetic structure of existence; they are not doctrines or propositions of this or that metaphysical speculation, but precede all metaphysics; and these problems of existence cannot be abolished by discarding this or that speculation as unsatisfactory or obsolete. In an age that has good reasons to doubt the validity of large parts of classic and scholastic metaphysics, it is therefore of the first importance to disengage from the metaphysical efforts of the past the truth of existence that has motivated and informed them.

I have again used the expression "truth of existence." We can now define it as the awareness of the fundamental structure of existence together with the willingness to accept it as the *condicio humana.* Correspondingly we shall define untruth of existence as a revolt against the *condicio humana* and the attempt to overlay its reality by the construction of a Second Reality.

Corollary: The analysis of existence here offered pertains only to the structural elements that have informed the demonstrations of classic and scholastic metaphysics. It does by far not exhaust the structure of existence; large areas, as for instance historical existence, have not even been touched.

IV

We have traced the problem of truth in reality as it appears in the strange-sounding formulations of Aquinas and Aristotle to its origin in the noetic structure of existence. We shall now resume the problem of debate as it presented itself to Aquinas.

The *Summa Contra Gentiles* defends the truth of faith against the Pagans. But how can one do that, if the prospective partner to the debate will not accept argument from Scripture? Let us hear Aquinas himself on the question. It is difficult to argue the truth of faith against the Gentiles, he admits, because they do not agree with us in accepting the authority of any Scripture by which they may be convinced of their error. And then he continues:

> Thus, against the Jews we are able to argue by means of the Old Testament, while against heretics we are able to argue by means of the New Testament. But the Mohammedans and Pagans accept neither the one nor the other. We must, therefore, have recourse to natural reason, to which all men are forced to give their assent.

The passage formulates succinctly the problem of debate in the thirteenth century and together with it, by implication the profound difference which characterizes the situation of debate in our own time. For every debate concerning the truth of specific propositions presupposes a background of unquestioned *topoi* held in common by the partners to the debate. In a debate with the Jews the unquestioned *topoi* are furnished by the Old Testament; in a debate with heretics, by the New Testament. But where do we find them in the debate with the Gentiles? It seems to me no accident when in the answer to this question Aquinas shifts from the earlier language of Intellect to the language of Reason, without further explaining the shift. We remember our analysis of existence: We had to distinguish between the various properties of Intellect, between Illumination, Transcendence, Ideation, and Reasoning. If Aquinas believes that

he can rely on the power of Reason to force the assent of the Gentiles, he tacitly assumes that the reasoning of the Gentiles will operate within the same noetic structure of existence as his own—a quite justified assumption in view of the fact that the Mohammedan thinkers were the very transmitters of Aristotle to the Westerners. For obviously—that is, obviously to us—the logical operations of Intellect *qua* Reason will arrive at widely different results, if Reason has cut loose from the *condicio humuna*. The unquestioned *topoi* which Thomas has in common with the Gentiles of his time, to whom he addresses his argument, so unquestioned that he does not even formulate them but can take them for granted, are the *topoi* of existence. He can justly assume that his opponents are just as much interested as he is himself in the Why and How of existence, in the questions of the nature of man, of divine nature, of the orientation of man towards his end, of just order in the actions of man and society, and so forth.

These however are precisely the assumptions that we can no longer make in the situation of debate in our time. Going over again the list of Aquinas, we must say that we cannot argue by the Old Testament, nor by the New Testament, nor by Reason. Not even by Reason, because rational argument presupposes the community of true existence; we are forced one step further down to cope with the opponent (even the word "debate" is difficult to apply) on the level of existential truth. The speculations of classic and scholastic metaphysics are edifices of reason erected on the experiential basis of existence in truth; they are useless in a meeting with edifices of reason erected on a different experiential basis. Nevertheless, we cannot withdraw into these edifices and let the world go by, for in that case we would be remiss in our duty of "debate." The "debate" has, therefore, to assume the forms of (1) a careful analysis of the noetic structure of existence and (2) an analysis of Second Realities, with regard to both their constructs and the motivating structure of existence in untruth. "Debate" in this form is hardly a matter of reasoning (though it remains one of the Intellect), but rather of the analysis of existence preceding rational constructions; it is medical in character in that it has to diagnose the syndromes of untrue existence and by their noetic structure to initiate, if possible, a healing process.

R. F. Baum

Sorokin, Popper, and the Philosophy of History

VOL. 8, NO. 1–2, 1972

Morris Cohen once called philosophy of history the chief intellectual matter of our time, and went on to observe that it was also philosophy's most neglected province. Few will deny that since the eighteenth century philosophies of history have exerted on Western minds an influence comparable to that exerted earlier by theology. At the same time, as Cohen implied, not only philosophers of history but equally their critics, among them respected historians and social scientists, have commonly displayed an embarrassing unfamiliarity with the canons and discriminations of rational thought.

The late P. A. Sorokin no doubt had that last in mind when, on his election in 1963 as president of the American Sociological Association, he proposed that at the Association's next general meeting he and Karl Popper, both notable for bracing sociological inquiry with a rigor drawn from natural science, present papers on philosophy of history and then engage in an open discussion. The proposal may also have reflected a belief that Sorokin's *Social and Cultural Dynamics* had made him the weightiest living champion of the idea that history is

open to predictive theory, while Popper's *Poverty of Historicism* and *Open Society and Its Enemies* had made Popper the same idea's weightiest critic.

The present essay attempts to pick up the opportunity which in the end the Association felt it had to drop. Comparing the positions taken by Popper and Sorokin on identical issues in philosophy or, as both might prefer to call it, theory of history, the essay attempts what a personal confrontation surely would have gone far toward achieving: joint puncture by both outstanding minds of fallacies that commonly turn discussions of historical theory into mere displays of temperament, a much needed illumination of predictive theory itself, and possibly, agreement on the conceptual framework, the limits, and the peculiar difficulties of predictive theory in the field of history.

Today the two theories of history most in vogue among laymen seem that pivot of popular thought, continual human Progress and what many consider its alternative, which we can call Decay. Although Decay seldom receives explicit assertion, much of the reaction to books like Orwell's *1984*, Seidenberg's *Post-*

Historic Man, and Ellul's *Technological Society* suggest that fear of an irreversible trend toward man's dehumanization or destruction is crystallizing.

Popper and Sorokin give us strong reasons for staying out of that embattled ring, and in so doing both effectively dispose of the hoary argument that, since some people take as evidence for Progress what others take as evidence for Decay, both theories elude objective criticism. Sorokin and Popper expose as a fallacy the conception of any irreversible or permanent trend whatever, which eliminates the question of such a trend's good or evil.

Sorokin adduces against supposedly permanent trends such as the increase of knowledge or population such familiar facts as the loss of knowledge that occurred with the crumbling of the Roman Empire and the decrease in population evidenced by uninhabited ruins, those at Angkor Wat, in the Middle East, or in the Rome of the Middle Ages, for example. Similar evidence bearing on the ingrained belief that technological advance, especially, presents us with a permanent trend now lies at hand in recent histories of technology. These remind us that, for example, technology reached a height in Darius's Persian Empire (overthrown 333 B.C.) which it later failed to reach in Hellenistic times or in the Roman Empire.[1] Facts like these reveal that the permanent trends asserted result from graphing straight lines from initial, pre-human zero points to present accumulations. That lines or trends so produced can be projected without limit into the future is open to serious question.

Tackling that issue analytically, Sorokin observes that the idea that historical change can proceed forever in a fixed direction usually arises from failure to ask a question that among physicists is routine: granted that certain causes or conditions produce certain results, within what limits does the correlation hold? Very ordinary considerations reveal the pertinence of this question. The harder one strikes a piano key, the louder the sound, until one breaks the piano. Improving the diet of half-starved people increases their stature and fertility, but once diet is adequate the correlation vanishes. Similarly, so long as conditions favor, population will continue to increase, but a finite habitat sets limits to which the increase must eventually yield. In the bare sense of information, natural knowledge may seem capable of unlimited accumulation, yet even here the unattainability of perfect knowledge of anything sets a limit no accumulation will transgress. Moreover, in the past both individuals and societies have often discarded natural knowledge as "foolishness with God" or as inimical to some ideology. Sorokin thus exposes in all notions of permanent or irreversible trends an unwarranted assumption that certain causal relationships, welcome or unwelcome, possess unlimited validity.

Going further to assert the positive error of the notion that a social system can change perpetually in a fixed direction, Sorokin observes that such change would require the following conditions: a) that the system perpetually retain the characteristics favoring the change, b) that the system not be susceptible of any contrary change, and c) perpetual non-interference by external forces capable of stopping the change. None of these conditions seem likely ever to obtain in social actuality.[2]

Popper, attacking the conception of permanent trends in such philosophies of history as Comte's and Marx's, puts his finger squarely on a central confusion: the confusion of trends with laws. Trends, he rightly emphasizes, are radically different from laws and cannot like laws be considered permanent. One can say straight out that a valid law will continue to hold, forever, but one cannot say equally unconditionally that a trend will continue to proceed. Whether cultural or social, or for that matter biological, a trend is a historical happening that has proceeded in accord with many laws, some no doubt unknown, and it depends for continuance on conditions, possibly also unknown, that are subject to change. As a simple example, a tide floods for hours but when crucial conditions change the tide begins to ebb, all in accord with unchanging laws. Likewise: the long biological success of dinosaurs, followed by their extinction,

Popper concludes that a trend that has persisted for centuries or millenia may change within a decade or even more rapidly than that. He also writes:

> This, one may say, is the central mistake of historicism. Its *"laws of development"* turn out to be absolute *trends:* trends which, like laws, do not depend on initial conditions, and which carry us irresistibly in a certain direction into the future. They are the basis of unconditional prophecies, as opposed to conditional scientific predictions. (Emphases Popper's)[3]

All of which brings Popper to a conclusion bearing with equal force on both Progress and Decay, a conclusion that seems to brook no challenge: "There can be no scientific theory of [permanent] historical development serving as a basis for prediction."

Confusing trends with laws and asserting that change in a fixed direction can go on without limit, all theories of permanent or irreversible Progress or Decay stand condemned by Popper and Sorokin both in what seem compelling appeals to fact and reason.[4]

Popper goes on in *The Poverty of Historicism* to make an observation crucial to the whole question of historical theory and identical with one Sorokin had made earlier. Popper observes that the possibilities for rational prediction in any field lie not at all where Progressivists and exponents of Decay look for them, in unprecedented developments, but instead, as in astronomical prediction, in the discovery of phenomena that are repetitive and "allow us to neglect any symptoms of historical development"(with such development again understood as permanent). Prediction becomes possible where similar events occur or can be made to occur again and again. In the orbitings of planets, in the (impermanent) developments of tadpoles and stars, in laboratory experiments, repetitious events occur and provide the essential condition for prediction. Contrariwise, predictive or nomothetic science does not concern itself with and cannot predict things novel or unique.[5]

That joint statement of a basic canon of science has this salient and perhaps surprising consequence: should a predictive theory of history prove possible, it would be a theory of historical recurrences. In accord with this, Popper has stated that history may be predictable, but only insofar as it is repetitive. Sorokin, a decade after emphasizing the same scientific canon, announced a discovery of sociocultural, which is to say historical, repetition and went on to elaborate a predictive theory.

But before summarizing Sorokin's often grossly misinterpreted theory to see if it survives a Popperian scrutiny, we first should mention Sorokin's and Popper's joint exposure of a methodological naïveté that robs Spengler's and Toynbee's recurrence theories of scientific status. In seeking to establish their theories Spengler and Toynbee adduce "examples," historical events that accord with their theories, without reflecting that one establishes a theory quite the other way around, not by adducing instances that accord with it, but by showing that no instances contradict it.[6] Further, as Thomas Aquinas long ago observed, a theory's complete agreement with facts cannot suffice to prove it true, because a totally different theory might also agree with the same facts. Recognizing this, scientists trying to establish a theory try to show that it is the only one from which the facts can be deduced. Spengler, Toynbee, and journalistic publicists without number ignore this basic canon.

Before summarizing Sorokin's theory we should also detail the reasons Sorokin and Popper give us for rejecting two arguments that historians and social scientists commonly urge against the very possibility of a scientific theory of history. The first argument draws on Croce, or on Marx and Freud, and asserts the inescapable subjectivity of all views of history. All assertedly are shaped by their champions' involvement in the issues of their own time, and thus all historiography or historical theory is "contemporary history" and none can be objective.

To this Popper and Sorokin oppose the Socratic reply that such an argument rebounds against itself. The Oxford philosopher W. H. Walsh has put this objection most concisely: "[It] asks us to believe, as a matter of rational conviction, that rational convictions are impossible. And this we cannot do."[7] Popper and Sorokin also adduce a counterargument more positive. As Popper puts it in his *Logic of Scientific Discovery*, the reason why a person, whatever his political or other persuasions, arrives at a theory or

idea has a merely psychological interest and does not bear on the question of the theory's truth. What counts in evaluating a theory or idea is not how or why it originated, but how it has been tested and if further tests by other people corroborate it. That this last can happen in historical as well as physical inquiry would seem sufficiently proved by the loud objections all historians would raise to the statement "Columbus discovered Japan."

That the burning issues of some particular time or, as Marx and Freud would have it, a person's economic situation or his upbringing may affect his view of history in no way necessitates that view's inability to survive the tests of logic and fact which determine any view's acceptability as truth. To clear the field of a persistent (and most sophistical) obstacle to rational inquiry, we need say only this: the subjectivity of an idea or theory cannot prove it subjective only. It may also be objectively true, which is the point worth finding out.

The second argument commonly levelled by historians against theories of history asserts that historical events are unique and that, as implied earlier in discussion of the conditions for prediction, about things unique it is impossible to generalize. Taken seriously, Sorokin writes, this argument from the uniqueness of historical events would render worthless everything historians themselves have written about "modern war" instead of about particular modern wars, everything they have written about "Roman Law" instead of particular Roman laws. It would also require us to discard all the laws and principles of physical science, because events in nature, too, occur at definite times and are therefore historical. Moreover all of them are unique. Popper has stated this last, regularly unperceived fact this way:

all the physical repetitions which we experience are approximate repetitions, and by saying that a repetition is approximate I mean that the repetition B of event A is not identical with A, or indistinguishable from A, but only more or less similar to A.[8]

In truth, no event or thing in nature, no passage of the earth around the sun, no planet, no atom, no tadpole completely resembles or repeats any other in all its aspects. All physical events and things are unique. Yet a physical theory as sweeping and predictive as $E=mc^2$ exists and scientifically succeeds.

The puzzle is pretty easily unraveled. The objection arises from a naiveté similar to the one that confuses trends with laws or the one that takes examples as proof of theories. The humanists who urge the objection overlook all scientific theory's abstract, which is to say partial, nature. Rightly convinced that no one will ever generalize or predict historical events in all their unique totalities, they fail to perceive that physical theory does not generalize or predict physical events in all their totalities. The law of inverse squares, for example, says nothing about a physical body's color, structure, origin and infinitely more. Scientific theory in any field surmounts whatever difficulty is posed by the indisputable uniqueness of all actual events, physical as much as historical, by taking notice only of those aspects which events of certain kinds have in common. Scientific theory is abstract; it explains and predicts only the typical and not the concrete uniqueness in which the typical unfolds.

For us, the principle involved above has large and wholesome significance. It means that an acceptable predictive theory of history, which we have earlier seen would have to be a theory of recurrences,

would not at all entail determinism. It would not claim that certain events repeat themselves or are predictable in their totalities.[9] Claiming only what predictive physical theories claim, that certain events repeat themselves and are predictable in certain aspects, it would leave ample room for human freedom and responsibility. It would indeed imply limits to that freedom, but so do the laws of physics and physiology and the dictates of common sense.

Now, with the field cleared of permanent trends, proofs by "examples," psychologistic assertions of the impossibility of objectivity, and blanket condemnations all theory, we can consider the theory of recurrences formulated by Sorokin in his masterwork, *Social and Cultural Dynamics*.

AT THE outset Sorokin exhibits an analytical competence unique among theorists of history. Rejecting the exaggerated organicism that finds all of history flowing systematically from some Prime Mover such as the mode of production (Marx) or the maturing of mankind (Comte), he points out also, contra Spengler and Toynbee, that whole civilizations are not organically growing and dying systems, since many of their parts, for example a people, may go on living while other parts, for example a culture, die.[10] He therefore begins by seeking system, which is to say intelligibility, in culture only, with this taken in the limited sense of a given people's art, law, religion, philosophy, and science. And instead of merely asserting or offering examples of cultural system he proposes it as an hypothesis for strenuous testing. Far from simple, but brilliant in its searchingness, his hypothesis is that at certain times the dominant principles of art, law, and thought have articulated—i.e., logically followed from—an identical conception of reality that has gained, held, and eventually lost dominance at the same time in all the fields named. In some cultures, the hypothesis continues, the common systematizing conception has been that reality is physical or sensory. Sorokin calls this type of culture Sensate. In other cultures, called Ideational, the conception has been that reality is supersensory or spiritual.

The following paradigm of characteristic Sensate and Ideational principles, all flowing logically from the opposed conceptions or "major premises" above, will give "Sensate," "Ideational," and the entire hypothesis more meaning:

Sensate

- Becoming, time
- art represents sensory reality
- law adjusted to circumstances
- ethics of worldly happiness
- observation, empirical scientists
- needs are physical, satisfied by changing environment

Ideational

- Being, eternity
- art symbolizes supersensory reality, law cleaves to principle
- ethics of spiritual principle
- revelation, priests, oracles
- needs are spiritual, satisfied by changing self[1]

Sorokin also hypothesizes the historical existence of a third integrated culture type, called Integral (or Idealistic). Again a unified system, not an eclectic compromise, this type conceives reality as both sensory and supersensory, but with the latter aspect predominant. Individual exemplars of this rare type—Socrates, Thomas Aquinas—employ reason to mediate between empirical observation and supersensory revelation. They view needs as both spiritual and physical, but with the former predominant.

To test and confirm the historical existence of these types of integrated culture *Dynamics* presents the results of an unprecedented effort of empirical research. Enlisting the assistance of a score of art, law, and other scholars, and keeping them ignorant of the hypothesis itself, Sorokin provided them with clearcut criteria of Sensate, Ideational, and Integral manifestations in their special fields. They then used these criteria to classify centuries and in some instances decades of various societies' art, law, and thought as dominantly Sensate, Ideational, Integral or unintegrated and mixed.

The criteria provided for the particular art of painting exemplified the definiteness and objectivity of the criteria generally. In painting, the major Ideational criterion was absence of concern for visible objects except as symbols of a supersensory reality. The crudely executed anchors, fish, and olive branches that in Christian paintings in the catacombs symbolized faith, souls, and salvation exhibit this trait perfectly. As minor Ideational criteria Sorokin included artistic anonymity, lack of commercial interest, and avoidance of the nude. The criteria for Sensate painting were the opposite: accurate representation of visible objects, attribution to individual artists, concern for the market, frequent and often erotic use of the nude.

While the specialists involved could not of course classify every manifestation in their fields, they covered their fields so thoroughly—one survey of painting classified over 32,000 works, another half as many—and showed such close agreement in their final classifications of periods that challenge of these results by neglected data was precluded. If, for example, some hitherto unknown early medieval painting fitting Sensate criteria should turn up, which in itself seems all but impossible, it still would not invalidate the conclusion that early medieval painting was predominantly Ideational. For practical purposes the final classifications of periods of art, law, and thought that were arrived at can be said to be based on and therefore, the point of this huge team effort, tested by all the relevant data—quite a different matter from an accumulation of selected examples. Scientists and scholars who soon endorsed *Dynamics*'s handling of the data included Karl Compton of M.I.T., the French sociologist Jacques Maquet, F. S. C. Northrop, and Crane Brinton.[12] And when the classifications in various fields had been put together, the initial hypothesis stood confirmed.

In the cultures studied, though all fields had occasionally, but at the same times, been mixed, all had at other times primarily articulated the Sensate premise and at still other times primarily the Ideational premise. Moreover, in changing premises all fields had moved together from the same old premise to the same new one. Severely compressed, the classifications of periods of Graeco-Roman and Western culture fell into the following order:

Greece

Mycenean culture ---------------------- Sensate
9th, 8th century------------------------- Mixed
7th, 6th century --------------------- Ideational
5th century-----------------------------Integral
4th–1st A.D. ---------------------------Sensate[13]

Rome

Etruscan---------------Mixed, but with strong
Ideational current
3rd, 2nd century ---------------------------Same
1st B.C., 1st A.D. -------------- Same, but much
imitation of Greek Integral
(By 1st A.D. cultural fusion occurs)
2nd, 3rd, 4th A.D. ---------------------- Sensate

Western

5th or 6th to 10th --------------------Ideational
11th to 16th----------------- Mixed, but strong
Integral current
17th to 20th---------------------------- Sensate

The diagram above reveals, instead of a permanent trend such as the one toward positivism that Comte attributed to continual maturing of the human mind, a trendless fluctuation. *Dynamics* also brings to light an equally trendless fluctuation in Egyptian, Chinese, and Indian culture, though in India, while Sensate currents have sometimes proved strong enough to require classifying some periods as mixed, the integrated cultures have always been Ideational.

Equally significant, in demonstrating that cultures corresponding to his abstract culture types not only have existed but have done so repeatedly, Sorokin appears to have uncovered the kind of repetitious events that both he and Popper have declared the first requisite for predictive theory. And by his focus on culture types rather than on particular historical cultures Sorokin clearly will be able to avoid looking for laws or generalizations where, as Hayek has said, they cannot in the nature of the case be found, in the succession of particular historical phenomena. Sorokin appears on the way, at least, to what Popper, in denying its realization elsewhere, has aptly called a "theoretical history . . . that corresponds to theoretical physics."

From this discovery of an apparently repetitive order in cultural history Sorokin went on to consider the extent of its influence on society. Avoiding what Popper calls "psychologism" (the notion that social manifestations are simply the results of human nature), Sorokin warns that though the culture of its members strongly influences any society's institutions and activities, these also respond to the actions of other societies and to affairs like economic success or failure, climate, and pestilence. This means that correlations between culture and its social matrix cannot prove as tight as those between the different fields of integrated cultures themselves.

Yet since an Ideational culture views its members as children of its god or gods, Sorokin observes that we might expect it to favor a familistic social organization. By similar token we might expect a Sensate culture, which denies gods, to favor a contractual organization. At the same time we might expect either type, when its bearers feel it threatened, to resort to compulsion. Severely compressed, Sorokin's research into the kind of bond that in the past has cemented Western society and enabled it to function bears out these expectations:

A.D. 800–1200------------------------familistic,
some compulsion
1200–1500 ---------------both compulsory and
contractual elements increase
1500–1750 -----------------notably compulsory
1750–1914 -----------------contractual element
gains dominance
post–World War I ------ - contractual element
declines, compulsory increases[14]

Here again *Dynamics* shows us a trendless fluctuation, marked by reversals of centuries-long trends. This clearly falsifies all notions of permanent trends toward freedom, justice, etc., or the opposite. Sorokin comes to another major conclusion in *Dynamics's* pioneering study of war magnitudes. While he finds the present century showing the greatest magnitude or burden of war proportionate to population, a finding Quincy Wright and later students of war endorsed, no permanent trend emerges. What does emerge is a clear tendency for war to decrease during periods when culture is integrated on either Sensate or Ideational premises—e.g., the Middle Ages or the nineteenth century—and to increase during periods of cultural disintegration and transition—e.g., the eighteenth and seventeenth centuries.

Since wars often involve alien societies who bear some of the responsibility for them, the tendency described should appear most clearly in internal rebellions and disorders, and Sorokin's research confirms this expectation. The fact should not surprise us, he remarks, because cultural integration provides common premises for argument whereas when premises themselves come into dispute the appeal is likely to be to force.[15] It seems a pity that present efforts to reduce war and other disorders proceed in disregard of these rational and well documented conclusions.

Making culture, which is to say men's minds, an "independent variable," and cutting to the marrow of men's minds with the Sensate-Ideational distinction, Sorokin's discovery of an intelligible order in cultural history, an order bearing significantly on social history, seems as pertinent to the ancient world as to the modern, to the Orient as to the Occident. It far surpasses any other historical generalization in the surprising deductions it allows us to make.

From the clear dominance in any society of an art portraying the visible world, as did European painting in the eighteenth and nineteenth centuries, we can deduce the simultaneous dominance of empiricism in thought, an ethics of wordly happiness, and reliance on bargaining and contract. If in art or thought we find basic principles more disputed than agreed on, as is the case today, we can deduce a similar dispute in law and a high incidence of war and internal disorders.

But despite these and other unparalleled results, Sorokin's theory as so far summarized is only descriptive and cannot claim predictive power. Here we return to Popper, who has pinpointed as a crucial element in any predictive theory one that he finds lacking in theories like Spengler's and Toynbee's: "valid reason to expect of any repetition . . . that it will continue to run parallel to its prototype"—in other words, valid reason to believe that it really is a repetition and not a superficial coincidence. Such a reason would of course be a universal principle or principles from which, as from Newton's gravity and inertia, the repetitions observed and similar repetitions in the future could be deduced.

Here Spengler offers only the metaphor that civilizations are organisms, which they are not. Toynbee attempts a universal principle with his Challenge and Response, but as several critics have noted this is not really universal; it does not apply, for example, when a people survives or triumphs through help from outside allies.

Sorokin begins his search for universal explanatory-predictive principles, a search that relativists would declare futile a priori, by considering the principle

or cause of historical change, of which cultural fluctuations and their social concomitants afford vivid instances. He observes that for generations the fashion has been to account for change via some external cause acting on the culture or society undergoing change. Occasionally this suffices, as with changes forced by an alien conqueror or a plague. But when taken as it has been, as a universal principle, this environmentalism carries with it the untenable and thoroughly deterministic implication that men and societies are purely passive objects incapable of initiating change. Further, when we are told that changes in the family, say, result from economic changes, we cannot help asking what changed the economy, If the answer is technology, we ask what changed technology? Trying to end such a regress, environmentalists can only point to some nonhuman Ur-cause or Prime Mover such as Marx's mode of production or the evolutionists' evolution. This not only involves a false organicism but, as Sorokin writes, appeal to a self-changing Ur-cause contradicts the central environmentalist contention that nothing initiates its own change. Appeal to evolution attributes social and cultural changes, among the most frequent and rapid known, to biological change, one of the rarest and slowest.[16]

Having exposed by these and other cogent arguments the untenability of environmentalism, Sorokin writes:

> Since any sociocultural system is composed of human beings as one of its components, and since any organism, so long as it exists, cannot help changing, the sociocultural system . . . cannot help changing, regardless of its external conditions, even [if they are] absolutely constant.

Sorokin therefore advances, as a universal principle accounting for sociocultural change and permitting prediction of its continuance, a principle of immanent change. This principle does not deny the sometimes powerful influence of external forces; it does consider change both normal and normality the result of forces or properties within a changing system itself.[17]

Here Sorokin has tried to satisfy the basic canon that demands not only that a theory be shown adequate to facts but that it be shown the only such theory possible. He has shown the alternative to immanent change, environmentalism, untenable,

As environmentalism does not, the principle of immanent change allows scope for a basic measure of human creativity and freedom, which are in many places affirmed by Popper. Critics of the principle have charged it with "anthropomorphism" or "mysticism" on the scientist ground that physical science recognizes only such principles as inertia and external force. But as Popper has pointed out, citing von Hayek, one does not err in thinking anthropomorphically about man.[18]

But with his principle of immanent change Sorokin has only partly solved his problem. To meet the essential requirement set forth by Popper above, Sorokin must do more than account for change itself; he must account for the recurrent nature of the sociocultural changes whose existence he has empirically demonstrated.

ONCE MORE he considers the alternatives, which are (a) change or development in a permanent direction, and (b) the emergence of systems *wholly* new. We have seen a) disposed of earlier in discussion of permanent trends.

With b) the key word is wholly. While Sorokin does not of course contend that actual, historical sociocultural systems repeat themselves in all respects, he does contend that wholly new systems do not occur. In support of this he notes that historians and social scientists habitually classify economic, political, familial, and other systems by means of a few basic categories—e.g., for economic systems: hunting and collecting, pastoral, agricultural, industrial. He also notes that in the long history of natural science a few basic thought systems such as atomism, vitalism, and mechanism emerge, vanish, and recur. Of course every atomism, just as every monarchy or marriage, or every historic culture fitting Ideational or Sensate criteria, has its novelties and peculiarities. Yet each repeats its forerunners in significant respects.[19]

Discovering cultural similarities between peoples so widely separated in time or space that inheritance or borrowing cannot explain them, anthropologists have come to recognize that many human activities have limited possibilities of variation. There are only a few generic ways of making a fire, regulating marriages, or ruling societies. Sorokin expands a similar insight into a universal principle of limits. Denying the tacit assumption of man's unlimitedness, which has profoundly influenced Western thought since the Renaissance (and much non-thought today), this principle reminds us that through all his changes man remains a son of Adam. The principle asserts limits not only to the possible extent of any given sociocultural change (as in Sorokin's discussion of permanent trends) but also to the number of possible sociocultural types, which his theory sets at four: Ideational, Sensate, Integral, and mixed.

From that last it follows that once a people has created those four possible types of culture and concomitant society, that same people can only repeat the same types—though not, Sorokin remarks, necessarily or even probably in the manner often called cyclical, that is, in the same sequence and over the same lengths of time. In combination with the principle of immanent change, which recognizes change's unceasingness, the principle of limits appears fully to meet the essential requirement of nomothetic theory that Popper has justly emphasized.[20]

It is not on a mistaken organicism or a mystic fatalism but on a rational and, be it said, elegant deduction from the undeniable unceasingness of change and the undeniable existence of limits to human possibilities and choices that Sorokin rests his theory of sociocultural, which is to say historical, recurrence.

TO CONCLUDE this necessarily thumbnail summary of a monumental intellectual achievement, a summary that ignores many illuminating facets of Sorokin's theory as well as a few noncrucial instances where his data or reasoning seem questionable:

The theory puts the contemporary West, hence most of the contemporary world, in a period of transition occasioned by the disintegration of a Sensate culture that achieved dominance in the eighteenth century and began to disintegrate around 1900. In art, the Sensate aim of representing visible objects has in many quarters been abandoned. In thought, the empiricism characteristic of Sensate culture has via instrumentalism, operationism, etc., created an increasing distrust in empirical science itself as a finder and repository of truth. In society at large, contracts, from marriage contracts to those involved in monetary policy and international treaties, are

taken by all parties as mere descriptions of situations which all regard as increasingly ephemeral. These and countless other indications of a Sensate culture's disintegration are massively supported by our century's high incidence of war and internal disorders.

It follows from Sorokin's principle of immanent change, and can be stated as a law, that no culture lasts forever. Historically, none has. Before he had fully elaborated his theory in *Dynamics'* four data-packed volumes, Sorokin observed twentieth-century culture and society in that theory's light and, to the amazement and sometimes lofty amusement of Progressivist social scientists, he predicted the continuance of a period of cultural confusion, wars, and disorders which he said had begun around the time of World War I. Before the Depression or Hitler's rise to power, let alone World War II and its aftermath, had disturbed Progressivists' dogmatic slumber, he predicted what everyone would agree has happened: namely, that a high incidence of confusion and disorder would persist and probably increase until, he went on, men achieved a fresh cultural integration on Integral or, more likely in view of Integral culture's rarity, Ideational premises.[21]

Most unfortunately, Popper has written not a word about Sorokin's theory, which, were Popper acquainted with it, might sharply qualify Popper's apparent hostility to historical theory in general. As we have seen, that hostility arises in large part from detection of the crucial flaws in permanent trend or development theories such as Comte's and Marx's and in recurrence theories such as Spengler's and Toynbee's—but Sorokin has described the same flaws in terms often identical with Popper's own, and Sorokin's theory is free of those flaws. Sorokin's theory seems unaffected by the various objections raised in Popper's *Poverty, Open Society,* and *Conjectures* to a "theoretical history . . . that corresponds to theoretical physics."

But mention of physics brings to mind a final, major objection to any theoretical history: the objects of historical study are not susceptible to isolation and controlled experiment in anything like the same degree as physical objects.

As I know from conversations with him, Sorokin himself would be the last to deny the force of that objection.[22] Also, it follows from the same impossibility of isolation and controlled experiment that Sorokin's predictions are not timed, and that his theory therefore lacks what Popper emphasizes as the high *degree* of testability and exposure to falsification of many physical theories.

Still, Copernicus's example reminds us that controlled experiments are not essential to scientific success. Moreover, if in their lack of timing Sorokin's predictions fall short of those made in laboratories or at Cape Kennedy, they do compare with the much looser but still significant predictions physical science makes about such un- or only slightly controlled affairs as weather, crops, and human health. And though Sorokin's theory does not tell us when the radical cultural reversal it predicts will stand completed, it does clearly define that reversal and offer abundant evidence that it has begun. That evidence and the theory generally satisfied the late A. L. Kroeher, who announced his broad agreement with Sorokin. Probably independently of Sorokin, but in agreement, Ortega y Gasset in his testamentary *Man and Crisis* also predicted modern man's eventual cultural "turnabout."[23]

Finally, Sorokin could not well be challenged if he remarked that on the basis of some theory of history, fragmentary or structured, both men and nations make many of their decisions and attempt to provide for the future. Does not provision interlock with prevision? Prevision absent, provision seems hardly possible. Practically, the question we confront is what theory of history we will use—and with what sense of such theory's difficulties and of all theory's limitations. As with all sound theory, Sorokin's predicts the recurrence of abstract types or forms only; it does not allow prediction of the sometimes huge novelties—e.g., the early church, modern technology—in which the typically Ideational or Sensate may unfold.

In conclusion, I submit that both Popper and Sorokin have dealt fatal blows to the linear or permanent trend theories of history, usually Progressivist but now tending toward pessimism, that have dominated Western thinking since the eighteenth century. I further submit that Sorokin and Popper have punctured the arguments commonly brought against the very possibility of a predictive theory of history. Finally, it seems to me that Sorokin, via brilliant mastery of empirical research and conceptual analysis, has made into a well defined and amply documented theory the perception of earthly history's significant recurrence that was common to the greatest Greeks, to Augustine and other Christian Fathers, and to Vico and the poets, dramatists, and scholars of the Renaissance.[24] Theirs was a perception and Sorokin's is a theory profoundly philosophic and poetic and, I venture, true. In this time of cultural conflict and disorder we can ignore it and pin our hopes on Sensate nostrums, be these political, educational, or whatever, only at our own and our children's growing peril.

Notes

1. Charles Singer, ed., *A History of Technology* (Oxford: Clarendon Press, 1954–58), 753. On the notion of permanent technological advance see also an essay by the present writer in *South Atlantic Quarterly,* Winter, 1972.

2. P. A. Sorokin, *Social and Cultural Dynamics* (New York: American Book, 1937–41), 894–99.

3. Karl Popper, *The Poverty of Historicism* (Boston; Beacon, 1957), 128.

4. The arguments cited do not of course assert the impossibility of man's destruction or, say, his mutation into a superman. They do deny that such events are foreordained by or predictable on the basis of permanent or irreversible trends.

5. Sorokin's similar statement appears in his *Contemporary Sociological Theories* (New York: Harper, 1928), 740–41.

6. No one would ever advance any theory unless a great deal seemed to agree with it. But so called examples only illustrate a theory, making clear what it asserts. Consequently, ten thousand examples cannot confirm a theory, whereas, as we know, one contradictory instance does upset it. Tests of theories are searches for such instances.

7. W. H. Walsh, *Philosophy of History* (New York: Harper Torchbook, 1960), 103.

8. Karl Popper, *The Logic of Scientific Discovery* (New York: Science Editions Paperback, 1961), 420.

9. Guicciardini, no determinist, put the matter concisely when he wrote that "things repeat themselves, but under changed names and colors." *Ricordi,* Domandi Translation (New York: Harper & Row, 1965).

10. Sorokin emphasizes that civilizations are "vast agglomerations of ideas, people, and artifacts, some of which merely happen to exist adjacent to each other." Such congeries may include integrated systems like those of law, mathematics, or individual works of art where all parts affect each other's functioning and change together, but entire civilizations are not such organic unities and hence not susceptible to organic processes like birth and death. See *Dynamics,* vol. 1, ch. 1, and especially Sorokin's *Modern Historical and Social Philosophies* (New York: Dover paperback, 1963), 209–17. Popper's similar rejection of a false organicism occurs in discussion of "holism," *Poverty,* 76–83. See also "organic theory of society" in index, *The Open Society and Its Enemies* (New York: Harper Torchbook, 1963).

11. *Dynamics,* vol. 1, ch. 2, especially 97–99.

12. Jacques Maquet, *The Sociology of Knowledge* (Boston: Beacon, 1951); Northrop's introduction to same; Brinton in an article otherwise critical of *Dynamics* in the *Southern Review,* 1937. (See Sorokin's reply to the last in the *Southern Review,* 1938).

13. L. Edelstein, *The Idea of Progress in Classical Antiquity* (Baltimore: Johns Hopkins Univ. Press, 1967) has brought striking support to this classification by demonstrating the pervasiveness of the characteristically Sensate idea of Progress in Greece and Rome. This upsets the long-accepted notion that the idea was an unprecedented creation of the eighteenth century.

14. *Dynamics,* vol. 3. See Index on contractual and familistic relationships. Also 185–92.

15. *Dynamics,* vol. 3, 375–80.

16. Actually, as Rudolph Virchow vainly noted in Darwin's day and as J. Huxley, C. C. Simpson, and other biologists and anthropologists recognize today, *Homo sapiens* has not changed his physical habit, which includes his brain, since his emergence.

17. *Dynamics,* vol. 4, 593–94 and entire ch. 12.

18. Karl Popper, *Conjectures and Refutati*ons (New York: Basic Books, 1962), 81 n. 29.

19. Especially with regard to physical theories, Progressivist often denigrate such partial repetitions as "merely formal." Scientists have spoken otherwise, Heisenberg's *Physics and Philosophy* (Gifford Lectures 1955–56, New York: Harper Torchbook, 1962) emphasizes at length the similarity between quantum theory and certain ancient theories. Popper has written that there can "no longer be any doubt about the astonishing similarity, not to say identity, of the aims, interests, activities, arguments, and methods of, say, Galileo and Archimedes, or Copernicus and Plato, or Kepler and Aristarchus" (*Conjectures,* 75 n. 16). When

scientists differ with Progressivists, it is a safe rule to side with scientists. And in siding with Popper here we can dispose of a conditional argument against historical prediction advanced in *Poverty*: "If there is such a thing as a growth of knowledge, then we cannot anticipate today what we shall know only tomorrow"—which means that insofar as knowledge influences events, we cannot predict them. True, but in the respects Popper has mentioned, growth of knowledge is often absent.

20. *Dynamics,* vol. 4, ch. 14.

21. P. A. Sorokin, *The Crisis of Our Age* (New York: Dutton paperback, 1957), 13–14.

22. See also *Contemporary Sociological Theories,* 754–55.

23. A. L. Kroeher, *Style and Civilizations* (Ithaca, NY: Cornell Univ. Press, 1957), 134, 180; José Ortega y Gasset, *Man and Crisis* (New York: Norton, 1958), 68–70, 152, 177; also P. A. Sorokin, *Modern Historical Social Philosophies* (New York: Dover paperback, 1963), ch. 14.

24. Augustine of course denies identical historical recurrence, but he endorses the idea of nonidentical or typal recurrence in earthly history in many places—e.g., when he calls Babylon the first Rome and Rome the second Babylon. Cf. *The City of God* (bk. 18, ch. 2).

John C. Koritansky

Democracy and Nobility: A Comment on Tocqueville's _Democracy in America_

VOL. 12, NO. 1, 1976

I. The Love of Equality and the Essence of Democracy

From the time of its first publication until the present, Alexis de Tocqueville's _Democracy in America_ has commanded the attention of social and political scientists who have wanted to understand modern democracy as a distinctive form of political society. Tocqueville has been such a mine of useful and apt quotations that his name and several of his observations have become common parlance among social scientists and historians— so much so that it is almost waggish for a member of those professions to admit not having read _Democracy in America_ at least once. Nevertheless, I think that the reasons for the continuing pertinence of Tocqueville's work are not understood nearly as widely as his reputation extends. For as Tocqueville himself asserts, the source of his power and insight is his grasp of the particular "political passion," the love of equality, that defines and animates democracy as distinct from other political forms.[1] I think that the centrality and the meaning of Tocqueville's statement on this point is not generally appreciated because modern social scientists tend to

have a more democratic understanding of democracy, so to speak, than that suggested by Tocqueville's statement. That is to say, democrats think democracy to be _the_ regime that is open to the widest variety of human types because it allows men their differences without interpreting those differences as differences in rank. Accordingly, if modern men appear to be a disturbingly homogeneous lot, modern democrats find the cause in the incidental features of our social life: e.g., bureaucracy and industrial routinization. Democracy is thought to be a set of procedures that do not necessarily lead to any substantive outcome, especially not regarding the _kind_ of human being that will be generated by democracy.[2]

Tocqueville, on the other hand, does think that democracy represents the victory of a certain kind of man and that democracy will regenerate that kind to the exclusion of others. The love of equality is a distinctive aspect of the human soul; it is but one selection from the wider variety of human types. It does not characterize all men as such, but rather the class of men who have become decidedly preponderant. Thus, Tocqueville's insight into the nature of modern democracy stems from a perspective that is different from democracy's own perspective—he has not forgotten or ignored the claims of those whose character democracy has effectively suppressed.[3] But Tocqueville's understanding of the necessarily repressive character of democracy does not mean that he judges democracy as an evil. In this essay I will attempt to show that Tocqueville does compare the traits of democratic man against the charactistics that were encouraged by the inegalitarian society that modern democracy displaced. On the basis of that comparison, I believe I will then be able to shed some new light on the way that Tocqueville attempts to strengthen democracy's own proper advantages.

II. The Meaning of the Inevitable Triumph of Democracy over the Pre-democratic Order

Democracy in America is not composed in the manner of a treatise. More specifically, it does not delineate a view of human nature and then proceed to derive consequences for the order of political society. Indeed, Tocqueville goes so far as to deny that he has presented any argument to show that democracy is the regime most conducive to the best in human nature, although he is not at great pains to hide his preference for democracy.[4] I suggest that the reason for this rather enigmatic feature of the book is not that Tocqueville really dispenses with the question of human nature. Rather it is that Tocqueville recognizes an ambiguity in his own understanding of human nature such that he is only able to set forth his view by way of a carefully drawn illustration instead of a definition. The illustration that he draws is contained in the eighteenth chapter of Volume I of the *Democracy*,

"Some Considerations Concerning the Present and Probable Future Condition of the Three Races that Inhabit the United States."

In support of the distinctive importance of chapter eighteen, it is noteworthy that this is the one chapter in the whole two- volume work where Tocqueville extends his gaze beyond the democratic order and considers man in a three-fold variety of conditions. The Reds, the Blacks, and the Whites seem to represent a comparison of the three fundamental alternative human conditions: aristocratic but barbaric freedom, abject servitude, and democratic equality. Tocqueville says that his remarks in this chapter are "like tangents to (his) subject being American, but not democratic, (while his) main business has been to describe democracy."[5] Nevertheless, while the chapter is strictly speaking tangential, it is not of marginal importance. Here and only here does Tocqueville go beyond the description of democracy and also beyond the recommendations for the improvement of democracy. In the comparison of the conditions of the three races, Tocqueville shows the natural primacy of the condition of democratic equality.

The displacement of the Indians by the Whites in America seems to be a clear parallel to the displacement of the feudal civilization by what would finally emerge as modern democracy. The Indians appear like a caricature of the feudal nobles. They suffer from too high an opinion of themselves, and this very pride makes for their weakness before the Whites. What is critical is that they consider it beneath their station to work. War and hunting are the only pursuits their sense of honor permits them. When the advance of the White farmer drives away the Indians' game, the thought of their tilling the soil never enters their heads, and so they flee with the deer. Were the Indians able to subsist on the wild fruits of the land, they might have successfully retained their proud refusal to labor even in the absence of game, but what is the deepest element of their tragedy is that the slightest touch with the White civilization fills the Indians with new wants that cannot be satisfied by means familiar to them. Their attempt to satisfy their new hungers by exchanging the booty of the hunt with Whites puts still greater strain on the game resources and deepens the scarcity. Both the Indians' social structure and the psychic structure are pathetically weak and vulnerable. Beyond the pathos generated by Tocqueville's touching description, we cannot help but conclude that the Indians are, literally, not fit to survive.

The advance of the Whites at the expense of the Indians is by no means simply a savage conflict. The Whites remove the Indians with the greatest show of deference to humanity, and under the color of legal form. Moreover, the Indians do not defend themselves in the manner of brutes. Tocqueville reproduces the essence of both arguments, and in so doing, he shows the weakness of both. As for the Indians, they make an argument in defense of their natural right to their property.

"From time immemorial, our common Father, who is in heaven, has given our ancestors the land we occupy; our ancestors have transmitted it to us as their heritage. We have preserved it with respect, for it contains their ashes. Have we ever ceded or lost this heritage? Permit us to ask you humbly what better right a nation can have to a country than the right of inheritance and immemorial possession? We know that the state of Georgia and the President

of the United States claim today that we have lost this right. But this seems to us a gratuitous allegation. At what time have we lost it? What crime have we committed which could deprive us of our homeland?" . . .

Such is the language of the Indians; what they say is true; what they foresee seems to me inevitable. [6]

The case of the Indians is eloquent and touching—and it contains the truth that "natural right" is on the side of the Indians. But Tocqueville's obvious sympathetic feelings for the Indians does not determine his final judgment. To grasp Tocqueville's final judgment, it is necessary to consider the case that is made by the Whites.

See inter alia the report of February 24, 1830, written by Mr. Bell on behalf of the Committee on Indian Affairs, in which on page five it is established by very logical arguments and most learnedly proved that: "The fundamental principle, that the Indians have no rights by virtue of their ancient possession either of soil or sovereignty, has never been abandoned either expressly or by implication."

Reading this report, written, moreover, by an able man, one is astonished at the facility and ease with which, from the very first words, the author disposes of arguments founded on natural right and reason, which he calls abstract and theoretical principles. The more I think about it, the more I feel that the only difference between civilized and uncivilized man with regard to justice is this: the former contests the justice of rights, *the latter simply violates them.*[7] (my emphasis)

The astonishingly cavalier hypocrisy

in the argument set forth by Mr. Bell should not obscure Tocqueville's concurrent admission that the Indians' argument is also, in its own way, hypocritical. The Whites assume an obligation to contest the justice of the Indians' claims—an obligation that they cannot possibly meet. But clearly, if the shoe were on the other foot, the Indians would feel no such compunction. More specifically, the Whites feel obliged to contest the justice of the Indians' argument because they are a property-holding civilization, and the very notion of property seems to presume a notion of natural right that must be honored even in the breach. But the Indians, Tocqueville says, own no property. He asserts that they "occupy" the land but they do not "own" it. It would seem, then, that in their appeal to the Whites in behalf of the natural right to their property they make a kind of argument that they have no occasion to make except vis-à-vis the Whites, and even then they are forced to make it only because they are the weaker party. This reflection shows the problematical grounds of the natural right argument employed by the Indians. The problem is that natural right has no meaning outside political society of a certain kind. If this is the case, then must we not conclude that the necessarily inevitable conquest of the Indians by the Whites has the sanction of nature? A few pages preceding the quotation cited above, Tocqueville also quotes Mr. Bell, and in view of the sense in which the Whites' property-holding civilization has been shown to be superior to the Indians' proud barbarism, it would seem that Bell expresses the hard truth that

> the practice of buying Indian titles is but the substitute which humanity and expediency have imposed in the place of the sword in arriving at the actual

enjoyment of property claimed by the right of discovery, and sanctioned by the natural superiority allowed to the claims of civilized communities over those of savage tribes.[8]

This harsh conclusion might be avoided if it were the case that the Whites might have resisted their own greed for land and preserved something of independence for the Indian nations through the exercise of their own self-control. But Tocqueville shows us that that would have been impossible. In another footnote he cites the examples of the conflict between the Americans and the French Canadians and also that between the Americans and the Mexicans, and he shows that the situation is similar. He concludes that, "If comparatively imperceptible differences in European civilization lead to such results, it is easy to see what must happen when the most fully developed civilization of Europe comes into contact with Indian barbarism."[9] Thus, the conflict between the Indians and the Whites is as inevitable as the outcome of that conflict. We are confronted with the example of a nation that necessarily vanishes at the slightest touch with a more vigorous competitor; unless we lack seriousness, can we turn from the conclusion that the Whites' civilization is superior?

Tocqueville continues his examination of the three races in the United States by examining the relationship between the Blacks and Whites in the American South. The point he makes here is that the Whites in the South have violated the principle of the fundamental equality of all men as such through the institution of Negro slavery. Whatever effect this institution may have on the Blacks, it is clear that the Whites have been corrupted by it. They begin to take on the contempt for labor and the glorification of hunting and war characteristic of feudal nobles. And what is critical, they have grown weak because of it. Tocqueville's comparison of the two sides of the Ohio River, slave and free, is proof of the corrupting and softening effects of the "reintroduction of inequality into the modern world."

What is perhaps most curious of all is that even the Southern Whites know that slavery is an uneconomic institution. They know that they are being impoverished through its effects.

> Increasing enlightenment in the South makes the people there see that slavery is harmful to the master, and the same enlightenment makes them see, more clearly than they had seen before, that it is almost impossible to abolish it.
>
> . . . Slavery is more and more entrenched in the lairs just where its utility is most contested.[10]

The Southern Whites know the cost of slavery, yet they retain it because to do otherwise would require that they mingle with the Blacks, and hence that they cast off those social distinctions that make them what they are. They would have to see themselves as other than members of the class that does not toil, but rather pursues the pleasures involved in hunting and war. The Southerners know that they are sacrificing something, but they willingly sacrifice the advantages of their Northern countrymen as beneath the dignity of men of honor. Their notion of honor is proven vain by the fact that the Southerners are doomed by it.

What we learn from the discussion of the three races is that Tocqueville is profoundly indebted to Machiavelli's view of human nature and politics. Indeed, there is much to suggest that Tocqueville is attempting to rejuvenate modernity by returning to the thought of that original modern philosopher. Tocqueville follows Machiavelli's rejection as politically irrelevant any "other worldly" standard for human life. A notion of human excellence that leads to contempt for the requirements of success in this world just cannot be consistent with nature's ordinances. Democracy is proved to be naturally superior to the inegalitarian order of the past because it is naturally stronger. And despite the fact that Tocqueville is not insensitive to certain brilliant features of the old order, it cannot be true that Tocqueville believed the old order to be better than the new, while resigning himself to its passing. What collapses of its own weakness cannot seriously and truly be called good.

It is this Machiavellianism that I think Tocqueville is suggesting to us when he asserts in his Introductory Chapter that, "God does not Himself need to speak for us to find sure signs of His will; it is enough to observe the customary progress of nature and the continuous tendency of events; I know, without special revelation, that the stars follow orbits in space traced by His finger."[11] Interpreted in this way, Tocqueville enjoys the irony of expressing his Machiavellian thought in a politely pious formula.

Just as Tocqueville agrees with Machiavelli that what is ultimately stronger must be ultimately better, he agrees too that this does not mean that whatever is is right. This is the difficult and important point. Like Machiavelli, Tocqueville holds that greatness (*grandeur*) goes with strength. The conflict with which the world abounds requires that we be concerned with success, but what makes the human conflict what it is is pride—and therefore any genuine success must contain the satisfaction of pride. Were it not for pride, pride in oneself and one's own conquests, the struggles of this world would lose their human meaning. Tocqueville's discussion of the races does not show that the Whites are superior because they have overcome pride. We should not forget that the central animus of the American civilization is the love of equality, and that, surely, is an expression of pride. What Tocqueville shows is that the democratic form of pride is superior to the older form which made an invidious and debilitating distinction between workers and warriors. The pre-democratic pride was self-defeating, the democratic form is self-vindicating; that is the core of the inevitable triumph of democracy. But for that triumph to be a victory for man, it must come to view as a victory. Democracy must see its own conquest and be swelled by it. If it does not lie in Tocqueville's power to avert or advance the cause of democracy, still he can try to generate the political conditions wherein the citizens of modern democracy will recognize that cause as their own.

III. The Poetic Interpretation of the Commercial Activities of Democratic Citizens—How These Can Be Interpreted as Revealing the Natural Greatness of Man

Tocqueville's recognition of the centrality of pride in all forms of political society has a decisive influence on his political thought. Pride is the root of the "political passion," the love of equality, that is distinctive of democracy. It is useful to note that here Tocqueville follows Rousseau as well as Machiavelli, for in this regard Rousseau is the more direct heir of Machiavelli's teaching than are the earlier modern philosophers, Hobbes and Locke. Rousseau had objected to Hobbes specifically because Hobbes had failed to realize the way in which civilized man

has been alienated from his natural self and his natural rights. The "self" that civilized man loves is a vain construct, maintained and measured through the eyes of others and conventions we share with others.[12] And Tocqueville follows the consequences Rousseau draws from this thought; namely, that it is not possible to derive social obligations from the rational extension of natural self-interest. Rather, the only way to reconcile social obligation with the happiness and freedom of vain men is to generate a public-spirited form of pride, whereby men can take pleasure in their duty. I suggest that what Tocqueville calls the "manly and legitimate passion for equality which rouses in all men a desire to be strong and respected" is intelligible only as a public-spiritedness that parallels Rousseau's idea of the "general will." [13]

For anything like a general will to arise in modern democracy, there must be a medium—a ritual—through which it can act. Various alternatives are possible, as Rousseau had indicated,[14] but the one that is most likely in the modern world is commercial activity. Commerce can be the medium through which democratic citizens feel themselves to participate in their nation's life; but if commerce is to serve Tocqueville's project in this way, it will have to be "poetically" interpreted so as to reflect a kind of splendor. Thus, it is a matter of critical importance for Tocqueville to find, as he does, that democracy is not devoid of the poetic instinct despite evidence to the contrary. In his chapter on poetry, he suggests that America exemplifies the form democracy's poetic inspiration can take.

> The Americans see themselves marching through the wilderness, drying up marshes, diverting rivers, peopling the wilds, and subduing nature. It is not

just occasionally that their imagination catches a glimpse of this magnificent vision. It is something which plays a real part in the least, as in the most important, actions of every man, and it is always flitting before his mind.[15]

This and similar expressions near the end of Volume I illustrate that Tocqueville's understanding of the relation between commerce and democracy is that commerce can be a medium through which a people gives expression to its "political passion." The Americans, he says, "put something heroic into their way of trading."[16] They see it as part of the proud conquest of man over nature.

Through poetry, commerce can be the medium through which a democratic people can express a public spirited and noble form of their love of equality. And poetry, in turn, can reflect the splendor of commercial activity only if poetry can appeal to the cosmic significance of the conquest of nature through commerce. Thus, again following the lead of Rousseau, Tocqueville cannot complete the ennoblement of democracy without calling in the aid of a civil religion. [17]

It is my contention that Tocqueville's discussion of "the idea of the indefinite perfectibility of man" is a sketch of a religion that is compatible with the love of equality and that answers the need for a civil religion outlined above. Here, as was the case with his discussion of the three races, Tocqueville does not make explicit the significance of his discussion—the reason being perhaps that according to him no new religions are possible in the democratic order. If the doctrine of indefinite perfectibility were to be introduced in democracy, it would have to be done indirectly, perhaps by way of a denatured and humanized form of Christianity.

The suitability of the idea of indefinite perfectibility to democracy is carefully drawn by Tocqueville in his discussion of the intellectual propensities of democracy. Democracy has a kind of instinct for general and simple ideas—for too facile generalizations. The tendency for democratic citizens to gather a whole range of things under a simple label or general formula derives, in turn, from the fact that men themselves appear to be more like each other than did the men of aristocracy. Equal men find it "hard to think about one branch of mankind without widening (their) view until it includes the whole."[18] From that they develop a habitual taste for generalizations in everything: "hence it becomes an ardent and often blind passion of the human spirit to discover common rules for everything and to include a great number of objects under the same formula, and to explain a group of facts by one sole cause."[19]

There is a danger in democracy's intellectual propensity towards generalization. Equal men may lose sight of the significance of their *own* individuality; they may think of themselves as interchangeable elements in a flat, atomistic order of things.

The conception of unity becomes an obsession. Man looks for it everywhere, and when he thinks he has found it he gladly reposes in that belief. Not content with the discovery that there is nothing in the world but one creation and one Creator, he is still embarrassed by this primary division of things and seeks to expand and simplify his conception by including God and the universe in one great whole.[20]

Tocqueville calls this general frame of mind "Pantheism," and he devotes a chapter to an indictment of its political consequences. Pantheism "destroys human individuality, (and) just because it destroys it, will have secret charms for men living in democracies."[21] He encourages all friends of liberty to unite their efforts in opposing this evil doctrine.

But under a different expression, the democratic intellectual propensity may be friendly to the idea of individual freedom. Indeed, Tocqueville suggests that the idea of genuine human freedom can only be grasped by a mind that is *able* to grasp the idea of mankind in general. Even the best products of the pre-democratic order were all but blind to the simple fact that characterizes all human beings as such namely, freedom itself.

> The profoundest and the most wide-seeing mind of Greece and Rome never managed to grasp the very general but very simple conception of the likeness of all men and of the equal right of all at birth to liberty.[22]

The conclusion from this is of the greatest importance for an understanding of the foundation of Tocqueville's thought; democracy is the condition suitable to the revelation of a supremely important truth.

What is necessary is an interpretation, in the form of a public teaching, about the order of the world and man's place within it that comports with democracy's instinct for a simple and general rule while at the same time supporting the idea of the individual and his freedom. I suggest it is in response to this need that Tocqueville addresses the chapter immediately following his indictment of Pantheism, "How Equality Suggests to the Americans the Idea of the Indefinite Perfectibility of Man."

Though man resembles the animals in many respects one characteristic is peculiar to him alone; he improves himself and they do not. . . . So the idea of perfectibility is as old as the world; equality had no share in bringing it to birth, but it has given it a new character.

When citizens are classified by rank, profession, or birth and when all are obliged to follow the career which chance has opened before them, everyone thinks that he can see the ultimate limits of human endeavor quite close in front of him, and no one attempts to fight against the inevitable fate. It is not that aristocratic peoples absolutely deny man's capacity to improve himself, but they do not think it unlimited. They think in terms of amelioration, not change . . . they assume in advance certain impassable limits to such progress. . . .

But when castes disappear and classes are brought together, when men are jumbled together and habits, customs, and laws are changing, when new facts impinge and new truths are discovered, when old conceptions vanish and new ones take their place, then the human mind imagines the possibility of an ideal but always fugitive perfection. . . .

Thus, searching always, falling, picking himself up again, often disappointed, never discouraged, he is ever striving toward that immense grandeur glimpsed indistinctly at the end of the long track humanity must follow.[23]

The discussion of the doctrine of human perfectibility shows that this idea opposes the bad consequences of Pantheism, but it does not do so as traditional Christianity does, through recourse to a dualism between the mundane and the transworldly realms. The idea of indefinite perfectibility seems to deny the significance of any transworldly perfection—any "ideal" human nature to which no individual human being can perfectly correspond. According to the doctrine of perfectibility, the essence of human nature is a kind of openness.

From the standpoint of rationality, this notion of indefinite perfectibility is subject to a host of questions and objections. Fundamentally, there seems to be a confusion in it between the potentiality and the actuality of human nature. But Tocqueville makes no attempt to give a rational defense for the doctrine. He says only that it accords with democracy's intellectual propensities and that it has the enormous practical advantage of giving sanction to the notion of freedom. The idea of indefinite perfectibility sanctions a *vision* of society wherein each man, through the pursuit of the betterment of his own material conditions, sees himself contributing to a more general advance and that he thus partakes of "the natural greatness of man." Indefinite perfectibility is the doctrine that ennobles the indefinite progress in material well-being to which democracy gives license, and thus it is "the general and systematic conception by which a great people conducts all its affairs."

> I once met an American sailor and asked him why his country's ships are made so they will not last long. He answered offhand that the art of navigation was making such progress that even the best of boats would be almost useless if it lasted more than a few years. [24]

Properly set forth, the doctrine of human perfectibility yields to democracy a vision of itself that can enlarge the heart and can provide sanction and opportunity for noble exertions. For while democracy can only value the labor of the mind if it produces material goods, this need not mean that the status of the intelligence is thereby demeaned. It will not be demeaned if men can be brought to interpret material improvement as the *sign* of the greatness of human nature.[25] Indeed, it is just because knowledge is seen by democracy to be useful that "no one easily allows himself to be confined to the material cares of life, and the humblest artisan occasionally casts an eager, furtive glance at the higher regions of the mind."[26] To pull several strands together into one formula, I interpret Tocqueville's discussion of the doctrine of the indefinite perfectibility of man to be the cardinal element of a public philosophy or civil religion whereby he transforms democratic envy that "leads the weak to want to drag the strong down," into a healthy and prideful belief that one shares in a political order that reveals the natural greatness of man. The resulting pride is what Tocqueville means both by the manly love of equality and by the spirit of freedom.

IV. Inequality, Ambition, and the Consequent Insufficiency of Commerce as the Medium for the Expression of Democratic Virtue— The Prospects for War in Democracy and for Democracy in War

A severe problem remains for the foregoing account of Tocqueville's attempt to reconcile nobility and democracy through a poetic interpretation of commerce. The problem stems from the fact that commerce tends to be universalistic. If commerce does not break down completely the cultural differences that exist among different nations, it tolerates such differences only to the extent that they do not interfere with productivity. Thus, while a nation may manifest a commercial kind of greatness, the very activity through which it does so tends to undercut the significance of that nation's independent existence. The poetic elaboration of commerce does not oppose democracy's own universalism—rather it is consistent with that universalism.

> [I]t is not only the members of a single nation that come to resemble each other; the nations themselves are assimilated, and one can form the picture of one vast democracy, in which a nation counts as a single citizen.
>
> The existence of the entire human race, its vicissitudes and its future, thus become a fertile theme for poetry.[27]

The poetic vision of every democratic people points beyond itself; it points, so to speak, to the conventionality of its own particular conventions.[28] But how can men lay claim to nobility by conforming to conventions *that they recognize as conventions*? How is honor possible where the very terms within which we honor are seen as false?

To understand fully the problem of nobility in democracy, we must understand that for Tocqueville, there is no such thing as a universal standard of honor. "If we can further suppose that all races should become mixed, and all peoples of the world should reach a state in which they all had the same interests and needs, and there was no characteristic trait distinguishing one from another, the practice of attributing a conventional value to men's actions would cease altogether. . . . [I]t is the dissimilarities among men which give rise to the notion of honor. . . ."[29] But we must also understand that Tocqueville does not

think that democracy necessarily leads to a universal society.[30] Were he to think so, the problem of reconciling nobility and democracy would prove impossible. Differences among democratic nations *can* persist. The problem stems from the fact the since equal men can *imagine* a single, planetary democracy, those differences will appear less significant than they once did.

Tocqueville's discussion of the particular problem before us here occurs in the second half of Book III, Volume II of *Democracy in America*. It is in connection with this problem that he draws attention to a distinction in mankind regarding ambition. The distinction is that while all men need to be able to esteem themselves, and thus require standards that supply the terms of self-esteem, only some men are driven exclusively by a yearning for public recognition and honor. As for the generality of men, Tocqueville's point is that they *can* accept the conventionality of their public conventions and even continue to conform to them, so long as those conventions are consistent with their own pursuit of material gain. Most men are willing and able to act as if they believed what they find convenient.[31] But those few who yearn for honor exclusively cannot be accommodated in this way. They take themselves too seriously. The next question is whether democracy is compatible with the happiness of such men, and whether such men can be tolerated by democracy.

The last eight chapters of Book III, Volume II of *Democracy in America* are devoted to the problem of the few ambitious men in democracy. These chapters are also the ones that contain Tocqueville's reflections on war and democracy. The connection needs to be carefully explicated. In chapter nineteen of Book III, Tocqueville asserts that, when despite all natural obstacles, [men of great ambition] do appear, they wear another face.

Under aristocracies the career open to ambition is often wide, but it does have fixed limits. In democratic countries the field of action is usually very narrow, but once those narrow bonds are passed, there is nothing left to stop it. As men are weak and changeable, and as precedents have little force and laws do not last long, resistance to innovation is halfhearted and the fabric of society never stands up quite straight or firm. As a result, when ambitious men have once seized power, they think they can dare do anything. When power slips from their grasp, their thoughts at once turn to overturning the state in order to get it again.[32]

It is impossible to follow Tocqueville's argument here unless it is recognized that, despite the dangers that broad ambition poses to free institutions, Tocqueville does not brand ambition an evil, and he does not wish to expunge it. He accepts ambition of this kind as a given, and he argues that "it would be very dangerous if we tried to starve it or confine it beyond reason . . . we should be very careful not to hamper its free energy within the permitted limits."[33] The question for Tocqueville is, therefore, how to make ambition "proportionate, moderate, and yet vast." Democracy must in some way find a substitute for the capacity of aristocracy to provide a legitimate field for the expression of ambition. But what sort of field for the ambitious is democracy able to provide?

Tocqueville further develops his discussion of the role of extraordinary ambition in democracy in chapter twenty-one of Book III, "Why Great Revolutions Will Become Rare." Near the opening of this chapter, Tocqueville issues the warning that this "subject is important, and I ask the reader to follow my argument closely." The central point of this chapter is that, contrary to the opinion Tocqueville attributes to many of his contemporaries, democracy is not an unstable and revolutionary condition. The great class of men in democracy who are owners of modest amounts of property are the natural enemies of violent conditions: "Their excitement about small matters makes them calm about great ones."[34] The consequence of what Tocqueville asserts here is that there is a disjunction between the great mass of citizens in democracy and the ambitious few, and on reflection it is this disjunction primarily that robs the ambitious few of a field of expression.

I am not suggesting that they resist him openly by means of well-thought-out schemes, or indeed by means of any considered determination to resist. They show no energy in fighting him and sometimes even applaud him, but do not follow him. Secretly their apathy is opposed to his fire, their conservative interests to his revolutionary instincts, their homely taste to his adventurous passion, their common sense to his flighty genius, their prose to his poetry. With immense effort he rouses them for a moment, but they soon slip from him and fall back, as it were, by their own weight. He exhausts himself trying to animate this indifferent and preoccupied crowd and finds at last that he is reduced to impotence, not because he is conquered but because he is alone.[35]

Though democracy is not incapable of being inspired by thoughts of public glory it is hard to get equal men to *sacrifice* much for it. The ambitious are frustrated and become the enemies of society. Given *this* restatement of the issue, what is principally required in order to civilize extraordinary ambition is that the generality of men somehow be rendered fit to recognize and appreciate the value of such ambition. They must not be allowed to remain wholly preoccupied with their private activity; they must rather be put within reach of "those great and powerful public emotions which do indeed perturb peoples but which also make them gross and refresh them."[36] With regard to this special problem of the role of the ambitious in democracy, we must conclude that the vision of the nation's glory that is conveniently conducive to the general pursuit of private satisfaction is *not* sufficient. The commercial glory of the democratic nation is an image that satisfies only the more modest form of political passion. It yields a sense of honor satisfactory only to those who are not driven by a yearning for honor above all else. A people that is fit to reward with appropriate honors the actions of those who are driven most by ambition must themselves enter the field of those "great and powerful public emotions" that drive men to the greatest heights. Having made this point, Tocqueville abruptly and without further explanation turns to the subject of the last five chapters of Book III, namely, the prospects for war in democracy and for democracy in war.

The most dangerous form of the danger to democracy from its most ambitious element is war. "All those who seek to destroy the freedom of the democratic nations must know that war is the surest and shortest means to accomplish this. That is the very first axiom of their science."[37] Nevertheless, just as Tocqueville does not think that the problem of ambition can

be resolved by purging democracy of its ambitious men, so Tocqueville does not think that democracy can purge itself of war and the concern with war. War would not be impossible unless there ceased to be distinct nations: a situation that is equivalent to the triumph of the worst prospects in democracy. For this reason Tocqueville takes it for granted that "war is a hazard to which all nations are subject, democracies as well as the rest."[38] The question, therefore, is how can the threat of war be *minimized* in conformity with the conditions necessary to the highest and strongest expression of public emotion?

Having said that all nations are necessarily subject to the hazard of war, Tocqueville goes on to say that war is not an unqualified evil. All too easily understressed is his statement that

> I do not wish to speak ill of war; war almost always widens a nation's mental horizons and raises its heart. In some cases it may be the only factor which can prevent the exaggerated growth of certain inclinations naturally produced by equality and be the antidote needed for certain inveterate diseases to which democratic societies are liable.[39]

With reference to the central issue that underlies all these last several chapters of Book III, Volume II, the significance of this qualified praise of war is as follows. The only way that a people can be brought within reach of those truly "great and powerful public emotions" is to involve them in thinking about war, A people that is fit to bestow with appropriate honors those who are most ambitious for honor must themselves know the nobility of the ultimate sacrifice a citizen can make for his country. The reader whose sympathy Tocqueville has won up to this point will have been prepared to draw the conclusion for himself, and Tocqueville, understandably, stops short of making it explicit. The people who are fit to honor their best citizens must combine the role of citizen and soldier, perhaps through the institution of something like universal military service.

The problem of reconciling nobility and democracy, which is *the* problem of democracy from Tocqueville's point of view, absolutely requires a combination of the roles of democratic citizen and soldier. This fact surely does not mean that Tocqueville recommends war and conquest as a way of life for modern democratic nations. But, like Machiavelli,[40] Tocqueville suggests that a free people must never believe that their freedom depends on any security other than their own military strength. A citizenry that is disarmed, and puts its trust in hirelings (Tocqueville's example here is the non-commissioned officer—the professional soldier) runs *an increased risk of war*; and moreover, it runs an increased risk of *defeat*. As Tocqueville describes him, the professional is susceptible to a reckless kind of ambition for war. War is the only condition in which rapid promotion is possible; therefore the professional soldier "wants war; he always wants it and at any cost."[41] Thus, Tocqueville would prevent the spirit of the professional soldier from characterizing the democratic army because he wants to civilize soldiery as well as to ennoble citizenship. The remedy for the army's vices can only be sought in the pacific and orderly habits of the private, citizen soldier."[42]

One question remains of Tocqueville's discussion of war and democracy. Is the citizen army that Tocqueville seems to be recommending really fit to fight and win in a contest with trained profession-als? Tocqueville considers this question in some detail, with the conclusion that democratic citizens *can* make excellent soldiers. There is, he notes, an often hidden connection between the spirit of democracy and the war passion.

> Moreover, there is a hidden connection which war uncovers between the military and democratic mores.
>
> The men of democracies are by nature passionately eager to acquire quickly what they covet and to enjoy it on easy terms. They for the most part love hazards and fear death much less than difficulty. It is in that spirit that they conduct their trade and industry, and this spirit carried with them onto the battlefield induces them willingly to risk their lives to secure in a moment the rewards of victory. No kind of greatness is more pleasing to the imagination of a democratic people than military greatness which is brilliant and sudden, won without hard work, by risking nothing but one's life.
>
> An aristocratic people which, fighting against a democracy, does not succeed in bringing it to ruin in the first campaigns always runs a great risk in being defeated by it. [43]

Tocqueville goes still beyond this statement in accounting for the excellence of the democratic army. Democracy's greatest advantage in war is that it is well constituted to recognize the glory that its citizens may win in battle. Aristocracy, by contrast, has difficulty seeing that it is a man's *own* life that he risks for his country.

> The [aristocratic] soldier has broken into military discipline, so to say, before he enters the army, or rather

military discipline is only a more perfect form of social servitude. So in aristocratic armies the private soon comes to be insensible to everything except the orders of the leaders. He acts without thought, triumphs without excitement, and is killed without complaint. In such a condition he is no more a man, but he is a very formidable animal trained for war.[44]

Democracy, however, is freer with its gratitude. Indeed, Tocqueville's discussion of the military advantages of democracy reads like a straightforward elaboration of what Machiavelli says regarding the vital differences between the people and the nobles; namely, the nobles are stingy with their gratitude.[45]

Marshal Rommel is alleged to have said on some occasion that the soldiers of the American democratic army are the fiercest and hence the best that he opposed—after the first battle. Whether Rommel actually said that tribute or not, it nicely accords with what Tocqueville reveals as the root of democracy's natural supremacy. Democracy fights only at first with instruments, but afterwards with men. Tocqueville's discussion of war and democracy reveals that what he means by the noble love of equality is in fact the warrior spirit. His central purpose in *Democracy in America* can be summed up as an attempt to keep that spirit alive.

Democratic peoples must despair of ever obtaining from their soldiers this blind, detailed, resigned, and equable obedience which aristocracies can impose without trouble. The state of society in no way prepares men for this, and there is a danger that they will lose their natural advantages by trying artificially to acquire this one. In democracies military discipline ought not to try to cancel out the spontaneous exercise of the faculties; it should aspire only to direct them; and the obedience thus trained will be less precise but more impetuous and intelligent. It should be rooted in the will of the man who obeys; it relies not only on instinct, but on reason too, and consequently will often grow stricter as the danger makes this necessary. The discipline of an aristocratic army is apt to relax in wartime; it is based on habit, and war upsets habits. But in a democratic army discipline is strengthened in the face of the enemy, for each soldier sees very clearly that to conquer he must be silent and obey.

Those nations that have achieved most in war have never known any other discipline than that of which I speak. In antiquity only free men and citizens were accepted for the army, and they differed but little from one another and were accustomed to treat one another as equals. In that sense the armies of antiquity can be called democratic, even when they sprang from an aristocratic society. As a result, in those armies a sort of fraternal familiarity prevailed between officers and men. To read Plutarch's lives of great commanders convinces one of that. The soldiers are constantly talking, and talking very freely, to their generals, while the latter gladly listen to what they say and answer it. Their words and their example lead the army much more than any constraint or punishment. They were as much companions as leaders to their men.

I do not know if the Greeks and Romans ever brought the small details of military discipline to such perfection as the Russians have done, but that did not prevent Alexander from conquering Asia, and the Romans the world.[46]

V. Conclusion

For the student whose outlook on politics has been influenced by Machiavelli, nothing seems more disappointing than the absence of *grandeur* from the modern materialistic world. The deglorification of modern politics had been performed by Hobbes and Locke, who extended but also perverted Machiavelli's arguments. Hobbes and Locke had learned from Machiavelli the vanity of man's concern with otherworldly pleasures, and they concluded that political society could be founded on the basis of men's willingness to support the conditions necessary to their pursuit of material gain. But with the rejection of the political relevance of otherworldly concerns, Hobbes and Locke rejected the possibility of men attaching glory to their political triumphs with reference to divine sanction—and hence the modern world was deglorified.

I believe that Tocqueville tries to renew men's instinct for greatness. He tries to rejuvenate modern political life by way of a return to the original thought of Machiavelli. What is central to this attempt is Tocqueville's recognition of the centrality of man's "political passion," rooted in pride, as against man's desire for material gain. Hobbes and Locke had erred because they had not seen that Machiavelli's denial of man's divine life does *not* mean that men are simply materialists. The desire for glory is central for man even though the divinity whose sanction is necessary for glory cannot become the object of human concern or activity.

Like Machiavelli, Tocqueville thinks man can escape the shadowy precariousness of his existence through worldly greatness—at least to whatever extent any escape is possible. From the perspective formed by Plato, what is denied by Machiavelli and Tocqueville is the *erotic* root of men's political passion; for Plato shows that *eros* necessarily longs for immortality and cannot be satisfied with the opinions or appearances of this world, however great. The consequences of this difference in perspective between Plato and Tocqueville can try to resist democracy's tendency towards atomistic homogeneity through an invigoration of its spirit; he does not argue, as does Plato, the necessity for moderating *eros*. Tocqueville's project is misdirected if the real problem of democracy is, as Plato warned, that democracy liberates an *eros* that destroys *all* restraints in law and decency that remind *eros* of its mortal condition, and in that way reduces society to a subhuman equality. I think that modern students can profit much from Tocqueville's reassertion of the centrality of "political passion" in political affairs. The most profitable result may be to tame that very political passion and to redirect our concern for "equal social justice" toward the question of nature and the human soul.

Notes

1. Alexis Tocqueville, *Democracy* in *America*, ed. J. P. Mayer and Max Lerner, trans. George Lawrence, (New York: Harper and Row, 1966), 2, 157, 475–76, 645.
2. Cf. David Spitz, *Pattern of Anti-Democratic Thought,* (New York: The Macmillan Company, 1949), esp. 255.
3. Tocqueville, *Democracy in America*, 163–65, 183.
4. Ibid., 643.
5. Ibid., 291.
6. Ibid., 311.
7. Ibid., 312, fn. 29.
8. Ibid., 300, fn. 8.
9. Ibid., 307, fn. 19.
10. Ibid., 351.
11. Ibid., 6.
12. Ibid., 477–78.

13. I sought to demonstrate the connection between Tocqueville and Rousseau asserted here in my article, "Two Forms of the Love of Equality in Tocqueville's Practical Teaching for Democracy," in *Polity*, vol. VI, no. 4, Summer 1974, 490–91.

14. J. J. Rousseau, *The Social Contract*, trans. Willmoore Kendall, (Chicago: Henry Regnery Company, 1954), 78.

15. Tocqueville, *Democracy in America*, 453

16. Ibid., 569.

17. But cf. Marvin Zetterbaum, who argues that religion is marginally related to Tocqueville's solution to the "problem of democracy." Zetterbaum clearly has a different understanding of the nature of that problem than is presented here. Marvin Zetterbaum, *Tocqueville and the Problem of Democracy,* (Stanford: Stanford Univ. Press, 1967), 120–23.

18. Tocqueville, *Democracy in America*, 403.

19. Ibid., 404.

20. Ibid., 417.

21. Ibid., 417.

22. Ibid., 404.

23. Ibid., 419–20.

24. Ibid., 420.

25. Ibid., 424–25, 518.

26. Ibid., 425.

27. Ibid., 454.

28. Cf. also Tocqueville, *The Old Regime and the French Revolution,* Stuart Gilbert, trans. (Garden City: Doubleday and Company, Inc., 1955), 169.

29. Tocqueville, *Democracy in America*, 602

30. The Lawrence translation of the passage in ch. eighteen of bk. III, vol. II, "Concerning Honor in the United States and Democratic Societies" is misleading on this point. Lawrence translates, ". . . as such differences become less, it [the notion of honor] grows feeble; and when they disappear, it *will* vanish too." *loc. vit.* 602, my emphasis. But the French is conditional, ". . . *et il dispouitrait avec elles.*" Honor *would* vanish in a universal society, but Tocqueville does not predict that that must come. Tocqueville, *Democratie en Amerique*, (London: Macmillan&Co., 1961). 247.

31. Tocqueville, *Democracy in America*, vol. II, bk. III, ch. 14–18.

32. Ibid., 606.

33. Ibid., 607.

34. Ibid., 613.

35. Ibid.

36. Ibid.

37. Ibid., 625.

38. Ibid., 621.

39. Ibid., 624.

40. N. Machiavelli, *The Prince,* esp. chapters 12 and 13, Luigi Ricci, trans. (New York: Modern Library, 1940).

41. Tocqueville, *Democracy in America*, 629.

42. Ibid., esp. 625 and 629.

43. Ibid., 632–33.

44. Ibid., 634.

45. Cf. N. Machiavelli, *The Discourses,* bk. I, ch. 19, Christian E. Detmold, trans. (New York: Modern Library, 1940). Note that Machiavelli is referred to by name in this section of *Democracy.*

46. Tocqueville, *Democracy in America,* 634–35.

Frederick D. Wilhelmsen

The Family as the Basis
for Political Existence

VOL. 26, NO. 2, 1991

To speak of the family as the basis for political existence could be totally drained of intellectual interest even before I began this essay if we meant by the title nothing more than the obvious fact that political life is peopled by people, and people are born of parents, other people.

Theoretically, of course, political philosophers can conceive of a situation such as the one detailed in Plato's *Republic* in which the family is systematically destroyed and children are born from mates who do not even know one another. In George Orwell's *1984* the family is reduced to a breeding ground pululating with helots governed by a small elite of rulers sworn to celibacy, living a kind of secularist, monastic existence. *1984* is a novel but the late Heinrich Himmler in reality conceived of a similar program in which superior Nordic types would breed youngsters like themselves altogether without benefit of clergy and totally bereft of any familial institution, the children—as in Plato and Orwell—being educated by the state. Himmler tried out his experiment in a few houses set aside for nothing more than copulation between paradigmatically muscular and beautiful blonds who would never see one another again after conceiving future Nordic supermen. He began the experiment too late for it to have anything of a future, and it died in the *Götterdämmerung* of the Third Reich.

Even Marxism, which in theory has a very jaundiced view of the family, does not try to suppress it as an institution. The early free love and easy divorce espoused in Russia in the first flush of the Communist takeover immediately after World War I produced a sexual anarchy that constrained Lenin and later Stalin to render divorce far more restrictive and difficult to obtain than in Western democracies, and which thus kept the family alive even if confined within a vise that turned children into spies on their own parents. The business still exists today in Red China. History teaches that even the most savage totalitarianisms in principle, those that claim all children for the service of the state, concede—if reluctantly—that the best way to ensure their own futures (no children, no future) is to permit to human nature the institution of the family. The alternative of the political brothel of Plato and Himmler does not seem to work.

That this last is a concession made by Marxist theoreticians and practitioners is an issue which is not foreign to the main thrust of my study. Modernity, be it Marxist or otherwise, has had to make some concessions with regard to the family, if only for the very crass reason that the family seems—at least at this moment—to be the best breeding ground for populating the gnostic paradise of the future, howsoever we might conceptualize the Golden Age promised us by totalitarians. The family does seem to be indispensable practically, and until science can breed youngsters out of test tubes, that practical necessity will remain to either trouble or bolster all political regimes. The family is a basic, indeed *the* basic, human institution. Individuals do not spring into existence out of nothing: they come out of families.

Reginald in his Supplement to the unfinished fourth part of the *Summa Theologiae* of St. Thomas Aquinas cites Aristotle to the effect that man is more a conjugal animal than a political animal.[1] But, he goes on, given that political life is perfectly natural, it follows that domestic life is even more natural to man. Familial life, that romance of domesticity sung so highly by Chesterton in his *What's Wrong with the World*, accentuates the political nature of man.[2] The student of politics can better understand his own subject if he bends back and scrutinizes domestic life. In Aristotle's conception of the social hierarchy governing human life, the household emerges as more fundamental than the city, and even that intermediate state he called the village or township is itself largely composed of families bound together geographically and by common interests. (Aristotle's hierarchy today is blurred by the abolition of space through electronic technology and by the immense mobility of the modern managerial class

with its subsequent suppression of roots. However I must abstract from these considerations which I have treated elsewhere for the sake of the march of the argument of this paper.)[3]

The Family Prefigures the Polity

Aristotle, in Book VIII of the *Ethics*, deepens his understanding of the ontological relations between politics and family by listing notable analogies between familial and political friendship.[4] Friendship is integral to both. The friendship between a father and his sons parallels the friendship between a king and his subjects. "A father is the cause of his son's existence (considered the greatest good in this life), rearing, and instruction—benefits that are attributed also to a man's ancestors."[5] Aristotle here sounds almost like a Roman—a living continuity binds together present, past, and future, all annealed by a *pietas*, a piety, towards a family extended in time. St. Thomas in his *Commentary* adds that "friendships of this type imply a kind of excellence in the ruler. For this reason parents are honored; and so justice is not the same for both parties but must be proportioned to their worth."[6] Aristotle then notes that whereas monarchy is reflected in the father-son relationship, aristocracy is reflected in the friendship between husband and wife. Aquinas comments that the roles of husband and wife are differentiated and engender virtues proper to each. "The husband being more worthy, is placed over the wife; however, the husband does not direct the affairs belonging to the wife."[7] If royal and aristocratic politics are reflected familially, as argued by Aristotle and Aquinas, so too is the form of government often called timocracy or good democracy. (These terms have, of course, a different meaning in Plato.) In the well-ordered family, brothers—due to their likeness in age and to the common education knitting them into unity—find often a kind of friendship rooted in equality and virtue, "the friendship of comrades" (Aristotle).[8] This friendship, antedating all political constitutions in the *polis*, is comparable to it. Brothers are like comrades in arms. Those of you reading these pages who might have known battle will recall the comradeship making friends out of soldiers, certainly among the higher forms of friendship. Aristotle finds this friendship necessary for the well-being of democracies, and he sees it as prefigured in the friendship between brothers within a household governed by parents.

These parallels between the political life of the regime and the more intimate life of the family adumbrate the tripartite division of governments into monarchy, aristocracy, and democracy. The family incarnates all of them spontaneously and naturally, prior to the conscious artistry needed to craft political constitutions into reality. Full political life demands constitutions, themselves works of art that fashion into being the ways in which political orders govern themselves. But the family is *not* like that. Whatever there be of art in a family operates totally within a natural society anterior to art. I once knew a man who wrote a constitution for the government of his family, one inspired by the American Constitution. Rarely in my life have I ever experienced such a sensation of irreality, comic absurdity. My spontaneous reaction was laughter. Families simply do not work this way, and even more, they *are not* this way.

But every political society does structure itself according to constitutions which vary from society to society. And—once again—Aristotle: constitutions do not grow on trees like apples. But give us human beings and, Platonic and Himmlerian perversity aside, we are going to have families. The family is deeper than constitutionality but most constitutions seem to find in the family a prefiguring of themselves. Constitutions are representative. A family, on the contrary, although it might be represented in political life—I will return to the issue—is not in and of itself representative. The family simply is. It exists. It does not represent some prior and more profound society.

Every political society represents something. I appeal here to Eric Voegelin's *New Science of Politics*.[9] Voegelin noted that the concept of "representative government" was little more than fact so far as theory is concerned: i.e., democratic governments do exist. But this fact does not exhaust the meaning of representation. *Every* government or polity is representative of the society that it governs.[10] The society in question either accepts this representation or it does not: in the latter case we encounter revolution or internal collapse. Both revolution and collapse give way to some new order, and hence, my thesis retains its validity.

We might suspect that the family—that without which there would seem to be no political orders at all—might well find itself represented in some formal constitutional structure. The family—I repeat the proposition for it is crucial to the argument—does not represent anything or anybody: it simply is. Could it, however, be represented *qua* family in political life? Permit me to suggest that the family can, indeed has been, represented politically in our Western history, but that this representation has been blurred by a deficient articulation of the forms of government in occidental philosophy. Often we do not see what is there to be seen because we approach reality through glasses cut by craftsmen who did not know their own trade. A refined theory of political representation is required to come to terms with this series of problems. Every regime or polity images forth the society that it represents. The political order is a mirror in which a social world can see itself but, being paradigmatic, it invites that same social world to be all the more itself. Both reflecting "back" and inviting "forward," a political regime is at once pulpit and picture. This is what we are as a people! This is what we wish to be! But we wish to intensify our own corporate existence. "I am what I am and that's all that I am." But even Popeye takes spinach in order to be more of what he is, "the sailor man."

Forms of Government

If "democracy" means the power of, and government by, a majority of individuals, then democracy is one among several ways in which mankind has organized its politics. But "democracy" can also mean the truth that every governmental form or regime represents the society that it leads. I am reminded of Sir John Fortescue's symbolism of the "king" as "erupting" (*erumpit*)[11] from society, the *corpus politicum*, as its *caput* or "head," its self-articulation, that without which a body is a corpse. From this angle, it would seem that every political society is "democratic" even though its governmental form might be very undemocratic indeed. Again, Plato: "The City Is Man Writ Large," which is the other side of the coin, "Every society gets the government it merits."

But very few political orders represent societies that are monolithic in their social composition. Aristotle noted that there were few democracies or monarchies

around in his own time, and no aristocracies at all—all this some five hundred years before the birth of Christ. Noting as well in the *Politics* the truth that compromise, not virtue, lies at the heart of most polities, Aristotle suggested that *most* existing regimes reflected an alliance between the many (hence the poor) and the few (hence the rich), democracy and oligarchy. Only the rich or those backed by the rich can be elected but the election pertains to the many, to the *demos*. Much of Aristotle's politics is obsolete but on this point he targeted a perennial truth. The Stagirite was dead right: try to get elected today if you have no money or are backed by nobody with money! And if you have the money needed to mount massive television and print campaigns, to set up the costly machinery of party politics, it is still the majority of the great unwashed that will vote you into office. Wisdom has very little to do with it. Money wedded to votes is the *usual*, which is not to say the *normal*, road to political power. Aristotle, noting all this, lost interest in the classical tripartite division of governmental forms. Without exactly denying it, he bypassed it because it did not seem to describe the political reality he knew. Professor Alvaro d'Ors in Spain has accused Aristotle here of "*pereza intelectual,*" and in the next few paragraphs I follow d'Ors fairly closely in his analysis.[12]

The old tripartite doctrine that Aristotle and Plato inherited contains an essential law, an inbuilt political tendency, even though that law was hidden by the historical vicissitudes of the times that saw the theory, if only imperfectly, come into existence. The arithmetical division of political forms into three was spoiled by Plato's introduction of the notion of legality versus illegality and Aristotle's introduction of a search for the common good as opposed to the egotism of the ruler. Hence the expansion of the original three into six: monarchy plus tyranny; aristocracy plus oligarchy; democracy plus mob rule. These moral considerations do not do justice to the original theory of the three. Plato and Aristotle failed to take into account the principle of representation and the origin of political power. d'Ors has argued:

> Give me a society formed overwhelmingly of individuals, and I will give you a democratic and liberal republic. Give me a society formed in part by prominent families and in part by individuals, and I will give you an aristocratic republic. Give me a society formed principally by families, represented juridically, and I will give you a traditionalist, dynastic monarchy. The principle involved is in no way moral or ethical, nor is it based on a personal preference. The principle justifying the tripartite division of governmental forms follows the curve of how societies are in reference to the role of the family discovered therein. The family is everything. The family is something. The family is nothing.

In a few words: a political order—and, as argued, every political order is representational—can represent families or it can represent individuals or a working compromise between them. In a liberal democracy everybody normally comes out of a family, but the family as such has no political role whatsoever. Familial authority is not recognized in an Upper House, and the vote is not given the family qua family. *One man—One Vote! That is the cardinal dogma of liberal democracy.* When the basis of a society, hence, is composed principally of individuals, liberal individualistic democracy is perfectly representational and normal.

Legitimacy and Legality

The orchestrating principle in the theory is that of *legitimacy* united with the *origin* of political power. Legitimacy is deeper than legality, positive law, and legitimacy finds its paradigmatic structure within the familial community. Legality is posterior to legitimacy, and it either recognizes or fails to recognize familial legitimacy in the three fundamental political forms under discussion.[13]

A society divided into a majority of men whose families do not count socially or politically counterpointed by an aristocratic minority based on families marked by their historical names, sometimes titles, sometimes not, represents itself naturally in an aristocratic republic. That the republic might be crowned ceremonially is irrelevant. The model here for d'Ors is the Roman Republic with its patrician and plebian classes. A plebian could rise to political pre-eminence but when he did so it was not as the representative of a family. The business is easily illustrated by the American experience: a Kennedy is elected because he is a Kennedy, the scion of an illustrious family. A Dukakis becomes governor of a state and a candidate for the presidency because of *what* he stands for, not because of *who* he is. Dynasties often emerge in liberal democracies because the formal structures of individualistic government have not yet eliminated familial and hence aristocratic pretensions. We live today in this country within an uneasy compromise. (Democracy seems to want happy and good family lives in its rulers but it is unwilling to represent the family politically.) To the example of Rome, we might add as well the experience of England in the past few centuries. A Churchill rises to prominence because he is a Marlborough. A Disraeli rises to power because he is himself. That both men were brilliant is beside the point for the thesis being argued. Senator Kennedy is not a particularly deep fellow and not even his friends would argue the contrary. But he represents an illustrious family: *that* is his ticket of admission to American political power.

A society in which every family is a dynasty unto itself represents itself naturally in a dynastic monarchy. Legality dominates democracy, legality balanced by legitimacy marks aristocracy, and legitimacy as anterior to and legitimative of legality seals monarchy. Monarchy thus is less government by one than government by a family. The dynastic monarchical principle has always been under attack historically from two different sources. Aristocracies resent royal power because one family is placed above the powerful and the rich and hence might well impose its will on their privileges. Thus aristocracy won in England but lost in Spain and France. But the dynastic principle is attacked by democratic individualism in another way. A sign of democracy is its permanent attack on the differences between legitimate and illegitimate children, its attempt to equalize them both *legally*. Democracy, when faithful to its essence, cannot recognize anything political which is not grounded in legality. Democracy does not defend illegitimate children out of any tender charity towards these unfortunate youngsters but out of a deep resentment for the family as an institution incapable of being really at home in a society that recognizes *legally* the existence of nothing more than the isolated individual. Where the family lacks political representation, monarchy is an unnatural form of government, the superimposition of a crowned mummy upon a body foreign to its essence. But where fathers are kings in their own

families, one of their own—a dynastic king—is father of all the fathers.

Filmer argued that same thesis from Scripture but he overstated his case.[14] Monarchy is *a* natural form of government but it is certainly not the only one. Aquinas, for example, preferred monarchy but he argued for the validity of both democracy and aristocracy. That there are very few traditionalist monarchies in existence, if any at all, is due to the decline in the social and political role of the family, a decline sometimes resisted and even reversed thanks to the aristocratic principle, but that principle, as suggested, tends to be hostile to monarchy. Aristocracy, with its network of blood relationships and its oligarchical financial base, resembles a broadly extended country club, and it has usually been uncomfortable with royalist pretensions.

The concept of Republic is not the contradictory of Monarchy. There have been transitional republics, crowned republics, and transitional monarchies. The enemy of legitimate monarchy is illegitimate monarchy, usurpation in the strict sense of the term.[15]

The moral considerations advanced by Aristotle to distinguish tyranny from monarchy do not truly reach the heart of the problem. A tyrant, *de facto,* might govern well and a "good" dynastic king poorly. The formal difference between the two of them must be sought elsewhere, *in the origin of their power* linked to its representative role. The legitimate king inherits from his father as does the legitimate son from his. When events go badly for the legitimate king—as well as for the legitimate father of any decent family—his own gather all the more around him, rally to him in his misfortune. Louis XIV had his back to the wall when the armies of the continental alliance threatened to push deeply into

France unless he withdrew his grandson's claim to the Spanish throne. The French King called a Council of the Blood Royal to advise him on his duty. When the guns were roaring and Marlborough was at his gates, Louis forgot his absolutist pretensions and remembered that his power was founded not in himself but in his family. After the Austrian defeat at Austerlitz the Austrian Emperor, Francis II, was cheered in Vienna by the populace but that very Emperor wondered whether the same reception would be accorded Napoleon in Paris had he lost such a crucial battle. The tyrant must go on from victory to victory—or die. We might evidence here as proof the late Adolf Hitler.

Factually, of course, every dynasty at its origin was imposed by violence but its legitimation does not depend on its founder but upon his descendents who inherit. I cite once again Professor d'Ors:

> The virtue of a king does not reside in his being one; unity can be achieved in other ways as well; that virtue reposes upon the king's being legitimate, in being the supreme incarnation, living and enduring, of all loyalty and every legitimacy.[16]

It follows that the classical tripartite distinction, although badly articulated by the Greeks, contained within itself principles of enduring truth for political philosophy. They are even insinuated in the very Greek words used to designate the three governmental forms. *Cracia* as in "demo*cracy*" or in the "auto*cracy*" of the tyrant, or even in aristo*cracy* simply means the fact of political power; *arquia* as in mon*archy* is essentially the origin of power, that is, familial legitimacy. Thus, in monarchy the power of the royal family; also in olig*archy* the power of families of noble or preeminent origin.

Possibly it might be wise to note here that familial legitimacy must not be identified with the sheer fact of blood succession. In the old Turkish Empire a new Sultan usually had all his brothers killed, often by strangulation. Born of a woman who belonged to a harem, the Ottoman Emperor had little in common with the Christian dynastic king whose power was thought to be housed in the very institution of the legitimate dynasty *qua* family. A Christian who murders his brothers is guilty of an abominable crime and yet the deed was common in the Islamic world and, much earlier, in the Roman Empire where succession to the purple by the son of the emperor was always precarious and never settled by a fixed principle of legitimacy. Claudius spent half his life ducking assassination from his own family. He died, finally, assassinated.

Family Legitimacy in America

Quite naturally we are concerned in a special sense with the role of the family in the United States. Political tendencies in reality rarely exist with the abstract purity proper to science or theory. These tendencies, each with its own law of growth, usually mingle and are often muted by their antithetical opposites. This Federal Union began two hundred years ago as a basically aristocratic republic with severe qualifications—economic and otherwise—placed on the right to vote or to enjoy the power of the magistrate. At its origin an aristocratic republic with, however, large doses of democracy, today—thanks to what Adlai Stevenson called "the catalyst of history," the watershed being the Civil War—the United States is basically a democratic republic with a quasi-monarchical executive and large doses of aristocracy which operate now outside the Constitution. It is important to note that aristocratic or oligarchical dynasties arise constantly in our time. Some of these dynasties last only a couple of generations. As the family wealth is dissipated when the clan scatters and converts itself into mere individuals, the dynasty dies. Others perdure, such as the Kennedys (the recent ministries on the "Kennedys of Mass" is a splendid confirmation of my thesis). Familial legitimacy grows out of oligarchical wealth in our country. We might think of the Cabots, the Lodges, the old Virginia Dynasties, the Fish. (For as long as I can remember there has been a Hamilton Fish in Congress, and I can recall Franklin Roosevelt's once famous quip, directed against his aristocratic Republican opponents, "Martin, Barton, and—Fish.") No longer legally represented in the affairs of state, *these men are elected to political power because of their last names,* familial legitimacy mocking democratic individualism. They balance the democratic individualism which today is sweeping the entire Western world, and apparently, the countries behind the Iron Curtain.

Aristotle's observation in his own time that most regimes are blends of oligarchy and democracy could not find a more vivid verification than in the United States of today.

Although a popular dynastic monarchy reposing upon a society formed principally of families that are both protected and represented politically would seem to be the most natural expression of familial politics, the family by no means shrivels into insignificance in aristocratic republics. In aristocratic England after the Protestant Settlement of 1688, which effectively destroyed royal power, the importance of the family in a large

minority of titled and untitled oligarchs was, if anything, accentuated. The door was always open to the commoner who, if rich or bright, could buy into the House of Lords. If distinguished, he was welcomed thanks to his merits. Nowhere were family relationships and ties more important for the filling of governmental and military posts and the execution of the business of state. Rich commoners marrying impoverished noblemen was a widespread practice, satirized by men of letters but eagerly sought after by both parties to the matrimony. Hilaire Belloc in his remarkable little book, *The Nature of Contemporary England,*[17] written sometime before the egalitarianism that swept Great Britain after World War II, noted that a mark of the success of the English aristocratic government was the truth that poor and rich men imitated the manners and the clothes of their "betters." Everyone wanted to be a "gent" and Charlie Chaplin early in the century exploited this with great success: the comic little Cockney with bowler hat and walking stick, a cartoon of the lower-class Englishman's attempt to mimic the aristocrat.

In the old Roman Republic, as indicated, the distinction between patrician and plebian was based on venerable ancestry in the one and the lack thereof in the latter, but the plebian could rise to power and eventually, in some cases, his family could be graced with the toga of the Senate.

But where the family lacks political representation, even if it be nothing more than an added vote given the head of a household, the family is resented by the regime that becomes increasingly individualistic.[18]

The Family Endangered

Liberal democracy can only give lip service to the family. That it does so at all is a mark that the family is a society deeper than all positive law. The attack on the family is easily noted by any reflective student of politics, and this altogether apart from his personal preferences. The causes are not exclusively political. Some reflect a decline in traditional Christian morality. Some reflect technological changes. Altogether they bring about the family under siege. Anybody can string his own rosary of individualistic beads buttressing my thesis: legal abortion; easy divorce; the widespread phenomenon of couples living outside wedlock and the social acceptance of this situation; the disappearance of a sense of shame in men and women who engage openly in adultery and fornication; the move to legalize sodomy; Gay Liberation; feminism and its flattening out the differences between men and women (differences upon which Aristotle and Aquinas based the intimate friendship which ought to exist between husband and wife); widespread violence in our schools; the disappearance of the family council and good conversation around the dinner table due to the invasion of television; the abolition, dictated by economics, of the family farm and the "Mom and Pop" corner grocery store, shop, or tavern; heavy confiscatory taxation on inheritances which in England, during the Labour Government, insisted on the ripping of roofs off old houses when the taxes could not be paid; heavy urbanization which makes children an economic liability rather than an asset; the fear fathers have of offending their own children; the reality of young people who do not know the names of their own grandparents—and who could not care less! All these factors, many of which are rooted in quite distinct causes, mix together in the individualistic and liberal democracies marking the West today. Some of these cultural changes can—I presume—be defended but all of them together run against the grain of family life as we have known it for millennia. All of them render it virtually impossible for the family to play a political role in society. Democratic individualism, when faithful to its own essence, must marginate the family and even mock its claims. When mankind is reduced to an aggregate of individuals, an amorphous mass with neither family traditions nor corporate memories, just about everything in my rosary of woes falls into place.

My role in this essay has not been that of a Jeremiah. I am not a moralist: the role makes me uneasy. I write here as a political philosopher who attempts to discover laws, living tendencies, a *nomos,* in political existence. The older Christian exaltation of the family, going back to the Holy Family and enshrined in all the poetry of Christmas, can never be at home in a political order that recognizes legally only isolated individuals. The question today is not can the family be at home in the modern world? The question rather is, can the family be at all?

Notes

1. St. Thomas Aquinas, *S.T., Supplementum,* Q. 41, a. 1.
2. G. K. Chesterton, *What's Wrong with the World* (New York: Sheed and Ward, 1956).
3. Frederick D. Wilhelmsen and Jane Bret, *The War in Man* (Athens, Ga.: Univ. of Georgia Press, 1970).
4. Aristotle, *Nichomachean Ethics,* Bk. VIII, 1160b–1161.
5. Ibid., 1161a, 15–16.
6. St. Thomas Aquinas, loc. cit.
7. Ibid.
8. Aristotle, loc. cit., 1161b, 25–26.

9. Eric Voegelin, *The New Science of Politics* (Chicago: Univ. of Chicago Press, 1952).

10. I have argued the thesis in an epistemological context that representation can be understood either substantively or verbally (*Man's Knowledge of Reality*, Albany, N.Y.: Preserving Christian Publications, 1988, 81–85). Substantive representation—what I called "ambassadorial representation"—is a representative who takes the place of the represented: it bespeaks an absence. Verbal or "existential" representation is a representing of that which initially exists in itself: this bespeaks a presence. Political representation is a blending of both: the regime acts for its citizenry and it represents, renders present politically to the world, the society that it represents.

11.. Sir John Fortescue, *De Laudibus Legum Anglie*, ed. and trans. with introduction and notes by S. B. Chrimes (London: Cambridge, 1949), 69 and passim.

12. Alvaro d'Ors, *Forma de Gobierno y Legitimidad Familiar*, "O Crece o Muere" (Madrid: Rialp, 1960); cf. my study, "The Political Philosophy of Alvaro d'Ors," *Political Science Reviewer* XX (Spring 1991).

13. For a Spanish opinion contrary to that of d'Ors on the nature of political legitimacy, *cf.* Manuel Fraga Iribarne, *La Monarquía y el País* (Barcelona: Colección Panorama, 1977), 31–35. Fraga understands legitimacy in terms of function, not origin. He does grasp, however, the strength of d'Ors' analysis, but he will not follow it through to its conclusions because he considers the thesis to be inapplicable today. A consideration of Fraga's thesis would require a study in itself.

14. Sir Thomas Filmer, *Patriarcha and Other Political Works* (Oxford: Basil Blackwell, 1949).

15. d'Ors, loc. cit., 36.

16. d'Ors, ibid., 41.

17. Hilaire Belloc, *The Nature of Contemporary England* (London and New York: Constable and Co., 1937).

18. Familial representation through the hereditary peers in the British House of Lords is restricted to the higher nobility, hence it is thoroughly aristocratic, but this situation mingles with membership by peers nominated for life and whose role in the Lords is not based on familial succession. The last "popular" or wide-spread political representation of the family in modern Europe was to be found in the regime of General Francisco Franco in Spain where heads of families were represented as such in the Cortes by their own elected "Procurators" or *procuradores*. Whether this political representation was effective or only ceremonial is a question from which I abstract. Indeed, to my knowledge the issue has never been studied thoroughly by political scientists. An interesting moral issue in regimes with a heavy familial politics is the imputation of guilt. In the Roman Republic shame tended to be more familial, corporate, than individual, as Professor Melvin Bradford has pointed out to me. Thus, Lucius Junius Brutus killed three of his sons for cowardice in battle. They had disgraced the family. Their punishment was meted out not by the magistrates of the regime but by the patrician head of the family. Resonances of this attitude can be found in the Scottish and Irish clan systems where individuals identified themselves by their clan name, by the blood that gave them birth.

Thomas Molnar

The Liberal Hegemony: The Rise of Civil Society

VOL. 29, NO. 2, 1994

There are now roughly two modern theories about the early structuralization of political society in the West. Both are merely groping in the darkness of pre-history, but both are plausible and conform to what is known with a reasonable certainty. One hypothesis holds that in "early times" the function of the king and high priest is found in a state of fusion: the king (or tribal chief, etc.) was an absolutely sacred figure, directly communicating with the deity or the pantheon of gods, at times even a god himself. There are many signs of such a state of affairs in the annals of mankind, from China to the Malabar coastal region of India and to the position of the Inca in ancient Peru. The other hypothesis, rather ill-received in scholarly circles but gaining ground, was proposed and documented in this century by Georges Dumezil who took Indo-European documents (archaeology, sagas, linguistics) to show that political structure in this basic "tribe" of the present-day European peoples was tripartite: the king and the warriors, the priestly class, and the artisans/peasants/tradesmen, what we call today civil society.

But even if we accept the first theory, historical records tell us that very early the royal and the sacerdotal function must have split up (Egypt, Mesopotamia, Hellas). We should bear in mind that both had their hands full of tasks in a society where royal authority was the fountainhead and sole possessor of power, and the priests were taken with extreme seriousness, for at least three reasons: through worship as well as through science (astronomy, irrigation) they guaranteed the community's survival and peace with the gods; they served as administrators and scribes at the royal court; and in that same capacity they raised taxes, oversaw the depots of food supply, and planned the construction of public buildings and monuments.

Throughout known history, the tripartite division into material, military, and spiritual functions existed in every part of the world, which is a good indication of the structure's validity well beyond the Indo-European tribe and the Middle East. The main theme is compatible with numerous variations: tribal chief and witch-doctor, pharaoh and priestly class, Roman consuls and sacerdotal colleges, and of course Hebrew kings and Levites, Christian kings or emperors and the Catholic Church. It is not the task of this article to examine each of these functions and their relationships of dependence or equality, although such an examination would be eminently useful in another writing. It is, however, important to outline very briefly the function of the third entity, the class of lower activities as they were always referred to, the peasants, the artisans, the miners, the sailors, the tradesmen, the personnel of caravans, the shepherds, the merchants, the bankers. If throughout history the king-and-warriors and the priestly castes were understood to form two distinct *institutions*, the third class just mentioned was never known by that name, it never had an internal cohesion or a function other than that of the "service sector." Without the latter, the life of the whole society would have come to a standstill; nevertheless it was not acknowledged as a political entity on its own, with a distinct political weight. In fact, whenever this service sector, or civil society, or parts of it attempted to organize into a coherent whole, a pressure group with recognized and asserted interests, the other two institutions of society moved against it or at least declared its dependence on them and their supervisory power and authority over it.

The general situation was, however, far from static. A characteristic feature of this tripartite arrangement was its dynamism, at least in the Western world and the world in which the later West had been politically and intellectually prepared. What we described above was valid for the non-Western world also, except that there—in the middle-eastern empires, African tribes, pre-Columbian America, the steppes of Asia—the tripartite system was and remained rigid, particularly with regard to the "third

class," civil society. Which leads us to the conclusion that it was the *mobility* of pre-Western and Western, particularly of Christian, society which allowed these historical actors—royal palace, temple, and civil society—to engage in their respective roles and thus create *history* in the Western sense of the word. The precondition of such an evolution may be detected in the clear cleavage between king and pope, the temporal and spiritual power. Such a cleavage is noticeable in the early history of some nations, although there are only indirect evidences. In the Hebrew kingdoms, there appeared, next to the Levites, the individuals called prophets who never ceased castigating the sovereign for his morals and policies. In Hellas, the *basileus,* the early king, is found again in the pre-classical centuries as being entrusted with the priestly function of sacrifice—clearly a power transfer about which we know little, but one through which political leadership, perhaps the *tyrannus,* accumulated all power in his hands, leaving only the shadow of it to the priestly class. In Rome, too, the function of the *pontifex maximus* was separated after a while from political power, although deep into the Caesarian world the religious label was still assumed by the newly sacralized imperial Caesar.

We spoke of the cleavage between king and priest, and just saw that it had been adumbrated in Judea, Hellas, and Rome—while in Egypt, for example, nominally at least, the priests remained subordinated to the pharaoh throughout a long and conflictual history. The cleavage became a central reality with the words uttered by Jesus Christ: "Render unto Caesar . . . render unto God" their respective due. The ancient Gordian knot was thus cut, and we may argue that "modern" history began with those words. It is also evident that these words had more than a religious significance, and that the political problem of legitimate rule also received a long-delayed solution. Granted, power has always been sacralized; but there is an essential and enormous difference between a regime which commands the citizen's mind, conscience, and transactions, and one which has competitors in this endeavor and where this endeavor is divided by two equally powerful institutions. (We shall see below how liberalism and the totalitarian regimes respond to this permanent Western dilemma of divided power.)

THE "ACTORS" being now in place, let us examine their reciprocal relationship in Western/Christian history. The words of Christ did not settle the issue of who rules in the practical order. The Constantinian association of state and church raised new problems. Was the church to be grateful and submit to the questionable solicitude of the emperors who wanted to restore the health of the empire with doses of a vital and dynamic religious faith? Or was the church to formulate a new relationship, something that Pope Gelasius attempted to do with his doctrine of the Two Swords: acknowledgment of two separate but cooperating areas, the spiritual and the temporal, pope and emperor, but papal supremacy nevertheless since the pope is also responsible for the salvation of the emperor's soul. Indeed, Bishop Ambrose of Milan practiced Gelasius's doctrine a century before the latter's promulgation when he stood up to Emperor Theodosius, forbidding him to enter the church for a massacre he had ordered in Thessalonika.

Ambrose, Gelasius, and subsequent popes were obliged to guard attentively the church's independence, prompted by the inclination of the state to encroach upon the ecclesiastical domain, as became so obvious at the Reformation, one thousand years later. The Empire (Eastern-Roman) also had reason to complain about the church, many of whose leading representatives were not willing to appreciate the imperial interests in a hostile surrounding, with German tribes and an advancing Islam taking the emperor between two mortal perils. The balance in the spirit of Gelasius was temporarily restored in the year 800 when, politically speaking, a new actor appeared on the stage, the Frankish power of Charlemagne. His crowning by the pope on Christmas night in Rome weakened the pope's dependence on the emperor in Constantinople, but prepared a series of new conflicts between the church and the European kings, conflicts lasting until the rule of Napoleon, and beyond, to this day.

The point here is not to deplore these conflicts, but to insist that in spite of them the basic cooperation of church and state continued, since their common interests were at least equal in importance with the built-in conflicts, skirmishes, and, not infrequently, wars. Christ's words lent themselves to more than one interpretation, and the state, too, could argue that, as an institution, it is much older than the church, derives its power directly from God (St. Paul's teaching), and that there can be only one power within a nation. Starting with the eleventh century, kings and emperors listened to jurists whose training in Roman (pagan) law predated that of ecclesiastical lawyers. They could argue for the king's temporal power over against the pope's and bishop's theses. (According to some historians, these Roman jurists had laid the foundations of Roman-oriented humanism and Renaissance paganism.) It must be emphasized, however, that these conflicts did not contradict the cooperation, since both church and state needed a common front vis-à-vis the believers' immorality and the citizens' lack of discipline and civic virtue, the ordinary penchant of all men in all ages.

We are speaking here of civil society. Let us state bluntly that while churchmen and state administrators are tempted by their closeness to power and the abuses derived therefrom, members of civil society are exposed to the temptations that their daily activities offer. Over and against the sacrality of temporal and ecclesiastical institutions, the profane transactions turning around material interests and money also offer a vast area for abuse. Put in a simplified way, state and church never quite trusted the agitation in the forum and the marketplace, the myriad intertwined interests, the greed, the occasions for immorality. The all-time consequence was (it still is, read the papal encyclicals) the insistence on the supremacy of church and state over civil society; the first two possessed clear institutions, outlines and structure; civil society by its very nature could not be called an institution, and its ambition always reached beyond previously set limits. In the non-Western, traditional world, these limits were not allowed to be trespassed; hence, civil society remained dependent on the will and decision of the two other institutions. In the West, state and church by and large granted civil society a large amount of independence and freedom of movement, and gradually as commerce went from the periodic markets supplied by Syrian and Jewish tradesmen (in the early half of the Middle Ages) to the large-scale commerce in the Italian and Flemish port cities—Antwerp, Venice, Genoa—beginning with the eleventh century.

Needless to say, the members of the civil society were just as devoted (or dissimulating) Christians, and just as loyal citizens, as the members of the two leading institutions. And it is merely a sign of the universality of church and state in the general environment that the two cooperated in the setting up of "bourgeois" institutions like guilds and corporations, whether for artisanship or learning. The proverbial butchers, bakers, and candlestick makers belonged to religious corporations with their chaplains, like the corporation called University of Paris, Oxford, or Bologna. In no sense a despotic way, state and church had a hand (light or heavy, depending on the circumstances) in the professional life of the citizenry, creating thereby a certain equilibrium—the absence of which we deplore today, without concealing, of course, the numerous drawbacks of that balanced structure.

From the eleventh to the fifteenth centuries, and then increasingly beyond, we witness the incredible growth of civil society, unthinkable in other civilizations. The measure of its growth is its increasing articulation and, naturally, its power. Civil society intelligently exploited the conflicts between church and state, taking generally the side of the king who was struggling against his own rivals, the anti-burgher feudal lords and the similarly feudal lord-bishops. His jurists, a reliable rampart around his power, were mostly of burgher origin themselves, and so were the personnel of his administration, blocking whenever possible the power of the nobility. The growing bourgeois power can be ascertained even today in every old European city and its architecture. Next to beautiful churches (Prague, Florence, Ghent, etc.), one finds magnificent city halls, the private palaces of merchants meant to compete (in Brussels, Florence, Bruges, Frankfurt) with the noble families' chateaux, the feudal fortresses, even the royal and episcopal residences. And what was true of buildings was also true of a whole branch of art, what could be called "bourgeois" or "third-estate" art: the burgher joined the courtier in having his portrait painted, in purchasing relics and having them encased in precious stone, in having magnificent prayer books, organizing splendid burials in churches to which they financially contributed.

These are only the outward manifestations of growing power and wealth. There was more. The vast network of commerce, industry, and banking increased the burghers' influence on policies. They lent money to the papal court, to the imperial court, they financed huge overseas operations and possessed entire fleets to carry them out with handsome profits. They endowed monasteries, sponsored book publishing, and had a hand in new religious movements, wars, and crusades against the Turks. They even had the beginnings of an *ideology,* starting with the fourteenth century, not surprisingly at a time when the church was going through a series of crises as a consequence of new battles against the growing royal power. And when royal power proved finally to be the winner in these conflicts with the church, the burgher class is found on the side of the former. The ideas of a Marsilius of Padua, whom we may call a disciple of William of Ockham (the nominalist philosopher), display daring novelties about bourgeois power—still dissimulated, of course, in the rhetoric of faith and doctrine, but revolutionary for the times, the middle of the fourteenth century. The burghers' cause was to derive enormous as yet theoretical benefits from these ideas: burgher participation at councils, increase of imperial power at the expense of the church, the pope's demotion to the rank of an imperial civil servant! The Gelasian doctrine was all but forgotten.

The ideology of civil society was still far from its later formulation, yet we should understand in advance the decisive role it was to play inside the still-Christian commonwealth of a Europe at least nominally united in its faith. This is a culminating moment, with the sixteenth and seventeenth centuries as a first zenith. It is evident that both church and state had a well-articulated and deepened "ideology." For the first, it was the admirable edifice of the Christian dogmatic and corpus of doctrine, jurisprudence, and moral teaching—which had assimilated the best of Hellenic philosophy and Roman law. There is no need here to enter into the details. The state similarly rested on natural and Roman law, on the old tribal custom, and ancient philosophy. Again, the details are documented in the huge literature of statecraft, law, financial policies, and the "wisdom of nations." The bourgeoisie faced the uncomfortable situation of not resting on a political theory of its own, of not being able to justify its power and interests. Political philosophy of past ages passed quickly over such chapters, such issues, attributing them to *alien* thought, that of state and church. Aristotle's *Politics* begins typically with the household, but only to establish the truth that the life of the *polis* obeys altogether different rules and considerations. Even the contemporary political literature took no notice of bourgeois interests, and speculated (Machiavelli, Jean Bodin, the English jurists) on the place that the new Prince must occupy at the head of a well constructed commonwealth. There was only an indirectly orientated literature that took bourgeois interests into account, with writers hiding their preoccupations in a humanistic garb. Only Protestantism was to produce a political literature wherein civil society's interests and ideological makeup were frankly displayed, and even there we must separate particles of the new political doctrine from philosophical considerations, as in the case of Hobbes and Spinoza.

In retrospect, it is important to note the need of civil society to formulate an ideology of its own, an indispensable instrument to bring about first, its *prise de conscience;* then, its equality with its age-old rivals, state and church; and finally, its (at the time unexpected) hegemony. The last four centuries appear then as the gradual acquisition of political hegemony by civil society, a historical first which still leaves all concerned open-mouthed. Let's spell it out: modern history is the history of the growth of civil society's hegemonic position within the framework of Western nations.

WHAT IS suggested here is not what Ranke believed historiography to be: "telling it as it actually happened." We are no longer claiming to be masters of all the parameters of events. Every day new disciplines are born which become auxiliaries of the study of history: archeaology, anthropology, the exploration of myths, beliefs, of archaic industry, and so on. What we offer here is a hypothesis: it *seems* that a new intelligibility may be acquired about the present if we arrange phenomena in a certain way. Society's tripartite division saves these phenomena (as Hellenic wisdom claimed science was about), makes them rational and plausible. There are, of course, those who contradict the hypothesis at its roots. The anthropologist Pierre Clastres, who studied Brazilian indigenous people, claimed that the tribe itself (in our terms, "civil society") decided about public matters, imposed its decisions on the chief, and sent into battle the warriors who by no means formed a class and did not depend

on the chief (our "king"). Needless to say, this description is contrary, for example, to things as we find them in the *Iliad*.

We learned from Marx, and also from pre-Marxian thinkers, that a social class becomes conscious of itself, its interests, cohesion, and power, and mounts an offensive against other classes which, in its own view, block its progress. Marx finds a correlation between the self-awareness of a class and the economic system at a certain stage. This is only one view of things, although it is part of social dynamics. We claim, on the other hand, that self-awareness by a vast ensemble like civil society evolves as a result of literature, psychological reactions, for example, to humiliation by upper classes—the desire to imitate (mimesis*),* wealth seeking power, and many other factors. Among these factors there are envy and resentment, at any rate, a long tradition of subordination. It was natural for civil society—as it witnessed the Reformation-caused split in the church, the consequent fragility of the monarch "by divine right," and, last but not least, the conquest of science and industry—to interpret these epoch-shaking events as its own success and future domination. It was not a conscious decision to reverse the course of history, since large masses of people are above all conservative and cannot envision things contrary to their habits and habits of thought. Rather, there were signs of changing times which ultimately coalesced in a philosophy and proved to be an extremely powerful battering ram against the rival forces, church and state. Some of these signs: If God is found to be bound by scientific laws, why shouldn't the king be, and, more generally, power? If the Bible is a mere moral tale (Spinoza), why hold that a moral society cannot exist without a religious superstructure, when newly discovered distant people live a normal life without a church, whether in civilized China or in the forests of Brazil? (This observation was based on ignorance, since all people had religion, even if it was very different from Christianity.) If there are such great differences between ways of organizing collective existence, why not look for the "natural man" ("noble savage") who must be virtuous since civilization and institutions have not yet spoiled him? In other words, there is a possibility of building a new world, without kings and noblemen, prelates and religious authorities, a world founded on the burghers' simple virtues.

THESE WERE some of the signs which strengthened civil society's self-confidence, and prompted philosophers like Mandeville, Montesquieu, Adam Smith, and a legion of others in the seventeenth and eighteenth centuries to systematize these thoughts. They become the leading thoughts (ideology) of modernity, justifications of the belief in progress and the conscious vision that civil society can and will emancipate itself from the shackles imposed on its natural dynamism and industry by two parasitical institutions. The central idea, the fuel of the social motor, was victory over church and state, their neutralization (the radicals said abolition) through separation. As it was later expressed, "the alliance of throne and altar" must be terminated.

What the philosophers of the bourgeoisie had theorized about, civil society proceeded to carry out through policies and concrete events. *Not* as a conspiracy—history is not a series of complots, except in the eyes of those too lazy to think—but as a network of theoretical and practical considerations, the way mankind moves in history. Briefly: there were the Huguenots, the free thinkers, the

neo-European materialists, etc., who, by no means agreeing between themselves, agreed that the old regime was rotten. The new moralists, Mandeville (of Huguenot origin) chief among them, wrote of the private vices turned into publicly useful social behavior. Montesquieu and Kant believed that bourgeois industry contradicts royal power, and that bourgeois republics, financially sober and anti-war, will establish public order inside the state and peace among nations. Adam Smith, fearful of the economic competition he foresaw and theoretically endorsed, preached the necessity of moral sentiments and of an internal censor against excesses. Thomas Hobbes, denying the classical and Christian teaching about man's social nature, based his philosophy on man's fear of his fellows, and wanted public order based on the social contract of property holders, guaranteed by the king's religion, whether it is the religion of the Stuarts or of Cromwell. Pierre Bayle, Spinoza, Locke, Lessing believed in a "natural religion," shorn of dogma, liturgy, and myth, corresponding to beliefs that can be shared by all mankind, a rational creed. These were the slowly emerging contents of what we called "bourgeois ideology," summarized, systematized, and promoted by thinkers, propagandists, politicians, and very often pastors and priests, all spokesmen for the new moral order.

Events seemed to prove correct the writings of the new theorists. Under Oliver Cromwell between 1640 and 1660, and under Robespierre two centuries ago, the bulk of the transformation took place, each time in the favor of the burghers, the moneyed and industrial class. Even though these were not complete victories since royal restorations followed, after Cromwell, then under Napoleon, the bourgeois claims were consolidated and bourgeois views prevailed in such areas as economic structure, the activation of commerce and industry, education, political reforms—and the disconnection of religion, at least in its doctrinal expression, from the life of the state and from decisively large sections of civil society. Without its uncomfortable but indispensable ally, religion, the state itself started to drift, partly because it was now completely desacralized, partly because it was now called upon to arbitrate, but without authority or power, among the religious substitutes we call ideologies. Without its uncomfortable but indispensable ally, state power, the church sank to the level of a mere pressure group inside civil society, and had no recourse against the new hegemony since it had also signed the "social contract," together with the other, myriad interest groups.

Thus a valid point may be made that civil society achieved its century-long, if not historical, objective of neutralizing its two great rivals, and placing its own ideology—liberalism and/or socialism (or various combinations)—at the center of the commonwealth. The separation of state and church has become a veritable *civil dogma,* at the pinnacle of the social contract and civil religion. Conservatives especially (but are they other than decently talking liberals and justifiers of the status quo as long as it favors them?) complain about the power of the state. Yet, we wonder if a very large number of phenomena we deplore, from abortion, sex education, drug addiction, sexual violence, and so on, are not the inventions and whims of civil society, inventions and whims that the state, under pressure, erects into laws. As Lorenz von Stein wrote: "The first practical application of the rule of capital [civil society] over the organs of the state consists in the formation of institu-

tions by which society controls the state: this is the Chamber of Deputies." We are warned that what the state promulgates as law may be under pressure by civil society, not the other way around.

The church is, of course, even more strictly controlled. In our age, the competition between state and civil society has not yet ended in the decisive victory of either. We see indeed a kind of rivalry-and-cooperation between the organs of the state and the semi-private bureaucracies and corporations of civil society—as it used to be the case between state and church in the Middle Ages. However there is no such rivalry-and-cooperation between civil society and the church. The latter is inaudibly but clearly warned that it is a parasitic organization, a myth-engendered institution, and that there are other myths to take its place, from ethical humanism, to psychoanalysis, to intergalactic communications, to sects. The church behaves according to these tacit instructions, and in the process takes on a "protective coloration": it declares for religious pluralism, curbs its mission to convert, it retreats on educational matters, democratizes itself, and its members begin to wear civilian garb, making them indistinguishable from the professionals of civil society.

Let us emphasize that neither state nor church have ceremonially, at one point, converted to civil society's ideology, habits, mentality, and way of dressing—the last example being important since people follow fashion at all times and adjust, in externals, too, to prevailing anonymous injunctions. It is thus not a coincidence that simultaneous to civil society's hegemony, heads of state, monarchs included, abandoned the military uniform, that is the externalia of the "warrior class," and appear in civilian clothing, including on their official portraits. In this, they were followed by the Bolshevik rulers, who no longer wore the worker's cap and overalls, but business suit and necktie. The last in bourgeois liberal accommodations were the prelates of the Catholic Church, after Rome officially signed the "social contract" at the sessions and in the documents of the Second Vatican Council. These are admittedly symbolic acts; nevertheless, symbols merely translate deeper changes of loyalty and function.

AS WE said above, there has not been any kind of ceremonial transfer of power from state and church to civil society, although there was undeniably such a transfer and ceremony when Charles I and Louis XVI were beheaded. Nor has there been any solemn declaration on the part of civil society to assume power and sovereignty. What did happen was that civil society, after centuries and millennia of presence in history, chose, as it were, *liberalism* as its best-furnished arsenal with which to fight its battles—and win the war. This does not mean at all that civil society necessarily opts for liberalism; we may indeed find other options in the future or in other geographical areas. In the case circumscribed by the last four centuries and in the northwest of Europe (by extension in the United States), liberalism was demonstrably the winning ideology, the organizing principle of civil society and the modern community. The future indeed is unknown. It may well happen that the triangular situation so typical of the West—state, church, and civil society—takes other turns, hegemony assumed by one of those that have lost it. The sign of ideological rigidity (reification) is when the powerful assumes that with his victory things become permanent and unchangeable. Western history is a long demonstration that it is not so.

In our days, too, there are many writers (Francis Fukuyama, Michael Novak, George Gilder) who like to dogmatize about the present shape of things and to build further programs on this, according to them, unilinear direction. More liberalism, its worldwide permanent conquest, the minimal state, the forever privatized church, and so on. All we can say is that none of this is certain.

In fact, our century has witnessed gigantic efforts at combating liberal society and its ideology. The Marxist undertaking may be interpreted in the following way: state and church tried to recuperate the old, preliberal power, not for the benefit of either of them, but in favor of a new political entity, the Party. The Party indeed confiscated the entire power of the state, and that of the church also—not in the form of the old religion, but as an ideology. In a way, we see in the totalitarian Party—and I emphasize its newness—the renewed but caricaturized "alliance of throne and altar." It logically followed that the third element, civil society, be reduced to a caricature of itself, and that even this caricature be absorbed by the omnipotent Party—once again, "omnipotent" because it possessed the respective powers of the three institutions.

Facing the Marxist enterprise, the liberal ideology tries to recuperate the entire civil society, and consequently to marginalize state and church. Not just marginalize, but, to be exact, partly to absorb them. The state becomes an economic agent of this enlarged and power-gorged civil society, and the church is warned each time it ventures to make morally motivated statements when such statements contradict civil society's own religion/ideology, for example, on the family, education, abortion, public ethos.

MARXISM AND liberalism thus occupy similar areas in the triangular relationship and institutional network congenial to the West. Both are expressions of hegemonic aspirations, thriving on the weakened structures of state and church; both intend to occupy the whole territory and unify it under their philosophical and political hegemony. The likelihood is that they will not succeed in the long run. The plurality of institutionalized power is typical of the West, and this situation presupposes functional differentiation and the rotation of hegemony. The ideal would be an equilibrium of state, church, and civil society, but this remains a paradigm, with no translation into reality. Yet even paradigms are useful—they serve as thermometers for things gone wrong. Man, Western man at least, needs life under the power, discipline, and loyalty we associate with the state; he also needs the moral insight and limitations that we associate with religion and the institutional church; and he needs the wide area of material and intellectual transactions that are provided by civil society—not only manual or mechanical work, but also education, the press, the associations, public debate. But man cannot give himself the law, the state can; he cannot be morally autonomous, outside religion; he cannot organize trade and other activities without help and endorsement by civil society.

In short, the individual is not as strong and independent as liberalism claims, and the collectivity is not as bold, unified, and forward-looking as Marxism asserts. The paradigm points at the historical balance discussed in these pages. It also points at the risk involved in the hegemony of any one component.

III.

AMERICA'S
CONSTITUTIONAL IDENTITY

M. Stanton Evans

THE STATES AND THE CONSTITUTION

VOL. 2, NO. 3, 1965

The genius of American freedom is the division of powers. In this our system corresponds to the British practice from which it sprang; yet it is different. The division of powers in America means at once something more extensive and more specific than Crown, Lords, and Commons once meant in Britain. There has never been before, and perhaps never will be again, a government so equilibrated as the American system in full working order. Our complexities have been celebrated by spokesmen, both domestic and foreign, astonished that through such a maze of governments and sub-governments we can successfully rule ourselves.

The present age, with its special insistence upon collective action that is quick and sweeping, has seen such commentary redoubled. The ineffable counterpoise of the American Constitution, we hear it said, results in wasted energies, inefficiency, and needless delay. The purpose of this essay is neither to affirm nor to refute such charges, but rather to inspect in one of its most important particulars the curious machinery which has given rise to them. Our object is to determine what the American system is, and why it

is; and although some of its merits will be implicit in what follows, a full discussion of them will have to await some other occasion.

The first point to be noted is that what seems to some critics to be confusion or sloppiness was quite deliberately arrived at. The Founding Fathers knew they were constructing a complex system, and themselves remarked on it. In an 1814 letter to John Taylor of Caroline, John Adams inquired: "Is there a constitution on record more complicated with balances than ours?" In the first place, he noted,

> eighteen states and some territories are balanced against the national government. . . . In the second place, the House of Representatives is balanced against the Senate and the Senate against the House. In the third place, the executive authority is in some degree balanced against the legislature. In the fourth place, the judiciary power is balanced against the House, the Senate, the executive power, and the state governments. In the fifth place, the Senate is balanced against

the president in all appointments to office and in all treaties. This, in my opinion, is not merely a useless but a very pernicious—balance. In the sixth place, the people hold in their own hands the balance against their own representatives by biennial which I wish had been annual elections. In the seventh place, the legislatures of the several states are balanced against the Senate by sextennial elections. In the eighth place, the electors are balanced against the people in the choice of the president. And here is a complication and refinement of balances which for anything I recollect is an invention of our own and peculiar to us.[1]

Not all of these balances have survived; election of senators by the state legislatures was ended by the seventeenth amendment; the independent role of the state electors in choosing the president has, with an occasional exception, fallen into disuse. Yet the major outlines suggested by Adams are on the whole familiar enough to modern Americans in theory, if not in practice. So familiar indeed, that the reasons for their being have long since receded into the mists of memory.

Why is the American system so intricate? The large answer is that the Founding Fathers believed that only through the diffusion of political power could liberty be maintained. The more particular answer is that, in their quest for liberty, they relied in equal portions upon what they understood as their heritage as Englishmen, and upon their experience in the new world. They sought to bring tradition to bear upon the facts of their daily existence. From their heritage they derived one set of balances; from their experience another. The two fused, interlocked, and married, so that balances were struck within balances,

and the system was equilibrated in every extremity.

From their English heritage—a heritage in which the absolute supremacy of Parliament à la Bagehot was not yet articulated—the colonists had derived the notion that governmental departments should in some wise be pitted against each other. The point of both exercises was given classic statement by James Madison in *Federalist* 51:

the great security against a gradual concentration of the several powers in the same department consists in giving to those who administer each department the necessary constitutional means and personal motives to resist encroachments of the others. . . . Ambition must be made to counteract ambition. The interest of the man must be connected with the constitutional rights of the place. It may be a reflection on human nature, that such devices should be necessary to control the abuses of government. But what is government itself but the greatest of all reflections on human nature? If men were angels, no government would be necessary. If angels were to govern men, neither external nor internal controls on government would be necessary. In framing a government which is to be administered by men over men, the great difficulty lies in this: you must first enable the government to control the governed; and in the next place oblige it to control itself.[2]

The insistence upon checks and balances was partly practical, of course; it had "worked," the colonists believed, to preserve liberty in Great Britain, and it had "worked" in America. But its main force was theoretical; it was the prevailing idea of the age, affirmed by all respectable political philosophers. Madison's disquisition is a brilliant statement of what all men of good sense in that era believed. No doctrine was more familiar to them than Adams's assertion that a republic was "a government whose sovereignty is vested in more than one person."[3] The separation of legislative and executive, Edmund Randolph said at the constitutional convention, was the "received maxim" of the day;[4] Madison called it "the sacred maxim of free government."[5] The doctrine fairly bristles from Madison's Notes on the convention and from the *Federalist Papers*. According to then-current theories, the division of government into legislative, executive, and judiciary, with the legislature divided into a popular branch and an "aristocratic" branch, was as much as mortal men could do to restrain the effects of "faction," while giving government its necessary powers. Had the American Constitution been a purely theoretical matter, things no doubt would have ended there.

But the founders were not dealing simply with theories; they were dealing with the facts of life in America in 1787, and those could not be encompassed by the Euclidean trisection of the supreme authority. Madison and his colleagues confronted, not a single nation to be disposed of by abstract design, but thirteen separate nations, each possessed of an independent sovereignty. Such was the brute reality of the American situation, the reality from which arose those characteristics of our system rendering us not merely a "republic," but a "federal republic," and a "compound federal republic" at that. It is the *federal* element in our system which makes it so much more intricate than the English—even if our standard is the British constitution prior to the rise of parliamentary absolutism. There can

be no adequate appraisal of the American government without recognizing this fact, without understanding that *the states* were the chief agents in founding the republic and maintaining its prolonged prosperity. The tension between local and general authorities, the diffusion of power, the necessity of a written constitution and of a pronounced legalism in the weighing of duties and prerogatives: these ingredients of American liberty are rooted in the institutions of federalism.

The Federal Idea

History affords perhaps two dozen clear examples of federations or confederacies prior to the founding of the United States. The Amphictyonic Council and the Delian League, the Ghibelline and Hanseatic Leagues of the Middle Ages, the Dutch Republic and the Swiss confederation, the sporadic fusions of Italian city states in the 15th and 16th centuries—all had been attempts to achieve concerted action with a maximum of local autonomy. Madison and Hamilton arrived in Philadelphia well read in the history of these experiments. Madison in particular stuffed himself with information about the Amphictyonic Council and the Lycian League, comparing their method of operation with the inadequacies of the Articles of Confederations.[6] *The Federalist* is replete with references to ancient confederations, and *Federalists* 18, 19, and 20 are given over to a case by case analysis of various attempts at federative association. The authors also note, in *Federalist* 19, that federalism in its modern form—as exemplified in the Holy Roman empire—owes much to the development of feudalism.[7]

In addition to this historical knowledge, the founders had a certain residue of information and sentiment from their British background. While the structure of the British government was effectively centralized—the sheriffs were chosen by the king—a strong tradition of local autonomy, bequeathed by England's own unusual variant of the feudal constitution, had nevertheless persisted. Edward Cheyney notes that "the ordinary Englishman in the seventeenth century had much more to do with local than with national government. The political institutions which surrounded him on all sides, insensibly controlling every action and forming the world to which his outward life conformed, were familiar to him and affected his habits and ideas, whether he remained at home or emigrated to the colonies, far more directly than did the political institutions of the nation."[8]

Both by study and by habit, therefore, the founders were predisposed to the idea of local autonomies under a federative system. But the federalism they evolved was different from either of its historical antecedents. The ancient and medieval examples, as Bryce noted, were most properly designated "leagues," in which the unit of government that counts is the small autonomous state; such a league "will . . . vanish so soon as the communities which compose it separate themselves from one another."[9] Such a league was the American Confederation. In the second case, the British system of local government, the central authority has all the effective power—whatever the state of popular sentiment; the local officials are its functionaries, and through them it acts directly upon the citizens; the intermediary agencies are in fact administrative subdivisions, and can afford no security to freedom if slippage toward despotism sets in.

In the first case, the dispersal of power among several communities forestalls the dangers of consolidation, but tends to pull the system apart. In the second, the government gains in efficiency, decentralizing administration while maintaining responsibility at the center, but affords no safeguard against the ingathering of power.

The American Federal Republic corresponds to neither of these two forms, but may be said to stand between them. Its central or national government is not a mere league, for it does not wholly depend on component communities which we call the states. It is itself a commonwealth as well as a union of commonwealths, because it claims directly the obedience of every citizen, and acts immediately upon him through its courts and executive officers. Still less are the minor communities, the states, mere subdivisions of the union, creatures of the national government, like the counties of England or the departments of France. They have over their citizens an authority which is their own, and not delegated by the central government. They have not been called into being by that government. They existed before it. They could exist without it.[10]

Thus did Bryce set about explaining the American commonwealth to his countrymen. "America is a common-wealth of commonwealths," he said, "a Republic of republics, a state which, while one, is nevertheless composed of other states even more essential to its existence than it is to theirs."[11]

The vigor of the American states, at least until the twentieth century, has seldom failed to impress foreign observers sensitized to the preconditions of freedom. It is no accident that the most notable friends of liberty in the nineteenth century—Tocqueville and Acton—were profoundly affected by the American variant of federalism. Tocqueville called it "the most perfect federal Constitution that ever existed";[12] Acton described it as America's great contribution to the theory and practice of government, saying: "It is the only method of curbing not only the majority but the power of the whole people, and it affords the soundest basis for a second chamber, which has been found essential security for freedom in every genuine democracy."[13]

How America came to create a federal union transcending both ancient forebears and the British system which nourished it must be the next object of our consideration.

The Realities of 1787

Federalism demands diversity within a framework of orderly association. The first condition of successful federation, A. V. Dicey tells us, is "a body of countries . . . so closely connected by locality, by history, by race, or the like, as to be capable of bearing, in the eyes of their inhabitants, an impress of common nationality. . . . It is certain that where federalism flourishes it is in general the slowly matured fruit of some earlier and looser connection. Second, the inhabitants of the territory to be governed must desire union, and must not desire unity."[14] These were exactly the sentiments which prevailed in 1787. The Americans were actuated by loyalty to a common set of principles as sons of England: From Massachusetts Bay to Georgia, they had for 150 years considered themselves citizens of England entitled to the rights of Englishmen. They all looked to the British heritage of liberty under law, of respect for popular freedom and the rights

of property. They all studied Coke and Locke and Blackstone and Montesquieu. And they all had state governments premised on English ideas: "The states were alike in structure; they had the same political inheritance; the fundamental ideas of English liberty and law, taking root in congenial soil, had grown strong in every section."[15] All of these common characteristics had led them to unite in the War for Independence, and clearly made them capable of bearing "an impress of common nationality."

But there were other factors. Within the framework of heritage, practice, and common cause there were strong motives toward diversity. During the war the colonies had reason to focus on values held in common, and to act in concert. War's end gave them occasion to consider their differences once more—which, indeed, was one of the privileges for which the war had been fought. They had staged a revolution to defend local prerogatives against a distant central authority—as Andrew McLaughlin put it, "to support local government against a general government"[16]—and were not anxious to surrender their hard-won privileges to some other distant authority. And the state governments were working governments in fact, with all the customary advantages of authority de facto and de jure.

Dicey notes that "in 1787 a citizen of Massachusetts felt a far stronger attachment to Virginia or to Massachusetts than to the body of confederated states"[17]—a fact which may be verified by noting that Jefferson referred to Virginia as "my country," and that John Adams, whose theoretical attention to states' rights was nil, used the same affectionate language toward Massachusetts. These "countries" conducted themselves toward one another very much as countries everywhere behave in international concourse—sometimes wisely, sometimes not so wisely. Harold U. Faulkner summarizes the boundary disputes, commercial warfare, boycotts, and punitive duties which the states inflicted upon one another, concluding they in effect dealt with one another as foreign powers.[18] Which in fact and in law is precisely what they were.

If all of this seems improbable to modern Americans, it is because we have forgotten the relative isolation of the states. It was then a four days' ride from Boston to New York on the best roads in America. "The highways of Pennsylvania were almost impassable, and travel on them was little less than misery. South of the Potomac the roads were still worse; there even bridges were a luxury."[19] Charleston, the largest city in the South, had in some ways more in common with Bermuda, which at least shared its global latitude, than it did with Richmond. "Of affairs of Georgia," Madison said in 1786, "I know as little as of those of Kamskatska."[20] Moreover, the fact that the colonies had been settled along the Atlantic seaboard meant each of them had its own coastline and harbors. The disputes characteristic of these foreign powers, while occurring frequently enough to stress the fact that they *were* "foreign," were therefore minimized. The colonies did not have to depend greatly upon one another, and did not have to struggle over vital seaports.[21] Prof. Francis Walker comments:

> Prior to the outbreak of the revolution, in 1775, hardly a trace of sentiment of American nationality had manifested itself among the colonies. Carolinians were content to be Carolinians; Virginians to be Virginians; New Yorkers to be New Yorkers. . . . The state governments had a real and vital existence. They were well organized, with compulsory powers. . . . The states dealt with the really larger interests of society, the care of the peace, the protection of person and property, the domestic relations, the ordinary course of private, social, and industrial life. . . .[22]

Such was the outlook and condition of the American colonies at the time of the revolutionary war; not one nation with thirteen administrative subdivisions, but thirteen nations, sovereign and independent. When the British government treated to end hostilities, it conceded independence not to "America," but to the states, calling each of them out by name. The Treaty of Paris, September 3, 1783, states: "His Britannic majesty acknowledges the said United States, viz., New Hampshire, Massachusetts Bay, Rhode Island and Providence Plantation, Connecticut, New York, New Jersey, Pennsylvania, Delaware, Maryland, Virginia, North Carolina, South Carolina, and Georgia, *to be free, sovereign and independent states*; that he treats with them as such."[23] This document is the legal basis for the existence of the United States—a ratification in international law of what had been achieved by the strength of American arms, a verbalization of sentiment and custom which prevailed among the fathers of our republic.

The Articles of Confederation

The Articles of Confederation, under whose sign the Revolution was concluded, had given full recognition to the particularism of the colonies. Richard Henry Lee's motion before the Continental Congress (June 7, 1776) urging a plan of confederation presaged the language of the Treaty of Paris: "these United Colonies are, and of right ought to be, free and independent states."[24] Debate on this motion raised some of the questions which were to become stumbling blocks to the confederacy, hazards upon which the Constitution was almost capsized, and perplexities which still confound students of the American government. "If a confederation should take place," John Adams wrote to his wife Abigail,

> one great question is, how we shall vote. Whether each colony shall count one? Or whether each shall have a weight in proportion to its wealth, or number, or exports and imports, or a compound ratio of all? Another is, whether Congress shall have authority to limit the dimensions of each colony, to prevent those, which claim by charter, or proclamation, or commission, to the south sea, from growing too great and powerful, so as to be dangerous to the rest.[25]

Events relentlessly pressed the Americans toward a solution. By the summer of '77, it was apparent a confederacy was needed to prosecute the war and to raise money to pay for it. Accordingly, the major impasse was broken and the dilemmas of sovereignty answered in favor of the states. The fathers agreed that: "In determining questions in the United States, in Congress assembled, each state shall have one vote."[26] The point was underscored in Article II, the first substantive paragraph of the document: "Each state retains its sovereignty, freedom, and independence, and every power, jurisdiction, and right, which is not by this confederation expressly delegated to the United States, in Congress assembled."[27] A principal disputed issue, that of levying taxes, was left in the hands of the states. The power of raising taxes for the common treasury was intrusted to the state legislatures—source of considerable difficulty in years to come.

The Articles of Confederation were a great achievement. They established the concept of dual sovereignties within a single system, even though they failed to make the idea fully workable. McLaughlin observes that "with remarkable care they separated the particular or local powers from those of general character . . . under no conditions, of course, would the states surrender all political authority to any central government; but by the Articles of Confederation they granted nearly every power that was really of a general or national character."[28] Farrand shows that the founders, while sensible of the Confederation's defects, nevertheless believed it a worthy form of government, needing improvement rather than radical reconstruction.[29] The conclusion of Merrill Jensen, although he has partially retracted the Beardian language about "radicals," is to the point:

> An analysis of the disputes over the Articles of Confederation makes it plain that they were not the result of either ignorance or inexperience. On the contrary, they were a natural outcome of the revolutionary movement within the American colonies. The radical leaders of the opposition to Great Britain after 1765 had consistently denied the authority of any government superior to the legislatures of the several colonies. From 1774 on, the radicals continued to deny the authority of a superior legislature whether located across the seas or within the American states.[30]

The Articles were, in short, designed to good purpose—to create sufficient power for essential national tasks, while preventing its excessive accumulation. They put diplomacy and commerce, the making of war and peace, the raising of a navy and the regulation of militia, and the establishment of rules for free internal trade, into the hands of the central government. They left all other powers to the states. In the first legal document of Union, two things were thus established: The sovereign independence of the states, as the legal entities creating the government; while some designated aspects of sovereignty were, for the good of the whole, transferred to a central authority.

With the exception of a few ardent nationalists like Hamilton and Gouverneur Morris, the founders did not repent the general formula; but they came to see that the apportionment of power they had achieved was not adequate to their purpose. The Confederation had trouble raising revenues, dependent as it was on the good will of the states for collections; it had a similar difficulty in enforcing other decrees, lacking as it did the power to act directly on the citizenry; and because of its financial distress, it proved too weak to uphold the interests and the honor of the United States abroad.

In 1787, after six years' experience had improved their understanding of the federal balance, the founders saw they had not given Congress the energy it needed to carry out tasks of national scope. Pressures mounted for correction and enlargement of the Articles, resulting in the Philadelphia convention of May, 1787. The founders gathered, not to spin a new order out of their imaginations, but to put into action the results of their experience, to combine what they had learned with the imperatives of tradition and of law. And in all they did, they reckoned at every step with the obdurate reality

enshrined in the custom and sentiment of America as in the legal framework of the Articles: They were dealing, not with a single nation, but with thirteen jealous and energetic sovereignties.

The Federal Convention

The American Constitution succeeded by making a virtue of hard necessity: it blended the formulae of Harrington and Montesquieu and Adams with the native conditions of American experience. The features of tripartite check and balance were interfused with the federal structure inherent in the existence of the states. The result was not one, but two securities for freedom, each interacting upon the other: The doctrine of divided powers within the federal authority, and the doctrine of enumerated powers which limited that authority in the aggregate. To compound matters, the states themselves were organized internally in terms of the tripartite balance, and were working agencies in various departments of the central authority.

In the convention, the states had one vote apiece. The burning question was whether they would emerge from the gathering with the same powers they carried into it. The large states, repeating arguments of ten years earlier, saw no merit in voting as states. Such things as population and wealth, they argued, would be more appropriate grounds for representation. The small states, concerned that they might be "swallowed up," insisted upon equality. There seemed little prospect of reconciling everyone to a common arrangement. But not all members were blinded by parochial interests. Some foresaw that the apparent nemesis of the convention might be its principal virtue. The framers, after all, were interested in two major objectives: to form a government vigorous enough to conduct the affairs of the nation, yet limited enough so that it did not endanger the rights of its citizens.

As early as June 2, John Dickinson, one of the great unsung heroes of American political theory, gave an almost perfect summary of the result which was to emerge from the convention three months later. "One source of stability," Dickinson said, "is the double branch of the Legislature. The division of the country into distinct states formed the other principal source of stability. This division ought therefore to be maintained, and considerable powers be left with the states. . . . If ancient republics have been found to flourish for a moment only [and] then vanish forever, it only proves they were badly constituted; and that we ought to seek for every remedy for their diseases." One of these remedies he conceived to be the accidental lucky division of this country into distinct states; a division which some seemed desirous to abolish altogether. As to the point of representation in the national legislature as it might affect states of different sizes, he said it must probably end in mutual concession. "He hoped that each state would retain an equal voice at least in one branch of the National Legislature."[31] Dickinson had attempted, in the early wrangling over the Confederation, to infuse greater strength into the central government; now he attempted to prevent that government from becoming too strong. Both efforts were correct, and both remarkable for the clarity with which they foretold the final equipoise of the Constitution.

A month and a half after Dickinson's statement, precisely these "mutual concessions" were adopted. The delegates had already decided the lower house of the legislature would be chosen through proportional representation—that is, with seats apportioned among the states according to population. On July 16, by a narrow 5 to 4 vote, it was agreed the upper house would be chosen by states—that is, with each state having an equal vote. This was the turning point of the convention. Though many details remained to be settled, the major danger was averted. The small states had won the day, and the principle of states' rights was welded permanently into the Constitution. "This is," Farrand tells us, "the great compromise of the convention and of the Constitution. No other is to be placed quite in comparison with it."[32]

The states now became vital agents in the operation of the new government. Subsequent to the guarantee of equal suffrage, they were accorded the major role in electing the president, through the machinery of the electoral college. "The election of the President and Senate," Madison later observed, "will depend, in all cases, on the legislatures of the several states."[33] And in further deference to small-state fears, it was made plain the new government would be one of severely limited powers. Its authority would extend only to matters given it in the Constitution, and would be barred from all matters not so designated. The powers of the federal government, as Madison put it, were to be "few and defined," those of the state governments "numerous and indefinite.[34]

The Constitution was not intended, as has been alleged by both its enemies and some mistaken friends, to reconstitute the nation according to a radically new design. Its purpose was to retain the original principle as nearly as possible, while *correcting* the system in the light of experience.[35] The fundamental rules of construction were not altered; instead, certain specific powers which the

Confederation did not give the central authority were to be vested in it. All such specific powers *not* transferred were, exactly as under the Confederation, to remain with the states.

This simple fact of our history, so important to assessing the founders' intentions, has been obscured both by those who picture the Constitution as a grand and necessary consolidation, and by those who want to disparage it as a conspiracy against the common man. It may be argued the delegates in Philadelphia exceeded their powers; yet if so, they did not seek to overturn the going system. They sought to improve it. "The truth is," Madison wrote,

> that the great principles of the Constitution may be considered less as absolutely new, than as the expansion of principles which are found the Articles of Confederation. . . . If the new Constitution be examined with accuracy and candor, it will be found that the change which it proposes consists much less in the addition of new powers to the Union, than in the invigoration of its original powers.[36]

Farrand repeatedly notes the reliance of the convention upon the formulae of the Articles, and adds:

> There is practically nothing in the Constitution that did not arise out of the correction of . . . specific defects of the Confederation. . . . However much the members of the federal convention may have prepared themselves by reading and study, and however learnedly they might discourse upon governments, ancient and modern, when it came to concrete action they relied almost entirely upon what they themselves had seen and done. They

were dependent upon their experience under the state constitutions and the Articles of Confederation . . . It is possible to say that every provision of the federal constitution can be accounted for in American experience between 1776 and 1787.[37]

When the Constitution emerged from the convention, however, many of its opponents claimed the system had been radically changed. The general government, they alleged, would engulf the states; the reserved powers cherished under the Confederation would be effaced. Madison, Hamilton, and James Wilson were at great pains to prove these accusations untrue; the Constitution like the Articles, they stressed, reserved all powers not specifically delegated to the several states.

Hamilton, the aboriginal centralist, was plain-spoken. "An entire consolidation of the states into one complete sovereignty," he wrote in *Federalist* 32, "would imply an entire subordination of the parts; and whatever powers might remain in them, would be altogether dependent on the general will. But as the plan of the convention aims only at a partial union or consolidation, the state governments would clearly retain all the rights of sovereignty which they before had, and which were not, by that act, *exclusively* delegated to the United States."[38] (Emphasis added.)

In *Federalist* 33, Hamilton declared that "acts of the larger society which are not pursuant to its constitutional powers, but which are invasions of the residuary authorities of the smaller societies . . . will be merely acts of usurpation and will deserve to be treated as such."[39]

Madison, in *Federalist* 45, gave the position its classic formulation:

The powers delegated by the proposed Constitution to the federal government are few and defined. Those which are to remain in the state governments are numerous and indefinite. The former will be exercised principally on external objects, as war, peace, negotiation, and foreign commerce; with which last the power of taxation will, for the most part, be connected. The powers reserved to the several states will extend to all the objects which, in the ordinary course of affairs, concern the lives, liberties, and properties of the people, and the internal order, improvement, and prosperity of the state.[40]

In *Federalist* 39, Madison put it that: "It is to be remembered that the general government is not to be charged with the whole power of making and administering laws. Its jurisdiction is limited to certain enumerated objects, which concern all members of the republic, but which are not to be attained by the separate divisions of any. The subordinate governments, which can extend their care to all other objects which can be separately provided for, will retain their due authority and activity."[41]

In the Virginia ratifying convention, Madison said the parties to the Constitution would be "the people—but not the people as composing one great body; but the people as composing thirteen sovereignties."[42]

Among the most frequent accusations against the Constitution was that it contained no Bill of Rights. Wilson, Madison, and Hamilton replied that, because the new government was one of enumerated powers, no Bill of Rights was necessary. Incursions against freedom of speech and press, etc., would be impossible, they argued, because no authority was given respecting such things. Moreover, a partial enumeration of "rights" could be highly dangerous, because it might create the presumption that rights omitted from the list were not secure from governmental interference. The *"enumerated powers"* doctrine provided far better security.

Madison wrote that he was not greatly concerned about enacting a Bill of Rights because "the rights in question are reserved by the manner in which the federal powers are granted. . . . The limited powers of the federal government, and the jealousy of the subordinate governments, afford a security which has not existed in the case of the state governments and exists in no other."[43]

Hamilton, in *Federalist* 84, argued: "bills of rights, in the sense and to the extent which they are contended for, are not only unnecessary, but would even be dangerous. *They would contain various exceptions to powers not granted*; and, on this very account, would afford a colorable pretext to claim more than were granted. *For why declare that things shall not be done which there is no power to do?*"[44] (Emphasis added.)

These reiterated arguments had their effect. Federalists and Anti-Federalists compromised on the proposition that the Constitution would go into effect, with certain desired amendments to follow. Preeminent among these was a clause putting into law the rule of construction elaborated by Madison and Hamilton. Among the states insisting upon this step were Virginia, Massachusetts, South Carolina, New Hampshire, New York, North Carolina, and Rhode Island. Each of these appended to its act of ratification either a demand that a guarantee of reserved powers be written into the Constitution, or a statement explaining that its act was based on the understanding that the powers were in fact reserved as the Constitution stood. Owing to the arguments of the proponents, it is safe to assume that in all the states—particularly in such smaller ones as New Jersey, Delaware, and Connecticut—the men who ratified the Constitution did so on the premise that the government they were establishing was one of enumerated, limited powers. But to make it certain, seven of them, or a clear majority, made the matter explicit.[45]

In 1823, Jefferson wrote: "I have been blamed for saying that a prevalence of the doctrine of consolidation would one day call for a reformation or revolution. I answer by asking if a single state of the Union would have agreed to the Constitution had it given all powers to the general government? If the whole opposition to it did not proceed from the jealousy and fear of every state of being subjected to the other states in matters merely its own?"[46] The question was well asked. Had not the "enumerated powers" construction been agreed upon, the Constitution would never have come into being at all. McLaughlin tells us:

> The Amendments which were asked for by the Massachusetts convention were intended to limit the powers of Congress and to assure the individual certain rights and privileges. The most important was the first, declaring that the Constitution should explicitly state that all powers not expressly delegated by the Constitution were reserved to the several states. The method of ratification had its influence in other states. Had the delegates been reduced to the alternative of rejecting the Constitution or accepting it without reasonable hope of amendment, their fears in some cases would have made rejection certain. But the conciliatory proposition met with favor. Of the

seven states acting on the Constitution after Massachusetts, only one failed to accompany ratification with amendments recommended for subsequent adoption.[47]

The consensus of these states was translated into the clear words of the Tenth Amendment, which follows the language emerging from the recommended changes: "The powers not delegated to the United States by the Constitution, nor prohibited by it to the states, are reserved to the states respectively, or to the people."

With that phrasing, and the legislative history which preceded it, there can be no serious doubt as to the severe boundaries the founders intended to impose on the federal government. It is not within the power of words to make things plainer.

The Tenth Amendment

With the Tenth Amendment, we reach the most visible and accessible evidence of the founders' intentions concerning federal-state relationships. People who may not have read *The Federalist* or looked up the debates in convention can quite readily get a copy of the Constitution itself, with all its amendments. And there, in black and white, is a tolerably clear statement of the states' rights position. It is not surprising, therefore, that the meaning of the Tenth Amendment has been by degrees explained away. The Amendment, we are told, is at best a statement of conditions as they existed in 1789, at worst a redundancy. On the one hand, it is suggested, strict confinement of federal power may have been proper for an agrarian society, but obviously cannot be proper for America today. On the other, it is argued that the Amendment is a truism holding merely that everything which pertains to the federal government pertains to it—a formulation which tells us nothing about appropriate lines of division.

A little investigation will prove both forms of this argument inconsistent with the evidence. We have seen that the doctrine of reserved powers, far from being an empty tautology, was fraught with specific meaning for the founders; they would not accept the Constitution until it was guaranteed to them. To suggest the fruit of their insistence was a mere word game comports neither with their expressed purpose nor with the careful economy of language which, as good legalists, they constantly affected.

Moreover, as legalists, they did not intend the Tenth Amendment to be merely a statement of the then existing balance between state and federal governments. Their intention was to govern that balance in the years to come—to lay down a *rule of construction* by which the dual sovereignties of state and nation could be held in proper equilibrium. Such a rule was and is necessary for the success of the federal enterprise. Federalism, yoking together two kinds of authority, must have ground rules for determining controversies. As one authority notes, "federalism, to be genuine, can never be completely one-sided. A balance of functions and authority, always precarious, must be maintained by the central and local authorities."[48] Without that balance, the project must inevitably slip into one extremity or the other, or else founder in dispute and eventual bloodshed. The Tenth Amendment was an effort to make clear the ground rules for avoiding such dangers.

The proper rule of construction under a federal system is so fundamental that, unless it is understood, the insights gained from other aspects of our study will profit

us little. It would be all too easy for everything otherwise established simply to be "interpreted" away. Concerning the Tenth Amendment, R. L. Ashley says:

> In this amendment we find given the means of determining whether a power is rightfully exercised by a state, and this is done by finding out what does not belong to the state. If a power is given to the central government alone, or if it is prohibited to the states by the Constitution, it cannot be used; all other powers belong to the states, and can be exercised by the state governments unless the state constitutions forbid. . . . Practically all matters belonging to the criminal and to the private laws are regulated by the states, including laws regarding property and the business and personal relations of one individual to another.[49]

The genius of federalism consists exactly in the fact that it balances units of government one against the other; should it yield to centralizing tendencies, the balance is upset. It must hew to strict construction or else relinquish its reason for being. A. V. Dicey gives an excellent summary of the federal logic:

> The constitution must necessarily be a "written" constitution. . . . The constitution must be a written document, and, if possible, a written document of which the terms are open to no misapprehension. . . . The constitution must be what I have termed a "rigid" or "inexpansive" constitution. The law of the constitution must be either legally immutable, or else capable of being changed only by some authority above and beyond the ordinary legislative bodies, whether federal or state legislatures, existing under the constitution.

. . . It is hard to see why it should be held inconceivable that the founders of a polity should have deliberately omitted to provide any means for lawfully changing its base. Such an omission would not be unnatural on the part of the authors of a federal union, since one main object of the states entering into the compact is to prevent further encroachments upon their several state rights; . . . The question, however, whether a federal constitution necessarily involves the existence of some ultimate sovereign power authorized to amend or alter its terms is of merely speculative interest, for under existing federal governments the constitution will be found to provide the means for its own improvement.[50]

The applicability of these words to our own Constitution is apparent. The founders, as Judge Cooley pointed out, did not want the fundamental law to be changed whimsically;[51] their object was to fix the relations of the state and federal governments with as much certitude as possible, and to insure as best they could that the central authority would not through improvisations gather state powers unto itself. Ability to change the fundamental law on the part of the ordinary legislature, Dicey writes

> would be inconsistent with the aim of federalism, namely, the permanent division between the spheres of the national government and of the several states. If Congress could legally change the Constitution, New York and Massachusetts would have no legal guarantee for the amount of independence reserved to them under the Constitution, and would be as subject to the sovereign power of Congress as is Scotland to the sovereignty of

Parliament; the Union would cease to be a federal state, and would become a unitarian republic. . . . The legal sovereignty of the United States resides in the states' governments as forming one aggregate body represented by three-fourths of the several states at any time belonging to the Union.[52]

And again:

> The distribution of powers is an essential feature of federalism . . . as it is not intended that the central government should have the opportunity of encroaching upon the rights retained by the states, its sphere of action necessarily becomes the object of rigorous definition. . . . Federalism, as it defines, and therefore limits, the powers of each department of the administration, is unfavourable to the interference or to the activity of government. Hence a federal government can hardly render services to the nation by undertaking for the national benefits functions which may be performed by individuals. . . . A system meant to maintain the status quo in politics is incompatible with schemes for wide social innovations. . . . The least observation of American politics shows how deeply the notion that the Constitution is something placed beyond the reach of amendment has impressed popular imagination. The difficulty of altering the Constitution produces conservative sentiment, and national conservatism doubles the difficulty of altering the Constitution.[53]

It must be granted that the founders' ideas were not quite so precise as Dicey's. Their theoretical approach to states' rights was somewhat halting, conducted without benefit of a working theoretical vocabulary. When they thought self-consciously about restraining power, they tended to slip into the more comfortable categories of checks and balances within the supreme authority, a theme on which men such as Adams and the early Madison were tireless virtuosos of eloquence. Their federalism, as we have indicated, was a practical matter, and the theory explaining it came tagging after the fact.

It was Jefferson who first formulated the full states' rights position, in the national bank controversy of 1791. Quoting the language of the Tenth Amendment, Jefferson said: "To take a single step beyond the boundaries thus specially drawn around the powers of Congress is to take possession of a boundless field of power, no longer susceptible of any definition." The reserved powers of the states, he said, formed "the foundation of the Constitution."[54] If they were violated, there could be no certain security for freedom.

The ultimate safeguard of liberty, under this interpretation, lay not in the tripartite division of federal powers, nor in the guarantees of free speech and free press, but in the aggregate limitation of the national power as a whole, implicit in the federal union. According to the theory and experience of the founders, and of their British forebears, power could not be checked (in Madison's phrase) by "parchment barriers." It could be checked only by an equal and opposite power. The single ready source of such power outside the federal government was the power of the states; unless that power were effectively husbanded and employed, there could ultimately be no restraint upon what the government might or might not do should its three branches become united in despotic intention.

It will be readily seen that this logic, if carried far enough, must result in the cul

de sac of secession, and thus in the dismemberment of the Union itself. Because it goes beyond the Constitution and beyond federalism it can properly be settled in terms of neither; the answer when the dispute reaches this stage must be the test of arms—precisely the test which precipitated the Civil War. But the fact that the doctrine cannot find its resolution in terms of the Constitution should not blind us to the fact that it is implicit in the Constitution, and—as Dicey suggests—*implicit in* the nature of federal union. By the Constitution, a boundary line *is* drawn around the powers of the federal government; but suppose the legislature, the president, and the courts mutually determine to carry federal authority *across* that line. How can it be repelled?

Insofar as this problem was considered at all by the drafters of the Constitution, it seems evident they envisioned some kind of concerted action by the states, even military action. Hamilton says in *Federalist* 28:

> It may safely be received as an axiom in our political system, that the State governments will, in all possible contingencies, afford complete security against invasions of the public liberty by the national authority. Projects of usurpation cannot be masked under pretences so likely to escape the penetration of select bodies of men, as of the people at large. The legislatures will have better means of information. They can discover the danger at a distance; and possessing all the organs of civil power, and the confidence of the people, they can at once adopt a regular plan of opposition, in which they can combine all the resources of the community. They can readily communicate with each other in the

different states, and unite their common forces for the protection of their common liberty.[55]

In 1798, when the Adams administration handed down the Alien and Sedition laws, the problem became all too real. Adams signed a law which made it a crime to engage in political opposition—as tyrannical a measure as ever enacted in America. Newspapers were closed and political dissidents sent to jail. Congress, president and judiciary joined in assenting to this siege of despotism. The balance of powers was not doing the job.

Jefferson turned to the more primeval safeguard of popular liberties, the reserved powers of the states. In the Kentucky Resolutions, he stated the first principles of liberty under the American system:

It would be a dangerous delusion were a confidence in the men of our choice to silence our fears for the safety of our rights; . . . confidence is everywhere the parent of despotism—free government is founded in jealousy, and not in confidence; it is jealousy and not confidence which prescribes limited constitutions to bind down those whom we are obliged to trust with power; . . . our Constitution has accordingly fixed the limits to which, and no further, our confidence may go, and let the honest advocate of confidence read the Alien and Sedition acts and say if the Constitution has not been wise in fixing limits to the government it created, and whether we should be wise in destroying those limits. Let him say what the government is, if it be not a tyranny, which the men of our choice have conferred on our President, and the President of our choice assented to. . . . In ques-

tions of power, then, let no more be heard of confidence in man, but bind him down from mischief by the chains of the Constitution.

Authority for the Alien and Sedition Acts, Jefferson said, was denied the federal government by the nature of the union, and by the Tenth Amendment. The answer sought was for state legislatures to declare the acts void, to refuse to enforce them, and to petition for their repeal. The language of the Kentucky Resolutions continues:

[T]his Commonwealth does therefore call on its co-states for an expression of their sentiments on the acts concerning Aliens, and for the punishment of certain crimes herein before specified, plainly declaring whether these acts are or are not authorized by the Federal Compact. And it doubts not that their sense will be so announced as to prove their attachment unaltered to limited government, whether general or particular, and that the rights and liberties of their co-states will be exposed to no dangers by remaining embarked on a common bottom with their own: That they will concur with this Commonwealth in considering the said acts as so palpably against the Constitution as to amount to an undisguised declaration, that the Compact is not meant to be the measure of the powers the General Government, but that it will proceed in the exercise over these states of all powers whatsoever; That they will view this as seizing the rights of the states and consolidating them in the hands of the General Government with a power assumed to bind the states (not merely in cases made federal) but in all cases whatsoever, by laws made, not with their consent, but by others against their consent; That this would be to surrender the form of Government we have chosen, and to live under one deriving its powers from its own will, and not from our authority; and that the co-states recurring to their natural right in cases not made federal, will concur in declaring these acts void and of no force, and will each unite with this Commonwealth in requesting their repeal at the next session of Congress.[56]

Madison gave utterance to similar sentiments in the Virginia Resolutions and his Report of 1799. He noted, as he had in *The Federalist,* that the rule of construction clearly understood to prevail under the Articles of Confederation also prevailed under the new Constitution.[57] He deplored the fact that "indications have appeared of a design to expound certain general phrases (which having been copies from the very limited grant of powers in the former articles of confederation were the less liable to be misconstrued) so as to destroy the meaning and effect of the particular enumeration which necessarily explains and limits the general phrases."[58] He added that "in all the contemporary discussions and comments, which the Constitution underwent, it was constantly justified and recommended on the ground, that the powers not given to the government were withheld from it; and that if any doubt could have existed on this subject, under the original text of the Constitution, it is removed as far as words could remove it, by the [Tenth] Amendment, now a part of the Constitution, which expressly declares 'that the powers not delegated to the United States by the Constitution, nor prohibited by it to the states, are reserved to the states respectively, or to the people.'"[59]

On this subject, there could hardly have been a better authority, since Madison had been both the moving force behind the creation of the new government (and a big-state man, at that), and the principal exponent of its virtues in the battle for ratification, in which he and his fellow Federalists of that day hammered home this very rule of construction.

The General Welfare

We come now to the practical fate of states' rights in the intervening century and a half. And when we do so, the most obvious fact which confronts us is that the outlines of the American system we have sketched above are nowadays barely visible. The fundamental emphases have been reversed; the standing rule concerning uncertain areas of power is no longer that the central government is denied what is not granted; it is instead deemed to possess what is not denied. The gray areas are no longer left to the authority of the states, but are ceded to the authority of Washington. The central government's powers are no longer "few and defined," but, as the state governments' powers were intended to be, "numerous and indefinite." Although the point is hardly in dispute, we may invoke the authority of Prof. Edward S. Corwin by way of illustration: "In general terms, our system has lost its resiliency and what was once vaunted as a Constitution of Rights, both state and private, has been replaced by a Constitution of Powers. More specifically, the Federal System has shifted base in the direction of a consolidated national power, while within the national government itself an increased flow of power in the direction of the president has ensued."[60] It is not our province here to trace the various causes of this transformation; but it is necessary to take note of certain devices used in bringing it about.

These consist primarily in phrases seized from the body of the Constitution, subjected to centralizing construction apart from the rest of the document, and then imputed to the men who wrote it. As it happens, these same devices were brought forward in the early days of the Republic, and effectively answered at the time. The founders were so far from accepting these verbal escape hatches that they anticipated and refuted them—a fact which has not, however, prevented modern-day centralists from resorting to them repeatedly.

The apertures through which most centralizing legislation has been thrust in the past three decades are the clauses which appear in Article I, Section 8, of the Constitution, wherein Congress is given power to lay and collect taxes to "provide for the common defence and general welfare of the United States," and "to regulate commerce among the several states," and "to make all laws which shall be necessary and proper for carrying into execution the foregoing powers . . ." It is nowadays argued that, under the general welfare clause, for example, Congress may enact all sorts of public subsidies and controls, engage in business enterprises, conduct vast programs of federal aid, dispense medical services, build housing, and whatnot. Under the commerce clause, it is deemed to have power to set wages and hours, regulate businesses, fix prices, establish regulations, control rents, etc. Indeed, the power of the federal government to do all of this and more is today taken so much for granted that the last argument anyone raises concerning any of them is to suggest that they are not constitutional. The all-conquering potency of "general welfare" and "commerce" is part of our jurisprudence, and of our folklore.

It would be hard to conceive of anything more directly opposed to the intention of the founders. While it apparently never occurred to the men of '87 that the commerce clause could be carried to such lengths, certain opponents of the Constitution raised both the "general welfare" and "necessary and proper" issues. The matter was thoroughly discussed and, it seemed at the time, conclusively settled. Moreover, Madison had occasion in later years to comment upon it further, so that we have rather extensive commentary on the subject from the Father of the Constitution himself, who had given long personal consideration to every phrase in the document, and who knew better than anyone else what the language emerging from the convention did or did not mean.

The fundamental point at issue concerning the "general welfare" clause is whether it was intended to be a separate grant of power, distinct from other grants contained in the Constitution, or whether it was intended to suggest the *purpose* of the specific powers which were listed below it. If the first interpretation is correct, then the vast powers imputed to the federal government under this phrase are legitimate; if the second is correct, then they are illegitimate.

As in most matters involving the legal and constitutional ideas of the founders, a glance at British experience will prove enlightening. One of the great endeavors of Englishmen in their centuries-long struggle to impose limits upon arbitrary power had been to insure that money granted the Crown could not be used for special and partial purposes, to the favor of one group and the detriment of another. The corollary of the principle that the king could levy taxes only with the consent of the whole realm was that the purposes for which they were spent should be for the good of the whole realm.

Each was an essential aspect of the rule of law. Among the great principles of British liberty, Professor Stimson tells us, is "that the object of all levies, the end for which all moneys are raised by law, must be the general good of the people, that is, the good of the people, not of any one person, even the king, nor of any particular class, such as the nobles or the merchants."[61]

In this sense, it will be seen that the "general welfare" concept is in fact a *limitation* upon the taxing and spending power; the purposes must be for the good of the polity at large, not simply to benefit some segment of it. Far from conferring unlimited authority through a general grant of power, it seeks to insure that *particular grants* will be used only for *general purposes*. That this meaning of the phrase was accepted by the founders may be readily established.

To begin with, it should be reiterated that the phrase "general welfare" occurred in the text of the Articles of Confederation; yet no one would have dreamed that the phrase conferred upon the Confederation unlimited power to do whatever it wished. When controversy on the point first arose, Madison observed:

> [T]he language used by the convention is a copy from the Articles of Confederation. The objects of the union among the states, as described in article third, are, "their common defence, security of their liberties, and mutual and general welfare." The terms of article eighth are still more identical: "All charges of war and all other expenses that shall be incurred for the common defense or general welfare, and allowed by the United States in Congress, shall be defrayed out of a common treasury," etc. A similar language again occurs in article ninth. Construe either of these

articles by the rules which would justify the construction put on the new Constitution, and they vest in the existing Congress a power to legislate in all cases whatsoever.[62]

The existing Congress under the Confederation of course did not possess such power; if it had, the Philadelphia Convention would not have been necessary. Madison's point was that the new Congress would have no such power either. The "general welfare" phrase was not an omnibus grant, but a statement of the purposes for which specific grants of power were to be used.

Serving in the first Congress, Madison again scored the device of using "general welfare" as an independent grant of power. "If Congress can employ money indefinitely to the general welfare," he said, "and are the sole and supreme judge of the general welfare, they may take the care of religion into their own hands; they may appoint teachers in every state, county and parish and pay them out of their public treasury; they may take into their own hands the education of children, establishing in like manner schools throughout the union; they may assume provision of the poor. . . . Were the power of Congress to be established in the latitude contended for, it would subvert the very foundations and transmute the very nature of the limited government established by the people of America."[63]

That statement is not only a good index to Madison's thinking and to the meaning of the Constitution; it is also, given the present scope of federal legislative activity under "general welfare," a pretty good piece of prophecy.

At about the same period, Madison wrote to Edmund Pendleton in rebuttal to Hamilton's construction of "general welfare" in his *Report on Manufactures*:

If Congress can do whatever in their discretion can be done by money and will promote the general welfare, the government is no longer a limited one, possessing enumerated powers, but an indefinite one, subject to particular exceptions. It is to be remarked that the phrase out of which this doctrine is elaborated is copied from the old Articles of Confederation, where it was always understood as nothing more than a general caption to the specified powers, and it is a fact that it was preferred in the new instrument for that very reason, as less liable than any other to misconstruction.[64]

In the controversy over the Alien and Sedition acts, Madison saw part of his prophecy come true. He again contested the wide interpretation given "general welfare" by the Federalists:

[W]hether the phrases in question be construed to authorize every measure relating to the common defence and general welfare, as contended by some; or every measure only in which there might be an appropriation of money, as suggested by the caution of others, the effect must be substantially the same, in destroying the import and force of the particular enumeration of powers, which follow these general phrases in the Constitution. For it is evident that there is not a single power whatever, which may not have some reference to the common defence or the general welfare; nor a power of any magnitude which in its exercise does not involve or admit an application of money. The government therefore which possesses power in either one of these extents, is a government without the limitation formed by a particular enumeration of powers; and conse-

quently the meaning and effect of this particular enumeration is destroyed by the exposition given to these general phrases.[65]

Thus Madison in 1799. In 1817, as president, he had cause to return to the subject again, in a message accompanying a veto of an "internal improvements" bill enacted by Congress. "To refer the power in question to the clause 'to provide for the common defence and general welfare,'" he said, "would be contrary to the established and consistent rules of interpretation, as rendering the special and careful enumeration of powers which follow the clause nugatory and improper. Such a view of the Constitution would have the effect of giving Congress a general power of legislation instead of the defined and limited power one hitherto understood to belong to them, the terms 'common defence and general welfare' embracing every object and act within the purview of a legislative trust."[66]

In 1830, in the midst of the nullification controversy, Madison set forward the fullest exposition of the "general welfare" clause ever ventured by any member of the federal convention. The letter is a long one, taking up some nineteen printed pages in Madison's collected works, and cannot be quoted at length here. It deserves, however, to be read in its entirety by anyone interested in this question. In essence, the letter recapitulates the proceedings at Philadelphia, the paternity of the phrase in the Articles of Confederation, the history of it under the Articles, and the fact that by the time of ratification the phrase was so universally understood to be harmless that the Anti-Federalists suggested no amendments concerning it, "which, if understood to convey the asserted power, could not have failed to be the power most strenuously aimed at."[67]

That Madison's view of the "general welfare" clause was faithful to the intent of the Constitutional Convention is suggested by the record of the proceedings there. Roger Sherman, for example, wanted to insert the words, "for the defraying the expenses that shall be incurred for the common defence and the general welfare," which would have made the status of the phrase as a statement of purpose rather than as a separate power clear beyond all peradventure.[68] The suggestion was rejected, not because it was incorrect—but *because it was unnecessary.*[69] Max Farrand records one bit of by play which makes things clearer still. "In the report of the committee of style," he says, "this clause was separated from the preceding and following clauses by semicolons, thus making it an independent power of Congress. This was not the way in which it had been adopted by the convention, but it was more in accordance with [Gouverneur] Morris's ideas. . . . In the Constitution as it was finally engrossed, the clause was changed back to its original form, and the credit for this Albert Gallatin gave to Sherman."[70]

In the struggle over ratification, the issue was raised explicitly by opponents of the Constitution. "The clause giving Congress power to lay taxes to provide for the common defence and the general welfare of the United States was termed the 'sweeping clause'; it would in the end bestow all authority on the central government. . . . These objections were met by the Federalists with good arguments. The 'sweeping clause' was shown to contain no new powers, but indicate only the purposes of taxation—to provide for the common defence and general welfare."[71]

The best of the good arguments occurs in *Federalist* 41, in which Madison refutes those who said the clause would be interpreted loosely, and that there-fore the Constitution should be rejected. This particular refutation is so well-stated, and so apposite to current misuse of the phrase, that it is worth quoting, and studying, at length:

> But what color can the objection have, when a specification of the objects alluded to by these general terms immediately follows, and is not even separated by a longer pause than a semicolon? If the different parts of the same instrument ought to be expounded, as to give meaning to every part which will bear it, shall one part of the same sentence be excluded altogether from a share in the meaning; and shall the more doubtful and indefinite terms be retained in their full extent, and the clear and precise expressions be denied any signification whatsoever?
>
> For what purpose could the enumeration of particular powers be inserted, if these and all others were meant to be included in the general power? Nothing is more natural nor common than first to use a general phrase, and then to explain and qualify it by a recital of particulars. But the idea of enumeration of particulars which neither explain nor qualify the general meaning, and can have no other effect than to confound and mislead, is an absurdity. . . . The objection here is the more extraordinary, as it appears that the language used by the convention is a copy from the articles of Confederation. The objects of the Union among the states, as described in article third, are, "their common defence, security of their liberties, and mutual and general welfare." The terms of article eighth are still more identical "All charges of war and all other expenses that shall

be incurred for the common defence or general welfare, and allowed by the United States in Congress, shall be defrayed out of a common treasury, etc." A similar language again occurs in article ninth. Construe either of these articles by the rules which would justify the construction put on the new Constitution, and they vest in the existing Congress a power to legislate in all cases whatsoever.[72]

All of which, Madison argued, proved how baseless were allegations that the "general welfare" clause could legitimately be employed as a separate grant of legislative power. It was instead a statement of purpose, which purpose was to be fulfilled by the particular grants of power stated below it. Nothing, indeed, could have been more logical, and the argument obviously had its effect in achieving ratification. Such was the published position of the Federalist Party and the direct commentary of the acknowledged classic on the meaning of the federal Constitution, proclaimed to Americans everywhere, without demur, as the meaning of the Constitution as conceived by its sponsors, accepted as its meaning when the Constitution itself was accepted.[73]

The same considerations which apply to the "general welfare" clause also affect "necessary and proper." If it makes no sense to enumerate particular powers in one paragraph only to bestow superseding general powers in another, then the "necessary and proper" clause can be no more elastic than "general welfare." Hamilton, in *Federalist* 33, took particular notice of the "necessary and proper" objection, saying: "It may be affirmed with perfect confidence that the constitutional operation of the intended government would be precisely the same" if the clause were omitted. It added noth-

ing except common sense, and "though it may be chargeable with tautology and redundancy, is at least perfectly harmless."[74] Madison made the identical argument in *Federalist* 44.

That even Hamilton, the father of loose construction, should have taken such a view of "necessary and proper" suggests how far afield modern centralists have strayed. The most ardent consolidator among the founders, Hamilton never attempted—even in the *Report on Manufacturers*—to argue that specific phrases within a limited constitution could be construed as unlimited grants of power. In his famous dissertation on "general welfare," he suggested the latitude granted to Congress by this phrase affects only the power to appropriate money, and "would not carry a power to do any other thing not authorized in the Constitution, either expressly or by fair implication."[75]

In his Report on the National Bank, which marked him out as Jefferson's supreme antagonist, his fidelity to the canons of limited government was even more obvious. In substance, he repeated his own interpretation from *Federalist* 33, acknowledging that the federal government could pursue only those ends assigned to it by the Constitution, and that "necessary and proper" was not, and could not be, a grant of power in itself. It was instead, he argued, a device empowering the government to take whatever *means* it required—provided they were neither illegal nor immoral—to fulfill the specific, enumerated *ends* assigned to it by the Constitution." At no point did Hamilton contend that either of the disputed phrases was in itself an autonomous delegation of constitutional authority to the federal government.

Madison's argument on "general welfare" and Hamilton's on "necessary and proper" amounted to this: The purpose of the Constitution is to grant certain designated powers, and to withhold others not designated. It makes no sense to grant certain *specific* powers by designation and then—in defiance of the agreed-upon construction—to turn about and grant a *general* authority exceeding and negating these specific powers by a catch-all commission to do anything and everything. What sense did it make, Madison was asking, to construe the document as barring unlimited government at the door but admitting it by the window?

If that logic be accepted, it extends to the commerce clause as well. If the document is intended to spell out specific, limited grants of power, then no isolated phrase in it can sensibly be construed as containing unlimited grants. In the case of the commerce clause, which did not attract as much attention as "general welfare," the Madisonian answer would obviously have to be that the unlimited government which is shut out by the front door of the Constitution and barred at the window of the "general welfare" clause is here simply being pulled in through the chimney.

The Fait Accompli

If it is granted that the founders meant our system to be decentralized, the advocates of consolidation suggest other grounds for disparaging states' rights: The question, it is said, concerns not what ought to be, but what is. And our system in point of fact *is* centralized, and, as Henry Adams argued, has become so through an inevitable progress from diffusion to compactness. Ever since Hamilton's *Report on Manufactures*, or at any rate since John Marshall ascended to the Supreme Court, we have been tend-

ing steadily toward greater centralization. The process was made irrevocable with the Civil War and the reconstruction, which settled the issue of "states' rights" forever. Anyone who wants to decentralize our system must undo the amendments, the war, Lincoln, Jackson, Marshall, Hamilton—a palpable impossibility.

The argument is two-fold. First, that our system is in fact centralized—a point made previously in this essay and about which there is no serious argument. Second, that this centralization has been a steady process down the years, part of our historical drift from the beginning. On this point, we shall find much evidence to the contrary.

To take the most centralizing of all the examples cited, we may acknowledge that the Civil War established beyond any peradventure that a state could not secede from the Union. And the Fourteenth Amendment established that a state could not rightfully deprive its citizens of the equal protection of the law. These are indeed powerful negatives concerning highly specific matters; but neither dictates a radical disruption of the federal system; neither implies that our form of government should become consolidated; and neither suggests that the Tenth Amendment has been repealed with respect to *undesignated* areas of federal-state disagreement. Two specified kinds of behavior were denied to the states in a test of strength. Nothing was thereby altered concerning unspecified kinds of behavior. The half-century following the Civil War found it definitely established that the rights of the states, short of secession and unequal legislation, were intact. It is no exaggeration to say that the South, in so far as it represented the cause of local autonomy, lost the battle for secession, but won the battle for states' rights. The victory is symbolized constitutionally in *Tarble's Case* (1872), politically in the transaction by which Rutherford B. Hayes became president and Reconstruction was brought to an end (1877). Felix Morley observes that "the Civil War did not of itself affect the federal structure of the Republic. . . . When the always dubious right of secession was effectively denied, all the other, less contestable, rights of the states were inferentially reaffirmed."[77] In *Tarble's Case*, vindicating, as it happened, federal law against an intrusion by the state of Wisconsin, the court suggested the persistence of the federal balance by stating that "there are within the territorial limits of each state two governments, restricted in their spheres of action, but independent of each other, and supreme within their respective sphere. . . . Neither government can intrude within the jurisdiction, or authorize any interference therein by its judicial officers with the action of the other."[78]

The Reconstruction amendments, of course, did impose limitations upon the powers of the states. The Thirteenth Amendment outlawed slavery, the Fifteenth guaranteed the right to vote. The troublesome amendment, the Fourteenth, said that "No state shall make or enforce any law which shall abridge the privileges and immunities of citizens of the United States; nor shall any state deprive any person of life, liberty, or property without due process of law; nor deny to any person within its jurisdiction the equal protection of the laws."

For the purposes of this essay, it is not necessary to go into the issue of whether the Fourteenth Amendment was properly ratified—although the evidence seems plain enough that it was not. The amendment has been treated as a part of the Constitution for 100 years and is to all practical purposes a settled part of

our system. The relevant question, since it exists and is part of our fundamental law, is what it means. According to current theory, the Fourteenth Amendment gives the federal government power to integrate public schools, order reapportionment of state legislatures, overrule the use of prayers in public schools, and even superintend the practices of private businesses operating within the states. In short, the Fourteenth Amendment has become, along with the "general welfare" and "commerce" clauses, a kind of philosopher's stone by which Washington can turn virtually anything into a federal case.

Was the Fourteenth Amendment intended to achieve such things? The answer, as with general welfare and commerce, is in the negative. The Fourteenth Amendment was meant to give constitutional sanction to the Civil Rights Bill of 1866, out of which it grew. In discussing that bill, certain members of Congress raised precisely the question we are here considering: To what subjects do its guarantees extend? What were the "civil rights" to be guaranteed by the federal government against the states? Senator Lyman Trumbull of Illinois, sponsor of the bill, gave this answer:

> The first section of the bill defines what I understand to be civil rights: The right to make and enforce contracts, to sue and be sued, and to give evidence, to inherit, purchase, sell, lease, hold and convey real and personal property. [79]

Trumbull added something emphasized by other speakers on the subject, by the practices of the northern states at the time, and by the practice of the federal government itself, that "the right to go to school is not a civil right and never was."[80]

Congressman Wilson of Iowa similarly remarked: "What do these terms mean? Do they mean that in all things civil, social, political, all citizens, without distinction of race or color, shall be equal? By no means can they be so construed. . . . Nor do they mean that . . . their children shall attend the same schools. These are no civil rights or immunities."[81] Going further toward the intent of the Congress which approved the Fourteenth Amendment was the fact that this same session passed a bill establishing segregated schools in Washington, D.C. The Congress also segregated Negroes and whites in its galleries. Similar practices prevailed in the states which ratified the amendment, Northern as well as Southern. New York, California, Illinois, New Jersey, Ohio, Pennsylvania, Indiana, Maryland, and Missouri all maintained segregated schools *after* they had ratified the Fourteenth Amendment. It is apparent the men who passed the Fourteenth Amendment did not mean to include the schools.

All of which is not to say the attitudes of these men were correct, or that they *should* have wanted to maintain segregated schools. The point is what they *did* want, and intended when they enacted the Fourteenth Amendment—to limit the prohibition against state action to such matters as laws preventing ownership of property. And it is the intention of the lawmaker, not what *should* have been his intention, which is the law.

Similar considerations prevail in the matter of reapportioning state legislatures, a political area which even Thaddeus Stevens did not place within the purview of the amendment. If anything, the intention of the legislators who drafted the Fourteenth Amendment is clearer on this point than on the question of segregated schools. Again and again, the congressmen and senators sponsoring the amendment pointed out that it did not empower the federal government to usurp state prerogatives in questions of suffrage. Stevens himself observed, unhappily, that the amendment allowed the states, where voting was concerned, "to discriminate among the same class, and receive proportionate credit in representation."[82] Congressman Bingham of Ohio, a principal author of the amendment said: "The amendment does not give, as the second section shows, the power to Congress of regulating suffrage in the several states. The second section excludes the conclusion that by the first section suffrage is subjected to congressional law."[83] And: "[T]he exercise of the elective franchise, though it be one of the privileges of a citizen of the Republic, is exclusively under the control of the states."[84] Congressman Broomall of Pennsylvania said: "It is known to every gentleman in this hall . . . we leave it to these states to grant or refuse suffrage without regard to the condition, the opinions, or the crimes of those claiming it. . . ."[85] Congressman Miller of Pennsylvania put it that "[t]his amendment will settle the complications in regard to suffrage and representation, leaving each state to regulate that for itself. . . ."[86]

On the Senate side, Senator Howard of Michigan said: "the first section of the proposed amendment does not give to either of these classes [Negro and white] the right of voting. The right of suffrage, is not, in law, one of the privileges or immunities thus secured by the Constitution. It is merely the creature of law. It has always been regarded in this country as the result of positive local law. . . ."[87]

And: "We know very well that the states retain the power which they have always possessed of regulating the right of suffrage in the states. It is the theory of the Constitution itself. That right has never been taken from them; no endeavor has ever been made to take it from them; and the theory of this whole amendment is, to leave the power of regulating the suffrage with the people or legislatures of the states, and not to assume to regulate it by any clause of the Constitution of the United States."[88]

Explaining the amendment, Senator Johnson of Maryland said: "It says to the states, 'If you exclude any class from the right to vote, we, admitting your power to make the exclusion, say it shall have no other effect whatever than to deduct the number excluded from the whole number which is to constitute the basis of representation [in the federal legislature]. . . .'"[89]

And: "*[N]obody dreams of interfering with the right of the states to regulate suffrage with reference to their own officers, or of interfering with the right of the states to appoint their own officers, and to prescribe the qualifications which the electors of their own officers are to have. Nobody has ever dreamed that this government was to tell the states how their legislatures shall be elected, how their officers shall be chosen . . .*"[90] (emphasis added).

In view of all that, it can hardly be suggested that the Congress which passed the Fourteenth Amendment intended to empower the federal government to intervene in matters of state apportionment. And if the Congress which sponsored the amendment did not so construe it, we may be certain the various state governments which ratified it—almost all of them consisting of legislatures chosen on precisely the basis the Supreme Court has attacked—did not understand their action to be aimed at declaring themselves unconstitutional.

In 1873, in the famous Slaughterhouse cases, the Supreme Court ruled that the Fourteenth Amendment did not apply

federal privileges and immunities to the states. To declare otherwise, the Court said, would have been "to transfer the security and protection of all the civil rights . . . to the Federal government . . . to bring within the power of Congress the entire domain of civil rights heretofore belonging exclusively to the states," and "to constitute this court a perpetual censor upon all legislation of the states, on the civil rights of their own citizens, with authority to nullify such as it did not approve as consistent with those rights, as they existed, at the time of the adoption of this amendment." The effect of such action, the Court added, would be "to fetter and degrade the state governments by subjecting them to the control of Congress, in the exercise of powers heretofore universally conceded to them of the most ordinary and fundamental character. . . . We are convinced that no such results were intended by the Congress . . . nor by the legislatures" which ratified the amendment.[91]

In succeeding years, this doctrine was modified and remodified as hundreds of cases involving state regulation of business were brought before the Court under the Fourteenth Amendment. But the basic conception, that there was no automatic application of federal privileges to the states, persisted. As late as 1959, the Supreme Court observed:

> We have held from the beginning and uniformly that the due process clause of the Fourteenth Amendment does not apply to the states any of the provisions of the first eight amendments as such. . . . The relevant historical materials have been canvassed by this court and by legal scholars. . . . These materials demonstrate conclusively that the Congress and the members of the legislature did not contemplate

that the Fourteenth Amendment was a shorthand incorporation of the first eight amendments making them applicable as explicit restrictions upon the states. [92]

Under the Fourteenth Amendment, it is true, the Court had on many occasions rebuked various of the states for procedural failings which interfered with the specific prohibitions of the amendment; but they had steadfastly refused to adopt the notion that the amendment automatically converted the internal affairs of the state into a domain ruled by the federal law, or fully covered by the federal Bill of Rights. In *Adamson v. California*—in which the Court had ruled that the "due process clause of the Fourteenth Amendment . . . does not draw all the rights of the Federal Bill of Rights under its protection"—Justice Felix Frankfurter commented: "The notion that the Fourteenth Amendment was a covert way of imposing on the states all the rules which it seemed important to eighteenth-century statesmen to write into the federal amendments was rejected by judges who were themselves witnesses of the process by which the Fourteenth Amendment became part of the Constitution. Arguments that may now be adduced to prove that the first eight amendments were concealed within the historic phrasing of the Fourteenth Amendment were not unknown at the time of its adoption. A surer estimate of their bearing was possible for judges at the time than distorting distance is likely to vouchsafe." [93]

Finally, the most evident misreading of the Fourteenth Amendment is contained in the current doctrine that its provisions can be applied to individuals, rather than to legislative actions by the states. There is no warrant for such a construction in any part of the history of the amendment. Thaddeus Stevens observed that Congress could not "interfere in any case where the legislation of a state was equal, impartial to all." The purpose of the amendment, he said, was "simply to provide that where any state makes a distinction in the same law between different classes of individuals, Congress shall have power to correct such discrimination and inequality." [94] And again, the amendment was designed to "correct the unjust legislation of the states, so far that the law which operates upon one man shall operate equally upon all." [95] Charles C. Tansill, Alfred Avins, Sam S. Crutchfield, and Kenneth W. Colegrove discuss this issue in a recent study, "The Fourteenth Amendment and Real Property Rights." They conclude that the problem contemplated under the amendment "was not one of forcing private individuals to deal with Negroes, but simply of removing state legislation which prohibited them from leasing or buying land from willing sellers. . . . Congress intended to restrict state legislation primarily, and state action exclusively. Private individuals were not restricted. [96]

Thus, in brief compass, the legal impact of the Civil War and the Reconstruction Amendments. Changes there were; radical consolidation there was not—a fact which may be confirmed by glancing back at American life in the latter part of the nineteenth century, well after the dust of war had settled and the amendments were established law. The picture we get is very much like the picture in Jefferson's and Madison's day—but unlike our own.

Walter Bagehot's famous contrast between the British and American constitutions (1867) did not fail to note the persistence of local autonomies, as the fundamentals of our system endured through the height of Reconstruction. "As each state fixes the suffrage for its own legislatures," Bagehot observed, "the states altogether fix the suffrage for the federal lower chamber. By another clause of the federal Constitution, the states fix the electoral qualification for voting at a presidential election. The primary element in a free government—the determination how many people shall have a share in it—in America depends not on the government but on certain subordinate local, and sometimes, as in the South now, hostile bodies."[97] And again: "The 'constitution' cannot be altered by any authorities within the constitution, but only authorities without it. Every alteration of it, however urgent or however trifling, must be sanctioned by a complicated proportion of states or legislatures."[98]

Two decades later, when Reconstruction had come and gone, Bagehot's countryman Lord Bryce journeyed to America, and remarked on the same phenomenon. In the *Commonwealth*, Bryce tells of a meeting of the American Protestant Episcopal Church, in which a prayer was proposed containing the words, "O Lord, bless our nation." So many protests were raised against this wording, he reports, "as importing too definite a recognition of national unity," that the phrasing was changed to "O Lord, bless these United States."[99] This was some 87 years after Marshall ascended to the Supreme Court and some twenty years after the Civil War—suggesting that neither John Marshall nor Abe Lincoln, despite their actions to maintain the unity of the United States, had transformed America into a monolith. Bryce described the America he saw in the following terms:

An American may, through a long life, never be reminded of the Federal government, except when he votes at presidential and congressional elections, lodges a complaint against the post-office, and opens his trunks for a custom-house officer on the pier at New York when he returns from Europe. His direct taxes are paid to officials acting under state laws. The state, or local authority constituted by state statutes, registers his birth, appoints his guardian, pays for his schooling, gives him a share in the estate of his father deceased, licenses him when he enters a trade (if it be one needing a licence), marries him, divorces him, entertains civil actions against him, declares him a bankrupt, hangs him for murder. The police that guard his house, the local boards which look after the poor, control highways, impose water rates, manage schools—all these derive their legal powers from his state alone. Looking at this immense compass of state functions, Jefferson would seem to have been not far wrong when he said that the Federal government was nothing more than the American department of foreign affairs.[100]

A decade later, things were still much the same. Describing "the system of government and liberty . . . in the United States in the year 1898," John W. Burgess gave these as the prevailing characteristics of the nation:

the doctrine of individual immunity against governmental power, the principle of the widest possible scope for free action on the part of the individual and of strict limitation in behalf of such action upon the powers of government . . . the requirement that local government shall have the maximum of powers which it is capable of exercising, and . . . that it shall be the recipient of the residuary powers, that is, of such governmental powers as may be assigned or recognized by the sovereign power back of all government, but not specifically assigned to either the general or the local government. . . .[101]

It was the well understood and universally appreciated principle of our constitutional law in the year 1900, Burgess goes on,

that the general government could exercise only such authority and power as had been expressly granted to it by the Constitution or by reasonable and necessary implication from such express grant, and that all other governmental authority was reserved to the states of the union, limited only by those immunities of the individual secured by the Constitution against *all* governmental power, national and local. . . . No part and nobody of any importance claimed residuary powers for the general government within the Federal organization. There were strict constructionists and liberal constructionists, but there was no party and nobody who claimed any powers for the general government not expressly vested in it by the Constitution or derived by reasonable, direct implication from express grants.[102]

Ashley gives us this description of the American system at the turn of the century: "The state has complete charge of all local government, of education, of elective franchise, of most corporations, police duties, marriage and divorce, the poorer and delinquent classes, and public health. It is constantly brought into close touch with the individual. Legislation on these subjects, and the administration of the laws made upon them, may be left by

the state to the state government or the local government; but in any case the control of the state over all of them is exclusive and absolute."[103] This was written in 1902.

In short, America's constitutional law was remarkably similar in 1900 to what it had been in 1800; there had been no long, slow descent into centralization, despite some particular acts which had a centralizing tendency, and despite some highly necessary efforts by the central government to prevent the entire system from descending into anarchy. Neither Hamilton nor Marshall nor Lincoln had reversed the basic conception of American constitutionalism—that in doubtful cases, the presumption is with the states. It remained for twentieth-century liberalism to accomplish that transformation.

Notes

1. Quoted by R. L. Ashley, *The American Federal State* (New York: Macmillan, 1902), 104.
2. *The Federalist,* (New York: Modern Library, 1937), 337.
3. Letter to Roger Sherman, July 17, 1789, George A. Peek Jr., ed., *The Political Writings of John Adams:* (Indianapolis: Liberal Arts Press, 1954), 165.
4. "Madison's Notes on the Federal Convention," Winton U. Solberg, ed., *The Federal Convention and the Formation of the Union of American States* (Indianapolis: Liberal Arts Press, 1958), 139.
5. *The Federalist, op. cit.,* 320.
6. Solberg, *op. cit.,* 152, 143.
7. *The Federalist, op. cit.,* 113 *et seq.*
8 Edward Potts Cheyney, *European Background of American History* (New York: Collier Books, 1962).
9. James Bryce, *The American Commonwealth* (New York: Macmillan, 1891), vol. 1, 13.
10. Ibid., 13–14.
11. Ibid., 12.
12. *Democracy in America* (New York: Vintage Books, 1955), vol. I, 172.

13. Quoted by F. A. Hayek, *The Constitution of Liberty* (Chicago: Univ. of Chicago Press, 1960), 184.

14. A. V. Dicey, *Law of the Constitution* (New York: Macmillan, 1920), 137.

15. Andrew C. McLaughlin, "The Problem of Imperial Organization," Alfred Bushnell Hart, ed., *Social and Economic Forces in American History* (New York: Harper and Bros., 1913), 150.

16. Ibid., 147.

17. Dicey, *op. cit.*

18. Harold Underwood Faulkner, *American Economic History* (New York: Harper and Bros., 1924), 178–79.

19. McLaughlin, op. cit., 149.

20. Letter to Jefferson, August 12, 1786, *Madison's Works* (R. Worthington, 1884), vol. I, 245.

21. Francis A. Walker, *The Making of the Nation, 1783–1817* (New York: Scribner's, 1898), 2.

22. Ibid., 2, 6.

23. The Treaty of Paris, 1783. Text reprinted in Samuel Flagg Bemis, *The Diplomacy of the American Revolution* (Bloomington, IN: Indiana Univ. Press, 1957), 259–60.

24. Merrill Jensen, *The Articles of Confederation* (Madison, WI: Univ. of Wisconsin Press, 1959). 103.

25. Ibid., 250.

26. Solberg, op. cit., 44.

27. Ibid., 42.

28. Andrew C. McLaughlin, *The Confederation and the Constitution* (New York: Collier Books, 1962), 45.

29. Max Farrand, *The Framing of the Constitution of the United States* (New Haven, CT: Yale Univ. Press, 1962), 127–28, 154, 202.

30. Jensen, op. cit., 239.

31. Solberg, op. cit., 94–95.

32. Farrand, op. cit., 105.

33. *The Federalist*, op. cit., 297.

34. Ibid., 303.

35. Cf. Farrand, op. cit., ch. II, X, 204.

36. *The Federalist*, op. cit., 255, 303.

37. Farrand, op. cit., 202–4.

38. *The Federalist*, op. cit., 194.

39. Ibid., 201–2.

40. Ibid., 303.

41. Ibid.

42. Alpheus Thomas Mason, *The States' Rights Debate* (Englewood Cliffs, NJ: Prentice-Hall, 1964), 72.

43. *Madison's Works*, op. cit., 424.

44. *The Federalist*, op. cit.

45. Cf. Solberg, op. cit., 366 *et seq.* Among the amendments agreed upon in Virginia the list was topped by the following: "That each state in the Union shall respectively retain every power, jurisdiction, and right, which is not by this Constitution delegated to the Congress of the United States or to the departments of the federal government."

The first amendment recommended by the Massachusetts convention was "that it be explicitly declared that all powers not expressly delegated by the aforesaid Constitution are reserved to the several states to be by them exercised."

The first amendment recommended by Rhode Island was that "the United States shall guarantee to each state its sovereignty, freedom and independence, and every power, jurisdiction ratify.\

46. Letter to Judge William Johnson, June 12, 1823, *The Writings of Thomas Jefferson* (Charlottesville, Va: The Thomas Jefferson Memorial Association, 1903), vol. XV, 444.

47. *The Confederation and the Constitution*, op. cit., 194

48. Alfred de Grazia, *Politics and Government* (New York: Collier Books, 1962), vol. II, 223.

49. Ashley, op. cit., 208.

50. Dicey, op. cit., 142, 114.

51. "A Constitution is not to be made to mean one thing at one time, and another at some subsequent time when the circumstances may have so changed as perhaps to make a different rule in the case seem desirable. A principal share of the benefit expected from written constitutions would be lost if the rules they established were so flexible as to bend to circumstances or be modified by public opinion. . . . The meaning of the Constitution is fixed when it is adopted, and it is not different at any subsequent time when a court has occasion to pass upon it."

52. Dicey, op. cit., 144–45.

53. Ibid., 147, 168–69.

54. *The Writings of Thomas Jefferson*, op. cit., vol. III, 146.

55. *The Federalist*, op. cit., 174.

56. Edward Dumbauld, ed., *Jefferson's Political Writings* (Indianapolis: Bobbs-Merrill,

1956), 161; *The Kentucky-Virginia Resolutions* (Richmond, VA: Virginia Commission on Constitutional Government, 1960), 8–9.

57. *The Kentucky-Virginia Resolutions, op cit.,* 26.

58. Ibid., 27.

59. Ibid., 18.

60. "The Passing of Dual Federalism," Robert G. McCloskey, ed., *Essays in Constitutional Law* (New York: Vintage Books, 1957), 186.

61. Frederic Jesup Stimson, *The American Constitution* (New York: Scribner's, 1914), 83.

62. *The Federalist,* op. cit., 269.

63. Quoted by Thomas James Norton, *Undermining the Constitution* (New York: Devin-Adair, Co., 1951), 188.

64. Letter to Edmund Pendleton, January 21, 1792, *Madison's Works,* op. cit., vol. I., 546.

65. *The Kentucky-Virginia Resolutions,* op. cit., 27.

66. James D. Richardson, ed., *Messages and Papers of the Presidents* (Washington: U.S. Government Printing Office, 1896), vol. I, 584–85.

67. *Madison's Works,* op. cit., vol. I, 546.

68. Solberg, op. cit., 302.

69. Farrand, op. cit., 177.

70. Ibid., 182–83.

71. *The Confederation and The Constitution,* op. cit., 199.

72. *The Federalist,* op. cit., 268–69.

73. This rather clear history of the "general welfare" clause has been attacked by historian Irving Brant, biographer of Madison. In a book published in 1936 (*Storm Over the Constitution,* Indianapolis: Bobbs-Merrill), Brant argued that, because Roger Sherman had submitted another more sweeping "general welfare" clause as well as that finally included in the document, he was covertly trying to add to the powers of the government. Even if this were true of Sherman (and it is not very clear on Brant's speculation that it is), that would not alter the understanding of the matter which prevailed in the Federal convention concerning the clause that was adopted, the clear and unequivocal expression by the sponsors of the Constitution in explaining it, or the intention of the various state assemblies that adopted it. Brant would have us dismiss the explicit statements of Madison, the asseverations of the *Federalist Papers,* the numerous arguments of Federalist partisans and the evidence on the matter of the semi-colon presented by Farrand, in order to drag in a second rather unclear general welfare clause never considered by the convention, never submitted to the states for ratification, and never debated between the contending parties—claiming this balances all other considerations and impels us to give the "broadest scope" to the clause that *is* in the Constitution. Each reader may assess the logic of this procedure for himself. A somewhat more restrained version of Brant's argument is contained in his biography of Madison (vol. III, *James Madison: Father of the Constitution,* Indianapolis: Bobbs-Merrill, 1950).

74. *The Federalist,* op. cit., 89–200.

75. John C. Hamilton, ed., *The Works of Hamilton* (New York: John F. Trow, 1850), vol. III, 250–51.

76. Jacob E. Cooke, ed., *The Reports of Alexander Hamilton* (New York: Harper and Row, 1964), 90–91.

77. *Freedom and Federalism* (Chicago: Henry Regnery Co., 1959), 59.

78. *United States v. Tarble,* 13 Wallace 397 (1872).

79. Quoted by James Jackson Kilpatrick, *The Sovereign States* (Chicago: Henry Regnery Co., 1957), 264.

80. Ibid., 277.

81. Ibid., 265.

82. *Congressional Globe,* 39th Congress, 1st Session, 2460.

83. Ibid., 2542.

84. Ibid.

85. Ibid., 2499.

86. Ibid., 2510.

87. Ibid., 2766.

88. Ibid., 3039.

89. Ibid., 3028.

90. Ibid., 765.

91. Edward S. Corwin, ed., *The Constitution of the United States of America* (Washington: US Government Printing Office, 1953), 966.

92. *Bartkus v. People of State of Illinois,* 358 US 676 (1959)

93. Corwin, op. cit., 1116.

94. C. C. Tansill, et al., "The Fourteenth Amendment and Real Property Rights," Alfred Avins, ed., *Open Occupancy or Forced*

Housing Under the Fourteenth Amendment (New York: The Bookmailer, 1963), 77.

95. Ibid., 81.
96. Ibid., 71, 87.
97. *The English Constitution* (New York: Doubleday, n. d.), 249.
98. Ibid., 252.
99. Bryce, op. cit., vol. I, 12.
100. Ibid., 411–12.
101. *Recent Changes in American Constitutional Theory* (New York: Columbia Univ. Press, 1933), 3, 6.
102. Ibid., 31–32.
103. Ashley, op. cit., 208–9.

Alexander Landi

Was the American Founding a Lockean Enterprise? The Case of James Madison

VOL. 10, NO. 2, 1975

The opinion that John Locke's writings shaped the political thought of America's founders has for some time been widely accepted by students of the republic's formative years. While this opinion does not have "biblical" status, it seems to have acquired the more unassailable authority of an old wives' tale: a story which the custodians of the national lore have repeated to one another so often that its truth is taken for granted.

The equation of the founders' political vision with Locke's has an important bearing on another opinion, shared by many critics and proponents of the American polity: that economic self-interest has been, from the outset, the central principle of the nation's public life. This belief has gained so much currency that Aleksandr Solzhenitsyn could casually remark in his letter to the Nobel committee, that one can't expect much from a people whose social foundation is the institutionalized clash of interests. Furthermore, some of the most sober and respectable students of the founding, such as Martin Diamond, likewise hold that the founders had such a "low"—indeed, "Lockean"—vision of politics in America. Given such opinions, it might appear that any effort to foster the ethically good life in the United States would be futile since a wholly "modern" politics is so deeply rooted in America's political heritage. Wisdom and virtue must find a private sanctuary; they have no place in public life.

The thesis of this article, however, is that the above interpretation of the American founders does not apply to the "Father of the Constitution," James Madison. Madison's politics, I shall argue, was more comprehensive than Locke's, and reflects a view of man and society more consonant with classical and medieval than with modern political theory. To see this will require attention to the traditional elements in Madison's strictly "political" teaching, and to his understanding of the non-govern- mental aspects of public life. The effort is worthwhile, for to reduce Madison's politics to its Lockean component is to do him an injustice, and to deprive contemporary Americans of an important part of their political heritage. But let us first consider the case that can he made for viewing Madison as a Lockean.

The Ends of Government

We may begin with Madison's affirmation that "the object of government . . . is the happiness of the people."[1] In speaking of the means by which government may achieve its object, he often adverts to the securing or protection of safety, property, and the unequal faculties of acquiring property. It is such statements that lead Professor Diamond to infer that Madison's anthropology is roughly congruent to that of the modern political theorists, especially John Locke. That is, Madison views the good life in terms of the bourgeois "ideal" of comfortable self-preservation.[2]

Diamond's interpretation merits serious consideration. It is true that Madison's political writings emphasize the importance of securing safety and property. Also, he has a good deal to say about encouraging commerce and promoting prosperity. In these respects, Madison seems much more in harmony with modern political thinkers than with the philosophers of classical antiquity and of the Christian centuries, for whom comfort and self-preservation are strictly subordinate to human excellence.

We must, however, bear in mind that Madison was writing as a statesman, and that a statesman may be constrained to emphasize the lower things, even if he is personally oriented toward the higher possibilities of human and political existence. Diamond himself, in speculating on the reasons why Madison "lowered the sights" of politics, speaks of considerations that are properly those of a statesman. Madison's reduction of the objects of government to the baser aspects of human happiness, Diamond contends, may be linked to his advocacy of popular government, inasmuch as popular government may require: a) that the desire for acquisition be given an outlet in economic activity, lest the republic be blown apart in the clash between avarice and envy; b) that the objects of government be reduced to a level commensurate with the capacities of most men.[3]

According to Diamond, then, Madison's public statements concerning the ends of government were written with a view to the *popular* notion of happiness. That is, he was writing as a republican statesman. His own understanding of political, let alone of human, happiness need not have been as limited as that emphasized in his public writings.

In fact, there are many indications that Madison's vision of the good political life does not end with satisfying human appetites, but extends to the moral and intellectual well-being of citizens. Though he emphasizes safety and property as the objects of government, he at times gives evidence of a broader vision. For example, in his notes for an early speech against paper money, the young statesman attacked the issuance of unsecured tender as "vitiating morals" and "reversing the [end] of Govt. which is to reward best and punish worst." In similar vein, he was later to define government as: "An institution to make men do their duty."[4] Although Madison does not often mention the virtue of citizens as a direct object of government, he evidently considers that object proper to the political sphere. Furthermore, he shows a keen concern for the moral *effects* of legislation which may have other objects.[5]

That Madison considered the intellectual as well as the moral welfare of citizens to be among the proper ends of government is evidenced by his lifelong support of public education (which would include "moral instruction"). In a letter to a prominent Kentucky advocate of public education, Madison makes it clear that moral and intellectual virtue belong to the very substance of the human good *in their own right*, and are properly of the highest public concern in precisely that respect. "Academies, Colleges, and Universities . . . establishments which give to the human mind its highest improvements," Madison proclaims, "also give to every country its truest and most durable celebrity." He closes his endorsement of public education with the following peroration:

> The American people owe it to themselves, and to the cause of free Government, to prove by their establishment for the advancement and diffusion of Knowledge, that their political Institutions are as favorable to the intellectual and moral improvement of Man as they are conformable to his individual and social rights. What spectacle can be more edifying and more seasonable, than that of Liberty and Learning, each leaning on the other for their mutual and surest support.[6]

We may conclude that Madison's frequent use of Lockean language concerning the ends of government does not imply that he understood "the happiness of the people" simply in terms of comfortable self-preservation. It includes moral and intellectual virtue—which government may properly promote.

While the latter aspects of Madison's politics should be kept in mind, he more often speaks of government in narrower terms: It secures the persons and property of men, and thus emancipates their faculties. But here we should consider what Madison understood men's faculties to be emancipated for. The question becomes: of the many human activities which the American republic would liberate from

the "despotism" of monarchy and aristocracy, which did Madison consider to be the most important? An answer is implied in his essay on property, which merits quotation at length:

> [Property] in its particular application means "that dominion which one man claims and exercises over the external things of the world, in exclusion of every other individual."
>
> In its larger and luster meaning, it embraces everything to which man may attach a value and have a right; and which leaves to every one else the like advantage.
>
> In the former sense, a man's land, or merchandise, or money is called his property.
>
> In the latter sense, a man has property in his opinions and the free communication of them.
>
> He has a property of peculiar value, in his religious opinions, and in the profession and practice dictated by them.
>
> He has property very dear to him in the safety and liberty of his person.
>
> He has an equal property in the free use of his faculties and the free choice of the subjects on which to employ them,
>
> In a word, as a man is said to have a right to his property, he may be equally said to have a property in his rights.[7]

Clearly, the activities to be protected by government are several. Although Madison does not make their hierarchy explicit, he does give indications of their relative importance. Intellectual activity is accorded first mention. Religious activity is said to be "of peculiar value." Note that Madison does not indicate the importance of religion in subjective terms. He might have done so, for example, by speaking of the peculiar value which a man *attaches* to his religious opinions, etc. Instead, he writes that the rights pertaining to religious activities are of peculiar value—without reference to the subjective feeling of the given individual, who may after all be indifferent to religion.

Madison's treatment of religion is then markedly in contrast to that accorded the remaining species of "property": a man's property in "the safety and liberty of his person," and his "equal property" in freely employing his faculties on the objects of his choice. When Madison attributes importance to the latter kinds of property, he does so in the subjective sense: These aspects of a man's property are "very dear to him." Although Madison's language does not deny their objective value, neither does it accord them the highest dignity.

Thus, it would appear that Madison understood the most important activities of man to be those pertaining to the intellectual and religious life. The same emphasis is present throughout the essay on property, as in the following passage:

> [T]he praise of affording a just security to property, should be sparingly bestowed on a government which, however scrupulously guarding the possessions of individuals, does not protect them in the enjoyment and communication of their opinions, in which they have an equal, and in the estimation of some, a more valuable property.

> More sparingly should this praise be allowed to a government where a man's religious rights are violated by penalties, or fettered by tests, or taxed by a hierarchy. Conscience is the most sacred of all property; other property depending in part on positive law, the exercise of that, being a natural and inalienable right.

Madison's focus on intellectual and religious liberty is not restricted to this one essay; rather, it is a theme that appears very early in his writings and to which he was to recur frequently throughout his life. For example, at the Virginia Convention of 1776 he proposed an affirmation of religious liberty that was to be incorporated into the sixteenth article of the Virginia Bill of Rights:

> That religion, or the duty which we owe to our CREATOR, and the manner of discharging it, can be directed only by reason and conviction, not by force and violence; and therefore all men are equally entitled to the free exercise of religion, according to the dictates of conscience; and that it is the mutual duty of all to practice Christian forbearance, love, and charity towards each other.

Finally, as evidence that Madison's devotion to religious liberty was neither transitory nor merely a matter of political expedience, consider the autobiography that he dictated in his old age. Nearing the end of a lifetime in which he had become justly celebrated as framer of the Constitution, congressional statesman, party leader, president, and wise elder of the nation, the aging Madison took care, in his brief autobiographical sketch, to point with pride to the fact that his "first political act" was to change the religious freedom clause in the Virginia Bill of Rights from the concept of toleration to that of "*natural and absolute right.*"[8]

What has been said thus far should establish that Madison considered religion and thought to be the most important kinds of "property" that government exists to protect. However, I do not mean to imply that Madison is the unappreciated St. Augustine of the eighteenth century. It would appear that he was rather insensitive to the highest aspects of religious life: holiness, communion with God, sharing in the very life of God. His understanding of religion seems to be restricted to the intellectual and the moral: religious convictions, the duties which men have to God, and their divinely ordained duties to one another. Consequently, in noting that Madison recognized a "peculiar value" in religion, perhaps no more can be inferred than that he saw a special dignity in the moral and intellectual realms.

Still, we may conclude that Madison saw a hierarchy in the human activities to be emancipated under the American regime: the intellectual and the moral rank above the appetitive. It follows that if Madison more often than not employed Lockean language regarding the purposes of government, he did not correspondingly "lower the sights" of politics. On the one hand, he at times speaks of the moral and intellectual well-being of citizens as direct ends of government. And when speaking of the protection of property as the object of government, he refers not merely to a man's material possessions, but rather, "in its larger and juster meaning," to his acts as well. Among the activities protected (and emancipated) by government there is a hierarchy which exists even though government does not enforce it, and many emancipated men may not recognize it in thought or in practice. The most eligible of human activities are the intellectual and religious (perhaps better read: intellectual and moral). As a corollary, the end for which Madison understands man to be emancipated is not *primarily* the life of comfortable self-preservation: Happiness is not achieved by mere acquisition. As Madison might well have said, to understand the human faculties, the protection of which is the first object of government, to refer solely to the faculties of acquiring

land, money, and merchandise, would be to take the term in its "more narrow and less just meaning."

The Effects of Government

Though the previous discussion shows that Madison's political vision was more comprehensive than Locke's, and reflects a view of the human good akin to the teachings of classical and Christian philosophy, it would be exaggerated to identify his politics with the premodern tradition. To go no further, why does Madison not say of government, as Aristotle did of the political community, that it is ordered to the good of man, especially to the highest good? There are several possible answers to this question. Some will require recognition that when Madison speaks of the government, he says nothing of what he expects to occur in the societal aspect of the public life.[9] But first, let us look into Madison's expectations concerning the *effects* of his limited government. For it may be that Madison's constitutional model, like Aristotle's favored practical regime, the polity, could be expected to have effects beyond the formally stated ends of the regime.

To begin with, a government which secures the rights of property is positively related to the good life, in that it permits the achievement of excellence by those of superior faculties. That Madison understood the very possibility of excellence to be problematic, and that he viewed the protection of that possibility as inextricably linked to protecting property, is argued convincingly in Paul Eidelberg's *The Philosophy of the American Constitution.* Eidelberg's reasoning is based largely on a rendering of *Federalist* 10, which locates the source of faction in the diverse and unequal faculties of men:

"The protection of these faculties," says Madison, "is the first object of government." Negatively stated, this means that the first object of government is to guard against any attempt to remove the latent causes of faction! It means that the first object of government is to guard against any attempt to bring about a massive uniformity of opinions, passions, and interests. But since the first object of government must be commensurate with the principal danger confronting civil society, and since the principal danger, for Madison, is none other than majority faction, it follows that to protect the diverse and unequal faculties of men is to protect men of superior advantages from any attempt to the many to render all men equal by reducing them to a level of mediocrity.[10]

A government which restricts itself to the protection of property, then, is nonetheless related to the excellence of its citizens as an enabling principle, as a necessary if not sufficient condition, as a means to an end (even though it does not promote that end explicitly and directly).

In the second place, Madison's limited government would do more than secure the possibility of human excellence, for the political arrangements which he proposes for protecting property could be expected to foster virtue and reason by their very operation. To see this aspect of Madison's politics, let us further consider his discussion of faction. Republics, Madison remarks in *Federalist* 10, have labored under opprobrium because they are prone to the rule of a factious majority, a majority actuated by a common motive adverse to the interests of the community, or to the rights of other citizens. His remedy for this vice of popular government is to establish a republic large enough

to embrace a multiplicity of interests (or potential factions), so that no single interest can form a majority and control the government. To the degree that the large republic succeeds in preventing the formation of a factious majority, it will frustrate the unbridled passion of any faction. The unbridled passions of a given faction will not persuade the majority, because the latter will not be actuated by the same passion. Each interest *will* have to present its claims in terms that the majority will find persuasive. Thus, anyone who hopes to be politically effective must learn to moderate his passions. In this way, the very operation of the large republic promotes the virtue of moderation. Moreover, the success of the extended republic would almost require justice and reason in the public life of the citizens. As Madison concludes in *Federalist* 51:

> In the extended republic of the United States, and among the great variety of interests, parties, and sects which it embraces, a coalition of a majority of the whole society could seldom take place on any other principles than those of justice and the general good.[11]

Finally, Madison's model for limited government provides a context in which high political virtue can flourish. Lest the great body of citizens lack the wisdom and virtue needed to secure private rights and the other ends of government, the Virginian's constitutional model includes the principle of representation. This may provide, in the Senate especially, a select body of men characterized by "wisdom patriotism and love of justice." To secure its objects, it seems, a republican constitution must provide for the exercise of high public virtue, the vindication of "reason, justice, and truth" by those citizens most capable of statesmanship.

Madison's republican constitution would promote the exercise of statesmanship: a) by establishing the principle of representation in a large republic, thus tending to center the public choice "on men who possess the most attractive merit, and the most diffusive and established character"; b) by establishing a legislative body, the Senate, with a tenure lengthy enough to provide its members with the requisite experience of the nation's affairs, and to insulate them from transient popular passions; and c) by establishing the separation of powers, which should check the propensity of the few to exercise their characteristic vices.[12]

Thus, even if Madison's understanding of government is taken only in the limited sense that he emphasized, one can see that he expects government to have effects on the activities of its citizens, beyond its explicit objects. It will protect the possibility of excellence. It will promote moderation in the great body of the citizens. And in addition, it will provide a context in which superior men may rise to public office, and be able to exercise the virtue of statesmen.

Religion in a Free Society

The above remarks should help to explain why Madison could comfortably state a doctrine according to which government has as its object something far less than the full human good as he understood it. But even taking into account the expected effects of his constitutional model, Madison's "government" is certainly more limited than Aristotle's polis. It does not follow, however, that Madison correspondingly "lowered the sights" of public life, since Madison distinguished in public life the governmental from the societal. Hence, to better comprehend

the relation between Madison's anthropology and his understanding of civil life (the member of "society" being, for Madison, "citizen"), we should go beyond his statements on the ends of government and consider his expectations regarding the use of freedom in society. Stated otherwise: with respect to those ends traditionally considered the highest concern of political society, but which Madison deemphasized as objects of government, what did he expect would be achieved by social institutions, informal associations, and individual citizens, acting without the direct support or guidance of government? For two reasons, it will be most instructive to look into Madison's expectations regarding religion: a) because the traditional Western polity had regarded the support of religion as a proper, if not the chief, object of government; and b) because Madison, like Locke, adamantly severed government from any connection with religious ends (which he did not do with regard to the moral and intellectual improvement of citizens).

Madison's predictions for religion in a free society were, in one word, optimistic. Religion, he remarked, is natural to man; there are causes in the human breast that secure the perpetuity of religion without the aid of law.[13] Madison attributed the desire for established religion to the opinion that government and religion rely on one another for mutual support. Repeatedly, he contradicted that opinion, which he called an "old error." Such a coalition, he claimed, is a corrupting influence on both parties. Often he would point with pride to the results of disestablishment in his native Virginia, especially to its effect on the previously established Episcopal Church:

> Prior to the Revolution, the Episcopal Church was established by law in this

State. On the Declaration of Independence it was left with all other sects, to self-support. And no doubt exists that there is much more of religion among us now than there ever was before the change; and particularly in the Sect which enjoyed the legal patronage. This proves rather more than, that the law is not necessary to the support of religion.[14]

Madison did not claim that disestablishment would favor the universality of orthodox religious opinion: Human opinions must be "various and irreconcilable concerning . . . doctrines of religion."[15] There may also appear religious extravagances injurious to both religion and social order. The proper remedy for such excesses, he counseled, is time, forbearance, and example. In such instances, reason will gradually gain its ascendancy, while the interference of government would more likely increase than control fanatic tendencies." Doctrinal differences among Christian denominations appear not to have concerned Madison very much; perhaps he considered them to be variants of those frivolous and fanciful distinctions, absurd to the philosopher, that arouse men to mutual animosity. But he did claim that disestablishment would promote reasonability in religious opinions, and moreover that it would foster the practice of the gospel virtues.

In conclusion, Madison expected religion to flourish in American society, without falling excessively into fanatic distortions, even though it is neither enforced, encouraged, nor guided by government. Thus, Madison's limited view of the objects of government must be understood within the context of this expectation: that the most sacred of human activities would find public support and expression in society, and that they would be better served by such means than by the "interference" of government.

Limited Government: The Dictates of Prudence and the Value of Liberty

Given that Madison's politics were more comprehensive than Locke's, and reflect a view of man and society more consonant with classical and medieval than with modern political theory, one might wonder why he advocated limited government. Why did he not see the full human good as an end belonging as fully to government as to social institutions? Was he so sanguine as to think that social institutions seeking to form men for the good life will always function well, and have no need for the public support and discipline provided by law? May not social agencies (family, church, academy, profession, local community) suffer decadence or degradation? And even if society could be relied on to function adequately at all times, why should the most common of public institutions, the government, have a minimal and muted role with regard to the highest of human activities?

Madison was not in fact sanguine regarding the use of autonomy under a limited government—men have a tendency to be dominated by their passions. But he had substantial reasons for advocating limited government. Some of his reasons were negative, and were rooted not in his view of the human good, but in his judgment of the "fallenness" of concrete men. Madison's positive reason for advocating limited government was also the major reason for his republicanism: the value he placed on human liberty.

First among the Virginian's negative reasons for narrowly defining the role of government was his lively awareness that power is subject to abuse. Rulers, under the guise of promoting the happiness of the people, may in reality use their power for tyrannical purposes. Such is the case with the very regimes which make wisdom and virtue the basis of their claim to rule: "In monarchies, the interests and happiness of all may be sacrificed to the caprice and passions of a despot. In aristocracies, the rights and welfare of the many may be sacrificed to the pride and cupidity of the few."[17] Madison saw similar dangers in popular government: The democratic majority may abuse its power, and the elected officials of a republic may apply to personal ends the powers delegated to them. This is not to say that Madison viewed men as radically corrupt; he saw in the generality of men qualities "which justify a certain portion of esteem and trust." He never forgot, however, that present in the creature is "a degree of depravity . . . which requires a certain degree of circumspection and distrust. . ."[18] Madison did not hold that such flaws in human character imply stringent limits on the powers of government. For example, against those who contended that the Constitutional Convention had framed a government which places too much confidence in men, he argued: "Where power can be safely lodged, *if it is necessary*, reason commands its cession. In such cases, it is imprudent and unsafe to withhold it."[19] However, Madison did not deny that there are reasons for distrust as well as confidence in those who will control government. Madison's qualified mistrust of popular majorities and of government officials, magnified to the degree that they might wield power, does much to explain why he emphasized only those functions of government that are strictly necessary.

A second reason for Madison's advocacy of limited government was alluded to earlier: His statesman's concern for establishing a regime fitted to concrete men, rather than to an unrealizable "nation of philosophers." Not inconsistent with Aristotle, Madison held that the aims of any government must be formulated with a view to the capacities of most citizens. His own application of this axiom was for given men, in a given place and time, with a view to a given regime. Thus, the fact that Madison focused quite so much on the narrower functions of government may be related to the individualist cast of mind prevalent among his fellow citizens. A more fundamental consideration may have been his judgment that this particular people would perform respectably in a free society. He did not advocate limited government for every time and place. But the most important consideration, in this context, is that Madison was a *republican* statesman—an advocate of popular government. Although he explicitly placed his confidence in the capacity of mankind for self-government, he at the same time averred that "there are subjects to which the capacities of the bulk of mankind are unequal."[20] This implies limited government for two reasons. First, the aristocrat's insistence on the primacy of virtue may not make much sense to everyman. Secondly, the far-ranging and complex activities of "positive government" are likely to place public affairs beyond the popular understanding—a piece of wisdom recently recaptured by contemporary social scientists, albeit at great expense.

The last point raises a further question: Why was Madison a partisan of self-government in the first place? To be sure, he was aware that the "genius of the American people" favored popular government. It may also be that he saw in the dynamic of mercantile and industrial capitalism the portents of a democratic age. Still, his advocacy of republicanism cannot be reduced to an accommodation to the spirit of the age (or of future ages). Madison was a genuine republican, whose republicanism was rooted in his deep regard for human liberty. His attachment to liberty gave him a positive reason for emphasizing only the most basic and necessary functions of government.

The importance which Madison attached to the principle of liberty is apparent in his reflections on the significance of American enterprise. Liberty, he writes, is "the great end, for which the Union was formed"; it should be the central object of the social system, having power as its satellite.[21] Madison's reasoning seems to be the following: men are naturally endowed with the faculties required to pursue the human good in its various dimensions. Among some peoples, those faculties may be at such a primitive stage of development as to require paternal rule. Madison no doubt recognized that even in the most civilized societies, there may be individuals whose mental incompetence or moral depravity requires that they be ruled by others. Most men, however, are sufficiently endowed with the specifically human faculties: the unequal distribution of those faculties may imply a difference in rank, but not a difference in kind. Since men are equal in this sense, men are naturally free: no man or group of men has the right to rule other men without their consent.[22] Human nature thus require that the sovereignty of the people be acknowledged. It is in her recognition of popular sovereignty and the liberty of man that America has, for Madison, a universal significance. This belief is expressed in the opening passage of his essay on "Charters":

> In Europe, charters of liberty have been granted by power. America has set the example and France has followed it, of

charters of power granted by liberty. This revolution in the practice of the world, may with an honest praise, be pronounced the most triumphant epoch of its history, and the most consoling presage of its happiness. We look back, already, with astonishment, at the daring outrage committed by despotism, on the reason and rights of man; we look forward with joy, to the period, when it shall be despoiled of all its usurpations, and bound forever in the chains, with which it had loaded its miserable victims[23]

Since liberty implies popular government, it also implies limited government, for reasons already mentioned. Yet the relation between liberty and limited government also has more direct and positive dimensions. Just as the people have a right to be governed by their own consent, so does the individual have a right to autonomy which may not justly be denied, even by popular consent. The areas of personal autonomy are listed by Madison in his essay on property, cited above. Liberty of action for each of the rights mentioned in that essay is, to be sure, limited by government's legitimate protection of the rights of others. The rights of conscience, however, "the most sacred of all property," are apparently to be subject to no further constraints. And, although "other property" may depend "in part on positive law," it is clearly Madison's sense that positive law should recognize that limitations on these rights, not their free exercise, are the exception rather than the rule.

Madison and the Western Tradition

Madison's advocacy of a free society returns us to the question of his "place" in the Western political tradition. While the previous argument has shown that he is not a "modern," neither is he an "ancient" in his emphasis on liberty. In this light, I would suggest the possibility that his political thought has specific roots in Christian political thought.

The idea of limited government is not specifically modern, but rather was original to medieval Christianity. In the medieval vision the church, the Body of Christ, is charged with the care of spiritual things, which are eternal, whereas the political community is concerned with the things which will pass away with time. Thus, the political community is inferior to the church, and must recognize the church's right to pursue its higher ends. That Madison assigns the most sacred rights to the conscience, rather than to the church, may be seen as simply an expression of the Protestant principle, each man his own priest. Similarly, a general emphasis on liberty, such as we find in Madison's thought, may well be implied by the Christian principle that each man has a personal responsibility freely to seek the good—a responsibility also encumbent on social institutions (the family, the academy, etc.) with regard to the particular goods appropriate to each.[24]

The importance that Madison attaches to liberty, especially the liberty of conscience, is difficult to square with the perspective of an Aristotelian statesman. It may better be interpreted as an expression of the Christian political mind, for it involves no irrevocable link with strictly modern politics. As noted earlier, Madison was not an apostle of the claims of the passions, nor was he a simple partisan of freedom, indifferent to the ways in which it would be used. He saw, and was concerned about, some of the vices which would be incident to a free society. Aware as he was of the "fallenness" of concrete men, Madison knew

that licentious behavior and extravagant intellectual error are possibilities implicit in the emancipation of the faculties. Yet such judgments did not lead Madison to assign plenary powers to government. Madison's advocacy of liberty, despite the danger of its misuse, may have been influenced by his lack of confidence that any class of "guardians" would govern justly, and by his belief that the free society, at least in America, would provide adequately for those things which would not be the focus of governmental activity. Madison did not advocate limited, republican government in every circumstance. In the case of the American Indian, he in fact proposed a paternal rule that would last until the Indians developed civilized institutions. It appears that the translation of man's natural liberty into a civil right must be proportioned to the capacity of a given people to use liberty well. Yet for a sufficiently mature, civilized people, the first principle of Madison's politics is liberty: the liberty of a people, and of persons, who are expected freely to order themselves to the higher things. We thus find in Madison a noble alternative to that Lockean liberty which is the emancipation of acquisition.

Notes

1. *Federalist* 62. (New York: The Modern Library, 1937), 404.

2. Diamond's treatment of the political teleology of the *Federalist Papers* can he found in his "Democracy and *The Federalist*: A Reconsideration of the Framers' Intent," *American Political Science Review*, vol. LIII, no. 1., 52–68. Also see his article on *The Federalist* in *History of Political Philosophy*, ed. Leo Strauss and Joseph Cropsey (Chicago: Rand McNally & Co., 1963), 573–93.

3. "Democracy and *The Federalist*," *Ibid.*, 63–64, et passim.

4. *The Writings of James Madison* (New York: G. P. Putnam Sons, 1900–1910), II, 281: Jonathan Elliott, ed., *Debates in the Several State Conventions on the Federal Constitution* (Philadelphia: J. B. Lippincott, 1896), III, 394.

5. *Writings,* Ibid., II, 88; IX, 126–27.

6. Ibid., IX, 107–08.

7. Ibid., VI, 101.

8. "Autobiography," 1692 (Library of Congress Manuscripts); reprinted in Douglas Adair, "James Madison's 'Autobiography,'" *William and Mary Quarterly,* Third Series, vol. ii. no. 2, 191–229.

9. The distinction between "government" and "society" is foreign to Aristotle's discussion of the political community. For an excellent discussion of Aristotle's concept of the polis, and its distinction from the modern concepts of government, society, or government and society, see Harry Jaffa, "Aristotle," *History of Political Philosophy,* op. cit., 65–72.

10. *The Philosophy of the American Constitution,* (New York: The Free Press. 1968), 153.

11. *Federalist* 51, op. cit., 340–41.

12. Citations from *Federalist* 10 and 63. See also *Federalist* 51 and 62; Eidelberg, op. cit., ch. 8.

13. *Writings,* op. cit., IX, 101, 126–27, 487.

14. Ibid., 126–27.

15. Ibid., V, 82.

16. Ibid., IX, 487.

17. Ibid., IX, 361.

18. *Federalist* 55, 365.

19. Elliott, op. cit., 394.

20. *Writings,* op. cit., V, 81.

21. Ibid., VI, 109, 120.

22. See Harry Jaffa, *Equality and Liberty* (New York: Oxford Univ. Press, 1965), 176–78, et passim.

23. *Writings,* op. cit., VI, 83.

24. *Vide* the papal teaching on the principle of subsidiarity, beginning with the encyclical of Pope Leo XIII, *Rerum Novarum,* collected in *The Social Teachings of the Church,* ed. Anne Freemantle, (New York: Mentor-Omega Books, 1961), 20–56.

M. E. Bradford

A Teaching for Republicans: Roman History and the Nation's First Identity

VOL. 11, NO. 2, 1976

The Federal District of Columbia, both in its formal character as a capital and also in its self-conscious attempt at a certain visual splendor, is, for every visitor from the somewhat sovereign states, a reminder that the analogy of ancient Rome had a formative effect upon those who conceived and designed it as their one strictly national place. What our fathers called Washington City is thus, at one and the same time, a symbol of their common political aspirations and a specification of the continuity of those objectives with what they knew of the Roman experience. So are we all informed with the testimony of the eye, however we construe the documentary evidence of original confederation. So say the great monuments, the memorials, the many public buildings and the seat of government itself. So the statuary placed at the very center of the Capitol of the United States. And much, much more.

But Roman architecture and sculpture were not the primary inspiration for America's early infatuation with the city on the Tiber. That connection came by way of literature, and particularly from readings in Roman history. What Livy,

Tacitus, Plutarch, and their associates taught the generation that achieved our independence was the craft of creating, operating, and preserving a republican form of government. For gentlemen of the eighteenth century, Rome was the obvious point of reference when the conversation turned to republican theory. The Swiss, the Dutch, the Venetians and (of course) the Greek city states sometimes had a place in such considerations. And in New England the memory of the Holy Commonwealth survived. Yet Rome had been *the* Republic, one of the most durable and impressive social organisms in the history of the world. Moreover, there was a many-sided record of how it developed, of how its institutions were undermined and of the consequences following their declension. This Rome was no construct issuing from deliberations upon the abstract "good," no fancy of "closet philosophers."[1] Public men might attend its example with respect, learn from its triumphs and its ruin. On these shores they did. And, once we were independent, with a special urgency. To explain why and with what results, I will first reconstruct a composite Roman model according to the understanding of those first Americans and then document that pointed synthesis with a limited selection from the wealth of supporting evidence left to us from the architects of our political identity. Only then will it be possible to account for the impetus given by this effort at emulation to the development of an indigenous American regime: account for and thus correct many now accepted readings of our early history, as that identification requires.

The best way to recover Roman history as it signified to the English Whig or likeminded commonwealthsman of the late eighteenth century is to ignore such diverting questions as what it meant to the republican historians themselves, to Polybius, to Plutarch, the Renaissance, or the leaders of the French Revolution. Or of what it means to Western man today. The distinction here is akin to the difference between the study of biblical influence and direct exposition of the scripture itself. Our fathers trusted the Roman historians rather well. To them, as to other late Augustans, history was a moral and political study, not a precise antiseptic science.[2] And especially Roman history. They found the truth of men and manners in its long and varied entirety. This enlightenment did, to be sure, include a deposition from life under the Caesars—even though that testimony was chiefly negative in character. But the deepest teaching of the full chronicle was concentrated in its first three parts: from 510–252 B.C., the rise of the Republic (in Livy and Book II of Cicero's *De Republica*); 262–202 B.C., the era of the Punic Wars (in Livy, Appian, and Polybius); and 201–27 B.C., the decline toward anarchy and despotism (in Sallust, Lucan, Tacitus, Suetonius, Plutarch, and others).[3] Admiration for the old order was a convention with the later, imperial authorities. Caesar allowed the sentiment, sometimes even officially encouraged it: Caesar as the only conceivable keeper of the republican fires. Yet the moral imagination of *Romanitas* continued its location in the memory of the Republic long after the subject of this recollection had forever disappeared. Nothing could be more republican than the wicked, arbitrary, and tumultuous princes drawn to life in Suetonius's *Twelve Caesars,* than Tacitus's portrait of Tiberius in *The Annals,* or the Galba and Otho of Plutarch's *Parallel Lives.* But these writings are republican only by implication. It is a presupposed knowledge of the Republic itself, and of the books where it is described and reported, that gives them an indirect resonance of bygone stabilities. Finally, it is *the history of the Republic* that is republican history proper.

Yet an even further narrowing of focus is in order. Beyond any doubt or question, the second of my divisions of the Roman record before Augustus is the most important. For its relation to the other two is almost as normative as that of the entire Republican period to the total history of Rome. Indubitably, the tale turned there, the action that embodied and implied the politics with which we are here concerned. In other words, the Rome that overcame Carthage was the perfection of pagan republicanism. Its merit, slow and certain in formation, corporate and all-absorbing in operation, was revealed in that test. Rome as a whole won a victory—won it with finality despite poor generalship, lack of sea power, and a terrifying adversary. That the consequence of successfully implementing this perfection was to be internecine strife is in no wise a necessary judgment upon the constituent particulars which worked toward its formation: is instead only evidence that traditional societies cannot recognize their own composition as something frail, in need of self-conscious husbandry, of protection from internal schism and the temptations of novelty and change. Imperial expansion, in conjunction with rearrangements within the Roman order—changes brought on by the exigencies of protracted conflict and unexpected, inadvertent conquests—disrupted the moral and economic balance of the Republic. Or at least set in motion the forces which brought that disruption to pass. How Rome at large became strong and then, by stages, lost that strength is what fascinated the generation which made a new republic in this new place.

Probably the best way to understand how the Roman Republic came to be is to consider the place occupied in its development by the Twelve Tables of the Law (449 B.C.). This codification made official and permanent the replacement of the ancient kings by a prescriptive, constitutional system. For the Law of the Tables was "essentially a codification of existing customs," the "funded wisdom" of the Roman people upon which all subsequent additions to their legal order drew for their authority.[4] It objectified their will toward existence as a community. To borrow language applied elsewhere, Rome was not *made* but *grew*. Despite the legend of Romulus and Remus and the myth of Trojan relocation, Romans did not connect their purchase on the favor of the gods with an original commitment to political "propositions" or a plan for improving the world. The ontological fact of Rome, rooted in familial piety, flourishing in patriotic zeal, was logically prior to any meaning it acquired. Out of the pull and push, the dialectic of a few tribes in central Italy, emerged a cohesive unity, bound by blood, place and history, slowly absorbing neighboring cities and peoples once these had earned their right

to absorption, periodically redistributing sources of power within itself whenever the amiable interaction of its constituent parts required such adjustment. For out of that remarkable oneness of spirit Rome had acquired its original hegemony. And out of it the city continued to grow and prosper under new and unexpected conditions: continued to augment the dignity of its name and the honor of having a share in that name's hieratic authority.

Said another way, the self-respect of every Roman depended upon his *being* a Roman. In a fashion which few of us would understand, the self in this system was derivative of the social bond and depended upon a common will to preserve that broad fabric of interconnection intact. A good Roman of the old school had personal pride and a considerable sense of honor. His was a shame culture, dominated by intense and personally felt loyalties to family, clan, and individual. Commitment to Rome had its root in, and was not separable from, these most primary attachments. They tell us what Rome meant. And why a true Roman was not an individual as we understand the term. Yet this frame of mind was not so statist or secular as such evidence would lead us to believe. For the fabled *virtu* of full citizens under the Republic had a ground in what Richard Weaver wisely denominated "the older religiousness."[5] Romans honored (and moved with them, as earth) the *manes* of their ancestors, the lares and penates of hearth and rooftree, the *genius loci* of groves and plains and waters, and the higher gods consulted through official augury: honored them privately and in the service of the state, itself always reverent toward the mysterious powers which touch the lives of men.[6] But Rome's tangential connection with the numinous entailed little of fable or theology, little suggestion of a divine plan for the city, only prescribed rites and ordinances. And this bond through custom only reinforced their social and political conservatism whose patterns were of a piece with the inherited religion. Respect for *all* the *mores majorum,* the tested ways, permeated everything in the *habitus* of this society. The will of the Fathers *was* the will of the gods.

The old Roman of good family had about him a continuous visual reminder of the history by which he had been personally defined. I make reference to the images of his ancestors which had a prominent place in the disposition of his household effects. According to Pliny the Elder:

> In the days of our ancestors [these images] . . . were to be seen in their reception halls . . . arranged, each in its own niche . . . to accompany the funeral processions of the family; and always, whenever someone died, every member of the family that had ever existed was present. The pedigree, too, of the individual was traced by lines to each of the painted portraits. Their record rooms were fitted with archives and records of what each had done. This was a powerful stimulus.[7]

Roman history proper began with these family annals, and with the linen rolls which recorded by year the names of office holders and a few events. These propitiary figures stood between the Roman and the higher powers, dictated the religious ritual by means of which that relation was negotiated, and could therefore dictate in conjunction with these rite a prescriptive law which was the political state as the customary forms of worship were the state religious. Rome *was* the prescriptive law; and that law had a sanction in religion.

Of course, the prescriptive culture of plebeians and of the ordinary free farmers in the countryside was less elaborate than what we found in Pliny or can discover in the glowing pages of Fustel de Coulanges.[8] Plutarch, however, in reporting a speech by the noble Tiberius Gracchus, leads us to believe that in the days of Roman glory the identity with the *antiqui moris* had been supported by the same ties with blood and place throughout every level of class and occupation. It is to the disappearance (during the Punic Wars and their aftermath) of these reasons for mutuality that the tribune objects. And for their reestablishment that he died.

> The savage beasts, in Italy, have their particular dens, . . . places of repose and refuge; but the men who bear arms, and expose their lives for the safety of their country, enjoy in the meantime nothing more in it but air and light; and, having no houses or settlements of their own [are subjected to an indignity when their commanders exhort them] to fight for their sepulchers and altars . . . [when they have neither] houses of their own nor hearths of their ancestors to defend.[9]

A general distribution of property, in at least thirty-one of the thirty-five tribes, was the strength-giving backbone of the Roman Republic. For, as one scholar has remarked, the original Roman was a farmer/soldier.[10] And his mind reflected his occupation. Roman literature, and especially its normative components, tells us nothing to the contrary. It warns reiteratively against the corruption of the cities, the urbanite intrusion of foreign values or notions, and praises the advantages, practical and spiritual, of rural life. I call this mood hard pastoral—as opposed to the Arcadian (escapist) or Dionysian (fierce) pastoral of the Alexandrian Greeks. Peace, health, and repose (as, for instance, in Horace) are a part of its benison, but not freedom from work or liberation from duty. Consider in this connection the *De Re Rustic* of Cato the Censor. Or the satires of Juvenal. Or the *Germania* of Tacitus (about the Romans, not the rough folk across the Rhine; for the Germans serve as reminders of the human excellence once possible in Rome's general population).[11] All locate Rome at its best with a regulated combination of honesty, thrift, patience, labor, and endurance—with the "home place," the routines of field, stream, and altar, where men and women of a predictable character may be formed out of a well-tested mold. The city was a place of general worship, a scene for politics, an armory and refuge in war, a point of contact with other societies. Rome is thus an arena, but not a seedbed for the original Roman sensibility. As was the case with Sparta, its firmest walls were the breastplates of its soldier/citizens so long as they could be expected to say (with Cato the Younger) in response to appreciation for service, "You must thank [instead] the commonwealth."[12]

But this Cato Uticensis (along with his great-grandfather the Censor, and perhaps Camillus, a cynosure of republican excellence) comes down to us as a byword because his rectitude was a dramatic, unbelievable anachronism when it appeared in the senate, the forum and the field. In Cicero, Lucan, Persius, Plutarch, Tacitus, Appian, Martial, Sallust, and Virgil, he is remembered as the exemplar in that he stood out in bold relief against the political and moral decadence of the social wars. And because the Republic breathed its last with him at Utica, there was only one Cato to resist Julius Caesar. To confront Hannibal there were thousands.

Which returns us to my centerpiece of republicanism in action, the Rome of the Punic Wars.

Public spirit had its heyday in these troubled times. Rome's future existence was at stake. Livy tells us that after Cannae Roman women were forbidden to weep, that no man (soldier, planter, or merchant) charged the state for his goods or service, that no one took political advantage of his country's distress.[13] And Sallust adds in support that "before the destruction of Carthage the people and senate of Rome governed the Republic peacefully and with moderation. There was no strife among the citizens for glory or power."[14] In the view of the prudent Polybius, the credit for this balance (his great theme) and thus for Rome's persistence belonged to its prescriptive, "organic" constitution: a constitution drawn by no lawgiver or savant but made "naturally," not "by purely analytical methods, but rather through experience of many struggles and problems; with the actual knowledge gained in the ups and downs of success and failure."[15] Of course, this is a slow process and certain to involve fierce conflict. Livy's first ten books give us a narrative of that evolution.[16] And a clear impression of the reluctance among the plebeians (when agitated by their tribunes) to accept any stable order which did not guarantee their absolute control. Or the patricians to distribute unoccupied or conquered lands to those landless and deserving in the ranks of the common soldiery. Formidable enemies (such as Pyrrhus and Brennus) taught both the necessary lessons, that "such being the power of each element [of Roman society] both to injure and to assist the others, the result is that their union is sufficient against all changes and circumstances."[17] Taught them just in time.

The history of the three wars with

Carthage is as stirring a tale as anyone could want. It is a story of repeated defeats and terrible casualties. Yet always the city stands and its citizens regroup. Hannibal seems to fear the physical proximity of Rome, even when it appears to be defenseless. He wanders south, attempting (with no success) to break the loyalty of Rome's satellite communities. Then the tide turns. Carthage is riven internally. A narrowly commercial city, it has no healthy yeomanry to call to arms. Its aristocrats lack public spirit and aspire to absolute dominion. Mercenaries finally falter before armed and patriotic citizens. The Romans learn war at sea, learn Hannibal's tactics and discover in their midst a captain to face him down. Scipio locates the weak link in the armor of his adversaries. The Africans lack dependable allies and cannot defend their city from siege.

Carthage does not frighten the Romans. Thereafter the end comes swiftly. For a summary, I must cite Titus Livius once again: "No other nation in the world could have suffered so tremendous a series of disasters and not been overwhelmed,"[18] does not exaggerate.

> Who, after this, will dare to jeer at those who praise olden times. If there were a city composed of sages such as philosophers have imagined in some ideal, but surely not actual world, I for my part cannot think that it would contain leaders with greater dignity of mind and less lust for personal power, or a populace more admirably conducted.[19]

But as we all know, the republican spirit of incorporation disappeared rapidly once Cato the Elder got his way and the ancient (and perhaps useful) enemy was no more. It is a commonplace that the

Roman Republic was ruined by success, both in the Punic Wars and in the East (Macedon, Parthia, etc.). It is more appropriate to say that the harm was done by the form of that achievement, and by the time that it required. External pressure had been necessary to the development of a balanced constitution and a cohesive interdependence of the classes, a community of older (patrician) and newer (plebeian) families.[20] Yet, contrary to many authorities, this dependence was in itself nothing ominous or unusual. Some of it is visible in the history of every healthy nation—an oblique proof that enemies can motivate a people to perform their best. Instead, the real problems were (1) removal of the Roman armies from the category of citizen-soldiers into the classification of fulltime military professionals; (2) the consequent decline of home agriculture and village life; (3) the growth of large slave-operated, absentee-owned estates; (4) the large concentration of wealth in a new group of imperial managers and international traders; (5) a great dependence on foreign food and the skills of educated foreigners; (6) a sharp decline in character among the plebeians of the city—the emergence of a useless, dishonorable proletariat. Without a rural nursery for virtue or a necessary role for all citizens, and with Romans in the army detached (and almost in exile) from the motherland, the ground had been cut from under the institutions of the old Republic.[21] Add to these harbingers of disaster the decline of the official Roman religion and the concomitant "passion for words flowing into the city," the foreign rituals and forms of speculation, and we can understand why old Cato drove out strange priests and philosophers.[22]

But to no avail. For Rome, though it had no imperial theory, had acquired an empire with a rapidity and ease which its social structure could not digest.[23] Moreover, conquest had given the imperialist temper of the city a momentum which its earlier struggles in Italy did not foreshadow. The spread of wealth unconnected with merit or the spirit of public service completes the pattern: the substitution of "nobles" (rich men) for patricians (men of good birth); of *proles* (faceless members of a mob) for plebeians (plain but solid fellows). Sallust draws us a painful picture of the results:

> The whole world, from the rising of the sun to its setting, subdued by [Rome's] arms, rendered obedience to her; at home there was peace and an abundance of wealth, which mortal men deem the chiefest of blessings. Yet there were citizens who from sheer perversity were bent upon their own ruin and that of their country.[24]

And with the mob even worse:

> For in every community [thus corrupted] those who have no means envy the good, exalt the base, hate what is old and established, long for something new, and from disgust with their own lot desire a general upheaval. Amid turmoil and rebellion they maintain themselves, without difficulty, since poverty is easily provided for and can suffer no loss.[25]

How different from the men who defeated "Pyrrhus, Hannibal, Philip and Antiochus, if not for [their] liberty and [their] own hearthstones [then for the] privilege of submitting to nothing but the laws."[26] I conclude my abbreviated Roman model with that potent conjunction. Liberty meant in this milieu access to one law, not freedom for "self-realization" (whatever that now signifies):

dignity meant incorporation in that law, but not equality. Sallust informs us that, once the old kings fell from disrespect for liberty in law, living with senate, consuls, tribunes, and people under that ancient, common and impersonal authority made "everyman to lift his head higher and to have his talents more in readiness."[27] This was the *concordia ordinum* of Cicero.[28] Its significance was not lost upon 1688 English Whigs who could see in the Roman balance what they had themselves achieved *with* and *through* a king. And it was the obvious burden of Roman history for the English colonials in North America who lived in constant fear of despotic subjection, burdened by a sense of general decline in the moral fiber of their world—a decline with its source in England.

But Americans, in creating a new republic, a modified Whig Rome, were proving to themselves that by sundering the link with England they were resisting despotism and arresting the corruption of their fellows: that is, such of their countrymen as were prepared to honor law, the unwritten prescription, and the *patria* (their lesser homelands, the chartered colonies *qua* states). *Virtu* was demonstrated in every assembly, on every battlefield. Personal honor and the unselfish keeping of oaths were both assumed. But responsible liberty was the precondition for all of these elements of character: liberty restricted by a given identity and channeled by a will to cohesion shared by a number of discrete political entities and kinds of people. And, as with the Romans after Lucius Junius Brutus had done his work, the law and the prescription were actually strengthened by removal of the king from the American Whig configuration. New arrangements among persons and states, to institutionalize what they were (and what they were becoming, by insisting on that character) seemed necessary. And especially after war. But no founding—any more than the Roman Republic had been an invention or creation out of whole cloth. As for confederation, Rome did a lot of that, absorbed to defend itself any who accepted its values, could reinforce its strength and needed the protection that combination could provide. Assuredly, Americans were a rural people, in the habit of governing themselves, with almost every freeholder a potential man-at-arms. Europeans, and especially the English who fought them, marvelled at the warlike firmness of these "embattled farmers." And soon enough they came to prefer such of their number as could be recruited to serve in red to the mercenaries George III sent over. Add to this a general commitment to inherited religion and the pattern is complete. Once the die was cast, among such a people—a community which "knew the literature of Rome far better than they did that of England"—it is no marvel that, in making the break official, "the young boasted they were treading upon the republican ground of Greece and Rome."[29]

I will not attempt to record all of the available expressions of self-conscious Romanism coming down to us from the original United States. For they are numerous enough to form a work of two large volumes. Indeed, they were so numerous, positive, or even assertive that Gouverneur Morris of Pennsylvania complained of the "pedantry" of "our young scholars . . . who would fain bring everything to a Roman standard."[30] Yet Morris grumbled in vain. For the analogy which he found to be oppressive informed the conduct of even so unintellectual and representative a public figure as the commander of our armies and then first President, George Washington. Consider for an instance Washington's manifesto

in answer to Burgoyne's demands for submission, August 1777: "The associated armies in America act from the noblest of motives, liberty. The same principles actuated the arms of Rome in the days of her glory; and the same object was the reward of Roman valor."[31] Pure Livy—and from a man who kept a bust of Sallust on his mantel, who loved to be identified as a Cincinnatus, and who quoted regularly from the *Cato* of Joseph Addison, his favorite play. And if Washington behaved in this way, what Romanizing would we expect to find among his more bookish, intellectually curious peers?[32]

But what surprises is not the Roman predominance in this early American passion for antiquity. For Augustan and later English neoclassicism was always principally an admiration for, and emulation of, Rome—not Greece. The difference on this side of the Atlantic was a matter of degree—of frequency and intensity in political application of the example. And especially outside of New England.[33]

However, though I cannot cite every offhand remark that confirms the pattern of allusion suggested by Washington, I must expand somewhat upon the echoes of Roman history distributed among the sayings of our political forefathers in order to establish a ground for my final arguments concerning their implications for the interpretation of our national beginnings. And to this end I will emphasize a representative set of "rebels": Patrick Henry of Virginia, John Dickinson of Pennsylvania, and John Adams, the Squire of Braintree, Massachusetts. I commence with Henry because his draft upon the Roman model was so homely and so completely of a piece with his American Whiggery. For these reasons, and because he represents the untroubled *romanitas* of the South, where that attitude put down its deepest and earliest roots. Dickinson

I include because he was one of the reluctant revolutionaries—a legalist or Erastian for whom the English Whig and Roman regimens coalesced into one (still predominantly English) instruction for American colonials. And also in recognition of his importance as a spokesman for the sensible Middle Colonies. John Adams is an obvious choice. For no colonial American was a deeper student of the history and political importance of earlier republics than this brilliant New Englander. Furthermore, he functions in pointed contrast to the perfectibilitarians so frequently spawned in the Zion of his nativity. Not one of this trio was an egalitarian, an optimist, or a devotee of "propositional, teleological politics." And not one was a *democrat* of the sort we are often led to imagine that such men must have been.

Though Patrick Henry was, with the possible exception of Washington, more frequently compared to the great figures of the Roman Republic than any American of his time, he was almost as little a scholar as his illustrious friend upstate. But what he did study, he knew well. Says William Wirt, his first serious biographer, Henry read "a good deal of history." And Livy "through, once at least, in every year during the early part of his life."[34] To what effect this concentration, we all know. But it is wise to consider the impact of Henry's vigor and *gravitas* on the leading men of his own era. Only there can we recognize the premeditation in his achievements as patriot *qua* orator, his emulation of Livy's heroes. St. George Tucker in recalling the performance before the Virginia Convention of March 23, 1775 ("Liberty or Death") asks us to "imagine this speech delivered with all the calm dignity of Cato of Utica; imagine . . . the Roman Senate assembled in the Capital when it was entered by the profane Gauls. . . ."[35] And George Mason, when recalling his great contemporary's total career as keeper of the common *virtus,* of the memory that makes for honor, could go so far as to write that ". . . had he lived in Rome about the time of the first Punic War, when the Roman people had arrived at their meridian of glory, and their virtue was not tarnished, Mr. Henry's talents must have put him at the head of that glorious commonwealth."[36]

So seemed Henry to the end of his life when he thundered against the ahistorical, impious ideology of the French Left. So even when, in 1788, he fought the ratification of the Constitution by summoning up the togaed exemplars of his boyhood dreaming, to say "nay" once more to power, to protect the hearth and rooftree.[37] Reasoning from the universality of his impact, we can assume with confidence that there was calculation in Henry's Roman posture, a sense of what could be accomplished by cultivating the Roman analogy running throughout his entire career. From his sort of working classicism we can defend the claim of Charles Mullen that the "ancient heroes" of early Rome "helped to found the independent American commonwealth . . . not less than the Washington and Lees."[38]

Unlike Henry, John Dickinson was a thorough classicist. And a deep student of the law, trained in England at the Middle Temple. The former intellectual *habitus* was subsumed within the latter. Against the usurpations of crown and Parliament, Americans had no better defender of their "historic" (as opposed to "natural") rights as Englishmen. And for such strictly prescriptive constitutionalism this pillar of the Philadelphia bar found much Roman precedent. In the late 1760s he could write with his beloved Sallust, *"Nihil vi, nihil secessioni opus est"* (No need for force, no need for separation).[39] Yet the promise of something more severe is just beneath the surface of his reasonable *Letters of a Farmer in Pennsylvania*: a determination epitomized in the words of Memmius as quoted by Dickinson from the *Jugurtha* in his final exhortation to his countrymen: "I shall certainly aim at the freedom handed down from my forebears; whether I am successful or not . . . is in your control."[40]

Indeed, Dickinson quotes as much Roman history as his purposes will allow. Like a good Whig, he insists that all Englishmen have their civil status (and are one) in the law, politically exist through that bond. King and Parliament have authority according to its dictates, not in themselves. Furthermore, the constitution (*prior to* and *the basis* of statute law) will be kept, even if some of the derivative elements of the transoceanic political structure surrender their connection to each other in its behalf. Dickinson's most recent editor is wise to set him over against "the rationalist view" of human justice which maintains that men are meaningfully "born" with "certain rights" on which they can insist, even if not specified in a particular social continuum.[41] That rights—even the most sacred—can be realized only in a specific history and are likely to disappear when the edifice which contains them is fractured, Dickinson never forgets. He invokes the bad examples of James II and of the Caesars of Tacitus who, by art, "ruined the Roman liberty" and practiced "dangerous innovation."[42] And especially in the matters of taxation, standing armies, and court manipulation. Two worlds, but one problem. In England there were, as Dickinson notes, men who denied that either English or Roman political history was of any significance in treating of the North American colonies,

men who prated of "indirect representation" and urged the King toward writs of fire and sword. But the Roman colonials, if citizens when they went out to form a new city, were still citizens once there—sometimes better citizens. And likewise American colonials, as secured in their charters binding on both King and Parliament. But he does insist, knowing with Cicero (Oration for Sextius) that never to be roused is to forget what honor demands.[43] His letters are the essential expression of that great middle body of Americans who continued to think and feel as a kind of Englishman, even when they had come with regret to join with their radical compatriots and insist on independence. And he continued to be the same kind of man as author of the original Articles of Confederation, and at Philadelphia in 1787.[44]

A discussion of John Adams in this context must be very restricted. For though a great "common law" man like Dickinson and a lifetime admirer of the "balanced" Roman constitution, a devout republican and *therefore* no democrat, his near stoicism causes him at times to plead universal law as a ground for rebellion: to plead as if he were a primitivist and theoretical uniformitarian like Jefferson (at his worst) and Paine, a meliorist with a habit of ignoring historic circumstance. These passages, *solus*, are, however, misleading. Adams pled "higher law" only in the spirit of Burke, as something sometimes visible and partially preserved in "the cake of custom"—and especially after regular English cooking; or as something obvious, like the right of self-preservation."[45] I identify this part of his politics with those of the not-too-Puritan, not antinomian members of the 1641 English Parliament: and with the authors of the 1689 Declaration of Rights. It was Adams's view that England, once the Stuarts were expelled, became through its constitution ". . . nothing more nor less than a republic in which the King is . . . first magistrate."[46] And that the situation of Americans changed very little when the King, as administrator of the given law ("a republic is a government of laws, and not of men" alone) failed in his duty, "abdicated," and had to be officially removed.[47] A republican is what Adams always was, even when loyal to George III.

But as American republican, Adams advocated consistently a "balanced constitution." And what he meant by this familiar language is, by reason of our ignorance of the classics, nothing like what we might imagine. Polybius is behind this facet of Adams's position, and also Livy. Particularly Polybius.[48] But more important (and encompassing these Roman instructions) is his view of how the English prescription, the great body of Whig theory, could be applied to the new situation created at Yorktown.[49] Adams in this respect clearly resembles Dickinson, combining English and Roman constitutionalisms, with the former retaining predominance: combining them in the quarrels before the Revolution; and, once the war was over, continuing with them in the effort to convert the resulting independence into a framework for sustaining a nationality already there. Adams had clearly a more rigorous mind, a more consistent theoretical position than his friend from Delaware and Philadelphia. Yet he is identical with him in refusing to accept Lockean or other rationalist conjectures about men in a pre-social state.[50] For him, a social contract was, if trustworthy, something worked out by a given people: worked out among themselves, over a period of time. Their existence as a people is, however, *a priori*. This is Polybius and Livy. No constitution, even if aimed at balance, could be better as a social bond than one "negotiated," whose develop-

ment itself was a source of mutual trust among the people whose unity it formalized. Adams understood balance in these terms and, in his *Discourses on Davila* (1791), said so: "While the [Roman] government remained untouched in the various orders, the consuls, senate, and people mutually balancing each other, it might be said, with some truth, that no man could be undone, unless a true and satisfactory reason was rendered to the world for his destruction." With this promise, liberty begins.[51]

Even in 1787, Adams's thought began with what was and had been, not with what might be. After the "tyrannical machinations" of George III had been forestalled, his fear was of the process well described by Livy, that by seeking perfect liberty Americans could well discover what real servitude is like.[52] Devotion to an inherited regime, as in the time-tested constitutions of the states, protecting legitimate holdings in property while securing to all citizens access to the same restricted body of laws, could hope to secure a general assent.[53] And if we were to go further with union, we should begin the process with a foundation in that devotion. Comity would be the result. *Inside* the American configuration, Adams struggled to conserve. In the year of the Declaration he could write a friend, "I dread the Spirit of Innovation."[54] What we often fail to see is that such dread is what *made* him a rebel and *still* a New England sort of American; an Englishman, once rebellion was done. Imbalance through foolish innovation should be expected, in a republic, to draw its support from the lower orders of society, as aggravated by ideologists and crafty demagogues. Not from the senatorial class, Adams's beloved republican gentlemen. And envy would be the cause. Titus Livius tells us nothing to the contrary. Nor the favorite of Adams's old age, gloomy Sallust. Following their example, he thundered against the "simple, centralizing schemes of Dr. Franklin and Tom Paine," defended the institution of senates, a strong elected executive, and a deference toward law in the conduct of popular assemblies.[55] And he cried out in alarm when certain of his countrymen conflated their own political inheritance with what had in 1789 begun in France.

But the best way to measure the indebtedness of John Adams to the history (and historians) of the Roman Republic is to look outside his published writings and beyond his public career: to the correspondence of his old age, and particularly his exchange with Jefferson. One scholar has observed that ". . . the greater part of Adams' historical investigations were devoted to studying governments which failed, he believed, because of their unbalanced structure."[56] This was true of his early preparations in response to the Stamp Acts. And it was true to the end.[57] Readings in Roman history were, however, only part of a larger, lifetime habit. As an aged man, he could claim that . . . classics, history and philosophy have never been wholly neglected to this day."[58] For the repose of his spirit, and the support of his judgment, he found these "indispensable."[59] The senectual epistles prove these words to be no exaggeration.

The Virginian, in contrast, was more Greek than Roman. His studies, like his experience, had made him sanguine. Above all else, Adams found in the classics warnings against men in the mass, unrestrained by precept or authority, corrupted by flattering politicians. Jefferson (especially in Tacitus, Suetonius, and other authorities on the Empire) saw more of a caution against concentration of power than an admonition to avoid egalitarian preachment, an "excess of words in the city." But finally, in the shadow of section-al conflict over the admission of Missouri as a state, the thought and language of the two old friends/old enemies came together. The end result of the centralizing that began in 1820 was both a concentration of power and triumph for the popular spirit of endless adjuration over "principles": the new founding of Abraham Lincoln, which Adams, as a New Englander, could spot on the horizon long before his Southern counterpart.[60] The French influence combined, in the years before secession, with the old Puritan montanism to undermine the civility and public spirit necessary to republican cohesion. In their place stood finally the politics of "continuing revolution" and capital-letter abstractions, the "Empire of *Equality* and *Liberty*" foreshadowed in Webster's reply to Hayne.[61] In consequence, the Roman republican teaching as a serious influence was thereafter generally confined to the nomological South. There survived the dream of ordered liberty saluted in the following lines, by an anonymous Charleston Whig of 1769:

Parent of Life! true Bond of Law!
From whence alone our Bliss we draw,
Thou! who dids'st once in antient
    Rome,
E'er fell Corruption caus'd its Doom,
Reign in a Cato's godlike Soul,
And Brutus in each Thought controul;
Here, here prolong thy wish'd for Stay,
To bless and cheer each passing Day,
Tho' with no pompous Piles erect,
Nor sculptured Stones, thy shrine is
    deckt;
Yet here, beneath thy fav'rite Oak,
Thy Aid will all thy SONS invoke.
Oh! if thou deign to bless this Land,
And guide it by thy gentle Hand,
Then shall AMERICA become
Rival, to once high-favour'd Rome.[62]

This vision of the political good I can trace from John Randolph's fulminations against bankers, cities, dole, and expediency *(alieni avidus sui profusus)* to Tom Watson's outcry against "A party for Pompey—A party for Caesar—No Party for Rome."[64] And beyond—i.e., until the South came to feel that the heritage of the Republic had become its exclusive possession, even in secession.[64] But that is another essay.

What then did Rome mean to the original Americans? What counsel did its early history contain? And what must we conclude about our forefathers from their somewhat selective devotion to the Roman analogue?

To begin with, in so far as the original national identity derives from a reading of early Roman history, our first Americans did not see in independence a sharp departure from the identity they already enjoyed. Rather, both of these developments were, above all else, necessities for the protection of an already established society: necessities like those behind Rome's own republican development. "Their respect for [that] past brought them to their rebellious and finally revolutionary posture."[65] Even in whatever they attempted that seemed new. All of which is another way of saying that *Romanitas* on these shores, to whatever extent that we may demonstrate its presence, is an indication that American Whiggery is (or was) closer to that of Edmund Burke than to the nostrums of Priestly and Fox. And is no relation whatsoever to the "virtue" preached by Robespierre. Burke's view of the ancient European orders transplants rather well in a locally structured commonwealth with no nobility and no established church. Indeed, as Burke himself discovered in conflicts with his King, it is perhaps more consonant with a pious, xenophobic republicanism under a specified tradition *qua* law than with monarchy."[66] A community of interdependent parts, inseparable and yet distinct, was the natural consequence of the growth of thirteen colonies as separate social, political, and economic units. The war with England had itself given the specific colonies unto themselves a new social maturity and cohesion, and to their citizens a horror of class conflict and internecine strife.

Roman history taught that all of this was natural: a commonwealth "grown," not made; a definition by history, not by doctrine or lofty intent; and a general recognition, negotiated in the dialectic of experience, that all Americans had together a corporate destiny and would henceforth depend upon each other for their individual liberties. Confederation for liberty: Roman history allowed for that one near-abstraction. But liberty, meaning collective self-determination and dignity under a piously regarded common law, is a check upon ideology, not a source.[67] For modern regimes the alternative is the hegemony of an ideal as end, not condition. And the arrangement becomes finally the hegemony of a man, a despotism which makes a noble noise. Between 1775 and 1787, we discovered no new doctrine. We left that to the English. Self-defense was our business. Courage and discipline were displayed. Also self-sacrifice. Furthermore, leaders filled with public spirit had appeared and had earned the confidence of their compatriots: leaders who would be available to call up, once again, the active virtue which had preserved "the walls of the city." King John and the Tarquins, Charles I and James II had together made Americans to know what was wrong with "emperors" and with George III. Once freed of his authority (and his provocations) they would aspire to no overseas dominion, employ no mercenaries, deify no administrator, and neglect no freeholding. Or, at least for a while, they would go from what and where they were, many and one, a culture of families, not so atomistic or commercial as *The Federalist* anticipates they were to become. Not deracinated, they would cherish the emotionally nourishing matrix of the unpoliticized communities to which they were primarily attached. And they would keep the "democratical" component of their position in perspective, tolerating no *Jacquerie* (*vide* Shay's Rebellion), no divisive feudal appointments—honoring their most deserving citizens with office and good repute, as in history. Their only innovative engagement would be in the creation of new states in the "open" lands to the west—states just like their own!

All of this composition and more our fathers could recognize in the history of Rome, in the "laboratory of antiquity" where lessons for their not-so-new science of politics seemed unmistakably clear. In between us and these self-evident truths stand the War Between the States and other, subsequent (and derivative) transformations. Plus a legion of historians from the party which triumphed in these "other revolutions." To penetrate their now accepted obfuscations and to see the elder Rome as did the first American citizens is an appropriate undertaking in these years of official self examination. Appropriate, painful, and surprising.

Notes

1. Hostility to Plato among colonial republicans was so great that it has puzzled all subsequent scholarship. But it is easily explained: Plato's politics are an *a priori,* theoretical creation, derived not from experience but from high doctrine and propositional truth. See 178–79 of Richard M. Cuminere's *The American Colonial Mind and the Classical Tradition* (Cambridge, MA: Harvard University Press, 1963).

2. This attitude toward history as a humane or ethical study was an Augustan commonplace. See for instance H. Trevor Colbourn's *The Lamp of Experience: Whig History and the Intellectual Origins of the American Revolution* (Chapel Hill, NC: University of North Carolina Press, 1965), 21–25; James William Johnson's *The Formation of English Neo-Classical Thought* (Princeton, NJ: Princeton University Press, 1967), 31–68; and Daniel J. Boorstin's *The Lost World of Thomas Jefferson* (Boston: Beacon Press, 1960), 218–19.

3. Cicero's *De Republica* was available only in fragments before 1820. But its arguments are suggested in the rest of Tully.

4. Cited in full, with the appended comment which I quote, in *Roman Civilization: The Republic* (New York: Columbia University Press, 1951), edited with an Introduction and Notes by Naphtali Lewis and Meyer Reinhold, 99–111.

5. *The Southern Tradition at Bay* (New Rochelle, NY: Arlington House, 1968), edited by George Core and M. E. Bradford, 98–111.

6. Hyperbolic but indispensable for the study of the full sweep of Roman piety is Fustel de Coulanges' century-old *The Ancient City.* I cite the Doubleday Anchor Books edition, New York, 1955, 38–40 and 136, *et passim.* Consider also the *Antiquities* of Vasso, the Stoic, as represented by Augustine in the *Civitas Dei.*

7. *Roman Civilization,* 482 (from *Natural History,* XXXV, 2). Polybius supports this view: *The Histories* (New York: Twayne Publishers, 1966), translated by Mortimer Chambers, with an introduction by E. Badian, 261–62.

8. But not in its essential impulse. Consider, for illustration, Horace's image of life on the Sabine Farm.

9. Plutarch, *Lives of the Noble Grecians and Romans,* translated by John Dryden and revised by Arthur Hugh Clough (New York: Random House, n.d.), 999. For support see Cicero's second oration against Verres, (*Roman Civilization,* 456).

10. R. H. Barrow. *The Romans* (Baltimore: Penguin Books, 1949), 11–14.

11. Tacitus is as often praised by Old Whigs, English and American, as any Roman historian. And his *Germania* has become infamous as a point of departure for various rhapsodies on the need for *gemeinschaft* and the merits of the organic (that is, unphilosophical) society. But his republicanism, apart from a few portraits, is too indirect for the purposes of this essay. It is, however, pervasive. See M. L. W. Laistner, *The Greater Roman Historians* (Berkeley, CA: University of California Press, 1966), 114; and Michael Grant, *The Ancient Historians* (New York: Charles Scribner's Sons, 1970), 271–305.

12. Plutarch, 928. From his life of Cato Minor, expressed by Cicero in response to the reduction by Uticensus, of the abusive orator Clodius.

13. See Livy, Book XXIV. I employ here the text as translated by Aubrey de Selincourt, *The War With Hannibal,* Books XXI–XXX of *The History of Rome from Its Foundation* (Baltimore: Penguin, 1970), 253. See also Laistner, 89, on the communal theme in Livy.

14. Sallust, "The War With Jugurtha," xli; I cite the Loeb Classical Library edition, edited by J. C. Rolfe (Cambridge: Harvard University Press, 1921), 223. See also Grant, 201–07.

15. Polybius, 222. See also 193.

16. Grant writes (228) that Livy's "account of the earlier Republic is largely one long narration of traditional Roman virtues."

17. Polybius, 229. In support see Livy, Book III, xvii. I cite the Loeb edition, edited by B. O. Foster (Cambridge, MA: Harvard University Press, 1939), 57–61: the speech of Publius Valerius. Also Grant, 240, *et seq.*

18. Livy, *The War With Hannibal,* 154–55.

19. Ibid., 385.

20. See Livy, Books III and IV; also Joseph M. Lalley, "The Roman Example," *Modern Age,* XIV (Winter, 1969–1970), 14.

21. I derive here (as did our fathers) from Baron de Montesquieu. See David Lowenthal's edition and translation of *Considerations on the Causes of the Greatness of the Romans and Their Decline* (Ithaca, NY: Cornell University Press, 1968), 91–92.

22. Plutarch, "The Life of Cato Major," 428.

23. In this connection I would recommend Arnold J. Toynbee's finest work, *Hannibal's Legacy* (Oxford: The Clarendon Press, 1965); and also Tenney Frank's *Life and Literature in the Roman Republic* (Berkeley, CA: University of California Press, 1956), 19–23.

24. Sallust, "The War With Catiline," xxxvii, 63 of the Loeb edition.

25. Ibid., xxxvii; still 63.

26. Sallust, "Speech of the Consul Lepidus," iv; 387 of the Loeb edition.

27. Sallust, "The War With Catiline," vii; 13 of the Loeb edition.

28. Cicero's vision of the social order depended upon his confidence in the "political manners" of the Romans, the force of the "public orthodoxy." Things in this *societas* were attempted in the way of political change only in an accepted fashion, a manner which postulated loyalty to Rome, regardless of personal success, or else the result would be forfeiture of status as citizen. On the difference between *societas* and *universitas* (nomological and teleological regimes) see Michael Oakeshott's *On Human Conduct* (London: Oxford University Press, 1975), 199–206. On Cicero see "Cicero and the Politics of the Public Orthodoxy," *The Intercollegiate Review* 5 (Winter, 1968–69), 84–100, by Frederick D. Wilhelmsen and Willmoore Kendall.

29. Gummere, 119 and 18.

30. Ibid., 14.

31. Ibid., 18.

32. Johnson, 91–105. Also Howard Mumford Jones's splendid chapter, "Roman Virtue," 227–72 and 96 of *O Strange New World* (New York: The Viking Press, 1964), Jones helpfully includes illustrations of Washington carved as a Roman senator.

33. See Charles F. Mullett, "Classical Influences on the American Revolution," *The Classical Journal,* 35 (November 1939), 92–104. Gummere admits (37) that the reformist temper, coming down from Puritanism, worked against the classical inheritance in New England. New England remained a *universitas,* even when Unitarian.

34. William Wirt. *Sketches of the Life and Character of Patrick Henry* (New York: McElrath and Bangs, 1835), 31. Henry also read one political theorist, Montesquieu,

whose constant text was Livy. See Richard Beeman, *Patrick Henry* (New York: McGraw-Hill, 1974), 116.

35. Jay Broadus Hubbell, *The South in American Literature, 1607–1900* (Durham, NC: Duke University Press, 1954), 120.

36. Quoted in Kate M. Rowland's *The Life of George Mason 1725–1792* (New York: G. P. Putnam's Sons, 1892), Vol. I., 169.

37. Gummere, 186.

38. Mullett, 104. Henry of course was not unique in this emulation. And it may have been unselfconscious, the reflex of an intense admiration like that of Charles Lee when he told Henry, "I us'd to regret not being thrown into the World in the glorious third or fourth century of the Romans" but changed when he could say that his classical republican dreams "at length bid fair for being realized." Quoted in Gordon S. Wood's *The Creation of the American Republic, 1776–1789* (Chapel Hill, NC: University of North Carolina Press, 1969), 53.

39. Gummere, 107,

40. In *Empire and Nation,* containing "Letters From a Farmer in Pennsylvania" and Richard Henry Lee's "Letters From the Federal Farmer" (Englewood Cliffs, NJ: Prentice-Hall, Inc., 1962) ed. with an Introduction by Forrest McDonald, 84.

41. Ibid., xiv.

42. Ibid., 35 and 10.

43. Ibid., 71.

44. The best description of this middle party, who made the Revolution possible and then controlled its results (away from Jacobinism) in drawing up the Constitution, is in Merrill Jensen's *The Founding of a Nation: A History of the American Revolution, 1763–1776* (New York: Oxford University Press, 1968). John Dickinson, as their spokesman, went so far as to oppose the Declaration of Independence as both too early and too ambiguous in its language. But he accepted the results and went out with his neighbors. Dickinson's greatest influence may have been toward the establishment of a Continental Congress and, in the Constitutional Convention of 1787, in the creation of a United States Senate with two seats for each state.

45. George A. Peck Jr., ed., *The Political Writings of John Adams* (Indianapolis:

Bobbs-Merrill, 1954), xxiv of the editor's "Introduction."

46. Colbourn, 96. Also *The Political Writings of John Adams,* 44.

47. Colbourn, 87. Adams was a chauvinistic New Englander and therefore blind to the differences between his own legalism and the antinomian, "revealed politics" of Cromwell and other Puritans. He seems not to know that many Erastians followed Charles I. But he is clear about the settlement of 1688–89.

48. Gilbert Chinnard, "Polybius and the American Constitution," *Journal of the History of Ideas,* 1 (January 1940), 38–58. See also Richard M. Gummere's "The Classical Politics of John Adams," *Boston Public Library Quarterly,* 9 (October 1957), 167–82, and Zoltan Haraszti, *John Adams and the Prophets of Progress* (Cambridge, MA: Harvard University Press, 1952). On the link between the Whigs and Polybius see Zera S. Fink, *The Classical Republicans* (Evanston, IL: Northwestern University Press, 1945). Colbourn, 102.

49. Colbourn, 102.

50. *The Political Writings of John Adams,* Peck's "Introduction," xv.

51. Jones, 260.

52. Livy, III, 121 of the Loeb edition. Also Peck's "Introduction" to Adam's *Political Writings,* xviii.

53. I refer to his *A Defence of the Constitutions of Government of the United Slates* (1786–87). Here and in his early *A Dissertation on the Canon and Feudal Law* (1765) Adams identifies New England as the perfection of the English tradition.

54. Colbourn, 87.

55. *The Political Writings of John Adonis,* 105, 119, and 132.

56. Colbourn, 87.

57. See Vol. VI, 12, 43, 86–87, 209, 217 and 243 of Adams's *Works,* the edition of Charles Francis Adams (Boston: Little Brown, 1850–56), 10 volumes. But the influence of Roman history is evident throughout his political writings. See especially the *Novanglus* (1774–75).

58. Colbourn, 85. By "philosophy" he meant, for the most part, ethics and "political philosophy."

59. Gummere, 193.

60. Adams in answering Governor

Hutchinson, 1773. Quoted by Colbourn, 98. The difference between this paper and the rantings of other Sons of Liberty is instructive. Such radicals, of course existed, but the Revolution was not finally their show.

61. See Richard Weaver's "Two Orators," *Modern Age,* 16 (Summer–Fall 1970), 226–42.

62. Hubbell, 161. Quoted front the *South Carolina Gazette.* I suspect that the author may have been William Henry Drayton. See Jones, 254, for a related passage from Richard Henry Lee.

63. This echo from Sallust's "The War With Catiline," iii, is quoted on 164 of Russell Kirk's *John Randolph of Roanoke: A Study in American Politics* (Chicago: Henry Regnery, 1964) and is part of an extended philippic against American declensions

from "republican virtue"; Watson's remark seems to come from Cato Minor's orations in Lucan's *Pharsalia.* See C. Vann Woodward's *Tom Watson: Agrarian Rebel* (Savannah: The Beehive Press, 1973), 109 and 353.

64. A good illustration is Major Buchan, the patriarch in Allen Tate's *The Fathers* (Denver: Alan Swallow, 1960).

65. Colbourn, 186.

66. Indeed, no society is likely to be as xenophobic as a racially homogenous republic. The only equivalent would he a monarchy uniting strictly patriarchal tribes.

67. See Richard Henry Lee, *An Additional Number of Letters from the Federal Farmer to the Republican* (Chicago: Quadrangle Books, 1962), 178. Reprint of the edition of 1788.

68. Wood, 51–52.

Charles R. Kesler

The Higher Law and "Original Intent": The Challenge for Conservatism

VOL. 22, NO. 2, 1987

It would not be much of an exaggeration to say that political debate in America today takes place between two camps—conservatives and liberals, realists and idealists—whose stock arguments are familiar to anyone who reads a daily newspaper. On the side of realism one expects to find the defenders of the national interest, skeptics of the welfare system and of social reformism in general, believers in the funded wisdom of the past (whether invested in the marketplace or in social customs or in the church). On the other side one expects to find defenders of transcendent international morality (human rights, the Law of the Sea, etc.), compassionate believers in the morality and efficacy of the Welfare State, and prophets of future progress who see the past as mere prologue, and its funded wisdom as poor if not, indeed, bankrupt.

To be sure, one doesn't always find what one expects in politics (there are those strange bedfellows, remember), and in any case these descriptions are only rough-and-ready sketches. But they are useful at least in a preliminary way, to suggest the intellectual and rhetorical disadvantage under which present-day conservatives force themselves to labor. For the truth is that many conservatives *like* to think of themselves as "fact" men— realistic, hard-nosed, practical—and are proud to leave "values" to the liberals. But in politics a good "value" will beat a plain "fact" any day. This is, after all, precisely the way that liberals explain President Reagan's political successes—his simplistic but nonetheless stirring invocations of "traditional American values" tend to win out over a Jimmy Carter's or Walter Mondale's mastery of the "facts." And up to a point, they are right.

As the case of President Reagan shows, however, conservatives do have "values," even if these "traditional American values" (President Reagan's favorite formulation) appear to be valuable only because of the "fact" that they are part of our tradition. Besides, the insistence on sticking to "facts" is itself a judgment of value. The assertion of value-judgments in politics is inescapable because politics is *about* "values;" more precisely, it is about which "values" or opinions get to rule. To some conservatives this is sufficient reason to shun politics altogether. To most conservatives this is a good reason to have as little as possible to do with politics, which is itself an easy excuse for the political failures that American conservatism has suffered in the past and may suffer again in the final years of the Reagan administration.

Take, for example, the important series of questions raised by Attorney General Meese under the rubric of "the jurisprudence of original intent." In the past, such questions would eventually have ascended from particular cases to general principles to the intention of the Constitution as a whole and hence to what earlier generations of constitutional scholars had learned to call the "higher law" above even the Constitution. Almost sixty years ago, Edward S. Corwin, in his classic little book *The "Higher Law" Background of American Constitutional Law*, traced the intentions of the Constitution and the source of the American people's abiding respect for those intentions to the idea that the Constitution was an "embodiment of an essential and unchanging justice." In Corwin's words:

> There are . . . certain principles of right and justice which are entitled to prevail of their own intrinsic excellence, altogether regardless of the attitude of those who wield the physical resources of the community. Such principles were made by no human hands; indeed, if they did not antedate deity itself, they still so express its nature as to bind and control it. They are external to all Will as such and interpenetrate all Reason as such. They are eternal and immutable. In relation to such principles, human laws are, when entitled to obedience save as to matters indifferent, merely a record or transcript, and their enactment an act not of will or power but one of discovery and declaration.

This admirable description might be applied to the American case by saying that the Constitution was thought to embody the principles of the Declaration of Independence—the "Law of Nature and Nature's God" and the "unalienable Rights" claimed under those laws. Respect for the Constitution was therefore understood to be part of a high obedience to the natural law, to the fundamental rules of justice ordaining, moderating, and limiting majority rule. The duties of judges under the Constitution were accordingly not radically different from the duties of citizens. Judicial review depended upon popular veneration of the Constitution (see *Federalist* 49), which as an embodiment of "the nature and reason of the thing" (*Federalist* 78) authorized experts in the law to review popular legislation for its consistency with the declaratory law. The judges' task was not to create law or to exercise their policy preferences, but to interpret and defend the Constitution that the people revered, and by preserving its justice, to render it worthy of continued reverence.

This understanding of the judges' task has not, alas, fared well in this century, either with liberals or, as we shall see, with conservatives. The symptoms of its breakdown are apparent even in Corwin's eulogy of the "'higher law' background" of the Constitution. The "higher law" is not the same as the natural law; and though his book is almost entirely concerned with the influence of the natural law tradition on American constitutionalism (he views divine and common law in the light of natural law), he seems to prefer the term "higher law" not so much because it is more comprehensive but because it is less controversial. It frees him from having to debate the theoretical presuppositions of the natural law, because the truth—and therefore the content—of it is not in question. Only its influence as a belief—the "fact" that it was a widely held "value"—is of scholarly concern.

"Natural" or "Higher" Law

Yet in the end it is not scholarly convenience that decides against the natural law. "It has become a commonplace," Corwin writes, "that every age has its own peculiar categories of thought; its speculations are carried on in a vocabulary which those who would be understood by it must adopt, and then adapt to their special purposes." This is in the first place not a hermeneutical but a rhetorical principle. To be understood by your time you must speak its language, but are free to use that language for your "own special purposes." Corwin does not clarify whether the objects of knowledge to which words refer have an existence independent of the conventions of language—and for good reason, as he soon reveals. "Nowadays," he continues, "intellectual discourse is apt to be cast in the mould of the evolutionary hypothesis. In the seventeenth and eighteenth centuries, the doctrine of natural law, with its diverse corollaries, furnished the basic postulates of theoretical speculation." Clearly, the dominance of what he is scrupulous enough to call the "evolutionary hypothesis" results in an acute problem for the natural law. If nature is forever changing, and toward no particular ends, then how can it have an unchanging law? It cannot, unless that law is itself a law of change. This is "'natural law' in the sense of 'the observed order of phenomena,'" commanding only the survival of the fittest; and it is this sense of the term, Corwin notes, that has crowded out the "rationalistic" or "Ciceronian" definition in modern times. Hence perhaps his preference for the "higher" law,

meaning (in particular) higher than the struggle for existence—though how such a law could exist (mythically? deontologically? miraculously?) is never made clear.

That the natural law is a law of progress would seem to be a dictum of the progressive view of politics—Woodrow Wilson said exactly that—and hence of modern liberalism. Strangely, however, it has come to be shared by many conservatives as well, and in particular by some of the most influential conservative jurists and philosophers of law, including many of those leading the charge for a return to "original intent." Corwin, writing in 1928, had already placed the "higher law" in the "background" of American constitutional interpretation, but the modern history of constitutional jurisprudence exhibits the increasing dominance of the foreground.

By foreground I do not mean the text of the Constitution. There have from time to time been legal positivists on the Supreme Court, eager to confine the meaning of the Constitution to its positive provisions, whether for purposes of restricting or enhancing judicial power. But they have been exceptional, and anyway the Constitution does not *say* that it is to be interpreted positivistically or literally; so jurisprudence that lives by positivism runs the risk of dying by positivism. Instead, the rule has been to interpret the Constitution by implicit or explicit reference to some extra-constitutional standard. Originally, this was the law and rights of nature: The debate between strict and liberal constructionists was over the extent of federal power, and ultimately over the kind of citizenship, required to secure men's rights and to conform to the natural law.

This debate seemed to have been resolved, at least politically, by the Civil War. With the advent of Darwinism and its philosophy of history in American intellectual life, however, the victory of strict constructionism proved to be temporary. With the "evolutionary hypothesis" firmly implanted in the judicial mind, the debate between strict and liberal construction was gradually transformed into the contemporary debate between judicial restraint and judicial activism. What the disputants in the current controversy have in common is the premise that since there are no natural ends that the law ought to serve—that man's reason can apprehend in the nature of things—the only question to be answered is whose *will*—the legislature's or the court's—should be the source of law. Although philosophically considered this would appear to be nothing more than a beginning question in the positive theory of law, practically it is a question that has required a theory of history to answer.

Why is this so? The positive theory of law requires a clear definition of sovereignty, but America has never had one. Or, to put it more precisely, the United States has had from the beginning a notion of sovereignty that is itself complicated and ambiguous, two things that the idea of sovereignty should not be. Indeed, much of the American argument against the British Parliament's efforts to exert authority over the colonies in the years after the Seven Years' War was dismissed out of hand by learned men on both sides of the Atlantic, as an attempt to divide the indivisible phenomenon of sovereignty, to construct an *imperium in imperio*—a fallacy in political reasoning so blatant as immediately to call into question the Americans' good motives. Of course, that didn't prevent our forefathers from continuing to press the argument, nor from redefining sovereignty to meet the argument's needs, nor from winning the war.

With the locus of sovereignty now moved from the Parliament (or the King-in-Parliament) to the people, in 1788 the American people approved the Federal Convention's choice of a new Constitution that seemed to express the people's sovereignty by bifurcating it between the national and state governments. Veterans of the losing side in the Revolution, not to mention other acute observers, could be forgiven the thought that the sin of *imperium in imperio* was about to be visited unto the seventh generation of Americans. But in the decisive respect, the division in the American understanding of sovereignty was not between the state governments and the Union, but between the people's liberty and the law that entitled them to liberty. The sovereignty of the people, after all, is a deduction from the rights and laws of nature. And so long as it was understood that in America, "the law is King," to use Thomas Paine's ringing phrase, then the people could be sovereign only in a subordinate and conditional way. But to say that sovereignty is subordinate, much less conditional, is, strictly speaking, nonsense. To that extent, America has gotten along without a strict theory of sovereignty for the very reason that it has adhered to the natural or higher law tradition.

The Problem of Sovereignty

Having denied, however, that the natural law or the dictates of prudence could be "sovereign" in the traditional (rational or pre-Darwinian) sense of the term, the critics of American constitutionalism were faced with a difficult question. Where *was* sovereignty located in America? In the people? the state legislatures? the national legislature? the Supreme Court? If sovereignty was understood purely from the standpoint of will, it was difficult to see where the supreme law-making power of the society was lodged, or even by whom it had been authorized. To meet this difficulty, theorists of American law—most famously, Oliver Wendell Holmes Jr.—turned to history. As Holmes declared on the opening page of his influential *The Common Law*: "The life of the law has not been logic; it has been experience. The felt necessities of the time, the prevalent moral and political theories, intuitions of public policy, avowed or unconscious, even the prejudices which judges share with their fellow-men, have had a great deal more to do than the syllogism in determining the rules by which men should be governed." If federalism, the separation of powers, and the constitutional obstacles to amendment make it impossible to determine where the supreme law-making will was meant to be vested in American government, then the only recourse was to the history of the actual distribution of power as a guide to the effective locus of sovereignty.

So "experience" became a better guide than reason or logic. But experience cannot be a guide to what ought to be done unless it revealed a regularity in events or a constant rule of action. In Holmes' formulation, the abstract question of the rules by which men "should be" governed becomes reduced to the historical question of the rules by which men have been governed. The "felt necessities of the time" tend therefore to become reified as the real necessities of the time: law becomes a product not of a reasonable will but of the historical state of a people—their "felt necessities," "prevalent . . . theories," "intuitions," and "prejudices" rolled into one. Not to mince words, Law is transformed into an expression of the "spirit of the age," and the task of govern-

ment—in particular, of the courts—is to see that the law does not depart from that spirit.

It is this understanding that has largely guided commentary and interpretation of the Constitution in the succeeding years. As a result, the Constitution has increasingly come to be seen as a species of common law, pronounced by judges (or, perforce, congressmen, presidents, and bureaucrats—but that is another story) not, however, according to the standards of the genuine common law—i.e., right reason or as a determination of the natural law—but according to some view of the nation's place in the stream of history. There are more progressive and more conservative interpretations of constitutional common law, but their disagreements concern the pace and timing of progress, not its sovereignty or even, properly considered, its beneficence.

Thus, in apostolic succession from Justice Holmes, the mantle of interpreting the "felt necessities of the time" has passed down to Louis Brandeis and (with a psychoanalytical twist) Jerome Frank and Earl Warren and now William Brennan. The pity is that conservative jurists seem to have no substantial alternative to offer. Judge Robert Bork, for example, holds (in his American Enterprise Institute lecture, "Tradition and Morality in Constitutional Law") that "our constitutional liberties arose out of historical experience. . . . They do not rest upon any general theory," including, of course, natural or higher law theory. Chief Justice Rehnquist, in his renowned essay on "The Notion of a Living Constitution," argues that if a democratic society

adopts a constitution and incorporates in that constitution safeguards for individual liberty, those safeguards do indeed take on a generalized moral rightness or goodness. They assume a general social acceptance neither because of any intrinsic worth nor because of any unique origins in someone's idea of natural justice but instead simply because they have been incorporated in a constitution by the people. Beyond the Constitution and the laws in our society, there is simply no basis other than the individual conscience of the citizen that may serve as a platform for the launching of moral judgments. There is no conceivable way in which I can logically demonstrate to you that the judgments of my conscience are superior to the judgments of your conscience, and vice versa.

There is, in other words, no right or wrong by nature, but only "a generalized moral rightness or goodness" that arises simply because a majority agrees to incorporate certain social value judgments into a constitution.

Whereas the doctrines of liberal jurists leave us with no defense against judicial supremacy or tyranny, the doctrines of the conservatives leave us with no defense—indeed, not even an argument—against majority tyranny. At the same time, paradoxically, they also undercut any moral argument for lawful majority rule; for if there is no rational basis for value judgments or judgments of conscience, why should the will of the majority be accepted as the rule? Because they are stronger? But it is often the case that a vehement minority is stronger than a quiescent majority; and besides, what kind of a moral or legal principle is the right of the stronger?

Sad to say, but these conservative jurists are only a part of a larger problem within the conservative intellectual movement in America. The return to a "jurisprudence of original intent"—like the genuine grounding of conservatism in the American political tradition—remains unconsummated, because it is perplexed by what it finds in the writings and speeches of the American founders. One will not find many leaders of the conservative intellectual movement ready to affirm that "We hold these truths to be self-evident, that all men are created equal, that they are endowed by their Creator with certain inalienable rights. . . ." And that is the nub of the problem. Our forefathers did not radically separate "facts" and "values," did not place their faith in the "facts" of progress as over against the subjective "values" of morality, did not try to wrap the dictates of history up in the guise of the dictates of prudence.

On the bicentennial of the U.S. Constitution, no approach to the original intentions of the founders is conceivable—hence no authentic American conservatism is possible—without realizing that for them, the facts of human life implied the rights of man, and man's natural rights in turn served as a standard to which the facts of political life had, gradually, prudently, democratically to be conformed. The "is" implied the "ought," and the "ought" was meant to guide the "is" to the fulfillment of its proper character or purpose. That was, and is, the meaning of the natural or higher law in the American political tradition. Recovering that meaning is the great intellectual and political challenge confronting conservatism in the Constitution's third century.

George W. Carey

How Conservatives and Liberals View _The Federalist_

VOL. 25, NO. 1, 1989

Conservatives—American and otherwise—have always held _The Federalist_ in extremely high regard. Virtually all would agree with Clinton Rossiter that it stands with the Declaration of Independence and the Constitution among the "sacred writings of American political history."[1] And some might even agree with the more lavish assessment of Chancellor Kent who wrote that he knew of no finer work "on the principles of free government," not even those of "Aristotle, Cicero, Machiavelli, Montesquieu, Milton, Locke, or Burke."[2] On the other hand, I think it fair to say, liberals would scarcely be as unified or laudatory in their appraisals.

Why are conservatives so attracted to _The Federalist?_ Why do they hold it in such esteem? Most answers to these questions would involve its complementary relationship to the Constitution and Declaration of Independence; that is, its role relative to the official documents of the founding era. Jefferson touched upon one side of this relationship when he wrote that _The Federalist_ is the work "to which appeal is habitually made by all, and rarely declined by any as evidence of the general opinion of those who framed and of those who accepted the Constitution of the United States, on questions as to its genuine meaning."[3] In this vein, numerous justices over the decades have almost elevated _The Federalist_ to the status of fundamental law. Still others see it as providing the theory and "constitutional morality"—i.e., a morality, not to be found by reading the Constitution with an innocent eye, that informs us how its institutions and processes should operate—that bridges the gap between the Declaration and the Constitution by spelling out, authoritatively and in greater detail than any other source we have, how the Constitution secures the goals and ideals of the Declaration.[4]

These reasons taken together point to the fact that conservatives see a continuity in our tradition in which _The Federalist_ performs an indispensable role. By contrast, as we will see shortly, liberals see no continuity. Indeed, quite the opposite: they are inclined to look upon _The Federalist_ as an elaborate justification for the derailment of our "true" tradition.

In what follows I want to develop and set forth other and more basic reasons—

228   _Four Decades of the_ INTERCOLLEGIATE REVIEW

quite apart from those that derive from any complementary relationship—why Publius's teachings are, or should be, inherently attractive to conservatives, and why, moreover, his approach and concerns transcend the particular circumstances surrounding the ratification struggle. To put this a bit differently, I want to indicate why *The Federalist*'s approach and teachings are enduring, still highly relevant to today's world, and why, to quote Washington, they will "always be interesting to mankind so long as they shall be connected with civil society."[5]

Oddly enough, a convenient way to come to grips with what I regard to be the more significant and enduring aspects of Publius's approach and teachings—and we may presume as well those of most of the founders—is to examine the dominant and persistent criticisms that have been leveled against them. Such an examination forms a splendid backdrop for an appreciation of Publius's lasting contributions.

Publius's Critics

Beginning in 1907 with the publication of James Allen Smith's *The Spirit of American Government*,[6] the Founding Fathers, the Constitution, and *The Federalist* (both critics and friends understandably tend to lump them together) have come under sustained attack from the academic or "intellectual" left. These attacks, as we will see, vary in approach by concentrating on different aspects of the founding era, but they all echo the same basic themes that Smith dwelt upon. The first of these, quite simply, is that the Constitution was not designed to provide for popular government. Smith found it difficult to see "how anyone who had read the proceedings of the Federal

Convention could believe that it was the intention of that body to establish a democratic government." On the contrary, he insisted, "Democracy—government by the people, or directly responsible to them—was not the object which the Framers of the American Constitution had in view."[8] What the delegates sought to do, he argued, was to draft a document "just popular enough" to avoid "general opposition" and to secure its adoption, but which would, in effect, give the people little by way of real political power.

With regard to what the Framers were "up to," Smith's work was soon eclipsed by Charles Beard's *An Economic Interpretation of the Constitution of the United States* published in 1913.[9] Beard's work possessed all the trappings of a scholarly inquiry, the heart of which was a partial, but original, inquiry into the economic interests of the members of the Philadelphia Convention. Beard concluded that "[t]he movement for the Constitution was originated and carried through principally by four groups of personality which had been adversely affected under the Articles of Confederation: money, public securities, manufactures, and trade and shipping."[10] But these findings, largely refuted by later scholarship, were really quite secondary to the main message of the book which reflected the contemporary frustrations of the left wing of Progressivism. As Douglass Adair remarked, on Beard's showing these "radicals and reformers" were denied the opportunity to transform America "into a land where social justice prevailed," "not" as they believed "by a usurping court" which had invalidated certain of their programs, "but by the sacred word of the Constitution of 1787." "Beard's answer" to this dilemma, according to Adair, "was to expose the nature of that Constitution, to unmask its hidden features in order to show that it deserved no veneration, no respect, and should carry no authority to democratic Americans of the twentieth century."[11]

A second and related theme set forth by Smith, and one which is still very much alive in one form or another, is that the Framers betrayed the principles and ideals of the Declaration of Independence. In his view, the Constitution was a deliberate effort to curb the democratic forces that had been unleashed by the Revolution. "The adoption" of the constitutional system, he contended, represented "the triumph of a skillfully directed reactionary movement."[12] In this regard, he noted the absence of "Samuel Adams, Thomas Jefferson, Thomas Paine, Patrick Henry, and other democratic leaders of that time" from the Philadelphia Convention. Indeed, he pointed out that although the Constitutional Convention convened "only eleven years after the Declaration of Independence was signed . . . only six of the fifty-six men who signed that document were among its members."[13]

While it is clear that Beard also believed the Constitution served to thwart "progressive" notions of social and economic justice, he did not elaborate on these notions or set forth his vision of a better society. This was a task undertaken by Herbert Croly, whose influence, albeit indirect, is still evident today in liberal quarters. Croly did subscribe to the Beardian thesis that "the Constitution was . . . 'put over' by a small minority of able, vigorous and unscrupulous personal property owners,"[14] but his major concern was to spell out the Progressive ends—the substance of what he called the "Promise of American life" or the "National promise"—and how they might be realized. Aware that to achieve these ends required a strong national government, he was not nearly as harsh on the Framers as Beard

or Smith. He could even find much to admire in Hamilton's efforts on behalf of "constructive national" policies because they demonstrated the potential of a strong national government to promote the common good.

Here we cannot treat of all the specifics of Croly's "National promise" because they involve far reaching changes in almost every aspect of the social, economic, and political fabric of society. As he acknowledged, he was advocating "a radical transformation of the traditional national policy and democratic creed." Yet certain key aspects of his program are noteworthy. He did not believe that a truly democratic nation should "accept human nature as it is, but . . . move in the direction of its improvement." (He accepts John Jay Chapman's assertion that "Democracy assumes perfection in human nature.")[15] Part of this improvement involved what Croly termed "individual emancipation" which, in turn, required that the individual be prepared and willing "to sacrifice his recognized private interest to the welfare of his countrymen." "Not until his personal action is dictated by disinterested motives," he contended, "can there be any such harmony between private and public interests."[16] And, at various places in his writings, he specifies means designed to produce this harmony. For instance, "selfish acquisitive motives" ought to be de-emphasized and replaced where possible in the economic field by encouraging "excellence of work."[17] He believed that the state, in assuming the responsibility "for the subordination of the individual to the demand of a dominant and constructive national purpose," should also assume the responsibility "for a morally and socially desirable distribution of wealth."[18]

Vernon L. Parrington in the first of his monumental three-volume *Main Currents in American Thought*—dedicated to James Allen Smith—embraces and develops the basic framework and propositions of the leftist critique of the founders. He accepted Beard's economic determinism and contended that Madison's tenth *Federalist*, with its emphasis on economic divisions and factions, represented "pretty much the whole Federalist theory of political science." With Smith, he held that "an honest appeal to the people was the last thing desired by the Federalists." Similarly, he bemoaned the Federalists' attacks on "the democratic machinery of recalls and referendums and rotations in office, which had developed during the war" by alleging that these were "factional devices" which would render "good government" impossible.[19]

More importantly, however, Parrington reconceptualized the essence of Croly's concerns about democracy and the American political experience by placing them in a broader historical and theoretical context. According to Parrington, the founders (and Publius) essentially accepted "English liberalism" which "was self-seeking, founded on the right of exploitation, and looking toward capitalism." In so doing, he argued, they rejected "French radicalism" embodied in Rousseau's philosophy whose "ultimate ends . . . were universal liberty, equality, and fraternity." This French radicalism, in Parrington's words, "was humanitarian, appealing to reason and seeking social justice," the outgrowth of Rousseau's conviction that "[a] ruthless social order is forever perverting the natural man; whereas if social rewards were bestowed on the social-minded, the innate sense of justice would speedily modify and control the impulse to egoism."[20] In sum, French radicalism pointed the way toward Croly's emancipated individual and, as Parrington would have

it, "a skillful minority"[21] (the Federalists) turned the majority away from his path.

Although a good deal has been written over the decades to counter the "good guy/bad guy" version of our founding era characteristic of the Progressive historians and commentators, its essential elements are still part of the intellectual mainstream,[22] particularly among the historians. Thus, Gordon Wood can write in his widely praised *Creation of the American Republic* that "through the artificial contrivance of the Constitution overlying an expanded society, the Federalists meant to restore and to prolong the traditional kind of elitist influence in politics that social developments, especially since the Revolution, were undermining" and that "The Constitution was intrinsically an aristocratic document designed to check the democratic tendencies of the period."[23]

More significantly, Wood writes of "a fundamental transformation" of the "political culture" which had "taken place" between "the Revolutionary constitution-making of 1776" and "the formation of the federal Constitution of 1787."[24] In this regard, he observes, "The sacrifice of individual interests to the greater good of the whole formed the essence of republicanism and comprehended for Americans the idealistic goal of their Revolution."[25] Alas, he contends, this classical view of "public virtue"—the "willingness of the individual to sacrifice his private interests for the good of the community"[26]—had all but disappeared by the time of the Constitutional Convention. What is striking in his account are the parallels between this "classical" public virtue, Parrington's "French radicalism," and the characteristics of Croly's "emancipated individual."

Publius and Human Nature

Let us put the foregoing to one side for the moment and briefly examine Publius's views on human nature (and presumably those of a majority of the founding fathers as well). Clearly these views are a critical component of his thinking and bear a very close relationship to the why's and wherefore's of our constitutional structure and processes. But I think they are particularly important in pointing up wherein Publius's teachings differ fundamentally from those of his critics. This, in turn, leads us to fundamental and abiding reasons why conservatives should feel at home with *The Federalist*,

We can profitably begin with perhaps the most famous passage of *The Federalist*: "If men were angels, no government would be necessary" (322).[27] This sentence is usually taken to mean that Publius held to a rather "low" or "pessimistic" view of human nature. In fact, this passage is noteworthy because it reminds readers in a rather striking way of their existential status—i.e., we are mortal, we are not perfect, we are prone to various kinds and degrees of conflict that necessitate the existence of earthly, superintending authority. The reminder is highly important, but the message is couched in terms that render it little more than a mild "put down."

That is not to say that Publius doesn't picture man in "dark" terms. Certainly one of his most straightforward accounts arises in connection with his estimate of the consequences of a rejection of the Constitution with the states remaining independent sovereigns or forming partial confederacies. Such a situation, he warns, would involve the states or confederacies in "frequent and violent contests with one another." To believe otherwise, to assume that the states or confederacies would

peacefully coexist, he argues, "would be to forget that men are ambitious, vindictive, and rapacious" (6:54). In this same vein, he cautions that "our political systems" should not be modeled "upon speculations of lasting tranquility" because this would be "to calculate on the weaker springs of the human character." "To judge from the history of mankind," he explains, "we shall be compelled to conclude that the fiery and destructive passions of power reign in the human breast with much more powerful sway than the mild and beneficent sentiments of peace" (34:208). Or one need only look as far as the famous *Federalist* 10 to appreciate the dangers of faction, particularly majority factions, the "causes" of which "are sown in the nature of man" (84). Scarcely anything could speak more directly to his views regarding human nature than this.

Publius gives us many examples of the darker side of human nature. But he alludes to the brighter side as well. The final portion of the last paragraph of *Federalist* 55 is the most widely cited passage to show that he was not totally pessimistic about man's nature. While scarcely a ringing affirmation of the innate goodness of man, he does write: "As there is a degree of depravity in mankind which requires a certain degree of circumspection and distrust, so there are other qualities of human nature which justify a certain portion of esteem and confidence" (346). Similarly, he asserts in *Federalist* 76 that "The institution of delegated power implies that there is a portion of virtue and honor among mankind," and that "[a] man disposed to view human nature as it is, without either flattering its virtues or exaggerating its vices, will see sufficient ground of confidence in the probity of the Senate" (458–59) to prevent its domination by the executive through use of his appointment power.

It is tempting to conclude from these and other passages that could readily be produced that Publius held to a "mixed" view of human nature—mostly "bad" but enough "good" mixed in to provide the basis for republican government. This, or one very close to it, would seem to be the prevailing understanding of Publius's position. Yet, whatever merit it may have in describing his general stance, it scarcely provides us with anything resembling a coherent view of human nature. In the words of James Scanlan, such a formulation is itself "theoretically functionless."[28] We know, for instance, that Publius makes a number of judgments and predictions throughout *The Federalist* concerning how individuals or institutions will behave in differing circumstances. But unless he did so on the basis of some coherent theory of human nature from which he systematically derived his judgments, we are left to guess about the bases for his conclusions. For instance, without a coherent theory, we would have no way of determining whether or not he was simply subscribing to whatever assumptions happened to serve his immediate purposes.

As Scanlan so ably points out, there is—as we would have every reason to expect—an underlying theory of human nature in *The Federalist*; a theory best expressed in terms of propositions relating to human motivation. Scanlan identifies three categories of motives that are central to Publius's thinking: passion, reason and virtue, and interest. While it is well beyond our purpose here to elaborate fully on Scanlan's analysis, one general finding merits our attention: Publius operates on the assumption that "immediate self-interest" will usually predominate over "reason and virtue," "true" interest, or long-term "common" interest when these motives come into conflict.[29] We see as

much in his treatment of the proposition, advanced by "visionary and designing men," that "commercial republics will never be disposed to waste themselves in ruinous contention with each other."

> Is it not (we may ask these projectors in politics) the true interest of all nations to cultivate the same benevolent and philosophic spirit? If this be their true interest, have they in fact pursued it Has it not, on the contrary, invariably been found that momentary passions, and immediate interests, have a more active and imperious control over human conduct than general or remote considerations of policy, utility, or justice? Have republics in practice been less addicted to war than monarchies? Are not the former administered by men as well as the latter? Are there not aversions, predilections, rivalships, and desires of unjust acquisitions that affect nations as well as kings? (6:56)

Publius does admit of exceptions to the domination of immediate interests. In *Federalist* 10, he acknowledges the existence of "enlightened statesmen," individuals who can "adjust . . . clashing interests and render them all subservient to the public good." But, he writes, such individuals "will not always be at the helm," thereby suggesting that at best they will be few in number. What is more, by way of indicating the strong pull of immediate self-interest, he points out that even if they were at the helm, such adjustments would be rare in those matters which require that "indirect and remote considerations" be taken into account. These considerations, he states, "will rarely prevail over the immediate interest which one party may find in disregarding the rights of another or the good of the whole" (80).

What is clear is that the Constitution is not built on the premise that subsequent generations are to count on enlightened statesmen. At least Publius operates on the assumption that immediate self-interest will prevail. This is evident in his conviction that no man (or party) ought to be judge of his (its) own cause. This is why, as a reading of Federalists 48 through 51 will reveal, reliance is placed upon "ambition counteracting ambition" to preserve the constitutional separation of powers. Primary reliance on the people for this purpose would, he believed, result in Congress—the likely trespasser—judging of its own action. Likewise, this is the basic reason why he regards legislation for states, rather than for individuals, to be the "great and radical vice" of the Articles: the states' compliance with national law will hinge, not on the common good, but on "their [the states'] immediate interest or aim; the momentary convenience or inconveniences, that would attend its adoption" (15:111).

Publius's Enduring Legacy

Much more could be said about how a recognition of these motivational propensities, and the corollaries that flow from them, influenced the form of our constitutional procedures and institutions. The critics' charges that the institutions are "undemocratic," I should note in passing, clearly fail to take into account Publius's concerns to neutralize these tendencies. Even so, as I have shown elsewhere,[30] contrary to what his critics maintain, Publius defends nothing that would impede deliberative majorities from ruling consistent with republican principles. But let us leave that matter for another day and turn straightaway to the basic issues that separate Publius from his critics.

As I have already intimated, these issues may be cast in terms of reasons why conservatives so readily and enthusiastically identify with *The Federalist* and its teachings.

One reason seems obvious enough: Publius recognizes the dark side of human nature and accommodates to this reality. For instance, a goodly number of his "selling points" consist of showing how the proposed Constitution will operate to resist the "downward pull" of men's motivational propensities. Beyond this, one of the most notable aspects of his theory is that these less than noble propensities can be pitted against one another for good ends. His claim that majorities will "seldom" coalesce on principles other than "justice and the general good" is credible precisely because it is not based on the assumption that "emancipated individuals" will predominate in keeping with the principles of "French Radicalism" or "classical republicanism." Put another way, Publius's approach is based on the proposition that adjustments must be made for motivational propensities of man if a political system is to survive and fulfill its ends.

This points to other reasons why conservatives can and do fasten to *The Federalist*. To begin with, while clearly recognizing the imperfections of men, Publius makes no claims that the new Constitution will provide the means for their perfection or "elevation" to new plateaus of reason and virtue. Though he does believe that good government might serve to alter the behavior of men for the better,[31] the thrust of his arguments would strongly suggest that he took human nature as a "given." In his mind, it seems clear, institutions had to be accommodated to human nature, if for no other reason than it would be impossible to fashion human nature to institutions.

He proceeds in his discourse as if human nature, at least in terms of motivation, has been constant over the centuries; that it is the same in all countries; and that, most significantly, it is unchangeable. He rejects the very idea of a "golden age" that holds out "promises of an exception from the imperfections, the weaknesses, and the evils incident to society in every shape" (8:59). He writes, too, of the "true springs by which human conduct is actuated" (15:110)—i.e., the passions, as well as immediate self-interest—that is everywhere to be observed and necessitates government. Whatever the case might be with regard to his general views, however, it is evident he presumed that we will never be free from the "downward pull."

On this score, Publius stands in sharp contrast to his critics who cling to an almost entirely different set of assumptions. They hold that, just as the Constitution served to corrupt a basically virtuous people by embracing "English liberalism," the people can be saved or redeemed, the "National promise" fulfilled, through social and political readjustments. Given an institutional and social setting—i.e., one instituted to impart and to reinforce virtue and reason—men can be made to abandon acquisitiveness, to place the general welfare above their individual interests, to curb their passions. Thus, man's nature is malleable—perfectible even.

The divide that separates Publius from his critics can be put in more striking and general terms. Publius never ventures far from existential reality. This fact alone is of enormous significance because we find none of the elements of gnosticism or utopianism of the Enlightenment in *The Federalist* that were to play such a significant role in the French Revolution. To borrow from J. L. Talmon's framework of analysis, Publius was caught up in what

can be termed a political enterprise; that is, his undertaking was concerned with the "concrete data of experience, by reference to logic and to the limitations inherent in any given historical situation."[32] As Talmon points out, "[p]olitics involves a choice between evils or, more charitably, an acceptance of the second best" because it deals with "very intractable material," that is, "men."

Quite different from "Politics," Talmon informs us, is "Utopianism," which simply "postulates a definite goal . . . for the attainment of which you need to recast or remold all aspects of life and society in accordance with some very explicit principle."[33] With the "Age of Reason," he continues, the belief in the goodness or perfectibility of man led to the conviction that "absolute justice based on the supremacy of reason could and would be achieved," that there could be, given a "rational order," "a harmonious reconciliation of all interests."[34] But Utopianism, Talmon writes, leads ultimately to "totalitarian coercion:" when the promised salvation—the harmony, peace, happiness—is not forthcoming, the culprit must be "evil forces" (not, of course, human nature) and "to frustrate" these forces requires "forceful intercession to lend a helping hand" so that "destiny" can "take its predetermined course."[35]

From Talmon's account, we can see just how wide the gulf is between Publius's teachings and Utopianism with its inevitable evils. In this respect, we may say that *The Federalist* reflected a fundamental American disposition, an uneasiness with the "isms" that hold out the prospects of earthly salvation, which is still very much with us. We can also better appreciate the significance of the distance that separates Publius from his Progressive critics. To be sure, Publius writes of "new" and "improved" "principles" of the "science of politics" and he urges his countrymen to abandon the classical teachings concerning the possibilities of republican government over an extensive territory. Yet he urges nothing which, given the sentiments and experience of the American people, is wild or chimerical. His concern, we may say, is to provide for an orderly and decent government, one better and more effective than the Articles, not one whose mission is to reconstruct society or the individual to conform more closely with objectives derived from some ideological construct. Moreover, and leaving to one side the question of the desirability of such objectives, *The Federalist* also asserts the truth of limited government: that is, the notion that there are things which government cannot do, no matter how hard it might try. Beyond this, of course, Publius's recognition of the imperfection of man, of those human propensities that could lead to wickedness and folly, clearly suggest that he also believed that there are any number of things government *should* not do.

Apart from the fact that these reasons tell us why *The Federalist* will always enjoy a warm spot in the hearts of conservatives, they constitute reminders that republican regimes are not free from the fundamental difficulties which arise from man's nature; that decent and orderly republican government requires more than merely elections, toleration, and a sufficient degree of "pluralism"; and, inter alia, that sweetness and light do not flow as a matter of course from self-government. Put another way, Publius's concern with existential reality, his awareness of the intractable nature of man and the need to make adjustments to it, stand in sharp contrast to the euphoric expectations frequently associated with every advance of "liberal democracy." This alone should have a sobering effect on the democratic globalists in our midst, particularly those who profess to use the American model as their guide.

Notes

1. Introduction to *The Federalist,* Clinton Rossiter, ed. (New York: New American Library, 1961), vii. All subsequent citations to *The Federalist* in the text are to this edition,

2. Quoted in Gottfried Dietze, *The Federalist: A Classic on Federalism and Free Government* (Baltimore: Johns Hopkins Univ. Press, 1960), 6. Chapter one of this work provides probably the most extensive review of general appraisals of *The Federalist.*

3. Quoted from introduction to *The Federalist Papers,* Roy P. Fairfield, ed., 2nd ed. (Baltimore: Johns Hopkins Univ. Press, 1981), xiii. On this point also see Danny M. Adkison, *"The Federalist* and Original Intent," *Political Science Reviewer* (1987).

4. An excellent book of essays which attempts to show how this gap is bridged in *Saving the Revolution,* Charles R. Kesler, ed. (New York: The Free Press, 1987).

5. Quoted from Rossiter, introduction, viii.

6. James Allen Smith, *The Spirit of American Government,* Cushing Strout, ed. (Cambridge, MA: Harvard Univ. Press, 1965).

7. Ibid., 31–32.

8. Ibid., 29–30.

9. Charles A. Beard, An *Economic Interpretation of the Constitution* (New York: Macmillan, 1913).

10. Ibid., 324.

11. Douglass Adair, *Fame and the Founding Fathers,* Trevor Colbourn (New York: W. W. Norton, 1974), 85.

12. Smith, 37.

13. Ibid., 33.

14. Herbert Croly, *Progressive Democracy* (New York: Macmillan, 1913), 49.

15. Herbert Croly, *The Promise of American Life* (New York: Macmillan, 1911), 418. He is quoting from John Jay Chapman's chapter on "Democracy" From his *Causes and Consequences.*

16. Ibid., 418.

17. Ibid., 415.

18. Ibid., 23.

19. *The Colonial Mind*, vol. I of *Main Currents in American Thought* (New York: Harcourt, Brace and World, 1927), 290.

20. Parrington, 276.

21. Parrington, 277.

22. We have, for example, Robert Dahl's elaborate and widely heralded critique, with which most political scientists are well acquainted, of Madison's major contributions to *The Federalist*, delivered some fifty years after the publication of Smith's book. Dahl concludes from his analysis that "Madison [understood to mean a majority of the Framers, as well] wished to erect a political system that would guarantee the liberties of certain minorities whose advantages of status, power, and wealth would, he thought, probably not be tolerated indefinitely by a constitutionally untrammeled majority. Hence majorities had to be constitutionally inhibited." *A Preface to Democratic Theory* (Chicago: Univ. of Chicago Press, 1956), 31. For a devastating and near definitive critique of Dahl's analysis see Ronald M. Peters Jr. "Political Theory, Political Science, and *A Preface to Democratic Theory,*" *Political Science Reviewer* (1977).

23. Gordon Wood, *Creation of the American Republic* (Chapel Hill, NC: Univ. of North Carolina Press, 1969), 513.

24. Ibid., viii.

25. Parrington, 53.

26. Ibid., 68.

27. All citations in the text are to the Rossiter edition.

28. James P. Scanlan, "The *Federalist* and Human Nature," *Review of Politics* 21 (October, 1959), 659.

29. Scanlan also points out that "antagonistic passions" (envy, jealousy, avarice) like "immediate" and "personal" interests will usually prevail over "amicable passions," "reason and virtue," "true" or "common" interests.

30. George W. Carey, "Separation of Powers and the Madisonian Model: A Reply to the Critics," 72 *American Political Science Review* (March, 1978).

31. He can see how forbearance might come about after the people have grown accustomed to the institutions and processes and are convinced of their fairness and judiciousness. See, for instance, Federalists 51 and 63.

32. J. L. Talmon, "Utopianism and Politics," George Kateb, ed. *Utopia* (New York: Atherton Press, 1971), 92.

33. Ibid.

34. Ibid, 94.

35. Ibid., 95.

M. E. Bradford

How to Read the Declaration: Reconsidering the Kendall Thesis

VOL. 28, NO. 1, 1992

Our collective confusion about the American experience begins at the beginning. Most Americans who think about such questions imagine that they understand the Declaration of Independence, though many of them may be puzzled that it did not (and does not) produce the results one might expect from the commitments which they believe it makes. After much misleading, they take the task of interpreting it to be a belaboring of the obvious, even though they know very little about its text, its content, or the moment in history that produced it. For by the spokesmen for one tradition in American politics they have been carefully taught to apprehend the document in a certain selective way: that is, by the tradition usually acknowledged by press and electronic media, pulpit and textbook maker; the tradition which is perhaps too confident of itself, even though it has brought forward nothing in the way of proof for its favorite assumptions. So much is indeed self-evident truth.

But it is likewise true that for the first one hundred years of our national existence the Declaration of Independence was usually understood in another way, according to a theory that reads its commitment to government based on "the consent of the governed" and to the aboriginal sameness of all men in their right to a certain order of political experience as a statement about citizens in their corporate character, as they enter the social state. In this tradition "all men" is taken as a statement about human nature that is made specific by subsequent language concerning the Creator. Men are formed to live under the authority of a particular sort of government. Or so the Signers maintained. The Marquis de Chastellux observed that they meant by "all men" primarily "all citizens or property holders"—substantial persons who owned land and probably slaves. Or all nations of men. The Marquis was attempting with this formulation to explain why almost no one among the colonial leaders of American society argued that the Declaration of Independence required of their country an internal social and economic revolution. In his opinion, by the word "people" they meant nothing so universal as the "half philosophers" among his countrymen sometimes intended when they spoke of humanity in general. He was quite correct in observing that the purpose of the American Revolution was to preserve (or restore) a known felicity, not to create a new one: not to transform and elevate mankind "in general," even though we might, after the fact of independence, congratulate ourselves for having done so. Certainly the forms taken by the declarations of rights adopted in most of the original thirteen states would seem to support his argument. For a majority of them speak of the status of men "once they enter into a state of society," or (like South Carolina) they refuse to speak of rights at all. The Virginia Declaration of Rights was drawn specifically so as to prevent misunderstanding about any disposition to free the slaves. Other documents are careful about suffrage. But I believe there is a better way of deciding what is meant by "all men are created equal" than by falling back upon circumstantial paraphrase of an astute French observer. For I think the Declaration can be read according to the canons of formalist literary criticism as a structure, as a literary artifact or system within which each component modifies and reinforces the implications of every other paragraph, phrase, or word operating within the whole.

FROM THE very beginning of the Declaration of Independence, the voice that addresses us is plural: issuing from one group of people toward mankind at large. It presupposes a "people," most of whom think of political life as occurring through their participation in some collectivity: or by way of several such identities operating simultaneously. And it presupposes other nations of men (and men within nations) as audience. The last sentence of the Declaration which encapsulates its form also speaks of a "we" who pledge "our lives, our fortunes and our

sacred honor." And throughout the text there is evidence that everything which is maintained subsists in the plural. Taken that way, the second sentence of the Declaration concerns the minimum grounds for the acceptance of a government by the people who live under it: that it not threaten the lives or properties or hopes for a future entertained by its citizen members; that it at least do better than the Great Turk. Taken this way, the human nature (and natural law) affirmed by the Declaration is the minimum expectation that may be assumed as the ground for the legitimacy of the state. God made men for civil life, but not for an absolute submission to a state that promises them no protection in return and denies them the hope of improving their condition. All men are created equal (i.e., are alike) in this respect. For such a total state to claim a right to obedience goes against the God-given qualities of human nature.

Part of the way of testing these assumptions about interpreting the Declaration comes from asking questions about what happens to the coherence of the text if its prologue is said to deal with the natural rights of pre-social individuals. Only thus is sentence two an epitome of the entire document. Understanding equality in the opposite fashion, however, creates fewer problems. Writes Daniel Boorstin, recently our Librarian of Congress, "[w]e have repeated that 'all men are created equal,' without daring to discover what it meant and without realizing that probably to none of the men who spoke it did it mean what we would like it to mean." Just before the adoption of the Declaration, the Virginia Convention on May 15, 1776, urged that the Congress "declare the united colonies free and independent states" on the grounds of "the eternal [i.e., natural] law of self-preservation." Hence a phrase concerning all men (i.e., human communities) and their expectations of any government not merely tyrannical. The list of offenses under English law charged against King George III and Parliament and the body of the Declaration work outward from the given elements of law to the necessity for a prologue concerning the collective reaction to tyranny in North America. The spirit of all this material derives from the Glorious Revolution of 1688, when James II had forfeited his crown after setting himself above the law that made him king—with the English constitution being sovereign, not the will of the prince.

Above and beyond English law is the tradition alive in all Christian civilization that legitimate authority, "government long established," should be obeyed, even though it is sometimes mistaken in its operations: that there should be no revolution for "light and transient causes." George III in his 1775 "Proclamation for Suppressing Rebellion and Sedition" had put his North American subjects beyond the protection of law and then made war on them. He had fostered servile insurrections, he had armed savages and had otherwise offended against "the common blood." These charges cannot logically co-exist with an egalitarian and universalist prologue of the kind usually assumed in the now conventional reading. If origin and history and belief make no difference, why is it wrong to hire German troops or to offer freedom to the slaves or the means of self-defense to the Indians? Only by maintaining (as Lincoln does) that most of the Declaration is unimportant can the advocates of the popular version of its meaning sustain their position. Lifting three or four words out of context, they sail along merrily. On the other hand, if the text means what Stephen Douglas and Jefferson Davis,

Henry Clay and Franklin Pierce thought it meant—that Americans are not inferior to Englishmen as a citizenry—then all of its parts work together to one effect, especially Jefferson's ironic comments about a "Christian King" who has "plundered our seas, ravaged our coasts, burnt our towns, and destroyed the lives of our people." As a matter of fact, we know that the bill of particulars maintained at law is what the signers of the Declaration thought to be important about it. Even though it is true that when representative government is established, and operates regularly over a period of time, it has as one of its side effects a degree of equalization, giving *incidentally* more liberty to more persons: true despite the fact that there is no design at work to effect such a purpose. About these republican developments no one complained—and no one but Charles Pinckney generalized, observing how rare were our "official" inequalities.

WITH SO much said concerning the formalist technique for reading the Declaration of Independence as a forensic whole, a political bill of divorce, I am now ready to make a few observations on the status of the document as it relates to the United States Constitution. Legal separation on grounds drawn from the English constitution was a necessary preliminary to independence, to the receipt of French and Dutch assistance, and to the Confederation of those erstwhile colonies who speak with the authority of their instructions from the various legislatures as a "we" joined in revolution and assembled in the Continental Congress. For that reason the Declaration is printed in the United States Code just before the Articles of Confederation. Independence and confederation were prologue to Union. And the Articles of

Confederation as a gloss upon the second sentence of the Declaration warn us not to make that sentence a promise of either equality of condition or equality of opportunity for all of the inhabitants of the new country. Mr. Lincoln at Gettysburg notwithstanding, Willmoore Kendall was correct when he maintained that "the Declaration of Independence does not commit us to equality as a national goal." The document creates no authority at law. It does not mandate any legislation or policy. It alters the status of no man or woman—except as it preserves to them a portion of their heritage under the now broken British constitution. It is not a prologue to the United States Constitution. For that instrument says almost nothing about equality of any kind.

The Declaration neither obligates nor binds Court or Congress in any way—as American statesmen specify repeatedly in the period running from 1790 through 1820. Moreover, the notion that the Declaration was designed to have one meaning in its own time and another one today, sometimes the doctrine of President Lincoln, goes against everything that we know about human nature in that it imagines Christian men obliging their children and grandchildren to conduct vast and potentially dangerous social and political experiments that they are unwilling to see attempted in their own time and place. That a decision to proceed in this way was made by an entire generation no sensible person can believe. I call this the "ticking bomb theory" of the Declaration. It is impressive only to those anachronists who have a special interest in discovering hidden meanings in materials that have heretofore seemed to be obvious in their burden; the expression of a sentiment that becomes a command. Since these theorists of unfolding meanings can find little to encourage them in

the speech, writings, or conduct of the Framers, we cannot take them very seriously. As for those who, in the tradition of abolitionist jurisprudence like that of Senator Charles Sumner and Thaddeus Stevens, would sift the Constitution back and forth through the Declaration of Independence until it is swallowed up by their view of that text, I can only respond with the language of Justice James Iredell, who in the 1798 case of *Calder v. Bull* observed that "ideas of natural justice are regulated by no fixed standard" and are no basis for setting aside the acts or decisions of legislative powers. The legislative process, he argued, was the place for revisions of the national identity, especially by way of amendment.

Modern scholars, jurists, and legal historians—such as are indeed chiefly interested in what the Constitution *ought to say*—are often surprised by its general silence on the laws of nature and the rights of man: its procedural, nomocratic character. Like Carey McWilliams in his afterword to the recent *Ratifying the Constitution*, they are often disturbed at not finding such an emphasis in our fundamental law or in the context which originally gave it force and authority. But if they are generally in search of the truth of things, they can do no other than agree with McWilliams that "the Constitution made no explicit appeal to natural right" and that this omission was functional since Governor Edmund Randolph maintained (on May 29, 1787), just before proposing what we now know as the Virginia Plan for replacing the Articles of Confederation, that the subject before the Great Convention was not "human rights" but how to get over too much democracy—"requisitions for men and money" and stable government.

As reported and summarized by Charles Warren, Randolph in Philadelphia says he is against "such a display of theory . . . since we are not working on the natural rights of men not gathered into society but upon those rights modified by society and interwoven with what we call the rights of the States." According to this teaching, "natural rights may be dangerous [to the entire social and political fabric of American life] . . . since the Constitution presumes the existence of and seeks to protect [i.e., secure] conventional rights." In the same spirit spoke Colonel Joseph R. Varnum of Massachusetts, who in that state's ratification convention, insisted that Congress, under the Constitution, had no right to alter the internal relations of a state; and Theophilus Parsons, famous attorney and judge from the same state, who "demonstrated the impracticability of forming a bill in a national constitution for securing . . . individual right." So also spoke Alexander Hamilton in the New York ratifying convention at Poughkeepsie: "Were the laws of the Union to now model the internal police of any state [or to] penetrate the recesses of domestic life, and control, in all respects, the private conduct of individuals—there might be more force in the objection [made against that Constitution]." And George Champlin of Rhode Island at South Kingston: "This Constitution has no influence on the laws of the States." But whether safe or potentially harmful, powerless or imperial in nature, according to Justice Iredell, the Constitution cannot be assumed to enact natural rights since these were meant to be defined under the police power of the states and localities: in the phrase of Edmund Pendleton, "our dearest rights in the hands of our state legislatures."

Of course, from time to time someone in Congress made reference to the Declaration before the War Between

States. Lincoln's allusions to that text are well known. And after the War, radical Republican spokesmen in the Congress appealed to the Declaration's statement about aboriginal equality whenever they were advocating Reconstruction amendments or legislation supposed to have special effect on the South. Other Republicans (and the Democratic minority) did not agree to act on such a basis. And the Chase, Waite, and Fuller Courts (to say nothing of those that followed) denied that metaphysical, a priori equality was part of the Constitution. The modern Court has of course made reference to the Declaration from time to time. Consider *Gulf C&S F Railroad v. Ellis*, 165 U.S. 150 (1897); *Butchers Union Co. v. Crescent City Live-Stock Co.*, 3 U.S. 746 (1884); *Northern Pipeland Co. v. Marathon Pipe Line Co.*, 458 U.S. 50, 60 (1982); *United States v. Will*, 449 U.S. 200 (1980); *Youngstown Sheet & Tube Co. v. Sawyer*, 343 U.S. 579, 641 (1952); *Nevada v. Hall*, 440 U.S. 410, 415 (1979); *South Carolina v. Katzenbach*, 383 U.S. 301, 359 (1966); *Parklane Hosiery Co. v. Shore*, 439 U.S. 322, 340 (1979); and *Faretta v. California*, 422 U.S. 806, 829 (1975). But these adversions to the Declaration in rulings by the Supreme Court are mostly of recent vintage. And none of the cases where they are found depend primarily on the Declaration for their authority. They merely drag it in for color.

Moreover, with legislative and judicial references to the Declaration there is always the problem of which version of that document, which reading, has been invoked—as when the Black Republicans on June 16, 1906, got a guarantee that the original state constitution for Oklahoma should contain nothing "repugnant to the Constitution of the United States and the principles of the Declaration of Independence" written into the Enabling

Act allowing that territory to take such steps toward statehood. And then, one year later, allowed the Sooner State to enter the Union under basic laws providing for the establishment of a segregated system of schools. It is not the simplistic version of the Declaration of Independence that played a part in these events. Though to this day—as witness Mortimer Adler's *We Hold These Truths*—the old Neoabolitionist convention for twisting the Constitution into a gloss and expansion upon the Declaration continues to hold its place in the political thought of the American Left and to function as an alchemical instrument for transforming the U.S. Constitution without legislation or amendment.

What the Declaration meant (and means) it achieved by way of its form. That significance is visible in what men did about its adoption. And in what they did not do.

Mark C. Henrie

Russell Kirk's Unfounded America

VOL. 30, NO. 1, 1994

In the very first *Federalist* paper, Alexander Hamilton claimed that at stake in the process of American constitution-making was a matter of world-historical importance. He wrote that the outcome of the American experiment would determine "whether societies of men are really capable or not of establishing good government from reflection and choice, or whether they are forever destined to depend for their political constitutions on accident and force."[1] From this perspective, the new American republic would constitute not simply a new nation among others, but a *novus ordo seclorum,* "a new order for the ages"; for the first time, the characteristically modern project of controlling fate through human ingenuity and craft would have been achieved. Furthermore, because of the principles made to prevail in the American Constitution, this country would emerge as the first "universal nation," a people bound not by blood, history, or divine election, but solely by political right. Indeed, the American people—as a people—would be a people without a past, a people with a future only. The progressive orientation of the American Revolution

illustrates how difficult it is to define an American conservatism.

Of course, the extent of America's liberation from the past has been exaggerated. The country surely does not lack some *pietas,* as any consideration of the temples built in Washington to honor the cult of the founders makes plain. Yet beyond the civil-religious piety for these particular ancestors, America perhaps inherits more of an older tradition than the patriotic narrative of the American founding, recounted above, reveals. And our forgetfulness of such an inheritance many constitute not only impiety, but injustice. Not least, we might notice that the style in which our new capital and its temples were constructed is not a "new" style at all, but a conscious imitation of classical Roman exemplars. What this and many other facets of our "way of life" indicate about the meaning of America was one of the most important questions explored by Russell Kirk.

Ever the conservative, Kirk attempted to demonstrate the *un*originality of the American Revolution. To him, ours was "a revolution not made but prevented,"[2] a conservative revolt against the novelty of George III's centralizing rule and Parliament's departure from past practice into direct taxation of the colonies. At a political level, Kirk was more impressed by the continuity between the arguments of 1688 (the "Glorious Revolution") and those of 1776 than by their differences, while he was more impressed by the discontinuity between 1776 and 1789 (the French Revolution) than by their similarities. Following Burke's implicit view and the arguments of such later conservative thinkers as Friedrich von Gentz,[3] Kirk distinguished the American experience from that of other nations during the so-called "Age of Democratic Revolution." What was truly *novel* about America's experience for Kirk was that it had undergone a political "revolution" precisely while escaping the ideological *novelty* of the age.

Furthermore, Kirk's view of the American Constitutional founding in 1787 was captured in his refusal even to speak of a "founding"—a word which conjures images of some Great Man, a Solon, Lycurgus, or Aeneas. A founding implies the quasi-divine legislation of an entirely new way of life, the *creation* of a people. Kirk, however, read the Constitution of 1787 as a reworking of traditional English and colonial American practice rather than anything new or particularly speculative. Certainly it is fanciful to imagine immediately deducing bicameralism, for example, from any postulate of natural right. For Kirk, just as the constitutions of the states were prudent revisions of colonial charters, so the 1787 U.S. Constitution was a slight adjustment of the Articles of Confederation. Kirk was surely correct that whatever the "intention" of the drafters of the Constitution, this was the "understanding" of the ratifying conventions of the states, whose consent established our political regime.[4]

Even if we can speak of an American founding, Kirk's conservative political science raised and attempted to answer questions which are otherwise begged in the patriotic narrative: Whence came that founding generation of Americans? Whence can we trace *their* "roots"? Some commentators ignore these questions, but only by presuming an ahistorical, "mythic" founding. On the other hand, to address such questions seriously, we cannot look only to the political order under which the founding generation were raised, for since the collapse of the unity of the ancient polis it is a mistake simply to equate the political regime with the totality of a way of life of a people. To determine who these men of the founding generation were—and who *we* are—we must look instead to tradition and culture, to all the elements of our civilization.

Here Kirk found his field, which was fitting. For conservative theorists have always been less interested in formal political institutions than in manners and mores. A fundamental proposition of conservative reflection on social matters is the supremacy of the "unwritten" constitution of a people to "written" political forms.[5] The many traditions that constitute a people are where we discover the meaning of our common life, for culture is deeper than politics. As Kirk put it, "Culture cannot really be planned by political authority, for much of culture is unconscious; and politics grows out of culture, not culture out of politics. . . ." Placing the American founding into the context of our cultural traditions yields quite a different understanding of the meaning of America.

Specifically then, Kirk insisted that America's is a "British Culture," one clearly continuous with that of our Anglo-Saxon forebears. We can speak of *our* Anglo-

Saxon forbears, for whatever a particular American's ethnic descent, our common life, Kirk believed, reveals a British heritage. Because Americans speak English, our most vivid common images and metaphors are the products of the British literary tradition. Politically, we inherit an attachment to the rule of law, a peculiarly Anglo-Saxon practice.[7] Kirk also drew attention to our appropriation of representative government and most fundamental of all, our heritage of Anglo-Saxon mores, manners, habits, and domestic institutions.[8] For Kirk, both our founders and we share this British culture, and this more than anything defines "us."

In arguing for America's foundation in British culture, Kirk was addressing only immediate antecedents. In an earlier work, he had explored at length the deeper roots of American order—roots which he traced down the ages to Jerusalem, Athens, and Rome, before they had reached London.[9] In each case, Kirk uncovered a decisive influence on the American way of life, though seldom was this a matter of political forms. Indeed, he observed that "America's political institutions owe next to nothing to the ancient world." More important, however, America is indebted to Jerusalem, Athens, and Rome for models of good character, theories of justice, and literary evocations of the human condition.[10] Together these form the horizon of our experience and establish the shared pre-theoretical understandings which generate a common agenda of philosophical questioning. Kirk emphasized what we share with Europe rather than what distinguished the New World from the Old. His recounting of an America bound to a particular past was meant to provide criteria for determining proper conduct as we faced a future which increasingly had no answer to that subversive question of ideological progressives: "why not?"

KIRK'S VIEW of an "unfounded" America has drawn perhaps more criticism than any other element of his thought, and the political theorist Harry Jaffa is only the most colorful of the critics. Jaffa champions an especially philosophical version of the patriotic narrative of the American founding. He has argued against Kirk that in fact "it *was* the paramount intention of the Framers of the Constitution, and of the people for whom they framed it, 'to institute new government' in the sense in which the Declaration of Independence speaks of instituting new government."[11] The sense Jaffa has in mind is in conformity with "the laws of nature and nature's God." He insists that "long before the decision for independence, it was clear that the ground of the American argument was not the English Constitution but 'the immutable laws of nature.'"[12] Thomas Jefferson thus emerges in Jaffa's writings as the quasi-divine Legislator who would found an American regime on "self-evident" truths requiring the rejection of "all traditions inconsistent with reason and nature." And Jaffa quotes George Washington to illustrate the intentional discontinuity of America's founding with European history: America's foundations were "not laid in the gloomy ages of ignorance and superstition; but at an epoch when the rights of mankind were better understood and more closely defined than at any other period."[13] The new American regime seems in Jaffa's mind to amount to the actualization of the life according to nature, a leap out of the traditional nomoi and into *physis*. In contrast to Kirk's America, where eighteenth-century gentlemen sought merely to protect their prescriptive "chartered rights" and continue unmolested in their way of life, for Jaffa ours is a regime committed to "abstract truth applicable to all men and all times."[14] For Jaffa, we are a nation "dedicated to a proposition."

Concretely, this dispute between Kirk and Jaffa reduces to a difference of opinion about the role of the Declaration of Independence in interpreting the character of the American regime. For Jaffa, the U.S. Constitution is only intelligible when understood as seeking to achieve the "abstract" aspirations of the Declaration. The propositions of natural right heralded in that document are the key to the regime.[15] Kirk on the other hand follows Willmoore Kendall: the Declaration is simply a political document designed to secure the support of France against England in the War of Independence. It does not articulate the central principles of our common life. Jaffa vehemently faults Kirk for thus "reading the Declaration of Independence out of the American political tradition."[16]

Jaffa objects to Kirk's depreciation of the Declaration's place in American history because as he understands the logic of natural law, the American regime is itself good *only* insofar as it secures the (equal) natural rights outlined in the Declaration. For Jaffa, the only serious alternative to such a Lincolnian understanding of the American regime is Calhoun's account of "states' rights," a view to which he finds conservatives like Kirk attached, and which he believes is philosophically indefensible.[17] At the heart of Calhoun's doctrine, Jaffa maintains, lies the *sui generis,* arbitrary power of the "sovereign" states, unrelated to, because underived from, natural law. Such political communities are at the deepest level "lawless"; not being products of "reason," they cannot be legitimate. Thus, to embrace their claims is to reject natural law.

But would Calhoun (or Kirk) recognize himself in Jaffa's recounting of this position? Without a teleocratic dedication to the (equal) rights of nature, Jaffa seems to believe that historically concrete communities amount only to collections of "mere will." Yet it is precisely this contention of the *philosophes* against which conservatives have so long marshalled their arguments. With their more modest view of the power of human reason to grasp the whole, conservatives find it reasonable to presume that the long historical existence of a practice or a community is itself evidence of its conformity to a Providential (rational) design. We know what the political good is by a reflection upon the historical experience of the community, rather than from a priori principles. Perhaps the most important thing we learn from history is that human living-together is for the good life in its totality and not merely for the securing of abstract rights with zealous single-mindedness. Yet without acknowledging the fact, Jaffa follows the moderns by holding the right absolutely prior to the good, while he strangely calls this "natural law." Indeed, sometimes Jaffa writes as if only the right were good. That for which Kirk would most fault Jaffa is his failure to acknowledge the genesis of his thought in the Enlightenment, and his failure to engage conservative arguments about the (meta-)rationality of tradition.

This dispute about the Declaration of Independence manifests a deeper philosophical point which Jaffa wants to press against Kirk. As suggested above, Kirk eschews "abstractions" concerning natural right and seeks to find guidance for political practice in history. Jaffa can only see this as straightforward "historicism." For without abstract principles, Jaffa finds it logically impossible to discern "guidance" in history: while the truth of natural right might from time to time be *found in* a tradition, natural right cannot be *founded on* tradition as such. For

Jaffa, "tradition" cannot be self-interpreting. Quite simply, tradition cannot tell you what parts of tradition are normative; only abstract principles can do that. Jaffa concludes that "modern liberalism" and "modern conservatism" (Justice Brennan and Judge Bork) "stand upon common ground"—both are "historicist" in believing that the truth of right emerges in history rather than remaining constant and beyond history. Both are "arbitrary."[18]

Two points must be made about this attack on Kirk's conservative methodology. First, Jaffa's argument rests on a controversial understanding of the powers and prerequisites of reason. Jaffa's view of reason strikes us as initially reasonable only because he has (arbitrarily) prescinded from, or presumed answers to, several key questions. He follows Jefferson in holding that "God hath created the mind free," thus ignoring the Christian account of an original sin which limits human reason. He identifies the evil of slavery in "a black man possess[ing] a rational will" rather than in his creation in the image of God or in the requirements of the common good.[19] Yet "reason" alone does not determine that the element of man which possesses dignity is "rational will," nor that the only means of respecting human dignity is the respecting of political right. The "reason" of eighteenth-century natural rights differs crucially from the reason which grounds the natural law; Jaffa gives us no reason to prefer his narrow account of reason to the older view. If he did, he would reveal his defection from the natural law tradition.

Second, Kirk is famous for his elegiac defense of "the permanent things." This fact should raise a suspicion about the adequacy of Jaffa's account of Kirk as a historicist. Kirk's adherence both to (changing) history and to (unchanging) natural law follows Burke, who was closer to the older tradition than is Jaffa.[20] Burke saw politics as "morality writ large." He seems to have believed that we have surer access to the commands of the moral law than we do to the laws of political right. We may deduce different ways to achieve justice politically—i.e., indirectly—under varying historical circumstances, but moral statesmanship remains primary, and a permanent obligation regardless of the regime. Thinkers in the Enlightenment tradition reversed this ordering. Confronted by differing ethics uncovered in exotic climes, their confidence in the truth of "Christian morality" waned. But they had also created the "new science of politics," a sure method, they thought, of achieving just political outcomes. Consequently, they were certain only of the rules of political right, and they were forced by the logic of their position to deduce a new morality of "politics writ small." This inversion is perhaps uniquely responsible for the moral revolution whose fruits are now universally lamented in our public oratory. When Jaffa focuses primarily on the political or constitutional implications of his natural law, he is following in a tradition which began with Hobbes. When Kirk ties together tradition and the moral law, he is at once both more traditional and more innovative than Jaffa. Above all, he is attempting in this synthesis to recognize that the right does not exhaust the good.[21]

FINALLY, IT must be admitted that Kirk's view of American order may be too optimistic. Kirk argues in effect that America is well-founded because it is not really "founded" so much as "grown"— from the healthy soils of Jerusalem, Athens, and Rome. But what then accounts for the obvious pathologies which have of late "grown up" in our society? Jaffa has a similar problem: If America is well-founded, because founded on natural right, and if the political regime determines the cultural order, then whence the pathologies which he, like Kirk, adduces and denounces? There remains the possibility that the American regime was ill-founded. If this were true, conservative *pietas* for Tradition would require selective impiety toward some traditions.

Looming therefore over these disputes about the American founding is the question of "the West." Throughout the Cold War, conservatives identified themselves as defenders of the West, but the meaning of that term was blurred for the sake of assembling a political coalition against Soviet communism. For Kirk, the West names a civilization tracing back more than three thousand years. The West is a name which succeeds the name of Christendom. It is the totality of *our* culture, *our* civilization, and therefore *our* identity. For another part of the conservative coalition, the West names only the "culture" of secular liberalism which emerged in the eighteenth century in repudiation of Christendom. For these, the West is that community which recognizes the priority of the right to the good, and which is organized around sovereign political institutions that express this priority. Jaffa appears to hold this view.

Concealed by his gentlemanly manner, Russell Kirk's piety for Jerusalem, Athens, and Rome is an act of impiety toward the eighteenth century's cult of the new. His work is in part an attempt to show that many of the good things which holders of the second view believe are attributable only to the Enlightenment's narrow horizons do not exhaust the political goods which we may seek, a fact which is obscured by the narrative of *novus ordo*

seclorum. Kirk's work is an attempt at the *recovery* of tradition from the diremptions of the eighteenth century. The success of the attempt remains uncertain.

Notes

1. *The Federalist Papers* (Penguin Books, 1987), 87.
2. *Modern Age,* Fall 1985, 295–303. Kirk's title is a phrase taken from E. J. Payne, summarizing Burke's interpretation of England's 1688 "Revolution."
3. Gentz (1764–1832), Metternich's secretary and a patron of the romantic conservative Adam Müller, translated Burke's *Reflections* into German, and he also wrote *The French and American Revolutions Compared*, a work translated into English by John Quincy Adams (Chicago: Regnery Books, 1955).
4. This observation Kirk owed to the late M. E. Bradford.
5. In typically bold fashion, Joseph de Maistre went so far as to claim that if a country attempts to give itself a written constitution, this demonstrates that it does *not yet* have a "constituted" people. The only constitutional peoples are those without written constitutions. Joseph de Maistre, *On God and Society—Essay* on *the Generative Principle of Human Constitutions* (Chicago: Regnery, 1959).
6. Russell Kirk, *Eliot and His Age,* 334.
7. It will be objected that there is nothing peculiarly British about the rule of law. But compare everything we mean by "the rule of law" to its analogue in the German-speaking world, the *Rechtstaat.* These concepts are similar but not identical, and our American intuitions concerning the requirements of political justice reflect the British understanding of these matters. Nor is either our "rule of law" or the German *Rechtstaat* identical with, though both derive from, Aristotle's idea of the sovereignty of law in *The Politics* (1282b).
8. Russell Kirk, *America's British Culture* (Rutgers: Transaction Press, 1993), 11.
9. Russell Kirk, *The Roots of American Order* (Malibu: Pepperdine, 1974).
10. Kirk, *America's British Culture,* 96, 103, 104.

Also fundamental are the divine revelations at the heart of the Jewish and Christian faiths. Judaism and especially Christianity are historical religions; their universalism is tied to a particular historical experience. They are not simply philosophies and, in the Christian case, not primarily Law.

11. Harry Jaffa, "What Were the 'Original Intentions' of the Framers of the Constitution of the United States?" *University of Puget Sound Law Review* 10:351, 355. Italics mine.

12. Ibid., 384.

13. Harry Jaffa, "Who Killed Cock Robin? A Retrospective on the Bork Nomination and a Reply to Jaffa Divides the House' by Robert L. Stone," *University of Puget Sound Law Review* 13:511, 527.

14. Jaffa, "Original Intentions," 377, quoting Abraham Lincoln's comment in Roy P. Basler, *Abraham Lincoln: His Life and Speeches* (Cleveland: World Publishing, 1946), 376.

15. Given that the equality and natural rights so dear to Jaffa have been achieved in American political life largely through the Bill of Rights, it might be thought that Jaffa's thesis would be strengthened by a discussion of the first ten amendments to the Constitution. The reason Jaffa must turn our attention instead to the Declaration is the inconvenient fact that the Bill of Rights was not part of the original intention of the founders, but a practical compromise—and a compromise demanded not by Madison and the Federalists Jaffa admires, but by the Anti-Federalists whose tradition leads to Calhoun, whom Jaffa is intent to diabolize.

16. Jaffa, "Original Intentions," 380.

17. Ibid., 364.

18. Ibid., 394, 395.

19. Jaffa, "Judicial Conscience and Natural Rights," *University of Puget Sound Law Review* 11: 219, 225, 229.

20. I believe, however, that it is a mistake to view Burke simply as a "natural law thinker." He departs from the tradition as well. But this is not the place to discuss comprehensively the complex problem of Burke's political thought.

21. These reflections are meant only to begin a line of inquiry, not to provide exhaustive answers. The question of how we are to understand tradition's normative character, for example, remains incompletely addressed. Jaffa's questions here are serious, and will have to be seriously investigated. Yet one hopes that Jaffa's dismissal of Kirk's coherence has now been revealed as not yet conclusive.

Ellis Sandoz

Philosophical and Religious Dimensions of the American Founding

VOL. 30, NO. 2, 1995

The foundation of the American regime was deeply influenced by the rationalist mood of Enlightenment thought, primarily in its English and Scottish aspects. But it began and remained more fundamentally an antimodernist recovery and rearticulation of Western and English constitutionalism on the classical and medieval patterns identified with the seventeenth century of Sir Edward Coke, a principal figure of the Elizabethan Renaissance, and of John Locke, himself a principal enlightener. Moreover, all aspects of the political, constitutional, and philosophical debate were strongly conditioned by an ethics and ontology grounded in the ample range of religious convictions of an American Protestant Christianity dominated by Dissenter or Nonconformist perspectives.

While (given the empirical evidence) all of these elements certainly cannot be homogenized or blended into a perfect harmony and generalized as such, there still remained significant consensus or near agreement on fundamental principles sufficient to sustain independence, fight the revolution, and conclude with the Constitution. This process soon was capped by adoption of the Bill of Rights (a condition of ratification in some states) that affirms natural and traditional liberties of persons and states by placing them beyond the ordinary reach of majorities. There is no attempt here to deny differences of many kinds, even multitudinous and profound differences. But one must concede that without some sort of effective consensus to structure the new community and to allow its organization for political action in history, there could have been no founding and there would be no United States of America. The thrust of this essay considers several aspects of this consensus and glances at its religious and philosophical underpinnings.

SINCE NOVELTY and revolution mesmerize contemporary consciousness, the relative lack of novelty in the American founding seems counter-intuitive and requires emphasis at the outset. The institutional forms were new in degree, but the underlying theory was often very old and highly traditional. There is thus a strong contrast with much of our contemporary world and its recent past.

To begin with, the conceptions of human existence and of comprehensive reality prevailing during the American founding were not *ideological* in the strict sense of the term. By this at least the following is meant.

The American founders (as a rule) did not hold out the promise of a humanistic *transformation* of time and the world as a goal within the reach of action and revolution—apart from the traditional Christian faith in the transfiguration of the world at the end of time as consistent with eschatological expectation of the Parousia, the Second Coming of Christ.

The founding was not significantly infected by the radical humanistic egophanic rebellion that supplants God through the apotheosis of "Autonomous Man" as the center and ground of reality. To the contrary, a transcendental-immanent worldview is reflected in the core of the American founders' thought, as is plainly expressed in the Declaration of Independence's proclamation that "all men are reated equal and are endowed by their Creator with certain unalienable rights." Perhaps the most persuasive expression of this orientation in reality is voiced in Alexander Pope's *Essay on Man* (1734). Evoked there is the millennial image of the great chain of being with man the middle link, an image whose genesis lies in the distant antiquity of Anaximander's *apeiron* as developed by Plato and Aristotle. Pope wrote so compellingly as to make the poem favorite reading for eighteenth-century Americans:[1]

> Vast Chain of being! which from God began, / Natures aethereal, human, angel, man, / Beast, bird, fish, insect, what no eye can see, / No glass can reach; from Infinite to thee, / From thee to nothing.

The founding was not "utopian" in expectation nor in the assessment of the world. Thus the reality of the American founders, while distinctly hopeful, was nonetheless considered a stable site of human striving in nature and in a process of history governed by beneficent and responsive providence, a time when fallible human beings might seek the joys of life and anticipate the bliss of salvation and eternal beatitude. *Reality* itself was conceived as the four-fold "Man, God, World, and Society" of classical philosophy and traditional understanding. To again illustrate from Pope's picture of human reality:

> Plac'd in this isthmus of a middle state, / A being darkly wise and rudely great, / With too much knowledge for the sceptic side, / With too much weakness for the stoic pride, / He hangs between; in doubt to act or rest; / In doubt his Mind or Body to prefer; / Born but to die, and reas'ning but to err; . . . / Chaos of Thought and Passion all confus'd. / Still by himself abus'd, or disabus'd; / Created half to rise, and half to fall, / Great lord of all things, yet a prey to all; / Sole judge of Truth, in endless error hurl'd; / The glory, jest and riddle of the world.[2]

Government under such conditions was pronounced (by James Madison in *Federalist* 51) the "greatest of all reflections on human nature." Because human beings are neither angel nor brute but in between, capable of virtue and inclined to vice, the first task of government is to control the governed; the second task is to oblige the rulers to control themselves. "Ambition must be made to counteract ambition."

We are thus reminded of the cautious view of man as flawed and sinful, graced with reason but inclined to follow passion and selfish interest. Madison's language in that place of all places in the *Federalist Papers* (51) may be more fully quoted. For there the core constitutional innovation of separation of powers and system of checks and balances is explained as the means of attaining a government of laws and not of men—even though, paradoxically, there are only human beings available to rule. The underlying analysis for the constitutional mechanisms is sketched as follows:

> The interest of the man must be connected with the constitutional rights of the place. It may be a reflection on human nature that such devices should be necessary to control the abuses of government. But what is government itself but the greatest of all reflections on human nature? If men were angels, no government would be necessary. If angels were to govern men, neither external nor internal controls on government would be necessary. In framing a government which is to be administered by men over men, the great difficulty lies in this: you must first enable the government to control the governed; and in the next place oblige it to control itself. A dependence on the people is, no doubt, the primary control on the government; but *experience* has taught mankind the necessity of auxiliary precautions.[3]

Finally—and deserving of utmost consideration—there is the ubiquitous criterion of *experience* just encountered in the passage from *Federalist* 51. Experience, illumining the present and future by the light and lessons of the past, is *the* cardinal touchstone of validity. It also is the one that indelibly distinguishes the American founders from those they ironically

helped greatly to inspire, the soon-to-appear Jacobin revolutionaries of France inebriated with utopian rationalism. By comparison the American founders were a sober lot. Thus, in August, 1787, during the Convention, John Dickinson famously observed that "experience must be our only guide. Reason may mislead us."[4] Perhaps nothing better marks the mind of the American founders than this conviction. It runs like a thread through all of their deliberations. Rule of law grounded in both natural and historical jurisprudence distinguishes American constitutionalism, as does also a political order devoted to *salus populi* and to the protection of every individual person's life, liberty, and property within the limits of possibility.[5]

What, indeed, may be possible can be decided only by prudential judgment anchored in experience. Briefly to dwell on this bedrock principle, we find Publius in the *Federalist Papers* using such phrases as these: "Let *experience,* the least fallible guide of human opinions, be appealed to" (*Federalist* 6); "the best oracle of wisdom, *experience*" (*Federalist* 15); "*Experience* is the oracle of truth; and where its responses are unequivocal they ought to be conclusive and sacred" (*Federalist* 20); "Let us consult *experience,* the guide that ought always to be followed whenever it can be found" (*Federalist* 52); "*experience* is the parent of wisdom" (*Federalist* 72).[6]

Alexander Hamilton concludes the *Federalist* (85) with a quotation from David Hume's *Essays* (1742) which underlines this good sense from our birthright. For Hume demonstrates the abject inability of reason *alone* to guide philosophy toward truth. He thereby finds himself compelled to take account of the whole experiential horizon as context, if reason is reliably to serve inquiry and direct men toward truth and happiness. To do otherwise would be to fall into the hubris of autonomous reason that ends either in the despair or in the ataraxy of radical skepticism—or (more frequently) in the disaster of evoking autonomous Man after the fashion of generations of immanentizing ideologues from 1789 into the present.[7] From this prudential perspective, then, Hamilton quotes Hume as follows:

> To balance a large state or society whether monarchial or republican, on general laws, is a work of so great difficulty, that no human genius, however comprehensive, is able by the mere dint of reason and reflection, to effect it. The judgments of man must unite in the work: *Experience* must guide their labour: *Time* must bring it to perfection: And the *feeling* of inconveniences must correct the mistakes which they *inevitably* fall into, in their first trials and experiments.[8]

These representative sentiments signal the sober, realistic, undogmatic yet hopeful outlook of American politics at its inception. Whatever the historical lapses, they supply the standards nurtured to this day.[9]

LIBERTY AND the truth which makes men free go hand in hand in the political and religious discourse of the American founding era. There was general agreement that political and religious truth are vitally intertwined: "Year after year the preacher reaffirmed from his high pulpit that both revelation and reason pointed to a single set of principles which outlined the best form of government."[10] Nor was this merely a Puritan or New England affair, as recent scholarship attests. Robert M. Calhoon stated in 1994

that "Evangelical political thought, discipline, and use of the Bible—among other expressions of its activity and vision—formed a coherent whole and functioned as a persuasion in the early South. It was an eclectic, improvised mixture of intellectual assumptions, behavioral norms, and Scottish common-sense teachings about the interconnectedness of all knowledge and revelation."[11]

The old interpretation is, with refinements, now becoming the new interpretation of scholars. Religion gave birth to America, Tocqueville long ago observed. On the eve of revolution, in his last ditch attempt to stave off impending catastrophe, Edmund Burke reminded the House of Commons of the inseparable alliance between liberty and religion among Englishmen in America. A recent student has echoed Tocqueville in dubbing America the nation with the soul of a church. Another has elevated the political sermon considered as *jeremiad* to the rank of primary symbolic form of the American mind. Yet another has exclaimed of the Americans on the eve of the Revolution, "Who can deny that for them the very core of existence was their relation to God?"[12]

Given modern predispositions, and despite new developments, our point of departure may still have to be negative. It requires that we abandon what Perry Miller over three decades ago called "obtuse secularism" as a reflexive habit of mind so as to enter into a quite different attitude.[13] Miller's bristling phrase as emblematic of the prevailing climate of opinion probably still is justified. God-centered existence is not the twentieth-century commonplace among literate Britons and Americans that it was among our eighteenth-century brethren. For all the differences among them, American preachers of the eighteenth century premise an unsurprisingly biblical vision that includes a stratified, differentiated reality, an ontological Whole experienced as the *community* of being articulated into the familiar four-fold structure of God, man, world and society.[14] The human and divine are tensional polarities of this reality, the one unintelligible without the other. The modern reductionist deformations of being into a contracted reality of autonomous man lodged in an equally autonomous nature do not reflect the intellectual horizon of any significant segment of the thinking public of the time, although radically secularizing influences of the French Enlightenment were pushing them that way. Thomas Paine and Ethan Allen, and the more ambiguous instance of Thomas Jefferson, rightly are adduced as evidence of the presence of such influences. But they plainly are exceptions. And even the so-called rationalistic elite probably can best be understood in *religious* terms, as historians recently have begun to argue—even from the vantage point of the ratification process near the end of the founding era. Thus, writes Stephen A. Marini in 1994,

> it was primarily among Anglicans and Congregationalists and the political, economic, military, and literary elites they dominated that a movement of Enlightenment religious liberalism burst into full flower. Thomas Jefferson, the Virginian who shared Voltaire's theological skepticism yet penned passionate defenses of an innate moral sense and committed the sayings of Jesus to memory, Benjamin Rush, the Philadelphia physician who embraced Unitarianism and Universalism while campaigning passionately for temperance reform and the abolition of slavery, and Benjamin Franklin, the transplanted Bostonian

who provided the new nation with a wealth of moral aphorisms and a model of toleration by contributing to all churches of Philadelphia, epitomized the sort of *religious liberalism* that swept through America's cultural elite during the late eighteenth century. ... In its advocacy of a benign Creator, a benevolent cosmos, human reason and free will, and a thoroughgoing moral optimism, Enlightenment religious liberalism supplied a powerful theological and philosophical foundation for the cosmopolitan republican culture of the 1780s. . . . The Deism of Paine and Ethan Allen failed dramatically to become the new American faith, especially after the French Revolution. In 1787, however, Enlightenment religious liberalism still flourished widely in America's urban churches, universities, and plantation parishes.[15]

Prevalent American ontology reflects the familiar biblical image of Creator and creation, of fallen and sinful men, striving willy-nilly in a mysteriously ordered historical existence toward a personal salvation and an eschatological fulfillment. These goals are themselves paradoxically attainable only through the divine grace of election, a condition experienced as the unmerited gift of God discernible (if at all) in the mode of hopeful human responsiveness called faith in Christ. The relationships are variously symbolized by personal and corporate reciprocal covenants ordering individual lives, church communities, and society as a whole in multiple layers.[16]

The bare externals of these relationships so regulate the visible community as to beckon everyone to open their souls to truth and thereby enjoy in appropriate measure more perfect participation as members of the mystical Body of which

Christ is Head. The communion of the faithful, those actuated by the love of God even to the contempt of self, comprises the invisible church of the regenerate (in America often the gathered, visible church itself) made one through love of God.[17] The picture that emerges is not parochially Puritan or Calvinist but palpably Augustinian, thoroughly biblical, and often Arminian. Even so, it will be salutary to avoid misgivings by recalling Ralph Barton Perry's indispensable admonition against the *Fallacy of Difference* as we reflect on American religious experience with one eye on its Puritan background. He writes, "Puritanism was an offshoot from the main stem of Christian belief, and Puritans, equally with Catholics, claimed descent from St. Paul and Augustine. [Thus, it can be defined as] theocratic, congregational-presbyterian, Calvinistic, protestant, medieval Christianity."[18] Even institutionally this was so. For, although Baptists and Quakers felt obliged to secede, orthodox New England Puritans gave allegiance to the Thirty-Nine Articles and remained within the national communion of the Church of England well into the eighteenth century. Although they might call themselves congregationalists, this was primarily descriptive of a form of church polity that they insisted was true to the New Testament and apostolic so that "in their heart of hearts [they] remained convinced that [theirs] was no more than the most reformed portion of the universal church."[19]

The intricacies of the varieties of belief cannot be much explored here, but at least a few hints must be given. For though our primary focus is on *political* dimensions—and thus exceptional expressions of the faith of a people who looked not primarily to history but to the eternal beyond—the spiritual root of that collaborative enterprise as directed by divine Providence requires clarification.

It has been persuasively argued that a revolution in the spiritual and social life of America began with what is called the (First) Great Awakening. There is considerable reason to suppose that religious and political lines of development are intimately, perhaps decisively, linked. Narrowly construed as occurring in the years 1739 to 1742, the Great Awakening designates the outburst of religious revival that swept the colonies in those years.[20] It reached from Georgia to New England and affected every stratum of society. There had been a quickening of religious impulses even earlier, but the First Great Awakening was a spiritual earthquake, one that, as Alan Heimert and Perry Miller argue, "clearly began a new era, not merely of American Protestantism, but in the evolution of the American mind."[21] A turning point and crisis in American society, it rumbled and echoed through the next decades. Colonial life was never the same again. American events could be seen as part of the general rise of religious sentiment traceable in Europe between 1730 and 1760, particularly in Great Britain where major catalysts were the itinerant Anglican priests John and Charles Wesley, the founders of Methodism, and their compatriot George Whitefield. These men played a large part in rescuing England from the social debauchery and political corruption associated with the Gin Age, aspects of the period portrayed in William Hogarth's paintings and prints and in his friend Henry Fielding's novels.[22] The so-called Second Great Awakening began around 1800 as revival camp meetings on the frontier and in the back country. The great political events of the American founding, thus, have a backdrop of resurgent religiousness whose calls for repentance and faith plainly complement the calls to resist constitutional corruption and tyranny so as to live virtuously as God-fearing Christians and, eventually, as responsible republican citizens.[23] It should be emphasized in this context, perhaps, that Stephen Marini argues for a surge in religiousness *during* the time of the American Revolution: religion prospered during the Revolution. Indeed, there was a "Revolutionary revival." This 1994 judgment merely confirms one that Perry Miller made in 1961: "The basic fact is that the Revolution had been preached to the masses as a religious revival, and had the astounding fortune to succeed." And in 1994 Patricia Bonomi in no way recants her 1982 and 1986 views on the thriving and increasing of religious consciousness in all parts of the American community during these same years, including the colonies and subsequent states of the Middle Atlantic and Southern regions of the country. These judgments challenge the old orthodoxy; to quote Marini:

> Far from suffering decline, religion experienced vigorous growth and luxuriant development during the Revolutionary period. It occupied a prominent place in public culture and a disproportionately large number of religiously active men served in the new nation's constituent assemblies. In a host of ways, both practical and intellectual, the church served as a school for politics.[24]

With this perspective on the Awakening and religious development during the remainder of the century in mind, understanding the earlier surge of religiousness becomes all the more urgent. In fact, the preeminent awakener in America throughout much of this whole period was the English evangelist George Whitefield, who first visited the colonies in 1738 and made six more preaching tours of the country, and who died in 1770 one September morning just before he was to preach in Newburyport, Massachusetts. Regarded as not only the most controversial preacher of his time but as "perhaps the greatest extemporaneous orator in the history of the English church," it is Whitefield's view of the human plight and its therapy that will best give a clue to the thrust of the awakening as formative of the American mind.

> The theme of his preaching is that of evangelicals in every age: in his natural state man is estranged from God; Jesus Christ, by his death and Atonement, has paid the price of that estrangement and made reconciliation with God possible; to achieve salvation man, with the guidance and the grace of the Holy Ghost, must repudiate sin and openly identify himself with Christ. To Whitefield, religion, when properly understood, meant "a thorough, real, inward change of nature, wrought in us by the powerful operations of the Holy Ghost, conveyed to and nourished in our hearts, by a constant use of all the means of grace, evidenced by a good life, and bringing forth the fruits of the spirit." There was, of course, nothing new in this belief. Its special appeal for eighteenth-century audiences lay partly in the fact that it answered an emotional need the established Church had for too long tried to ignore, and partly in the charismatic personality of the man who revived it.[25]

It is worth stressing in a secularized age that the *mystic's ascent* and the *evangelist's call,* although conducted in different forums, have a common root and purpose.

For each seeks to find the responsive place in a person's consciousness where vivid communion with God occurs. The consequence is that such communion becomes the transformative core of personal existence for the individual person who therewith feels himself a new man. Initially this is manifested in the conversion experience (understood as a spiritual rebirth) and subsequently in the continuing meditative nurture of the soul pursued by every means but chiefly, in the American Protestant horizon, through prayer, sermons, and study of the Bible. Thus, Whitefield's words—those of an Oxford graduate and ordained Anglican priest, we may remember—can in some respects be compared with a remarkable passage in Augustine's *Confessions* (bk. 7. 10. sec. 16) where a great mystic tells of finding his way to God:

> And being thence admonished to re-
> turn to myself, I entered even into my
> inward self, Thou being my Guide:
> and able I was, for Thou wert become
> my Helper. And I entered and I beheld
> with the eye of my soul, (such as it was,)
> above the same eye of my soul, above
> my mind, the Light Unchangeable.
> Not this ordinary light, which all
> flesh may look upon, nor as it were a
> greater of the same kind, as though the
> brightness of this should be manifold
> brighter, and with its greatness take up
> all space. Not such was this light, but
> other, yea, far other from all these. Nor
> was it above my soul, as oil is above
> water, nor yet as heaven above earth:
> but above to my soul, because It made
> me; and I below It, because I was made
> by It. He that knows the Truth, knows
> what that Light is; and he that knows
> It, knows eternity. Love knoweth it.
> O Truth Who art Eternity! and Love
> Who art Truth! and Eternity Who art

> Love! Thou art my God, to Thee do I
> sigh night and day. . . . And I heard, as
> the heart heareth, nor had I room to
> doubt, and I should sooner doubt that
> I live, than that Truth is not. . . .[26]

The appeal of the evangelist is analogous to the quest of the mystic. It is to stir response to the actualizing attraction of the divine pull as far as he can, both in himself and in those with whom he communicates. The intent is to steadily find in the soul the place of communion with the divine and, thereby, eagerly to vivify the life of the spirit through ever better—more perfect—participation in the transformative experience of transcendent divine Being. Such living communion with God that is experienced as a passion in Whitefield and in the awakened Americans no less than it is in Augustine—himself a matchless preacher—lies at the heart of the Awakening and revivalism more generally as mass phenomena in eighteenth-century Britain, America, and elsewhere. Hence its power and effectiveness both personally and socially as well as historically.[27]

The cry was for a converted ministry able to revive religious communities lacking vitality and zeal, to make the presence of God with his people a palpable reality. Such hortatory preaching and intent were the hallmarks of the so-called New Side Presbyterians and New Light Congregationalist clergy, along with the Baptists, Quakers, Anglican-Methodists, and other evangelicals, as contrasted with their opposites who eschewed emotion and experimental religion. Many of the former, like Whitefield himself, had no church of their own but traveled the country preaching in homes and pastures or wherever they could. *Conversion,* as the criterion of election, involves a personal experience of regeneration at least somewhat along lines classically drawn by Augustine. The individual is flooded with a sense of divine presence and intense participation or union with God such as that intimated by Augustine's words: "'I am the food of grown men; grow, and . . . be converted into Me!'" A further mark is complete assurance of blessing and of feeling the embrace of Truth itself, so that the moment becomes supremely authoritative for whomever it befalls. Thus, Augustine's words convey all the energy language can bear and fall like hammer blows: "I heard, as the heart heareth, nor had I room to doubt, and I should sooner doubt that I live, than that Truth is not. . . ."

Such robust experiences made the Awakening what it was. And it cannot be too surprising that its sociological dimensions manifested emotionalism, sometimes rising to the level of frenzy, we are told. Comparable intensity lies close to the surface of the account of such experience by the likes of an Augustine, a spiritual virtuoso of world historic stature. Such *experience,* one Virginian explained, came with surrender or an abandonment of his own efforts at reform, and with the consequent realization that "my guilt was gone, my conscience at rest, and my soul at liberty." As a church covenant stated in matter-of-fact language, the power of this freeing came through "faith" understood not as "an act of man's free will and power but of the mighty, efficacious grace of God."[28] The criterion, thus, was "an experience of grace" which both made faith possible and succored the soul through liberation and forgiveness.[29] As Robert Calhoon writes, quoting George Whitefield: "The immediacy of Christ's sacrifice brought ecstasy and the 'indwelling of the spirit' into the consciousness of the convert; evangelical Christianity combined Calvinist assumptions about

human depravity and divine majesty with the Arminian appreciation of God's desire to flood all humanity with grace; evangelical converts felt and communicated a contagious desire to be bonded spiritually to others."[30] At the core of the evangelical political theology, Stephen Marini writes, "was 'the necessity of the New Birth,' the requirement that all true Christians experience an episode of conscious spiritual regeneration modeled on the accounts of the New Testament."[31]

One concern of the preachers, however, was to maintain a balance between reason and emotion so as to avoid the opprobrium of being seen as *enthusiasts.* What concretely resulted from the kind of evocative discourse that Whitefield and his fellow evangelists practiced in proclaiming the Word, then, was a strengthening of conviction regarding fundamental truth, righteous resolve, and palpable moral reform. First encountering him in Philadelphia in 1739, Benjamin Franklin not only found Whitefield's preaching personally moving beyond all expectation but became his printer and testified to the good he did:

> [Whitefield] was at first permitted to preach in some of our Churches; but the Clergy taking a Dislike to him, soon refus'd him their Pulpits and he was oblig'd to preach in the Fields. The Multitudes of all Sects and Denominations that attended his Sermons were enormous, and it was matter of Speculation to me who was one of the Number, to observe the extraordinary Influence of his Oratory on his Hearers, and how much they admir'd and respected him, notwithstanding his common Abuse of them, by assuring them they were naturally *half Beasts and half Devils.* It was wonderful to see the Change soon made in

the Manners of our Inhabitants; from being thoughtless or indifferent about Religion, it seem'd as if all the World were growing Religious; so that one could not walk thro' the Town in an Evening without Hearing Psalms sung in different Families of every Street.[32]

It is against the experiential background of such preaching that the political teaching of the eighteenth-century preachers is to be seen as it came into powerful display in the crisis of conflict and revolution. A sketch of their views might begin with the representative statement of the famous lexicographer and biblical scholar Noah Webster, who was himself caught up in the fervor of the Second Awakening. He wrote:

It is extremely important to our nation, in a political as well as religious view, that all possible authority and influence should be given to the scriptures; for these furnish the best principles of civil liberty, and the most effectual support of republican government. They teach the true principles of that equality of rights which belongs to every one of the human family, but only in consistency with a strict subordination to the magistrate and the law. The scriptures were intended by God to be the *guide of human reason.* The Creator of man established the moral order of the Universe; knowing that *human nature,* left without a divine guide or rule of action, would fill the world with *disorder, crime and misery.* . . . The principles of all genuine liberty, and of wise laws and administrations are to be drawn from the Bible and sustained by its authority. . . . [T]here are two powers only which are sufficient to control men, and secure the rights of individuals and a peaceable

administration; these are the *combined force of religion and law,* and the *force or fear of the bayonet.*

The Bible is the chief moral cause of all that is *good,* and the best corrector of all that is *evil,* in human society; the *best* book for regulating the temporal concerns of men, and the *only book* that can serve as an infallible guide to future felicity.[33]

This biblical perspective can be illustrated, then, by a representative exposition of the human condition and its political implications such as that sketched in Rev. Gad Hitchcock's anniversary sermon at Plymouth on December 22, 1774. He began from the premise that man is a moral agent living freely in a reality that is good as coming from the hand of God: "And God saw every thing that he had made, and behold, it was very good."[34] His responsibility is to live well, in accordance with God's commandments and through exercise of one's mind and free will. Thus, man longs for knowledge of God's word and truth and seeks God's help to keep an open heart so as to receive them. Among the chief hindrances to this life of true liberty is the oppression of men, who in service to evil deceive with untruth and impose falsehood in its place proclaiming it to be true. Man, blessed with liberty, reason, and a moral sense, created in the image and likeness of God, a little lower than the angels, and given dominion over the earth (Genesis 1:26; Psalm 8; Hebrews 2:6–12), is the chief and most perfect of God's works. Among his perfections is his capacity freely to hold communion with God and, through this intercourse, improve in natural and moral science and perfection, controlling appetites by his superior principles and growing into full personality through acts of love, gratitude, and obedience towards God and fellow human beings. Pursuit of these authentic goods, then, defines responsibility.

Liberty is an essential principle of man's constitution, a natural trait which yet reflects the supernatural One whose image man is, and who freely created him and the world. The growth of virtue and perfection of being depends upon free choice, in response to divine invitation and help, in a cooperative relationship. Liberty is most truly exercised by living in accord with truth and is, therefore, the correlate of responsibility. Man's dominion over the earth and other creatures therein, his mastery of nature through reason, is subject to no restraint but the law of his nature which is the perfection of liberty; his obligation to obey the laws of the Creator is only a check to licentiousness and abuse. Liberty is thus God-given. However, this gift of freedom to do right and live truly carries the opposite possibility as well, i.e., rebellion and rejection. This, in turn, leads to the necessity of government to coerce a degree of right living and justice from a mankind fallen from the high road of willing obedience to the loving Father. Moreover, coercive law can be inflicted in ways not merely just and conducive to truth, righteousness, and union with God but frequently to their very opposites. This biblical understanding of the human condition is reflected, as we have seen, in the most famous passage of the *Federalist Papers* (No. 51), which turns on the sentiments that, if men were angels there would be no need for government, for what is government but the greatest of all reflections on human nature? It remains true, however, James Madison went on, that "Justice is the end of government. It is the end of civil society. It ever has been, and ever will be pursued, until it be obtained, or until liberty be lost in the pursuit."

Hence, the Royal Psalmist prays (Psalms 119:134): "Deliver me from the oppression of man: So will I keep thy precepts." The prayer is that he be delivered from human oppression *so that* he can keep the truth of God. This is thus a prayer for just and free government wherein responsibility to the civil laws conduces to the perfection of virtue and truth in concrete lives of concrete societies of men. The psalmist does not endorse, but rather he condemns, enforcing evil in the name of justice and propagating lies as truth, thereby perverting reality and the lives of a people who would, then, imbibe and embody corruption. Such perversion would create an abomination standing in the holy place. It would deform everything it touched. Indeed, by such misrule not liberty but slavery is enforced, inasmuch as living in accordance with an evil will necessarily results in being enslaved to the passions of *libido dominandi,* the lust for power that is the nadir of pride (*superbia vitae,* I John 2:16) productive of tyranny or dictatorship. So to live is to abandon both God and our true selves, forfeit liberty while proclaiming it, and mutilate the divine image that animates the noble conception of man and reality reflected in Psalm 8, which is rightly called the Magna Carta of humanity. Hence, Thomas Jefferson's personal seal carried the famous motto: *"Resistance to Tyrants is Obedience to God!"*

While it seems to be true that the federal Convention did not embrace the aged Benjamin Franklin's suggestion for prayer, there is little doubt that Franklin evoked the sentiment of the country no less than of the clergy when he remarked to that great assembly, presided over by George Washington himself that

> I have lived, Sir, a long time, and the longer I live, the more convincing

proofs I see of this truth—*that GOD governs in the affairs of men.* And if a sparrow cannot fall to the ground without his notice, is it probable that an empire can rise without his aid? We have been assured, Sir, in the sacred writings, that "except the Lord build the House they labour in vain that build it." I firmly believe this; and I also believe that without his concurring aid we shall succeed in this political building no better than the Builders of Babel.[35]

Nathan O. Hatch has remarked that "the right to think for oneself became . . . the hallmark of popular Christianity" in America. Such pre-Revolutionary figures as the Presbyterian Rev. David Caldwell in North Carolina and the Baptist Rev. Richard Furman in backcountry South Carolina sought political truth in history and in the Bible all the while emphasizing "the autonomy of the individual conscience."[36] At the heart of this autonomy lay the conviction of the individual's capacity to read and understand the Bible. The consequences are incalculable. As Hatch has emphasized, for example:

> Deep and powerful undercurrents of democratic Christianity distinguish the United States from other modern industrial democracies. These currents insure that churches in this land do not withhold faith from the rank and file. Instead, religious leaders have pursued people wherever they could be found; embraced them without regard to social standing; and challenged them to think, to interpret Scripture, and to organize the church for themselves. Religious populism, reflecting the passions of ordinary people and the charisma of democratic movement-

builders, remains among the oldest and deepest impulses in American life.[37]

A prime example is the message of the popular Baptist Elder John Leland, friend of Thomas Jefferson and James Madison, who joined them—or they him—in arguing that the *conscience* ought to be "free from human control," and insisted that "religion is a matter between God and individuals," and who roundly dismissed as snobbery and worse the contention that "the ignorant part of the community are not capacitated to judge for themselves." On the contrary, Leland asked:

> Did many of the rulers believe in Christ when he was upon earth? Were not the learned clergy (the scribes) his most inveterate enemies? Do not great men differ as much as little men in judgment? Have not almost all lawless errors crept into the world through the means of wise men (so called)? Is not a simple man, who makes nature and reason his study, a competent judge of things? Is the Bible written (like Caligula's laws) so intricate and high, that none but the letter learned (according to the common phrase) can read it? Is not the vision written so plain that he that runs may read it? [38]

Confidence in the "natural" clarity and unity of the Bible to the ordinary intelligence is not merely a theme of the eighteenth and nineteenth centuries. It is as old as the English Bible itself, as John Wyclif stressed in the Prologue to his translation (ca. 1380).[39]

Unity and intelligibility of the Bible to the average person was increasingly a motif of major importance in subsequent centuries. It also was reflected in the preachers' approach to textual exegesis from the pulpits. The assumption and basic principle, following Augustine and Calvin, was that the Bible is reflexive in the sense of providing its own explanation of its meaning in an overall consistent whole. The key to finding that unity according to William Perkins's manual entitled *The Arte of Prophysying* (1592, translated in 1607) was to begin the mastery of the Bible by first mastering Paul's Letter to the Romans, then, and only then, ought the student move to the remainder of the New Testament and subsequently to the Old Testament. The result of this, because of the emphases in Romans, is a stress on justification, sanctification, and true faith. Meaning is to be found through the three methods (which cannot be entered into in detail here) called circumstance, collation, and application. Thus, it is the task of the preacher as interpreter to place any text into its circumstances and context, collating it with similar texts elsewhere in the scriptures, and to find consistent meaning—then to finish the text of the sermon by conforming it and his preaching to the "analogies of faith." This means that any statement made had to be in harmony with or contained in the Apostle's Creed.[40]

For the ordinary believer and individual person the consequences of habitual Bible reading were enormous. The reliance upon individual judgment of the terms of eternal salvation largely based on private Bible study may be said to lie at the heart of the formation of the civic consciousness of responsible individuals. It greatly contributes to the rise of the American republican ethos and citizenry during the period leading up to independence and in the decades subsequent to it. As George Trevelyan more generally remarks, "the effect of the continual domestic study of [the Bible] upon the national character, imagination, and intelligence for three centuries—was

greater than that of any literary movement in the annals, or any religious movement since St. Augustine."[41]

THE POLITICAL implications outlined by Alice Baldwin remain serviceable today:

> Southern Presbyterian ministers based their political concepts upon the Bible. The idea of a fundamental constitution based on law, of inalienable rights which were God-given and therefore natural, of government as a binding compact made between rulers and peoples, of the right of the people to hold their rulers to account and to defend their rights against all oppression, these seem to have been doctrines taught by them all . . . in the South as in New England, the clergy helped in making familiar to the common people the basic principles on which the Revolution was fought, our constitutional conventions held, our Bills or Rights written and our state and national constitutions founded.[42]

These views are reinforced and amplified by Patricia Bonomi in 1994 in the following language:

> To be sure, religious differences alone did not bring on the American Revolution. . . . But the striking thing about the dissenting mentality is how easily it flowed in with the emergent republican understanding of the political radicals. Habits inculcated over more than 150 years by such Nonconformist practices as the gathering of congregations, electing of leaders, and then sharing power with them under the principle of majority rule proved far more congenial to re-

publican forms than to the imperial alternative. . . . We may stop well short of proposing religious differences as the primary "cause" of the American Revolution. It may nonetheless be asserted that the state of mind in which American colonials moved toward separation is nowhere better seen than in the realm of religion.[43]

The complexities are not to be minimized for the good reason, as Jonathan Clark has stated, that "early-modern societies [are] far more theoretically articulate than the societies which succeeded them, and their social relations were expressed to a much larger degree in terms of grand theory." Furthermore, Clark states that, "In America a new and programmatic civil religion provided an evangelical impetus for society unlike any the world had seen before: at once more ethical and more materialistic, more libertarian and more deferential to the sovereignty of collective opinion."[44]

Finally, as I recently have tried to summarize a part of this subject elsewhere:

The great frame of biblical symbolism is comprehended in Exodus, Covenant, and Canaan. That the American Israel understood itself as continuing this history through its pilgrimage to the American wilderness in analogy with the Mosaic adventures is well known but bears repeating. The fact that Americans organized themselves by covenants for civil as well as religious purposes and even in federations of covenants is clear; and that the Constitution itself is framed in the spirit of the covenant, compact, contract symbolism is evident. That this symbolism is indebted to Christian theory is also acknowledged, "Without the strong link that Augustine forged between consent and will, social contract theory would be unthinkable, since it defines consent in terms of will" [writes Patrick Riley]. But then, the whole sequence of biblical covenants linking consent and will lay behind Augustine. That the symbolism of Exodus can be applied to the departure of America from the British Empire through independence also is clear and in keeping with the tenor of the religious literature of the period. That the Revolution was theorized as a just war is explicit in the resolutions of the Congress and even in Tom Paine's writings. That the fulfillment of time in the dawn of the millennium in America by establishment of *novus ordo seclorum* of Constitution and republic is a palpable hope of a faithful people and a theme that has played a role in American consciousness into the present century. Who could doubt that America is a special and favored nation? Could this not be the beginning of time transfigured into the eternal Sabbath of the Eighth Day? Such apocalyptical enthusiasm, however, was generally kept in check by the robust good sense of the Founders, and the watchful, hopeful waiting typified by President Ezra Stiles [of Yale] seems to be consonant with general sentiment.[45]

It is from some such general perspective, one emphatically open to the horizon of being, that not only the ringing lines of the Declaration of Independence are to be read and understood, but also the Constitution and Bill of Rights and the order they represent—*if* we mean to understand them as Americans of the time did. Or at least so it seems to me. This, in turn, might serve to direct our inquiry toward the philosophical and natural law foundations of the American political and constitutional order so as to trace its sources into Renaissance, Medieval, and perhaps still earlier times. As Harold Berman lately wrote, from the religious perspective on law and Constitution, "history is a revelation of divine providence, a spiritual story of the unfolding of God's own purposes, and more particularly [it teaches] that God works in history, in part, through his elect nation . . . which is historically destined to reveal and incarnate God's mission for mankind."[46] Then, when we are satisfied that we have the story straight as to origins and meaning, we still have to face the question of the importance of even an essentially true account for present and future concerns—the famous *So what?*—i.e., the theoretical, political, and existential consequences for the conduct of life in truth.[47] But these are tasks for another day.

Notes

1. Pope's *Essay on Man* was favorite reading: see Forrest McDonald, *Novus Ordo Seclorum: The Intellectual Origins of the Constitution* (Lawrence, KS, 1985), 164n; Agnes Marie Sibly, *Alexander Pope's Prestige in America, 1725–1835* (New York, 1949), 23–56.

2. Alexander Pope, *Essay on Man,* in Charles W. Eliot, ed., *English Poetry, vol. I: Chaucer to Gray* (New York, 1910), *Harvard Classics, XL,* 417–18, 424, 425. Cf. discussion and literature cited in Ellis Sandoz, *A Government of Laws: Political Theory, Religion, and the American Founding* (Baton Rouge, 1990), 223–25.

3. John Jay, Alexander Hamilton, James Madison, *The Federalist,* ed. Jacob E. Cooke (Middletown, CT: Wesleyan Univ. Press, 1961), 349. Italics added.

4. Max Farrand, ed., *Records of the Federal Convention of 1787,* Rev. Ed., 4 vols. (1937; rpt. New Haven, CT, 1966), 2:278.

5. Cf. Sandoz, *A Government of Laws,* 116, 174, 197, 227. See also Ellis Sandoz, ed., *Political Sermons of the American Founding*

Era, 1730–1805 (Indianapolis: Liberty Press, 1991), xiii–xxiv and passim; Ellis Sandoz, ed., *The Roots of Liberty: Magna Carta, Ancient Constitution, and the Anglo-American Tradition of Rule of Law* (Columbia. Mo., 1993), 1–21; and J. C. D. Clark, *The Language of Liberty, 1660–1832: Political Discourse and Social Dynamics in the Anglo-American World* (Cambridge, England, 1994), 296–391.

6. *The Federalist,* ed. Cooke: 32, 96, 128, 355, 489. Emphasis added.

7. The large question of autonomous Man is discussed from a range of perspectives in the following places: Ellis Sandoz, "The Politics of Poetry," *Modern Age,* 34 (Fall 1991):16–23; with respect to Hume in Donald W. Livingston, *Hume's Philosophy of Common Life* (Chicago, 1984), 20–33 and passim; Donald Livingston, "Notes and Discussions: A Sellarsian Hume?," *Journal of the History of Philosophy,* 29 (April 1991): 281–90; with respect to socialism in F. A. Hayek, *The Fatal Conceit: The Errors of Socialism,* vol. I, *The Collected Works of F. A. Hayek,* ed. W. W. Bartley III (Chicago, 1988), 21–28, 66–88; and broadly with respect to modern political and economic liberalism in John Gray, *Beyond the New Right: Markets, Government and the Common Environment* (London, 1993), esp. 66–123.

8. From "The Rise of the Arts and Sciences" as quoted by Publius in *The Federalist,* ed. Cooke: 594; emphasis and italics as in original. Cf. David Hume, *Essays Moral, Political, and Literary,* ed. Eugene F. Miller (Indianapolis, 1985), 124.

9. The preceding four paragraphs are drawn from my "Philosophical Foundations of Our Democratic Heritage: A Recollection," *Presidential Studies Quarterly,* 24 (Summer 1994): 669–73.

10. Harry P. Kerr, "The Election Sermon: Primer for Revolutionaries," *Speech Monographs,* 29 (March 1962): 18. Quoted from Mark A. Noll, *Christians in the American Revolution* (Washington, DC, 1977), 152.

11. Robert M. Calhoon, "The Evangelical Persuasion," in *Revolution in a Revolutionary Age,* ed. Ronald Hoffman and Peter J. Albert (Charlottesville, 1994), 156–83 at 176. Calhoon thus generally confirms the

much earlier interpretation of the influence of religion on the politics of the South provided by Alice M. Baldwin, "Sowers of Sedition: The Political Theories of Some of the New Light Presbyterian Clergy of Virginia and North Carolina," *William and Mary Quarterly,* 3rd Ser., 5 (1948): 52–76. Basic to any study of religion in the American founding remains Alice M. Baldwin, *The New England Clergy and the American Revolution* (Durham, NC, 1928).

12. Alexis Tocqueville, *Democracy In America,* trans. George Lawrence, ed. J. P. Mayer, 2 vols. in 1 (Garden City, NY, 1969), II, 432; cf. Ibid., 46–47, 288–91; Edmund Burke, "Speech on Moving His Resolutions for Conciliation with the Colonies, March 22, 1775," in Burke, *Selected Writings and Speeches,* ed. Peter J. Stanlis (1963; rpt. Chicago, n.d.), 147–85 esp. 158–60; Sidney E. Mead, *The Nation with the Soul of a Church* (New York, 1975); Sacvan Bercovitch, *The American Jeremiad* (Madison, Wis., 1978), 176–210 and passim. The quotation is from Carl Bridenbaugh, *Spirit of '76: The Growth of American Patriotism Before Independence, 1607–1776* (New York, 1975), 117.

13. Perry Miller, "From the Covenant to the Revival," in *Religion in American Life,* ed. J. W. Smith and A. L. Jamison, 4 vols. (Princeton, NJ, 1961), 1:336n.

14. Cf. Voegelin, *Order and History,* vol. I, *Israel and Revelation* (1956), 1, for this "primordial community" and its "quaternarian structure" which was clearly intact in the American eighteenth century, as the documents demonstrate.

15. Stephen A. Marini, "Religion, Politics, and Ratification," in *Religion in a Revolutionary Age,* ed. Hoffman and Albert, 184–217 at 196. *Emphasis added.*

16. The "law of liberty" or "perfect law of freedom" [*nomon teleion eleutherias*] of James 1:25 (cf. James 2:12 and I Peter 2:16) echoes the Johannine Christ: "Ye shall know the truth, and the truth shall make [set] you free [*eleutheroosei*]" as given in John 8:32 and reiterated in subsequent verses (8:33, 36) culminating in the great declaration: "If the Son therefore shall make you free, ye shall be free indeed."

17. For the bold account of the distinction between love of self and love of God *(amor sui, amor Dei),* symbols of the radical reorientation in reality marked by a person's conversion, see the classic passage in St. Augustine, *The City of God,* trans. Marcus Dods, intro. by Thomas Merton (New York, 1950), 477 [Bk. XIV, Chap. 28].

18. Ralph Barton Perry, *Puritanism and Democracy* (New York, 1944), 82–83; cf. Sandoz, *A Government of Laws,* 98–101.

19. Perry Miller, *The New England Mind: From Colony to Province* (1953; rpt. Boston, 1961), 464.

20. See Alan Heimert and Perry Miller, eds., *The Great Awakening: Documents Illustrating the Crisis and Its Consequences* (Indianapolis, Ind., 1967), xiii. A generally contrasting perspective to that of Miller, Heimert, and of the present essay is given in Jon Butler, *Awash in a Sea of Faith: Christianizing the American People* (Cambridge, MA, 1990). Valuable for the canvass of some of the historiographic perspectives at issue here is the review of Clark's *The Language of Liberty* by Jack P. Greene, "Why Did They Rebel?" in *Times Literary Supplement* (June 10, 1994): 3–6.

21. Ibid., xiv; cf. Perry Miller, "The Great Awakening from 1740 to 1750," *Encounter* (The Divinity School, Duke University, Durham, NC, March 1956), 5–9.

22. See the biographical notes and sermons numbered 4, 13, 14, and 18 in Sandoz, ed., *Political Sermons of the American Founding.*

23. A fine concise account of the relationship of the Great Awakening to political developments is given by William G. McLoughlin in "'Enthusiasm for Liberty': The Great Awakening as the Key to the Revolution," in Jack P. Greene and William G. McLoughlin, *Preachers & Politicians: Two Essays on the Origins of the American Revolution* (Worcester, MA, 1977), 47–73.

24. Marini, "Religion, Politics, and Ratification," in *Religion in a Revolutionary Age,* ed. Hoffman and Albert, 188, 193. Perry Miller, "From the Covenant to the Revival," in *Religion in American History: Interpretive Essays,* ed. John M. Mulder and John F. Wilson (Englewood Cliffs, NJ, 1978), 145–61 at 157.

25. James Downey, *The Eighteenth Century Pulpit: A Study of the Sermons of Butler, Berkeley, Secker, Sterne, Whitefield and*

Wesley (Oxford, 1969), 155, 157, internal quote cited from J. Gillies, ed., *Works of Whitefield*, 6 vols. (London, 1771–72), 5:161.

26. *The Confessions of St. Augustine*, trans. E. B. Pusey, with a foreword by A. H. Armstrong, Everyman Ed. (London, 1907), [Bk. VII, Chap. 10], 132–34; cf. 219–27 [Bk. X, Chaps. 17–26]. The "It" of Augustine's meditation receives powerful development in Eric Voegelin's late writings when he speaks of the "It-reality": "To denote the reality that comprehends the partners in being, i.e., God and the world, man and society, no technical term has been developed, as far as I know, by anybody. However, I notice that philosophers, when they run into this structure incidentally in their exploration of other subject matters, have a habit of referring to it by a neutral 'it.' The It referred to is the mysterious 'it' that also occurs in everyday language in such phrases as 'it rains.' I shall call it therefore the It-reality, as distinguished from the thing-reality [apprehended through sensory perception.]" Voegelin, *Order and History*, vol. V, *In Search of Order* (1987), 16.

27. The spiritual depth of American religion generally is so often passed over in favor of defining the various doctrinal beliefs and disputes that emphasis must be placed on it here, even if it cannot be widely illustrated. Whether New Light or Old Light, the eighteenth-century clergy (and their audiences) imbibed scripture with great thoroughness and profundity. They widely read such meditative literature as Augustine's *Confessions*, whose spiritual discipline they took to heart and practiced day and night. Among other "popish divines," Pascal was a favorite author of the Scottish Presbyterian John Witherspoon at Princeton, for instance; and Ezra Stiles at Yale was reading PseudoDionysius as much as he was the New Testament at the end of his life, we are told. Jonathan Edwards the Elder, the greatest American mind of the age and a leading New Light, was himself a mystic.

28. The Virginian Edward Baptist and the John Corbly Memorial Baptist Church "Declaration of Faith in Practice, Being a Covenant, . . . November 7, 1773, " quoted

by Robert M. Calhoon, "The Evangelical Persuasion," *Religion in a Revolutionary Age*, ed. Hoffman and Albert, 157.

29. Lemuel Burkitt and Jesse Read, *A Concise History of the Kehukee Baptist Association* (Halifax, NC, 1803) as quoted in Marini, "Religion, Politics, Ratification," *Religion in a Revolutionary Age*, ed. Hoffman and Albert, 211.

30. Calhoon, "The Evangelical Persuasion," 160, quoting George Whitefield, *The Indwelling of the Spirit, the Common Privilege of All Believers* (London, 1739), 1–2.

31. Marini, "Religion, Politics, and Ratification," *Religion in a Revolutionary Age*, ed. Hoffman and Albert, 215. Internal quotation unattributed.

32. *The Autobiography of Benjamin Franklin*, intro. by R. Jackson Wilson (New York, 1981), 132.

33. Noah Webster as excerpted in Verna M. Hall, ed., *The Christian History of the American Revolution* (San Francisco, 1976), 21; Noah Webster, preface, *The Webster Bible* (1833; facsimile rpt. Grand Rapids, MI, 1987), v. Italics as in original.

34. Genesis 1:31. This and Psalm 119:134 (quoted below) were the texts for the Plymouth Anniversary Sermon by Gad Hitchcock of Pembroke that was preached at Plymouth, Massachusetts, on December 22, 1774; it is the principal source of the summary given in the following three paragraphs. This sermon is reprinted in Hall, ed., *The Christian History of the American Revolution*, 30–43.

35. Benjamin Franklin in Farrand, ed., *Records of the Federal Convention*, 1:451.

36. Calhoon, "Evangelical Persuasion," *Religion in a Revolutionary Age*, 159, 162–63. Hatch is quoted from his "In Pursuit of Religious Freedom: Church, State, and People in the New Republic," in *The American Revolution: Its Character and Limits*, ed. Jack P. Greene (New York, 1987), 391.

37. Nathan O. Hatch, *The Democratization of American Christianity* (New Haven, CT, 1989), 5.

38. John Leland's 1790 and 1791 statements, principally from *The Rights of Conscience Inalienable . . . or, the High-flying Churchman, Stripped of his Legal Robe, Appears a Yaho* (New London, 1791), 8, 15–16, as quoted in Hatch, *The Democratization*

of American Christianity, 98. For the full text of Leland's pamphlet see Sandoz, ed., *Sermons of the American Founding Era,* 1079–99.

39. Wyclif's Bible was the first complete English version, a translation from the Latin Vulgate completed around 1384, the year of his death; it was largely the work of his pupils, Nicholas of Hereford and probably John Purvey, who did a revision. But the first complete printing of Wyclif's Bible occurred only in 1850 in the edition by Forshall and Madden. See the prologue to Wyclif's Bible, Josiah Forshall and Sir Frederic Madden, eds., 4 vols. (Oxford, 1850), I, 2, 3. Wyclif's teachings inspired certain aspects of the later Reformers' efforts and political theory; they are suggestive, also, of themes of the New Light preachers of the eighteenth century.

40. Cf. Teresa Toulouse, *The Art of Prophesying: New England Sermons and the Shaping of Belief* (Macon, Ga., 1987), Chap. 1.

41. Trevelyan as quoted by H. Richard Niebuhr, "The Idea of Covenant and American Democracy," *Church History,* 23 (1954), 126–35 at 130. Cf. Henning Graf Reventlow, *The Authority of the Bible and the Rise of the Modern World,* trans. John Bowden (Philadelphia, 1985), 211–14.

42. Baldwin, "Sowers of Sedition," *William and Mary Quarterly* 3rd Series, 5 (1948), 76. Cf. *The New England Clergy and the American Revolution,* 168–72.

43. Bonomi, "Dissent and Exceptionalism", in *Religion in a Revolutionary Age,* ed. Hoffman and Albert, 50–51.

44. Clark, *The Language of Liberty,* 36, 384.

45. Sandoz, *A Government of Laws,* 160–61. The internal quote is from Patrick Riley, *Will and Political Legitimacy: A Critical Exposition of Social Contract Theory in Hobbes, Locke, Rousseau, Kant, and Hegel* (Cambridge, MA, 1982), 5.

46. Harold J. Berman, "The Origins of Historical Jurisprudence: Coke, Selden, Hale," *Yale Law Journal,* 103 (May 1994):1651–1738 at 1722. The ellipsis omits the word *England,* but the sense equally applies to America as heir to English historical jurisprudence and common law.

47. A start is made in Ellis Sandoz, "Foundations of American Liberty and Rule of Law," *Presidential Studies Quarterly,* 24 (Summer 1994): 605–17.

James R. Stoner Jr.

Is There a Political Philosophy in the Declaration of Independence?

VOL. 40, NO. 2, 2005

Is there a political philosophy in the Declaration of Independence? One step toward answering this question—not the only step, but from the philosopher's point of view the most fundamental—is to ask whether the "self-evident truths" of the Declaration are really true after all. Another way of putting it, which I once saw in a conference title, is to ask whether the "self-evident truths" are fact or fiction.

I have to admit that "fact or fiction" struck me at first as an odd way of questioning the authenticity of truths, but on reflection I decided it was a particularly felicitous turn of phrase. Living in a pragmatic age, we tend to equate fact with truth, and fiction with falsehood. There is something characteristically American about such a way of thinking. Still, it is important at the outset to recognize that this frame of mind is not universal. No less an authority than Aristotle writes that fiction (poetry) is "more philosophic and more serious" than fact (history), because it speaks of universals rather than particulars; there is more truth in understanding the soul of a man like Homer's Odysseus than in knowing, to

quote Aristotle, what "Alcibiades did or had done to him"[1]—or even, did *not* do or have done to him, as students of Plato's *Symposium* will understand. I will return to the question of fact and its relation to truth, but my point at the outset is that part of the question of whether there is a political philosophy in the Declaration is whether what the Declaration proclaims as self-evident truths really are true.

But that is not the whole of the question. As others have pointed out, the Declaration does not say, "These truths are self-evident. . . ." It says, instead, that "we hold" them to be so. If we understand "philosophy" as it is often understood, in the sense of a doctrine, and if we understand "political philosophy" as political science departments often do, as a synonym for political theory, then the question of whether there is a political philosophy in the Declaration is the question of whether the Declaration binds us to a particular political creed.

I say "binds" because the Declaration is treated, even today, as authoritative law in one sense: It is printed at the head of the *United States Code,* where it is considered the first of our organic laws.

More to the point, politically today the Declaration of Independence has no open enemies; it is the touchstone of our political arguments rather than an object of advocacy any more. Even those who dismiss the American founders as racist or sexist want to keep the Declaration. They accuse the founders of hypocrisy rather than mistaken principle. It is not only that no one wants to be on the wrong side of the Declaration, but that even the charges made against the Declaration's authors seem to be anchored in the Declaration's own principle of equality. Whether or not that principle and the other purported truths that accompany it are true, they would seem in fact to be the first principles of our regime.

And this leads to my third concern. If the "self-evident truths" of the Declaration are either true or fundamentally ours, how should they affect our political life? While loyalty to the original Constitution is often dismissed as hopelessly anachronistic or conservative, loyalty to the Declaration might seem to have the opposite consequence: to mandate support of those movements that seek to extend the reach of equality in America. Abraham Lincoln seems to have thought so. He wrote that the assertion of human equality in the Declaration provides

> a standard maxim for free society, which should be familiar to all, and revered by all; constantly looked to, constantly labored for, and even though never perfectly attained, constantly approximated, and thereby constantly spreading and deepening its influence, and augmenting the happiness and value of life to all people of all colors everywhere.[2]

At the very least, Lincoln's use of the Declaration's principle of equality in the controversy over slavery set a precedent for its use to reform the regime from within.

Still, however important Lincoln's achievement or however appropriate the use of the Declaration in its support—Jefferson himself understood the implications of his principles for the question of slavery, as evidenced by the clause condemning the slave trade that he would have included but that Congress cut out—it still ought to be legitimate to ask whether the Declaration today commits Americans to a particular program of development.

These then are my questions. I want to ask whether the self-evident truths are true, whether we believe they are, and how we ought to act on them. First, however, I want to ask what they *mean* and to answer by paying attention to the document as a whole.

The Short Version and the Long

Suppose the Declaration had been written as it is usually read today. It would be only about a page in length, edited down to the first two paragraphs and then the last, where the actual declaration of independence is made. No one would deny that these paragraphs—especially the famous second one, with its elegantly simple account of the first principles of natural rights and just government—contain the most memorable phrases in the document, indeed precisely the phrases that have fired the imagination of generations of Americans and of reformers and revolutionaries around the globe. Nor is it only frequent repetition that gives these phrases their ring of self-evidence, even several centuries after they were penned. Jefferson crafted them with care, and he drew upon a rich tradition of political theory that had developed in the previous century or so in England, most especially as conveyed in the *Two Treatises of Government* by John Locke.

Though echoes of Locke's phraseology can be heard in Jefferson's language, Jefferson claimed that the Declaration did not reflect any single man's ideas but rather "the harmonizing sentiments of the day, whether expressed in conversation, in letters, printed essays, or in the elementary books of public right, as Aristotle, Cicero, Locke, Sidney, etc."[3] Insisting that political reflection must begin with equal natural rights, that government is itself not naturally given but rather is formed through the consent of those who acknowledge it, that government has the limited purpose of securing rights, and that abusive government can be cashiered, the theoretical paragraph of the Declaration sketches a political doctrine that today we recognize as classically liberal—in contradistinction, I might add, despite Jefferson's claim, to Aristotle's teaching that the polis exists by nature and has the promotion of virtue as its highest end. Whether out of personal conviction or because liberty cannot be secure unless the people believe—remember his famous remark a decade later, "can the liberties of a nation be thought secure when we have removed their only firm basis, a conviction in the minds of the people that these liberties are of the gift of God?"[4]—Jefferson states more clearly than Locke that what I have called equal natural rights are an endowment of the Creator, presumably the same "Nature's God" mentioned in the Declaration's first sentence. But that government itself has a human rather than a divine origin is clear. Indeed, in a sense, that is the whole point—for the Declaration is written to justify political change.

Still, the famous paragraphs of the Declaration are but a part of the whole. Looked at by an age enamored of political theory and ideology, they appear to be its most important passages; but at the center of the document is a list of grievances against the king and Parliament that make the case for independence there and then. These are, the Declaration says, "Facts . . . submitted to a candid World" to "prove" that the British are intent upon "the Establishment of an absolute Tyranny over these States."

These central passages of the Declaration's bill of indictment are conveniently grouped in three divisions. The first is concerned with constitutional violations and abuses of constitutional powers by the king. Here, twelve different complaints are lodged, accusing the king of threatening the public good by the use of his veto, dissolving colonial assemblies, obstructing justice, keeping standing armies among them in peacetime, and the like. The thirteenth grievance introduces the second division, the "Acts of pretended legislation" that the king has passed by "combin[ing] with others to subject us to a Jurisdiction foreign to our Constitution, and unacknowledged by our Laws." Referred to here are nine acts of Parliament, described not by name but by their effects—imposing taxes without consent, suspending trial by jury, abolishing colonial charters, and so forth. Finally, there are five statements introduced by an implicit reference to the King's Proclamation of Rebellion of August 23, 1775, under which "He has abdicated Government here, by declaring us out of his Protection and waging War against us." Here, his acts of war are summarized and denounced.

From the point of view of the theoretical paragraphs with their "self-evident truths," these many statements in the middle of the Declaration are the "facts" which prove that the king has in mind a despotism over America and that the colonists had better act now. As a reading of the middle section, this is sound, but not sufficient. To be sure, if revolution has to be made for a reason, then there has to be a way of proving that the king is becoming tyrannical; this is precisely what the various facts are meant to show. But unlike the first principles of politics, the tyranny in these rather general facts—which never name names or dates or places—is not immediately self-evident. The outrage comes from a hidden premise: the English constitutional tradition, or at least the common law rights and liberties of that tradition, which the Americans claim as their rightful heritage.

Here is the source of the principle of no taxation without representation, the independence of the judiciary, trial by jury, the priority of civil to military authority, and much else. That scholars today no longer tend to read these parts of the Declaration is some measure of how far we have lost touch with that tradition, but that does not mean the complaints were not taken seriously by our founding generation. To speak only of the federal level, nearly every grievance detailed in the Declaration is addressed and prevented by a specific provision of the Constitution and the Bill of Rights. The bill of grievances, in other words, adds gravity and substance to the abstract principles formulated in the "self-evident truths," and thus guards against arbitrary recourse to rebellion.

The Declaration justifies a political revolution, to be sure, but the constitutional dispute with England gave our revolution its distinctive form and contributed to its success. That revolution was not without its lawless moments, but on the whole its spirit was to reinvigorate old forms of self-governance and to reinforce protection for property and social order. Its self-evident first principles were soon to challenge some of these forms—restrictions on the suffrage, for example, and in some of the states, slavery, itself unknown at common law—but it is no more an accident that these challenges were approached in a spirit of constitutional compromise than that the revolution culminated in a Constitution. There, after all, in the middle division of the middle part of the Declaration, is mention of an unwritten "Constitution" which the Americans *already* assert to be their own.

What Is *Not* Self-Evident about the Self-Evident Truths

The self-evident truths of the Declaration, then, garner much of their specific political significance for the American Revolution from the evidence offered by the facts of Anglo-American constitutionalism; these measure the violations (and later the remedies) as well as moderate the radical potential in the revolutionary language taken by itself. Stripped of this context, the first principles enunciated by Jefferson are not self-evident at all—at least, not to anyone raised in the tradition of Western virtue or in a world formed by Judeo-Christian belief.

Let me give an example. The "self-evident truths," it seems to me, do not give an adequate account of the family, the fundamental institution of social life. First, whatever might be said of the relation of husband and wife, the family is built not around equality, but around the inequality of parent and child. Precisely the most basic meaning of Jefferson's statement of equality—that no man is the natural ruler or the natural subject of another—is *not* true of this relation, for the parents are surely the natural rulers of their dependent children. Second, the family is first and foremost not about rights, but about duties; even the right of children to care and education is abstract and vague compared to the duty of parents to provide and instruct and the duty of children to obey and learn. Third, the origin of the family is not exactly consent. In some cultures, including our own, spouses choose for themselves whom to marry, but even then the roles they assume are largely socially defined. Except in cases of adoption, and very rarely then, children do not choose their parents, and (leaving aside brave, new technologies and, again, adoption) parents do not choose their children. Fourth, the end of the family is only incidentally the security of rights; it is principally provision and nurture in an environment formed by love. And fifth, when family becomes destructive of its ends, it cannot be altered and abolished without in most instances inflicting further wounds that never heal.

Now about this counterexample to the self-evident truths of the Declaration, allow me to make two points. First, Jefferson and his fellows were altogether aware that families were not formed upon their principles. Precisely what they objected to in Tory political theory was *political* patriarchalism, the effort to form *the state* on analogy to the family. Natural equality meant that the king was not to act as father in relation to his people— not that fathers were not kings in their own homes. Government by consent meant that the commandment to honor one's father and mother could not be invoked by a political nobility demanding homage. That abusive government can be changed was not seen to undermine the indissolubility of marriage nor the lifelong attachment between parent and child.

But secondly, there is no denying that, since as long ago as John Locke's *Two Treatises* and even Thomas Hobbes's *Leviathan,* liberal philosophers have sought to reconceive the family on liberal terms, and of course in our own day a vast social experiment has been undertaken to remodel the family on egalitarian principles and to reorient authority within it on the basis of consent. Though opinions about the success of this effort are bound to differ, allow me to say for my own part that I am more impressed by the resilience of old patterns against all the force of dominant opinion than I am by evidence that abuses have been diminished and familial happiness more commonly achieved. The fundamental equality of the sexes may be self-evident, but their equality in the sense of their having no relevant differences even from the point of view of the family is not. And unless one is driven by a personal or ideological commitment to nontraditional family forms, I do not see how one can argue that the current regime with regard to the family in Western society is self-evidently the best, at least with respect to children. One might note that almost nowhere in the West today are native populations even reproducing their numbers, and in some countries those populations are on the verge of precipitous decline. It is a matter in which we certainly need, and all have difficulty sorting through, the facts.

What, Then, *Is* Self-Evidently True?

My point in raising the counterexample of the family is not to deny that what the Declaration calls self-evident truths are true, but to show, first, the grounds that might be raised in objection to them (and so, I concede, to call into question their self-evidence), and second, to suggest how they need to be understood so as not to place their authors under the charge of hopeless contradiction.

Of course a contradiction between our founders' words and practices was much noted and commented on in the country's first four-score years and seven in regard to the institution of slavery. Justice can hardly be done to this topic in a brief mention, but I would say that on the whole the founders recognized the contradiction and hoped, in Lincoln's terms, that they had placed slavery on a course of ultimate extinction—even though they excised the condemnation of slavery from Jefferson's draft. When a generation came along that defended slavery as a positive good, that generation either denounced the Declaration or interpreted its universal language in narrow ways.

With regard to the family, however, I see no contradiction within the Declaration's theory, though perhaps there is a certain ambiguity. It is easy enough to understand the pressure of analogy that would make the hierarchical family entail an authoritarian state, or make an egalitarian state demand an egalitarian family. But it also makes sense to see the relation as, I would argue, our Founding Fathers did: The patriarchal state had to go because it makes children of real fathers, refusing to allow them the manly responsibility of governing themselves and those with whose care they are charged. In this way, the issue resembles the related theological question of God's kingship. On the one hand, divine kingship might seem to entail by analogy a divine right to rule in a human, hereditary king. On the other hand, if God is king, then every human king is a usurper. Would not the true believer say: "We have no other king but God"?

What the Declaration and the revolution it articulated did establish was *political* liberty. So wrote John Marshall to a correspondent in his later years; in fact, his letter was to the redoubtable Edward Everett, Unitarian minister, Harvard Professor of Greek literature, then a U.S. Representative, later president of Harvard, Governor of Massachusetts, U.S. Senator from the same, and the man who shared the platform with Lincoln at Gettysburg in 1863. Wrote Marshall to Everett:

> Our resistance was not made to actual oppression. Americans were not pressed down to the earth by the weight of their chains nor goaded to resistance by actual suffering. . . . The war was a war of principle against a system hostile to political liberty, from which oppression was to be dreaded, not against actual oppression.[5]

In other words, Americans already knew political liberty, or at least had tasted some part of self-government, through their experience with the practices and rights, the privileges and immunities, of England's common law constitution. And they could see that Parliament and the king were committed to a colonial policy that would henceforth keep them subordinate. The relation of mother country to dependent colonies, however appropriate in the early years, was fast becoming a fiction as a rising generation of Americans learned they had the wisdom, the skills, the confidence, and the solidarity to govern themselves.

The British ministry understood this development, too, and when they moved to foreclose it, the colonists struck back. Because the Americans soon realized that the conflict was irreversible, they could not merely invoke traditional liberties.

Besides, they had learned over the course of a decade of constitutional dispute that their ability to resist Britain depended on their concert of action, and there was no established continent-spanning government to whose traditional authority they could make appeal. Thus it is not quite true, as Lincoln later said, that "the assertion that 'all men are created equal' was of no practical use in effecting our separation from Great Britain"; it was necessary to make intellectually coherent the appeal to *traditional* liberties that would now have to be embodied in *innovative* forms—a federal government that spanned the length of the Atlantic coast and reconstituted governments in "free and independent states."

In asserting a right of self-government, the Americans in the Declaration appealed to a universal principle, political liberty, which against the fictions of the time had a radical meaning, but which they themselves knew from actual experience, as Marshall's letter makes plain. Even when Lincoln suggests its radical potential, in the passage I quoted above, he implicitly clings to its specifically political connotation. The founders, he adds, "knew the propensity of prosperity to breed tyrants, and they meant that when such should reappear in this fair land and commence their vocation, they should have at least one hard nut to crack."[6] At least in the nineteenth and early twentieth centuries, every extension of the principle of equality in American constitutionalism—from the extension of the franchise coupled with an attack on politically entrenched economic privilege in Jacksonian times, to the extension of basic economic and then political rights to blacks and to women—involved an expansion of the class who could claim political liberty, not its replacement with a contrary ideal.

Read in the light of the document as a whole, then, the self-evident truths of the Declaration of Independence constitute an understanding of political liberty that is the basis of our constitutional order. Precisely because they commit us to liberty on political questions, they swear us to no allegiance to a political creed beyond a willingness to support the Constitution. Because the political things are not the whole of things, or even the noblest things, the truths about the political things cannot pretend to capture the whole of truth: political liberty can be a good, even a noble good, without being the comprehensive good.

But the whole truth is more complex than these Aristotelian propositions alone would indicate. Under the theory of the Declaration, politics is instrumental in its origin and limited in its ends, but this is precisely what makes it possible for us to act freely in political life, to bring truth as we understand it and goods and interests as we experience them into the public square. In other words, political liberty is good *because* it is not the comprehensive good. Since human beings are limited beings, we can only be just if we are also moderate.

Liberalism and Republicanism

It was fashionable a couple decades ago to debate the revolution and the founding in terms of a dichotomy between liberalism and republicanism. Since my foregoing remarks might seem to align me with the republican camp, let me clarify the dispute as I understand it and explain where I mean to be.

On this dichotomy, liberalism describes a political philosophy, traceable to Hobbes and Locke, that makes individual rights fundamental and government derivative and instrumental to their security. Despite their differences, both Hobbes and Locke thought men equal in a pre-political state of nature, and both thought that equality was necessarily compromised when society was formed. Men are equally subject to government, according to Hobbes, or to "settled, standing rules," according to Locke, but substantial inequalities in property and in all the other rewards of civil society are allowed—indeed, through commerce they would be encouraged to develop. Hobbes made the sovereign the judge of what religion would be publicly taught in the commonwealth, while Locke famously argued that all tolerant sects ought themselves to be tolerated, but both agreed that religion could raise no claim to political authority. In almost no other respect could Hobbes be thought a champion of political liberty. Locke could, but political life was narrowly circumscribed by making its end the preservation of property; there is a place for great politics in Locke, but only at the moment of an "appeal to heaven," when the people need to call their government to account for having changed its form illegitimately or for having transgressed its end.

The republican alternative to liberalism sketched by historians is variously attributed to Aristotle, Machiavelli, and Harrington, and ought perhaps to refer as well to the early books of Montesquieu's *Spirit of the Laws* or even to the *Social Contract* of Rousseau. Here, the emphasis is on selfless devotion to the common good, military service, education in citizenship, and the active exercise of virtue in the public realm. Property is not ignored, but it is the precondition of citizenship: One needs to own to have the independence to act freely, and perhaps one needs to own much to know how to command. The republican tradition is less philosophical than the liberal, for the latter

was theoretical in nature—it was, after all, imagining something new—while the former generally had its eyes on Rome. While liberalism made its peace with human vices, such as avarice and ambition, republicanism stressed the danger of corruption and the need for vigilance and renewal. As for religion, republicanism prudently retired it to a subordinate theater or boldly made it civic, consecrating the republic. If the proof texts of this civic republicanism are elusive, its monuments are unmistakable. Most obviously, they define the architecture of Washington, D.C., and the capitols of many of the states.

In recent years, the liberal-republican dichotomy has been challenged in several ways. First, scholars such as Paul Rahe, Thomas Pangle, and others have argued that there is a distinctively modern republicanism that bridges the gap between the two schools of thought.[7] In Michael Zuckert's formulation, liberalism dictates that the end of the polity is the security of rights, while republicanism designs the political science by which a government might be constructed to keep rights secure.[8] Second, historian Gordon Wood has argued that the true alternative to republicanism is not liberalism but democracy; republicanism was simply an ideology that facilitated the transition between two relatively stable, if not natural, social and political regimes, monarchy and democracy.[9] The republican founders meant to reject monarchy, in which they had been raised, but they did not intend to establish democracy; despite their intention, the changes they initiated in their revolution necessarily entailed democracy, once men bred under monarchy passed from the scene.

While I find some cogency to both of the critiques just outlined, I do not think that they show the Declaration to be either staunchly liberal or increasingly democratic in its implications. Instead, it seems to me that the common law constitutionalism sketched at the center of the Declaration defines the form and the limits of political liberty as it was understood by those who made the revolution and preserves an influence in the American regime that should be called Aristotelian. The form of government it supposes has a mixed character; the goods it secures are multiple and not readily commensurable; its adversarial process invites rhetorical dispute; its attitude toward change is wary, but not dismissive; it makes room for equity, without surrendering government by law to rule of the wise.

Common law is unwritten law—like that unwritten "Constitution" mentioned in the middle of the Declaration—and the friends of common law would hold with Aristotle that "[l]aws based on unwritten customs are more sovereign, and deal with more sovereign matters, than written laws."[10] Moreover, it is the unwrittenness of common law and its consequent openness to truth that made possible its concurrence or coexistence with the Christian religion, and later with different varieties of that religion and with Judaism and even with other faiths—and this, without the dogmatism of liberalism's separation of church and state.

My point is not to deny classical republican influences in the American founding or in the subsequent history of the regime or especially in its military traditions; nor to deny that liberalism laid the basis for our dynamic economy and its engine of technological development and change, nor that liberalism has influenced the course of our political development, especially in overcoming racial slavery. But I think that our constitutionalism and the spirited political

liberty that gives it shape depend, if they are to be fully understood historically and analytically, on other things.

Conclusion

In looking at the Declaration of Independence, then, I am saying that we can accept a few basic political principles that undergird our constitutional order without having to insist on an orthodoxy of first principles. We can hold the self-evident truths to be self-evidently true precisely because the principles they articulate do not offer a comprehensive account of human life. Perhaps no one would disagree if the issue is put in this way, but it entails, to my mind, an agreement not to press the argument of the Declaration beyond its proper bounds. When the Declaration is stretched, it becomes a partisan tool, not an anchor of consensus. As there is room in the American polity for one who believes in rights but not in the Creator who endows us with them, so there ought to be room for one who thinks that rights derive from duties to just such a Creator, or even to a nature that distinguishes better from worse.

To be true to the spirit of the Declaration means, from my perspective, not that we are bound to the most radical reading of its most abstract truth, but that we ought to recover the spirited aspiration to self-government that gave the American Revolution its force and its justification. Rather than look to an unelected judiciary for the formulation of our ideals—or to the liberal philosophers who want to rule through them—we should neither shy away from free debate on important social questions nor demand that every consensus work out its derivation from first things in order to count. Let us hold, then, to the principles of the Declaration as constitutive of our fundamental law, but let us not mistake them as adequate to every exigency in our personal, our religious, or even our political lives. Political philosophy of different sorts influenced the Declaration, but the Declaration itself is not, nor was it meant to be, a philosophical text. That by its terms it points us beyond itself, to political philosophy and to other things, is no small measure of its greatness and no little element of its success.

Notes

1. *Poetics,* 1451b1 ff.
2. Speech at Springfield, Illinois, June 26, 1857, in Abraham Lincoln, *Selected Speeches, Messages, and Letters,* ed. T. Harry Williams (New York: Holt, Rinehart, and Winston, Inc., 1957), 72–73.
3. "Letter to Henry Lee," in *Jefferson: Writings,* ed. Merrill Peterson (New York: Library of America, 1984), 1501.
4. Jefferson, "Notes on the State of Virginia," Query XVIII, in *Writings,* 289. The passage continues: "That they are not to be violated but with his wrath?"
5. Letter to Edward Everett, August 2, 1826, quoted in R. Kent Newmyer, *John Marshall and the Heroic Age of the Supreme Court* (Baton Rouge: Louisiana State Univ. Press, 2001), 1.
6. Op. cit., 73.
7. Paul Rahe, *Republics Ancient and Modern* (Chapel Hill, NC: Univ. of North Carolina Press, 1992), and Thomas Pangle, *The Spirit of Modern Republicanism* (Chicago: Univ. of Chicago Press, 1989).
8. Michael Zuckert, *The Natural Rights Republic* (Notre Dame: Notre Dame Univ. Press, 1997).
9. Gordon Wood, *The Radicalism of the American Revolution* (New York: Knopf, 1993).
10. Aristotle, *Politics* III, 1287b1

IV.

EDUCATION & ITS ENEMIES

Richard M. Weaver

Education and the Individual

VOL. 2, NO. 1, 1965

The greatest school that ever existed, it has been said, consisted of Socrates standing on a street corner with one or two interlocutors. If this remark strikes the average American as merely a bit of fancy, that is because education here today suffers from an unprecedented amount of aimlessness and confusion. This is not to suggest that education in the United States, as compared with other countries, fails to command attention and support. In our laws we have endorsed it without qualification, and our provision for it, despite some claims to the contrary, has been on a lavish scale. But we behold a situation in which, as the educational plants become larger and more finely appointed, what goes on in them becomes more diluted, less serious, less effective in training mind and character; and correspondingly what comes out of them becomes less equipped for the rigorous tasks of carrying forward an advanced civilization.

Recently I attended a conference addressed by a retired general who had some knowledge of this country's ballistics program. He pointed out that of the twenty-five top men concerned with

our progress in this now vital branch of science, not more than two or three were Americans. The others were Europeans, who had received in their *European* educations the kind of theoretical discipline essential to the work of getting the great missiles aloft. It was a sad commentary on a nation which has prided itself on giving its best to the schools.

It is an educational breakdown which has occurred. Our failure in these matters traces back to a failure to think hard about the real province of education. Most Americans take a certain satisfaction in regarding themselves as tough-minded when it comes to successful ways of doing things and positive achievements. But in deciding what is and is not pertinent to educating the individual, far too many of them have been softheads.

An alarming percentage of our citizens, it is to be feared, stop with the word "education" itself. It is for them a kind of conjuror's word, which is expected to work miracles by the very utterance. If politics become selfish and shortsighted, the cure that comes to mind is "education." If juvenile delinquency is rampant, "education" is expected to provide the remedy. If the cultural level of popular entertainment declines, "education" is thought of hopefully as the means of arresting the downward trend, People expect to be saved by a word when they cannot even give content to the word.

SOMEWHAT BETTER off, but far from sufficiently informed and critical, are those who recognize that education must, after all, take some kind of form, that it must be thought of as a process that does something one can recognize. Most of these people, however, see education only as the means by which a person is transported from one economic plane to a higher one, or in some cases from one cultural level to another that is more highly esteemed. They are not wholly wrong in these assumptions, for it is true that persons with a good education do receive, over the period of their lifetime, larger earnings than those without, and it is true that almost any education brings with it a certain amount of cultivation. But again, these people are looking at the outward aspects and are judging education by what it does for one in the general economic and social ordering. In both of these respects education is valued as a means of getting ahead in life, a perfectly proper and legitimate goal, of course, but hardly one which sums up the whole virtue and purpose of an undertaking, which, in a modern society, may require as much as one quarter of the life span. Education as a conjuror's word and education viewed as a means of insuring one's progress in relation to his fellows both divert attention from what needs to be done for the individual as a person.

Education is a process by which the individual is developed into something better than he would have been without it. Now when one views this idea from a certain perspective, it appears almost terrifying. How does one go about taking human beings and making them better? The very thought seems in a way the height of presumption. For one thing, it involves the premise that some human beings can be better than others, a supposition that is resisted in some quarters. Yet nothing can be plainer, when we consider it, than this fact that education is discriminative. It takes what is less good physically, mentally, and morally and transforms that by various methods and techniques into something that more nearly approaches our ideal of the good. Every educator who presumes to speak about his profession has in mind some aim, goal, or purpose that he views as beneficial. As various as are the schemes proposed, they all share this general concept of betterment. The teacher who did not believe that his efforts contributed to some kind of improvement would certainly have lost the reason for his calling. A surface unanimity about purpose, however, is not enough to prevent confusion and chaos where there is radical disagreement about the nature of the creature who is to be educated.

If man were merely an animal, his "education" would consist only of scientific feeding and proper exercise. If he were merely a tool or an instrument, it would consist of training him in certain response and behavior patterns. If he were a mere pawn of the political state, it would consist of indoctrinating him so completely that he could not see beyond what his masters wanted him to believe. Strange as it may seem, adherents to each of these views can be found in the modern world. But our great tradition of liberal education supported by our intuitive feeling about the nature of man, rejects them all as partial descriptions.

THE VAST majority of people conscious of this tradition agree that the purpose of education is to make the human being more human. Every generation is born ignorant and unformed; it is the task of those whom society employs as educators to bring the new arrivals up to a certain level of humanity. But even with this simple statement, we find trickiness in the terms. The word "human" is one of varying implications. In estimating what constitutes a complete human being some persons today are willing to settle for a pretty low figure. To some of them, as previously noted, he is nothing more than an animal in an advanced state of evolution. His brain is only a highly developed muscle, useful to him in the same way that the prehensile tail is to the monkey; his needs are a set of skills which will enable him to get his sustenance from nature, and his purpose is to enjoy himself with the minimum amount of anxiety and the maximum amount of physical satisfaction. Others go somewhat beyond this and insist that in addition to his requirements as an animal, man has certain needs which can be described as social, intellectual and aesthetic, and that these in turn require a kind of education which is not limited to practical self-survival. Others go beyond this and say that man is an incurably spiritual being—that he is this even when he says he is not—and that he cannot live a satisfying sort of life until certain ends which might be called psychic are met. Man has an irresistible desire to relate himself somehow to the totality, to ask what is the meaning of his presence here amid the great empirical fact of the universe. Many feel that until this question receives some sort of answer, none of the facts of life can be put in any kind of perspective.

We will not pause to weigh the opinion of those who consider man merely an animal. This view has always been both incredible and repugnant to the majority of mankind, and is accepted only by the few who have bound themselves to a theoretical materialism.

All others agree that the human being has a distinguishing attribute in mind. Now mind is something more than brain. Many anatomists and surgeons have seen a brain, but nobody has ever seen a mind. This is because we believe that the mind is not merely a central exchange of the body's system, where nerve impulses are brought together and relayed; it is a still mysterious entity in which man associates together the various cognitive, aesthetic, moral, and spiritual impulses which come to him from the outer and inner worlds. It is the seat of his rational faculty, but it is also the place where his inclinations are reduced to order and are directed. Most importantly for the concerns of education, mind is the place where symbols are understood and are acted upon.

MAN HAS, in fact, been defined as the symbol-using animal. This definition makes symbol-using the distinguishing characteristic which separates him from all the other creatures with which he shares animal attributes. Even though the definition may be a partial one, it points to the faculty which has enabled man to create cultures and civilizations. The significance of the symbol is that it enables us to express knowledge and to communicate in an intellectual and not in a sensate way. Even in the matter of economy, this gain is an enormous one. If a man wishes to indicate six, he uses the symbol "6"; he does not have to lay out six pieces of wood or other objects to make his meaning clear to another. If he wishes to indicate water, he does not have to go through the motions of drinking or some other pantomime. If he wishes to express his insight into a wide complex of physical phenomena, he can do this by means of a mathematical formula, like the now famous $E=mc^2$. This is a highly symbolic form of expression, in the absence of which, it is hardly needful to point out, man's power to deal with nature would be very much smaller than it is at present. But symbolism is not used only to convey information about the physical world. Through the use of symbols man expresses those feelings and states of being which are none the less real for being subjective. His feelings of love, of delight, of aversion have been put in forms transmissible from generation to generation through the use of symbols—letters in literature, notation in music, symbolic articles in dress and in ceremonials, and so on. It is impossible to realize how poor our lives would be without the intellectual and emotional creations which depend upon this symbolic activity.

It might seem that all of this is too obvious to need a case made for it. But there exists a crisis in education today which forces all who believe in the higher nature of man to come to the defense of those subjects which discipline the mind through the language of sign and symbol.

FOR SOME while now there has been a movement among certain people styling themselves educators to disparage and even do away with the very things that were once considered the reason for and the purpose of all education. There has been a bold and open attempt to deny that man has a nature which is fulfilled only when these higher faculties are brought into play, educated, and used to make life more human in the distinctive sense. Oddly enough, the movement has

arrogated to itself the name "progressive." That seems a curious term to apply to something that is retrogressive in effect, since it would drag men back toward the pre-symbolic era. In preempting the adjective "progressive" for their brand of education, these innovators were trying a rhetorical maneuver. They were trying to give the impression that their theory of education is the only forward-looking one, and that the traditional ones were inherited from times and places that sat in darkness.

Now it is quite true that "progressive" education represents a departure from an ideal that has prevailed ever since the ancient Hebrews, the people of the Bible, thought about religion, and the Greeks envisioned the life of reason. This new education is not designed for man as an immortal soul, nor is it designed to help him measure up to any ideal standard. The only goal which it professes to have in view is "adjustment to life." If we examine this phrase carefully, we will see that it, like a number of others that these educational imposters have been wont to use, is rather cleverly contrived to win a rhetorical advantage. "Adjustment" has an immediate kind of appeal, because no one likes to think of himself as being "maladjusted"; that suggests failure, discomfort, and other unpleasant experiences. And furthermore, "adjustment to life" may be taken by the unwary as suggesting a kind of victory over life—success and pleasure and all that sort of thing. But as soon as we begin to examine the phrase both carefully and critically, we find that it contains booby traps. It is far from likely that the greatest men of the past, including not only famous ones but also great benefactors of humanity, have been "adjusted" in this sense. When we begin to study their actual lives, we find that these were filled with toil, strenuousness, anxiety, self-sacrifice, and sometimes a good bit of friction with their environment. In fact, it would be much nearer the truth to say that the great creative spirits of the past has been maladjusted to life in one or more important ways. Some kind of productive tension between them and their worlds was essential to their creative accomplishment. This indeed seems to be a necessity for all evolutionary progress, not merely on the organic level but on the cultural level as well. This must not be taken to mean that such persons never achieve happiness. "Happiness" as employed by today's journalism is a pretty flabby and misleading word. Certain distinctions must be made before it can be safely used. The moments of happiness of creative people, though perhaps comparatively rare, are very elevated and very intense. This is characteristic of the life of genius. And when a culture ceases to produce vital creative spirits, it must cease to endure, for these are necessary even to sustain it.

Now let us look carefully at the second term of this formula. The prophets of the new education say that they are going to teach the young to adjust to *life*. But when we begin to elicit what they have in mind, we begin to wonder what kind of thing they imagine life to be. They seem to have in mind some simulacrum of life, or some travesty, or some abstracted part. They do not contemplate adjusting students to life in its fullness and mystery, but to life lived in some kind of projected socialist commonwealth, where everybody has so conformed to a political pattern that there really are no problems any more. Adjustment to real life must take into account pain, evil, passion, tragedy, the limits of human power, heroism, the attraction of ideals, and so on. The education of the "progressives" does not do this. It educates for a world conceived

as without serious conflicts. And this is the propaganda of ignorance.

Furthermore, nearly all of the great lives have involved some form of sacrifice for an ideal; nearly all great individuals have felt the call for that kind of sacrifice, But sacrifice does not exist in the vocabulary of "progressive" education, since for them everything must take the form of "adjustment" or self-realization. Were Buddha, Socrates, and Jesus "adjusted to life"? The way in which one answers that question will reveal whether he stands with those who believe that man has a higher self and a higher destiny or whether he is willing to stop with an essentially barbaric ideal of happiness. The adjustment which the progressive educators prate of is, just because of its lack of any spiritual ideal, nothing more than the adjustment of a worm to the surface it is crawling on.

WHEN WE turn to the practical influence of their theorizing, we find that it has worked to undermine the discipline which has been used through the centuries to make the human being a more aware, resourceful, and responsible person. As would be expected, the brunt of their attack has been against those studies which, because they make the greatest use of symbols, are the most intellectual—against mathematics and language study, with history and philosophy catching a large share also of their disapproval. (There are excellent reasons for terming certain subjects "disciplines" and for insisting that the term be preserved. For "discipline" denotes something that has the power to shape and to control in accordance with objective standards. It connotes the power to repress and discourage those impulses which interfere with the proper development of the person. A disciplined body is one that is developed and trained to do what its owner needs it to do; a disciplined mind is one that is developed and trained to think in accordance with the necessary laws of thought, and which therefore can provide its owner with true casual reasoning about the world. A person with a disciplined will is trained to want the right thing and to reject the bad out of his own free volition. Discipline involves the idea of the negative, and this is another proof that man does not unfold merely naturally, like a flower. He unfolds when he is being developed by a sound educational philosophy according to known lines of truth and error, of right and wrong.)

Mathematics lies at the basis of our thinking about number, magnitude, and position. Number is the very language of science. So pervasive is it in the work of the intellect that Plato would have allowed no one to study philosophy who had not studied mathematics. But these are the very reasons that mathematics is calculated to arouse the suspicion of the "progressives"; it works entirely through symbols and it makes real demands upon the intellect.

Language has been called "the supreme organon of the mind's self-ordering growth." It is the means by which we not only communicate our thoughts to others but interpret our thoughts to ourselves. The very fact that language has the public aspect of intelligibility imposes a discipline upon the mind; it forces us to be critical of our own thoughts so that they will be comprehensible to others. But at the same time it affords us practically infinite possibilities of expressing our particular inclinations through its variety of combinations and its nuances. Most authorities agree that we even *think* in language, that without language thought would actually be impossible. Those who

attack the study of language (whether in the form of grammar, logic, and rhetoric or in the form of a foreign language) because it is "aristocratic" are attacking the basic instrumentality of the mind.

HISTORY HAS always been a sobering discipline because it presents the story not only of man's achievements but also of his failures. History contains many vivid lessons of what can happen to man if he lets go his grip upon reality and becomes self-indulgent; it is the record of the race, which can be laid alongside the dreams of visionaries, with many profitable lessons. Yet the modern tendency is to drop the old-fashioned history course and to substitute something called "social science" or "social studies," which one student has aptly dubbed "social stew." What this often turns out to be is a large amount of speculation based on a small amount of history, and the speculation is more or less subtly slanted to show that we should move in the direction of socialism or some other collectivism. Often this kind of study is simply frivolous; the student is invited to give his thought to the "dating patterns" of teenagers instead of to those facts which explain the rise and fall of nations. There is more to be learned about the nature of man as an individual and as a member of society from a firm grounding in ancient and modern history than from all the "social studies" ever put together by dreamy "progressive" educators.

Philosophy too is an essential part of liberal education because it alone can provide a structure for organizing our experience and a ground for the hierarchical ordering of our values. But under "progressive" education there is but one kind of philosophy, that of experimental inquiry in adapting to an environment.

This has no power to yield insight and no means of indicating whether one kind of life is higher than another if both show an adjustment to the externals around them.

Thus with amazing audacity the "progressive" educators have turned their backs upon those subjects which throughout civilized history have provided the foundations of culture and of intellectual distinction.

If this has been stressed at some length, it is in order to deny the claim that "progressive" education fosters individualism. It may have the specious look of doing so because it advocates personal experience as a teacher and the release of the natural tendencies of the person. Yet it does this on a level which does not make for true individualism. *Individualism in the true sense is a matter of the mind and the spirit; it means the development of the person, not the well-adjusted automaton. What the progressivists really desire to produce is the "smooth" individual adapted to some favorite scheme of collectivized living, not the person of strong convictions, of refined sensibility, and of deep personal feeling of direction in life.* Any doubt of this may be removed by noting how many "progressive" educators are in favor of more state activity in education. Under the cloak of devotion to the public schools, they urge an ever greater state control, the final form of which would be, in our country, a federal educational system directed out of Washington and used to instill the collectivist political notions which are the primary motives of this group.

NO TRUE believer in freedom can contemplate this prospect with anything but aversion. *If there is one single condition necessary to the survival of truth and of values in our civilization, it is that the educational system be left independent enough to espouse these truths and values regardless of the political winds of doctrine of the moment.* The fairest promises of a hands-off policy on the part of federal educational authorities would come to nothing once they were assured of their power and control. If education were allowed to become a completely statist affair, there is no assurance that the content of even science courses would be kept free from the injection of political ideas. The latter might seem a fantastic impossibility, yet it has actually occurred in the Soviet Union. This is a case well worth relating as a warning to all who would put faith in centralized education under a paternalistic state.

Some years ago the leading Soviet geneticist was one T. D. Lysenko, who occupied the post of president of the All-Union Lenin Academy of Agricultural Science. Lysenko claimed that he had disposed of the genetic theories of Mendel and Morgan, his motive being that these were "reactionary" and counter to the theories of socialism. Western scientists exposed the fallacies in his work and denounced him as an ignorant quack. But Lysenko, working through a stooge named Michurin, established what he called "Michurin science" in genetics, to which Soviet geneticists still have to bow because it is in accord with the Marxist political line. How far the Communists are willing to go in perverting science to the uses of politics may be seen in the following excerpts from an article in the *USSR Information Bulletin* written by Lysenko himself.

> It was the great Lenin who discovered Michurin and the great Stalin who launched Michurin's materialistic biological theories on the highroad of creative work.

Not only has the great Stalin rescued the Michurin teaching from the attempts of reactionaries in science to destroy it; he has also helped to rear large forces of Michurinist scientists and practical workers, His guiding ideas have played and are playing a decisive role in the triumph of the materialistic Michurin teaching over the reactionary, idealistic Weissmannism-Morganism in the Soviet land.

The works of Joseph Stalin are an invaluable and inexhaustible fount for the development of theoretical Michurinist biology. His classic work, *Dialectic and Historical Materialism,* is an indispensable general theoretical aid to all agrobiologists, which helps them to gain a correct understanding of biological facts. Only when examined in the light of dialectical and historical materialism, the principles of which have been further developed by Stalin, does the Michurinist biological teaching gradually reveal its full depth and truth to us.

Where education is under the control of collectivist fanatics, not only is the individual's loyalty to truth despised, but the objective findings of science may be thus perverted to serve the ends of a political ideology.

Even though this may be regarded as an extreme case, we are living in a world where extreme aberrations occur suddenly, so that "It can't happen here" may be followed rather abruptly by "Now it has happened here." Dangers are always best met at the frontier, and the frontier in this instance is just where the state proposes to move in on education. Education's first loyalty is to the truth, and the educator must be left free to assert, as sometimes he needs to do, unpopular or unappreciated points of view.

EDUCATION THUS has a major responsibility to what we think of as objectively true. But it also has a major responsibility to the person. We may press this even further and say that education must regard two things as sacred: the truth, and the personality that is to be brought into contact with it. No education can be civilizing and humane unless it is a respecter of persons. It may be that up to a certain utilitarian point, everyone's training can be more or less alike. But in a most important area, no educational institution is doing its duty if it treats the individual "just like everybody else." Education has to take into account the differing aptitudes produced by nature and individual character, and these differing aptitudes are extremely various. Physiologists are just beginning to understand how widely men differ in their capacities to see, to taste, to bear pain, to assimilate food, to tolerate toxic substances, and in many other physical respects. On top of this are the multifarious ways in which individuals differ psychologically through their nervous systems, reflexes, habits, and patterns of coordination. And above this are the various ways in which individuals differ psychically in their ways of intuiting reality, their awareness of ideals, their desires for this or that supersensible satisfaction, and so on. When all of these factors are brought into view, it is seen that every individual is a unique creation, something "fearfully and wonderfully made," and that the educator who does not allow for special development within the discipline which he imposes is a repressor and a violator.

NOW THE educator who is aware of all the facts and values involved in his difficult calling will recognize in the individual a certain realm of privacy. Much of present-day education and many of the pressures of modern life treat the person as if he were a one-, or at best two-dimensional being. They tend to simplify and indeed even to brutalize their treatment of the person by insisting that certain ways are "good for everybody." Yet it is a truth of the greatest importance that our original ideas and our intuitions of value form in certain recesses of the being which must be preserved if these processes are to take place. The kind of self-mastery which is the most valuable of all possessions is not something imposed from without; it is a gestation within us, a growth in several dimensions, an integration which brings into a whole one's private thoughts and feelings and one's private acts and utterances. A private world alone is indeed dangerous, but a personality whose orientation is entirely public is apt to be flat, uncreative, and uninteresting. The individual who does not develop within himself certain psychic depths cannot, when the crises of life have to be faced, meet them with any real staying power. His fate is to be moved along by circumstances, which in themselves cannot bring one to an intelligent solution.

Most people have marvelled how Abraham Lincoln was able to develop such a mastery of logic and such a sense of the meaning of words while growing up in a society which set little store by these accomplishments. Yet the answer seems easy enough; Lincoln had a very real private life, in which he reflected deeply upon these matters until he made them a kind of personal possession. He was an individual—keeping up a train of personal reflection, even while mingling in friendly and humorous way with the people of his frontier community. Lincoln paid a price for this achievement, of course, the rule of this world being

"nothing for nothing." But no one who believes in greatness will say that the price was out of proportion to what was gained. If it is true that Lincoln "belongs to the ages," it is so because he learned to think about things in a way that enabled him to transcend time and place. This is what is meant by developing a personality.

HOW FAR modern theorists have drifted from these truths may be seen in the strange remarks of the "progressive" educator John Dewey.

> [T]he idea of perfecting an 'inner' personality is a sure sign of social divisions, What is called inner is simply that which does not connect with others—which is not capable of full and free communication. What is termed spiritual culture has usually been futile, with something rotten about it, just because it has been conceived as a thing which a man might have internally—and therefore exclusively.

For Dewey an inner consciousness is exclusive, aristocratic, separative. What Dewey denies, what his spurious system forces him to deny, is that by achieving a depth of personality, one does develop a power and a means of influencing the community in the best sense of the term "influence." To speak personally is to speak universally. Humanity is not a community in the sense of a number of atoms or monads, knocking together; it is a spiritual community, in which to feel deeply is to feel widely, or to make oneself accessible to most of one's fellow members. In consequence, it cannot be too forcefully argued that the education which regards only development with reference to externals is not education for a higher plane of living, for the individual and for the society of which he is a part, but for a lower—for an artificially depressed level of living which, were it to be realized, would put an end to human development.

Although it may at first seem paradoxical to insist both upon discipline and the development of private and inner resources, the cooperative working of the two is a proved fact of education. Nothing today more needs recovering than the truth that interest develops *under pressure*. Man is not spontaneously interested in anything with an interest that lasts or that carries him beyond attention to superficial aspects. Natural interest which is left to itself nearly always proves impermanent, disconnected, and frivolous. It is only when we are made to take an interest in something that we become exposed to its real possibility of interesting us. It is only then that we see far enough into its complications and potentialities to say to ourselves, here is a real problem, or a real opportunity. We need not suppose that institutions are the only source of this kind of pressure. The situation a person finds himself in when he must earn a living or achieve some coveted goal may exert the necessary compulsion. But here we are talking about what formal education can do for the individual, and one of the invaluable things it can do is face him with the necessity of mastering something, so that he can find the real richness that lies beyond his threshold indifference to it. An interest in mathematics, in music, in poetry has often resulted from an individual's being confronted with one of these as a "discipline"; that is, as something he had to become acquainted with on pain of penalties. The subject there by its own powers begins to evoke him, and before long he is wondering how he could ever have been oblivious to such a fascinating world of knowledge and experience.

From this point on his appreciation of it becomes individual, personal, and creative.

As individuality begins to assert itself in the man or woman, we realize that its movement is toward a final ethical tie-up of the personality. Individuality should not be equated with a mere set of idiosyncrasies. Idiosyncrasy is casual, fortuitous, essentially meaningless. No enlightened believer in individualism rests his case on anything as peripheral as this. To be an individual does not mean to be "peculiar" or somehow curious in one's outlook. It does, however, mean to be distinctive.

Individuality as a goal must be explained by men's inclinations toward the good. All of us aspire toward something higher, even though there are varying ways in which that something higher can be visualized or represented. Whether one is prone to accept an ethical humanism, a tradition of religious principles, or a creed having its authority in revelation, the truth cannot be ignored that man is looking for something better both in himself and in others. But because different persons have, through their inheritance, nurture, and education different faculties, they have different insights into the good. One man is deeply and constantly aware of certain appearances of it; another of others; and sometimes these differences are so great that they lead to actual misunderstanding. Nevertheless, the wisest have realized that such differences express finally different orientations toward values, and that the proper aim of society is not to iron them out but to provide opportunity for their expression. Variations appearing in these forms do not mean simply that one man is right and another wrong; they mean that the persons in question are responding according to their different powers to apprehend an order of reality. In this kind of perception, some persons are fast movers; others are slow but deep; some have to see things concretely; others are more successful in working out ideas and principles; some people are profoundly sensitive to place; others would do about the same kind of thinking anywhere; some do their best work while feeling a sense of security; others require the excitement and stimulus of uncertainty to draw forth their best efforts.

Such a list of differences could be extended almost endlessly. But what it comes down to is this: the reason for not only permitting but encouraging individualism is that each person is individually related toward the source of ethical impulse and should be allowed to express his special capacity for that relation. This is at the same time the real validation of democracy. Democracy cannot rest upon a belief in the magic of numbers. It rests upon a belief that every individual has some special angle of vision, some particular insight into a situation which ought to be taken into account before a policy is decided on. Voting is perhaps only a rough way of effecting this, but the essential theory is clear: every person is deemed to have something worthy to contribute to decision-making, and the very diversity and variety of these responses are what makes democracy not indeed a more efficient, but a fairer form of government than those in which one, or a few men at the top assume that their particular angle upon matters contains all the perception of the good that is needed.

Yet there is a very true sense in which one does not become such an individual until he becomes aware of his possession of freedom. One cannot act as a being until one is a being; one can not *be* a being unless he feels within himself the grounds of his action. The people in this world who impress us as nonentities are, in the true analysis, people whose speech and actions are only reflections of what they see and hear about them, who have no means of evaluating themselves except through what other people think of them. These are the "other directed men," the hollow men, the men who have to be filled with stuffing from the outside, of which our civilization is increasingly productive. The real person is, in contrast, the individual who senses in himself an internal principle of control, to which his thoughts and actions are related. Ever aware of this, he makes his choices, and this choosing is the most real thing he ever does because it asserts his character in the midst of circumstances. Then the feeling of freedom comes with a great upsurging sense of triumph: to be free is to be victorious; it is to count, whereas the nonentity by his very nature does not count.

A LIBERAL education specifically prepares for the achievement of freedom. Of this there is interesting corroboration in the word itself. "Liberal" comes from a Latin term signifying "free," and historically speaking, liberal education has been designed for the freemen of a state. Its content and method have been designed to develop the mind and the character in making choices between truth and error, between right and wrong. For liberal education introduces one to the principles of things, and it is only with reference to the principles of things, that such judgments are at all possible. The mere facts about a subject, which may come marching in monotonous array, do not speak for themselves. They speak only through an interpreter, as it were, and the interpreter has to be those general ideas derived from an understanding of the nature of language, of logic, and of mathematics, and of ethics and politics. The individual who is trained in these basic disciplines is able to confront any fact with the reality of his freedom to choose. This is the way in which liberal education liberates.

Finally, therefore, we are brought to see that education for individualism is education for goodness. How could it be otherwise? The liberally educated individual is the man who is at home in the world of ideas. And because he has achieved a true selfhood by realizing that he is a creature of free choice, he can select among ideas in the light of the relations he has found to obtain among them. Just as he is not the slave of another man, with his freedom of choice of work taken from him, so he is not the slave of a political state, shielded by his "superiors" from contact with error and evil. The idea of virtue is assimilated and grows into character through exercise, which means freedom of action in a world in which not all things are good. This truth has never been put more eloquently than by the poet Milton.

I cannot praise a fugitive and cloistered virtue unexercised and unbreathed, that never sallies out and sees her adversary, but slinks out of the race, where that immortal garland is to be run for, not without dust and heat. Assuredly we bring not innocence into the world; we bring impurity much rather; that which purifies us is trial, and trial is by what is contrary.

Freedom and goodness finally merge in this conception; the unfreeman cannot be good because virtue is a state of character concerned with choice, and if this latter is taken away, there is simply no way for goodness to assert itself. The moment we judge the smallest action in terms of right and wrong, we are stepping up to a plane where the good is felt as an imperative, even though it can be disobeyed. When education is seen as culminating in this, we can cease troubling about its failure to accomplish this or that incidental objective. An awareness of the order of the goods will take care of many things which are now felt as unresolvable difficulties, and we will have advanced once more as far as Socrates when he made the young Athenians aware that the unexamined life is not worth living.

Mark Blitz

The Place of the Liberal Arts

VOL. 14, NO. 2, 1979

WE begin our discussion of the place of the liberal arts by putting the liberal arts in question. Consider the everyday perspective of activities and interests, of business and practical affairs. These may include patriotic celebration and the music and poetry connected to it. They may include religious ceremony. But they do not include the liberal arts as such. How do the liberal arts make their entrance? Why, from the practical perspective, do we need them? How can they justify themselves?

The central element of a justification concerns understanding the insufficiency of the practical activities in their own terms. This insufficiency reveals itself most starkly in the impossibility of defending the purpose and ends of such activities through the activities themselves. The physician as such cannot—with his profession and skill—show why health is good, when and where: where is death to be risked and where not? The producer of goods at any level from a shoemaker to a Ford cannot—through his distinguishing skill—show the propriety of the goods he produces. What purposes do they serve, how defensible are these purposes, do they serve these purposes appropriately? The lawyer learns legal technique within a judicial system; but he cannot say what justice genuinely is.

The necessity of thought about and consideration of these questions therefore emerges. But are they simply unconsidered in practical life? No: they are at root answered in any time and place by the way of life of the community—by its political understanding of the common good and the place of activities, professions and individual citizens in this good. Practical affairs in general, professional affairs in general, receive their justification within the common good. This priority of the political is less obvious in liberal democracies such as ours than in other regimes, but it is clear enough here. Yet, do the citizens, the root rulers of a regime—let alone passing administrations—genuinely grasp what is just or good? Can they defend their opinions from challenge? Are they aware of the possibility of challenge? Is a life devoted to pleasure best—or one devoted to productive work, or one devoted to politics? Is justice equal to equals? Unequal treatment based on ability? From each according to his abilities, to each according to his needs? Here we see that the political community as such—and, therefore, all the practices and professions within its ambit—falls short of knowing what it most of all needs to know. The liberal arts can, therefore, first defend themselves, and demonstrate their meaning and significance, as reasoned thought and discussion about the fundamental purposes and goals from which all other activities take their meaning.

BUT SUCH a defense is insufficient because it understands liberal education to be ministerial. The school of law, the school of medicine, the school of business, the school of public policy do, indeed, all require an education which gives them direction, and the elements of this education can be found in the liberal arts. But if we leave it at this, the liberal arts are only a servant, even if they serve by guiding: they are at best the first servant of the practical world and of the education devoted to the practical world. A higher defense must show how and that liberal education is its own reward, an end in itself, indeed the highest end. A proper defense must show that liberal education is the most beautiful, most attractive, of human possibilities and therefore the most eminently—if not most concretely—useful. A proper defense of the liberal arts in education is no longer merely a defense.

Here we see that the liberal arts distinguish themselves from all practical activity by being that which considers, reflects, and exercises the distinctively human. All other education primarily makes up for our insufficiency as animals—for our lack of concretely assigned limits in food, sex, clothing, shelter. The professions and technical education are the chief contemporary way of turning our distinctive reason to these non-dis-

tinctively human necessities. And, as we have said, liberal education must inform these activities through its reflection on the ends, purposes, and limits which are given neither instinctively not by technical education itself. But the chief defense of liberal education is that it is *itself* the proper employing and exercising of our distinctively human traits. It is the training of reason in its own right; it is the experiencing of the fundamental causes and structures; and, further, it is the cultivation of the leisured enjoyment of the passions, the feelings, as they are informed by our reason and speech, that is, as they are human. Liberal education is both the shaping of reason for its own sake and the shaping of our most unique passions, the love of the beautiful, the sense of the mysterious and awesome, the sense of the ridiculous.

Liberal education therefore defends itself in the last analysis because it itself is the proper employment of playful leisure, which is superior to all serious activity, even great statesmanship. And it defends itself in the next to last analysis by guiding the serious activities and serious techniques—all seriousness is for the sake of something beyond itself. To put this in the most accurate traditional sense: liberal education is the forming of man's distinctive liberality or openness; it is the shaping of the soul. In this sense, to continue to educate oneself liberally is the central goal of a lifetime; and we today are uniquely fortunate that it can be the most immediate and urgent task for so many for at least a few years.

BUT HAVE we not made liberal education too consistent? After all, liberal education comprises the humanities, the social sciences and the natural sciences; and at some schools we have decreed that this trio become a quartet so that the biological sciences become a separate quadrant. But these elements do not obviously belong to a well formed whole. The first and most thoughtful raising of this question of disharmony belongs to those ancients who first discovered liberal education: it is the question of the relation—the quarrel between poetry and philosophy, where philosophy comprises the subjects of mathematics, physics and biology as well as its own unique subjects. This quarrel is most beautifully and most amusingly developed in Aristophanes' *Clouds* and Plato's *Symposium*. In its general form it is a question considered by leading physicists of our own century; and it is familiar to us as the debate between the two cultures. The elements of the quarrel concern the relative rank of the activities which constitute the distinctively human. But this is to say that in their most intelligent form the contenders never dream of debunking one or the other side completely. Any debunking of the theoretical study of the root purposes of humans—any debunking of the philosophical elements of politics and morality, or the historical and literary experience of human greatness—runs up against the same problem of self justification which shows the limit of technical education. The natural sciences, and those social sciences which more or less perfectly ape the natural sciences, are themselves human activities standing in need of human justification. Any debunking of the physical study of nature, or of mathematics, thoughtlessly eliminates both a whole range of distinctively human activity and an entire area of love and experience of the beauty of truth and form. The possibility of the pure encountering and discovery of what is not human is a unique human gift; properly speaking the sciences are not inhuman. Now, we can-

not defend each and every organization of the academy, nor each and every "discipline." This becomes a practical matter to be dealt with prudently. But the chief consideration is that the divisions among those who love knowledge and beauty do not detract from the essential unity of the life of the mind, nor from the justification of liberal education as the attempt to express and develop our excellent and distinctive capacities.

Despite the fact that the organization of any given faculty of arts and sciences is a matter for prudent judgment, it is important to see that a defense of liberal education cannot properly—at the most general level—defend each and every activity that goes by the name liberal education. For the chief danger to liberal education lies within liberal education itself. Its current internal loss of direction arises from the inadequacy of the self understanding of the liberal educators; this in turn arises from the implicitly dogmatic attachment to opinions which derive from the greatest thinkers. These thinkers themselves are—as such—in no way dogmatic. Liberal educators often defend their enterprise as valuable, but only because we value it traditionally and values are in principle equal. Liberal educators often defend their enterprise as the expression of one culture which allows us to be open to other cultures. But by this understanding all cultures are in principle equal; the Greeks are at best a slightly higher form of Hottentot; the Renaissance Florentines are at best an inexplicably more interesting version of the "culture" of the ward heeler. At worst there is simple theoretical equality. Such an understanding cannot in fact defend liberal education because it does not consider the genuine necessity of educated understanding nor the genuine dignity of the cultivation of the human mind.

But this understanding, which talks in terms of the central and highest human abilities, faces its own danger. Its danger is the danger of degeneration to rigid philistinism or narrow political control. The understanding of equality in value and culture, which is inadequate because it leaves liberal education without a ground, is, at least apparently, more faithful to our openness, our contingency, our indefiniteness. Yet, cannot this openness be saved in a liberal education which defends itself properly as the expression of reason and its distinctive relatives? For if liberal education, among other things, puts into question the fundamental human purposes; if it deals with the radical openness of human choice; and if it expresses what is distinctive to man in its variety, it cannot properly become dogmatic and authoritarian. The search for knowledge of fundamental causes, and the discovery of what is beautiful, are, as such, a continual awareness of our incompleteness. But this search cannot know itself, the liberal arts cannot be truly open and liberal, without also recognizing the limits and distinctions between the human and the nonhuman. The liberal arts cannot be themselves without asserting their own dignity; and their own dignity is a kind of superiority. For they exercise the distinctive in man and therefore exercise the freest in man. And they do this by studying the highest—the fundamental natural possibilities. The liberal arts at best, therefore, do teach one to be moderate, and not improperly dogmatic, but also not excessively modest or timid.

THE DANGER to the liberal arts which arises from the excessive modesty of its defenders is not the only danger. If it is true that the liberal arts are essentially playful, if it is true that they are dedicated to knowledge and beauty but not dedicated to serious use, then we see that they face the danger of being and being seen as essentially frivolous. Liberal studies become perceived as the peculiar playthings of those lacking the talent to bowl with pleasure, not to say bowl for a living. Liberal studies are therefore of no more importance than any other frivolity. Here one might be tempted to concede the point and merely argue that serious pursuits—earning a living, ruling a country, fighting a war, securing health—are all ultimately for the sake of leisure and the use of leisure. But this is not sufficient. The playful and the leisured is superior to the serious but only if it properly exercises our capacities of reason and speech, and employs the senses—hears the music and views the art—most informed by these capacities. The liberal arts cannot be themselves without defending their superiority to frivolous entertainment. They are entertaining, but only to a certain audience which their very study forms. The liberal arts form a taste for the beautiful and excellent—the liberal arts generate a taste for more of themselves. By studying the liberal arts we learn to love the love of the beautiful, and to admire those who love the truth. In this way we hope ourselves to become those who love what is beautiful and what is true.

The liberal arts are also distinguished from the merely frivolous because what is studied in them is, among other things, the meaning and extent of the goals practical activity serves. Only what is considered by the student of the liberal arts can serve as a sufficient justification of practical affairs. Indeed: only in terms of the powers, possibilities, and capabilities of the human soul uncovered in the liberal arts can the practical skills and pursuits be properly appreciated in their own excellence. The merely frivolous activities furnish no grounds for such defense; and in terms of what the liberal arts uncover they are less significant, less human, than properly informed practice. This is the answer of the liberal arts to what is frivolous. It is also the answer—as we suggested at the beginning—to the serious and technical. The liberal arts can defend themselves from the danger arising from their apparent lack of utility by demonstrating the secondary nature of the useful, however urgent it is. Such a defense, of course, cannot outline the specific relations between what is urgently practical and the study of the significant but playful. But it does clarify the proper order of things, just as the liberal arts themselves clarify the proper order of things for all who pursue them, including those who become dominant in practical affairs.

THIS ARGUMENT does not overcome the fact that, in principle, the study of the liberal arts is not wholly compatible with political and moral life. Although the political community—as the ordering of serious affairs—takes for granted questionable opinions about justice, it is healthy that it do so, within limits. Individual morality requires that certain principles of right and wrong be taken for granted; practical affairs require artificial limits for their successful conduct. The political community and its reigning opinions are the chief among these limits. But the liberal arts challenge these limits. Are they not, then, destructive?

The problem of the meaning of the liberal arts is, therefore, a species of the traditional problem of the relation between philosophy, taken in its broadest sense, and politics, taken in its broadest sense. Here we must say that the study of the liberal arts leads to the salutary

moderation of dogmatic political and moral opinion, salutary precisely because these are mere dogmas and opinions. But such moderation is indeed destructive unless the study of the liberal arts also moderates the possible contempt for, and destruction of, what politically and morally must be practically taken for granted. The liberal arts open the limits of everyday opinion; they moderate them, but also threaten simply to overcome them. But, when thoughtfully pursued, they also moderate our expectations concerning political and moral perfection here on earth. At best, they allow a reunion with what is best within the life of a community, now understood more fully. Perhaps a similar argument could be made concerning the connection of liberal education and the religious education it has largely replaced.

But does this not suggest that the liberal arts are the province of the few, whom we today call the elite? This cannot be simply denied, nor should it be simply denied, if a proper defense of liberal education ought not to fear making distinctions. But then, even if the study of liberal arts is salutary when engaged in properly is it not diseased when studied by those not fit? One might suggest that those improperly exposed to too much liberal education will more likely be harmed than harm—that the vague unease with the ordinary and acceptable will sour appreciation of the ordinary and acceptable but not threaten what is desirable in it. Be that as it may, the greater danger to the liberal arts is that they lose the rigor connected to their dignity once they become too popular. This is one half of the ancient problem of the distinction between philosophy in the broadest sense and sophistry in the broadest sense. The liberal arts in a democracy such as ours must welcome all who are capable of them and many who are not, but as much as possible they must welcome them on their own terms. Democracy at its best wishes universal excellence, the universal equality of the best, the aristocratic. Proper study of the liberal arts teaches the practical limits of this dream; but democratic openness in principle allows a greater entrance to the liberal arts and therefore a possibly greater expression of and awareness of the distinctively human than do other regimes here and now. This is a beautiful opportunity. But it makes it peculiarly difficult for genuine art and thought to hold their own here and now. What responsible teacher of the liberal arts—and the teachers are only students a bit further along—has not considered this danger in his own teaching and work?

THIS MENTION of democracy leads to the final problem of the liberal arts today. This problem is that they, or some of them, have become too useful. Rather than simply appearing to be a danger to political and moral life, to serious concerns; and rather than needing or being able to validate themselves as the studies which consider the sources of the meaning of practical affairs, they appear to be extraordinarily useful—extraordinarily useful but still subordinate. This is the other half of the ancient quarrel between philosophy and sophistry. Not only must serious study be distinguished from the concerns and products of the journalists and intellectuals; it must also be distinguished from the concerns and products of the advisors, the research organizations, the translators of liberal studies to technical utility. The distinctive educational feature of liberal democracy is not only that it desires to spread a version of the liberal arts but also that it seeks to,

and must, make use of their products. Liberal democracy is coordinate with enlightenment. And by revolting against the old authorities, it has no choice but to make reason a new kind of authority. When reason becomes an authority, when the products of reason and art are measured by utility calculated by reason, the genuine independence of reason and art is threatened—their dignity and their highest employment are threatened. Such a threat can be met. But it is particularly difficult to meet. For we all fall into justifying liberal arts along the lines of practical results; and we all fall into justifying these results through more or less sophisticated echoes of the dominant liberal experience of goods as values which satisfy our in-principle equal desires. Here we return to the problem the liberal arts face because of their own practitioners. Natural and social science must be defended from becoming mere technique, and the arts must be defended from becoming mass productions and the outlandish idiosyncrasies which are merely the negations of these productions. The liberal arts today face the unique dual danger of being useless—and, in another way, too useful.

WE CONCLUDE by surfacing from these dangers and restating the meaning of the liberal arts, in their highest form. The liberal arts are the fullest expression of man's distinctive powers and have as their proper objects the most fundamental, most permanent, most beautiful, of human and natural possibilities. They necessarily stand in need of defense before urgent and serious practical considerations but at root they are superior to such considerations. They at once lead us to step boldly outside of ordinary limits and return us to the moderate understanding of ordinary and extraordinary limits. The task of the student of the liberal arts—of the lover of the arts and the sciences—is to make what is most important in itself—the objects of these arts and sciences—most immediately important for him. The task is to make the truly important the most urgent. This task cannot be perfectly fulfilled because of practical exigencies. But the student's moderate—if you will ironic—understanding of his own inability to give to the objects of the liberal arts what they genuinely deserve is but another gift given to their students by the liberal arts themselves.

Gerhart Niemeyer

The Glory and Misery of Education

VOL. 18, NO. 1, 1982

Let us put before our inner eye five young men in the process of being educated: a teenage Australian aborigine, a fifth-century Athenian youth studying with Hippias the Sophist, the same youth after he later had become a disciple of Socrates, a young Russian intellectual in the first half of the nineteenth century, and his great-great-grandson, in our century.

What in each case is happening, and why? The Australian boy is being initiated into manhood by instruction in all that grown men know about the higher forces or powers or beings that either cause or govern birth and death, growth and decay, fertility and barrenness. This knowledge makes him a full-fledged member of his society, the order of which consists in myth, symbol, ritual and lore. The Greeks, in the course of two astonishing centuries, "discovered the mind," opening the possibility of truth that transcended the traditions of society. It immediately gave rise to two approaches: that of "enlightened" Hippias who saw the mind as an instrument for the pursuit of private utilitarian ends of power and wealth, and that of Socrates who

"desired knowledge" from a sense of wonder, thinking himself ignorant and philosophizing in order to escape from ignorance, and not for any utilitarian end. (This sentence is practically a copy of Aristotle's words in *Metaphysics* I 982b 11–27.) Francis Bacon turned his back on this "free science" by taking from Renaissance "white magic" the objective of power and declaring it the chief end of knowledge; Thomas Hobbes sought so to define his terms that he could manipulate men into a society centered on power; and less than three hundred years later the Russian intellectual pursued this very aim by means of studying Fourier, Hegel, Proudhon, Bakunin, and Marx. The emphasis now was no longer on understanding the world but on changing it, and this teleology of education was not confined to revolutionary ideologies but characterized the approaches to natural science, psychology, and sociology. The product of this kind of education is the modern self, characteristically split into self-pity and self-deification or magnification.

The sequel to these three hundred years is another phase of education exemplified at present primarily by the modern totalitarian regimes but lagging yet in the major societies of "democracy and capitalism," an education designed to produce docile instruments useful to the totalitarian rulers alone. It may be that these five types exhaust the possibilities of educational variety, in the same way in which the Christian heresies of the first four centuries of our era have set patterns that recur again and again in later periods.

The picture still includes another feature, which, born out of the concept of "free science" (Aristotle, ibid., 982b 27), has been embodied in an enduring type of institution, the Western-type universities. Born at the height of medieval Latin-Christian culture, they were and are unique in human experience, functioning as centers of learning that were in large degree free from requirements of utility, either private or collective. Such institutions could occur because at the time of their founding there were available large bodies of knowledge not relative to, or dependent on, any given political society, its power and needs: Greek science in the form of philosophy, Roman law, and the *doctrina Christiana*. Moreover, there existed an equally non-relative set of "tools of learning" defined, in the medieval syllabus, as grammar, dialectic, and rhetoric. At the universities, young men

> learned a language, not just how to order a meal in a foreign language, but *the structure of a language, and hence of language itself*-what it was, how it was put together and how it worked. Secondly, he learned how to use language: how to define his terms and make accurate statements; how to construct an argument and how to detect fallacies in argument [his own argument and other people's]. Dialectic,

that is to say, embraced Logic and Disputation (Dorothy Sayers, "The Lost Tools of Learning").

All tools, and the handling of tools, were useful. The utility of the medieval *trivium* had probably the widest spread of any hitherto known human skill, a skill useful to knowledge which in itself was free from utilitarian limitations.

The new departure linked to the names of Bacon, Descartes, and Hobbes brought forth also its own mental tool, "analysis," the taking apart and putting together again of reality, in one's own mind. It was conceived in close connection with mathematics, which in turn appeared no longer as the paradigm of eternal verities but rather as a powerful instrument useful to dominate nature. Henceforward human reason lost its character of the "discovery of the mind" by the great Greek philosophers and came to be conceived as a practical and useful faculty, an instrument of human power. Bacon and Descartes envisaged the conquest of nature as man's "chief and great end," the practical justification of all endeavors of theory. Socrates, Plato, and Aristotle looked on reality in wonderment, and their wondering included the very reason by which man could participate in divine transcendence. Descartes, in order to launch his new enterprise, first "closed" his mind in systemic and absolute doubt. That in turn entailed a systemic suspicion of "prejudices," i.e., anything not having been produced by the instrument of reason in the form of "clear and simple ideas." From there arose a new notion of "free science," or liberty defined as "stripping away" whatever had grown, or had been known or believed on past authority, replacing it with what one had made oneself. From this beginning in turn came the later growth of positivism, the dictatorship of a single method, as a quantitative approach of the physical sciences was declared the sole permissible key to all kinds of knowledge. Hence this exclusivity of one method governed relevance, the object, truth, and even reality itself. It bred the fact-value dichotomy and the exclusion of value from the realm of knowledge, entailing the replacement of philosophy by the supposedly positive science of sociology.

These developments occurred within the institutions of learning which since the Middle Ages had been dedicated to "free science" in Aristotle's sense, "which alone exists for its own sake." The instrumental view of reason, however, imposed on science an inescapable utilitarian goal, the utility being conceived as either private or social, either as pragmatism or as revolutionary remaking of reality. Greek and Christian philosophy were at the same time rejected as "uncertain sciences," and philosophers planted the claim of *certainty* as their distinctive banner, culminating in Hegel's *Phenomenology of the Mind*. The quest for certainty entailed the removal of the *doctrina Christiana* and exclusive reliance on the positive sciences or pseudo-sciences. Education began to lose its core of unity, as universality was replaced with multifariousness. The ideal of a liberal education lived on, but in the curiously meaningless version of a wide collection of as many specialized disciplines as possible. Where philosophy could not be replaced by sociology, it gave way to the history of a subject. Thus there are taught the history of ideas, the history of culture, the history of literature, the history of art or music. The more smatterings of such information, the broader and better an education was supposed to be. This winetasting approach entailed a necessary neglect of any widely applicable tools of learning, so that the dropping of

the medieval *trivium* was followed by the decline of the study of language, of logic, and finally even of reading and writing. In the midst of highly efficient technology and social organization one can thus observe a rapidly increasing barbarism. As one contemporary teacher reported:

> The students are woefully undereducated, and before I can discuss philosophical theories I usually have to explain the meanings of basic English words. The number of students who have some idea of what the Incarnation is remains at the normal level of approximately one per class (i.e., one out of fifty). The number of students who find it incredible that anyone could ever have believed the utterly ridiculous ideas put forth by Plato and Aristotle seems higher.

Entire chunks of knowledge drop into oblivion. People of today cannot communicate anymore with the people even of the previous generation. Allusions are no longer understood. Language shrinks in scope and power of differentiation. Still, the modern barbarian is no savage, since he is not privileged to the savage's education in myths, ritual, skills, and lore. He is more dangerous than the savage because of his well-nigh unlimited gullibility which puts him at the disposal of any charismatic Anti-Christ. Hence the misery of education redounds to the advantage of the demagogue, the feasibility of terroristic enterprise, the power of mobs, and the disposition for dictatorship.

In that kind of situation one might even wish for a return to a previous age, one without colleges, without high schools, one in which education at a mother's knee and by a father's example sufficed for an ordered human life, in which the feats of heroes and the competence of master craftsmen served as measures of excellence, and decency came with proverbs. No such return is possible or even desirable. From the level of complex technology, an all-engulfing bureaucratization, specialization of all jobs, computerization replacing human labor, there is no falling back on earlier versions of self-sufficiency. Since the education we have pushed millions into barbarism, and since barbarism no longer possesses any redeeming primitive order for us, we cannot evade the task of re-winning what it was that made meaningful education possible.

A cat learns, a bird learns, a wolf learns. Is human education, then, essentially nothing more than what occurs between animals? An animal is prodded into imitation, but instinct supports the learning process. Instinct holds together the complex societies of ants or bees. Are we to infer that human order, too, is basically instinctual? The question should be raised, since it comes close to the hidden premise of anarchism, and, in our time, libertarianism. Many sociologists have taken to establishing animal models for human education. Men, too, learn to some extent by imitation. Still, beyond this there extend the vast reaches of education dominated by human self-reflective consciousness. Man is aware of himself as a learner as well as a teacher, and most learning is the subject of disciplines articulated in language and communicated by concepts as well as by example. Human consciousness not only orders that which is to be taught, it also overflows the formulae of discipline and points beyond it, and beyond the teacher, by virtue of its capacity for infinity. Thus the work of civilization is an artifact not merely of things but also of human beings. "Man is made" is the phrase used by Werner Jaeger (*Paideia*, xxxiii).

This phrase may be confused with the saying of Karl Marx, "man makes himself," meaning emphatically that man is nobody's creature but the "creator" of his own life. The difference between Jaeger and Marx is a watershed of worldviews. Jaeger's central concept, *paideia*, is not so much a "making" but a *bringing out* of a given essence, out of the potentiality into actuality. The Greeks looked on education as a process of "becoming what you are." The Latin word *educare* is akin to *ducere*, thus carrying the notion of "leading out." Marx, by contrast, saw human history as a process of "coming-to-be," an emancipation from non-being, the emancipation conceived as man's own enterprise, unaided, uninspired, and unguided.

A third view implying "making" is that of Giambattista Vico:

> In the night of thick darkness enveloping the earliest antiquities . . . there shines the eternal and never failing light of a truth beyond all question: that the world of civil society has certainly been made by men, and that its principles are therefore to be found within the modifications of our human mind (*The New Science*, #331).

Vico obviously uses "making" not in the sense of "producing," like "making a clock," but rather in the sense of "emerging in the stream of human actions," using the latter term with Aristotle's meaning of "acting" as contrasted to "making" (*Nicomachean Ethics*, VI, 4). If history is the "making" of men in that it consists of "the modifications of the human mind," education is properly concerned with this latter subject. That places Vico on the opposite side from Marx who denies that consciousness has a history (Feuerbach, "The German Ideology"). If education is the bringing out of something that is already given, then Marx cannot see anything like human nature, order, or cosmos as given. The place of education is taken by revolution, the "changing of the world." Nor can Marx see anything like Heraclitus's *koinos*, that which people have in common: "To those who are awake, there is one ordered universe common (to all), whereas in sleep each man turns away (from this world) to one of his own" (Diels-Kranz, fr. 89). Again, if the realm of the common is not yet, but is merely a coming-to-be, there could be no subject of education. Aristotle made it clear that men have in common a "desire to know" which in turn he traces back to the experiences of "seeing" the cosmos as a whole. This "seeing," this sense of wonder without any admixture of utilitarian cupidity, is the core of a freedom predicated of science as well as of man. Here is the concept of liberal education, the education of free men in the setting of a "free science," subject to nobody and to no passion. Without a "free science" there can be no liberal education, as without the "desire to know," which is a common trait of all men, there can be no *koinos*, no reality experienced as essentially common, something that it would be the task of education to "bring out."

These considerations should have thrown sufficient light on Werner Jaeger's phrase, "man is made," to ban every confusion with Marx's superficially similar utterance. It is precisely the experience of a reality common to all men, an experience had in the process of "discovering the mind," which accounts for such concepts as *paideia* and "free science." Today, Aristotle's language in the first chapter of the *Metaphysics* is either forgotten or has moved beyond the scope of common understanding. We have inherited the institutions of liberal education but cast away its premises and its spirit. Under the circumstances, the institutions will operate but not to the end of freedom, either of science or of man. Their effect will be disorder rather than order, asphalt barbarism rather than culture, dissociation rather than community. Still, as the name of democracy keeps before us an ideal which men will again and again try to realize, the name of liberal education will also maintain some sense of obligation that will refuse to die. Given the history of the last three hundred years of Western civilization, are there still any possibilities of regaining an education that deserves the predicate "free"? Putting it differently one may assert that regardless of college catalogues and curricula, a school of liberal education, as soon as it opens its doors, makes to the student an implicit promise, even though neither students nor teachers may be explicitly conscious of it. Still, the promise is grasped by the student retrospectively, in his maturity, when he tries to sum up what his education has given to him. He may wonder what help his education has been in his endeavor to recognize the possibilities of life, along with the requirements for making good use of them. He will rummage through the sediments of his education, looking for tools to help him discern the character of the time in which he lives. Most often, though, mature alumni will ask what visions their college has **opened** for them regarding the meaning of **the** whole. Any thinking person needs purpose and insight. If his mind remains unprepared to cope with such questions, it has simply failed him.

This inquiry we have just conducted demonstrates that humans cannot engage in any project, least of all education, without beliefs that cannot be proved right or wrong. All the same, they can be discussed and criticized, and there is a discernible distinction between beliefs rational and beliefs irrational. Prominent scientists have written histories of science showing that all great advances of sciences have relied on beliefs and would not have occurred without beliefs. Whatever one thinks about positivism and quantitative methods, then, its categorical exclusion of beliefs from critical examination is not only untenable but demonstrably most harmful. Educators who are resolved to protect students from this harm therefore must make room in the curriculum for courses dealing seriously and critically with beliefs. One need not go to the opposite extreme of banning any courses using the empirical approach, and even courses dealing with human problems through quantitative methods. Quantitative research will always have its usefulness. Its error lies in the tyranny with which it makes that method into the sole criterion of relevance. That kind of criterion of relevance can in no way be empirically established: it, too, is a belief that cannot be falsified, thus does not belong to science, and as a belief is irrational in that it claims scientific rank in an area where no positive science applies. Thus the exclusion of beliefs from the liberal arts curriculum is a part of positivism which should be vigorously resisted by deans of arts and letters. As beliefs are once again carefully and systematically examined in education it becomes useful to distinguish between beliefs that are hypotheses and other beliefs beyond proof or refutation. These latter, "transcendent beliefs," are the really important ones. They transcend man's subjectivity, both personal and collective; they also transcend nature and history. They regard the whole of which we acknowledge ourselves to be a part. Assuming that we are part of a whole is an integral part of our thinking. Witness, for example, the recurring

attempt of the great physicists of our time to sketch a portrait of the universe as a whole; witness also the acknowledged need of astronomers for a concept of that within which the ultimate processes of this universe of galaxies occur. The whole, then, has no context: there is no place beyond on which we could stand, even in imagination, to look on the whole as if it were an object. Our wonderment about the whole therefore can have no end. The whole has inescapably the character of a mystery, and our place in it likewise must remain mysterious. Questions concerning it cannot be answered by way of experiment, nor can they be silenced by any compelling proof. If there were such proof our questioning would be stopped once and for all; we would be enclosed by a confining wall of "fact" imprisoning us beyond endurance.

Against this latter possibility, "You must submit because twice two make four . . . that's mathematics) Just you try to find an objection," Dostoevsky rebelled in the name of human freedom. His rebellion took an indeterminate, even dangerous, form: "I agree that twice-two-is-four is a very fine thing; but, after all, twice-two-are-five is rather nice, too." Let us not forget that Dostoevsky puts these words in the mouth of the "underground man," the man produced as a result of modernity, with its claim to "the tower of Babel," "the Crystal Palace," and "the Man-God." Dostoevsky's own work, however, makes clear that he in no way asserted that any belief would suffice if it only averted the prison of sheer fact. We are creatures endowed with reason. The inescapability of beliefs in our thinking and action does not require the silencing of the intellect. Tertullian's *credo quia absurdum* (I believe because it is unreasonable) was superseded by Augustine's *credo ut intelligam* (I believe that I may understand). Beliefs must not be confused with contempt for experience. Arguments about beliefs testify to the seriousness of the believer, and to the compatibility of beliefs with rational critique, always bearing in mind that there are also those kinds of critique which in themselves root in irrational beliefs. Liberal education, then, must focus its main efforts on thinking about and examining our beliefs, studying them not as if they were alien objects, but rather from within, the beliefs as well as their study being seen as an integral part of the "serious play" of life in which we are involved.

That brings us to a second requirement of re-founding liberal education in our day and age. This one has to do with the historical past, both in the narrow sense of "handing down the tradition," and in the wider sense of history as the symbolic form of our consciousness. When "tradition" is mentioned, the modern mind associates the term with past "quaintness," with primitive mentalities, characters, and ideas, with crudity in manner and feeling. This is the kind of prejudice generated by *The Whig Interpretation of History*, (the title of a seminal book by Herbert Butterfield), the view that history resembles an escalator, moving steadily upwards, so that its apex is identical with the present for which all the past has been nothing but an unavoidable preparation. The Whig concept of history is only one variety of the "stopping or freezing" of history (Eric Voegelin, *From Enlightenment to Revolution*, 84) which means the fallacious establishment, in history, of a point or age to which absolute validity is attributed. This became the hallmark not only of Marx's view of history, but also of Auguste Comte's, and it is this latter version that dominates our thinking about history and engenders the preju-

dices characteristic of it. Here we have an example of a critique based on irrational beliefs. Thus deans of arts and letters must be able to find teachers of history who are aware that history has meant not only growth, but also, at times, decline, decay, and perversion, so that "later" does not automatically mean "higher."

Life, in a sense, is indeed a movement toward what is new, but no innovation occurs in empty space. A dimension of our environment is the past, the public memory, the tradition. All newness is a *re*-newal. Human beings are members of one another, not merely in the plane of the present (roughly what we mean by the useless cliché of "humanity") but also in the dimension of past and future. Every new religion has deep roots in an older one which are not only modified but also preserved in their newness. Every scientific progress relies on work already done and appropriated. Every moral action is taken in the presence not merely of contemporaries, but also of our fathers and our descendants. He who believes he can cut himself off from tradition is not a free man but rather a naked and isolated "self," drifting in icy solitude, debarred from any signposts of direction or hints of possibilities. The *New Yorker* once published the cartoon of a clock which, instead of numbers, only had twelve spots, each saying "NOW!" Rebellious movements of our age have embraced a critique based on irrational belief, a critique elevating that "NOW!" to a substitute for history. As they thought to destroy the past, they also destroyed the future, ending up in nihilism.

Thinking, as many eminent philosophers have pointed out, is largely memory. No memory is purely subjective and individual. What is more, tradition is a public memory, replete with signs and symbols, a memory that undergirds a common culture and political order. Therefore, the passing on of tradition is not an exercise in nostalgia but a solemn obligation of parents, schools, colleges and universities, churches, governments, and judges. As in the case of beliefs, tradition must be transmitted not blindly but critically, being imperceptibly changed in the process of examination. This must not be perverted in an invidious, rebellious, and hostile undertaking. Rather, the critical task must be performed in the spirit of ancient Roman *pietas*, reverently, "as one approaches the wounds of a father," to use Burke's words. Nor must that "piety" be confused with bigotry. Rather it manifests respect, love, and loyalty for everything that bears a human face, for all human questing for the ground, the end, and the way.

This brings us to a third requirement of liberal education regained, and this one most controversial. It concerns the place of Christianity in liberal studies. In a sense, the transmission of the tradition cannot avoid dealing with Christianity. Beyond that, however, there must be courses available that teach Christianity not merely in the context of literature, art, politics and past culture, but in its own right. In other words, such courses must embrace Christianity in its fullness and study it "from within." Such studies must embrace the body of Scripture, the proclamation of the Gospel, dogma as well as kerygma, the developing of the liturgy and of theology, the errant movements of heresy, and constructive ones of monasticism, the mystics and the doctors of the church, its institutions of moral discipline and its enterprise of mission.

One can readily hear the objections: "Why just Christianity? Why not religion in general, if at all?" "All right, if Christianity is to figure in the curriculum, equal time must be given to other religions, including atheism." "Since Christianity claims to be the true religion, how can you avoid dogmatic indoctrination?" "No, better risk loss of truth than chance of error" (this latter being William James's description of the skeptic's position). To which one may respond as follows: a) "religion" as such is no subject matter; at most it is a branch of psychology which, however, has had great difficulty in grasping what religion is; b) as for comparative religion, it is a legitimate subject, and an important even though very difficult one. It may well be added to Christian studies, but it will not do as a substitute because Christianity has been the source and center of our culture, the ultimate truth that has shaped our past and is still shaping our present, regardless of what attitude to it particular persons may have. We cannot realistically step out of this truth into "another one," we cannot in truth become Hindus or Buddhists. Western civilization came into existence through the unifying impulse of Latin Christianity, and no other religion has played a similar role among us. The historical metamorphoses of our culture can be understood only in their relation to their Christian origins, even where these metamorphoses have emerged as bitter enemies of Christianity. The Hegelian and Marxian systems are nothing if not perverted schemes of the Christian salvation. Finally, as for the skeptic's option, "better risk loss of truth than chance of error," one can put against it the believer's option, "better risk chance of error than loss of truth," but in any case this is a decision which cannot be made in the context of class assignments, tests, and grades, but only in the solitude of each person's heart.

Another objection might point to the traditionally secular concept of the liberal arts college. This may well be granted, but in spite of this admitted secularism, Christian studies have formed, up to the end of the last century, not only an integral part but the crowning part of liberal education. The objection, then, will in fact come from contemporary hostility to Christianity, a hostility which is effective also against liberal education as a concept. All the same, it is a fact that students entering a liberal arts college today come with a different intent than those seeking a Bible college. In some cases this intent is interpreted by the faculty as a kind of general taboo of even the word "God," which, if mentioned by someone in conversation within the college, may lead to an abrupt change of subject or of the conversation itself.

Thus the introduction of Christian studies into the liberal arts curriculum requires a most careful effort of justification. It must be vigorously defended against the fallacious view that sees transcendent beliefs as a denial of thinking. That defense can hardly be successful until the Cartesian concept of reason itself can be shown false. Fortunately, there is much first-class contemporary philosophy that will support such a demonstration. Even then, however, there remains the limitation that the character of liberal education prohibits the offering of Christian studies with a proselytizing intent. One may ask, however, whether that is a limitation of liberal studies or does it not really belong to all studies proceeding by means of lectures, recitations, tests, and grades. Some time ago, the dean of one of the foremost Anglican seminaries addressed a parish meeting at my church. Our director of religious education rather heatedly assailed the dean's talk with the demand that religious education should have as its subject "experience." The dean, with great firmness, replied: "Life, indeed, consists largely of experience, but the subject of education is tradition."

Let us say, then, that Christian studies in the framework of liberal education are part of the handing down of tradition. Our entire culture with all its works of art and artifacts bears so much testimony to the Christian religion that without knowledge of what Christianity is about it can never be understood. Beyond this, however, there is another reason for Christian studies; one may also classify it among the utilitarian reasons. Ours is a culture of life in tension. Between time and eternity, nature and transcendence, the world and heaven, the sacred and the profane there are experiential tensions which cannot and should not be resolved. They are the hallmarks of our civilization. Our time is fortunate in the sense that a number of great scholars have brilliantly understood these tensions and have furnished us with a vocabulary for the philosophical articulation of the attendant problems. One who is not even aware of the problem easily becomes the prey of demagogic leaders who collapse the tension into a fallacious identity of God and man, salvation and politics, religion and revolution. Hence the multitude of movements in our time which enlist mass support by holding out the promise of a heaven on earth, a perfect social harmony, an identity of political power and authority. No positivist can grasp the nature of these movements and their totalitarian regimes, since he has barred his mind from understanding transcendent beliefs in general, and the Christian religion in particular. Likewise the student shaped by a liberal education that knows nothing of Christianity, faith, mysticism, and "words adequate to God" (St. Basil's definition of theology), will remain unable to grasp the nature of our time and its political pitfalls.

As one looks at the curricula of our

colleges and universities, and the patterns of thinking of our educational leaders, one realizes that the kinds of changes proposed on these pages are not easy to come by. Even the skeptical reader, however, cannot help grudgingly admitting that all three, or even one of them, would go far to restore to liberal education the core of meaning which the cafeteria-type curriculum is lacking. There is also the evidence of small colleges who have boldly set out to devise their own education around a core concept, be it Greek philosophy, or Christian religion, or the great books,—all three, incidentally, parts of the grand tradition which educators have a sacred duty to pass on. There is also the evidence of the recent attempt to restore some modicum of liberal education at Harvard College. These are manifestations of a "great refusal," if one may dare to baptize a concept of

unholy intent, a refusal to put up any longer with the muddle that today passes for education in so many institutions. In all probability the misery will have to become more sharply unbearable, the suffering personal and yet wide-spread before people begin to run after a real teacher, seize him by the hem of his overcoat, and beg him to take charge of their children. Let us not say that then it will be too late. It may be too late for some of us. But Augustine, finishing the *City of God* in a town besieged, and eventually conquered, by Vandals, was not completing his work "too late." Nor was his master, Jesus of Nazareth, abandoned by his disciples and rejected by his compatriots, crucified "too late." Our civilization has lived in the knowledge that "the future is open, and it is God's." There is no "too late."

Ewa M. Thompson

Body, Mind, and Deconstruction

VOL. 23, NO. 1, 1987

In her commentary on Plato's *Parmenides*, the Greek scholar Edith Hamilton said: "The argument runs on and on in words that appear to make sense and yet convey nothing to the mind"[1]

My feeling is that many academics feel the same way about deconstruction. It is not that they do not understand it; they do, but the knowledge seems to evaporate almost as soon as it is acquired. An unwillingness to retain an understanding of deconstruction derives, I think, from the radicalism with which it practices what Jacques Martain has called the "denaturing of human reason"[2] To master the language of deconstruction, to acquire that special understanding of "nonconcepts" such as *difference, trace, supplement*, or verbs such as *to inscribe, to defer, to open up a text*, one has to assume an intellectual posture that is deeply unnatural within the culture in which we live. To practice deconstruction means to achieve the ultimate degree of separation between the reading of texts and the experience of life. Writing and thinking deconstruction involves constant switching of the levels of discourse, from discourse proper to meta-discourse to meta-meta-discourse.

This is why it is easy, having understood what deconstruction is all about, to forget it promptly.

A deconstructionist pays an exorbitant homage to time. He starts with a rather trivial observation that there is a difference between the *fact* that something is, and our *thinking* or *writing* that something is.[3] A time lapse always occurs between the event and our thinking about it. Nothing happens in the present; everything is "always already" behind us, from the standpoint of time. There is no present tense, and therefore there is no *presence*. Deconstruction invokes the notion of deferral, of "being late" in regard to "what is": our thought about it occurs after the "being" itself. On this notion of deferral, of being late, Jacques Derrida built his system of interpretation of literary texts whose central thesis is that nothing really *is*, that "being" as construed by Western metaphysics is an illusion. There exists only a system of writing, a printed page, a set of traces of something that apparently *was* but in fact never was. There *is* only "space" between concepts.

A deconstructionist assumes that the world changes continuously and radically, and that there occur in every culture "paradigm shifts," or irreversible and fundamental changes in the consciousness of men. He seeks to effect a "paradigm shift" in the explication of literature, and to place thought in a sealed world in which it is no longer in contact with anything but itself. Deconstruction is a manifestation of the post-Cartesian retreat of the human mind upon itself, and it arguably represents the ultimate intellectualism which its predecessors managed to avoid. In a sense, it is a form of lust for pure spirituality which a physical person inhabiting a physical world is incaple of achieveing.[4]

In his book *Three Reformers*, Jacques Maritain made a distinction between two kinds of rationalism: one which goes back to Plato and Aristotle and relies on syllogism, and the other which goes back to Descartes and relies on intellectual intuition. The first is cognizant of the limitations and powers of the human intellect and of its dependence on the body. The second is "independent of external objects,"[5] makes no distinction between "speculative order and historical sequence," and is contemptuous of the body and the limitations of knowledge which it implies. It makes men into angels or mystics, that is to say, into thinking intellects independent of their bodies and independent of "time, movement, generation and corruption" in acquisition of knowledge. It sees cognition as intuitive, innate and independent of things. Maritain subscribes to the first kind of rationalism, and he argues that what has passed for rationalism since Descartes is responsible for much of the sterility and pedantry of modern philosophy. He charges that the first move of Cartesian rationalism was to "disown reason," and that Cartesianism produces men who ignore the testimony of the senses and their own physical naure.

An understanding of Maritain's critique of Descartes seems to me essential for the understanding of what deconstruction is all about, and whence it comes, and where it is heading. Deconstruction travels backward into Eastern philosophy and the negative theology of late Plato by way of Cartesianism.

Deconstruction Looks East

Jacques Derrida once said that deconstruction operates on the margins of philosophy. He should have said, on the margins of European philosophy. For it fits comfortably in the philosophy of the East and the wisdom of Lao-Tzu. This affinity with Asian thought deserves more attention than it has so far received.[6] Both deconstruction and Taoism reject any philosophical system that accommodates Western metaphysics and the notion of a transcendent and personal Being. The antonym of deconstruction is not construction but being, in the sense in which scholastic philosophers used that word. In Derrida's writings, thought finally breaks with being, and there is no positive reality that underlies the world of change. Like the philosophers of the East, the deconstructionists claim that there is nothing permanent in the empirical self. They seek to proclaim a rupture between the paradigm of postmodernity and the culture that preceded it. Derrida's goal seems to be a post-Western, or post-European culture which will look toward the East rather than West for phil-osophical affinity. In the deconstructionist paradigm, meaning is "generated over time, by means of convention, and within particular contexts . . . [it] is ultimately language-bound, perception-bound, and bound to a given worldview or ideology."[7] And it dies alongside the ideology which gave it birth.

What are the common points between the intuitions of Taoism and Derrida's theory of texts? Taoism's way of looking at the world involves deleting from the philosopher's vocabulary any idea of a center, of a personal God, or of the rules of logic. Lao-Tzu and other Taoist thinkers used a concept which in English is rendered by the expression "the way." It comprises both the meaning of Taoism and the instructions on how one should live. "The way" of Lao-Tzu is like Derrida's absent center: it is impossible to speak of it in words. One can grasp "the way" only by divorcing oneself from the idea that language, with its temporal and spatial dimensions and its grounding in the analogical imagination, is our only way of experiencing the world and expressing our experience. The fundamental anonymity and non-referentiality of texts which Derrida postulates is also characteristic of Lao Tzu's view of the ultimate text: reality itself. Lao-Tzu says that reality is "nameless, indescribable, beyond telling; and therefore anything said about it is faulty. . . . [I]t cannot be defined by word or idea. . . . [Before it] words recoil."[8] The goal of "the way" is to make the subject and the impersonal reality coalesce. Reality here is like *presence* in Derrida's discourse; it is "always already" gone, absent, impossible to describe or come into contact with. A person who thinks he has mastered "the way" finds it slipping away; a person who tries to hold on to presence finds that he holds on to nothing.

A student of Taoism, Herrlee Creel, says that "The Tao is unknowable in its essence. . . . Morally, Taoists philosophy is completely indifferent. All things are relative. Right and "wrong" are just words which we may apply to the same thing, depending upon which partial viewpoint we see it from."[9] The use and definition of the word "Tao" excludes any idea of

intelligent cause.[10] Like deconstruction, Taoism is a philosophical perspective that encourages what the Chinese scholar Da Liu calls, descriptively rather than reproachfully, "a completely aimless life."[11] For that reason, it is "an unlikely basis for social organization."[12] An adherent of Tao will probably not take interest in social problems or participate in a political debate. A struggle for political liberty is unthinkable within the confines of Taoism. In the best of all conceivable worlds, a Taoist would be left alone to cultivate his garden. But our world is arguably not the best of all conceivable ones, and a society whose members practice Taoism in large numbers is likely to be taken over by those who thirst for power rather than for peace of mind.

In Taoism and in deconstruction, I perceive a way of approaching "what *is*" that is fundamentally alien to European, or Western culture. The latter has displayed activism, a desire to improve things, an absence of fatalism or of passivity. Taoism is pessimistic about "what *is*" and about man's ability to come into contact with it. The notion of empirical verification does not exist within the confines of Taoism. In contrast, the post-Socratic Greeks, the Jews and the Christians (and through them, European culture) have been rather upbeat about the possibilities of understanding reality. The philosophers of the East and Derrida thus stand on the opposite pole from the European tradition. They reject the notion of a center-bound intelligibility of the world. They voice an extreme pessimism in regard to the center, and abandon not only the idea of approaching it but even of conceiving of it. It is true that in European thought starting perhaps with Hegel, the center of *what is* also began to lose contours, was depersonalized and declared to be unapproachable. But until recently, philosophers still spoke of a *conception* of a center (e.g., Nietzsche). In confessing his inability to conceive of a center, in shifting the discourse onto the margins of the debate about the center, Derrida turns out to be the ultimate pessimist of modern times.

In Derrida's metaphysics *à rebours*, language does not refer to any presence. It is a shadow incapable of conveying any essence, a trace of something that is no more and that never was, properly speaking. Knowledge travels by intuitive leaps. For Taoists and deconstructionsts, there is nothing more wrong than to say, "At the beginning was the Word."

The bleakness of the landscape from which Derrida removed presence and which Lao-Tzu identified as the civilization of men can hardly be doubted. Man's hold on language turns out to be illusory, and a proclamation of linguistic impotence is issued.[13] This is a materialistic and fatalistic view. In deconstruction and in Taoism, undecidability is all. The linguist B. L. Whorf has conjectured that the non-Indo-European languages embody a non-linear and atemporal conception of the world.[14] Derrida wants to convince us that such a conception is applicable to the Indo-European languages as well. *In Derrida, we get for the first time a distinctly non-Western, non-European theory of texts.*

A crucial part of this non-Western approach is Derrida's attempt to dislocate the joint which links speaking and writing, and undermine the ease with which we pass from speaking to writing and then back to speaking. The goal is to show the artificiality of our conception of writing as a record of speaking (and of *presence*), and thus to de-couple speaking and writing. *Of Grammatology* is largely devoted to this task. But in European experience, there first was Socrates and then the *Dialogues* of Plato. There first was Christ and then the New Testament. Writing came after speaking as a way of preserving speaking and holding on to presence. In the European tradition, writing has been a way of holding on to the quiddity of things which Derrida wants to excise from our understanding. His is truly a negative philosophy, or negative theology if you wish, and it has been articulated centuries ago by some Eastern religious thinkers.

Souls without Bodies

In contrast, in the European tradition writing has been regarded not only as a record of speaking but as a way of confirming the physical *and* intellectual nature of man. Men gain understanding and a grasp on reality not by means of wordless mystical revelations but by a physical and mental effort combined. Every effort of the mind is also an effort of the body, and it requires the senses alert enough to provide the grounds for thinking and understanding. The deconstructionists pay little attention to the cooperation of man's physical self and his mind in the activity of speaking and writing. They insist that texts have unnamable and non-rational beginnings, and that in a sense they produce men rather than the other way 'round.

In the deconstructionist paradigm, language has no direct connection with reality because reality is "always already" gone before it reaches language, and because language itself is only a play of differences. The corporeal world disappears from deconstructionist philosophizing. The deconstructionists reject the method of a patient production of certitude through a chain of syllogisms, and they do not see concepts in the light of one another. They say that in order to understand language, one first has to look at writing and see it as an instance of a productive, if ontologically empty relationship between the sign resources and the writing non-subject who makes partial use of these resources. They go farther than either Nietzsche or Freud in their denial of center. While Nietzsche and Freud taught us caution and advised against an overconfident use of language, they postulate that language is a means of mystification, a game that plays itself out through men. Deconstruction implants in us a notion of discontinuity between language and the testimony of the senses, between speaking and writing. As the critic Floyd Merrell rightly observed, Derrida wants to destroy the notion of language on which Christianity has been built.[15] Derrida's vision of writing and speaking is directly opposed to that of St. Paul. St. Paul warned us that the letter is deadly to the spirit, and European culture took him seriously. According to Derrida, the letter created the Spirit, and thus the Spirit is dead while the letter is alive—it is, in fact, the only reality of civilization.

While denying the spoken heritage of the letter, the deconstructionists trivialize its civilizing power and its invariable tendency to lead away from itself and toward the Spirit. They speak contemptuously of the "fetishism of the letter." Their vision of the world outside the written letter is Rousseauistic: in feminist deconstructionsim, the clerical letter is the law and authority, castrating and repressive, while orality is life-giving, anarchic and erotogenic.[16]

Jacques Derrida has antecedents not only in the East but also in the Western tradition. Plato's *Parmenides* and *Sophists* should be counted among these antecedents. However, until recently, European thought did not pay much attention to *Parmenides*. Undoubtedly this was due largely to Christianity which strongly affirmed a center, a being, a presence that was both personal and transcendent, and which discouraged speculation on such esoteric topics as the being of non-being.[17] For most of the time during which our civilization has existed, we have ignored the eastward-looking *Parmenides* and instead have followed Plato's and Aristotle's models of syllogistic reasoning and their habit of seeing one truth in the light of another. The Socratic model of thinking was spiritualized by Christianity and it became the cornerstone of European and later Western civilization. Derrida urges us to abandon it and acquiesce to the possible consequences of his non-Western model of thinking and of texts.

Thus in a way, deconstruction pursues the idea that language is dependent on a transcendent and personal reality which exists beyond empirical reality. It pursues this idea in order to repudiate it. When such repudiations first became common over a century ago, it seemed that they would not necessitate a change in our approach to language. But recently, a perception began to develop that this repudiation has profound consequences for language itself, and that Taoist writings, *Parmenides*, and *Sophist* must replace Aristotle and the Bible as arch-models of discourse. Derrida and his American followers realize that removal of the notion of the Deity from European languages will necessitate reformulating the definition of each and every word. When the personal and transcendent God ceased to be the rock-bottom premise of philosophers, when a wave of agnosticism rolled over the Reformation, it seemed at first that language as such was not affected, and that one could still use it in the same way in which it had been used when the Deity was the center. The deconstructionists realize that this is not so, and this realization may be their most important contribution.

The relation between deconstruction and Marxism has been clouded by a common but erroneous perception of the situation of Russian letters in the 1920s and 1930s. At that time, the so-called formalists and structuralists were in disfavor in Soviet Russia, and so-called "orthodox" Marxists dominated the scene. Thus a perception arose, later perpetuated by the professors of Russian literature in the United States, that there existed in Russia and elsewhere a fundamental hostility between the literature-oriented formalists and structuralists, and the politics-oriented Marxists. Since deconstruction is in some ways related to the first two trends, and since it has been declared a bourgeois invention by the Party propagandists in Russia, an antagonistic relationship between Marxism and deconstruction was assumed to exist.

However, it has to be remembered that even though the Russian formalists and structuralists were silenced, they too were Marxists. (The situation was more complex in the English-speaking countries where the "formalists," or "the new critics" as they were usually called, ranged from Marxist fellow travelers such as Kenneth Burke to traditionalists such as T. S. Eliot.) They did, however, subscribe to a version of Marxism which happened to lose ground in their country. Their anti-metaphysical orientation was implicit rather than explicit: ostensibly, they were only interested in explicating poems and stories. They insisted that the word "intentionality" be removed from a critic's vocabulary; that poetic language is non-referential; and that the "old" interpreters of literature confused words with things. In formalist criticism, ideas were downgraded, and "verbal texture" was upgraded. There were no rules in the formalist game; it was limited only by a critic's imagination and his sense of intellectual honesty. Formalism eventually transformed itself into structuralism, and the new trend treated philosophical ideas as part of verbal texture. The deconstructionists further refined these propositions, and they appropriated for their own purposes the habits of the formalists. In deconstructionist criticism, ideas are used as crutches to traverse texts, or as makeshift tools of analysis produced by social circumstances, but their ennobling power is dismissed as illusory.

The Exploitation of Texts

While the formalists and the structuralists have succeeded in correcting some abuses of the *fin-de-siècle* literary criticism, their hastily formulated credos bred acceptance of studies which looked at the margins of words rather than at the words themselves.[18] What in formalism was a technique for an appreciation of poetry, in deconstruction became a means of asserting the hollowness of culture. What the victorious Russian Marxists have been unable to achieve—the eradication of traces of the spiritual from language and literature—the deconstructionists have set out to do in earnest. The formalist and structuralist schools prepared the ground for Derrida's assertion that, "The reading must always aim at a certain relationship, unperceived by the writer, between what he commands and what he does not command of the patterns of the language that he uses."[19] A reading should not protect or explicate, because there is nothing there to be protected or explicated. A reading can only produce. Deconstruction offers proof that the seemingly innocuous postulates of the formalists helped to open up texts to limitless exploitation.

The deconstructionists replaced "intentionality" by "ideology," and thus further distanced themselves from the assumption that a reading should attempt to recover a meaning rather than create it. The Frankfurt school notion of ideology as a worldview beyond the control of an individual and arising out of his life situation fits comfortably in the deconstructionist context, and its contingency corresponds to the spiritual emptiness of discourse in Derrida's interpretation of it. Another Marxist-influenced view, that of Karl Mannheim, says that ideology is deprived of such attributes as falsity or truthfulness and is dependent on social conditions, on the historical moment and psychological proclivities of the subject, or on factors which render the subject powerless to decide about his own fate. "Total" ideology is a product of "false consciousness" which Mannheim arbitrarily assigned to those who disagreed with him. It is a trap into which entire epochs of human history are said to have fallen. This total ideology has nothing to do with human motivation but consists in the "structural differences in minds operating in different social settings."[20] Marxism and deconstruction share this concept of ideology and ignore the fact that our present knowledge depends on the correctness of our past knowledge, and is unthinkable without it. In deconstruction and in Western Marxism, thought knows itself not by empirical verification but by an immediate grasp of itself.[21]

Deconstruction has been appropriated by Western Marxists as a tool to help explain the problem of "superstructure" posited but not explored by Marx. While the Russian Marxists tend to attribute cultural developments directly to the economic base of society, Western Marxists shun such simplistic explanations and opt instead for a relative autonomy of superstructure. They acknowledge indefinite delays in the influence exerted by the base and the dependence of superstructure on factors not directly traceable to economics. Viewed from this vantage point, the deconstructionist vision explains some of the mysteries of culture without linking them directly either to the GNP or to metaphysics. For that reason, some Marxist thinkers welcome deconstruction not as a marginal investigation but as a central one. Richard Terdiman said that deconstruction can be used to "evade and deconstruct the institutional mechanisms producing signification" and thus to accomplish "an ideological critique" of bourgeois society,[22] and Terry Eagleton hailed deconstruction as an ally in the struggle against that society.[23] In his view, deconstruction can be a means of "subverting" the existing culture. Eugene Vance said that the goal of deconstruction is to show that Western logocentrism has made writing "the primal instrument of power."[24] If one can deconstruct Western writing and persuade the readers of its hollow insides, then the ancient power base of the exploiting classes will crumble and power will presumably change hands.

Leo Trotsky was Vance's predecessor in making this kind of argument. In *Literature and Revolution* (1924), he mounted an attack on those Russian literary critics who in his opinion diverged too far from the goal of social change by assigning permanent value to words instead of class struggle. He accused these critics of a "fast ripening religiousness," of being "the followers of St. John" and believing that "In the beginning was the Word." "But we believe that at the beginning was the deed. The word followed, as its phonetic shadow," proclaimed the creator of the Red Army.[25] Like the deconstructionists, Trotsky despised the logocentric tradition in language.

Language, for him, was a tool that could be appropriated by the leaders of society in order to manipulate the human material, a part of superstructure that had no *presence* in it. The deed, the power, the flexing of the muscle; this is what Trotsky saw in human civilization. Language appeared later as a "trace," a "shadow," or an "instrument of power."

It is to be noted that both the philosophy of passivity such as the Tao, and the philosophy of activism such as Marxism, proclaim the emptiness and marginality of language. Deconstruction takes a further step in the same direction and attempts to show that language can be "opened up" like an unoccupied house and displayed to the public as containing nothing save an imagined metaphysical ballast. Out of this nothingness, Trotsky wanted to shape a weapon to help the revolution. He felt that language could be molded indefinitely, that newspeak was indeed possible because language could be purged of concepts such as identity and non-contradiction. Granted that the leading deconstructionists in this country such as J. Hillis Miller, Geoffrey Hartman or the recently deceased Paul de Man have not been political activists. However, the deconstructionists certainly have done the homework for Trotsky's followers by providing them with sophisticated arguments against *presence* and by their wholesale opposition to "the natural, the given, the taken-for-granted" in language.[26]

Not that the deconstructionists have not been helped in some ways by the traditional historiography. For instance, in the knowledge which Western culture has of itself, Eastern Europe is conspicuously missing. The importance of these eastern marches for the very existence of the center has slipped the attention of all major cultural historians of the West.

The knowledge of the Eastern European component of Western culture was suppressed by such German historians as Heinrich von Treitschke in the nineteenth century and by historians sympathetic to Russia in the twentieth. So it is easy for a Marxist deconstructionist to show that in the Second Reich, or in Tsarist or Communist Russia, writing was and is an instrument of power. He of course does so not in order to defend Eastern Europe but to de-center the center. For instance, in *The Invention of Tradition* (1983), Eric Hobsbawm traces the way in which Bismarck's Germany attempted to provide historical legitimacy for the merging of the Prussian and German states, and to that effect invented cultural "traditions" which ranged from music and architecture to public ceremonials and rituals. [27]

The Opportunity for Conservatives

Which brings us to the problem of attitudes to deconstruction of those scholars who see its basic assumptions as wrong and are skeptical of its professed goals. Does deconstruction offer any opportunities to a conservative critic? I would like to answer with a qualified "yes." An observation made by T. S. Eliot in *After Strange Gods* seems to me relevant: "The essential of any important heresy is not simply that it is wrong; it is that it is partly right."[28] On occasion, deconstruction succeeds in refining and correcting interpretations that need laundering, and as such it deepens our understanding of written texts. Hobsbawm's study of nationalist symbolism in nineteenth-century Germany, and Hugh Trevor-Roper's analysis of the invented Highland tradition of Scotland tolerated by the English to prevent a revival of Scottish separatism,[29] are examples.

While the conservative critics too often engage in refutations and borrow terms of discourse from others, the deconstructionists succeed on occasion in forcing texts to reveal their multiple meanings. While the conservatives too often pretend that the history of Western politics coincides with the history of Western values, the deconstructionists leave the familiar grooves of thought in order to explore areas that need to be explored. Some part of the deconstructionist effort can be diverted from its original aim and used by those whom the deconstructionists mean to render obsolete: the logocentric critics. Some part of the deconstructionist work can be treated as a fitting session, as trying on new clothes on old concepts. Rather than being dreadfully provoked by the deconstructionist sinners, one can follow them along a bit, and discover the methods by which they propose to sew reality's new clothes.

The phenomenon of literary interpretation is traceable to many causes. One of them is the educated man's desire to get beyond the *Mother Goose* stage of reading, to analyze as well as enjoy a rhyme or a story. Before it is reflected upon, imaginative literature is not unlike *Mother Goose* in the effect it has on us: it charms and fascinates us, and it attracts our attention by means which we cannot clearly articulate. Interpretation makes one aware of the soft underbelly of meaning; it makes the subconscious conscious and the inchoate, expressible. Some deconstructionist interpretations do not achieve what Derrida wants them to achieve; they are just interpretations, and thus part of the hermeneutic tradition that can be traced back to what Scripture scholars did in the Middle Ages and what they still do today. While the goal of deconstructionism is "[to release] the signifier from the semantic restraints

of the logocentric tradition,"[30] and is as such unacceptable, the way it goes about accomplishing its goal has to be mastered if one is serious about logocentrism.

The beginning and end of language are shrouded in mystery, and the logocentric critics have accepted this fact with too much docility. A degree of inexactitude is characteristic of language; we always see through a glass darkly. Some deconstructionists point out that the meanings which have been imposed on words by imprudent thinkers fall into pieces under scrutiny. One has to "get to the other side" of this kind of deconstruction. A suspension of belief in the transcendent core of language is deadly only if one makes it a habit and a foundation of one's thinking. I would recommend to anyone the reading of journals such as *Diacritics,* not because I agree with their goals but because I see in the ways therein explored a fountainhead of new apologies for the old logocentrism. While the letter without the spirit becomes deadly, the spirit without the letter becomes flabby.

Like Marxism, deconstruction is not internally falsifiable, and is thus immune to criticism on its own terms. M. H. Abrams and Gerald Graff have tried to refute it, only to be dismissed as either not rigorous enough in their arguments,[31] or as committing an error due to the limitations of their first principles.[32] But while deconstruction cannot be internally disapproved, it can be partially absorbed and by-passed, as has been the case with other significant theories. Some deconstructionist works may eventually be looked upon in the way in which an educated Greek must have looked upon the paradoxes of Zeno: while he was unable to demonstrate that Zeno was wrong, he *knew* that he was wrong. In *The Open Society and Its Enemies*, Karl Popper spoke of a nineteenth-century doctor who could unerringly diagnose tuberculosis but was unable to define it. Popper's conclusion was that we need not always produce definitions of things in order to know what they are. A similar point can be made about some deconstructionist claims. Others can be digested and assimilated.

The final lesson which deconstruction offers may paradoxically be this: it is impossible to fully master a language without recognizing its analogical structure and its metaphysical dimension. Most people do not draw the ultimate conclusions from their use of language, and deconstruction offers an opportunity to come to these conclusions. More than any other trendy philosopher, Derrida has shown how inconsistent and complacent are not only the ordinary users of language but also critics and thinkers. Without transcendence, language indeed seems to be merely a set of multivocal traces of socialization and historicization of man; the analytical strain of the Enlightenment turns out to be a delusion, just as Adorno thought; the "warring forces of signification" invite endless manipulation. Contrary to his declared intentions, Derrida has shown that the great works of literature are either a means of deception which can and must be deconstructed, or they are mysteriously linked with something that transcends them. The Russian poet Nikolai Gumilev expressed this dilemma in a poem entitled "The Word" *("Slovo,"* 1921) with which I would like to conclude these remarks:

In those primal days when God Almighty
Bent His face over the fresh world—then
The Word made the sun stand still in
   heaven,
The Word tore apart the towns of men.

• • •

We forget that only the word is haloed
Here where earthly cares leave us
   perplexed.
In the Gospel of St. John is written
That the Word is God: that is the text.

We have put a limit to its meaning:
Only to *this* life, *this* shallow shell.
And like bees in an abandoned beehive,
Dead, deserted words have a bad smell.[33]

Notes

1. Edith Hamilton, introduction to "Parmenides," *Plato: The Collected Dialogues,* Edith Hamilton and Huntington Cairns, eds. (Princeton, NJ: Princeton Univ. Press, 1978), 920.

2. Jacques Maritain, *Three Reformers: Luther, Descartes, Rousseau* (Port Washington, NY: Kennikat Press, 1970), 79.

3. Floyd Merrell, *Deconstruction Reframed* (West Lafayette, IN: Purdue Univ. Press, 1985), passim.

4. Maritain, op. cit., 78.

5. Ibid., 66; see also Thomas Molnar, *God and the Knowledge of Reality* (New York: Basic Books, 1973), x.

6. Merrell, op. cit., 32–35.

7. Ibid., 10.

8. *Tao Te Ching: The Way of Lao Tzu*, by R. B. Blakney (New York: The New American Library), 29.

9. Herrlee G. Creel, *What is Taoism? and Other Studies in Chinese Cultural History* (Chicago: Univ. of Chicago Press, 1970), 3.

10. Stanislas Julien, *Le livre de la voie et de la vertu* [1842], trans. by Herrlee Creel, op. cit., 30.

11. Da Liu, *The Tao and Chinese Culture* (New York: Schocken Books, 1979), 17.

12. Ibid., 18.

13. The adherents of deconstruction might invoke here Hegel's distinction between speculative and ratiocinative uses of language. But human beings do not compartmentalize thought in this fashion, as Karl Marx proved shortly after appropriating some of Hegel's important insights.

But even without invoking this example, it can be stated that experience indicates that both uses of language mingle in human thinking about all subjects, from practical to abstract. For a distinction between speculation and ratiocination see G. W. F. Hegel, preface, *Phenomenology of Spirit*, A. V. Miller, trans. (Oxford: Oxford Univ. Press, 1977), especially 36, 43.

14. B. L. Whorf, *Language, Thought and Reality: Selected Writings,* Carroll, ed. (Cambridge, MA: MIT Press, 1956), 134–59.

15. Merrell, op. cit., 118. This notwithstanding such deconstructionist theologians as Mark C. Taylor and his recent *Deconstruction in Context* (Chicago: Univ. of Chicago Press, 1986).

16. Peggy Kamuf, *Fictions of Feminine Desire: Disclosures of Heloise* (Lincoln: Univ. of Nebraska Press, 1982).

17. Molnar, op. cit., 5.

18. Jacques Derrida, *Of Grammatology,* trans. Gayatri Spivak (Baltimore: Johns Hopkins Univ. Press, 1976), 141–64.

19. Ibid., 158.

20. Karl Mannheim, *Ideology and Utopia: An Introduction to the Sociology of Knowledge* [1936] (London: Routledge & Kegan Paul, 1948), 51.

21. Maritain, op cit., 70.

22. Richard Terdiman, "Deconstructing Memory: On Representing the Past and Theorizing Culture in France since the Revolution." *Diacritics* (Winter 1985), 33–34.

23. Terry Eagleton, *The Function of Criticism: From 'The Spectator" to Post-Structuralism* (London: Verso, 1984), 97–100; 123–24.

24. Eugene Vance, "Medievalisms and Models of Textuality," *Diacritics, (*Fall 1985), 60.

25. Leo Trotsky, *Literature and Revolution* [1924] (New York, 1957), 183. Trotsky was wrong: the critics whom he had in mind very soon abandoned their "metaphysical" interests and began to march to the tune of the Revolution. Eventually, both Trotsky and the critics he had criticized were repudiated by the winning faction.

26. William E. Cain, *The Crisis in Criticism: Theory, Literature, and Reform in English Studies* (Baltimore: Johns Hopkins Univ. Press, 1984), 246.

27. Eric Hobsbawm, "Mass-Producing Traditions: Europe, 1870–1914," Eric Hobsbawm and Terence Ranger, eds., *The Invention of Tradition* (Cambridge: Cambridge Univ. Press, 1983), 273–79.

28. T. S. Eliot, *After Strange Gods* (New York: Harcourt, 1934), 26.

29. Hugh Trevor-Roper, "The Invention of Tradition: The Highland Tradition of Scotland," Eric Hobsbawm and Terence Ranger, op. cit., 15–42.

30. Donald Pease, "J. Hillis Miller: The Other Victorian at Yale," *The Yale Critics: Deconstruction in America,* Jonathan Arac, Wlad Godzich, Wallace Martin, eds. (Minneapolis: Univ. of Minnesota Press, 1983), 70.

31. Paul A. Bové, "Variations on Authority: Some Deconstructive Transformations of the New Criticism," *The Yale Critics,* 3.

32. *The Yale Critics,* 11–12, 70–71, 81–82, 181.

33. *Modern Russian Poetry,* Vladimir Markov and Merrill Sparks, trans. and eds. (Alva, UK: McGibbon & Kee, 1966), 245, 247.

Cleanth Brooks

Means and Ends:
Education in a Secular Age

VOL. 25, NO. 2, 1990

The serious writer of today lives in a very much secularized world, a world of measurable objects, a world of space and time considerations, a world that must be studied not only rationally, but scientifically. Now, this situation did not suddenly come about in the middle of the seventeenth century. It has been developing since that time, and I think if we wanted to be very careful we could push it far back of the seventeenth century. But many people agree that a very important part of the process becomes evident in the seventeenth century.

An important man in this process is the French mathematician and philosopher, René Descartes (1596–1650). Descartes distinguished, you will remember, the mind from matter, and thus split the world into two different realms. On one side there was the realm of mental activity, the world of ideas, fancies, and all kinds of subjective things. And outside of the human head was the world of objects and things. God alone, Descartes thought, knew how to relate the two worlds, the world of time and space and the world of mental activity. And Descartes, it ought to be said, certainly had no intention of

removing God from the process (he was a Christian), or of attacking a religion. Nevertheless, the dualism that Descartes set up worked steadily through the decades to clear the path for a more careful study of the world of things. It cleared the highway for the marvelous development of the so-called hard sciences like physics, chemistry, and biology. They have grown magnificently, particularly in our own twentieth century.

Think, for instance, how fast and how far chemistry and physics have gone since even 1915, how far medical science has gone since 1900. I am convinced that if it had not been for these wonderful developments and changes, I would have been blind long before this time, and probably dead. So I have a real personal gratitude to register for the marvelous things that have happened in the hard sciences.

We do not operate on a person's body because of hunches and blind instincts. We used to. I'm told sometimes we do it now, but we try to avoid it as much as possible. Instead, we try to examine the body, make the most meticulous of tests, so as to know what we're doing when we perform the operation. We develop the tools and machines that allow us to make incredibly finer measurements.

I expect that most of you have heard that among Descartes' accomplishments, was "to cut the throat of poetry." But again, that was not in the least his intention. In any case, how could his dualism have possibly brought about that? In the early stages of mankind, the man of religion, the man of science, the seer, and the prognosticator, frequently were all bound up in one single person. He was the truth-teller, the man you went to for advice about everything. And he frequently wrote in poetry. Originally, it was he who would tell the truth about us and our activities and beliefs. But what was the truth? With the triumph of science, which clearly could convey some very powerful and exact truths about how the world we live in makes out, and how our bodies can be best cured of disease, and how we can build skyscrapers, or build a vehicle that can go faster than the speed of sound, we are driven to ask, what was the nature of the truth that poetry, on the other hand, told us? Surely it was a highly subjective truth. Much of it was fantasy, or could be questioned as fantasy, or was merely an imaginative suggestion, or a set of rhetorical flourishes, matters which obviously could not be objectively true.

Now, I don't want to overstate matters, that with Descartes in the middle of the seventeenth century, the throat of poetry was cut, poetry was dismantled, the subjective world was demolished—not at all! Poetry did not suddenly become worthless. The kind of truth that worked in the world did, however, seem to lie more and more in the hands of the scientists. And poetry and fiction and drama, too, more and more were thought of as providing entertainment or an escape from the world of fact. Indeed, insofar as the poet has in the eyes of the public been dislodged from his position as the great truth-sayer, speaking the living word of truth, he has been left by some simply to play among the pretty flowers of life.

I do not mean to say that this state of affairs appeared all at once. It did not. As late as the Victorian period a hundred years ago poetry was still regarded by many people, sometimes by the poets themselves, as the dispenser of wisdom. Though a close examination of the process will show even then, significant changes in the nature of poetry.

In the late nineteenth century, for example, Wordsworth and Coleridge were much concerned to accommodate poetry to science, to relate it to science, and to insist that poetry still had very important things to say. Yet if the problem was not solved by Coleridge and Wordsworth (I don't think it was really solved), it was at least more and more recognized to be a problem, a serious problem.

In the twentieth century the character of what literary artists may say and whether they engage truth at all has come under more rigorous examination. One of our popular, though serious novelists, engages the problem in most of his novels. I am thinking here of Walker Percy. He deals with the problem quite directly, and he has written in addition to his novels, two books on semiotics, and tells us that he has a third one that he is working on now.

His Jefferson Lecture, the lecture chosen by the National Endowment for the Humanities to be delivered each year, was given in May. It begins with a reference to Cartesianism. Percy calls this split made by René Descartes: "the San Andreas Fault in the modern mind." For three centuries this fault line has been visible to scholars of what we sometimes call the science of man, sociology, say, or psychology. They work uneasily, he thinks, on one side of the crevice, sometimes attempt to straddle it, and often try to deny that the fissure even exists. Thus they talk about things which can often be measured, such as synapses between the nerves, or electric currents which run along nerve pathways. These all belong to the realm of things—these electrical energies, nerve patterns and so on.

But scholars set down beside them mental events, emotional, transcendental values, and these are not things at all. For can you measure a thought, or weigh an emotion? You can do it metaphorically—we say that all the time—but can you really in any scientific sense? Transcendental values as such are not "things," but something very different. Thus, Percy says that the social scientists sometimes talk about the mind, that is, the mental activity, as a function of the brain. The brain is indeed a solid thing made up of a very complicated mass of nerves. But Walker Percy doesn't believe that the phrase, "it's a function of," tells us much, or helps explain anything about mental activity, as he puts it. Who would say that the particular vision given to us by a madonna painted by Raphael is a function of the pigments and canvas that Raphael used? In some sense it is, but so what? How is a mental impression related to those physical things that Raphael used to produce it? How can "function of" tell us very much about the nature of the changes over from things to certain activities that we all experience in viewing the painting, or in reading in poetry, or experiencing in our daily emotional lives?

In any case, what does a twentieth-century American, the typical man in the street, make of the situation? Much of it will depend, of course, upon his upbringing and his education, taking that term in its fullest sense. If he knows the work of Walker Percy or of T. S. Eliot or of Flannery O'Connor, he may be fully aware of the "San Andreas Fault" that runs through the twentieth-century mind, and may have found his own way of dealing with it. He will have met that sophisticated problem, one hopes, with an answering sophistication of his own. If, however, if he is, let's say, a fundamentalist, he will scarcely understand the issues that his very ignorance of the new ideas, and his habitual nurture do so much to obscure from him. Nevertheless, ignorance and confusion are never the best defenses against the new and advancing intellectual ideas. A few years in college will probably tell the son or daughter of the fundamentalist a good many things that he had not understood before and may dislodge him from his ignorance. I say "a few years in college" because I am talking in largely general, institutional, and statistical terms. Obviously there are colleges and colleges, and obviously what the individual student may get from any college may be very different from what another receives from it.

To return to the typical American citizen of our time; what impresses him powerfully is not the fact of theoretical constructions. Even his own college may have given him only a very vague notion of what kind of truth the hard sciences give. What does impress him is what applied science has done and proposes to do further. A citizen knows—well or perhaps more vaguely, but he knows—that theoretical and experimental science undergirds our vast technological establishment, and he is much impressed with the power and mighty accomplishment of that technological achievement.

Now, I would be the last to distract from it. It has been admirable and its powerful good has been immense. But I hardly need to say that its powerful evil has been immense also. Witness the Second World War and the other wars that we have fought since. We Americans have been brought up to praise and even venerate our great technical accomplishments. We speak day-in and day-out of dollar values and winning. Our very university system taken as a whole powerfully expresses this view of the world. The praise of a winning football or basketball team, the salary paid to the coach and to his retinue of assistant coaches, the scandalous revelations about what sometimes really goes on in putting prize athletes through college, not so much to educate them as to allow them to use their talents for athletic fame.

Such evidence convincingly shows the way in which the highest educational ideals are often trampled on in our will to win anything, everything, at any cost. To win success of any sort becomes a national badge of honor. If you doubt this, read the advertisements in your newspapers and magazines, or listen occasionally to the pleas for your attention that come over our radios or on our television screens.

A great corporation relates every morning as I turn on my spot news coverage: "Americans want to succeed, not simply to survive." And a great national newspaper signs off its TV achievement by telling us that it is "the daily diary of the American dream." And what is the American dream? It would seem to be one of worldly success. That is trumpeted all day long and every evening long in dozens of revelations of that dream as it expresses itself in clothing, motor cars, houses, clubs, travel, and hundreds of other ways. But the terms are always material terms. "Well," somebody says, "What of it? You don't ask our great corporations to praise poverty, do you?" No, I don't. I'm not arguing that we should forbid such ads, even if we could. What

I am calling to your attention is the impact of that kind of exhortation on every American citizen. It is powerful, it is very pervasive, but much of it appears to be non-Christian, if not actually anti-Christian. I am particularly concerned here with how a populace, so thoroughly secularized as ours seems to be, can be profitably addressed by an author who is a Christian or is even simply sympathetic with Christian ideas. I am also concerned with the prospect for the study of the humanities in a world that is more and more devoted to—perhaps more and more obsessed by—a certain kind of truth, and which regards more and more suspiciously claims to authenticity that cannot be tested by scientific means.

Before moving on to other topics, I would like to set forth another judgment on what happens when a culture comes to regard as truly consequential truth only that kind which can be validated by scientific testing. I want to read a paragraph from a statement made by Professor Eric Voegelin a number of years ago in a book called *From Enlightenment to Revolution*.

Existence has the structure of the In-Between, of the Platonic *metaxy* [*Metexa* is the Greek word meaning "in-between"] and if anything is constant in the history of mankind, it is the language of tension between life and death, immortality and mortality, perfection and imperfection, time and timelessness, between order and disorder, truth and untruth, sense and senselessness of existence, between *amor Dei* and *amor sui*, *l'àme ouverte* and *l'àme close*; between the virtues of openness toward the grounds of being such as faith, hope and love, and the vices of infolding closure such as hubris and revolt; between the moods of joy and despair; and between alienation in its double meaning of alienation from the world and alienation from God. If we split these pairs of symbols, and hypostatize the poles of the tension as independent entities [that is, if we split the tension between earth and heaven and simply say, we will just talk about earth—that's the important thing, or just talk about heaven—that's the important thing], we destroy the reality of existence as it has been experienced by the creators of the tensional symbolisms; we lose consciousness and intellect; we deform our humanity and reduce ourselves to a state of quiet despair or activist conformity to the "age," of drug addiction or television-watching, of hedonistic stupor or murderous possession of truth, of suffering from the absurdity of existence or indulgence in any divertissement (in Pascal's sense), that promises to substitute as a "value" for reality lost. In the language of Heraclitus and Plato: Dream life usurps the place of wake life. [I think we would say "waking life."][1]

Voegelin writes a very compact, highly compressed style. Moreover, his ideas are new and unfamiliar to a great many of us, or else, they are so old and traditional that they impress us as radically fresh and strange. The statement that we live in an "in-between" may seem indeed very strange and puzzling. But we can take the expression quite literally. Man is indubitably an animal, but while any other animal that we know of has a short memory and can hardly foresee the future, man can become interested in proposals and institutions that will go on long after his own death, and on the contrary, he can immerse himself in customs that go back for five thousand years. Mankind can thus have some sort of intimations of

immortal life, something possessing the range of interests of a god. In short, man is an animal who has in a very limited way, a godlike range of interests. But if he takes a notion that he really is a god, he usually turns into something like a demon. Man may have heroic possibilities, but he is definitely not a god. There will be lamentable failures also if he tries to be simply an animal. He lacks the other animals' safeguards and inhibitions. Man trying to be just a good-animal always turns out to be so much worse than any other animal.

So mankind is always in an uncomfortable posture, neither a self-contained, self-regulated wild creature, nor a wise and beneficent god who occupies a realm of endless time, or a realm outside of time. But if man has lived fruitfully in this state of being in which he is in tension with two finally opposed realms, there lies the prospect of glory and joy, as well as the prospect of horror and despair. Moreover, as Voegelin says, if we try to fixate on either of the opposed poles, we do become indeed alienated from full human life. We do, then, indeed, as Voegelin says,

> deform our humanity and reduce ourselves to a state of quiet despair or activist conformity to the "age," of drug addiction or television-watching, of hedonistic stupor or murderous possession of truth. . . .

Let me break into the quotation here at this point to call the names of Hitler and Stalin as special appropriate illustrations of the "murderous possession of truth." Both of them were quite satisfied about how history was coming out, and they were very quick on the job to kill a few million people in order to help history on with its proper task. But back to my quotation:

suffering from the absurdity of existence or indulgence in any divertissement . . . that promises to substitute as a "value" for reality lost. In the language of Heraclitus and Plato: Dream life usurps the place of wake life.

Few of us moderns are receptive to being admonished in language drawn from Heraclitus or Plato. Try it out. You'll find it doesn't help much. But after all, Voegelin's radical modernism is based squarely on the ancient Greek philosophers, and on the testaments of the Judeo-Christian tradition. Moreover, when Voegelin mentions as ways of leading a dream life, rather than the wide-awake life, drug addiction and television-watching, we can be quite sure that he has in mind, among other things, our own America.

I had promised to talk about some of the ways in which the modern author and the serious author of our day may deal with an audience that is as thoroughly infected with secularism as ours is. When I first began teaching English, I was told immediately that English was a service department. Our job was to help with the grammar and punctuation of students who were studying objects of real importance, such as chemical engineering, anatomy, or city government. Even so, fifty years ago the universities were already moving away from the classics and from the arts to the sciences, theoretical and applied. They were concerned to teach means, how to do things, how things work, and not ends, goals, purposes. As the machinery developed by the culture became more and more complicated, pressure needed to study such subjects was tremendously increased. I am thinking here not so much of what happened to a few old and privileged schools, but of the great state universities and their allied institutions,

including the many more who were described as universities, but whose studies, frankly, were those meant to teach people how to get trained for a job. It's been one of the great fallacies of the American system to call things by the wrong names.

To the average student the liberal arts seem peculiarly unqualified for guaranteeing the student entry into a good job in a highly technological society. You miss my point entirely, however, if you think that I believe the matter of getting a job is unimportant. It is, of course. But for the masses in a secular age, the liberal arts have seemed to qualify the recipient for only one special job—that of teaching other liberal arts—not as the equipment for any good citizen who ought to know what the proper goals of life are.

The point that I want to make then, is not a disparagement of work or even work in a highly technological society. It is rather just this: technical training and much of the theoretical science that lies behind it has to do with means, how to do a job most efficiently, how to carry out this particular quest cheaply, and so on. But important as the problem of means is, the problem of ends is even more important. We have comparatively little education in the matter of ends and purposes. The institutions that once nurtured such ideas and interests were the church, the usual course of study at the college, the teaching of manners and morals in old-fashioned schools, and so on. These institutions have become more and more disparaged. In actual practice our civilization is top-heavy with machinery, and flushed with pride at what that has accomplished. Society has allowed the advertising industry to tell us what we ought to aspire to win. Thus, what success really means is the kind of house you ought to live in, the kind of car you ought to drive, the restaurants you should patronize, and the kind of underwear, refrigerator, or book you ought to buy. Look at the TV for an hour or so each morning and note the prevailing notion of what the good life is or ought to be in modern America. The message is, work hard, get the means that allow you to acquire these rich bundles of delightful prizes.

How have some of our writers responded to this state of affairs? Many of them by providing simply more entertainment. Writing becomes a trade, a craft, and sometimes it is done very successfully. But the serious artist has a more difficult job. How is he going to address himself to a secularized society? How is he going to get a hearing? How is he going to make even those few serious readers see what he is talking about? One of my old teachers at Vanderbilt, John Crowe Ransom, a poet, was well aware of the general situation. I want to present a poem of his that describes very accurately what has happened and to show one of the kinds of methods that the serious artist has used.

Ransom called his poem "Persistent Explorer."

The noise of water teased his literal ears
Which heard the distant drumming and
    thus scored:
Water is falling—it fell—therefore it
    roared.
But he cried, that is more than water I
    hear.

He went still higher, and on the dizzy
    brink
His eyes confirmed with vision what he
    had heard:
This is but tumbling water. Again he
    demurred:
That was not only water flashing, I think.

But listen as he might, look fast or slow,

It was water, only water, tons of it
Dropping into the gorge, and every bit
Was water, the insipid chemical, H_2O

The sound was tremendous, but it was
    no voice
That spoke to him. The spectacle was
    grand
But still it spelled him nothing, nothing
    and spell
Forbade him whether to cower or rejoice.

What would he have it spell? He scarcely
    knew;
Only that water and nothing but water
    filled
His eyes and ears, nothing but water that
    spilled;
And if the smoke and rattle of water drew

From the deep thickets of his mind the
    train,
The fierce fauns and the timid tenants
    there
That burst their bonds and rushed upon
    the air,
Why, he must turn and heat them down
    again.

But he, as a modern secularized man knows that images of a goddess or fauns and nymphs coming out of the froth of the water, are simply fantasy. As a rational man, he has to dismiss them.

So be it. And no unreasonable outcry
The pilgrim made; only a rueful grin
Spread over his lips until he drew them in;
He did not sit upon a rock and die.

This modern poet is not doing what the Romantic poet would do, grief-stricken, tempted to commit suicide, finding out that nature, its reverence gone, has nothing to say to him. He grins. The joke's on him finally. The joke is on modern man.

There were many ways of dying; witness,
  if he
Commit himself to the water, and descend
Wrapped in the water, turn water at the
  end,
And flow with the great water out to sea.

But there are many ways of living, too.
And let his enemies gibe, but let them say
That he would throw this continent away
And seek another country—as he would
  do.[2]

Well, did Mr. Ransom find another country? A world that truly fulfilled him—that existed beyond the world depicted by science? I don't know. If his explorer's search turns out to be futile, why had he expected anything more than what happens? So much for Ransom's explorer, but did Ransom himself ever discover that other country? One qualified to satisfy the whole man, the emotional man as well as the scientific man? Again, I don't know. But my interest in quoting this poem is not to try to settle that question. I read the poem primarily for its account of what modern learning has done to the world in which most of us live and what it is likely to do to a great deal of Romantic poetry.

Here's another poem, which again does not reveal Allen Tate's conception of what an endurable world would be like. I read it, however, because he beautifully describes the anguished state in which some of the sensitive observers of our time have found themselves. You will note that the poem does not end with a description of a complete world, but rather an anguished prayer to be allowed to return to an earlier world.

Tate's poem is called the "Last Days of Alice." He doesn't identify Alice, but part of the educated reader's job is to see who Alice is.

Alice grown lazy, mammoth but not fat,
Declines upon her lost and twilight age;
Above in the dozing leaves the grinning
  cat
Quivers forever with his abstract rage:
Whatever light swayed on the perilous
  gate
Forever sways, nor will the arching grass,
Caught when the world clattered,
  undulate
In the deep suspension of the looking-
  glass.

Surely this is the Alice of *Alice in Wonderland,* and the cat who dissolves away until finally there is nothing left but his abstract grin, and surely the Alice who went through the looking glass and found that curious, strange, inhuman, logical world, a whole world laid out as upon a chess board—all of these things tell us this is Alice of *Alice in Wonderland* and *Alice Through the Looking-Glass.*

Mr. Tate is suggesting that modern man has become Alice. He's looking at himself in a mirror and trying to get into the mirror. He's creating a world out of his own mind. And so he goes on to say

Turned absent-minded by infinity
She cannot move unless her double move,
The All-Alice of the world's entity
Smashed in the anger of her hopeless love,

She tries to find herself completely
  in that world, the world completely
  knowledgeable to her, understood fully.

The poet has described a person who has broken into a world which is beautifully logical, where everything fits together perfectly and is beautifully adjusted, but it is just an inhuman world.

Alone to the weight of impassivity,
Incest of spirit, theorem of desire,

Without will as chalky cliffs by the sea,
Empty as the bodiless flesh of fire:

All space, that heaven is a dayless night,
A flightless day driven by perfect lust
For vacancy, in which her bored eyesight
Stares at the drowsy cubes of human dust.

Alice would see all of you before me here as just "drowsy cubes of human dust" because you have become in this world of pure things, merely things, perfectly measurable and so on. But then the poet changes suddenly and says

—We too back to the world shall never
    pass
Through the shattered door, a dumb
    shade-harried crowd
Being all infinite, function depth and
    mass
Without figure, a mathematical shroud
Hurled at the air—blessd without sin!
O God of our flesh, return us to Your
    wrath,
Let us be evil could we enter in
Your grace, and falter on the stony path![3]

It's a passionate poem, all right. The bleakness of the world that modern man has created out of his own brain, as he looks at himself in the mirror, is brilliantly, but balefully described in stanza six, "Alone to the weight of impassivity, incest of spirit, theorem of desire." Those of us who have remained human finally long for flesh that is not bodiless, not "empty as the bodiless flesh of fire," but it is a world that more and more seems to control us rather than one that we can ourselves control. After all, we've constructed it, but unfortunately we worry that we are unable to control ourselves. And if we are correct, then Alice's world becomes infinitely more terrifying now that we have such marvelous instruments in our hands.

The poem says that we human beings are blessed without sins, but the reason is not that we have become saints. We have simply agreed that sin does not exist. And so to be blessed without sin does not amount to very much of a coup after all. If there is any sin, then surely we are all sinners. So the poet, speaking in the poem, would rather be returned to God's wrath and to be dealt with as a sinner than live in the new dispensation. It is an anguished prayer, one that begs God to return us to His wrath. Yet why is He appealed to as "God of our flesh"? We ordinarily think of God as a spirit, but remember that the issue here is not spirit and flesh in the usual senses, but the concrete as against the abstract.

It is important to call this problem to your attention, for it is not merely a problem that concerns the literary artist. It bears powerfully on the whole problem of college education—the need to study the ends of life as well as the means for making a living. The vaunted term "liberal education" becomes meaningless if our study is to be no more than how to manipulate mechanisms and how to manipulate our fellows. That kind of training cannot possibly "liberate" anyone's mind.

Notes

1. Eric Voegelin, *From Enlightenment to Revolution*, John H. Hallowell, ed. (Durham, NC: Duke Univ. Press, 1975), viii.
2. John Crowe Ransom, *Two Gentlemen in Bonds* (New York: Knopf, 1927), 43–44.
3. Allen Tate, *Poems, 1922–1947* (New York: Scribner's, 1948), 115–16

R. V. Young

Distinct Models: Why
We Teach What We Teach

VOL. 26, NO. 2, 1991

In his commendatory poem in the first folio edition of Shakespeare's *Comedies, Histories, and Tragedies* (1623), Ben Jonson addresses the Bard as "Soul of the age!" (17); however, a couple of dozen lines later, Jonson proclaims, "He was not of an age, but for all time" (43).[1] I must confess to having taken a perverse delight over the years in watching students squirm when asked to resolve the apparent contradiction. We may then surmise that a certain poetic justice, a certain perversity of the Fates, has come into play as I find myself squirming at the spectacle of learned and distinguished colleagues, scholars of literature and the other humane disciplines, quite as nonplussed by the Jonsonian paradox as the most callow sophomore. According to the reigning heterodoxy, absolutely nothing is "for all time"; and works of literature do not bespeak the "soul of the age," so much as they conceal, even while embodying, its ideological agenda and economic imperatives. Hence the current clamor from certain quarters within the academy and other intellectual institutions for the "opening up" or dismantling of the "canon" of "classic" works, for the abolition of

the very notion of "great books." Should this view prevail, then the question, "Why we teach what we teach?," would be no longer moot, but merely meaningless. Although *pretexts* for teaching this or that *text* would abound, there could be no *reasons,* since rational discrimination among the "products" of deterministic cultural hegemonies is impossible. It is, therefore, important to attempt an understanding of how Shakespeare—or Plato, or Dante, or Jefferson, or Carlisle can be both "Soul of the age" and "for all time." Although in the remarks that follow I shall speak principally about poetry, that is largely a matter of my own convenience. As Cicero points out, "All the arts, which pertain to humanity, have a certain common bond and are joined together among themselves as it were by a certain kinship."[2] I wish to suggest that this element of common humanity is crucial in our curricular decisions and is, indeed, the only basis for our integrity as scholars and teachers.

Perhaps the one conceivable benefit of the current assault on Western culture from among its ostensible conservators is that we are forced to reflect upon what it is and why it is worth conserving. And make no mistake, we are not confronting merely an urge to modify or expand the canon, or an argument over criteria for the admission of authors and titles to the curriculum, much less over the inclusion or exclusion of this or that particular work. What is at stake is whether a hierarchy of works can be established at all, whether rational (and hence just) norms for determining intellectual, moral, and aesthetic excellence are possible. A negative answer to this question entails not "opening up" the curriculum, but eviscerating it; and if there is no canon of intrinsically great works, then professors of the humanities will seem less like scholars than vultures and jackals feeding on the cadaver of the liberal arts. Hence Barbara Herrnstein Smith was somewhat disingenuous when she used the occasion of her 1988 MLA Presidential Address to sneer at "members of the association who still regard women as members of another species and are still waiting for the theory fad to blow over," and to insinuate that distress about the present state of affairs in the academic world arose from "the comparison of Oedipus with Sherlock Holmes or the assignment of *The Color Purple* alongside *The Scarlet Letter*."[3]

The Exalted Critic

The revolutionaries who currently dominate academic discourse in the humanities are not really interested in gaining acceptance for *The Color Purple* as a great book, or in gaining a new theoretical purchase on *The Scarlet Letter*. Revision of the literary canon—both by addition and revaluation—has been old news for a long time. The concept is available, for example, in T. S. Eliot's 1919 essay, "Tradition and the Individual Talent," where he remarks, "The existing monuments form an ideal order among themselves, which is modified by the introduction of the new (really new) work of art among them."[4] Determining the criteria for and the identity of the "really new" work and assessing its precise effect upon the canon are undertakings subject to reasonable, tolerant, and even fruitful debate. But this is *not* the nature of the current disputes, and Barbara Herrnstein Smith could have found this out on her own by stepping down the hall and conferring with her Duke colleagues. "Literature is inherently nothing," Frank Lentricchia avers; "or it is inherently a body of rhetorical strategies waiting to be seized."[5] In another context Professor Lentricchia illustrates the practice of ideological appropriation by treating Wallace Stevens's "Anecdote of the Jar," a brief poem written about seventy-five years ago, as an attack on American intervention in Vietnam.[6]

Jane Tompkins, another member of the Duke literature faculty, furnishes an even more efficient model of political hermeneutics in her minute analyses of the "Western" fiction of such writers as Zane Grey and the late Louis L'Amour (that's "Western" as in bang-bang, you're dead; not as in Western culture). If literature is merely a bundle of rhetorical strategies anyway, it would hardly seem to matter what bundle of verbal material the critic begins with. In fact, the Western offers a distinct advantage: part of the greatness of great literature is precisely the resistance it offers to ideological reductivism and ordinary oversimplication (Professor Lentricchia is really not very convincing about Wallace Stevens). Much popular literature, however, has insufficient substance of its own to put up a real fight and can be made to say pretty much whatever the critic wishes. Jane Tompkins rather manhandles *Hondo* and

Riders of the Purple Sage, which submit with hardly a whimper: "What I want to argue for specifically here is the idea that the Western owes its essential character to the dominance of a women's culture in the nineteenth century and to women's invasion of the public sphere between 1880 and 1920." This essay in the *cherchez la femme* school of literary interpretation concludes triumphantly in this wise: "The Western doesn't have anything to do with the West as such. It isn't about the encounter between civilization and the frontier. It is about men's fear of losing their hegemony and hence their identity, both of which the Western tirelessly reinvents."[7] Call this hegemony envy if you wish, but I am reliably informed that there is no truth to the rumors that Jane Tompkins once worked as a sportswriter for the *Boston Herald* on special assignment to the New England Patriots. Zane Grey and Louis L'Amour might be baffled by the array of semantic doves and rabbits she pulls out of their ten-gallon hats; however, anyone familiar with current academic discourse will recognize the sleight-of-hand and the semiological stage properties, as the ideological buckboard rumbles across the textual plain, scattering signifiers like so many tumbleweeds.

What unties the approaches of Tompkins and Lentricchia is the *privileging* of the work of the interpreter over the text—the putative object of interpretation. Such an exaltation of the role of the critic has been a major project of Duke's English Department chairman, Stanley Fish, who assures us that abandoning the notion that any piece of writing embodies inherent truth or meaning will provide us with "a greatly enhanced sense of the importance of our own activities." It is the critic's own activity, Professor Fish maintains, "that brings texts into being

and makes them available for analysis and appreciation. The practice of literary criticism is not something one must apologize for; it is absolutely essential not only to the maintenance of, but to the very production of the objects of its attention."[8] Under this new dispensation, then, neither *The Scarlet Letter* nor *The Scarlet Pimpernel,* neither *The Color Purple* nor *Riders of the Purple Sage* has any intrinsic significance; indeed, they only exist as a result of the critic's conjuring. If this interpretive theory were given credence, then the canon of great books could scarcely be more than a record of the ideological impositions of regnant "cultural hegemonies." But if such is "the practice of literary criticism," then apologies are certainly in order: in this schema the critic is no more than an illusionist—a huckster noisily calling attention to his own contrivances (Penn & Teller, call your office). Or the critic is Humpty Dumpty: works, like words, mean exactly what he says they mean. And we all know what happened to Humpty Dumpty.

Such a critical practice is not without its practical consequences. Two years ago the English Department at Syracuse University issued a manifesto entitled "Not a Good Idea: A New Curriculum at Syracuse." The authors (all eleven of them) point out the difficulty of designing a curriculum in a vacuum, literally not knowing what you are talking about:

> The first element that allowed our discussions to maintain collectivity with neither the support of a common canon nor the envelope of an indifferent critical pluralism was the recognition that we had to live, uncomfortably, with our pedagogical object as somehow displaced. Whether in the language of alienation, of repression, of loss, or of self-division, we faced a com-

mon awareness that the assumption of a self-evident object of study disappeared along with the closed canon that once incarnated it.[9]

Having lost the "object" of their work, the professors were forced to fall back on their own predilections; and "the construction of a new curriculum" was expressly an exercise in self-interest: "By 1985 it had become clear that the actual teaching and research interests of the department were no longer adequately served by the curriculum as it stood" (2). The impact upon students of substituting their teachers' hobbies for a genuine curriculum is predictable and made quite explicit by the Syracuse document:

> For those committed to understanding and resisting the role of texts in producing oppressive race, class and gender relations, the end of an education in literature will be, not the traditional "well read" student, but a student capable of critique—of actively pressuring, resisting and questioning cultural texts. The consequences for a curriculum will be a shift from privileging a particular body of culturally sanctioned texts to emphasizing the modes of critical inquiry one can bring to bear on any textual object and the political implications of such modes. (1)

If "textual objects" are "inherently nothing," if their very existence is a result of interpretation, naturally the task of the literature professor is to guide the student in the formation of politically correct attitudes, and liberal education is reduced to training in fashionably sanctimonious carping. That students might learn more about their professors' prejudices than the substance of their courses has heretofore been regarded as one of the pitfalls of

the university; now inculcation in *odium academicum* would seem to be the *sole purpose* of courses utterly devoid of substance in themselves.

The Heart of the Curriculum

In order to see fully the implications of such curricular sans-culottism, we must recall that curriculum—what we teach—is ancillary to education; and that *education* ought to be understood in the root sense of the word. The Latin *educare* means to "rear or bring up (children or young animals)," and it in turn derives from *educere,* "to lead forth" or "to lead out." Implicit in the term is the idea that education consists in leading the young *out* of something, and the something out of which everyone must be led is the peculiar, self-interested ego; for to be self-centered is the common predicament; narrow, stifling subjectivism, the universal prison of all human beings. A great work of literature is, then, a book that extends our horizons, that alters our perspective, that makes us take notice of something beyond our immediate needs and desires. Note well that the new curriculum at Syracuse encourages students to question "cultural texts" and apply a pervasive skepticism to virtually everything except themselves. Similarly, the editors of a new collection of essays on seventeenth-century poetry promote their book as "deeply skeptical of the received ideas about a literature that is itself sensitive to the disruption of epistemological, social, and economic certainties." The essays constitute "a skeptical interrogation," they say, "of numerous received ideas along a variety of fronts."[10] Notice that again what gets questioned or "interrogated" is the literature itself, or at least the "received ideas" about it (and this amounts to the same thing, since postmodern theory does not allow for the existence of literature apart from interpretations).

Now I do not mean to suggest that every piece of literature that is subjected to critical scrutiny in the classroom, much less in the scholar's library carrel, is a deathless classic, embodying the perennial wisdom of Western culture. Such works should be at the heart of the curriculum, but they are not the whole story. Students in my American literature survey, for example, read the poems of Anne Bradstreet. Although she is by no means a great writer, her competent, if undistinguished verse provides an invaluable window into the daily life of colonial Massachusetts, a matrix of American culture; moreover, the poems reveal a great deal about the fortitude and generosity of Bradstreet's own wholly admirable character.

If I teach Anne Bradstreet in spite of her literary mediocrity, then Michael Wigglesworth's *Day of Doom* finds a place because of its ineptitude. I generally ask the class to consider the stanzas where Christ explains to the souls of unbaptized infants why they are justly adjudged to hell, along with hardened sinners, only for having inherited the guilt of Adam's original sin:

Would you have griev'd to have receiv'd
through Adam so much good,
As had been your for evermore,
if he at first had stood?
Would you have said, we ne'r obey'd,
nor did thy Laws regard;
It ill befits with benefits,
us, Lord, so to reward?

Since then to share in his welfare,
you could have been content,
You may with reason share in his treason,
and in the punishment. (Stz. 174–75)[11]

Several stanzas later (the poem runs to more than 200 just like these) the souls of the unbaptized infants trudge ruefully off to hell, though with this small consolation:

A crime it is, therefore in bliss
you may not hope to dwell;
But unto you I shall allow
the easiest room in Hell.
The glorious King thus answering,
they cease, and plead no longer:
Their consciences must needs confess
his reasons are the stronger. (Stz. 181)

There is some value in exposing students to a negative exemplum and to a worldview that is eccentric and unpalatable by modern standards, but it is still more important to show how an awkward style and logic that is somehow both obtuse and hair-splitting are the marks of a superficial mind failing to come to grips with a profoundly serious, if terrible, doctrine. *The Day of Doom* was incredibly popular in colonial New England, but I suspect that its appeal to seventeenth-century youth was akin to the effect upon their modern counterparts of that series of horror films featuring a dreadfully disfigured villain in desperate need of a manicure: Christ the Judge as Freddy Krueger.

There are, then, sound pedagogic reasons for teaching the poetry of Bradstreet and Wigglesworth in undergraduate literature courses, but the same ends could be attained with, say, the prose of William Bradford and Thomas Shepard. The exact composition of a syllabus often depends on what is included in the most conveniently available anthologies. But there are some writers who should be included in every American literature anthology and on every syllabus. Consider the following poem, written some two centuries after *The Day of Doom,* and dedicated to the same theme of our eternal destiny:

Because I could not stop for Death—
He kindly stopped for me
The Carriage held but just Ourselves—
And Immortality.

We slowly drove—He knew no haste
And I had put away
My labor and leisure too,
For His Civility

We passed the School, where Children strove
At Recess—in the Ring
We passed the Fields of Gazing Grain—
We passed the Setting Sun

Or rather—He passed Us
The Dews drew quivering and chill—
For only Gossamer, my Gown—
My Tippet—only Tulle

We paused before a House that seemed
A Swelling of the Ground
The Roof was scarcely visible
The Cornice—in the Ground

Since then—'tis Centuries—and yet
Feels shorter than the Day
I first surmised the Horses' Heads
Were toward Eternity—[12]

This of course is Emily Dickinson, who turns the common meter hymn stanza, the same verse form that Michael Wigglesworth reduces to jog-trot doggerel, into as subtle a vehicle for poetry as Death's elusive "Carriage." While Bradstreet and Wigglesworth are important largely because of when and where they lived, Dickinson's poetry manifests an intrinsic literary value; that is, she is both "soul of the age" and "for all

time." If Anne Bradstreet were a twentieth-century suburbanite rather than a colonial housewife, her poems would be of interest only to her friends. If Michael Wigglesworth were alive today, he would probably be a televangelist rather than a poet. It is difficult to imagine a civilization, however, in which "Because I could not stop for Death" would not find at least a few responsive readers. In derivative and unimaginative, though by no means contemptible verse, Bradstreet states respectable (I mean the term sincerely) commonplaces. From the commonplaces of her own rather diminished world, Dickinson fashions a poetry that speaks to the essential human condition.

If we consider the two women as individuals, the life of the pioneer woman, Anne Bradstreet, is certainly richer and more capable of sustaining interest than that of Emily Dickinson, who spent most of her life as a recluse in her father's house in Amherst. To be sure, the conditions of Dickinson's life generate a good deal of attention from feminists nowadays; but, whatever the merits of this perspective, the revival of interest in her poetry preceded the rise of academic feminism, and it will surely outlast it—even as Sappho's poetry has survived 2,600 years of turmoil in literary and political fashion. While almost nothing is known about her life, there is still no doubt that Sappho merits authentic canonical status as a poet. By the same token, Emily Dickinson's importance as a poet does not depend upon the circumstances of her life as a repressed, frustrated spinster in a "patriarchal" society—with all the grist thereby generated for the "dark satanic mills" of ideology.

Or perhaps I should say that her biography is important insofar as there is a repressed, frustrated spinster in all of us. To put it another way, it is part of the human condition to feel dependent, even helpless, unfulfilled, and at the mercy of what seems a senseless, arbitrary fate. The situation of an unmarried woman of Emily Dickinson's class in nineteenth-century New England can be taken as a special case of what is, ultimately, everyone's situation. We can all respond to her poems because she enjoys a unique perspective on what is an element pervasive in human life, but not so evident to most of us. Consider the particular instance of "Because I could not stop for Death"—we are all going to die. In the face of this inevitability, we all experience fear, hope, and just plain curiosity. Dickinson's poem draws upon a virgin's apprehensive yet fascinated imaginations of the wedding night: death is the ineluctable suitor who will have every maidenhead. This trope, that can be traced to the poet's own peculiar experience, converges with broadly public symbolism of Christian tradition: all of us, men and women alike, are intended as brides of Christ; before God we are all feminine. Yet before that consummation, devoutly to be wished, we must lie down in the marriage bed of the grave. The poem thus plays off the reassuring typology of the Bible against the individual's immediate perplexity and terror in order to dramatize a universal human ambivalence toward death.

But the power of the poem is not limited to a brilliant initial conception. A judicious selection and careful placement of every word, of every syllable, effect a tone of delicate irony, of subtle equivocator. The gossamer gown and tippet of tulle, cherished adornments of a diminutive, feminine world (and the sort of details that need explaining to undergraduates), enhance by contrast the stark, immense mystery of death. There is a delicious irony in the way the poem comments on its own not-quite-successful attempt to domesticate death: the tulle and gossamer prove inadequate for "The Dews drew quivering and chill." Then there is the wry conceit that the grave is merely another "House," only it is almost completely buried: "The roof was scarcely visible—/The Cornice—in the Ground." The startling appropriateness of "Cornice"—an architectural ornament that serves as a synecdoche for all the "useless" though precious details that enhance our lives—defies comment. It is matched by the use of "surmised" in the closing stanza:

Since then—'tis Centuries—and yet
Feels shorter than the Day
I first surmised the Horses' Heads
Were toward Eternity

The poem as a whole is an evocation of all that is implied in this improbably perfect word *surmised*: we are not told but reminded by way of an elusive verbal structure, delicate as the gossamer gown, that all our notions of death and "Eternity" lie in the realm of surmise.

Distinct Models

There are various legitimate reasons for teaching a diversity of works in college classrooms, but at the heart of our curriculum should be the canon—a list of classic works that embody in a universally significant manner the common experience of men and women and enable us, by studying them, to grow into the full humanity that we share with others. Almost all the reasons for reading poetry are summed up in Cicero's *Pro Archia Poeta*, where the crafty lawyer promotes his old teacher's claim to Roman citizenship with every argument he can think of. Some of his reasons are practical: as an adult Cicero finds relief and relaxation for his "weary ears" after "the noise of the forum,"[13] and as a boy it was literary study that taught him that praise and honor only were worthy of pursuing with great effort in the face of every difficulty and danger. So his friends owe his success in defending them to poetry.[14] Some of his reasons border on vulgarity: Archias has celebrated Roman achievements in the past, and it is poetry that holds out the hope of future immortality for those now living.[15] But Cicero also perceives that poetry is valuable because of its intrinsic qualities. In a justly celebrated passage, he explains how literary education becomes a permanent part of the individual's inner life:

> Other occupations are not suitable for all times and places and ages; but these studies nourish youth and delight old age; they furnish the ornaments of prosperity and refuge and solace in adversity; they please at home without hindering us in public affairs; with us they pass long nights, lighten our journeys, and remain with us in the country.[16]

What the Greek and Latin writers have left us, Cicero explains, are "distinct models of gallant men, not only for contemplation, but even for imitation."[17] The key phrase here is "distinct models" (*imagines . . . expressas*); that is, models or figures or images finely crafted or shaped or squeezed out. If they are also for imitation, they are initially for contemplation; and indeed, that is *how* they are imitated, by assimilation into our souls—into our rational and imaginative being through study and contemplation. We teach such works because they help us to discern the order and purpose in human existence. It is a paradox of our nature that we must learn from others to be what we are, to

attain an authentic individual freedom. The most valuable educational service we can offer our students, as they strive to find themselves, is, in Matthew Arnold's still acute phrase, *"a disinterested endeavor to learn and propagate the best that is known and thought in the world."*[18]

Notes

1. "To the memory of my beloved, the AUTHOR, MASTER WILLIAM SHAKESPEARE, AND what he hath left us," in William Shakespeare, *The Complete Works*, Stanley Wells and Gary Taylor, eds. (Oxford: Clarendon Press, 1988), xiv.

2. *Pro Archia Poeta Oratio* 1.2, *Selections from Cicero*, ed. Charles E. Bennett (1922; rpt. Boston: Allyn & Bacon, 1968), 93: "Etenim omnes artes, quae ad humanitatem pertinent, habent quoddam commune vinculum et quasi cognatione quadam inter se continentur."

3. "Limelight: Reflections on a Public Year," *PMLA* 104 (1989), 286, 287.

4. *Selected Essays* (New York: Harcourt, Brace & World, 1960), 5.

5. *Criticism and Social Change* (Chicago: Univ. of Chicago Press, 1984), 152.

6. "Anatomy of a Jar," *South Atlantic Quarterly* 86 (1987), 395–401.

7. "West of Everything," *South Atlantic Quarterly* 86 (1987), 375, 376.

8. *Is There a Text in This Class? The Authority of Interpretive Communities* (Cambridge, MA: Harvard Univ. Press, 1980), 368.

9. P. 3. "Not a Good Idea: A New Curriculum at Syracuse" is a six-page, typed document by Steven Cohan et al., members of the English Department at that university, dated December, 1988. Page numbers of subsequent quotations appear parenthetically in the text.

10. Elizabeth D. Harvey and Katherine Eisaman Maus, eds., *Soliciting Interpretation: Literary Theory and Seventeenth-Century English Poetry* (Chicago: Univ. of Chicago Press, 1990), xxi.

11. Wigglesworth is quoted from *Seventeenth-Century American Poetry*, Harrison T. Meserole, ed. (New York: New York Univ.

Press, 1968). This volume also includes selections from Anne Bradstreet's poems.

12. *The Complete Poems of Emily Dickinson,* ed. Thomas H. Johnson (Boston: Little, Brown & Co., 1957), #712.

13. VI.12: "Quia suppeditat nobis, ubi et animus ex hoc forensi strepitu reficiatur et aures convicio defessae conquiescant."

14. VI.14: "Nam, nisi multorum praeceptis multisque litteris mihi ab adulescentia suasissem nihil esse in vita magno opere expetendum nisi laudem atque honestatem, in ea autem persequenda omnes cruciatus corporis, omnia pericula mortis atque exsili parvi esse ducenda, numquam me pro salute vestra in tot ac tantas dimicationes atque in hos profligatorum hominum cottidianos impetus objecissem."

15. IX–X passim.

16. VII.16: "Nam ceterae neque temporum sunt neque aetatum omnium neque locorum; at haec studia adulescentiam alunt, senectutem oblectant, secundas res ornant, adversis perfugium ac solacium praebent, delectant domi, non impediunt foris, pernoctant nobiscum, peregrinantur, rusticantur."

17. VI.14: "Quam multas nobis imagines non solum ad intuendum, verum etiam ad imitandum fortissimorum virorum expressas scriptores et Graeci et Latini reliquerunt!"

18. "The Function of Criticism at the Present Time," *Poetry and Criticism of Matthew Arnold,* A. Dwight Culler, ed. (Boston: Houghton Mifflin, 1961), 257.

Peter Augustine Lawler

The Dissident Professor

VOL. 34, NO. 2, 1999

To begin with a whine worthy of a country song: It's hard to be a conservative professor in America today. And it's a self-righteous whine! We conservatives are those who prefer truth and morality to success and popularity. And it's a whine that reflects a most confusing state of affairs. Conservatives, in principle, long for a world where they could celebrate a vital communal tradition or culture, and leftists, in principle, love to be antiestablishment dissenters. But in the American academic community today, the liberals or leftists are the establishment, and the conservatives are the dissident critics of the community's view of morality and justice. This strange situation presents conservative professors with the opportunity and the duty to stand by the principles that made them conservative. If living the virtuous life truly is more important than mere careerism, then our time has come. In standing with the dissidents against the tyranny of imposed opinion, we conservatives are in good company.

LEFTIST PROFESSORS preach the virtues of dissent. Tenured radicals tell moving stories about their youthful demonstrations on behalf of civil rights and against the War in Vietnam, and so against racist populism and patriotic chauvinism. And they praise today's efforts by the feminists and gays to emancipate themselves from the repression of the moral majority. Intellectual leftists have also preached against capitalism's vulgar love of success at the expense of culture. But despite the best efforts of alleged postmodernists to integrate leftism with the philosopher Martin Heidegger's anti-Americanism, cultural leftism remains in a period of decline. The pragmatist Richard Rorty, probably America's most influential professor of philosophy, reminds postmodern snobs that cultural leftism is an oxymoron.[1] The Left has no perspective by which to privilege cultural over banal human aspirations, and so leftist writers should be wholly devoted to achieving a classless society, one without cruel repression and in which everyone has an equal opportunity to fulfill his or her private fantasies. Rorty observes that the fall of communism has discredited political revolution as the route to that society. So the leftist method should now become the therapy of politically correct propaganda. Professors and other writers should work to purge our language of cruel, humiliating words, in order to eradicate cruel, humiliating experiences. They dissent from and work to change ordinary language and ordinary experience, but to make them more ordinary or banal. Rorty is confident that racism, sexism, and classism, not to mention metaphysics and theology, can be talked out of existence; and doing so in the name of justice, we are led to believe, should be regarded as the goal of American education today.

Leftist professors now tend to identify intellectual excellence with political correctness, with thought and action on behalf of the true or wholly consistent or egalitarian understanding of justice. Only they are completely free from popular and traditional racism, sexism, classism, and so forth. Only they are wise and moral enough to understand all that is implied in (and to be wholly devoted to) a classless society. They often claim to be devoted to diversity, but this means nothing more than diversity of physical appearance, clothing, and sexual orientation. Banished is diversity of opinion about fundamental human questions. Nor are these professors really "multiculturalists," if culture means devotion to some inegalitarian or illiberal religious morality. Multiculturalism properly understood is a tool used to devalue one's own culture, meaning one's own religion, with the equal and incompatible claims of others. Today's leftist professors are not really anti-Western, for they use the generic non-Western perspective to level the imperial or inegalitarian features of the West. They criticize the West's past according to a Marxian/Hegelian or a radically Western view of the world's future. Multiculturalism really defends egalitarianism or permissive democracy against the claims of all cultures, even as it empties culture of its content by separating it from intense devotion to a particular country or religion. Culture becomes a weightless whim, and so incapable of providing a moral point of view from which to resist dominant opinion.

Leftist professors are proud enough to believe they are wise. They say that everything is political, and that they understand the true purpose of political life. They believe they know what justice is, and that most people do not. The strength of popular racism, sexism, and heterosexism are exaggerated to distinguish their own wisdom more clearly. Wisdom, for leftist professors, is the privilege of our time, for even the best thinkers of the past were tainted by sexism and classism and so unjust and unwise. They identify wisdom with justice to ensure the superiority of themselves and their time and to negate the thought that Plato, the Bible, or Shakespeare might still have something fundamental to teach human beings today about, say, love and death. They believe they know and must teach that there is nothing for us to learn about our human condition from dead white males, more because they are dead than white or male. And their view of history is purely pragmatic or ideological; history is useful only as a weapon to legitimate the present and project for the future.

The chauvinism of our professors is impossible to exaggerate. In the past, they assert complacently, all human beings were deluded and cruel—with cruelty defined as all moral restraint that did or does not contribute to progress toward justice. Despite calling themselves Nietzschean relativists, they exhibit an astounding certainty that their justice and wisdom exceed the virtues of any human beings before them. Of course, if they really possessed the relativist's open-mindedness, they would encourage students to think about and choose cruelty (that is, morality) if they pleased.

MOST PROFESSORS today understand their educational task as the correction of the diverse, vulgar (Rorty's word is "redneck"), and obsolete prejudices of their students. I teach at a small college where most professors are leftist and some students come to college with strong fundamentalist or evangelical religious convictions. The faculty connect such conviction with closed-mindedness and injustice. And so they aim to expose the students to "uncomfortable" thoughts, to put them on the road to wisdom and justice. But for conservatives, the goal is to deprive the students of any perspective by which they can resist the comprehensive claims of the classless society, or prefer love, personal responsibility, and living well with death to the pursuit of perfect justice. Those who proudly dissent from popular prejudice aim to keep ordinary students from dissenting from professorial wisdom. The wise cannot be made uncomfortable by the opinions of others. On that point, "secular humanist" professors and "fundamentalist" students agree, for the last thing either wants to do is engage in a "Socratic dialogue" about the naturalness or goodness of homosexuality or women's liberation, much less about the competing claims of reason and revelation. And the fundamentalist whose mind is closed by certainty about God's will is at least more conscious of his human limitations than the professor who sees himself as replacing God with his wisdom.

Today's politically correct professor often recognizes no limits to efforts to bring racism, sexism, and classism to an end. As Alan Kors and Harvey Silverglate report in *The Shadow University*, many universities now openly pursue the "progressive" goal of assuming absolute control over the thought and action of students. The administrators believe they can use almost any means necessary to create a classless society—one which does not recognize the distinctions between men and women and gay and straight, and which has no place for the soul or conscience or unapproved personal association at all—incorporating all of campus life, from the classroom to the dorm room to the bathroom.[2] What can be achieved for the students is a prelude to what can be done for all Americans. Religion, for example, must be judged not by its truth or its adequacy in addressing ineradicable and transpolitical human longings, but for its contribution to inculcating devotion to a rights-based understanding of justice. The family must be judged according to the same principle, and so according to its egalitarian socialization of children. The danger of a child being raised well by two heterosexual parents is believing that his or her form of family is better than others, and so the school must correct the historical and anthropological narrowness of that opinion.

Dissenting leftist professors, in the name of correcting the cruel tyranny of ordinary life, tyrannize the American academic community. They dislike dissent in their realm as much as they imagine ordinary Americans do in theirs. As the establishment, they are comfortable in their preference for conformity. Their confusion of their fashionable dogmatism with wisdom is the greatest threat to freedom of thought in America today. The libertarian argument that American free thinkers must be rescued, above all, from stultifying rural (or suburban) idiocy was never more than partly true and now makes no sense at all.

But a more fundamental assault on freedom is the leftist professors' contempt for common decency and moral virtue. They regard traditional claims for virtue—which include the thought that men and women have sacred duties to each other, their families, their country, and to God—as a rationalization for repression. And so education for virtue—both by parents and schools—is also regarded as tyranny to be remedied through their expertise. They aim to liberate individuals to choose their own destinies without dogmatic constraint, even as they undermine the conditions under which responsible choice can be made. A choice that is wholly lacking in constraint is impossible for a merely human being.

Virtue—the disciplined exercise of personal responsibility—is what allows human beings to resist impersonal determination by either the market (meaning the expert manipulation of the needs of consumers) or the contemporary state (meaning big, bureaucratic government). And that exercise must be cultivated by personal institutions such as the family, neighborhood, and church. When functioning effectively to inculcate and support moral virtue, such institutions will not conform to the egalitarian view of justice that experts call wisdom. So the defense of American virtue is really the defense of human beings who are responsible enough to be free and to resist impersonal or expert determination. The leftist professors incoherently both work against and deny the possibility of that personal resistance.

CONSERVATIVE PROFESSORS are those who do not identify devotion to the classless society with wisdom or human happiness. So they are not leftists, although they are not necessarily on "the Right." Some reasonable conservatives believe that the very distinction between Left and Right—or between progressive and reactionary—depends on the leftist view of history and is intended to make the Left look good and its victory inevitable. Conservatives are not justly defined as those who are *for* racism and sexism! And some professors proud to stand with their conservative colleagues, such as defenders of the continuing relevance of classical education, still brag that they never vote Republican.[3]

Conservative professors, in my view, are those who dissent from the reigning intellectual tyranny. By opposing the impersonal, responsibility-denying lie that animates the community in which they work, they resemble anticommunist dissidents such as Aleksandr Solzhenitsyn and Václav Havel. But conservative professors, like the anticommunists, are united far more by what they oppose than by what they favor.[4] They all are for living responsibly in light of the truth, but they differ on exactly what the truth is and on what social and political conditions best support it.

It seems to be whining beyond belief to connect the oppression and isolation of American conservative academic dissidents with the time in prison of Solzhenitsyn and Havel. The American dissidents live in freedom and prosperity, and they are usually secure in their jobs once they are awarded tenure. But the philosopher-novelist Walker Percy argued that a situation worse than the Gulag is that of having no influence. The Soviet Communists feared Solzhenitsyn's truth-telling, and with good reason. But our leftist establishment seems to have little to fear from conservative dissidents, and so it is free to dismiss them, in Rorty's words, as know-nothings, blinded by greed or animosity, or just insane. It is hard to think and live well in ineffective isolation. According to Percy, truth-telling American writers suffer from Solzhenitsyn envy.[5]

CONSERVATIVE PROFESSORS must use the lip service the Left pays to intellectual freedom to their advantage. To be sure, leftist professors preach liberation while also saying, quite incoherently, that most or all opinion is determined by race, class, and gender. And so they are for both intellectual freedom and political correctness. But most intellectuals—with the notable exception of the pragmatist Rorty—are embarrassed to be caught in contradictions, and conservatives must use that embarrassment to get them to put their class interest—freedom—before justice. They can almost always be counted on to be too confused to say that the time for freedom is over because we are now wise. More generally, taking a stand on behalf of freedom of thought is the best way to win liberal allies, such as the card-carrying members of the ACLU.

Conservatives should favor the impartial application of standards of excellence for hiring, promotion, and tenure decisions. They should support leftist professors who meet them and demand the same consideration in return. No set of standards, of course, is ever perfect, and complete impartiality is impossible. But the goal should be standards solid enough to keep careerist radicals from using fashionable dissent and disgruntled conservatives from using the excuse of unfashionable dissent to mask a real absence of achievement. For conservative professors, something close to the rule of

law is usually much better than the rule of men (and surely better still than the rule of women).

Conservatives should favor tenure, on the traditional grounds that it protects the teaching of the truth. Tenure sometimes protects incompetent leftists who teach nonsense with impunity. But its abolition would endanger tenured conservatives in many more cases than tenured radicals. Radicals would usually be protected and conservatives cast out by the tyranny of the community's majority.

Conservative journalists and politicians who oppose tenure in the name of competence and accountability do so in ignorance of who really rules most programs in the social sciences and the humanities and of the character of most college and university administrators. According to Paul Cantor, "Some critics of tenure think that abolishing it will provide a means of bringing to bear the less radical views of society as a whole on the academy. But the more likely outcome would be to give new power to a subset within the academy, namely the educational establishment or perhaps even the education school establishment—which is generally more radical than the academy as a whole."[6] The tightening stranglehold schools of education have over administration, assessment, and accreditation is a far greater threat to intellectual liberty than the foolishness of tenured professors of literature. Too many of those schools' leading professors work to replace the pursuit of truth and excellence with ideological rigidity, the mindless use of technology, promiscuous sensitivity, and unearned self-esteem. "Reform the schools of education!" not "Abolish tenure!" should be the conservative cry.

Conservative professors should also, in most contexts, present themselves as the true partisans of diversity. The leftist professors identify diversity with increasing the numbers of black and female faculty and students, and they usually contribute to diversity by hiring African Americans and women who agree with them. Conservatives should say that the true Socratic would put a greater premium on diversity of opinion, and so on hiring those who dissent from the leftist establishment. The Socratic argument for a faculty with diverse opinions is that no mere mortal is wise, and all good professors are likely to see part, but only part, of the truth. The intellectual argument for uniformity of opinion can only come from the wise.

What should conservative professors do with their academic freedom? They cannot, in most cases, use it to reform their institutions, and they sometimes join the old fogies in resisting initiatives such as expanded core requirements and standardized syllabi that might be beneficial under different circumstances. Dissidents must often defend their freedom against efforts at communal integration. Even most tenured conservative professors are marginalized. They disagree with their colleagues too fundamentally to have much to say to them, and their colleagues, in turn, view their lack of wisdom with contempt. Conservative and leftist faculty cannot laugh at many of the same jokes about politics and religion, for what one takes seriously, the other finds ridiculous. Conservative professors at various institutions must talk with each other to fend off isolation and the obsessions it can produce. Whining less, they should share the pride and fun in taking a rebel's stand.

Conservative faculty should teach and write with the intention of influencing others in the name of the truth. In the context of most American colleges and universities today, their task is to

form countercultural communities. They should not make the mistake of Rorty or Allan Bloom of believing that the formation of such communities is becoming impossible. They should have a reasonable faith in the moral realism of ordinary people, and so should not hesitate to make populist appeals and attack the moral irresponsibility of the intellectual elite. But even privileged and sophisticated Americans are not really becoming flat-souled and lamely apathetic. They still long to know and love each other, the truth, and God.

Americans, it seems to me, live particularly deranged and angry lives today. They are restless, as Alexis Tocqueville observed, in the midst of prosperity, and they are particularly disoriented because they have so little clue why. The politically correct experts tell them that their misery and confusion can be cured through linguistic, economic, or political reform. Yet that ineffective advice only confuses them more. Experts have largely deprived them of the metaphysical and theological language that corresponds to their human longings. And their mouthing of politically correct therapeutic platitudes barely suppresses the fury that corresponds to that deprival. They can live less angrily and more reasonably and responsibly only to the extent that they have a true understanding of their longings, which includes a true account of human joys, miseries, and limitations. Such self-understanding is a prelude to a renewal of all forms of human community.

As Solzhenitsyn and Havel have explained, Americans are unhappy because they cannot really live the lie of the ideology of the classless society. The best educational antidote to the lie today is the study of literature.[7] According to the old-fashioned liberal Lionel Trilling, literature is the result of "the human activity that takes the fullest and most precise account of variousness, possibility, complexity, and difficulty."[8] It is a corrective to every attempt to understand human beings according to some ideology or to reduce the problem of self-understanding to theory. Literature, in this view, includes not only novels, plays, and poems, but Platonic dialogues, St. Augustine's *Confessions*, and such subtle, elusive, yet stunningly comprehensive accounts of the human condition and political order as Tocqueville's *Democracy in America*. Works of literature are rightly judged according to both their fullness and their precision in describing the way human beings are. So characteristically "modern" or "existentialist" or too theoretically influenced writers who describe the abstract or unconnected individual invented by liberal theorists as if he were a real human being rank low.[9] Writers from our time perhaps especially to be recommended are the most personal and penetrating critics of the ideological tendency of American democracy who wrote both philosophic prose and novels, such as Solzhenitsyn and Percy.

Not so long ago, American leftist intellectuals often assumed that great literature supported their cause. Simply reading the best books with an open mind frees the human being from the complacent philistinism of the middle class and for revolutionary thought. Liberal education is liberating and so anticapitalist education. Or so at least is *liberal* education in FDR's sense. But now leftist professors prefer reading literary theory to literature itself. They say that politically correct theory should determine the manner and the extent to which we should read nontheoretical books. So they often insist that we judge works of literature solely according to our contemporary wisdom concerning race, class, and gender. Rorty and Martha

Nussbaum recommend novels only insofar as they sensitize the reader to the cruel suffering caused by classism.[10] They use novels to achieve the political goal that they impose upon them in their tyrannical and futile attempt to reduce human greatness to theory.

Today only conservatives accept the truth of the traditional dissident claim of liberal education that the best books take the thought and imagination of human beings beyond the constraints of the dominant opinion of their time and place. Read with open minds and on the terms set by the authors, the best books are an indispensable beginning in an age of theory for understanding and accepting the personal responsibilities of free, rational, and limited beings who love and die.[11]

Notes

1. Richard Rorty, *Achieving Our Country: Leftist Thought in Twentieth-Century America* (Cambridge, MA: Harvard Univ. Press, 1998).
2. Alan Charles Kors and Harvey A. Silvergate, *The Shadow University: The Betrayal of Liberty on America's Campuses* (New York: The Free Press, 1998).
3. Victor Davis Hanson and John Heath, *Who Killed Homer?* (New York: The Free Press, 1998), 258.
4. See Mark C. Henrie, "Rethinking American Conservatism in the 1990s: The Struggle Against Homogenization," *Intercollegiate Review* (Spring 1993), 8–16.
5. Walker Percy, *Lost in the Cosmos: The Last Self-Help Book* (New York: Farrar, Straus and Giroux, 1983), 158.
6. Paul A. Cantor, "It's Not the Tenure, It's the Radicalism," *Academic Questions* 17 (Winter 1997–98), 34.
7. But because most literature courses in college are now so bad and because what natural scientists teach really is part of the truth, I am not saying that students should take only literature courses—English, polit-

ical philosophy, theology, and so forth—in college. Natural science professors, in fact, typically are smarter, better role models, less ideological, harder and fairer graders, and often more religious than those in the social sciences and humanities. Their admirable love of the truth, if not the whole truth, ought to shame their politically correct colleagues.

8. Lionel Trilling, *The Liberal Imagination: Essays on Literature and Society* (New York: Harcourt, Brace, Jovanovich, 1979), preface (no page number).

9. According to Pierre Manent, "modern literature has sought to unmask the falsity of all human relationships, the illusory character of love, and the ludicrousness or fraudulence of language. The upshot is an exploration of what it means to become an individual" (*Modern Liberty and Its Discontents* [Lanham, MD: Rowman and Littlefield, 1998], 152.) So modern literature attempts to describe the truth of Rousseau's theoretical insight. It is wrong on friendship, love, and language, and by showing that all that is distinctively human or social is a worthless illusion, it can justify pragmatic self-surrender. But as an attempt truthfully to describe and so defend the individual, it remains an antidote, if the weakest one, to the conformism of politically correct theory.

10. Richard Rorty, *Contingency, Irony, and Solidarity* (Cambridge: Cambridge Univ. Press, 1989); Martha Nussbaum, *Poetic Justice: The Literary Imagination and Public Life* (Boston: Beacon Press, 1995).

11. For more than a beginning, see Ann Hartle, *Self-Knowledge in an Age of Theory* (Lanham, MD: Rowman and Littlefield, 1997).

Louise Cowan

The Necessity of the Classics

VOL. 37, NO. 1, 2001

In _Kagemusha,_ the Japanese film director Akira Kurosawa portrays a beggar called upon to impersonate a powerful warlord. About to be put to death for thievery, this lowly figure is snatched from execution by royal officers who detect in him an uncanny physical resemblance to their chief. They hide him in the palace to understudy the great man and to master the ways of the court. On the death of the warlord, the officers pass this double off as the ruler himself, hoping by this deception to conceal from their enemies their vulnerability. The beggar learns to act the part of a noble and fearless leader and, as he grows in his understanding of his role, acquires its internal as well as external dignity. He successfully continues the impersonation until—after the monarch's death has been discovered and the ruse is no longer useful—he is driven away from the palace, a beggar once more.

But a strange thing has happened: this pretender has developed a genuine sense of responsibility that cannot so lightly be dismissed. The burden of leadership, with its peculiar blend of selflessness and pride, has become his own. Despite his low sta-tion, he follows along after the troops in battle and stands at the last defending the banner of his defeated people, exposing himself to the enemy's onslaughts when all others have fallen. The film makes us question: Is this heroic gesture still part of the act? Where does it come from, this apparent greatness of soul that finally re-quires in a counterfeit role an authentic death? Kurosawa implies that it issues from the depths of human nature itself. But if so, as the film makes clear, it hardly arises naturally. On the contrary, its real-ization has come about through schooling in a tradition. Such magnanimity, we are shown, requires _mimesis_—imitation. To remake oneself in the image of some-thing that calls to greatness demands a heroic tradition displaying heroic models. _Kagemusha_ is, in fact, despite its Japanese subject matter, in the line of the Western and Roman epics, an extension of the Greek heroic code. Like these classics, it uncovers the innate nobility of the soul as a driving force that issues in noble action. _Kagemusha,_ a modern classic, speaks to us with a peculiar power in a time when all energies seem to be devoted to self-preser-vation and to bodily comfort.

THE WORD *classics*, if used with strict accuracy, refers to academic studies in Greek and Latin, though it is frequently applied to a list of great books, largely philosophical, that have been assembled for their ability to promote dialectic. Further, *classics* is sometimes employed in reference to a curricular syllabus, under whose auspices works such as *To Kill a Mockingbird* and *Catcher in the Rye* come to assume inordinate importance. These meanings are related of course, and even somewhat overlapping—though they also have clearly different implications. But one use of the word classic in our society is often considered to be a kind of idealistic pretentiousness, despite the truth, the reality, that it conveys. I am speaking of the meaning Matthew Arnold ascribed to the term in his effort to identify poetic works of unquestioned quality that deserve a place in what is simply "the class of the best." Despite any appearance to the contrary, these masterpieces, Arnold thought, would never lose "currency."

Some forty years after Arnold, from a position of high modernism, T. S. Eliot further extended the idea of the "best" in literature when he spoke of an identifiable ideal body of texts from Homer to the present, having what he called a "simultaneous existence" and a "simultaneous order, " and making up a tradition that can be acquired only through hard labor. Eliot was speaking within and to a world in which, as he well knew, this tradition *had* lost currency. Hence, addressing himself to poets, he reminded them of their need for its retrieval.

What Eliot wrote at that crucial moment we should now be ready to acknowledge as applicable to us all. We have begun to see a world in which the classics have virtually disappeared—though they have been woven so tightly into the patterns of our culture that *meaning*, for us, is hardly separable from them. For a while we may be able to get by on the echoes of their past glory; but when they finally have become perfectly silent, what sort of world shall we inhabit? To lose the classics is to lose a long heritage of wisdom concerning human nature, something not likely to be acquired again. Yet most college curricula now remain sadly untouched by their august presence, or at best make a gesture in their direction with a few samplings for select students. Such neglect is one of the most serious threats our society faces today.

IN SPEAKING of the classics as the primary curricular need in our time, then, I prefer to designate them not as *literature* but as *poetry,* the generic term used by the ancients for mimetic (fictional) writing. Since the advent of Renaissance humanism this kind of writing has been thought of as *belles lettres,* or in English as *literature,* and given until fairly recently a privileged if narrow position—along with proper speech and table manners—in the education of the few. But since the Enlightenment, *literature* has been increasingly marginalized as the "real work" of the university came to be dominated by analysis, measurement, factuality, competition: the sciences.

But when the Greeks spoke of *poetry,* they meant not so much a graceful polish of style, an artful use of language, as an entire cast of mind. *Poiesis* was considered to be a making process governed by mimesis, the envisioning, or imagining, of fictional analogies, a kind of *knowing* different from philosophy or history and yet occupying an irreplaceable position in the quest for wisdom. "Poetry is a more philosophical and a higher thing than history," Aristotle tells us in his *Poetics.* "For poetry tends to express the universal, history the particular." Hence, "it is not the function of the poet to relate what has happened, but what ought to happen."

Poetry appeals to the imagination, that faculty of the mind which enables the intellect to know the things of the senses *from the inside*—in other words, to experience by empathy things other than ourselves and to make of that experience a new form. This is the action that Coleridge calls the primary imagination ("the repetition in the finite mind of the infinite I AM"). In contrast, the rational intellect, musing on things from above, sees the structure of a phenomenon with a certain detachment that prevents any knowledge of objects on their own terms. It must abstract from them, reason about them, analyze them in order to reach its conclusions. Only through the agency of the imagination, which begins always with cherishing the things of sense—with finding a fullness of being in such lowly acts as seeing and touching—can the intellect know what John Crowe Ransom has called "the true *dinglichkeit,* the thinginess of things." This active functioning of the imagination is not the act of a child, a kind of make-believe; nor is it fantasy; nor is it fancy. It is a mature and vigorous act of the mind and heart, oriented toward reality, expanding the cosmos within which the knowing mind dwells.

Yet this mode of knowledge—poetry ordering the passions so as to make them "philosophical" and hence matters for reflection—is increasingly dismissed in higher education. Consequently, American colleges and universities have ceased performing one of their most important functions: not to be simply a repository of past thought or a sponsor of the new, but to serve as a guide for the otherwise wayward poetic impulse al-ways present in the human community. For if this energy is unchanneled, it tends to flow in one of two directions: toward a dionysiac frenzy or toward the banality of *kitsch. Poiesis* is part of the human make-up, ineradicable and yet vulnerable to debasement in the absence of tradition. We rightly sense that this wildly creative faculty, if ungoverned, will end by making golden calves or bronze serpents—or, as in Dostoevsky's *The Possessed,* burning down the city.

Thus, if we could imaginably discover the *telos* of liberal education, the underlying purpose for which communities sponsor so impractical and expensive an endeavor as a university, we might find, surprisingly, that it is not so much to further individual success or to produce "new knowledge" or even to preserve the monuments of the past. Rather, it is to give form to this creative impulse in human culture. As we have always secretly suspected, democracy has imposed upon us from the beginning an obligation to provide a liberal education for every citizen—a charge that implies not simply literacy but an ability to judge the high from the low, the genuine from the shoddy. We are now failing to perform this task, largely because our schools have discarded the great staple of our education, the poetic mode of thought.

THE TWO fountainheads of poetic wisdom for the West have been the Greek and Hebrew writings. One speaks of nobility; the other of humility. Both are necessary. And in both it is primarily in poetry that they communicate their hearts and enable us to find our own. The Hebrew heritage looks inward, seeking the hidden God; the Greek heritage looks outward, aspiring to divinity. Greek poetry thus shows forth—in symbol, in *mimesis,* in the *eikon*—what it is that lies behind appearances. I have written at another time *(IR,* vol. 36, nos. 1–2) of the splendor of our Hebrew legacy and the necessity of including it in today's curriculum. What I want to emphasize now is the importance of the Greek *paideia,* the leading out of the soul and directing it upward.

For it was unmistakably the Greeks who discovered *eros,* desire and aspiration, as the path toward the highest good. It was the Greeks who saw both the poverty and the profundity of the soul, and who proclaimed, as Aeschylus put it, that we must "suffer into wisdom." It was the Greeks who intuited the underlying generic patterns of poetry: who gave us epic, tragedy, and comedy. Homer, in inventing the epic, invented an entire civilization; and Aeschylus, Sophocles, and Euripides produced the most profound tragedies in existence at the moment of that civilization's greatness, just before the decline. It was an encounter with the Greeks (through Rome, and later, Constantinople) that led diverse European peoples to know themselves and that taught the American founders the meaning of the polis. It is a return to the Greeks from time to time in history that reanimates those same peoples and allows them to remember who they are.

And the poetic process goes on. The sublime Greek writings have attracted to themselves others from various places and epochs and in response to new additions reveal fresh insights, transforming all sorts of heterogeneous texts into an organic, if polyphonic, whole. Diverse works from various cultures, such as *The Divine Comedy, Hamlet, Paradise Lost, Faust, The Scarlet Letter, Moby-Dick, Madame Bovary, The Brothers Karamazov, Go Down Moses, One Hundred Years of Solitude,* and *Beloved,* among many others, strike sparks from the earlier works,

revealing nuances hitherto concealed. Then these later texts themselves, after they have settled into the community of immortals, select their associates and invite them in, continuing to unlock within themselves meanings inaccessible without their fellows.

This body of writing, until recently considered the very center of European and American education, has stood guard over the march of Western civilization, preserving its ideals of truth and justice, whatever its lapses may have been. And the later writers included in this remarkable group of texts have continued the unsparing examination of conscience that the Greeks inaugurated three thousand years ago. Hence, the Greeks make up the unmistakable foundation of our body of classics. To be ignorant of Homer, Aeschylus, and Sophocles is to be ignorant of the range and depth of human possibility.

IN *THE Oldest Dead White European Males,* Bernard Knox, one of our foremost classical scholars, recounts the story of how the Greek texts survived for the Western world: "When in the third and second centuries B.C. after the great age of Greek literary achievement, the scholars and critics of the Alexandrian library set to work to establish the texts of the classical authors and equip them with commentaries," he writes, "they also established select lists." They did not use the word *canon,* though it is a Greek word, meaning a carpenter's rule; rather, they spoke of the writings they chose as *hoi enkrithentes,* "the admitted," or "the included." Knox goes on to say,

> In the final, desperate centuries of classical civilization, the years of civil wars and massive foreign invasions,

the vast bulk of ancient Greek literature [vanished], including, to our
everlasting loss, most of the work of
the nine lyric poets. . . . Only those
works transferred to the more durable
(and expensive) material of parchment
could survive . . . Homer, Hesiod,
Herodotus, Thucydides, seven tragedies each for Aeschylus and Sophocles,
ten for Euripides, eleven comedies
of Aristophanes; . . . all of Plato and
much of his successor Aristotle.

It is strange, Knox comments, to
find these works today attacked as reactionary and to hear the charge that they
dominate the curriculum by "enforced
conformity." For as he points out, their
role in the history of the West has always
been "innovative, sometimes indeed subversive, even revolutionary." Surely this is
so. The list of rebels is long: the lonely
hero Achilles, challenging the authority
of the warlord Agamemnon; the swine-
herd Eumaeus, whose wisdom and honor
the poet respects so greatly as to address
him directly in the *Odyssey;* Antigone,
defying the tyrant Creon; Dionysus, destroying the narrow-minded Pentheus;
the Titan Prometheus ignoring the prohibitions of Zeus himself for love of the
human race. One thinks, also, of the
comic takeover by women in *Lysistrata*
when they deny their beds to their husbands and put a stop to war—and of the
lonely little old men—the *poneroi*—who
are the heroes of Aristophanes' comedies.
All of these instances represent something like putting the bottom rail on top,
hardly a vindication of some conservative
establishment.

This is most plain in comedy. In
contrast to only seven plays each from
the tragedians, eleven of Aristophanes'
comedies survive—all naughty and all
subversive (and all much beloved by the

early Church Fathers). We sometimes
tend to underplay the importance of
Aristophanes' remarkable comic genius,
primarily, one supposes, because the genre
of comedy seems inherently less important and—of course, mistakenly—less
serious. It is the distinguishing mark of
comedy that, as Aristophanes argued in
his choruses, it sifts the truly degrading
from the merely shocking and protects the
health of the city. Obscene, bawdy, risqué
matters have their rightful place in the
purifying heart of the comic; pornography dwells only in deadpan seriousness.

The primacy of the Greeks in the Western curriculum, then, as Knox insists,
is not a result of any decree by a higher
authority; neither church nor state has
imposed them, nor even men of money
and power. The Greek texts hardly compose a "master narrative" enforced by
conservative tradition. Nor has any ethnic
group gained power or prestige from their
study. They have had their effect, quite
simply, from their intrinsic quality: and it
is that quality—to which the classics call
us all—that makes them immortal.

THE LATE Professor Cedric Whitman
of Harvard maintained that it is from the
ancient classics that our culture inherited its idea of the heroic. "The notion
of the hero," he writes, is "the center of
one of the most powerful clusters of ideas
that ancient culture has bequeathed to
Western literature and art." We could
probably with justice maintain that without poetry, we would have no real notion
of the heroic. Admittedly, in America
we are heirs to multiple traditions of the
hero. Every group of people migrating to
this continent brings with it legends and
myths of heroes; and these imported stories and ideals have combined with the
myths and tales of the native Americans

to make up a complex mixture perhaps unique in human culture. But two major strands of heroic ideals composed the Founding Fathers' heritage when our nation came into being, the Greek and the Roman, and these, along with the biblical view, have shaped the fabric of our society for more than three centuries.

A recent poet, Robert Creeley, in a work entitled "Heroes" replies to the challenge of the Latin poet Virgil across the centuries:

> In all those stories the hero
> is beyond himself into the next
> thing, be it those labors
> of Hercules, or Aeneas going into death.
>
> I thought the instant of the one
>   humanness
> in Virgil's plan of it
> was that it was of course human enough
>   to die,
>   yet to come back, as he said, *hoc opus,*
>   *hic labor est* [here the work, here is the
>   labor]
>
> That was the Cumaean sibyl speaking
> This is Robert Creeley, and Virgil
> is dead now two thousand years, yet
>   Hercules
> and the *Aeneid*, yet all that industrious
>   wis-
>
> dom lives in the way the mountain
> and the desert are waiting
> for the heroes, and death also
> can still propose the old labors.

Creeley is referring to the sixth book of the *Aeneid,* when the sibyl tells Aeneas that to go to the underworld is fairly easy (everyone has to do so eventually), but "to retrace your steps and return to the upper air, this is work, this is labor." And, the poem implies, this is as difficult in the

twentieth century as in the first. Yet the *Aeneid* calls us to it; and "the mountain and the desert" are still waiting for the heroic action. All the "industrious wisdom" of the *Aeneid* reminds us that we are destined to something beyond death, harder than death, requiring heroic labor.

We might call this the Roman view of the heroic life, one that had immense influence on the West. The *Aeneid* was for centuries the most popular book in Europe, the book for the formation of Europe during the development of Christian culture. T. S. Eliot considered it "our classic"; it has been woven into Western thought and institutions. The *Aeneid's* two great features are *pietas* and *fatum,* duty and mission, as we might translate the Latin. No two words could more accurately describe America's deepest sense of what some have pejoratively called "manifest destiny," but which others have believed to be a true mission.

In America, as in Europe, the *Aeneid* has been our dominant classic; until the 1920s it was taught to every schoolboy and schoolgirl. It offers us the image of the person of duty, of *pietas,* who lives not for his own self-fulfillment but for others: for the gods, for the city, for family. Aeneas loses city, wife, father, and the beautiful Queen Dido in his quest to do the will of the gods—to found a new Troy, which will be the great Rome. Virgil does not spare us Dido's suffering; she is a noble queen, with her own city, tricked by the cruel goddess Aphrodite into an infatuation with Aeneas. Yet Aeneas is a man of duty and responsibility who cannot relinquish his god-given task of founding Rome. Part of the poem's power lies in its ability to own up to the dreadful cost of civilization: the damage that has to be done to the family and to women in order to move on to the new: "Such hard work it was to found the Roman city." As his father's shade tells him in the underworld, his is a demanding calling: "Remember, Roman, these will be your arts / To teach the ways of peace to those you conquer / to spare defeated peoples, tame the proud."

Hence, as Thomas Greene wrote in *The Descent from Heaven*: "The loss of Virgil to the modern world is an immeasurable cultural tragedy. . . . [F]ar more than Homer, Virgil has been the classic of Western civilization. This has been true partly because he is more fitly a poet of maturity than of youth, because his work continues to educate as the understanding ripens. Fully to know him one must know him long. If he teaches the schoolboy style, to the man he imparts nobility." Western man has found his ideal of the public virtues in "pious Aeneas," the man of destiny chosen for a great task: strong, brave, generous. He is resolute enough to turn his back on personal happiness; he fights skillfully and bravely; he is in fact a great hero. But he is a hero for a cause, for others, having accepted his role in life, his duty. Virgil taught the Western world the civilizing arts and incorporates the softness of our hearts (our Trojan ancestry) into the dynamism of civilization. As T. S. Eliot has reminded us, the prophecy of the *Aeneid* has not failed; we are still in a sense citizens of that city, the eternal Rome. But many current readers cannot accept the poem's ambiguity; perhaps the loss of the ability to bear subtle distinctions stems from the loss of the poem itself in our culture.

BUT THERE is another strain of the heroic that we inherit from antiquity, the one that I quoted Cedric Whitman as commending: the Greek, which, as Whitman writes, gives us that "inviolable lonely singleness, half repellent because

of its almost inhuman austerity, but irresistible in its passion and perfected selfhood." Another twentieth-century poet, William Butler Yeats, captures this quality in a poem written about Major Robert Gregory, "The Irish Airman Foresees his Death":

I know that I shall meet my fate
Somewhere among the clouds above;
Those that I fight I do not hate,
Those that I guard I do not love;
My country is Kiltartan Cross,
My countrymen Kiltartan's poor
No likely end could bring them loss
Or leave them happier than before
Nor law or duty bade me fight,
Nor public men nor cheering crowds,
A lonely impulse of delight
Drove to this tumult in the clouds;
I balanced all, brought all to mind,
The years to come seemed waste of breath,
A waste of breath the years behind
In balance with this life, this death.

This choice of a short life lived in pursuit of heroic achievement is a twentieth-century parallel to the classic decision of Achilles, chief protagonist in Homer's *Iliad*, to enter the Trojan war and risk everything on a short but glorious life. It is this tragic choice that makes his situation so unendurable when, at the beginning of the poem, Agamemnon insults him and engenders the famous "wrath of Achilles" which is the focus of our horrified admiration. Achilles becomes so merciless in his wrath that many readers cannot forgive him; in fact, they find it hard to consider him noble when he puts his own honor above the good of his fellow men. But it is an interior quality above all else that concerns Achilles: that *arete*, excellence of soul, which is the mark of the Greek hero—a heroic achievement sought not for mortals but for the gods. And readers are led into enduring the almost unbearable contradiction in Achilles' choice, the "terrible beauty" of his monstrous wrath.

Despite whatever inordinate deeds the hero commits, the poet knows that true heroism is the most glorious thing that can be passed down in memory through poetry. The novelist Caroline Gordon has commented that the writer has his eyes fixed on the hero, sees him when he is about to take that fatal step—the step that will hurl him into the abyss. For the hero as Homer conceived of him (and then the later Greek dramatists) is too large to be contained by the civic order; he is excessive, must go beyond codes. The other warriors in the *Iliad* fight bravely and nobly, but they do not enter into that realm of heroic paradox that is the true abode of the hero. Nor will they, we feel, enter into *kleos*, heroic memory, the only immortality known to Homer's readers. The basis of the Greek heroic paradox is that human beings must aspire to divinity and yet because of their mortality fail to achieve it. "No Greek ever became a god, and no true Greek ever gave up trying," Professor Whitman observed.

Heroism is one of the fundamental patterns built into all of us, a universal potentiality that must, however, be ignited to be realized. America has been steeped in the classical heroic tradition. But it can easily remain merely latent if each generation simply starts over again without the guidance of the classics. Admiration for the heroic principle will surface from time to time in surprising ways; but without a tradition of reverence it is likely to be deformed and misplaced. A godlike aspiration, a selfless desire for a commitment to a calling, a sense that honor is far more valuable than life—these are aspects of the soul that must be awakened by a vision of the high and the noble.

And herein lies one of the great values of studying the classics: our poetic heritage gives imperishable form to the heroic aspiration. Shakespeare's *Henry V,* Melville's *Moby Dick,* Conrad's *Lord Jim,* Crane's *The Red Badge of Courage,* Faulkner's *The Unvanquished,* Hemingway's *The Sun Also Rises*—these and other works enter into a dialogue with the Greek and Roman classics to kindle the image of the hero within the individual soul. The heroic thus becomes not a set of rules but a living ideal, incarnated in the lives of us all.

A RECENT book entitled *Who Killed Homer?* takes up this very topic. Written by two classics professors, Victor Davis Hanson and John Heath, this book gives a clear and unequivocal answer to their question: the professors have killed Homer. Their argument is that the academic world has finally "killed" the body of ancient poetic knowledge that had survived sturdily if somewhat precariously for centuries. By fostering a detached and impersonal scholarship, adopting a methodological sophistication, and marking off the territory as fit solely for specialists, the professors have sought to triumph over the texts they teach and write about, without witnessing to the wisdom and vitality of their contents.

What Hanson and Heath say about the demise of the Greek and Roman writings may be declared as well about all the classics—all those works that have depth, that avoid the simple recitation of what people think they already know, that manifest such difficulty that readers, left to their own devices, avoid them. In this way, all the genuine classics, all poetry, is being "killed." By detaching themselves from the texts and yet mastering their every detail, by avoiding assertions, generalizations, and affirmations, by scorning anyone who dares to speak of one of these works without himself being an expert—and, more recently, by purporting to find in these works exclusions, stereotypes, and subterranean messages of dominance—scholars have turned the classics into philological and semiotic quarry. The classics are thus hunted down by specialists who can kill from a great distance by a single shot—kill, that is, by negating their intrinsic meaning, quibbling about esoteric details, rendering it impossible for anyone but fellow specialists to read the texts in question. These masterpieces are thus off limits for the general reader. And certainly the ordinary college student cannot even obtain the license to hunt.

Our loss of the Greeks and Romans is symptomatic of our loss of the idea of *quality* and of *aspiration*, our loss of the heroic which is known in poetry. Yet we need the classics as never before in our history. For what is happening in our time is the making of a new synthesis, much like that large encompassing pattern of culture constructed in the High Middle Ages or in the period we know as the Renaissance. Ours is a time when the human schema and indeed the total world picture are being redefined. Ours is a "postmodern" age, and we live in a time of "globalization." We are called to respond to our *fatum*: to begin the task of sifting from the poetic traditions of the whole world those works that reflect and extend the meaning of our literary tradition.

This process has gone on at various junctures in civilization: European writings have been added to the Greeks and Romans, as have those representing America. Now that there is indeed one world for us, in which economic, educational, and cultural systems are linked as closely as were the different countries of Europe from the Renaissance onward, we are obligated to include writings from the rest of the world in our curricula and our concern. We need not be afraid that by extending generosity to worthy things outside the Western tradition, we shall be debasing our heritage. As Bernard Knox wrote, nothing short of totalitarianism will admit unworthy things into the canon. Placed beside the works that have long been there, the shallow and merely political pieces will gradually fade away, as did the minor works of the past. But we need an active and lively sense of our own heritage if the widening of the Western heritage to the world is to occur. When our society does indeed become "globalized"—when West and East do stand together as equals in the exchange of ideas as well as goods—we had better be ready by having something left to preserve.

Our need for the classics is intense. Yet any defense of them in our time must come from a sense of their absolute necessity—not from a desire to inculcate "cultural literacy," or to keep alive a pastime for an elite, but to preserve the full range of human sensibility. What is needed is to recapture their spirit of high nobility and magnanimity, of order and excellence, but to recapture that spirit in a framework of democracy engendered by a biblical culture of radical openness. The things worth preserving, the things we ought to be passing down, far transcend any single heritage: they partake of the fundamental structures of being itself. Melville called them the "heartless, joyous, ever-juvenile eternities." And if our children do not encounter these realities in their studies, they are not likely to encounter them at all. As *Kagemusha* makes clear, greatness of soul is an aspect of human being as such, but it is not a quality that comes naturally. It must be taught. The classics have become classics because they elicit greatness of soul. Far from being a particular province of the specialist, they are the essential foundation of our educational process and the impulsion toward that forward movement of the human spirit for which schools exist. In an unpoetic age, we have to learn all over again what and how to teach our own children. We need to re-read the Greeks.

V.

FREE MARKETS & CIVIL SOCIETY

Patrick M. Boarman

Bread and the Spirit

VOL. 2, NO. 1, 1965

For the better part of the last one hundred and fifty years, Western man has been obsessed with his body. He has anguished over the problem of how to keep his body properly fed, clothed, sheltered, and amused. And the spectre which has held more terrors for him than any other is the spectre of want. Want, so runs the maxim of this materialistic age, is the root of all evil, from juvenile felony to Communist revolution. Banish the fear of want—in the big city slums or in underdeveloped countries—keep people's bellies filled, increase economic "growth" everywhere, and most of the world's problems will be solved.

It is in the light of this theory that the mass unemployment which afflicted Germany in the early 1930s is still regarded—and not only by Germans—as a prime explanation (if indeed it is not held to be the exclusive one) for Hitler's rise to power. And that the prospects of communism for success vary directly with the poverty of a country is considered so self-evident as to be beyond discussion. It would be futile to deny the partial truth of the "poverty leads to communism (or Nazism)" thesis. For though man does not live by bread alone, he must have bread before he can think about the other things by which he lives. Unfortunately, many in the Western world, including not a few Christian experts on the "social question," have allowed obsession with "bread" to crowd out consideration of the "other things," and have apparently succeeded in transmitting the obsession to most of the non-Western peoples of the world. More and more, man has forgotten that he has a soul; and forgetting his soul, he has forgotten that hunger of the soul can be just as agonizing and just as evil, as hunger of the body.

In many places of the still free world, people pay little heed to God. Religion is something which is more honored in the breach than in the observance. In certain Western countries, for example, there are probably millions of Christians, Protestant and Catholic, who are not unwilling to pay their church taxes (to be excused from which requires a formal declaration of atheism) but who otherwise, and apart from the customary invocation of God at births, marriages, and deaths, lead a-religious lives. An unwillingness to be counted an atheist (for a variety of reasons) is coupled with a practical atheism in what amounts to a classic case of a "cultural lag." The present state of religion in the West has been well put by C. F. Ramuz:

At the present time bourgeois society is in a state of extreme confusion. A part of it believes that God exists; for the rest, God does not exist. The foundation of all ethics and indeed of any possible sociology is sometimes denied, sometimes affirmed, but most of the time is deliberately ignored. Bourgeois society today is an incoherent aggregate of individuals only saved from total collapse by an extremely complicated armature of law—not to mention armies, police, courthouses, custom houses, and monetary systems. It may be—and this is a more profound reason—that what still holds it up, though very precariously and only for a short time, is its rooted indifference, the total incapacity of most of its members to make up their minds to choose and therefore to love and therefore to hate. . . . It is a society, crystallized on the outside, but containing the elements of decomposition . . . in which no one believes that his personal faith should mean anything to anyone else—a weak manner of believing, for he who believes strongly, believes in a truth which is not only true for himself but for everyone.[1]

It is not the intent here to try to trace the reasons for the religious erosion which has been going on for a long time in many traditionally Christian countries. It is sufficient for our present purposes to note the fact. What is of immediate significance is that despite the decline in the active practice of religion, man's hunger for the things of the spirit has remained as acute as it ever was. In the very act of rejecting the spiritual food which his church, Catholic, Protestant, or other, offered him and which was his birthright, modern man created a spiritual vacuum in his own heart.

Wrote Edgar A. Mowrer, an American correspondent in Germany in 1932: "Nothing is more dangerous than the void left by a lost religion."[2] The void left by the erosion of Christian belief made men say: "If I can no longer love God, I can love the nation; if I can no longer love the nation, I can love the proletariat."[3] Suffice it to say that as Christianity has lost influence, new religions—principally nationalism and communism—have taken its place. The recent rapid westernization of underdeveloped countries has similarly shaken the structure of traditional religion or tribal beliefs, dynamited the established organization of society, instilled contempt in the intelligentsia of these countries for the faiths of their fathers, and created a vacuum into which Communist or crypto-Communist doctrines have moved. In the richer non-totalitarian countries, it is sometimes merely a vulgar materialism (in which the progress of the human race becomes a simple function of its standard of living), but more often a "faith" in democracy or, in the case of the intellectuals, in science which becomes the core of a new mystique. A question of some moment is whether Christianity or any traditional religion can win back those who find the lures of these new false gods irresistible or even prevent still others from succumbing to idolatry.

One thing, at least, seems clear: a specifically Christian revival will be handicapped to the extent that some Christians continue their naive connivance with these false religions by accepting their declared premises. Consider, for example, the matter of social justice. Some Christian zealots in the area of social reform still talk as if there had been no change in the material condition of the worker since the days of Manchesterism, the sixteen-hour day, and the employment of children in the coal pits. Hence, they see the solution to the social problem almost exclusively in terms of higher wages, shorter hours, and better working conditions. But these measures constitute only half, and today probably the least important half, of the solution to the contemporary social problem.

The real social problem of our time is, to use the noble words of Pius XI in *Quadragesimo Anno,* the *redemptio proletariorum*—the redemption of the proletariat. Of what does this redemption consist? Of rendering to the worker only what is due him in wages and other material sustenance?

The real wages of workingmen in the "affluent society" are high beyond the dreams of their fathers and of most of the population of the world. Their working hours are shorter than ever before and getting still shorter; they have more clothes, food, automobiles, television sets, and amusements than ever before. If higher wages and shorter hours were the solution to the social problem, this problem should by now, in the United States at least, be largely solved. And yet in spite of this fat living, in spite of a solicitous security which follows the average citizen from the cradle to the grave, strikes are a predictable annual phenomenon. Unrest and discontent are the recurrent illnesses of industrialism regardless of how successful it may be in terms of its material output. In Samuel Gompers's day, the cry for "more" would seem to have had a certain justification. But the cry is more vehemently heard than ever. And this outcome puzzles those who, accepting the premises of the stimulus-response school

of psychology, believe that the contented mouse is the one who finally gets the cheese. The concept of social justice continues to be discussed, even by some who should know better, in terms reducible in one way or another to dollars and cents. There seems to be a general pur-blindness (indicated by the elevation of "freedom from want" to the level of the freedoms enunciated in the Bill of Rights) to the fact that hunger is a condition found not only in the stomach or even primarily there, but in the heart and in the soul.

II

It is not very difficult to explain the emergence of communism as an ersatz religion in many countries of the world, developed and underdeveloped. The Industrial Revolution which took place at the beginning of the nineteenth century, and industrial revolutions of the type now underway in many non-Western countries, must be regarded, obviously, not as technological or economic occurrences merely but as social upheavals in the fullest sense. Ancient ways are destroyed, the established structure of values and goals is shattered, and for a long time there may be nothing to fill these empty spaces except goods and services. It is not necessary to follow the almost universal practice of looking upon the onset of the Industrial Revolution in Europe as a period of unrelieved misery in order to understand how it could have helped to pave the way for false religions. In fact, living conditions in English towns in the nineteenth century, bad as they were by today's standards, probably represented a substantial improvement over eighteenth-century conditions. And in any case, the disease, dirt, and ugliness of the nineteenth-century factory town were certainly not due exclusively, as is often assumed, to free enterprise as such. As T. S. Ashton has pointed out

> some at least of the responsibility lay with legislators who, by taxing windows, put a price on light and air and, by taxing bricks and tiles, discouraged the construction of drains and sewers. Those who dwell on the horrors that arose from the fact that the products of the sewers often got mixed up with the drinking water, and attribute this, as all other horrors, to the Industrial Revolution, should be reminded of the obvious fact that without the iron pipe, which was one of the products of that revolution, the problem of enabling people to live a healthy life together in towns could never have been solved.[4]

Moreover, it does not make sense from the standpoint of economics to attribute the improvement in the physical lot of the worker merely to the enactment of factory legislation, as is done repeatedly. The passing of laws of itself cannot cause the quantity of goods and services to increase; but it is such an increase which ultimately is required if an improvement in the average standard of living is to be realized. Thus, it is rarely recalled that "rising productivity of male labor had something to do with the decline of the number of children exploited in the factories or the number of women degraded in the mines."[5]

It is not the alleged poverty and sufferings of the early industrial development of Europe which constitute the fundamental explanation of the success of the *Communist Manifesto*—itself a product of well-to-do bourgeois intellectuals—so much as the spiritual aenemia which marked the increasingly impressive material achievements of nineteenth-century capitalism.

And this progressive spiritual anemia appears to be related in a not insignificant way to the radical social and economic transformations in the life of the West, in particular in the life of its working classes, which were brought about by the Industrial Revolution.

What were the features of pre-revolutionary life which were transmuted or destroyed in the post-revolutionary period? Three, at least, may be distinguished:

(1)Work itself had a meaning-content. The shoemaker saw the operation of shoemaking through from beginning to end. He made the last, the heels, and sewed the leather. The finished shoes were the product, in a sense, of his own personality.

(2)The meaningfulness of his work and hence the workman's own value to the community were clearly visible. The instinctive urge in man to seek approbation from his fellows, the primal desire for the feeling of self-worth was fulfilled. This element in the life of the individual craftsman has been strikingly portrayed in the French film classic "La Femme du Boulanger" (The Baker's Wife). Raimu, the great French tragi-comedian who played the role of the baker, had just married a young and pretty wife. One day, the young wife runs off with another man. Raimu leaves his bakery in pursuit of the truant. His ovens grow cold. There is no bread for the villagers. To end this distressing state of affairs, the whole village, including the *curé*, turns out to join the chase. Clearly, the usefulness of the baker to his fellowmen was not in doubt. Then, too, the community itself was a tightly knit group whose life revolved around the significant activities of not alone the baker, but the butcher, the farmer, the carpenter, the smith, the dressmaker, etc. It revolved around the church, which gave the final and transcendent meaning to these in themselves meaningful activities. Life in such a community was, to use Ramuz's famous phrase, "made to the measure of man."[6]

(3) There was an element of economic and psychic security in this pre-factory life which is almost totally lacking in the great industrial centers of the world, whether East or West. If, for instance, wars or other disturbances over which the village carpenter had no control, caused a fall in the demand for chairs, the carpenter could always spend less time making chairs and more time growing beans in his garden. He may not have been able to buy a Chevrolet or a Volkswagen (or their equivalents at that time) but it was unlikely that he would ever be thrown on the dole. To this extent he was independent of the system, he was rooted in his own resources.

Consider, by way of contrast, the mode of life which emerges *after* the Industrial Revolution. How has the factory (white or blue collar) affected man's life? Malthus notwithstanding, the most striking feature of the new system—and surely a positive one—is the tremendous increase in the amounts and kinds of goods which are now produced with only a fraction of the human effort required in the afore-mentioned village. In effect, the so-called capitalist system succeeded not only in making possible an unexampled increase in the world's population but in lifting the average living standards of these new millions to undreamed-of heights. But it is necessary to consider the costs of this change. Part of the price that has been exacted has been an enormous increase in the interdependence of all units operative in the economic system and hence in the susceptibility of the whole system to crisis and upset—the familiar alternation of prosperity and depression. Moreover, the very specialization which mass production makes possible and requires reduces

the *economic security* of the specialists. A slump in the demand for their product may mean loss of a job with little possibility because of their specialized training, of such individuals switching to the production of something for which demand has increased.

Finally and most importantly, the extreme specialization of a highly developed economy tends: to stunt and deform the personalities of those who do most of the work. This cost of technological progress has been graphically described by Ralph Borsodi in his *This Ugly Civilization:*

> special machines can be devised for each operation and the worker instead of having to perform all the operations involved in making the product from beginning to end can be confined to the endless repetition of a few simple operations. Amazing economies, as Henry Ford and others have shown, become possible. . . .[7]

Originally, the assembling of the Ford automobile chassis required twelve hours and twenty-eight minutes. But

> [t]his operation was finally cut down by the principle of division and sub-division of labor to one hour and thirty-three minutes. The sub-division of operations in the Ford factory is almost incredibly fine; the man who places a part does not fasten it—the part may not be fully in place until after several operations later; the man who puts on the bolts does not put on the nuts; the man who puts on the nuts does not tighten them Thus division and sub-division of labor go on, in the factories and in the offices, not only in the automobile industry, out in all industries, and thus the economies of the factory system are fully realized.[8]

Since Borsodi wrote these words in 1929, the idea that it is always and under all circumstances good to pursue alleged economies of scale (i.e., for individual firms to get bigger and bigger, provided lower costs of production can be realized thereby) is more than ever regarded by economists and businessmen as axiomatic. That untrammeled pursuit of bigness may eventuate in monopoly does not cut much ice with those who regard economic concentration not only as desirable but as the inevitable concomitant of an advancing technology. When pressed on the possible threat to free enterprise posed by the existence of monopoly and oligopoly power, they will point to the existence of "countervailing power": "big labor" is available to counteract the power of "big business," and "big government" (make the monopoly a public utility, set up a system of wage and price controls) is available to offset both. Apart from the purely economic objections that may be raised against capitulation to the onward rush of giantism,[9] the question of the human and social cost involved has hardly begun to receive adequate attention.

III

It is obvious, in the first place, that modern work has largely been robbed of its content. And it is by no means certain that further automation will not aggravate this process even while turning over the more monotonous motions to the machine. Indeed, automation is a word invented to describe merely the intensification and acceleration of the mechanizing process. Thus, in hearings before Congress, D. J. Davis, vice president of Ford Motor Co., affirmed that

[i]n planning and executing this program (the use of inline or transfer machines and mechanical handling devices between them) we feel that we are doing no more than our predecessors did when they utilized new technology to mass produce the model T. We do not believe that automation, as we use it, is a revolutionary development in production techniques; rather it is just another evolutionary phase of our advancing production technology.[10]

In the wake of continuous and even accelerated mechanization, the opportunities a craftsman once had for creative expression and for the fulfillment of his personality are drastically reduced and in some instances entirely lacking. The worker is ten times, a hundred times removed from the final consumer of his output. And if he himself is unable to see the ultimate significance of the bolt or the nut which he has fastened in place or of the button which he has pushed, how can it be expected that his neighbors will see the meaning of his work or give to him that recognition as an individual which he craves?

Because the work itself has little meaning-content, the worker concentrates on the only other thing which is available—money. Hence, the continuous agitation for higher wages. Lacking genuine love of his work and perhaps even finding it distasteful most of the time, he seeks to reduce the time spent on it to a minimum. Hence, the constant pressure for shorter hours.

Not finding meaning in his work, the modern job-holder seeks away from his job, and it is precisely at this juncture that he collides with new discouragements. At the very moment when the stability and security and spiritual content of the pre-factory, church-centered, God-oriented community are most needed, they have vanished. The worker finds himself instead to be just one more atom in the shifting sands of the intensely mobile urban and suburban populations of our day. He cannot send down roots into the good earth from a tenement or an apartment house. Even the movement of workers to suburbia does not always represent a nearer approach to the good life. One finds he has been rescued from the total anonymity of city life only to be submerged like a bee in a hive in the excessive "togetherness" of a suburban housing project. Nor can the modern proletarian always find that meaning, that justification for his existence, in a church to which his relationship has become entirely impersonal, and of which he may not even know the pastor's name. Increasingly, he is told by the sociologists that he is one of the dependent millions, one of the "masses," and he numbly endeavors to accept this fact even while deeply resenting it.

In part, the union movement itself constitutes a kind of rebellion against the atomization of industrial society. To an extent of which the membership is perhaps not consciously aware, unions—as Frank Tannenbaum has suggested—come into being in answer not only to the monopsonistic power of employers but to the need for identification and self-worth in a world where the principle of association is chiefly the cash nexus. The great moral tragedy of the industrial system, writes Tannenbaum, is that

> it destroyed the symbolic and meaningful world that had endowed the life of the individual with an ethical character. The individual worker now had no recognizable place that he could call his own, no society to which he

"naturally" belonged, and no values by which he was expected to live. The ordinary meanings that make life acceptable had evaporated. His economic insecurity was but part of a larger perplexity. . . . It is against this background that the role of the trade-union must be examined. In terms of the individual, the union returns to the worker his "society." It gives him a fellowship, a part in a drama that he can understand, and life takes on meaning once again because he shares a value system common to others. . . . [Trade unionism] is a social and ethical system, not merely an economic one. It is concerned with the whole man. Its ends are the "good life." The values implicit in trade-unionism are those of an older day, antedating the grating modern political slogans. It is an unwitting effort to return to values derived from the past: security, justice, freedom, and faith. It is in those values, explicit and inherent, that man had found his human dignity.[11]

From this point of view, unions may be regarded, paradoxically, as foci of conservative resistance to the social disintegration produced by a rapidly evolving technology.

IV

Candor requires the admission that few workers would be willing or able to view their malaise in the terms used here. In the language of psychoanalysis, the modern worker's unease, his unhappiness is experienced for the most part unconsciously. He believes consciously that he works for money and he is abetted in this belief by his employer and by his union chief who din into his ears day-in and day-out that higher wages are the answer to all his problems. But since man does not live by bread alone, the discontent and the frustration remain, unappeasable by the highest wages. Strikes and slowdowns become the concrete manifestations of his unconscious grievances and the union the willing vehicle of his unconscious rebellion. Significantly, recent surveys conducted in many American industrial plants reveal that increasing numbers of workers are beginning to rank recognition of individuality and personal worth above money income. Perversely, however, unions often elect to support programs and objectives which deny the feeling of self worth. For example, the structure of wage rates should logically be a highly differentiated one to correspond to the very different talents of the individuals who compose the labor force. But it is precisely the elimination of such differentials which many unions, especially those of the "industrial" type, will set as their long-run objective on the grounds that they are "undemocratic," or that the complexities of wage administration thus introduced make it more difficult for the union to get everybody's wages lifted, or simply that the results of union activity under such a system will be less dramatically evident to the membership. The end effect of wage uniformization anyhow is to aggravate the general process by which the individual is smothered in the mass. Thus is the original evil of the age compounded, and the seething spiritual discontents; of modern man magnified until, ignited by the proper dose of demagoguery, they explode.

The implications of the foregoing are clear. Mankind in the nations of the West—and his plight is extending ever more rapidly to the non-Western nations—has increasingly lost his stature; he has been torn out of the context in which life had value and purpose. It is alleged that America has lost its sense of "national purpose," an observation which, if true, reveals the emptiness not of the national mind or the national soul—there is no such thing—but of countless individual minds and souls. Science goes forward with huge strides; every week, every day sees new and astonishing progress in the microscopic and the macroscopic measurement of the universe. On the one hand is the scientist who probes the immensities of space with his telescope and prepares to explore it with his person; on the other, the scientist who probes the immensities of the atom with his cyclotron and plays like a fearful child with its titanic forces. But where, as C. F. Ramuz asks, does man fit in this universe of cold immensities without beginning or end? Thus science as well as the industrial system which it fosters have combined to inject a large measure of futility into the life of modern man. They have cut him loose from all that was stable and traditional in his life; they have set him adrift on an uncharted sea without rudder or compass to guide him to the shore for which his soul hungers.

V

It is easy to understand now why growing numbers of men, in their frantic search for spiritual nourishment, have created for themselves the false, the ersatz gods of nationalism and communism. The surface appeal of communism lies in this: that it promises to end the present misery, the sole cause of which is capitalism. Only overthrow capitalism, so runs the dogma, and happiness will follow. This is a lie for communism is, if anything, even more determinedly committed to industrialism, to the factory, to uniformization, to giantism, to the destruction of the individual by the mass. Nevertheless, men have turned to communism and to its less robust brother, socialism, because they are dimly aware that these religions put a meaning into an existence barren of meaning. Lower wages, even longer hours and onerous working conditions become endurable where there is a purpose. If man cannot love God, let him love the proletariat, let him love society, let him work, live, and die for society. Clearly, it is necessary to guard against the self-deception which may result from denouncing communism as "atheistic" and "materialistic." For this alleged philosophy of materialism responds to something in man's nature profoundly moral and spiritual. The bourgeois too, notes Ramuz, is often an atheist, though a passive one.

> He does not believe strongly enough in his atheism to make it a principle of action. His atheism remains passive, whereas Soviet atheism goes into action, for it is an anti-faith, in other words another kind of faith (and therein lies its superiority). Bourgeois atheism is based on tolerance; it is perfectly willing to exist at the side of faiths that contradict and oppose it; it says, "I do not believe, but I do not prevent you from believing." The bourgeois does not even believe strongly enough that he does not believe. . . (Communist ethics) although meticulously anti-Christian, completely the reverse of Christian, make a wonderfully symmetrical parody of Christian morality, or rather of Christian moralizing. For they, too, are busy "reforming" drunkards or "reclaiming" those who have strayed from the path of virtue—not for the sake of God, however, but for the sake of society. Society replaces God. . . .

> This atheism . . . is giving man once more a stature—where he had lost all stature.[12]

Marxism has a pretended scientific content. It offers a theory of society and of economics. But it is not the scientific part of this doctrine which arouses enthusiasm but the very part which transcends science. The fallacies and obscurities of *Das Kapital* have not hindered the onward march of communism, because the march of communism has very little to do with logic. And this is why it will not be sufficient merely to expose Marx' errors in economic reasoning in order to defeat communism. Communism knows that man has a soul and it wishes to feed this soul. To this end, it even supplies the paraphernalia of traditional religion: it has its high priests, Lenin and Stalin; its prophet, Marx; its Bible, *Das Kapital*; its devil, capitalism; its faithful, the proletariat; its kingdom to come, the classless society; and its god, mankind *en masse*.

What of nationalism? In his fine study of *National Consciousness* Walter Sulzbach has noted the essential conflict between nationalism and Christianity:

> For Christianity, there is God and the individual soul; nations, groups, and classes count for nothing. For nationalism, the nation is everything and the individual has value only insofar as he takes part in the collective life of the group. This contradiction of goals accounts, more than anything else, for the conflict between the Catholic Church and the doctrine of National Socialism.[13]

Nazism, too, liked to robe itself in the mantle of science, or more accurately, pseudo-science. It is easy enough to expose Hitler's race theories and his geopolitics as the ravings of a megalomaniac; and not much sophistication is needed to realize that *Mein Kampf* is a boring mixture of half-baked logic, pathetic ignorance of history, and essential vulgarity. And yet the Fuehrer's ideas, oral and written, moved millions to frenzy. The truth is that both communism and Nazism are faiths beyond logic; they offer a mystique, they offer ideals, however perverted, and ideals are not material but spiritual. They fill a vacuum in the soul of modern man, they assuage his spiritual emptiness.

Can the twin demons of nationalism and communism be exorcised from men's hearts? "Every moral association of men," states the Encyclical *Mystici Corporis* (Pius XII), "is in the end directed to the advancement of all and of every single member. For they are persons." These words offer a key to what Christian reformers and Christian social scientists can do to halt the drift to the aggrandizement of society and to the degradation of man. Obviously it is not possible to return to the conditions of the eighteenth-century village. The food requirements alone of the world's vastly increased population would make this a suicidal venture. But in a manner suitable to the present age, to the developed and to the underdeveloped countries, we need to do whatever is necessary to enable man to become once again *a person*. For Christ comes to the person, not to the nation, nor to the class, nor to the mass.

VI

Because socialism (both of the weaker as well as of the more robust type) is to be condemned is not necessarily a reason why old-style capitalism should be embraced. Both are pernicious: old-style capitalism because it denies man his soul, socialism because it indeed allows man a soul—the sham-soul of the mass man. But in rejecting old-style capitalism it is important that we avoid throwing out the baby with the bath-water. The market economy must be the core of any economic and social system which in our day proposes to provide maximal amounts of the material things man requires and yet to leave him the freedom without which material plenty is a bitter fruit. A system without freedom is one which lacks the very wellspring of true morality and of true spirituality. The precise institutional framework which is needed to make the market method of organization the servant and not the master of man has been competently described elsewhere

What must in any case be avoided as equally futile and destructive approaches to the tasks of social reconstruction are, on the one hand, an economically ignorant "moralism" which tries to shape the good society in ignorance of or even in opposition to economic verities, and, on the other, a morally and spiritually obtuse "economism" (Röpke), uncaring or contemptuous of the things which lie beyond supply and demand.

It is most strange and ironic to find that economism has infected many Christian discussions of the social question and that Christians often appear increasingly concerned with man's stomach whereas the Communists are increasingly concerned with his soul. Those in the Christian camp who keep talking of social justice as a process whereby the proletariat rises ever higher on the material scale must acknowledge that in so doing they are every bit as much in the grip of *homo economicus* as any Manchesterian. There would seem to be some point at this juncture in interrupting our preoccupation with economics and with morals—disciplines of this life—long enough to recall that the redemption of the proletariat, the redemption of man, is not to be found in bread alone, or in any given distribution of the available bread, but in every word that comes from the mouth of God.

Notes

1. C. F. Ramuz, *What Is Man?* (New York, 1948), 94–95.
2. Edgar A. Mowrer, *Germany Puts the Clock Back* (New York, 1932), 48.
3. Harold D. Lasswell, *World Politics and Personal Insecurity* (1934), quoted in Walter Sulzbach, *National Consciousness* (Washington, DC, 1943), 122.
4. Cf. T. S. Ashton, "The Treatment of Capitalism by Historians" in *Capitalism and the Historians,* ed. F. A. Hayek (Chicago, 1954), 52,
5. Ibid., 57.
6. C. F. Ramuz, op. cit., 54–61.
7. Ralph Borsodi, *This Ugly Civilization* (New York, 1929), 187.
8. Ibid.
9. Cf. Wilhelm Röpke, "Klein- Und Mittelbetriebe in der Volkswirtschaft," *ORDO, Jahrbuch für die Ordnung von Wirtschaft und Gesellschaft,* Helmut Küpper vormals George Bondi Verlag, vol. 1 (Bad Godesberg, 1948), 153–74. Cf. also Lawrence Abbott, *Quality and Competition* (New York, 1955).
10. Testimony of D. J. Davis, vice president, Ford Motor Co., in *Automation and Technological Change,* Hearings before the Subcommittee on Economic Stabilization of the Joint Committee on the Economic Report, 84th Congress, 53 ff., quoted in *Automation* by Almarin Phillips (Washington, D. C, 1957), 6.
11. Cf. Frank Tannenbaum, *A Philosophy of Labor* (New York, 1951), 7–11.
12. C. F. Ramuz, op. cit., 93–97.
13. Walter Sulzbach, op. cit., 119.
14. Cf. Wilhelm Röpke, *A Humane Economy* (Chicago, 1960).

Israel M. Kirzner

Divergent Approaches in
Libertarian Economic Thought

VOL. 3, NO. 3, 1967

The writings of the great majority of economists over the past thirty years have supported the powerful currents that sweep the modern world toward centralized authority, interventionism, and statism. The teachings of these economists led generations of students and laymen to believe uncritically that an economy based on unhampered individual enterprise and the institution of private property must breed unemployment, instability, resource misallocation, stagnation, and an unjust distribution of income. And yet, there has consistently been a dissenting minority whose voices are not completely drowned out by the teachings of their colleagues,

These economists, arguing on strictly technical grounds, defend the efficiency of the unhampered market economy, and point out again and again how measures put into effect by governments must lead to consequences worse than the evils that they seek to avoid. Apart from the strictly technical questions involved, these writers also point to the value judgments implicit in many of the conclusions of their colleagues. They show how many of the welfare proposals offered in the name

of economics merely reflect arbitrary opinions concerning such matters as the ethical status of private property, the ability of an individual to choose for himself, and the like.

In recent years this minority view among economists has gained considerable strength. Our younger economists are no longer persuaded that the old interventionist dogmas are beyond criticism. The benefits arising from the free interplay of market forces are more and more coming to be recognized. The views of free-market economists are becoming less and less easy for the still-dominant "mixed-economy" exponents to ignore.

This change in climate is being felt by the more inquiring of our undergraduate students around the country. Ten or fifteen years ago it was commonplace for an intelligent student to complete his undergraduate studies—often with even a major in economics—and yet gain no inkling of the very existence of a respectable minority free-market view in the contemporary economic literature. This has changed; the existence of an economic literature that formulates policy recommendations with full consciousness of the relevant market consequences and their implications for individual welfare and freedom of choice is now a matter of common knowledge.

THE ECONOMISTS who have contributed to this literature in the United States have written as individuals, not as members of a single "school," and there have been significant differences of opinion among them, both on theoretical questions and on policy issues. It is, of course, always a hazardous undertaking to classify independent writers. However, it seems widely recognized that most of the economists who have emphasized the efficiency and other advantages of the free market can be associated with either one or the other of two intellectual sources. On the one hand there is an academic tradition strongly associated with the University of Chicago, embracing in particular the work of the late Henry Simons, of F. H. Knight, and of younger scholars such as Milton Friedman, Yale Brozen, and George J. Stigler. On the other hand there has since the 1940s been felt in this country an expanding, well-articulated influence that clearly traces back to the Austrian subjectivist school. This influence is almost synonymous with the work of Ludwig von Mises, and has inspired significant similar work by others in the same tradition. It is idle to speculate on the appropriateness of the term "schools" to describe these two intellectual sources. While the term school is widely applied to Chicago economists,[1] it would probably be inaccurate to refer to the writers most strongly influenced by Professor Mises as a "school."[2] Nonetheless, it remains a fact that there exist significant differences between the "Austrian" literature, in which the works of Mises are the most

important and influential, and the writings of the economists whom we will, for the sake of brevity and convenience, call the "Chicago" economists.

It is, of course, important not to exaggerate the differences between the two streams of writing, the Misesist and the "Chicago." While, as we shall discover, there exist sharp differences in methodology and in perspective between the two trends, there is an almost surprising coincidence between their views on most important policy questions. This is especially true with respect to issues having to do more narrowly with the operation of the price system. The truth is that whatever differences exist between the two approaches, both have basically the same sound understanding of how a market operates, and this is responsible for the healthy respect which both approaches share in common for its achievements. It is this common denominator which provides the rationale of this essay, the purpose of which is to describe clearly the more important points of distinction that set apart their two approaches to the market. And for this reason this essay does not take up some important differences between these two streams of thought that occur in monetary economics and business cycle policy—areas in which the basic denominator common to both trends has far less direct relevance.

But whatever the similarities displayed in these two approaches, it does seem a useful task to enunciate with some care the more fundamental matters of method and perspective upon which agreement is absent. In what follows the writer presents the controversial issues as he understands them; he makes no claim to represent the distilled "official" views of any particular writer.

ONE WAY of presenting the difference between the two approaches under consideration might be as follows: The price theory that underlies the contributions of the "Chicago" writers is not fundamentally different from that accepted by American economists generally, including those holding the efficiency and justice of the market system in deep mistrust. It is merely that the Chicago economists apply their price theory more consistently and more resolutely, assigning to it a scope of relevance far wider than that granted by others. On the other hand, the Misesist approach involves a theory of price that differs in important respects from that taught and applied by others.

This admittedly oversimplified way of stating the difference between the two approaches, among other advantages, enables us to perceive the intellectual roots of their divergence from one another. Chicago price theory, like that taught in most United States economics departments, is solidly in the Anglo-American neoclassical tradition associated most importantly with Alfred Marshall. The profound influence exercised by Marshall upon American price theory, in spite of its modification at the hands of Edward H. Chamberlin (a modification that is, from the point of view of this essay, yet on Marshallian lines), is clearly visible as the central thread in Chicago-type textbooks on price theory."[3]

On the other hand the price theory associated with Mises, nourished from the stream of Austrian thought going back to Carl Menger, has entered American economics as a distinctly alien element. (The only comparable influence, and that a rather muted one, is that deriving from the writings of Philip H, Wicksteed.) While Walrasian general equilibrium ideas made their strong impact early on American economics in the 1930s and

1940s with the growing vogue of mathematical economics, it was not until much later, when Mises's writings came to be known in their American editions, that his ideas were seriously discussed in this country.

While there are numerous smaller points of difference that separate the two approaches—the dominant neo-Marshallian microeconomics of Chicago, and the Austrian-type theory of the Misesist—it will prove convenient to concentrate on three rather major sources of disagreement. We will discuss in turn the following: (1) the role of equilibrium; (2) the role of empirical investigations; and (3) the concept of monopoly. A clear understanding of these matters will go a long way towards an understanding of what sets the two approaches apart, and the degree of the separation.

The Role of Equilibrium

In Marshallian economics, as in Walrasian, the concept of equilibrium plays a major, if not a permanent role. Considering the various forces at work in a market, the price theorist asks himself what conditions would have to be fulfilled before one can pronounce these forces to be in balance. The initial data governing a situation determines the conditions needed to reach equilibrium. Since a situation in which these conditions are absent is not in balance, it cannot be assumed to be a lasting situation; market forces will bring about change. Because the direction of motion of a disequilibrium market was more or less uncritically assumed to lead toward the fulfillment of the conditions for equilibrium, the latter situation came to be looked upon as "the solution." In other words, whenever one is provided with a list of existing conditions, and is asked to use price theory to explain "what will happen" as a result of these initial conditions, the answer is seen to be provided by *the description of the equilibrium situation appropriate to the initial data.* This procedure of equilibrium analysis has become, through the method of "comparative statics," the principal means of analyzing the consequences of changes in the data. One simply compares the equilibrium conditions appropriate to the new set of data with those appropriate to the older set. The change in data can then be said to bring about a change in the market situation from the "old" equilibrium configuration to the new one.

The concept of equilibrium is one which has been applied, mutatis mutandis, to different market structures. In particular, the changes in neo-Marshallian price theory that resulted from the work of Harvard's Professor Chamberlin in the 1930s did not affect the use of the equilibrium method. For Chamberlinian theory as for that of his predecessors, the important objective is the description of the equilibrium situation corresponding to the postulated data. Whereas pre-Chamberlinian theory had operated in a world in which only two patterns of market structure could occur, Chamberlin argued for a view of the market that should accommodate an entire spectrum of different structures. With respect to each kind of market structure there will then be sought the corresponding equilibrium configuration.

THE EQUILIBRIUM notion as applied to the market refers to the particular pattern of decisions on the part of the market participants that permits all the decisions to be successfully carried out. The particular market structure prevailing in a given situation determines the range of possible decisions open to each participant. The theorist's insight into how an individual participant reaches his decisions enables explanation of which possible decision will be selected as the best opportunity in given circumstances. It is thus possible to list the set of decisions that will have to be made by the various participants in a given market situation if one is to be able to say simultaneously (a) that each participant is making the best decision possible from his point of view; and (b) that all the decisions can be carried out at the same time.

As a result of this emphasis on the situation at equilibrium, consideration of the neo-Marshallian approach led naturally to a rather special view by economists of the method appropriate to their task, and this tendency was reinforced by the strong influences of Leon Walras. This methodological view emphasized the strictly formal character of the search for the equilibrium conditions. Given the structural conditions assumed for the market, the tastes of the consumers and the technological constraints governing production, we find that discovering the set of price offers and bids, the set of product quantities and qualities, and the set of inputs to be employed in production assumes a character amenable to mathematical attack. It became easy for price theorists to set up the appropriate equations that would have to be satisfied simultaneously in order to pronounce the market to be in equilibrium; it became easy to emphasize the task of examining the conditions under which a solution of these equations is formally possible.

In addition, the stress on equilibrium situations facilitated yet a further tendency (one that was reinforced by the work of Chamberlin), that is, a persistent pattern of analyzing markets on the assumption that *the structure of the market is a da-*

tum. While this tendency has begun to wane in recent years, the more traditional approach, including that followed by "Chicago" economists, has been to specify the particular character of competition or monopoly believed to be relevant to a particular market, and to seek the corresponding equilibrium solution. Little attempt was made to understand how the relevant competitive structure of the market has been itself forged out of the dynamic process of the market, and how out of the continued operation of this process there may be expected, perhaps, an evolving market structure.[4]

Before turning to consider how different a role is assigned to the equilibrium notion in the Misesist system, it will be useful to notice one further implication of the dominant neo-Marshallian approach shared by "Chicago" economists. This is the seriousness with which the perfectly competitive model is treated. In the 1930s the hitherto widespread use of this model by economists generally came under sharp attack on the grounds that it lacked realism, but not in terms of its internal formal adequacy. ("Chicago" economists, in fact, have tended to defend continued wide use of the perfectly competitive model, arguing that it provides a workable approximation to the real world.)

And yet, as F. A. Hayek has pointed out, the perfectly competitive model suffers from the severe defect that it *is restricted to a situation that already satisfies the conditions for equilibrium.*[5] The perfectly competitive market is one in which conditions exist that by definition assume that no decision made need be disappointed. Each buyer and each seller in the perfectly competitive market is assured of being able to buy or to sell as much as he wishes at the going price; no possibility exists for analysis of a perfectly competitive market that is *not* in

equilibrium. The astonishing willingness of economists to restrict so much of their work to analysis of a model that from the start rules out consideration of disequilibrium possibilities can clearly be ascribed only to the prevalent exclusive concern with equilibrium situations. With little interest attached to any but equilibrium solutions, with no awareness of the dynamics of market structure, there need be little compunction in raising the perfectly competitive model to a paramount position.

All this contrasts very starkly indeed with the role assigned to the equilibrium notion in the Misesist system. Here the emphasis is *not* on the configuration of decisions necessary to ensure that all of them can be carried out. The emphasis is, instead, on the *process* generated by the forces of the market. The focus is not on the set of prices, output and input quantities, that must prevail if a market is to be in equilibrium. Instead it is upon the manner in which prices, outputs, and inputs *change* from one period to the next as the logic of the market forces adjustments to be made in the decisions of the participants.

To the Misesist the problem to be solved is not the specification of equilibrium conditions corresponding to different market structures. The economist is called for, instead, to understand how one disequilibrium situation generates the pressures that lead toward a new situation in which disequilibrium maladjustments have, to some degree, been corrected.

Of course, for Mises too the position of equilibrium is a unique one. But its uniqueness consists not in its providing the solution, the outcome determined by the data. Its uniqueness is simply that the equilibrium position, were it to prevail, would be characterized by the *cessation* of the market process, all relevant market forces having successfully spent themselves. Analysis of equilibrium conditions provides a useful *contrast* to the process of market agitation that marks a state of disequilibrium, but it is this agitation itself which is the focus of analytical attention.

It follows that, for the Misesist view, the enumeration of the equations whose simultaneous solution is required for equilibrium and the examination of the possibilities for such a solution to exist, are activities of profoundly subsidiary importance. These activities do not provide the answers the Misesist economist is seeking. For this reason the elaborate techniques marshalled by the mathematical economists leave the Misesist totally unimpressed. Not only are they not addressing themselves to the problems the Misesist considers important, but they are confining themselves to analysis of conditions in which the market has nothing further to contribute.

For similar reasons the Misesist has little patience for the elaborate consideration of the perfectly competitive model. He objects to this model, not primarily on the Chamberlinian grounds of realism, but on account of the model's irrelevance to the market *process* set in motion by disequilibrium conditions. The perfectly competitive model has nothing to say about such a process; by definition such a process can occur only in the *absence* of perfectly competitive conditions.

In fact the entire concept of market structure has little relevance for the Misesist. From his point of view competition is not a condition of the market that indicates a certain pattern of decisions as being an equilibrium pattern. Rather, competition is seen as the driving force behind the adjustment process taking place in the market. Since only competition provides this driving force,

analysis of different market structures boils down, in this view, to analysis of the strength of this drive. And since market structures are themselves *produced* by the process of market adjustment, it is hardly useful to take them as given, as data that independently determine the course of the market process.

One further implication of the Misesist approach may be mentioned in concluding this section, and that is the role of the entrepreneur. For a theory of price concerned primarily with states of equilibrium, the entrepreneur is a somewhat peripheral figure. He has no role at all in the central scheme of things, at least until we are ready to postulate changes in the data. Despite the careful attention which so original a "Chicagoan" as Professor Knight has devoted to the theory of uncertainty and profit, the entrepreneur hardly occupies the center of attention in "Chicago" economics. It is otherwise in the Misesist approach. Here the entrepreneur, the initiator of change, searching for the profit opportunities spawned by disequilibrium conditions, performs the most essential role of all. It is his competitive pursuit of profits which sets the market process in motion. It is he who occupies the center of analytical attention.

The Role of Empirical Investigations

The contemporary dominant view of economics is one in which important roles are assigned both to the theorist and to the empirical research worker. The general attitude is somewhat as follows: In earlier days, when economics was rather primitive, there was disagreement on the method appropriate to the discipline. At the close of the last century there were those who stressed theory to the exclusion of empirical investigation, and there were others who believed it possible to acquire economic knowledge only through the methods of historical research. In the enlightened present we have come to realize that both kinds of investigation are required and that they complement one another. Theory and empirical research, in this dominant view, are closely intertwined. One is willing to deplore contemporary institutionalist attacks on theory; one is equally willing to deprecate armchair theorists who disdains to muddy their hands with down-to-earth statistics.

"Chicago" economists are in general strongly in agreement with the mixed approach, While they vigorously emphasize the power and usefulness of theory, they subscribe to the requirement that theory be "operational," and watch for "implications" of theory that can be tested against empirical data. Because "Chicago" economists have *more* faith in the power of theory than other (non-Misesist) economists, and because, as a result, they apply theory to many neglected facets of economic activity (e.g., many kinds of non-pecuniary motivations), they are in fact frequently engaged in a *wider* range of empirical investigations than other economists are. In this kind of approach a theory is a tentative "guess" whose validity must await confirmation by the evidence. While "Chicago" economists are probably more aware than other econometricians of the subtle difficulties of extracting watertight confirmations, or even refutations, of theories from observational data, they nonetheless tend to look upon these difficulties as merely a need for more refined statistical, observational and computational techniques, rather than as a problem ineradicably inherent in the nature of the material under investigation.

In this view, the investigator writing down market prices, measuring output volume, or describing the degree of concentration in industry may be engaged in exactly the same kind of activity—that of helping to acquire economic knowledge—as is the theorist whose models suggest the particular sets of statistics to be collected.

The view is rather different when considered from the Misesist perspective, however, and some of the most extreme literary disagreements between the two approaches have to do with this issue. In the Misesist view the role of empirical investigation is an altogether different one, and knowledge obtained by the empirical investigator is of an altogether different character from that discovered by the theorist. In this view empirical confirmation of the theorems obtained by abstract logic is neither possible nor necessary. It is not possible, because there are no constants in the realm of human actions; it is therefore impossible to investigate the consequences of changes in one variable with assurance that no disturbance is at the same time being caused by changes in other variables. On the other hand, confirmation of economic theorems is not necessary, because the theorems themselves describe relationships logically implied by hypothesized conditions. The validity of these relationships can be tested by examining the reasoning employed to establish them.

Empirical work in the Misesist system has the function of establishing the *applicability* of particular theorems, and thus of *illustrating* their operation. Factual measurement and description provide information which can be used in applying theory. Economic theory postulates certain relationships under specific conditions. Only concrete observation, therefore, can tell the applied economist which particular theorem is of relevance in a given situation. But the discovery that the facts fit perfectly with the predictions of a theory does not provide the economist with knowledge that he did not possess before; nor would the failure of the facts to fit with theory cause him to abandon a valid theorem—this might merely indicate inapplicability of the theorem. The world of facts is too complex to permit simple hypothetical relationships to be directly perceived or refuted; with only variables to be observed, the real world market can only be understood with the help of theory, not the reverse. Direct observation does indeed provide knowledge, possibly important knowledge, but of a different kind from that embodied in an economic theorem. Observation provides the material to be understood by applying the appropriate theory.

The skillful theorist well acquainted with real market phenomena may be in an ideal position to illustrate the validity of theory by reference to well-chosen concrete facts. He may in this way convince laymen of the far-reaching truth of price theory far more powerfully than by direct teaching of the theory itself. But this is a matter of pedagogy, not of establishing the substantive truth of the theory in a manner satisfactory for science.

It will be seen that we have here a fundamental and profound difference in outlook between the too approaches being examined in this essay.

The Concept of Monopoly

The last example of disagreement between the "Chicago" and Misesist views we shall consider here concerns the notion of monopoly. We have had occasion earlier in this essay to draw attention to

the different concepts of competition that characterize the two approaches. The disagreement about monopoly that we shall consider here is not unconnected with the different outlooks noted earlier.

In the dominant Anglo-American tradition in price theory, monopoly is invariably associated with a particular pattern of decision possibilities seen facing the *firm*. In technical jargon, the firm enjoying some degree of monopoly power faces a downward-sloping demand curve, i.e., it can sell any of a wide range of different volumes of output, but can sell the larger outputs only by charging lower prices. This is contrasted with the "perfectly competitive" firm, which is able to sell the amount it wishes, within reason, without having to lower its price.

This view of monopoly is the one upon which the Chamberlinian theory of monopolistic competition is predicated; it is the view upon which economic analysis of anti-trust policy is almost invariably based. The distinguishing features of this monopoly concept are, first, that monopoly power is possessed by the producing firm, and second, that it is evidenced by the power of the firm to raise its price by being willing to sell smaller quantities of output. This is the monopoly concept used as a matter of course by "Chicago" economists.

In the Misesist system, however, the term monopoly is used to denote a quite different concept. And there is in this system little significance attached altogether to the downward-sloping demand curve that faces a firm. In this system, with its utter disinterest in the perfectly competitive model mentioned earlier, the demand curve facing *any* firm is understood—at least in disequilibrium—to be more or less downward-sloping. This is not seen as in any way interfering with the dynamic process of competition which we earlier found to be central to the Misesist view of the market.

Moreover, in the Misesist emphasis on the process rather than on the result, the concept of monopoly is inseparable from the explanation of the source of monoply power. To contend that a firm enjoys monopoly power one must be able to account for the existence of this power. Since a firm is merely the interim resource complex assembled by the entrepreneur, its possession of exclusive selling power can only be ascribed to possession of unique resources. Entrepreneurship is viewed as being by definition competitive in a free unhampered market. With no restriction on buying or selling, no one entrepreneur is able, without having already captured unique resources, to control any one branch of production. Clearly in the long-run view, monopolistic control over production cannot be ascribed to firms as such, but only to the fortunate owners of unique resources.

This is not the occasion to examine more thoroughly the implications of this view of monopoly for judgments on the efficiency of resource allocation, or for one's opinions on antitrust policy. It is not difficult to see that these implications must be considerable. We return to appraise very briefly the significance of the distinctions which we have drawn between the "Chicago" and Misesist approaches.

With such deep-seated differences separating the foundations of Misesist economics from that of "Chicago," it is, for the libertarian, reassuring to discover that so many policy questions seem to lead to the same answers in both approaches. Clearly there is some common ground possessed by the two, on which the cited differences do not make a great deal of direct practical difference. For the pragmatic policy-maker, less concerned with philosophical underpinnings than with ready-to-use conclusions, the distinctions setting apart the two approaches may not seem of great moment. On the other hand, for the student and scientist, these differences will seem of far greater importance. For the student of the history of ideas, the matters of disagreement are similarly of considerable interest. While there are, as we have seen, many policy questions on which both are in agreement, there can clearly be no guarantee that this will always be the case. Only careful, dispassionate study of both approaches can enable one to choose intelligently between them, and to be able to perceive the truth where the two views do in fact lead to divergent conclusions.

Notes

1. For an academic discussion of this usage, see *Journal of Political Economy,* February, 1962.
2. And despite the fact that Professor Mises teaches at New York University, it would be quite incorrect to talk of a Misesist "New York University School."
3. The dissatisfactions with the theory of monopolistic competition that have been voiced by "Chicago" economists do not affect the validity of the statements in the text.
4. For a perceptive discussion of this point see J. M. Buchanan, "What Should Economists Do?", *Southern Economic Journal,* January, 1964.
5. Cf. F. A, Hayek, *Individualism and Economic Order* (Chicago: Univ. of Chicago Press, 1948), 92–106.

Ludwig von Mises

Capitalism versus Socialism

VOL. 5, NO. 3–4, 1969

Most of our contemporaries are highly critical of what they call "the unequal distribution of wealth." As they see it, justice would require a state of affairs under which nobody enjoys what are to be considered superfluous luxuries as long as other people lack things necessary for the preservation of life, health, and cheerfulness. The ideal condition of mankind, they pretend, would be an equal distribution of all consumers' goods available. As the most practical method to achieve this end, they advocate the radical expropriation of all material factors of production and the conduct of all production activities by society, that is to say, by the social apparatus of coercion and compulsion, commonly called government or state.

The supporters of this program of socialism or communism reject the economic system of capitalism for a number of reasons. Their critique emphasizes the alleged fact that the system as such is not only unjust, a violation of the perennial God-given natural law, but also inherently inefficient and thus the ultimate cause of all the misery and poverty that plague mankind. Once the wicked institution of private ownership of the material factors

of production will have been replaced by public ownership, human conditions will become blissful. Everybody will receive what he needs. All that separates mankind from this perfect state of earthly affairs is the unfairness in the distribution of wealth.

The essential viciousness of this method of dealing with the fundamental problems of mankind's material and spiritual welfare is to be seen in its preoccupation with the concept of distribution. As these authors and doctrinaires see it, the economic and social problem is to give to everybody his due, his fair share in the endowment that God or nature has destined for the use of all men. They do not see that poverty is "the primitive condition of the human race."[1] They do not realize that all that enables man to elevate his standard of living above the level of the animals is the fruit of his planned activity. Man's economic task is not the distribution of gifts dispensed by a benevolent donor, but production. He tries to alter the state of his environment in such a way that conditions become more favorable to the preservation and development of his vital forces. He works.

Precisely, say the superficial among the critics of social conditions. Labor and nothing but labor brings forth all the goods the utilization of which elevates the condition of men above the level of the animals. As all products are the output of labor, only those who labor should have the right to enjoy them.

THIS MAY sound rather plausible as far as it refers to the conditions and circumstances of some fabulous nonhuman beings. But it turns into the most fateful of all popular delusions when applied to homo sapiens. Man's eminence manifests itself in his being fully aware of the flux of time. Man lives consciously in a changing universe; he distinguishes, sooner and later, between past, present,[2] and future; he makes plans to influence the future state of affairs and tries to convert these plans into fact. Conscious planning for the future is the specifically human characteristic. Timely provision for future wants is what distinguishes human action from the hunting drives of beasts and of savages. Premeditation, early attention to future needs, leads to production for deferred consumption, to the intercalation of time between exertion and the enjoyment of its outcome, to the adoption of what Boehm-Bawerk called round-about methods of production. To the nature-given factors of production, man-made factors are added by the deferment of consumption. Man's material environment and his style of life are radically transformed. There emerges what is called human civilization.

This civilization is not an achievement of kings, generals, or other *Fuehrers*. Neither is it the result of the labors of "common" men. It is the fruit of the cooperation of two types of men: of those whose saving, i.e., deferment of consumption, makes entering upon time-absorbing, round-about methods of production possible, and of those who know how to direct the application of such methods. Without saving and successful endeavors to use the accumulated savings wisely, there cannot be any question of a standard of living worthy of the qualification human.

Simple saving, that is, the abstention from immediate consumption in order to make more abundant consumption at a later date possible, is not a specifically human contrivance. There are also animals that practice it. Driven by instinctive urges, some species of animals are also committed to what we would have to call capitalistic saving if it were done in full consciousness of its effects. But man alone has elevated intentional deferment of consumption to a fundamental principle of action. He abstains temporally from consumption in order to enjoy later the continuous services of appliances that could not have been produced without such a postponement.

Saving is always the abstention from some kind of immediate consumption for the sake of making an increase or improvement in later consumption possible. It is saving that accumulates capital, dissaving that makes the available supply of capital shrink. In acting, man chooses between increasing his competence by additional saving or reducing the amount of his capital by keeping his consumption above the rate correct accountancy considers as his income.

Additional saving as well as the non-consumption of already previously accumulated savings are never "automatic," but always the result of an intentional abstention from instantaneous consumption. In abstaining from instantaneous consumption, the saver expects to be fully rewarded either by keeping something for later consumption or by acquiring a capital good, by acquiring the *property* of a capital good.

Where there is no saving, no capital goods come into existence. And there is no saving without purpose. A man defers consumption for the sake of an improvement of later conditions. He may want to improve his own conditions or those of definite other people. He does not abstain from consumption simply for the pleasure of somebody unknown.

There cannot be any such thing as a capital good that is not owned by a definite owner. Capital goods come into existence as the property of the individual or the group of individuals who were in the position to consume definite things but abstained from this consumption for the sake of later utilization. The way in which capital goods come into existence as private property determines the institutions of the capitalistic system.

Of course, today's heirs of the capitalistic civilization also construct the scheme of a world-embracing social body that forces every human being to submit meekly to all its orders. In such a socialist universe everything will be planned by the supreme authority and to the individual "comrades" no other sphere of action will be left than unconditional surrender to the will of their masters. The comrades will drudge, but all the yield of their endeavors will be at the disposal of the high authority. Such is the ideal of socialism or communism, nowadays also called planning. The individual comrade will enjoy what the supreme authority assigns to him for his consumption and enjoyment. Everything else, all material factors of production, will be owned by the authority.

SUCH IS the alternative. Mankind has to choose: On the one side—private property in the material factors of production. Then the demand of the consumers on the market determines what has to be produced, of what quality, and in what quantity. On the other side—all the material factors of production are owned by the central authority and thus every individual entirely depends on its will and has to obey its orders. This authority alone determines what has to be produced and what and how much each comrade should be permitted to use or to consume.

If one does not permit individuals to keep as their property the things produced for temporally deferred utilization, one removes any incentive to create such things and thus makes it impossible for acting man to raise his condition above the level of nonhuman animals. Thus the anti-property (i.e., socialist or Communist) authors had to construct the design of a society in which all men are forced to obey unconditionally the orders issued from a central authority, from the great god called state, society, or mankind.

II

The social meaning and the economic function of private property have been widely misunderstood and misinterpreted because people confuse conditions of the market economy with those of the militaristic systems vaguely labeled feudalism. The feudal lord was a conqueror or a conqueror's accomplice. He was anxious to deprive all those who did not belong to his own cluster of any opportunity to make a living otherwise than by humbly serving him or one of his class comrades. All the land—and this means in a primitive society virtually all the material factors of production—was owned by members of the proprietary caste and to the others, to those disdainfully called the "villains," nothing was left but unconditional surrender to the armed hereditary nobility. Those not belonging to this aristocracy were serfs or slaves, they had to obey and to drudge while the products of their toil were consumed by their masters.

The eminence of the inhabitants of Europe and their descendants who have settled in other continents consists in the fact that they have abolished this system and substituted for it a state of freedom and civic rights for every human being. It was a long and slow evolution, again and again interrupted by reactionary episodes, and great parts of our globe are even today only superficially affected by it. At the end of the eighteenth century the triumphal progress of this new social system was accelerated. Its most spectacular manifestation in the moral and intellectual sphere is known as the Enlightenment, its political and constitutional reforms as the liberal movement, while its economic and social effects are commonly referred to as the Industrial Revolution and the emergence of modern capitalism.

The historians dealing with the various phases of this up-to-now most momentous and weighty period of mankind's evolution tend to confine their investigations to special aspects of the course of affairs. They mostly neglect to show how the events in the various fields of human activity were connected with one another and determined by the same ideological and material factors. Unimportant detail sometimes engrosses their attention and prevents them from seeing the most consequential facts in the right light.

The most unfortunate outcome of this methodological confusion is to be seen in the current fateful misinterpretation of the recent political and economic developments of the civilized nations.

The great liberal movement of the eighteenth and nineteenth centuries aimed at the abolition of the rule of hereditary princes and aristocracies and the establishment of the rule of elected representatives of the people. All kinds of slavery and serfdom ought to be abolished. All members of the nation should enjoy the full rights and privileges of citizenship. The laws and the practice of the administrative officers should not discriminate between the citizens.

This liberal revolutionary program clashed very soon with another program that was derived from the postulates of old Communist sects. These sects, many of them inspired by religious ideas, had advocated confiscation and redistribution of land or some other forms of egalitarianism and of primitive communism. Now their successors proclaimed that a fully satisfactory state of human conditions could be attained only where all material factors of production are owned and operated by "society" and the fruits of economic endeavors are evenly distributed among all human beings.

MOST OF these communist[3] authors and revolutionaries were convinced that what they were aiming at was not only fully compatible with the customary program of the friends of representative government and freedom for all, but was its logical continuation, the very completion of all endeavors to give to mankind perfect happiness. Public opinion was by and large prepared to endorse this interpretation. As it was usual to call the adversaries of the liberal[4] demand for representative government the parties of the "right" and the liberal groups the parties of the "left," the Communist (and later also the socialist) groups were considered as "more to the left" than the liberals.

Popular opinion began to believe that while the liberal parties represent only the selfish class interests of the "exploiting" bourgeoisie, the socialist parties were fighting for the true interests of the immense majority, the proletariat.

But while these reformers were merely talking and drafting spurious plans for political action, one of the greatest and most beneficial events of mankind's history was going on—the Industrial Revolution. Its new business principle— that transformed human affairs more radically than any religious, ethical, legal, or technological innovation had done before—was mass production destined for consumption by the masses, not merely for consumption by members of the well-to-do classes. This new principle was not invented by statesmen and politicians; it was for a long time even not noticed by the members of the aristocracy, the gentry, and the urban patricians. Yet, it was the very beginning of a new and better age of human affairs when some people in Hanoverian England started to import cotton from the American colonies; some took charge of its transformation into cotton goods for customers of modest income; while still others exported such goods to the Baltic ports to have them ultimately exchanged against corn that, brought to England, appeased the hunger of starving paupers.

The characteristic feature, of capitalism is the traders' unconditional dependence upon the market, that is, upon the best possible and cheapest satisfaction of the most urgent demand on the part of the consumers. For every kind of production human labor is required as a factor of production. But labor as such, however masterfully and conscientiously performed, is nothing but a waste of time, material, and human effort if it is not employed for the production of those goods and services that at the instant of their being ready for use or consumption will best satisfy in the cheapest possible way the most urgent demand of the public.

The market is the prototype of what are called democratic institutions. Supreme power is vested in the buyers, and vendors succeed only by satisfying in the best possible way the wants of the buyers. Private ownership of the factors of production forces the owners—enterprisers—to serve the consumers. Eminent economists have called the market a democracy in which every penny gives a right to vote.

III

Both the political or constitutional democracy and the economic or market democracy are administered according to the decisions of the majority. The consumers, by their buying or abstention from buying, are as supreme in the market as the citizens through their voting in plebiscites or in the election of officers are supreme in the conduct of the affairs of state. Representative government and the market economy are the product of the same evolutionary process, they condition one another, and it would seem today that they are disappearing together in the great reactionary counter-revolution of our age.

Yet, reference to this striking homogeneousness must not prevent us from realizing that, as an instrument of giving expression to the genuine wants and interests of the individuals, the economic democracy of the market is by far superior to the political democracy of representative government. As a rule it is easier to choose between the alternatives which are open to a purchaser than to make a decision in matters of state and "high" politics. The average housewife may be very clever in acquiring the things she needs to feed and to clothe her children. But she may be less fit in electing the officers called to handle matters of foreign policy and military preparedness.

Then there is another important difference. In the market not only the wants and wishes of the majority are taken into account but also those of minorities, provided they are not entirely insignificant in numbers. The book trade publishes for the general reader, but also for small groups of experts in various fields. The garment trades are not only supplying clothing for people of normal size, but also merchandise for the use of abnormal customers. But in the political sphere only the will of the majority counts, and the minority is forced to accept what they may detest for rather serious reasons.

In the market economy, the buyers determine with every penny spent the direction of the production processes and thereby the essential features of all business activities. The consumers assign to everybody his position and function in the economic organism. The owners of the material factors of production are virtually mandatories or trustees of the consumers, revocably appointed by a daily repeated election. If they fail in their attempts to serve the consumers in the best possible and cheapest way, they suffer losses and, if they do not reform in time, lose their property.

FEUDAL PROPERTY was acquired either by conquest or by a conqueror's favor. Once acquired, it could be enjoyed forever by the owner and his heirs. But capitalistic property must be acquired again and again by utilizing it for serving the consumers in the best possible way.

Every owner of material factors of production is forced to adjust the services he renders to the best possible satisfaction of the continually changing demand of the consumers. A man may start his business career as the heir of a large fortune. But this does not necessarily help him in his competition with newcomers. The adjustment of an existing railroad system to the new situation created by the emergence of motor cars, trucks, and airplanes was a more difficult problem than many of the tasks that had to be solved by enterprises newly started.

The fact that made the capitalistic methods of the conduct of business emerge and flourish is precisely the excellence of the services it renders to the masses. Nothing characterizes the fabulous improvement in the standard of living of the many better than the quantitative role that the entertainment industries play in modern business.

Capitalism has radically transformed all human affairs. Population figures have multiplied. In the few countries where neither the policies of the governments nor obstinate preservation of traditional ways on the part of the citizens put insurmountable obstacles in the way of capitalistic entrepreneurship, the living conditions of the immense majority of people have improved spectacularly. Implements never known before or considered as extravagant luxuries are now customarily available to the average man. The general standard of education and of material and spiritual well-being is improving from year to year.

All this is not an achievement of governments or of any charitable measures. More often than not it is precisely governmental action that frustrates beneficial developments which the regular operation of capitalistic institutions tends to bring about.

Let us look upon one special case. In the precapitalistic ages, saving and thereby the betterment of one's economic condition was really possible, apart from professional money-lenders (bankers), only to people who owned a farm or a shop. They could invest savings in an improvement or expansion of their property. Other people, the propertyless proletarians, could save only by hiding a few coins in a corner they considered as safe. Capitalism made the accumulation of some capital through saving accessible to everybody. Life insurance institutions, savings banks, and bonds give the opportunity of saving and earning interest to the masses of people with modest incomes, and these people make ample use of it. On the loan markets of the advanced countries, the funds provided by the numerous class of such people play an important role. They could be an important factor in making the operation of the capitalistic system familiar to those who are not themselves employed in the financial conduct of business affairs. And first of all—they could more and more improve the economic and social standing of the many.

But unfortunately the policies of practically all nations sabotage this evolution in the most disgraceful manner. The governments of the United States, Great Britain, France, and Germany, not to speak of most of the smaller nations, were or are still committed to the most radical inflationist policies. While continually talking about their solicitude for the common man, they have without shame, again and again through government-made inflation, robbed the people who have taken out insurance policies, who are working under pension plans, who own bonds or savings deposits.

IV

The authors who in Western Europe at the end of the eighteenth century and in the first decades of the nineteenth century developed plans for the establishment of socialism were not familiar with the social ideas and conditions in Central Europe. They did not pay any attention to the *Wohlfahrtsstaat,* the welfare-state of the German monarchical governments of the eighteenth century. Neither did they read the classical book of German socialism, Fichte's *Geschlossener Handelsstaat,* published in the year 1800. When much later—in the last decades of the nineteenth century—the nations of the West, first among them England, embarked upon the Fabian methods of a temperate progress toward socialism, they did not raise the question why continental governments whom they despised as backward and absolutist had long before already adopted the allegedly new and progressive principles of social reform.

But the German socialists of the second part of the nineteenth century could not avoid dealing with this problem. They had to face the policies of Bismarck, the man of whom the pro-socialist *Encyclopaedia of the Social Sciences* says that he was "with reason regarded as the foremost exponent of state socialism in his day."[5] Lassalle toyed with the idea to further the cause of socialism by cooperation with this most "reactionary" paladin of the Hohenzollerns. But Lassalle's premature death put an end to such plans and, very soon, also to the activities of the socialist group of which he had been the chief. Under the leadership of the disciples of Marx, the German socialist party turned to radical opposition to the Kaiser's regime. They voted in the Reichstag against all bills suggested by the government. Of course, being a minority party, their votes could not prevent the Reichstag's approval of various pro-labor laws, among them those establishing the famous social security system. Only in one case could they prevent the creation of a government-supported socialization measure, viz., the establishment of a governmental tobacco monopoly. But all the other nationalization and municipalization measures of the Bismarck age were adopted in spite of the passionate opposition of the socialist party. And the nationalization policy of the German Reich that, thanks to the victories of its armies, in those years enjoyed all over the world an unprecedented prestige was adopted by many nations of Eastern and Southern Europe.

IN VAIN did the German socialist doctrinaires try to explain and to justify the manifest contradiction between their fanatical advocacy of socialism and their stubborn opposition to all nationalization measures put into effect.[6] But notwithstanding the support the nationalization and municipalization policy of the authorities got from self-styled conservative and Christian parties, it very soon lost its popularity with the rulers as well as with those ruled. The nationalized industries were rather poorly operated under the management of the administrators appointed by the authorities. The services they had to render to the customers became highly unsatisfactory, and the fees they charged were more and more increased. And, worst of all, the financial results of the management by public servants were deplorable. The deficits of these outfits were a heavy burden on the national treasuries and forced again and again an increase in taxation. At the beginning of the twentieth century, one could no longer deny the obvious fact that the public authorities had scandalously failed in their attempts to administer the various business organizations they had acquired in the conduct of their "state socialism."

Such were conditions when the outcome of the First World War made the socialist parties paramount in Central and Eastern Europe and also considerably strengthened their influence in Western Europe. There was in those years in Europe practically no serious opposition to most radical pro-socialist plans.

The German revolutionary government was formed in 1918 by members of the Marxian social-democratic party. It had no less power than the Russian government of Lenin and, like the Russian leader, it considered socialism as the only reasonable and possible solution to all political and economic problems. But it was also fully familiar with the fact that the nationalization measures adopted by the Imperial Reich before the war had brought unsatisfactory financial results and rather poor service, and also that the socialist measures resorted to in the years of the war had been unsuccessful. Socialism was in their opinion the great panacea, but it seemed that nobody knew what it really meant and how to bring it about properly. Thus, the victorious socialist leaders did what all governments do when they do not know what to do. They appointed a committee of professors and other people considered to be experts. For more than fifty years the Marxians had fanatically advocated socialization as the focal point of their program, as the nostrum to heal all earthly evils and to lead mankind forward into the new garden of Eden. Now they had seized power and all of the people expected that they would redeem their promise. Now they had to socialize. But at once they had to confess that they did not know what to do and they were asking professors what socialization meant and how it could be put into practice.

It was the greatest intellectual fiasco history has ever known and it put in the eyes of all reasonable people an inglorious end to all the teachings of Marx and hosts of lesser known utopians.

Neither was the fate of the socialist ideas and plans in the West of Europe better than in the county of Marx. The members of the Fabian Society were no less perplexed than their continental friends. Like these, they too were fully convinced that capitalism was stone dead forever and that henceforth socialism alone would rule all nations. But they too had to admit that they had no plan of action. The flamboyantly advertised scheme of Guild Socialism was, as all people had to admit very soon, simply nonsense. It quietly disappeared from the British political scene.

But, of course, the intellectual debacle of socialism and especially of Marxism in the West did not affect conditions in the East. Russia and other Eastern countries of Europe and China turned to all-round nationalization. For them, neither the critical refutation of the Marxian and other socialist doctrines nor the failure of all nationalization experiments meant anything. Marxism became the quasi-religion of the backward nations which were anxious to get the machines and, first of all, the deadly weapons developed in the West, but which abhorred the philosophy that had brought about the West's social and scientific achievements.

The Eastern political doctrine asking for immediate full socialization of all spheres of life and the pitiless extermination of all opponents gets rather sympathetic support on the part of many parties and influential politicians in the Western countries.

"Building bridges to the Communist sector of the world" is a task rather prevalent with many governments of the West. It is fashionable with some snobbish people to praise the unlimited despotism of Russia and China. And, worst of all, out of the taxes collected from the revenues of private business some governments, first of all that of the United States, are paying enormous subsidies to governments that have to face tremendous deficits precisely because they have nationalized many enterprises, especially railroads, post, telegraph and telephone service, and many others.

In the fully industrialized parts of our globe, in the countries of Western and Central Europe and Northern America, the system of private enterprise not merely survives, but continually improves and expands the services it renders. The statesmen, the bureaucrats, and the politicians look askance upon business. Most of the journalists, the writers of fiction, and the university teachers are propagating various brands of socialism. The rising generation is imbued with socialism in the schools. Only very rarely does one hear a voice criticizing socialist ideas, plans, and actions.

But socialism is for the peoples of the industrial world no longer a living force. There is no longer any question of nationalizing further branches of business.[7]

NONE OF the many governments sympathizing with the socialist philosophy dares today seriously to suggest further measures of nationalization. On the contrary. For example, the American government as well as every reasonable American would have reason to be glad if the new administration could get rid of the Post Office with its proverbial inefficiency and its fantastic deficit.

Socialism started in the age of St. Simon as an attempt to give articulation to the ripeness of Caucasian man's Western civilization. It tried to preserve this aspect when it later looked upon colonialism and imperialism as its main targets. Today it is the rallying cry of the East, of the Russians and the Chinese, who reject the West's ideology, but eagerly try to copy its technology.

Notes

1. Bentham, *Principles of the Civil Code* (in *Works*, ed. Bowring, vol. I), 309.
2. About the praxeological concept of "present" see *Human Action*, 3rd ed., 100f.
3. The term "socialism" was fashioned only many decades later and did not come into general use before the 1850s.
4. "Liberal" is here used in its nineteenth-century meaning that still prevails in European usage. In America "liberal" is nowadays used by and large as synonymous with socialism or "moderate" socialism.
5. See W. H. Dawson in the *Encyclopaedia of the Social Sciences,* vol. II, 573.
6. About the lame excuses of Engels and Kautsky, see my book *Socialism,* J. Kahane, trans., 1951 edition, pages 240 ff.
7. The British Labour cabinet paid homage to its party ideology in dealing with the steel industry. But everybody knows that this is merely a facade to conceal a little the great failure of all that the various British left-wing parties were aiming at for many decades.

Götz Briefs

The Janus Head
of the Welfare State

VOL. 7, NO. 3, 1970–71

In a truly surprising vision, Alexis de Tocqueville foresaw the consequences of what goes today by the term of "welfare" state in his *De la Démocratie en Amérique*, (vol. 1, Paris 1951, 1st edition 1839–40): "I have always felt that this regular, mild and seductive kind of vassalage might be associated more easily than one is apt to assume with the exteriors of freedom and so becomes established in the name of the sovereignty of the people."

In proportion to the degree to which the welfare state extends the scope of its services and administration, it loses in legitimate sovereignty and authority; but because it evolves—in that same proportion—towards a public assistance and public ownership state, it compensates for what it loses. In this way the Janus head of the welfare state makes its appearance. Its development is ominous; the wholesomeness of society itself as well as of the social structure is endangered. But it does not seem ominous to those who enjoy its fruits: for as long as the "fiscal" state continues to bestow welfare and security more and more widely, and as long as the beneficiaries have faith in its promises to go on doing so, they are perfectly con-tent. Who are the "they" that have to pay for it? Superficially, "they" can be identi-fied by means of steeply progressive taxes on income, wealth, and inheritance; it is possible, at first, to bleed the "haves" for the benefit of the "have nots." But there are limits to this process. As early as 1950, the British Chancellor of the Exchequer, Sir Stafford Cripps, felt obliged to warn his own Labour Party, which was then in power, that whatever wealth it was possi-ble to skim off from the well-to-do to use for social purposes had already been ex-hausted, so that henceforth anything that Labour wished to allocate for welfare and social security would have to be paid by the beneficiaries themselves. In Sweden the same thing has repeatedly been said by the governing party's Minister of Finance and the president of the Central Bank. It has been expressed, yet again, in the warning given by the German Federal Chancellor and the President of the Federal Bank in reference to the "summer sales" during the election year 1965.

Let us not overlook either, though these are less obvious, the consequences of the redistribution occurring in the Western welfare state. Whether by taxation or by inflation, our wealth and incomes cannot be looted without creating the risk that the sources of saving and the means of capital development run dry. Governmental extensions of credit cannot substitute for private building of capital, for here it is a question of *Real-Kapitalbildung*: something impossible to achieve other than through restraint in consumption. Credit facilities by way of the central bank have, indeed, some limited purpose insofar as unused capacity of productive capital and labor exists, otherwise such credit merely constitutes a focal point for inflation and leads to deficits in the balance of payments. When, therefore, the saving capacity within the private sector is weakened by over-consumption and by redistribution, the state itself becomes obliged to take measures for reducing consumption so as to make it possible for sufficient real capital to be formed.

The involvement of governments in general welfare and security policies, in particular, in their being faced today with the alternative of either inflation or unemployment, accounts for the hectic eagerness and efforts of governments to intervene. Professor Samuelson (in *Full Employment, Guidepost and Economic Stability*, American Enterprise Institute, Washington, D.C., 1967) observes very aptly: "Every time the economy showed signs of flagging other programs were introduced. . . . Now almost in a hypochondriacal way, the minute the economy begins to flag the least little bit, the stops are pulled out in favor of expansion" (97). And in view of the time lag between action and success, there lie the implicit difficulties of those hectic efforts. To quote Professor Samuelson once more: "If what our right hand does today had its effect upon the economy tomorrow, we would have limited need of accurate

forecasting. If what our right hand does today has actions nine months from today and nothing along the way can change that action, then it's quite obvious that we must have some notion of what things are going to be like nine months from now" (100).

ONCE AGAIN we are brought back to the essential question of whether capital formation by saving is to be a function of the state or be left to private initiatives. One might opt for the state, and as regards the formation of social capital—what is called the social overhead—it would be right to do so; but anything beyond that will tend to give the state excessive responsibility and power. Incidentally, the experience of the Communist economy, especially in the agricultural sector, supplies us with examples of the monstrous miscarriages that are bound to ensue from a centralized, state-planned economy with its accompanying state monopoly of capital formation.

What is in question is not the transfer of responsibilities actually unable to be borne by individuals or social groups but the transfer of responsibilities which individuals or associations would in fact be able to bear, though they find it more convenient to transfer them to the state. Consequently the state may in fact accept these responsibilities, but it is not itself an initiator of production. It has to obtain from somewhere the means for meeting the costs of those responsibilities it has taken over. For reasons easy to understand, the legislative bodies are very willing to distribute welfare, but naturally they shy away when it comes to covering the costs. Experience to date shows that one way of escaping this is through inflation. In the opinion of some authoritative writers, inflation is built into the mechanism of a pluralistic policy and into the compromises which associations arrange, whether in the form of "low fire inflation" (Röpke) or as an accepted necessity for economic growth (Slichter). The institutional attraction of inbuilt inflation is also unmistakably evident in the fact that conflicts between associations are easier to resolve when inflationary trends exist than when prices and exchange rates are stable.

Responsibility for dependents used to bear too heavily on individuals, who have now been relieved by transferring much of it to their associations, which follow suit by largely transferring it to the state, which turns it back again by way of taxes or credit expansion. These processes of transfer back and forth are only partly deliberate and planned; the rest is happening out of necessity. In either case the incidence of the responsibility is largely unrecognized, if not anonymous, for there are temporary bearers of it who later transfer it to others or return it back whence it came. The responsibility may partially devolve upon anyone.

Thus, responsibility for the welfare of every possible kind of social group is largely split up and scattered. It is true that welfare taxation appears as one of the visible bearers of the responsibility, as do all the agents of monetary and credit policy, but they are no more than interim agents for the purpose. The anonymity of responsibility is a consequence not only of shifts in power relationships and of fortuitous transfers back and forth, but also results from the dynamics of the economic process itself. Often a particular group may not even know what consequences have ensued from its own handling of a matter, because these consequences may not be immediate, and they may not affect the group itself. They may have repercussions in any direction. Who is in a position to affirm with cer-

tainty just where protective duties, price increases, wage increases and reduction of working hours will ultimately hit? The pluralistic groups do not have to think about the general welfare; they are not founded for that purpose, they look after their own interests over periods of time that are relatively short because from their own points of view, prices, wages, interest rates and conditions of sale are their short-run problems. The range between the short and the long-term is perhaps the most questionable aspect of modern laissez faire pluralism because by far the most extensive components of society are the strata that calculate and think in the short-term. The reasons for this are easy to understand, for it is inevitable that the associations to which they belong should be preoccupied with short-term policies.

Here the danger increases in proportion to the belief that, partly through applied science, progress must inevitably continue to open up wider horizons and scope for better and more secure living. Knowledge or intuition of the tragic side of human and social life is all too easily lost when the *carpe diem* sentiment of individuals, of groups or of society itself becomes the predominant ethos. "The man in the street does not notice the devil even when the devil is holding him by the throat" (Goethe).

THE SHIFTING pattern of the pluralistic and of their repercussions on the welfare state provide so many points for attack on the general welfare, ethically submarginal thrusts and practices, that warnings of responsibility remain unheard even by those who would gladly hear them. This explains how it is that leaders of groups, even some whose personal integrity is beyond any doubt, are apt to display almost incredible moral laxity when they are representing organized interests. National socialism and communism are not alone in having supplied shocking examples of this prostitution of private by institutional morality. It seems, indeed, that in a direct proportion, as personal values become absorbed and dominated by the collectivities, there is a general tendency for private ethics to decay and be replaced by ideological empire building. And when this happens, who is to be blamed? Under such conditions it is only to be expected that the private ethos, threatened and overwrought, will be tempted to identify itself with the collective ethos. That is understandable; and so, likewise, is the seizing of opportunities to creep in underneath the collective ethos.

It is well known that all totalitarian systems, whatever particular form they take, suffer from a proliferation of illegal actions and private greed even though it has to be clandestine. The basic falsity of collectivism in its relationship to people and things collides head-on with the reality of human nature; and if people are prevented from rebelling openly they will do so illegally by way of black markets, racketeering, information, etc. *The immorality inherent in forced collectivism is the acid that disintegrates the personal conscience.*

When it happens that a special kind of collective ethos takes shape alongside and competing with the private ethos, the question arises what form and features it actually has. In considering this, we are led to perceive, it is precisely in the pluralistic phase of society that the term "social" has come into use as the designation of something which has now acquired the status of a dominant ethos. Now that the "social" evaluation outweighs any other, nobody can avoid being "social." The employer obviously cannot; neither can the state, public opinion, or the private household; still less can any kind of association do so. But what does "social" actually mean? In the nineteenth century there was no problem: The "social question" was taken to mean simply the "labour question." Beyond this there was no occasion to ask what it meant until the beginning of recourse to the state as guarantor of social demands, which gave rise to the ideas of a "social state." A lively controversy then ensued which has instigated some very valuable critical analyses. The popular saying that "social" means to get something for nothing describes it more graphically than any academic statement.

THE CONCEPT denoted by "social" was examined by Hayek (*Was ist und was heisst Sozial?* In: *Masse und Demokratie*, edited by Albert Humid, 1957, Zürich). Hayek appositely draws a distinction in scope between "the social" and "the moral." Ethical principles, he says, are not the result of discoveries but are the outcome from a process of growth and selection whereby experience begets discernment. Moral propositions "have acquired their authority through having proved more successful than other propositions, having stood the test better within the groups of people to whom they applied." His definition of "social" is a very precise one: The requirement that we should behave in a social manner involves, he says, "consciously taking account of very remote consequences for our actions and basing our decisions on knowledge of the particular consequences likely to ensue from them" (75).

During the last few decades, however, the word "social" has come to be used ever more frequently in the place of "moral," or even in the place simply of "good." In compound expressions it nowadays retains little connection with the special characteristics of social forces; in particular, the contrast previously drawn between evolved structures and ad hoc organizations has completely disappeared. Hayek did not deal with the question of why the ambiguous word "society" has come to be preferred to the concrete designations "people," "nation," or "citizens," although obviously it relates to the last mentioned. "The important point, as I see it, is that all these uses of the word 'social' imply that actions are performed with common and known aims but what those aims are is never stated" (79). "Thus, the obligation to behave socially loses its force because it undermines the rules of simple morality which are its own foundation" (78).

The primacy of the social ideal as a dominant ethos is anti-moral; its prevalence erodes the feeling of individual responsibility. "True social service does not consist of exercising authority or leadership, not even of sharing in a common effort directed towards a common goal. It consists of contributing to the general good which is greater than ourselves and which is able continuously to bring forth new benefits within a free environment." (84). "Dominance by the social ethos is something to be fought against, because it weakens those forces that in actual fact promote the improvement of society. In this sense, much of what nowadays purports to be socially positive appears to me as anti-social in the deeper and truer sense of the word" (84).

THE SUPREMACY of the social ethos raises the question of how far it satisfies the needs of a dynamic economy; for the essence of what is "social" is not something that can drift freely about in economic space: It remains subject to economic preconditions insofar as it gives rise to costs. Or should this be put the other way around, by regarding what is "economic" as a dependent variable of what is "social?" As long as the social problem was identified with the labor question and treated accordingly—as it happened in the nineteenth century and continued into the beginnings of the twentieth—it enjoyed no higher status than that of a special problem encountered by governments and parties. The limits to the possible solution of the problem were clearly staked out by phases of liberalism, especially those of liberal capitalism. Since then, "social" has changed from designating a special case to designating the general case and the position has become such that many authors define the problem as being one of socio-political concern.

Professor H. Achinger thinks he has solved the hitherto baffling puzzle of what the word "social" in popular use is intended to mean—the solution being found quite simply in a resigned acknowledgment that "social is what social bureaucracies say it means" (*Sozialer Sicherheit*, Stuttgart 1953, 58 ff.). We have reached a point where the social apparatus is itself the embodiment of social advancement and determines its direction (Achinger, *Sozialer Fortschritt*, No. 10, October, 1959). He refers to what Alva Myrdal has called the "new era" in which every one of us will subject himself to the system and depend on it for his security from the cradle to the grave; social policy having risen in status from being the servant of society to being responsible for it; from being no longer merely an agency for rectifying undesirable conditions of life but the power that determines them. Here Mrs. Myrdal's assumption seems to be that if a social security system is given precedence and authority over the economic process it can be conducive to harmony and agreement. But the epitome of "the social" as now displayed to us is in no position to offer itself as an economically rational, independent system. To justify calling it a system, its elements and modes would need to be assembled in accordance with some controlling principle in order to form a logically coherent whole, but without surrendering their separate identities.

EVERYONE MUST surely agree that the "social idea" as now presented lacks any sort of claim to be regarded as a system. It is in fact no more than a haphazard growth of miscellaneous institutions and measures, influenced by historical accidents and resulting in a pattern which is as full of internal contradictions as of economic and social irrationalities. Its officialdom suffers from institutional rigidities and interdepartmental jealousies engendered by vested interests in functions and powers, and its implementation supplies us with a classic example of Parkinson's Law promoting bureaucratic parthenogenesis. None of this amounts to a denial that present-day social policies and institutions also have positive features, such features certainly exist, but their effects are far below the optimum in nation to their cost. Moreover, they provoke to a certain extent the seeds of diseconomies and injustice. Whatever Gunnar and Alva Myrdal may say, this is true even in Sweden.

Why in fact has the ethos described by the adjective "social" become the dominant one? As a concept it was unknown both in classical antiquity and in the Middle Ages, as—by the way—was the concept corresponding to the modern term "society." In both those eras the centers around which thought revolved were the *polis* and the *res publica*, what we call "social order" being taken for grant-ed as something sacred which existed in obedience to natural law, something hierarchical, founded upon reverence (*pietas*) and righteousness (*dike*). The idea that society is open-ended and pliable did not occur either in classical or medieval times. There were, indeed, reforms attempted such as Solon's *seisachteia* in Athens and the land reform by the Gracchi in Rome; another example is the exodus of the Roman plebs (*secessio in montem sacrum*), but all such movements either postulated or endeavored to discern the existence of an objective order supported by a framework of rules. The urge towards *dike*, towards *jus et justitia*, was felt permanently; the urge to create a "new order," to bring about a "revolution," was not felt at all.

IN THE late nineteenth century and well into the twentieth, the "social" meant a different sort of picture. Its origins may be recognized in the fragmentation of the Christian tradition and in that of liberalism as a worldview and equally so of collectivism. Today, "the social" signifies a compromise between liberal capitalism and revisionist collectivism; in an age which has lost what Eric Voegelin called the "gnosis of salvation" it represents a pragmatic equation for the loss of hope in the transcendent. "The social" is in fact the designation of what remains as the terminal moraine of the nineteenth century: liberalism and socialism. Nowadays it has become accepted as the current coin even though no definite standard exists for its purchasing power.

"The social" is a category *sui generis* which belongs under the heading of what Toennies described as "society," using that word in its precise sense. It is not personal but functional. The political environment in which it arises is that of egalitarian democracy, pragmatically inclined. Pragmatic democracy and laissez faire pluralistic society correspond with and qualify one another.

We recall Goethe's saying: "Edel sei der Mensch, hilfreich und gut"—"O that man be noble, helpful and good." Can this be shortened to "O that man be social?" Linguistically, such a phrase rings hollow and is pointless. No child would describe its father as being "social." Nor would that word be used by workers referring to a patriarchal or good employer; they might consider him a good or bad master, but not as being a "social" one. There is obviously no logical connection between being "noble, helpful and good," and being "social." It may be granted that the quality denoted by "social" has some sort of moral root and there may be a transition; but in present circumstances what matters is that to be "social" does not mean the same thing, save by accident, as being "noble, helpful and good." Goethe's saying applies at the personal level: "social" applies in contexts that are functional and impersonal. From the standpoint implicit in the use of the word "social," human beings are not primarily persons, but rather individuals characterized by the fact that he or she happens to belong to some particular collective category—the fact that he or she is one of the workers, one of the aged, one of the sick, one of the accidentally injured, one of the unemployed, one of the expectant mothers, etc. Here too runs the dividing line between being "social" or being "charitable."

ON ONE side of that line benevolent helpfulness is extended to persons each of whom is recognized as a particular, irreplaceable entity. On the other side, certain sums of money are set aside by firms or by the state through its welfare agencies for "social purposes," against which individuals have claims arising from the circumstance that they belong to certain designated groups—claims which they are entitled to make repeatedly, as of right, even if the grants in question are of a free and private nature (such as Christmas bonuses, tea or coffee breaks). The depersonalizing of relations that occurs in an associatively organized society is nowhere more clearly highlighted than in the devaluation of private acts of kindness from man to man. In this context acts of charity no longer fall into the same category as arrangements for promoting assistance and welfare.

If something helpful is performed with even a minimal degree of regularity it is thereby recategorised as "social," in the sense that its beneficiaries are regarded as having acquired a right or claim to it. This tendency is reinforced by the interest of the association concerned which feels that private acts of welfare threaten its corporate integrity or even the loyalty of its members. The effect is that interpersonal relations, and to a great extent charity, goodness, trust, even normal respect between persons, mutual obligation, and helpfulness by man to man, yield precedence and significance to the promotion of what is "social" as an entitlement.

Here lies the profoundest reason for that undermining of the foundations on which all human society rests, that erosion of its common values, so often deplored. In the long run this will shatter also the validity and meaning of "the social," which ultimately also is dependent on values and virtues fostered and cultivated by directly interpersonal relationships (Max Scheler, *Formalism in Ethics and Material Value Ethics*, Halle, 1916).

Ernest van den Haag

Justice and the Market: The Present System

VOL. 10, NO. 1, 1975

The Present System

The economic system produces the pie which makes moral justice possible; the market system produces more of it, by far, than any other. By producing the pie, the economic system necessarily produces the moral problem of just distribution as well. Distributive justice concerns apportionment of the pie—a problem raised, and all too circumscribed, but not decided by producing the pie. No economic system as such can yield the moral justification required for its "distributive justice." Thus, no amount of production engendered by the incentives of the market could morally justify the income distribution linked to it. The incentives for production, which the market criteria for distribution of income create, are independent of distributive justice. In the words of Friedrich A. Hayek:

> [I]t is meaningless to describe the manner in which the market distributes the good things of this world among particular people as just or unjust. . . .[1]

Meaningless? Not quite. Irrelevant, yes. For the market provides incentives, not moral justice. These two are not the same (*pace* John Bates Clark, or Ayn Rand) unless the production of market value, economic merit, is simply defined as moral merit. Such a definition confuses the historical de facto (if you please, natural) conditions of generation—or of legal entitlement, or appropriation, or of actual possession—with their justification; it identifies what is to be justified with its moral justification. Even if historical conditions were shown to be not only advantageous but also unavoidable they would not, therefore, become just. But history, though never avoided, is never unavoidable.

Whatever independent definition of "moral desert" is chosen, it is certainly not to be identified with "economic desert"; wherefore, the morally and the economically justified distribution may differ as well as coincide. A sexy movie actress, a shrewd promoter, a successful manager, or advertising man, or inventor, or oil discoverer are not morally superior to a faithful nurse or worker, to a courageous lifesaver or veteran, to a needy child, a great poet, or philosopher. The former may earn much more for good enough economic reasons (what they offer has more market value), but not because they are regarded as morally more deserving than the latter who are less well paid. To argue otherwise, to regard the movie actress as necessarily more deserving than the nurse, is to identify the market value of the two activities with their moral value, or with that of the two persons. This identification of moral and economic desert does not express what ordinary people, or, for that matter, philosophers, mean by either.

It is because they do not identify moral and economic value that people wish to link them. For the fact that on the market the services of the morally less deserving can be more valuable economically than those of the more deserving outrages the sense of justice—although the very people outraged by it bring this result about by their willingness to pay more for the economically more valuable services; which is why those who render them get more, regardless of their moral desert. But people also want to change this result to make it reflect their sense of justice, at least in some degree.

Yet if only for the sake of efficiency, rewards must be distributed according to the market value of services. Critics, who have conflated their warranted moral objections to the moral injustice (better, the non-justice) of the market with objections to its efficiency in calling forth production, are surely wrong. A look at the alternatives is altogether persuasive here. Further, the socialist systems which aim directly at justice have not been notable so far for achieving more of it than market systems; and they certainly grant less, if any, freedom; they are also less efficient by far.[2]

If resources are to be allocated to produce the total output valued most highly by the allocators (in a free market, ultimately, consumers) and if production is to be maximized, inequalities of income, status, and power are unavoidable. Work must be rewarded by income, and the incomes earned by each worker must depend on how much work he does, on his skill, and on the value placed on it. Ability, skill, the inclination, and the opportunity to work differ—as does the economic value of the work done, and therefore, the reward. Market value depends on scarcity, on how much is available relative to demand. Scarcities differ.

So do, therefore, the incomes earned for performing services. Wherefore, the social structure—the distribution of inequalities—arises independently of any moral criteria used to judge it.

Functional requirements and institutionalized historical traditions determine what personal qualities will help individuals to attain or to keep the social positions which require or allow them to perform specific services and to earn the incomes associated with them. Some qualities may be ignored (e.g., physical size within the normal range); while others (e.g., intelligence, managerial ability, ruthlessness, knowledge, docility, experience, imagination, judgment, skin color, or family membership) are judged relevant to the attainment and to the retention of unequally rewarded positions. (Their relevance may be functional or traditional or both.) The qualities judged relevant are as unequally distributed among individuals as those which are not. Nature distributes its gifts unequally, granting more intelligence, health, ability, or beauty to some than to others. Ambitions differ, and so do the efforts individuals are willing to make to fulfill them. Society and chance, in turn, offer unequal opportunities to people to utilize their gifts and make efforts for advancement.

If legacies are neglected,[3] and if the acquisition of property *vita natural durante* is treated as a skill or opportunity, the size and the distribution of social inequalities (of status, power, and income) reflect unequal innate gifts, different inclinations, unequal social opportunities, chance, and, finally, different social rewards for the gifts granted by nature, the skills acquired, and the services performed. As Christopher Jencks[4] has lately demonstrated, inequalities of parental background or of educational opportunity play a very minor role in explaining the inequality of earnings in the U.S.— so minor that unknown factors (which Jencks summarizes as "luck") and talent seem responsible for most of it.

The Marxian Alternative

In Marx's time, origin—social class— played an overwhelming role in determining careers and earnings in Europe. It does not in the contemporary U.S. Still, could the Marxian scheme produce more justice in the U.S. if it were applied now? Would socialism, as a first step, at least reduce inequalities? Unlike many of his followers, Karl Marx did not rest his case on justice or equality. He thought those who did were moralistic Utopians, and he never ceased ridiculing their "verbal rubbish." Nonetheless, it is because Marx tried to tie together moral and economic merit in his elaboration of the ideas of the classical economists that Marxism appeals to so many people. He separated economic merit ("value") from price, and defined labor as the ultimate source of economic value. However, the definition is otiose: once economic value is separated from the actual market price, economic value can be no more than a metaphysical category, a synonym or disguise for moral value, which fails altogether to explain prices or distributions, and merely asserts a preference for redistribution. "Value" as defined by Marx attributes creation to workers (a quite arbitrary definitional imputation), and tells us that distribution is wrong (Marx would say contradictory). Marx strenuously denied the cryptomoral function of his definitions. He attempted to reduce moral to economic argument but succeeded only in collapsing the latter into the former.

Marx's socioeconomic determinism predicted and advocated a reorganization of production and a change in the role of workers to which justice would be incidental, since it "can never be higher than the economic structure of society," i.e., has no independent status. Yet side by side with his usual diatribes against idealistic rhetoric about justice, in his *Critique of the Gotha Program*, Marx explicitly adopts Louis Blanc's "from each according to his ability to each according to his needs" as an ideal of a higher Communist (post-socialist) social organization. It is an ideal of justice which rejects equal distribution (advocated by some socialists) and distribution according to merit (advocated by others). Indeed, the ideal rejects justice altogether in favor of charity. Its possibility rests on three propositions.

(1) The ability to exercise the right to buy and sell is unevenly distributed in a "capitalist" market system, owing to private ownership of the means of production. Proletarians, who have nothing to sell but their labor, become wage slaves.[5] Public ownership would free them; it would give them more and more equal power. They would have higher incomes and more to say about production and about their work.

Experience so far indicates that socialism is unlikely to bring about the desired equalization of the ability to exercise rights. Socialist societies with public ownership of means of production have not increased the freedom or power of workers. Nor their income. Workers actually are less free to bargain about wages and conditions with management than they are in capitalist societies. They are often less free to choose their work, and they are far more restricted by management identified with the government. One reason why they do not earn more, although public ownership eliminates private profits, is quite simple: even gross profits, under capitalism, are only a small percentage of payrolls. After deduction of what goes for taxes—nearly half in the U.S.—and for investment (which a socialist society would have to continue), there remains but the excess consumption expenditure (above the average) of profit recipients. Where it is not needed as an incentive, it would be available for redistribution. But the amount available would be too insignificant to make any difference to the great mass of workers or low-income recipients. As for the inequalities of power linked to private ownership, they actually would be likely to increase with a public monopoly of means of production. Power holders would be government officials rather than private individuals—but they would probably have more rather than less power.

(2) Marx generously mistook innate differences in ability for differences in acquired skills which he attributed to unequal opportunities. However evidence since accumulated shows convincingly that many differences of ability and talent are inborn. (Ability, or its utilization, seems also to depend on infantile environments. But these too are nearly impossible to equalize.) Because abilities differ, equalization of the opportunity to acquire skills could only redistribute social inequalities in accordance with innate or quasi-innate differences. This might slightly increase efficiency, but it would not reduce inequalities.[6]

(3) One might try to distribute income without regard to abilities or market values. Marx believed that a Communist society ultimately would not have to reward services according to their economic (labor, or scarcity) value. He thought that those who render services, as well as those who do not, could—at least ultimately—receive incomes according to their needs. But it seems unlikely that distribution according to need (however defined and determined) could maximize the quantity and optimize the quality of production. Even a highly ascetic society, however technologically advanced, is unlikely to he satisfied by the production called forth without direct economic incentives.

Yet economic incentives necessarily lead to an unequal distribution in accordance not with need, but with market value. The moral criterion of need is independent of distributive incentives. It would separate monetary reward from allocation and from performance. Non-monetary rewards would be required to spur both. But none have come into view to effectively replace the monetary incentives now used in all industrial societies. Kibbutzim and communes have tried to do without, and in some cases they have succeeded. But only when the membership is small, homogenous, and bound together by a common ideology. Except in temporary states of exaltation, these conditions could not be reproduced in large societies—not even with an enforced totalitarian ideology. The Chinese are about to painfully learn as much.

Regardless of moral advantages or disadvantages, neither altruism nor compulsion appears an efficient enough alternative to economic incentives—despite marginal or occasional success. To be sure, if people were different, a different system could work. This frequent objection is not entitled to be taken seriously as long as no serious grounds are advanced to believe either that the future will offer effortless abundance, so that all goods could be free, like air (or at least like air was at one time), or that people in the future will be different enough to give efforts freely, independently of rewards.

The Resentment of Intellectuals

Intellectuals and moralists all too often volubly resent the market, because through it people pay for *economic*, as though indifferent to *moral* value, which is left out in the cold; worse, *they* are. Since they do not feel at home in the market, intellectuals have designed socioeconomic organizations which would reward moral rather than economic values. But they are unlikely to succeed—although it is easy to mobilize dissatisfaction with market distribution. However, once the impersonal criterion of economic distribution by the market is abolished, it must be replaced by political (government) distribution. Political distribution is most likely to reward political and, perhaps, managerial services, since it depends on political power, which is as independent of moral desert as the market is. We might be stuck with a distribution felt to be morally as irrelevant and arbitrary as that of the market, but which leaves us all poorer by providing more incentives for political than for economic services.

And less free. For the government can distribute income effectively only if it deprives individuals (or groups: corporations) of the right to produce and sell what buyers are willing to pay for. What is to be produced would depend upon government planners and, therefore, would be likely to serve them rather than consumers. Unable to choose what to produce or sell, at what price, and what to buy, we would have lost one aspect of freedom. To keep us bereft of it, the government would have to deprive us of political freedom (civil rights) as well; as sole producer and employer, it would find it easy to do so. Shorn of all institutional defense, individual liberty could not long survive.

The Task Before Us

It is fairly clear, then, that Marx and many others who resent the market would lead or push us from the frying pan into the fire. Yet, although the fire is certain to be worse, the frying pan is still an uncomfortable place. No social system can endure unless people think it just and not merely efficient. And however much philosophers disagree, the popular sense of justice now demands further reduction, if not of wealth, at least of poverty. Because it does not satisfy the sense of justice, our economic system has already lost, if not its usefulness, its moral authority.

If the sense of justice, of morality, cannot be satisfied through the market—and it cannot—it must be satisfied independently, for unless justice is served elsewhere in the social system, the market cannot last. Hence the distributive incentives, which necessarily lead to social inequalities, must be reconciled with whatever moral objections to these inequalities are accepted. Such a reconciliation cannot ignore or assume away (as Marx did) what is to be reconciled to morality: the need for economic incentives leading to inequality based on non-moral criteria. Else social analysis is replaced by eschatological speculation. But moral sentiments cannot be ignored either.

Can sufficient redistribution occur, then, independently of the market to satisfy the sense of justice? Can such a redistribution obviate poverty without impairing the market which it must supplement? The answer now seems obvious: it is possible to supplement the market through fiscal measures so that without impairing incentives we can provide for those left miserable by nature, society, or misfortune. One can argue about how much should and can be done, and by what means. But not about our ability to supplement market distribution with some degree of redistribution—or about the need to do so.

Notes

1. *The Constitution of Liberty.* F. H. Knight held the same view.

2. "Socialist systems" here excludes China, about which little is known at this time.

3. Legacies now are the main source of income for only one family in a thousand. If they were socialized instead of enriching the few people who now receive them, the amounts available for redistribution (after appropriate deductions for what now goes into taxes or reinvestment) could not significantly alter the inequalities of income affecting 999 out of 1000 families.

4. *Inequality: A Reassessment of Family and Schooling in America,* (Basic Books, New York, 1972).

5. For the relation between rights and ability to exercise them, see my *Political Violence & Civil Disobedience* (Harper Torchbooks, New York, 1972).

6. Jencks (op. cit.) has shown that unequal educational opportunity plays an insignificant role in explaining income differences.

Paul Craig Roberts

The Political Economy of Bureaucratic Imperialism

VOL. 12, NO. 1, 1976

A person born before the turn of the century was born a private individual. He was born into a world in which his existence was attested by his mere physical presence, without documents, forms, permits, licenses, orders, lists of currency carried in and out, identity cards, draft cards, ration cards, exit stamps, customs declarations, questionnaires, tax forms, reports in multuplicate, social security number, or other authentications of his being, birth, nationality, status, beliefs, creed, right to be, enter, leave, move about, work, trade, purchase, dwell.

He was born into a world in which a person could travel anywhere on the face of the earth, excepting Russia and Turkey, without need of a passport, visa, or identity card. He was born into a world of freedom of movement of people, money, and ideas. A confident nineteenth-century futurology predicted that the twentieth century would find him freer still.

But by the time of the First World War, the world into which he was born was on its way out. And the period since has been one of the growing autonomy, not of the individual, but of the state. He was born in a century that pulled down walls and lived out his life in the century of the wall builders. Twentieth-century walls, whether made from iron, or barbed wire, mine fields, and machine-gun towers, or from paper—the barbed wire of documents—twentieth-century walls are by-products of the universal bureaucratization of life. In place of the nineteenth century's autonomous individual, to whom some romantics romanticized all things were permitted, we have the twentieth century's autonomous state to which, as Dostoevsky predicted and Lenin declared, all things _are_ permitted.

The private individual is an extremely recent and precarious invention. A central question of our century is whether he is a mere momentary caprice of history.

Many people take private individuals for granted, and they will find what I am saying farfetched. But private individuals do not exist in the Soviet Union or in China where the claims of the state are total and even art and literature must be subservient to the interests of the state— as the recent expulsion of Solzhenitsyn reluctantly reminds the wistful hopes of a weakened West. Neither do private individuals exist in many of the emerging nations where change consists only of replacing the subordination of the person to tribe or caste with subordination to the modern activist state.

But my topic is not one of communism versus democracy. My argument does not turn on the form of political system but on the self-interest of bureaucrats and their beneficiaries and allies, whatever the form of the political system.

Just as private individuals do not exist today in the Soviet Union or in China, they did not exist in ancient Egypt. Nor were they prevalent in the Europe of the Middle Ages. Private individuals were the creation of the social revolution that created private property.

I do not use the term social revolution lightly, as do academic sociologists who find a social revolution every time students change their hair styles or sex habits. I am speaking of a social revolution which, along with the reaction to it, comprises the social, economic, political, and intellectual history of Western civilization from the twelfth century through the present.

The Rise and Fall of the Private Individual

The Social Revolution through which private individuals were created hand-in-hand with the creation of private property began with the Inclosures in the twelfth century and attained its greatest flowering in the nineteenth century. Prior to the appearance of private property, private individuals did not exist. There existed only the rulers and the ruled, lords and serfs.

A serf was a person who did not own his own labor. Although he was not himself owned by another, that is, he could not be bought and sold like a slave, the feudal nobility, the state of that time, had rights over the serf's labor. When we say that a peasant was enserfed, we mean that he owed a certain amount of his working time to the state. Over time and regions this obligation seems to have averaged about one-third of a serf's working life.

In turn the serf had use-rights in the land. The same social revolution which abolished the serf's use-rights in the land abolished the state's use-rights in the serf's labor. The same social revolution which created private property in land and capital created private property in labor. Serfdom disappeared as wages appeared. As Karl Marx recognized, "Wages and private property are identical."

Reaction to this great social revolution began with it, and over most of the course of this revolution, reaction was identified with conservatism. But what was really happening was that as different groups—landowners, merchants, capitalists, and laborers—attained specific private property rights—in land, trade, capital, and labor—each group had an incentive to gain control of the state as a means of advancing its specific property rights at the expense of others. A "reactionary" was merely whoever had control of the state at a point in time and was defending his interest against the interests of others. As different groups in different times gained control of the state, each in turn passed from the offensive to the defensive and were automatically turned into conservatives, which meant they wanted to conserve their interests. But no group trusted the state as such. No group felt its property rights secure unless it controlled the state. Each identified progress with the advancement of its property rights.

Historians have often confused this strife between different property interests with an alleged reaction of property against democracy. But whichever property group was in power, it would tend to see democracy as the right of others to vote away its property. Democracy was thus confined to voting by members of the group whose property interest was dominant. This greatly limited the power of government because any claim to act in the public interest was quickly recognized for what it was.

Although each property group had an accurate assessment of the threat of government to its interests, each group mistakenly saw its interests as divergent from the interests of others, and each preferred to unite with government against the property interests of others. However, in spite of the strife among its beneficiaries, the social revolution of private property was inexorable, and the real reactionaries were swept aside.

But the revolution was never quite completed. Just as the various property groups began to realize, under the influence of Adam Smith and others, their common interests and to unite against government per se, the greatest reactionary of them all, Karl Marx, appeared and began a new counter-attack against the on-going social revolution. Like some of the earlier reactionaries, Marx knew exactly what he was reacting to. He was reacting to private individuals. According to Marx, man is only individualized through the creation of private property: "Man originally appears as a generic being, a tribal being, a herd animal." Private property "makes the herd animal superfluous and dissolves the herd."

Marx's counter-attack was a work of genius. According to Marx, the private individual is rootless, powerless, alienated, and unfree. He only appears to be free, but as an individual actor he must bear the consequences of his own action; yet as an individual actor he has no control over his life because he is affected by, but

has no control over, the actions of others. Thus, the divergent actions of private individuals produce consequences beyond the control of all, and a private individual is the victim of his own individuality.

Marx's solution is to do away with the private individual and return to the herd animal. Herd animals do not act as individuals and therefore they do not have to bear uncontrolled consequences of private actions. Instead they act as a community, or the state acts for the community. Marx's genius launched the career of a new class of professional rulers—the bureaucrats. In the Soviet Union and China this class is known as the Communist Party and in the United States and Europe it is known as the civil service.

As Marx and his followers translated his esoteric argument for the masses, it came out: "It is not government that exploits, but private property." To Lenin, to Mussolini, to Hitler, to European socialists and statists of all hues and colors, and to their counterparts in the United States who go under the name of liberals—a curious perversion of a name that originally designated one who stood for the interests of private property against the interests of the state—to all of these this meant that progress could be realized only through government. The strife this century between the various statists has overshadowed their common agreement that government action is the instrument of progress.

My liberal acquaintances are generally proud of what they see as the progressive nature of their view that government is the instrument of social progress. It is unknown to them that they share this view with the great reactionaries of history. My liberal acquaintances become annoyed when I quote from Mussolini and from Camelot liberals on the state as the instrument of social progress, and they find that they cannot tell them apart. But I generally lose their friendship when I point out that Alexander Herzen published an open letter to Tsar Alexander of Russia in 1857 protesting the Tsar's idea that government action is the instrument of progress.

Many people are not aware of the extent of bureaucratic involvement in private life. Usually I find that people, whether my students, my academic colleagues, or my mailman, see themselves under the thumb of big business and multinational corporations. They generally look to government for protection, which means that each wants government to overrule any private action that each does not see in his interest. Government, of course, is anxious to oblige because in this way it gains power over all private actions. Let me give two recent examples which have left even some statist liberals shaken.

A female student at the University of Georgia failed in her efforts to be chosen by her fellow students as sports editor of the student newspaper. In petty spite she filed a discrimination complaint with HEW, and this cabinet-level agency quickly involved the United States government in the matter of the students' selection of the sports editor of their newspaper.

U.S. District Judge Wilbur Owens instructed the Board of Regents of the University System of Georgia to use involuntary transfers of faculty members between system institutions to achieve racial balance among the faculties. As long as the involuntary transfers of teachers was infra-city and confined to elementary and high school teachers, my liberal colleagues saw it as social progress. But once they faced inter-city involuntary transfers, they called it fascism. It is true that until the liberal progress of the 1960s, government direction of labor in this cen-

tury was unique to the Hitler and Stalin regimes. As is often the case, people realize the consequences of statist ideas only when their own private individualities are touched.

But examples such as these are unlimited and many are so horrific that they are unbelievable until they touch us individually. Let me instead sum up the success of the reactionary forces in this century in simple economic terms. At the turn of the century government in the U.S. had a claim to only one-eighth of the national income. By 1970 government had a claim to one-third of the national income. In relative terms our position is no different from that of a medieval serf who owed the state one-third of his working time.

Serfdom and the Bureaucratic State

It is true that the statists owe their success partly to technological change which raised national income through time. If people are better off in absolute terms, they may not notice that they are worse off in relative terms. But statists mainly owe their success to the power of reaction in the twentieth century. It is striking that it has required little more than a half century to reverse a social revolution that had been on-going since the twelfth century. When you hear a liberal say that you cannot repeal the twentieth century, all he is saying is that in the twentieth century statist reactionaries have repealed the nineteenth and eighteenth centuries and have us on our way to re-enserfment.

Many may reject this parallel. They may say that we have a democratic government controlled by the people, and that high taxes and big government merely reflect the voters' demands for public goods in the public interest. Such an argument is reassuring but problematical. The income tax was voted in under one guise and retained under another. Furthermore, it was the action of a past generation. For us it is an inherited obligation, as were feudal dues, and it is seen that way by the Internal Revenue Service. All of us have been born to the statist gospels. Any clamors for tax reduction are translated into proposals for tax reform, which are further transformed into proposals for securing more revenues for government.

The public interest remains what it has always been—the interest of those who speak in the name of the public. Few who understand the workings of democracy, or any form of government, will claim that a public interest can prevail over divergent special interests. Individual citizens find that their time is spent in going about their jobs and ordinary affairs. The cost is large to any single individual of organizing a constraint on bureaucratic power, and the gains to him are not clearly identifiable. He tends to hope it will be done by someone else because in that event he shares the benefits without incurring the costs.

But precisely because they do have special interests offering them identifiable gains, bureaucrats and their beneficiaries have incentives to enlarge the scope of government. Today legislation is originated by bureaucrats who unlike politicians are life peers and cannot be voted out of office.

Since the bureaucracy's position is the strongest, and since the benefits to its members of more government are large and easily identifiable, it is unlikely that a democracy offers the ruled any more control over the rulers than did feudal serfdom. In fact the medieval serf may have been in a stronger position than the ruled of today. The feudal state was constrained by custom and tradition, and the medieval serf was more intelligent than his twentieth-century counterpart. He would immediately see through any king or noble who might claim he was raising taxes in the public interest. This is the reason that the power of government in a kingdom is less than the power of government in a democracy. No king could claim to speak in the name of the people or to act in the public interest without arousing suspicion. The power of governments which historians cavalierly term autocratic was extremely small. No king ever had draft laws at his disposal. The universal draft originated with the democrats of the French Revolution and has ever since been a feature of democracy. Perhaps the only case in which the rulers can be controlled by the ruled is when government is small, and if government is small, its form is of little consequence.

Bureaucratic Undermining of the Market

Our founding fathers were products of the great social revolution of which I have spoken. As such, they believed that God had created people as private individuals and not as herd animals. Not trusting governments with God's handiwork, they attempted to design a political system that would preserve the private individual against the self-interest of government. But any viable federalism as a means of checking the power of government was destroyed by the Civil War. Since that time bureaucratic power has been limited only by an on-going market system. To the extent that markets work, there is no need of government. Once this was realized by bureaucrats and their allies, they saw their vested interests in arguments that markets do *not* work and in policies assuring that indeed they did not work. The Great Depression launched their battle to beat back the constraint that a market system placed on bureaucratic power. All of economic and social policy and the predominant economic and social theory since that time can be explained in these terms.

This is a new explanation of social and economic theory and policy, and it may be difficult for people born to statists gospels to follow. After all, it is taught in every college and university in the country, and it is printed in virtually every economics textbook, that government economic policy is conducted in the public interest to achieve economic stability, to prevent recessions and inflations, to protect the public from monopolies and from unemployment and eroding purchasing power. It is true that many have noticed that the record of government social and economic policy is one of dismal failure, but the general conclusion has merely been that bureaucrats make errors like anyone else and lack sufficient power, that better minds are needed in positions of more power.

Such a conclusion is possible only if the assumption is that bureaucrats attempt to act in the public interest and merely fail. But if we assume that bureaucrats act in their own interest, as do other groups and individuals, public failures are transformed into bureaucratic successes.

Some people are sufficiently sophisticated to notice that bureaucrats are quick to use every opportunity to feather their nests and enlarge their budgets and powers. But I am saying more. I am saying that there is no coincidence whatsoever between the interest of bureaucrats and the public interest. I am saying that government social and economic policy is the tool of bureaucrats for self-aggrandizement and is inimical to the public interest.

Before we had activist government economic policy, we had small government and lots of little ups and downs called the business cycle. These ups and downs were used as an excuse for an activist government economic policy to smooth them out and replace the business cycle with uniform stability. With activist economic policy not only came big government but the worst long-term depression and inflation in our history, that is, chronic economic instability. Many people have puzzled why the Federal Reserve and the Treasury always do the wrong things— even when they are run by Milton Friedman's teachers and colleagues.

But the trouble with this way of puzzling over the matter is that it assumes the bureaucracy has an interest in economic stability. Whereas any given president has an interest in economic stability for the period of his re-election campaign, no one else in government has an interest in economic stability. Put simply, economic stability does not increase the demand for bureaucrats and their services, or for pork-barrel legislation to deal with the consequences of instability.

It is easy for government to cause economic instability, and it can always rely on its allies among the liberal academics to blame the instability that government causes on the private sector. All government needs to do is intervene in markets and disrupt them, or shrink the money supply, or increase the money supply faster than business and labor can produce goods. The resulting instability becomes the excuse for increases in government programs and in the supply and power of bureaucrats. If government wishes to take control over an industry and to facilitate the takeover by placing the industry in a bad light with the public, it can begin by causing inflation. Then on the grounds of fighting inflation, government can impose price controls and cause shortages. At this point its academic allies can begin alleging conspiracy among the businessmen. The result will be rationing and government determined production schedules, followed by a decline in profitability, subsidies, and then nationalization.

If government wishes to increase its share of the national income relative to the private sector, all it needs to do is cause inflation. Inflation allows government to increase its share of national income in three ways: (1) with the progressive income tax system, inflation drives people into higher tax brackets, thus increasing government's claim on their income and the government's relative share of national income, (2) the inflation that government causes can be blamed on excessive consumer spending, and an increase in taxation can masquerade as a scientific economic policy to fight inflation, and (3) through the inflation tax on money.

The reason all countries suffer inflation is not because it is not known how to prevent it, but because inflation increases the powers and incomes of governments.

The Academic Allies of the Bureaucratic State

My references to the academic allies of the bureaucracy may annoy some, although others may be proud of the connection. The subject of the academic alliance with the bureaucracy is an essay in itself. I have shown how economic policy since the Great Depression can be understood in terms of the bureaucracy's interest in inefficacious markets, that is, in markets that do not work. As I said, also, that economic theory itself could be understood in these same terms, I must now provide some argument in support.

Many believe the popular misconception that economists are class-biased lackeys of capitalists whose science is an ideology for the market, and they may even misinterpret what I am saying as evidence in support of this misconception. Indeed, many economists themselves prefer this misconception because it provides a disguise that conveniently masks whose lackeys they really are.

On the surface it may look like economists are not sufficiently relevant to be anyone's lackeys. Large expanses of modern economics are inscrutable even to many economists. But if one strips away the reified jargon and mathematical symbols and looks at what the economists who dominate the profession have been doing for the last forty years, one sees that they certainly have not been providing an ideology for the market. Rather, they have been providing a rationale for big government, whose handmaidens they are.

The two subjects which have dominated theoretical economics during this period are externalities and Keynesian macroeconomics. The externality literature is replete with the concepts of "market failure" and "social costs." The purpose of this literature is to discredit the efficacy of the market on a microeconomic level. The Keynesian literature is replete with unemployment equilibrium. The purpose of this literature is to discredit the efficacy of private saving and investment decisions and the market on a macroeconomic level. The justification of big government as scientific economic policy is precisely the purpose of the most famous diagram in postwar economics—the "Keynesian cross"—a diagram that is familiar to every student who has had an economics course during the last quarter century. This diagram is devoid of economic content and is solely a propagandistic rationale for the efficacy of big government.

It does not surprise me that economists fashion their theories to serve the interest of the state rather than the interests of private enterprise. After all, it is in their self-interest. Private enterprise does not provide the research grants that are the bread and butter of the influential social scientists. These grants come from the National Science Foundation, the National Endowment for the Humanities, the U.S. Department of Health, Education and Welfare, the U.S. Department of Labor, and so forth. Neither can private enterprise provide the positions of power which academics enjoy as cabinet ministers and presidential advisors. Any social scientist who can discover a social problem that can be parlayed into a new federal program is set for life.

The conspiracy of bureaucrats and their alliance with academia is unwittingly protected by the naive worldview of liberals who believe that all good follows from public actions and all evil from private actions. The liberal is the easy dupe of the bureaucrat because the liberal's outlook is highly simplified: On the one hand he sees the public interest, identified with government, self-evident and beyond questioning by any upright person; on the other hand he sees private interests, selfish, sinister, and illegitimate. As a result of the pervasiveness of this outlook, the public learns in schools, colleges, universities, and from the news media to be suspicious of the private businessman and to look with favor upon government interventions as acts in the public interest. I expect that the informal inculcation of this attitude will soon become official educational policy in the U.S., just as it is today in Sweden—a country totally ruled by bureaucracy.

The Bureaucratic State in Sweden and West Africa

This conspiracy and alliance is far from being unique to the U.S. and can be found in most every country. I will conclude with remarks on its manifestations in Sweden and in West Africa.

In Sweden the "new left" is subsidized by the bureaucracy to discover social imperfections, because each imperfection justifies an increase in state power to correct the imperfection. The Swedish "new left" may have convinced itself that it is revolutionary, but in fact it is either an agent or a dupe of the bureaucratic state.

The imperialistic rule of the Swedish bureaucracy has been established since the late eighteenth century when King Gustaf III, under the influence of the French Enlightenment, toyed with the idea of a nation of private individuals and was promptly assassinated by his bureaucracy, which felt its prerogatives threatened. The imperialistic rule of the Swedish bureaucracy is the standard to which our own aspires. But it is in the lands that most shrilly accuse the West of imperialism that the imperialistic nature of indigenous bureaucracy stands out most starkly. The voluminous writings about imperialism are just another mask behind which hide the real imperialists. Let me strip away the mask.

In some nations of West Africa there are state export monopolies, or marketing boards as they are officially described, that extend their control over practically all agricultural products. These boards were set up ostensibly to stabilize the prices received by private farmers. African farmers, if they wish to sell their crops, must sell to the state marketing boards at prices set by the boards. The boards in turn sell the crops on the world market. The original idea supposedly was that during years of high world market prices, the boards would hold back part of the proceeds from the producers in order to provide a reserve for years when world market prices were low. In this way incomes were to be stabilized.

When these state monopolies were introduced, categorical, formal, official assurances were given that the marketing boards would serve as trustees and agents for the private producers and that no money would be withheld overall from the farmers. In the words of the supporters of the marketing monopolies:

> There will be no question of the boards making a profit at the expense of West African producers. On the average of a period of years, the average price paid to the producers will be equal to the average net price realized on world markets, and the boards' buying and selling transactions will, therefore, approximately balance.

By 1962 the state marketing monopolies had withheld between one-third and one-half of the commercial values of their crops from the producers in Nigeria and Gold Coast-Ghana. The total sum withheld exceeded two billion dollars! The political changes and upheavals in Nigeria and Ghana in the 1960's stopped the publication of consistent statistical information on the operations of the marketing boards, but the evidence indicates that the state marketing monopolies continue to be the instrument of exploitation of those whom they were ostensibly set up to help. What was supposed to be state help to private producers has resulted in prolonged large-scale confiscation of their incomes.

What has become of this huge sum stolen from the poorest elements of the populations by their own governments? Some of it was lost in currency devaluations,

but much of it was transferred to cover current operating expenses of the governments. In effect, a productive sector of the population, whose money income is minuscule, has been kept poor by being taxed at rates equivalent to those levied on American annual incomes of $50,000 to $140,000! The consumption and investment of West African farmers have been throttled in order that civil servants and government officials can enjoy relatively high incomes.

This makes it clear why West African governments have been such vociferous consumers of the anti-Western imperialist diatribes that originate in the West. It is always in the interest of indigenous imperialists to support the argument that the country is exploited by foreigners.

Indigenous imperialism has been obscured by an assumption underlying the economic theory of public goods which asserts that governments act not in their own interests but in the interests of others—the "public interest." Economists who use the "public interest" assumption to analyze the state sector simultaneously assume that other organized groups and individuals act in their self-interest. This dichotomy in the economists' assumption about behavior protects indigenous imperialism under the mask of benevolence.

Such exploitation of agricultural export producers as has occurred in West Africa retards economic development. The lack of progress is then taken as evidence of the need for greater amounts of foreign aid. The government-to-government grants that characterize "foreign aid" allow the recipient governments to consolidate and extend their control over their citizenry. The situation is made even worse by the fact that many of the African government leaders have been products of Western universities and have little sympathy for the culture of those they govern.

The real beneficiaries of foreign aid are the international organizations, those who control political power in the recipient countries, those who staff the foreign aid agencies of the giving countries, and the Western professors who advise on economic development schemes. I once served in a state university as the academic replacement for a professor who had just purchased a $60,000 home and gone on an AID mission to India for two years. His pay for his mission to the poor was $30,000 per year plus expenses, and it allowed him to pay off his mortgage on his return. One of his colleagues had gone on a similar mission to South America and bragged to me that he had "salted away $30,000." Such "missions" which let academics save at annual rates of up to twice their normal incomes explain the great popularity among professors of foreign aid and all arguments that justify it. He who hasn't got' his yet can hope to in the future. Western taxpayers who are assuaging "guilt" for the poverty of underdeveloped countries are fattening the pocketbooks of others, but the others are not the exploited farmers of West Africa.

It is clear that the state marketing monopolies are supported not by the producers whose incomes they confiscate, but by officials of governments and international organizations and their academic handmaidens. As the boards came to accumulate huge reserves by exploiting the farmers, price stabilization gradually receded as the argument for their existence. Now it is laid that the boards are necessary to raise taxes to finance economic development and to control inflation. In other words, the agricultural producers are going to be imperialized to the end.

The rationale for the marketing boards is clear. They are one more result of the cult of state power which serves the material interests of a new class of planners, academics, state functionaries, and international civil servants—a class which appropriates the wealth of others under the guise of the "public interest." These salaried do-gooders are the new imperialists.

Conclusion

I hope what I have said will be interpreted as a call to arms and not as a counsel of despair. There are still some intellectually honest men and women. Within the limits of their talents they can do much. Those who cannot be bought can analyze the lack of coincidence between the public interest and the interest of government. They can strip away the various moral guises behind which hides the self-interest of government and leave the statists unmasked, naked in their greed.

We can learn to apply the logic of skepticism universally, and not just toward the private sector. When John Kenneth Galbraith, Ralph Nader, Common Cause, and the Secretary of HEW claim to speak in the public interest, we can be just as suspicious as we would be if the presidents of General Motors and U.S. Steel claimed to speak in the public interest. If we can increase the sophistication of the public just a bit, we can have them jump the gap between amusement over the idea that "What is good for General Motors is good for the country" to amusement over the idea that what is good for HEW is good for the country. One day we may have the modern democrat as sophisticated as the medieval serf who, when told by his noble master that his taxes were going up in the public interest, thanked his lordship for his concern but told him no thanks, the public be damned.

Robert Higgs

The Sources of Big Government

VOL. 20, NO. 1, 1984

We must have government. Only government can perform certain essential tasks successfully. Without government to defend us from external aggression, maintain domestic order, define and enforce private property rights, few of us could realize our individual objectives. In recognition of its immense potential for oppression and destruction, some have called government a necessary evil. But Ludwig von Mises, a devoted libertarian, disputed this characterization. "Government as such," he declared, "is not only not an evil, but the most necessary and beneficial institution, as without it no lasting social cooperation and no civilization could be developed and preserved."[1] Mises understood that a strong but limited government, far from suffocating its citizens, enables them to be productive and free.

For more than a century after its formation, the United States had such a government. It created a political and legal environment conducive to rapid economic progress, fostering what Willard Hurst, the eminent legal historian, has called a "release of energy."[2] Inventiveness, capital formation, and organizational innovation flourished as never before. Specialization and trade increased prodigiously. And during the nineteenth century the nation grew from an internationally insignificant outpost into the world's richest and freest society.

The twentieth century has witnessed a decline of American commitment to limited government and extensive private property rights. As the century began, our government still approximated a minimal state. We did not practice pure laissez faire—no society ever did—but we still placed severely binding restraints on government and allowed few intrusions of its potentially awesome power into the economic affairs of individual citizens. That long-established restraint has largely dissolved during the past seventy years. Government now suffuses every aspect of economic and social life. Merely to list its numerous powers would require a large volume: our farms and factories, our homes and schools, our health care, even our recreation—all feel its impact. Virtually nothing remains untouched by the myriad influences of governmental regulation, taxation, and expenditure.[3]

Several explanations of the growth of Big Government have been advanced. Too often, however, the proponent of a particular hypothesis touts it as if no other wheel will roll. In fact, most of the proposed explanations contain valuable insights, and they are not necessarily mutually exclusive. Nothing is gained, and much is lost, by attempts to locate a single source of Big Government. Accepting this stricture against a monocausal approach, one must try to comprehend clearly what the various hypotheses can and cannot explain and employ them so that they provide maximum illumination of the historical record.

Unfortunately, some explanations of the growth of Big Government have an abstract quality that obscures essential attributes of the reality of government itself. Some speak of government as if it were One Big Nonhuman Thing, a gigantic man-eating machine. The Spanish philosopher José Ortega y Gasset, for example, said that

> In our days the State has come to be a formidable machine . . . set up in the midst of society . . . anonymous . . . a machine whose existence and maintenance depend on the vital supports around it . . . sucking out the very marrow of society. . . .[4]

But of course any government is, for better or worse, human; it is simply the collectivity of persons who exercise legal authority.

Treating government as One Big Nonhuman Thing, distinct and apart from the people, encourages misleading characterizations of governmental motives and behavior. Real governments cannot survive without the sustenance and support, or at least the tolerance, of nongovernmental people. Moreover, some people

are always circulating between the ruling group and the ruled group. In part because the American government includes several levels—federal, state, local, and hybrid—and several branches—legislative, executive, judicial, and hybrid—it does not operate as if its component human actors were of one mind. Conflicts *within* government are as common and significant as conflicts *between* the rulers and the ruled. We would do well to bear constantly in mind that the American government is, and always has been, not One Big Nonhuman Thing, but rather many coexisting human institutions of varying function, scope, and authority.

Modernization

Reading between the lines in many historical works, one encounters what I shall call the Modernization Hypothesis. This rather foggy notion suggests that a modern urban-industrial economy simply *must* have an active and extensive government. Declamations about horse-and-buggy government in the Space Age or the impossibility of turning back the clock give rhetorical support to this idea. Exactly why a modern economy must have Big Government usually remains obscure.

Some supporters of the Modernization Hypothesis argue that a modern urban-industrial economy must have considerable governmental activity because it is so complex. "That the increased complexities and interrelationships of modern life necessitate this extension of the power of the state," insisted Calvin Hoover, "is no less true because it is such a well-worn cliché."[5] No one denies that the economy has become more complicated over time. New products, technologies, and industries have proliferated. Population has grown and concentrated in urban areas. Interregional and international flows of goods and funds have multiplied. Greater specialization has made individuals less self-sufficient, more dependent on a vast network of exchange.

Yet one cannot correctly infer that merely because of these growing complexities the people's economic affairs *required* more governmental involvement for their effective coordination. Indeed, as many economists—from Adam Smith in the eighteenth century to Friedrich Hayek in the twentieth—have argued, an open market is the most efficient system of socioeconomic coordination, the only one that systematically receives and responds to the ever-changing valuational signals transmitted by millions of individual consumers and producers.[6] Anyone who witnessed the artificial shortages and gasoline lines of the 1970s will be skeptical that governmental directives can perform better than the market in coordinating economic activities in a complex world.

How well a market economy operates, of course, depends on the character of the competition that propels it. Some observers believe that the emergence of large corporate firms in the late nineteenth century substantially altered the character of the economy's competitiveness and ushered in a new era. "This transformation of competition into monopoly," wrote V. I. Lenin in 1916, "is one of the most important—if not the most important—phenomena of modern capitalist economy. . . ." Accepting this allegation as factual, one may interpret the growth of government during the late nineteenth and early twentieth centuries as a reaction, a development of "countervailing power," by which the public resisted the inefficiencies and distributional distortions that Big Business would have entailed under unregulated conditions.

Representative events include the enactment of antitrust laws and the creation of the Federal Trade Commission and the various independent industrial regulatory commissions such as the Interstate Commerce Commission and the Federal Communications Commission. In short, according to this interpretation, economic modernization fostered the growth of private monopoly power, and government grew more powerful in order to resist, control, and neutralize this threat.[7]

The buttresses of this explanatory edifice are weak in both theory and fact. Though many large corporate enterprises developed after the Civil War, and the turn of the century certainly did witness a spate of mergers, crowned in 1901 by the creation of the giant United States Steel Corporation, no one has ever established that the *overall* economy became substantially less competitive. Neither huge firms nor high industrial concentration ratios necessarily imply an absence of effective competition. The decisive elements of the competitive process are dynamic—chiefly technological and organizational innovation—and under conditions of dynamic competition neither a firm's bigness nor an industry's high concentration poses a serious threat to the welfare of the public.[8]

Further, the government's efforts have tended more to preserve weak competitors than to assure strong competition. In this respect, the historical performances of the FTC and many of the independent industrial regulatory commissions are notorious. As George Stigler has said,

Regulation and competition are rhetorical friends and deadly enemies: over the doorway of every regulatory agency save two should be carved: "Competition Not Admitted." The Federal Trade Commission's doorway should announce, "Competition

Admitted in Rear," and that of the Antitrust Division, "Monopoly Only by Appointment."[9]

In fact, it would be more accurate to describe these governmental activities as creating or sustaining private monopoly power than precluding or reducing it. Of course, this result may have been exactly what some or even most interested parties desired from governmental regulation, though it would have been impolitic for them to have said so. But antitrust activities and the regulation of prices and services within industries, however one views their motivation and results, constitute only a minor element among the multifarious activities undertaken by modern government.

Sometimes arguments in support of the Modernization Hypothesis make much of the population's growing physical proximity. People living cheek by jowl inevitably cause spillover costs; economists call them "negative externalities." Where these occur, third parties unwillingly share the costs of others' transactions. Pollution of air or water is a familiar example. If the legal system fails to define and enforce a private property right over every valuable resource, including air and water, then negative externalities may entail a socially inefficient pattern of production and resource use in the free market. For example, smoke from your factory smokestack may dirty the laundry hanging on my clothesline, yet I cannot make you pay for the damages. From a social point of view, the activity of your factory is excessive because a portion of its true social cost of operation is shifted without consent onto third parties.

Government regulation conceivably can ameliorate such situations. Whether historically it has done so depends on how the government has framed and enforced

its regulations, which has partly determined the magnitudes of the costs and benefits of its interventions. Proponents of the Modernization Hypothesis seem to take for granted that negative externalities historically have been commonplace and significant, that much government activity has been motivated by a desire to rectify such conditions, and that these interventions routinely have succeeded in bringing about a socially more efficient pattern of resource use. Each of these suppositions may be questioned.

No doubt, some significant negative externalities have existed, and some governmental interventions have been motivated by a desire to rectify these situations. Public health regulations furnish the most compelling examples. Contagious diseases generate external costs in a most literal manner; historically they wrought tremendous harm; and government's public health regulations were generally framed and enforced to bring about a socially more efficient condition.[10] In recent decades, anti-pollution laws and enforcement bureaus such as the Environmental Protection Agency provide examples of the governmental attack on negative externalities, though the framing and enforcement of these environmental regulations raise many questions about their exact intent and the degree to which they have succeeded or failed from a comprehensive social point of view.

In sum, the Modernization Hypothesis has some merit as an explanation of the emergence of Big Government, but its explanatory power is quite limited. Regulation of industrial competition, public health, and environmental externalities account for only a small part of what modern governments actually do. Most of their activities have no plausible connection with the increased complexity of the economy, maintenance of competition, or the spillover costs that attend population concentration.[11] Especially in application to the federal level, where governmental expansion has been most prodigious in the twentieth century, the Modernization Hypothesis has little to offer.

Public Goods

A somewhat related idea—related because it also may involve nonexclusivity or spillover effects—has to do with public goods. A "public good," in the language of economists, is not simply or necessarily one supplied by a government. Rather, it has the peculiar property that its enjoyment by one consumer does not diminish its enjoyment by another. As economists put it, once the public good has been produced, it has a zero marginal cost of additional use. National defense is the most familiar example. If more protection from external aggression is provided, all citizens share the benefit of enhanced protection equally. My enlarged security does not entail diminished security for any other citizen.

Public goods create an economic problem because, as all consumers share their benefits fully, each consumer has an incentive to avoid paying for them. Each wishes to be the "free rider." Normally, of course, consumers who will not pay for a good cannot enjoy it, because those who do pay can exclude others from sharing in its benefits. For some public goods, however, exclusion is either impossible or prohibitively costly. One cannot defend a nation without defending every citizen in it. Left to provide such nonexclusive public goods in the market, people would provide little or nothing. As everyone held back, hoping to become the unexcludable free rider, no provision at all would be made.

Government can break the stalemate created by the free rider problem. By taxing all—or at least many—of the beneficiaries of a public good, it can obtain the funds to pay for the good. Some thorny issues remain even after government intervenes, because the appropriate level of provision and the apportionment of the tax burden cannot be determined by any straightforward procedure. In practice, the political process determines how much is provided and how the costs are shared by the citizens.

The Public Goods Hypothesis asserts that during the twentieth century the demand for nonexclusive public goods—chiefly national defense and the technology associated with warfare—has grown and, as only government can meet this demand effectively, government has grown correspondingly. The argument has considerable merit, particularly in relation to the federal level of government where the provision of national defense is concentrated. Certainly, the twentieth century has witnessed extraordinary international instability and hostility. Two world wars, a host of smaller international conflicts, and the Cold War have elevated the demand for national security far above its nineteenth-century levels. The development of modern military technology has made this enlarged demand enormously more costly to satisfy. Indeed, since World War II an ongoing arms race has meant that the demand for national security can never be satisfied once and for all, as each round of action and reaction alters the requirements for effective deterrence.

Still, notwithstanding its obvious cogency, the Public Goods Hypothesis provides only a partial explanation of the growth of Big Government. Even at the federal level, most expenditures have no direct relation to national defense. The massive outlays for old age pensions, unemployment benefits, medical care, agricultural subsidies, school lunches, and so on and on—not to mention the hydra-headed regulation of everything from children's pajama fabrics to commodity futures contracts—have no connection with national defense or other nonexclusive public goods.

The Welfare State

The counterexamples just mentioned remind us that the United States has developed not simply a Big Government but a welfare state. One may employ still another variant of the Modernization Hypothesis to account for this aspect of the rise of Big Government. Economic growth and the concomitant socioeconomic transformation have tended in various ways, many of them subtle and indirect, to diminish the social service roles formerly played by such private institutions as families, churches, and voluntary associations. Victor Fuchs has hypothesized that

> The fruits of the market system— science, technology, urbanization, affluence—are undermining these institutions which were the foundation of the social order. . . . With the decline of the family and of religion, the inability of the market system to meet such needs becomes obvious, and the state rushes in to fill the vacuum. [Hence] . . . the growth of government can also be viewed as a substitute for family or church as the principal institution assisting individuals in time of economic or social misfortune.[12]

No doubt the substitution of governmental for private social services has occurred on a wide scale. But Fuchs's remarks leave one wondering about the exact workings of the process by which this vast substitution has been effected, including such critical matters as who benefits, how much and in what forms, and who pays.

Wilhelm Röpke, like Fuchs and many others, viewed the modern welfare state as "without any doubt, an answer to the disintegration of genuine communities during the last one hundred years." But he also recognized that "[t]oday's welfare state is not simply an improved version of the old institutions of social insurance and public assistance." Rather, it has evolved into "the tool of a social revolution" where "taking has become at least as important as giving," and "it degenerates into an absurd two-way pumping of money when the state robs nearly everybody and pays nearly everybody, so that no one knows in the end whether he has gained or lost in the game."[13] Thus, by a natural, almost inevitable progression, the welfare state has become the redistributional state. Governmental policies for the limited purpose of rescuing the most unfortunate citizens from destitution have merged into governmental policies for the unlimited purpose of redistributing income and wealth among virtually all the groups, rich as well as poor, that constitute society.

Political Redistribution

An attempt to explain how "the state rushes in to fill the vacuum," transforming the welfare state into something vastly more comprehensive and penetrating, is the Political Redistribution Hypothesis. This argument views government as an instrument for the coercive redistribution of wealth. It sees the voters as knowledgeable and self-interested, and the elected officials as highly responsive to clear messages sent them by the voters. The argument has taken various specific forms.

In Allan Meltzer and Scott Richard's version, it maintains that

> Big Government results from the difference between the distribution of votes and the distribution of income. Government grows when the franchise is extended to include more voters below the median income or when the growth of income provides revenues for increased redistribution.[14]

This version of the hypothesis fits the historical facts poorly. Evidently, extensions of the franchise have had no independent effect on the growth of government, and the most dramatic extensions of governmental power have occurred in periods of stagnant or falling real civilian income, as during the world wars and the Great Depression. Further, to assume, as this version of the hypothesis apparently does, that all governmental redistributions transfer income to lower-income recipients flies in the face of facts too numerous and familiar to require recitation.

Sam Peltzman's version of the Political Redistribution Hypothesis holds that "governments grow where groups which share a common interest in that growth and can perceive and articulate that interest become more numerous." Here the process of governmental growth is seen as driven exclusively by citizen demands, governmental response being taken for granted. Peltzman further maintains that

> the leveling of income differences across a large part of the population . . . has in fact been a major source of the growth of government in the developed world over the last fifty years [because this leveling created] a broad-ening of the political base that stood to gain from redistribution generally and thus provided a fertile source of political support for expansion of specific programs. At the same time, these groups became more able to perceive and articulate that interest . . . [and] this simultaneous growth of "ability" served to catalyze politically the spreading economic interest in redistribution.[15]

Unlike the Modernization, Public Goods, and Welfare State Hypotheses, which seem implicitly to assume that government grows by automatically serving a broad but changing "public interest," the Political Redistribution Hypothesis explicitly views the growth of government as the outcome of a political process. That perspective is its chief virtue. But in many of its detailed formulations it characterizes the political process in a highly stylized, grotesquely oversimplified way. It assumes that the size of government is determined exclusively by elected officials seeking reelection. Where are the Supreme Court and the fundamental restraints of the Constitution and conservative public opinion? What roles are the permanent "civil service" officials of the executive branch and the independent regulatory agencies presumed to play?

Certainly the assumption of fully informed voters is untenable and fundamentally misleading. The assumption that the average voter is completely ignorant would approximate the truth more closely. To suppose that the political actors know precisely how an electoral outcome will be linked to a specific policy action and hence to a particular redistribution of wealth is to push the assumption of complete knowledge to absurdly fictitious lengths. As James Buchanan has observed, "The electoral process offers, at best, a crude disciplinary check on those who depart too much from constituency preferences." Elections occur infrequently. Few citizens possess much accurate information about political issues or the actions of politicians; nor do many citizens have much incentive to inform themselves better. Hence, "almost any politician can, within rather wide limits, behave contrary to the interests of his constituents without suffering predictable harm."[16] Indeed, it is virtually inevitable that the politician will behave contrary to the interests of his constituents even if he wishes to serve them faithfully. Apart from the heterogeneity of constituents' interests, the information problem is simply overwhelming.

The slippage between the interests of constituents and the actions of their elected officials is readily confirmed. The conservative former-Congressman, David Stockman, provided a wonderful example in his notorious confessions: "I went around and cut all the ribbons and they never knew I voted against the damn programs." Congressman Pete McCloskey recently made the same point in recalling his first congressional victory, in a special election in 1967. A post-election survey, designed to demonstrate the victorious candidate's mandate, revealed "that 5% of the people voted for me because they agreed with my views; 11% voted for me even though they disagreed with my views, and 84% didn't have any idea what the hell my views were."[17]

Because so much of the political process takes place in a supercharged atmosphere of ignorance, misinformation, posturing, and emotion, interested elites and strategically placed leaders play much more decisive roles than the mass of voters. And ideology probably drives the entire process far more than is admitted by the proponents of hypotheses based on the assumption of well-informed, rationally maximizing actors.

Ideology

Indeed, many scholars maintain what I shall call the Ideology Hypothesis to explain the modern growth of government. Supporters of this hypothesis make strange bedfellows. They include John Maynard Keynes, the patron saint of today's liberals, who asserted that

> the ideas of economists and political philosophers . . . are more powerful than is commonly understood. Indeed the world is ruled by little else. . . . [S]oon or late, it is ideas, *not vested interests*, which are dangerous for good or evil. [18]

Another firm believer in the force of ideas is Friedrich A. Hayek, a leading intellectual mentor of today's conservatives. He has located the ultimate cause of the abandonment of the market system in "certain new aims of policy," in particular a conviction that government should "determine the material position of particular people or enforce distributive or 'social' justice" by means of "an allocation of all resources by a central authority."[19] Thus, Keynes, who argued in favor of a "somewhat comprehensive socialization of investment," and Hayek, who has devoted a long professional life to combatting socialism of any sort, seem to agree that the growth of government depends ultimately on ideas or, perhaps more accurately, ideologies.[20]

Ideology, or what some observers more vaguely refer to as public opinion, must have played an important part, at the very least a decisive *permissive* role. As Ortega y Gasset has said, and many others have recognized, "there can be no rule in opposition to public opinion."[21] If people generally had opposed Big Government on principle, free markets could scarcely have been abandoned as they have been during the past seventy years. One can easily document the drift of public opinion toward the left during the twentieth century.

Public opinion being intangible and immeasurable, one must hypothesize about its effects with extreme caution. Yet something can be said, especially when one recognizes that opinion *leaders* have the ability to reshape and guide the opinions of the masses. "Public opinion," a political scientist has observed, "is often vague, transitory, and inconsistent. . . . In so far as the public is aware of issues, it focuses frequently on issues and topics which have been promoted or popularized by politicians and the media." The opinions of a Walter Lippmann or a Walter Cronkite may do more to shape the prevailing climate of opinion than the opinions of millions of less respected and less strategically situated observers of society and polity. "[I]n a mass democracy," as Röpke has said, "policy has to withstand . . . the pressure of . . . mass opinions, mass emotions, and mass passions," but these are "guided, inflamed, and exploited by pressure groups, demagogy, and party machines alike."[22] By concentrating on the ideas broadcast by strategically located elites and specific influential persons, we have a more defensible basis for generalizations about the prevailing ideologies that matter. (Whether the historical twists and turns of ideology among opinion leaders themselves can be explained I consider, at least on this occasion, a moot question.)

Even if the dominant ideologies can be identified, however, one must recognize that, as William Letwin has

expressed it, a legislature "is not a factory that mechanically converts opinion into statutes."[23] Just as there is much slippage, as noted above, between the material interests of constituents and the actions of their political representatives, so there is much slippage between the opinions or ideologies of constituents and the actions of legislators or other governmental officials. To understand this slippage would be to understand a great deal of the reality of the workings of modern representative democracy.

A further difficulty is that ideology is not simply an independent variable in the sociopolitical process. Joseph Schumpeter perceived this when he observed that

> whether favorable or unfavorable, value judgments about capitalist performance are of little interest. For mankind is not free to choose. . . . Things economic and social move by their own momentum and the ensuing situations compel individuals and groups to behave in certain ways whatever they may wish to do—*not indeed by destroying their freedom of choice but by shaping the choosing mentalities and by narrowing the list of possibilities from which to choose.*[24]

Some may object that this statement goes too far, that it is unjustifiably deterministic, leaving no room at all for ideological voluntarism.[25] Still, in this tantalizing reference to the sociology of knowledge in relation to the growth of government, Schumpeter identified a critical question and laid down an analytical challenge that any fully satisfying account will have to answer.

Crisis

A final explanation of the growth of Big Government is the Crisis Hypothesis. This maintains that, under certain circumstances, periods of national emergency call forth extensions of governmental control over or outright replacement of the market economy. Supporters of this hypothesis assume that national emergencies markedly enhance *both* the demand for and the supply of enlarged governmental activity. "At the time of economic crisis," observed Calvin Hoover,

> when critical extensions of governmental power are likely to occur . . . there is little opportunity for a meaningful vote on whether or not, as a matter of principle, the powers of the state should be extended. Instead, there is likely to be an insistent demand for emergency action of some sort and relatively little consideration of what the permanent effect will be.[26]

In American history the most significant crises have taken two forms: war and business depression. At the outbreak of war, a suddenly heightened demand for governmental provision of a public good, national defense, leads immediately to displacement of market processes of resource allocation in favor of greater taxation, government expenditure, and regulation of the remaining civilian economy. The larger and longer is the war, the greater is the suppression of the market economy. Modern "total" war, widely regarded as a test of the nation's very survival, also encourages a lowering of the sturdiest barriers—primarily constitutional limitations and adverse public opinion—that normally obstruct the growth of government. In severe business depressions, many people come to

believe that the market economy can no longer function effectively and that an economy more comprehensively planned or regulated by government would operate more satisfactorily. Hence, they give greater support to political proposals for enlarged governmental authority and activity. Though to a lesser degree than during wartime, changes in public opinion during depressions may also operate to enhance the supply of new governmental interventions by demanding, approving, or at least condoning facilitative reinterpretations of the Constitution. (Note that once constitutional barriers have been lowered during a crisis, a legal precedent has been established giving government greater potential for expansion in subsequent *non*crisis periods, particularly those that can be plausibly described as "crises.")

Governmental expansion historically has been highly concentrated in a few dramatic episodes, especially the world wars and the Great Depression. A major virtue of the Crisis Hypothesis, a virtue that it alone appears to possess, is that it fits well the main contours of the historical record. To employ the hypothesis to best advantage, however, one must look beyond the crises themselves. One must discover why the expansions of governmental power during the crisis do not disappear completely when normal socioeconomic conditions return. And one must explain why crises led to upward racheting governmental powers in the twentieth century but not in the nineteenth, which had its own crises. Accounting for this difference requires that some of the other hypotheses be brought into play as complements of the Crisis Hypothesis.

Conclusion

Big Government in the United States has various sources. Obviously, not all are equally important, but scholars have yet to develop analytical procedures for determining with any precision their relative importance. Given the intricate interdependencies among the various sources, such a determination may not make sense even conceptually, much less in empirical application. Ameliorating negative externalities, providing nonexclusive public goods, stretching a safety net beneath the most unfortunate citizens, redistributing income and wealth, pursuing the elusive goals of influential ideologies, reacting to crises—such are the activities of modern Big Government. These manifold activities respond differently to any particular stimulus or obstruction. Those who believe that government has grown too big cannot combat it successfully with any single weapon. And unless they come to appreciate better its historical sources, they are unlikely to deflect its future evolution very much.

Notes

1. Ludwig von Mises, *The Ultimate Foundation of Economic Science: An Essay on Method* (Kansas City: Sheed Andrews and McMeel, 1978 [1962]), 98.
2. James Willard Hurst, *Law and the Conditions of Freedom in the Nineteenth-Century United States* (Madison, WI: Univ. of Wisconsin Press, 1956), 3–32 and passim. See also Lawrence M. Friedman, *A History of American Law* (New York: Simon and Schuster, 1973), passim.
3. Useful general accounts of the growth of American government in the twentieth century include Solomon Fabricant, *The Trend of Government Activity in the United States since 1900* (New York: National Bureau of Economic Research, 1952) and

Jonathan R. T. Hughes, *The Governmental Habit: Economic Controls from Colonial Times to the Present* (New York: Basic Books, 1977), 126–242. The most revealing descriptions of the vastly enlarged scope of modern government, however, have been produced not by scholars but by the authors of "helpful guides" for citizens seeking governmental benefits. Two mind-boggling examples are William Ruder and Raymond Nathan, *The Businessman's Guide to Washington* (New York: Collier Books, 1975) and Roy A. Grisham Jr., and Paul D. McConaughy, eds., *The Encyclopedia of U.S. Government Benefits* (New York: Avon Books, 1975).

4. José Ortega y Gasset, *The Revolt of the Masses* (New York: Norton, 1957, twenty-fifth anniversary edition [1932]), 119–21. Ortega y Gasset recognized (122) that "for all that the State is still composed of the members of that society," but a few lines later he wrote of "what State intervention leads to: the people are converted into fuel to feed the mere machine which is the State." Perhaps these passages illustrate only the dangers inherent in highly metaphorical writing.
5. Calvin B. Hoover, *The Economy, Liberty, and the State* (New York: Twentieth Century Fund, 1959), 373.
6. Adam Smith, *An Inquiry into the Nature and Causes of the Wealth of Nations* (New York: Modern Library, 1937 [1776]), passim; F. A. Hayek, *Law, Legislation and Liberty: A New Statement of the Liberal Principles of Justice and Political Economy. Vol. I. Rules and Order* (Chicago: Univ. of Chicago Press, 1973), 35–54, esp. 50–51, and passim. See also Thomas Sowell, *Knowledge and Decisions* (New York: Basic Books, 1980), esp. 214–23.
7. This thesis is developed by John Kenneth Galbraith, *American Capitalism: The Concept of Countervailing Power.* 2nd ed. (Boston: Houghton Mifflin, 1956), esp., 135–53 on "Countervailing Power and the State." Lenin's statement is from *Imperialism: The Highest Stage of Capitalism.* new rev. trans. (New York: International Publishers, 1939), 17.
8. Joseph A. Schumpeter, *Capitalism, Socialism, and Democracy,* 3rd ed. (New York: Harper and Row, 1950), 81–106;

Israel M. Kirzner, *Competition and Entrepreneurship* (Chicago: Univ. of Chicago Press, 1973), esp. 125–31.

9. George J. Stigler, *The Citizen and the State: Essays on Regulation* (Chicago; Univ. of Chicago Press, 1975), 153 and passim. For a survey of studies of a wide variety of regulatory programs, see Thomas K. McCraw, "Regulation in America, A Review Article," *Business History Review* 49 (Summer 1975), 159–183 and Bernard H. Siegan, *Economic Liberties and the Constitution* (Chicago: Univ. of Chicago Press, 1980), 283–303.

10. Edward Meeker, "The Social Rate of Return on Investment in Public Health, 1880–1910," *Journal of Economic History* 34 (June 1974), 392–421,

11. Thomas E. Borcherding, "The Sources of Growth of Public Expenditures in the United States, 1902–1970," in Thomas E. Borcherding, ed., *Budgets and Bureaucrats: The Sources of Government Growth* (Durham: Duke Univ. Press, 1977), 53. See also the sources cited in note 3 above, especially the "helpful guides."

12. Victor R. Fuchs, "The Economics of Health in a Post-Industrial Society," *Public Interest* (Summer 1979 10, 13. For some provocative variations on this theme, see Robert Nisbet, *Twilight of Authority* (New York, Oxford Univ. Press, 1975). esp. 230–87.

13. Wilhelm Röpke, *A Humane Economy: The Social Framework of the Free Market,* trans. Elizabeth Henderson (Chicago: Henry Regnery, 1971), 156, 164–65. See also Mancur Olson, *The Rise and Decline of Nations: Economic Growth, Stagflation and Social Rigidities* (New Haven, CT: Yale Univ. Press, 1982), 174.

14. Allan H. Meltzer and Scott F. Richard, "Why Government Grows (and Grows) in a Democracy," *Public Interest* (Summer 1978), 116. See also, by the same authors, "A Rational Theory of the Size of Government," *Journal of Political Economy* 59 (October 1981), 914–27. The latter article measures the size of government by the share of income redistributed. Given the multitude of indirect as well as correct ways that governmental policies effect redistributions, this measure is obviously non-operational and hence the hypothesis cannot be tested empirically.

15. Sam Peltzman, "The Growth of Government," *Journal of Law and Economics* 23 (October 1980), 285.

16. James M. Buchanan, "Why Does Government Grow?" in Borcherding, ed., *Budgets and Bureaucrats,* 13. See also Buchanan's *Limits of Liberty: Between Anarchy and Leviathan* (Chicago: Univ. of Chicago Press, 1975), 156–161; Siegan, *Economic Liberties and the Constitution,* 91, 265–82; Olson, *Rise and Decline,* 52; Graham K. Wilson, *Interest Groups in the United States* (Oxford: Clarendon Press, 1981), 110, 117, 125; Thomas R. Dye and I. Harmon Zeigler, *The Irony of Democracy: An Uncommon Introduction to American Politics* 5th ed, (Monterey: Duxbury Press, 1981), 193, 196, 362, 364, 367; Brian Barry, *Sociologists, Economists and Democracy* (Chicago, Univ. of Chicago Press, 1978), 127, 135.

17. William Greider, "The Education of David Stockman," *Atlantic Monthly* 248 (December 1981), 30; "Pete McCloskey: Trying to Run on the Issues," *Wall Street Journal* (June 3, 1982), 22.

18. John Maynard Keynes, *The General Theory of Employment, Interest and Money* (New York: Harcourt, Brace and World, 1936), 383–84 (emphasis added).

19. Friedrich A. Hayek, The *Constitution* of *Liberty* (Chicago: University at Chicago Press, 1960), 231–32.

20. For further discussion of ideology in relation to the changing role of government, see Douglass C. North, *Structure and Change in Economic History* (New York: Norton, 1981), 45–58 and passim. For some interesting, if not entirely compelling, econometric tests of the Ideology Hypothesis, see James B. Kau and Paul H. Rubin, *Congressmen, Constituents and Contributors: Determinants of Roll Call Voting in the House of Representatives* (Boston: Nijhoht, 1982), passim. For a painstaking scholarly treatise on the concept of ideology, see M. Seliger, *Ideology and Politics* (New York: Free Press, 1976).

21. Ortega y Gasset. *The Revolt of the Masses,* 128. See also 126.

22. Wilson, *Interest Groups,* 11; Röpke, *A Humane Economy,* 142. Ortega y Gasset agreed that "The majority of men have no opinions, and these have to be pumped

into them from outside. . . ." Also, "Under universal suffrage, the masses do not decide, their role consists in supporting the decision of one minority or another." See *The Revolt of the Masses,* 128–29, and 48.

23. William Letwin, *Law and Economic Policy in America: The Evolution of the Sherman Antitrust Act* (Chicago: Univ. of Chicago Press, 1965), 54.

24. Schumpeter, *Capitalism, Socialism, and Democracy,* 129–30.

25. Hendrik Wilm Lambers, "The Vision," in Arnold Heertje, ed., *Schumpeter's Vision: Capitalism, Socialism and Democracy after 40 Years* (New York: Praeger, 1981), 120; Herbert K. Zassenhaus, "Capitalism, Socialism and Democracy, the 'Vision' and the 'Theories,'" in Ibid., 189–91.

26. Hoover, *The Economy, Liberty and the State,* 326–27. See also Robert Higgs, "The Effect of National Emergency," *Pathfinder* 4 (April 1982), 1–2.

James Gwartney

Private Property, Freedom, and the West

VOL. 20, NO. 3, 1985

THE ARCHITECTS OF Western civilization believed that protection of private property was essential for the preservation of individual freedom. When individuals do not possess secure property rights, dependency on kings, lords, and governments for the essentials of life is inevitable. But freedom and dependence are antithetical; one cannot be free and simultaneously be dependent.

In recent decades, appreciation of private ownership has been declining in the West. High taxes, welfare transfers, regulatory restraints, and bureaucratic edicts are eroding private property. Increasingly, the political process—that is, government ownership and control—is being substituted for private property and the market process which is a natural outgrowth of private ownership.

Paradoxically, the decline in appreciation for private ownership is coming at a time when both theoretical advances and economic outcomes are strengthening the case for private ownership. Evidence is mounting that private ownership not only protects liberty, as our forefathers recognized, but it also provides for superior economic performance. In contrast, government ownership creates a perverse incentive structure which leads to a Hobbesian world of political infighting and waste of valuable resources.

Three Types of Ownership Rights

Property ownership denotes who has the right to control and benefit from a thing. There are three types of property rights: (1) communal, (2) private, and (3) state (or government).

Communal property rights grant everyone the right to use a resource as intensely as they desire. No one has exclusive ownership—the right to prohibit unauthorized use by others. Since individual resource users bear little of the costs accompanying resource exploitation, each has an incentive to use the resource before someone else does. Thus, over-utilization and failure to conserve for the future characterize communal ownership. The case of buffalo in the early West illustrates the impact of communal ownership. Each hunter knew that a buffalo that was not captured today would probably be captured tomorrow by someone else. Since exclusive ownership was absent, so too was the motivation to exploit the buffalo in a manner that provided for the future posterity of the animal. The outcome: mass slaughter of buffalo for their hides and virtual extinction of the species. While communal ownership may appear attractive to a utopian, the system fails to make individuals accountable for their actions. Economic waste and destructive behavior are the result.

In contrast with communal rights, private ownership grants individuals and private groups the exclusive right to control, benefit from, and transfer property as long as their actions do not harm the property of others. Each party is free to do what he wants with his private property as long as his use does not violate the property rights of another. While often associated with selfishness on the part of owners, private ownership would more properly be viewed as a means by which owners are protected against the selfishness of others. Private ownership provides legal protection against the seizure of one's property via theft, violence (or threat of violence), or fraud by another party.

Finally, property may be owned by governments. The government ownership may involve either direct title to property or indirect ownership via taxation and regulation of property nominally owned by private parties. While state-owned property technically belongs to all, this does not mean everyone has the right to use it. In contrast with communal property, government ownership provides for exclusive use by designated parties. The political process determines how, by whom, and under what conditions government property may be used. Essentially, government ownership substitutes the decision-making of government officials and the political process for the choices of private owners.

Individual Freedom, Private Ownership, and the Intellectual Roots of the West

As the population of Europe grew in the sixteenth century, land became increasingly scarce. The communal ownership of grazing lands and the destructive impact of overgrazing which accompanied it eventually led to the enclosure movement. About the same time, changes in military technology expanded the optimal size of geographic area defensible against potential intruders and plunderers. This led to the nation-state as a replacement protective agency for the prior feudal order.[1] Simultaneously, the influence of the Reformation began to sweep across Europe. By the seventeenth century, the idea that individuals had certain God-given rights that should not be violated by anyone gained popularity.

It was against this background that people like John Locke and David Hume began to think seriously about human freedom, private ownership of property, and the role of government. They propagated the view that all individuals, not just those born of noblemen, were entitled to the fruits of their labor and enjoyment of their property. However, private property was constantly threatened from, as Locke put it, "the invasions of others." As a result, in his *Second Treatise of Government* (1690), Locke argued:

> [An individual] seeks out and is willing to join in society with others, who are already united, or have a mind to unite, for the mutual preservation of their lives, liberties, and estates, which I call by the general name, property.[2]

Hume, too, perceived that the major function of government was to protect the possessions of individuals and thereby provide for freedom and order. In his *Treatise* written in 1740, Hume stated:

> No one can doubt, that the convention of the distinction of property, and for the stability of possession, is of all circumstances the most necessary to the establishment of human society, and that after the agreement for the fixing and observing of this rule, there remains little or nothing to be done toward settling a perfect harmony and concord.[3]

These early English philosophers exerted a profound influence on the thinking of Thomas Jefferson, John Adams, James Madison, and other early American political leaders. The architects of the U.S. political system also believed that private property was the foundation of human freedom and that the function of government was to protect and secure the possessions of individuals from both foreign (national defense) and domestic intruders. It was John Adams's opinion that:

> Property is surely a right of mankind as real as liberty. . . . The moment the idea is admitted into society that property is not as sacred as the laws of God, and that there is not a force of law and public justice to protect it, anarchy and tyranny commence.[4]

The early American intellectuals were keenly aware of the interdependency of personal freedom with one's right to own property. Labor and saving are the foundation of physical property. Without physical possessions, individuals would be unable to store up the fruits of their labor or pass along gifts to family and other loved ones. Denial of one's rights to possessions justly acquired (without the use of violence, theft, or fraud) is equivalent to denying one the fruits of his labor—the very subsistence of livelihood.

Thus, without protection of one's private property other rights would have little meaning. Recognizing this point, James Madison argued that protection of private property was interwoven with the protection of other personal freedoms. While still a congressman from Virginia, he stated:

> In its [the right to own property] larger and juster meaning, it embraced everything to which a man may attach a value and have a right, and which leaves to every one else the like advantage. In the former sense, a man's land or merchandise, or money, is called property. In the latter sense, a man has a property in his opinions and the free communication of them. He has a property of peculiar value in his religious opinions, and in the profession and practice dictated by them. He has a property very dear to him in the safety and liberty of his person. He has an equal property in the free use of his facilities, and free choice of the objects on which to employ them. In a word, as a man is said to have a right to his property, he may be equally said to have a property in his rights.[5]

Wisdom of Our Forefathers

Even with the benefit of the last two hundred years of history, serious scholars must be impressed with the insight possessed by the early proponents of private ownership. Even though they did not understand fully how a private-property based economic system worked, they recognized that it minimized social conflict and protected individual freedom.

Private property and market organization permit individuals to choose different occupations, consumer goods, and even lifestyles without interfering with the freedom of others to do likewise. Market organization based on private property is a system of proportional representation. Each individual casts his dollar votes for the consumer goods of his choice and receives them. Similarly, each individual is free to sell productive services to whomever he or she chooses without having to obtain permission from a king, lord, or political majority. The result is both freedom and diversity as various minorities, directed by market prices, choose varying bundles of goods and supply differing types of productive services.

Contrast this with a system of state property rights and political allocation. In the political arena the majority decides for everyone. For example, when schooling, retirement pensions, housing, and land management are provided through the political process, we all must pay for and subscribe to the program or service favored by the dominant political coalition. The will of the individual must give way to the will of the majority. Unnecessary social conflict results as minority views are suppressed.[6]

Simultaneously, private property also protects individual freedom by keeping economic power dispersed. Of course, power accompanies ownership. The owner of a plot of land determines whether it will be used for a housing development, wheat farm, parking lot, or some other use. The owner of each oil pool determines whether the resource will be exploited now or preserved for the future. However, with private ownership this power is spread among literally millions of people, no one of whom has much power over another. The power of even the wealthiest property owner is limited by the presence of other property owners willing to provide similar products and services. If the Hunt brothers decide to quit selling oil or David Rockefeller gets out of the banking and real estate business, neither the earning ability nor consumer alternatives available to Americans would be altered significantly.

A recent survey by the Federal Reserve Board indicated the wealthiest two percent of American households own twenty-eight percent of the nation's physical property. At first glance, this appears to be enormous power in the hands of a few people. However, reflection should cause one to question this view. This wealth, enormous as it is, is in the hands of 1.6 million households, representing diverse political, religious, ethnic, and personal interests. Unless it is used to provide services *to others* in exchange for income, the wealth of these property owners will shrink. Compare the power of these wealthy households with the power of 536 elected federal office holders. This latter group, comprising just .0000025 percent of our population, determines how one-quarter of our national output is allocated. They tax approximately one-fifth of our national income away from earners and allocate it to nonearners. They set the dollar value of the social security benefits received by thirty-six million Americans. The regulatory power under the jurisdiction of the 536 individuals holds a life or death grip on the economic health of literally millions of businesses. In contrast with private owners, members of Congress have the power to take property, a portion of your earnings for example, without your consent. One could go on and on, but the point is clear. When government ownership is substituted for private property, enormous power over the lives of others is bestowed upon a small handful of political figures. One of the major virtues of private property is its ability to check the excessive concentration of economic power in the hands of the few. Widespread ownership of property is the enemy of tyranny and abusive use of power. This proposition is just as true today as it was a couple of hundred years ago.

Economic Progress and Private Ownership

While the early defenders of private ownership emphasized its importance as the cornerstone of individual liberty, economic theory indicates that private property also provides the foundation for efficient use of resources and rapid economic growth. Production does not just happen. Human decision-makers must be motivated to undertake productive activities, use resources wisely, and discover better (less costly) ways of doing things. There are five major reasons why a system of well-defined, secure private ownership rights promotes economic progress.

1. *Private ownership encourages wise stewardship.* More than 2,300 years ago Aristotle noted, "What is common to many is taken least care of, for all men have greater regard for what is their own than for what they possess in common with others." Here, as in many other areas, his insight has stood the test of time. Private owners pay close heed to how their property is used because if it is damaged, abused, or misused, they will bear the costs of the depreciating action. Simultaneously, improvements that add more to the value of their property than their costs will increase the wealth of the owner. Thus private owners have a strong incentive to undertake cost-effective property improvements.

It is often observed that private housing is better maintained than public housing, private campgrounds better cared for than public grounds, and private lands more efficiently utilized than public lands. This should not be surprising. Private owners take good care of things because they both bear the costs of irresponsible use and reap the benefits of wise stewardship.

2. *Private ownership makes people accountable for their actions and thereby promotes the general welfare.* A system of well-defined, secure private ownership rights allows individuals to reap the benefits of the positive things they do for others and simultaneously holds them responsible for costs they impose on others.[7] With private ownership, producers incur costs when they use resources and simultaneously they are in a position to capture the benefits (through the sale of products and services) their actions bestow upon others. When an activity generates more benefits than costs, profit-seeking entrepreneurs have an incentive to discover and undertake it. On the other hand, they have an incentive to avoid counterproductive activities for which costs exceed benefits. Private ownership makes *decision-makers* accountable. As Adam Smith noted long ago, this accountability is the genius of a private property-based system because it brings individual self-interest and social welfare into harmony.

3. *Private ownership encourages individuals to develop and employ resources in a manner that is most advantageous to others.* When private property rights are protected, people get ahead by selling productive services in exchange for income. The exchange process leads to mutual gains stemming from specialization, division of labor, and mass production methods. Positive-sum economic activities—actions that generate mutual gain

for trading partners—are encouraged. Social cooperation and expansion in the size of the economic pie results.

Individuals have a strong incentive to (a) develop skills for which the demand of *others* is strong and (b) employ their resources in a manner that is most beneficial *to others* because such employment generates more income. With private ownership, the link between providing services *others* deem beneficial and personal income will be a close one. Individuals who provide large amounts of productive services *to others* will earn large incomes. In contrast, those who provide few productive services *to others* will experience lower incomes. In a very real sense, one's income will be directly related to one's ability to provide services that enhance the welfare of other people.

4. Private ownership brings the widest possible range of knowledge to bear upon the problem of scarcity. Improved knowledge and innovations provide a vital impetus for economic progress. In fact, the major difference between the modern man and the early gatherer-hunter is the amount of knowledge that we possess with regard to how resources can be transformed into desired goods. Our ancestors possessed virtually the same resources available today. But the superior knowledge we possess today permits us to squeeze a vastly larger output per person from the available resources.

No individual or elite group knows everything. Genius often comes from unexpected sources. Private property and economic freedom permit a wide variety of individuals, reflecting different combinations of creative talents, ideas, and market perceptions, to contribute knowledge to the production process. While this attribute of a free economy is often overlooked, unquestionably it is an important contributor to the dynamic growth of production under the system.[8]

5. Private ownership encourages current resource owners to conserve for the future. Since the current market value of property will reflect its expected future income, private ownership encourages wise conservation. Any time the present value of using a resource in the future is more valuable than the use of the resource now, the resource will be preserved for the future. For example, suppose one believes the price of a barrel of oil (or any other resource) is going to rise ten percent annually. When the expected increase in price is greater than the interest rate, resource owners (or potential purchasers who think the price of the resource will rise more rapidly than the interest rate) will gain by conserving the resource for the future.

As long as private property is transferable, even current decision-makers who do not expect to *personally* reap the future harvest of an asset will have strong incentive to take the preferences of future generations into account. Suppose a sixty year-old tree farmer is contemplating whether or not to plant Douglas fir trees which will not reach optimal cutting size for another fifty years. When ownership is transferable, the market value of the farmer's land will increase in anticipation of the future harvest as the trees grow and the expected day of harvest moves closer. Thus, the farmer will be able to capture his contribution at any time, even though the actual harvest may not take place until well after his death.

Doomsday commentators who fear we are going to use up vital minerals, cut all the trees, or eliminate all the wilderness areas do not understand the conservation ethic of the market. Should any of these things become relatively more scarce in the future, *when they are owned privately,* their prices will rise more rapidly than the interest rate. The rising price will induce individuals to cut back on their current use, preserve more of the resource for the future, and search more diligently for additional supplies of the resource (and good substitutes for it). As Dwight Lee, Professor of Economics at George Mason University, recently stated, "No social institution does more to motivate current decision-makers to act *as if* they cared about the future than the institution of private property."[9]

Private Ownership— The Economic Record

The linkage between private property and economic progress has been illustrated under a broad range of circumstances. First of all, there is the economic miracle of the West during the last 250 years. Since Americans tend to lack a sense of history, most fail to recognize just how well the political economy of the West has worked. Improved living standards are not something that started with, say the discovery of the wheel 5,000 years ago. Quite the contrary, the historical record is the story of a nip-and-tuck race between subsistence and starvation. Periods of economic growth have been rare exceptions. Our ancestors were keenly aware of this point. As Phelps Brown has shown, the real income of a typical English tradesman was virtually unchanged between 1215 and 1798, a period of nearly six centuries. Just as human beings had worked sun-up to sun-down to eke out a minimal living for 6,000 years, so too did our ancestors just 250 years ago.

However, all of this began to change about the time the new ideas on property rights and the role of government were transformed into public policy. Human creativity developed ideas that transformed the way people lived and worked. Improved farming techniques (e.g., crop rotations, fertilizers, and miracle grains) permitted our ancestors to squeeze much larger outputs from the land. Machines were developed that improved our ability to produce agriculture products and transformed resources into manufacturing goods. Petroleum, electricity, and later nuclear power replaced human and animal power as the major source of energy. Eventually, we figured out how to construct engines that revolutionized our ability to power machines and transport both people and cargo. Not only did we achieve these things, but simultaneously quality food, warm clothing, comfortable houses, and diversity of entertainment were brought within the budget constraints of the mass population. For the first time in history, millions of human beings attained living standards far above subsistence. The economic history of the West is a story of progress far beyond even the imagination of our ancestors.

Just as private ownership based systems delivered economic progress in the past, a check of recent economic performance indicates they continue to do so in the present. During the 1960–81 period, the annual growth rate of per capita GNP of only four countries exceeded six percent. Those four countries were Japan, Hong Kong, South Korea, and Singapore—all private ownership based economies. Compare the economic record of South Korea with North Korea, West Germany with East Germany, Kenya with Ethiopia, or Taiwan and Hong Kong with mainland China. In each case, the record paints the same picture—economies that rely more fully on private property rights grow more rapidly.

Even in the Soviet Union, private ownership is associated with high productivity. Soviet families living on collective farms are permitted to cultivate a private plot, the area of which is not to exceed one acre. Although these private plots constitute only about one percent of the land under cultivation in the Soviet Union, the Soviet press reports that approximately one-quarter of the total value of agricultural output is generated on these plots.

State Property—The Alternative to Private Ownership

One cannot adequately judge the case for private ownership without considering the alternative—government ownership of property. Public ownership means the substitution of the political process for market allocation. Until recently, traditional economists and political scientists held what might be called the "benevolent despot" model of government. According to this view, government decision-makers always choose the alternative that is best for society. The political process was simply viewed as a corrective device.

Recognizing the naiveté of this view, a group of economists—they are now referred to as "public choice" economists—set out to enhance our understanding of how the political process really works. While the work has not attracted wide media exposure, it may prove to be the most revolutionary breakthrough of economic analysis during the postwar era.[10] Public choice analysis provides insight as to what we can expect from the democratic collective decision-making process. For our purposes three of the implications are particularly important.

First, there will be a strong tendency for politicians to support positions favored by well-organized, easily identifiable special interest groups. When the cost of special interest legislation is spread widely among the voting populace, most non-special interest voters will largely ignore the issue. In fact, they are likely to be uninformed as to how the issue impacts their welfare. In contrast, special interest voters will be vitally concerned. They will let candidates (and legislators) know how strongly they feel about the issue. Many special interest voters will vote for or against politicians, almost exclusively, on the basis of this issue. Given the intensity of special interest voters and the apathy of other voters, politicians will be led as if by an "invisible hand" (to borrow Adam Smith's expression) to promote the positions of special interests.

Second, the political process will be biased toward the adoption of short-sighted policies, actions which yield payoffs prior to a forthcoming election while generating costs that are not readily observable until after the election. The pre-election benefits will enhance the politician's image with voters while the negative side effects will not generally be observable on election day. Since politicians neither capture benefits nor experience costs beyond their tenure in office, they have a strong incentive to choose alternatives that are attractive in the short run even though the long run effects may be quite different and highly inefficient.

Finally, allocation via the political process encourages individuals and groups to engage in redistributive and protective activities rather than production. When the government moves beyond the protection of private property and actively reallocates income and other property rights, more resources will flow into favor-seeking (economists use the term "rent-seeking"). Individuals, businesses, and interest groups will invest more heavily in political resources (lobbying, contributions, etc.) designed to yield government action that promotes their personal interest. The political ethic of "taking from others in exchange for votes and political "resources" replaces the market ethic of helping others in exchange for income. However, just as sheep do not stand still while they are sheared, neither do individuals deprived of their property. Citizens will respond to higher tax rates by expanding their tax avoidance activities.[11] Similarly, additional regulation will lead to additional protective action. The more a society relies upon tax, transfer, and regulatory activities to determine income shares, the closer the society will approach the Hobbesian world of political infighting and economic stagnation. As individuals and interest groups allocate more resources to fighting and clawing for a larger slice of the economic pie, the absolute size of those slices will decline. The American experience with the tax-transfer society is not inconsistent with this view.

The Invalid Charge— Private Ownership Favors the Rich

Even while recognizing many of the positive attributes of private ownership, critics often charge that it promotes inequality and works to the advantage of the rich. "The rich get richer and the poor get poorer," we are told. When analyzing the validity of this view, it is important to keep several facts in mind. First, ownership of physical property, particularly inherited property, is not a major source of income inequality. Between eighty-one percent and eighty-three percent of national income in the United States is allocated to labor, and the share has been amazingly constant during the last fifty years.[12] Income differences stemming from the provision of labor services are the major

source of inequality in the United States. The share of national income going to physical capital in the form of interest, rents, and corporate profits is only seventeen to nineteen percent of our national income.[13] Not only is the fraction of income derived from physical wealth small, most owners of physical wealth acquire it by saving from their labor income rather than inheritance. The share of aggregate income derived from inherited property is estimated at two percent. Thus, even complete elimination of the inheritance of property would do little to promote income equality.[14] Given that leaving wealth to whomever one chooses provides a valuable stimulus to productive effort and that such bequeaths contribute little to inequality, the case for the elimination of inheritance is weak.

Second, we live in a dynamic world, one where there is considerable movement both up and down the economic ladder. A recent study found that of the top twenty percent of income recipients in 1971, more than half had fallen from their prior lofty position seven years later. Similarly, nearly half of those among the bottom quintile of income recipients in 1971 had moved up the income ladder by 1978.[15] Studies of intergenerational income data find even more mobility—both upward and downward—in the comparative economic position of fathers and sons. Private property rewards achievers from all socioeconomic backgrounds. When property—including one's property right to the fruits of his labor—is protected from oppressive taxation, achievers from all economic backgrounds have the opportunity to create, expand their wealth, and climb to the top of the economic ladder.

Third, those who charge that private ownership favors the rich generally fail to recognize that the market process is a powerful force for uplifting the mass of population. Blinded by the illusion of a static world, like Marx, they fail to understand the dynamics of economic growth and income generation. As we previously discussed, the major difference between our modern standard of living and that of our ancestors hundreds of years ago is the amount of knowledge we possess with regard to how resources can be transformed into desired goods. When property rights to innovations are protected, a market economy not only provides a strong incentive for entrepreneurs to innovate, but it also provides *a premium reward for innovations that improve the living standard of the mass population.* Successful entrepreneurs will focus on how they can bring a product or service within the grasp of the typical consumer—how they can serve markets where sales units are tabulated in the millions rather than the hundreds.

Most products go through two rather distinct phases. At first, they are quite expensive and purchased only by the very rich. During this phase, producers experiment with alternative designs and methods of production. The high initial price, paid primarily by the rich, serves to cover developmental costs. Entrepreneurs iron out complications and acquire valuable experience which will permit either them or their emulators to succeed in the next phase. During the second phase, production techniques and product modifications are developed making the product attractive and affordable to more and more consumers. Mass production and market penetration are the keys to success in this phase. Of course, entrepreneurs who serve a mass market often earn a fortune. But in the process of doing so, they improve the standard of living of numerous people (remember, exchange is a positive-sum activity).

You cannot have mass production without also having economical products for the mass of consumers. No one understood this point better than Harvard economist Joseph Schumpeter. Summarizing his ideas on this topic, Professor Schumpeter noted:

> [T]he capitalist engine is first and last an engine of mass production which unavoidably also means production for the masses. . . . It is the cheap cloth, the cheap cotton and rayon fabric, boots, motorcars and so on that are the typical achievements of capitalist production, and not as a rule improvements that would mean much to the rich man. Queen Elizabeth owned silk stockings. The capitalist achievement does not typically consist in providing more silk stockings for queens but in bringing them within the reach of factory girls in return for a steadily decreasing amount of effort.[16]

Entrepreneurs do not make fortunes by selling just to the rich. Large-scale entrepreneurs must bring their products within the budget constraint of the mass market. In the process of doing so, they uplift the living standards of the mass of consumers. This is a tremendously important point that both Marx and modern egalitarians totally fail to grasp.

Finally, it makes no sense to compare economic equality under private ownership with an unattainable standard such as perfect equality. The relevant comparison is with what one would expect from the political process. Perhaps surprising to some, there is little reason to believe that allocation via the political process promotes equality. Politicians find redistribution from widely dispersed, disorganized groups (e.g., taxpayers and consumers) to easily identifiable, concentrated interests (e.g., labor, business, farmers, and the elderly) far more attractive than egalitarian transfers. Similarly, politicians are attracted to transfers that provide (or appear to provide) readily identifiable current benefits at the expense of costs that are difficult to observe. These are the types of reshuffles one should expect from the political process and there is little reason to believe they will be egalitarian.[17]

At the individual level, persons who develop persuasive skills (i.e., lobbying, public speaking, public relations, media exposure), organizational abilities, finances, and political knowledge will be rewarded handsomely with income, prestige, and power when resources are allocated via the political process. There is little reason to believe that the poor will possess relatively more of these characteristics. In fact, the entrepreneurs and managers in a politically dominated society are likely to be pretty much the same people as those who would excel under market organization. The people with better ideas, more creative minds, and more energy will rise to the top of a socialist bureaucracy just as they will rise to the top in the business world. Those who fare poorly under market organization are unlikely to do better, either relatively or absolutely, under socialism.

The empirical data are consistent with this view. Despite the enormous increase in the tax-transfer sector, the distribution of income in the United States has changed little since World War II. Similarly, there is little evidence that income transfers have reduced the incidence of poverty. In fact, one can build a strong case that the transfers have confronted the poor with a perverse incentive structure and have thereby actually retarded progress against poverty.[18]

Concluding Thoughts

Our current situation is beset with irony. The twentieth century has been characterized by the growth of government and the weakening of private ownership. Government expenditures now total nearly forty percent of our national income. More than one out of every five dollars is taxed away from its earner and transferred to another in the form of either cash payments or noncash benefits. Far from protecting property rights as envisioned by the political architects of the West, government has become the major source of attenuation in private property.

Nonetheless, the intellectual case for private ownership is stronger today than at any time in the past. History illustrates that, just as its early defenders perceived, private ownership minimizes social conflict and provides a shield against oppressive concentration of power. Where private property is most widely respected on this planet, personal freedom is most secure and the presence of the domineering state is least observable. In addition, the evidence of a positive link between private ownership and economic progress is most impressive. Against the historical record of man's struggle for survival, clearly the development of widespread private ownership in the West was associated with something of an economic miracle. The superior performance of private-property based systems continues today as the rising living standards of modern-day capitalist economies compared to their socialist counterparts illustrates. Recent work in public choice has made us more fully aware of the defects of even the democratic political process—why political allocation leads to economic stagnation while failing to promote economic equality. Only the naive continue to cling to the notion that the political process is the friend of the mythical common man.

An old Chinese proverb states: "Societies are like fish; they always begin to go rotten in the head." History illustrates the wisdom of private ownership. To the extent we fail to realize it, it merely illustrates we are going "rotten in the head."

Notes

1. See Douglass C. North, *Structure of Change in Economic History* (New York: Norton, 1981), for an excellent account of this period.

2. John Locke, *Treatise of Civil Government,* Charles Sherman, ed. (New York: Appleton-Century-Crofts, 1937), 82.

3. David Hume, *Treatise of Human Nature,* book III, part II, para. II.

4. John Adams, "Defense of the Constitutions of Government of the United States of America" in Charles F. Adams, ed., *The Works of John Adams* (1850–56), VI, 8f.

5. Statement made March 27, 1792, from *The Works of James Madison,* vol. IV, 478–79. Also see John Locke, A *Letter Concerning Toleration* for similar views.

6. The case of schooling vividly illustrates the unnecessary social conflict that emanates from political provision. Views vary as to what constitutes a quality education. Some parents would like schools to focus on the basics; others favor a broad curriculum. Some favor highly structured organization; others prefer the open school concept. Some want their children to attend schools that emphasize moral values and religious beliefs; others oppose even so much as a moment of silent meditation. When schooling is provided in the private sector, all of these diverse views can and are satisfied. In contrast, each of the differences promotes division and conflict within the public school system.

7. Of course, in some cases it is difficult to assign property rights in a manner that permits decision-makers to capture fully the benefits of their actions and make them accountable fully for the costs they impose on others. Migrating animals and use rights to rivers, oceans, and the atmosphere provide examples. Under such circumstances, ideal economic efficiency breaks down. See James Gwartney and Richard Stroup, *Economics: Private and Public Choice,* 3rd ed. (New York: Academic Press, 1983), ch. 30 for additional detail on this topic.

8. Thomas Sowell, *Knowledge and Decisions* (New York: Basic Books, 1980), clearly articulates the importance of this factor.

9. Dwight Lee, "Patience is a Market Virtue," *Reason* (January 1985), 44. Through the ages, some previous writers, including Aristotle, have argued that private parties should be granted exclusive use rights while the government still maintains ownership. While maintaining government ownership, several state governments granted use rights to land in early America. Fortunately, this policy was soon abandoned. As our analysis indicates, the problem with use rights without ownership is that the arrangement fails to provide an incentive to maintain and improve the property for the future since, lacking transferability rights, users are unable to capture the benefits of wise stewardship. Also see Richard Stroup and John Baden, *Natural Resources: Bureaucratic Myths and Environmental Management* (Cambridge, MA: Ballinger, 1983), for additional detail on the efficiency of private ownership as a protector of natural resources and the environment.

10. For those desiring additional information on the economics of public choice see Gordon Tullock, *The Vote Motive* (London: The Institute of Economic Affairs, 1976); Henri Lepage, *Tomorrow, Capitalism* (LaSalle, IL: Open Court Publishing Co., 1978) chapters 5 and 6; James and Richard Stroup, *Economics: Private and Public Choice*, chapters 4, 29, and 30; and Mancur Olson, *The Logic of Collective Action* (Cambridge, MA: Harvard Univ. Press, 1971).

11. See James Gwartney and James Long, "Tax Rates, Tax Shelters, and the Efficiency of Capital Formation," in Dwight Lee, ed., *The Political Economy of Capital Formation* (San Francisco: Pacific Institute, 1985), for evidence on this point.

12. Labor income is composed of employee compensation plus the earnings of self-employed workers.

13. As egalitarians are fond of pointing out, the richest twenty percent of income recipients own approximately fifty-nine percent of the physical wealth, while the poorest twenty percent own only eight percent of the wealth. In interpreting the significance of data on the inequality of physical wealth holdings it is important to recognize that such wealth generates less than one-fifth of our national income.

14. See Alan S. Blinder, *Toward an Economic Theory of Income Distribution* (Cambridge, MA: MIT Press, 1974), for additional detail on this topic.

15. Greg J. Duncan, et al., *Years of Poverty, Years of Plenty* (Ann Arbor, MI: Institute for Social Research, Univ. of Michigan, 1984), Table 1.1.

16. Joseph Schumpeter, *Capitalism, Socialism, and Democracy*, 3rd ed. (New York: Harper and Row, 1962), 62.

17. Less than twenty percent of the income transfers in the United States are means-tested—that is, targeted toward the poor. If one includes transfers stemming from regulatory actions such as trade restrictions, occupational and business entry restraints, and export subsidies, the share of transfers targeted toward the poor would be even smaller.

18. For a comprehensive analysis of this issue, see Charles Murray, *Losing Ground: American Social Policy, 1950–1980* (New York: Basic Books, 1984).

Samuel Gregg

Markets, Morality, and Civil Society

VOL. 39, NO. 1–2, 2003–4

The free market has always occupied an uneasy place in conservative thinking. Conservatives have generally proven better at identifying the economic systems they oppose rather than any one economic theory they can wholeheartedly support. While most conservatives identify themselves as supporters of free market institutions, others harbor considerable reservations. Some have advocated corporatist economies. Others, such as some European Christian Democrats, have searched for a "third way." Indeed, beyond a commitment to private property rights and opposition to statism, it is often difficult to find common ground among conservatives on economic matters, either at the level of principle or of policy.

At the root of this uneasiness is *not* primarily a concern about inequalities of wealth. The drive to radically equalize economic outcomes is largely opposed by conservatives as wrong in itself. Nor since communism's collapse have many self-identified conservatives questioned the market's capacity to produce material wealth more effectively than any other economic system. Instead, the con-

cerns of many conservatives about the market reflect a deeper, more fundamental unease with certain basic aspects of modernity.

During the Cold War, conservatives could avoid dwelling on these matters. Many were willing to form strategic alliances with classical liberals and libertarians on the grounds that the political priority in such circumstances had to be the rallying of those forces opposed to the patent evil of Marxism-Leninism. Now, however, with the exception of a handful of maverick states, Marxist-Leninist and centrally planned economic systems have been rejected across the globe. And many on the center-left acknowledge the market's superior wealth-creating capacities. This being the case, conservatives now find themselves freer to debate the virtues of the market among themselves, as well as with classical liberals and libertarians, and to assess where the market fits into conservative thought about the moral culture and civil society of free political orders.

The Ascendancy of Planning

Standing at the beginning of the twenty-first century, it is difficult to imagine the omnipresent hostility towards the market which prevailed in left-wing, modern-liberal, and even some conservative circles at the end of World War II. The commitment to Keynesian economic planning went largely unchallenged, save by figures such as Friedrich Hayek and other intellectual pariahs. Though the British conservatives did oppose the Labour Party's socialist program during the 1945 general election, that party's shattering electoral defeat contributed to the eventual dominance of "One Nation" Tories within the Conservative Party.

One exception to this trend was the market-liberalization program pursued in postwar West Germany by Ludwig Erhard and the *Ordo* liberal school of economics associated with figures such as Wilhelm Röpke, Alfred Müller-Armack and Walter Eucken. These reforms were undertaken largely against the wishes of the Allied Military Occupation authorities (advised by John Kenneth Galbraith among others) and were realized via administrative fiat before the first postwar elections. Erhard was later to remark that had his proposals been subject to the approval of political parties, their implementation (and West Germany's "economic miracle") would never have happened.

The secret of the *Ordo* liberal program's success may be found in its distinction between competitive market processes and the institutional framework within which free economic activity occurs. While insisting that the state should help to shape the social and economic order, *Ordo* liberals believed that price-determination and economic exchanges should be generally left to competing individuals. On the one hand, they stressed that market economies are premised upon widespread acceptance of certain rules and institutions, such as the law of contract and private property. These in turn presuppose the existence of public order guaranteed by state authority.[1] At the same time, the *Ordo* liberals underlined a reality about markets that many, including a number of conservatives, often failed to appreciate. Too often "the market" is spoken of as if it is an anonymous amoral conglomerate that exerts its own will. Markets, however, actually consist of literally millions of people making free choices in the buying and selling of goods and services. To subvert this process through centralized planning, the *Ordo* liberals stressed, was bound to distort prices and eventually the process of supply and demand itself.

From the standpoint of the history of ideas, one should note that the postwar intellectual opposition of many conservatives to economic planning and burgeoning welfare states was never solely based upon arguments about efficiency. Many who favored market economic orders stressed the connection between the suppression of economic liberty and a resulting diminishment of political and civil freedom. It was not coincidental that the determination with which Communist regimes sought to suppress liberty in the commercial realm was only exceeded by the intensity with which they attempted to crush religious freedom. Marx, Lenin, and other luminaries of Communist thought had always stressed that institutions such as private property, processes such as free exchange, private entrepreneurship, and the subsequent growth of a commercially based middle class, were among the prime obstacles to the implementation of their vision of the future.

The conservative insistence upon the link between economic and political liberty was not new. It was pivotal to Edmund Burke's criticisms of the British government's policies toward its American colonies. But it was also, and remains, an argument about the moral imperative of allowing the free human choices and free human acts of free human persons to be expressed in economic life. In short, the conservative argument about the proper structuring of economic life is less concerned with efficiency than it is about the market as a moral requirement of a society that takes the idea of freedom *seriously*. This point lies at the heart of Wilhelm Röpke's insistence that only a market order is able to give individuals the necessary scope for free choice in the material realm. As Röpke explained in 1953, "my opposition on technical grounds is that socialism, in its enthusiasm for organization, centralization, and efficiency, is committed to means that simply are not compatible with freedom."[2] "My fundamental opposition to socialism," Röpke continued, "is to an ideology that, in spite of all its 'liberal' phraseology, gives too little to man, his freedom, and his personality; and too much to society."[3]

Market Revivals and Conservative Doubts

Given the immediate postwar ascendancy of socialist and Keynesian economics in the academy and in government, it remains surprising just how suddenly these became discredited by the end of the twentieth century. Communism's collapse, of course, removed command economies as an alternative to the free market. But perhaps more startling was the pace at which a growing number of governments beginning in the late 1970s—a decade before the fall of the Berlin Wall—adopted measures with the intention of making their economies freer, more open, and less regulated. In many instances, this development transcended traditional "left-right" categories. For example, some of the more radical and far-reaching market-oriented reforms were pioneered by Labour governments in New Zealand and Australia in the 1980s.

Admittedly, the picture is a muddled one. In even the most market-directed countries, the state continues to control large proportions of national GDP. Taxation levels in some of the same countries have barely altered over the past twenty years. There also remains a long list of countries in which only limited shifts in economic policy have occurred. Sweden, for instance, remains largely frozen in a postwar Social Democrat time-warp. In those countries that have sought to embrace market economic policies, the process has usually occurred erratically and has experienced restrictions and reversals. Nonetheless, on balance, the past thirty years have seen national economies becoming more market-oriented, and international transactions less subject to restrictions.

For many people, the material and technological advances facilitated by this expansion of the market and private enterprise are enough; they are conclusive evidence for the incontestable superiority of free market economics. There are, however, others who—while acknowledging the material progress flowing from this expansion of economic liberty—have not regarded the spread of markets with unmitigated joy. For those who aspire to be reasonable, no set of economic arrangements makes sense unless it is grounded in a theory that identifies the purposes that the economy is supposed to serve. It is the posing of this question that has resulted in considerable conservative anxiety about the market.

One conservative concern has been the association of free markets with modernity. From the standpoint of most conservatives, modernity has proven a deeply mixed blessing. The mixture of modernity's deliberate abstention from reflection upon the proper ends of human action with the tremendous scope for choice offered by the market is bound to alarm those conservatives who hold certain high views of ethical life and cultural life. In this connection, conservatives have noted that the dominant philosophical justifications currently offered for free market arrangements, be they evolutionist (Hayekian), positivist (Friedmanite), or utilitarian (Misesian), are all rationalizations. The essential unreasonableness of these explanations, they suggest, leaves the market economy presently bereft of all but the weakest of moral justifications.

Other conservatives have expressed unease at the current application of free market thinking to a range of areas from which it has traditionally stood aloof. The reason for this concern was, ironically enough, perhaps best outlined by a committed libertarian, Murray Rothbard:

> In recent years, economists have invaded other intellectual disciplines and, in the dubious name of science, have employed staggeringly oversimplified assumptions in order to make sweeping and provocative conclusions about fields they know little about. This is a modern form of "economic imperialism" in the realm of the intellect. Almost always, the bias of this economic imperialism has been quantitative and implicitly Benthamite, in which poetry and pushpin are reduced to a single-level, and which amply justifies the gibe of Oscar Wilde about cynics, that they (economists) know the price of everything and the value of nothing. The results of this economic imperialism have been particularly ludicrous in the fields of sex, the family, and education.[4]

Conservatives familiar with the ideas promoted by some adherents of the Law and Economics School (most notably, Richard Posner) will immediately recognize that Rothbard's concern was not misplaced. Insofar as conservatives believe that utilitarian arguments have only a minor role to play in explaining why freedom ought to prevail, they are bound to take issue with the application of market logic to those spheres of human existence that do not lend themselves to utility calculations, such as the good of beauty or the value of human life.

A twentieth-century economist and social philosopher who anticipated such difficulties was Wilhelm Röpke. One suspects that Röpke would probably have resisted the label "conservative." Yet the extent to which his ideas have been embraced by many conservatives indicates, at a minimum, that they regard Röpke as a fellow traveler. Röpke is especially instructive precisely because of the development in his own thought about the place of markets in free societies. Prior to being exiled from Nazi Germany, Röpke was very critical of pre-Enlightenment European thought. His philosophical defense of the market at this early point in his career remained very much rooted in the late-Enlightenment emphasis on utility.

The factors which caused Röpke to repudiate the instrumental-rationalist defenses of the market that remained central to the thought of some of his colleagues (most notably, Ludwig von Mises). First,

Röpke's experience of liberal democracy's collapse throughout continental Europe when confronted by the profoundly anti-Christian movements of Nazism, fascism, and communism awakened him to the indispensability of Christianity's contribution to Western civilization. Another factor was his acceptance of many insights of Old Whigs such as Edmund Burke (like Röpke, a deeply religious man who had a youthful flirtation with rationalism) concerning the importance of tradition in preventing tyranny.

Another important influence in the development of Röpke's integration of the market economy into "conservative" thought was his experience of living in Switzerland from the 1930s until his death in 1966. Many have been critical of Röpke's somewhat romantic vision of rural life and small villages. Whatever the validity of such criticism, there is no question that in Switzerland Röpke discovered a multi-ethnic society in which economic liberty flourished, but did so embedded in a culture emphasizing personal responsibility and within an institutional framework that encouraged the growth of genuinely free associations. From this, he drew the conclusion that market economies had to be embedded in a flourishing range of intermediate associations, bounded by a limited state, and grounded in a culture that emphasized an objective hierarchy of values.

Röpke is perhaps even more important today insofar as, unlike some market-orientated economists, he did not dismiss moral-cultural matters as something too ephemeral or insubstantial to be taken seriously. Röpke was increasingly perturbed in his later years by what he described as Western society's "proletarianisation": a mounting uniformity and monotony of social life. But he did not identify commerce or the market as being primarily

responsible for these developments. Nor did he maintain any romantic illusions about the conditions of material existence that prevailed in the premodern world until the spread of economic freedom began to liberate man from poverty. Nonetheless, as a Christian humanist, Röpke sought to remind his audiences of the insight of Judeo-Christian revelation, which is confirmed by right reason: that man is much more than *homo economicus.* "Above all," Röpke wrote, "man is *Homo religiosus.*" Thus, Röpke stressed the futility of modern man's attempt to get along without God, and he maintained that atheistic and agnostic anthropologies of man were inadequate foundations for free societies—including even the economic component of free societies. At the core of man's identity, Röpke stressed, is a spiritual and moral essence. This, by definition, means that man is destined for greater things than being a mere pleasure-machine.

Commerce and Human Flourishing

This brings us to the nub of conservative worries about the market's place in society. To the extent that conservatism embodies a sense of awe before the transcendent or adherence to the principle that the moral and the spiritual necessarily enjoy primacy over the material, then conservatives are bound to be uneasy about the market's potential (shared by all other economic systems, insofar as they in fact "deliver the goods" of material life) to facilitate an inversion of this priority.

If conservatives regard the purpose of human existence as human flourishing (in the sense that figures such as Aristotle and Aquinas understood this expression), then they are likely to be alert to any sign that a commercial order might contribute to the diminishing of those conditions that facilitate human flourishing. One obvious danger in market systems is that their very success in wealth-creation may encourage some to view this as an end in itself. This is a problem, or an error, since wealth is only instrumental to the fulfillment of persons. Wealth in itself does not represent the actualization of any intrinsic moral goods. Another difficulty is that everyone in the marketplace is exposed to calculations of utility. There is always a risk that this will encourage people to objectify or instrumentalize other persons.

There is, however, another way for conservatives to look at this matter, and that is to consider how markets might actually facilitate conditions that *favor* human flourishing. Admittedly, this is an area in which much reflection is still required. Conservatives may, however, be uniquely positioned to think through the possible connections between human flourishing and the market in a way that many classical liberal and libertarian thinkers are not. For conservatives generally purport that their philosophical commitments compel them to be morally concerned about the ends that people choose to pursue with their freedom, whereas most classical liberals and libertarians (if they are consistent with the premises of their philosophies) cannot.

Of course, the nature of market competition is such that it cannot be expected to replicate the life of a religious order. (Any conservative who imagines it should is forever doomed to regard markets with profound distaste.) It is true that commercial relations tend not to embrace the degree of self-giving that occurs, for example, in family life. Different forms of communities do, however, have naturally different purposes. A commercial business has different immediate ends than

that of a marriage. The purpose of marriage is the participation of a man and a woman in the same good of an exclusive and lifelong self-giving to each other, consummated through sexual acts of the reproductive type. The same cannot be said of a business relationship in which two or more people may cooperate in order to attain monetary resources that enable them to pursue somewhat dissimilar ends.

Nonetheless, conservatives should not underestimate the capacity of market economies to promote the realization of non-material goods. Commercial life demands, for instance, that people take prudential risks, trust others, and be diligent, industrious, and reliable. In other words, living within a market economy encourages certain forms of virtuous behavior. Careful reflection upon the nature of contracts underlines this point.[5] When people make a contract, they are engaging in a commercial convention and a recognized legal practice. Such an activity presupposes a basic exercise in promise-making in which we make a reasoned choice to commit ourselves to performing certain actions. Contracts are in fact null and void without such prior commitments. They thus enlist our willingness to be truthful and act upon the reasonable promises we make. In this sense, they require us to act in a practically reasonable manner. To this extent, the very act of entering into a contract can directly facilitate human flourishing.

Then there is the calming, almost civilizing potential of commercial activity. The market brings people from very different backgrounds into contact with one another, while simultaneously reducing the possibility for conflict. Echoing Montesquieu's earlier reflections on the effects of commercial life, Alexis de Tocqueville wrote,

Trade is the natural enemy of all violent passions. Trade loves moderation, delights in compromise, and is most careful to avoid anger. It is patient, supple, and insinuating, only resorting to extreme means in cases of absolute necessity. Trade makes men independent of one another . . . it leads them to want to manage their own affairs and teaches them how to succeed therein. Hence it makes them inclined to liberty but disinclined to revolution.[6]

What Type of "Civil Society"?

For all the conservative's potential appreciation of the market's ability to create conditions that encourage human flourishing, some vital questions concerning the market's place within the wider social order remained unresolved. These concern the effects of commercial life on a society's intermediate associations, often referred to as "civil society." Educational, religious, cultural, and charitable associations have the capacity to assist people to look towards those higher ends of truth, beauty, and the good that many conservatives believe reflect the Divine within man. Drawing people out of their immediate family without subsuming them into the state, these "little platoons" have long been defended and promoted by conservatives.

Here, we should recall that the modern use of the phrase "civil society" owes much to the tradition of reflection on social questions that began only with the growth of commercial societies in some eighteenth-century European countries. Prior to this period, the term "civil society" was usually employed to distinguish the secular realm from that of the ecclesiastical, or else as a synonym for the political community. Aquinas spoke, for example, of *communitas civilis sive politica*. The coterminous use of the expressions "political society" and "civil society" forms part of a European tradition traceable back through medieval thinkers to Cicero's idea of *societas civilis*.[7]

The concept began to undergo significant change in the eighteenth century. The Physiocrats used the term *société naturelle,* meaning economic relations, to distinguish their area of interest from *société politique*. Likewise, the Scottish Enlightenment scholar Adam Ferguson noted that by promoting a multiplication of wants and a more complex division of labor, the spread of commercial relations facilitated the growth of a range of non-caste-based intermediate groups whose impact upon society could not be ignored.

Moreover, such was the power of this commercial dimension of what the post-Enlightenment era calls "civil society" that even among the earliest observers of the spread of commerce we can discern concerns about its implications for a society's moral culture. Ferguson himself expressed distinct anxieties about the effects of commerce upon what he called "civic virtue." He drew attention to commerce's potential to narrow man's horizons, coarsen his moral habits, and diminish his taste for the sublime.

The phenomenon of consumerism is, of course, not new. Nor is it something limited to market economic orders. The profound shortage of material goods that prevailed in Communist countries, for example, contributed to making them among the most materialistic societies known to history. The ongoing dilemma for the conservative is that while he usually respects the importance of free will, he also holds that what is good for each and every person is not a matter of arbitrary taste. Markets celebrate and seek to enhance choice. They are, however, rather less good at providing moral guidance as to what people *ought* to choose.

Some might argue that as long as the moral culture is in sound condition, people are more likely to make economic choices that will reinforce rather than damage that culture. The fact remains, however, that throughout much of the West, the moral culture is *not* in good shape. In many Western nations, access to pornography is regarded as a right of free speech, abortion is justified on the strange basis that choice in itself "outweighs" the value of human life, and autonomy and tolerance are widely regarded as the only legitimate moral reference points. Throughout these societies, the cultural influences that might encourage consumers to buy Thomas More's *Utopia* instead of the latest offering from *Playboy* are weak. In the wake of the biotechnological revolution, moreover, the stakes have become even higher: businesses anxious to pursue the potential profits to be made from practices such as embryonic stem-cell research (which involves the intentional destruction of embryonic human beings) increasingly appeal to consumer choice to justify experimental practices that both reflect and contribute to what some have aptly described as a culture of death, understood as an array of outlooks and practices indicating a willingness to *intend* the death of others for the sake of individual expediency, utility, or self-satisfaction.

Conservatives therefore find themselves in a bind. While Western moral culture remains immersed in the quicksands of utilitarianism, a willingness to detach liberty from truth, and a mindset of what Plato described as "practical atheism" (when people live and act as if God does not exist), then the market is

likely to reflect the choices of many for a culture that does not aspire to be authentically human, and in which many intermediate associations cannot even begin to understand why "having" ought to serve "being." Conservatives, one hopes, will regard themselves as compelled to resist this. But can they do so in ways that do not emasculate the market, the material prosperity it generates, and its potential to help people to acquire particular virtues?

One way for conservatives to grapple with this matter is to examine whether it is possible to ground key market institutions, such as contracts and the rule of law, in a human anthropology that does not take its inspiration from emotivists such as David Hume or utilitarians such as Jeremy Bentham. To put it another way: is it possible to base purportedly "liberal" market-economic arrangements upon "nonliberal" understandings of man? At this point in history, the answer is not yet clear.

Conservatives nevertheless need not be daunted by such intellectual challenges. After all, the moral validity of private property was firmly established by some of the finest minds produced by Western civilization centuries before John Locke penned his thoughts on the matter. Likewise, the practices of commerce, free trade, and markets were not foreign to the world of the High Middle Ages. Neither, one imagines, were materialism or mindsets that we would describe today as consumerist. Yet conservatives, one suspects, are likely to recognize the pre-Enlightenment reasoning underpinning these arrangements as more true to the nature of man as *homo religiosus, homo creator, homo dignus, homo rationalis,* and *homo peccatus* than the emoting pleasure-maximizer that Bentham and other moderns would have us believe humans to be. Retrieving and renewing these older traditions and introducing them to contemporary reflection about the market economy is surely an appropriate endeavor for conservatives, and a genuine contribution to civilizational renewal.

Notes

1. See, for example, Walter Eucken, *Grundsätze der Wirtschaftspolitik* (Tübingen: Mohr Siebeck, 1952); Franz Böhm, "The Rule of Law in a Market Economy," in A. Peacock and H. Willgerodt (eds.), *Germany's Social Market Economy: Origins and Evolution* (London: Macmillan, 1989), 115–31.

2. Wilhelm Röpke, "The Economic Necessity of Freedom," *Modern Age* 3 (Summer 1959), 230.

3. Ibid., 230.

4. Murray Rothbard, "The Hermeneutical Invasion of Philosophy and Economics," *Review of Austrian Economics* 3, (1989), 45.

5. See John Finnis, *Natural Law and Natural Rights* (Oxford: Clarendon Press, 1980), 298–308.

6. Alexis de Tocqueville, *Democracy in America*, ed. J. P. Mayer, trans. G. Lawrence (New York: Perennial Classics, 2000), 637.

7. See John Keane, "Despotism and Democracy: The Origins and Development of the Distinction between Civil Society and the State 1750–1850," in John Keane (ed.), *Civil Society and the State: New European Perspectives* (London: Verso, 1988), 36.

VI.

THE LONG, TWILIGHT STRUGGLE

Gerhart Niemeyer

National Self-Defense
and Political Existence

VOL. 2, NO. 5, 1966

Our existence as a nation is threatened today, not only from without but from within, by moral erosion and civic disintegration. Two decomposing forces are at work the Marxist condemnation of our entire social structure, and the pacifist rejection of our right to national self-defense. Both attacks compel us to rethink problems to which we have given little attention for many, many years. The problem of modern war is confusing enough in its technological aspects. It is also maintained that the technology of modern war has totally changed the relation between war and political order, so that now political order could no longer be maintained if the price of its maintenance is war. On the other hand, our time has revived the doctrine of just war, both on the Communist side and on our own, although the two doctrines are quite different. At any rate, clarity about the problem of war in its moral aspects belongs to the intellectual equipment the modern citizen needs.

A footnote first: One does not consider the problem of morality and war in timeless abstraction but rather in the setting of a singular historical situation. Our

situation is singular in that we are living in a political order created by Western civilization under assault by the hostile force of communism. Both sides are armed with nuclear weapons. There are those who would also mention the United Nations among the features making up the singularity of our historical situation. I personally would not do this, on the grounds that the UN, while designed to alter the nature of international politics, has in fact not done anything of the kind and has played, by and large, a minor role in contemporary affairs. That leaves Western civilization, communism, and nuclear weapons as the salient features, as far as the problem of war is concerned. One more prefatory remark concerning the approach to morality: We take it for granted that nobody today thinks of morality in the terms of that caricature drawn up in the eighteenth century, a body of cut-and-dried abstract principles valid unchangeably for all times and places. Rather, we approach moral problems as Aristotle suggested: as the mature man's rational response to reality, both the fundamental reality of being and his own nature, and the changing reality of time and place. (Cf. Eric Voegelin, *Das Rechte von Natur, Zeitschrift für Öffentliches Recht*, XIII, 38–51.)

As children of Western civilization, who cannot cut ourselves off from our own shadows, we cannot overlook what the great minds of the West have found out about war and morality. Among the remarkable products of this civilization of ours is a doctrine of just war, or, as Paul Ramsey suggests, "justifiable war" (Paul Ramsey, *War and the Christian Conscience*, 1961). There is no need to study the history of this doctrine in detail, but it may be useful to recall that there are at least three different versions of it and that the distinction between them may help us considerably. Augustine, the originator of the doctrine, did *not* say that war was justified if and when one side defended a just cause. He had too low an opinion of the justice of human causes to take that position. We remember his argument against Cicero who had claimed that a people was constituted by "common interests and a common acknowledgement of right," i.e., "true justice." Augustine demolished this view, pointing out that "true justice" is the property of God rather than of fallen man and that a people was held together by "a common agreement as to the objects of their love," as were, e.g., the Romans by their common love for liberty and the praise of men. Augustine's definition of a people is a far more existential one. Whatever it is that a people may love, they are a people in so far as they agree on a common object of love. Furthermore, a people and the government that it produces are the existential foundation of peace and order and justice, "such as this mortal life can afford." This peace, imperfect as it may be, all the same participates in the perfection of God's peace. Any created nature requires peace and seeks peace even through strife.

Augustine clinches this point by observing that even bandits maintain peace in their gang, but then hastens to add that the peace of the wicked "does not deserve to be called peace."

These are the conceptual elements from which Augustine shapes his doctrine of the justification of war, i.e., of military action aimed at killing enemies for the sake of public defense. His justification of war is remarkable in that he denies justification of killing to which a private person may resort in individual self-defense. Confronted with an armed robber who threatens my life, I may still not seek to kill him, says Augustine, for this would put an inordinate value on my own life, something that should not be loved more than it is worth, i.e., more than God. Augustine remarks that the law permits killing in individual self-defense but points out that the virtuous man is not enjoined by the law to kill under such circumstances. The soldier, however, is in a different situation. The law bids him kill the enemy and punishes him if he does not do so. Moreover, when engaged in military action, the soldier acts not in his own interest but as an "agent of the law." He takes life not for his own good but for the common good, the peace and order that is endangered by the enemy. And his is an action prompted by the common love through which he is a part of his people. Thus it is in the spirit of service to good and sacrifice for others that killing is justified. The background of all this, of course, is the assumption that wars will occur, for, as Augustine says, "It is the wrongdoing of the opposing side that compels the wise man to wage just war." This is no cause for moral celebration, for the war is caused by wrongdoing but not justified by one's own high justice, and both war and wrongdoing are occasion for deep grief for all of us.

THE TYPE of doctrine of just war of which all of us tend to think automatically was not developed until the sixteenth and seventeenth centuries. It is linked with the names Victoria and Grotius who developed the concept that a nation can be justified in going to war only if it acts to punish a wrong or vindicate a right. All nations together were assumed to constitute one legal community in which the enforcement of justice lay within the particular nations (Cf. Walter Schiffer, *The Legal Community of Mankind,* 1954). In a sense this is a return to Cicero's idea. But it also amounts to the idea that wars arise over cases which can be catalogued and handled in terms of particular rights and particular wrongs and that wars are necessary because there is no supranational agency to adjudicate these cases and enforce the judgments. This idea came to the fore again after World War I when it served as the foundation for the League of Nations and, later, the United Nations. The new concept was that of "disputes" which, if not settled, presumably forced nations to go to war. Accordingly, the League of Nations established machinery for the "peaceful settlement of disputes" and sought to make use of this machinery obligatory for all nations. The doctrine of just war in the sense of Grotius was now converted into another one in which war in defiance of this international machinery was termed "aggression," and resistance to aggression was called "sanctions." As we know, the peaceful settlement machinery of the League, or that of the UN, was never fully accepted and thus the sole concrete substance of the concept of "aggression" was removed. All the same, the concept has played a major role in modern times as a general term of condemnation in connection with military action.

Between Grotius's doctrine and the modern idea of "aggression" and "sanction"

another view of war was developed. It stemmed from Vattel's observation, in the eighteenth century, that since there was no objective way of determining the justice of either side in a war, and since both sides claimed that they fought for a just cause, in effect both sides were equal in that respect. Accordingly, the nineteenth century no longer was interested in justifying war on the basis of just causes but rather talked of power conflicts and the requirements of the balance of power. We have here not so much a justification as a characterization of war. Wars will occur when several units of order and political existence rub shoulders with each other and occasionally find themselves in a conflict that to each side appears as a clash of existences. This is a late formulation of an insight that can be found in much earlier writings, even though in not fully elaborated form: while actions are subject to moral judgments and are appropriate matters for judicial contention and verdict, existences as such are not. There is no way to adjudicate the claim of one people to exist as compared with that of another, and a conflict, once it has arisen, is not resolved by the observation that both have an equal claim. What is more, a clash of political units involves existence which for many people constitutes the setting of peace, order, justice, that is, the representation of the good and true in their lives. If we look closer, it is this same insight that prompted Augustine to justify action in defense of a people which he characterized as no more than a group in agreement on a common object of love, i.e., an existential community.

There is one other, ultra-modern version of the doctrine of just war (let the reader note that I use the word "modern" without the usual overtones of praise) many people doubt the right of our country to go to war, to "impose our will on others" unless and until our society has become perfect. This notion is ideologically complex, for it stems from the background of the total critique of society as taught by communism, anarchism, and other radically revolutionary movements of our time. Society, so it is implied, has no right to do anything, including engaging in war, maintaining public order through judges and police, and levying taxes, as long as it has the marks of imperfection upon it. While faulty, everything that a society does lacks title of authority. This implies that once perfect, a society could do no wrong. We must remember that the Communist and anarchist ideologies postulate that whatever society will emerge from the destruction of the present-day society will by definition be perfect.

Enough of the doctrines by which war has been justified. None of these doctrines can be ignored when we make up our mind on morality and war. That does not mean that all of them are equally valid. I may have already indicated that I regard Augustine's view as free from self-righteous pretenses as well as clearly aware of political realities and thus to be preferred, even though the part of truth that is contained in the others must not suffer neglect. The doctrine of just war represents our participation in Western civilization. We must now turn to the second great reality of our time, the Communist attack on our society.

THE CRUCIAL question about communism is whether we are or are not to regard it as simply one government among others, a government, let us say, with a peculiar economic system. The organization of communism calls itself a party. A party normally is a group of persons standing ready to run a government.

A government, as we have seen, procures peace, establishes order, and administers justice within its realm. In that sense, the Communist Party is misnamed, for rather than running a government it substitutes for government a conflict operation which knows no peace and respects no justice. For Communists postulate the continuation of a bitter struggle against a more powerful class enemy even after they have assumed power in a country. They expect this struggle to continue for an indefinite time to come. They regard themselves as a minority surrounded by people whose instincts, habits, and traditions are alien and injurious to Communists and whose resistance they cannot possibly conquer by force. They assume that they and their subjects are *not* bound by a common love. Thus the co-existence of Communists with these elements is not peace, even though the struggle may be conducted with the instruments of government rather than those of armies. Lenin coined the concept of "protracted struggle," a struggle that would continue during the entire "period of transition" between the overthrow of capitalism and the emergence of the new society. Stalin characterized this period as "an entire historical era, replete with civil wars and external conflicts, with persistent organizational work and economic construction, with advances and retreats, victories and defeats." During this period, there could be no government. What the Communists put in place of government carries the name of "dictatorship of the proletariat." Lenin emphasizes the difference quite consciously. "The dictatorship of the proletariat," he says, "is not the organization of order but the organization of war," Stalin, too, speaks of this regime in terms of military conflict: "general staff," "strategy," "tactics," "reserves," and so on. The purpose of this regime is not to maintain peace but to wage the "protracted struggle," to combat an enemy with whom one has to co-exist and whom one cannot "vanquish" by force, to maintain the spirit of irreconcilable struggle within the ranks of the Revolution. As the regime does not serve peace, neither does it look to justice. On Lenin's showing, the regime is "based on force and not limited by law." Justice, he insisted, must be subordinated to the requirements of the class struggle.

The Communist power organization closely adheres to these ideological concepts. War-like operations have characterized the Communist regime from the outset. The police is organized and operates as an army. It has all kinds of weapons, is housed in barracks, and trained to fight in military formation. The regime maintains a host of spies against its subjects. It engages in activities designed to break the spirit of its subjects. It takes life among its subjects not on the grounds of wrongdoing but on the grounds of hostility. If the Communist regime resembles a government, it is a military government conducted by an occupation force, in the midst of a hostile country. Military government is part of a general combat operation, and so is the regime of the Communist enterprise. As no Communist regime yet has brought peace to the people it controls, so Communist foreign relations have aimed at conflict rather than peace. The avowed chosen instrument of Communist foreign policy is a type of conflict defined as "wars of liberation and popular uprisings." In spite of the definition, these movements of subversion and unrest are not confined to the cause of liberation from colonial rule. They continue even in countries that have already won their independence, until they submit to a Communist regime. Once under a Communist regime, they

do not enjoy peace but continue subject to the official warfare waged on them by those in authority.

The reason for the "peacelessness" of communism lies in the ideology which has focused the Communist's attention exclusively on the destruction of the "inhuman" present-day society. Unlike so-called "utopian socialism," Marxism-Leninism does not comprise a blueprint of an ideal society. It does, however, contain a strategy for the revolutionary destruction of what now exists. Its faith in the ultimately beneficent "laws of history" claims that nothing but good can follow from the radical tearing down of the house we now inhabit. In that it believes that total destruction to be salutory, communism, along with anarchism, should be called an ideology of destruction. Neither communism nor anarchism has developed theories of a future order. There is no Communist political theory or a Communist economic theory. There is no theory of a Communist culture or of a Communist world order. Some pathetic attempts to lay the foundations of such theories were made by Stalin but did not go beyond the stage of hints. Communists literally "do not know the things that belong to their peace" and could not know them if they wanted to, since their ideology has defined only the struggle, the enemy, and the forces of the Revolution. The precepts of the protracted struggle, of combat organization, and of revolutionary strategy are clear, emphatic, and consistent—but nothing in his ideology tells the Communist when and how to come to rest.

This inability of communism to arrive at peace is what gives the Communist assault on existing societies its peculiar character. That assault fits into no available pigeon hole. Should it be characterized as "aggression" in the sense of the League of

Nations concept? Communists, at least those following Lenin, do not consider war a decisive and preferred instrument of their struggle, although they also reject pacifism as bourgeois reaction. Should one look upon it as great-power aggrandizement in the sense of nineteenth-century politics? Communists are not primarily interested in territory but rather in the control of people and will trade territory for other means of manipulation if necessary. The crux of the matter is that a regime of Communists is a perpetual combat operation and thus an instituted condition of "peacelessness." Societies, which now have governments in the normal sense, pass into the Communist peacelessness if they succumb to Communist forces in any way whatsoever, with or without "aggression" in the form of military invasion. The struggle of "free," i.e., not Communist-controlled societies against communism is thus essentially in defense of such peace as these societies have achieved. One can hardly grasp this situation with the help of concepts of international relations such as "aggression," "great power conflicts," or "international disputes." Augustine's peace as the supreme common good of peoples and his justification of fighting for the sake of this good is more to the point, even though Augustine could not have foreseen the present situation. communism, not only through military action but through its embattled regime, assails that peace on which decent men everywhere depend for their human potentialities.

Now the question arises to what extent the entire justification of war and fighting has been eliminated by nuclear weapons and the indiscriminate destruction to which they are supposed to commit future belligerents. The crux of the discussion in this regard has been the death of "innocents," i.e., noncombatants. Innocents have always fallen victims to warfare. All the same, their death has not affected the justification of war, on the theory of the "double effect." This concept, originated by Thomas Aquinas, distinguishes between the intended effect of an action and secondary or unintentional effect. It is only the intended effect which should be taken into consideration in judging the morality of an action. Thus if military action aims at combatants, seeking to conquer and possibly even kill them, this action is covered by the general justification of the war, if any. On the other hand, the intentional killing of noncombatants is not covered, although if noncombatants are unintentionally killed in the course of justified military action, the whole action does not thereby become unjust. In the case of nuclear weapons, and even in that of obliteration bombing, the argument now goes, this distinction can no longer be made. The death of innocents *must* be intended. The military action thereby turns, at least partly, into murder. War is no longer justifiable.

Another argument is based on the concept of proportionality, also stemming from Thomas Aquinas. He argues for "moderate defense" so that the evil of the remedy should not exceed that of the original wrong. Such proportionality, we now hear, is no longer possible in the age of nuclear armaments. Their use means the mutual destruction of the combatant countries, plus the destruction of other countries, and in the extreme even the depopulation of the earth.

What conclusions are drawn from these assumptions? Some recommend that we rid ourselves of atomic weapons so as to make just wars possible once again. Others would commit us to never using the nuclear arms we possess. Still others want unilateral disarmament. And a few do not tire of repeating "Rather red than dead." The conclusions seem to fall into two categories: either a wish that conditions were not what they are or else a refusal to defend the political order under which we live. Neither can be called a moral solution. One is mere wishing for what cannot be. The other is the destruction of the extant common good for fear of some alleged common evils. An apparently moral critique of war turns into an immoral subversion and disruption of society.

The rationale of subversion says that a society that permits war is not worth having, however, it is not the worth or unworth of societies that tenders wars possible but the fact that human beings live in many societies that differ from each other in language, culture, and the common love around which they are constituted. Reaching deep into historical roots, each of these societies is a given setting of human life: that makes activities, love, purpose, and growth possible. Each of them is particular in the sense of not constituting a class with others, except insofar as it belongs to the class of social orders. "That among particularities accidents will occur is not accidental but necessary," said Rousseau, and Hegel restated the idea in Paragraph 324 of his *Philosophy of Right* (cf. K. N. Waltz, *Man, the State, and War,* 1959). Among the particularities of historically grown societies, war is a possibility on which one must count, just as one must count on accidents in traffic in which many cars are driven by particular drivers. Self-defense is thus necessarily an integral part of political existence in a world of many nations, a necessity that could be obviated only by a world state which in turn would make civil wars and uprisings an almost daily occurrence.

When the will to self-defense dies, the "common love" that holds a people together dies along with it. Citizens become fear-struck demi-animals, each scrambling for whatever small tangible possession has the strongest hold on him at the moment. The impression of the disintegration of France in the spring of 1940 must have been General de Gaulle's overriding experience. He perceived then that without the readiness to self-defense there can be no people and no political order and that without a vigorous participation in a common political existence men fall into total disarray. Whatever mistakes de Gaulle may have made subsequently, this insight rather than any cheap nostalgia for past glories of totalitarian design has been his basic motive.

THE IDEOLOGICAL rejection of self-defense by those whose minds are totally obsessed with the fear of nuclear war amounts to a version of nihilism. To say, "In the atomic age, no society is worth defending" is tantamount to saying that sheer physical existence is preferable to the love of the good that constitutes a people. "We lose our values which are worth defending and then lose our arms and language, and with loss of civilizational identity become incapable of governing ourselves" said Vico, in the eighteenth century, and in the twentieth Raymond Aron adds this comment: "The costs of servitude for a people and a culture may be higher than the costs of a war, even an atomic war." The renunciation of a society's self-defense becomes one prong in a multi-pronged nihilistic subversion, others being the tearing down of sexual inhibitions, the undoing of a common religious orientation, the moral condemnation of the entire economic system, the rejection of anything that speaks of authority, of up and down, more important and less important, sacred and profane.

The attempts to establish the immorality of nuclear war have turned out to stem from either wishful or immoral roots. That, of course, does not alter the fact that the deliberate mass killing of innocent people, either through atomic or conventional weapons, cannot be morally condoned. The answer, however, is not the decomposition of political order but rather the elaboration of weaponry and strategy which, to speak in Paul Ramsey's terms, makes "just war possible." Efforts in that direction have been made and have proceeded quite far. We have moved along three paths: one toward more diversified and sophisticated weapons enabling us to control nuclear force more and more and to subject it to a clear-cut military purpose; the second toward a strategy of nuclear war that has turned its back even on the practices of World War II and is more strictly geared to a "counterforce" concept; third, toward a doctrine of conflict management which has sought to increase and enlarge the situations offering us choices and to avoid situations in which the sole choice is a nuclear strike against an entire country.

No man in his right mind can do anything but grieve at the thought of any war. A "just war" is not something to be sought and celebrated. But the defense of one's peace for the sake of the "common love" which unites men in peoples is so much an integral aspect of our humanity that to deny it to men, insofar as it is defensively justified, means to put nothingness above the good.

Joseph Schiebel

Convergence or Confrontation? The Future of U.S.–Soviet Relations

VOL. 5, NO. 2, 1968–69

I. Soviet Foreign Policy

Those who do not heed the lessons to be learned from the past history of Soviet foreign policy and of Soviet-American relations are doomed to learn them the hard way. This fact may be entirely satisfactory to those who, by philosophy or temperament, are disposed to deal pragmatically with the problems posed by the Soviet Union, but the cost of this approach and the high risk contained in it suggest that we would do well to draw on some of the achievements of Western man in analysis and reasoning which permit us to be more rational, critical, and prudent.

The Soviet system of power is as clear an example as we have of an enterprise operated by people who act consistently with their beliefs—and who act consistently and systematically because their beliefs are consistent and systematic. Throughout its history, the Soviet Union has conducted its affairs on the basis of firmly held and well-structured assumptions and concepts, which have permitted a maximum of resourcefulness and flexibility in practical decision-making. This flexibility is readily apparent in the con-

tinuous and often startling changes and elaborations that have characterized the political behavior of the Soviet regime—behavior which, it should be stated at the outset, has led many observers of Soviet affairs to infer that Soviet foreign policy is arbitrarily formulated and executed more or less in response to the international situation at any given moment in time.

Notwithstanding this kind of mistaken analysis, it is essential to bear in mind that the assumptions and concepts which undergird Soviet foreign policy have traditionally been, and continue to be, remarkably evident in Soviet foreign policy decision-making. These assumptions and concepts have been internally consistent both ideologically and metaphysically and have been neither ignored nor compromised during the first five decades of Soviet rule.

Unless—or at any rate, until—the Soviet leadership ceases to act politically in conformity with its established ideological vision and conceptual political framework, or changes substantially its ideological and operational principles, these will also provide the basic premises with which Soviet international political behavior must be consistent in the future. When employed as one of the constant factors in trying to predict Soviet behavior, an awareness and understanding of them is one of the essential ingredients of successful analysis.

Not only have the basic and currently unrepudiated concepts and principles of Soviet foreign policy been consistent since their earliest formulations, which makes an understanding of the history of that policy relevant to its current analysis and to the anticipation of its future, but Soviet foreign policy has also been, throughout, dynamic and outgoing, not to mention aggressive. This fact has crucially affected the dynamics of international relations because the Soviets have taken initiatives and created realities which have necessitated responses by the other powers.

Fundamentally, Soviet foreign policy has been unlike that of most noncommunist states whose interest in international politics is basically regulatory, mainly concerned with relations among states and with stabilizing those relations. It has, rather, been concerned not with preserving the existing order, but with transforming it—on three levels. The first level of this transformation of the international order was to make room in it for the Soviet Union as a state of conventional form but unconventional purpose, to defend it and to secure acceptance for it. The second level comprises the struggle for strategic power in the world. On the third level, Soviet foreign policy is concerned with the fulfillment of the visionary rationale of the Soviet system, the transformation of not only the world state system, but of the very structure and nature of the social order, from its pluralism of evolved forms to the so-called socialist form—that is, toward the ideal of the totally rational, perfectly managed society.

Historical materialism, which expresses pseudo-scientifically but sincerely the Communist understanding of the world social revolution, not only states that communism exists because the irrational old order is doomed to be replaced by the new order—whose only legitimate master is the "proletarian vanguard"—but makes the pursuit of that vision the sole reason and condition for being a Communist. All this is meant to suggest that it was the Soviet Union which exercised the bulk of the initiative in its relations with other states and societies in the past, that not only political realities but also a fundamental ideological commitment made the Soviet dynamic and aggressive initiatives expectable and necessary, and that any analysis of Soviet foreign policy is likely to be sound only when it is assumed that nations or groups of nations, in their relations with the Soviet Union, over the long run do not *act,* but *react* to Soviet initiatives, subtle though some of these may be.

This view of Soviet foreign policy as the systematic implementation of a firmly held, long-range vision and as an aggressive contributor to the dynamics of international relations is, of course, only one of several interpretive frameworks. It will be necessary to make a case for this interpretation, and to present it along with a critical discussion of other existing approaches. This having been done, it will be possible to identify the main features of both the theory and practice of Soviet foreign policy over the past fifty years. Finally, a correlation of what the Soviet leadership has done, and is now doing in its foreign enterprises, to its stated primary goals and concepts will allow of some careful surmises of what may be expected of it in the near future, and of what place the United States occupies in the Soviet scheme of a transforming world order.

II. Other Views

Since our academies have so far withstood the assaults of those who wish to whip them into goose-stepping conformity with *the* social revolution, and the essential institution of controversy has thus been preserved, differing interpretations are not only expectable but also creative. But the savage competition of ideas bordering on academic civil war has deeper roots. Consuming passions and ambitions are involved in the elaboration of interpretations because they are often meant to serve as operational doctrines for official policies and because they inescapably must engage both our understanding of the world and our hopes for it.

It is fair to say that the bulk of scholarly production on Soviet foreign policy expressly denies that there is any significant consistency in Soviet political behavior, either in time or with ideology, or that there is a fundamental aggressiveness in Soviet policy, or that it has provided the major initiatives in international political relations.

Challenging the contention that Soviet foreign policy can be understood by taking seriously the ideological beliefs of the Soviet leadership are the cynics—those who, professing to live and act according to no beliefs and principles of their own, find it impossible to accept that anyone else does. The cynics see in the Soviet leadership an essentially good-natured group of problem-solvers, reasonable and intelligent though fallible men who pragmatically do the best they can in maintaining the Soviet position in international relations from one day to the next, with no more than a normal attachment to the past and to ideology, and with no more concern for the future than is absolutely necessary. One can start with the *New York Times* in looking for such views.

Whether or not human behavior in fact consists of only conditioned reflexes or whether ideas are a basic prerequisite for action are questions which are too ambitious in this context. They are, at any rate, irrelevant, since neither the Marxists nor the authentic pragmatists (i.e., those who have thought about pragmatism) claim ideas to be superfluous or of secondary importance. To project onto the Soviet leadership an indifference to ideology which one mistakenly attributes to oneself is an error. This projection may very well be the basis for rejecting the notion of fidelity to ideology among the Soviet leaders, since the pose as a non-ideological problem-solver has become very fashionable in American and European politics of late. It is no more than a pose. Even our own leading politically ambitious "problem solver," Senator Charles Percy, once organized the compilation of "Goals for America."

James Burnham, as long ago as the Eisenhower administration, identified the earnest, decent, competent men who could grasp every problem except that of communism as something more than another conventional nation-state. It is, indeed, astonishing that intellectuals have been able to attribute enormous ideological obsessions to Germans, Catholics, Arabs, Ku Klux Klanners, Rhodesians, Gaullists and to almost everyone else except to the Soviet leadership. If the test of any proposition is to be found in practice, those who maintain that the Communists are not only pragmatic but also intelligent ought to consider the possibility that the Soviet leadership crushed Czechoslovak reform, imprisoned intellectuals, and produced cliché-ridden propaganda, among other things, not because these are the least offensive and most effective ways to win friends and influence people, but because

Communist ideas and beliefs are at stake, not their political prosperity.

ANOTHER SCHOOL of thought appears to believe that the kind of ideological and political single-mindedness and toughness which makes a foreign policy both consistent and aggressive can appear only in a monolithic system. One meets them at cocktail parties, among other places, terminating even the most carefully hedged warnings against certain Soviet objectives with the grand phrase that "of course everyone knows that the Soviet Union is no longer a monolith," expecting thereby to have proven beyond the shadow of a doubt that it is sheer insanity to consider the Soviet Union as anything other than peaceful and progressive, or to think about her at all. One might argue that what is said at cocktail parties is irrelevant, but then there is more than a presumption of evidence that a considerable amount of diplomacy is conducted through this institution, and a good deal of foreign policy is formulated there.

To say that the Soviet system is no longer monolithic, whatever is meant by that, is neither startling nor original. It never has been monolithic; if anything, the intraparty and intramovement struggles are better managed now than they were in the past. Perhaps Trotsky, the Purges, and the dissolution of the Comintern have been forgotten. Nor does the breakup of a monolith turn political wolves into sheep. The Hitler-Mussolini-Tojo axis was nonmonolithic but was able to create considerable damage nevertheless. National Socialism became most bestial and war most total after one axis partner broke away and the relationship with the other had become virtually meaningless and after the empire began to fall apart from the inside. The maintenance of the established pattern of Soviet foreign policy requires a very high concentration of command functions in the Soviet Union and within the Communist state system, but disintegrative events and processes have so far not limited Soviet behavior or objectives, though they obviously affect Soviet capacity.

More credible is the position of those who maintain that Soviet foreign policy was, indeed, at one time nothing less than systematic aggression, but that the character of the leadership and the institutional nature of the system have changed, that the ideological obsessions and the revolutionary élan have disappeared as the Soviet Union has moved from revolution to restoration and has become a status quo power which has taken its proper place in the world community of conventional states. Thus, the interests of the Soviet Union in its early years are no longer its interests today, or so it is said, and even though claims and ideologies have not been jettisoned, reasonable men in the Soviet Union are bound to see that their interests are served best when the interests of the world community are served, or so it is hoped. This view appears to be taken for granted by the establishment, i.e., the Democratic (and probably the Republican) administration, their ideological mentors, and the mass of newspaper writers and readers. Official documents, expert opinion, scholarly studies, newspaper comment, and political rhetoric make it clear that a large part of the public and of the policy-making establishment is convinced that profound changes have occurred in Soviet thought and practice (which ought not to be denied), and that these changes have led to the unilateral cancellation of the Cold War by the Soviet Union (which ought to be questioned). One prominent newspaper, in fact, termed the invasion of Czechoslovakia a Soviet declaration of Cold War II, implying that Cold War I had ended sometime before. From this view emerges the conclusion, fuelled by fear of nuclear war, that a period of cooperation and détente between the United States and the Soviet Union has become possible, a period which will result in a mutual interrelatedness and in a political stabilization of world politics (the Tehran-Yalta-Potsdam vision of Big Power peacekeeping appears at long last in view), assuring a general peace.

Détente and cooperation are, of course, highly desirable. The question is how one goes about achieving both, and what conditions and terms of such a reconciliation and mutual moderation of goals and power will have to be accepted. The attempt has already been made in the Soviet-American partition of the world at the end of World War II, and in an explicit commitment at Tehran, Yalta, Potsdam, and elsewhere to cooperate in the maintenance of world peace, guaranteed by (choose one:) two, three, four, five big powers. That attempt has failed. The Soviet Union has, since 1945, projected her power far beyond her "assigned" sphere of influence, particularly into the third world, and has promoted international conflict rather than reducing it.

More important, since those facts could be explained as necessary actions in international balance-of-power politics, there has been no change whatsoever in the basic Soviet theoretical statements which describe any state of cooperation and détente as necessarily temporary. Peaceful coexistence loses its meaning, according to every relevant Soviet statement, when the achievement of a preponderance of Soviet power and a shift of the nuclear balance favorable to the Soviet Union make it possible to proceed with the "unfinished business of the revolution"—the social transformation of the world and the elimination of inferior, i.e., noncommunist, social systems. If a preponderance of power is achieved by the Soviet Union sometime in the future, those Communists who wield that power will not be compelled and, therefore, not inclined to discuss any terms of détente (no more than the Germans were asked in 1945 under what terms they would be willing to normalize their relationship with the rest of the world).

UNTIL THE Soviet leadership conclusively, in theory and practice, makes a presently temporary commitment to détente and coexistence permanent, it would be well to discuss and scrutinize the terms severely to avoid another disappointment when a program of international cooperation once again turns out to have promoted Soviet power rather than world peace. No one, at any rate, here or in the Soviet Union, really knows whether certain temporary Soviet commitments to international cooperation, nonviolent competition, and the maintenance of the status quo will in fact become permanent. It is simply too early to tell whether the presently cooperative aspects of Soviet policy will ultimately turn from a tactical and strategic expedient into a permanent posture. While such a transformation must be hoped for and promoted, premature and careless initiatives toward détente and cooperation ought not to be permitted to provide a sanctuary for Soviet strategic growth and encouragement for renewed aggression.

It is also too early to tell whether, as is often claimed, the Soviet leadership has abandoned its original revolutionary posture, whether the Soviet Union can now be characterized as a conventional nation-state, and whether Soviet international behavior is, therefore, no longer irrational, aggressive, and inscrutable, but rational, cooperative, and predictable.

For historical reasons—the Soviet Union does occupy somewhat the same territory and confronts somewhat the same powers as did the Russian Empire—and for ideological reasons, Soviet theory holds that in the time between the assumption of power by the Communist Party and the consolidation of domestic and worldwide control, Socialism must have a fatherland and conventional political institutions must be maintained. There is more than a surface resemblance between much of Soviet political behavior and, on the one hand, traditional tsarist patterns and, on the other, the international political behavior of other nation states. Here again, it is a question of whether the Soviet Union will ultimately abandon political practices temporarily taken over from the old order which it was otherwise determined to repudiate and annihilate, or whether these patterns will significantly alter Soviet political behavior against original goals. It is also a question of whether the fact that the Soviet Union is forced by the realities of power and international environment, as is ideologically acknowledged, to behave according to established patterns of international relations for as long as it does not enjoy a preponderance of power over all other nations will in time produce permanent changes in the goals and methods of Soviet foreign policy.

The Soviet leadership has clearly stated that during this phase (the length of which cannot be predicted) of forced coexistence and competition with conventional nation states, the Soviet Union is required to behave in some essential respects like such states. It has stated just as clearly that it intends, during that phase,

to continue to pursue its advantage until a sufficiency of power permits the liquidation of this stage and the establishment of an ideological world hegemony and a worldwide social transformation. The ultimate outcome can only be ascertained and verified by historians, and they can do so only when this historical episode has come to a close.

The political and academic analysts of Soviet foreign policy who appear to have been most influential are those who share the basic belief that the Soviet Union pursues power in the conventional sense, and that this power is pursued and maintained by means of rational politics. They insist that the study of Machiavelli, the correlation of Soviet behavior with that of other nations, and the observation of that behavior will yield a correct understanding, while ideological statements are irrelevant and their evaluation misleading.

The Soviet leadership, in short, is said to have limited or abandoned proclaimed Communist objectives, to have accepted the principle of a multi-centered world political structure, and to have adopted a disposition towards cooperation because these are reasonable.

Aside from reiterating the view that the permanent character of these postures cannot now be established, it is necessary to state that the concrete evidence for this analysis is not conclusive and frequently contrary. Since empirical and immanent analysis is therefore problematical at best, while statements of policy and theory are unambiguous, it would appear to be wise for the purpose of scholarly investigation and essential for the purpose of policy determination to rely primarily on the latter as indicators of Soviet objectives and guides to analyzing and predicting Soviet international behavior.

WHILE MANY of those who question relevance of ideological and conceptual commitments to the formation of Soviet foreign policy concede that Soviet behavior can in fact be characterized as having been aggressive and dynamic, there are others who reject that premise as well. Prominent among them are people with affinities either for the convergence school of thought or for the theory of the capitalist encirclement of the Soviet Union. Basic to the convergence view is the assumption that developmental laws or changing realities are inexorably moving the Soviet Union away from those patterns of politics which require of her leadership an aggressive, expansionist posture and are making a defensive, cooperative attitude not only worthwhile but indeed inevitable. While it is necessary to point out that the convergence theory is completed by insisting that the United States inexorably moves in the opposite direction until all contradictions (and, therefore, if Marx is correct, tensions) between them disappear in the resulting institutional homogenization, one does the theory no favor by doing so. One can, for instance, inquire why two social systems should develop in exactly opposite directions (one toward pluralism, the other toward centralism) for exactly the same reason: increasing industrial complexity. One could also wonder why the United States should move to converge at all because, if the movement of Soviet society in the American direction will render the Soviets more cooperative, then presumably an American drift in the Soviet direction will render the United States less cooperative and more aggressive. Since the prospects for any kind of significant convergence are, at any rate, exceedingly dim, and since the history of mankind is replete with many fearful wars between states which appear institution-

ally to have been highly compatible (or "converged"), we need do little more with the theory than to state its existence.

Another view is that advanced in a sizable body of literature, both Communist and revisionist, which has its roots in the assumption that the Soviet Union has, from its inception, been surrounded by enemies bent on its destruction and that any Soviet diplomatic or military action which exceeded purely domestic aims has been preventive or defensive in nature. This, like the view that the United States has never sought to force her influence on any outside state or society, is essentially a metaphysical proposition which is believed not because it has been proven to be true but because it stills ideological thirsts, however pretentious the scholarly apparatus of the supporting arguments may be. One does not dispute statements of faith; one either accepts or rejects them. Since even those Soviet statements which characterize the first fifty years of Soviet foreign policy as an attempt to break out of the capitalist encirclement are advanced within the context of arguments that the successful defense of the Soviet Union must necessarily be followed by Communist expansion, there is no reason whatsoever for accepting this interpretation.

III. Ideological and Institutional Mainsprings

It is one thing to insist that Communist theory provides a broader and more meaningful basis for analyzing Soviet foreign policy than the observation of political behavior alone. It is another to define and describe that theory. Our concern must be with ideology as the metaphysical basis for all political action and with the operational aspects of Communist theory, that is, those propositions which directly determine and delimit concrete goals and action.

It appears unreasonable to assume that the Soviet leaders, alone among all men who have ever held political power, plan their political roles solely as the servants of the Soviet state and the promoters of universal tranquility and prosperity or that, in the Machiavellian sense, they exercise that power because it is there and someone has to do it. Power is sought and held either for the sake of that power and the psychological appetites its possession creates or fills or for the sake of a non-immanent vision of a more or less perfect, more or less universal social order. Usually it is both vision and power which provide the drive and basic incentive.

While it is necessary to say that the sweep of the vision and the claim for power can be satisfied only by the so-called world revolution, it is also, alas, necessary to insist that the Communist world revolution is very much more sophisticated and real a matter than the notions of bomb-throwing anarchists, Trotskyite rabble-rousers, sinister spies, shoe-pounding missile-wavers, and martial conquerors maliciously or naively associated with that term. The Soviet leadership pursues power for the sake of a vision of a perfect universal social order in which it believes. It is in this respect that ideology is important. The Soviet leaders believe themselves to be acting not by preference, but according to the ineluctable process of history, a proposition which has not changed in any respect from Marx's earliest writings to the most recent official Soviet formulations. They believe themselves to be in possession of the scientifically verified laws of history according to which the entire old order (i.e., noncommunist world) is doomed and deserves to be doomed because it is

not rational and therefore has prevented mankind from achieving full happiness. Man will be perfectly happy, they believe, in a rationally and scientifically regulated social and political environment which satisfies all his material and physiological wants (or at least needs), and from which the element of competition and tension has been removed. The means for achieving this millennium, Communists believe, have been placed in their hands, and with it they claim to have been charged with the duty to bring this utopia into being, regardless of human or other cost. From this certainty that they are the saviors of mankind, they derive their militancy and their stubborn pursuit of world revolutionary goals in almost every corner of the globe—even at this point in time, when it would be clearly to their advantage to abandon them and to consolidate the enormous gains they have made in the past fifty years.

This was Lenin's vision. All Soviet leaders since 1924 have claimed to be Leninists—and we may take them at their word. Virtually all analysts agree that Lenin took his ideology seriously, applied it creatively and flexibly to changing conditions without changing its basic tenets, pursued Soviet power for the sake of the utopian vision, and left to the Soviet leadership a legacy and trust which has to this day not been repudiated, not even in China.

As a social and political system, the Soviet Union represents a unique type. If the word is to be left with any meaning at all, the Soviet state is most decidedly not a socialist state, whatever may be meant by that in Sweden, Yugoslavia, Great Britain, or in the Great Society. It is also far from being either a conventional, multi-centered nation-state or a modern totalitarian manifestation of dictatorship. It combines, instead, three major historical trends in the organization of political power which give it an inner cohesiveness, a concentration of power and resources, and an outer toughness never before achieved by any state. Its base is the structure of an Asiatic despotism, that is, a political system in which a single ruler, with the assistance of a ruling bureaucracy, dominates a society which is politically, socially, and economically atomized. This society does not have the institutions through which it can effectively limit the power of the state. Added to this are techniques of dictatorship developed in Western Europe partly from enlightened absolutism and modern forms of dictatorship. Finally, the motivating element behind this system of power is a messianic ideology which makes a total claim on the allegiance of man.

THERE ARE undoubted signs of disintegration evident within the Soviet Union, and the Soviet leadership faces domestic crises of enormous magnitude. But the anticipation of an imminent collapse of the Soviet system, or its even less likely transformation into an open, cooperative society must be tempered by the realization that systems of total power far weaker than the Soviet Union have withstood challenges far more serious than those confronting the Soviet leaders at the present time. Experience indicates that internal opposition to a centralized state can be successful only if the system is also assaulted from without. There exists no significant outside threat to the Soviet system today; those who are disposed to challenge the Soviet Union are unable to do so effectively, viz., Czechoslovakia or perhaps Communist China. And the policies of the leading noncommunist powers, including the United States, are based on the assump-

tion that the interest of world stability is best served by promoting the stability of the Soviet system.

Because of these policies, which may be defended on other grounds, the Western powers are, as they have been on several previous occasions, providing crucial support to the Soviet leadership in maintaining the integrity of its system. They may, ironically, be preventing those changes from taking place which convergence and evolution theorists have noted or predicted. To be fair, a body of unilateralist opinion, private and official, has advanced the theory that in time the Soviet leadership will have to, or want to, respond positively to such generous concern for its own welfare and for unilateral stability. These unilateralists propose that Western initiatives will be predictably responded to by a rational Soviet leadership, that exchanges of signals will reveal to each side what the other expects of it and is prepared to accept, and that out of a period of signal-communication there will emerge a modus of mutual cooperation.

The signal-calling, which has been in progress since 1961, has revealed some truths, among them some highly unexpected ones. The outlook, particularly since 1965, has become dimmer rather than brighter for Soviet-American cooperation as indicated by Soviet responses and actions. The Soviet Union has dramatically increased, not reduced, its role in Vietnam, has been hell-bent on the development of sophisticated arms systems while talking of nuclear controls and limitations, has penetrated, not left, important strategic areas such as the Middle East, and has crushed institutional and artistic liberalization and reform at home and in the satellites. While our signal-callers have prophesied an end to Stalinist aggression and oppression, the Soviet leaders have restored not only the memory of Stalin but much of his outlook and statecraft as well.

The Stalinist period has been mistakenly identified as shaped by Stalin's personality rather than Communist theory and structure. It will be equally misleading to interpret the new Soviet course or mood as the expression of the personalities of this or that faction. Soviet theory embodies long-range planning and objectives, and Soviet operational doctrines and institutional realities strongly bind and influence succeeding generations of leaders. Style and tactics may reflect personality and factional politics. Concepts and objectives reflect Soviet ideology and institutions.

IV. Fundamental Strategic Concepts of Soviet Foreign Policy

The fundamental thing . . . is the rule which we have not only mastered theoretically, but have also applied practically, and which will, until socialism finally triumphs all over the world, remain a fundamental rule with us, namely, that we must take advantage of the antagonisms and contradictions between two capitalisms, two systems of capitalist states, inciting one against the other. As long as we have not conquered the whole world, as long as, from the economic and military standpoint, we are weaker than the capitalist world, we must adhere to the rule that we must know how to take advantage of the antagonisms and contradictions existing among the imperialists."[1]

Here, and in the remainder of this speech, given in September, 1920, Lenin bares what have been the two major premises of Soviet foreign policy since 1920. The first is the assumption that, for a considerable period of time, the socialist powers will be weaker than the noncommunist states, and will, therefore, in order to defend the revolution and to create opportunities to advance it, have to operate within the existing international order. The second is the assumption that during this "third stage," as Stalin called it, a strategy of promoting and inciting major international conflicts among noncommunist states must divert the energies and efforts of noncommunist states and peoples to serve Soviet ends. I would call this the jiu jitsu style of foreign policy: the technique of turning political energies of noncommunist states against themselves. This makes diplomacy, propaganda, and political manipulation the primary means of securing and advancing Communist power.

Reliance on theoretical statements here does not constitute citatology, or the custom of finding an explanation for Soviet behavior in this or that obscure quotation from Communist scriptures. Not all Communist statements are of equal weight, nor do they refer to matters of equal magnitude. The Leninist concepts referred to here, which have been constantly reiterated ever since his time by other Communist leaders, established principal goals for a major period of Soviet policy. Every significant concrete initiative in the past fifty years has reflected them, which alone would indicate that they should be taken seriously. Disregarding these concepts, Soviet policy may be interpreted in many different ways. With them, the task of evaluating Soviet behavior becomes not only more manageable, but the likelihood that our analysis reflects actual immanent goals, rather than imputed motivation, becomes very much greater.

OBSERVING BOTH theory and practice, and departing from Lenin's 1920 formulations, these have been the major sets and levels of contradictions around which the operational basis of Soviet foreign policy has been constructed.

1. An actual and potential conflict between the United States and Japan over strategic mastery of the West Pacific and East and Southeast Asia was identified early. While there is no justification for arguing that Soviet policy is solely responsible for the U.S.–Japanese war, though it had been called for by the Communists, more thorough investigations of the prewar Soviet apparatus in Japan and the work of Communist and procommunist elements in the Japanese government and army (and in other states) may well yield indications that, along with known Soviet political activities, the diversion (and even development) of Japanese initiatives toward the United States and China and away from Siberia and the Soviet Union was influenced by them. The Moscow-initiated Communist-Nationalist united front of 1937 in China did engage Japan in China, the Soviet-Japanese Neutrality Pact of April, 1941, did leave the latter free to prepare for her confrontation with the United States, and the Japanese occupation of large areas of East and Southeast Asia did provide the Communists with the opportunity to establish Communist Party hegemony over the various national-liberation movements which laid the basis for the successful as well as unsuccessful postwar takeover attempts. Soviet interest throughout was both defensive and expansionist. With the exception of the hoped-for major tensions between Great Britain and the United States, Soviet expectations materialized to a great degree. If it goes too far to credit Soviet diplomacy with responsibility for conflicts which might have come about

without it, it nevertheless did play a role at crucial junctures in maximizing, rather than minimizing conflict when the Soviet Union had an opportunity to do the latter.

2. Stalin had characterized Germany as the "mine under Europe." This phrase reflects the earlier Leninist and present Communist conviction that the latent conflicts between Germany and the major Western powers, and among the latter over Germany, have the greatest potential for intra-capitalist wars from which the Soviet Union can gain, and for the prevention of that general solidarity among the major noncommunist powers which would be disadvantageous to the interests of the Soviet Union and the Communist movement. Lenin and Stalin foresaw a magnificent opportunity to exacerbate deep hostilities between "vanquished" and "semi-colonial" Germany and the victorious and domineering Western powers into a general world conflagration, preferably with the Soviet Union as an uninvolved bystander. The main results of this posture were expected to be the prevention of an anti- or noncommunist alliance against the Soviet Union, the greatest possible perpetuation of European political, social, and economic instability, a general European war providing the Soviet Union with a variety of opportunities for political and territorial expansion, a weakening of the Western powers to reduce their ability to resist Communist advances into dependent and semi-dependent non-Western areas (decolonization) and a preoccupation with Germany as the major problem of world diplomacy to divert attention from the problems and challenges posed by the Soviet leadership. All these expectations were fulfilled to a remarkable degree. While the Japanese policy has had to be downgraded after World War II for

a number of reasons, Germany remains today the principal focus of the Soviet strategy of maintaining, to its advantage, a divisive worldwide concern with that country.

The Soviet German policy could not have been more consistently applied in the past fifty years. It began with Soviet support for German revisionist anti-Versailles interests and the secret rearmament of Germany in the Soviet Union after World War I, was reflected in the Communist efforts to undermine the Weimar Republic, explains the crucial assistance provided by the German Communist Party to the National Socialists in their struggle against the republic and German social democracy from 1928 to 1933, was behind the Soviet efforts in the formation of an anti-German alliance in the nineteen-thirties, and reached its peak in the Soviet-German nonaggression pact and partition of Poland which permitted the commencement of the tragic chain of events leading to World War II from which the Soviet Union, despite her own destructive and unanticipated involvement, emerged as a major world power.[2] After an initial postwar attempt to mobilize hoped-for German resistance to integration with the Atlantic powers, the Soviet Union returned, with the Twentieth Party Congress of 1956, to a persistent policy of promoting, through diplomacy and propaganda, anti-German postures among her potential and actual partners, with the goal of perpetuating Germany's position as an object of big-power competition and of undermining her role as a productive partner in a general rapprochement and integration. Concrete gains are expected from external tensions over Germany and from internal disintegration and radicalization, both of which are actively being promoted.

3. While the strategy of dividing the principal noncommunist powers has been primarily defensive and only occasionally expansionist, a strategy was devised for expanding into the strategically weak area of the so-called third world of underdeveloped, backward, or neutral nations while the main powers were being limited, co-opted, or paralyzed. Lenin drew on the experience of the Russian October Revolution which, as organized by him, had placed a small Communist elite at the head of a general anti-autocratic movement of liberation with the mass support of the peasantry whose adherence had been gained by offering them a fraudulent land reform program. The road to Paris was said to lead through Peking, a formulation which expresses the Communist judgment that the prospects for major revolutionary gains are for the time being greater in the so-called colonial countries than in the capitalist societies which had unexpectedly withstood the revolutionary tide which had emerged in 1918, and that the establishment of Communist control over colonial areas—on which the Western powers were believed to depend for economic survival—would weaken those powers in preparation for a later direct confrontation.

The class struggle was now redefined as including antagonisms between oppressor nations and all the peoples, including the national bourgeoisie (the class enemy of tomorrow), of the colonial countries, and the presence of a mass revolutionary force was seen in the peasantry whose land-hunger was noted. The strategy of the Communist movement now had become the organization and control of movements of national liberation which were, when they had succeeded, to be converted into Communist regimes. As particularly exemplified by Comintern efforts in China, the expectation in the

1920s was that a Communist-infiltrated nationalist movement would achieve independence and power, whereupon a coup would convert the new regime into a Communist dictatorship, with those having ridden the tiger ending up inside. In the 1930s, Communist movements frantically attached themselves to nationalist movements and regimes to remain viable, and to influence national policies as much as possible to contribute to the polarization of the world that was desired, namely the emergence of opposing blocs of "fascist-militarist" and "democratic-imperialist" states. In the 1940s, Moscow-led Communist parties "became" anti-fascist resistance movements and "leaders" in the struggle for national liberation from fascist and militarist oppression, a strategy which resulted not only in a great number of outstanding recruits and much good will, but in the political and military base essential to the postwar efforts to establish Communist regimes wherever conditions permitted them. During that time also, "agrarian reform" became an important strategic factor through which was won not only great support among the masses, but from Western intellectuals, propagandists, and governments as well. In the 1950s, the third-world strategy was attached to the so-called process of decolonization, and noncommunist nationalist regimes were enlisted in a general posture of neutralism which, while it was not particularly helpful to Communist expansion, was immensely harmful to the strategic position and moral prestige of the West. The offensive to form Communist-led national-liberation movements and to convert extreme nationalist regimes through Communist coups was resumed in the late 1950s and continues into the 1960s. While hitherto there has been a cannon-fodder approach to such movements and regimes, with the

Soviet Union providing little concrete assistance, or pretending not to, the 1970s quite likely will see an increase in both the militancy of national-liberation wars and movements, and in direct strategic Soviet support for them. The anticipated result will be a far-reaching Soviet hegemony over a substantial portion of the world's territory and population which, together with major advances in Soviet strategic military power and a disintegration of the cohesiveness, power, and will of the noncommunist nations, will decisively tip the balance in favor of the Soviet Union and permit it to proceed with the next two points on the original Leninist agenda, the mobilization of another round of intracapitalist confrontations, and the final showdown between the "two camps."

4. Lenin and Stalin had identified the latent tensions between the United States and her democratic allies as the fourth major set of contradictions which would weaken the noncommunist world and provide expansionist opportunities for Soviet power. Clearly documentable applications of this strategy of driving wedges between them can be found consistently since the 1920s, and its intensification, and success, in the past few years are so evident as to scarcely require mention. The thrust of the bulk of Communist propaganda, Communist-led opposition movements, and bona fide dissident expression has been that the United States is morally and strategically unfit for leadership of the noncommunist world. The aim has been to create a crisis of confidence between the United States and other states and peoples leading to the isolation of the United States as a world power. Opposition to the Vietnam War, to the American strategic and developmental presence in various parts of the world, the denigration of American culture, exposure of American racial and

social problems have centered around the point that the United States must not be emulated, followed, cooperated with, or respected. Ironically, American inability or unwillingness to provide decisive assistance or leadership has also been used in propaganda intended to convey the message to some nations that dependence on an unreliable super-power is unwise. There is a multitude of ways, some simple and others very subtle, to promote discord and distrust among noncommunist nations, and the Soviet leadership has missed few opportunities to seek to alienate the United States from the rest of the world.

V. Prospects for Soviet Foreign Policy and Soviet-American Relations

The fifth major set of contradictions identified by Lenin in 1920 was the struggle for strategic power between the United States and the Soviet Union, in which the issue over which social system prevailed would be finally decided. Available evidence would indicate that it is premature to assume the Soviet Union to now be determined to avoid such a clash. At the same time, the existence of nuclear and other horror weapons has made a direct confrontation improbable and the experience with Communist China has indicated the strong likelihood that communism, once established worldwide, will promptly break up and disintegrate. I believe that the Soviet leadership has adjusted to these realities by aiming now at absolute strategic hegemony over the world, but not a political and military conquest or occupation.

Highly effective systems of rule over large foreign areas have been maintained in the past through select and largely remote controls rather than by a physi-

cal mass presence. One such historic "occupation by strategic controls" was experienced by the Russians in the Mongol period; the most recent example of a state which achieved virtual world hegemony through a highly limited apparatus of strategic, military, economic, and cultural controls was nineteenth-century Great Britain. I see strong indications that the new Soviet style of world politics is going to resemble more and more the old British style of empire-building. The Soviet leaders have been slow to push for the establishment of bona fide Communist regimes in various areas of the world, creating instead a whole series of dependent relationships as if aware that hegemony is, in the long run, more effectively maintained by control than by occupation. A whole array of military and particularly naval developments and the imminent succession by the Soviet Union to strategic bases (especially those which would permit the Soviet Union almost total domination over the Near and Middle East) vacated by Great Britain point to a preoccupation with techniques of empire by strategic control. The emergence of the Soviet Union as a substantive provider of developmental aid (with strategic strings attached to much of it), as a marketer of major competitive goods (oil, advanced airplanes, etc.), and as a factor in the international money market indicate a growing capacity in this medium of political controls. Finally, and there is no British corollary here, while various arms limitation agreements were sought under the assumption that both the capacity and the willingness to develop further major weapons had leveled off here and in the Soviet Union, it is no longer denied even by the Department of Defense that the Soviet Union has made major developmental and production advances in strategic military capacity.

The long-range aims seem, for the moment, to be reasonably evident. The Soviet Union will pursue, in every way possible, strategic, political, economic, psychological, and every other advantage in order to achieve a monopoly or such a preponderance of power over all other nations that, without a worldwide occupation, which would be self-destructive, and without a direct confrontation with the United States, which would be even more so, an ideological and political hegemony, a *Pax Sovietica,* can be established in the shadow of whatever social transformational goals remain to be accomplished.

To compare this concept of empire to the British example is not, of course, meant to obscure the fact that enormous differences existed between pluralistic, democratic England and the single-centered, despotic Soviet system, and that the result of British rule was often (as Marx, for one, acknowledged) progress and the export of democratic institutions and ideals, while no such gains will accrue to the beneficiaries of the new Soviet imperialism.

The German strategy, the national-liberation strategy, and the strategy of isolating the United States as a world-power will dominate operational aspects of Soviet foreign policy in the foreseeable future.

AFTER NEARLY a century of incessant anti-German propaganda in the West, and after the Hitler period, Communists have no difficulty in finding responses to propaganda aimed at persuading people, for perfectly good reasons of their own, to undermine German-Allied cooperation in the interest, unknown to them, of the Soviet Union. But there is more to it than propaganda. It has been suggested that

the Soviet occupation of Czechoslovakia in August, 1968, amounted to a major Soviet strategic troop deployment in preparation for an attack on West Germany. If American guarantees for the defense of Germany were to wither and if political disintegration within Germany were to render the constitutional government impotent, such an invasion would not only be possible, but likely. Soviet leaders, at any rate, have said so. While I do not believe the German option to have the highest Soviet priority, I do believe it to be active, because it is reasonably possible. There are political candidates in the United States who a) could be elected and b) would reduce the American commitment in Germany. And Communist agitational work in West Germany has become so effective and organized that the Bonn Republic may well go the way of the Weimar Republic, which was undermined by smaller groups of political and ideological degenerates and wreckers than are today assembled in West Germany—which, if anything, is more permissive of such things than the old republic.

Wars and movements of national liberation will intensify and promise to be particularly rewarding to the Soviet leaders in Africa and the Middle East. There, they can be supported far more directly and effectively than in Vietnam, the slogan "No more Vietnams, especially in Africa" will paralyze American response for a long period, and if initial national-liberation wars are directed against regimes which the United States is presently pledged to isolate and eliminate, such as Rhodesia and Angola, the Communists can also have their forces supported by the United States.

There has been a concentration of attention on developments and events within the Soviet Union which point to the making of a serious internal crisis of control. communism is popular only where it is either unknown or misunderstood, and the Soviet people are no doubt fed up with the system at a time when the disparity between Soviet life and the outside world becomes not only greater but also better known to them. To conclude, however, that a dramatic crisis, which at any rate is limited to a challenge by men and women with convictions and ideals (which leaves out the cynics and managers who may complain but who have neither the guts for nor the interest in revolt at the peril of their status), can only lead to a deliberate loosening up of control and more cooperative international behavior is to overlook the abundant power and potential for domestic repression and foreign expansion.

THE SOVIET system of today is, indeed, not the crude and blundering revolutionary and expansionist enterprise of yesterday. Its apparatus for analysing and appraising social and political conditions around the world is highly sensitive and sophisticated. Soviet foreign policy is opportunistic in the best sense of the word. Equipped with overall analytic concepts and strategic goals, every

discontent, every conflict, every manifestation of unintegrated power is evaluated and creatively exploited. The Soviet leadership, in addition to its troubles, also has a good many things in the world today favoring it, not the least of these being the fact that no Soviet initiative has been and will be resisted when it is not recognized or understood. The Soviet leaders are not omnipotent supermen. They owe their successes to the fact that they were able to so organize and arrange their advances that there would be no enemies.

Notes

1. Lenin, V. I., *Selected Works* (New York, International Publishers, 1943) vol. VIII, 279–80. Cf. also Lenin, *Collected Works*, vol. 31 (Moscow, 1966), 448–50 and Stalin, J., *Works*, vol. 6 (Moscow, 1954), 98–110, 267–95.

2. In anticipation of one objection, let it be understood that, whatever may be said to minimize Soviet culpability in the origin of World War II, the Soviet Union did not have to support Hitler's ambitions at this point by signing the pact. And whatever may have been said about this matter in the Soviet Union subsequently, the Soviet leadership clearly stated its interest in a revisionist, i.e., anti–Western Germany and a general capitalist war before 1939.

James E. Dornan Jr.

The Search for Purpose
in American Foreign Policy

VOL. 7, NO. 3, 1970–71

I

Few commentators on current affairs would challenge the assertion that the present period is one of uncertainty and confusion in American foreign policy. The United States is involved with the external world to a greater extent than ever before in its history, yet at few times in the nation's history has there been more debate and disagreement among leaders and public alike concerning the purposes of American foreign policy and the means appropriate for the realization of these objectives.

In retrospect, I believe, it will become apparent that the present debate over ends and means in foreign policy is an inevitable culmination of the post–World War II revolution in America's relations with the outside world. Prior to the twentieth century, the internationalist and interventionist thrust implicit in the American self-vision lay concealed behind a hard-headed realism in the choice of foreign policy objectives and in the actual conduct of diplomatic relations with other nations;[1] hostility and conflict among real or potential adversaries cou-

pled with a fortuitous geographic position made possible a policy of isolationism or, more accurately, nonalignment, which concealed from the American people the importance of an effective foreign policy to the survival of nations in a world of anarchy. Thus it was, as Charles Burton Marshall has noted, that the United States "came to maturity without having, in Whitman's phrase, to 'learn to chant the cold dirges of the baffled and sullen hymns of defeat.'"[2] Neither did the various international adventures of the early twentieth century or even Wilson's "great crusade" of 1917 mark any significant departure from the earlier tradition. There is little evidence suggesting that the nation as a whole fully appreciated the significance of the Spanish-American War, especially the territorial acquisitions which followed in its wake; and surely neither Mr. Wilson nor his constituents viewed World War I as marking a permanent commitment by the United States to active participation in international politics. Indeed, for Wilson himself, as his critics are fond of noting, America fought the Great War out of a conviction that "the world must be made safe for democracy,"³ and in order to usher in a new era in world history in which an institutionalized rule of law would replace war as the final arbiter of disputes among nations.⁴ The rapidity and fervor with which the nation re-embraced nonalignment when it became apparent that Wilson's dream bore little relationship to reality is fitting testimony to the twentieth-century strength of the isolationist tradition, however transmogrified in inspiration that tradition may have become since its origins in the eighteenth century.

It was not until after World War II, therefore, that the United States came to regard its own vital interests, not to mention its ultimate hopes and expectations for mankind, as depending upon the nation's assumption of an active role in world affairs. This was the ultimate significance of the much-discussed "revolution in American foreign policy:"⁵ the operational vistas of United States policy began to encompass the globe. The contrast with the decade of the thirties was particularly sharp, as more than one commentator has observed:

> In the 1930s the United States had retracted into a pathological isolation: Americans had rejected even the non-compulsory jurisdiction of the World Court, made the decision to retire from the Philippines, refused to build up fortifications on Guam, and abandoned their neutral rights at sea. . . . Yet during the following decade Americans fought a global war, led the mightiest coalition in history, became deeply involved politically in all parts of the earth, made the pivotal decisions that affected the future everywhere, and an American President bestrode the world like Caesar Augustus of old. In the light of its traditional foreign policy this sudden stupendous global

influence of America constituted a veritable revolution, one of the most dramatic in history.⁶

The consequences of this rather sharp change in the operational pattern of America's relations with the external world have been many, and in fact are only beginning to be understood. But surely among the most important is one which until recently has been little observed: For the first time in its history, the United States has been compelled in recent decades to act on the basis of its traditional, imperfectly examined and articulated understanding of international politics, and for the first time as well has been forced to confront the consequences and implications of its classic definition of national purpose. Is the United States in its principles and behavior fundamentally different from the other national units which participate in international relations? Is the American political system the embodiment of the natural rights of man, and thus of a set of political values felt to be the legitimate political inheritance of all mankind? Is the United States destined to help other men to achieve that inheritance? How—by what means is it to accomplish this end?

NEEDLESS TO say, these are difficult questions, involving ultimately nothing less than the self-vision of the nation itself and the relationship between the vision and the nation's behavior in world affairs. It was therefore inevitable that as the United States sought to implement its newly assumed global role in the late 1940s there would be errors at the level of design and reverses at the level of execution, and it was no less inevitable that these errors and reverses would stimulate a reaction at home. Indeed, from the beginning of the nation's postwar involvement in international relations there have arisen frequent charges that our policymakers have acted unwisely in one particular or another, and dissatisfaction with the results of policy has also led from time to time to a questioning of the general sweep of the nation's global strategy itself.

Resistance to the postwar "revolution" in American policy, it is worth remembering, came from both ends of the political spectrum.[7] The Henry Wallace Democrats of the middle and late 1940s, rejecting the mounting evidence that Roosevelt's "grand design" for postwar cooperation with the Soviet Union was doomed, bitterly denounced the gradual development of the containment policy, and anticipated as well the central thesis of later New Left critics in insisting that the United States bears the principal responsibility for the onset of the Cold War. Taft Republicans, on the other hand, although harboring few illusions concerning the goals of Soviet foreign policy, strongly opposed any advance military guarantees to the nations of Western Europe, while appearing to suggest at the same time that the United States ought to have done more to prevent Mao's accession to power in China.[8]

The discontent in both camps was fed by the rather ambiguous outcome of the Korean War, and it is clear that public dissatisfaction with our initial efforts to "contain" communism in Asia had a considerable impact on the foreign policy of the Eisenhower-Dulles administration the much-maligned policy of "massive retaliation" included within its operating assumptions the thesis that native forces should be used wherever possible in conflicts abroad, with the primary American role to be that of providing ancillary sea and air power.[9] If American foreign policy during the Eisenhower years seemed

to suffer—as many critics from all points on the political spectrum have charged—from a severe case of muscle paralysis, it is not only the faulty understanding of the nation's leaders which must be blamed: that faulty understanding only mirrored the state of mind of the nation at large. Indeed, there is little indication that matters have improved much in the interim.

To be sure, the Kennedy era was to have changed all this. The torch of leadership, we were told, had been passed to a new generation, more wise and more able than that which it had succeeded, and we could thenceforth anticipate in the period ahead a foreign policy at once relevant and efficacious. The rhetorical seeds of the 1961 Inaugural rather quickly fell on the stone ground of Cuba, Laos, and the Vietnam quagmire, however, and it soon became apparent to most interested observers that the seemingly vast military and economic power of the United States was succeeding neither in improving American security nor in promoting international order and stability. Increasingly, then, a new kind of criticism of American foreign policy began to be heard: the motives and intentions of our policymakers began to be called into question, and a gap discerned between the end desires of the national leadership and those of the people at large—or, at least, of the more informed and intelligent among them.[10] Our elected officials, according to these critics, have betrayed the national purpose. They have been corrupted by exposure to power, and turned arrogant in its exercise. Indeed, in many respects they have become only mirror-images of the adversaries whom they oppose, and consequently their policies have not only helped create enemies where none exist, but moreover constitute a significant cause of disorder and war in contemporary world politics as well. Such criticism, of course, logically should culminate in a call to replace that leadership with a new group more in harmony with both the desires of the populace and the ultimate purposes for which the nation stands. Some such view as this seems to have constituted part of the inspiration of both the Robert Kennedy and the McCarthy presidential campaigns prior to the Democratic convention of 1968.

FINALLY, THERE has emerged of late still another class of critics whose attacks on foreign policy are far more comprehensive than any which have received a serious hearing in the past. These critics, most of whom are associated with the New Left, have challenged at the foundation the entire sweep of recent American diplomacy,[11] denouncing both the definition of national purpose and the view of international reality which inspires it. Not only are the issues thought to be vital by the nation's leadership said to be false issues, but our historical view of national purpose and even our traditional self-image are asserted to be false as well. There are no universally valid moral principles which constitute the basis for action in international politics, nor is there a vision of political life which provides a meaningful standard against which to measure the behavior of other nations and political movements. Attempts to conduct foreign policy on the basis of such principles and standards, therefore, constitute exercises in futility and self-delusion. Indeed, far from pursuing noble motives in a benevolent manner in its international relations, the United States has commonly acted the part of an imperial state of a rather classic type, trampling on the rights of small nations in pursuit of economic and political power. According to these critics, then, the nation needs far more than a mere

change of leadership; what is required to end the crisis of American foreign policy is nothing less than a radical change in the very lifestyle of the nation itself. The radical critics appear by no means certain, incidentally, that such a change is possible.

In any event, it is clearly a mistake to believe that the present debate and discontent over the American role in world politics is a totally new phenomenon. While some of the current criticism may be more far-reaching in scope than has been the case in the past, debate over American policy has occurred throughout the postwar period, and even earlier. Moreover, it remains uncertain just how widespread and how deep is the current discontent among the citizenry at large. As many commentators have observed, there is no clear tradition of public involvement in foreign policy decision-making in the United States. Americans are normally quite content to allow "politics to stop at the water's edge," and to trust the national leadership to define and implement the nation's international policy. The public, in fact, has rarely joined in any of the "great debates" over foreign policy, except perhaps to protest a real or apparent defeat or to object to the protracted or costly nature of some of the nation's international involvements. Several reasons have been suggested to explain this fact, from the enduring appeal of the isolationist tradition to the political immaturity of the American people (which may be another way of saying the same thing).

But there may be deeper reasons, related to the traditional American understanding of world politics and of the nation's place in it. Until our series of confrontations with the many faces of international communism after World War II, there was little reason to question the twofold conviction of the Founding Fathers that the political systems of the world were destined to evolve over time in a democratic direction, and that the United States was intended to make a significant contribution to that end. At the same time neither the thinking of the nation's early statesmen, however internationalist-interventionist its thrust, nor the American diplomatic tradition itself, until the twentieth century largely isolationist in character, offered much guidance concerning the means and methods through which this contribution would be made.

Considered in this light, the reluctance of the public to become deeply involved with foreign policy issues becomes more understandable: such involvement did not appear necessary, nor, given the general uncertainty concerning how the nation was to fulfill its international destiny, did it seem possible for the citizenry to make a relevant contribution to the process. What *would* be a new phenomenon in the history of civic discourse in the United States, therefore, would be a penetrating reexamination of the fundamentals of American foreign policy which involved large segments of the body politic, and which extended beyond means and tactics to embrace the ends and purposes of foreign policy itself in a world of anarchy. It is far from certain that the pervasive dissatisfaction with the outcome of our Southeast Asian policy will stimulate such a debate; indeed, the evidence thus far would appear to be to the contrary. Should it do so, however, the war in Vietnam might indeed come to be regarded as a turning point in American foreign relations, but not for the reasons considered important by most of the war's critics.

II

A debate of this kind, it would surprise most Americans to learn, took place at the very beginning of our history as a unified national state, during the Philadelphia Convention of 1787. A brief analysis of that debate is instructive for the light it sheds both on the foreign policy concerns of the Founding Fathers and on the whole problem of defining purpose in the making of foreign policy.

The exchange referred to involved Charles Pinckney of South Carolina and the redoubtable Alexander Hamilton of New York, and arose as part of the Convention's debate over the nature of the upper house of the national legislature. Pinckney opened the discussion by expressing his concern over proposals to create an upper house similar to the British House of Lords. Such a step would be disastrous, he argued, because it would do violence to the principle that a government "must be suited to the habits [and] genius of the people it is to govern, and must grow out of them."[12] The people of the United States, he asserted, are "the most singular of any we are acquainted with":[13] they are "not only very different from the inhabitants of any State we are acquainted with in the modern world," but moreover "their situation is distinct from either the people of Greece or Rome, or of any State we are acquainted with among the ancients."[14] The reason has to do with the equality of station characteristic of social life in America: Among Americans, there are "fewer distinctions of fortune and less of rank, than among the inhabitants of any other nation."[15] And this social fact, Pinckney believed, was of singular significance for American political institutions:

Every freeman has a right to the same protection and security; and a very moderate share of property entitles them to the possession of all the honors and privileges the public can bestow: hence arises a greater equality, which is more likely to continue—I say this equality is likely to continue, because in a new Country, possessing immense tracts of uncultivated lands, where every temptation is offered to emigration and where industry must be rewarded with competency, there will be few poor, and few dependent.[16]

Consequently, no one will be excluded by birth and few by fortune from full participation in the political life of the nation. "The whole community," he concluded, "will enjoy in the fullest sense that kind of political liberty which consists in the power the members of the State reserve to themselves, of arriving at the public offices, or at least, of having votes in the nomination of those who fill them."[17]

IT FOLLOWS, then, that the United States cannot draw any useful lessons in constructing a political system from the experience of Great Britain: the English Constitution, although in many respects "the best Constitution in existence"[18] has its roots deep in the history of the Anglo-Saxon peoples and in the political institutions which arose during the course of their social development. There are no "orders" nor rigidly distinct social classes in America comparable to those of England, and hence the basis for establishing a system of checks and balances on the British model did not exist. The architects and builders of American political institutions, therefore, must look elsewhere for their inspiration, and keep foremost in mind the goal of "preserving

that equality of condition which so eminently distinguishes us."[19]

The distinctive nature of America's social and political situation, Pinckney was moreover persuaded, had great significance for the conduct of foreign policy as well. The republican simplicity of one nation's social mores, he argued, was the very antithesis of "the military habits [and] manners of Sparta"; and this in turn meant that our policy would be "perfectly different" as well:[20]

Our true situation appears to me to be this—a new extensive Country containing within itself the materials for forming a Government capable of extending to its citizens all the blessings of civil and religious liberty—capable of making them happy at home. This is the great end of Republican Establishments. We mistake the object of our Government, if we hope or wish that it is to make us respectable abroad. Conquest or superiority among other powers is not or ought not ever to be the object of republican systems. If they are sufficiently active and energetic to rescue us from contempt and preserve our domestic happiness and security, it is all we can expect from them,—it is more than almost any other Government ensures to its citizens.[21]

In Pinckney's view then, the purpose of American foreign policy ought to be the preservation of the nation's domestic political institutions. Asserting the political and moral uniqueness and superiority of the American people and their way of life, he argues that our social mores render us unsuitable for the pursuit of glory in world politics, and implies that if, in defiance of all reason and logic, we pursue an adventuresome policy abroad, our own social system will be endangered.[22] "We cannot pretend to rival the European nations in their grandeur or power," he asserts, and in any event when we secure "civil and religious liberty" at home, "we secure everything that is necessary to establish happiness."[23]

The Pinckney speech stimulated several replies, most of them dealing with his thesis concerning the equality of condition which he asserted was characteristic of social life in America.[24] Hamilton, however, took up directly his views concerning the goals of foreign policy in a democratic republic. He begins by asserting that foreign nations were already observing closely the political difficulties of the new nation. "Foreign nations having American dominions are and must be jealous of us," he stated. "Their representatives betray the utmost anxiety for our fate, and for the result of this meeting, which must have an essential influence on it."[25] Unless the thirteen former colonies can solve the problem of unity in diversity and avoid the dissolution of the confederated state which many were predicting, involvement in the wars of Europe and possible reconquest were real possibilities. These facts, in turn, pointed to the more basic problem confronting the nation:

> It had been said that respectability in the eyes of foreign Nations was not the object at which we aimed; that the proper object of republican Government was domestic tranquility and happiness. This was an ideal distinction. No Government could give us tranquility and happiness at home, which did not possess sufficient stability and strength to make us respectable abroad.[26]

HAMILTON IS arguing, then, that nations do not exist in a vacuum. It is perfectly unexceptional to assert that among the essential purposes of foreign policy is the preservation of the nation's domestic political institutions and the happiness and tranquility of its people, although in fact few of the Founding Fathers believed that this was the sole purpose of diplomacy; but even if this point is conceded, the discussion has at that point only begun. How in fact are the security of the state, the integrity of its institutions and the quality of its way of life to be preserved in an alien international environment? To what extent is a foreign policy which focuses primarily on domestic ends possible, even if desirable? The answer, of course, depends on the changing contingencies of time and place, on the particular threats to its national interests which arise to challenge the state in given historical periods. It is instructive to observe that Pinckney nowhere asserts that, if subject to serious threats from external sources, the United States should pursue a policy of self-abnegation; he merely fails to reflect sufficiently upon the consequences of the fact that the United States exists in a world populated by other political units, each pursuing interests of its own which may run athwart those of the American nation. His definition of the purposes of foreign policy in short is an effort to define away the problem of foreign policy. To Hamilton's credit, he confronts this problem head on, if failing—at least here—to provide much direction toward its solution.

To be sure, neither Pinckney nor Hamilton in their arguments deal, at least directly, with the moral dimensions of policy of so much concern to others among the founders.[27] Neither was this a public debate, engaging large segments of the citizenry in a common quest for answers to one of the great questions of politics. To a far greater extent than most debates since, however, Pinckney and Hamilton directly confront one of the most fundamental problems of foreign policy, and their discussion is thus of relevance still.

III

What, then, may be said of the quality of the current debate over ends and means in American foreign policy? In particular, what of the critics of recent United States activities in world politics: Have their analyses illuminated the essential dilemmas involved and in the process assisted in the quest for purpose in foreign policy? Or are they guilty of fundamental errors of their own, errors which in many cases bear striking similarity to those inherent in the policies which they so vigorously denounce? This, of course, is a large question, which can only partially be dealt with within the scope of an essay such as this. By selecting a few of the more prominent opponents of contemporary American policy for brief analysis, however, it is possible to indicate the principal analytic categories in terms of which the critics can be classified, and thus to examine the "models" of international politics and foreign policy on which their positions rest.

Few schools of thought have had more influence upon the teaching of international politics in the United States than the so-called Realist school, which first achieved prominence in the years immediately following World War II and is generally associated with men such as Reinhold Niebuhr and Hans J. Morgenthau. The Realists, indeed, spearheaded the revolt against moralism and legalism in thinking about problems of interstate relations, and contributed significantly to deepening and also popularizing the attack on the Wilsonian era in American foreign relations which was already gaining currency in academic circles.[28] Among Wilson's most bitter Realist critics, in fact, has been George F. Kennan, whose lengthy career has combined both theory and practice and whose work, therefore, offers us an especially valuable opportunity to study the Realist position.

Kennan attacks Wilson in terms familiar to most students of twentieth-century American diplomacy. Wilson, he tells us, ignored the effects of human weakness and frailty upon the realm of politics, and failed to appreciate the largely intractable nature of conflict among nations. He thus fell victim to a naïve utopianism which led him to define the purposes of American foreign policy almost exclusively in moral terms, and which inspired his belief in the efficacy of legal and organizational solutions to the problems of world politics.[29] Ultimately, Kennan argues, such an "idealist" approach to international relations leads inexorably to a crusading internationalism which is as futile as it is dangerous for even the most powerful of states under modern international conditions.[30] Over against the constellation of idealists, internationalists, and utopians whose policies he believes are primarily responsible for the misfortunes and disasters which have beset American diplomacy in the twentieth century—and most of the nation's statesmen fail to meet his standard in one way or another—Kennan proposes a foreign policy seemingly rooted, Burke-like, in an understanding of politics as the art of the possible. Given the world as we know it, it is quixotic to postulate either perpetual peace or universal democracy as the purpose of American diplomacy, he argues; rather, we require a foreign policy which is "modest and restrained," with "its sights . . . leveled on fixed and limited objectives, involving only the protection of the vital processes of our life."[31] There is "no room in such a policy" for either "international benevolence" or "lofty pretensions," but plenty of room indeed for an understanding of power realities and a willingness to manipulate them in the service of national interests.[32] In terms reminiscent of passages from Burke's *Reflections,* he sets forth his analysis of international conflict:

> The sources of international tension are always specific, never general. They are always devoid of exact precedents or exact parallels. They are always in part unpredictable. If the resulting conflicts are to be effectively isolated and composed, they must be handled partly as matters of historical equity but partly, also, with an eye to the given relationships of power.[33]

Surely, one rushes to respond, here is analysis in the finest tradition of the conservative statesman; here is wisdom in the classic manner of a Metternich or a Talleyrand. The mind boggles: why has his writing not found an honored place in the pages of *National Review,* or at least *Modern Age*? For an explanation it is necessary to look much deeper than conservative opposition to Kennan's often-expressed belief that the Cold War with the Communist bloc is a fading memory, and that the time has long since arrived for decisive action on the part of the United States to set Soviet-American relations on a new course. Neither does it stem essentially from Kennan's bitterly critical attacks on recent United States policy in Southeast Asia.[34] Keenan cannot

place himself or be placed in the ranks of conservatism because he does not accept, at the level of philosophy, the validity of the Western ethical-political tradition:

> We Americans have evolved certain concepts of a moral and ethical nature which we like to consider as being characteristic of the spirit of our civilization. I have never considered or meant to suggest that we should not be concerned for the observation of these concepts in the methods we select for the promulgation of our own foreign policy. Let us, by all means, conduct ourselves in such a way as to satisfy our own ideas of morality. But let us do this as a matter of obligation to ourselves, and not as a matter of obligation to others. . . . But let us not assume that our moral values, based as they are on the specifics of our national tradition and the various religious outlooks represented in our country, necessarily have validity for people everywhere. In particular, let us not assume that the *purposes* of states, as distinct from the methods, are fit subjects for measurement in moral terms.[35]

He concludes with the observation that "I doubt that even for individuals there are any universally applicable standards of morality."[36]

For Kennan, therefore, what is wrong with American foreign policy is not merely that it has been inspired by a moralism divorced from the world of reality and by a legalism which ignores the intractable nature of international conflict; what is ultimately wrong with American foreign policy is that it has presumed to aspire to moral purpose and the defense of ethical-political values at all. Kennan's political philosophy is that of the ethical relativist, who can find no basis on which to propose action in the political realm, except personal or group preference. The latter, appropriately transformed and dressed in the language of the great practitioners of the continental tradition in statecraft, is Morgenthau's concept of national interest.

The logic of such a position, in Kennan's view, leads directly to an assertion of the primacy of domestic over foreign policy, except when serious threats to the survival of the nation compel us to give attention to the world beyond our borders.[37] Thus, students of American foreign policy who were familiar with Kennan's thought should not have been surprised at the essentially reactive and defensive nature of the containment policy as Kennan conceived it: Containment was not likely to lead to the defeat of the Communist enterprise because, in his view at least, it was not necessary that it do so. Never as persuaded as many students of international affairs that ideology in and of itself is a factor of great importance in shaping Soviet behavior, he believed that an essentially minimal effort on the part of the United States would be sufficient to persuade the Soviet Union to assert the primacy of domestic over foreign policy also, and thus bring to an end the East-West confrontation which had begun implicitly with the revolution of 1917.

THESE OBSERVATIONS bring us face to face with aspects of Kennan's thought which his philosophic outlook alone cannot explain. There is surely nothing inherent in a relativist epistemology which necessarily blinds a man to the power realities of two decades of world politics, and which makes him impervious to evidence that the goals of Soviet foreign policy have remained essentially unaltered throughout the postwar period. For all of his professed skepticism,

for all of the idiom of Machiavellian hardheadedness in which his positions are couched, Kennan remains at heart a Wilsonian, who dreams of the day when the world will be transformed in his own image of the good society.[38] Interestingly enough, when he contemplates the mode of transformation his thinking is, if anything, even more magical than Wilson's. Soviet power, he tells us, "is something we have it in our power to counteract by the quality of our leadership and the tone of our national life generally."

> If these were what they should be, they would radiate themselves to the world at large, and the warmth of that radiation would not only represent the best means of frustrating the design for further Soviet expansion—it would also be the best means of helping the people behind the Iron Curtain to recover their freedom.[39]

By the power of example, then, the United States can change the world. Jefferson at his most utopian was never more irrelevant: A policy of skepticism and moral despair, sufficiently scratched, is discovered to conceal yet another example of the American penchant for "talking of foreign policy in a frame of reference akin to the wishful tales of childhood."[40]

I have dwelled at length on Kennan's philosophy of foreign affairs not only because of the significant position he has occupied both as theoretician and practitioner in the postwar history of American foreign policy, but also because of the highly representative character of his thought. Considered superficially, the attacks mounted from the Left on America's Vietnam policy appear imbued with the same "realistic" spirit which is found in Kennan's critique of Wilsonianism. The

United States, these critics argue, has mistakenly become involved in an interminable conflict in an area of the world only tangentially related to the nation's vital interests; indeed, our global strategy itself is rooted in the same false assumptions about the nature of world politics and the purposes of foreign policy as animated the "Great Crusade" of 1917. As a result, a worsening imbalance exists between our international commitments and our power capabilities, and retrenchment is essential if the nation is to avoid disaster.[41]

It is a mistake, however, to assume that the contemporary liberal critics of American policy have been any more able than Kennan to abandon either the vision of the world's future which is so essential a component of their *Weltanschauung,* or the traditional view concerning America's role in the creation of that future. What is renounced is not America's global mission, but rather the means recently adopted in order to fulfill that mission.[42] A careful analysis of the statements of the man usually denounced on the Right as the leader of the Senate "neo-isolationists" makes this point perfectly clear. Even more explicitly than Kennan, Senator William Fulbright has attempted to identify his analysis of the purposes of foreign policy with those of the great European practitioners of statecraft. "The kind of foreign policy I have been talking about," he writes,

> is, in the sense of the term, a *conservative* policy. It is an approach that accepts the world as it is, with all its existing nations and ideologies, with all its existing qualities and shortcomings. It is an approach that purports to change things in ways that are compatible with the continuity of history and within the limits imposed by a fragile human nature."[43]

His "realistic" demand that American foreign policy rest on an understanding of the world as it is, however, has not destroyed the Senator's belief that the United States should continue to seek the political regeneration of mankind. It is through the power of example, however, and not the power of arms, that the regeneration can best be achieved. "The world has no need," he has written, "in this age of nationalism and nuclear weapons, for a new imperial power, but there is a great need of moral leadership—by which I mean the leadership of decent example."[44] And that kind of leadership will be sufficient to accomplish great things:

> Favored as it is, by history, by wealth, and by the vitality and basic decency of its diverse population, it is conceivable, though hardly likely, that America will do something that no other great nation has even tried to do—*to effect a fundamental change in the nature of international relations. It has been my purpose . . . to suggest some ways in which we might proceed with this great work.* All that I have proposed . . . has been based on two major premises: first, that, at this moment in history at which the human race has become capable of destroying itself, it is not merely desirable but essential that the competitive instincts of nations be brought under control; and second, that America, as the most powerful nation, is the only nation equipped to lead the world in an effort to change the nature of its politics.[45]

In Senator Fulbright's definition of the purposes of foreign policy none of the millenarianist hopes of Woodrow Wilson—or the Founding Fathers—concerning the American role in world affairs are lacking. What has been abandoned is the conviction, which Wilson and the Framers both shared, that the exercise of power might at some point be necessary if these goals were to be achieved. Neither the Senator nor any of the other prominent liberal critics of American policy have faced up to the problems involved in defining and achieving purpose in the complex world of international relations.

SUCH IS also the case, it should be unnecessary to add, with the critics located further leftward along the ideological spectrum. One of the symptoms of the utopian mentality is the continued reaching for the scapegoat, upon whom is to be fixed all blame for the failure of the world to progress in accordance with the millenarianist theory of history. Periodically during the course of America's transformation from isolationist nation to global participant in world politics, observers disappointed with the inability of the United States to create the millenium have focused on something called the military-industrial complex as the cause of our—and thus the world's—ills. There is, in fact, little to distinguish the contemporary attack on American policy from this perspective from the long-discredited "devil theory of imperialism," so beloved of liberal isolationists during the 1930s, which sought to fasten the blame for World War I upon the so-called "merchants of death."

One of the more sophisticated variants of this thesis now current is that offered by Richard J. Barnet, of the New Left–oriented Institute for Policy Studies, in a series of widely published articles and a much-publicized book.[46] Barnet's particular fixation is someone called the "National-Security Manager" and his largely autonomous role, free from accountability to either legislature

or people, in the nation's foreign policy-making apparatus. According to Barnet, the National-Security Manager (the term is meant to archetypify the State or Defense Department functionary) views the world through a series of prisms, the product of his World War II–shaped political "socialization," which renders him incapable of dealing effectively with the realities of the present. "Coming to power in the midst of World War II," states Barnet, "he formed his view of international politics from his experience in the struggle with Hitler. The primary problem is aggression. The principal cause of aggression is weakness and instability."[47] Thus, the National-Security Manager takes it as an article of faith that the purpose of United States foreign policy is conflict management on a global scale, especially in the so-called Third World.[48] The United States has assumed the mantle of Rome in the modern world and has become "increasingly outspoken in claiming the unilateral right to make a determination whether a conflict anywhere in the world constitutes a threat to its national security or international order and what should be done about it."[49]

But the National-Security Manager, according to Barnet, is motivated by drives more fundamental than concern about American security or fear of the consequences of international disorder. Whether because he has become jaded or corrupted due to overly long exposure to the responsibilities and temptations of power or due to his inherent psychological make-up (here Barnet appears uncertain, and in any event is not deeply concerned about the problem), the American decision-maker believes that "the acquisition of power is both a necessity and an end in itself."[50] Barnet here presents us with the Hobbesian vision of man: Absorbed with the potential of the instruments at his disposal, he seeks opportunities to employ them, regardless in the last analysis of the necessity to do so:

> The ultimate bureaucratic dream is the perfect freedom of unlimited power. It is the ability to push a button, make a phone call, and know that the world will conform to your vision. The capacity to control, or, as he might put it, to have options, is a much clearer objective for the professional statesman than the purposes to which he would put such power. The guiding stars of the working bureaucrat are not cosmic goals.[51]

It is on this basis that Barnet explains the various American involvements in Greece, Lebanon, the Dominican Republic, Cuba, Guatemala, and especially Vietnam.

While he has never spelled out in any detail his own prescriptions for American policy, his thesis appears to be that our quest for power has distracted us from a larger vision of politics, and prevented us from paying true homage to moral principle and the rule of law on the one hand, and assisting with the economic and social development of disadvantaged peoples on the other. Like Kennan and Fulbright, Barnet accepts the view that if the United States leaves the world alone, not only will the world be a better place, but the United States itself will be more secure. He resolves the problem posed by attempts to reconcile force and justice by asserting that the occasions on which it is necessary for a nation to use force are few, and that in any event the use of force is self-defeating. In his single-minded search for an explanation of the evil which he sees about him as he surveys international politics, moreover, Barnet's simplism far exceeds that of Kennan and Fulbright.

IV

Even the preceding abbreviated survey of some of the prominent critics of recent American foreign policy should be sufficient to indicate the extent to which both the "liberal establishment" and its radical critics have failed to make a cogent contribution to the contemporary quest for purpose in American foreign policy. The "realism" of the Kennan school, when deeply probed, is discovered to consist in actuality of an uneasy combination of skepticism and optimism which ignores as many problems as it attempts inadequately to solve. The "conservatism" of Fulbright is of a similar character, amounting essentially to an undemonstrated—because undemonstrable—claim that the United States can continue to aspire to all of the magnificent dreams of the American political tradition, without fear that great effort will be required for their fulfillment. The more radical criticism of Barnet and his New Left confreres, inspired by a roseate vision even more obvious than that of Fulbright, usually amounts to little more than a search for a scapegoat, whose elimination from the scene would restore the historical process to its proper course. Political "realism" which is not grounded in an accurate understanding of the human condition is, of course, utopianism.

Contemporary critics, thus, have far surpassed Charles Pinckney in their inability to come to terms with the problem of purpose in foreign policy. Like Pinckney, the contemporary critics seek to solve the dilemma of foreign policy by denying its existence, but with far less excuse. In the late eighteenth century it was at least plausible to speculate about the possibility of escaping the problems posed by the "expand or perish" thesis by avoiding involvement in world affairs, although Hamilton had the better of that argument even in the context of that time, at least until 1823. The present period affords no such luxuries, and the need for a "great debate" on the purpose of American foreign policy remains. That debate, should it begin, must contain a dual focus. On the one hand, it is necessary to define once again, with contemporary meaning and relevance, the content of the values of our civilization, and define them particularly in the context of interstate relations. What does the Western tradition have to tell us about the reasons for the division of man into separate political societies, about the reasons for conflict among them, about the possibilities of controlling these relations? What is the role of the "just regime" in that kind of political system? Is peace possible, and if not, how can the use of force best be limited? And on the other, it is essential that these values be related adequately to the complicated international political system which exists in the final third of the twentieth century, and a hierarchy of interests identified which does justice both to principle and to reality.

What the nation needs, in short, is precisely the sort of political wisdom and awareness, grounded in the tradition of the West, which only conservatism can supply. Unfortunately, the work of elucidating a "conservative theory of international relations," and of establishing the relevance of such a theory for contemporary American foreign policy, has only hardly been begun: The Right has largely restricted its work in this area to expounding and defending a rather uncritical anticommunism. If contemporary conservatism is to make a contribution to the forming of the national opinion on this most vital of issues, it must do much more, and do it much better—or the field will be left to the likes of those whose

positions have been partially dissected in this essay.

Notes

1. For a somewhat unconventional analysis of the meaning of the early American diplomatic tradition, see the author's "The Founding Fathers, Conservatism, and American Foreign Policy," *Intercollegiate Review*, VII, 1–2, (Fall 1970), 31–43.

2. Marshall, *The Limits of Foreign Policy* (rev. ed.; Baltimore: Johns Hopkins Univ. Press, 1968), 53.

3. The phrase is from Wilson's Address to Congress, April 2, 1917, Ray Stannard Baker and William E. Dodd (eds.), *The Public Papers of Woodrow Wilson* (8 Vols.; New York: Doubleday, Page & Co., 1927–1939), V, 14.

4. It should be unnecessary to observe that not all Americans were so naïve. Theodore Roosevelt and Alfred T. Mahan on the one hand, and their anti-imperialist critics on the other, were fully aware that the Philippine adventure, at least, presaged something brand-new under the sun for the United States. For a perceptive discussion of the "great debate" over the purposes of American foreign policy which occurred during this period, see Robert L. Beisner, *Twelve Against Empire* (New York: McGraw-Hill Book Co., 1968).

5. See, e.g., William G. Carleton, *The Revolution in American Foreign Policy* (New York: Random House, Inc., 1963), Chap. 1.

6. Ibid., 17

7. For a not-altogether satisfactory analysis of post–World War II isolationist sentiment in the United States, see Selig Adler, *The Isolationist Impulse: Its Twentieth Century Reaction* (New York: The Free Press, 1966), chaps. 14–16, and Norman A. Graebner, *The New Isolationism: A Study in Politics and Foreign Policy Since 1950* (New York: The Ronald Press Company, 1956), chaps. 2–3.

8. Taft's own views, by no means as severe as some of his fellow Midwestern senators, and thus perhaps for that reason not altogether free from ambiguity, are best found in his *A*

Foreign Policy for Americans (Garden City, NY: Doubleday & Company, inc., 1951).

9. The most thorough study to date of the "new look" in national security policy instituted under Eisenhower is found in Warner R. Schilling, Paul Y. Hammond, and Glenn H. Snyder, *Strategy, Politics, and Defense Budgets* (New York: Columbia Univ. Press, 1962), 379–524. Professor Snyder, who is the primary author of this section of the volume, specifically calls attention to the isolationist sentiments that at least partially inspired some of the administration's thinking. Incidentally, it is remarkable that almost no one has called attention to the similarities between Dulles's "new look" and the so-called Nixon Doctrine, at least where nonnuclear aspects of national security policy are concerned.

10. To be sure, some critics of the policies toward the U.S.S.R and toward Chinese communism pursued by the United States during and immediately after World War II have attributed the disastrous nature of those policies in part to the influence of Communist agents over American decision-makers, and to the importance which certain Communists achieved in the decision-making apparatus. But the present assault on American policy, even that which emanates from the tame moderate elements on the Left, appears far more sweeping in its analyses than did that of the old rightists of the late 1940s, it was only in the mid-fifties and later, after the intellectual maturing of American conservatism, that critics on the Right began to interpret the failures of American foreign policy as products of the *Weltanschauung* of liberalism itself.

11. Indeed, efforts are under way to reinterpret the whole of American history from a similar perspective. See, e.g., the essays in J. Bernstein (ed.), *Towards A New Past* (New York: Pantheon, 1968), as well the earlier treatise by William Appleman Williams *The Tragedy of American Diplomacy* (Cleveland: World Publishing Co., 1959).

12. Gaillard Hunt and James Brown Scott (eds.), *The Debates in the Federal Convention of 1787 Which Framed the Constitution of the United States of America* (New York: Oxford Univ. Press, 1920), 160.

13. Ibid., 156.

14. Ibid., 159

15. Ibid., 156.

16. Ibid.

17. Ibid. These quotations are taken from Madison's notes. Robert Yates, in his more terse version of the Convention debates, has Pinckney merely state that "there is more equality of rank and fortune in America than in any other country under the sun; and this is likely to continue as long as the unappropriated western lands remain unsettled." See Yates, *Secret Proceedings and Debates of the Convention* (Albany, NY: Websters and Skinners, 1921), 161.

18. Hun and Scott, op. cit., 156.

19. Ibid., 158.

20. Ibid., 159.

21. Ibid., 159–60.

22. Here, of course, is the essence of one of the more common arguments for the policy of isolationism, an argument employed from time to time by Paine, Jefferson, and John Adams: if the nation wishes to maintain the integrity of its political system, we must avoid contaminating contact with the degenerate policies of the Old World.

23. Yates, op. cit., 162,

24. Of these replies, Madison's is far and away the most cogent, anticipating as it does many of the arguments of *The Federalist* No, 10. See Gaillard and Hunt, op. cit., 166–71.

25. Ibid., 187.

26. Ibid. For an analysis of Hamilton's argument within the context of this theory of foreign policy, see Gerald Stourzh, *Alexander Hamilton and the Idea of Republican* Government (Stanford, CA: Stanford Univ. Press, 1970).

27. Thus, I cannot agree with Stourzh's judgment that the Pinckney-Hamilton debate contained the seeds of the later great debates between "idealists" and "realists" over the purposes of American foreign policy. See Stourzh, op cit., 126.

28. For general statements of the Realist position, see Hans J. Morganthau, *Scientific Man and Power Politics* (London: Latimer House, 1947); *In Defense of the National Interest* (New York: Alfred A. Knopf, Inc., 1951); and George F. Kennan, *American Diplomacy 1900–1950* (Chicago: Univ. of Chicago Press, 1951). For the critique of Wilson's foreign policy, see Robert

E. Osgood, *Ideals and Self-interest in American's Foreign Relations* (Chicago: Univ. of Chicago Press, 1953), and Harley Notter, *The Origins of the Foreign Policy of Woodrow Wilson* (Baltimore: Johns Hopkins Univ. Press, 1937).

29. Kennan, op. cit., chap. IV. Like many of the Realists, Kennan is convinced that Wilson's utopianism represents a radical departure from the nation's early diplomatic tradition. See, e.g., his *Realities of American Foreign Policy* (New York: Oxford Univ. Press, 1954), 6–12. For a different view, see. Dornan, op. cit.

30. The Realists have denounced the foreign policy of the Johnson administration in similar terms. See, e.g., Morgenthau's *A New Foreign Policy for the United States* (New York: Frederick A. Praeger, 1969), chap. 2.

31. *Realities,* 12.

32. Ibid. Cf. Morgenthau's hyperbolic assault on the Johnson administration's hostility to "that middle ground of subtle distinctions, complex choices, and precarious manipulations which is the proper sphere of foreign policy," and its denial of "the existence of priorities in foreign policy which are derived from a hierarchy of interests and the availability of power to support them." *A New Foreign Policy,* 14.

33. *Realities,* 36.

34. See Marcus G. Raskin and Bernard B. Fall (eds.), *The Viet-Nam Reader* (rev. ed.; New York: Random House, Inc., 1967), 15–31.

35. *Realities,* 47.

36. Ibid.

37. To be sure, it might be pointed out that the relativist position can cut both ways. If it becomes possible, under a given set of international conditions, for a nation to pursue, e.g., imperial grandeur without seriously threatening its own survival, and if it deliberately chooses this course of action, relativism does not offer any standard, moral or otherwise, by which to object.

38. See, for example, *Realities,* 104–7. "We recognize," he writes, "that the advance of our society along the lines of its traditional ideals is no longer something that can be realized just within the framework of our national life itself . . . we must be prepared to make real sacrifices and painful adjustments; in our domestic life for sake of the health, of our world environment."

39. Ibid., 91.

40. The phrase is C. B. Marshall's, in op. cit., 28.

41. See, e.g., Raskin and Fall, op. cit., Parts I and V.

42. For a perceptive discussion of this point, see Robert W. Tucker, *Nation or Empire? The Debate Over American Foreign Policy* (Baltimore: Johns Hopkins Univ. Press, 1968), 130–37.

43. Fulbright, *The Arrogance of Power* (New York: Random House, Inc., 1966), 255. He continues: "I think that if the great conservatives of the past such as Burke and Metternich and Castlereagh, were alive today, they would not be true believers or relentless crusaders against communism. They would wish to come to terms with the world as it is, not because our world would be pleasing to them—almost certainly it would not be but because they believed in the preservation of indissoluble links between the past and the future, because they profoundly mistrusted abstract ideas, and because they did not think themselves or any other men qualified to play God."

44. Fulbright, "The Great Society is a Sick Society," the *New York Times,* August 20, 1967, 90, quoted in Tucker, op. cit., 131.

45. *The Arrogance* of *Power,* 255–56 (italics added).

46. See especially *Intervention and Revolution: The United States in the Third World* (Cleveland: The World Publishing Company, 1968).

47. Ibid., 25.

48. Ibid., 27.

49. Ibid., 258.

50. Ibid., 25.

51. Ibid., 29. For an even more damning indictment of the foreign policy bureaucrat—and indeed of all of recent American diplomacy—see Noam Chomsky, *American Power and the New Mandarins* (New York: Pantheon Books, 1969). As an exercise in sheer hysteria, this collection of essays is unrivaled in the recent history of foreign policy debate in the United States.

Alan Ned Sabrosky

An Imperial Recessional:
The "Domino Theory" Revisited

VOL. II, NO. 2, 1976

Few concepts in contemporary world politics have been the center of as much controversy as the ubiquitous "domino theory." The domino theory was first publicly articulated in 1954 by President Dwight D. Eisenhower, although oblique references to such an idea had occasionally appeared earlier. This concept, which was developed concurrent with the globalization of the doctrine of containment during the Cold War, largely reflected an assumption that any defeat incurred by the United States or its allies in one part of the world would necessarily have adverse consequences for the West elsewhere. In its original (and most restricted) form, the domino theory was applied to Southeast Asia in general, and to the noncommunist states of Indochina in particular. Thus, it was first argued that if any of the Indochinese states "fell" to communism, the others (and ultimately the remainder of Southeast Asia itself) would topple in rapid succession like "a row of dominoes." Therefore, in order to safeguard American interests in Asia, the United States undertook to oppose the extension of Communist power into Laos, Cambodia, and South Vietnam.[1] Eventually, as the fighting in South Vietnam intensified, and as the American military involvement in that country expanded in the mid-1930s, the survival of noncommunist Indochinese regimes came to be seen as a test of the credibility of American policy.[2] Even after the withdrawal of all U.S. combat forces from Indochina in 1973, there remained a strong belief in many circles that the character of the eventual settlement in Indochina would have a major impact on the future shape of American foreign policy.[3]

That settlement has now been reached, and the "final solution" of the Indochina Question is being put into effect. With the Communist victories in Cambodia and South Vietnam in the spring of 1975, the "peace" once heralded by Henry Kissinger became a reality.[4] For the United States, however, and especially for its Indochinese allies, the coming of that "peace" meant bitter defeat. The extreme precariousness of the political-military situation throughout Indochina, of course, had long been apparent to most observers. Whatever else they may have accomplished, neither the 1973 Paris accords nor the Nobel Peace Prizes awarded two of their principals had produced anything more substantial than a poor caricature of stability in the region. In the end, the final settlement of the Indochina conflict was wrought not by negotiations, but by force of arms. And in fact, that is the only way that a settlement there *could* have been reached, given the unabated aggressiveness of the Communist forces and the war-weariness that prevailed in Washington.[5] We had finally reached the long-sought "light at the end of the tunnel." Unfortunately, that light turned out to be, as Warren Demian Manshel succinctly put it, a "funeral pyre."[6] The United States had lost its first war.

Despite the passing of overt dissension over the U.S. involvement in Indochina, it is likely that the *dénouement* there will be the subject of an extensive (if not necessarily intense) debate, at least within the academic community.[7] And in many respects, the central issue therein is not *why* that defeat occurred. It is rather what impact the Indochina debacle has had on the American role in, and conducting of, world affairs. On this point, however, nothing approaching a consensus has yet begun to appear. Some have suggested that American power remains intact, and that our Indochina experience can only adversely affect U.S. policy elsewhere if we convince ourselves that such an outcome is inevitable.[8] Others have argued that although what happened in Indochina is likely to have profound implications for U.S. foreign policy, events there were really "only part of a larger process of change" that would have taken place regardless of how the Indochinese conflicts were ultimately resolved.[9] And still others have echoed the assertion that, with the surrenders of Phnom Penh and Saigon, "a full thirty years of American policies lie in ruins,"[10] with all of the con-

sequences for the United States and the world that such a ruination would entail.

Each of these general positions, as well as their several variants, basically reflects different assumptions about the importance of the Indochina conflict for a wide range of developments in the international system. In addition, however, each is also a critique of the validity of the domino theory itself. Other factors are certainly involved as well. But since so much of the debate on the U.S. role in Indochina was expressed in terms of the relative validity of the domino theory, it seems appropriate to assess the ramifications of the U.S. defeat in Indochina within the context of that concept. The precise implications of Indochina for the future role of the United States in world affairs may well not become clear for some time, or at least until this country faces its *next* major international crisis. Some "dominoes" which now seem to be tottering may demonstrate an underlying degree of strength, while others which now appear firm may collapse. But in the interim, we cannot simply await later developments. If we are to improve our understanding of the parameters within which the United States will be conducting its foreign policy in the coming years, it is imperative that we (a) assess the validity of the "domino theory," and (b) explore its meaning for American foreign policy. Only by doing so can we begin to draw from the Indochina experience those "lessons" of the past[11] that must be learned if U.S. foreign policy is to be conducted effectively in coming years.

The "Dominoes": What They Were, How They Fared

There is little doubt that the most immediate, and most obvious consequences of the Indochina debacle have been felt in Southeast Asia itself. In general, there now seems to have been considerably more substance to the original interpretation of the much-denigrated domino theory than some critics of American foreign policy had been willing to grant. In the wake of the collapse of the pro-American regimes in Phnom Penh and Saigon, the Pathet Lao assumed control of Laos virtually without a struggle. Australia and Japan have raised serious questions about the credibility of U.S. defense guarantees, despite continued reassurances by the highest American officials. The Philippines and South Korea have expressed similar reservations, but in a sharper manner, with the Philippines in particular taking steps to "correct" its image as an American client state. Indonesia, one of the staunchest anticommunist states since the abortive Communist coup in 1965, has moved toward an accommodation with Hanoi, as have Malaysia and Singapore. Thailand has undertaken both the withdrawal of all U.S. forces by 1976 and a political accommodation with Hanoi and other Communist states. Finally, the Southeast Asia Treaty Organization (SEATO)—once considered by many to provide a framework for both regional security and the projection of U.S. power—is being phased out in accordance with what have been called "the new realities of the region."[12]

Even with these developments, however, it is clear that (except for Laos) military defeat in Cambodia and South Vietnam did not mean, and had never really meant, that the remainder of Southeast Asia would be militarily overrun by Communist forces. Moreover, there is little doubt that the defenders of U.S. policy in Indochina weakened their own case over the years by raising such

an increasingly implausible spectre. The image of Southeast Asian states toppling like a "row of dominoes" in the aftermath of a U.S. defeat in Indochina was always too simplistic to be truly credible. It was, at best, a poor metaphor for what would at least initially be only a shift away from the United States by the remaining non-communist states in the region, as they adjusted to the changing balance of power there. Yet even if the "falling dominoes" analogy *was* overdrawn in its literal interpretation, there was certainly an element of truth even in that restricted sense. It is undeniable that there has been a substantial deterioration in the U.S. position in South-east Asia. And while the states there may not all be falling like that proverbial row of dominoes, it is clear that the United States is no longer the preferred player in the game in that region.

In addition, it seems that there were other dominoes at stake besides those in Southeast Asia proper, and that the fate of those perhaps less obvious but more fundamental dominoes was closely tied to the outcome of the fighting in Indochina. That is, the domino theory was always more complex than most of its detractors would accept. It was even more complex than many of its supporters recognized, although there is little doubt that its broader implications became increasingly clear to some of them as the end of the war approached in Indochina. Correctly or not, both the credibility of U.S. foreign policy and the legitimacy of U.S. leadership in world affairs had come to be linked in large part with the successful defense of American interests in Indochina. But one of the problems with linkage politics at any level is that failure in one geographical or functional area is even more likely than success to spill over into other areas, especially when that failure occurs in what is generally perceived to be a "test case" for American policy. In other words, while success in such a test case may increase the possibility of successes elsewhere, either the anticipation or the fact of failure in that instance will almost certainly have adverse effects in other areas as well.

The scope of the "domino effect" attending the American failure in Indochina, then, is considerably more substantial than a "mere" toppling of pro-Western governments in Indochina, or even an erosion of the pro-American stance of other Southeast Asian states. Broadly speaking, the other dominoes that are involved fall into four principal categories. First, there are two *psychological* dominoes: the political will of the American people, and the perceived credibility abroad of the steadfastness and the sense of direction in American foreign policy in general. Second, there are two *military* dominoes: the ability of the United States to wage limited war, and the barrier of self-restraint against the further proliferation of nuclear weapons. Third, there are three *diplomatic* dominoes: the viability of détente, the validity of the "Nixon Doctrine" (or, as many have called it, the Nixon-*Kissinger* Doctrine), and the stability of the American system of alliances. And finally, reflecting the combined impact of the first three sets of dominoes in addition to being a domino in its own right, there is a single *geopolitical* domino: the American leadership in world affairs: These dominoes will be discussed *ad seriatim* in the following pages. Each one, of course, could easily be the subject of a major study in and of itself, although such treatment is well beyond the scope of the present essay. Thus, what follows should be seen as but a preliminary assessment of an important set of issues that will be dealt with at greater length at a later date.

The Psychological Dominoes

The psychological dominoes are at one and the same time the most important and the least amenable to precise analysis, for they reflect a subjective assessment of sometimes ill-defined and often unstable perceptions of probable U.S. responses to future events. Nevertheless, it seems likely that the stability of the domino labeled "American political will" has been badly eroded. It is not that the will of the American policy community has been irrevocably weakened by the U.S. failure in Indochina, although the consensus and sense of purpose that once obtained within it has yet to be reconstituted. On the contrary, there are some indications that many of those who comprise the American foreign-policy elite are determined to reassert this country's credibility and influence in the world, if only to forestall a precipitous unraveling of the American-led structure of international security.

A quite different situation obtains, however, among the public at large. Put bluntly, the will of the American people was tested in Indochina, and in the long run—found wanting, with all of the consequences that experience has for Americans' understanding of the United States and its place in the world.[13] The political will of the American people was always, as Leslie Gelb aptly put it in 1972, "the essential domino,"[14] and it remains so in any future engagement. But in reality, that domino had fallen long before the end in Indochina in 1975, even though American inaction and near-indifference as its Indochinese clients collapsed served to illuminate its fall. In fact, the earlier toppling of the "political will" domino largely made possible the defeat of the United States and its allies. Had it not fallen, the United States would not have abandoned its allies. And had the Communist forces not been certain that, in the words of one North Vietnamese officer, "the Americans had lost the will, if not (the) capability, to intervene militarily,"[15] it is doubtful that their spring offensive would have been pressed as vigorously as it was. The erosion of the power of the U.S. presidency in the wake of Watergate certainly contributed to Communist confidence that the United States would not reintroduce its forces to stave off defeat. In the spring of 1972, for example, the North Vietnamese thought that the United States would not bring its air and sea power against them if they attacked; but when they began their offensive, they "found that Mr. Nixon had not been bluffing."[16] In 1975 there was a different president in office, constrained both by his own inexperience in foreign affairs and by a lack of support within the Congress for any further aid to Indochina. But the American incapacity to act decisively in support of its Indochinese allies in 1975 was rooted in a more fundamental problem: the virtual absence of any substantial support among the general public for *any* reintroduction of U.S. forces, regardless of the fate of our erstwhile allies. The American people had become disenchanted with the war, and wanted it finished; they had been beaten, and wanted no more of it. The raw power to intervene was still available to the United States in 1975, but not the political will to employ it.

The apparent erosion of American political will during the "end-game" in Indochina also has implications for the second psychological domino: the perceived credibility abroad of the steadfastness and sense of direction in American foreign policy in general. This, of course, goes well beyond an assessment of the apparent ability of the United

States to sustain its formal commitments to other nations. It also includes judgments on the willingness of this country to act in a manner commensurate with the status of a leading world power, on behalf of the much broader set of interests that such a power has in the international community. But on what are those evaluations based? By and large, it is much more a matter of perceptions of American political will than it is of this country's objective capability, although the latter consideration is certainly not ignored. Yet for a nation such as the United States, which either has or can mobilize great power, the crucial question for all other nations is not whether this country *can* act when and where its interests are involved. It is whether it *will* do so with a high degree of reliability.

Here, however, it seems clear that the perceived credibility of American foreign policy has suffered significantly. As late as the spring of 1975, as the Communist offensives gained momentum, a member of a senatorial fact-finding committee asserted in his report to the U.S. Senate that "If the United States does not fulfill its responsibility to South Vietnam, there may be a domino effect of our lack of credibility throughout the world."[17] Now that it is generally (and in most circles, *accurately*) perceived that the United States did not "fulfill its responsibility" in Indochina, even the most constant U.S. ally must entertain more reservations than before about the consistency and the reliability of U.S. foreign policy, while the perceived credibility in all nations of an American response to challenges has likewise declined. It is not so much a concern that the United States might fail to initiate actions in support of its friends or interests overseas. It is rather that there are serious and wide, spread doubts about the willingness of the United States to *sustain* those policies over time, especially under conditions of protracted adversity.[18] And in the light of the Indochina experience, it must be acknowledged that those doubts have some basis in fact.

Yet there is one additional element that influences the perceived credibility of American policy, especially outside of Western Europe. And that is linked to the idea, "Do the Americans *care* about the people they choose to help?" It must be scant comfort to many peoples that the United States proclaims its willingness to stand by Western Europe, Israel, or a wealthy and useful ally such as Japan (or Korea, on the route to Japan). After all, the United States may well support those countries, at least for a while, if for no other reason than an interest in minimizing the negative consequences of the Indochina affair. But many states must now realize that they have no such claim on American assistance, while even those whose protection is still nominally guaranteed cannot help but wonder at what point that protection will be withdrawn. The remark on April 2, 1975, of Tran Kim Phuong, the last South Vietnamese Ambassador to the United States, to the effect that "Probably it is safer to be an ally of the Communists and it looks like it is fatal to be an ally of the United States"[19] must haunt many decision-makers whose nations depend, either directly or indirectly, on the United States for their security. Nor is this situation altered significantly by the Mayagüez affair of May 1975, despite the general acclaim which the U.S. actions received. For all that was really demonstrated in that instance was that the United States *may* act against *de facto* pirates in defense of U.S. citizens and property, but that at least some other peoples tend to be seen in Washington as Kiplingesque "lesser breeds without the Law" who are more or less expendable.

Until that image can be altered, there is little likelihood that our credibility will be enhanced in the "world arena."

The Military Dominoes

The first of the military dominoes is itself linked to the apparent decline in the credibility of U.S. foreign policy. That domino is the ability of the United States *to wage and to win* a limited war, if it chose to commit its power to the conflict. And here, there can be no doubt; it is now clear that the United States cannot successfully wage a protracted limited war. Nothing in the American political culture prepares Americans for, or makes them receptive to the demands of, a limited war. Despite the late President John Fitzgerald Kennedy's inaugural claims in 1961, Americans are simply not good (in anything short of a crusade, at least) at paying prices, bearing burdens, and meeting hardships when the price becomes high, the burden heavy, and the hardship great. Military intervention, it seems, is really only possible in those circumstances in which (a) there is a "clear and present danger" to American interests, (b) there is a strong public consensus as to the immediacy of that danger, and (c) it is diplomatically and militarily feasible for the United States to intervene forcefully and directly with overwhelming strength. Otherwise, success is unlikely.

The problem here, of course, is that the first two pre-conditions for the successful use of military force by the United States appear to be incompatible with the third in all but isolated cases such as the Mayagüez incident of May 1975. Few threats to American security that are so great and so immediate as to give rise to a strong public consensus that action is necessary are likely to be manageable in a limited-war context. But those potential conflict situations which might be resolved within that context are unlikely to command the degree of popular support required for the limited use of force in a protracted war. Thus, for an American government to adopt a "limited war" strategy in virtually any foreseeable situation is tantamount to accepting the near certainty of eventual defeat, barring the rapid and credible attainment of easily identifiable successes that may bring the war to a close.

This development places the United States at significant disadvantage in a confrontation, particularly when that confrontation occurs in a potential limited-war conflict situation. For in the absence of a viable limited-war option during such a confrontation, the United States essentially has a choice between waging (or threatening) a general war with the risk of Armageddon, or withdrawing from the dispute and accepting a diplomatic defeat. Neither option is desirable, and the fact that this is, in virtually all possible instances, a Hobson's choice weighted heavily in favor of the latter option underscores this point. We may proclaim once again, as we did after the Korean War, that we will not (because we know now that we *cannot*) wage another limited war. But it is precisely this type of war which is *most* likely to occur in the future,[20] aside from the fact that our potential adversaries are unlikely to oblige us by allowing us to wage those wars that favor us. Our Achilles' heel is now all too obvious, and future challenges are all too likely to take advantage of that weakness. And this our allies, our adversaries, and "neutral" nations also know.

A second military domino that has been weakened, but not yet toppled, is the barrier against the further proliferation of nuclear weapons.[21] Other considerations will certainly influence a nation's decision to cross the nuclear threshold, but it is also quite possible that the events in Indochina, plus the now-doubtful long-term credibility of American foreign policy, will prompt several threshold nuclear powers to proceed with the development and deployment of their own nuclear weapons systems, non-proliferation treaty or no. Caught between the unlikelihood that the United States would risk a nuclear holocaust to defend at least some of its interests or its allies, and the inability of the United States to wage limited war successfully, a number of states may see in the possession of a national nuclear deterrent force a more reliable guarantee of their own security. After all, the belief that a nation could not entirely rely on the American nuclear deterrent was a key factor behind France's development of an independently controlled nuclear capability (or *force de dissuasion,* as it came to be called), and there is no sound reason to assume that other states will feel differently in the future. It is not that the proliferation of nuclear weapons would necessarily pose a direct threat to the security of the United States. But it will have an adverse effect on the stability of the nuclear balance, and thereby increase the uncertainties with which the United States must deal in international affairs.

The Diplomatic Dominoes

The end in Indochina also shook three diplomatic dominoes which were key pillars of U.S. foreign policy: (1) détente with the Soviet Union (and, in a modified form, with China); (2) the so-called "Nixon Doctrine"; and (3) the stability of the American alliance system. None of these dominoes has yet fallen, of course, although the viability of each has become increasingly uncertain. This is perhaps most apparent in the case of détente. It seems that the utility to the United States of détente—already called into question because of developments in the Middle East and Portugal—received a serious blow with the collapse of the U.S. clients in Indochina. Détente all too clearly means an agreement by the United States to restrain itself and its allies, coupled with a willingness by the Soviet Union and China to take advantage of that restraint. Perhaps the Soviet and Chinese actions are part and parcel of Realpolitik; but if so, the American apostle of Realpolitik who now heads the Department of State would do well to take note of the lesson.[22] In its present form, détente is little but an illusion, all but devoid of substantive value for the United States. If the fact that this domino has been shaken prompts the United States into taking a more realistic policy toward its principal rivals, then at least some good may come of it all. But if the United States continues to hold to the policy of détente as it is currently practiced, despite increasing evidence that it is detrimental to the interests of this country, then the United States' inability to act decisively where its own welfare is directly concerned will underscore both its failure in Indochina and the erosion of its position in the world.

Whereas the détente domino tottered as Indochina fell, the "Nixon Doctrine" domino began its own fall before the United States had even ended its own active military participation in the war. That doctrine, which essentially declared that hence-forth the United Stales would assume a lower profile in many conflict situations, rested (as one scholar has put it) on Nixon's perception of the decline of American power, external and internal.[23] That is, the Nixon Doctrine was both

based on the partial erosion of American power, and a contributing factor in the further erosion of that power.

In some respects, the Nixon Doctrine symbolized the decline or fall of many of the other dominoes. It was simply an attempt to rationalize the loss of a sense of mission, a decline in our credibility, and an inability to wage limited wars. Had the outcome in Indochina been more favorable from the American perspective, it is possible that the Nixon Doctrine could have become the basis for a more realistic structure of peace in Asia. But with the collapse of the pro-U.S. Indochinese regimes, the viability of that doctrine could no longer be assured. Indochina had been, or least had *become*, a test case for the Nixon Doctrine as well;[24] and in Indochina, that doctrine had failed its test.

The last of the diplomatic dominoes to be shaken, but not yet knocked over, was the American system of alliances. There is little doubt that both American security and the stability of the global balance of power have been, and would continue to be, enhanced by a strong alliance system centered on the United States, however much that might inconvenience the politburos in Moscow and Peking. Thus, there is much wisdom in arguments to the effect that maintaining such an alliance system would provide the soundest possible basis for future U.S. foreign policy.[25] Yet as the unwillingness of the United States to sustain its commitments over time became apparent when Phnom Penh and Saigon capitulated while an American task force stood offshore, the value of our system of alliances to our allies and to international stability declined substantially.[26] Secretary of State Kissinger might well assert that: "We will permit no question to arise about the firmness of our treaty commitments. Allies who seek our support will find us constant."[27]

It would be surprising, however, if our remaining allies, reflecting on similar assertions made for years on behalf of South Vietnam (and, later, Cambodia), would unskeptically accept that "guarantee" at face value. Once shaken, an alliance system is difficult to revitalize.

In a number of ways, the entire Indochina experience provide American allies with a chilling lesson—one that makes an offer of U.S. military assistance in time of need nearly as fearful as its being withheld. For the possibility that the United States may initially assist, then tire, and finally withdraw would mean only that the allied nation's demise would be postponed, while the costs sustained by it would be multiplied. In such circumstances, the threatened state could well consider accommodation—even surrender—preferable to a fruitless defense. After all, neither the lack of steadfastness demonstrated by the American people in the case of Indochina nor the shift in what Gabriel Almond has called the prevailing "moods" in the American body politic[28] toward a post-Vietnam amalgam of pessimism, cynicism, and a variant of neo-isolationism are likely to reassure our allies of the worth of our guarantees of support. America's remaining allies in Asia (and elsewhere) may continue to stand by it, if only for lack of a more attractive alternative. Still, all of them are likely to take a more cautious view henceforth of the value to them of U.S. support. Their own interest will require it, for few countries will see any advantage in relying on a "protector" whose dependability is, in the final analysis, problematical at best.

The Geopolitical Domino

The net effect of the Indochina experience on the psychological, military, and diplomatic dominoes has been an erosion of the stability of the principal domino: the paramount position of the United States in the international arena. When the United States entered the Vietnam conflict, it was clearly the most powerful and influential nation in the world. By the time this country withdrew from Vietnam and, later, saw its entire Indochina policy collapse into ruins, that was no longer the case.[29] The war that had been undertaken in large part to contain the expansion of Communist power, reaffirm that credibility of American security commitments, and maintain U.S. influence in Asia had ended with Communist power in the ascendancy, U.S. credibility badly shaken, and American influence on the wane. It was, in retrospect, unwise of the United States to have staked so much of its prestige as a world leader on the outcome of a conflict in an area of secondary importance to its security. But once that was done, failure inevitably meant a contraction in the boundaries of American influence, and a diminution of the U.S. role in world affairs.

In some ways, the American intervention in Indochina (and especially in South Vietnam), however costly it ultimately became, was fully in keeping with the country's assumption of the same responsibilities accepted by *every* imperial power for the maintenance of order in the world.[30] Put colloquially, the United States *was* acting in Indochina as a self-ordained "world policeman." But it would be well to consider what the post-1945 years would have been like without such an America, and to reflect on whether or not the world would have been well served by an equally strong but more steadfast "cop" in the 1930s. The real criticism of the United States is not that it waged the "wrong war, in the wrong place, at the wrong time." Few events that challenge the stability of the existing international order occur at a time and a place favorable to the defender of that order, and Indochina was no exception. It is rather that the United States waged that war ineptly, thereby failing to preserve either the stability of the international order or its own position in it. Viewed from this perspective, the forced American withdrawal to an offshore strategy in the Pacific Basin, the passing of U.S. strategic superiority, and the legitimization at Helsinki in 1975 of Soviet hegemony in Eastern Europe are simply manifestations of the decline of the U.S. position in world affairs.

One must, of course, take care not to overreact to the defeat in Indochina, thereby magnifying the damage that has been done already.[31] Much of our physical power is still intact, and many of our allies—although more apprehensive now than in the past—pin much of their faith on a continuation of American support. It is also possible that if the bitterness and divisiveness that once attended our intervention in Indochina is replaced by a great public awareness of the increased precariousness of the American situation in the world, a strong and more assertive consensus may be reforged. And such a consensus, being indicative of a renewed American self-confidence, would do much to strengthen our credibility and to reassure our allies.

Some might well be comforted by this scenario, but a more realistic assessment of the combined impact of falling and shaken dominoes suggests that even a renaissance of American political will might not suffice to rectify the situation. Our power *is* in retreat, despite some

prospects in the Middle East and elsewhere for some short-term gains, and we cannot simply wish away that fact. By losing in Indochina, the United States did not "merely" acquiesce in a new order of things, or even in a slight modification of the old order which allowed it to retain its paramount position. Instead, this country served notice that it was in the ebbtide of its power, although less from a lack of *means* than from a lack of *will*, both of which are essential for the exercise of world power. Those who declaim against that reality are, for a variety of reasons, largely unwilling to reconcile themselves to a future world order in which the United States can no longer dominate the course of international affairs. Indochina has been a watershed in world history; both the structure of, and the trends in, the international system have been changed significantly by the U.S. defeat there. Further, those changes—needless to say—have not worked to this country's advantage.[32] Assertions to the effect that the defeat in Indochina was really not as great as it might have been, and that we still possess the lion's share of our former power, are partially true and largely trivial. Such assertions, after all, are the hallmark—indeed, the clarion call—of every state that has experienced an imperial recessional.

A Final Assessment: Whither America?

To ask, "Whither America?" is really to ask what lessons have been learned from the conduct and the consequences of the U.S. involvement in Indochina. And in addition to the specific lessons that flow from the discussion of the individual dominoes, there are three general conclusions to be drawn here. First, it seems that the domino theory was hardly what one writer labeled a "small, rhetorical image"[33] except in its narrowest sense: that which envisioned the rapid capitulation of neighboring countries to Communist forces in the aftermath of Communist successes in Indochina. The *real* dominoes at stake were (and remain) psychological, military, diplomatic, and geopolitical, and the impact of the U.S. defeat on those dominoes cannot lightly be explained away. In fact, the initial preoccupation with the "dominoes" that might be endangered in Southeast Asia drew American attention from these other dominoes, and especially from the most important domino of all: the geopolitical paramountcy of the United States.

Second, the relative position of the United States in the international community has declined from what it was before this country escalated its involvement in Indochina in the mid-1960s. It is now acting under greater constraints than before. Its principal rival, the Soviet Union, is increasingly strong; China's power in Asia is growing; the Western alliance is weakened, buffeted by a wide range of military, economic, and political problems; and the United States itself cannot overlook the reality of its own recent defeat. This does not mean, of course, that disaster is imminent; the fall of an imperial power is likely to be as slow or slower than its rise. But it does suggest that the situation of the United States is becoming increasingly precarious, while there is little—if any—chance that American power will undergo a renaissance in the coming years.

Finally, it seems that the central problem for those who direct American foreign policy in the aftermath of Indochina is not how best to maximize our gains in the global dialectic of power. It is, instead, how best to minimize our losses, making

advances where possible, but by and large trying to conserve our remaining power as much as possible. By undertaking to lead the international order after the end of the Second World War, the United States performed a largely beneficial function. There *were* excesses by the United States, particularly in Central America, although on balance this country was an agent of progress as well as stability. Perhaps, on reflection, it would have been wiser for the United States to have pursued a less ambitious goal. Nevertheless, once America had set out on the path of paramountcy, its choices were sharply constrained by the parameters of the world order it had helped to create, and whose maintenance had become a cardinal principal of U.S. foreign policy. In the future, American policy may recover a sense of direction and purpose, but a substantial part of this nation's prestige and credibility is gone.

Notes

1. For summaries of the origins of the "domino theory," see Saul B. Cohen, *Geography and Politics in a World Divided* (2nd ed.; New York: Oxford Univ. Press, 1973), 59–63; John M. Collins, *Grand Strategy: Principles and Practices* (Annapolis, Maryland: Naval Institute Press, 1973), 240–41; and Lawrence L. Whetten, *Contemporary American Foreign Policy* (Lexington, MA.: D. C. Heath and Company, 1974), 43–53.

2. See, for example, Maxwell D. Taylor, Responsibility and Response (New York: Harper and Row, 1967), 16: and Franz Michael, "The Stakes in Vietnam," *Orbis*, vol. XII, no. 1 (Spring 1968), 121–31.

3. James Chase, *A World Elsewhere* (New York: Charles Scribner's Sons, 1973), 73; and Robert L. Pfaltzgraff Jr., "American-Asian Relations in Global Perspective," *South-East Asian Spectrum*, vol. 3, no. 2 (January 1975), 5.

4. For a summary of the events attending the final defeat of the anticommunist govern-

ments of South Vietnam and Cambodia, see the author's unsigned "Reflection" in *Orbis,* vol. XIX, no. 1 (Spring 1975), 20–24.

5. The likelihood that this outcome would obtain was explored in an analysis prepared before the deterioration of the situation in Cambodia and South Vietnam in early 1975. See Alan Ned Sabrosky, "The Indo-China Question: An Analysis of Policy Options," *South-East Asian Spectrum,* vol. 3, no. 3 (April 1975), 1–11.

6. Warren Demian Manshel, "Judas and the Scapegoat," *Foreign Policy,* no. 19 (Summer 1975), 147.

7. For selected opening statements in this debate, see Alastair Buchan, "The Indochina War and World Politics." *Foreign Affairs,* vol. 53, no. 4 (July 1975), 638–50; Manshel, op. cit., 146–54; Robert W. Tucker, "Vietnam: The Final Reckoning," *Commentary* (May 1975), 27–34; Earl C. Ravenal, "Consequences of the End-Game in Vietnam," *Foreign Affairs,* vol. 53. no. 4 (July 1975), 651–67; Frank N. Trager, "After Vietnam: Dominoes and Collective Security," *Asian Affairs: An American Review,* vol. 2, no. 5 (May/June 1975), 267–75; and Walter F. Hahn, "American Introversion Post-Vietnam," *Strategic Review,* vol. III. no. 4 (Fall 1975), 18–26.

8. See, for example, Stanley Hoffmann, "The Sulking Giant," *New Republic,* May 3, 1975; Henry Brandon, "The Sources of U.S. Power Are Intact," *New York Times,* April 13, 1975; and Richard Holbrooke, "Escaping the Domino Trap," *New York Sunday Times Magazine,* September 7, 1975.

9. Buchan, op. cit., 638.

10. Editorial, *Far Eastern Economic Review,* April 4, 1975.

11. Ernest R. May, *"Lessons" of the Past: The Use and Misuse of History in American Foreign Policy* (New York: Oxford Univ. Press, 1973).

12. *New York Times,* March 25, 1975. Indonesia and the Philippines have been among the more outspoken critics of U.S. policy in the last days of the Indochina conflict. Indonesia's Foreign Minister Adam Malik, anticipating the defeat of the pro-American regimes in South Vietnam and Cambodia in the absence of further U.S. aid, remarked in late March 1975 that "the Saigon Government expected too much of the Americans . . . but others would not make the same mistake [in the future]" (*New York Times,* March 27, 1975). After that defeat had occurred, President Ferdinand Marcos of the Philippines observed that "it doesn't pay to appear to do the bidding of the United States" (*New York Times,* September 7, 1975). Both nations have since been pursuing more independent policies with less reliance on the United States than had been the case in the past. For a summary of the shifts in Asian states since the Indochina debacle, see Trager, op. cit., 274–75: Hahn, op cit., 19–21; *Time,* May 12, 1975, 30–33; and *Far Eastern Economic Review,* May 2, 1975, 28–33.

13. Cf. Buchan, *op. cit.,* 649–50; and a symposium entitled "A Failure of Nerve?" in *Commentary,* July 1975, 16–87.

14. Leslie H. Gelb, "The Essential Domino; American Politics and Vietnam," *Foreign Affairs,* vol. 50, no. 3 (April 1972), 459–75.

15. Quoted in Nayan Chanda, "Suddenly last spring," *Far Eastern Economic Review,* September 12, 1975, 35. See also the concurring view expressed earlier by North Vietnamese Generals Vo Nguyen Giap and Van Tien Dung, as reported in the *New York Times,* July 11, 1975.

16. Henry Brandon, *The Retreat of American Power* (Garden City, NY: Doubleday and Co., 1973). 333–339.

17. U.S. Congress, Senate, *Report of Senator Dewey F. Bartlett, March 14,1973.* 94th Cong., 1st Sess., 1975.

18. A theoretical distinction has been made between (a) the probability of an action being *initiated,* and (b) the probability of that action being *sustained,* as elements in assessing the credibility of a given response. See J. David Singer, "Inter-Nation Influence: A Formal Model," *American Political Science Review,* vol. LVII (1963), 420–30.

19. *New York Times,* April 3, 1975.

20. Andre Beaufre, *Strategy for Tomorrow* (New York: Crane, Russak and Company, 1974), 2–4.

21. I am indebted to Robert A. Schadler for raising this issue in private correspondence.

22. See James Dornan, "The Works of Henry A. Kissinger," *Political Scence Reviewer* V (Fall, 1975) for a thorough examination of this point.

23. James Dornan, "The Nixon Doctrine and the Primacy of Deténte," *Intercollegiate Review*, vol. 9, no. 2 (Spring 1974), 89.

24. Sabrosky, "The Indo-China Question," op. cit., 9–10.

25. See, for example, Eugene V. Rostow, *Peace in the Balance: The Future of American Foreign Policy* (New York: Simon and Schuster, 1972), 334–35.

26. For an excellent discussion of this point, see Ravenal, op. cit., 657–60.

27. Address to the Japan Society, June 18, 1975, as quoted in the *New York Times,* June 19, 1975.

28. Gabriel A. Almond, *The American People and Foreign Policy* (2nd ed.; New York: Praeger, 1960), 53–65.

29. See Raymond Aron, *The Imperial Republic: The United States and the World, 1913–1973*, Frank Jellinek, trans. (Englewood Cliffs, NJ: Prentice-Hall, 1973), 93–108, 148–57; Chase, op. cit., 9; and Whetten, op. cit., 43, 59.

30. See George Liska, *Imperial America: The International Politics of Primacy* (Baltimore: Johns Hopkins Univ. Press, 1967), ch. I–II.

31. Cf. Manshel, op. cit., 154.

32. Cf. Ravenal, op. cit., 660; and Aron, op. cit., 326.

33. The term appears in Holbrooke, op. cit., 17.

Gerhart Niemeyer

Détente and Ideological Struggle

VOL. 14, NO. 1, 1978

Those whose business it is to conduct foreign policy must have in their minds some picture of the reality in which they are acting, as well as some kind of broad principle that guides their action. When Britain and France tried to deal with Italy's war on Ethiopia in 1936, when Roosevelt delivered his "Quarantine Speech" in 1937, when Truman initiated a "police action" in Korea, the prevailing picture was evidently that of a world which by common agreement had renounced war, so that "aggression" could be looked upon as a kind of atavistic-abnormality that must be contained lest it spread like a contagious disease. That brave hope did not survive the Korean War, after which there was a return to the imagery and principle characteristic of the nineteenth century, which went under the name of "balance of power." The choice was made somewhat uncritically. Nobody seemed to have considered that the international realities of the mid-twentieth century might possibly be as far from nineteenth-century power rivalry as the nineteenth century had been from the foreign affairs of the Middle Ages. The "balance of power" concept

seemed to be the sole available alternative to international idealism.

Could the "balance of power" principle fit the politics of ideological conflict? Balance of power was essentially conceived as an equation with two variables. The first consisted in the comparative and somewhat quantifiable ratio of power instrumentalities (weaponry, manpower, resources, and terrain) which, secondly, was assessed in view of the intuited relation of what Bismarck called "The imponderables," i.e., elements of judgment, intention, and emotion influencing leading statesmen. This much is elemental. There is, however, still one more aspect of the "balance of power" which one may call "the externality" of foreign policy. Nineteenth-century statesmen were able to take the solidarity of their nations pretty much for granted, so that their decisions could confine themselves to the instrumentalities of external power and the imponderabilities of external relations. One's nation's unity for purposes of external action was taken for granted, which meant that foreign affairs were one thing and domestic politics another. *This externality of foreign policies was mutu-*

ally sustained. Thus the makers of foreign policy could be specialists in "external affairs," i.e, in relations in which nations figured as given integers, as if they were persons, and the problems of which were characteristically *inter*national.

In an age of ideologies the solidarity of states and peoples can no longer be considered a given. We have been late in acknowledging this fact, even though we had considerable early warning. New ways of looking at politics were proclaimed as early as 1848 when Marx declared that the relevant concept of political unity was not a people but class, that workers have no country, that revolution ignores all boundaries. Lenin's *Imperialism,* published in the year before he came to power, projected Marx's concept of class struggle into world politics. Lenin described capitalism as a single worldwide system, to which he opposed, three years later, a single system of Communist parties bound to the Soviet center in the loyalty of common defense. Lenin distinguished between wars made by imperialist countries for "The distribution and re-distribution of the world" and wars between capitalist and colonial countries, the latter conflict assuming the functions of Marx's revolution. Lenin attributed different "class" characteristics to wars, and called for the conversion of an "imperialist war" into a civil war. Lenin thus construed the known facts of world politics as aspects of a revolutionary process in which power between nations was seen not as a problem of equilibration but rather as a means for turning societies, cultures, and human beings upside down.

Another fact of contemporary life is that the Russian Revolution brought to power not a group pursuing the interests of its own state and people, but rather one engaged in a global enterprise and claiming authority beyond its national boundaries, like a church though not being a church, then again, like a government though not being a normal government. This enterprise has followers in other countries who in turn prepare themselves to seize power over their state. This means that an expansion of Soviet power is both something like an international sphere of influence yet also the subversion of another people's way of life, and the conversion of another state into a venture to "build a Communist society resembling the Soviet model." Soviet foreign policy, then, remains "external" only in the sense that Soviet rulers, relying on their monopoly of power, can afford to take the unity of their subjects for granted. On the other hand, any successful expansion of Soviet influence amounts to moral, cultural, and human disasters for the people unfortunate enough to fall under Communist control, so that these results are not merely in the realm of external power, but mainly in the internal order of a state and even of human personalities. The foreign policies of the ideological group controlling the Soviet Union are therefore *subjectively external but objectively internal.*

Communist-controlled countries are not all the ideological reality there is in the world today. Ideological notions clustering around both the Marxist and the anarchist model are widely spread among the peoples of the world. They give rise to loyalties other than to country and state, yardsticks other than the humanistic respect for life, liberty, property, and dignity. They have aroused extraordinarily intensive passions for disruptive organization and action. Ideologically motivated people no longer care for the order of a common life but give their loyalty to a cause of irreconcilable struggle against the world. A total critique of society, a sweeping condemnation of everything that exists, is characteristically attached to any and every grievance caused by concrete failings or shortcomings. In the eyes of ideologically infected groups, all actions by society's representatives are tainted by what one may call "systematic suspicion." The on-going existence of a people in a system of order and peace is constantly and unfavorably compared with some "possible reality" that has no existence, past or present, except in the heated fantasy of the ideological mind. This attitude gives rise to both an activist-militant and a passive-lethargic variant. The activists see it their duty to join their own country's enemies, display the enemy's symbols, visit the enemy's leaders, support the enemy's cause rhetorically and politically. Thus an internal alienation produces external effects, a domestic dissension becomes a power factor in international conflicts. The politics of ideologies in noncommunist countries are *subjectively internal but objectively external*.

This situation has further domestic consequences affecting the nation's power to act, in that representative leaders, unable to distinguish between ideological subversion and legitimate political argument, become unsure of themselves and tend to suffer from what has been called a "loss of nerve," guilty conscience destroying the ability for action. With the combination of alienation among the citizens, attraction of ideological causes based on foreign countries, and the weakening of leadership, a nation may well decompose to the point of no longer being capable of any external action, and that not for want of power instrumentalities. The manpower may remain the same, the arsenals may be full, the resources available; but in the absence of national one-mindedness the instrumen-

talities cannot be put to use. Under such circumstances it no longer makes any sense to conceive foreign policy as "the right use of power." Policy then ceases to be amenable to an understanding as an equation with two variables. One may still continue to see a "balance" of external power as desirable, but that can no longer be considered an end of the matter. The various aspects of external power are interlocked, in the Free World, with the complexities of generating and protecting the very condition of that national unity which underlies national power.

LET US now attempt a brief sketch of how the Soviet Union and the West handle themselves in this situation. Soviet strategy combines four aspects: (1) "Peaceful coexistence" (or détente), a complex of limitation and reduction of armaments, trade and cultural exchange pacts, regional declarations of peace, gestures of mutual consultation and apparent goodwill; (2) expansion of Soviet influence through the use of "national liberation" movements and wars, and "popular uprisings," and including unsettling deliveries of Soviet arms, active support of native military or paramilitary forces aiming at the creation of leftist regimes, inciting of conflicts between such forces and the United States; (3) stepping up the increase of armed strength of the Soviet Union and its satellites, including conventional forces, nuclear armaments, and acquisition of new bases in various parts of the world; (4) the continuation and intensification of "ideological struggle." Others have written and spoken sufficiently on the first three aspects of this strategy, even though there is a tendency to deal with them separately rather than as a whole. The fourth aspect, however, is usually passed over in silence. Brezhnev said recently: "Détente does not in the slightest way abolish, and cannot abolish or change, the laws of class struggle." Other Soviet leaders have emphasized that the "Spirit of Helsinki" does not apply to ideological struggle. For twenty years the Soviets have insisted that "peaceful co-existence" is a form of class struggle, and that the ideological struggle must be intensified in the presence of peaceful external co-existence.

What does "ideological struggle" mean? Why has this aspect of Soviet policy been passed over in silence by the West? Could it be because one believes that one can dismiss the phrase as windowdressing? That assumption can be made only by neglecting what social science knows about the continuing identity of cultural structures. Henri Frankfort[1] has introduced the term "form" to designate the enduring principle of unchanged identity that maintains civilizations for very long periods and through changing internal and external circumstances. Frankfort's research, it is true, deals with civilizations. Norman Cohn's work[2] on medieval millennarian movements, however, has shown that such movements also have a "form" and maintain their principle of identity over long periods, and that this identity comes to an end not as a change of the "form" but rather through extermination or attrition of the membership. The "form" of the Communist movement is its universal and uncompromising hostility to the entire existing world, in the name of an alleged new world that must replace the existing one, the replacement to be effected by a protracted but irreconcilable struggle. As historical movements go, the Communist Party is not yet old. All the same, it has gone through considerable internal and external changes while its "form" has continued the same. From it flows the raison d'être of the Party. The

Soviet insistence on the combination of "peaceful co-existence" with "ideological struggle" is nothing but a manifestation of the enduring "form" of the Communist movement. The Party manifests its concern with dangers threatening its "form" in a period of "peaceful co-existence" which to some might suggest the cessation of class struggle. This concern cannot be dismissed as mere rhetoric. "Ideology" in Communist eyes means not so much attention to a formula but rather a way of existence, existence in hostility to the class enemy and in protracted struggle led by the Party. That existence is predicated on the attribution of the world's evils to the class enemy, and on the presumption that Communists constitute that part of mankind which possesses the alternative to those evils. It is an existence positioning "high terms of separation between such and the rest of the world" (Richard Hooker's words analyzing the sixteenth-century Puritans) so that between the two parts of mankind no common obligation is conceived. It is dangerous to dismiss such attitudes as "mere mythology." Class is, indeed, the Communists' myth, but so was "race" the Nazis' myth, and Dachau still bears gruesome witness to the evil deeds spawned by a "mere myth."

"Ideological struggle," then, means that the axiom of ultimate and universal hostility to the class enemy, meaning us, continues as the background to even the Soviets' peaceful moves, by virtue of the "form" of the movement's continuing identity. Circumstantial evidence corroborates this thesis. We notice, for instance, that the policy of détente has been adopted not only by the Soviet Union, where one could attribute it to reasons of state security, but also by the Communist parties of Italy, France, the U.S., and Japan. These parties are not defending a position but rather aspiring to get into power and to control the government. The new strategy calls for a public image of Communists implying reasonableness, respectability, and demonstrative dedication to the people's daily well-being. That image would go far to dispel the strong emotional resistance that so far has blocked Communist ruling power in those countries. On the other hand, one finds that the new strategy is obviously more than a mere expedient to help this or that Communist party to the seats of power, with a view to help solving its own country's problems. Such conferences as those of chairman Miyamoto of Japan's Communist Party with Secretary General Carillo of the Spanish Communist Party (March 30, 1976) and Secretary Marchais of the French Communist Party (April 8, 1976) indicate an international orchestration of the various Communist parties' domestic policies.

"Ideological struggle," we must conclude, means that Communists in the Soviet Union and Communists in Western countries agree in their ultimate expectation of Communist regimes to be established in the leading countries of the world. In that perspective all more immediate policies take their place as partial moves toward a grand objective. It also means that the Communists are giving top priority to the political aspects of power, on the premise that the measure of their power is but a function of our resistance. Their strategy envisages a combination of such pressures and illusions acting on the West as will melt the residue of anticommunist resistance. It was anticommunist attitudes which in the past generated NATO, Western re-armament, the deployment of U.S. troops in defense of allies in various parts of the world, and sufficient programs of internal security. Solzhenitsyn has remarked that he, Sakharov, and other dissidents enjoyed a modicum of safety in the Soviet Union because of the pressure of aroused public opinion in the West. If we should ask ourselves in astonishment, what would the Soviets have to fear from the West if they killed Solzhenitsyn, Sakharov, and others who think like them, the answer is that the Soviets have reason to fear a re-kindling of that Western indignation that flamed up when Czechoslovakia was first raped in 1948, when Greece seemed on the point of succumbing to invading Communist guerrillas, when South Korea was invaded, when the West's access to Berlin was blocked. That indignation was the sap of our strength. It provided a will to maintain armaments in such quantity that the Soviets could not afford to disregard them, to set limits to Soviet expansion, to confront them even at the risk of war. Later that Western indignation was officially pronounced obsolete by the same American president who had drawn strength from it in order to force Khrushchev to remove his missiles from Cuba. During the Vietnam War, President Johnson and his advisers, failing to understand the ideological dimension, took deliberate steps not to arouse it again, and thus conducted the war from the outset in a twilight of ambiguity that prevented the people from grasping its meaning. In the climate of well-orchestrated propaganda against America's "imperialism" the Vietnam War was lost primarily on the political home front. "Ideological struggle," in sum, turns around the Soviets' determination to keep their own hostile will at high pitch while weakening ours to the point of ineffectiveness. That requires both steps creating the illusion of "peace in our generation" and avoidance of steps that would renew anticommunist indignation. The dispelling of anticommunism as a political force in the West is a matter of highest priority, so stated in the 1961 Program of the CPSU. To that end, the Soviets have officially renounced or postponed both a military showdown between their forces and those of the West, and the overthrow of Western governments by violent revolution. They are willing to seek intermediate changes from which they could hope for better conditions favoring their political operations. "Ideological struggle" in the short run aims at removing institutional, organizational, legal, and emotional obstacles to Communist propaganda and organization. They are convinced that with much patient political preparation, they will need neither an international war nor civil war to pluck the fruit of power in the world's leading industrial countries.

One interpretation of "ideological struggle" seems to be absolutely excluded: it does *not* mean that the Communists, having renounced international war and violent revolution, have placed their reliance wholly on persuasion. They remain aware that the Communist Party is not a ruler one might eventually accept as legitimate, respect, cherish, and willingly obey. They know that a deep gulf separates them not merely from capitalists, but also from socialists in the West, or rather, the Free World. They see that their cause cannot recommend itself to the world by virtue of the justice it might be seeking. They have declared themselves at war with everything that has traditionally made for order in human life. Thus they cannot escape operating on fear and force, falsehood, terror, guile, blackmail, dictatorship, and penal servitude. Persuasion presupposes belief in a humanity participating in common reason by virtue of its participation in a common order of being. That idea is one which no Communist can understand, let alone accept.

NOW LET us likewise examine the conduct of the West. Our policy goes under its own name: détente. In asking ourselves what that is, we are facing greater difficulties than in the case of Soviet policy. Kissinger himself has provided a brief formula: "To create the maximum incentives for a moderate Soviet course." This is admirable, but not very clear. The Truman Doctrine, after all, was a maximum incentive for a Soviet moderate course, so was the Berlin airlift, Dulles' "massive retaliation," and Kennedy's partial mobilization to counter Khrushchev's Cuban missiles. What is more, these and similar measures had the desired results. They manifested our capabilities and signaled our determination to use them, so that while we held this firm course, no major power position was lost, none was added to the Soviet Union, and Azerbaijan and Austria were even recovered. Détente, having begun before the Nixon era, hit its full stride with the opening to Peking, truly a landmark event. That was followed by the liquidation of the Vietnam War and the subsequent indifference of the United States to Hanoi's violation of the agreements which made the eventual Communist conquest of all of Indochina inevitable. Next came the opening of trade relations with the Soviet Union, leading to the sales of vital wheat and, more important, advanced technology. This went hand-in-hand with Brandt's *Ostpolitik*, implying the West's acceptance of the status quo in Central Europe. The chief attraction to the West was the prospect of an eventual agreement with the Soviet Union limiting and reducing armaments both strategic and deployed, a hope kept alive by a series of conferences the main purpose of which seemed to be precisely to keep alive a hope. The same may be said of the Helsinki Pact, an agreement the nature and meaning of which has remained most unclear, Soviet interpretations differing sharply from those in the West. The entire policy was underscored by the willingness of the United States to lower its requirements of national security, abandoning the criterion of "superiority" and falling back on the standard of "sufficiency," again a term without precision.

The key to the logic holding these main pieces together may be locked forever in the secretive mind of Henry Kissinger. Taken by themselves, the pieces do not fit into a self-evident pattern. We know that containment consisted in the judicious combination of various types and locations of tangible pressures to prevent further Soviet expansion. Détente has claimed to be the opposite of containment. Still, the opening of relations with Communist China may also be seen as the creation of new pressure on the Soviet Union, almost like the opening of a Second Front in World War II. Only in that the new pressure was created wholly by diplomatic means was it novel, a bold and imaginative step. That step, however, did not call for subsequent détente with the Soviet Union. Détente, in that it relieved the Soviet Union of pressures, even nullified the benefits the West had received from Nixon's trip to Peking. Similarly, the policy of negotiations which Nixon proclaimed had no need to include either direct or indirect approval of Soviet practices, power, and aims. Other countries had previously negotiated and maintained fairly close relations with the Soviet Union while continuing an unwavering opposition to communism as a potential regime. Again, a moderation of the arms race is an undeniably worthwhile objective, but it does not necessarily entail a lowering of national security requirements for the United States. If, then, the pieces of dé-

tente do not fit easily together, there must be an additional and intangible element, probably a psychological element, which has not been expressed but contains the unifying principle. Kissinger's and Sonnenfeldt's presentation to the meeting of American ambassadors in London has been read as a revelation of this so far hidden rationale of détente. The unraveling of détente, however, is not our problem here. We are engaged in an examination of its ideological dimensions.

If détente is the opposite of containment, and if containment relied on tangible pressures, then détente would consist in removing pressures, or at least irritations. One might even surmise that it would seek to create attractions for the other side, which brings to mind the title of one of Pirandello's plays: *As You Desire Me.* Again, if containment operated on conditions under one's own control, trying to shape those conditions into a complex that would give one the most potent leverage in response to the other side's potential actions, détente would amount to a self-adjustment to the other side's moods in an attempt to change the other side's attitudes and priorities. It would operate, then, on the basis of psychological speculations. That would give us a clue to the West's ultimate expectations underlying the policy of détente: it must be an expectation to see an emerging Communist Party of the Soviet Union that is worthy of the West's trust and friendship. Let us keep in mind that the Soviets' ultimate expectation is to see Communist regimes in the leading nations of the world. Détente, then, roots in the psychological speculations that it may be possible to have Communists give up the notion of class struggle, of the class enemy, and of the redeeming mission of communism, or, alternatively, on the speculation that the Soviet leaders may already have abandoned those notions (a speculation as wishful as conflicting with the record of Soviet conduct).

Détente is a relationship, and thus it must affect both sides. Each side, however, seems to be sure that itself will be immune against any ill effect and that only the other side will be subject to far-reaching changes. There is this difference, however: The Soviets did take positive measures to counteract potentially weakening effects of détente on themselves, precisely their new emphasis on "ideological struggle," while no need for similar precautions seems to have been perceived by Western leaders. Yet it is the West which is ideologically more vulnerable, since it publicly tolerates any degree of ideological dissent including open subversion, while the Communist Party has built into it a principle of ideological discipline. It would seem that the most undesirable effects on the West would occur by way of mutation in its public assessment of communism.

A parenthetical remark is in order here. In the course of normal foreign relations no moral judgment of other nations is required, because of that mutually sustained "externality" of foreign policy that was earlier mentioned. If such a judgment does take shape among citizens or leaders (as it did, for instance, in Britain regarding Turkey, at the beginning of this century), that is a kind of private self-indulgence of little or no consequence. In the presence of such phenomena as communism or Nazism, however, the formation of a judgment about them must be called a political necessity. For these movements appear in the world with a claim to universal authority which implicitly sets them up as a potential alternative to every political order in the world. That means that the evil they practice as their official policy of ruling must also be seen as the potential lot of any nation, nay, as a potential personal fate of every man, woman, and child in the world. Thus approval or disapproval of this potentiality is inescapable. By comparison, no moral judgment is a political necessity in relations with, let us say, the Stroessner dictatorship in Paraguay, or the Park regime in South Korea, both of which may be viewed as mere givens in the realm of external affairs, without any actual or potential reach beyond their own boundaries.

Détente, a policy of accommodation to Soviet moods and aspirations, expecting eventually to attain full trust and friendship with Soviet leaders, is bound to affect the public's judgment of communism. Détente inclines to ignore or even deny the fact that the Communists to this day have not yet learned to live in peace with their own subjects. The decrease of media reporting about the treatment of intellectual dissidents in the Soviet Union, and President Ford's snubbing of Solzhenitsyn are cases in point. In 1963, the term "Communist threat" was declared taboo in the United States; now détente has added any notice of Soviet terror to the taboo. The pattern of public actions under détente implies an image of the Soviets as a normal, respectable, reasonable, peace-loving, right-thinking government. That image is bound to remove the emotional and moral rejection of communism which has prevailed in the West and has mobilized Western nations to both internal and external resistance. In the course of time, it will become more and more difficult to utter any objection to the admission of Communists into the government, which means that Communists will come into demand as political partners of legitimate parties, and will be able to attain positions of power as members of a coalition. Czechoslovakia in 1948 shows how such ventures end.

Among others effects there would be a growing unwillingness to vote appropriations for armaments and armed forces, to maintain troops at foreign bases, and to shoulder the responsibilities of sharing defense with one's allies. The most serious effects, however, would come through situations in which the requirements of détente would move our leaders to sacrifice the freedom and lives of other peoples to Communist expansion. A case in point is the so-called Sonnenfeldt doctrine which says that in the interest of peace with the Soviet Union the United States favors the conversion of a presently crude presence of Soviet force in Eastern Europe into an "organic relationship." Eventually, dramatic situations would produce themselves, for instance, if we should similarly favor the abandonment of 16 million peaceful, orderly, and prosperous Taiwan Chinese to "an organic relationship" with mainland Communist rule. Two or three precedents of this kind, each reeking with official cynicism, will cause a real erosion of Western citizens' trust in the protective nature of their society. If today trusting allies can be sacrificed to the expediency of power relations, why would not I be the next? There might emerge a kind of Watergate psychosis in reverse, as everybody feels that he is potentially in line to die on the altar of god Moloch, which in the government is officially called "peace." A peace agreement with evil demands human sacrifices. Since that evil is not confined to its state boundaries but potentially reaches right into our living room, it is clear that the accommodations of détente may well bring about a protracted crisis of civil confidence in government—any Western government. In the presence of universal, potentially world-conquering ideologies foreign policy has thus an inescapable moral dimension, so that a foreign policy of principled compromise can directly affect the moral foundation of our country.

Into this situation President Carter's emphasis on human rights introduced a moral note which seemed equally suited to protect us against the erosive effects of détente as are the Soviet efforts to maintain "ideological struggle." That new emphasis would once again fan the flames of public indignation about any Communist regime which, never achieving something like peace with its own subjects, and never enjoying the intangible benefits of legitimacy, had to rely on the limitless efforts to attain total power enforced by a lawless police terror. Détente and public emphasis on human right in U.S. foreign policy therefore are in tension with each other. If the American president insisted on noting the endemic disregard for human rights by the Soviet regime, he would contribute to forces apt to increase Western armaments, strengthen the West's will to resist communism, and determination to fight if necessary. The test of this policy was identified with the concept of "linkage," i.e., a quid-pro-quo relation between Soviet conduct and either disarmament negotiations or U.S. policies in the Mideast or Africa. Officially, "linkage" has been denied; unofficially it has been effective. Its effect has been ambiguous, so that one must assume that both President Carter's insistence on human rights and his efforts to obtain a SALT agreement will be negatively affected and U.S. policy will be denied success across the board.

The Soviets, reacting sharply to criticism of their domestic policies, have been able to force the voice of criticism to become muted and, indeed, intermittent, with the result that the full weight of American moral censure has fallen not on the Soviets but on America's allies who have no leverage by which to tone us down. In one respect this has produced a warping of our foreign policy perspective, in that Rhodesia, South Africa, and post-Allende Chile now appear to be dangers outranking the Communist threat. On the other hand, however, relations with the Soviet Union have not been restored to the openness of the Kissinger period. The impression of confusion in U.S. foreign policy is thus not an assessment of President Carter's personality but rather the observation of several wills conflicting with each other in the design and execution of our foreign conduct. In spite of a declared moral intention, U.S. foreign policy has given the impression of less moral substance than the preceding détente, which had in its favor the doubtful but yet single-minded logic of a "peace-in-our-time" morality.

It was the moral substance of Rome which enabled the Senate, in one hopeless situation after another during the Punic wars, to rise to that supreme effort by which they eventually turned seemingly fatal defeats into an ultimate victory of Rome. Centuries later, a morally drained Roman empire no longer could muster such determination, and helplessly watched the barbarians take over, bit by bit, the empire's territory and government. "You have the impression," Solzhenitsyn says to us, "that democracies can last. But you know nothing about it. Democracies are lost islands in the immense river of history. The water is always rising. . . . The existence of the civilization the West created is going to be at stake in the next years. I think it is not aware of this."

Notes

1. Henri Frankfort, *Before Philosophy* (Harmondsworth, UK: Penguin, 1951).
2. Norman Cohn, *The Pursuit of the Millennium* (New York: Oxford Univ. Press, 1970).

Philip F. Lawler

Just War Theory and
Our Military Strategy

VOL. 19, NO. 1, 1983

Since hope is a theological virtue, one continues to hope—despite all the dismal evidence—that the current debate on the morality of nuclear armament will generate some useful ethical insights. Certainly we need some original, sophisticated arguments, to break the deadlock of a debate that has degenerated into empty rhetoric and emotional posturing. But the outlook is indeed bleak. During the past year, while innumerable ideologues proclaimed the need for a moral approach to nuclear defense, there was a marked decline in the public understanding of the moral issues at stake. And perhaps this is not surprising. During the same period, while the debate over nuclear weapons has raged within the American Catholic Church, there has been a similar marked decline in the appearance of arguments that bear the stamp of a long, impressive, and distinctly Catholic intellectual tradition. The tradition I have in mind is, of course, based on the theory of just war.

Elsewhere I have written a great deal about the particular controversy that is afflicting American Catholics.[1] In this essay, however, I shall set aside that church dispute to concentrate more generally on the theory of just war and its relevance for contemporary defense problems. I take this broader approach for three reasons. First, because the dispute arming Catholics touches on a number of theological and ecclesiological points that will not hold much interest for non-Catholics. Second, because the just war theory can be grasped and endorsed apart from the doctrines of Roman Catholicism; its essential principles can be accepted with equal fervor by a Protestant, a Jew, an agnostic, or even a Jesuit. Third, because after 1500 years of elaboration and refinement, the just war tradition provides an unparalleled guide through the moral dilemmas of military strategy.

Modern technology has changed the face of warfare. Political leaders of past generations could never have dreamed of holding the destructive potential that their successors now hold. But human nature has not changed, and the fundamental ethical problems confronting military strategists are still the same: the need for peace and security, the protection of innocent civilians, the delicate balance of arms increases and arms control. All of these ethical problems have been explored by the proponents of just war theory, and most of them have been discussed in detail by generations of theorists.[2] Perhaps some day the ideologues who have "discovered" the moral problem of nuclear weaponry will realize that their discovery came several hundred years late. At the very least, it would seem fair to expect that, before dismissing the just war theory, they should try to understand it.

I

St. Augustine is generally recognized as the originator of the theory of just war, but the fundamental premises on which the theory is based can be traced further back, to the establishment of Christianity itself. The message of the Gospels contained two stunning breaks with the ancient understanding of war and peace, life and death. First, Jesus proclaimed Himself a peacemaker and insisted that His disciples should be the same. Of course, the peace of Christ is not the peace accepted by this world, as the Gospels very clearly point out.[3] Nevertheless, the Sermon on the Mount left no doubt as to the dignity of those who work for peace here on earth.[4] Second, Jesus emphasized with equal vigor that His kingdom was not of this world, and that consequently the values of this world must be subordinated to those of the heavenly kingdom. Again the Sermon on the Mount made the point clear, and thousands of Christian martyrs took the message literally.[5] All human desires, even the desire for life itself, must be downgraded in the light of Christ's eternal kingdom.

To say that Christianity is a religion of pacifism, then, is to distort the faith—almost to render it trivial.[6] A Christian nation confronts a paradox: every hu-man life is immeasurably valuable, and yet some other things are more valuable still. Death is preferable to apostasy, or to sin. It is better to die than to be robbed of human dignity. By the same token, there are circumstances when the use of violent force may be justifiable (as in self-defense) or even obligatory (as in the defense of one's children). When those circumstances arise, the ordinary Christian preference for nonviolence may evaporate.

A recurrent argument in the contemporary debate claims that the early Christians refused to take up arms in the defense of Rome, thereby revealing themselves as pacifists.[7] For the most part, it is indeed true enough that Christians refused military service. But it is also true that the Roman army, during that era, expended a portion of its energy in the task of throwing Christians to the lions. The fact that Christians refused to serve does not prove that they rejected military service on principle; it merely proves (in case anyone doubted it) that they considered the regime unworthy of their full support.

After the conversion of Constantine, and with the gradual emergence of the Holy Roman Empire, the situation changed radically. St. Augustine, in *The City of God*, emphasized the discrepancies between life in the sinful City of Man and in the eternal Kingdom. Nevertheless, he pointed out that earthly kingdoms do enjoy certain authorities in their own proper sphere, and that it might be necessary to invoke civil authority and civil force to repair injustices. The power of the state is certainly not the power of God, but if the state can improve man's lot here on earth, then that too is a part of God's work.

II

From that basic understanding, just war theory arose, to be developed by each succeeding generation of Christian thinkers. Although a history of the development of just war theory would be beyond the scope of this essay, two points bear mentioning. First, so far from being pacifist, within a few centuries after Augustine the church was advocating holy wars: the Crusades.[8] Second, as the march of technology brought increasing deadly power into the hands of warring nations, Christians repeatedly raised the question of whether or not warfare had become too horrible to be guided by the precepts of just war theory. With the invention of the crossbow, the cannon, the rifle, and the airplane, a controversy arose that is remarkably similar to the controversy raging today. Time and again, some scholars claimed that just war theory was obsolete. Time and again, others recognized that the theory was more important and more relevant than ever.

To say that just war theory was useful, of course, is not the same as to say that it was always observed. Over the centuries, the church has been no more successful in enforcing observance of its prescriptions in the realm of military theory than it has been in its quest to rid the world of greed or of lust. Wars have always been—and have never ceased to be—occasions for the grossest sort of inhumanities. Nevertheless, one can still draw some lines and make some moral discriminations. Surely the age of chivalry, in which (in the ideal "Knights of the Round Table" formula) knights fought each other according to a strict code of warfare, was morally more advanced than our own century, with its glorification of the *Blitzkrieg*. Nor is it a coincidence, presumably, that the age of chivalry came

at a time when the precepts of just war theory, however much they might have been abused, were at least taken quite seriously.

Over the years, and despite the multiple restatements of just war theory, the skeletal framework of the theory has remained constant. A just war must conform to two sets of conditions: those that define the circumstances under which a war may be waged *(ius ad bellum),* and those that define the permissible standards for the conduct of war *(ius in bello).* Each of these categories is itself subdivided into individual moral tests,

Ius ad bellum describes the conditions under which a nation may override the usual precept against the taking of human life. Essentially, *ius ad bellum* demands the fulfillment of five requirements:

First, just cause. The war must remedy or prevent a real injustice. In the past, just war theory also allowed punitive wars, to extract vindictive justice for past transgressions. Recent developments of just war theory have discarded this interpretation.[9]

Second, right intention. A war must be waged for some ostensible moral purpose. That is, self-defense is justifiable, but the imperial acquisition of territory is not.

Third, exhaustion of peaceful means. War cannot be morally justified if any other recourse is still available.

Fourth, reasonable prospect of success. An individual might choose to fight to the death against impossible odds; a ruler cannot require his subjects to make the same sacrifice.

Fifth, competent authority. The war must be declared and waged by a sovereign public authority, not by an individual citizen.

Today's debate over the morality of nuclear warfare does not center on the *ius ad bellum* category, but concentrates on the *ius in bello*. That focus is ironic, since modern warfare raises several very knotty problems for anyone interested in *ius ad bellum*. For instance: In an all-out nuclear war, can anyone advance a reasonable prospect of success, by any plausible definition of that term? In guerilla warfare, what is a sovereign authority? In an era of lightning-quick offensive weapons, what constitutes a valid declaration of war?

And the present preoccupation with *ius in bello* is doubly ironic, since a just cause is the first and indispensable requirement for moral warfare. If a nation goes to war for an unjust cause, nothing can salvage that war from moral condemnation, no matter how scrupulously the fighting is conducted. If the cause is just, *then* one turns to consider the morality of the warfare itself. If the cause is unjust, no further discussion is required.

III

Today, as we formulate our national defenses in response to the growing Soviet threat, we must contemplate the primary question of *ius ad bellum*. Could we, under any conceivable circumstances, have a just cause for warfare against the Soviet Union? To put the question in a slightly different form, is human freedom a worthy moral value, when placed on the scales opposite a ruthless totalitarian ideology? That question is rarely addressed today, perhaps because the answer seems obvious to most Americans. Yet it is important to articulate that answer, since without an answer we cannot begin to plan our strategy. Yes, under certain circumstances we could—and should—justly engage in warfare against the Soviet Union. Given the character of the regimes involved, and the relentless denial of human rights under Soviet domination, it is reasonable

to envision a cause that would justify warfare even at the cost of severe human suffering.

(Perhaps some Christian pacifists would argue that the United States today is as corrupt—as unworthy of support—as was ancient Rome to the early Christians. That argument would at least be internally consistent. But could it be taken seriously?)

We turn, then, to *ius in bello*: the moral guidelines for ethical warfare. These can be summarized in two categories. First, proportionality: the damage inflicted must be proportionate to the goal sought. Thus, one could not justly obliterate a city if the military goal were to stop a single sniper. Second, discrimination: the warring party must make every effort to avoid damage to civilians and non-military targets. A just war does not make noncombatants into targets. So terrorism is by its very nature morally indefensible.

In just war theory, the argument in favor of warfare must overcome a strong presumption in favor of peace. In the case of nuclear warfare, that argument must be overwhelming: the presumption against a nuclear strike is especially strong. On the grounds of both proportionality and discrimination, it is very difficult to justify the use of nuclear devices. The awesome destructive powers of these weapons are disproportionate to any normal political or military goal. And all nuclear weapons (at least all of the ones currently stockpiled by the major powers) would inflict massive civilian casualties. Consequently, some analysts claim that *ius in bello* prohibits any use of nuclear weapons, whatever the circumstances. And no respectable theorist denies that a premeditated first-strike attack would be inexcusable.

IV

Yet these conclusions do not address the real question of nuclear defense. No strategist in his right mind contemplates the offensive use of nuclear weapons. Quite the contrary, the primary purpose of a nuclear weapon is to remain unused. This is the paradox of nuclear strategy: the paradox of intention in nuclear deterrence. The United States owns a huge strategic force of nuclear warheads, ready for use. Our national defense planners proclaim their readiness to use those warheads if necessary in defense of freedom. The Pentagon devises scenarios for fighting a nuclear war. And yet we do *not* intend to use our weapons. Or, to be more precise, the real use of those weapons lies in their non-use. If our missiles—poised quietly in their silos until they become obsolete—deter the Soviet Union from its aggressive plans, then they have fulfilled their purpose. We say that we intend to use our weapons if we must. But our *real* intention is to leave those weapons unused.

So do we, or do we not, intend to use our nuclear weapons? For the just war theorist, that question is absolutely crucial.[10] If we intend to use them in battle, then we are contemplating a type of warfare that would violate the principles of proportion and discrimination. But if we intend to use them solely as a deterrent, then our purposes are defensive and our moral stature is undiminished.

The paradox of deterrence does not yield simple solutions. It is not enough, for instance, to use nuclear weapons purely as a bluff. If we have no intention of using our strategic power under any circumstances, and our adversary realizes this, our deterrent immediately collapses. For that matter, if our adversary has any question about our willing-ness to respond *in extremis*, he will be sorely tempted to test our will—thereby bringing us repeatedly to the brink of a nuclear holocaust. Only a firm, credible determination to use nuclear force can provide a meaningful deterrent. To bluff is not enough. We must be prepared for the worst. We must *intend* to do the very thing that we so dearly hope we will *never* do.

In the last analysis, then, we must face the horrible question of how we would respond to the ultimate provocation. If the Soviet Union launched an all-out attack on the United States, would we respond in kind? To say Yes is to plan the annihilation of millions of innocent Russian civilians. To say No is to surrender before the fighting begins. There is no satisfactory solution. Our nuclear deterrent is based on an irrational premise, and proceeds from that premise to an equally irrational conclusion. So in the extreme position—faced by a Soviet willingness to launch nuclear warfare—we would be faced with two choices, each totally unacceptable.

No one is satisfied with this strategic posture. While there are widely differing opinions on how to resolve our dilemma, there is at least a universal agreement that the United States must amend its military policies. Some counsel disarmament; others, a better war-fighting capacity. Which of these options is more congruent with just war theory?

V

Before answering that question, one must understand the genesis of our present strategic policy. In the aftermath of World War II, the U.S. deterrent was unquestioned; we alone had the atomic bomb. But when the Soviet Union developed its own thermonuclear weapons, to complement its overwhelming superiority in conventional armed forces on the European continent, American planners were forced to devise a new policy for deterring Soviet aggression. To match the Soviet conventional threat would have been prohibitively expensive, and for political reasons (the difficulty of persuading the American people to spend that sum on defense, and forego government spending on other domestic programs), our government adopted a new strategic policy, which came to be known as the doctrine of Mutually Assured Destruction (MAD). According to the terms of MAD, any Soviet aggression against ourselves or our allies would be met with immediate, massive, nuclear retaliation.

As MAD developed, strategic planners saw stability in the very insanity of the posture. If both the U.S. and the USSR faced annihilation—so the argument ran—then both sides would be forced to behave responsibly, and to avoid any possible conflicts that might prompt the dread confrontation. By that reasoning, planners concluded that a greater threat made for a stronger deterrent—the more horrible the weapons, the better. At its height of popularity, MAD proscribed any defensive measures to protect civilians against nuclear attack. The two superpowers (in theory, again) were to confront each other naked, totally vulnerable to attack, and therefore totally unwilling to risk situations that would make attack more likely.

So the theory ran. But the theory was wrong. Gradually, American planners realized that the Soviet Union did not share our belief that nuclear war was unthinkable;[11] the Kremlin had embarked on an ambitious campaign of diverse weaponry and civil defense, obviously contemplat-

ing strategic nuclear superiority. Nor did the Soviet Union avoid confrontations. Instead—secure in the knowledge that Americans would not resort to nuclear overkill—they pushed forward with their policies of subversion, intimidation, and outright invasion. In Hungary, Poland, Czechoslovakia, Afghanistan, Iraq, Laos—again and again the Soviets tested the Western will. In each case, it was palpably irrational for the U.S. to respond with a strategic nuclear strike, and fruitless to contemplate a conventional response against overwhelming odds, MAD failed.

Perhaps not coincidentally, MAD was also a failure from the perspective of moral judgment. Instead of a rational, proportionate defense, MAD held out one single, blood-chilling possibility: if provoked, we would touch off a conflagration that would destroy civilization as we know it. MAD failed the test of proportion, and—even more miserably—that of discrimination. As if that were not enough, it was also difficult to conceive of a victory in all-out nuclear war, and so MAD failed to satisfy the conditions of *ius ad bellum* as well.

Finally, the moral and strategic difficulties of MAD became impossible to ignore. First under the Carter administration, and then under President Reagan, the United States has begun to move away from MAD. Instead of fixing our bombsights on Soviet cities, we have begun to aim for military installations. Instead of insisting that nuclear warfare would mean an all-out attack with the full force of our arsenal, we have begun to devise weapons and strategics that might limit nuclear conflict at a relatively low level. In effect, we are moving toward a more flexible posture, and one more in keeping with the criteria of just war theory. And we can do much more.[12]

Bishops and theologians, however, are not by nature astute military or political analysts. So today, just as the tide is turning against the MAD doctrine, moralists have suddenly discovered that MAD is immoral. Just as the Pentagon is beginning to consider just war criteria (under different names, admittedly), the clergy has announced that just war theory is outmoded. Just as the U.S. begins to establish a morally defensible strategy for nuclear deterrence, the moral seers have revealed that nuclear deterrence is immoral.

VI

To a certain degree, the condemnation of nuclear weaponry is both understandable and even laudable. Clerics should always be peacemakers; those who represent Christianity should always exercise a countervailing influence to balance the ambitions of political opportunists. And in the tradition of just war theory, peace is always strongly preferred, and every form of warfare is naturally suspect. Still, the opponents of nuclear deterrence face a moral obligation of their own. If deterrence is unacceptable, what are the alternatives? On that score, the critics have failed miserably in their search for an ethical solution.

Consider the possible alternatives to nuclear deterrence:

1. The United States could dismantle its nuclear warheads unilaterally, leaving the Soviet Union with an effective monopoly on thermonuclear power. The historical record leaves very little doubt that the Soviet Union would use that monopoly to enforce its conquest of the world, leaving human freedoms in the dustbin of history. In effect, this choice would be the choice of martyrdom—the decision to die as a civilization rather than face the threat of warfare. For individuals, such a choice might be praiseworthy. For a government, it is not.[13]

2. We might severely reduce our nuclear arsenal, leaving a minimal deterrent against Soviet strategic attack, but making our own posture unthreatening to the Soviet Union. In other words, we could retain a nuclear deterrent useful only in case of a direct attack on our country. But this option leads to two companion dangers. First, our remaining deterrent could only be aimed at the most vulnerable targets in the Soviet empire: the cities. So we would be perpetuating the city-heisting strategy that makes MAD morally indefensible.[14] Secondly, we would be sacrificing the security of our allies in NATO and around the world. Uninhibited by American deterrence, the Soviet Union could conquer the other, weaker countries at their leisure—leaving the U.S. as the last domino, awaiting the inevitable final assault. In the process of these serial conquests, the Soviet Union would certainly inflict massive casualties in many different conflicts, and after the Soviet conquest there would be more lives lost in the Gulags that would spring up around the globe. In other words, by our efforts to avoid the danger of nuclear war with its massive casualties, we would be guaranteeing the occurrence of many smaller wars, each with its own casualties.[15] The toll in human suffering would probably be quite similar; the cost in human freedom would be incalculably higher.

3. We could bluff, retaining our weapons but abandoning our intention to use them even under the most extreme provocations. But this choice would run the risk of inviting Soviet adventurism. As repeated tests met with repeated passive responses from the West, the Kremlin would become increasingly

aggressive and provocative. At best, the result would be an eventual piecemeal conquest of the free world. At worst, we would abandon our passive intentions, and launch a nuclear war in response to one such test.

4. We could negotiate an arms-control agreement, whereby both sides would make their strategic forces less threatening and more stable. Theoretically, this solution would be ideal from every perspective. But the practical difficulties are considerable. After a generation of negotiation on arms limitations, we are no closer to a lasting peace; few Americans would say that they are more comfortable now, in the wake of the SALT talks, than they were a decade ago. The arms race continues, unabated. Each side improves its military power, within whatever constraints the agreements enforce. (In fact, the Kremlin has shown few scruples about violating established agreements when they prove incompatible with Soviet plans.[16]) Indeed, a glance through history suggests that arms controls work only as long as the powers involved find them useful.

Even if the Soviet Union and the United States did somehow achieve a workable arms-control agreement, our problem would not be solved. How long would it be before a new set of nuclear powers threatened the same sort of worldwide destruction? Several other nations already belong to the nuclear "club"; several more are on the threshold. Having unlocked the secret of thermonuclear might, mankind cannot now make that power disappear, however attractive that dream might appear. Like it or not—and very few people like it—we are faced with the probability that nuclear weapons will exist for years if not forever.

VII

That sobering realization should add a fresh perspective to the current argument about armaments. Is an arms race per se immoral? While we are pouring billions of dollars into the development of weapons that remain unused, the price is not too exorbitant if the result is an honorable peace. Nor are arms races in themselves likely to increase the danger of war. Most historians agree that an arms race in Europe contributed to the causes of the first World War; on the other hand, most historians also agree that the failure of the Allies to match Hitler's weapons build-up made World War II possible.[17] Arms races, like weapons themselves, are neither moral nor immoral. Morality is determined by the motives and strategies of the human beings who guide government policy.

An arms race in today's Cold War could—if guided by the proper consideration for nuclear morality—lead us out of the ethical morass that MAD has occasioned. With our spectacular technological capacities, we can create defenses that make nuclear attacks less likely to succeed, and therefore less threatening.[18] We can design missiles and other weapons—both nuclear and conventional—that possess a higher degree of accuracy, thereby guaranteeing a greater discrimination between military and civilian targets. We can increase our ability to meet conventional attacks with conventional defenses, so that we do not invoke a nuclear threat against a small-scale offense. We can devise an overall military strategy that meets each potential challenge with a proportionate, convincing deterrent.

Just war theory is not outdated; it is merely out of fashion. And the results of that change in fashion are evident all around us: we are simultaneously frightened by the morality of our defensive posture and the possibility that it might not be secure enough to save our lives and our freedoms. Still it is not too late to begin thinking once again in terms of just war theory. Perhaps it is even possible to hope that, once the present confusion is abated, moral theorists will shed some new light on the need for a sane and sound strategic defense.

In one respect, a just war is just like any other war it cannot be successfully prosecuted by someone who is not prepared for the battle. We cannot assume that the United States and its allies would conjure up a morally upright defense during the heat of battle. And if the appropriate weapons and strategic plans are not available in time, neither just nor effective defense is possible. We hope never to fight a war, but if we must fight we should fight justly. The time to begin planning a just strategy is now.

Notes

1. *The Bishops and the Bomb: The Morality of Nuclear Deterence*, Heritage Lecture Series no. 16 (Washington, DC: The Heritage Foundation, 1982); *"Regina Pacis, Ora Pro Nobis," Catholicism in Crisis*, I, no. 2 (January 1983); "Draft's Assumption Questionable," syndicated column appearing in *Sacramento Union, Philadelphia Inquirer*, etc., November 1982. See also *Justice and War in the Nuclear Age*, Philip F. Lawler, ed. (Washington: Univ. Press, 1983).

2. The single indispensable book, for anyone interested in just war theory, is *The Conduct of Just and Limited War,* by William V. O'Brien (New York: Praeger, 1981). All but the must serious students will find that O'Brien answers all their questions even those who want to know more will find O'Brien's footnotes and bibliography exhaustive. Also helpful are: James

T. Johnson, *Just-War Tradition and the Restraint of War* (Princeton, NJ: Princeton Univ. Press, 1982), and Paul Ramsey, *War and the Christian Concience* (Durham, NC: Duke Univ. Press. 1961). An interesting viewpoint is expressed by Michael Walzer in *Just and Unjust Wars* (New York: Basic Books. 1977). With particular reference to the Catholic bishops and their Pastoral Letter, see Lawler (ed.), *Justice and War in the Nuclear Age.* One of the bishops drafting that Pastoral has himself written a fine introduction to the topic: John J. O'Connor, *In Defense of Life* (Boston: St. Paul Edition, 1981).

3. The biblical references are numerous: Luke 12:51; Rom. 3:17; I Thes. 5:3; I Peter 3:11. And this is the peace that "passes all understanding" (Phil. 4:7). Nor is this theme absent from the Old Testament, as witness Jeremiah complaining against those who cry "Peace, peace, when there is no peace" (Jer. 6:14, 8:11, 12:12).

4. Matt. 5:9; James 3:18.

5. Matt. 5:11; Rom. 12:14.

6. Matt. 10:34; Luke 12:51.

7. There is some irony in hearing Catholic clergymen cite the early Christian church as a model from which modern developments have departed. Until quite recently, that was the standard criticism made by Protestants against the Roman Church.

8. Frequently, today's pacifists cite St. Francis of Assisi as an exemplar of Christian pacifism. That is absurd. St. Francis preached a crusade. See Regine Pernoud, *The Crusaders* (New York: Putnam, 1962), 221–23; or Omer Engelbert, *St. Francis of Assisi* (London: Burns Oates, 1950), 207–11 and passim.

9. This development was made fairly explicit by Pope Pius XII. See the interpretation placed on that pope's thoughts by Father John Courtney Murray, "The Uses of a Doctrine on the Uses of Force," in *We Hold These Truths* (New York: Sheed and Ward, 1960), 255–256.

10. This "paradox of intention" in nuclear deterrence has been explored most productively by Michael Novak.

11. Richard Pipes, "Why the Soviet Union Thinks It Could Fight and Win a Nuclear War," *Commentary* (July 1977), 21–34. See also Kenneth Adelman, "Beyond

MADness," *Policy Review* 17 (Summer 1981), 79–80.

12. Angelo Codevilla. "Justice, War, and Active Defense" In Lawler (ed.), *Justice and War in the Nuclear Age*, 83–98.

13. Rev. James V Schall, S. J. "Intellectual Origins of the Peace Movement," in Lawler, *op. cit.*, 27–61.

14. This argument has been forcefully made by Ambassador Edward Rowny, chief negotiator at the START talks, in discussions with the American bishops.

15. See Edward Luttwak, "How to Think About Nuclear Weapons," *Commentary* 74 (August 1982), 21–28.

16. Jake Garn, "Soviet Violations of SALT I," *Policy Review* 9 (Summer 1979), 11–32.

17. George Weigel Jr., *The Peace Bishops and the Arms Race* (Chicago: World Without War Council, 1982), 21.

18. One such hopeful possibility is spelled out in great detail in Lt. Gen. Daniel Graham's *High Frontier: A New National Strategy* (Washington: High Frontier, 1982).

Robert R. Reilly

Atheism and Arms Control: How Spiritual Pathology Afflicts Public Policy

VOL. 24, NO. 1, 1988

What causes war and what causes fightings among you? Is it not your passions that are at war in your members? You desire and do not have; so you kill. And you covet and cannot obtain; so you fight and wage war.

—The Epistle of St. James (4:1–2)

The great enthusiasm for the flurry of nuclear arms reduction offers from Mr. Gorbachev and the recently concluded INF agreement seems to be based on the idea that a diminution in weapons, in and of itself, will necessarily increase stability and promote peace. And why not? It would seem that with fewer weapons, fewer threats could be made and fewer people could be hurt. There is certainly a surface appeal and plausibility to the idea that fewer weapons mean a safer world, but it can be true only if weapons are themselves the source of conflict. Such a notion, however, is difficult to maintain either logically or historically. War requires not only weapons, but the will to use them and a purpose to do so. Given the will, men will use whatever weapons are at hand. A sword, for instance, may be a museum piece or material for a plowshare. It becomes a weapon only in the hands of a person who intends to use it as a forceful means to advance or defend a particular cause.

In fact, people with no weapons to speak of have done incalculable damage. The recent slaughters in Cambodia were largely carried out by fanatics with crude wooden clubs. In 1964, African tribal strife between the Tutsi and the Hutu in Rwanda and Burundi resulted in a large number of people being eaten. No one would suggest that these disasters were precipitated by a failure in arms control. Rather, such examples clearly demonstrate that weapons do not constitute the source of conflict. In other words, weapons do not give rise to threats, but are mere expressions of them.

However, when it comes to nuclear weapons, some have sought to invert the relationship between the weapons and the causes of conflict. This same inversion occurred before World War II with respect to aerial bombardment, spoken of at that time with exactly the same rhetoric as nuclear weapons are today, and before World War I with respect to naval power. In each case, the weapons were described apocalyptically as the principal source of danger. In each case, the danger was addressed by arms control treaties which were heralded as harbingers of peace. ("Peace in our time.") In each case, war followed because the underlying political and moral realities which would have preceded any possible use of these weapons were ignored.

Eugene Rostow wryly remarks that the world has not really seen a successful arms control pact since the Rush-Bagot Convention of 1817 between the United States and Great Britain which demilitarized the Great Lakes. Actually, the Convention succeeded because it reflected the political realities which preceded it and was not itself used as the means to achieve an otherwise unobtainable peace. Even without the treaty, the warships would have disappeared from the Great Lakes because the underlying conflict of which they were an expression had been resolved.

Likewise, today's political realities are not shaped by the nuclear bomb. Rather the bomb's significance flows exclusively from political realities. France and Great Britain possess enough atomic bombs to destroy every American city with a population of over 50,000. But this does not leave us in trepidation, nor impel us to arms control efforts, because the political realities of our relationships make the use of these weapons against us inconceivable. We worry about the bomb because the Soviet Union has it, and because of the moral character of the Soviet regime. These political and moral realities give nuclear weapons their relevance, not the other way around.

However, this simple truth is being forgotten by those who focus on the symptoms of conflict to the exclusion of its real causes. More importantly, this inversion reflects a more fundamental error. The notion that weapons are the basic problem in human relations arises from confusion about even more important things. What conception of human nature assigns to weapons and their control such paramount importance in human affairs?

A careful analysis of this question reveals a view of man that is secular and materialist, with roots going back to the ancient heresies of the Manicheans and the Pelagians—both fundamental misunderstandings of the nature of evil. The Manicheans thought the cosmos was radically split between good and evil and that the two were absolutely distinct. Within this dualistic vision they demonized material things. The Pelagians thought man was untainted by any fundamental disorder within himself, and, therefore, was capable of complete self-perfection. Today's new Manicheans embrace a radical dualism according to which weapons are evil, people are good. As a corollary, the new Pelagians deny the assertion of St. James that man's passions are at war with his own members. Therefore, they believe that peace requires only a rearrangement of things external to man (e.g., weapons), rather than an internal transformation or right ordering of the soul. Man is already good; therefore, the requirements for peace are purely secular.

The Management Approach to Evil

Yet the daily experience of man is that there is little if any peace. The crime page of any newspaper, the divorce statistics, the regional wars throughout the world testify that something is profoundly wrong. In each case, whether the strife be domestic or foreign, those who view man as thoroughly good assign the source of these problems to external factors. Thus the solution to these problems must be external as well. If there is growing neighborhood crime—build a housing project or begin a literacy program. If armed conflict threatens in some Third World area—send food or enforce an economic embargo. If tension with the Soviet Union increases—decommission several submarines and send the New York Philharmonic to Moscow. In other words, peace is a management problem requiring no moral choices, but rather social engineering skills. Various peace institutes have sprung up where apparently these engineering skills can be learned in courses called "crisis management and conflict resolution." Arms control is at the top of the curriculum.

The management approach to the causes of conflict, whether it is applied to Vietnam or to sex education, ultimately fails because it discounts the spiritual disorder in man's own soul. In other words, the fault is not in our arms, but in ourselves. In his *Epistle to the Romans*, St. Paul explained at length what St. James meant by saying "your passions . . . are at war in your members." He stated that there was a struggle within himself, that though he knew in his mind what the good required of him, he nevertheless did evil: "For the good which I will, I do not; but the evil which I will not, that I do." Why? Because, he said, even "when I have a will to do good, evil is present with me." Therefore, "I see another law in my members, fighting against the law of my mind and captivating me in the law of sin that is in my members." Every person who has not killed his conscience knows this as the interior condition of his own soul and experiences simultaneously the knowledge of the good and the attraction of evil. It may be called concupiscence or some other thing. But the fact that man can choose evil over good constitutes the central human problem in every great faith and moral philosophy.

The Western tradition has assigned the origin of this spiritual disorder to the dislocation in the relationship between God and man which is usually called "original sin," or "fallen nature." Fallen nature sets the parameters within which man seeks his betterment. He must face the moral imperfections of himself and of his world with the realization that there will be no end to wars and "fightings" without a resolution to the spiritual war within his own soul. If he prefers, like the Pelagians, to deny the existence of original sin and of the struggle it occasions, he must find another culprit for the evil he sees. If sin is no longer personal in the sense that individuals are spiritually responsible for it, then it must be social in the sense that the structures of society produce it.

Therefore, the fight against sin becomes political, and politics becomes the vehicle for salvation. One can then march for peace or pass laws against war (e.g., the Kellogg-Briand Pact of 1929, which outlawed war as an instrument of settling international disputes). Or one can engage in arms control. It is all part of the same spiritual pathology which, while denying the interior struggle between good and evil in each person's soul, actually externalizes it by projecting it onto society. An obsessive concern with arms control is simply another manifestation of this denial of human culpability and another element in the externalization of the spiritual struggle it implicitly denies. In fact, faith in arms control as the solution to conflict increases in direct proportion to the decline of belief in original sin. The more adamantly one refuses to acknowledge the source of disorder as internal to man, the more blindly one will believe in and insist upon an external resolution to conflict, such as arms control. This is why arms control as a subject of study in peace institutes is a uniquely modern phenomenon. Only in modernity have we seen the wholesale rejection of original sin, which likewise makes it possible for politicians regularly to proclaim the utopian goal of "peace for all time."

However, any scheme for peace that does not refer evil back to a disorder in the human will is bound to founder upon the enormous distortion of reality which it creates. Peace which is based upon arms control is such a distortion because it proposes to remove evil by making weapons the scapegoat of human guilt. This has not and will not work because arms control is a secular solution to a problem that is spiritual. Arms control does not remove evil; it simply recasts it in another form—in fact, in a far more dangerous form, because it makes evil harder to recognize. The arms control treaties preceding World Wars I and II made it far more difficult to see the gathering forces of evil that caused the Wars and that the Wars subsequently unleashed.

But this does not shake the modern belief in arms control, because arms control has become an item of faith in a secular religion in which arms control agreements are transformed into secular sacraments, semi-liturgical rites performed to reinforce the faith of its Pelagian practitioners and adherents. Its pseudo-ecclesiastical character is evident in the reaction of those devoted to arms control when anyone points to violations of arms control treaties by the Soviet Union and argues against any such future arrangements. One may as well suggest to a clergyman that sinners should not go to church. One would be quickly informed that if a person sins it is all the more reason for him to go to church. In fact, he should go more often. Likewise, violations of arms control are simply seen as reason for more arms control. Any attempt to stop the arms control "process" is seen as the secular equivalent of sacrilege.

The ultimate version of this secular view of the causes of conflict, however, sees the source of the problem so deeply embedded within the existing social and political structures that the actual elimination of these structures is required for a cleansing of the earth and the dawning of a New Age. No amelioration of our existing institutions will do. Since they are the source of the problem, any solution is predicated on their complete destruction. This destruction will presage the construction of a new man. Ironically, this utterly secular view now often goes under the label of "liberation theology." It used to be called Marxism.

Marxism is the most powerful answer to the spiritual problems of the world posed in material terms. It is superior to less radical forms of secularism because it has the logical force of consistency and has boldly reached the conclusion from which the lazy materialist of the West shies away: arms control will not change the world, man-control will. This clarity of vision and the pseudo-religious dedication it inspires give the Marxist a natural superiority in any negotiations with the obsessive arms controller who thinks a community of interest exists based upon his own fear of extinction. Since the obsessive arms controller sees the source of disorder as external to man, peace for him is simply the absence of external conflict, predicated upon fewer weapons. The Marxist sees the source of disorder in the material forces of history which have shaped man in a malignant way. The Marxist therefore does not share in the neo-Pelagian illusion of the Western secularist: for the Marxist, man is not basically good. Man must be changed. To change man, command of those historical forces must be obtained. The path to that command is total power. Peace for the Marxist is predicated not upon the absence of conflict, but upon the extinction of all opposing forces. Arms control is simply another tool for that purpose. That is why Marxists are better at using arms control to gain relative advantage than are the mild materialists of the West for whom peace is solely a question of disarmament.

Of course, the truly theological view of conflict, as already adumbrated in the quotations from St. James and St. Paul, recognizes that there is a war within man's own soul and that the nature of this war is a spiritual one because it primarily involves man's relationship to God. This is why that great warrior, General Douglas MacArthur, said: "The problem (of peace) basically is theological and involves a spiritual recrudescence. . . . It must be of the spirit if we are to save the flesh."

The Revolt Against God

The proper relationship to God is achieved only through a favorable resolution to that conflict within man's soul by which he prefers himself to God. To confront the central dislocation in life between man and God requires either reconciliation or revolt. Reconciliation through the grace of God is the answer of Judaism and Christianity. Revolt is the answer of modern totalitarian ideology. Both require sacrifice and discipline. But while one commands a reordering of one's will to the will of God, the other commands the reordering of the world to one's own will.

That act of reconciliation between man and God is the true theological source of peace because it is the only means by which man can be at peace with himself. It is the conjunction of the knowledge of good with good acts that ends the moral schizophrenia diagnosed by St. Paul. Vertical harmony between man and God is also the prelude to and necessary condition for horizontal peace between men. A man who is at war within himself is not likely to make true peace with his neighbor. In fact, as Aristotle pointed out in *The Ethics*, such a man is naturally prone to disrupt the social and political order: "Men start revolutionary changes for reasons connected with their private lives."

There is no greater act of revolt than the denial of God's existence. Atheism is not only a disorder in the God-man relationship, but a denial of it. Since God is the source of the transcendent standard by which the distinction between good and evil is ultimately made, His removal erases the recognition of the moral struggle in man's soul. If there is no firm foundation for the knowledge of the good with which man ought to bring his acts into conformity, then man is free to reorder or to reconstruct himself in any way he wishes. Man can live "beyond good and evil." Man can be made over—not in the image of God—but in a new image conceived by man. But in what image? Who is man without God? And, if there is to be no relationship between man and God, what shape will the relations between men take?

The problem is that, by denying the possibility of a relationship between God and man, atheism also denies the possibility of a just relationship between men. In other words, atheism removes the grounds for the recognition of, and therefore respect for, another person as a fellow human being. Before one can know what is justly due a man, one must know what a man is. But in the absence of God, it is impossible to know it. Nicolas Berdyaev put it this way: "If there is no God, there is no man either." He meant that atheism strips man of his nature and transforms him into a material product of historical circumstances. Human life is sacred only if there is a God to sanctify it. Otherwise, man is just another collection of atoms and can be treated as such.

How does one treat a collection of atoms? Paul Eidelberg pointed out the logic and consequences of this loss of human nature: "Unless there is a being superior to man, nothing in theory prevents some men from degrading other men to the level of the subhuman." If man does not have an immortal soul, the very standard by which one would judge the degradation of a human being is gone, because no fundamental distinction remains between a man and a dog. The degradation of man thus follows as a natural course from the denial of God. The consequences of this could not be more profound for the relationship between men. If a man dehumanizes another person, how does he then love him as a fellow human being and vice versa? Degradation removes the grounds for love between human beings because, as Pope John Paul II has said, "there can be no love without justice."

Karl Marx was one of the first thinkers to grasp the consequence of atheism for human relations and he concluded from it that "exploitation" is necessarily the fundamental relationship between alienated human beings. However, without love as the animating principle among men, what will serve as a basis for human relations? Lenin followed Marx's ideas to their inevitable conclusion. "We must hate," Lenin counseled; "hatred is the basis of communism." It is extremely important to note that, for Lenin, hatred is not so much a passion as it is the theoretically correct solution to the philosophical problem arising out of a world without God. As Khrushchev later said, "hatred of class enemies is *necessary*" (emphasis added). Soviet textbooks teach this as well by informing students of "the *principal class enemy* against whom it is essential to concentrate class hatred."

Within his own soul each individual is, and always has been, faced with the fundamental choice between reconciliation with God or revolt against Him. These moral choices are bound to affect not only the individual making them, but, to various extents, those with whom the person comes into contact. A morally depraved person, for example, hurts not only himself but most likely his family as well. However, it is seldom that such damage spreads to society as a whole. Modern, totalitarian ideology, however, is the twentieth century's unique contribution in collectively organizing the choice of revolt against God in the form of political institutions that affect everyone. It is one thing for a single individual to deny God and hate his neighbor. It is quite another to attempt to use that denial and hatred as the founding principles for a political enterprise the purpose of which is to bring the consequences of the revolt against God to all mankind.

The spiritual disorder within man's soul of which St. James wrote has become, in the modern age, institutionalized. In other words, the moral disorder of the individual soul has become the principle of a general, public disorder: first as it was articulated in the teachings of Nietzsche and Marx, and then incarnated in the Nazi regime and in the various Marxist-Leninist states of today.

Of course, no political order is perfect, but at least most publicly acknowledge *in principle* the transcendent moral standards by which to judge their imperfections in practice. What happens in a regime based upon the public denial of a transcendent principle of justice? As Lenin said, "For us, 'justice' is subordinated to our interest in overthrowing capitalism." In the absence of a transcendent standard of justice, there is no recourse from injustice since the means of distinguishing between the two have been removed. Force then becomes the adjudicator. Totalitarian ideology is the very philosophy of force. As John Paul II said, it "sees in force the source of rights." In other words, force or unlimited power becomes its own justification. By definition "the stronger is the right," as Hitler put it. Injustice therefore reigns, not as it has at other times in history in the tyranny of a single person or persons, but *by principle* and through the institutions embodying that principle. It is a systematized injustice. That is why *who* rules in the Soviet Union is largely irrelevant to any fundamental reform. So long as the principles of the Soviet Union remain unchanged, *glasnost* can only be, as it has been since its inception by Lenin, a change in window dressing. As the former Polish ambassador to the United States, Romauld Spasowski, said of the Soviet Union, "it cannot change, because it is based upon power."

The institutionalized disorder of modern totalitarian ideology has both vertical consequences for the relationship between man and God and horizontal consequences for the relationship between men. The consequences of the Nazi regime in both respects are now obvious, but only with the hindsight of history. In the 1930s people seemed to have had as much trouble grasping the true dimensions of Nazi ideology as we do today in realizing the real nature of the Soviet enterprise.

Religion as the Enemy

First of all, the attempt to snap man's vertical relationship to God has had the consequence of making religion the number one enemy of totalitarian ideology. Mikhail Borodin, Stalin's agent in China, once explained to Madame Chiang Kai-shek that the greatest threat to communism is the Christian concept of forgiveness because it so undermines Lenin's notion of inevitable class struggle and class enemies. As Lenin said: "Every religious idea of a god, even flirting with the idea of god, is unutterable vileness of the most dangerous kind, 'contagion' of the most abominable kind. Millions of sins, filthy deeds, acts of violence, and physical contagions are far less dangerous than the subtle spiritual idea of a god."

This virulent condemnation has translated into incredible devastation for religious life in the Soviet Union. Before Lenin's coup d'etat in 1917, Russia had 77,767 Russian Orthodox churches and 112,629 clergy. By 1975, according to estimates by Natalia Solzhenitsyn and material from Keston College, there were only 7,062 churches left, and 8,500 clergy. Today, there are only 5,994 priests in all of the USSR and a currently estimated number of 6,500 Orthodox churches. Of the 25,000 mosques that existed in the Caucasus and Central Asia, only some 400 to 500 remain today. Without being too crudely quantitative, if one wishes to measure *glasnost* as a standard of fundamental change, keep count of the churches. While Mr. Gorbachev may be willing to give up his SS-20s, he is unremitting in his call for "a determined and unbending struggle against religious tendencies" with a necessary "reinforcement of atheistic propaganda" (*Pravda Vostoka*, March 4, 1987). According to the March, 1987 *CSCE Digest*, "Fewer political activists are being arrested, but the rate of arrests of religious believers remains the same." However, Natan Shcharansky claims that "attacks against religious observers are [now] larger in scale." At an October 6th press conference after his release from the USSR on September eighteenth, forty-four year-old Yosyp Terelya, who has spent over twenty years in Soviet prisons, concentration camps and psychiatric hospitals, testified: "Christians in Soviet prisons receive the worst treatment. They are punished for praying. . . . The suppression of the Church in the Ukraine is worse than it was." Nonetheless, without flinching, Mr. Gorbachev proclaimed in his TV interview with Tom Brokaw that the Soviet Union is preparing to celebrate the millennium of Christianity in Russia during 1988.

As one would logically expect, the severance of the vertical relationship between God and man spread devastation to the horizontal relationship between men. Thus were ruptured the relations between the rulers and the ruled, the relations among the ruled, and the relations between nations. Totalitarian regimes do not differentiate between the reactionary elements within their own societies and those without. Both must be either forced into conformity with the totalitarian ideology or destroyed. Thus a state of permanent revolution and implacable hostility exists, in which it is impossible to distinguish between war and peace, except as different facets of the same struggle for total victory. This disorder takes its toll even in so-called times of peace. Stalin revealed the ideologue's inability to distinguish between internal and external enemies, and between war and peace. In a conversation at the Moscow Conference in 1943, Churchill asked Stalin whether the stresses of the war had been as great as those experienced with the forced collectivization of Soviet agriculture. Stalin responded: "Oh, no, the collective farm policy was a terrible struggle." It involved, he added, not just a million people, but "ten millions." Indeed, the civilian casualties from the forced collectivization of the Ukraine eclipsed the total body count of all combatants in World War I.

In fact, more people have died from this horizontal rupture, in the various gulags and concentration camps of totalitarian regimes in the twentieth century, than have died from all the wars of this century. While the casualties from war have, been estimated at 45.7 million people, well over twice that number of innocent people have fallen victim to totalitarian state violence during the same period. Stalin typified the totalitarian perspective in which murder is a logical necessity: "One traffic death, that is a tragedy; a million executions of counterrevolutionaries, that is a statistic." The most recent "statistics" are from Southeast Asia where, since the end of the Vietnam War in 1975, more people have lost their lives to the victorious communists than during the entire course of the war. In Cambodia, only several thousand of the 60,000 Bhuddist monks survived the religious extirpation efforts of the Khmer Rouge.

The consistency of the Soviet regime in its internal and external affairs was recently reaffirmed by Mr. Gorbachev in the introduction to one of his books of speeches: "Our foreign policy is an organic and logical extension of our domestic policy." As Lenin said, "there is nothing more nonsensical than the separation of international from domestic policy." These statements should worry anyone familiar with the internal history of the Soviet Union since 1917. Of course, it will not disturb those who accept Mr. Gorbachev's claim in Paris during his 1986 visit that there are no political prisoners in the Soviet Union. In an early example of *glasnost*, he told *L'Humanité*: "They do not exist in our country, just as persecution of citizens for their belief does not exist."

The predominant feature of world politics today is the struggle between the United States and the Soviet Union. To focus upon weapons in isolation from the moral character of that struggle with the hope that such discussions might lead to peace is a dangerous delusion. Change in the fundamental nature of the Soviet regime is the only realistic basis upon which to judge arms control or reduction proposals. Otherwise one will fall victim to the secular illusion that the weapons themselves are the danger. It is, of course, in the Soviet Union's interest to foster this illusion because it diverts attention from its true character and purpose. At the same time it induces a disposition in the West actually to cooperate in the Soviet Union's own efforts to strengthen itself in ways which would shift the "correlation of forces" decisively in its favor. Nazi Germany nearly succeeded in this same "peace" strategy. Winston Churchill had to win the war precipitated by this false peace. Ironically, victory in that war led to nothing but the transfer of half of Europe from one totalitarian power to another, precisely because nothing had been learned about the true nature of totalitarian ideology.

Should the Soviet Union ever succeed in its often proclaimed goal of global hegemony—a goal to which it is far closer today than ever before—it will do so on the basis of a series of inversions, all of which are intimately related: the inversion within man's own soul according to which he thinks of himself, rather than God, as the ultimate arbiter of the universe, codified into a plan for secular salvation (Marxist-Leninist ideology); the institutionalization of that inversion in a regime based upon its principles and dedicated to its universal application (as in the Soviet Union); and the inversion of the relationship between weapons and politics, which addresses the material effects rather than the spiritual causes of conflict (a secularized West incapable of seeing that the true source of peace is justice, founded upon the sanctity of each individual). These inversions may lead to a war which the West may lose. Far more

likely, they will not. Rather, they will lead to a defeat without war. But the "peace" which follows that defeat will have more casualties than the war that never was. Pax Sovietica.

This is not an argument against arms reductions per se. It is an argument against those who cry "peace, peace," when there is no peace, and who, by doing so wittingly or unwittingly, perpetuate the underlying injustice which makes true peace impossible. The antidote to these dangers to peace is the truth. Until recently, President Reagan consistently insisted on telling the truth about the nature of the Soviet Union despite the upset his "evil empire" remarks caused. As he unrepentantly told Barbara Walters on March 24, 1986, "I thought it was necessary to establish reality; to let them see that, no, we definitely saw what they were doing as evil. . . . I wanted them to know that I saw them realistically." The president has repeatedly said to Mr. Gorbachev: "We have distrust between us, not because of arms; we have arms because there is distrust." In other words Mr. Gorbachev, if you give up your totalitarian ideology, we can give up our arms; short of that, we must proceed even in our arms negotiations on the basis of the mistrust caused by that ideology. Justice requires nothing less.

The danger of arms control is that it disguises the evil it purports to cure. Even someone as wary as President Reagan has been so affected by the INF Treaty that he actually suggested that the Soviet Union now may no longer insist upon its universal claim to rule. Unfortunately, as in the past, this new era of arms control presages greater danger, not less. We can avoid the danger of arms control only by seeing clearly the false view of man of which it is a part and by recovering a full sense of who man is and how he finds true peace.

Rett R. Ludwikowski

Glasnost as a Conservative Revolution

VOL. 25, NO. 1, 1989

The origin of the idea of a "conservative revolution" is not clear. The term was used by the Austrian writer Hugo von Hofmannsthal to describe a countermovement to the intellectual upheaval of Renaissance and Reformation. Hermann Rauchning reexamined this idea in his book *The Conservative Revolution*[1] in which he portrayed German Nazism as a countermovement to the nihilistic Revolution that originated during the intellectual upheaval of the sixteenth century and unveiled itself in political form through the French and Russian revolutions.[2] Rauchning did not deny the material or the intellectual achievements of the revolutionary movements. He wrote:

> Beyond question, both sides of this one great revolution, which may justly be described as a process of human liberation, have had their salutary effects and will continue to have them. It is neither possible nor desirable that this revolutionary emancipation should be eliminated from the history of mankind. If, nevertheless, groups of us in all countries set ourselves against this

revolutionary current, attempting to stem it, such primitive motives should be not imputed to us as a desire to return to the Middle Ages and to reintroduce moral and political serfdom.[3]

Rauchning claimed that revolutions albeit they set out to burst oppressive limitations, brought also undesirable and destructive side effects. These side effects have to be eliminated by counter-movements which he referred to as "revolutions of reconstruction" or "conservative revolutions."

In the late seventies the term "conservative revolution" became popular in Poland through historians who reexamined the legacy of the French Revolution.[4] These effects yielded a fascination with such self-contradictory notions as "ahistorical historicism" or "realistic utopia."[5] The term "conservative revolution" was used also to describe the message of the famous film *Danton* by the Polish director Wajda. It was commented that the French Revolution was, in fact, presented by Wajda as a metaphor of the conservative revolution of Polish Solidarity. Rafael Krawczyk wrote:

West European socialists wanted to see Solidarity as their ideological child. This view survived longer than Solidarity itself. In 1982, Andrzej Wajda, a well known Polish film director with an international reputation, presented in Paris a first-night performance of his new picture 'Danton.' His work had been sponsored by the ruling French Socialist Party. France's President, Francois Mitterand, left the theater immediately after the performance refusing to comment. Surprisingly to all socialists, Wajda's view of the French Revolution appeared entirely conservative. In a historic contestation between Danton and Robespierre, Wajda took the side of Danton putting in his mouth explicit condemnation of the revolutionary rule of terror.[6]

It was often argued that terror was an unnecessary by-product of the Revolution and that, in fact, the Revolution preserved the imperial position of France. Using the same controversial term to portray Polish Solidarity Krawczyk concluded, "if Solidarity has been a 'revolutionary challenge' to the system called 'the real socialism,' it has been at the same time the first 'conservative revolution' in the world's history."[7] Quite recently the application of this term was extended to *glasnost* and *perestroika* which were portrayed, on the one hand, as "revolutionary" in comparison to the stagnation of Brezhnev's era. On the other hand, they were depicted as "conservative" in the sense of "transformation from within" which could solidify and preserve the power of the Communist Party elite. In his report of June 28, 1988, Mikhail Gorbachev declared:

The basic question facing us, delegates to the nineteenth All-Union Party Conference, is how to further the *revolutionary restructuring* launched in our country on the initiative and *under the leadership of the Party* and to make it irreversible.[8]

To call the current Soviet reconstruction plan a "conservative revolution" provokes a number of questions. Is *glasnost* going to "preserve" the pillars of the socialist system and protect it from collapse? Is it truly revolutionary? What is a conservative revolution? Is not the very idea self-contradictory?

"Preservative" Effects of *Glasnost*

Glasnost is defined by Russian-English dictionaries as publicity or openness. *Glasnyi* means "open," "public." Both the Western and the Soviet press characterize *glasnost* as a policy of change that replaced a policy of stagnation typical of the Brezhnev era. The student of socialist law and politics who wants to find out what really changed in socialist domestic and foreign policy will, however, experience some difficulty.

"Socialism," argues Professor Leslaw Paga of the Catholic University of Lublin, Poland, "is a transitory period from capitalism to . . . capitalism."[9]

Passing along the streets of Polish cities, one can easily notice large inscriptions on the walls of houses: "Proletarians of all countries, forgive me—Karl Marx."[10]

If we were to assess *glasnost* from the thousands of similar inscriptions, leaflets and statements we would have to acknowledge that its most striking characteristic is open *criticism* of communism.[11] In an article entitled "Sources" in *Novy Mir* even Lenin comes under criticism for abolishing private property and creating a system of forced labor camps.[12]

A recent article in *Pravda*, mostly a compilation of letters from readers, leveled serious charges against former Kremlin officials like Suslov and Brezhnev.[13]

This is an important reflection that should be borne in the minds of those who admire the changes of the *glasnost* era. The real change rests in the possibility of discussing problems that were for decades prohibited topics in the socialist countries. Unfortunately this change is limited to criticism of key elements of the socialist economy and social life, with current politics remaining an almost 'taboo' topic. The Western observer, impressed with this change, often confuses this "criticism from within" with "reform from within" and is inclined to forget that the core of the totalitarian system is still unchanged. He forgets that the mere possibility of exposing the distresses of the system from within does not change the system ipso facto. It has, however, new international implications that have to be carefully analyzed in the West.

The leaders have begun to notice that restructuring the system is a tremendous task. They have found that a successful *perestroika* requires time, funds, patience and public support, and the Soviet leadership has run short of these goods. In the past, their predecessors had tried to conceal the symptoms of internal crisis. To stifle criticism and subordinate the populace of Communist countries to the dictatorship of the party, the leaders used several techniques that have been employed interchangeably: the strategy of terror used most effectively by Stalin, the appealing promise of economic success through communism used by Stalin's successors, and the ideological or nationalist euphoria that was exploited during the postrevolutionary era and World War II. None of these strategies can be used as successfully as before. Ideological or na-

tionalist clichés do not appeal to people who want to live on the level of civilized societies. Terror is still effective, but its blatant application does not fit the liberal disguise of Gorbachev's leadership during the *glasnost* period, and *glasnost* is a prerequisite to Soviet relations with the West. It has become obvious to the Soviet leaders that without cooperation and technology from the West, the economies of the bloc countries will deteriorate further, just at the time when Western economies are on the mend. Continuation of "détente and cooperation" seems to be viewed by the Soviet leaders as the condition *sine qua non* of *perestroika*. *Glasnost* is the price paid for the successful restructuring of the socialist economy.

Admittedly, *glasnost* has dramatically changed the way of life of people in the Soviet Union. Henry Kissinger commented after his visit to the Soviet Union:

> The seediness of the accommodations had not changed, nor the backwardness of what in the West are considered life's amenities. One remains amazed that a country subsiding on so marginal a standard of living should conduct so assertive a global policy. Yet the surface impression of stagnation was misleading. There is clearly unprecedented ferment underneath the gloomy surface of wintry Moscow. The new leadership is different. It displays a vigor, dynamism and flexibility inconceivable ten years ago.[14]

Even those experts on Soviet domestic policy who believe in the seriousness of the reform program admit that liberalization is only a by-product of *perestroika*, and the achievements of *glasnost* should be checked carefully. "The purpose of that reform is not to spur democracy or freedom; it is to encourage efficiency and industrial progress, hence to make the Soviet Union more powerful."[15]

So far the "preservative" effects of *glasnost* and *perestroika* are not highly visible. *Glasnost* undermines rather than enhances the foundation of the socialist system. Public discussion of the distresses of communism reveals that in spite of the attempt at reforming the system, Soviet politics in the early 1990s will be shaped by economic crisis, and the Soviet bloc will face unprecedented shortages of energy, capital, and food. For the first time it is clear, even to the people living within the Communist structure, that in spite of the efforts of the Soviet leadership, the technological gap between the socialist economies and the other industrialized countries will increase. The Communist paradise promised by Khrushchev will not come true.

The reforms have already endangered the position of the middle ranks of the Party bureaucracy and have resulted in the considerable conservative reaction within the Communist Party. Undoubtedly, the economic distresses will further stagnate the standard of living and cause a decline in the growth rate of mass consumption. *Glasnost* will shatter the chance of hindering the economic slowdown and the growing gap between the rulers and the ruled. Watchful Western commentators often warn that full-fledged *glasnost* may open a Pandora's box of social distress and result in more serious social turbulence than the Hungarian events of 1956, the "Prague Spring" of 1968, or the Polish Solidarity crisis of the 1980s. The 1987 Polish referendum, the 1988 strikes, the reports on public dissatisfaction with the Communist leadership in Czechoslovakia and Hungary, the development of the nationalist and ethnic movements in the Soviet Republics, and the most recent revolt against communism in China confirm the seriousness of this danger.[16]

The deteriorating economies of satellite countries will make the bonds between the Soviet Union and Eastern Europe less and less profitable. Obviously Moscow's relations with its satellites in the last few years are highly political in nature. These military and political determinants of the Soviet interest in the Eastern Europe buffer zones will probably remain constant, but the future will show to what extent the Soviet Union will be able to afford costly commitments in this region. Economic decay may erode Moscow's dominance in the Soviet bloc as well as Soviet involvement in risky and expensive international ventures.[17] The Soviet troop pullout from Afghanistan confirms these prognoses.

Internal turbulence and a decline in Russian nationalism combined with an increasingly anti-Russian nationalism in the non-Russian regions[18] may force the regime to follow Poland's example and seek military leaders who would be able to deal with the situation. It is possible that the isolated Party may experiment with military coups, and the regime may relapse into a modified Stalinist form of dictatorship, which proved suitable in a state of emergency but useless in the face of serious and permanent social and economic problems.

Instead of "conservation" the West can expect destabilization of the system and a sort of zigzag policy with typical strategies based on both calculated and some irrational motives. The failures of Reykjavik-type meetings might be followed by successful summits, and the friendly relationships and disarmament gestures may be intertwined with incidents as dangerous as the shooting down of the Korean airliner or the ramming of American ships on the Black Sea by Soviet warships. The policy of liberalization and democratization might be replaced by the reign of terror similar to China's crackdown.

Glasnost as a "Revolution"

Even the most enthusiastic commentators on Gorbachev's attempt at restructuring the Soviet economy admit that the system does not show many "revolutionary" signs of a quick economic recovery. Gorbachev's *glasnost* and *perestroika* are being tested in an atmosphere which resembles more the Sisyphean Labors than the noisy hurrah-enthusiasm of the Khrushchev era.[19] The situation stands as follows:

The Soviet system has forever destroyed the so-called collective mentality, which was supposed to be a basic component of Communist political culture.

The crisis within Communist ideology is irreversible. The belief of the masses in Marxism-Leninism cannot be reconstructed, yet socialist leaders will not give up obsolete dogmas because they do not know how to function without them.

The ideological crisis has undermined the rudiments of Communist morality and corroded all Marxist-Leninist values, including the key dogma of common ownership.

The moral and ideological crisis has killed all healthy incentives among workers and managers.

The double standard of morality, together with massive economic dis-locations, has created a black market and corruption, which have been tolerated for so long that they are now irrevocably integrated in the way of life of Communist countries.

The need to create a relatively open party elite forced the party to build a system of "negative selection" that promotes compliant, conformable "yes" men who care far more about their careers than about the system of Communist values.

The lack of competence, and accountability, and widespread corruption on the part of decision-makers, are incompatible with the basic principles of economic efficiency.

The lack of information, coordination, and proper control over the implementation of productive decisions, coupled with a form of decentralization that is more apparent than real, cripple the socialist system's central planning and decision-making effort. These factors also work against the attempts to introduce market mechanisms into the socialist system. The combination of central planning and a market economy, totalitarian power of the party and the socialist democracy resembles the woman who is only "half pregnant." This kind of reform may result in the creation (using Kolakowski's expression) of a sort of "boiling ice."

The concept of "socialist pluralism" is meaningless when combined with control by the Party. The recognition of opposition within socialism should not be confused with pluralism. The attempt to put "Western" and "socialist" pluralism on the same footing reminds one of the argument that "slaves and their owners are equal because all of them have two legs, two hands, and one head."

The functioning of the double legislative body composed of the huge Congress and the smaller but still bicameral nucleus organ (Central Executive Committee or Supreme Soviet) had been well tested in the twenties and thirties. These Congresses of several thousand delegates, handicapped by their size, were typically more responsive to the party rhetoric. They were organized carefully in advance and held in an atmosphere encouraging no dissenting debate. Recent signs suggested that the new Soviet Congress would be something more than a huge manifestation of support for the Party.

The Congress, however, followed the well-anticipated Gorbachev scenario.

The modified system did not introduce elements of political pluralism. The Constitution guarantees that one-third of the deputies are elected from the all-union social organizations controlled by the Communist Party. The remaining two-thirds of the candidates are nominated by labor collectives, and there are no indications that the majority of them will not be selected from the Party-controlled electorate. In this situation the new USSR Supreme Soviet might accept only nominal dissent and be in fact an institution with the same profile as the old Supreme Soviet which was called to applaud the party's decisions.

The evolution of the electoral system should be watched carefully. So far, multi-seat electoral districts have been introduced only in local elections and the experience of other socialist countries shows that they are not ipso facto a guarantee of democratization of the electoral process. Double and multiple nominations were theoretically possible under the old electoral Soviet laws. In practice however, candidates or the organizations that nominated them dropped their names when alternative names were submitted and single candidates ran for each seat uncontested. Without public control of the election process the slogan "free elections" is meaningless in light of the socialist record.

The nomination of Gorbachev to the position of president of the Supreme Soviet enhanced his power under the new constitutional law. This law limits the tenure of this position to ten years (two five-year successive terms) but extends the functions of the president to head of state, who chairs the powerful Defense Council and names candidates to the posts of chairman of the USSR Council of Ministers, USSR general prosecutor, chairman of the USSR Supreme Court, and also chooses other high officials. The combination of the position of General Secretary of the Party with the presidency and the announced combination of the equivalent positions on the local level hardly can favor the announced reversion of power to the soviets.[20]

The new law raised great concern especially in the Northern Republics of the Soviet Union. The widely heralded, yet vaguely implemented shift of power from the party to the legislature was accompanied by restrictions on public demonstrations and the freedom of association.[21]

It is worth repeating after Andrei Sakharov that "the West should be genuinely interested in the success of *perestroika* and interested in supporting it," yet he observes that so far "this is *perestroika* only from above."[22]

The changes in the Communist way of life are visible but *by no means revolutionary*. The massacre on Tiananmen Square in Beijing followed by a wave of arrests proved that the West should not be deluded by the symptoms of liberalization and democratization. At least the core of the system remains unchanged. It can be characterized by several main traits.

First, the existence of an official ideology which sometimes causes leaders to act, but serves at other times to disguise the cynicism of the ruling elite and to rationalize actions that in fact are uncoordinated and ineffectual.

Second, control by a single party, which is represented as a mass organization, but is in fact an elitist structure that co-opts into its top ranks individuals who are conformable to and compliant with the official party line. The party is headed by a small group of activists and often by a single autocrat (although not as omnipotent as Stalin) who is presented as the charismatic leader of a nation, a class, or even all mankind. The party is able to survive for a comparatively long period of time because its lower ranks are relatively open and ready to accept anyone who blindly follows party orders.

Third, operation of the party through a party bureaucracy and various intermediary associations devoted to the ruling elite. These numerous cadres, subordinate to top party leaders, help to maintain military control over the country, as well as monopoly control of all economic activity and of all means of communication and education.

Fourth, the use of an extremely widespread system of police control which helps to keep individuals obedient and almost completely deprived of an independent personal life. The domination of society by the state and the minimization of the private and individual sphere are not limited by law. Rather, the law serves only to enhance the power of the ruling elite. The extended penetration of all spheres of social life by the state—including the ethical, religious, economic, and legal—distinguishes this system from all other dictatorships and autocratic regimes.[23]

The system has created its own "vicious circle," without its key ingredients, ideological rhetoric, bureaucracy, the party centralized leadership, the system of police control, the system cannot function; but with them, no reform is possible. These key ingredients can be crushed but not reformed. They are an inseparable part of the system.

The above observations bring us to several conclusions:

First of all, although this author does not have a great liking for definitional disputes he admits his almost instinctive aversion to showy but gimcrack plays

on words. The concept of "conservative revolution" is self-contradictory and has never proven to be true. Revolutions do not change all elements of the existing reality, and all social transformations have some "preservative" consequences. In this sense the Great Socialist Revolution extended the authoritarian model of power in Russia, and the French Revolution revitalized and prolonged the life of the French monarchy which would be restored after the Napoleon era. The exposition of "preservative" elements of revolutionary change is as confusing as the exposition of elements of socialism in "national socialism." Conservatism is a negation of revolution. A revolutionary world is a world of destruction, emotions, and irrational hopes. A conservative world is one of prudence, peace and reasonable compromise. Revolutions often promise a rapid liberation from present oppression and misery. Conservatism promises continuity and reasonable progress. Conservatism may be anti-revolutionary but it cannot be ipso facto revolutionary or counter-revolutionary. It has to be clearly observed that the concept of a "conservative revolution" is alien to a conservative mind and has always been challenged from a conservative point of view.

Secondly, the movement of Polish Solidarity is neither revolutionary or conservative. On the contrary, the leadership of the movement has tried to avoid as strongly as possible any violent challenge to the system; on the other hand, the movement is oriented toward change, not toward the preservation of the foundations of the establishment. *Solidarity* is neither conservative or liberal. As Andrze Waljcki wrote,

Solidarity is a product of socialism. It might be furiously critical of socialism on the conscious level, but it is deeply socialist on the unconscious level—if by socialism we mean egalitarianism and collectivism; the primacy of politics over economics, cancelling the objective laws of the market; belief that political power can and should regulate everything in social life—in this sense, belief is an unlimited political power.

If all these things characterize socialism, then Solidarity must be seen as a socialist mass movement, one striving for at least a share of political power, but not one seeking to limit political power in the name of individual freedom. It is a movement aiming not so much at the separation of economics from politics, but rather at the democratization of politico-economic decision making. It is a democratic movement, but it can hardly be called liberal because it opposes authoritarian bureaucratic collectivism not in the name of individualistic values, but in the name of a democratic collectivism of the masses. It wants to *divide* political power, but it is not sufficiently aware of the desirability of *limiting* the scope of all political power, including democracy. In this sense we can even say that the political thinking of the leaders of Solidarity (not to mention that of its ordinary members) is contaminated to some extent by the spirit of socialist totalitarianism—in spite of their verbal condemnations of all kinds of totalitarian power.[24]

The "round table accords" in Poland confirmed the readiness of Solidarity to reach agreement with the Party to avert crisis. The accords and the recent elections proved a coexistence in Poland of totalitarian and democratic forces. In voting for Solidarity the voters voted for the democratic program of reforms of the organization which was portrayed as anti-totalitarian and anti-revolutionary. The Solidarnosc Civic Committee's Election Program reads:

> Why do we say "yes" to elections? We ask everyone to participate in the elections because we see what Poland can gain by having independent representatives in the Diet and the Senate. . . . Participation does not mean closing our eyes or granting legitimacy to the non-democratic political system prevailing in our country. It reflects the desire to change that system in an evolutionary way, using parliamentary mechanisms.[25]

Finally, we also tried to prove that *glasnost* is not a "conservative revolution." *Glasnost* is a distress signal within the system. Being "revolutionary" it is more destructive than "protective" of the system. If *glasnost* were "conservative" it could not be revolutionary.

At the end of his book Hermann Rauchning wrote about German Nazism, "Thus it was a mistake to propose to make a conservative revolution. What we want and what we failed to achieve, and what will be the aim of the peace to come, is the *end of the revolution.*"[26] This conclusion ideally fits the *glasnost* era. The leaders of this movement must realize that a "conservative revolution" is not the solution to their ills. What their people really want and clearly need is *the end of the socialist revolution.*

Notes

1. Hermann Rauchning, *The Conservative Revolution* (New York: Putnam, 1941).
2. Ibid., 50–62.

3. Ibid., 53.

4. It was often used by the historians who followed the well-known Polish historian of ideas Jan Baszkiewicz. Baszkiewicz wrote *Historia Francji* [History of France] (Warsaw, 1974); *Robespierre* (Wroclaw, 1976), *Canton* (Warsaw, 1978).

5. This author strongly opposed this tendency in his review of W. Karpinski and M. Krol's book *Sylwetki Polityczne XIXw,* [Political Figures of the Nineteenth Century] (Cracow, 1974), review in 3 *Kwartainik, Historyczny* (Historical Quarterly] (1975), 669–674.

6. Professor Rafael Krawczyk is a Bradley Scholar at The Heritage Foundation in Washington. D.C. The quotation is from his unpublished paper, *Conservative Reflections on Eastern Europe* (1988), 3.

7. Ibid., 10.

8. Report by Mikhail Gorbachev, in: *Documents and Materials,* (Moscow: Novosti Press Agency Publishing House, 1988), 5, emphasis added.

9. Leslaw Paga, unpublished lecture at the Catholic Univ. of America, Department of Economics, April 15, 1988.

10. See Rett R. Ludwikowski, *The Crisis of Communism*: *Its Meaning, Origins and Phases* (Washington: Pergamon, 1986), vii.

11. *Przeglad Tygodniowy* (March 1988).

12. "Even Lenin Now Comes Under Criticism," *Washington Post,* 7 June 1988.

13. "Article *Pravda* Assesses Difficulties for Gorbachev," *Washington Post,* 8 June 1988.

14. *Newsweek,* 2 March 1987, 39.

15. Ibid.

16. See *Washington Post* 20 November 1987, 1 December 1987, 224–226; February 1988; see also "Multiple Ethnic Conflicts Challenging Gorbachev," *Washington Post,* 29 February 1988, A1, A12.

17. See Marshall Goldman, *USSR in Crisis: The Failure of an Economic System* (New York; Norton, 1983, xi).

18. See "Reports on Growth of Ethnic Nationalism in Lithuania, Latvia and Estonia," *Newsweek,* 29 February 1988, 39.

19. See Rett R. Ludwikowski, "Gorbachev and His Reform," *Modern Age* (Spring 1986), 120–30.

20. "Changes to Enhance Democracy" (Moscow: TASS, 22 October 1988).

21. See "Angry Estonians to Discuss Changes in Constitution," *Washington Post,* 4 November 1988.

22. "Sakharov Sees Threat to Soviet Reform," *Washington Post,* 8 November 1988; "Sakharov's Fears," *Washington Post,* 7 November 1988.

23. See Rett R. Ludwikowski, introduction to Victor A. Kravchenko, *I Chose Freedom* (New Brunswick, NJ: Transaction Publishers, 1989, xix–xx).

24. "Liberalism in Poland" *Critical Review* (Winter 1988), 8–9.

25. *Solidarnosc News,* no. 133, May 1–15, 1989.

26. Rauchning, *Conservative Revolution,* 280.

VII.

CRISES, CONTROVERSIES
& CURIOSITIES

Russell Kirk

THE UNIVERSITY AND REVOLUTION:
AN INSANE CONJUNCTION

VOL. 6, NO. 1–2, 1969–70

Already the reaction is upon us. Political leaders, college presidents, and syndicated columnists join in condemnation of violence on the campus. Yesterday's fashionable prattle about revolution in the university and revolution in the United States and revolution in the world is reproved piously by those very liberals who, such a short while ago, beamed upon the ferment of the rising generation. Mr. Irving Howe, editor of *Dissent*, wanders over the face of the land reproaching the more vehement dissenters and reminding them of the delightful benefits of Social Security. One thinks of Edward Gibbon, so progressive at the commencement of the French Revolution, observing from his Swiss retreat the course of that movement; reflecting, presently, that revolutionaries kill people like Edward Gibbon; and then promptly taking another tack.

For my part, however, I do not propose to deliver another sermon about the naughtiness of ungrateful undergraduates. Whatever the silliness of revolutionary slogans and methods, one does not deal with them by mere smug remonstrance. We need to address ourselves, rather, to the real causes of our present discontents

in the university and in this nation; and my observations are of that character.

The principal cause of some people's revolutionary mood is the decay of community—the decadence of academic community, and the decadence of urban community. In the phrase of Miss Hannah Arendt, "The rootless are always violent." Until community is restored, certain students and considerable elements of our urban population will continue to detest the existing order.

Having been for two decades a mordant critic of what is foolishly called the higher learning in America, I confess to relishing somewhat, as Cassandra might have, the fulfillment of my predictions and the present plight of the educationist Establishment. I even own to a sneaking sympathy, after a fashion, with the campus revolutionaries. Consider, by way of illustration, the recent experience of Mr. John A. Hannah, president of Michigan State University, recently chosen to be director of the federal government's foreign-aid program.

Called to relieve the miseries of Kerala and to improve the lot of Bolivia, President Hannah delivered his farewell address to the members of his faculty on February 10, 1969. In three decades as master of Michigan State, Dr. Hannah (the doctorate honorary, conferred by his own university on the day he became its president) had built up a student body now exceeding forty thousand, with expectation of seventy thousand, or more, before from his eyes the streams of dotage flow. In the process, somehow Mr. Hannah himself had grown rich. On the branches of his university, the sun never sets: they flourish in Okinawa and in Nigeria. Doubtless President Hannah, on this day of leavetaking, felt that he deserved well of the rising generation. Certainly he knew that he had done well out of the education business—having risen so far when his earned degree was that of bachelor of science in poultry husbandry—and he was determined that those national institutions which had facilitated his success should not perish from the earth.

True, he was departing from Michigan State in the nick of time. Having passed the retirement age set by himself, he was in an awkward situation when certain hostile trustees of the university hinted that he might not be altogether indispensable. The Attorney-General of Michigan had looked into charges that Dr. Hannah might have engaged in activities constituting "conflict of interest"; and though President Hannah himself was exonerated—more or less—his close associate, the chief financial officer of the university, with whose affairs those of Hannah were curiously plaited—had been discovered busy in certain enterprises very much in conflict of interest with the concerns of the university, and had found it prudent to retire from the scene. Moreover, some of the students (members of the biggest undergraduate body in the world, on one campus) were ungrateful.

As President Hannah addressed his professors for the last time, riot-police—gas-masks and all—stood guard in the auditorium. Several hundred students, a discharged instructor with a bullhorn, and a number of outsiders—among these, Carl Oglesby, of Students for a Democratic Society—were chanting unpleasantly outside the auditorium. It was found prudent to cancel the reception that had been scheduled to follow President Hannah's speech.

"A small coterie," the masterful chickenologist told his faculty, "has declared social revolution against America. America's universities have been marked as the first fortress that must fall. We've been warned of the weapons to be used and the tactics to be employed." He exhorted his professors to resist to the last blue-book these enemies of civilization. Then, meaning to do high deeds beside the Potomac, he departed from their midst.

John Hannah had been a brick-and-mortar president. His university has become an intellectual cafeteria, or rather a vocational cafeteria, offering every serious discipline from fly-casting (for physical-education majors) to Afro-American studies (after all, he had been chairman of the Civil Rights Commission, even if in his early years in office the only Negro employee of Michigan State had been the president's own errand-boy). Unceasingly he had recruited students, qualified or unqualified, telling them and their parents that a college graduate earns much more money in his lifetime than does a barbarian of the outer darkness. He had offered students the nexus of cash payment—and what else is there to a university, after all?

Yet the gentry of the New Left remained unappreciative. One of them, James Ridgeway, has published a book containing lively references to Dr. Hannah: *The Closed Corporation—American Universities in Crisis*. Here we must content ourselves with one passage:

> From 1950 to 1958 more than $900,000 in MSU construction contracts went to the Vandenburg Construction Company. The president of this firm was Hannah's brother-in-law, who subsequently went out of business and turned up as construction superintendent at MSU. Hannah was quoted as saying at the trustees' meeting, "It's true that Vandenburg is my brother-in-law, but I didn't know he was employed by the university." He also said, "As far as I know he never did a job for this institution. I was surprised by the figure. . . . I smell what's coming on. This is an attempt at discrediting the university by discrediting me."

Really? Or is it the Hannahs of our time who have discredited the university, and so raised up a turbulent generation of students, at once ignorant and passionate, who still sense somehow that Hannah's idea of a university is not quite John Henry Newman's idea of a university? Having established academic collectivism, having overwhelmed academic community, having severed the intellectual and moral roots of the higher learning, people like John Hannah are chagrined to discover that the proles are restless.

NO LESS a public figure than Miss Joan Baez remarked recently that if one desires to be a revolutionary, the campus is an unlikely place to commence; that she is disgusted with the antics of campus radicals; and that she will have no more to do with them. One wishes that certain professors might share her wisdom. But

they will, eventually—they will: for revolutions devour their children, and also their fathers.

Dr. Bruno Bettelheim, the psychologist, who has had unpleasant personal experience with revolutions, says that the crowd of campus revolutionaries—the violent folk, he means—are paranoiacs, though led by shrewd ideologues intent upon personal power. Paranoiacs may belong in an institution, but that institution is not the university; ideologues have no stopping-place short of heaven or hell, and so they ought not to be permitted to convert the university into a staging-ground. We need to recall the principal purpose of a university. The university is not a center for the display of adolescent tempers, nor yet a fulcrum for turning society upside down. It is simply this: a place for the cultivation of right reason and moral imagination.

From its beginnings, the university has been a conservative power. The principal schools of Athens, particularly the Academy and the Stoa, had for their end the recovery of order in the soul and order in the commonwealth. The medieval university was intended to impart wisdom and temperance to a violent age. My own higher studies were undertaken at St. Andrews, a university founded by the inquisitor of heretical pravity in Scotland, expressly to confute the errors of Lollardry.

So it is not in the nature of a university to nurture political fanaticism and utopian designs. The professor rarely is a neoterist, and one cannot expect the university to harvest a crop of exotic flowers annually. Dr. Robert Hutchins observes, with only a little exaggeration, that few of the Great Books were written by professors. If one would be a mover and shaker in his own hour, the forum is preferable to the grove of Academe. In a small way,

I have done some moving and shaking myself; but I found myself much freer and more effective once I had withdrawn from the shadow of the Ivory Tower.

Only in our century, indeed, has the plague of ideological passion descended upon the quadrangle and the campus. To some degree, in previous times, all universities ordinarily were, after the fashion of Oxford, sanctuaries of lost causes: conservative to a fault, if you will. So far as they aspired to influence the bustling world, it was to tug at the check-rein, not to use the spur: of ungoverned will and appetite, the average sensual man in the civil social order needs no larger endowment. The university tried to teach the rising generation how to rise superior to will and appetite.

Yet temporarily, at least, throughout the world, many a campus has fallen into the clutch of ideology, ours being a time of ideological infatuation. What the university used to offer was freedom; what some zealots seek there, just now, is power. Freedom and power are in eternal opposition. To demand that the university devote itself to the *libido dominandi* is to demand that the university commit intellectual and moral suicide.

A good many entering freshmen tell me that they desire to be on a campus "where the action is." But of action, we all have plenty in the course of life. A university is a place not for action, but for leisure—that is, for reading and good talk, for dialogue between scholar and student, and for a reflective preparation. Few people ever find again, after they enter upon the hurly-burly of the world, time enough to study and to think. The four or five or seven years of college and university life are precious, then; they are a period of self-discipline and self-examination; and, as Socrates put it, the unexamined life is not worth living.

Even a young person who aspires to turn the civil social order inside out is foolish if he occupies his university years in "activism." Marching, demonstrating, shouting, sitting-in, he squanders the time he might have used to prepare himself for effective action after graduation. He could have been a member of an academic community; instead, he has chosen to become a face in an academic mob; and in later years, intellectually undisciplined, he must be virtually worthless as a partisan of radical reform. The systematic Marxist, incidentally, is well aware of this difficulty; and though he may make use of the anarchic student for the immediate purposes of his movement, mere perpetual activism scarcely is the course he commends to the initiates of a Marxist study-group. The labors of Marx were accomplished in the British Museum, not in Trafalgar Square.

ALL THIS said, nevertheless, I think I apprehend the causes of the New Left mentality on the campus, and in part sympathize with the mood of rebellion. For two decades, I have been declaring that most colleges and universities are sunk in decadence. Against that decadence, the confused outcries of the New Left people are a reaction. For a university, as for the human body, the power of reaction is a necessity, and often a sign of latent health: the body that no longer can react is a corpse.

Against what does the radical student rebel? Against a crass and boring and "oppressive" society, he declares; but more immediately, he rebels against what James Ridgeway calls "the closed corporation": the university that has decayed into a vast impersonal computer, serving big government and big industry, neglecting wisdom for isolated facts and skills, routinely conferring degrees that are mere certificates of introduction or employability, at best; the university that has forgotten quality in the appetite for quantity, that exalts "service"—which is to say, the gratification of the whims and material desires of the hour—above learning; the university that has made some professors affluent, and some administrators more than affluent, but which leaves the typical undergraduate intellectually and morally impoverished.

Were I to indulge my taste for Jeremiads, indeed I might succeed in out-lamenting the New Left people at the Ivory Tower's wailing-wall. Though they might not use precisely these words, in effect the New Left zealots are proclaiming that today's university offers next to nothing for mind and conscience. Amen to that. I am not sorry that the radicals have fluttered academic hencoops like Dr. Hannah's, for I have long been endeavoring to do precisely that myself.

What I do regret is the proclivity of the New Left to pull down. Demolition is simple enough; but the craft of the architect is something else. The university, and the modern world, require the torch: not the arsonist's torch, however, but the torch of learning. "Revolution" means violent and catastrophic change. Of catastrophe, we have experience enough already in this century. Revolution—political and technological and moral and demographic—is upon us in this century, whether we like it or not; we have no need to flog the galloping horses of the four spectres of the Apocalypse. Reconstruction, renewal, reinvigoration, are the real necessities of this hour; we require creative imagination—which the university is supposed to cultivate—not the sapper's petard, that so frequently hoists its pioneer.

Our present discontents in the Academy, I repeat, are not difficult to describe. Foremost among their practical causes is the problem of scale. Behemoth University is too big; it has been inundated by, or has lured in, an academic crowd; and a crowd easily is converted into a mob. When community dies, collectivism succeeds, in the university or in the state. No man rejoices at finding himself merely an IBM number. At the institution where I spent my undergraduate years—Michigan State—a great many new graduates complain that they cannot obtain job-recommendations from any professor, because they never have met a real professor, in four years of course-taking: their converse was not with Mark Hopkins, but (at best) with an obscure teaching-assistant, who meanwhile has proceeded to greener pastures. At the early medieval universities, the student was an acolyte; now he has become a cipher.

Nowadays the typical student is bored. Mankind can endure anything but boredom. It is by boredom, actually, that the student is oppressed—not by "the administration" or "the establishment." Revolution always is attractive to the man intensely bored: anything for a change. But of revolution inspired by boredom, one must say what Bierce said of suicide: a door out of the prison-house of life. It opens upon the jail-yard. Undoubtedly the domination of King Log was boring. Yet as for the new regime of King Stork—why, exiled students from the University of Havana, many of them Fidelistas once, may attest to that.

Why bored? Why, on the typical campus nowadays, the majority of students don't know why they have enrolled, and probably never should have enrolled at all. Nearly eight years ago, Mr. Christopher Jenks—who later investigated, for the regent of the University of California, the background of the first Berkeley riots—published in Harper's an article entitled

"The Next Thirty Years in the Colleges," in which he said what he could in defense of the higher learning in this land. He then estimated that on the typical campus, one percent of the students desire a serious scholarly or scientific training; two percent seek a more general intellectual education; perhaps five percent want an introduction to upper-middle-brow culture and upper-middle-class conviviality; twenty percent are after technical training; another twenty percent desire merely certification as ambitious and respectable potential employees. That leaves more than half of the students; and, as Mr. Jenks put it, the majority don't know what they desire from college, and never take degrees. What with the added inducement of postponing or escaping military service, and increased recruiting by universities and colleges, matters are somewhat worse now, eight years later.

Bored students, quite aimless in the university, will embrace any university rag for diversion from the dreary routine of classes; and no inconsiderable part of the "revolutionary" students are merely idle young people, looking for a moment's excitement not to be obtained from folios. But also a good many of the more genuine students—say those in Mr. Jenks's uppermost eight percent—are no less bored than are the fun-and-games undergraduates, and considerably more indignant.

"Irrelevance" is their battle-cry; and there is some substance in their protest, even though most of them possess only a dim notion of what really is relevant to the higher learning. I cannot digress here concerning Relevance; I remark merely that the grievances of these better students are concerned with the curriculum and the administration of the university itself, really, though their dissent may take the form of a general denunciation of modern society. Although I am not unresponsive even to this latter distaste for the dominations and powers, the fads and foibles, of the moment, I venture to observe that the assault by students upon American institutions scarcely is so relevant as is the uprising of Czech or Yugoslav students against the grim regimes by which they are ruled.

NOW ADD to this mood the personal grievances of most undergraduates and graduate students against military conscription; add to it the burning discontent of the proletariat of Academe—that is, the overworked and underpaid graduate assistants and teaching fellows. Add to it the resentment and bewilderment of Black Power students, impelled to "do their thing"—even though, as Tocqueville said of the French Revolution, "halfway down the stairs we threw ourselves out of the window to reach the ground more quickly." With these conditions in mind, one does not wonder that an impulse to pull down is at work upon the typical campus.

People with real grievances, but ignorant of political theory and institutions, are the natural prey of the ideologue. The terrible simplifiers appear, and an energumen with a tawdry set of yesteryear's anarchist or Marxist slogans can find some following on any campus. Those slogans are even less relevant to the present difficulties of the American university, or of American society, than are the dreary courses of study to which the radical students so vehemently object, but any ideology will serve as an apology and a focus for an academic mob. Parallels with Nazi and fascist and Communist student movements, more than a generation ago, are ignored by the more violent student activists, sure of their own virtue and vision.

Consider an eminent ideologue of New Leftism on the campus—Mr. Tom Hayden, with whom I have debated. Hayden, principal founder of Students for a Democratic Society, yearns to ride the whirlwind and direct the storm; for painstaking reform, he has only contempt; practical remedies he disdains. His rhetoric—and his program, so far as he possesses one—are those of Jack London's pseudo-proletarian romance *The Iron Heel.* He would organize the poor and the uprooted, whom he would have rise in righteous wrath to turn the rascals out, forever. What happens when the revolution is consummated, Hayden does not inform us. Actually, when any old order has fallen, persons like Hayden—rebels by nature against any regime, craggy and impractical—promptly are disposed of by persons like Stalin and Mao and Castro. (The anarchists of Cuba are dead or imprisoned.)

When first I shared a platform with Tom Hayden, that evangel of Pull Down was organizing the poor of Newark. He spoke from a platform at the University of Michigan; and I happened to comment upon the causes and conditions of social decay and poverty in Corktown, the old Irish district of Detroit. Now Tom Hayden had been editor of the *Michigan Daily,* the student newspaper of the University of Michigan, and had held in Michigan the first convention of Students for a Democratic Society. Yet Hayden then confessed that he never heard of Corktown, though for years he had lived about twenty-five miles distant from that slum.

It is so dull to brighten the corner where you are; so pleasant, initially, to carry a secular gospel to the gentiles of Newark, say. But presently Newark is aflame; alarmed, one seeks less perilous centers for the revolution—the ivied halls of Columbia University, say; or one flies to Hanoi, to Dar-es-Salaam, anywhere the funds of the movement will carry one for a well-publicized conference or interview. One impedes political conventions in Chicago; one taunts police; one mocks at everybody in either regular political party; one utters obscenities, complacently, at a Congressional hearing. What a charming vision of the future, chums— a revolution led by the sullen perpetual adolescent, unable to govern, unable even to dream any dreams except Londonian nightmares of violence! While the novelty endures, before the inevitable public reaction sets in, such a career is not at all unpleasant for those who like that sort of thing. But as a means to the reform of the university, or to the reform of the civil social order—why, one need not labor this point.

Some months ago I saw a painting, rather in the manner of Daumier, by Renee Radell. It is called "Doing Their Thing." In the foreground stand two young men bearing placards, barring the way. On the placards is no inscription at all. The young men are grinning; and their mirth is the laughter of hyenas, for they are smug and well-fed and well-dressed nihilists. They bar the way to everything traditional and everything decent.

Renee Radell has caught perfectly the tone and temper of certain youthful anarchists, protesting against the affluent society that produced them. Their schooling, one gathers, has been costly and bad; their suburban environment has kept them from real knowledge of the world. Such sneering "revolutionaries" merely play a disagreeable game when they do their thing, and from them cannot conceivably come the intellectual and moral regeneration of the university, let alone the revitalizing of the civil social order. They are merely one side of the academic coin which bears the visage of John Hannah on its other face.

There exists a moral order, says Edmund Burke, to which we are bound, willing or not—the "contract of eternal society" joining the dead, the living, and those yet unborn. There exist certain conventions and institutions that we must accept, if the civil social order is not to dissolve into the dust and powder of individuality, where every man's hand would be against every other man's. For very survival, in any society, in any age, we must submit to the traditions of civility, if you will. "But if that which is only submission to necessity should be made the object of choice, the law is broken; nature is disobeyed; and the rebellious are outlawed, cast forth, and exiled, from this world of reason, and order, and peace, and virtue, and fruitful penitence, into the antagonist world of madness, discord, vice, confusion, and unavailing sorrow."

Into that antagonist world, the terrible simplifiers, the frantic ideologues, would cast us; and by revolution, they would make reform impossible. Stir the molten bronze in the cauldron, with Danton, and presently you slip, and are consumed in one agonizing moment.

YET EVEN if one cannot resist the temptation to stir the cauldron—even if the young revolutionary cries that one crowded hour of glorious life is worth an age without a name—still the university is a curious place to play at being a revolutionary. The perennial university student, the swaggering university instructor who cries havoc from the sanctuary of the Ivory Tower, the intemperate professor who hankers after power rather than freedom—these are shabby and self-re-

garding revolutionaries, deserving of Joan Baez's scorn. "He that lives in a college," wrote the young-Burke, "after his mind is sufficiently stocked with learning, is like a man, who having built and rigged and victualled a ship, should lock her up in a dry dock." Those who mean to direct the world must enter the world.

We are incessantly assured by our comforters that the great bulk of American students do not participate, even on the most radical of campuses, in massive demonstrations or radical organizations—and doubtless this is true. But apathy and indifference are no reasons for a society to congratulate itself. The passive average student does not assault his university; yet neither does he defend it against the revolutionary zealots. Time was when every university served as a locus of affections, and then—not long ago, either—the typical student would have dealt summarily with any Comus's rout of eccentrics—many of them "street people" not members at all of the academic community—that might have ventured to invade the quadrangle and interrupt—perhaps by arson—the university's ways. Today, on many a campus, the average student shrugs and watches indifferently: pull devil, pull baker. Clearly, an institution that can command no more loyalty than this is far gone in decadence. It remains little more than a dull apparatus for conferring meaningless certificates upon the lonely and faceless crowd of pesudoscholars. When loyalty has trickled away, when the concept of a community of scholars is forgotten, the energumen and the fantastic may play what games they will.

Ideologues' pranks may injure a university irreparably, though they cannot improve it. In Egypt, in India, in much of Latin America, the universities have been unable to recover from the damage inflicted by student fanatics, whose concept of "student rights" is chiefly the right to be idle. Stifling free discussion, intimidating all opposition, abolishing standards of scholarship, the triumphant radical students in those lands have put an end to academic freedom and to academic attainment. In postwar Japan, the student political factions have so blighted scholarship that any intelligent young Japanese really desiring to learn something of his own culture must enroll at the University of Chicago's Oriental Institute, or at the Oriental schools of Harvard or Princeton or some other still-reputable American university. The logical culmination of such "progress" occurred a few years ago in Burma, when the army used heavy artillery against the University of Rangoon, leveling the campus to the ground that it might no longer shelter the Communist apparatus.

"Revolution" within the universities of Egypt, India, Latin America, Japan, and Burma has not overthrown the governments of those countries; it has only overthrown right reason and moral imagination within the universities; it has only given the death-blow to the academic community; it has only invited retaliation by the state; it has only injured those real students who know that the university is a place for reflection and preparation, not for theatrical violence. The results of play-revolution within American universities—even were the zealous minority of radicals to prevail on many a campus—would be no less disastrous for the intellect, and no more agreeable to the rebels.

For the American civil social order, with all its faults, is broad at its base, prosperous, and still strongly supported by the overwhelming majority of its citizens. It cannot be overthrown by any cabal of radical utopians. If sufficiently irritated, the American public is quite capable of

taking steps to terminate indefinitely the play-acting of campus radicals. And such steps might postpone for a great while, or prevent permanently, those reforms of the American college and university so urgently needed.

IN A democratic age, dissidents must endeavor to win public opinion to their side; if they cannot persuade—if they alienate public opinion by their extreme measures—they must be crushed by general disapproval. In any society, organized protest must employ one of two methods. On the one hand, the dissenters may demonstrate and petition with the object of informing those in power (or the responsible public) that injustice or bad policy exists—thus, in effect, pleading visibly for a redress of practical grievances. Or on the other hand, the dissidents may endeavor to mount a massive revolt—beginning with civil disobedience, perhaps, but soon growing incivil—meant to overthrow the existing powers; this method presupposes that the great mass of the public dimly sympathizes with the dissidents, or at least will remain inactive.

The latter undertaking would be absurd, in America today; five or ten percent of a student body cannot permanently capture a university (though they may disrupt it for some time), let alone capture the American nation. There remains the first approach, that of calling attention, through peaceable means, to justified discontents. But for a petition of grievances to be heeded, the petitioners must be sensible in their requests and decent in their methods. In that, most of the student radicals have failed. Most of all, they have failed in shallow talk of "revolution," when what they really require—and all they can possibly get, with luck—is prudent reform.

"The Sensual and the Dark rebel in vain," Coleridge wrote, "slaves by their own compulsion." The neglect of right reason and moral imagination on the typical campus may account for the un-reasoning and violent character of much student protest; but also that decay makes it impossible for students them-selves to plan a real improvement of the Academy—until they first emancipate themselves from the oppression of the sensual and the dark. "In God's name," said Demosthenes to the Athenians, "I beg of you to think." Strange though it may seem, the American university is supposed to be a center for thought. Though lacking, among administrators, professors, and students, there remain only two possibilities: the dreary domi-nation of people like John Hannah, or the destructive antics of people like Carl Oglesby. Neither can succeed in restor-ing academic community and academic vigor—for, as Talleyrand put it, you can do everything with bayonets except sit upon them.

In American society at large, it is the uprooted and dispossessed who turn to violence: as Governor George Romney pointed out (somewhat tardily), the pri-mary cause of the Detroit riots was the federal bulldozer—the dislodging of hundreds of thousands of people by an urban "renewal" which created urban desolation. Those dispossessed cannot work an urban revolution, let alone a national revolution; yet they can make a city dangerous and miserable. True com-munity shattered, men cannot live in security and peace.

So it is with the academic community. Revolution cannot mend it; only patient labor and the employment of imagina-tion can restore its loyalties. Frivolous "revolutionary" gestures by students will have no other effect than diminishing the serious voice in a university's affairs that responsible students ought to have. At Indiana University, very recently, a mock election was held to nominate a chancellor for the Bloomington campus. (Actually, the post is appointive, being under the jurisdiction of the regents, of course; but this election was to be an ex-pression of students' concern.) And what candidates were nominated? Why, Paul Boutelle of the Socialist Workers Party, Staughton Lynd the militant pacifist, and William Dennis, the Black Power revolu-tionary. (One conservative student placed his own name in nomination, justly feel-ing himself no less qualified than these gentlemen.) What sensible undergradu-ate reformers!

I do not mean to express contempt for all the suggestions of the New Left peo-ple, where university reform is concerned. Some of them recommend, for instance, that the alumni be given a much larger power in the university's affairs; and I agree that it would be well to interest the alumni in something besides season tickets for the football games. But this scarcely is "revolution": indeed, it is one of the most conservative features of the old British universities, where much au-thority reposes in the "university court," or similar body, in which all alumni may vote annually, if they bother to attend. I am surprised that the New Left folk do not seem to have thought of proposing for American universities a kind of students' tribune, after the fashion of the rector (elected by the students, as representative of their interests) at each of the Scottish universities. (At three of the four ancient Scottish universities, I confess, the stu-dents usually choose some mountebank or passing [and absentee] celebrity as rec-tor; but at least they have the chance to be heard in the university's deliberations.)

The revolutions of our time have not

brought liberty and peace: from Moscow to Peiping, from Accra to Jakarta, they have conferred power upon squalid oligarchs—to be overthrown in turn, perhaps, by military juntas. Revolution has not brought security to Nigeria, nor fraternity to Columbia. At best, revolutions have brought such a hard master as would be anathema to intransigent professors and students. Revolution in America (per impossible), within the university or without it, would hideously disillusion the very utopians who talk sanguinely and sanguinarily, of such possibilities.

To recognize at last that something is amiss with the higher learning in America, and with American society, is some considerable gain—worth, perhaps, the price we have paid for this knowledge through disruption. This tardy awareness may impel us to humanize the university again. Yet the university is not the Bastille, to be taken by frantic storm and razed to the ground; nor ought we to massacre the Invalides, dull dogs though some professors may be. The university is not a prison or a fortress, but a community of scholars—and not a community of one generation only. If you would reform it, understand its past greatness and its surviving promise—and, to quote Joan Baez one last time (her words in the first turbulence at Berkeley), "Do it with love."

Henry Hazlitt

In Defense of Conformity

VOL. 7, NO. 1–2, 1970

I cannot remember ever having read any essay, article, or book in defense of conformity. From my earliest days, I have found it disparaged or derided. Two of my favorite writers, in my teens and early twenties, were John Stuart Mill and Herbert Spencer. Spencer was the son of a Nonconformist (in the religious sense); Spencer's first article was even written for a magazine called the *Nonconformist;* and Spencer constantly lauded nonconformity in thought and action. Nonconformity was also one of the key virtues in John Stuart Mill's code of ethics. His essay, *On Liberty* (which appeared in 1859), is a paean in praise of variety, diversity, even eccentricity, in both behavior and thought. "In this age, the mere example of nonconformity, the mere refusal to bend the knee to custom, is itself a service. . . . It is desirable . . . that people should be eccentric."

Mill and Spencer, in their time, were really expressing a minority view, even among intellectuals. But their disparagement of conformity has become a deeply embedded part of our literary and philosophical tradition. It is now, ironically, the fashion; and it has been the fashion for at

least the last quarter century. It would be hard to recall a college commencement address in all that time which has not deplored and warned against conformity. The only judicial opinions which we ever hear praised are the dissents. The highest honor which his admirers could think of bestowing upon the late Justice Holmes was to dub him The Great Dissenter.

What we find extolled and rewarded today seems to me to be more and more dissent for its own sake. The college president or the commencement orator assures himself a reputation for liberality and sagacity by suggesting that the students who riot, seize administration buildings, smash windows, burn files, and kick deans down stairs are more to be praised than those who are trying seriously to pursue their studies, because the rioters are Dissenters, alive to the new revolutionary tides in the world, resentful of the injustices going on everywhere, and determined to bring about—ah! magic word—Change. So the youngsters who get adult attention and newspaper headlines are not the quiet students who do well, even extraordinarily well, in their studies, but those who dress filthily, refuse to get haircuts or shaves, and make nonnegotiable demands.

I should like to put forward what may today seem the perverse suggestion that there is a case for conformity—conformity in dress, speech, manners, morals, action and thought. I would go even further, and suggest that without this basic conformity civilized society could hardly survive.

The essence of society is cooperation among individuals for the achievement of their common purposes. And conformity to accepted rules is an indispensable element of all cooperation.

I do not here attach to the word conformity any unusual or strained definition. The first definition of "conform" in the Random House Dictionary is: "to act in accord or harmony; comply."

If we want concrete illustrations we could hardly do better than begin with traffic rules. The purpose of traffic rules is to maximize the flow of traffic and to minimize snarls and accidents. All such rules demand conformity: conformity to accepted and specified speed limits, to the rule of driving on the right side of the road (or the left in Britain), to the rules on right, left, and U-turns and one-way streets, to all legal signals and signs. When any driver insists on deciding for himself just which rules to conform to, he increases the probability of an accident. If every driver insisted on deciding for himself which rules, if any, to conform to, there would be traffic chaos.

But the traffic rules, in addition to their own inherent importance, symbolize all the rules by which society works and lives. As Henry Sidgwick remarked a century ago: "The life of man in society involves daily a mass of minute forecasts of the actions of other men." These forecasts are necessary to human cooperation. We can make them correctly in so far as oth-

ers conform to generally accepted rules. Every automobile driver depends on his ability to forecast accurately what the other fellow is going to do. This forecast is most often based on the assumption that the other fellow is going to conform to the established practice or rule applying to that situation.

Such conformity is indispensable for most of our daily actions. It makes life smoother and pleasanter even in trivial matters. The actions of men in modern society are synchronized by clocks and watches and set schedules. We depend on each other's punctuality. A worker gets to the factory at 8:00 and stays till 4:00 on the understanding that his co-workers and foreman will be there from 8:00 to 4:00.

The enormously increased efficiency and productivity brought about by the synchronization and division of labor are made possible only by this conformity to set time schedules. When a man takes the 8:17 to the office and the 5:26 home he depends on the railroad's conformity to this pre-advertised schedule; the railroad depends in turn on a sufficient number of commuters' adhering to it. If a dinner invitation is for 7:00, you get there at 7:00. If the symphony concert begins at 8:15 everybody is supposed to be in his seat by then.

IN SHORT, a great society can function, in its diversions and pleasures no less than its work, only by the daily, hour-by-hour, and often minute-by-minute cooperation of its constituent members, their willing subordination to a common time-schedule that will enable them to synchronize their individual contributions. A business firm—a large newspaper, for example—can function and succeed only if each employee, reporter, re-write man, photographer, editor, printer, columnist, copy-boy, proofreader, advertising solicitor, artist, layout man, delivery truck driver, newsstand operator, carries out his special function on schedule.

This is what it means to be that now much derided creature, an Organization Man. The performance of any great constructive work whatever, the very survival of society, depends on the organization men and women. Modern society functions by the division of labor. The division of labor is only possible through cooperative organization. Cooperative organization is only possible through the mutual voluntary meshing and conformity of one man's contribution with that of others.

This must occur on both the largest and smallest scale, in university life, scientific research, business, sports, amusements. If a symphony concert is to give pleasure to anyone, then every player of every instrument in the orchestra must conform with the utmost precision of tempo and note to both the score before him and to the conductor's baton. Every performer, in addition to having the skill and training to do so, must willingly subordinate his individual contribution to the collective result that all the performers are trying to achieve. Each instrumentalist must be, not least of all, a superb Organization Man.

Conformity in manners, though the tendency of so many of the young today is to deride it as adherence to a needless and silly ritual, also makes daily life enormously smoother and pleasanter than it would otherwise be. Take the understood rules for precedence through a doorway: the guest before the host, the lady before the man, the older before the younger, and so on. Or take even the rules of dress: Most of us dress not merely to please ourselves, but to please others, and even to show respect for others; so that if we accept an invitation to a formal dinner we put on the conventional formal wear. General recognition of these and similar rules obviously makes for more harmonious human relations.

Many readers will readily grant that such conformity to establish rules, written or unwritten, is necessary or at least generally desirable in matters of behavior; but surely, they will protest, not in matters of thought and opinion. Yet here it is necessary to make some very imporant distinctions.

PROGRESS IN any of the sciences is only possible, of course, if at least some individuals make discoveries that changed a hitherto accepted view. But these discoveries are not made by those who dissent simply for dissent's sake. They are made, in the overwhelming majority of cases, by men who have arduously studied what has already been learned or discovered by their predecessors. It is only then that a thinker, however original, is in a position to understand the problems and difficulties and to propose or achieve a new solution. When he does this, he may be said to be "dissenting" from the previously accepted view, though "disagreeing" would be a more appropriate word. His disagreement, moreover, is merely incidental to his discovery. (Perhaps from here on out we should adhere strictly to the vital distinction recently made by Daniel J. Boorstin: "People who disagree have an argument, but people who dissent have a quarrel. . . . A liberal society thrives on disagreement but is killed by dissension.")

What has been said about the conditions for true progress in the sciences applies also in the arts. The architects of the ancient Greek temples, and of the cathedrals of the Middle Ages, had none of the uneasy struggle for "originality" that marks the architects of our own age. They were not determined that this year's temple or cathedral should be strikingly different from last year's. Architectural styles did change; but by centuries rather than by years, and one style almost imperceptibly evolved out of its predecessor. El Greco, the archetype of the great original painter, began as a student of Titian, and mastered the style of Titian before he developed his own daring innovations. The earlier compositions of another great innovator, Beethoven, were in the style of Haydn, one of his teachers. True originality usually grows out of the mastery of a tradition.

The modern penchant for innovation for its own sake, in art, science, and philosophy, is mainly a symptom of restlessness. As Morris R. Cohen pointed out in 1931: "The notion that we can dismiss the views of all previous thinkers surely leaves no basis for the hope that our own work will prove of any value to others."

Even the most independent and original thinker in his own field is compelled to assume provisionally the truth of the prevailing opinion in areas in which he is not an expert. It is absurd, even impossible, to challenge every accepted belief at once.

One fundamental reason why we follow custom is that we cannot make a fresh, original, and unique decision for every situation or contingency. We must economize our time and thought to meet situations for which no tested and customary response has been established. This applies to our conclusions as well as our behavior. As Bertrand Russell once remarked: "The average man's opinions are much less foolish than they would be if he thought for himself." And there is a limit to the number of subjects on which even the most brilliant man has time and knowledge to bestow independent thought, or challenge the accepted opinion.

I hope that at this point I may be allowed a personal note. I have thought of myself in the past as primarily a libertarian, but not as a conservative. And if the conservative position is interpreted as saying: Whatever is, is right; let us keep the old ways, the old institutions, the old beliefs, whatever they are; let us not change—then I am certainly not a conservative. But this picture is a caricature. The conservatism I have come to accept says, rather: Let us change our moral codes, our laws, our political institutions, when we find this to be necessary, but let us do so cautiously, gradually, piecemeal, making sure at each step that the change we are making is carefully considered and really represents a progress, not a retrogression. Let us beware always of sudden and sweeping change, of "wiping the slate clean," of "making a completely fresh start," of root and branch upheaval. That way lies chaos.

I will offer only a single illustration, from the field of law. There prevailed for generations, in the courts not only of this country but in responsible courts everywhere, the doctrine of *stare decisis:* "Stand by what has been settled": Let the principles of law established by previous judicial decisions be accepted as authoritative in cases similar to those from which such principles were derived. When the Warren Supreme Court contemptuously disregarded *stare decisis* it was at sea; and the Court is still at sea. Without this doctrine no one knows what the courts will decide or what the law is.

It is the increasing disregard of *stare decisis,* or its equivalent, in nearly all social areas today—in morals, manners, dress, in the legal, political, and economic field—that is now leading to such a chaotic result, to the disappearance of standards, to immorality, confrontations, riots, and crime. The glorification of "dissent" has turned into glorification of "protest," and finally into a glorification of lawlessness and nihilism.

Nothing is easier than to destroy. The tree that has taken half a century to grow can be sawed down in less than an hour. The cathedral that took generations to build can be demolished by a bomb in a minute. And without having a single building demolished, a great university can lose within a few months, by capitulating to some senseless student demand, everything that made it worth respecting. But when the problem comes of supplanting what has been destroyed, the rebels have only a hollow rhetoric for answer.

Ironically, what emerges is a new conformity, less tolerant than the old, and without redeeming social utility. As the sociologist Charles Horton Cooley was pointing out more than forty years ago, there is "nothing more sheep-like than a flock of young rebels." This is glaringly evident in the hippies of today: the prescribed dress—uncut hair, untrimmed beards, boots, tight jeans with paint splotches, dirty oversized sweaters, bodily filthiness, pot, guitars, rock, free sex, mutual imitation in everything; and ridicule and intolerance of good manners, neatness, cleanliness, patriotism, work, saving, self-discipline, responsibility, and everybody over thirty.

And in the realm of ideas (as Cooley was also pointing out forty years ago) young radicals, trying mainly to be unlike others, fall into "a subservience of contradiction." They take their cue from their "orthodox" opponents, and grab the other end of the same rope, so that in every age the conspicuous radicals are likely to be contradictors and hence subservient, while real changes gestate in obscurity.

LET ME not be misunderstood. This essay is in defense of conformity because, to repeat, a prevailing conformity is essential to mutual cooperation, and cooperation is essential to the achievement of our common ends. But in pointing to the indispensableness of conformity I am not trying to disparage nonconformity, or diversity, or independence, and certainly not individuality or originality. It is mainly a question of emphasis. What I am suggesting is that, in a turbulent and revolutionary era like the present, it is not especially helpful to keep praising nonconformity, dissent, and protest as if they were absolute virtues in themselves, regardless of what belief or practice is being protested or dissented from. We must always try to judge each belief or practice (if it lies within our own individual sphere of competence) on its own merits, rather than in conformity or nonconformity with what other people think or do. It may possibly have been true, when Mill wrote it more than a century ago: "That so few now dare to be eccentric, marks the chief danger of our time." But that so many now try to be eccentric, marks one of the chief dangers of *our* time. Nonconformity, dissent, and protest are in themselves disintegrative. True individualism and originality can flourish only within a basically cooperative system.

In sum, in the interests of social harmony and genuine progress, conformity must be the rule, and nonconformity the exception.

Thomas Molnar

Islam on the Move

VOL. 21, NO. 1, 1985

The rise of Islam and of Islamic countries in the twentieth century resembles in certain aspects that of Russia. Both were first "put on the map," that is, integrated within Western historical consciousness, by a Napoleonic invasion. In Russia it had awakened the progressively minded young officers by the 1820s. And it was in Egypt, in 1799, when Arab intellects first began asking two questions caused by contact with the French military and members of the scientific expedition: Why are we deep in decadence? What are the conditions of a rebirth? The first question was easily answered, whether the answer was valid or not. The Arab world decayed under the long Ottoman rule (as early Russia had been ruled by the Tartars) which stifled its aspirations, art and science; even the religious expressions were jealously supervised by Istanbul. It was Napoleon's expedition which awakened the Middle East from its long slumber, by giving the first jolt to the Turks in their own domain.

What about the rebirth? Now, almost two centuries later, these questions and their answers have awakened Islam, from Morocco to Indonesia, as well as the Arabic heartland. Again, like pre-Bolshevik Russia, the intelligentsia of the Muslim world is divided between the "Westernizers" who want to adopt the techniques of modernization, and the "fundamentalists" who seek first the religious/political kingdom. We may yet see, as in Russia, the emergence of a third movement, a synthesis of these trends, which would forge some kind of Islamic unity, or at least vast regional units, like the khalifates in the Middle Ages—which for Baghdad, Cairo and Cordoba were not "middle ages," but a first renaissance. Let us not fool ourselves: people who have known grandeur in their past keep dreaming of its restoration.

In Europe today there are large numbers of islamologists, political observers of Islam, refugees from Iran and journalists based in Arab countries, whose works, articulating Islam's aspirations, are of the utmost interest. Names like Henry Corbin and Jacques Berque illustrate islamology on the highest academic level; the first-class journalism of Bernard Levine, Péroncel-Hugoz, and George Manoulakis penetrate the Islamic political mentality to its deepest layers; a philosopher like

Dariush Shayegan writes analyses of Persian intellectual history of the highest caliber. All this mirrors the importance of the phenomenon which arouses passion and intellectual curiosity, political interest and erudite focus on the past.

I shall try to outline here the multifaceted present and to make intelligent guesses about the future.

The Islamic Perspective

On October 3, 1983, I gave a lecture in Buenos Aires about the situation in the Middle East. Answering a question, I remarked that Anwar Sadat's regime, indeed his life, were in danger. On October 6, the press and the airwaves brought the news of his assassination, and I received phone calls in my hotel, calling me a wizard for having predicted this violent end. Or at least people thought I had some special sources of information.

Yet, it was not so difficult to look ahead to that day when exactly four years before, October 6, 1979, I was watching the military parade in Cairo—commemorating the war of 1973 with Israel—where Sadat, accompanied by Mubarak, took the salute. I talked at the time with Egyptian and other Arab journalists, unanimous about Sadat's unpopularity for having gone to Israel. That gesture represented, in the eyes of Arabs, a sell-out of the Palestinians, and through them, of the causes of Islam. Israel was and is regarded as American real-estate, and America is regarded as the dog wagged by the Israeli tail. The visit thus meant, for example in the judgment of the Nasserite officers and the new bourgeoisie, the potential colonization by Israeli/American interests.[1]

There was more to it, however, than Sadat's visit. For decades, let us say since the 1930s, the Muslim world had come to understand a few realities about the modern West. In the early thirties, king Ibn Saud had told Hungarian Islam scholar, Gyula Germanus,[2] in Mecca, that the Western world was corrupt and decadent, and that Islam would soon have a chance of asserting itself. It was believed for a while that Mussolini and Franco, both of whom were anti-British, were conducting a realistic policy of recognition vis-à-vis the southern shores of the Mediterranean, and would redress the Western course. Others saw in various leftist revolutionary movements some unexpected turn. At any rate, Islam became increasingly anti-Western: for religious reasons first and always, that is from hostility to the infidel; for political reasons more and more, for resentment at foreign rule and the import of an alien culture.

Whether called capitalism or Marxism (the latter also a Western ideology), Western influence was judged to be contrary to the concept of the *umma*, the Islamic community transcending separatisms, and to the *sharia*, Islamic law based on the Koran and on the harsh justice inherited from the desert way of life that Mohammed had refashioned. Add to the pride of great achievements the memories of history and culture, when largely through Syria—first Greek, then Christian, finally Muslim—Hellenic philosophy and science spread as far as Spain, and fertilized speculation in Western universities from Padua to Oxford. Another decisive element was injected into the rich Muslim culture by Iran (Persia), a special chapter in this historical sketch, to which we will return.

All this must be kept in mind when we consider the present. Strictly speaking, there is no Muslim nationalism, rather a permanent inner pressure to fuse all the faithful into one community. Yet, a unifier has still not come, although candidates have not been lacking. He is cast as a typically Semitic messiah-figure: a religious-political savior. Note that the candidates so far—Nasser, Khadafi, now the militant ayatollah—have regarded themselves as the "sword of Islam," but they were not Mohammed-like enough to fill the immense role. The West is misled when it assumes that these and other potential candidates are "socialists" or "Marxists." These are Western terms, utilized by Arabs and by the entire Third World to partly imitate, partly scare the outsiders. Rather, they are desert raiders whose dream is to put together an empire which may, incidentally, fall apart the day after, as Mohammed's and Omar's religious-political construct soon divided into *caliphates*.

More important than modernist aspirations and ideologies are the integrist movements, emanating from several centers and rolling inexorably over the Muslim world. The process may take decades, and it will not be halted by political rivalries and dissensions, nor by the failure of unity (*umma*). It is a sui generis crusade, a basically religious movement that does not even claim it brings the masses closer to material well-being, and does not use slogans of political freedom, human rights, emancipation and progress. The strange thing is that while all profess allegiance to *umma* (Nasser, Khomeini, Khadafi have tried it by conquest, regional alliance, or the fusion of two or more "Islamic republics"), the Muslims accommodate themselves with life under separate sovereignties, somewhat like the kingdoms of medieval Europe which thought of themselves as members of one *respublica christiana*. And since all Muslims are supposed to be part of *umma*, it is not even surprising that after 1945 the first leaders were secular-nationalists, Mossadegh, Jinna, Nasser.

Only now, since the war with Israel has crystallized the religious aspect, has a new leader appeared, in the person of Khomeini. The secularized tendency did not seem to work out: it may have died with Sadat, and the coup de grace will be administered to it when Bourguiba too disappears from the scene.

In other words, religious fanaticism has returned, but, according to the color of the times, it has nationalist overtones and a vocabulary borrowed from both Left and Right. Politically, whether fundamentalists or reformists, Muslims are united on a certain number of propositions: the executive power in the hands of a "just despot," himself controlled by an elected assembly with limited powers; the party-system is unacceptable; law is based on the sharya; usury is outlawed, taxes are limited to *zakat*, a charitable contribution. This system, with variations, is on the point of prevailing in an increasing number of Muslim countries (Sudan, Saudi Arabia, Iran, Pakistan, Malaysia), and where it is not officially confirmed, there the general tendency moves in that direction. Indonesia and Malaysia have declared themselves "Islamic States," Pakistan promotes the idea through a referendum, Algeria, at the beginning a secular republic, has now an Islamic basic law, Senegal and Egypt are predicted soon to follow.

Iran: The Special Case

One may see from this list already that Iran is a special case. Of all Muslim countries occupied by the early conquerors, Persia fell most reluctantly under Islamic rule. It had had a long Zoroastrian tradition, which at the time was a remarkably purer religion than that of any of its neighbors to the east, south and west (we speak of the pre-Christian era), such as Egypt, Hellas, Brahminism, Buddhism. There is little doubt, Joseph Campbell writes in his *Oriental Mythology* that Zoroastrian Persia influenced the religious concepts of all its neighbors.[3]

The highly civilized and religiously refined Persians were compelled, in their military and imperial decadence, to submit to the faith brought along by barbarians from the desert. The submission was accomplished and Persia became a Muslim country—but with a difference. It remained rebellious to the generality of Islam, and preserved much of Zoroastrian spirituality and mysticism.[4] The fact that in the Islamic world it is a sectarian Shiite nation, over against a Sunni majority, that it is racially not Semite but Aryan, and that its art, philosophy, and poetry do not blend with those of the surrounding Arab correligionists, suggests a separate course for Iran. In the context of what we are here describing, that is contemporary political choices, the separate way of Iran means a more radical attitude, more integrist and also less conformist. It is true, however, that the special role Iran plays in the Islamic world sets it somewhat apart and isolates it under Khomeini as it was isolated under the Shah. Hence, Khomeini's Shiite revolution is not likely to have a durable impact on the sunnite Muslims in other countries—except where shiites are a strong minority, as in Iraq, Syria, Lebanon, and Afghanistan.

This is the real cleavage in Islam, politically speaking, but as we saw, this is inseparable from the basic religious choice. We may foresee that Iran's theocratic regime will turn increasingly towards its Asian neighbors whom it will try to detach from Moscow's dominion. This, in addition to geopolitical considerations, has determined the Soviet invasion of Afghanistan, the buffer zone between

militant Shiism and the Soviet Union as an Islamic power, having now some sixty million Muslims on its territory, a restless and self-assertive community with a high birth rate.

Meantime, Sunni, mostly Arabic, Islam, from Iraq to Morocco, tries to consolidate its secular regimes, but finds itself divided and weakened by the conflict between modernizers and fundamentalists, and also between those who put their card on a rapprochement with America and those who thoroughly distrust and dismiss the West, together with its values. The social base here, but also among the Asian Muslims, is the peasantry, with its solidly built tradition around the motherland, the family, the *umma*. It rejects individualism, the life for profit and pleasure, and suspects all leftist revolutionary movements. No ideology is strong enough to dislodge these deep-seated sentiments; the peasant base could only be enrolled under the integrist flag in the cause of Allah, and this is precisely what is being done. If, as is probable, the Khomeinists will not succeed, then the Muslim Brotherhood might; their sword is now double-edged: against the Washington-Tel Aviv axis, and simultaneously against the immoral Western/Christian infidel.

Cultural Confusion

Let me repeat that neither the Khomeinists, nor the Muslim Brotherhood aim at what we call a "revolution," an action suggesting in the West a socioeconomic betterment. This does not mean that the objectives of either movement may not produce a tremendous upheaval below Europe's "soft underbelly." What the Iranian philosopher, Dariush Shayegan, now in Parisian exile, writes about it, is worth our attentive reading.[5] I have had the opportunity to confirm some of his theses during visits in universities across Islam, in conversations with Arabs and Iranians, in interviews with politicians and journalists. Shayegan, considerably westernized, and a student of Corbin in both Tehran and Paris, believes that the intellectual contact of the Muslim intelligentsia with the West has confused several generations and has resulted in indecision between the ancestral tradition and Western nihilism. The latter's influence has eroded the Muslim "myth" and turned religion into an ideology, but an ideology with nostalgia for a partly, lost spiritual home. Therefore this modern spirit may create a new formula, a cry for justice in Allah's name, but also a mission to destroy through a jihad (holy war) the fortresses of Western capitalism and unbelief. This formula whose application we are witnessing, is not a Marxist one, although Moscow may exploit it here and there for its own purposes. The comparison may seem far fetched, but the diagnosis at the back of the religious revolution is similar to Solzhenitsyn's analysis of communism and the remedies he has suggested in several of his works: return to national and religious traditions and values, refusal of dehumanizing industrialization, and despotism if necessary, but not the atheistic, oppressive kind. In other words, the above-mentioned theme of "despotism with justice" and supervised by wise men, elected or spontaneously emerging from the community.[6]

Visits to Muslim capitals and big cities—Cairo, Fez, Tunis, Baghdad, Tehran, Dahran, Karachi, Kuala-Lumpur, Jakarta, Damascus, Amman—create the impression of an abandonment of tradition (in architecture, religious ritual, etc.) and chaotic "modernization" on the Western model, only with even less preoccupation with adequate urban planning. On the other hand, the countryside has remained by and large untouched, and its teeming millions very often present images as if taken from the Old Testament or anyway, from an immemorial past. One is tempted to meditate with fourteenth-century Arab historian, Ibn Khaldoun, on the process of conquest of the opulent but aimlessly hedonistic city by the wild and penurious country. (Mao may have taken his own thesis from Ibn Khaldoun). The attractiveness of the Khaldounian model stops when we take a new phenomenon into account: the Muslim intelligentsia, which is Western-educated and city-dwelling, increasingly desperate and turning to militant formulas. It is a fact that they too are torn between the Western, mostly American slogans and gadgets, and a revolution á la Khomeini. Yet, we should not misjudge this apparent confusion. The new Arab countries which have started out as secular, or even half-Christian States (Senegal, Nigeria, Sudan, Syria, Lebanon), are changing their legislation toward more conformity with the sharya, even when this means a drastic restriction of secular modes and freedoms. The chador may be resented by women of sophisticated background who used to make their purchases in Paris and New York. Mrs. Sadat, now isolated, used to play a feminist role. But they are a minority, and the "revolution," under whatever flag, will blow them away as a class, as it did under Marxist regimes. While the days of the individual speculators and baksheesh-takers—in a word, the days of large scale corruption—are by no means over, the bourgeoisie, a small class considerably westernized, is on the way out. The new generation now in schools and universities may wear blue-jeans, but by and large it accepts the chador (used here as a symbol) as a restored contact with traditional ways. Its militancy is rather purely Islamic, as it witnesses the failure of the Western panaceas, secularism, liberalism, and socialism.

Lessons for the West

Are there any lessons in this for the West, notably in the field of foreign policy?

First, we must realize, when we look at the new Islamic consciousness, that we are not dealing with a "Communist conspiracy," nor with an "old man's paranoia," nor yet with a "terrorist nest"—three comfortable labels that Western opinion-makers, lacking imagination and political intelligence, usually glue on phenomena they do not understand. On the contrary, we are witnessing a historic mutation, the re-emergence of a fighting race, always easy to fanaticize, but which, in its intellectual elements, is able to produce out of its entrails important political figures and sharp-eyed visionaries.

In the second place, we should give due regard to the fact that the dispersion of Islam into many Arab and non-Arab nations is not necessarily a permanent obstacle to an eventual unity, unity at least for large-scale action. This has been possible even on the national level: Mossadegh's standing up to British oil interests, temporarily a failure, became, twenty-five years later, a brutal upheaval by the religious class, able to succeed precisely because the action was not conducted for economic interests, but in spiritual terms. Another example was Nasser's nationalization of the Suez canal, then Syria's emergence as the key power in the Middle-East. These successes were those of nationalism, combined with Islamic inspiration.[7]

The third point is the Muslim world's humiliation by Israel's repeated victory against one, two, or three Arab neighbors. Whether the PLO will remain the spearhead of the anti-Israeli struggle is not the point; all observers agree that the Palestinian issue has become the focus of Muslim militancy, now too late to dismantle. From this nucleus; all sorts of consequences will arise, perhaps the emergence of a unifying figure, a leader of holy wars. It is too easy to dismiss Muslim unity as a dream, and argue that the West, together with the Soviet Union, is able to "divide and rule." We said, on the other hand, that in the case of Islam, unity does not mean the same thing as in other parts of the world. Here the common religion serves as an overarching communal attitude; a religious/national leader may activate and mobilize the masses, just as, in another context, "socialism" has been able to do so elsewhere.

This remark leads to the last point. The Western world has so completely evacuated any unifying myth and energizing belief from its mental structure, that it has lost the faculty of understanding psychological-religious motivations, whether among allies or enemies. Our governments are run by lawyers and businessmen of a positivistic mindcast, so that other issues are reduced and spelled-out by and for them on the lowest mentality-level in order to be dealt with. A symptom of this loss of comprehension is the Western assumption that "Arab politics is motivated by the oil interests," and that the various power centers: Damascus, Rabat, Ryad, Tehran, and Cairo are intent only on grabbing the loot.

In the age of decadence, empires—in this instance the "West"—always tend to misapprehend other people's nature, because that is the comfortable way of seeing it. In the case here discussed, Western governments, unlike serious Western scholarship, are blind to Islam's religious component. In a recent interview,[8] Pakistani president, Zia-ul-Haq, underlined once more the fact that the Shah had fallen under the influence of Western mirage-makers when he accelerated his country's process of industrialization and modernization. He took no account, Zia says, of the religious nature of the Iranians, who in their mass repudiate the secular mode of thinking and living. It must be repeated that Islamic religion is perfectly compatible with warfare, terrorist raids (think of the eleventh-century hashishim), savage campaigns and crusades. Integrism, holy war, return to tradition, and the Muslim Brotherhood are stronger than the modernizing policies timidly pursued (after the fall of the Shah) by the various regimes. These policies, emanating from the cities, are now increasingly shaped by the countryside and the tribes, thus at least indirectly by the *mullahs, marabouts, ulemas, imams*—and integrist intellectuals. The modernizing, even technological trends are not absent; but it seems that the fundamentalists whose domination will be gradually asserted in the coming decades are determined to take from the West the machines, not the values.[9]

Notes

1. In Cairo, at a journalist's office, I was handed with ironical laughter Harvard Law Professor Roger Fischer's book, *Dear Israel, Dear Arabs*, in which this naive "solver of conflicts" advises the antagonists to just settle and fall into each others' arms. Fischer has already so "advised" blacks and whites in South Africa, and Moscow/Washington too.

2. The great scholar had converted to Islam, and made his pilgrimage at this time.

3. The second volume of *The Masks of God* (New York: Viking, 1962).

4. This aspect has been brilliantly studied by the dean of Islamo-Iranian studies, the recently deceased (1978) Henry Corbin.

5. *Qu'est-ce qu'une révolution religieuse?* (Paris: Les Presses d'aujourd'hui, 1982).

6. In John B. Dunlop's book, *The Faces of Contemporary Russian Nationalism* (Princeton, NJ: Princeton Univ. Press, 1983), there is a detailed description of the channels through which Russian nationalism has found expression under the Bolshevik regime: religion, the preservation of artistic patrimony, the protection of nature from vandalism by the state.

7. Make no mistake about it: what for Lebanon and Lebanese Christians is a tragedy today, is counted as a huge achievement by Islamic integrism, namely, the advance of Syria and Iran.

8. In *Politique internationale*, Paris, no. 26, Winter 1984–1985.

9. It is hardly known that American oil company employees in Saudi Arabia are contractually obliged to send away their teenage children to school, so that they do not spread bad influences among Arab children.

Clyde Wilson

GLOBAL DEMOCRACY
AND AMERICAN TRADITION

VOL. 24, NO. 1, 1988

If we are to achieve the kind of world we all hope to see—with peace, freedom, and economic progress—democracy has to continue to expand. Democracy is a vital, even revolutionary force.

—*Secretary of State George Shultz, Congressional testimony in favor of establishment of a National Endowment for Democracy, 1983.*

The terms liberty, equality, right and justice, used in a political sense, are merely terms of convention, and of comparative excellence, there being no such thing, in practice, as either of these qualities being carried out purely, according to the abstract notions of theories.

—*James Fenimore Cooper,* The American Democrat, *1838.*

When we leave our door and go out among our fellows, we carry with us a certain self-image of what we are or ought to be. This image may or may not correspond to our real character or to the way others perceive us. The same is true of nations when they go among their fellows.

Of course, relations between nations are chiefly relations between governments, and given the vast apparatus of the modern state, whether in the free or the unfree world, this is bound to become a complicated encounter—as if we went onto the street accompanied by a bodyguard and a publicity agent.

For Americans, how we rationalize our relations with other nations has always involved a certain amount of abstractness. While we were long secure behind our oceans, there was more choice than necessity in the face we presented to the world, compared to less favored peoples. Unlike most European states, we had no frontiers bristling with fortifications and barriers of language or religion and competing dynasties or forms of government. And we were not, to the same degree, compelled to go abroad in search of markets, raw materials, and colonies for surplus or discontented populations.

Having made several preliminary forays into an active role in the world, Americans found themselves at the end of World War II, unwittingly and somewhat unwillingly, cast in the role of an imperial people with worldwide powers and responsibilities. There are examples in history of other peoples who achieved this status without deliberate design. What was unique about the American situation was the ease and suddenness with which world dominance was acquired. For the average American World War II was an experience of economic gain, not sacrifice. By world standards, casualties were minor. In contrast, Roman territory was devastated several times before Cato's imperative was achieved. And the graves of British soldiers, seamen, merchants, missionaries, and officials, who expended their lives over two centuries or more in building an Empire, circle the hot zones of the globe.

We are concerned here with the history and present condition of the image which Americans have of their role among the nations, with the implicit assumptions which are a starting place for their actions. We are not concerned directly with the facts and events of the world, a subject on which there are vast libraries of contending data and theory. In the next block we may meet a mugger, a con man, a panhandler, or a street-corner evangelist. These will not make any fundamental alteration in our self-image. However, how we handle ourselves in these encounters will be determined by our character and our idea of how we *ought* to behave.

The twentieth century has been marked by cataclysmic events. It has also been marked by a continuing struggle of articulate Americans to understand and to define satisfactorily their role in the world. We need only remember the intensity of the debate over the League of Nations after World War I, the strife between isolationists and internationalists before World War II, or the heat of the struggle between policies of containment and liberation during the long course of the Cold War.

Yet, since World War II, the predominant rationale of American involvement with other peoples, the character we have aspired to, has been some version of that given by Secretary Shultz in the passage quoted at the head of this essay. It is the goal of America in the world to expand the self-evident benefits of democracy. Sometimes this has been presented as a military mission, as in Korea and Vietnam. At other times it has been seen as a process of peaceful involvement through such ventures as the Peace Corps, Alliance for Progress, the Fulbright program, or the Reagan administration's "Project Democracy," for which Shultz was seeking support.

The only principled opposition to this view has been the postwar conservative movement, a movement that gathered strength steadily in the 1960s and 1970s, and, so it was thought, achieved power and validity during the Reagan reign of the 1980s. (Many leftward movements objected to particular aspects of American intervention in the world, but not to the vision of a democratic mission.) It was a truism that the postwar conservative movement rested upon allegiance to tradition, to the free market, and most of all to a principled anticommunism. One of the tenets of this anticommunism was that the Cold War was a life-and-death struggle between Western civilization and a godless totalitarianism. The history of the Cold War seemed to prove that the mild democratic platitudes and benevolent social-worker approach of the liberals were inadequate to the occasion and certain to lead to defeat. Something of the spirit of conservative anticommunism was summed up in the title of a book by James Burnham, *Containment or Liberation?*, and by Russell Kirk's remark that peoples did not fight and die for a standard of living.

How did a conservative president, who was thought to have been the heir and spokesman for Cold War hardliners, come to rest the foreign policy motives of his administration upon a philosophical base of "revolutionary" global democracy? Is the idea of a democratic mission a workable concept for guiding American actions in the world? To what extent is the self-image of America as the active exporter of democracy in keeping with the best of American traditions?

I wish to provide speculative explorations of these three questions as a contribution to the ongoing effort of Americans to visualize adequately their role and goal in the world. The last question is explored in this essay. A succeeding essay, "Global Democracy and Conservatism," will take up the first two. The historical scheme presented is suggestive of a possible line of interpretation. To "prove" it, in a strict scholarly sense, would take several lifetimes of research.

Preserving Domestic Happiness: The Founders' Vision

The tradition of debate on the American role in the world began at least as early as the end of the Revolution. In the Philadelphia Convention, during a discussion of the treaty making powers of the Senate, Charles Pinckney of South Carolina remarked:

> Our true situation appears to me to be this—a new extensive Country, containing within itself the materials for forming a Government capable of extending to its citizens all the blessings of civil and religious liberty—capable of making them happy at home. This is the great end of Republican Establishments. We mistake the ob-

ject of our Government, if we hope or wish that it is to make us respectable abroad. Conquest or superiority among other powers is not or ought not ever to be the object of republican systems. If they are sufficiently active and energetic to rescue us from contempt and preserve our domestic happiness and security, it is all we can expect from them—it is more than almost any other Government ensures to its citizens.[1]

Alexander Hamilton, who fancied himself a realist of power, but who was out of step with most of his fellow members and adopted countrymen, replied that Pinckney's distinction between domestic tranquility and prestige abroad "was an ideal distinction. No Government could give us tranquility and happiness at home, which did not possess sufficient stability and strength to make us respectable abroad."[2] Hamilton was really more concerned here with getting in a plug for "energetic government" than in defining a stance for foreign policy, but he took the opportunity to suggest the need for greater realism in regard to the world and activism in national defense than Pinckney had called for.

Both advocates and critics of later "idealistic" American intervention in world affairs have seen a precedent or portent in Pinckney's attitude toward later events which they approved of or deplored. Pinckney did, obviously, endorse a species of "American exceptionalism." But his view of the world can by no means be called utopian. He wanted the United States to be strong and secure from "contempt," and did not have a high opinion of what governments in general could aspire to, even "republican systems."

American commentators, especially conservatives, have often resorted to a theory that the debates of the early republic on foreign policy were carried on between Jeffersonian "idealists" (such as Pinckney, who was an incipient Jeffersonian Republican) and Hamiltonian "realists."[3] Somewhat under the domination of Henry Adams, whose spell has never been broken by American students of this period, we have thought that the Jeffersonians expressed a failed and misguided softness, and the Hamiltonians a hard-headed toughness in dealing with the dangers of the world. By this calculation, anticommunist conservatives and advocates of strong national defense should look to the Federalists as their forebears and to Jefferson and his friends as having spawned the over-trusting liberalism of a later day.

However, statements of American exceptionalism and "idealism" can be found in abundance among *all* the founders, Federalists as well as Republicans. If anything, the Federalists were not only more activist but a good deal more missionary and utopian in their view of the American role than were the Jeffersonians. For instance, Hamilton himself had remarked on an earlier occasion that the cause of America was "the cause of virtue and mankind."[4] And John Adams had described the settlement of America "as the opening of a grand scheme and design in Providence for the illumination of the ignorant, and the emancipation of the slavish part of mankind over the earth."[5]

The view expressed by Pinckney may or may not have been "realistic," but it offers a good deal more comfort to an isolationist than to a global-democratic and missionary image of the American place in the world. Even so, there is very little precedent for any notion of active democratic expansionism on either side of the division between the founders. There is a vast qualitative difference between en-

visioning America as an example to the world and feeling a mission to implement and enforce that example across the sea.

These early statesmen all had a quite natural belief in the superiority and value of their own hard-won republican institutions. They hoped these would set a precedent for mankind, suffering under the weight of arbitrary governments. This did not suggest (as all of American history up to at least the late nineteenth century proves) a proselytizing mission for the quotidian American republic. And while the rhetoric was often high-flying, it was mostly conscious self-assertion in response to the official wisdom of the Old World, which professed to scorn the viability and durability of republican institutions. *Nothing* in American actions for the next century indicated a belief that those institutions were intrinsically applicable to every people, place, and time, much less that there was a duty to impose them.

Such an attitude did reflect a belief in American exceptionalism, which from the point of view of jaded and cynical thinkers of the Old World (except for German metaphysicians) represented a delusionary claim to immunity from the realities of sin and sorrow. But such exceptionalism was, at that time, historically based and laced with realism and practicality. Exceptionalism rested on an apprehension that the English-speaking New World was free of certain built-in defects of the Old—rival nationalisms, hardened class interests, scarce resources. American society had enjoyed widespread ownership of property, vast unoccupied lands, the unmixed heritage of the best parts of British law and liberty, a fortuitous experience of colonial self-government, a successful war of independence, and a nearly unprecedented opportunity of constitution-making.

When Jefferson quoted with approval the wish of Silas Deane, who had preceded him as a representative in Europe, for "an ocean of fire between us and the Old World,"[6] he dreamed not of utopia but of the preservation of a real historical opportunity. He realized that what Americans had achieved rested upon fortuitous circumstances and was not necessarily repeatable. The New World could serve as an inspiration and example for the better spirits of the Old, but had no mission to impose its pattern beyond North America. The "policy" side of this belief was expressed in Washington's farewell address and Jefferson's first inaugural, in the warnings against entangling alliances which were taken to heart by generation after generation of Americans.

This general view was shared by all sensible Federalists and Republicans, despite the abortive forays of Hamilton into power politics. By its very nature republicanism called for non-intervention, not proselytization. Rather than free institutions being a license to reform the world, they were, on the contrary, a command for the maximum non-involvement. By republican theory, the involvements of free governments in the world were likely to be fewer and more honorable than those of other states, not because of any particular virtue on the part of Americans, but because such governments were restrained by the necessity that their wars and treaties be undertaken by open deliberation and supported by the sense of the community. This was still an important idea some decades later when James Fenimore Cooper, a conservative and Democrat, commented that "democracies pay more respect to abstract justice, in the management of their foreign concerns, than either aristocracies or monarchies."[7] This was a purely descriptive statement, not a moralistic assertion, and would not have

been disputed by Cooper's contemporary conservative, Tocqueville.

Those of the founders who hoped to preserve America immune from the ills of the Old World were realistic enough to know that their desires would be imperfectly realized. Said Jefferson in 1785:

> The justest dispositions possible in ourselves, will not secure us against it [war]. It would be necessary that all other nations were also just. Justice, indeed, on our part, will save us from those wars which would have been produced by a contrary disposition. But how can we prevent those produced by the wrongs of other nations? [8]

"We must make the interest of every nation stand surety for their justice, and their own loss to follow injury to us, as effect follows its cause," he wrote some years later.[9]

We were, after all, still a relatively weak power with hostile colonies on our borders and a partly mercantile economy that was vulnerable to European tumults. Yet republican non-involvement remained a sound *point of departure* for conceiving the American role in the world. It might be argued that that role long reflected a healthy synthesis of Pinckney's optimism and isolationism and Hamilton's realism and concern for national prestige. Possibly this still constitutes the basic, instinctual view of most of the American people, if not of their leaders.

Non-interventionist Realism: The Nineteenth Century

We cannot really find the principles of Reaganite global democratic revolution in Washington or Jefferson or anywhere else before this century. We will have to look for more exotic sources and a different and curious family tree. Nothing in the mainstream course of American history in the nineteenth century provides any precedent for a missionary role in the world, although certain lesser intellectual currents were portentous.

The advance westward, including the War of 1812 and the Mexican War and territorial acquisitions, were by no stretch of the imagination foreign interventionism or the pursuit of global democracy. The movement of an exuberant agricultural people into nearly empty and undeveloped lands on their own frontiers is different in kind from ventures overseas for profit, ideology, glory, or power. "Manifest Destiny" meant the conquest of new spaces for Americans and their democratic institutions, not the imposition of these institutions on other peoples.

An optimistic, non-interventionist realism is clearly seen in the attitude of Americans toward the Latin American revolutions of the early nineteenth century, as symbolized by the Monroe Doctrine. Americans, in general, were delighted that other peoples of the New World sought to throw off the oppressive system of the Old World and copy their republican institutions. But Americans also had realistic doubts, strengthened by the passage of time, about the possibility of success among other peoples. Except for a few volunteer military adventurers, there was no thought of American involvement. Americans were in fact quite content to acquiesce in the de facto maintenance of Latin American independence by British maritime power. They continued to observe a realistic detachment in their dealings with these countries, insisting on strict enforcement of the rights of American citizens. They looked upon Latin American republics, in other words, with friendly but skeptical detachment.

Anyone who will read the primary documents of Americans' experiences in and reflections on Latin America in the nineteenth century will see that they were pleased whenever evidences were shown of successful republican self-government, but understood that democratic ideals were not fully applicable to the situation. They did not think that democratic process in itself was intrinsically the magic cure for all the ills of those societies. They realized, in fact, that authoritarian features, uncongenial to American taste, were often the lesser evil in those circumstances. Nor did they feel, unlike their twentieth-century successors, any need to undermine the more reactionary features of life, such as the army, church, or great landowners, or assume foolishly that an American-style democracy would appear if they could be overthrown.[10]

Of course, this non-interventionism can be partly attributed to an awareness of America's relative weakness, that would not allow too much intermeddling in the world. But nowhere can we find any evidence that the future achievement of unassailable American strength, which all anticipated, would be a grant of power to alter the world. It would merely make more secure the republican example.

The French Revolution and the wars of Napoleon required realism from American statesmen, as Hamilton had anticipated. While we were relatively secure beyond the Atlantic, some involvement was inevitable because of the colonial powers still on our borders and because a substantial portion of the American economy—that of New England—was mercantile—which inevitably brought national interests and honor into conflict with Europe.

Undoubtedly, also, the French Revolution had an impact, positive and negative, on American thought. Some

Americans, notably in New England, recoiled in horror and professed to see the dangers of the same in America. Other Americans delighted in the possibility of republican principles gaining a lodgement in the heart of Europe. Relations with Britain and France, ideological, diplomatic, and economic, were a source of sharp controversy in the later eighteenth and early nineteenth centuries. Yet these were basically domestic disputes. Almost no responsible native American sympathized with the Revolution after its excesses became apparent. While competing parties labeled each other as Jacobins and monarchists, in the final analysis Americans realized that both the reactionaries and the revolutionaries of Europe were operating in a different context. This conclusion, that American republicanism was as distinct from the revolutionary movements of Europe as it was from the monarchical establishments, was a standard convention of American discourse in regard to Europe throughout the nineteenth century.

Jefferson, often thought to be the most optimistically universalist of American democrats among the early statesmen, always took a hopeful but cautious attitude toward French developments, at which he was present as an observer during the early stages. He advocated sensible reforms appropriate to the European situation, not revolution, and was quick to apprehend that no American or European interest would be served by radicalism.[11]

The Federalist election propaganda which imagined Jefferson, who was living peacefully among his books, farms, and 200 slaves, as plotting to guillotine the clergy, was a product of hysteria which had much to do with religious and economic dislocations in domestic New England society and nothing to do with Jefferson's beliefs or actions. Jefferson

wanted the New World to be an example to the Old, not vice versa. European revolutionaries no more provided a guide for America than did European reactionaries. He knew that the long-range cause of liberty was not served by the form which the Revolution took. "I was a sincere well-wisher to the success of the French Revolution, and still wish it may end in the establishment of a free and well-ordered republic," he wrote at the time he was being pilloried in the northern press as a Jacobin, "but I have not been insensible under the atrocious depredations they have committed on our commerce. The first object of my heart is my own country."[12]

Shortly before his ascension to the presidency he remarked on the rise of Napoleon: "On what grounds a revolution has been made, we are not informed, and are still more at a loss to divine what will be its issue; whether we are to have over again the history of Robespierre, of Caesar, or the new phenomenon of an usurpation of the government for the purpose of making it free.[13]

Much the same can be said for the general American reaction to the European revolutions of 1848. There was satisfaction that our example was being honored and sympathy with national independence movements, but no felt mission to promote the event and a certain amount of skepticism as to the possibilities of success. Americans understood that movements of social revolution were different in kind from their own revolution in favor of republican institutions. If for no other reason than the strength of the establishments that they had to overcome, European revolutionaries were bound to run to excesses of radicalism or militarism rather than follow the American example of a stable government of the people.

Yet seeds were planted for a later day. An influx of German refugees with universalist ideas swelled the ranks of the new Republican party in the 18"50s. In New England, the reaction to the French Revolution had a course similar to that of Germany—an adoption and transformation of the revolutionary impulse into a native form. One could see in John Adams something of the Puritan idealism that many have found to be a historical source of the peculiar abstractness and self-righteousness which they have found in American foreign policy. But when Transcendentalism had been added to the secularized remnants of this "City upon a Hill" ideology that had figured in the founding of Massachusetts, the ground was being cleared to erect a new temple of universalized aggressive Americanism.

For Emerson, the American was not simply something to be celebrated as an example in which we could take national pride—he was a model for the future of the world. The world was to be seized—by a new type who was a universal model for the future (and at the same time remarkably Bostonian). By filtering American "exceptionalism" and the Declaration of Independence back and forth through Transcendentalism, a subtle but lasting transformation was made in concepts of the American role in the world. This was projected not only forward, but backward in American history, so that later historians thought they saw precedents in the American Revolution for a global democratic revolution in the twentieth. From Emerson's new man it was but a short step to Whitman and the conversion of democracy from the stern and manly republican principles of the founders into an amorphous, universalistic egalitarianism.

These tendencies gained their first high-level political expression in John Quincy Adams, who wrote, in an official document: "The general history of mankind, for the last three thousand years, demonstrates beyond all contradiction the progressive improvement in the condition of man, by means of the establishment of the principles of International Law, tending to social benevolence and humanity." He also predicted a future world free of colonialism, "unfair" trade restrictions, and monarchy.[14] But Adams was not a typical American figure of his time, nor did these mystical aspirations interfere with his hard-headed nationalistic diplomacy.

Certain tendencies were thus evident to the discerning, but these remained, politically and in public morale, a lesser key throughout the nineteenth century. The American democracy of the nineteenth century was a rooted optimism about American conditions and the American common man, essentially isolationist and telluric, if not, indeed, xenophobic. There is nothing in the substantial history of the (largely Southern and Western) movements of Jeffersonian and Jacksonian democracy—their leaders, their rank and file, their policies, their social impulses—to provide a precedent for participation in a universal global democratic revolution. The same can be said for Lincoln, whose domestic revolution brought absolutely no change in the American role in the world. As Tocqueville remarked of the American democracy: "The foreign policy of the United States . . . consists more in abstaining than in acting."[15]

The Rise of Internationalism

One does not have to be a foolish economic determinist—a believer in the supremacy of abstract economic laws, whether the free market or Marxism—to note the impact of economic factors on the relationships of nations. Two developments took Americans, or rather a portion of their leadership class, out of their traditional benevolent isolationism at the end of the nineteenth century. First, a growing awareness of a substantial though still somewhat marginal economic interest in Latin America, Asia, and the islands of the Pacific—trade and investment which brought contact with native peoples and potential rivalry with European powers. This was not an over-riding necessity for America, as it was for Britain, which depended upon overseas markets and raw materials. Nor did imperialism ever become a widespread popular program of national self-assertion as it did among the German and French publics.

But by the end of the nineteenth century there were signs among the leadership class of an internationalist philosophy. This had two sides, whose unrecognized incompatibility has confused American foreign policy and the American self-image ever since, right down to late-twentieth-century Reaganism and its critics. On the one hand was a kind of realistic assessment, anticipated by Hamilton and typified in part by Theodore Roosevelt, that we were, whether we will or no, a power in the earth, and as such we had no choice but to take a vigorous and well-thought-out role. One could see this, possibly, as no more than traditional prudent national interest extended to new circumstances.

The other face, analytically distinguishable thought often mingled in the same minds, was a proselytizing version of American exceptionalism. It drew not from traditional impulses and understandings but from new ones—Progressivism and the degenerate form of Protestantism known as the Social Gospel. It sought a militant American role in reforming the world—in exactly the same spirit as the reformation of American slums, corrupt city governments and renegade corporations. It was an enthusiastic adoption, with an American twist, of the late imperialistic philosophy of the "white man's burden."

These combined tendencies were to have their culmination in Wilson's program to make the world safe for democracy, a formula from which Americans, or at least American intellectuals, have never escaped, and which provides our basic way of looking at the world, right down to the Reaganite obsession with the export of "vital," "revolutionary" democracy.

This new imperialism had in its origins a basically Anglo-Saxon cast. Not all imperialists were sympathetic to the new immigration, but in fact, the vast immigration of new peoples into the United States in the late nineteenth and early twentieth centuries and imperialism reinforced each other by making America seem more international than ever before. The idea of the "melting pot," which appeared at this time, was the domestic face of the international mission.

Even so, the new American imperialism was in neither respect really universalistic or egalitarian. It involved bringing the law to the natives, who were not, or at least not yet, ready for Americanization—it was paternal, not brotherly, just as the melting pot was really more conformist than pluralistic. In regard to European powers one could still see something of the old detachment and suspicion. Henry Cabot Lodge, though an early imperialist, would have agreed with Cooper's comment a half century earlier: "An opinion is seldom given in Europe of anything American, unless from impure motives."[16] But there was also a considerable movement toward coalescence with the other Western democracies, particularly Britain.

It would be too easy, though a great temptation to conservatives, to make a distinction between "realistic" internationalists like Roosevelt and "utopian" ones like Wilson. But, in earlier periods, the two aspects were inextricably confused everywhere. Roosevelt viewed World War I a good deal more enthusiastically and in some respects more blindly than did Wilson. It is misleading to blame on a particular political party or figure tendencies that are in fact widespread and deeply reflective of our national character as it has evolved.

Opposition to the new internationalism of the turn of the century took two forms. One, which has been less emphasized, but which has continued to run inarticulate and unrecognized through the American consciousness, was reflected by Bryan. It was traditional and Jeffersonian: exceptionalism with non-entanglement. It continued to believe in a benevolent but largely non-exportable American democracy. It felt that to imitate European powers in foreign ventures would lead to imitating them in domestic oppressions as well. Traces of this can be found, along with other elements, among the America Firsters of the 1930s, in figures as diverse as Charles A. Beard and Charles A. Lindbergh. Such a feeling was neither utopian nor pacifist, but it was non-interventionist. Possibly this strain of native belief and tendency has been more important than has generally been recognized. We have tended to characterize American opinion that was hesitant in such situations as the Korean and Vietnamese wars in terms provided by liberal historians, as rooted in the other, leftist form of opposition that was developing to American imperialism in the early twentieth century rather than in traditional non-interventionism.

Less important before the thirties but portentous for the future was the socialist critique of imperialism, which was curiously both isolationist and internationalist. It believed in the desirability, often the inevitability, of "world democratic revolution." Its view of the world drew from European socialism, not traditional republicanism. It opposed American internationalism because it was contaminated by big business and Christianity—it was insufficiently universalist and utopian.

As always, the actual political situation was more ambiguous than this analysis suggests. Most people do not see all the time all of the implications of their positions, and all parties and movements resort at times to convenient vagueness in order to broaden their appeal. Further, unexpected historical events tend to override formulations of foreign policy and upset ideal patterns of conflict—events like TR's sending of the fleet to the Philippines in anticipation of a war with Spain over Cuba, like nationalist unrest in the Balkan portion of the Austrian empire in 1914, like Hitler's invasion of Russia, or the overthrow of the Iranian emperor by militant Muslims.

After World War I, Americans, in the traditional phrase, "retreated into isolationism." That is, they exhibited a certain regret that they had defied all the teachings of the fathers and abandoned their splendid isolation for entangling alliances. Yet a transformation had been made in the American self-image, the Rubicon had been crossed.

America then settled into a kind of grudging and limited activity in the world. Republican administrations in the twenties busied themselves with international economic and naval agreements, and intervened in Latin America when necessary—all very Anglo-Saxon and Protestant enterprises and moderate and realistic versions of Wilson's failed fantasies. It was not so much a repudiation as a dilution of Wilsonism. Such internationalism was not universalist, however. The Third World, except for Latin America, China, and Japan, hardly entered into American consciousness. The European empires were the de facto keepers of world order. And Europe had been able to contain the new and frightening element of Bolshevism. Unlike the Kaiser, this posed no immediate threat to Western life.

Project World Democracy: The Postwar Era

From the fall of the League of Nations to the rise of fascism in American consciousness there were no serious conflicts over foreign policy, but there was also little real consensus or clarity in regard to the American role in the world. Roosevelt accomplished recognition of the Soviet Union in 1933 with only muted criticism. The old self-image having been abandoned in 1917, and the new Wilsonian one having been found to be disillusioning, nothing had yet replaced it. Americans were without a concept of their place in the world, and, except for the diehard Wilsonians, hardly felt the lack.

When war was renewed in Europe, Americans divided into three groups. The isolationists, centered in the Midwest and fuelled somewhat by Anglophobia and anti-New Deal discontents, could see no reason for American involvement in the troubles of the Old World and could discern no difference between fascist and Communist totalitarianism.

Another large segment of opinion was not eager for involvement but watched with increasing uneasiness the threats posed by aggressive and indecent regimes to the Pacific, to Western Europe, and to a tolerable world. They came slowly to face the necessity that rearmament was in order and that some involvement might be inevitable.

The third segment of opinion, developed on the Left during the 1930s and brought to full fruition during and after the war by massive official and unofficial propaganda, assumed the global democratic mission of America. (Remember, we are concerned less with events and real conditions than with how Americans were molded to conceive of their role in the world.)

The prewar period saw the first appearance in America of the Popular Front. Large segments of the Left, of various hues of red and pink, promoted an internationalist philosophy disembodied from the American national interest and the traditional guiding principles. We were the arsenal of democracy, which was threatened with extinction by aggressive fascist regimes (though apparently not by Stalinism). Already well-established in the 1930s, this philosophy had no principled opposition, and very little intelligent criticism, after the German attack on Russia, which silenced its critics to the Left, and Pearl Harbor, which ended isolationism.

In the view of the global democrats, an alliance with Soviet Russia was not a distasteful necessity—it was a glorious opportunity to be enthusiastically embraced, a mingling of the two major constituents of the future world order. Anyone who looks through the official statements, the news media, and the film entertainment of the time cannot escape this impression. Global democrats largely controlled the interpretation of the war from the news media and Washington bureaus, all of which teemed with plans for the postwar construction of world democracy. The fighting and dying in the air, the seas, and the lands was a sideshow being carried on by expendables. Indeed, for Eleanor Roosevelt, American fighting men should not return as heroes but should be quarantined for fear they had developed fascist tendencies while serving their country.

While Wilson had visualized a postwar order of nations, bound by legal agreements and deliberative institutions, global democracy was something new for Americans. It looked to a merging of peoples and an international order in which power would be as real but as amorphous and "democratic" as in the Soviet Union. The "right-wing extremism" which began to rise in the early 1950s, and was so decried by the intellectual class, rested to a considerable extent upon the inarticulate fear of many Americans that there were plans afoot to deprive them of their traditional self-government in favor of an anonymous world government. There is little doubt among scholars that FDR felt that a new world order would be constructed by himself and Stalin, with Churchill, representing the old order, curtailed as much as possible.

This line was less a mobilization of morale for the war, though it took on that aspect occasionally, than it was a plan for the postwar world. The war became a step in the global democratic revolution. The defeat of the fascist powers was only the first goal in an ongoing transformation of the world. While many or most Americans thought in terms of defeating their enemies, reestablishing a degree of order and decency in the world, and going back to peaceful pursuits, by this view the end of the war would be but a beginning.

For the first time America had become not an end but a means, expendable material for construction of a new world order (although the new order often curi-

ously resembled America writ large). Lip service was given to American values and ideals, but these were portrayed as nearly interchangeable with the Soviet variety. Curiously, not only were the defeated powers to be reconstructed, but also the victorious powers! While the guns still roared, the reform of the Western Allies was already projected—as a war goal—welfare state expansion in Britain, civil rights in the U.S. For the first time this was put not upon grounds of domestic justice but grounds of world opinion—the necessity to conform to an egalitarian world order. All of this was determined and proclaimed by the New Deal elite as *war goals.* Victorious American society must alter itself to please world opinion. The European empires would be liberated and form themselves into democratic constituents of the new world. The men who were fighting the war and the people who sustained them were expendable not only for the defense of their country but for the vision of their internationalist elite, which had pre-empted the meaning of the victory. Nor were they consulted. World peace was to be imposed by the elite through the regimentation of wartime.

Without the intensity of psychological stress and the pervasiveness of regimentation brought on by the war, so radical a break with American traditions could never have played in Peoria. As it was, this program would have gotten nowhere if it had not met a certain receptivity, if it could not have been given a plausible coincidence with the more modest and sensible goals of the masses of citizens and made to seem a fulfillment of traditional democratic ideals. But there was a rather tenuous connection between these schemes and the real aspirations and needs of the peoples of the world. The firm, serious role that Americans would be called upon to play when the fantasy of Soviet cooperation collapsed was nowhere anticipated, with the result of vast confusion, suspicion, and resentment when the Cold War impinged upon the victory and peace.

Those who grew up in the fifties can remember the unqualified and uncritical promotion of the United Nations in the schools and media in those days. The dying of Americans in the snows of Korea to stem Communist barbarism was portrayed as a United Nations police action, as if it were some disembodied exercise of world brotherhood. The pro-UN propaganda reached every hamlet in America with an intensity that was not even matched by the world wars. Its disappearance in recent years is an unexpected phenomenon which has hardly been noticed. The glorification of the United Nations continued until it became evident that the UN was intransigently anti-Zionist, which the American public could not accept. (The American public did not realize and the American intelligentsia did not care that the UN was almost as intransigently anti-Western.) Having failed of the vision, the UN was increasingly abandoned for unilateral American initiatives for the world democratic revolution, of which the Reagan "Project Democracy" is only the latest of quite a long line.

The application of the global democratic vision to relations with the Communist world was a disaster mitigated only by belated realistic actions of the early Cold War, which still stand as models of American generosity and good sense. But the American elite were reluctant to abandon their global democratic ideology, which no longer fit the circumstances.

In terms of intellectual rationalizations, there were two significant responses to the Cold War. One was the evolution of an American conservative anticommunism which insisted on strong military and moral mobilization against a threat to civilization and religion. Its criticisms of American policy during the 1960s and 1970s mainly concentrated on the need to view the world realistically as an arena of conflict rather than as a ground for the building of democratic utopia. Democratic societies, desirable as a long-term goal insofar as they were feasible, were not the measure of the emergency.

The second response was Cold War liberalism, summed up, as has so often been the case, most cogently and persuasively by Arthur Schlesinger Jr., in *The Vital Center.* The gist of this philosophy was to steer a course between the hateful extremes of communism and anticommunism, both of which were threats to the evolution of the world toward universal democratic norms. This view has clearly remained supreme in good times and bad. It has dominated public expression and controlled both parties, and even the conservative wing of the Republicans when in power, both in regard to the Soviet world and the Third World.

The application of the concept of world democratic revolution to the Third World was also a disaster, which American policy makers and opinion molders have clung to till this day. The American stumbling in Indochina and Central America stemmed directly from the concept of a democratic mission, which caused continual misconceptions of the needs and possibilities of the societies being defended and crippling disillusionment when the concept proved fantastic and inapplicable.

Possibly the American people at large did not share fully in either the philosophy of conservative anticommunism or that of Cold War liberalism. Perhaps they shouldered the burdens of World War II and the Cold War in a reluctant and defensive effort to restrain aggressive and indecent dictatorships, not to reduce the world to the American model or any other model. Perhaps all they wanted was a government, in the words of Charles Pinckney, "sufficiently active and energetic to rescue us from contempt and preserve our domestic happiness and security. . . ." For this they did not need any philosophy. All they needed was a normal and traditional faith in their country and its institutions.

Notes

1. Gaillard Hunt and James B. Scott, eds., *The Debates in the Federal Convention of 1787* (New York: Oxford, 1920), 159–60, (Madison's notes).

2. Ibid.

3. This was one of the arguments developed in two otherwise excellent and stimulating articles by James E. Dornan in the *Intercollegiate Review:* "The Founding Fathers, Conservatism, and American Foreign Policy" (vol. VII, nos. 1–2, Fall, 1970, 31–43) and "The Search for Purpose in American Foreign Policy" (vol. VII, no. 3, Winter 1970–71, 97–110).

4. Quoted with source in Dornan's first article cited above, 39.

5. Quoted with source in Ibid., 38.

6. To Elbridge Gerry, May 13, 1797, in Adrienne Koch and William Peden, eds.,

The Life and Selected Writings of Thomas Jefferson (New York: Modern Library, 1944), 543.

7. Cooper, *The American Democrat* (Baltimore: Penguin Books, 1969), 123.

8. To John Jay, August 23, 1785, in Koch and Peden, 378. In *The Federalist* nos. 3 and 4, Jay pursued Jefferson's distinction between unjust and just wars, affirming that the Union would be efficacious in avoiding the former.

9. To Edward Rutledge, June 24, 1797, Koch and Peden, 544.

10. For purposes unrelated to this essay, I have read hundreds of despatches from American ministers and consuls in Latin America in the mid-nineteenth century, including Democrats and Whigs, Northerners and Southerners. I have above summarized a nearly unanimous attitude.

11. It is necessary to read over all of Jefferson's correspondence with American and French friends as he followed the course of events. A small but good selection appears in Koch and Peden's collection, 414–556 passim.

12. To Elbridge Gerry, January 26, 1799, in Koch and Peden, 546.

13. To Dr. William Bache, February 2, 1800, Ibid., 556.

14. George Lipsky, *John Quincy Adams: His Theory and Ideas* (New York: Crowell, 1950), 279; W. C. Ford, ed., *Writings of John Quincy Adams* (New York: Macmillan, 1913–17), vol. 6, 396.

15. Alexis Tocqueville, *Democracy in America* (New York: Anchor Books, 1969), 228.

16. Cooper, *American Democrat*, 209.

Robert Royal

1492 AND MULTICULTURALISM

VOL. 27, NO. 2, 1992

Despite its widespread currency, the term multiculturalism remains a murky concept. In theory, it suggests a substantive pluralism, a quintessentially modern American culture of cultures in which no voice predominates—save the voice that says no voice shall predominate. But in fact, as it is widely used on campuses and at other cultural venues, multiculturalism means promoting certain elements in the American mix—primarily black, Hispanic, feminist, and homosexual elements—while demoting what is thought of as a white male heterosexual monolith. Multiculturalism, properly understood, then, has little to do with culture or cultures, and quite a lot to do with special interest politics.

There is perhaps no better confirmation of this analysis than some of the phenomena surrounding this year's Columbus Quincentenary. One hundred years ago, in 1892, Columbus was celebrated as a modern man liberating himself from the theological inhibitions of Catholicism and the feudal restraints of Spain to help create Protestant and democratic America. This interpretation had gained prominence earlier in the century primarily through Washington Irving's popular but skewed biography, which aimed at making Columbus into the embodiment of nineteenth-century American optimism and progress. This year, however, Columbus is being revised by many writers whose vested interest lies far from seeing him as a white progressive—that issue is long dead. Now he is the prototype of early white European capitalist oppression whose victims—blacks, Native Americans, women (communitarians and environmentalists all, of course)—are a veritable multicultural litany.

There is a profound historical distortion common to 1892 and 1992, however: the facile and myopic identification of Columbus with all white, more or less modern European males. Columbus may in fact have been Italian and late medieval, but for the multiculturalists, who for all their championing of other cultures care little for history and its complexities, that will do just as well as American and modern. Columbus was a European, and as one of the primary revisionists clarified for the record when accused of bias, "[My book] was written to indict not

Columbus, the Spanish or the Roman Catholic nations, but the thoroughgoing evils of the culture of Europe as a whole, whose enthusiastic inheritors we Americans have been."[1]

Yet the very focusing of attention on the events surrounding 1492 may cause some unintended consequences. Every school child today not only knows about Columbus, but has had drummed into his head revisionist theories about Columbus's shadowy predecessors and the unsavory aspects of the European conquest of the Americas. By detracting from claims that Columbus was here first, and by adding to the record the negative sides of European conquest, progressive historians think they are putting things in their proper perspectives. But once we begin to look seriously into the historical record some other, unexpected discoveries may await us.

Take the situation in the Caribbean just prior to Columbus's arrival. For much of the fifteenth century, the Taíno tribe that Columbus first encountered was being driven to the Northeast in the Caribbean Sea (out of what is now South America) because of raids by a fierce native tribe known as the Caribs. The Caribs were not only conquering territory: as one modern historian puts it, the Taínos, or Arawaks, were terrified of the Caribs because they were "then expanding across the Lesser Antilles and literally eating the Arawaks up."[2]

The Taínos (Arawaks) were, by Columbus's account, a gentle people, but they became even more hospitable when they learned that the Europeans abhorred cannibalism.[3] Columbus and his men, they thought, would make vigorous allies in warding off the Caribs. Thus began a process often submerged by oversimplified contemporary readings of noble savages versus ignoble Europeans: the Indian use

of Europeans for inter-Indian political and military purposes. One of the reasons that the 550 *conquistadores* who came ashore in Mexico with Cortés were able to conquer the Aztec Empire, for example, is that 20,000 Indians joined the Spanish in order to liberate themselves from Aztec control and tribute, including the obligation to send young men to the capital Tenochtitlán for sacrificing to the gods. The technical advantage to the Spanish of possessing clumsy rifles and a few horses against a million-person empire with a fierce warrior class pales in comparison to the support of native allies.

Opportunities for easy multicultural gains in other areas are likewise difficult to come by in studying 1492. In fact, some of them, such as the feminist agenda, do not get much of a boost at all. In modern multicultural alliances, women, gays, blacks, and Native Americans may align themselves against what they perceive as the dominant culture. But any attempt to show historical roots of these alliances soon trips over some rather large facts. Some relatively simple Indian tribes may have had societies in which women and men were roughly equal—in their differences. But if we turn to the pre-Columbian Caribbean again, we may also see some other elements in native cultures. The Caribs, according to mainstream scholarship, not only were cannibals but made it a habit to capture and make concubines of the women from the Arawak tribes. The women were segregated from the men to such an extent that they spoke two separate languages. Only the men spoke Carib; the women, even Carib women, spoke Arawak because of the large numbers of Arawak women captive among them.[4]

Furthermore, the Caribs were not an isolated instance of male domination in the New World. The modern Mexicans refer to Malinche, the Indian woman who served as Cortés' interpreter, as "the Traitoress." Yet her history, even by feminist standards, may give us pause. She was sold into slavery some years before the Spanish first made contact with the American mainland by a tribe allied with the Aztecs. When the Spanish arrived, she knew several Indian dialects and quickly mastered Castilian. It does not take a profound feminist hermeneutic to understand why this talented and independent woman may have felt less than full solidarity with the Aztec nobles when the conquistadores offered her a chance for liberation from their rule.

Among North American tribes, the generally simpler organization of the tribes did not allow large gaps to open up among "gender roles," but the constant warfare among tribes and the natural division of labor between domestic tasks and hunter/warrior concerns would seem to offer little for the modern feminist agenda. Women often suffered torture and humiliations because of war, but rarely, if ever, had "combat roles" as these might be conceived in modern terms.

In any event, there can be little comfort for the feminist agenda in touting native peoples as a readily available antidote to an allegedly unique European patriarchy.

In similar fashion, an odd habit has developed of considering Native Americans as ecological models for a staggering industrialized America. The evidence for this is, to say the least, slender. Usually, all we are told as proof of this contention is that Indians believed it was necessary to ask a tree's pardon before cutting it, or to ask an animal's pardon before killing it. Among North American Indians, this did occur, but not quite because of identifiably environmentalist reasons. Gods and goddesses ruled over nature, were jealous

of their dominions, and their acquiescence in the human taking of food or raw materials had to be gained. It might be an amusing sight if, following Indian customs, modern environmentalists prayed to a god or gods. But whatever good this might do for our secular and desacralized culture, we also have to recognize the widespread evidence that Indians often exhausted the resources of a certain area, then moved on. The difference between them and, say, a modern paper company was that they were few enough and land plentiful enough—that their actions led to no major, long-term disaster.

Higher native civilizations, however, fared far worse. The great Mayan city-states in Mesoamerica, for instance, abruptly collapsed about six hundred years before Columbus arrived in the Americas. Scholars are not sure exactly why, but the evidence seems to point to endemic warfare, deforestation, epidemics, and political turmoil.[5] Similarly, about the time Columbus arrived in the Caribbean, the great Mound Builder culture of Southern Illinois simply dispersed itself, probably for similar reasons. It would not be unreasonable to speculate that the more primitive Native American tribes were ecologically benign from weakness, and the more advanced Native American civilizations showed pathologies as bad as, or worse than, those in other developed civilizations.

And these could be very bad indeed, Modern Westerners blithely invoke the idea of indigenous peoples as examples of a "harmony with nature." Often, Christianity and Judaism are viewed as having inherited from the Bible a uniquely evil injunction to "subdue and dominate" the Earth.[6] Other cultures, we are told, "live in harmony" with nature. But harmony is not an unequivocal term. The Algonquins, Iroquois, and other groups, for example, tortured and sacrificed to war gods captives from other tribes to maintain "harmony."

But the most terrifying example of what the bare search for a natural harmony can mean, absent other considerations, occurred among the Aztecs. Like other Mesoamerican high cultures, the Aztecs thought the universe was created from the blood of the gods. Blood—human blood—was continually needed to prevent the original energy from getting out of kilter. Jacques Soustelle, an admiring but honest historian of Aztec ritual, describes the special sacrifices made to keep the heavens revolving:

> The astronomer priest made a sign: a prisoner was stretched out on the stone. With a dull sound the flint knife opened his chest and in the gaping wound they spun the firestick, the *tlequauitl*. The miracle took place and the flame sprang up, born from this shattered breast; and amid shouts of joy messengers lit their torches at it and ran to carry the sacred fire to the four corners of the central valley. And so the world had escaped its end once more. But how heavy and blood-drenched a task it was for the priests and the warriors and the emperors, century after century to repel the unceasing onslaughts of the void.[7]

This too is harmony with nature, after a fashion. Even a multiculturalist may think, however, that there are limits to modern pluralism in the face of such practices.

Black slavery is perhaps the most serious moral failure in the entire history of the Americas, but instead of being content to explore that failure, some of the revisionists feel obliged to go further. They affirm Afrocentric perspectives that

the historical data cannot support. The constant warfare among African tribes, for example, was no worse than other tribal feuds. But tribal cultures cannot be recommended as much of an alternative, even to our increasingly violent urban civilization. Afrocentric curricula are unlikely to report such facts or, for example, the extent of Islamic involvement in the subjugation of black Africans. Islam is often presented in the United States as a black African alternative to white European Christianity. But this is true only in a relatively recent historical sense. North Africa in St. Augustine's time was pagan and Christian, and had acquired its Christianity without the military imposition of the faith often decried by contemporary writers. Islam, by contrast, arrived later, as masses of zealous Muslim crusaders conquered North Africa and much of Spain. In other words, Islam was a colonizing force in Africa, about half a millennium earlier than medieval Christianity. This earlier Islamic conquest is lost to the multicultural vulgate, however, because it has no use in contemporary partisan politics.

In addition to this early conquest, however, as any good historian knows, late medieval Islamic countries were far more active in the African slave trade than were Europeans. The comparative size of its atrocities does not absolve Europe in the slightest, since European principles should have resulted in better institutional safeguards against such sins"[8] Yet recalling the unsavory facts about all parties involved serves the purpose of reminding us of the common human nature we all share. Northern "ice peoples"[9] were not more inhumane than the people coming from the sun and heat of the Middle East; nor, for that matter, were they any worse than African chiefs who themselves captured and sold members of other tribes to the European and Middle Eastern slave traders. Sin and savagery are equal opportunity employers in the true sense of the terms.

One of the greatest distortions of the European record occurs because many contemporary scholars find it hard to understand how anyone ever sincerely believed in Christianity. Columbus, for example, was hardly a saint, but in him, as we might observe today among American businessmen, the religious impulse coexisted along with a drive toward wealth and glory. These three elements—God, gold, glory—contradict one another at certain points, but reinforce one another as well. Late in life, Columbus sincerely believed that he had been called by God to become an instrument of universal evangelization. Furthermore, he believed that the wealth of the New World would make it possible for Europe to mount another crusade to recapture the Holy Land, leading to the end times. By some modern lights, this may not seem a wholly laudable aim, but to understand Columbus it is necessary to understand that religion was for him not simply a justification for his other ambitions, but a motive in its own right.[10]

In his own time, Columbus was hardly alone in this. We know that Isabella, unlike her Machiavellian[11] husband Ferdinand, took religious and moral principles seriously in regulating activities in the New World. In fact, when natives started arriving in Spain to be sold into slavery the moral outcry, and concern for her own role in an immoral practice, impelled her to forbid the trade before a decade had passed since the first New World landfall. Moral reflection on the responsibilities of Christian rulers went on continually in Spain.

In 1550, Charles V did something no other emperor in history has done: he called a halt to military action in the New World until theological and moral questions could be settled. At the famous debates in Valladolid, Bartolomé de las Casas, a Dominican friar who defended the natives, and the theologian Juan Ginés de Sepulveda argued whether Indians were sufficiently rational to govern themselves. Sepulveda believed they were not, but even he justified Spanish paternalism only as an instrument for promoting the good of the native tribes. In practical terms, these efforts had little immediate effect. In addition, many modern commentators see in this only European arrogance and blindness, but the degree of detachment from self-righteousness these Spanish debates suppose should come as the true surprise. There is probably no comparable philosophical and theological sensitivity to alien rights in any other civilization, high or low, at the time, or for long after.

Facts such as these should return us all to a much higher appreciation for the culture of Europe, despite its many terrible misdeeds in the New World. But much of the historical record has so far gone unreported or been willfully misread. Multiculturalist accounts of these events constantly contradict themselves for ideological reasons. For example, first we are told that European "culture was not higher" than Native American or African cultures, which had a richness and justification of their own. In a sense, of course, this is true because different cultures are not strictly comparable. But almost in the same set of arguments in favor of the indigenous Americas and Africa, European culture is usually denigrated because Medieval Islam and China were supposedly higher cultures than Europe. The National Gallery of Art's exhibit "Circa 1492," for example, strives in the best multicultural fashion to show the high artistic level of all parts of the globe around 1492. But, in an unexplained non-sequitur, it announces in its descriptive materials that Cathay and the other civilizations of eastern Asia were "among the world's oldest, wealthiest, and most advanced."

A similar process takes place when trade is discussed. After the fall of Constantinople in 1453, Europe had to seek new routes to the East. The Portuguese began to work their way down the African coast to find a direct water route; Columbus, sailing under the banner of Castile, proposed that a shorter route lay directly West. In either case, however, the revisionist historian looks upon this European desire for trade as a disreputable money lust, reflecting further Europe's appreciation of the superiority of Eastern luxuries. Yet one of the very defenses of other civilizations, often by the same revisionists, are their extensive trade routes. North American tribes in the Great Lakes region, we are told, participated in trade networks extending to Central Mexico. The Incas are praised for the extensive road network they created to conduct the business of empire and of trade. The principle behind this double standard seems to be this: when Europeans sought to expand trade, it was out of greed, but indigenous peoples elsewhere developed trade because of their high degree of civilization.

One undeniable impulse behind the promotion of Indian culture under the aegis of redefining 1492 is a perceived lack of spirituality in modern life. Joseph Epes Brown, for example, describes the difference between our lives and those of Native Americans in which "religion:"

> is not a separate category of activity or experience [but] is in complex interrelationships with all aspects of the peoples' life-ways. Shared principles underlie sacred concepts that are specific to each of nature's manifestations and also to what could be called sacred geography. In addition, a special understanding of language in which words constitute distinct units of sacred power. Sacred forms extend to architectural styles so that each dwelling . . . is an image of the cosmos. Mysticism, in its original and thus deepest sense, is an experiential reality within Native American spiritual traditions.

As is clear from this quotation, however, the interest in Native American spirituality actually reflects a Western sense of discontinuity with our own cultural background. The ideal describes something close to a Holy Roman Empire and its sacred art and architecture.

In fact, much of the current revisionist agenda, properly understood, comes dangerously close to endorsing the mainstream European culture that the multiculturalists abhor. When Robert Maynard Hutchins and Mortimer Adler were criticized for not including masterpieces from the East in their Great Books series, they argued that they had to draw a limit to the volumes somewhere. But then they pointed out that the works that many people suggested for inclusion (out of a kind of proto-multiculturalism) were far more similar to ancient and medieval European literature than their modern proponents might have suspected. The same is, mutatis mutandis, true of the promotion of certain indigenous, or supposedly indigenous, cultural elements against the modern Western world.

Native-American culture may not have much to say directly to our current crises, but it may teach us something. It would be far better for us, physically and spiritually, to do Corn Dances or Rain Dances on Saturdays or Sundays instead of spending so much time at shopping malls, for instance. A certain exuberance about nature and about the spiritual, properly understood, would open some windows in our climate-controlled world.

But perhaps the profoundest lesson we may hope to learn from contemplating 1492 is that it is important for every people to have a vigorous culture. A multiculturalist will admit this in every case save one, that of so-called Western culture. Like it or not, Western culture, with its own particularities and its openness to light from the outside, is the cultural matrix upon which the world has become, if not unified, then set on a path of something like universal mutual intercourse.

The Western tradition is debased, cut-off from, or in uncertain relation with its own roots. But those roots are what make an authentic multiculturalism possible at all. At its best, the West has integrated what is good and true into itself without losing its own momentum. As we look back at the last five hundred years of world history, we should be grateful that even this poor excuse for Western culture—and not some monolithic political or theological system—presides over all of our cultural futures as we approach the second millennium.

Notes

1. Kirkpatrick Sale in a letter to the *New York Times*, July 25, 1991. See his *Conquest of Paradise* (New York: Knopf, 1991) for the most vigorous presentation of this simple morality tale.

2. Guillermo Céspedes, *Latin America: The Early Years* (New York: Knopf, 1974), 10.

3. Actually, the Europeans were horrified at the thought of the anthropophagoi, the Greek term for man-eaters. The term "can-

nibal" derives from Columbus's garbled transcription of the name of the offending tribe as Caribs or Canibs (the latter in the hope that they were subjects of the Great Khan).

4. Though hotly contested by revisionists, no convincing evidence has emerged to discredit the general lines of this history.

5. For a sympathetic but reliable guide to the current state of knowledge about the Maya see Linda Schele and David Freidel, *A Forest of Kings: The Untold Story of the Ancient Maya*, (New York: William Morrow and Company, Inc., 1990).

6. This way of reading Genesis is clearly tendentious, but a powerful temptation. Even as fair a man as Albert Camus, who though not a Christian, was generally fair to Christianity, argued in *The Rebel*, "For the Christian, as for the Marxist, nature must be subdued. The Greeks are of the opinion that it is better to obey it. The love of the ancients for the cosmos was completely unknown to the first Christians," (New York: Vintage Books, 1956), 190. This is mistaken in several ways, but deserves some attention as an indication of how easy it is to identify incorrectly modern industrialism with the deep Judeo-Christian roots of Western culture.

7. Jacques Soustelle, *Daily Life of the Aztecs On the Eve of the Spanish Conquest* (trans. by Patrick O'Brien) (Palo Alto: Stanford Univ. Press, 1970), 101–2.

8. Although it took a while to develop, the respect for basic human rights that exists in international law today owes a great deal to the questions confronted by the Spanish in the face of the new discoveries. For this process see James Brown Scott, *The Spanish Origin of International Law* (Washington, DC: Georgetown University, 1928).

9. Leonard Jeffries, the chairman of the Afro-American Studies Department at the City University of New York, has invented the theory of "ice people" and "sun people." In this view, the harsh climate of northern countries causes their peoples to become violent, individualistic, xenophobic. By contrast, the sun peoples, owing to the chemical influence of melanin in their skin, are gentler, communitarian, and open to others. Jeffries's theory does not seem to explain much about the comparative social

habits of, say, Swedes and Sicilians, but has gained widespread public notoriety all the same.

10. Of the many new books on Columbus that have appeared in anticipation of 1992, the most temperate is Felipe Fernández-Armesto, *Columbus* (New York: Oxford Univ. Press, 1991). John Noble Wilford's *The Mysterious Christopher Columbus* (New York: Alfred A. Knopf, 1991) is a sober history, but not nearly as sophisticated as Fernandez-Armesto. The Genoese historian Paolo Emilio Taviani tries, and occasionally succeeds, in giving a heroic interpretation to his material in his *Columbus: The Great Adventure: His Life, His Times, and His Voyages* (New York: Orion Books, 1990) and is worth reading as a now true

minority position. Kirkpatrick Sale's anti-Columbus screed *The Conquest of Paradise* has already been mentioned. Columbus's growing preoccupation with apocalyptic religious motifs is explored in Delno C. West and August Kling, *The "Libro de las profecias" of Christopher Columbus* (Gainesville: Univ. of Florida Press, 1991).

11. Actually Ferdinand was Machiavellian before the fact. Machiavelli wrote the *Prince* in 1513 (Ferdinand had been ruling Spain since 1492 and was to die in 1516 only a few years after Machiavelli's text appeared). In that little work, the Florentine pointed to the Spanish king as a modern example of how a ruler who wishes to be effective must appear to be good while doing what is necessary.

Andrew Kimbrell

Second Genesis:
The Biotechnology Revolution

VOL. 28, NO. 1, 1992

"We can hold in our minds the enormous benefits of technological society, but we cannot so easily hold the ways it may have deprived us, because technique is ourselves. All descriptions or definitions of technique which place it outside ourselves hide from us what it is."

—*George Parkin Grant in* Technology and Empire

A technological revolution has begun. This revolution could affect each of us in the most intimate, yet permanent, fashion. It could indelibly change the destiny of mankind and the other members of the biotic community. The growing technology revolution is being made a reality by dizzying advances in the biological sciences and the application of that knowledge to a variety of techniques, most importantly recombinant DNA technology. It is now becoming possible to insert, recombine, rearrange, edit, program, and produce human and other biological materials just as our ancestors were able to heat, burn, melt, and solder together various inert materials. A growing group of engineers are in the process of manipulating, and creating, new combinations of living matter just as the machine makers of the past centuries created new shapes, combinations, and forms of inanimate matter. We are in a historical transition from the Age of Pyrotechnology to the Age of Biotechnology.

Over the last decade, the achievements of biotechnology seem more like science fiction than science fact. The accomplishments of the engineers of life have triggered visions of a utopia on earth, and concerns over the creation of a "brave new world." Consider just a few recent successes:

• Researchers at the University of Texas announce that they have produced genetically duplicate cattle from the biological information contained in a single body cell. This "cloning" of cattle is viewed as a significant step towards cloning human beings.

• Scientists at the National Institute of Health (NIH) gains approval for first experiments in gene engineering of somatic human cells. Many call for approval of germline genetic "surgery" that is aimed at altering the genetic makeup of future generations.

• Surgeons in Denver, Colorado perform the first U.S. transplant of fetal organ parts into the brain of a victim of Alzheimer's disease. Meanwhile, researchers in California report successful transplants of fetal organs into laboratory mice. Fetal organs and tissues suddenly become valuable commodities.

• Congress approves a massive three-billion-dollar scientific effort to map the entire human genetic structure. Researchers claim that diagnostic tests will soon be able to determine an individual's genetic traits and predispositions to physical and emotional disorders. Critics raise the specter of a new form of social discrimination based on genetic make-up. Corporate employers and insurance companies express an interest in mandatory genetic screening of workers and insurance applicants. Prenatal screening increases sex selection and other "eugenic" abortions.

• Researchers successfully place human growth genes into the permanent genetic code of mice and pigs. Other scientists create hundreds of transgenic animals including cows and fish containing human genes. In one bizarre experiment, researchers insert the gene that emits light in a firefly into the genetic code of a tobacco plant. The leaves of the plant glow twenty-four hours a day.

• U.S. patent officials announce that all genetically engineered animals, including those with human genes inserted into their permanent genetic code, are patentable. Under the Patent Act the legal status of these new species is that of "manufactures" indistinguishable from non-living commodities. Over 160 genetically engineered animals are now patent pending. Moreover, prompted by the patent decision, several U.S. institutions apply for patents on genetically engineered mammals, including humans, which are engineered to produce valuable proteins in their mammary glands.

• Corporations and universities are releasing genetically engineered viruses and bacteria, as well as genetically engineered plants and animals into the open environment. If one of these new genetically engineered organisms becomes dangerous, the results could be catastrophic—since these living organisms mutate, reproduce, and have extraordinary mobility, they cannot be recalled.

• As part of its biological warfare research program, the Department of Defense is using new genetic technology in experimenting with virtually every known dangerous microorganism in 129 university, corporate, and military laboratories across the country. Scores of these experiments involve controversial gene-splicing technology.

• Dozens of "baby brokers" have set up shop in the U.S., contracting with women to become surrogate mothers. Amniocentesis and other pre-natal genetic tests are used to ensure that the child contracted for is "fit." Under the contract, "abnormal" children are aborted upon request of the paying client. Since the famous Baby M case over two dozen law cases have been filed challenging the controversial business.

As societies scramble to cope with each new techno-dilemma, the new cadre of biological technicians and decision-makers are slowly beginning to assume a novel, though controversial, role in the natural scheme. Scientists and engineers, often with the best of intentions, are assuming the roles of creator and designer of the biotic community, from microbe to man. They are using their new-found abilities to alter the very blueprint of life—to apply traditional engineering values such as efficiency, utility, quantifiablity, predictability to the manipulation of life forms. Driven by billions of research dollars and massive profit possibilities, these techniques, whether in the areas of human health and childbearing or in the manipulation of animals, plants, and microbes, are invading the most intimate aspects of human life, and the most hidden areas of the natural world.

There can be little question that extension of the techniques and ideology of the industrial age to the living kingdom, including the human body, is among the most significant technological and philosophical transitions in recorded history. The question of whether we should embark on a long journey in which we become the architects of life is among the most important technological issues ever to face humanity.

Those overseeing and promoting biotechnology assure us that the consequences of the technological revolution can be managed. The *New York Times* in a recent editorial noted that; "Life is special, and humans even more so, but biological machines are still machines that now can be altered, cloned, and patented. The consequences will be profound but, taken a step at a time, they can be managed."[1] Biotech's supporters also point out that, whatever the short term dislocations, these novel techniques

and practices will bring dazzling social benefits. The engineers and salesmen of biotechnology confidently predict cures for cancer and AIDS; they hail the coming abolition of man's most pernicious hereditary diseases; they pronounce an end to human infertility; they herald a new biotech "green" revolution that will help end world starvation.

Those questioning the new technology are skeptical of these claims. As part of the generation brought up with a plethora of techno-booster bromides (i.e., that "Progress Is Our Middle Name," that we would have "Better Living Through Chemistry," "Cheap and Clean Nuclear Power," and even that "DDT Is Good for Me"), they find the promises of utopian technologists hollow, even tragicomic. Certainly, for a society viewing a new genre of social threats, including the destruction of the family, disintegration of communities, urban blight, growing crime; and a new genre of global environmental threats, including ozone depletion, deforestation, species extinction, and global warming, it is now painfully evident that every new technological revolution has both benefits and costs. Society's experience with industrial technology demonstrates that the more powerful a technology is at expropriating and controlling the forces of nature, the greater the disruption of our society and destruction of the ecosystems that sustain life.

The biological revolution is no exception to the technological rule. Though less than two decades old, it has spawned unprecedented environmental, economic, and ethical concerns. Environmentalists have raised alarms about biological pollution as the prospect of the release of thousands of genetically engineered microbes, plants, and animals comes closer to reality. Farmers, researchers, and workers around the world anxiously await the economic consequences of corporate controlled genetic engineering techniques and novel life forms replacing more traditional production methods and native plant and animal species.

Perhaps most compelling, the bio-revolution is creating an upheaval in the way in which we define, understand, and use life. As we transplant and engineer human organs, tissue, and genes into other animals, we blur the line between human and nonhuman. As we engineer, patent, and clone life forms as if they were "biological machines," we obscure the line between life and non-life. In our haste to better harvest human materials including the newly defined "brain dead" and fetuses, we throw into confusion traditional concepts of life and death. As we seek to cure infertility with in vitro fertilization, egg and sperm donors, and surrogate mother contracts, we no longer have clear lines on what constitutes motherhood or fatherhood. As we screen our unborn for abnormalities, we force eugenic decisions on what constitutes a life worth living. As we patent life forms, we turn the biotic community into corporately owned commodities. As we open up a market for "contract" children and human body parts, we initiate a bio-slavery for the economically disenfranchised who are lured into selling the irreplaceable. The human body itself, once held "sacred," or at least reverable, is rapidly becoming the raw material for the new bio-industrial age. The body has become commodity.

We are, today, unprepared to cope with the myriad ethical, economic, and political consequences of the biotechnology revolution. Clearly, the questions raised by the manipulation and marketing of life are among the most important ever to face the human family, yet we have done little to establish adequate bio-policies

to guide us through the moral morass. Furthermore, despite its epochal impact, biotechnology's chief decision-makers are not world leaders or elected officials. The issues surrounding the technology are not decided by democratic decision-making or popular opinion. Rather, the managers of biotechnology are a haphazard group of researchers, bureaucrats, doctors, businessmen, scientists, and judges. Their decisions are, more often than not, made through corporate board decisions, arcane bureaucratic regulations, and local and federal court opinions. They do not constitute a conspiracy, nor do they all share the same political ideology. In fact, they are generally guided in their decision-making by the narrowest of notions concerning efficiency and marketability.

Unfortunately, then, those now authorized to make decisions on regulating or limiting the genetic engineering are not inclined, or able, to guide society in addressing the policy challenges of biotechnology. Often goaded by scientific curiosity, the drive to cure disease, or raw personal profit, current actors in the forefront of the biorevolution do not seem to have the breadth of vision to confront the implications of what they are bringing to society. Perhaps it should not surprise us that those who spend their lives looking through microscopes tend to develop microscopic vision.

Even those employed as so-called "bioethicists" seem to be incapable of saying no to any new advance in the marketing of life, no matter how questionable. As the ethicists line up in favor of the continuing extension of biotechnology into the body's organs, cells, genes—even offspring—they seem intent on guiding the unthinkable on its passage to becoming debatable, and then toward being justifiable, and on to finally becoming routine. We are in an ethical free fall.

How will society limit biotechnology in order to reduce its risks and still reap its benefits? The prospect is far from reassuring. After all, we have never limited a technology to its beneficial uses. And, so far, there are no new answers. The biotechnology revolution is being managed and regulated in the same manner as have the other major technological breakthroughs of the last several decades. Author Langdon Winner has termed this mode of dealing with technology the "utilitarian-pluralistic" approach. The problem of technology is primarily seen as a question of benefits and costs. The utilitarian-pluralistic approach attempts to assess the possible risks of a technology as against the benefits it provides. Questions arising from this approach are routine public policy fare. What are the trade-offs between eliminating various sources of air pollution and possible productivity costs for industries affected by the restrictions? What are the trade-offs between preserving wilderness areas and the loss of jobs to the lumber industry? What are the trade-offs between the environmental threat of nuclear power as against the need for more energy?

Biotechnology is following the pattern. Regulating biotechnology now involves various federal agencies in the U.S., and similar international bodies, preparing a variety of risk assessments on sundry actions involving the use of genetic engineering techniques. Environmental agencies assess the risks of releasing genetically engineered organisms into the environment. Other regulators gauge potential health risks of genetically engineered foods (some of these foods border on the bizarre—tomatoes with flounder genes to enhance resiliency, pork produced by engineering human genes into pigs to create "leaner" meat). Advisory panels look into the risks posed by engineering the human germline. The Department of Defense evaluates the dangers of using biotechnology to create new biological warfare weapons as against possible advantages for national security.

Once risks and benefits of a technology are assessed, the next major regulatory issue required by the utilitarian pluralistic approach becomes distribution. The pluralistic approach to technological regulation attempts to ensure that the benefits of a technology be distributed equally and that the costs be allocated so that no sector of the population is overly burdened.

The utilitarian-pluralistic approach has been the dominant approach to technology by government and social activists alike. The environmental, consumer, and social justice movements have all taken this route. Social and environmental legislation are based in this approach to technology. Congress, scientists, and regulatory decision-makers use this approach almost exclusively. Even Marxism is primarily based in the pluralistic mode of viewing technology. The central social question as presented by Marxism becomes the relationship of various classes to the ownership of the means of production.

The utilitarian-pluralistic model of technology controls is woefully inadequate to the task. The major difficulties about technology are not its side effects, or projected "tradeoffs" necessitated by its introduction, but rather the fact that technologies ultimately become controlling influences on the very fabric of human thought and activity.

Man does not only reshape nature through technology. Technology shapes man and his thinking. The discovery of the clock gave us the "clockwork universe" of the early enlightenment thinkers, and it also gave us the idea that living organisms including our own bodies are machines. "Living bodies, are even in the smallest of their parts, machines ad infinitum," noted Gottfried Wilhelm von Leibniz. As technology developed into the great motors of the industrial age, experts in thermodynamics such as Helmholz assured us that "The animal body does not differ from the steam engine." In more recent times, we see our ourselves as computers. Computer mavin Marvin Minsky has compared the brain to a "meat-machine." Scientists see genes as information chips that can be manipulated as if they were parts of a computer. The utilitarian-pluralistic approach to technological thinking cannot deal with the tendency of technology to embody, and even create, social and political beliefs. Indeed, the utilitarian approach is merely another technological solution to the problems of technology. As noted by author Langdon Winner:

> The utilitarian pluralistic approach sees that technology is problematic in the sense that it now requires legislation. An ever-increasing array of rules, regulations, and administrative personnel is needed to maximize the benefits of technological practice while limiting its unwanted maladies. Politics is seen as the process in representative government and interest group interplay whereby such legislation takes place. . . .[2]

The alternative approach to understanding technology, an approach necessary if we are to control the biotechnology revolution, begins with the crucial awareness that technology is legislation. That technology and its bureaucratized forms of human regulation and control determine a large majority of what we are and what we believe. Technology is

itself a political, social, and theological phenomenon.

As such, technology is not in any sense neutral. A nuclear power plant, for example, regardless of how efficiently its risks are dealt with or how democratically it is owned or operated, contains certain political suppositions in the technology itself. For the technology to be used, a society must be capable of amassing large capital expenditures in the building of the facilities; a society must have centralized control of energy production and dissemination, either state-controlled or utility-controlled or both (no individual or smaller community could or would use such a large and potentially hazardous power source). There must be a massive bureaucracy to ensure safety of facility operations and disposal of nuclear waste. A scientific elite is required to build and supervise the plant. A military elite is necessary to guard against sabotage and use of the nuclear by-products. The social vision inherent in nuclear power involves a society that is capital-intensive, committed to centralized control of resources, extensive bureaucracy, and scientific and military elites. Compare this with the politics of solar power. This technology involves low capital accumulation, individual or community control of energy, no bureaucracy of risk assessment, and no need for a scientific or military elite. Clearly, every technology encodes a vision of the individual and of society. Different technologies realize different concepts of social and political life.

But that is not all. The biotechnology revolution demonstrates that technologies can also have a metaphysical content. A pig genetically engineered to contain the human growth hormone gene in order to make it a leaner, larger pig for the production of pork (a pig then patented as a "manufacture") reflects a view of life as machine and genes as information chips that can be inserted in the same manner as changing the program of a computer. Genetic screening of the newborn to find and abort those with abnormalities encodes the belief that the value of life is in "quality" of life, not in the eternal life of the soul. The genetic engineering and use of fetal tissue reflects a non-sacred view of the unborn.

But the biotechnology prospect is even broader. The biotechnologists are attempting to recreate nature in the image of efficiency. In fact, the genetic engineers envision little less than a second genesis—a genetic mixing and matching of the biotic community to create more useful and efficient life forms. This time the genesis is not of sacred origin but rather a secular creation based on the technological imperative. The view that life can be remade through biotechnology is the most breath-taking example of the tendency of the technological ethos itself to challenge traditional religious and cultural understandings of life—and life as a given good. As Gregory S. Butler argues:

> [T]he unlimited application of science and technology . . . involve[s] the intelligent control and manipulation of both human and nonhuman nature so that the material ends of the collective are better served and the deficiencies of nature finally overcome. A necessary part of the unbridled technological ethos, furthermore, is a conscious act of rebellion against the traditional moral authority given in classical and Christian metaphysics, especially insofar as the authority posits limitations on the creative powers of man by a claim to a knowledge of the nature of things. If a deficient creation is to be overcome or recreated, one must break free from those who persist in talking about eternal justice of a benevolent creator-God, or about the inherent worth and dignity of the individual before that God. The will to recreate is strong; it tends to eschew any understanding of man or God which might limit the progressive building of the future.[3]

The biotechnology revolution tends strongly in the direction of an anti-sacred, mechanistic view of life and the human. The biblical understanding that we are created in the image of God falls by the wayside. Scientists see the new technology as reifying the mechanistic worldview set out centuries ago by René Descartes and his critic/follower Julien Offray de La Mettrie. Dr. Robert Haynes, a keynote speaker at, and president of, the 16th Congress of Genetics, firmly reminded his audience that the doctrine of mechanism is a key organizing principle for the age of biotechnology.

> For 3,000 years at least; a majority of people have considered that human beings were special, were magic. It's the Judeo-Christian view of man," said Haynes. "What the ability to manipulate genes should indicate to people is the very deep extent to which we are biological machines. The traditional view is built on the foundation that life is sacred. . . . Well, not anymore. It's no longer possible to live by the idea that there is something special, unique, even sacred, about living organisms.[4]

Advances in biotechnology will further embody this mechanistic view of life. The new medical and genetic engineering technologies of the last few decades have and will save lives and perhaps will provide new cures for humanity, but, without resistance, these technologies and the ideology behind them will also lead to the devaluation and commercial exploitation of the human body, and the biotic community of which it is part. Biotechnologies are becoming ever more sophisticated. Additionally, extraordinary profits on body elements and processes are awaiting the scientists and biotechnologists who are pushing the new technologies. Unless checked, these advances in biotechnologies will, without doubt, significantly accelerate current trends. Advances in utilization of fetal parts for curing disease or for enhancement therapy will make the unborn ever more valuable commodities for the medical marketplace. As reproductive technologies become refined and increase the percentage of successful births via artificial insemination, egg donation, and embryo transfer, sperm, eggs, embryos, and children will be subject to increased marketing and will soon be legally defined as property by the courts and legislatures. As genetic screening of the unborn allows prospective parents to know a wide range of genetic traits of their offspring, eugenic abortions based on sex and other non-disease characteristics will expand. Greater understanding of the location and functions of genes will accelerate the marketing and patenting of valuable genes. Discoveries in genetic links to undesirable physical or social traits will also continue to lead to increased genetic manipulation of humans, including proposals to permanently change the genetic code of certain individuals through germ-line genetic surgery. Genetic engineering will also allow for even more transfer of human genes into animals, animal genes into plants, and plant genes into foreign species. Finally, breakthroughs in cloning could change the modes of reproduction

for all members of the living kingdom, including the reproduction of humans. The warning is clear. Unless human choices control biotechnology, biotechnology will control human choices.

As biotechnology begins to change our traditional views of central aspects of our being—life, death, birth, our bodies, motherhood, nature—we are shocked into a revelation about the history of our politics over the last century. During that time, the near cataclysmal struggle was between the market system and the Communist economic vision. The great cold war was essentially fought over different views about the ownership of the means of production. As the market system triumphed, some view the end of that struggle as the "end of history" itself.[5] However, the extraordinary issues surrounding biotechnology, and our other modern technologies, now demonstrate, to paraphrase Burke, that Marxism was not a revolution made, or failed, but rather one avoided. By fighting over the ownership of the means of production, society neglected the real political duty of our time—namely, the struggle over the means of production themselves. Each technology encodes an ideology. The technology becomes the embodiment of the ideology. As that technology becomes part of the means of production, it brings with it the full plethora of theological and social suppositions contained within it. Those suppositions then become an inherent and inextricable part of the social structure. Different ideas of God, what man is or is not, what a community is, or what is sacred require different technologies for their realization. The politics of technology is therefore the real politics of the next century.

Technological politics cannot be fought in the utilitarian-pluralistic framework—inside the regulatory forum. There is little reason to hope that current government agencies, themselves the product of a spiritually impoverished enlightenment liberal culture, will recant from the development and use of technologies that encode their basic beliefs, and begin constructing technologies resonant to a sacred view of life. Clearly, the major force behind reshaping our technological future and limiting biotechnology will have to be those whose religious and cultural beliefs respect the sacred over the efficient, those who see life not as a commodity but as divine gift. They must re-inhabit the "naked public square" and have the vision to begin supporting technologies that reify their beliefs. G. K. Chesterton noted that every revolution is

a revival. The task of remaking the technology of our culture in a sacred image is daunting but urgently required.

Notes

1. *New York Times,* February 22, 1988, "Life Industrialized," Editorial,

2. Langdon Winner, *Autonomous Technology,* (Cambridge, MA; MIT Press,1967).

3. Gregory S. Butler, "George Grant and Modern Justice," *Humanitas,* vol. 4, no.2, Spring 1990, 1.

4. Quoted in Virginia Morris, "Human Genes Not So Special," *New Haven Register,* 28 August, 1988.

5. Francis Fukuyama, "The End of History?" *National Interest* 16 (Summer 1989), 3–18.

John R. E. Bliese

THE CONSERVATIVE CASE
FOR THE ENVIRONMENT

VOL. 32, NO. 1, 1996

One of the strangest phenomena in the realm of public discourse of the last two or three decades is the extent to which conservatives have avoided the debate over environmental issues. Air and water pollution and other environmental problems affect everyone, regardless of politics, and many of the problems are acute and critical. But by and large conservatives have ignored these issues, during the very period when the environment was becoming a major political concern throughout America and the world. If, for example, one looks through *Modern Age* or the *Intercollegiate Review* one will find virtually nothing on the environment. *National Review* comments on practically everything in the political and social realms—and yet one finds there only a handful of not very thoughtful articles, almost all of which merely condemn some extremist fringe group or idea. The one major exception is The Heritage Foundation, which has published a few serious articles on the environment in *Policy Review* and in its *Mandate for Leadership* books.

Conservative politicians have done no better. As the federal government and the states were tackling pollution using bureaucratic systems of regulation proposed by the Left, conservatives in Congress and the legislatures have offered nothing more than ineffective opposition. The Heritage Foundation's *Mandate for Leadership III* summed up the Reagan administration's record this way:

> The Reagan Administration . . . had a rare opportunity to offer an alternative policy model for environmental controls: to place greater emphasis on developing property rights and on other solutions using market incentives. It has failed to do so and has provided absolutely no vision for a tough environmental policy based on market mechanisms. Without this vision and with its ill-chosen appointments at EPA, the Reagan Administration has lost the initiative on environmental issues. . . . It has appeared simply to offer lower budgets, federal inaction, and fewer restrictions on polluting industries. When dealing with highly charged political issues with moral and even religious overtones, a philosophy that seems to consist only of doing less

cannot compete effectively with statist activism.[1]

By and large, the Bush administration and the current Republican congress have given us more of the same.

There is nothing inherently liberal about environmental concerns. In fact, as *The Economist* observed, "the environment is an issue without any obvious political home."[2] A Roper poll that ranked Americans on their environmental awareness and commitment found that the group of the most active environmentalists contained the highest share of conservatives as well as of liberals.[3]

Yet, conservatives have largely abdicated the field, so environmental policy has been made with very little serious contribution from the Right. The results have been misguided policies that have not been nearly as effective as some possible alternatives, and in some cases have left our environment in worse shape than before.

It is not my purpose here to advocate any specific policies. The problem for conservatives at this point in time is more fundamental than that: we need, in the first place, to get conservatives thinking about environmental issues at all, and thinking about them in positive and constructive ways. When we do so, I believe one conclusion is inescapable: conservatives should be environmentalists.

There is a fairly well-defined and widely recognized split in the ranks of postwar American conservatism, between "traditionalists" and "libertarians" or "free-market"conservatives. George H. Nash explains "the gap between the two streams of thought":

While libertarians tended to emphasize economic arguments against the State, the new conservatives [traditionalists] were more concerned with what they saw as the ethical and spiritual causes and consequences of Leviathan. On the whole, the new conservatives were little interested in economics. . . . Instead, they were fundamentally social and cultural critics, for whom conservatism meant the restoration of values, not the preservation of material gains. . . .[4]

Nevertheless, certain bonds did link the two independent wings of the conservative revival. Both abhorred the totalitarian state and collectivism; both tended to support private property, decentralization, and (at least in a general way) a free economic system.

It is not my purpose to advance or mediate between these two perspectives. Rather, I will argue that both philosophical positions should lead conservatives to be at the forefront in the public debate on the environment, not merely in opposition but as activists with serious proposals of their own.

When considering the implications of the libertarian position on environmental issues, I am not concerned with a radical, anti-government philosophy, but rather with those who focus primarily on economics and the virtues of the free-market. For the libertarian, the free market system is believed to be not only the most efficient means of improving mankind's standard of living, but also the only sure foundation and protection for political freedom. From the free-market perspective, there should be great interest in solving many of our environmental problems—and indeed, there is a small group of free-market environmentalists, primarily associated with the Political

Economy Research Center (PERC) in Bozeman, Montana.

In a free market, producers and consumers negotiate their sales and purchases with no outside interference and without affecting third parties. The market price of a product, which the consumer pays, includes all of the costs of making it and some profit for the producer.

However, the real cost of production in the modern world often includes "externalities," costs that are not reflected in the price of goods and which must be paid by others, rather than by the consumers of the products. All forms of pollution are just such costs. If, for example, a factory does not properly dispose of its waste but saves money by dumping it untreated in a river, its customers get the products more cheaply, but downstream users of the river suffer damages. Perhaps they cannot use the river any more (say, for fishing or swimming). Or perhaps to keep using its water, they have to pay extra to clean it up first. If the factory processed its waste properly, the cost of doing so would be included in the price of its products and would be paid by their consumers, not by innocent third parties downstream.

As mentioned, the libertarian values the free market as a source and protection of freedom—freedom from interference by government and by others. But your freedom is decreased if someone can impose on you some of the cost of his production, or can invade your property with his pollution. Nothing in the theory of the free market justifies a producer and a consumer forcing an outsider to pay part of their costs. And your payment may be much more than just a few dollars; it may be in the form of acute suffering (e.g., illness from breathing polluted air or drinking polluted water). Wherever there is pollution, the libertarian should be devising ways to make sure

that the market works properly. The costs of production need to be "internalized" in the market price of goods in some way that also maximizes liberty.

The liberals who have dominated environmental policy attempt to force producers to bear the full costs of production by means of governmental regulation, enforced by ever growing bureaucracies. But a command and control system, besides infringing on freedoms, is seldom the most efficient or effective means of accomplishing the goal.

> Command-and-control generally delivers less clean-up per penny than more sophisticated alternatives. . . . Regulations tend to load high costs onto some producers, low costs onto others. . . . Command-and-control often means telling polluters what technology they must use to clean up. But government rarely knows best. As regulations are often tougher for new entrants to an industry than for existing firms, they may discourage new investment—even if it is cleaner than the old.[5]

We obviously, then, should look for the most efficient and least intrusive means of getting all costs included in market prices. There are several possible mechanisms: effluent taxes, treating pollution as an invasion of property rights (giving owners proper legal recourse for environmental "trespassing"), tradeable pollution permits, as well as many other "market-based environmental policies [to] give businesses and individuals an incentive not just to meet regulatory requirements but to go beyond them."[6] However, this is not the place to advocate any specific approach to particular problems, but the concern for those problems needs to be there, on the part of libertarians above all.[7]

Many other kinds of environmental problems should also be of direct concern to the libertarian. Libertarians are, on principle, opposed to subsidies and governmental regulations in general. But many of the environmental problems we face are the direct result of governmental actions, and would not have developed otherwise. Here we can look at only a few examples.

Government agencies systematically mismanage natural resources, often with devastating effects to the environment. Perhaps the most obvious evidence can be seen in the mismanagement of our public lands. The Bureau of Land Management (BLM) and the Forest Service control hundreds of millions of acres, mostly in the western United States, and for many years they have allowed these lands to be plundered and even destroyed at the taxpayers' expense. "The federal land bureaucracies have used taxpayer funds to subsidize economic activity that would never have taken place in the absence of subsidies. Perversely . . . American taxpayers have been financing the destruction of environments they increasingly value."[8]

As with many regulatory agencies, an "Iron Triangle" develops, with a relatively few rich and powerful people who want subsidized use of public resources, some powerful Congressmen beholden to them who get control of the relevant Congressional subcommittees, and the agency that happily does the bidding of the other two groups and is rewarded every year at appropriations time.

And what happens to the resources being managed? Look, for example, at the national grazing lands. The Forest Service and the BLM have allowed them to be devastated, "cow bombed," by massive overgrazing for many years. For this privilege, the ranchers pay less than a fourth of the going market rate to lease

similar private land, and the government loses money on the deal every single year. Congress makes sure that the grazing fees are kept low and the agencies kept properly subservient[9]—for which the agencies will get their rewards through appropriations and new projects, and individual bureaucrats will get their promotions.

Likewise, the Forest Service loses hundreds of millions of dollars every year in below-cost timber sales. With its system of "idiot forestry" (as the late Senator Herman Talmadge called it), the Forest Service is destroying our national forests by cutting timber too cheap to cover its costs.[10] The result is a devastated forest, erosion from the cleared land which then pollutes the rivers and destroys them as fisheries and for recreation, and damages water supplies downstream as well. For years, Congress even subsidized, with a specific annual appropriation, the systematic destruction of America's last great rain forest, the Tongass in Alaska.

The system works just fine, as long as no outsider figures out how much the taxpayers are losing and how much damage is being done to the land. But, as has so often been noted, those who benefit from the system have an intense and constant interest in maintaining it, while the individual taxpayers being fleeced have only a very limited motive even to learn what these mostly obscure agencies are doing, let alone to fight to stop the raid on the federal treasury. The system also distorts markets by giving subsidies to some producers (e.g., western ranchers) but not to others (ranchers in states without federal lands). So, the Iron Triangle system mismanages resources and subsidizes the destruction of nature, which obviously ought to be stopped.

These are just a couple of instances where governmental policies distort markets, add to pollution, and damage natural resources. There are many other cases. Overall, the *Economist* concluded, "in all sorts of ways American policy rigs market incentives in favour of pollution."[11] Free-market enthusiasts should search out all those policies and work to get them changed.

Another area of great concern today is hazardous waste disposal, and here, too, market-oriented proposals would be much better than the current system of regulation. Modern industry uses large amounts of toxic materials, which have to be safely disposed of somehow. "It is in hazardous waste management, if anywhere in environmental policy, that the infamous 'command and control' approach is to be found."[12] The result is a burdensome system that is not the most effective, and could only be made effective with an enormous and very expensive enforcement effort. A market-based system would be an attractive alternative.

> Rather than fining a generator or transporter for instances of detected improper disposal, why not pay for proper disposal?. . . If the amount of the payment is tuned correctly, the source should have an incentive not to try to conceal its waste . . . but rather to work to collect the reward. Presto! The terribly difficult monitoring problems seem to be solved. Toxic wastes all end up in the right places. [13]

And to keep the reward system from being a drain on taxpayers, it could be instituted as a deposit and refund system.[14]

Finally, from the market perspective, we may take a quick look at tax structures. Current taxes raise revenue but often do economic harm because they penalize jobs and profits. Shifting to "green" taxes (e.g., on effluents or on use of certain raw materials) could raise revenue and do some good at the same time, by protecting resources and making polluters pay the costs that they now pass on to others. [15]

Libertarians should be interested in environmental policy not just because market mechanisms can be effective in reducing pollution, but because pollution itself is evidence that the market is not working correctly. Pollution is also evidence that our freedom is being infringed.

Granted, market mechanisms may not work to protect the environment everywhere. "The bits of the planet that have no single owner (the sea, the rain forest, clean air) are the most vulnerable. Only governments have the power to protect them."[16] Governments, for example, may still have to control fishing and whaling in the open seas to keep commercial operations from completely wiping out all these creatures. [17]

But wherever possible—and that includes the vast majority of our environmental problems—libertarians should be guiding the public debate and proposing ways to use market incentives rather than command and control to solve our problems. This will be even more important in the future, because "the most intractable sources of pollution will increasingly be small companies and individuals, not big firms. It is easier to police a big power station or chemical company than lots of garages, farmers or shoppers. The best hope of getting small polluters to clean up will be to give them the right price signals."[18]

One major objection that business interests always raise against any and all efforts to protect nature or clean up our environment is that they will harm economic growth. Several observations here may put this objection into proper perspective, and lead us into a consideration of the traditionalist position.

In the first place, "not all growth is good. Metastasis is growth too"—even *National Review* was willing to print that.[19] Moreover, in order to preserve the ability of our economy to grow in the future, it is critical that we protect the environment now. "The real limits to growth are (a) the capacity of the environment to deal with waste in all its forms, and (b) the threat to resources which play no direct part in world commerce. These 'critical' resources—the ozone layer, the carbon cycle, Amazonia—are treated as free goods when in reality they serve the most basic economic functions: that of enabling people to survive."[20] If we have to give up producing a few more gadgets in order to preserve them, we obviously should do so.

In some ways, cleaning up the environment can even help economic growth. The technology needed to clean up our environment and keep it clean will itself be "one of the fastest-growing sectors of the global economy well into the twenty-first century."[21] The country that is at the forefront of developing this technology will reap huge benefits in jobs and income for its citizens. "America's fast-growing environmental-services industry is already worth $130 billion a year—and its capital is California," which "has the toughest environmental rules in the world."[22]

Finally, a clean environment, while expensive, may be considered the latest in a series of added costs that have successively contributed to our quality of life. Not many years ago, the same arguments were made that reasonable working hours and safe workplaces would be a burden on business and barriers to growth. But now they are universally accepted as proper expenses. So, too, must a reasonably clean environment be accepted as worth the cost, and a good in itself.

American conservatism of the traditionalist perspective is in many ways quite different from the free market one.

> Shocked by totalitarianism, total war, and the development of secular, rootless, mass society during the 1930s and 1940s, [these conservatives] urged a return to traditional religion and ethical absolutes and a rejection of the 'relativism' which had allegedly corroded Western values and produced an intolerable vacuum that was filled by demonic ideologies.[23]

From this traditionalist perspective as well, conservatives should be environmentalists.

Conservatives have all too often been willing to go along with business interests when they opposed environmental protection. The free-market position, we have seen, does not justify such passivity. Traditionalists provide an important corrective from a very different perspective.

> Many "traditionalist" conservatives are quite critical of unregulated capitalism. They view unregulated capitalism as an integral part of the materialism and hedonism they so dislike in the modern Western world; they spurn the civilization that has grown up around the capitalist order. They believe that unregulated capitalism has placed great burdens on the way of life they think necessary for the development of human freedom along virtuous lines. . . . [Their] primary concern is to emphasize the importance of culture and virtue.[24]

Russell Kirk is perhaps foremost among the traditionalists. He adopts Edmund Burke's "concept of society as joined in perpetuity by a moral bond among the dead, the living, and those yet to be born—the community of souls. . . . And Burke, could he see our century, never would concede that a consumption-society . . . is the end for which Providence has prepared man."[25] Likewise, Richard Weaver "was profoundly concerned by the growth of 'mass plutocracy'—the 'greatest danger' America confronted. He distrusted advertising and lamented the popular views that man was a being of merely 'appetitive function' and that material goods . . . could save us."[26] He praised the old South, because it was "the last non-materialist society in the Western World."[27]

Kirk decisively rejects the "practical conservatism [which has] degenerated into mere laudation of 'private enterprise,' economic policy almost wholly surrendered to special interests."[28] He "Indignantly denie[s] . . . that his conservatism could or should be identified with businessmen."[29] Other leading traditionalists concur. Peter Viereck admonishes conservatives to "conserve the humane and ethical values of the West rather than the economic privileges of a fraction of the West."[30] Stephen Tonsor contends that the traditionalist conservatives "are not now, nor will they be, identified with the American business community. They are clearly identified with natural law philosophy and revealed religion."[31]

From a traditionalist perspective, just as we have inherited our culture and must preserve it for future generations, so have we inherited this earth, and we have to take proper care of it as good stewards. As Margaret Thatcher stated when she announced her conversion to environmentalism, "No generation has a freehold on this earth. All we have is a life tenancy—with a full repairing lease."[32] The principle of stewardship, and consequently of "sustainable development," should

lead conservatives to accept their duty to design our economy so that we produce our goods in a way that does not impair the planet's ability to provide for future generations.

Closely related to the notion of stewardship is one of the cardinal virtues for the traditionalist conservative: piety, which includes a proper veneration for this earth. For Richard Weaver, nature is one of the things we should "regard with the spirit of piety."[33] One of the reasons he defends the older South is because the "ancient virtue of *pietas*" dominated its thinking.

> There existed veneration for the transcendent and the order of things; there was reverence for nature. . . . Man was the creature, not the Creator, and it was that most ancient vice, hubris, that contended man was self-produced and thus entitled to war on creation and the nature of things.[34]

A sense of piety should also lead the conservative to be in the front lines of the battle against the wanton destruction of nature by man, which Weaver thought was nothing less than a "sin."[35] We should condemn, with Russell Kirk, "the modern spectacle of vanished forests and eroded lands, wasted petroleum and ruthless mining . . . [as] evidence of what an age without veneration does to itself and its successors."[36]

For the traditionalist, the highest political virtue is prudence. Russell Kirk calls prudence "that transcendent conservative virtue . . . which Burke so often commends."[37] William Harbour explains:

> Prudence is supposed to be the guide by which the political leader is to mediate general principles by practical

considerations in order to deal with the specific considerations of the moment. . . . Prudence is the key word for the Conservative whenever it comes to dealing with specific political problems. [38]

Prudence should also lead the conservative to take the vanguard in confronting some of our most daunting ecological challenges.

We are, for example, pumping enormous quantities of "greenhouse" gases into the atmosphere, which may alter the world's climate far more rapidly than nature's own cycles. Of course, we do not now have conclusive proof of what the ultimate effects will be. But "environmental policy . . . often requires that decisions be made on the basis of incomplete knowledge, because of the grievous risks posed by lack of action."[39] Atmospheric scientists say it may take another decade of study before we will have anything close to certain knowledge. But it is virtually impossible to remove those gases from our atmosphere. If we do not change our ways in the meantime, we will simply compound the risks with another decade's generation of greenhouse gases. Prudence would dictate that we should follow Stephen Schneider's advice:

The prospect of climatic change occurring on a global scale ten to fifty times faster than typical natural average rates of change is not one we should relish. The possibility of major environmental surprises increases with the rate at which climate changes. Moreover, if there are things we can do to slow down this rate of change that simultaneously will provide multiple benefits, then it would seem logically compelling to take them seriously. . . . The prudent course to follow would

be making high-leverage investments, a common business practice that seeks to earn multiple benefits on the same investment. Using fuel efficiently not only reduces CO_2 injection, but also cuts acid rain, reduces the health effects of air pollution in cities, reduces the dependence of our energy security on unreliable resources, and improves our long-term competitiveness by cutting the energy cost of manufactured products.[40]

Likewise with species preservation. Our attack on planet earth is destroying habitat at such an enormous rate that entire species of plants and animals are becoming extinct at an ever accelerating rate. Preserving diversity of species and the necessary habitat is another matter of good stewardship. We do not know what roles most of those organisms play in the ecosystem. We do not know what benefits we might be able to obtain from them. In the often-quoted words of Harvard biologist E. O. Wilson, "the catastrophic reduction of species diversity throughout the world is the crime future generations are least likely to forgive us for." Again, sheer prudence would dictate that we should follow the first rule of the mechanic: when you take something apart, save all the pieces.

In many ways, modern technology has put an enormous premium on the traditionalists' virtue of prudence. Robert Solo warns:

Throughout his habitat on earth, man's technologies have been formed on the assumption that the autonomous system that produces the environment needed for life cannot be reached by what we do nor destroyed by us. And here, I think, a crucial change has come. The life system itself is no longer beyond the reach of man's technology nor beyond his power to disarrange, degrade, and destroy. This is a danger no age has ever faced before.[41]

It is a danger that cries out for conservatives to take the lead in advocating prudence.

The traditionalist should be active in efforts to preserve nature, especially in our parks and wilderness areas, for other reasons as well. The traditionalist wants to conserve our heritage, or at least the good parts of it, including those that make America unique. One significant factor in developing the American character was wilderness. As one of its foremost advocates contends, "wilderness is a fundamental constituent of the national culture, an indigenous part of Americanism, bearing qualities that set it apart as a contribution to civilization."[42] Now that our wilderness is virtually all gone, conservatives should be involved in preserving what little remains, just as we would want to preserve any major historical building.

The very concept of a national park is an American invention. The traditionalist with a concern for virtue should be at the forefront of efforts to preserve these and other natural areas for recreation. Michael Frome, an advocate for wilderness, calls the contemplation of nature "the most ennobling kind of recreation."[43] Richard Weaver shows how important it is in the modern world:

> What humane spirit, after [exposure to modern journalism and advertising] has not found relief in fixing his gaze upon some characteristic bit of nature? It is escape from the sickly metaphysical dream. Out of the surfeit of falsity born of technology and commercialism we rejoice in returning to primary data and to assurance that the world is a world of enduring forms which in themselves are neither brutal nor sentimental.[44]

And he wrote that before the age of television!

The traditionalist perspective perhaps suggests fewer specific remedies for environmental challenges than the free market one. But both are authentically conservative positions. "Both implicitly accept, to a large degree, the ends of the other" and they fight together "against the collectivist Leviathan state of the twentieth century."[45] The traditionalist would perhaps be more willing to advocate actions by the government to preserve the natural areas that have historically belonged to it. Since the market by itself might not be able to preserve a sufficient amount of natural habitat, the libertarian should be willing to accept that.[46] If, on the other hand, the libertarian can devise market mechanisms to solve pollution and protect the environment, the traditionalist might well be disposed to endorse them.

As we have seen, there are good philosophical reasons for conservatives of both kinds to be in the forefront of the public debate on environmental policy, devising proper measures to solve all of the different kinds of environmental problems we face.

Moreover, it is dangerous to leave these issues to be dealt with exclusively by the Left. Their propensity for governmental control and bureaucratic regulation, besides infringing ever more on our freedom, is seldom the best or most efficient way to solve environmental problems.

It is lamentable that more conservative intellectual activity has not been directed toward conservation of our environment. If conservatives had been engaged in environmental issues from the very first, we might have avoided a lot of dead ends and been spared much bureaucratic meddling. All of us would now be better off politically, economically, and environmentally.

Notes

1. Nolan Clark, "The Environmental Protection Agency," in Charles L. Heatherly and Burton Yale Pines, eds., *Mandate for Leadership III: Policy Strategy for the 1990s* (Washington, DC, 1989), 217–18.

2. "Costing the Earth, A Survey of the Environment," *Economist* (Sept. 2, 1989), 5.

3. Marshall Ingwerson, "On the Environment, Americans' Words Are Louder Than Deeds," *Christian Science Monitor* (Aug. 2, 1990), 2.

4. George H. Nash, *The Conservative Intellectual Movement in America Since 1945* (Wilmington, DE: ISI Books, 1996, 2007), 73.

5. "Costing the Earth," 7.

6. Robert N. Stavins, "Clean Profits," *Policy Review* 48 (Spring 1989), 59.

7. For an excellent analysis of many possible market-based environmental policies, see the two volumes of *Project 88* (Washington, DC, 1988, 1991), sponsored by Senators Timothy Wirth and the late John Heinz.

8. John Baden, "Crimes Against Nature," *Policy Review* 39 (Winter 1987), 36.

9. Just how subservient these agencies have been can be seen in an instance discovered by the General Accounting Office. "They reported the case of a BLM area manager who caught a rancher cutting trees without authorization in a sensitive riparian zone and ordered him to stop. Word came down through political channels that the BLM manager was to apologize to the rancher—and deliver the wood to his house" Robert Conniff, "Once the Secret Domain of Miners and Ranchers, the BLM Is Going Public," *Smithsonian* (Sept. 1990), 34.

10. Jeremy Kalmanofsky, "Subsidized Timber Sales Raise Public-Benefit Issue," *Christian Science Monitor* (June 20, 1991), 10–11.

11. "Green My Lips," *Economist* (Feb. 17, 1990), 19.

12. Clifford S. Russell, "Economic Incentives in the Management of Hazardous Waste," *Columbia Journal of Environmental Law* 13 (1988), 262.

13. Ibid., 265–66.

14. Ibid., 267.

15. "Money from Greenery," *Economist* (Oct. 21, 1989), 16–17.

16. "Costing the Earth," 4.

17. See Garrett Hardin, "The Tragedy of the Commons," *Science* 162 (1968), 1243–48, for the classic explanation of why a resource no one owns, a commons, will be rapidly depleted.

18. "Money from Greenery," 16.

19. David Horowitz, "Making the Green One Red," *National Review* (Mar. 19, 1990), 40. Gross national product figures can be misleading here. For example, the costs of trying to clean up the oil spill in Prince William Sound were added to the gnp, so would mathematically appear to be "growth."

20. "Costing the Earth," 5–6.

21. Joan Berkowitz, quoted by Brad Knickerbocker, "Green Conservatives," *Christian Science Monitor* (Feb. 4, 1992) 13.

22. "California Cashes in on Cleaning Up," *Economist* (Nov. 16, 1991), 79.

23. Nash, op. cit., xv.

24. William R. Harbour, *The Foundations of Conservative Thought* (Notre Dame, IN, 1982), 109–10.

25. Russell Kirk, *The Conservative Mind*, 7th ed. (Chicago, 1986), 10–11.

26. Nash, op. cit., 189.

27. Richard Weaver, *The Southern Tradition at Bay* (New Rochelle, NY, 1968), 391.

28. Kirk, op. cit., 455.

29. Nash, op. cit., 183.

30. Peter Viereck, *Conservatism Revisited* (New York, 1949), x.

31. Nash, op. cit., 123.

32. "Costing the Earth," 3.

33. Richard Weaver, *Ideas Have Consequences* (Chicago, 1948), 172.

34. John P. East, *The American Conservative Movement: The Philosophical Founders* (Chicago, 1986), 64–65.

35. Weaver, *Ideas Have Consequences*, 171.

36. Kirk, op. cit., 44–45.

37. Ibid., 184.

38. Harbour, op. cit, 62–63.

39. Strock, "Putting Our Habitat in Order,"

Policy Review 45 (Summer 1988), 40.

40. Stephen H. Schneider, *Global Warming: Are We Entering the Greenhouse Century?* (San Francisco, 1989), 283–84.

41. Robert Solo, "Problems of Modern Technology," *Journal of Economic Issues* 8 (1974), 863.

42. Michael Frome, *Battle for the Wilderness* (New York, 1974), 49.

43. Ibid., 89.

44. Weaver, op. cit., 112.

45. Frank S. Meyer, "Freedom, Tradition, Conservatism," *Modern Age* 4 (1960) 356, 360.

46. Stavins, "Clean Profits," 62.

Elizabeth Fox-Genovese

Severing the Ties That Bind: Women, the Family, and Social Institutions

VOL. 34, NO. 1, 1998

On the whole, at the opening of the twenty-first century, Western women enjoy a power, education, and privilege unprecedented in human history. And much of this unprecedented power and freedom has resulted from women's political activism on behalf of themselves and other women. Just as the social institutions of the West have both impeded and facilitated women's political activism, so has women's political activism caused both progress and decline in those institutions. Much depends upon your perspective and upon the historical moment you are considering.

Let us begin with the political context: there can be no doubt that the political institutions of Western Europe and the United States have played a role in the emergence of modern feminism and of women's growing role in the social, economic, and political life of Western nations. The ideals of individual freedom and political democracy are distinctly Western) and without them it is hard to imagine that women would have moved as readily into political life as they have. The political vocabulary of freedom, equality, and democracy has provided women with the principal justification for their campaign to enjoy the full status of citizenship, especially since there were never principled political justifications for their exclusion from it.

Many women remain dissatisfied with the results of women's access to political life, usually on the grounds that formal equality with men has not netted women an equal share of wealth, power, and prestige. But these days, most activists are likely to focus their attention upon social rather than political institutions and to view political activism as a weapon to effect lasting social change. The impact of women's political activism upon social institutions has been momentous, but its ultimate consequences still remain unclear.

In this essay, I shall briefly consider the current state of the balance sheet and then focus more closely on the specific institution of the family. On the positive side of the ledger, women's political activism of the past few decades has decisively improved the independence and dignity of women as individuals. Women today enjoy opportunities to fulfill their talents, attain an education, pursue a career, run for and win political office that most of our mothers and grandmothers could not have dreamed of. On the negative side, social institutions, especially in the United States, have been decisively weakened, most of all the family.

A word of caution is, however, in order: One of the major consequences of feminist political efforts during the past three or four decades has been decisively to blur the boundary between public and private and, by extension, between political and social institutions. You may recall the early slogan of Second Stage Feminism, "the personal is political." That slogan called for the systematic politicization of personal relations, and many of its goals have been attained. Historically, social institutions have usually been viewed as, in some measure, distinct from political life. During the early nineteenth century, Alexis Tocqueville visited the new United States and wrote a famous account of what he observed. In *Democracy in America*, Tocqueville commented that many American social institutions were voluntary, which is to say they lacked the legal identity of many European social institutions. He further commented that the egalitarian ideology of Americans and the fluidly of their democratic political institutions made social institutions all the more necessary to the health of the country.

The general situation that Tocqueville described persisted for decades, although specific social institutions changed along the way. Most, however, retained a measure of autonomy from political life. Throughout the nineteenth century and much of the twentieth, the family ranked as the main social institution, and, as an institution, it did enjoy a significant measure of autonomy. In effect, the principles of democracy stopped at the threshold of the private home—a man's castle, as

it was proverbially known. As a kind of corporate enclave within the surrounding bustle of competitive individualism, capitalism, and democracy, the family remained tied to hierarchical principles that placed the man, husband and father, in authority over all, including his wife, and placed both parents in authority over their children.

From the beginnings of the woman's movement in the mid-nineteenth century, feminists focused on the injustice of women's subordination to men within the family, and they gradually secured a number of reforms, beginning with a married woman's right to own property in her own name. Second wave feminists even more sharply condemned the family as the cradle of women's oppression, and they successfully campaigned for no-fault divorce, recognition of marital rape, and other forms or assistance for the wives of abusive husbands. Many of these changes represented significant progress for women, many of whom had previously lived in dependence and without any resources they could call their own. As recently as the 1960s it was often extremely difficult for a married woman to get credit in her own name.

Few today would, I think, dispute the positive value of these and related changes, but some are also beginning to worry that they have come at an exorbitantly high price. Their impact has been all the greater because they occurred in conjunction with—and arguably partially because of—a massive movement of married women and mothers of small children into the labor force. Thus, just as the formal bonds of the family were being weakened by legal reforms, women's presence in the family was decreasing because of the time they were spending at work, and women's economic independence from the husband was increasing because of the wages they were earning. And, as more and more people are acknowledging, the most serious casualty of the family's dissolution was children, who are increasingly being turned over to others or left to their own devices.

Feminist political rhetoric has tended to target men as the main obstacles to women's independence and equality, but much feminist political activism has, directly or indirectly, targeted the ties that bind women to children. The campaign to secure and defend abortion on demand is especially revealing in this regard. First, a woman's right to abortion has been defended in political language as an individual right—frequently as a woman's right to sexual freedom. No less significantly, it has been defended on the grounds of privacy. Consider the implications of these two positions. In the first instance, a woman has a right to be liberated from children—the possible consequence of her sexuality. This strategy effectively divorces children from any social institution by labeling them the concern of the woman rather than of a woman and a man. The second argument points in the same direction by reducing privacy to the privacy of the individual rather than the privacy of the couple or the family. As Mary Ann Glendon has argued, this interpretation of the right of privacy is a radical innovation in American law, and it represents a significant departure from the legal norms of Western European nations. Symbolically, the reduction of privacy to the privacy of the solitary individual effectively sounds the death knell of social institutions, especially the family, as organic units with claims upon their members.

Other features of the abortion campaign similarly chip away at the family as a social institution. Feminists have, for example, strongly resisted the idea

that a minor should have the consent of a parent or guardian before having an abortion. They argue that since the father or guardian may be the one who has caused the pregnancy in the first place, the requirement that the girl obtain consent simply exposes her to punishment or further abuse. Western European countries handle this danger by allowing a minor to obtain the consent of a judge, but feminist activists have opposed that solution as well, arguing that even a young woman's sexuality is a purely individual matter. Such a radical concept of individualism further weakens the notion that children constitute a social responsibility and not simply an individual possession to be disposed of at will. In a bitter irony, the largest business interests tend to concur with feminist activists in this regard, and in *Casey v. Planned Parenthood of Pennsylvania*, a majority of the Supreme Court argued that women had become accustomed to the free disposition of their sexuality and labor and that unplanned pregnancies should not be allowed to interfere with their ability to support themselves. The opinion amounted to recognition that social institutions, notably the family, have so far decayed that no woman or child can automatically count on their support.

Women's political activism in the United States has disproportionately focused upon securing and defending women's liberation from the binding ties of family and from traditional—or stereotyped—expectations about women's roles. As a result, many feminists have rejected the idea of maternity leave on the grounds that child rearing is as much the man's responsibility as the woman's. Maternity leave, they reason, would officially sanction a woman's special responsibility for children and accordingly reinforce the persisting inequalities between women and men. As a result, the United States stands as one of the few countries in the world that does not offer new mothers some form of Maternity leave. All of the Western European countries do so, some quite generously. They also make more generous provisions for state subsidized day care than we do in the United States.

In contrast, the European pattern has been to be generous to women by being generous to children and the reverse. European countries, with the Scandinavian countries in the lead, are also witnessing some weakening of traditional social institutions, especially the family, but none match the United States in divorce and illegitimacy rates—or in the number of abortions performed. Nor do any match our reluctance to subsidize the care of children. Of eight industrialized nations—Sweden, the Federal Republic of Germany, France, Canada, Australia, Israel, and the United Kingdom—the United States stands alone in neither providing maternity leave nor any universal child allowances. To compound the problems, we do less to support child care and are much less flexible and innovative in the kinds of child care we license than other Western, and many developing, nations. Some of these countries, notably Sweden, also provide housing allowances and health care benefits. And it is worth noting that none of these countries has as high a proportion of children either born to or living with single mothers, or as high rate of infant mortally. For the richest nation in the world, our record is nothing to boast about.

Sad and intuitively improbable as it may seem, women's political activism has much to answer for with respect to the current state of our social institutions. On this point I am emphatically not implying that blame should be laid entirely at the feet of one or another group of women. What I am arguing is that the political agenda of various women's groups has contributed to our current situation if only by failing to campaign vigorously for alternative solutions. Feminist opposition to maternity leave, as I have already suggested, has eased the pressure on business to face up to its responsibilities in this regard. The feminist leadership has also strongly favored policies that encourage women to work full-time throughout their children's early years. This preference has led feminists to campaign for federally-funded day care, but not for child allowances or even for an increase in the tax deductions for children that would make it easier for some women to work part-time or stay home for a few years while their children are young. Nor have feminists mounted a vigorous campaign against the penalty that our tax code imposes upon marriage, presumably because they wish single motherhood to enjoy the same status as marriage. No fault divorce has benefited some women, but it has harmed many others, and its very existence has tended to weaken both women's and men's willingness to make marriage and family a priority that justifies compromise or even sacrifice in other areas of life.

Conservative women, in contrast, often campaign vigorously for "family values," but more often than not they show no inclination to pay for services that might help less affluent Americans to hold families together. For better or worse, we have moved well beyond the point at which it is realistic simply to exhort people to do the right thing. For numerous and complex reasons, at least half of American marriages may be expected to end in divorce; barely half of adult Americans live in heterosexual marriages (54.4 percent); barely a quarter of all households includes a married couple and children; almost a quarter of all American children are born to a single mother (the figure jumps to almost 70 percent among African-Americans); and a quarter of American children live in a family headed by a single mother. All of these figures represent substantial changes within the last thirty-five years. During that period, women's fertility dropped dramatically, while out-of-wedlock births increased by 26 percent and families headed by single mothers by 13 percent. Nothing suggests that these patterns will automatically reverse themselves in the immediate future, and we may reasonably assume that without substantial support and incentives neither marriages nor two-parent families will regain their standing as foundational social institutions.

There is a disturbing message in all of this: American social institutions today are weaker than those of other Western countries, but elite American women enjoy more advantages and opportunities than women in any other Western nation. (Throughout Western Europe, the rapid rise in immigration and ensuing ethnic diversity is exerting great pressure upon the strength and cohesiveness of social institutions, but has not yet eroded them.) And this hard truth confronts us with a painful question: Must women's gains as individuals come at the expense of social institutions?

Social institutions, by definition, exist to link people into groups. Typically, they possess less authority than the state but more than the isolated individual. Their main purpose and justification lie in their ability to effect goals and facilitate social relations, and in their appropriate sphere they do both better than either the individual or the state. It is further worth noting that, in their absence, the state frequency takes over their functions—often with a marked loss in both social vitality and individual freedom.

Historically, social institutions have often legitimated or reinforced men's advantage over women—an advantage, sad to say, that too many men have abused. No less sad, feminist political struggles have too often sought to correct that imbalance by liberating women from social institutions which, we are learning, tend to crumble without women's commitment. Conservative women's campaigns simply to restore social institutions to some mythical state of normality have singularly failed, primarily because the vitality of social institutions always depends upon their ability to adapt to changing circumstances.

Somewhere between destruction and sterile perpetuation lies the opportunity to modify and revitalize our social institutions to meet the crying needs they were always intended to meet. Of this much, however, we may be sure: No society retains its health and vigor without robust social institutions to draw people into common commitments and to mediate between individuals and the state.

Keith Pavlischek

Just and Unjust War
in the Terrorist Age

VOL. 37, NO. 2, 2002

Americans have always sought to fight "moral" wars, and this is true once more in the war against terrorism. After September 11, rather than prosecuting an indiscriminant and disproportionate Western counter-jihad against the Muslim world, American political and military leaders have conducted—and the American public has supported—a limited, proportionate, and discriminating attack on terrorist organizations and on the nations that aid and abet them. Whether they realize it or not, Americans have been guided in forming their moral intuitions by a long tradition of Christian reflection on the moral questions that surround the use of force—the just war tradition.

This mainstream teaching in Christian moral theology has perennially faced two competing moral views. The first might be called Machiavellian realism, which rejects the idea that war can be a just and moral enterprise. For the realist, the resort to war, when all is said and done, is justified by the requirements of Realpolitik and is merely an extension of day-to-day politics. And for the realist, the conduct of war is, in principle, subject to no moral limitation. The other challenge to the just war tradition is pacifism, which involves the moral renunciation of violence tout court. Between pacifism and realism lies the just war tradition, an understanding of statecraft in which the use of force in the service of justice, order, and peace is both permitted and restrained.

While historically, at least in the past four centuries, the main challenge to the just war moral position has come from some shade of Machiavellianism, in recent decades the challenge to the tradition has come from the pacifist side. Ironically, pacifist objections have frequently been raised by those one might expect to be the principal guardians of the just war tradition—namely, Christian theologians. Here, I will discuss the fundamental contours of the classic just war teaching, suggest why it is relevant to the contemporary war on terrorism, and then defend the tradition against its principal contemporary competitors.

The classical Christian teachings on the use of force are known by the Latin terms *ius ad bellum* (literally, justice toward war) and *ius in bello* (justice in war). The *ius ad bellum* criteria provide guidance about the resort to war. The *ius in bello* criteria place restraints on the means used to wage even a justified war.

Classically, the *ius ad bellum* requires that before war can be waged there must be legitimate authority, just cause, and right intention. Each of these criteria is related to a fundamental political good: *right authority* is related to the political good of order, *just cause* is related to the political good of justice, and *right intention* is related to the political good of peace. As the tradition developed, other criteria were added to the *ius ad bellum* criteria as prudential considerations to guide statesmen when they contemplated the use of force: Is there a *reasonable chance for success*? Will the overall good exceed the harm done (*proportionality*)? Have other means to redress a harm been attempted (*last resort*)? Can peace among the combatants really be achieved (*the end of peace*)?

Traditionally, the criteria for just cause explicitly included one or more of three possibilities: defense against wrongful attack, retaking something wrongly taken, or the punishment of evil. Since the Peace of Westphalia (1648), just cause has been understood in international law almost exclusively as just defense—although in recent years a more expansive concept of just cause has been developed in light of attempts to justify humanitarian intervention for particularly egregious human rights abuses. Right intention has since the time of St. Augustine meant, negatively, that war should not be undertaken on account of implacable hatred, personal glory, or bloodlust. Positively, right intention has insisted that the aim of war is to bring about peace—not a utopian peace, nor the peace of the new heavens and the new earth, but as Augustine called it, a tranquility of order (*tranquillitas ordinis*) in international relations. Legitimate au-

thority classically meant that the right to employ force was reserved to persons or communities with no political superior—that is, to sovereign entities.

Ius in bello consists in the criteria of proportionality of means and discrimination (or noncombatant immunity). The criterion of proportionality of means places restrictions on gratuitous and otherwise unnecessary violence. The criterion of discrimination prohibits the direct and intentional targeting of noncombatants.

In light of September 11, we may ask what makes terrorism, from the just war perspective, a particularly grave evil. The answer would seem obvious. Unlike trained and disciplined soldiers on the traditional battlefield, terrorists deliberately attack innocent and defenseless civilians. Those tutored in the just war tradition will denounce terrorism because such actions are morally forbidden by the principle of discrimination of *ius in bello*. What makes the September 11 attack even more egregious than the attack on Pearl Harbor is that the focus of the Japanese attack was at least on a military target. If war against Japan was justified in the former instance, how it is not justified in this one is hard to see. Thus, from a just war perspective, the call for justice—in the form of retribution by the U.S. government against the perpetrators and their allies—is entirely warranted. President Bush's declaration, "whether we bring our enemies to justice, or bring justice to our enemies, justice will be done," should be applauded.

But the moral judgment against terrorism must not remain confined to the violation of the principle of discrimination and the targeting of civilians. In fact, to understand the evil of terrorism exclusively through the prism of noncombatant immunity is to make a dangerous moral and political concession. Here, we must turn to the *ius ad bellum* criterion of right authority. In recent years, the criterion of legitimate authority has almost entirely been neglected by theologians advancing claims in the just war tradition. At least among American theologians and philosophers, discussions have centered on such peripheral questions as whether the president can use force without the consent of Congress or whether a nation must first seek international approval for the use of force. While these may be important questions, they fail to address the most fundamental issue and thus obscure the full moral significance of the fight against terrorism.

In asking whether war could be waged justly, St. Thomas Aquinas began not with just cause, but with legitimate authority, citing as biblical support Romans 13:1–6. By legitimate authority, Aquinas (and classical Christian thought, more generally) was referring to a political authority to which there was no superior. Beginning with St. Augustine and developing throughout the Middle Ages, Christian thinkers sought to curb violence by declaring illegitimate any use of force by subordinate nobles, private soldiers, criminals, and the church. When confronted with a militaristic Germanic culture in which princes frequently engaged and gloried in combat for private ends, Christian thinkers repeatedly insisted that warfare was a *public* issue. War could not merely be an extreme tool of private parties but had to be a legal instrument, a part of the coercive power of law itself. Historically and theoretically, securing a public monopoly on the use of force was a necessary (though not sufficient) precondition for a peaceful and civilized society. From this perspective, the freelance terrorism of our time is nothing less than a direct assault on this achievement of civilization. Failure by the

United States to act decisively against terrorism in a publicly authorized way may encourage the proliferation of disorder and barbarism of a kind far worse than the private wars of the so-called "dark ages."

This is why—contrary to those who want terrorism to be handled exclusively as a criminal matter—we should not hesitate to embrace the term war to describe our fight against terrorism, especially when governments actively support terrorist groups in their sovereign territory. As James Turner Johnson, the most important contemporary scholar of just war theory, maintains, the tradition

> never distinguished between the use of force by the political community to combat disturbers of justice, order, and peace at home or abroad. The critical distinction made there was between use of force for the public good *(bellum)* and private use of force *(duellum)*. . . . It is, in just war terms, a proper *bellum* for the use of all levels of force as appropriate by the national authority to respond to this profound form of evildoing.

This distinction between *bellum* and *duellem* suggests why, if left unchallenged, the rise of terrorism may foreshadow a return to the barbarism of private war. In fact, a return to private warfare in the twenty-first century is far more ominous, since vengeance is no longer fueled merely by distorted notions of private glory and honor. Today the motive is ideological, ethnic, and a religious fanaticism that knows no bounds. And it is now equipped with technologies capable of inflicting truly inhuman carnage.

But it is not just the potential destructiveness of modern terrorism which raises heightened moral concern. Rather, terrorism by its nature aims to undermine the goods of justice, order, and peace which are secured by political authority. In attacking these political goods, terrorism thus attacks every human being who benefits from them. Johnson writes:

> While the tradition has allowed for the possibility of a war between two states both seeming, because of the complexity of the issues involved, to be just, the kind of violence we today call terrorism is evil in its very nature, because it attacks the foundations of political community itself. The authority to use force to curb and punish terrorism is thus the same authority that seeks to protect the goods of the political order as such. There is no justice in terrorism, only injustice.

Terrorism comes about as close as is possible to what the old moral theologians called *malum in se*—evil in itself. Thus, we should have no qualms when our political leaders refer to terrorists as evildoers. Far from being irrelevant to the war on terrorism, the classic just war tradition developed in large measure precisely to confront and contain the sort of private violence or private war currently practiced by terrorist organizations of all sorts.

Two forms of pacifism constitute the major contemporary moral challenges to the just war tradition. The first is expressed by the "seamless garment" metaphor made popular by the late Cardinal Bernardin of Chicago. This metaphor is intended to convey the notion that Christian opposition to violence must be all of one piece. It is morally inconsistent, the argument goes, to oppose abortion and euthanasia without also opposing capital punishment and war. After September 11, this form

of thinking was evident in a document issued by the Dorothy Day Catholic Worker House in Washington, DC. The statement declared, "Any bombing, anywhere, is a tragedy. Any bloodshed, anywhere, is a tragedy. No war is holy. All war is evil. If we kill as a response to this great tragedy, we are no better than the terrorists who launched this awful offensive. Killing is killing, and killing is wrong."

The problem with the seamless garment argument is that it fails to recognize a moral distinction between quite different types of coercive force. Conceptually, we can distinguish between three distinct uses of force, whether lethal or non-lethal. First, an act that originates or initiates harm of one's neighbor is simply illegitimate violence. When such violence is lethal it is called "murder." This first type of force stands in marked contrast to the two other possible uses of force. The second type involves a personal response to an initial act of violence against one's self, one's family, or one's neighbor. When force is employed in this case, whether lethal or non-lethal, it is typically called vengeance. On one level, such force is reprehensible because it is likely to start a spiral of violence, reprisals, and blood feuds. Nonetheless, it also can be understood to have a certain juridical character. A forceful response to violence is a form of retribution, distinguishable from the original act of violence. The third type is an act of force, either lethal or non-lethal, by a political system with established police and military forces. Rather than allowing the personally offended party to exact vengeance, an established political system makes it possible both to prevent or punish those who originate acts of violence and to halt acts of personal vengeance. This is why political authority is a human good.

The seamless garment position expressed in the Catholic Worker statement makes no moral distinction between the act of a cold-blooded murderer; a vigilante lynch mob formed in response to a murder; and a deputized sheriff's posse that sets out to arrest and if need be kill the murderer. Because they acknowledge no moral distinction between these different types of violence, the proponents of the seamless garment are led to the morally reductionist conclusion that if "we"—the United States—kill in response to terrorist acts, then "we" are just as evil as the terrorists.

This pacifist moral understanding dissents not only from the tradition of just war thinking but also, in important ways, from classical Christian pacifism as well. The classical Christian pacifist position is best articulated in Article 6 of the Schleitheim Articles of 1527, widely regarded as the theological consolidation of Anabaptism and an early expression of Mennonite theology:

> Concerning the sword we have reached the following agreement: The sword is ordained by God outside the perfection of Christ. It punishes and kills people and protects and defends the good. In the law the sword is established to punish and to kill the wicked, and secular authorities are established to use it.

Unlike seamless garment pacifism, classical Christian pacifism affirmed that public authorities have a mandate from God to do what Christians otherwise are supposedly prohibited from doing. While most versions of orthodox Christianity—Catholic, Lutheran, Calvinist, Anglican—entirely rejected pacifism for good biblical and theological reasons, the Schleitheim version of

Christian pacifism at least avoids moral and intellectual incoherence and thus deserves a modicum of moral respect.

The fundamental difference between classical Christian pacifism and the just war views both of the magisterial Reformers and of Roman Catholicism was not whether public authorities were authorized to punish evildoers by capital punishment and by waging war. The biblical witness was simply too perspicuous for any of them to doubt it. Contemporary pacifists are fond of quoting Romans 12:14,19, "Bless those that persecute you; bless and do not curse. Do not take revenge, my friends, but leave room for God's wrath," and then leaving it at that. But classical Christian pacifists understood that Romans 13 holds governing authorities to be agents of God's wrath, ordained by him to "bring punishment on the evildoer." Moreover, Christian believers are enjoined to submit to the governing authorities not out of fear, but for conscience' sake (Romans 13:5). As a result, classical Christian pacifists never suggested that a single word, violence or killing, could be used equivocally to refer both to an initiation of harm to neighbor and to a retributive response to such an act by public authority. By the reasoning of classical Christian pacifism, no moral equivalence exists between acts of terrorism and the response to such acts by legitimate public authority.

Classical Christian pacifists did teach that individual Christians, bound to the higher law of Christ-like love, could not themselves wield the sword. They could maintain a certain degree of moral and intellectual coherence because their pacifism was part of a broader rejection of all political activity for Christians. The classical pacifist prohibition against Christians wielding the sword was part of their general prohibition against

Christians holding judicial and political office of any kind. By making clear distinctions between the responsibilities of Christians and the divinely ordained responsibilities of political rulers, classical pacifists avoided the moral reductionism of the modern seamless garment position. Contemporary seamless garment pacifists, however, reject the implications of this radical dualism, usually out of an interest in "being prophetic." To the extent that contemporary pacifists want to breach this dualism and align the state with the gospel requirement of reconciliation expressed in the Sermon on the Mount, to that extent their policy prescriptions are morally incoherent.

Many contemporary theologians and activists want to reject the apolitical, avowedly sectarian stance of classical Christian pacifism but simultaneously want to reject traditional just war teaching as too bellicose. They have thus sought to create a hybrid out of pacifism and the just war tradition, which has variously been described as "just-war pacifism," "modern-war pacifism," "crypto-pacifism," or the "presumption against war" interpretation of the just war tradition.

This view has gained widespread acceptance in liberal mainline Protestant denominations and among some evangelical Protestants, but it is also reflected in much contemporary Roman Catholic teaching. In their influential 1983 statement *The Challenge of Peace*, for instance, the Roman Catholic bishops of the United States repeatedly asserted that pacifism and just war have equal standing in the tradition of the church. Moreover, that statement claims that the just war tradition shares with pacifism a common "presumption against war." Those who defend a more classical interpretation of the just war tradition insist that this claim is historically mistaken and that, practically, it introduces a perverse logic into moral reflection concerning war.

The first problem with the presumption-against-war view is that as an historical matter it simply has no precedent among the authoritative exponents of the Christian tradition, whether Catholic or Protestant. In *Contra Faustum* 22.74, St. Augustine asks rhetorically, "What is the evil in war?" He responds by rejecting the notion that war's evil is "the death of some who will soon die in any case," adding that, "this is mere cowardly dislike, not any religious feeling." The real evil of war lies in any evil intent of the warriors or of the political authorities who wage war: "love of violence, revengeful cruelty, fierce and implacable hatred of the enemy, wild resistance, the lust of power, and such like." But Augustine immediately adds that "it is generally to punish these things, when force is required to inflict the punishment, that, in obedience to God or some lawful authority, good men undertake wars, when they find themselves in such a position as regards the conduct of human affairs, that right conduct requires them to act, or to make others act in this way."

St. Thomas Aquinas discusses the question "Whether it is always sinful to wage war?" in a section of his treatise on theology devoted to love—*Summa Theologiae* 2-2, Q. 40. Aquinas, summarizing the medieval tradition, argues that war is not intrinsically sinful, and he holds, as we have already seen, that three things are required to justly wage war: legitimate authority, just cause, and right intention. In agreement with just war theorists before and after him, Aquinas moves from the responsibility of political authorities to guard the peace domestically to their responsibility to protect the commonwealth from external threats. "And as the care of the common weal is committed to those who are in authority, it is their business to watch over the common weal of the city, kingdom, or province subject to them. And just as it is lawful for them to have recourse to the sword in defending that common weal against internal disturbances, when they punish evil-doers (Romans 13:4) . . . so too, it is their business to have recourse to the sword of war in defending the common weal against external enemies."

The magisterial Protestant Reformers were in complete agreement on the moral responsibility of political authorities to use lethal force when necessary. Commenting on the Sermon on the Mount, Martin Luther asks, "What does it mean, then, to be meek? From the outset here you must realize that Christ is not speaking at all about the government and its work, whose property is not to be meek . . . but to bear the sword (Romans 13:4) for the punishment of those who do wrong (I Peter 2:14), and to wreak a vengeance and a wrath that are called the vengeance and wrath of God."

John Calvin is even more explicit concerning the obligations of the "civil magistrate." While "the law of the Lord forbids killing," Calvin observes, in order "that murderers may not go unpunished, the Lawgiver himself puts into the hands of his ministers a sword to be drawn against all murderers. . . ." Citing several biblical examples, Calvin argues that since the "true righteousness" of the civil magistrate is "to pursue the guilty and the impious with drawn sword," then if magistrates should rather "sheathe their sword and keep their hands clean of blood, while [in a passage most relevant to contemporary terrorism] abandoned men wickedly range about with slaughter and massacre, they will become guilty of the greatest impiety. . . ." For the same

reason, kings and their peoples must take up arms to wage lawful wars, "for if power has been given them to preserve the tranquility of their dominion . . . can they use it more opportunely than to check the fury of one who disturbs both the repose of private individuals and the common tranquility of all?" (*Institutes* 4, 20, 10 –11)

It should be evident from these (and countless other) classic texts that the Christian just war teaching does not begin with a "presumption against war" but rather with a presumption against injustice focused on the need for responsible use of force to confront wrongdoing. Force, according to the just war tradition, is a neutral instrument that can be good or evil depending on the use to which it is put. The classical Christian writers confirm George Weigel's observation that from its beginning "just-war thinking has been based on the presumption—better, the classic moral judgment—that rightly constituted public authorities have the moral duty to pursue justice, even at risk to themselves and those for whom they are responsible." Indeed, the criteria classified under *ius ad bellum* does nothing else than specify the terms under which those in political power are authorized to resort to force.

But the problem with the presumption-against-war position is not merely historical. More importantly, it introduces a certain perverse logic into moral reflection on the use of military force, a perversity that helps account for the irrelevance of most recent academic and ecclesiastical teaching on the ethics of war.

As we have seen, the resort to military force in the just war tradition has historically come to be defined through the following moral concepts: just cause, competent authority, right intention, reasonable hope of success, last resort, the goal of peace, and overall proportionality of good over harm. However, both historically and in terms of the inner logic of the just war idea, the criteria are not all of equal importance. Just cause, competent authority, and right intention have priority because they are immediately oriented to fundamental political goods. The remaining concerns—last resort, proportionality, reasonable chance for success, and the prospects for peace—must be taken seriously; but being prudential tests, they are, as James Turner Johnson says, "of a qualitatively different character from the deontological criteria" of the first three. Contemporary writers advancing the presumption-against-war position, however, tend to invert these priorities, so that prudential criteria such as last resort (probably the least helpful of the criteria) are presented as being at the center of the tradition.

To draw attention to this inversion of priorities is no mere splitting of academic hairs. The purpose of the just war tradition is not to provide publishing opportunities for academic philosophers, nor is it to provide course material for seminary professors teaching social ethics. Rather, the just war teaching has three quite serious and practical purposes. First, the tradition provides a normative grounding for statecraft, subjecting the use of force to a higher-law ethic. Second, the tradition provides guidance to military commanders, placing their role within the larger context of the moral ends of statecraft. Third, the tradition offers moral guidance for individuals as they conscientiously weigh the question of participation in the use of force and the degree of such participation. For most Americans, it is that last purpose which is most immediately relevant: the just war tradition illuminates the responsibilities of citizens in a self-governing democracy under God.

By inverting the logical priority of the criteria, the presumption-against-war interpretation of the tradition ends up presenting just war as a jumbled collection of abstract moral ideals, utterly disconnected from political and military judgment. Both historically and conceptually, however, the just war approach to the use of force is already in dialogue with the spheres of statecraft and military expertise. Indeed, just war reasoning belongs to, and properly resides with, military commanders and statesmen considering the use of force, not academics. If the mere use of military force is conceived in the first instance as the "problem" to which avoidance is the preferred solution, then just war reasoning is reduced to little more than a moralistic checklist brought in from the outside, external to the task of statecraft.

Properly, therefore, the judgment as to whether a military operation will be successful (the criterion of reasonable chance for success) or will result in greater good than harm (the principle of proportionality) rests with those who have the competence to render such judgments. Put bluntly, it resides with those who know what they are talking about. In almost every instance, that does not include bishops, theologians, and professors. It is the disorienting inversion of logical priorities in the presumption-against-war teaching that explains why, in recent years, we confront the maddening spectacle of theologians who know virtually nothing about military strategy, force structure, and weapons capability holding forth confidently on the likely or unlikely success of a military operation. It accounts for the frequently heard assertion that pacifists and just warriors share a common commitment to military force as a "last resort," the only purported difference being that pacifists believe a last resort is never reached—as if that were a minor difference. It also explains how it can be that so many intellectuals can support the use of force in theory, but also always oppose it in practice.

It is thus unsurprising that statesmen and military commanders who must make responsible and speedy moral judgments simply ignore the posturings of the modern pacifists who would be their moral guides. Modern pacifists offer a blanket moral advice that inevitably counsels "nonviolence" or extreme caution in the use of military force. History, of course, is full of examples of nations that have suffered catastrophes by being overly aggressive and over-extended militarily. This is a lesson from Thucydides' Peloponnesian War; it is arguably a lesson America learned from Vietnam. So, the modern pacifist or cryptopacifist will sometimes get something right. But history also tells us that an insufficiently forceful policy can have disastrous results as well. The classic case is the failure of appeasement in the 1930s, which led to the carnage of the Second World War. The pacifist will always get this wrong.

The moral and strategic limitations of pacifism are again evident in our contemporary war on terrorism. It is plausible that the terrorist attacks on September 11 resulted from the United States' failure to respond aggressively after the first attack on the World Trade Center in 1993, or after the bombing of our embassies in Africa in 1998, or after the attack on the U.S.S. Cole in 2000. In each instance, you needn't do a lot of research to discover what military response—or rather, lack thereof—the pacifists were urging. It is precisely the "seamless monotony" of the pacifists' moral advice that renders their advice morally useless.

A serious debate is now underway concerning national strategy after the conclusion of the Afghan campaign. How aggressively do we pursue terrorists elsewhere using military forces? Do we seek regime termination in nations that continue to sponsor terrorists, such as Iraq? These decisions must be made by wise, prudent, and moral statesmen. But our statesmen are not likely to heed the policy advice of pacifist professors and clerics who believe, by definition, that military forces should be eliminated, who know little or nothing about military capabilities and doctrines, and who misrepresent or misunderstand the core teachings of the just war tradition.

Ultimately, the intellectual source of this pastoral confusion lies with the novel contemporary effort to synthesize the two mutually exclusive moral positions of pacifism and just war. All such attempts fundamentally distort both traditions and render them logically, morally, and theologically incoherent. Just war thinking begins with the belief that in a fallen world, the use of coercion and force, including the use of lethal force by legitimate public authority, is not only permitted but also morally required under certain circumstances. For governments not to use lethal violence to protect the innocent is unjust and dishonors God. The classical pacifist believes that to use force is evil, perhaps in the case of the modern crypto-pacifist a necessary evil, but still an evil. Between these positions, no middle ground exists, and yet that is where the presumption-against-war thinkers have sought to build their intellectual house. Because their resulting hybrids are incoherent, they cannot do the practical political and military work that the just war tradition is designed, precisely, to do.

Which leaves us to suggest that St.

Augustine (and the Augustinians), St. Thomas Aquinas (and the Thomists), Luther (and the Lutherans) and Calvin (and the Calvinists) are, despite their diverse theological perspectives, more reliable guides to reflection on this great contemporary problem than are the vast majority of our contemporary academic experts. A recovery of the authentic just war tradition should be among our first tasks in these perilous times.

VIII.

PEOPLE, POETRY & PROSE

Robert Penn Warren

RELEVANCE WITHOUT MEANING

VOL. 7, NO. 4, 1971

This is the moment of crisis we are constantly being told—the crack-up of the Western World, of the Judeo-Christian tradition, of the American success story. In such a moment, what are we doing here—on this—or any other literary occasion? Are we—to use the sacred word—relevant?

When I first entered the library of Congress in 1944, I didn't come in feeling relevant. A couple of years earlier, in that time of crisis, I had offered my services to the United States Navy, and they had politely declined the offer. Defective vision, they said. So as time passed I got irrelevanter and irrelevanter until I reached the nadir of relevance—which was being the Consultant in Poetry at the Library of Congress.

But one morning my phone rang and a Captain X introduced himself and asked if I was the Consultant in Poetry. Yes, I said. Well, he said, General Y was writing the lyric for a song to inspirit our boys—that was the word he used, "inspirit"—and the General wanted to consult the Consultant in Poetry on a matter of meter. So at one end of the line the General read his lyric and tapped out the meter, and at my end, while he read, I tapped it out with my finger. We did this several times, and I told him it was fine meter. Meanwhile I had memorized most of his lyric, but now all I can remember is two lines:

We are the boys who don't like to brag,
But we sure are proud of our grand old
    flag.

The episode was a great comfort to me. If, in the middle of World War II, a general could be writing a poem, then maybe I was not so irrelevant after all. Maybe the general was doing more for victory by writing a poem than he would be by commanding an army. At least, he might be doing less harm. By applying the same logic to my own condition, I decided that I might be relevant in what I called a negative way. I have clung to this concept ever since—negative relevance. In moments of vainglory I even entertain the possibility that if my concept were more widely accepted, the world might be a better place to live in. There are a lot of people who would make better citizens if they were content to be just negatively relevant.

But, in general, this brand of comfort isn't quite comforting enough. The awareness of crisis has penetrated to the furthest reaches of society. The most illiterate and pot-ridden of dropouts mumble about their identity crises, along with the poets. Stickup men on heroin plead alienation. Time was when the bad news of Spengler's *Decline of the West* was restricted to the more romantic alumni of the University of Heidelberg, the heavy-thinkers of Greenwich Village, and disillusioned graduate students, but now an erstwhile humor magazine spreads the glad tidings of great gloom according to Charles Reich and Lewis Mumford among suburban housewives on the cocktail circuit and investment bankers grieving because their children are apathetic toward hard money and the Republican (or Democratic) Party.

I am not implying that Reich and Mumford are overestimating the gravity of our crisis—pollution, war, race, the cities, bad schools, irresponsible leadership, and all the rest. In fact, I am inclined to think they are underestimating the gravity, in that their diagnosis is not radical enough and their proposed solutions overlook some important aspects of our relation to technology, and at times are not far from old-time revivalism and snake-oil remedies. In brief, they seem to neglect the nature of the human animal—what we used to refer to as Original Sin. In other words, the need for "relevance" is greater than even the prophets of doom, the Black Panthers, Billy Graham, Martha Mitchell, and the Students for a Democratic Society, imagine. But what is relevance?

The most obvious question concerning literature is: What subject matter is appropriate for our time? Almost a hundred and fifty years ago, the young Nathaniel Hawthorne sat in an upper room, totally withdrawn from the real world, and wrote stories. No doubt writing stories was bad enough, but his stories were about the distant past. Later on, still brooding over the past, Hawthorne moved to Concord. But there he had a neighbor who was really relevant. The neighbor certainly didn't write stories, he told people how to live, and he took a very dim view of the past. He was a prophet with a crystal ball and his crystal ball did, as a matter of fact, show some important things about the future. It seems only natural that Hawthorne did not think very highly of his prophet neighbor, any more than the neighbor did of him. Hawthorne and Emerson met on the wood paths of Concord, and passed on, Emerson with his head full of bright futurities and relevances, Hawthorne with his head full of the irrelevant past. As Henry James was to say of them: "Emerson, as a sort of spiritual sun-worshipper, could have attached but a moderate value to Hawthorne's cat-like faculty of seeing in the dark."

We revere Emerson, the prophet whose prophecies came true. But having once come true, those prophecies began to come untrue. More and more Emerson recedes grandly into history, as the future he predicted becomes a past. And what the cat's eye of Hawthorne saw gave him the future—and relevance. He died more than a century ago, but we find in his work a complex, tangled, and revolutionary vision of the soul, which we recognize as our own. Emerson spoke nobly about relevance but Hawthorne *was* relevant.

The moral is that it is hard to tell at any given moment what is relevant. The thing so advertised is likely to be as unrelated to reality as the skirt length is to the construction of the female anatomy. To be relevant, to change our metaphor, merely to a symptom and not to the disease. The question is not that of the topicality of a subject. It is that of the writer's own grounding in his time, the relation of his sensibility to his time, and paradoxically enough, of his resistance to his time. For there must be resistance, and the good work is always the drama of the writer's identity with, and struggle against, his time. John Milton was in the profoundest way a man of the seventeenth century, but writing *Paradise Lost*, under the reign of Charles II, was he in tune with his time?

The relation of topicality to relevance is fascinating. Will *Naked Lunch* or *Portnoy's Complaint* really turn out to be the *Aeneid* of our new Rome? But let's push on to the more radical question: Is poetry per se—taking that as the inclusive term for imaginative literature—relevant in our time?

One could simply state that poetry is unavoidable in any age, that people inevitably demand poetry of one kind or another, and then argue about what *kind* of poetry would make sense now. And indeed, if we take poetry at its broadest meaning of emotive language, there has never been so much poetry as in our age of mass communication. The air waves are full of it, it is heard on the hustings, a million albums of so-called folk-ballads (being sung by some famous voice) are sold every year. Without poetry the advertising copy writer's typing fingers would be paralyzed and the tongue of the P.R. man would cleave to the roof of the mouth. The Congressional Record would, in fact, shrink to the translucent thinness of a dragon fly's wing in bright sunlight.

Let us meditate for a moment on the poetry sometimes to be heard in the Capitol. Marianne Moore has said that her kind of poetry deals with real toads in imaginary gardens. The kind of poetry in the Capitol might often seem very similar to hers. It deals with real solutions to imaginary problems. Sometimes, however, it deals with imaginary solutions to real problems. When genius begins to be inflamed, it deals with imaginary solutions to imaginary problems. But occasionally it ascends beyond the pitch of mortal thought and deals with imaginary solutions to imaginary problems of imaginary people, i.e., the people who are supposed to give the poll-takers their information, creatures more ectoplasmic even than the Economic Man.

But if that kind of poetizing, like that of the Rod McKuens and such, can scarcely touch us where we live—what can? The answer is easy. Any kind that is "real"; for the disease of our time is the sense of being cut off from reality. Man feels that a screen has descended between him and nature, between him and other men, between him and the self. Hence we have the hippie commune, the group grope, drug culture, et cetera.

Let us not think now of topicality and subject matter but of a thing inherent in the very nature of poetry, of imaginative literature, when it realizes its potentialities.

Any kind of poetry is "real" in which there is an awareness of the real stuff language. In our communication-numbed society we are buffeted and drowned in a flood of language, but it is a language that is debased, with the make-do word taking the place of the right word. Worse even, language is used as merely a convenient way of pointing. It becomes bleached out, not a thing expressive in itself. It is no longer a part of experience and an index of the speaker's own reality; and of the reader's or the listener's, too, as he senses the ripple of language in the throat, the deep and complex bodily response. "Rapid reading"—however useful it may be for certain practical purposes—represents the final corruption of language. Poetry—all imaginative literature of any quality—resists "rapid reading;" for here, to subvert Marshall McLuhan's slogan to our purpose, of which he might not approve, the "medium" is indeed the "message," and the "massage" to boot.

For primitive man, the word was not an abstract thing, a device of pointing. If he uttered whatever sound was his word for *tiger*, he was not merely pointing at (literally or symbolically) some remote ancestor of the creature of our time known as *Panthera tigris*, but was also expressing awe, fear, admiration. Nor is William Blake merely pointing at an example of the species *Panthera tigris* when he exclaims:

Tyger, tyger, burning bright
In the forests of the night

It is true that only by specializing language, by developing it to manipulate abstraction, have we gained the vast body of knowledge that is implied, for instance, in the very label *Panthera tigris*, and the vast power that enables us to go purchase a high-powered rifle at Abercrombie and Fitch and fly to Nepal and, as a civilized man, free from awe, fear, admiration, or personal risk, shoot a tiger. But for these and similar advantages we have forfeited a language that would nourish the relations that we now complain of having lost to nature, to others and to ourselves.

But can we have both languages? In so far as a writer is an artist, he creates a new language that unites the primitive density of meanings and depth of feeling with the civilized man's power of abstraction. So Blake, in the next two lines of his poem, can ask the sophisticated theological question:

What immortal hand or eye
Could frame thy fearful symmetry?

In the simplest metaphor of a poem or in the most developed scenes of a fiction, we find another instance of this strange and healing union of regression and sophistication. Here, in a parallel way, we find not merely a verbal language, but a primary language of imagery (the image of metaphor or the image of scene), the pre-verbal "language" that reaches back to infancy and the primitive dark; but it still remains the naked language of our emotional life by which we envisage the object of desire, hate, or fear. At the same time, poetry not only utters itself in such a language that reminds us of our deepest being, but embodies ideas and values; and so its images are, in one dimension, a sophisticated dialactic. The poem or fiction eventuates in "meaning"—no, *as* "meaning."

Literally, the process of composition is, in one degree or another, a movement toward meaning. The writer (like any artist) is not a carpenter who builds the chicken-coop according to a blue-print. If the carpenter has a blue-print he knows exactly what kind of chicken-coop will be forthcoming. But the writer, no matter how clear his idea or strong his intuition of the projected work, can never know what it will "be" or "mean" until the last word is in place—for every word, every image, every rhythm participates in the "being," and the "being" is, ultimately, the "meaning." And the reader is made to share in this process.

We are bombarded all day long by abstractions, by the "truths" of the advertising man, the politician, the preacher, and suddenly we are reminded that every truth that is not lived into, not earned out of experience, either literally or imaginatively, is a lie. We are redeemed from all our would be redeemers—especially from those who would redeem us for their own profit or power—and reminded that we must, after all, redeem ourselves. How? By learning to respect the self and respect experience. Chastened by a keener awareness of human possibility of salvation or disaster, we may be a little more certain of the terms by which the individual fate will be determined. If our current civilization would cut us off from ourselves as well as from nature and other men, we may remember what Henri Bergson says of fiction, and what may be said of all imaginative literature: It "returns us into the presence of ourselves."

Am I offering my own version of old-fashioned revivalism and snake-oil? Not quite. I am not saying that if we read a few good books we can save the country. But I am saying that they might help wake us to the fullness of our own nature, for good and for evil. To wake us, that is, from the torpor in which we now rest—from what Blake called the "single vision and Newton's sleep."

Edmund A. Opitz

THE DURABLE MR. NOCK

VOL. 10, NO. 1, 1975

Albert Jay Nock died too soon, but not before he had nailed to the mast several of the paradoxes which make living in our age so intriguing. He took great delight, for example, in pointing out that American colleges and universities are generally hostile to education and learning. In conversation one day with several college presidents, Nock laid down a number of stringent guidelines for running a college. One of the presidents, somewhat shocked, said, "Why Mr. Nock, if my college were to follow your advice we'd lose most of the faculty and all but about five of the students." Nock pondered this for a moment, and then replied, "That would be just the right size for a college."

The lifelong concern of this man was with the quality of life lived in our civilization; he found the quality poor. Institutions of higher learning, so called, were by no means his only target. Nock was a staunch defender of capitalism, but he was unsparing in his criticism of capitalists for distrusting the free market and for trotting down to Washington begging for handouts. "Businessmen don't want a government that will let them alone," he

wrote; "they want a government they can use." This is not to blame businessmen for being what they are; what they are is simply a reflection of the standards and values held in common by a significant number of people in our society. This is the age of materialism, or the age of Economism, as Nock preferred to call it. Economism is the doctrine that the production and consumption of material wealth is the chief end of man; it is the notion that if only everyone were well-housed, well-clothed, and well-fed, who could ask for anything more? No wonder we suffer from cultural deprivation! We exhibit just that kind of life, Nock remarked, that one would expect to find if he turned over a plank which has been rotting in the muck of Economism!

Every society constructs its institutions in its own image, and thus we get the schools we deserve, the economy we deserve, and the churches we deserve. Albert Jay Nock did his graduate work in theology, and before he joined the staff of *American Magazine* in 1908 he had served Episcopal parishes in three states. In later life he wrote that "when Christianity became organized it immediately took on a political character radically affecting its institutional concept of religion and its institutional concept of morals; and the same tendencies observable in secular politics at once set in upon the politics of organized Christianity." And just as schools offend against education, so churches offend against high religion.

But this is not all; he had other complaints. Universal literacy has been the ruination of literary standards; the rise of mass man has cost the average person much of his zest for life; and every extension of the franchise means that more people vote themselves into serfdom. We have spawned a culture which has made such men as Albert Jay Nock feel superfluous, and we've learned to live so well with what's ailing us that the mere prospect of a cure gives us the jitters!

Nock's "Peculiar" Politics

Nock's aversion to politics is well known. He came by it early, as he tells the story in one of his essays and again in the *Memoirs*. His childhood was spent in Brooklyn not far from an oddly shaped building known as the Wigwam, a political club—"an evil looking affair, dirty and disreputable, and the people who frequented it looked to me even more disreputable than the premises." His distaste for politics never left him, although he was a keen observer of public affairs. I cannot imagine Nock attending a political convention, even as a reporter, as his friend Mencken did. Nock actually did go to the polls once or twice to vote for the candidate of his own choice, Jefferson Davis, of Mississippi. "I knew Jeff was dead," he said, "but I voted on Artemus Ward's principle that if we can't have a live man who amounts to anything, by all means let's have a first class corpse."

Nock was, in one sense of the word, completely a-political, or even antipolitical. He distrusted all forms of social machinery and discounted all mechanical remedies for the ills which bedevil mankind. But in another sense, Nock was what Jacques Barzun called him, "a genuine political mind," in the sense that Nock adhered to the conviction that the only way any person can improve society is by presenting society with one improved unit. Every time Nock was buttonholed by a reformer, planner, socialist, single-taxer, or whatever, he would put one question to him: "Suppose you get your system all set up, what kind of people can you get to administer it—except the kind you've got?" And he answered his own question: "There ain't any!"

Libertarians understand Nock's position because this is the libertarian position, and it is the only sound position—in the long run. It is not a popular position, and there aren't many libertarians around—whatever the label—but numbers don't count. Now, numbers are important to the census taker and the opinion pollster, but numbers do not play the role of a "critical mass" in societal change. The opinion poller wants your opinion, yes or no, on various questions; he has no way of measuring the clarity and the intensity of your convictions. A small number of men and women whose convictions are so sound and so clearly thought out that they will go through hell and high water for them are more than a match for the multitude whose ideas are too vague to generate convictions. A little leaven raises the entire lump of dough; a tiny flame starts a mighty conflagration; a small rudder turns a huge ship. And a handful of people possessed of ideas and a dream can change a nation—especially when that nation is searching for new answers and a new direction.

The idea of a Remnant comes out of the Old Testament; it occurs in several passages, but Nock found the context he wanted and wrote his essay, "Isaiah's Job." The prophet Isaiah began his career around 740 B.C. toward the end of the reign of King Uzziah, which period coincided with the end of an era. The nation was going to the dogs and loving it; but not Isaiah. This young nobleman possessed a brilliant mind, foresaw the decline and fall of his country, and felt impelled to warn his fellow citizens of the impending ruin. Well, this was the last thing they wanted from Isaiah or anyone else, for there's no time for having fun like the mellow period of a nation's decline. Isaiah, discouraged, came to the Lord and asked for a new assignment. "You don't get the point," the Lord told Isaiah; "there is a Remnant out there. They are obscure, unorganized, inarticulate, each one rubbing along as best he can. They don't know each other, and they won't make themselves known to you. But it is they who keep things from going completely to pot, and it is the Remnant who will build society afresh after the collapse. They are listening to you, Isaiah, and your job is to minister to the Remnant." This was also Nock's job, as he himself conceived it.

Nock had an ample but refined capacity for enjoying life, even though he believed that he was living in the last days of a dying civilization. Nock believed he was experiencing the "imperatorship and anarchy" Henry George had predicted. But human nature is resilient, and once the pessimist assures himself that doom is certain, then that's settled and cheerfulness breaks in—like the man in the tumbril en route to the guillotine winking at the pretty girls in the rabble. Or—as Murphy puts it in one of his laws—"If you're sailing on the Titanic you might as well go first class!"

The only way he could serve the Remnant, Nock concluded, was to work for the advancement of his own understanding, which he did. Once he had unearthed a precious nugget of truth and put it on display where all who wished might see, he dropped the matter and went on to the next question. Training reinforced temperament to turn him away from even the slightest propaganda efforts; he never badgered anybody about anything. "Never argue; never explain," he would say with infuriating detachment. Nock believed, correctly I think, that he had uncovered the plain truth of things in the several areas of his interest, and he painstakingly set forth his elucidations in impeccable English, serene in his faith that this fully discharged his duty. The assumption back of this faith is that truth has an internal energy of its own enabling it, if we don't stand in its way, to cut its own channels and gain acceptance in minds ready for it. Trying to make truth palatable for minds not ready for it is no service to the people involved, for it clogs whatever thought processes they have; and truth tampered with is truth lost.

The hard truth is what Nock is talking about; truth with the bark on it, truth unsophisticated by even good intentions, undiluted by ulterior considerations. Are there minds ready for this kind of truth? Nock believed that every society has such minds else it would fall apart. Every society is held together by a select few—men and women who have the force of intellect to discern the rules upon which social life is contingent, and the force of character to exemplify those rules in their own living. These were Nock's chosen people, The Remnant. All else is mass man.

It's a lovely notion, runs the thought, but is it practical? will it work? Well, it appears to be working in Mr. Nock's case, although not all the returns are in and one can't say for sure. Albert Jay Nock's reputation while he lived was limited, and none of his books had much of a sale, except his *Jefferson* and the *Memoirs*. Nock's death, in 1945, passed relatively unnoticed. But then things began to happen; the posthumous publication of a *Journal,* two volumes of letters and a volume of essays; a new edition of the *Memoirs,* the reprinting of five of his out of print books, and the formation of The Nockian Society which has published *Cogitations from AJN.* And in addition to the ten titles and one anthology now in print, there are two books about Nock and two books edited by him. Not bad for a superfluous man!

Person and Legend

You may have gained the impression from what I have said that Albert Jay Nock was a man of monumental likes and dislikes. Indeed he was; and there's more! We have it on good authority that "a man who hates children and dogs can't be all bad." The authority is not W. C. Fields, who is usually credited with this sentiment, but Leo Rosten who used it on one occasion to introduce Fields. Nock's two sons had distinguished academic careers, so Nock had to make up for liking his children by disliking canines. "As against the dog I am in favor of the cat," he wrote to his friend B. I. Bell.

> The dog is nature's prize collectivist and authoritarian; he has the slave mentality and can't be happy out of servitude, a natural-born New Dealer, you know, utterly loveable and given to good works, y'understand, but a ding-busted fool, like your friend Henry Wallace. . . . He has no respect

for himself, no dignity. The cat, on the other hand, has oodles of self-respect and is bungfull of dignity. He is an individualist, and has no illusions about the social order.

Caustic, crotchety, witty, cantankerous; Nock was every one of these, but he was also a lot more. He was a formidable scholar and possessed immense erudition. Van Wyck Brooks worked on the old *Freeman* and says this about Nock:

> He had visited half the universities of Europe . . . (and) could pick up at random, with a casual air, almost any point and trace it from Plato through Scaliger to Montaigne or Erasmus, and I can cite chapter and verse for saying that whether in Latin or Greek he could quote any author in reply to any question. . . . "A diligently forgotten learning is the mother of culture," he once remarked, but he seemed to have remembered everything.

This portrait is drawn a little larger than life, but it is noteworthy that Nock was a legendary figure even to his staff. Nock, was social, but he was not gregarious; his passion for privacy inspired the quip that if you wanted to reach Mr. Nock when he wasn't in his office you had to leave a note under a certain rock in Central Park!

Someone praised Nock for the good things he had done for the bright young people who worked under him on *The Freeman.* "Nonsense," said Nock; "all I've done was to let them alone." "That may be so," the friend responded, "but it would have been different if some one else had been letting them alone!"

In person, Nock was elegant and aloof. One cannot imagine anyone calling him "Al!" Frank Chodorov told me he called him Albert Jay. Paul Palmer edited *The*

American Mercury in the 1930s and published Nock regularly. It was "Mr. Nock" for several years, Palmer tells us, even though the two men had frequent contact. "The first time I called him Albert to his face was somehow like my first cigar, my graduation from boot camp in the Marine Corps, my first hour at a desk marked EDITOR. I was a man." Nock certainly inspired respect among his associates, but those who knew him well, said a friend, found him "tender, sympathetic, and kindness itself." A select few were lifelong friends, both men and women, here and abroad.

Five Criteria of Culture

As the man, so the style. It appears simple, but try to imitate it! "It's not so much *what* you say," his friend Mencken told him, "It's *how* you say it." Nock's lucid style mirrors the clarity and coherence of his thought. This critic of the quality of life attained in our culture had worked up a set of precise measuring rods to determine where our civilization falls short, and by how much. Nock surveyed the high points of the human drama throughout history and concluded that the finest cultures were those which encouraged a full and balanced expression of the five fundamental social instincts of man; or, as we might prefer to say, the five basic urges, drives, or potencies of human nature. What are these five claimants for expression? Let's begin with the most familiar, with what Nock referred to as the instinct for accumulation and expansion; that is, the desire to make money and to exert influence, to turn a profit and wield power. Now this instinct represents but one-fifth of the horsepower latent in human nature, but it has crowded out the other four, Nock charges, and has con-

structed our lopsided society in its own image. What are the neglected instincts? They are, as Nock lists them, the instinct of intellect and knowledge, of religion and morals, of beauty and poetry, of social life and manners. These four, Nock says, have been "disallowed and perverted."

The charge that our civilization— since the Enlightenment—has permitted full expression to only one instinct is but another way of phrasing Nock's allegation that this is the Era of Economism, a period when people attach the highest value in life to the production and consumption of wealth. Take my word for it, Nock is not attacking the market economy; he is telling us that the market alone cannot sustain the market economy. The market is a universal human institution; trade and barter is as old as mankind. Wherever the human community exists there is a division of labor and a swapping of goods. So long as mankind survives on this planet there will be markets, and this will be true even under authoritarian regimes. The market, yesterday, today, and forever; but not the market economy. The market economy is a contingent thing; it has come into being in certain areas of the globe at certain periods and chunks of it now disappear daily before our eyes. There's no miracle of parthenogenesis by which the market can give birth to the market economy all by itself; the market does not institutionalize itself as the market economy without help from moral values and the law.

We live on a planet where almost everything is scarce relative to human demand, and therefore we must economize. To "economize" means to conserve scarce resources, which we do by attempting to diminish inputs while maximizing outputs. In other words, the more-for-less mentality is built into economic action, and that's the danger. Unless this frame of mind is counterbalanced by noneconomic forces, the more-for-less attitude degenerates into the something-for-nothing mentality—as has happened to us. When a nation is permeated by the something-for-nothing spirit it will invariably set up a corresponding power structure designed to transfer wealth legally from producers to pressure groups. Taxation for all, subsidies for a few. This power structure is the state, which Nock labelled The Enemy, and which he clearly distinguished from government. "My point is," he wrote in 1944, "that if the State were limited to purely *negative* interventions which I enumerated, and had no oversize power beyond that, then it wouldn't be the State any more. It would then be *government* only. . . . The point is only that when Society deprives the State of power to make positive interventions on the individual—power to make positive coercions on him at any point in his economic and social life—then at once the *State* goes out of existence, and what remains is government."

How do we put the state out of business? Well, of course, we need the correct analytical tools in economic and political theory; but these won't carry us very far if the prevailing view of human life and human nature is warped and one-sided. In a culture where every other facet and drive of our nature is subordinated to the instinct for accumulation and expansion the market economy is bound to give way. If we deny a balanced and harmonious expression to all sides of our nature—to the claims of intellect and knowledge, religion and morals, beauty and poetry, social life and manners—then these repressed and frustrated drives will have their revenge. Mass man will come to the fore and run the show, while The Remnant is driven underground.

Three Influences on AJN

Three men played a large role in Albert Jay Nock's life: Francis Rabelais, Thomas Jefferson, and Henry George. The first two pose no problem. Rabelais was a literary man of genius whose appetite for life helps us keep the human comedy in proper perspective. Jefferson was a man of integrity, about as a-political as a politician can be, and a champion of human liberty. It's the third name that's somewhat of a puzzler. How could Nock, the arch-individualist, be attracted to a scheme which, beginning with the finest intentions in the world, ends up with a blueprint for a society in which the agency which already wields the police power now assumes the enormous power inherent in the authority to allocate sites and resources?

Nock called himself a Single Taxer, but as we might expect, he was a maverick here too. Shortly after the appearance of *Our Enemy, The State*, Leonard Read wrote to Nock to compliment him on his marvelous book; but how, Read asked, "can an intelligent man like yourself advocate the Single Tax"? To which Nock responded, "Dear Mr. Read: I do not advocate the Single Tax; I merely believe in it."

In a letter to Henry Mencken, Nock wrote, "Henry George was mighty near the world's ablest man of the nineteenth century, and his economics are sound to the core." Now, George was without doubt the most eloquent economist who ever wrote—which is not to say a great deal; many of his writings are models of English prose. George embraced the economics of Smith and the Manchester School, put great emphasis on Ricardo's law of rent, adopted the anti-Statist ideas of the early Herbert Spencer, and suffused the whole with a passionate concern that the inherent, natural rights of each individual to life, liberty, and property be given full expression. The rights of persons are being impaired, George argued, from two directions: first, there is the unjust use of the taxing power to transfer money from one set of pockets to another; and, secondly, there is the power of the landowner to deprive the producer of a percentage of all he produces as the price of being allowed to produce anything at all! George proposed to remedy both these ills at once by abolishing taxation and paying for the costs of government out of the monies received by the political appropriation of the full rental value of land.

This reminds one of feudalism, where all land is held of the king, as a condition of his sovereignty and becomes a prime source of his revenue. It is not difficult to perceive that George's remedy is a kind of neofeudalism. Human beings occupy space, and the sites and resources they need are scarce. The allocation of these scarce goods is a function of ownership, for it is the owner of a good who determines how it shall be used and by whom. If the ownership of land is not private and multiple, then it must be political and unitary; but ownership there must be. The system of private, multiple land ownership is not perfect, but individuals within this scheme do have the opportunity to haggle, bargain, negotiate, and contract vis-à-vis millions of private owners; whereas, under any conceivable alternative it is individuals versus the omnipotent political apparatus.

So much, then, for AJN, our genial critic of life and manners. Some sound instinct kept Nock from ever becoming a reformer, in the usual sense. He was never a tub thumper for some system; never an organization man. He was, to the contrary, a lifelong learner. And because he spent a lifetime educating himself he is able to open all sorts of doors for us. With some help from Albert Jay—and a little bit of luck—we, too, may become superfluous!

Jere Real

THE PLAYWRIGHT AS BOHEMIAN TORY

VOL. 11, NO. 2, 1976

ONE does not usually think of the late Sir Noël Coward, that ubiquitous eminence of the British theatre for five decades, as being particularly a "political" dramatist. More often than not, public recollection of this playwright tends to recall his international celebrity, his status as world traveller and *bon vivant*; others remember his composition of witty ("Mad Dogs and Englishmen") or sentimental songs ("I'll See You Again" or "Someday I'll Find You"), or his stage and screen appearances. Even critics and students of the theatre appraising his career generally begin by acknowledging his wide-ranging versatility and then tend to concentrate their attentions on his major, most frequently staged comedies. Those plays (*Hay Fever, Private Lives, Blithe Spirit, Design For Living*, and *Present Laughter*) are characterized by their clever dialogue, a lightning-fast repartee, and the sparkling, yet blasé, sophistication with which they dispatch the stylish indulgences of the clever, such little pleasures of life as a menage a trois, adultery, spiritualism, or general Bohemian nonconformity. Even his final play, the three-part *Suite in Three Keys*

(recently produced in abbreviated form in New York), which dealt in part with homosexuality, was voted by the Outer Critics Circle as the "best comedy" of the 1974 season. Although Coward achieved his first great success in the 1920s with a controversial play about mother fixation and drug addiction (*The Vortex*), the critical propensity in the years since has been to categorize him as a comic playwright of superficial concerns.

Yet, an examination of the dramatist's total canon of work reveals him as an author who frequently questioned, and often set himself against, the prevailing social and political tides of his times. For example, Coward commented unfavorably many times about those in British political life who, through their policies, reduced his nation's power and influence in international affairs. Indeed, this writer of sophisticated comedy also wrote often commending nationalism, endorsing patriotism and tradition, praising the class system, and favoring the "common sense" approach of an enlightened middle class to that of pretentious intellectuals of the progressive Left in solving social ills. He also saluted bravery in battle in an era when most influential voices in the theater (and the arts, generally) were becoming increasingly anti-military. His views, coming when the world's theater espoused one school after another of despair and nihilism—from the Marxist-oriented social realism of the 1930s through the Existentialists up to the Absurdists, mark Coward as either a brave eccentric among the fashionable playwrights of his time or as a writer with a distinctly individualized, but nonetheless conservative, point of view.

Professor Robert Schuettinger, in his book, *The Conservative Tradition in European Thought,* suggested that the essence of true conservatism lies in its being an attitudinal disposition rather than a consistent ideology; thus, a conservative may desire simultaneously order in society and the toleration of personal nonconformity, he can doubt the existence of equality in the abstract but hope for the greatest variety in human experience. This combination—the orderly society combined with considerable expression of individual eccentricity—exists in our time, almost as nowhere else, in the England of a writer such as Noël Coward.

IN 1930, after several years of success in the theater had already granted Coward both fame and wealth, he wrote a drama of World War I, *Post Mortem,* which remains one of the more curious plays of our century in its theme. Although *Post Mortem* never received a major production on stage, it deserves attention because of its message among the war plays of the 1930s. Set in the trenches of World War I in its opening scene, the play is constructed in what must be termed reverse flashbacks; that is, the characters introduced as soldiers in the opening moments are shown

a sequence of scenes of their future lives after the war has ended. Soldiers and their families are visited by the spirit of John Cavan, a comrade fatally wounded in the first scene. The dying man's spirit goes forward in time to see if the ideals the war allegedly was fought for have been carried out in the peace that followed. Although the play is bitter in its tone, it does endorse ultimately some aspects of human behavior during war, suggesting that man often aspires to and attains higher levels of individual morality—superior levels of personal idealism—during the pressure of combat than he is capable of achieving in peacetime. When wars end, Coward argues in this play, man quickly reverts to his naturally baser instincts: greed, stupidity, the inability to love, and the failure to show compassion for others. The play is a curious switch on most anti-war drama of the period which tended to argue that war was evil and that if man could overcome his capacity for violence and aggression, humanity might be improved or saved. As Coward sees it, war is futile not because of its inherent evil but because, as one character in his play suggests, no one ever learns anything from it. The flaw is not in the act, but in the man. Given man's inherently flawed nature, an individual's conduct in wartime generally is more highly motivated than that of peacetime. "War is no evil compared with this sort of living," he has his hero say after viewing the petty existence of the war's survivors:

> War at least provides the opportunities for actions, decent instinctive clear actions, without time for thought or scariness, beyond the betrayal of fear and common sense, and all those other traitors to humanity which have been exalted into virtues.[1]

Obviously, the dramatist was not praising war, per se, however, he was attacking the manner in which peace allows complacent men to forget the ideals for which they have fought and sacrificed.

Coward again stressed this idea some thirty years later in a poem entitled "The Battle of Britain Dinner, New York, 1963." The poem marks the occasion of an annual memorial salute to the participants of the 1940s air war. There are toasts, a raising of glasses by the survivors "trying to make believe that their sacrifice was worthwhile. . . .":

> They flew out of life triumphant,
> leaving us to see
> The ideal that they died for humiliated
>   and betrayed
> Even more than it had been betrayed at
>   Munich
> By those conceited foolish, frightened old
>   men.[2]

This attack on postwar leadership by Coward is coupled with an equally scathing literary assault on the "angry young men" of British letters who, as the author sees it, "disdain our great heritage" and who were

> Seeking protection in our English sanity
> And spitting on the valiant centuries
> That made the sanity possible.[3]

This strong strain of nationalism is found elsewhere in Coward's work. His spectacular chronicle play-with-music, *Cavalcade,* produced in 1931, often has been cited as his most fervently nationalistic work. That huge production did performed for the stage the same function that Galsworthy's nine-novel *Forsythe Chronicles* had for the novel by tracing the growth and changes in a family against the backdrop of historical events

from the end of the nineteenth century to the 1930s. Coward's play included scenes coinciding with the Boer War, the death of Queen Victoria, the sinking of the Titanic, World War I and the Armistice, and, finally, a depressing nightclub locale in the thirties where there was sung the despairing "Twentieth Century Blues." The attribution of nationalism in this work derived primarily, from its final scene in which a gigantic illuminated Union Jack filled the stage while the entire cast (and the audience) sang "God Save the King."

Perhaps the most overtly nationalistic work in which the dramatist presented his innate conservatism is his *This Happy Breed,* a drama of middle-class life, written in 1939 just prior to the outbreak of World War II. It is the story of the Gibbons family set in a London suburb between 1919 and 1939, from the end of one war to the eve of another. Like *Cavalcade,* actual events serve as backdrop to fictional incidents: the General Strike of 1926, the Abdication of Edward VIII, the Munich Crisis of 1938, and, of course, the final summer of peace before the invasion of Poland. The focal character is the head of the family, Frank Gibbons, who gives us his views on everything as it happens—war, peace, love, human nature, traditional British liberties, the Germans, the Japanese, the League of Nations, and communism (a consideration necessitated by his son's flirtation with radicalism). Through Gibbons, Coward develops two themes: first, human nature is responsible for most of the world's evils and, second, lofty idealism, although sincerely motivated, is a poor substitute for common sense in solving most of the crises in one's life, whether domestic or political.

Gibbons is, naturally, the symbolic "common man," not unlike that character who kept changing costumes in

Robert Bolt's more recent drama, *A Man for All Seasons.* Gibbons, however, is a good deal more admirable. He is an affirmation of the best in the average man, the enlightened as opposed to the narrow-minded middle-class citizen. In several conversational exchanges with his son, he dismisses the "Bolshie business": "That's what all these social reformers are trying to do, trying to alter the way of things all at once."[4] At another point, he tells the young man that "it's up to us ordinary people to keep things steady."[5] When his son blames the existing order for social injustices, Gibbons tells him:

> where I think you go wrong is to blame it all on systems and governments. You've got to go deeper than that to find out the cause of most of the troubles of this world, and when you've had a good look, you'll see likely as not that good human nature's at the bottom of the whole thing.[6]

Elsewhere in the play, Gibbons is highly critical of the appeasement of Germany, scoffs at isolationism when someone suggests the threat of Japan is very far away, and suggests the League of Nations has been completely ineffectual in curbing aggression. He hopes "we shall never find ourselves in a position again when we have to appease anybody!"[7] He is equally blunt about pacifism; to him, a pacifist is merely someone trying to bring down his own country from within:

> People who go on a lot about peace and good will and the ideals they believe in, but somehow don't believe in 'em enough to think they're worth fighting for . . . the trouble with the world is, Frankie, that there are too many ideals and too little horse sense.[8]

This play's bold conviction about the stabilizing role of the British middle class—a group secure in its habits, traditions, attitudes and ideals—show Coward to be a dramatist squarely in the tradition of such earlier writers as Edmund Burke or Samuel Johnson.

His distrust of intellectuals and their solutions to problems is clearly revealed again in Coward's 1947 production, *Peace in Our Time,* a play taking its title from Neville Chamberlain's notorious reference upon his return from Munich. This drama is a study of the attitudes of a populace facing enemy occupation. In this instance, Britain has been occupied by Nazi forces, Parliament is being opened by Hitler, Goering, and Goebbels. Churchill has been executed, and the Royal Family is isolated at Windsor Castle. The play's attention is centered, however, on average citizens again, a cross-section of types who encounter one another in a pub, the *Shy Gazelle.* The question of how a conquered people confront their situation is posed. Coward juxtaposes an idealistic, emotional response (patriotism) against a cynically detached, intellectual view (reason). Should a citizen be "reasonable," adjust, accept, compromise, in other words, collaborate? Or should a person respond emotionally, accepting the more sentimental appeal of idealism and patriotism, the appeal of "King and Country"?

The choice of intellectual cynicism or emotional involvement was one Coward had posed for himself early in the war years. In his second volume of autobiography, *Future Indefinite,* he described how he found himself safe in America in 1940 at the time England faced Germany alone. He was naturally concerned about family and friends and their safety, but he wrote that he had to consider for the first time how he felt about England itself. His reflections and final resolution is one of the more ringing affirmations of national patriotism by a literary figure of the period:

> I had no cynical detachment where my emotions were concerned. . . . I did love England and all it stood for. I loved its follies and apathies and curious streaks of genius; I loved standing to attention for "God Save the King"; I loved British courage, British humor, and British understatement; I loved the justice, efficiency, and even the dullness of British colonial administration. I loved the people, the ordinary, the extraordinary, the good, the bad, the indifferent. . . .[9]

This same consideration—intellectual pragmatism or emotional idealism—is argued in the pub in *Peace in Our Time*. The chief spokesman for collaboration is Chorley Bannister, the editor of a small, intellectual journal pretentiously entitled *Forethought*. He tells those who wish to oppose the Nazi occupation that sentiments like patriotism are "conditioned by environment and education and habit and propaganda. Patriotism is not an inevitable, fundamental part of human nature."[10] Chorley has been a pacifist in the thirties and derides all expressions of nationalism. He is rebuked, however, at one point by a woman who detests the idea of an Englishman bargaining with his conquerors. She despises Bannister's political relativism (he has moved from pacifism in the 1930s to a procommunist position of anti-imperialism to, ultimately, that of a pro-Nazi sympathizer):

> You and your kind pride yourselves on being intellectuals, don't you? You babble a lot of snobbish nonsense about art and letters and beauty. You consider yourselves to be far above such primitive emotions as love and hate and devotion to a cause. You run your little highbrow magazines and change your politics with every wind that blows.[11]

The play's patriots are further enhanced in their position when at the end of the drama Britain is being liberated and the persons in the pub who have always opposed Bannister are united in an anti-Nazi underground movement.

Coward's other dramatic statement about national pride in war time was in a motion picture he wrote, the impressive *In Which We Serve,* in which Coward acted, co-directed, produced, and also wrote the music. The film embodied many of the same elements as *This Happy Breed* and *Peace in Our Time.* For a wartime film, it is characterized by a remarkable understatement dramatically. Ostensibly, it is the story of a destroyer and its crew who recall past experiences in their lives and naval service in a series of flashbacks as they cling to a raft after their ship has been sunk. Again, the views and life of a cross-section of the English public are given, and an admirable image of humans enduring real crisis emerges. Of course, the ship on which they served was more than a wartime vessel; it was the ship of state, the symbolic microcosm of Britain in duress. There were scenes of everyday people enduring the terrors of the Luftwaffe raids, and of the evacuation of Dunkirk, but the image that emerged was of a people grimly determined to save their nation, a picture unlike the super-heroics of many World War II films. Coward's film remains a moving document even when viewed today, a statement that cannot always be made of many Hollywood films of the period.

In the postwar years, Coward's dramatic work turned again to comedy, but many of his plays tended to be more topical in their humor than the well-known comedies of the twenties and thirties. Many critics during the fifties attempted to write Coward off as a playwright whose day in the limelight had passed; although some of his plays still commanded commercial success, he was dismissed by many as a "dated" commodity. Quite possibly, part of the critical animosity during the postwar years stemmed from Coward's tendency to satirize in these new comedies many of the sacred cows of contemporary political liberalism. For example, in his play, *South Sea Bubble* (written in 1949 and also staged in some places as *Island Fling*), he humorously attacked the notion that all colonial possessions ought to be given their independence. In this drama, the little island of Samola is about to be given control of its own affairs, but its citizens do not want this break with the imperial tradition. Doubtless, the playwright used Samola—an actual island possession—as his setting because he knew that in 1855, the ruler of Samola, King Kefumalani II, personally wrote to Queen Victoria begging her to allow his islands to have the privilege of belonging to the British Empire. In any event, *South Sea Bubble* pits a liberal-minded colonial governor, Sir George Shotter, against a British-educated (Eton) native leader who resists his islands' being given "self-government." As the governor's aide explains the situation:

> Most Samolans are still Empire minded. You see they've been happy and contented under British rule for so many years that they just don't understand when they're suddenly told that it's been nothing but a corrupt, capitalist racket from the word go.[12]

The old native leader, Punalo, who opposes independence, regularly argues with the governor telling him that minor economic gradations of caste provide the natives with incentives to work by allowing those who succeed the privileges of their improved social status. The governor has proposed the removal of coin-operated facilities in public conveniences of buildings of the island as his latest assertion of complete democracy. Punalo refutes the governor's theories by pointing out that the removal of first and second class distinctions in favor of an overall tourist class on the island's boat service has caused such a decline in business that the service has been forced into liquidation. About the governor's scheme to democratize the lavatories, Punalo says:

> Even in the most Utopian Welfare States, privilege is accepted as a natural perquisite of authority. In the Soviet Union itself, that Marxist paradise of Left-Wing Intellectuals, there is no recorded instance of the late Mr. Stalin queueing up for a public lavatory.[13]

The play's plot did have some romantic complications, but its thrust throughout was on the political folly of postwar "progress." Coward also managed to work in many of his famed one-line witticisms; at one point, a visiting novelist, Boffin, discusses the day's political realities with a native leader, Hali, who favors self-determination:

> HALI: It is most dismal to lose something of sentimental value.
>
> BOFFIN: Yes. Like India.[14]

IN HIS 1951 comedy, *Relative Values,* similar conservative questions were raised, that time about the possibility of social equality. That drama is a comedy about a young man of good family and high social standing who is about to marry a Hollywood actress who is both vulgar and outrageous in her conduct. The marriage ultimately is defeated by the efforts of the servants in the young man's household who are horrified at the idea of social equality. At the end of the play, the butler, Crestwell, who has been active in opposing the marriage makes a toast to "the final inglorious disintegration of that most unlikely dream that ever troubled the foolish heart of man—Social Equality."[15]

Earlier in his career, Coward had visited the Soviet Union and recorded his impression of that visit in his autobiography. In a passage that must have severely distressed Marxist-inclined intellectuals of the 1930s, he denounced the dulling conformity of the socialist state and praised the benefits of a society with class distinctions:

> [I]t was evident that there was something sadly lacking in me, some missing core of human understanding, that debarred me from sharing, with so many intelligent and thoughtful people, the belief that communism, as practiced by the Russians, was progressive and hopeful for the future of mankind.[16]

To the visiting playwright, the Soviet Union appeared to be both a physical and mental prison:

> Here, in this vast territory through which my train was carrying me, there seemed to be no semblance of freedom for the ordinary citizen. He was spied upon, regimented, and punished, frequently without even being aware that he had committed a crime.[17]

The dramatist's approval of a social order based on qualitative distinctions followed:

> Personally I have always believed more in quality than quantity, and nothing will convince me that the levelling of class and rank distinctions, and the contemptuous dismissal of breeding as an important factor of life can lead to anything but a dismal mediocrity.[18]

When viewed against such earlier statements as these, the satiric comedy of *Relative Values* takes on far greater impact.

In his other postwar works, Coward does not touch as obviously on political and social issues. Nevertheless, in his 1952 drama, *Quadrille,* he wrote in a admiring way about the virtues of the United States, a land he had come to view as a second home. In an era of "Yankee, Go Home!" he once more was striking a contrary mood. In that play, an American railroad man urges an English woman to visit the United States, saying she would recognize "its valour and forgive its young vulgarities."[19]

His 1954 comedy, *Nude With Violin,* also saw Coward poking fun at a prevailing artistic fashion, "modern" painting. In this play, the comic plot was built on the possibilities for charlatanism provided by such painting.

If the political views of Noël Coward, as they are variously revealed in his writing, were so conservative, one may ask, how then can his penchant for endorsing nonconformist behavior be explained? After all, he treats marriage and adultery in a cavalier fashion in several plays, notably in *Private Lives*: he presents an amusing and delightful *ménage* of Leo, Otto, and Gilda in *Design for Living*; and he argues for the legalization of homosexuality for consenting adults in *Suite in Three Keys*. The answer lies, I think, in the manner in which these acts are presented. In every instance, such nonconforming behavior is shown to be individualized; true, it is the individual's right, but it is also his or her responsibility. In other words, the problem—if there is one—is the individual's, not society's. Coward may seem to endorse a "new morality," but he also implies that personal morality is ultimately just that, personal. That might be seen as a kind of libertarian position. This attitude, coupled with his usual praise of common sense, is seen clearly in his long poem, *Not Yet the Dodo,* in which some middle-class parents, General and Lady Bedrington, discover that their son, who has entered the theater, is a homosexual living in London with a young Irish boy. After several meetings with the pair and a lot of rumors cause natural parental anguish, Lady Bedrington determines to come to grips with the problem. She confers with a servant who has worked for the family for years (and who has been Barry's "Nanny"), and they proceed to talk out the situation, one they had never once considered a possibility. Maggie, the servant, again is an endorsement of down-to-earth common sense. She embarks, Coward says, "upon her speech for the defense" to her worried employer:

"If you want my opinion," she said, "I think
We're both of us wasting our breath,
You can't judge people by rule of thumb
And if we sit gabbing till Kingdom Come
We'll neither one of us sleep a wink
And worry ourselves to death.

People are made the way the're made
And it isn't anybody's fault.
Nobody's tastes can quite agree
Some like coffee and some like tea
And Guinness rather than lemonade
And pepper rather than salt."[20]

She concludes her long speech saying she ultimately is more interested in the son, Barry, as a person than she is in his sexual predilections.

In summary, therefore, it might be said that Coward's attitude was one of maximum toleration of independence and nonconformity for the responsible individual. However, on larger societal issues of order, patriotism in times of crisis, tradition, national loyalty, skepticism about man's perfectability, and the inherent flaws of human nature, he was consistently conservative. Because of these views and his accompanying total trust in the intelligence of many average men, he qualifies, perhaps as much as any literary figure of our time, for that appellation Russell Kirk so frequently invokes, the Bohemian Tory.

Notes

1. Noël Coward, *Post Mortem* (Garden City, New York: Doubleday, Doran & Co., Inc., 1931), 96.
2. Noël Coward, "The Battle of Britain Dinner, New York, 1963," in *Not Yet the Dodo and Other Verses* (New York: Doubleday and Co., Inc., 1968), 82.
3. Ibid., 83.
4. Noël Coward, *This Happy Breed*, in *Play Parade*, vol. IV (London: William Heinemann Ltd., 1954), 462.
5. Ibid., 480.
6. Ibid., 479.
7. Ibid., 542.
8. Ibid., 553.
9. Noël Coward, *Future Indefinite* (New York: Doubleday & Co., Inc., 1954), 146.

10. Noël Coward, *Peace in Our Time,* in *Play Parade,* vol. V (London: William Heinemann, Ltd., 1958), 153.
11. Ibid., 211.
12. Noël Coward, *South Sea Bubble* (London: William Heinemann, Ltd., 1956), 3.
13. Ibid., 22.
14. Ibid., 114.
15. Noël Coward, *Relative Values,* in *Play Parade,* vol. V (London: William Heinemann, Ltd., 1958), 371.
16. Noël Coward, *Future Indefinite,* 36.
17. Ibid., 36–7.
18. Ibid., 37.
19. Noël Coward, *Quadrille* (Garden City, NY: Doubleday & Co., Inc., 1955), 138.
20. Noël Coward, *Not Yet the Dodo,* 106.

Marion Montgomery

The Poet and the Disquieting Shadow of Being: Flannery O'Connor's Voegelinian Dimension

VOL. 13, NO. 1, 1977

Out of the formless stone, when the artist
   united himself with stone,
Spring always new forms of life, from the
   soul of man that is joined to the soul of
   stone.
—T. S. Eliot, "Choruses from The Rock"

It has not been popular in our recent literary criticism to bring the arguments of the historian of ideas or the philosopher or theologian to bear centrally upon literary concerns, since it is supposed that such emphases must distort the aesthetic center of art. Like the student who resists the analysis of a poem on the ground that analysis destroys poetry, his teacher may resist the introduction of problems of epistemology, except as they may be thematic materials of a particular poem like Wordsworth's "Tintern Abbey." We become uneasy before the possible threats to aesthetic integrity. We would prefer to limit our concern to an encounter of sensibility with art in an arena removed from the larger context of mind's varied address to the problem of being. But concerns other than the strictly aesthetic are inescapable; the aesthetic moment cannot be sustained as timeless, a moon feast of sensibility in art's Eden. Disquieting

shadows intrude, willy-nilly. Yet intruding argument is not necessarily the defeat of aesthetic's value. It may be rather that an enlargement of argument offers one—the student of literature, for instance—the excellent advantage of enlarging upon those aesthetic virtues of art which he may have learned of in such specialties as the New Criticism. The aesthetic purity of a work considered in and of itself, valuable and necessary as that consideration is, must yet prove too limiting upon the work, as close reading of Croce and Eliot and Ransom and a host of critics must demonstrate. It is inadequate because the work necessarily encroaches upon provinces of thought separate (or seemingly separate) from the aesthetic the moment the work becomes more than the poet's or reader's exercise in craftsmanship. In the literature of "alienation," as we see it stretching from Milton to the newest *New Yorker* story, alienation is not simply a theme upon which the poet practices variation. It is an idea of an experience in whose depths stirs a devouring problem, growing to the point that it threatens not only individual sanity, but the whole community of mind. The aesthetic experience of *Paradise Lost* or *The Dubliners* or *The Waste Land* gives rise to a disquiet which a term paper or critical article on images and motifs will not allay. That disquiet begins to elicit the aid of all the faculties of the intellect and all the disciplines of the mind, turning the mind outward from its restricted attention in the work toward questions of being itself. The dissociation of sensibilities, the problem of objective correlatives in plays and poems—these do not yield comfortably under the authority of aesthetics alone, neither to poet nor reader.

One begins, then, to discover that Keats's concern for "negative capability" is a concern in him beyond the demands of art; what is at stake for Keats is mind itself, and the mind's vision. The individual object, whether it be an object of his aesthetic sensibility or of his senses alone, impinges upon that complex continuity of mind in time (which we certify as tradition) and upon its deepest hungers for the timeless. The poet finds that his word, in spite of his intentional or innocent attempt to protect it from deeper terrors, bears marks of the secret hunger of mind and heart. One encounters in the poet's word the drama of mind and heart in quest of some Word in the word, of some sustaining will, human or immortal or both. We may observe, almost as a measure of the poet's greatness, his troubled engagement of questions larger than the aesthetic. When Faulkner chooses to stand at the center of our attention, whether we be aesthetician, philosopher, scientist, or simply the mythical "general reader," we find he addresses himself as poet to a metaphysical inclusiveness in his desire to restore the community of mind. He speaks of art in its moral and spiritual dimensions. The poet's duty, he says in his Nobel acceptance speech, is to the complexity of man's "soul," to man's "spirit," which is "capable of compassion and sacrifice and endurance." The poet's voice "can be one of the props, the pillars to help [man] endure and prevail."

Faulkner makes a very large claim for the poet, or rather he enunciates a very large responsibility in the poet. We may be hesitant before this claim because we hear in it a continuation of that old "romantic" invasion of the provinces of intellect whereby, since the Renaissance, the poet increasingly assumes the responsibilities of the priest, philosopher, prophet, and politician. But the suggestion of inordinate usurpation does not make the claim absolutely invalid, any more than it proves the poet to have abandoned his responsibilities to aesthetics by his presumptions. Alas, the position Faulkner announces requires the considerable analysis of the metaphysician to set the relation of the poet to philosopher or prophet, an analysis freed of the specialized thinker's territorial concerns. Our world has scant respect for metaphysics. The "place" of the mind, Lucifer argues, is its own; since Milton, each mind's place has increasingly shrunk in the sometimes desperate and usually arrogant establishment of specialized sovereignties. And nowhere is that civil war more evident in the community of mind than in what used to be supposed the proper place for the preservation and nurture and propagation of mind, the academy—a realization the poet came to early in this century.

The poet, of course, is no less susceptible to the dangers of territorial jealousy than any other mind, as his war with science at this moment may show, quite often to the embarrassment of his position. Still, his concern for the technical side of his craft, and for craft's relation to an encompassing aesthetics, is likely to be a private concern, one considered in the company of his peers, his fellow craftsmen. One studies James and Joyce and Flaubert if one's vocation is poet, exercising one's peculiar gift in relation to the gift revealed in James and Joyce and Flaubert. But understanding the "quaint devices" of art (in Sidney's phrase) is still a limited way to the fullness of gift. The greatness of the poet, as he learns in pursuing his vocation, lies in his vision, made accessible by art, and it is that vision of man to which Faulkner addresses himself in his Nobel Address. If art is that which hides art, art is also that gift whereby the artist rises to the level of a vision which aesthetics alone will not fully explain.

We have lost this old truth, I suspect, in consequence of that very fragmentation against which Faulkner argues. And because we are always tempted to elevate our weaknesses to virtues, our failures to successes, we take a refuge in a "professionalism," a further narrowing of the vocation of mind and soul within our inherent limits. The decline of the academy itself, a growing subject of concern and controversy, is, as we see more and more, an effect of our fragmentation. Now the poet, if he develop beyond the limits of the lyric cry, comes to feel rather desperately the need of some metaphysics to sustain his vision. Keats remarks in a letter, rather naively, that perhaps Hazlett can name three or four books that will answer his necessity, uncloud his vision. In contrast, the typical college president feels the need of some system of accounting which will name fragmentation in an illusion of order; he is understandably confused by the chaos of disciplines and goals in the fragmented "professionalism" of mind. He settles for a "vision" which may balance resources and still somewhat a multitude of disparate and raucous demands. The academy, the medium of mind in history, flounders, and we have the poet's own raucous response to that

tragic comedy of mind, from Pound through the Beat poets. Very occasionally we have a mind who struggles to exorcise Lucifer from the Prometheus he wishes to appear, to establish the limits of the finite intellect as a protection against such possession. Less occasionally that mind is the poet's, and such a rarity, I contend, is Flannery O'Connor.

FLANNERY O'CONNOR speaks of herself as a "realist of distances," as a "prophetic poet," and the complexities of such a claim in a specialized age such as ours, in which intellect is fragmented and the fragments seized and elevated to absolute authority, points to the difficulty of valuing not only her claim but her accomplishment as artist as well. She reminds us that the prophet she means to be is the one who recalls us to known but forgotten truths, to the necessity of our casting backward in our thought to some point where thought went astray. The relation of poetry to truth is a vexing one in itself, not so easily satisfied by paradox as we desire. That beauty is truth, truth beauty, is itself a claim that arrests, though it is with difficulty riddled. But for a poet to complicate the problem by engaging reason in prophecy, as a guard against the poet's old easy dependence upon intuition and a too easy comfort in paradox, well nigh confounds the attempt to value the poet. In Miss O'Connor we have interesting and helpful assistance beyond this prophetic poet herself, to which she gives us clues. She asserts a kinship in her thinking with a variety of minds in whom common problems are addressed, minds as various as Hawthorne and Aquinas, Faulkner and Eric Voegelin. We may discover through her suggestions of such kinships at least what she understands to be the relation of truth to beauty and her role as prophetic poet in revealing that relationship.

Like Eric Voegelin, Flannery O'Connor is particularly interested in the effect of Enlightenment thought upon the "popular spirit of each succeeding age." That erosive process is, as she sees it, a force integral to her fiction, a force against which her protagonists come at last to set themselves with a violence that speaks the heroic. For that reason, a work such as Eric Voegelin's *From Enlightenment to Revolution* or Josef Pieper's *In Tune with the World: A Theory of Festivity* reveals a vitality and an intellectual dimension to Miss O'Connor's fiction as yet insufficiently acknowledged by her more strictly literary critic. It is evident that she knew neither of these particular works, the first appearing in 1975 and the second in 1965, but she knew other work by the two. Pieper's *Leisure: The Basis of Culture* is in her library. Voegelin's tribute to the Western mind, *Order and History,* is conspicuously present—the first three volumes—heavily marked in her hand. (These volumes she reviewed for the *Bulletin,* a diocesan periodical).

There are a number of reasons, however, that I should prefer to use the later works, which appear only after her death, a principal one being to suggest the importance of a community of thought, rather than be led too easily astray into the cause-effect oversimplification which one is tempted to in the study of "influences." Independent minds do often agree. Another advantage of using Voegelin's recent book is in particular that it addresses itself systematically to that tangled intellectual background which Miss O'Connor studies in a variety of critical minds, a background to which she repeatedly alludes, often cryptically, and which she carefully involves in the dramas of her fiction. In that growing in-

tellectual confusion since the Renaissance, as Voegelin says, "The Christian *credo ut intelligam,* which presupposes the substance of faith, is reversed into an *intelligo ut credam.*" It is against this change that Miss O'Connor develops the assurance in her "intellectual" agents of their own purchase upon the truth, in characters like Rayber in *The Violent Bear It Away* or in Asbury and Hulga and Mrs. Turpin of the stories. The comedy of her self-assured psychologists and sociologists and would-be writers, however, is also accompanied by the pathos of their emptiness. Not seeing the relation, a critic may too hastily conclude that she is anti-intellectual, that she calls reason in question, when in truth it is inordinate or inadequate reason that she rebukes. Through the pathos in such characters one begins to recognize them, in Miss O'Connor phrase, as "Christ-haunted." They know, though not intellectually, a spiritual disorientation such as results when (in Voegelin's words) "[t]he transcendental constitution of mankind through the pneuma of Christ is replaced by faith in the intraworldly constitution of mankind through 'compassion.'" Though such a replacement still requires the assurance of some authority, the only authority remaining after the attrition of authority is the individual's belief in the sufficiency of his own feelings, a new faith buttressed as well as intellect can manage with the sciences of the intraworldly.

It is against the chaos of such thought, born and bred in the Enlightenment and grown up to dominate the present moment, that the resonance of her fiction takes dramatic form—not against the local "Southern" materials she adeptly turns to the service of her art. Haze Motes, of *Wise Blood,* may appear an ignorant Georgia country boy, but appearance is shockingly deceptive. Thus one finds on reflection that the semi-literate Haze has certain origin in Locke's position that "Good and evil are nothing but pleasure and pain, or that which occasions or procures pleasure and pain to us," a proposition Voegelin sets in its historical perspective. We read in this light also her Misfit's sad words that "It's no real pleasure in life" except in "killing somebody or burning down his house or doing some other meanness." So often in her fiction, wherever the hunger for spiritual food is thwarted by a substitute appeal to what Voegelin calls the "intramundane spirit of man," violence and destruction ensue, though not always without some triumph for the spirit in its hunger, as with Hazel Motes and Tar-water, Julian, Mrs. Turpin, Mrs. Cope.

Locke's central point, distorted in its dissemination, infects Western thought and festers in it. It does so because it is a principle pragmatically convenient to individual and collective appetites for power, serving as well the lowest dimension of being, both social and private, reducing life to the primitive and thence to the animal. At the same time natural wit, through which the principle is exercised, creates a complicated facade of civilization exhibiting the orders of power—commercial or political or social. The result is the now famous "machine in the garden." Haze has his machine, his Essex, which he attempts to transform into an immortal God, though Miss O'Connor's humor makes the Essex rather a machine in the zoo of the city than in any garden. The contemporary products of our natural wit are exhibited in a spectrum from the advertising of deodorants to the advertising of political programs, each of which must be convincingly *new* to attract the satiated, whose pleasures have been increasingly anchored in the senses alone, since the

time of Locke, by the entrepreneurs of power. (For the development of the intellectual program, in the interest of power, see particularly Voegelin's "Helvetius and the Genealogy of Passions" and "Helvetius and the Heritage of Pascal" in *From Enlightenment to Revolution*.) The meaning one finds in Miss O'Connor's "wise blood," as explored through Haze Motes and Enoch Emory, is very much a commentary on this strain of Western thought.

Speaking of this secularization of Western thought, Voegelin remarks that "with Voltaire begins . . . the concerted attack on Christian symbols and the attempt at evoking an image of man in a cosmos under the guidance of intraworldly reason." The crucial shift is in the meaning of virtue so that virtue is concerned not with the individual soul's relation to God but to social man. In his *Dictionnaire Philosophique*, Voltaire speaks prophetically: "Virtue among men is a commerce of good deeds; who has not part in this commerce should not be counted." As Voegelin remarks, "Behind the phrase that a man who is not socially useful in this restricted sense does not count looms the virtuous *terreur* of Robespierre and the massacres by the later humanitarians whose hearts are filled with compassion to the point that they are willing to slaughter one half of mankind in order to make the other half happy."[1] Miss O'Connor comments on the same idea in ironic references to the easiness of compassion on modern lips, a compassion much changed in the interval since Voltaire's remark toward Voegelin's logical extension. It is "popular pity," through which (Miss O'Connor says) "In the absence of . . . faith, we govern by tenderness. It is a tenderness which, long since cut off from the person, is wrapped in theory. When tenderness is detached from the source of tenderness, its logical outcome is terror. It ends in forced-labor camps and in the fumes of the gas chamber." And Miss O'Connor's "tender" characters whose compassion is "wrapped in theory" reveal again and again, in her sharp reading of the narrowing of vision, our heritage from the Enlightenment. One notices particularly such characters as Rayber and Sheppard and those scattered characters whose religion is social man.

VOEGELIN'S ANALYSIS of the texts of recent Western thought throws a helpful light upon Miss O'Connor's artistic devices no less than upon the history held as background to her drama. There is, for instance, her concern for Christian symbol. Of the conflict between Christian symbols and the rational historical critique of them, Voegelin says:

> The language of Christianity becomes a "myth" as a consequence of the penetration of our world by a rationalism which destroys the transcendental meanings of symbols taken from the world of senses. In the course of this "de-divinization" . . . of the world, sensual symbols have lost their transparency for transcendental reality; they have become opaque and are no longer revelatory of the immersion of the finite world in the transcendent. Christianity has become historicized in the sense that a universe of symbols that belong to the age of myth is seen in the perspective of categories which belong to an age of rationalism.

And when symbol is reduced to the perspective of category, when rationalism governs symbol absolutely, the effect upon the popular spirit is predictable, since ideas do have such consequences. One sets beside Voegelin's remark a statement Miss O'Connor made in an interview, in response to questioning about her distortions of "reality." She found it necessary to shake up, in so far as art may do so, the comfortable categories settled in the popular spirit:

> If I write a novel in which the central action is a baptism, I know that for a large percentage of my readers, baptism is a meaningless rite; therefore I have to imbue this action with an awe and terror which will suggest its awful mystery. I have to distort the look of the thing in order to represent as I see them both the mystery and the fact.

To replace Christianity, there emerges that new religion we have been talking of, which concentrates its worship upon secular man to the general exclusion of the spiritual, a deficiency in the rationalistic version of being through which in Voegelin's words, "the symbolic expressions of spiritual experiences become opaque and are misunderstood as depending for their validity on their resistance to rational critique." That is the inevitable consequence of severing reason from faith and of casting faith in the category of superstition, the province often visited by our "folk" critics. Thus, Voegelin continues, in the process "the principles of ethics are severed from their spiritual roots, and the rules of conduct are determined by the standard of social utility." What is prepared thereby is the grounds for that "mobocracy" against which Kierkegaard was to rail. The mob, in the name of humanity, appropriates not only the natural world, but individual lives, on the strength alone of a vaporous desire multiplied by *number*. And so community becomes a matter of statistics, as does the quality of life itself. The *person* becomes an *individual,* well on the way to becoming an *integer,*[2] but always, of course, in the name of that abstraction in whose name power is gathered and exercised: humanity, a generalization erected on man's biological nature. Thus, ultimately, the mystical body of Christ has substituted for it the "mystical bodies of nations," since some symbolic focus is necessary to the appropriation of force, through the alchemy of numbers. A new symbology emerges, a new calendar of holy days to satisfy the mysterious desire in the blood for an object of devotion greater than the self. For without such symbols the accretion of numbers to the uses of power disintegrates.

The necessity of festival, public devotions, as Josef Pieper points out in his *In Tune With the World,* requires a shifting of the very grounds of festival in the new religion. For, "to celebrate a festival means: to live out, for some special occasion and in an uncommon manner, the universal assent to the world as a whole." But if the celebration of festival is a sacrifice to the whole of creation—"a festival without gods is a non-concept," Pieper says—then the reduction of creation to mechanical law denies, even in the seasons themselves, the presence of deity. The real hunger must be met by synthetic substitute. Thus one arrives at Comte's reformed calendar which establishes festivals of Humanity, Paternity, Domesticity, and the like. One may assume the necessity of festival as simply psychological. That was Jean Jacques Rousseau's solution: "Plant a flower-decked pole in the middle of an open place, call the people together—and you have a fete!" And thus "altars of the fatherland" were erected, at that Festival of Reason celebrated at Notre Dame in the 1790s. The rituals in celebration of the

mystical body of the state are legislated ones, the citizenry coerced to participate: "When the bells ring, all will leave their houses, which will be entrusted to the protection of the law and the Republican virtues. The populace will fill the streets and public squares, aflame with joy and fraternity. . . ." The "liturgist" of this celebration of the Mass of the mystical body of the masses is St. Robespierre.

Such a celebration of "fraternity" is, of course, wildly divorced from the reality of creation. Its symbols are also opaque, so that the individual is not only free to, but must, find his particular desire reflected in those symbols. The accomplishment of that desire depends in the last analysis upon his skill in the accumulation of power to the service of his own desire turned into appetite, whether the magnitude is that of a Robespierre or Flannery O'Connor's Mr. Shiftlet. The seeming complexity of the modern world is in considerable degree an effect of the fragmentation of the old sense of community into pockets of power, larger and smaller, according to the combination of wit and ruthlessness in individuals who accumulate that power. The accumulation is in the form of an accretion of "citizenry" in the support of particular shibboleths, advertised in a rhetoric that conceals its enslaving powers.

One sees a brief history of the evolution of secular festivals in Pieper's survey of May Day. Its connection is not with Spring festivals out of a pagan world, but rather with "moving day, the usual date when leases and other economic agreements ran out." The International Labor Congress in 1891, a hundred years after the elevation of Reason as God under the guidance of Robespierre, proclaimed the first of May a festival, "in order to preserve its specific economic character." The placards read "[t]his is the day the people made" and "Socialism, thy kingdom come!" And again, "Our Pentecost, when the power of the Holy Spirit of Socialism rushes through the world, making converts." Pieper concludes from his survey of the perversion of festival that even so, "[t]wo extreme historical potentialities have equal chances: the latent everlasting festival may be made manifest, or the 'antifestival' may develop in its most radical form," a development far advanced in both China and the Soviet Union at this point in time. (Lest we feel too much relieved, we might observe the same spirit long at work in our own nation; birthdays of Founding Fathers are easily shifted on the calendar to the general utility inherent in such shifts, and our celebration of the Bicentennial has more than the casual presence in it of attempts to erect altars to the fatherland.)

Our digression into secular festival throws light on Flannery O'Connor's concern for the recovery of that "latent everlasting festival" which she attempts to make manifest in its power to heal the fractured world of the self and the community, through the mystical body of Christ. That is her message as prophet. The fruit of festival, says Pieper, "is pure gift." It is a sacrifice in no way affected by temporal goals, though it is a temporal sacrifice. A definite portion of one's life, says Pieper, quoting ancient Roman usage, is made "the exclusive property of the gods." It is an act "in affirmation of the world." A tradition in the strictest sense of *traditum,* "received from a superhuman source, to be handed on undiminished, received, and handed on again." As St. Thomas Aquinas asserts, "The sacrifice is the soul of festival," so that exclusion from communion was called by the early Christians "banishment to unfestivity." Festival then involves one in a sacrifice which is a renunciation of the world, a free giving of the world to the source of the world, through love. In such openness of surrender, grace answers, and in the context of such reflections, it will occur to one that the Mass is itself the highest festival, in which one freely receives that incommensurate gift through which creation is reconciled to its Creator. It is with this particular gift that Miss O'Connor's fiction is always dramatically concerned, the drama lying between her character's resisting the gift and the threat of that gift. In her characters' struggles with festival sacrifice, one discovers how intimately related in her thinking is the concern for manners, in whose healthful recovery lies the possibility of an encounter with mystery and the recovery of that joy implicit in the whole of creation. But she sees that, as Pieper says,

> [t]here can be no festivity when man, imagining himself self-sufficient, refuses to recognize the Goodness of things which goes far beyond any conceivable utility; it is the Goodness of reality taken as a whole which validates all the particular goods and which man himself can never produce nor simply translate into social or individual 'welfare.' He truly receives it only when he accepts it as pure gift. The only fitting way to respond to such gifts is: by praise of God in ritual worship.

That seeing of the "Goodness of reality" is very close to what Miss O'Connor affirms in calling her vision that of a "realist of distances," seeing the created world, in Voegelin's phrase "immersed in the transcendent." For her, as for Voegelin and Pieper, "[e]xistence [in Pieper's words] does not 'adjoin' the realm of Eternity; it is entirely permeated by it." This is the vision that is lost to us, the vision she would recover to us.

AND THAT is why she was disturbed on occasion by misreadings of her work. A critic like Isaac Rosenfeld, from his perspective as a late child of the Enlightenment, must inevitably conclude that "[e]verything [O'Connor] says through image and metaphor has the meaning only of degeneration." For Rosenfeld, Haze Motes is "nothing more than the poor, sick, ugly, raving lunatic that he happens to be." Yet we see when we look closely at the images and metaphors of *Wise Blood* that whole larger world of which Pieper speaks. It is implicit in them, a world denied to such a mind as Rosenfeld's. His is a mind we shall see dramatized—not without sympathy from Miss O'Connor, though it is an uncompromising sympathy—in the figure of Rayber in *The Violent Bear It Away*. Meanwhile, it is well to remember that Miss O'Connor herself sees and speaks of that gnostic election of rationality which excludes the spiritual dimension of being, that election which Voegelin adumbrates in his work. We repeat her words:

> Since the eighteenth century, the popular spirit of each succeeding generation has tended more and more to the view that the ills and mysteries of life will eventually fall before the scientific advances of man.

To which she adds that such grotesque characters as she makes into her heroes "carry an invisible burden; their fanaticism is a reproach, not merely an eccentricity." They are stumbling prophets out of the intellectual desert we call the modern world.

One final general reminder concerning her use of images and metaphors: Voegelin, surveying the destruction of our symbols of belief and finding them increasingly opaque to the dim eye of an increasingly gnostic world, suggests the necessity of new symbols, requiring "a new Thomas rather than a neo-Thomist." But Miss O'Connor is confident of those symbols' continuing vitality since they are anchored in that ground of being which is unchanging. What is necessary, in her view of our problem, is a healing touch upon the diseased eye. It is a touch she intends to perform through those very symbols, in her "incarnational" art. The healing power lies in the fact that her symbols are fed continuously by the reality of the Crucifixion, Resurrection, and Redemption which those symbols make manifest. The world, one says, *is* created, not *was* created. And most important to her fiction, her symbols are fed by the witness of creation itself, by the natural world and by such revitalized persons as her fiction imitates. The created world is to her, as it was to Pascal, "an image of grace," a continuing witness of and medium for the incarnation's access to the created soul. When seen in its reality, the meanest leaf sparkles in the sunlight, revealing the constancy of grace in nature; to her, as to St. Bonaventure, the sun casts a more than symbolic light upon the struggling characters of her fiction.

We remarked earlier that when the metaphysical defenses of hierarchy were reduced to the intramundane, hierarchy becomes an instrument in the hands of the lords of worldly power. The displacement becomes possible through an assault upon the old scholastic authority, particularly as symbolized by the *Summa Theologica*. But authority in any of its forms becomes fair game once it is reduced to the arena of the intramundane, the justification of revolution resting upon the successful use of accumulated power. The uses of power accelerate, particularly in the intellectual sphere, though we speak of the development (in its empirical effect upon a mankind reduced to the "masses") as devoted to "humanity," that ultimate object of secular worship. Yet we best measure our progress in this line symbolically from the cannon to the atomic bomb. And if mankind is reduced, so too is the general body of nature, having expelled from it that authority St. Thomas found inherent in it, the authority of its Cause and Creator. It is by that expulsion that the poet robbed of his visionary authority which he once exercised through visionary symbol and metaphor. "How happy is he," says Donne in a couplet Miss O'Connor marks in her text of his poems, "which hath due place assign'd / To'his beasts, and disaforested his minde!"

Donne is not longing, of course, for mere imposition of order upon the world by the reason; he is lamenting the loss of vision, such vision as has led the poet since Donne to struggle in holding creation to a recovered vision, through the yoking of disparates by violence together. As the authority of the mind and of nature was increasingly called in question, the role of the poet was no less so. And what results from that questioning by the popular spirit of each succeeding age is a settling symbol to Voegelin's residual status. Eventually it settles to the murky region of the "subconscious," in which symbol becomes subjectively opaque. The question becomes whether art has any call upon the intellect. That is the question Miss O'Connor addresses herself to, seeing that the decay is not necessarily in symbol and metaphor but more likely in the mind that uses and abuses them. And that is why she does not call, as Voegelin does, for a new symbology. For nature does not lack authority merely by the mind's declaration that it does. It is for her still the present signature of its Creator, as St. Augustine and St. Thomas

argue, in which the poet finds his own authority. Thus there may be a special relationship established by art between the Creator and his creature, so long as the limits of art are recognized.

Not, of course, that authority is abandoned in the overthrow of the transcendent, a point by now sufficiently made but here hopefully repeated. It is rather that the claims of authority multiply as particular minds establish individual satrapies in the country of the mind, from which position nature and the mind are foraged upon. Engels, says Pieper, "infers from productibility of artificial things the possibility of exhaustive knowledge of all natural reality." But St. Thomas distinguishes between the "nature" of man and the "nature" of a letter opener as Engels does not. That is a distinction generally lost to us, to which Miss O'Connor speaks in her metaphors of mechanical art, in Haze's Essex or Rayber's can opener or hearing aid and glasses. In the confusions following the separation of grace from nature and of reason from faith, one sees a most particular effect upon the prophetic poet, caught up as he is in that long confusing war between the authority of beauty and of truth, a civil war in which Miss O'Connor does not take sides. Perhaps a speculative comment may be in order here, to suggest why she finds that conflict futile, the antagonists supporting only partially sound positions through inadequate authority. It may enlighten as well her own contentment with traditional symbology and its sources in Thomism, as well as suggesting why she anticipates an effect through art beyond the aesthetic, a partial healing at least of that breach made by the mind between grace and nature, reason and faith.

WHEN THROUGH the reason one establishes a ladder for an ascent of the mind to being (for whatever purposes), as Hegel does in his *Aesthetics* (art, music, poetry, philosophy are an ascending order, each absorbing the earlier), one is engaged in mythologizing man's experience of being. That procedure leads to an address to the world through category. The effect is a de-divinization, de-humanization, de-naturalization of being through the autopsy of category. Such an autopsy is a limited necessity, given the discursive nature of the mind, a burden some of us hold consequent to Original Sin. The philosopher as pathologist of being, however, must remember the *whole* nature of hierarchy, whether of mind or of any creation separate from the mind. That hierarchy requires of one's faith in being that it remember always the parts as members one of another. The strong temptation to gnosticism lies in forgetfulness at this point of the rational "X-raying" of the world's body by reason, for in that very activity is exercised a certain control over being which to the incautious or prideful appears to provide an avenue to the domination of being. It is against this temptation that Wordsworth protests when he charges the modern mind with murdering to dissect. Though they do not share the same terms, there is a sympathy between Wordsworth's and O'Connor's thought here. For Miss O'Connor, it is through faith and the support of grace, given the Enlightenment's insistent autopsy, that some recovery of our sense of the unity of being is possible. And in such a new spiritually sensitive state, the question of beauty's relation to truth as an analytic topic becomes irrelevant to the experience of being. In our recovered sense of being, we perceive beauty and truth participating ordinately, not experienced as separate.

Thus one has not reached the fullness of St. Thomas's definition of beauty—that which when seen pleases—if he separates the pursuit of the good from the contemplation of the beautiful. What remains to be said is that, to our fallen nature, the beautiful is a sign of the good. When one sees and is pleased, he is not pleased by an accident of the being. There is a mystical relation between the object as art and the perceiver of its beauty, as there is a mystical relation between the object as art and the Cause of all beauty, of which art is in imitation according to the rules of nature. As for the relation between the object and the beholder, what is experienced is a revelation through beauty, activated by that suspension of the will which makes one open to the beautiful, or by a consent of the will which draws one to the beautiful. (Coleridge's argument for the "suspension of disbelief" may be said to call for that openness to beauty of which we speak.)

The experience of beauty is of the nature of a revelation, the effect of which upon the beholder is (in a very real and not simply metaphorical way) that the perceiver is "realized" by the experience. But the disposal of the will to the possibility of beauty is an active disposal, though one's more immediate experience of beauty seems a passive one, as if one is acted upon by the object. That is the mystery of a spiritual aestheticism such as Wordsworth, once more, attempts to describe in speaking of the mind's relation to the object, with the image a medium in that relationship. Thus in speaking of "the mighty world / Of eye, and ear," that world is said to be "half created" and "half perceived," a union of "nature and the language of the sense" which the discursive mind feebly attempts to rationalize. In that experience, the mind is aware of a certain "feeling" which is realized in the experience—a feeling latent, potential. By virtue of the experience, through which one is changed, we recognize *in* the object and *through* the object—the work of art—a feeling we did not know we possessed as a part of our being. This "feeling" is an action toward the world, a reaching in us by that which has been waiting to reach.[3] In the aesthetic experience there is analogy to that experience of nature one comes to through a more active rational address to the external world. When St. Thomas says that "[i]t is natural for a man to tend towards the divine by the apprehension of sense-objects" or that "[a] perfect judgment of the mind obtains through turning to sense-objects which are the first principles of our knowledge," he is speaking to this experience in which one recognizes as undivided the true and the beautiful. Whether one's experience leads him to the poem or to E = mc², the arresting moment is that in which the perception of a truth and an aesthetic pleasure in that truth are wedded in the experience. Wonder and awe mingle, before one's falling away from that experience through a pride in possessing a new advance in one's own being. That pride is the gnostic temptation of which we have so often spoken, an inclination to understand the experience as if it were drawn from the object, abstracted by the intellect, so that the object becomes warped as a creature of man's intellect.

The supposition that "feeling" is either poured into the perceiver or drawn by him from the object is the error underlying and making possible that sentimentality practiced by artist and perceiver alike, either supposition being in effect a distortion of being in the perceiver on the assumption of a neutralized will, on the assumption that the perceiver is the passive object of the aesthetic experience. The tacit assumption is that the feeling

is an additive related to a beauty which itself is conceived as an accident of being. The attempt to acquire or to produce the "aesthetic experience" in this manner is a short-circuiting of the currents of being, of the relationship between the perceiver and the beautiful (the beautiful: being which is seen). It easily develops the assumption in the "popular spirit" that one grows "culturally" through a mechanism of senses, or of purely rational perceptions—of any partial relation of the perceiver to that which is perceived. But as we have said, to grow culturally is not the same as to grow a culture on a host as the pathologist does, though the dominant belief in our age that such is the case accounts for the modern mania for "cultural" overlays of "society," that spawn of courses and programs of cultural indoctrination usually provided as "outreaches" (in the popular jargon) of the academy.

The popular spirit, in so far as it has become separated from being, can only be further distorted, made more grotesque, by the supposition that culture is super-added to one's being, as when in the name of cultural education, night classes in classical music are given for ten weeks to whatever elements of society may be drawn together in the name of culture. Such vaccinations, if they take at all, take in ways quite different from the expected.

For a long harboring of beauty as it speaks being through the senses is required. Beauty is a devotion of a lifetime, because the cultural experience which is desirable is a coming to be, as when the flower opens to the sun and moves on toward seed. In that continuing and continuous experience, one is continuously awakened by awe. We speak of this awe when we try to describe the experience of "finding ourselves" through beauty. (Again, we say *through* beauty.) When Rilke says of that experience with the partial bust of Apollo that the perceiver must change his life, it is of this opening as the flower to the sun of which he speaks. When Hopkins considers the "inscape" that is his poem, he considers the *freshest deep down things* as the experience to which we are brought, the experience of the cause of all beautiful things, through which one draws and is drawn. Just as spiritual growth is a slow construction of the good in us, pervasive of our undivided being, so too is the aesthetic sensibility, which is but another of the categories which we use to talk of our coming to be. A spiritual growth through beauty is one of the modes of grace whereby our being is realized and all existence celebrated, in its multiplicity, as yet a body. For, in seeing that which is, accompanied by the pleasure of seeing it, one's being is moved toward that sacramental relationship with being in which we discover that the beautiful and the good are inextricable. One goes from strength to strength in the perception of being through the senses, when the will is ordinate in its reverence for being. "Seeing" in the aesthetic sense and "seeing" in the mystical sense are separations by our analytic minds before the mystery of being as we attempt to understand why we are moved or what it is that moves us to awe in the presence of what is. The answer to the *what* and *why* is deep down things: the uncaused Cause, which causes that we may be.

Notes

1. Voegelin, a refugee from Hitler's "compassion," is in a position to speak of the consequences of such ideas as he examines. In this connection we should remember as well another refugee, Karl Stern, who in his autobiography *The Pillar of Fire* recalls an effect of Enlightenment thought upon the Jewish community of Europe, which in Stern's view contributed to the attempt to annihilate that community. He speaks particularly of the effect of a decay of orthodoxy in that community. His grandfather, who practiced the formalities of his religion, did not want his grandchildren to do so, since they were to be part of a "generation of enlightenment" which was to follow the loosening effects of religious tolerance and political liberalism after World War I. Judaism as "tolerant eclecticism" led to an anemia in the Jewish community which Stern feels became a sort of death wish. Stern's own progress in reaction to the decay bears striking analogy to the progress of Haze Motes. His recollections might also cast a somewhat different light upon the liberal's *evidence* of "anti-Semitism" in Eliot and Pound. The grandfather practices his spiritual commitment in gestures without motion. Pound's comment on his Brennbaum, in *Hugh Selwyn Mauberley,* seems of a Jew such as Stern's grandfather;

   > The heavy memories of Horeb, Sinai
   >   and forty years,
   > Showed only when the daylight fell
   > Level across: the face
   > Of Brennbaum "The Impeccable."

2. See Maritain's analysis of Descartes's angelism, in *Three Reformers,* in which he examines Descartes's denial of the mind's discursiveness, thus separating mind from nature, a drift of thought which falls to the uses of Locke and Kant and helps establish an isolation of mind from nature.

3. Eliot, before the time of "Ash-Wednesday," is highly suspicious of the feelings, especially as such a term is used by Wordsworth: in "Tradition and the Individual Talent" he expresses those reservations, and in his concern for the "objective correlative," he is acutely concerned with the danger of feeling. But in 1929 he writes Dobre: "I doubt myself whether good philosophy any more than good criticism or any more than good poetry can be written without strong feeling. . . . I am sure that any prose I have written that is good prose, is good because I have strong feelings (more than adequate knowledge). . . ."

Robert Conquest

But What Good Came of It at Last?
An Inquest on Modernism

VOL. 16, NO. 1, 1980

I will not venture here a full conspectus of the modernist movement, tracing all the schools through cubism and vorticism and expressionism through suprematism and constructivism and De Stijl, through Valéry and Kafka and Gertrude Stein, through *Merz* and *Blast* and *Transition*, describing the interactions, the sectarian strife, the manifestos, the denunciations. Nor will I deal with modernism in every field—for instance, in music or in architecture (though much of that, unfortunately, seems to be more lasting than bronze). I will, therefore, restrict myself largely to literature, though with reference to broader trends. For all the arts were deeply affected; and it is even the case that painters like Picasso, for example, wrote a number of "poems." Moreover, the condition of painting may sometimes illuminate that of the other arts. For painting is, in its very nature, more dependent than the written word on the apparatus of culture-pushers—patrons, galleries, and so on. Again, it is probably easier to inflict a striped rectangle on the consumer, who only has to give it a casual look, than to make the same consumer read a damned thick book or even a fourteen-line poem. And this is apart from the perhaps partisan estimate made by Auden, that,

> those who feel most like a sewer
> Belong to painting not to literature.

More broadly, in dealing with modernism, any approach is bound to be a reflection of the reading, viewing, and experience of the lecturer: yet I do not think that any other selection of experiences would lead to general conclusions different from what I suggest.

But first let us consider our terms. When one speaks of movements and of modernism, one is using great general words. In practice there are individual books, written by men with their own characters and idiosyncrasies, not mere ectoplasm of the Zeitgeist. But I take it that I will not be held to any precise definition of modernism; in this sort of sphere above all we are surely entitled to rely on Aristotle's dictum that words should be used with the precision or generality suitable to the field. With that in mind, we may start by defining modernism in an illustrative rather than a formal way: modernism is what makes the Tate Gallery buy and exhibit a pile of bricks.

Now, when some supposed novelty of this sort is criticized, one finds to this day the rhetoric put forward that the critic is evidently a shocked and uncomprehending fuddy-duddy faced with something beyond his ken. But of course this is, generally speaking, nonsense. Modernism has been with us for some seventy years. In 1913, to take an example from poetry, Marinetti published the following lines of a type which has long since become so tediously familiar that none of us would be surprised to see them today in a state-subsidized "little magazine":

plombs + lave 300 + Puanteurs + 50
  parfums
pave matelas detritus crottin charognes
flic-flac entassement chameaux bourricots
tohubohu cloaque.

No, the critic of modernism is criticizing a tradition which has been established now for generations, which has been boringly familiar to all of us since childhood. It long ago received the seal of academic approval, which Housman calls "the second death"; its lumpish sculpture has been taken to the heart of the most establishmentarian corporations and government departments; its half-dimensional stripes and squares masquerade as paintings on the mantlepieces of New York stockbrokers. It is a paradox unique to our time that a traditionalism which has long lost its energies and spirits should yet contrive to pose as "new," so that we still have to insist that it is a postmodernist rather than a premodernist generation which now points out its deficiencies. It is the younger and fresher writers in the architectural journals who are now insisting that American Victorian architecture is better than the post-Gropius stuff. It is

Tom Wolfe, from the heart of the New York art world, who (in *The Painted Word*) destroys the pretensions of the cycle of schools of pseudo-art which followed the—already bad enough—American neoexpressionists. And likewise with literature, I should perhaps add that you can check my own case in *The Penguin Book of Surrealism and Verse*, where a poem of mine, written in my teens, is displayed for all to see.

Delimiting Modernism

Modernism does not appear to be a literary movement in the older sense. The relation between it and the sensibility of the age seems quite different from anything that has preceded it. A special disjunction has taken place. But at what point does this occur?

I think we can, if only roughly, set up a criterion by asking ourselves whether the changes in scope as seen in the novels of Proust, James, Lawrence, Svevo, and the early Joyce were broader and more radical than, or even as broad and as radical as, those of the novels of Dostoevsky and Tolstoy as compared with *their* predecessors. We must surely answer no. So let me first of all distinguish between the "modern," naturally different from the art of previous periods, in reflecting a different sensibility, and the "modernist"—something, in principle, total and revolutionary, which in prose one may associate with *Finnegan's Wake* and Gertrude Stein. In painting, I would place it at Kandinsky and Picasso, at the point they had reached in 1914, (when they were so nominated by Pound)—or, possibly a little earlier, with Braque's first formulation of the idea of painting without content, around 1910.

In poetry . . . but first let us remember

the deplorable state of English poetry in the first decade of this century. While the freshest prose reading, or seeing, of the man of cultural fashion was Wells and Bennet, Ibsen and Nietzsche and Shaw, in our poetry the leading names were, William Watson and Stephen Phillips.

A specific modernism set prior to World War I: the conscious setting up of Imagism around 1913, and the imported impact of Futurism (founded around 1907, but reaching Britain in 1912). All the ideas which were to infest poetic modernism for generations were present. Above all, what Wordsworth speaks of as a "degrading thirst after outrageous stimulation." Thus, from all these dates, it will be seen that modernism was not the product of a violent period, but of a peaceful period seeking violence.

So much for its birth. What about its life and, I would argue, its recent death? But, you will say, is it yet time to have an inquest? Modernism is more pervasive than ever among a huge semi-educated class. At the Tate, in the English Departments, its momentum is not yet spent. Yet it is dead, or nearly dead, as a live idea inspiring worthwhile work.

Modernism is sometimes distinguished from other movements in literature by its greater programmatic self-consciousness. This might be disputed: one could put forward such documents as the *Introduction to the Lyrical Ballads*, to say nothing of the poetic manifestos of French and other schools long preceding Mallarmé and Rimbaud. We may feel, rather, that it is not so much the existence as the totality, the omnipresence of the programmatic side of modernism, that makes the difference. In Ortega's extraordinary essay "The Dehumanization of Art" he takes the line that the urge behind modernist visual art was to deny the public any pleasure but the purely aesthetic. But

once such over-conscious ploys are adhered to, a great change has taken place. Neither Cezanne nor Van Gogh painted according to theory. It was the complex unarticulated directions given them by their own psyches which formed their work, rather than any program.

The role of the explanation of the painting became more and more important. The aim in the first place was to stop painting from having any "literary" appeal. First, of course, story and situation were removed; then human beings; then any physical object whatever. And so on, until in the world of neo-expressionism it was thought that some colors were more sentimental than others—so only harsh shades were permitted; then it was felt that the texture still gave a sentimental result—so only smooth brush strokes of a single uninteresting color were permitted. As Tom Wolfe says, these paintings gradually became nothing more than illustrations of verbal instruction—in fact, paradoxically, "literary" to an infinite degree. This sort of enterprise implies a knowledge we do not have. It follows that theory must base itself on what we do know; which is, on comparatively superficial aspects of the subject.

Readers of poetry too often seemed by long training to have suppressed their direct responses and replaced them by an unnatural set of automatisms drawn from critical theory. However, no critical machinery has yet been devised which can take over from the intelligent sensibility the job of deciding which poems are good—readable, moving, and felicitous. If you go on wearing a straitjacket long enough you lose the use of your arms. At any rate, theory became the main driving force. Critics abounded. That ours is an age of criticism and at the same time of frigid inventiveness is surely no coincidence.

One new phenomenon of our time was the establishment of English schools and English departments in the universities, at about the same time as modernism arose. For the first time we had a specific and separate group certified as exceptionally qualified to judge literature, as against that larger, more heterogeneous set of people constituting the cultural community.

Academic critics claimed to be the only people competent to discuss poetry properly and indeed to prescribe its forms, methods, and contents. This is as if a claim should be put forth that cricket should only be discussed by professors of ballistics. The American poet Karl Schapiro remarks that though he has known scores of poets, he has almost never heard from them the adulation of Eliot that is found in the textbooks. His awesome reputation may be the result of a vast effort by academics and others rather than by his colleagues and reasonable admirers.

If I may quote a recent book of mine:

In the old days no one paid much attention to the low-level critics. They knew their place: Grub Street. But in the first decades of this century the foundation of English schools and departments in the universities suddenly gave them status. Alf Shagpen, wheedling the price of a pint of porter from the editor of Blackwood's, became Doctor A. Shagpen, D. Litt., author of *Texture and Tension in Thomas Traherne*. The increase in sophistication was not accompanied by any improvement in taste, and the greater systematization of his delusions was far from representing an improvement in sanity, but the fellow was now an Authority.

Soon he found himself envying the other "disciplines." Perhaps he too could be a scientist and achieve rigour. Perhaps he too could imitate the philosophers and speak for the ultimate springs of human life. The trouble was that he was trained in neither the scientific nor the philosophical disciplines.

We may thus feel that a central fault in all the various attitudes of modernism lay in pursuing an aesthetic half-truth, or quarter-truth, to extremes. As a result, Philip Larkin pointed out some twenty years ago, poetry:

lost its old audience, and gained a new one, This has been caused by the consequences of a cunning merger between poet, literary critic and academic critic (three classes now notoriously indistinguishable): it is hardly an exaggeration to say that the poet has gained the happy position wherein he can praise his own poetry in the press and explain it in the classroom, and the reader has been bullied into giving up the consumer's power to say I don't like this, bring me something different . . . [i]f the medium is in fact to be rescued from among our duties and restored to our pleasures, I can only think that a large-scale revulsion has got to set in against present notions.

ONE GREAT delusion which has added to our troubles is that every country and every period now believes itself entitled to its share of great poets, authors, painters, and so forth. This is obviously untrue. There have been important periods in important countries which have produced nothing worthwhile. The rationing of talent is grossly unfair. Two great poets and one pretty good one in a century in the tiny Duchy of Ferrara and nothing to match them in the whole of Italy put together over the next two or three centuries is a typical story. Today the United States in particular feels entitled to its share of Great Creativity, so we get Jackson Pollock and de Kooning—and I say nothing of the painters that follow them—treated as though they were Rembrandt and Cezanne.

A further point is the mere proliferation of "artists." There are now, for example, more professional painters in the West than have existed in the whole world throughout previous history. None, unfortunately, is up to art apprentice of an assistant of Fra Lippo Lippi. When it comes to poets. . . .

By about 1920, modernism had become *fashionable*. Modernism in the visual arts was overwhelmingly institutionalized by 1929—that is exactly half a century ago—when the New York Museum of Modern Art was founded in John D. Rockefeller's living room, as Tom Wolfe puts it, "with Goodyears, Blisses, and Crowninshields in attendance." Soon the Container Corporation of America was commissioning Leger and Henry Moore, and then undertook a long-running advertising campaign in which (as Wolfe says) "it would run a Great Idea by a noted savant at the top of the page, one of them being 'Hitch your wagon to a star'—Ralph Waldo Emerson. Underneath would be a picture of a Cubist horse strangling on a banana."

We finally reached the absurdity of alienation being rewarded by the establishment: Picasso, the Lord Leighton of the period, approved by academics and patrons alike; of big-time Bohemianism; of knighthoods accepted by anarchists and surrealists—Sir Herbert Read, Sir Ronald Penrose.

Modernism's Audience

At first it had been only the academics and the duchesses who admired the new art. José Ortega y Gasset remarks:

> Modern art . . . will always have the masses against it. It is essentially unpopular; moreover, it is antipopular. Any of its works automatically produced a curious effect on the general public into two groups: one very small, formed by those who are favorably inclined towards it; another very large—the hostile majority. (Let us ignore that ambiguous fauna—the snobs.)

But this description is no longer recognizable, or alternatively the "snobs" have proliferated to an inordinate degree. Starting about the twenty-five years ago came a second phase of modernism. Surrealism found a new audience: this time not an innovative elite but a mass-culture phenomenon. It need hardly be said that its quality catastrophically declined in the process.

A. E. Housman decries the soul which "commands no outlook upon the past or future, but believes that the fashion of the present, unlike all fashions heretofore, will endure perpetually, and that its own flimsy tabernacle of second-hand opinions is a habitation for everlasting." Nor should we imagine that even the most impressive-looking Kulturtraeger are exempt from the appeal of mere fashion. As ever, they are the product of their time and their experience. If they can go wrong even more spectacularly than their predecessors, it is because modernism, and in particular modernist pseudo-aesthetics, opens up such a wide range of pointless or meaningless effort.

The crux, the main and major disjunction in all fields, was when the artist took the decision to abandon the laity.

It may be argued that artistic alienation had been around for a century ever since the "superfluous man" of Lermontov, the Byron of continental imagination, the romantic idea of the mad or maddish poet, grandly isolated from the rest of mankind. With this notion of artistic alienation came the similar, but logically distinct element of the existential human in his condition; and with the twentieth century, though deriving from earlier thought, came Angst.

It has often been said that the decline of religion led to the idea that art could undertake, in some obscure way, the salvation of mankind. This is an idea which preceded modernism, and which was not in this form generally accepted by modernists. Nevertheless, they did regard their work as in some sense transcending any other. And this could not but add to their self-importance.

At a less pretentious level, it is natural that an artist becomes bored with doing what he can do, and goes on to try to do what he can't do, or what can't be done at all. But the writer and artist pressed his autonomy too far, into the direction of almost total independence from an audience.

Even if modernism's proponents did not say that all obscurity is profound— and they came near to saying that—they certainly said that all profundity is obscure. But a muddy puddle may pretend to any depth: a clear pool cannot. Coleridge writes somewhere that he read one of Dante's shorter poems every ten years, always finding more in it. This did not mean that it lacked comprehensibility at first reading; merely that in this comprehensibility there were resonances which did not immediately declare themselves.

Mallarmé, the first true modernist, did not write poems "difficult" as to meaning. They have no meaning, in any ordinary sense, beyond what is there, given, in their words. They have, it is true, other *effects*, but these are effects which are also seen, in addition to, or fused with, ordinary meaning in poems of all types. His poetry is, in fact, ordinary poetry with one of its components omitted. This is not, in itself, to say that it is inferior. And the Mallarméan argument would, of course, admit the point, claiming that its poetry is "pure"—claiming, that is, that the extra content of ordinary verse constitutes a dilution.

Even on this argument, it cannot be said that his poetry has some extra level of meaning, as against an omissive technique which may or may not give some different illumination. "Symbolism" is a misleading word. Something like Penumbrism, or Obliquism, should have been selected.

The point in favor of these procedures is that a different and possibly rewarding effect may be gained by looking from a different angle at the object of one's attention. The counter argument is obvious—do both.

Mallarmé provided velleity, but further development of the principles which the next generation drew from his work led to Marinetti and worse, to poets of whom it could be complained, in Housman's words, "you treat us as Nebuchadnezzar did the Chaldeans, and expect us to find out the dream as well a the interpretation."

Modernism often got by on the simple argument that people had (or so modernists said) laughed at Beethoven. There is of course a logical fallacy involved. But more to the point is the fact that people with the highest reputation as innovators at a given period—Klopstock for example—are often regarded with horrified boredom by posterity. But it is also relevant that the "controversial" side of a "new" artist often has little to do with any real quality he may exhibit. Indeed, when the novelty is little more than novelty pure and simple, reputations die with astonishing speed. An example is Epstein, whose once immensely famous "Genesis" is now lying in a rubbish heap in one of the keeper's compounds in Battersea Park.

When the modernist mode began the most visible talker and writer was Ezra Pound. In examining his supposed novelty we find two main components. First, verse which is apparently "free" but which is usually a sort of resolved Whitmanesque hexameter—and right through his career we find his allegedly "new" artifacts crammed with "thou" and "didst" and all that. On the other hand (leaving aside economic and other nonsense), the main run of the more admired portions of the *Cantos* is little more than that imagism which Hilda Doolittle and others developed from their notion of Japanese verse. The original conception was clearly limited to fairly unified lyrics, and would have been better if it had been left there.

As to free verse, once it had established itself in the 1920s in England it became pervasive. No more than a decade later, school magazines of expensive girl's schools—always keener on "creativity" than boy's schools—were full of vague pieces of chopped up prose with vaguely emotional content. This may remind us that one notoriously bad effect of "free" verse is that large numbers of people educated during the last half century no longer understand the structure of real verse.

W. H. Auden was to remark in his later years "I cannot settle which is worse, / The anti-novel or free verse . . ." The truly astonishing discovery made by free versifier and anti-novelist alike was how much they could get away with. People have taken seriously, in recent times, novels consisting of loose pages in a box which the reader is invited to shuffle in any order he likes. It was of such things, and the many worse ones which will be familiar to all of you, that Philip Larkin writes, "The adjective 'modern,' when applied to any branch of art, means 'designed to evoke incomprehension, anger, boredom or laughter'" and defines modernism as "tending towards the silly, the disagreeable and the frigid."

In a fuller context the same writer tells us:

> I dislike such things not because they are new, but because they are irresponsible exploitations of technique in contradiction of human life as we know it. This is my essential criticism of modernism, whether perpetrated by Parker, Pound or Picasso: it helps us neither to enjoy nor endure. It will divert us as long as we are prepared to be mystified or outraged, but maintains its hold only by being more mystifying and more outrageous: it has no lasting power.

The Influence of Freud and Marx

No account of modernism can be complete without some reference to Freud. The extent to which Freudianism was taken as the last word on the human mind, the huge influences of the psychoanalytic myth, may surprise us nowadays. Yet it is worth remembering how fresh—and indeed shockingly so—was the Freudian concentration on sexuality. In particular every "advanced" young man and woman was able to point to what were still viewed as disreputable motives in all the actions of their elders or rivals. The idea of the Unconscious as a major—in fact senior—partner in the personality led directly, of course, to surrealism. But it also led in a less doctrinaire way to a treatment of images, in verse and prose, on a far more self-conscious basis than had yet been seen.

And then there was Marxism, which purported to give more or less final and definite answers to all matters of human society and behavior. To this attraction was added the fact that (like Freudianism) its mechanisms were so flexible that anything whatever could be fitted in somehow.

Is there then a connection between political radicalism and the aesthetic radicalism we call "modernism"?

The appeal of Marxism and in general of theories implying that "history" was on the verge of its final conclusion in the form of a perfect order, exhibited a certain parallel with the views taken by sponsors of modernist aesthetics—that an entirely new form of liberated art was now available, and that there would be no looking back. In both cases the predictions were false, and false for similar psychological reasons—a taste for novelty raised almost to a metaphysic, and a failure to consider that the intellectual fashions of any period, including one's own, eventually give way to something else.

Except for satire in its narrowest sense, there is remarkably little good political poetry in English. Even really good causes, far from being productive of good poetry, seem to have been sources of bathos, and this is true even of our greatest poets. As J. C. Furnas remarks in his scholarly and sensitive study of slavery, *The Road to Harpers Ferry*, "When touching on slavery, Cowper, Blake, Wordsworth and Southey produced drivel." Less good, or at any rate less straightforward causes, handled by greatly inferior poets, are more characteristic of our own time.

Few English poets have much *experience* of the political. They have generous impulses, no doubt, and well intended concern for humanity. These can be expressed in various ways and are not sufficient for a poem involving facts. On political issues it is extremely rare for the facts to be so clear, and the human involvement so direct and simple, as to approach the immediacy and undeniability of experience.

Even those few poets with some political knowledge and experience find it difficult to produce political poems. Laurence Durrell, one of those few, has dealt directly with political events in prose, in *Bitter Lemons*. But in the poem which concludes this book, as soon as he approaches the subject he has the modesty, a sense of the subject's intractibility, to write: "Better leave the rest unsaid." Excellent advice, for several reasons.

The Mexican painters like Rivera well illustrate one aspect of political modernism. And it is clear that an important part of the impact and the effect of their 'new' art was due far more to the political type of content than to the quasi-cubism involved in the forms chosen. In the palace at Chapultepec, one may see romantic revolutionary paintings of a century ago, showing liberators like Juarez and Diaz crushing venomous foes, etc., to the applause and enthusiasm of romantically conceived peasants and of "The People" in general. The difference between these and the more modern Mexican paintings is not great, and indeed the later generation owes a good deal not merely to this political inheritance but also to an element of primitivism already seen in their predecessors.

In fact, art with a "revolutionary" component of the political sort is very much a traditionalist form. The only exception I have come across, where a genuine new impulse seems visible, is in the strange statuary of Kemalist Turkey with its earthy New Turks pushing up out of the soil. Here, perhaps, the novelty may be due to the absence of any previous representational art.

One should also note a sentiment which is not exactly political but is strongly linked to attitudes on politics: the attraction avant-garde art had for those among the rich and privileged who felt guilty about their status. Just as with supporting or appeasing enemies of the bourgeoisie from Lenin to the Viet-Cong, there was (as Tom Wolfe puts it) "a peculiarly modern reward that the avant-garde artist can give his benefactor: namely, the feeling that he, like his mate the artist, is separate from and aloof from the bourgeoisie, the middle class."

This enmity of artists to "capitalism" and the "bourgeoisie" is a projection of mere temperament. (The notion that "capitalism" is hostile to art is in itself absurd. In fact, capitalist or bourgeois patronage has often marked a great flowering of art: the Medicis; Venice and Holland; or, to go further back, the great merchant-republic of Athens.)

In the first and second decades of this century there was an immense ferment of revolutionary-sounding attitudes, and these attracted some of the aesthetically radical—Marinetti into fascism, Mayakovsky into Bolshevism. Lenin himself disliked the futurists, and referred to Mayakovsky's views as "hooligan communism," but his cultural Commissar Lunarcharsky supported them. It is hard to remember now that political posters by Chagall were plastered on the trams in Vitebsk after the revolution. And outside Russia, a rather typical figure of the time was Ernst Toller, modernist playwright and revolutionary prisoner.

The revolutionary temperament emerged vis-à-vis a pre-revolutionary society, and this involved sharp and continual criticism of everything. But when a revolution comes, the ruling party is committed to a single truth, and thus to the destruction of the hitherto powerful critical faculty within its own ranks. So it was of course wholly misleading when the Nazis denounced modernism as *Kulturbolschewismus*: official Soviet art, by the mid-'20s, had become clearly Victorianized. Even so, some Soviet attraction remained.

Surrealism, of course was, in its origins, a highly doctrinaire and tight little movement, and one with a political commitment to communism. Andre Breton, as its chief theorist, led the movement in a more Trotskyite, anti-Soviet direction. But many of its adherents turned to Stalinism, in particular Louis Aragon but also to some degree Eluard.

And, even though orthodox communism repudiated modernist principles, there were plenty of "modernists" from Picasso to Neruda, who happily went along with it even in its most Stalinist phase.

On this issue, Brecht, whose intense artistic commitment to extremes of honesty is spoken of in the most lachrymose fashion in the drama departments of universities around the West, was totally dishonest at every level when it came to politics. No one, not even Sartre, has such a despicable record; and yet, politics formed a decisive element in his aesthetics. There is a certain paradox in the comparison between the subtlety and complexity sought by such writers in the structure of their prose and verse, and the complete crudity of the politics they embraced.

A Concluding Assessment

And what good came of it at last? When we look back we can surely say that the great revolution that the modernists thought they were bringing about simply failed.

But that is not the whole story. First of all, even if they were not as world-shaking as they imagined, they may still have left us some valuable, if peripheral, work. Such a modest contribution, after all, is all that Mallarmé claimed.

It is a remarkable fact that despite the opposition of well-established academics (a real priesthood of modernism) the more recent works which have against these odds forced themselves on the educated mind as the best writing of the last two or three decades are almost entirely "non-modernist." In Britain the novels of Anthony Powell and Graham Greene have little resemblance to *Finnigan's Wake* or *To the Lighthouse*. The poetry of Eliot, Auden, Larkin, is almost ostentatiously "unmodern" and mostly in traditional forms. But is there something of value that these writers of our generation have after all inherited from modernism?

I think there is.

Our rhythms have been loosened; our rhyme and assonance scheme has broadened; obliqueness—in verse or prose—is available on those occasions where it seems to work.

Such things as the attempt, in painting, to disentangle pattern from content may have its point in providing some sort of partial insight into why a great painting of the Quattrocento produced its effects, even if it failed as a prescription for present work.

The inventiveness sometimes produced charming or interesting results as with a "poem" of Arp's consisting of a square or oblong with, instead of pictorial detail, the words describing each part of a presumed painting, nicely phrased.

There was also an element, and often a very attractive one, of joking in the early avant-garde. Dada showed this to a very high degree. But the Dadaists for the most part went on to Surrealism. And although the latter contained an element of rather heavy-handed wit, this was largely a matter of aging charlatans like Salvador Dali, embraced by, instead of shocking, the bourgeois taste. On the whole, surrealism and its derivatives were merely solemn. As Auden writes:

With what conviction the young man
  spoke
When he thought his nonsense rather a
  joke:
Now, when he doesn't doubt any more,
No-one believes the booming old bore.

Still one finds the saving note of the comic not only in e.e. cummings, but also in Dylan Thomas for example— even at his most portentous he seems to fit Lautréamont's description of Byron: "L'hippotame des jungles infernales", more sympathetic, even as a monster, than the tyrannosaurs then infesting the continental countries.

Then we are (of course) much freer on sexual themes, and in the use of obscene words—which are to be found even in such works as *A Dance to the Music of Time*. But it is hard to believe that the uptightness which came into its own round at the end of the last century and went on in publishing circles for another 30–40 years, would not have given way to a more liberal view as previously puritanical episodes have always done. In fact the "modernist" contribution proper, whether associated with Freud, with radical anti-bourgeois notions, or with verbal theory, seems if anything to have been comparatively harmful—in that a gross excess of obscenity was thrust upon us in such things as the works of William Burroughs.

When it comes to a general consideration of modernism, was there another way open, back in the years following the turn of the century? Perhaps not. The arts were, it seems, driven in new directions at least in part by the mere exhaustion of the old at that particular time.

I think we should recognize the freshness and the excitement that affected the young as they came in contact for the first time with these new works that their elders found shockingly imcomprehensible. I still recall, while in my teens, the first surrealists, the first copies of *New Verse* and *Twentieth Century Verse*. (It is true that one found almost equal excitement in science fiction and jazz, both of which reached on through more ordinary channels: Wells and Verne preceding *Astounding Stories*, ragtime preceding swing.)

Of our reading of the time, what has survived? First of all, I think one should say that the victory of modernism in the minds of the young was never that total, that totalitarian sweep envisaged by its true believers. We (along with Auden and Eliot) continued to read Housman and Kipling.

But whom would we regard as a "modernist" poet in English? To us, today, Eliot, Yeats, and Auden appear traditionalists. With Dylan Thomas one may perhaps think that something wholly novel has been achieved. His poems, or many of them, are indeed the declamatory output of images scarcely connected at any conscious level. Still, there is nothing new in this idea of merely incantatory poetry, with little obviously "rational" content. It was no less a product of classicism that Gibbon himself who spoke of

the alternative aims of poetry being to "satisfy or silence our reason." Moreoever, incomprehensibility and pointlessness are not the same thing. There is nothing "incomprehensible" about a pile of bricks or a "concrete" poem.

What I am suggesting is that many writers claimed as modernist were merely modern. This is not to say that they were not affected by modernism, or experimentalism, proper, to various degrees. Thomas can properly be regarded as at least heavily charged with modernism: and we can add that it is his more "modernist" verse ("altar-wise by owl-light") which fades most quickly from our view—together, to be fair, with some of his slacker and later poems. Yet much remains—as can also be said of that true surrealist Kenneth Allott, though it may be noted that in both these cases disjunction of sense is matched by considerable rigor of form.

We have indeed been enriched by modernism; though, as I have suggested, the damage its attitudes have done in deadening both audience and mass sensibility by mere excess remains with us still.

In 1960 Pasternak, himself a modernist of the Russian Silver Age, said that

> all this writing of the twenties has terribly aged. . . . [o]ur works were dictated by the times. They lacked universality. . . . I have never understood those dreams of a new language, of a completely original form of expression. Because of this dream much of the work of the twenties which was stylistic experimentation has ceased to exist. The most extraordinary discoveries are made when the artist is overwhelmed by what he has to say. Then he uses the old language in his urgency and the old language is transformed from within.

That seems a very good summing up. Modernism was above all an attempt to create something which was not merely new in the sense that previous movements have been new, but rather a commitment to total and endless modernizing and re-modernizing—a Permanent Revolution.

When what this produced was the pointless and the meaningless, it became the main mission of the modernist type of mind not so much to produce or even procure this rubbish, but to explicate endlessly on its supposed value. The small benefits of modernism have long since been absorbed into the main body of the arts. What remains, claiming always to spontaneity, sensitivity, and liveliness, appears merely forced, apathetic, and moribund.

Mary P. Nichols

Whit Stillman's Comic Art

VOL. 35, NO. 2, 2000

Whit Stillman has claimed that he does not want to make serious dramas, only comedies. This does not mean, however, that his work has no serious intention. Critics have classified his three films, *Metropolitan* (1990), *Barcelona* (1994), and *The Last Days of Disco* (1998), as comedies of manners, and are reminded of Jane Austen. And well they might be, for Stillman has admitted that Austen, along with Tolstoy and Samuel Johnson, are the authors he loves most. A comedy of manners, according to the dictionary definition, is a satirical treatment of conventional or fashionable society. Satire arises when an author places an outsider among those who take the fashions, customs, and attitudes of their class for granted, allowing the audience to see conventional society from the outsider's perspective. In Austen's *Pride and Prejudice*, for example, we watch along with Mr. Bennet the absurdities of his wife's efforts to introduce their daughters into fashionable society. Comedy lies in the discrepancy between that society's understanding of itself and what the outsider sees. In a way, a comedy of manners portrays fashionable society itself as

a version of the classic comic figure, the boaster, at whom the audience laughs when the discrepancy between his pretensions and the truth comes to light.

Comedies of manners, however, need not be simply critical of the manners they satirize. While the English society of *Pride and Prejudice* offers us the hypocritical Miss Bingley, it also offers us Mr. Darcy, whose character and life reveal a sensitivity and moral worth inconceivable without society. Elizabeth Bennet may be an outsider whose keen perception penetrates Miss Bingley, but then so is Elizabeth's sister Lydia whose scorn for conventions leads to disgrace. Nor is it possible to understand Stillman's comedy without exploring the ambiguity of his attitude toward his characters, captured by one reviewer as "mocking affection."

In *Metropolitan*, we see a group of Manhattan socialites through the eyes of outsider Tom Townsend (Edward Clements), a Westsider among the Eastsider elites, a disciple of the French socialist Charles Fourier, a reader of Thorstein Veblen, and one opposed to debutante parties on principle. One of the debutantes of the group, Audrey

Rouget (Carolyn Farina), is herself a kind of outsider, due in part to her love of Jane Austen. When Tom objects that "everything Jane Austen wrote seems ridiculous from today's perspective," Audrey is quick to respond: "Has it ever occurred to you that today, looked at from Jane Austen's perspective, would look much worse?" By the end of the movie, Tom comes to appreciate Austen, Audrey, and his new friends.

In *Barcelona,* Ted and Fred Boynton (Taylor Nichols and Chris Eigeman) are American innocents abroad, one in the office of an American company in *Barcelona,* the other a naval officer on a diplomatic assignment there. However much they try to belong to the Spanish social scene, they are bourgeois Americans trying to negotiate European culture and corruption as well as anti-American political sentiment. Their unsophisticated tastes and sexual mores, their capitalist values, their American patriotism, and even old-fashioned piety at first appear as ridiculous, especially in the eyes of their Spanish friends, but ultimately constitute their solid human decency. The movie suggests a bridge between the two cultures when Ted's business requires commuting between Barcelona and Chicago, and eventually both Ted and Fred marry foreign women and bring them to the States.

The preppies of *Metropolitan* have become yuppies in *The Last Days of Disco,* and they frequent an exclusive Manhattan disco club. They are all now more or less outside, constantly trying to get into the Club. Even the Club's underboss occupies a precarious status, constantly risking his job by admitting friends through the backdoor. Stillman presents the conventions of disco culture, and the social craze it represents, as ridiculous, and certainly as morally questionable as the fashionable

society of Austen's novels. But while the fashions of any age may be limited and timebound, Stillman lets us see the human aspirations moving his characters' attraction to disco, just as Austen herself illustrates the moral benefits of social conventions. In this essay, I shall explore Stillman's comic standpoint in his three films—one that makes Stillman himself a mocking but affectionate critic, an outsider who is not simply an outsider.

METROPOLITAN SHOWS us Manhattan debutantes and their escorts home for Christmas vacation from their ivy-league schools. Scenes occur primarily at all-night "afterparties" in the affluent living rooms of the "urban haute bourgeoisie," or the UHB, a term coined by the group's theoretician, Charlie (Taylor Nichols). The film is well described as one of "preppie angst." Stillman shows us Spengler's *Decline of the West* by Tom's bedside as he dresses in his tuxedo. Another of the escorts laments the changing social conditions that foretell the "last deb season as we know it." Another senses that their whole preppie class is "doomed" to failure and extinction. Or perhaps their angst must be understood in less world historical terms, for as they themselves recognize, they are "at a very vulnerable point in their lives."

Metropolitan opens with the tears of its heroine, insecure deb Audrey Rouget, who is having difficulty with the fit of her new evening dress. Her mother tries to comfort her with the thought that her younger brother is no authority on female anatomy. Mrs. Rouget can at least take in the dress where "it is a bit full." As Mrs. Rouget knows, her daughter's dress may be altered, not so that it hides defects but so that it allows strengths to appear to best advantage. Hers is an art motivated by love.

Audrey comes to like her group's newcomer Tom, although he claims that Austen's *Mansfield Park* is "a notoriously bad book." Tom is initially the critic not only of Austen, but of the whole debutante scene. Falling in with the snobbish and sophisticated SFRP (the Sally Fowler Rat Pack, as they call themselves after one of their group), Tom is a less "haute" bourgeois. He rents rather than owns his tuxedo, and intends to go to no more dances—until Nick Smith (Chris Eigeman) changes his mind.

Nick also advises Tom about the dress code, defending the use of detachable collars in men's formal evening dress—"a small thing, but symbolically important," he informs Tom, observing that "our parents' generation was never interested in keeping up standards." Although such collars "look much better," like many things they "have been abandoned for supposed convenience." Although Stillman encourages us to smile at Nick's concern with detachable collars, he lets Nick's remarks about standards echo later in the movie when Nick himself has to admit he "failed to live up to [the standards of the UHB]."

Nick's failure lay in telling a story about Polly Perkins—a young woman whom Nick claims was mistreated by the movie's cad Rick Von Sloneker. But Polly Perkins is "a fabrication," and Von Sloneker accuses Nick of lying. Even Nick's friend Charlie tells him "this looks really bad." Nick insists that Polly Perkins is a composite rather than a fabrication, for while there is no one Polly "they're many of them." But Von Sloneker's view prevails with the rat pack. While Frank Sinatra's rat pack, from which Sally Fowler's takes its name, was more style than substance, Sally's pack has standards that uphold the truth. The film's defender of appearance seems to have strayed too far: the

invention of the detachable collar makes evening wear "look better," but Nick's invention of Polly Perkins that makes Von Sloneker look bad makes Nick look even worse.

On the other hand, appearances can deceive. When Nick presents the story of Polly Perkins, Cynthia defends Von Sloneker, claiming that she knew Polly and it wasn't Rick's fault. Because there is no one Polly Perkins, Cynthia's response proves, Nick argues, "that Von Sloneker is doing those kinds of things all the time." The film's exploration of the question of truth emerges in other ways as well.

At one after party, Sally Fowler proposes the game "Truth," in which players answer questions with "absolute honesty" and "openness." Audrey objects that "there are good reasons why people don't go around telling each other their most intimate thoughts" and that is why there are "convention[s]," but Cynthia accuses her of having something "to hide." Audrey, the reader of Jane Austen, is overruled in her reluctance to play "Truth," and the game proceeds. But we might ask, with whom does Stillman side? In this instance, not only are two players, Jane and Audrey, hurt by "truths" that others reveal, it is not clear that a simple answer to a question can reveal the truth in all its complexity. When Cynthia reveals the "truth" that the last person she slept with was Nick, for example, its meaning is open to various interpretations, as the subsequent discussion demonstrates. As to Tom's declaration of his crush on Serena Slocum and his lack of interest in anyone else, events prove that Tom, for all his honesty, was far from understanding his real feelings. The strictures on excessive candor may not be "just a social convention," as Cynthia insists, or even an awareness that the truth may hurt, as Audrey realizes, but a recognition that the truth may not be so simple a matter that it emerges with mere "honesty and openness."

It is Cynthia's ready acceptance of Nick's fabrication about Polly Perkins, after all, that Nick takes as proof that his fabrication was indeed a composite. And what looks like hypocrisy to Nick's accusers (his answering "yes and no", when asked if he made it all up) is in fact the truth, even if Nick's friends do not understand it, and even if Nick may be faulted for applying the device of poetry too simply to life. To say, as Nick does, that *New York Magazine* also creates composites is no justification. Poetry's composites do not speak about individuals, as Nick's does about Von Sloneker.

As Christmas vacation approaches its close, the group dissolves. Curiously, it is the initially critical newcomer Tom who seems most distressed. He has also come to appreciate Jane Austen, for now he is actually reading her, rather than getting her second hand through literary critics. He even wonders if "Fourier was a crank." Lest we suppose that the social critic has been co-opted by the system he criticized, we should note that Tom is less concerned by the disintegration of the Rat Pack than by the disappearance of Audrey, for a date with his idealized Serena has opened his eyes to his affection for Audrey. He is even more distraught when he discovers that she has gone with Cynthia to Von Sloneker's house party in Southampton and thinks that she has "turned her back on [Austen]." He and Charlie go on a rescue mission, but of course Audrey's virtue is safe. Von Sloneker is only too glad to have the "flat-chested goody-goody, pain-in-the-neck" leave with her rescuers.

When Nick says good-bye to Tom before heading upstate, he "leave[s] counting on [him] and Charlie to maintain the standards and ideals of the UHB," for "[Tom] and Charlie are the only ones who understand this kind of thing." Although Tom seems perplexed, Nick may again speak the truth, if in fact it takes someone who retains the perspective of the outsider to appreciate and maintain a society's standards and ideals. As they leave Von Sloneker's, Audrey asks Tom if he really thinks she is flat-chested. Tom has learned something about excessive candor, or about UHB ideals as well as behavior, for he answers, "Well, I shouldn't say that. The thing is, you look great—and that's what important. You don't want to overdo it. " These are the last words of the movie, and we witness "a small thing, but symbolically important," words that might apply to Stillman's film itself.

BARCELONA REVOLVES around two young Americans in Spain, and the women they meet, date, and love. Ted Boynton is a sales manager for the Barcelona office of the Illinois High-Speed Motor Corporation, and his cousin Fred a naval lieutenant doing diplomatic work there during "the last decade of the Cold War." The relation of the cousins is close, but not without friction. Fred drops in on Ted unannounced and takes his prolonged stay for granted. Fred also thinks his cousin "a prig." We see why. Because the "inordinate concern for physical beauty has wrecked . . . lives," Ted tells his cousin, he has decided to go out only with "plain or homely women." Fred, definitely interested in meeting "terribly attractive women" in Barcelona, and not at all put off by Ted's description of Spanish girls as "really promiscuous," claims that Ted's idea about homely women is "pathetic" and "crazy." No wonder Ted tells his cousin less than he tells us in a "voice-over" (film's substitute for stage's soliloquies) about his "aspiration . . . to free romance from the chains of physical beauty and carnality," and how he reads Old Testament books for "advice on romantic matters." If the character of Ted is a development of the virtuous Audrey (Fred refers to Ted as a "goody-goody," as Von Sloneker had Audrey), his virtue, as seen through Fred's eyes, appears ridiculous. It is no wonder that Fred cannot resist confiding in Ted's women friends that Ted "is not at all how he seems"—in fact, Ted admires the Marquis de Sade, and "under the apparently very normal clothes he's wearing these black leather straps, drawn so taut that while he dances. . . ." No wonder that Ted fails to appreciate Fred as "the best P.R. guy [he'll] ever have," or "get down on his knees and thank God [he has] a cousin who makes up interesting stories about [him]."

Ted looks ridiculous enough even without Fred, as he hides his Bible, filled with yellow Post-it notes, inside a copy of the *Economist* and reads the Holy Writ while swaying to the music of Glenn Miller. Perhaps, however, there is good reason to be circumspect about one's faith in a culture where it can be said matter-of-factly, as one of their "cool" women friends Montserrat (Tushka Bergen) does, that "'all the old gods are dead,'—there is no God. That we know." Montserrat seems quite sympathetic to the discovery made by her Spanish lover Ramon that "the idea of physical beauty . . . is the closest thing that remains to divinity in the modern world."

Apart from religion and sex, the other passion in Ted's life is his work. He is devoted to his job in "sales," which he views as "more than just a job. . . . It's a culture, a whole way of thinking about experience." Along with the Old Testament, Ted believes in "the genius of Carnegie's theory of human relations." In this film, *How*

I Raised Myself from Failure to Success in Sales and *The Effective Executive* have replaced *Mansfield Park* and *Persuasion*. Its moral lesson for sales is Ben Franklin's: "to bluntly tell the truth" about one's product, for honesty is "always safe and best." Stillman may have more elevated examples than Ted about what constitutes "the classic literature of self-improvement," but Ted's honest practice results in more than sales: "many [of his customers] also became his friends."

If the old gods are dead, however, Fred's patriotism is not. Fred insists on scratching out insulting anti-American graffiti, even if it takes "paint[ing] the whole wall with a ballpoint pen." He also proudly wears his naval dress uniform—to Ted's chagrin—as he and Ted make the rounds of Barcelona's social scene, although it provokes the outcry of "fascist" from the locals. Anti-American feeling intensifies in the course of the film, culminating in Fred's being shot by terrorists. The last quarter of the movie is dominated by Ted's vigil in the hospital at comatose Fred's bedside, keeping up a steady stream of one-sided conversation or reading aloud in the hopes of bringing Fred back to consciousness.

For all the tension between these cousins—at least since they were ten, when Fred, without asking, borrowed and accidently sunk Ted's kayak—their differences are more cosmetic than real. Like Fred, Ted is also a patriot, who not only defends hamburgers, but calls Ramon a liar to his face regarding his anti-American statements. Fred, for his part, is not as liberated from bourgeois ideals as his mockery of Ted might indicate. He is astounded when Marta (Mira Sorvino) expresses the view that wanting to get married is "[thinking] in extremist terms." And he desires to meet "the one [woman] in the world he was meant to be with."

By the third day of Fred's unconsciousness, Ted confesses that Fred, the stronger swimmer, may have in fact saved his life by going down in his kayak in his place. Ted speaks honestly, although it puts his own long-held grudge against Fred in a petty light. However much Ted understands his honesty in the style of Ben Franklin, his honesty here comes closer to George Washington's. American virtue may be enlightened self-interest, as Tocqueville said, but it occasionally reaches beyond itself.

At Ted's confession, Fred briefly opens his unbandaged eye. But no more than the words of the novel Ted has been reading to Fred do his words of regret by themselves revive his cousin. Only when Ted gets on his knees to pray, asking God to bring Fred back "to full consciousness" and to forgive his "doubting, vainglory, and unworthiness," does Fred speak. "Oh, give me a break," he responds to Ted's prayer, and turns away. One way or another, Ted's prayer has brought Fred out of his coma. "[Fred's] going to have a complete recovery," the ecstatic Ted proclaims to everyone.

A number of brief scenes conclude the movie, including plans for Ted's promotion and transfer back to Chicago and for his marriage to Greta. Ted met Greta in the hospital, when Aurora brought her along to help read to Fred. Ted is evidently not put off by her beauty, asking why wasn't she in any of Ramon's articles about beautiful women. There is a hint that it takes more than physical beauty to capture Ramon's interest when Greta confides that she "loathes" Ramon, and thinks he is "repelente." She also draws sketches of "hovering angels."

In the last scene of the movie, set in the United States, Greta is with Ted, Montserrat with Fred, and Aurora has been introduced to Ted's business associate Dickie Taylor. They are grilling hamburgers and hot dogs, and bourgeois life in America never looked so good, at least to the European women who earlier had contempt for hamburgers and other signs of American "culture." Dickie is perplexed that Aurora keeps smirking about his underwear. Ted, who may even be the cause of her smirk, plays along. He has gained enough distance from himself to become playful, and enough confidence to acknowledge Fred's perspective. Ted has not entirely forsworn the romantic illusions he tried earlier to reject. This does not mean that he is any less accepting of bourgeois life than he was earlier in the film. That rejection the film leaves to Ramon. But Ted makes bourgeois life interesting through art, just as Stillman does through his film.

THE LAST Days of Disco returns to Manhattan and to preppies who have graduated to jobs in business, publishing, and law. They frequent an exclusive Manhattan disco club—a place they "always dreamed of. Cocktails, dancing, conversation, exchanges of ideas and points of view. Everyone's here." Little, however, is as it seems in *Last Days*. Alice (Chloë Sevigny) and Charlotte (Kate Beckinsale), who attended college together and now work in the same publishing firm, turn out not to be the friends they seem. Nor is club manager Des (Chris Eigeman) the homosexual he claims to be in order to extricate himself from affairs with women. And the "clients" whom Jimmy Steinway (Mackenzie Astin) gets into the Club through his friendship with Des, turn out to be federal investigators. The Club itself, and its culture, encourages the cultivation of appearance: Alice suggests they she and Charlotte will be more likely to get into the Club if they arrive in a cab rather than on foot. Jimmy tries to hide his boss's garish clothes under his own stylish overcoat so that he will more likely be admitted. Tom (Robert Sean Leonard) advises Josh (Matt Keeslar) to "try to avoid eye contact" with the doorman as they go by. Whereas Fred's naval uniform in *Barcelona* is not a costume, even if Marta understands it that way, Des gives his friends costumes to sneak into the Club unknown. Other patrons dress as the Cowardly Lion and the Tin Man. Before the movie is over, the glitter of the Club gives way to its seamy underside—drug dealing and money laundering—followed by arrests and prosecutions.

As in Stillman's other films, *Last Days* has its virtuous heroine. Alice reads, and has better judgment and more refined tastes than some of her contemporaries. But her hero is J. D. Salinger rather than Jane Austen. She is also plagued with self-doubts, and tempted by the experience with men that she lacks. Alice is weaker than Audrey, lacks her moral resources, and is burdened by the advice of Charlotte who feeds her insecurities under the guise of building her self-esteem. "For most guys, sexual repressiveness is a turnoff," Charlotte confides. But when Alice succeeds in getting Tom into bed, she also loses his respect. Like the Club itself for so many, Alice is for Tom a vision or ideal that disappoints. Unlike the Club, however, Alice suffers, learns, and matures.

In spite of her susceptibility to Charlotte's advice and pressure, Alice makes two choices in the course of the movie that demonstrate her developing strength of character. She accepts Josh, despite his manic depression and Charlotte's contempt for him as a "sick-o." Alice also supports the publication of a manuscript on Tibetan Buddhism that

Charlotte recommended rejecting. When the author turns out to be a fraud—a writer from Los Angeles rather than the brother of the Dalai Lama he claimed to be, she is able to save "a really good book" by transferring it from nonfiction to the "self-actualization" category. Alice's ability to appreciate the virtue in what others find defective reaps her a promotion to associate editor by the end of the film, whereas Charlotte is laid off. Charlotte of course is hardly crushed, for she has no "devotion to the written word," and thinks she will find "a better job in television, . . . where [her] interests really lie."

Whereas Alice finds worth in a rejected manuscript, Josh criticizes the moral effect of a movie. *Lady and the Tramp* is "a primer for love and marriage directed at very young people, imprinting on their little psyches the idea that smooth talking delinquents recently escaped from the local pound are a good match for nice girls from sheltered homes." The cartoon "program[s] women to adore jerks." The only sympathetic character, the little Scotty who is loyal and concerned about Lady, "is mocked as old-fashioned and irrelevant." Josh not only knows the moral danger of art, he would be able to appreciate Jane Austen. And we have seen his attraction to Alice from the moment he is introduced into the movie.

As assistant district attorney, Josh pursues the arrests and indictments that lead to the demise of the Club he loves. He also warns Des to clean up his act (he is taking cocaine) before the DA's office moves against the Club. In spite of the success of the prosecutions, Josh is laid off for giving "preferential treatment to a friend." He appears to have no regrets, although he must also have that friend's passport confiscated at the airport to force him to do the right thing, to stay to testify. Des for his part is trying to run away, he admits, "like a rat," aware that the "Shakespearean admonition, 'To thine own self be true'" cannot apply to him, for his own self is "pretty bad." Integrity alone is not enough, there are standards by which to measure integrity. It is fitting that he and Charlotte in the end form a couple, as do Josh and Alice. Both couples in the end violate Charlotte's earlier stricture against "ferocious pairing off" from the group, a stricture she used to keep Alice away from Jimmy until she could grab him for herself. Like integrity itself, pairing off is not simply good. Pairing off cannot be judged apart from the character of the pair.

Religion makes an appearance in *Last Days* in a more muted form than in *Barcelona,* where there is mention of the Bible, prayer, and angels. Nor does religion receive the serious attention it does in *Metropolitan,* when Charlie argues at an afterparty that most of us as we mature lose our innate belief in God, which we later "regain only by a conscious act of faith," although he has not yet experienced such an act. We do see Charlie's utter faith in Audrey by the end of *Metropolitan,* perhaps foreshadowing *Last Days.* There, Alice not only finds value in a religious book and promotes its publication, she overcomes her hesitancy about Josh, whose "mania" became manifest in college by singing a hymn asking God's forgiveness. Charlotte, who originally criticized Alice's interest in Josh, later attacks her for being "weirded out" when Josh "sang a hymn" on the street. Charlotte claims that she herself has sung hymns on the street, and she breaks into "Amazing Grace." The words of the hymn continue to follow Alice as she walks along Manhattan streets. Charlotte's defense of singing hymns is only one more way to attack Alice, and to make her feel bad about herself under the guise of good advice. But this time she does give good advice, which Alice follows. Stillman does not mock the hymn, any more than he mocks the advice, by putting it in the mouth of such a defective character as Charlotte. The hymn is not less beautiful in being sung by Charlotte, nor the advice less good by being ill-intentioned. Greater the power of divinity when it works through imperfect means. As the words of "Amazing Grace" suggest, religion is less the conscious act of faith Charlie supposes than an acceptance of grace that permits one to find the *good* even in its imperfect forms.

AT THE end of *Last Days,* the Club has been destroyed, new owners cannot resurrect it, and more generally, the bottom has dropped out of disco record sales. The former doorman at the Club, now turned prosecution witness, announces that disco is dead. Josh delivers a final paean to disco: "[it] will never be over. It will always live in our minds and hearts. [It] was too great and too much fun to be gone forever. It's got to come back, someday." Josh recognizes not inevitable historical decline, as in theories about the decline of the West, but the necessary reemergence of the good because it is good. At the end of his speech in praise of disco, the group stares at him in silence, and we wait for some contemptuous comment by Des about Josh's manic phases. But Josh recognizes that he is making himself ridiculous, and becomes his own critic before Des can speak: "Sorry," he apologizes, "I've got a job interview this afternoon. I was just trying to get revved up. " By finding a way to call attention to his own absurdity, Josh prevents his praise of disco from being negated with laughter: "most of what I said, I believe."

In his description of the end of disco, Josh sounds a theme that we have heard in other forms: "for a few years, maybe for many years, it will be considered passé, and ridiculous. It will be misrepresented, and caricatured, and sneered at, or worse, completely ignored." Stillman hints at the difficulty he faces in writing comedy in the modern world, when the old gods have become passé and ridiculous, caricatured and ignored. In a world in which Ramon can be thought not only "fascinating" but godly, and where disco clubs substitute for churches in giving meaning to life, can religion do anything but hide itself—or peep out in ridiculous form from between the covers of *The Economist*? And if comedy presents the old gods only in comic guise, would it not simply contribute to their absurdity?

There are different kinds of comedy. There is a comedy that Stillman criticizes, seen in Cynthia's description of Nick as someone who looks down "from such lofty heights [that] everything below seems a bit comical." So too, everything high may seem ridiculous if one looks from too low a perspective, as suggested by the words of the limbo that Nick and Ted dance when they meet Ramon: "How low can you go?" Stillman's comic perspective is not one of ridicule, either of the low or of the high. Ted speaks for Stillman in *Barcelona* when he objects to a "perceptiveness" that ridicules rather than comprehends. Stillman's films ask us, as Audrey asks Tom, to look at ourselves from Jane Austen's perspective. But asking is not enough. For denizens of the modern age, Austen is an acquired taste, as she was for Tom. Tom's coming to know and eventually love Audrey was a precondition for his liking Austen. Stillman's films, including the one in which we too meet Audrey, function for us as Audrey does for Tom. Appreciating

Austen—or Stillman—is a metaphor for something important today—attaining a comic standpoint of mocking affection rather than of ridicule and cynicism. Ramon, we have seen, attempts to remind his readers of divinity through his stories and photographs of women of extraordinary physical beauty. Stillman suggests that Ramon has had some success; at least he has a following who is listening to him intently whenever we see him. Stillman's films are a better version of Ramon's journalism, for they reveal an inner beauty that reminds us of our connection with something higher than ourselves. We may be laughable, but we are not contemptible. "Mocking affection" fits, even for the bourgeoisie.

In *Metropolitan*, Charlie says that when he first heard of Bunuel's *The Discreet Charm of the Bourgeoisie* he "thought, 'finally someone's going to tell the truth about the bourgeoisie,'" but it is "hard to imagine a less fair or accurate portrait." Giving a more fair and accurate portrait—"the bourgeoisie does have a lot of charm," Charlie insists—is presumably how Stillman understands his task. But the task is a difficult one for an artist, not only because like the old gods the bourgeoisie has been discredited, but also because the bourgeoisie has been discredited for being prosaic. Charmless. If Stillman shows the charm of the bourgeoisie, as critics recognize, perhaps he can make the old gods credible as well. He does so in part by incorporating into his movies the doubts of even those who believe, as well as criticisms, such as Fred's criticism of Ted's search for a homely woman to marry in *Barcelona*, or Tom's of debutante parties in *Metropolitan*, or even Josh's criticism of himself in *The Last Days of Disco*. And then Stillman shows life triumphing over those doubts and criticisms.

Last Days ends when Josh and Alice meet on the subway on their way to an exclusive midtown restaurant to celebrate Alice's promotion to associate editor. At the sound of disco music coming from we know not where, Josh and Alice spontaneously start dancing, and soon everyone in the subway car, and even everyone on the platform waiting for the train, is dancing—rich and poor, young and old. Like the vision Stillman captures in his film, the joy from the music spreads from the couple, not to those admitted to an exclusive club, but to everyone. Stillman ends, however, like Josh before him, on a note of self-mockery, for the disco music blends into the words of "Amazing Grace." Maintaining through the end the distance from his film that preserves its charm, Stillman allows the hymn-singing Charlotte to deliver his film's final message.

Earlier in *Last Days*, the publishing staff where Alice and Charlotte work discuss an "outline" for how to write a best-seller: "create sympathetic characters with whom readers identify, give them problems, make those problems big." One member of the staff is disgusted, finds the outline "completely formulaic," and prefers nonfiction to fiction. Stillman, of course, opts for fiction, but he creates characters who evoke our laughter as well as our sympathy. And while he gives them problems, it is to his credit that he never makes those problems bigger than they are. Nor are their solutions out of reach. Such is his comedy of manners.

Robert R. Reilly

The Music of the Spheres, or the Metaphysics of Music

VOL. 37, NO. 1, 2001

"[In] sound itself, there is a readiness to be ordered by the spirit and this is seen at its most sublime in music."

—*Max Picard*

Despite the popular Romantic conception of creative artists as inspired madmen, composers are not idiots savants, distilling their musical inspiration from the ether. Rather, in their creative work they respond and give voice to certain metaphysical visions. Most composers speak explicitly in philosophical terms about the nature of the reality that they try to reflect. When the forms of musical expression change radically, it is always because the underlying metaphysical grasp of reality has changed as well. Music is, in a way, the sound of metaphysics, or metaphysics in sound.

Music in the Western world was shaped by a shared conception of reality so profound that it endured for some twenty-five hundred years. As a result, the means of music remained essentially the same—at least to the extent that what was called music could always have been recognized as such by its forbearers, as much as they might have disapproved of its specific style. But by the early twentieth century, this was no longer true. Music was re-conceptualized so completely that it could no longer be experienced as music, i.e., with melody, harmony, and rhythm. This catastrophic rupture, expressed especially in the works of Arnold Schoenberg and John Cage, is often celebrated as just another change in the techniques of music, a further point along the parade of progress in the arts. It was, however, a reflection of a deeper metaphysical divide that severed the composer from any meaningful contact with external reality. As a result, musical art was reduced to the arbitrary manipulation of fragments of sound.

Here, I will sketch the philosophical presuppositions that undergirded the Western conception of music for most of its existence and then examine the character of the change music underwent in the twentieth century. I will conclude with a reflection on the recovery of music in our own time and the reasons for it, as exemplified in the works of two contemporary composers, the Dane Vagn Holmboe and the American John Adams.

ACCORDING TO tradition, the harmonic structure of music was discovered by Pythagoras about the fifth century B.C. Pythagoras experimented with a stretched piece of cord. When plucked, the cord sounded a certain note. When halved in length and plucked again, the cord sounded a higher note completely consonant with the first. In fact, it was the same note at a higher pitch. Pythagoras had discovered the ratio, 2:1, of the octave. Further experiments, plucking the string two-thirds of its original length produced a perfect fifth in the ratio of 3:2. When a three-quarters length of cord was plucked, a perfect fourth was sounded in the ratio of 4:3, and so forth. These sounds were all consonant and extremely pleasing to the ear. The significance that Pythagoras attributed to this discovery cannot be overestimated. Pythagoras thought that number was the key to the universe. When he found that harmonic music is expressed in exact numerical ratios of whole numbers, he concluded that music was the ordering principle of the world. The fact that music was denominated in exact numerical ratios demonstrated to him the intelligibility of reality and the existence of a reasoning intelligence behind it.

Pythagoras wondered about the relationship of these ratios to the larger world. (The Greek word for ratio is logos, which also means *reason* or *word*.) He considered that the harmonious sounds that men make, either with their instruments or in their singing, were an approximation of a larger harmony that existed in the universe, also expressed by numbers, which was "the music of the spheres." As Aristotle explained in the *Metaphysics*, the Pythagoreans "supposed the elements of numbers to be the elements of all things, and the whole heaven to be a musical scale and a number." This was meant literally.

The heavenly spheres and their rotations through the sky produced tones at various levels, and in concert, these tones made a harmonious sound that man's music, at its best, could approximate. Music was number made audible. Music was man's participation in the harmony of the universe.

This discovery was fraught with ethical significance. By participating in heavenly harmony, music could induce spiritual harmony in the soul. Following Pythagoras, Plato taught that "rhythm and harmony find their way into the inward places of the soul, on which they mightily fasten, imparting grace, and making the soul of him who is rightly educated graceful." In the *Republic*, Plato showed the political import of music's power by invoking Damon of Athens as his musical authority. Damon said that he would rather control the modes of music in a city than its laws, because the modes of music have a more decisive effect on the formation of the character of citizens. The ancient Greeks were also wary of music's power because they understood that, just as there was harmony, there was disharmony. Musical discord could distort the spirit, just as musical concord could properly dispose it.

This idea of "the music of the spheres" runs through the history of Western civilization with an extraordinary consistency, even up to the twentieth century. At first it was meant literally, later poetically. Either way, music was seen more as a discovery than a creation, because it relied on pre-existing principles of order in nature for its operation. It is instructive to look briefly at the reiteration of this teaching in the writings of several major thinkers to appreciate its enduring significance as well as the radical nature of the challenge to it in the twentieth century.

In the first century B.C., Cicero spelled

out Plato's teaching in the last chapter of his *De Republica*. In "Scipio's Dream," Cicero has Scipio Africanus asking the question, "What is that great and pleasing sound?" The answer comes, "That is the concord of tones separated by unequal but nevertheless carefully proportional intervals, caused by the rapid motion of the spheres themselves. . . . Skilled men imitating this harmony on stringed instruments and in singing have gained for themselves a return to this region, as have those who have cultivated their exceptional abilities to search for divine truths." Cicero claims that music can return man to a paradise lost. It is a form of communion with divine truth.

In the late second century A.D., St. Clement of Alexandria baptized the classical Greek and Roman understanding of music in his *Exhortation to the Greeks*. The transcendent God of Christianity gave new and somewhat different meanings to the "music of the spheres." Using Old Testament imagery from the Psalms, St. Clement said that there is a "New Song," far superior to the Orphic myths of the pagans. The "New Song" is Christ, the Logos Himself: "it is this [New Song] that composed the entire creation into melodious order, and tuned into concert the discord of the elements, that the whole universe may be in harmony with it." It is Christ who "arranged in harmonious order this great world, yes, and the little world of man, body and soul together; and on this many-voiced instrument he makes music to God and sings to [the accompaniment of] the human instrument." By appropriating the classical view, St. Clement was able to show that music participated in the divine by praising God and partaking in the harmonious order of which He was the composer. But music's end or goal was now higher, because Christ is higher

than the created cosmos. Cicero had spoken of the divine region to which music is supposed to transport man. That region was literally within the heavens. With Christianity, the divine region becomes both transcendent and personal because Logos is Christ. The new purpose of music is to make the transcendent perceptible in the "New Song."

The early sixth century A.D. had two especially distinguished Roman proponents of the classical view of music, both of whom served at various times in high offices to the Ostrogoth king, Theodoric. Cassiodorus was secretary to Theodoric. He wrote a massive work called *Institutiones*, which echoes Plato's teaching on the ethical content of music, as well as Pythagoras's on the power of number. Cassiodorus taught that "music indeed is the knowledge of apt modulation. If we live virtuously, we are constantly proved to be under its discipline, but when we sin, we are without music. The heavens and the earth and indeed all things in them which are directed by a higher power share in the discipline of music, for Pythagoras attests that this universe was founded by and can be governed by music."

Boethius served as consul to Theodoric in A.D. 510. Among his writings was *The Principles of Music*, a book that had enormous influence through the Middle Ages and beyond. Boethius said that

> music is related not only to speculation, but to morality as well, for nothing is more consistent with human nature than to be soothed by sweet modes and disturbed by their opposites. Thus we can begin to understand the apt doctrine of Plato, which holds that the whole of the universe is united by a musical concord. For when we compare that which is

coherently and harmonious joined together within our own being with that
which is coherently and harmoniously
joined together in sound—that is, that
which gives us pleasure—so we come
to recognize that we ourselves are
united according to the same principle
of similarity.

It is not necessary to cite further examples after Boethius because *The Principles
of Music* was so influential that it held
sway for centuries thereafter. It was the
standard music theory text at Oxford until 1856.

THE HIERATIC role of music even
survived into the twentieth century with
composers like Jean Sibelius. Sibelius
harkened back to St. Clement when he
wrote that "the essence of man's being is
his striving after God. It [the composition of music] is brought to life by means
of the logos, the divine in art. That is the
only thing that has significance." But this
vision was lost for most of the twentieth
century because the belief on which it
was based was lost.

Philosophical propositions have a very
direct and profound impact upon composers and what they do. John Adams,
one of the most popular American composers today, said that he had "learned
in college that tonality died somewhere
around the time that Nietzsche's God
died, and I believed it." The connection is
quite compelling. At the same time God
disappears, so does the intelligible order
in creation. If there is no God, nature no
longer serves as a reflection of its Creator.
If you lose the Logos of St. Clement, you
also lose the ratio (logos) of Pythagoras.
Nature is stripped of its normative power.
This is just as much a problem for music
as it is for philosophy.

The systematic fragmentation of music was the logical working out of the
premise that music is not governed by
mathematical relationships and laws that
inhere in the structure of a hierarchical
and ordered universe, but is wholly constructed by man and therefore essentially
without limits or definition. Tonality, as
the pre-existing principle of order in the
world of sound, goes the same way as the
objective moral order. So how does one
organize the mess that is left once God
departs? If there is no pre-existing intelligible order to go out to and apprehend,
and to search through for what lies beyond it—which is the Creator—what
then is music supposed to express? If
external order does not exist, then music
turns inward. It collapses in on itself and
becomes an obsession with technique.
Any ordering of things, musical or otherwise, becomes simply the whim of man's
will.

Without a "music of the spheres" to
approximate, modern music, like the
other arts, began to unravel. Music's self-
destruction became logically imperative
once it undermined its own foundation. In
the 1920s, Arnold Schoenberg unleashed
the centrifugal forces of disintegration
in music through his denial of tonality.
Schoenberg contended that tonality does
not exist in nature as the very property of
sound itself, as Pythagoras had claimed,
but was simply an arbitrary construct of
man, a convention. This assertion was
not the result of a new scientific discovery
about the acoustical nature of sound, but
of a desire to demote the metaphysical
status of nature. Schoenberg was irritated
that "tonality does not serve, [but] must
be served." Rather than conform himself
to reality, he preferred to command reality to conform itself to him. As he said,
"I can provide rules for almost anything."
Like Pythagoras, Schoenberg believed

that number was the key to the universe. Unlike Pythagoras, he believed his manipulation of number could alter that reality in a profound way. Schoenberg's gnostic impulse is confirmed by his extraordinary obsession with numerology, which would not allow him to finish a composition until its opus number corresponded with the correct number of the calendar date.

Schoenberg proposed to erase the distinction between tonality and atonality by immersing man in atonal music until, through habituation, it became the new convention. Then discords would be heard as concords. As he wrote, "The emancipation of dissonance is at present accomplished and twelve-tone music in the near future will no longer be rejected because of 'discords.'" Anyone who claims that, through his system, the listener shall hear dissonance as consonance is engaged in reconstituting reality.

Of his achievement, Schoenberg said, "I am conscious of having removed all traces of a past aesthetic." In fact, he declared himself "cured of the delusion that the artist's aim is to create beauty." This statement is terrifying in its implications when one considers what is at stake in beauty. Simone Weil wrote that "we love the beauty of the world because we sense behind it the presence of something akin to that wisdom we should like to possess to slake our thirst for good." All beauty is reflected beauty. Smudge out the reflection and not only is the mirror useless but the path to the source of beauty is barred. Ugliness, the aesthetic analogue to evil, becomes the new norm. Schoenberg's remark represents a total rupture with the Western musical tradition.

The loss of tonality was also devastating at the practical level of composition because tonality is the key structure of music. Schoenberg took the twelve equal semi-tones from the chromatic scale and declared that music must be written in such a way that each of these twelve semi-tones has to be used before repeating any one of them. If one of these semi-tones was repeated before all eleven others were sounded, it might create an anchor for the ear which could recognize what is going on in the music harmonically. The twelve-tone system guarantees the listener's disorientation.

Tonality is what allows music to express movement—away from or towards a state of tension or relaxation, a sense of motion through a series of crises and conflicts which can then come to resolution. Without it, music loses harmony and melody. Its structural force collapses. Gutting music of tonality is like removing grapes from wine. You can go through all the motions of making wine without grapes but there will be no wine at the end of the process. Similarly, if you deliberately and systematically remove all audible overtone relationships from music, you can go through the process of composition, but the end product will not be comprehensible as music. This is not a change in technique; it is the replacement of art by ideology.

Schoenberg's disciples applauded the emancipation of dissonance but soon preferred to follow the centrifugal forces that Schoenberg had unleashed beyond their master's rules. Pierre Boulez thought that it was not enough to systematize dissonance in twelve-tone rows. If you have a system, why not systematize everything? He applied the same principle of the tone-row to pitch, duration, tone production, intensity and timbre, every element of music. In 1952, Boulez announced that "every musician who has not felt—we do not say understood but felt—the necessity of the serial language is USELESS." Boulez also proclaimed, "Once the past has been got out of the way, one need think only of oneself." Here is the narcissistic antithesis of the classical view of music, the whole point of which was to draw a person up into something larger than himself.

The dissection of the language of music continued as, successively, each isolated element was elevated into its own autonomous whole. Schoenberg's disciples agreed that tonality is simply a convention, but saw that, so too, is twelve-tone music. If you are going to emancipate dissonance, why organize it? Why even have twelve-tone themes? Why bother with pitch at all? Edgar Varese rejected the twelve-tone system as arbitrary and restrictive. He searched for the "bomb that would explode the musical world and allow all sounds to come rushing into it through the resulting breach." When he exploded it in his piece *Hyperprism*, Olin Downes, a famous New York music critic, called it "a catastrophe in a boiler factory." Still, Varese did not carry the inner logic of the "emancipation of dissonance" through to its logical conclusion. His noise was still formulated; it was organized. There were indications in the score as to exactly when the boiler should explode.

WHAT WAS needed, according to John Cage (1912–92), was to have absolutely no organization. Typical of Cage were compositions whose notes were based on the irregularities in the composition paper he used, notes selected by tossing dice, or from the use of charts derived from the Chinese *I Ching*. Those were his more conventional works. Other "compositions" included the simultaneous twirling of the knobs of twelve radios, the sounds from records playing on unsynchronized variable speed turntables, or the sounds produced by tape recordings of music that had been sliced up and randomly reassembled. Not surprisingly, Cage was one of the progenitors of the "happenings" that were fashionable in the 1970s. He presented concerts of kitchen sounds and the sounds of the human body amplified through loudspeakers. Perhaps Cage's most notorious work was his *4'33"* during which the performer silently sits with his instrument for that exact period of time, then rises and leaves the stage. The "music" is whatever extraneous noises the audience hears in the silence the performer has created. In his book *Silence*, Cage announced, "Here we are. Let us say Yes to our presence together in Chaos."

What was the purpose of all this? Precisely to make the point that there is no purpose, or to express what Cage called a "purposeful purposelessness," the aim of which was to emancipate people from the tyranny of meaning. The extent of his success can be judged by the verdict rendered in the prestigious *New Grove Dictionary of Music*, which says Cage "has had a greater impact on world music than any other American composer of the twentieth century."

Cage's view of reality has a very clear provenance. Cage himself acknowledged three principal gurus: Eric Satie (a French composer), Henry David Thoreau, and Buckminster Fuller—three relative lightweights who could not among them account for Cage's radical thinking. The prevalent influence on Cage seems instead to have been Jean Jacques Rousseau, though he goes unmentioned in Cage's many *obiter dicta*. Cage's similarities with Rousseau are too uncanny to have been accidental.

With his noise, Cage worked out musically the full implications of Rousseau's non-teleological view of nature in his *Second Discourse*. Cage did for music what Rousseau did for political philosophy. Perhaps the most profoundly anti-Aristotelian philosopher of the eighteenth century, Rousseau turned Aristotle's notion of nature on its head. Aristotle said that nature defined not only what man is, but what he should be. Rousseau countered that nature is not an end—a *telos*—but a beginning: man's end is his beginning. There is nothing he "ought" to become, no moral imperative. There is no purpose in man or nature; existence is therefore bereft of any rational principle. Rousseau asserted that man by nature was not a social or political animal endowed with reason. What man has become is the result, not of nature, but of accident. And the society resulting from that accident has corrupted man.

According to Rousseau, man was originally isolated in the state of nature, where the pure "sentiment of his own existence" was such that "one suffices to oneself, like God." Yet this self-satisfied god was asocial and pre-rational. Only by accident did man come into association with others. Somehow, this accident ignited his reason. Through his association with others, man lost his self-sufficient "sentiment of his own existence." He became alienated. He began to live in the esteem of others instead of in his own self-esteem.

Rousseau knew that the prerational, asocial state of nature was lost forever, but thought that an all-powerful state could ameliorate the situation of alienated man. The state could restore a simulacrum of that original well-being by removing all man's subsidiary social relationships. By destroying man's familial, social, and political ties, the state could make each individual totally dependent on the state, and independent of each other. The state is the vehicle for bringing people together so that they can be apart: a sort of radical

individualism under state sponsorship.

It is necessary to pay this much attention to Rousseau because Cage shares his denigration of reason, the same notion of alienation, and a similar solution to it. In both men, the primacy of the accidental eliminates nature as a normative guide and becomes the foundation for man's total freedom. Like Rousseau's man in the state of nature, Cage said, "I strive toward the non-mental." The quest is to "provide a music free from one's memory and imagination." If man is the product of accident, his music should likewise be accidental. Life itself is very fine "once one gets one's mind and one's desires out of the way and lets it act of its own accord."

But what is its own accord? Of music, Cage said, "The requiring that many parts be played in a particular togetherness is not an accurate representation of how things are" in nature, because in nature there is no order. In other words, life's accord is that there is no accord. As a result, Cage desired "a society where you can do anything at all." He warned that one has "to be as careful as possible not to form any ideas about what each person should or should not do." He was "committed to letting everything happen, to making everything that happens acceptable."

At the Stony Point experimental arts community where he spent his summers, Cage observed that each summer's sabbatical produced numerous divorces. So, he concluded, "all the couples who come to the community and stay there end up separating. In reality, our community is a community for separation." Rousseau could not have stated his ideal better. Nor could Cage have made the same point in his art more clearly. For instance, in his long collaboration with choreographer Merce Cunningham, Cage wrote ballet scores completely unconnected to and independent of Cunningham's choreography. The orchestra and dancers rehearsed separately and appeared together for the first time at the premiere performance. The dancers' movements have nothing to do with the music. The audience is left to make of these random juxtapositions what it will. There is no shared experience—except of disconnectedness. The dancers, musicians, and audience have all come together in order to be apart.

According to Cage, the realization of the disconnectedness of things creates opportunities for wholeness. "I said that since the sounds were sounds this gave people hearing them the chance to be people, centered within themselves where they actually are, not off artificially in the distance as they are accustomed to be, trying to figure out what is being said by some artist by means of sounds." Here, in his own way, Cage captures Rousseau's notion of alienation. People are alienated from themselves because they are living in the esteem of others. Cage's noise can help them let go of false notions of order, to "let sounds be themselves, rather than vehicles for man-made theories," and to return within themselves to the sentiment of their own existence. Cage said, "Our intention is to affirm this life, not bring order out of chaos or to suggest improvements in creation, but simply to wake up to the very life we're living, which is so excellent. . . ."

That sounds appealing, even humble, and helps to explain Cage's appeal. In fact, Cage repeatedly insisted on the integrity of an external reality that exists without our permission. It is a good point to make and, as far as it goes, protects us from solipsists of every stripe. Man violates this integrity by projecting meanings upon reality that are not there. That, of course, is the distortion of reality at the heart of every modern ideology. For Cage, how-

ever, it is the inference of any meaning at all that is the distorting imposition. This is the real problem with letting "sounds be themselves," and letting other things be as they are, because it begs the question, "What are they?" Because of Cage's grounding in Rousseau, we cannot answer this question. What is the significance of reality's integrity if it is not intelligible, if there is not a rational principle animating it? If creation does not speak to us in some way, if things are not intelligible, are we? Where does "leaving things as they are" leave us?

From the traditional Western perspective, it leaves us completely adrift. The Greco-Judeo-Christian conviction is that nature bespeaks an intelligibility that derives from a transcendent source. Speaking from the heart of that tradition, St. Paul in his Letter to the Romans said, "Ever since the creation of the world, the invisible existence of God and his everlasting power have been clearly seen by the mind's understanding of created things." By denigrating reason and denying creation's intelligibility, Cage severed this link to the Creator. Cage's espousal of accidental noise is the logically apt result. Noise is incapable of pointing beyond itself. Noise is the black hole of the sound world. It sucks everything into itself. If reality is unintelligible, then noise is its perfect reflection, because it too is unintelligible.

HAVING ENDURED the worst, the twentieth century has also witnessed an extraordinary recovery from the damage inflicted by Schoenberg in his totalitarian systematization of sound and by Cage in his mindless immersion in noise. Some composers, like Vagn Holmboe (1909–1996) in Denmark, resisted from the start. Others, like John Adams (b. 1947) in America, rebelled and returned to tonal music. It is worth examining, even briefly, the terms of this recovery in the works of these two composers because their language reconnects us to the worlds of Pythagoras and St. Clement. Their works are symptomatic of the broader recovery of reality in the music of our time.

In Vagn Holmboe's music, most particularly in his thirteen symphonies, one can once again detect the "music of the spheres" in their rotation. Holmboe's impulse was to move outward and upward. His music reveals the constellations in their swirling orbits, cosmic forces, a universe of tremendous complexity, but also of coherence. Holmboe's music is rooted and real. It reflects nature, but not in a pastoral way; this is not a musical evocation of bird songs or sunsets. Neither is it an evocation of nature as the nineteenth century understood nature—principally as a landscape upon which to project one's own emotions. To say his work is visionary would be an understatement.

Holmboe's approach to composition was quite Aristotelian: the thematic material defines its own development. What a thing is (its essence) is fully revealed through its completion (its existence)—through the thorough exploration of the potential of its basic materials. The overall effect is cumulative and the impact powerful. Holmboe found his unique voice through a technique he called metamorphosis. Holmboe wrote, "Metamorphosis is based on a process of development that transforms one matter into another, without it losing its identity." Most importantly, metamorphosis "has a goal; it brings order to the process and enables it to create a pattern of the same perfection and balance as, for example, a classical sonata." Holmboe's metamorphosis is something like the Beethovenian method of arguing short motives; a few hammered chords can generate the thematic

material for the whole work.

Holmboe's technique also has a larger significance. Danish composer Karl Aage Rasmussen observed that Holmboe's metamorphosis has striking similarities with the constructive principles employed by Arnold Schoenberg in his twelve-tone music. However, says Rasmussen, "Schoenberg found his arguments in history while Holmboe's come from nature." This difference is decisive since the distinction is metaphysical. History is the authority for those, like Rousseau, who believe that man's nature is the product of accident and therefore malleable. Nature is the authority for those who believe man's essence is permanently ordered to a transcendent good. The argument from history leads to creation ex nihilo, not so much in imitation of God as a replacement for Him—as was evident in the ideologies of Marxism and Nazism that plagued the twentieth century. The argument from nature leads to creation in cooperation with the Creator.

Rasmussen spelled out exactly the theological implications of Holmboe's approach:

> The voice of nature is heard . . . both as an inner impulse and as spokesman for a higher order. Certainty of this order is the stimulus of music, and to recreate it and mirror it is the highest goal. For this, faith is required, faith in meaning and context or, in Holmboe's own words, "cosmos does not develop from chaos without a prior vision of cosmos."

Holmboe's words could come straight from one of Aquinas's proofs for the existence of God. For Holmboe to make such a remark reveals both his metaphysical grounding and his breathtaking artistic reach. This man was not simply reaching for the stars, but for the constellations in which they move, and beyond. Holmboe strove to show us the cosmos, to play for us the music of the spheres.

Holmboe's music is quite accessible but requires a great deal of concentration because it is highly contrapuntal. Its rich counterpoint reflects creation's complexity. The simultaneity of unrelated strands of music in so much modern music (as in John Cage's works) is no great accomplishment; relating them is. As Holmboe said, music has the power to enrich man "only when the music itself is a cosmos of coordinated powers, when it speaks to both feeling and thought, when chaos does exist, but [is] always overcome."

In other words, chaos is not the problem; chaos is easy. Cosmos is the problem. Showing the coherence in its complexity, to say nothing of the reason for its existence, is the greatest intellectual and artistic challenge because it shares in the divine "prior vision of cosmos" that makes the cosmos possible. As Holmboe wrote, "In its purest form, [music] can be regarded as the expression of a perfect unity and conjures up a feeling of cosmic cohesion." Arising from such complexity, this feeling of cohesion can be, he said, a "spiritual shock" for modern man.

JUST AS Holmboe, whose magnificent works are finally coming into currency, represents an unbroken line to the great Western musical tradition, John Adams is an exemplar of those indoctrinated in Schoenberg's ideology who found their way out of it. Adams ultimately rejected his college lessons on Nietzsche's "death of God" and the loss of tonality. Like Pythagoras, he "found that tonality was not just a stylistic phenomenon that came and went, but that it is really a natural acoustic phenomenon." In total repudiation of Schoenberg, Adams went on to write a stunning symphony, entitled *Harmonielehre* ("Theory of Harmony") that powerfully reconnects with the Western musical tradition. In this work, he wrote, "there is a sense of using key as a structural and psychological tool in building my work." More importantly, Adams, explained, "the other shade of meaning in the title has to do with harmony in the larger sense, in the sense of spiritual and psychological harmony."

Adam's description of his symphony is explicitly in terms of spiritual health and sickness. He explains that

> the entire [second] movement is a musical scenario about impotence and spiritual sickness; . . . it has to do with an existence without grace. And then in the third movement, grace appears for no reason at all . . . that's the way grace is, the unmerited bestowal of blessing on man. The whole piece is a kind of allegory about that quest for grace.

It is clear from Adams that the recovery of tonality and key structure is as closely related to spiritual recovery as its loss was related to spiritual loss. The destruction of tonality was thought to be historically necessary and therefore "determined." It is no mistake that the recovery of tonality and its expressive powers should be accompanied by the notion of grace. The very possibility of grace, of the unmerited intervention of God's love, destroys the ideology of historical determinism, whether it be expressed in music or in any other way. The possibility of grace fatally ruptures the self-enclosed world of "historically determined forces" and opens it up to the transcendent. That opening restores the freedom and full range of man's creativity.

Cicero spoke of music as enabling man to *return* to the divine region, implying a place once lost to man. What is it, in and about music, that gives one an experience so outside of oneself that one can see reality anew, as if newborn in a strange but wonderful world? British composer John Tavener proposes an answer to this mystery in his artistic credo: "My goal is to recover one simple memory from which all art derives. The constant memory of the paradise from which we have fallen leads to the paradise which was promised to the repentant thief. The gentleness of our sleepy recollections promises something else. That which was once perceived as in a glass darkly, we shall see face to face." We shall not only *see*; we shall *hear*, as well, the New Song.

Daniel J. Mahoney

WHITTAKER CHAMBERS: WITNESS TO THE CRISIS OF THE MODERN SOUL

VOL. 37, NO. 2, 2002

Whittaker Chambers's *Witness* was published fifty years ago during the coldest days of the Cold War. It tells the story of a brilliant man driven by despair over the "crisis of our time" into the arms of the Communist Party. After playing a prominent role in the Communist underground in Washington, DC, in the 1930s, Chambers painfully broke with communism in 1938, rejecting all its works and ideological presuppositions. He resurfaced to become a distinguished writer and editor for Henry Luce's *Time* magazine.

The story of Chambers's descent to the Communist underground and return to the human world is told with remarkable eloquence. The most famous part of the book is Chambers's gripping account of the two perjury trials of Alger Hiss in 1949 and 1950, which pitted the cerebral if somewhat disheveled Chambers against the worldly Hiss, a man who had been Chambers's friend and protégé in the Washington Communist underground. The former State Department official and sometime president of the Carnegie Endowment for International Peace categorically denied Chambers's allegations that he had faithfully served the cause of

Stalin and the Soviet Union during many years of government service. Chambers provided abundant documentation, including the so-called "Baltimore" and "Pumpkin" papers and the most detailed personal information, to support his charges. Despite everything, Hiss would go on lying for half a century—right up to his death in the late 1990s. The collapse of the Soviet empire and the resulting revelations from Soviet bloc archives and the so-called Venona intercepts, however, would finally make Hiss's guilt clear enough even to his most determined partisans.[1] These recent revelations confirm what Chambers's initial testimony and evidence ought to have made clear: Hiss had been a faithful Communist, a spy for Stalin's tyranny, and an inveterate liar, all of his adult life. Chambers, who despised the role of informer, testified reluctantly and only from a sense of duty to an imperiled free world. He would pay mightily for his witness. Chambers was subjected to calumnies by the sorts of journalists and intellectuals who thought—and still think—that McCarthyism was a far graver threat to human liberty than Communist totalitarianism ever was.

But Whittaker Chambers believed that his witness was about much more than an espionage case or the sordid realities of Communist subversion, no matter how much the dramatic details of the "Hiss Case" engrossed his readers. If the Hiss Case were merely about espionage, then "it would not be worth my writing about or your reading about," he wrote in the "Letter to My Children," which provided the thematic introduction to *Witness*.[2] In *Cold Friday*, his posthumously published collection of essays, letters, and book fragments, Chambers wrote that "two points . . . seemed to me more important than the narrative of unhappy events" which preoccupied his readers. These two capital points dealt with "the nature of communism and the struggle against it." For Chambers, the "crux of this matter is whether God exists. If God exists, a man cannot be a Communist, which begins with the rejection of God. But if God does not exist, it follows that communism, or some suitable variant of it, is right."[3] This thesis is at the center of Chambers's understanding of the conflict between communism and Western freedom.

The second proposition follows from the first. The West must either "develop or recover" those spiritual and moral resources that constituted its superiority over communism or risk irrevocably losing its soul.[4] Even if the West turned out to be successful in its secular struggle with totalitarianism, it still risked revealing itself to be a mere *frère-ennemi* of its great rival. For Chambers, this seemingly lucid proposition was no simple matter. He did not proffer a simple-minded religious orthodoxy as the alternative to the secular religion of communism. Nor did he ignore the degree to which the West had already lost its soul and was deeply complicit in the great movement that he, like so many others, called "the crisis of our time."

According to Chambers, communism itself was symptomatic of a much larger crisis—a "total crisis," as he called it—that was convulsing the entire world. The crisis was simultaneously spiritual and social. Its defining trait was the West's loss of confidence in its animating principles. What were the original principles that no longer called forth the loyalty or assent of the enlightened elites of the Western world? Above all, the "advanced" thinkers of the West had forgotten that political freedom presupposed the reality of the soul. Properly understood, "external freedom is only an aspect of interior freedom." For Chambers, "religion and freedom are indivisible. Without freedom the soul dies. Without the soul there is no justification for freedom"—there is only the positing of *necessity* as the governing principle of the human world. Chambers believed that political freedom "as the Western world has known it" is best understood as "a political reading of the Bible." Only the Christian account of the soul could make sense of the human aspiration to responsible freedom. There can be no coherent defense of freedom without a recognition of the integrity of the human soul. The soul, irreducible in its mystery, transcends necessity and the understanding of causality put forward by a mechanistic science. And the soul cannot ultimately be explained without an appreciation of the created character of the world.[5]

At the heart of Chambers's moral vision is a rejection of the fundamental conceit of the Enlightenment: the self-sovereignty of "autonomous" man. This is the "revolutionary heart of communism" that grounds its revolutionary fervor and makes sense of its Promethean desire to remake human nature and society radically. Communism rejects the givenness of the world. For Communists, the goal of thought is not to understand but rather to "change the world," as Marx famously put it in the eleventh of his *Theses on Feuerbach*. This desire to transform the world, to conquer the soul, to overcome creation, is what allowed Communists to "move mountains." It gave them what was lacking in the democratic West, namely, "a simple, rational faith that inspires men to live or die for it." In his "Letter to My Children" Chambers links the Promethean faith of communism both to the enlightenment project of a world directed solely by "rational intelligence" and to man's original or primordial revolt against the Lordship of God. The promise of the serpent in Genesis that "Ye shall be as gods" is older than enlightenment philosophy, older than the so-called modern project. "It is, in fact, man's second oldest faith." The Communist "vision of Man without God" is a transformation and intensification of the age-old pride of man, who imagines a world without God. The project of human self-deification is a means of restoring man "to his sovereignty by the simple method of denying God." Atheism is at the core of radical modernity, a modernity that is broader and deeper than the Communist revolution.[6]

A precondition for Communist subversion is the distinctly modern confidence that rational intelligence can master the whole of reality, that "thought and act" can be united in one Promethean impulse. communism's "secret strength" lay in the "positivism" and "materialism" of modern life. Chambers argues in *Cold Friday* that the heart and soul of modernity is "Comtean," or was at least codified by the nineteenth-century French philosopher August Comte: positive science is the ultimate measure of reality, and the "religion of humanity," the sovereignty of acting man, is the moral principle of the

modern world. It was the stranglehold of this vision on the intellectual life of the democracies that allowed Communists to take advantage of the modern crisis—both by radicalizing the modern principle and by capitalizing on the self-doubts of the Western liberals. The liberal intellectual posits a godless universe but cannot tolerate the means—at least the most brutal revolutionary means—for actualizing human self-sovereignty. In light of this analysis, Chambers shared Ignazio Silone's view that the great struggle would be between Communists and excommunists. Only the excommunist could put forward a coherent and truthful "reason to live and a reason to die" which had a fighting chance of rallying the wills of free people. Otherwise, the West might win its battle with communism while being content with a more moderate but nonetheless insidious version of the claim that "Man is the measure of all things."[7]

In this case, any defeat of communism would at best be a Pyrrhic victory. The ultimate resolution of the modern crisis would be determined by whether the West could reconnect with the moral foundations of liberty or would it be content with a more livable version of "autonomous" freedom. In *Cold Friday*, Chambers went even further than asking if by joining the West he was, in fact, joining the losing side. This question haunts *Witness* and contributes to the pathos that informs every one of its pages. In *Cold Friday*, Chambers raises the more daring question of whether the West deserves to be saved. Is it sure enough of its principles to merit victory in its struggle with Communist tyranny? Is its principle in any significant way anything but a less confident and more tepid version of the scientism and materialism, the atheistic humanism, which provided communism with its remarkable sense of purpose?

Chambers hoped against hope that the titanic ideological struggle between communism and freedom would remind the West precisely what was worth fighting and dying for. But he had little confidence that such spiritual illumination would result from the protracted struggle.

In a remarkable fragment in the first section of *Cold Friday*, Chambers explores these unnerving questions with great penetration. His discussion is an amplification of the themes presented in the foreword to *Witness* and is, if anything, more pessimistic than the original. Chambers relates a discussion with a Catholic chaplain, Father Alan, in a Maryland hospital after Chambers's first heart attack in 1952. Chambers asked the priest how he should respond to those who wrote him after the publication of *Witness* to chide him for claiming in that work that he had left the wrong side for the losing side. His well-meaning critics chastised him for succumbing to pessimism, for believing "that evil can ultimately overcome good." Father Alan's response stirred Chambers to depths of meditative reflection. The priest quietly asked Chambers: "Who says that the West deserves to be saved?" In Chambers's view, Father Alan's remarks "cut past the terms in which men commonly view the crisis of our time." His remark went beyond questions of geopolitical rivalry or even ideological disputation. His question did not ask whether the West had "the physical power" to survive, but rather if it was justified in doing so. Chambers did not dwell on this question because he had some perverse desire to join the losing side. Rather, he believed that the question went to the very heart of the modern crisis. In his view, the West had lost a sense of its purpose and could not provide men with a compelling reason to live or to die.[8]

The West had once embodied a "certain truth" about God, the soul, and human freedom. But that truth was now at odds with the materialism that was the common faith of East and West alike. Communism was in Chambers's view only "a secondary manifestation" of the modern crisis—a crisis rooted in the West's inability to defend itself with anything resembling principled self-confidence. "The success of communism . . . is never greater than the failure of all other faiths." Chambers was no reactionary or obscurantist, and he vigorously defended modern political freedom and the achievements of modern science. But technological progress was strictly speaking soulless—and "unheard of abundance" was "perhaps the sole justification for the existence of" technological civilization. In the long run, this would not do. The West needed to offer itself and the world more than "more abundant bread" or it was "already half-dead." The social crisis marked by disrupted traditions, tentacular cities, inflation, unemployment, and class conflict, needed to be addressed both through economic development and through a renewed sense of spiritual purpose. But the spiritual crisis that accompanied the modern social crisis could not be so readily addressed. Chambers feared that the West stood "under the oldest and ultimate judgment," one "which could be lifted only in terms of more suffering than the mind can bear or measure."[9] He ended his discussion by citing Revelation 3:14–17:

> And unto the angel of the church of the Laodiceans write; These things saith the Amen, the faithful and true witness, the beginning of the creation of God; I know thy works, that thou art neither cold nor hot: I would thou wert cold or hot. So then, because thou art lukewarm, and neither cold nor hot, I will spue thee out of my mouth.

Because thou sayest, I am rich, and increased with goods, and have need of nothing; and knowest not that thou art wretched and miserable, and poor, and blind, and naked.

Chambers's vision can appear apocalyptic and far from politics in the ordinary sense of that term. But it is important to recognize that Chambers did not reduce the crisis of the West to a merely spiritual one. In a remarkable letter to his friend Duncan Taylor, dated September 14, 1954, and reprinted in *Cold Friday*, Chambers perfectly expresses the tension between a theoretical critique of modernity and the need for a political response to modernity's discontents. Chambers writes: "Of course, it is the duty of the intellectuals of the West to preach reaction, and to keep pointing out why the Enlightenment and its faults were a wrong turning in man's history. But it was a turning, and within its terms, we must maneuver at the point where to maneuver is to live."[10]

Chambers could be a hard-headed social and political analyst. He believed, for example, that a thoughtful conservatism must "accommodate itself to the needs and hopes of the masses." That meant, first and foremost, accepting the imperatives of technological society while trying to moderate and humanize them. A conservatism that cannot accept the dynamism of a market society and the relentless technological development that accompanies the modern revolution was one that was destined to irrelevance. Such romantic or nostalgic conservatism is a "literary whimsy." It is incapable of addressing the modern crisis in any kind of intellectually or politically compelling way. Chambers believed that an active and energetic state was destined to play a significant role in addressing the dislocations that proliferate in the age of machines. As his biographer

Sam Tanenhaus has stressed, by the late 1950s Chambers felt increasingly uncomfortable with the rigid orthodoxies of the conservative movement and what he saw as its relative blindness to the true nature of the modern social crisis. In Chambers's view, it was silly and irresponsible to try to put a stop to history. The relentless modern revolution needed to be tamed, but it could not be stopped or ignored. Chambers feared that his fellow conservatives could not accept the irrevocability of the modern revolution, that they were prisoners of stale political and religious orthodoxies.[11]

For all his genuine affection for and friendship with William F. Buckley Jr., Chambers felt somewhat uncomfortable with the spirit of orthodoxy that infused *National Review*, a magazine he wrote for between 1957 and 1959. In a letter written to Buckley in September 1954, shortly before the founding of *National Review*, he denied standing within any religious or political orthodoxy.[12] He was, to be sure, a man of genuine Christian faith and of a generally conservative political persuasion. But he had become an unorthodox (i.e., non-pacifistic) Quaker whose Christianity was "paradoxical" and existentialist in character. His theological and philosophical heroes included Dostoevsky, Niebuhr, and Barth, thinkers whose affirmation of God had little or nothing to do with traditional Christian rationalism. It was the absence of God, the dark night of the modern soul, which confirmed the reality of God for Chambers. In Chambers's view, this paradox was beyond any merely doctrinal formulation. As he argued in a moving and elegant tribute to Reinhold Niebuhr published in *Time* in 1947, the smug optimism of modern man, his groundless confidence in human perfectibility through science, politics, or revolution, had led to the great civilizational crisis of which the Communist threat was the most radical symptom. The failure of modern "progress" was everywhere in evidence. Technological achievement had paradoxically aided the prospects for military destruction. Abundance and mass production had led to spiritual confusion and could not even eliminate scarcities. Science cured diseases, but men killed each other at the service of destructive ideologies. Chambers wisely observed that "Men have never been so educated, but wisdom, even as an idea, has conspicuously vanished from the world."[13]

Against "the blind impasse" of optimistic liberalism and rationalism, Chambers turned to the "great religious voices of our time." Dostoevsky's powerful novels revealed that the denial of God led to political tragedy and to the self-immolation of the soul. This profound diagnostician of nihilism and prophet of redemptive suffering was perhaps Chambers's greatest teacher. The German theologian Karl Barth had recovered the radical otherness of God against the complacent this-worldliness of liberal theologians. The American Reformed theologian Reinhold Niebuhr had highlighted the palpable reality of original sin and the paradoxical faith—beyond all logic and rationality—that could make sense of human suffering and limn the path of redemption. For Chambers, the choice for God against deified Man was not primarily a choice for orthodoxy or tradition. Faith could never abolish the essential solitude of the human soul. An affirmation of paradoxical faith could not stem the modern revolution or provide certainties to rival the Promethean dogmatism of secular religion. Nor could it substitute for the political action by which the dislocations of our time could be addressed and perhaps healed. Chambers was a critic of "progres-

sivism" and enlightenment thinking, but he was not a partisan of the orthodoxies that in his view had been permanently shattered by the modern revolution. This paradox is not always appreciated by Chambers's conservative admirers.

Chambers, then, was no doctrinaire traditionalist. But he was a lucid critic of the voluntarism that undergirds almost every current of modern thought—the illusion that the human will, self-sufficient and rejecting all divine and natural limits, could build an earthly home worthy of man. He knew that the modern crisis preceded the rise of totalitarianism and would likely survive its fall. The West, too, was "dazzled" by a "materialist interpretation of history, politics, and economics."[14] This explains why so many intellectuals were disarmed before the challenge of communism and could not see it for the radical evil that it was. For many, it was simply a more brutal means for achieving the desired ends of industrial modernity and social equality—"the New Deal in a hurry," in Harry Hopkins's notorious formulation. That explains in part the divide between ordinary Americans, who tended to side with Chambers in the Hiss case and hated communism for its atheism as well as for its brutality, and elite opinion, which tended toward anti-anti-communism and refused to believe in the guilt of one of its own.[15]

Chambers believed that mainstream anticommunism, so-called liberal anticommunism, was superficial because it could not even begin to fathom the nature of the disease that threatened the modern world. This ailment was nothing less than what the French theologian Henri de Lubac termed "atheistic humanism" and what the great Russian writer Aleksandr Solzhenitsyn was to call in his 1978 Harvard Address "anthropocentric humanism": a vision of human progress that severed faith from freedom and initiated an age of spiritual and moral indifference.[16] Sam Tanenhaus rightly notes the profound kinship between Solzhenitsyn's and Chambers's analyses of the "modern crisis."[17] Both saw a direct relationship between communism and enlightenment humanism. Both believed that authentic freedom must be rooted in what Solzhenitsyn calls the "moral heritage of the Christian centuries with their great reserves of mercy and sacrifice." Both were convinced that a West that fought communism in the name of "autonomous, irreligious consciousness" could not provide a humanly compelling alternative to the more consistent and self-conscious humanism of the Communist world.[18]

It is undoubtedly the case that Chambers and Solzhenitsyn underestimated some of the internal resources of democratic societies. They rightly feared that modern liberalism could not generate or even defend the need for civic courage. But as both recognized, the modern West could still draw on moral resources that predated enlightenment humanism. The West's practice, rooted at least in part in common sense and the moral law, turned out to be better than the modern theory that increasingly defined its self-consciousness. As both Chambers and Solzhenitsyn suggest, modern societies give rise to, and are predicated on, a dangerous emancipation of the human will. But in practice, the tension between a multitude of individual wills and the collective sovereignty of the people prevents the development of tyranny in the Western world. This "neutralization" of competing sovereignties helps explain much of the remarkable energy and vitality of liberal societies.

Yet there is no doubt that our liberal societies increasingly confront a moral abyss: unsure of their purpose, plagued by a debilitating cultural and moral relativism, increasingly contemptuous of moral limits, and faced with scientific and technological innovations, such as cloning, that threaten the very humanity of man. In light of these challenges, our elites are unable to stand up to the specter of nihilism. As Irving Kristol has eloquently noted, they can give no adequate answer to the simple query, "Why not?"

Ten years after the collapse of Soviet despotism, few appear to have learned the real lesson of totalitarianism. The profound insight of a host of thinkers such as Dostoevsky, Chambers, de Lubac, Kolakowski, and Solzhenitsyn is that all efforts at human self-deification necessarily lead to what Aurel Kolnai called "the self-enslavement of man." "Progressive democracy," like communism and National Socialism, is one of the "Three Riders of the Apocalypse": it is, in fact, the precondition for the totalitarian adventures of the twentieth century.[19] Chambers may have been too pessimistic about the West's prospects in the Cold War, as some of his critics have charged over the years. His deepest fear, however, was not that the West would lose the military and political struggle with the Soviet Union, but that it would win it while losing its soul—by forgetting the reasons why victory was desirable in the first place. It would be premature to pronounce Chambers unduly alarmist in this regard.

After reading *Witness*, André Malraux famously wrote to Chambers that he had not "return[ed] from Hell with empty hands."[20] Malraux was one of the few who appreciated the spiritual depth that accompanied Chambers's witness against communism. Chambers was not only a courageous fighter against Soviet communism; he was, more profoundly, one of the few serious writers and thinkers of the age to bear clear witness to the nature of the modern crisis and the path of temporal salvation. He knew that there could be no enduring faith in freedom without faith in God and belief in the irreducible mystery of the human soul. As with Solzhenitsyn, Chambers's defense of faith in God and freedom was too often confused with political reaction. He was despised by most intellectuals (although he had impressive defenders such as Lionel Trilling and William F. Buckley) and his message was too often dismissed as irrelevant, or pathetic, or both.

With few exceptions, Chambers's critics missed the subtlety and depth of his reflection. He transcended the usual political and intellectual categories. Like Solzhenitsyn, Chambers recognized that there could be no turning back from the modern world. Instead, there could only be an *ascent* from modernity, one that accepted its principal achievements while rooting them in a more truthful account of God and man. As Solzhenitsyn suggests in his magisterial Liechtenstein Address, delivered in 1993 on the eve of his return to a post-Communist Russia, "human knowledge and human abilities continue to be perfected: they cannot, and must not be brought to a halt." Solzhenitsyn wisely adds that progress must be seen not "as a stream of unlimited blessings" but rather "as a gift from on high, sent down for an extremely intricate trial of our free will." Our task in a post-totalitarian age is to "harness" progress "in the interests of the human spirit . . . to seek or expand ways of directing its might towards the perpetration of good."[21] These words perfectly capture Chambers's message to a post-totalitarian world. Fifty years after the publication of *Witness*, Chambers now belongs to that small group of modern witnesses who combine spiritual wisdom with political judgment and provide in-valuable insights about the nature of the modern crisis. These insights will endure long after the world has forgotten the details of the most controversial espionage case of the twentieth century.

Notes

1. See Sam Tanenhaus's excellent *Whittaker Chambers: A Biography* (New York: Modern Library Paperback, 1998), 518–20. Hereafter cited as Tanenhaus.
2. Whittaker Chambers, *Witness* (Washington: Regnery Gateway, 1952, 1980), 3.
3. Whittaker Chambers, *Cold Friday* (New York: Random House, 1964), 68, 69.
4. *Cold Friday*, 70.
5. *Witness*, 7, 16.
6. Ibid., 9, 10.
7. *Witness*, 10, *Cold Friday*, 157–58, *Witness*, 462.
8. *Cold Friday*, 11, 12.
9. Ibid., 12–16.
10. Ibid., 227.
11. *Cold Friday*, 232–36, Tanenhaus, 499–501, 506, 512.
12. *Cold Friday*, 236–238.
13. "Faith for a Lenten Age" is summarized in *Witness*, 505–507, and reprinted in *Ghosts and the Roof*, Terry Teachout, ed. (New Brunswick, NJ: Transaction, 1996), 184–93.
14. *Witness*, 17.
15. See *Witness*, 793.
16. *Witness*, 17.
17. Tanenhaus, 469.
18. See Aleksandr Solzhenitsyn, "A World Split Apart," in *East and West* (Harper Perennial, 1980), 66, 69.
19. See Aurel Kolnai, "Three Riders of the Apocalypse," in Kolnai, *Privilege and Liberty*, ed. by D. Mahoney (Lexington Books, 1999), 105–18.
20. Tanenhaus, 502.
21. All quotes are from Solzhenitsyn's Address to the International Academy of Philosophy, Liechtenstein, September 29, 1993. The speech is printed as an Appendix to *Solzhenitsyn, The Russian Question at the End of the Twentieth Century* (New York: Farrar, Straus & Giroux, 1995), 112–128.

Roger Scruton

T. S. Eliot as Conservative Mentor

VOL. 39, NO. 1–2, 2003–4

T. S. Eliot was indisputably the greatest poet writing in English in the twentieth century. He was also the most revolutionary Anglophone literary critic since Samuel Johnson, and the most influential religious thinker in the Anglican tradition since the Wesleyan movement. His social and political vision is contained in all his writings, and has been absorbed and reabsorbed by generations of English and American readers, upon whom it exerts an almost mystical fascination— even when they are moved, as many are, to reject it. Without Eliot, the philosophy of Toryism would have lost all substance during the last century. And while not explicitly intending it, Eliot set this philosophy on a higher plane, intellectually, spiritually and stylistically, than has ever been reached by the adherents of the socialist idea.

Eliot attempted to shape a philosophy for our times that would be richer and more true to the complexity of human needs than the free-market panaceas that have so often dominated the thinking of conservatives in government. He assigned a central place in his social thinking to high culture. He was a thorough tradi-tionalist in his beliefs but an adventurous modernist in his art, holding artistic modernism and social traditionalism to be different facets of a common enter-prise. Modernism in art was, for Eliot, an attempt to salvage and fortify a living artistic tradition in the face of the corrup-tion and decay of popular culture.

ELIOT WAS born in St Louis, Missouri, in 1888, and educated at Harvard, the Sorbonne, and Merton College, Oxford, where he wrote a doctoral thesis on the phi-losophy of F. H. Bradley, whose Hegelian vision of society exerted a profound influ-ence over him. He came, as did so many educated Americans of his generation, from a profoundly religious and public-spirited background, although his early poems suggest a bleak and despairing ag-nosticism, which he only gradually and painfully overcame. In 1914 he met Ezra Pound, who encouraged him to settle in England. He married during the follow-ing year, which also saw the publication of his first successful poem, "The Love Song of J. Alfred Prufrock." This work, together with the other short poems that were published along with it as *Prufrock and Other Observations* in 1917, profoundly altered the course of English literature. They were the first truly *modernist* works in English, although the most visible influences on their imagery and diction were not English but French—specifically, the *fin-de-siècle* irony of Laforgue, and the symbolism of Rimbaud, Mallarmé and Verlaine. They were also social poems, concerned to express a prevailing collective mood, even when dressed in the words of a specific protagonist. The wartime generation found themselves in these poems, in a way that they had not found themselves in the pseudo-romantic literature of the Edwardian period.

Shortly afterwards Eliot published a book of essays, *The Sacred Wood*, which was to be as influential as the early poetry. In these essays, Eliot presented his new and exacting theory of the role of criticism, of the *necessity* for criticism if our literary culture is to survive. For Eliot, it is no accident that criticism and poetry so often come together in the same intelligence—as in his own case, and the case of Coleridge, whom he singled out as the finest of English critics. For the critic, like the poet, is concerned to develop the "sensibility" of his reader—by which term Eliot meant a kind of intelligent observation of the human world. Critics do not abstract or generalize: they *look*, and record what they see. But in doing so, they also convey a sense of what *matters* in human experience, distinguishing the false from the genuine emotion. While Eliot was to spell out only gradually and obscurely over many years just what he meant by "sensibility," his elevated conception of the critic's role struck a chord in many of his readers. Furthermore, *The Sacred Wood* contained essays that were to revolutionize literary taste. The authoritative tone of these essays gave rise

to the impression that the modern world was at last making itself heard in literature—and that its voice was T. S. Eliot's.

THE SACRED Wood turned the attention of the literary world to the "metaphysical poets" of the sixteenth and seventeenth centuries, and to the Elizabethan dramatists—the lesser predecessors and the heirs of Shakespeare, whose raw language, rich with the sensation of the thing described, provided a telling contrast to the sentimental sweetness that Eliot condemned in his immediate contemporaries. There is also an essay on Dante, discussing a question that was frequently to trouble Eliot—that of the relationship between poetry and belief. To what extent could one appreciate the poetry of the *Divine Comedy* while rejecting the doctrine that had inspired it? This question was a real one for Eliot, for several reasons.

Eliot was—like his fellow modernists and contemporaries, Ezra Pound and James Joyce—profoundly influenced by Dante, whose limpid verse-form, colloquial style, and solemn philosophy created a vision of the ideal in poetry. At the same time, he rejected the theological vision of the *Divine Comedy*—rejected it with a deep sense of loss. Yet in his own poetry the voice of Dante would constantly return, offering him turns of phrase, lightning flashes of thought, and—most of all—a vision of the modern world from a point of view outside it, a point of view irradiated by an experience of holiness (albeit an experience that he did not then share). And when Eliot did finally come to share in this vision, he wrote, in the last of the *Four Quartets*, the most brilliant of all imitations of Dante in English—an imitation which is something far finer than an imitation, in which the religious vision of Dante is transported and translated into the world of modern England.

One other essay in *The Sacred Wood* deserves mention—"Tradition and the Individual Talent," in which Eliot introduces the term which best summarizes his contribution to the political consciousness of the twentieth century: *tradition*. In this essay Eliot argues that true originality is possible only within a tradition—and further, that every tradition must be remade by the genuine artist, in the very act of creating something new. A tradition is a living thing, and just as each writer is judged in terms of those who went before, so does the meaning of the tradition change as new works are added to it. It was this literary idea of a living tradition that was gradually to permeate Eliot's thinking, and to form the core of his social and political philosophy.

"Prufrock" and *The Sacred Wood* already help us to understand the paradox of T. S. Eliot—that our greatest literary modernist should also be our greatest modern conservative. The man who overthrew the nineteenth century in literature and inaugurated the age of free verse, alienation, and experiment was also the man who, in 1928, was to describe himself as "classical in literature, royalist in politics, and Anglo-Catholic in religion." This seeming paradox contains a clue to Eliot's greatness as a social and political thinker. For Eliot recognized that it is precisely in modern conditions—conditions of fragmentation, heresy, and unbelief—that the conservative project acquires its sense. *Conservatism is itself a modernism*, and in this fact lies the secret of its success. What distinguishes Burke from the French revolutionaries is not his attachment to things past, but rather his desire to live fully in the concrete present, to understand the present in all its im-

perfections, and to accept the present as the only reality that is offered to us. Like Burke, Eliot recognized the distinction between a backward-looking nostalgia, which is but another form of modern sentimentality, and a genuine tradition, which grants us the courage and the vision with which to live in the modern world.

IN 1922 Eliot founded *The Criterion*, a literary quarterly which he continued to edit until 1939, when he discontinued the journal under the pressure of "depression of spirits" induced by "the present state of public affairs." As the title of the journal suggests, the project was animated by Eliot's sense of the importance of criticism, and of the futility of modernist experiments when not informed by literary judgement and moral seriousness. The journal also contained social philosophy of a conservative persuasion—although Eliot preferred the word "classicism" as a description of its political outlook.

The Criterion was the forum in which much of our modernist literature was first published, including the poetry of Pound, Empson, Auden, and Spender. Its first issue contained the work which established Eliot himself as the greatest poet of his generation: *The Waste Land*. This poem seemed to its first readers to capture completely the disillusionment and emptiness that followed the hollow victory of the First World War—the conflict in which European civilization had committed suicide, just as Greek civilization had done in the Peloponnesian War. Yet the poem hardly mentioned the war, had none of the vivid imagery of battle that English readers knew from the works of Wilfrid Owen and Siegfried Sassoon, and was choc-a-bloc with references to and quotations from a scholar's library. Its ostensible subject-matter was drawn from works of armchair anthropology—in particular, from Sir James Frazer's *Golden Bough*, a work which had also provided the title of *The Sacred Wood*.

The Waste Land was later republished with notes in which Eliot explained some of his references and allusions, such as that contained in the title, which alludes to the Fisher King of the Parsifal legend, and the waste land over which he presides, awaiting the hero who will ask the questions that will destroy winter's bleak enchantment and renew the world. The allegory of modern civilization contained in this reference to the medieval fertility cults, and their literary transformation in Arthurian romance, was not lost on Eliot's readers. Nor was it the first time that these symbols and legends of medieval romance had been put to such a use—witness Wagner's *Parsifal*, to which Eliot refers obliquely, by quoting from Verlaine's poem.

Nevertheless, there was a peculiar poignancy in the very erudition of the poem, as though the whole of Western culture were being brought to bear on the desert landscape of the modern city in a last effort to encompass it, to internalize it, and to understand its meaning. The use of anthropological conceptions parallels Wagner's use of the Teutonic myths. (In *The Waste Land* there are more quotations from Wagner than from any other poet.) Eliot is invoking the religious worldview—and in particular the sense that life's renewal depends upon supernatural forces—but as a fact about human consciousness, rather than an item of religious belief. In this way, he was able to avail himself of religious ideas and imagery without committing himself to any religious belief. As he was rapidly discovering, without religious ideas the true condition of the modern world cannot be described. Only by describing modernity from a point of view outside of history can we grasp the extent of our spiritual loss.

After *The Waste Land* Eliot continued to write poetry inspired by the agonizing dissociation, as he saw it, between the sensibility of our culture and the available experience of the modern world. This phase of his development culminated in a profound Christian statement—the poem "Ash Wednesday," in which he abandoned his anthropological manner and announced his conversion to the Anglo-Catholic faith. By now Eliot was ready to take up his own peculiar cross: the cross of *membership*. No longer playing the part of spiritual and political exile, he threw in his lot with the tradition to which his favorite authors had belonged. He became a British citizen, joined the Anglican Church, and wrote his great verse drama, *Murder in the Cathedral*. In a series of essays, he praised the writings of sixteenth-century Anglican divines and attacked the secular heresies of his time.

This phase of Eliot's development at length led to *After Strange Gods*, a "primer of modern heresy," in which he expressed his conservative antipathy to secular doctrine. It was Eliot's first of several attempts at social philosophy, of which the two most famous are *The Idea of a Christian Society* (1940) and *Notes Towards the Definition of Culture* (1948). Both these works are marked by a tentativeness and anxiety about the new condition of Europe, which make them far less clear guides to Eliot's vision than the great poem which he wrote at the same time, a poem which has been, for many of my generation, the essential account of our spiritual crisis—and the greatest message of hope that has been given to us. *Four Quartets* is a profound exploration of spiritual possibilities, in which the poet seeks and finds the vision outside time in which time and history are redeemed. It is a religious work, and at the same time a work of extraordinary lyric power, like the *Cimetière marin* of Valéry, but vastly more mature in its underlying philosophy.

ELIOT'S LIFE began with a question: the question of modern life and its meaning. His literary work was a long, studious, and sincere attempt to provide an answer. In the course of this enterprise, Eliot reshaped the English language, changed the forms of English verse, and produced some of the most memorable utterances in our literature. Although an impressive scholar, with a mastery of languages and literatures that he reveals but does not dwell upon in his writings, Eliot was also a man of the world. He worked first as a teacher, then in a London bank, and then in the publishing house of Faber and Faber, which he made into the foremost publisher of poetry and criticism in its day. His unhappy first marriage did not impede his active participation in the literary life of London, over which he exerted an influence every bit as great as André Breton over the literary life of Paris.

His refusal, through all this, to adopt the mantle of the bohemian, to claim the tinsel crown of artist, or to mock the "bourgeois" lifestyle, sets him apart from the continental tradition which he otherwise did so much to promote. He realised that the true task of the artist in the modern world is one not of repudiation but of reconciliation. For Eliot, the artist inherits, in heightened and self-conscious form, the very same anxieties that are the stuff of ordinary experience. The poet who takes his words seriously is the voice of

mankind, interceding for those who live around him, and gaining on their behalf the gift of consciousness with which to overcome the wretchedness of secular life. He too is an ordinary bourgeois, and his highest prize is to live unnoticed amidst those who know nothing of his art—as the saint may live unnoticed among those for whom he dies.

To find the roots of Eliot's political thinking, we must go back to the modernism that found such striking expression in *The Waste Land*. English literature in the early part of the twentieth century was to a great extent captured by premodern imagery, by references to a form of life (such as we find in Thomas Hardy) that had vanished forever, and by verse forms which derived from the repertoire of romantic isolation. It had not undergone that extraordinary education which Baudelaire and his successors had imposed upon the French—in which antiquated forms like the sonnet were wrenched free of their pastoral and religious connotations and fitted out with the language of the modern city, in order to convey the new and hallucinatory sense of an irreparable fault, whereby modern man is divided from all that has preceded him. Eliot's admiration for Baudelaire arose from his desire to write verse that was as true to the experience of the modern city as Baudelaire's had been to the experience of Paris. Eliot also recognized in Baudelaire the new character of the religious impulse under the conditions of modern life: "The important fact about Baudelaire," he wrote, "is that he was essentially a Christian, born out of his due time, and a classicist, born out of his due time."

Eliot's indictment of the neo-romantic literature of his day was not merely a literary complaint. He believed that his contemporaries' use of worn-out poetic diction and lilting rhythms betrayed a serious moral weakness: a failure to observe life as it really is, a failure to feel what must be felt towards the experience that is inescapably ours. And this failure is not confined, he believed, to literature, but runs through the whole of modern life. The search for a new literary idiom is therefore part of a larger search—for the reality of modern experience. Only then can we confront our situation and ask ourselves what should be done about it.

Eliot's deep distrust of secular humanism—and of the socialist and democratic ideas of society which he believed to stem from it—reflected his critique of the neoromantics. The humanist, with his myth of man's goodness, is taking refuge in an easy falsehood. He is living in a world of make-believe, trying to avoid the real emotional cost of seeing things as they are. His vice is the vice of Edwardian and "Georgian" poetry—the vice of sentimentality, which causes us not merely to speak and write in clichés, but to *feel* in clichés too, lest we should be troubled by the truth of our condition. The task of the artistic modernist, as Eliot later expressed it, borrowing a phrase from Mallarmé, is "to purify the dialect of the tribe": that is, to find the words, rhythms, and artistic forms that would make contact again with our experience—not my experience, or yours, but *our* experience, the experience that unites us as living here and now. And it is only because he had captured this experience—in particular, in the bleak vision of *The Waste Land*—that Eliot was able to find a path to its meaning.

He summarizes his attitude to the everyday language of modern life and politics in his essay on the Anglican bishop Lancelot Andrewes, and it is worth quoting the passage in full:

To persons whose minds are habituated to feed on the vague jargon of our time, when we have a vocabulary for everything and exact ideas about nothing—when a word half-understood, torn from its place in some alien or half-formed science, as of psychology, conceals from both writer and reader the utter meaninglessness of a statement, when all dogma is in doubt except the dogmas of sciences of which we have read in the newspapers, when the language of theology itself, under the influence of an undisciplined mysticism of popular philosophy, tends to become a language of tergiversation—Andrewes may seem pedantic and verbose. It is only when we have saturated ourselves in his prose, followed the movement of his thought, that we find his examination of words terminating in the ecstasy of assent. Andrewes takes a word and derives the world from it. . . .[1]

For Eliot, words had begun to lose their precision—not in spite of science, but because of it; not in spite of the loss of true religious belief, but because of it; not in spite of the proliferation of technical terms, but because of it. Our modern ways of speaking no longer enable us to "take a word and derive the world from it": on the contrary, they veil the world, since they convey no lived response to it. They are mere counters in a game of cliché, designed to fill up the silence, to conceal the void which has come upon us as the old gods have departed from their haunts among us.

That is why modern ways of thinking are not, as a rule, orthodoxies, but heresies—a heresy being a truth that has been exaggerated into falsehood, a truth in which we have taken refuge, so to speak, investing in it all our unexamined anxieties and expecting from it answers to questions which we have not troubled ourselves to understand. In the philosophies that prevail in modern life—utilitarianism, pragmatism, behaviorism—we find that "words have a habit of changing their meaning . . . or else they are made, in a most ruthless and piratical manner, to walk the plank." The same is true, Eliot implies, whenever the humanist heresy takes over: whenever we treat man as God, and so believe that our thoughts and our words need be measured by no other standard but themselves.

ELIOT WAS brought up in a democracy. He inherited that great fund of public spirit which is the gift of American democracy to the modern world, and the cause of so much ignorant hatred of America. But he was not a democrat in his sensibility. Eliot believed that culture could not be entrusted to the democratic process precisely because of the carelessness with words, this habit of unthinking cliché, which would always arise when every person is regarded as having an equal right to express himself. In *The Use of Poetry and the Use of Criticism* he writes:

> When the poet finds himself in an age in which there is no intellectual aristocracy, when power is in the hands of a class so democratised that while still a class it represents itself to be the whole nation; when the only alternatives seem to be to talk to a coterie or soliloquize, the difficulties of the poet and the necessity of criticism become greater.[2]

Hence, the critic has, for Eliot, an enhanced significance in the modern, democratic world. It is he who must act to restore what the aristocratic ideal of taste would have spontaneously generated—a language in which words are used with their full meaning and in order to show the world as it is. Those nurtured on empty sentiment have no weapons with which to deal with the reality of a god-forsaken world. They fall at once from sentimentality into cynicism, and so lose the power either to experience life or to live with its imperfection.

Eliot therefore perceived an enormous danger in the liberal and "scientific" humanism which was offered by the prophets of his day. This liberalism seemed to him to be the avatar of moral chaos, since it would permit any sentiment to flourish and would deaden all critical judgement with the idea of a democratic right to speak—which becomes, insensibly, a democratic right to feel. Although "human kind cannot bear very much reality"—as he expresses the point, first in *Murder in the Cathedral*, and then in *Four Quartets*—the purpose of a culture is to retain that elusive thing called "sensibility": the habit of right feeling. Barbarism ensues, not because people have lost their skills and scientific knowledge, nor is it averted by retaining those things; rather, barbarism comes through a loss of *culture*, since it is only through culture that the important realities can be truly perceived.

ELIOT'S THOUGHT here is difficult to state precisely. And it is worth drawing a parallel with a thinker whom he disliked: Friedrich Nietzsche. For Nietzsche, the crisis of modernity had come about because of the loss of the Christian faith. This loss of faith is the inevitable result of science and the growth of knowledge. At the same time, it is not possible for mankind really to live without faith; and for us, who have inherited all the habits and concepts of a Christian culture, that faith must be Christianity. Take away the faith, and you do not take away a body of doctrine only, nor do you leave a clear, uncluttered landscape in which man at last is visible for what he is. Rather, you take away the power to perceive other and more important truths, truths about our condition which cannot, without the benefit of faith, be properly confronted—such as the truth of our mortality.

The solution that Nietzsche impetuously embraced in this quandary was to deny the sovereignty of truth altogether—to say that "there are no truths," and to build a philosophy of life on the ruins of both science and religion in the name of a purely aesthetic ideal. Eliot saw the absurdity of that response. Yet the paradox remains. The truths that mattered to Eliot are truths of feeling, truths about the *weight* of human life. Science does not make these truths more easily perceivable: on the contrary, it releases into the human psyche a flock of fantasies—liberalism, humanism, utilitarianism, and the rest—which distract it with the futile hope for a scientific morality. The result is a corruption of the very language of feeling, a decline from sensibility to sentimentality, and a veiling of the human world. The paradox, then, is this: the falsehoods of religious faith enable us to perceive the truths that matter. The truths of science, endowed with an absolute authority, hide the truths that matter, and make human reality imperceivable. Eliot's solution to the paradox was compelled by the path that he had taken to its discovery—the path of poetry, with the agonizing examples of poets whose precision, perception, and sincerity were the effects of Christian belief. The solution was to embrace the Christian faith—not, as Tertullian did, *because* of the paradox, but rather in spite of it.

This explains Eliot's growing conviction that culture and religion are in the last analysis indissoluble. The disease of sentimentality could be overcome, he believed, only by a high culture in which the work of purification was constantly carried on. This is the task of the critic and the artist, and it is a hard task:

And so each venture
Is a new beginning, a raid on the
    inarticulate
With shabby equipment always
    deteriorating
In the general mess of imprecision of
    feeling,
Undisciplined squads of emotion. And
    what there is to conquer
By strength and submission, has already
    been discovered
Once or twice, or several times, by men
    whom one cannot hope
To emulate—but there is no
    competition—
There is only the fight to recover what
    has been lost
And found and lost again and again: and
    now, under conditions
That seem unpropitious. . . .[3]

This work of purification is a dialogue across the generations with those who belong to the tradition: only the few can take part in it, while the mass of mankind stays below, assailed by those "undisciplined squads of emotion." The high culture of the few is, however, a moral necessity for the many, for it permits human reality to *show itself*, and so to guide our conduct.

But why should the mass of mankind, lost as they are in bathos, "distracted from distraction by distraction," be guided by "those who know" (to use Dante's pregnant phrase)? The answer must lie in religion, and in particular in the common language which a traditional religion bestows, both on the high culture of art and on the common culture of a people. Religion is the life-blood of a culture. It provides the store of symbols, stories and doctrines that enable us to communicate about our destiny. It forms, through the sacred texts and liturgies, the constant point to which the poet and the critic can return—the language alike of ordinary believers and of the poets who must confront the ever-new conditions of life in the aftermath of knowledge, of life in a fallen world.

For Eliot, however, religion in general, and the Christian religion in particular, should not be seen merely in Platonic terms as an attitude towards what is eternal and unchanging. The truth of our condition is that we are historical beings who find whatever consolation and knowledge is vouchsafed to us in time. The consolations of religion come to us in temporal costume, through institutions that are alive with the spirit of history. To rediscover our religion is not to rise free from the temporal order; it is not to deny history and corruption, in order to contemplate the timeless truths. On the contrary, it is to enter more deeply into history, so as to find in the merely transitory the mark and the sign of that which never passes: it is to discover the "point of intersection of the timeless with time," which is, according to *Four Quartets*, the occupation of the saint.

Thus there emerges the strangest and most compelling of parallels: that between the saint and martyr of *Murder in the Cathedral* and the meditating poet of *Four Quartets*. Just as the first brings, through his martyrdom, the light of eternity into the darkness of the people of Canterbury (represented as a chorus of women), so does the poet "redeem the time," by finding in the stream of time those timeless moments which point beyond time. And the attempt by the poet to rediscover and belong to a tradition that will give sense and meaning to his language is one with the attempt to find a tradition of belief, of behavior, and of historical allegiance, that will give sense and meaning to the community. The real significance of a religion lies less in the abstract doctrine than in the institutions which cause it to endure. It lies also in the sacraments and ceremonies, in which the eternal becomes present and what might have been coincides with what is.

FOR ELIOT, therefore, conversion was not a matter merely of acknowledging the truth of Christ. It involved a conscious gesture of *belonging*, whereby he united his poetical labors with the perpetual labor of the Anglican church. For the Anglican church is peculiar in this: that it has never defined itself as "Protestant"; that it has always sought to accept rather than protest against its inheritance, while embracing the daring belief that the truths of Christianity have been offered in a *local* form to the people of England. It is a church which takes its historical nature seriously, acknowledging that its duty is less to spread the gospel among mankind than to sanctify a specific community. And in order to fit itself for this role, the Anglican church has, through its divines and liturgists, shaped the English language according to the Christian message, while also bringing that message into the here and now of England. In "Little Gidding," the last of the *Four Quartets*, the poet finds himself in the village retreat where an Anglican saint had retired to pray with his family. He conveys what to many is the eternal truth of the Anglican confession, in lines which are among the most famous that have ever been written in English:

If you came this way,
Taking any route, starting from
  anywhere,
At any time or at any season,
It would always be the same: you would
  have to put off
Sense and notion. You are not here to
  verify,
Instruct yourself, or inform curiosity
Or carry report. You are here to kneel
Where prayer has been valid. And prayer
  is more
Than an order of words, the conscious
  occupation
Of the praying mind, or the sound of the
  voice praying.
And what the dead had no speech for,
  when living,
They can tell you, being dead: the
  communication
Of the dead is tongued with fire beyond
  the language of the living.
Here, the intersection of the timeless
  moment
Is England and nowhere. Never and
  always.[4]

Later, returning to this theme of communication with the dead—*our* dead—and
referring to those brief moments of
meaning which are the only sure gift of
sensibility, Eliot completes the thought:

We are born with the dead:
See, they return, and bring us with them.
The moment of the rose and the moment
  of the yew-tree
Are of equal duration. A people without
  history
Is not redeemed from time, for history is
  a pattern
Of timeless moments. So, while the light
  fails
On a winter's afternoon, in a secluded
  chapel
History is now and England.[5]

Much has been written about "Little
Gidding," the atmosphere of which
stays in the mind of every cultivated
Englishman who reads it. What is important, however, is less the atmosphere
of the poem than the thought which advances through it. For here Eliot achieves
that for which he envies Dante—namely,
a poetry of belief, in which belief and
words are one, and in which the thought
cannot be prized free from the controlled
and beautiful language. Moreover, there
is one influence throughout which is inescapable—the King James Bible, and the
Anglican liturgy that grew alongside it.
Without being consciously biblical, and
while using only modern and colloquial
English, Eliot endows his verse with the
authority of liturgy, and with the resonance of faith.

THESE LINES take us back to the core
belief of modern conservatism, which
Burke expressed in the following terms:
Society, he wrote, is indeed a contract;
but not a contract among the living only;
rather, it is a partnership between the living, the dead, and those yet to be born.
And, he argued, only those who listen
to the dead are fit custodians of future
generations. Eliot's complex theory of tradition gives sense and form to this idea.
For he makes clear that the most important thing that future generations can
inherit from us is our culture. Culture is
the repository of an experience which is
at once local and placeless, present and
timeless, the experience of a community
as sanctified by time. This we can pass
on only if we too inherit it. Therefore,
we must listen to the voices of the dead,
and capture their meaning in those brief,
elusive moments when "History is now
and England." In a religious community,
such moments are a part of everyday life.

For us, in the modern world, religion and culture are both to be *gained* through a work of sacrifice. But it is a sacrifice upon which everything depends. Hence, by an extraordinary route, the modernist poet becomes the traditionalist priest: and the stylistic achievement of the first is one with the spiritual achievement of the second.

To many people, Eliot's theory of culture and tradition is too arduous, imposing an impossible duty upon the educated elite. To others, however, it has been a vital inspiration. For let us ask ourselves just what is required of "one who knows." Should he, in the modern world, devote himself like Sartre or Foucault to undermining the "structures" of bourgeois society, to scoffing at manners and morals, and ruining the institutions upon which he depends for his exalted status? Should he play the part of a modern Socrates, questioning everything and affirming nothing? Should he go along with the mindless culture of play, the postmodernist fantasy world in which all is permitted since neither permission nor interdiction have any sense?

To answer yes to any of those questions is in effect to live by negation, to grant nothing to human life beyond the mockery of it. It is to inaugurate and endorse the new world of "transgression," a world which will not reproduce itself, since it will undermine the very motive which causes a society to reproduce. The conservative response to modernity is to embrace it, but to embrace it *critically*, in full consciousness that human achievements are rare and precarious, that we have no God-given right to destroy our inheritance, but must always patiently submit to the voice of order and set an example of orderly living. The future of mankind, for the socialist, is simple: pull down the existing order, and allow the future to emerge. But it will not emerge, as we know. These philosophies of the "new world" are lies and delusions, products of a sentimentality which has veiled the facts of human nature.

We can do nothing unless we first amend ourselves. The task is to rediscover the world which made us, to see ourselves as part of something greater, which depends upon us for its survival—and which still can live in us, if we can achieve that "condition of complete simplicity / (Costing not less than everything)," to which Eliot directs us.

We shall not cease from exploration
And the end of all our exploring
Will be to arrive where we started
And know the place for the first time.

Such is the conservative message for our time. It is a message beyond politics, a message of liturgical weight and authority. But it is a message which must be received, if humane and moderate politics is to remain a possibility.

Notes

1. For Lancelot Andrewes (London; Faber, 1970[1929]), 20.

2. *The Use of Poetry and the Use of Criticism* (Cambridge, MA: Harvard Univ. Press, 1886[1961]), 22.

3. *Four Quartets* in T. S. Eliot, *The Complete Poems and Plays* (London: Faber and Faber, 1969), 182.

4. Ibid., 192

5. Ibid., 197.

IX.

ARGUING CONSERVATISM

Willmoore Kendall

How to Read Richard Weaver: Philosopher of "We the (Virtuous) People"

VOL. 2, NO. 1, 1965

"Richard M. Weaver of Chicago (but a devoted son of western North Carolina) . . . [bespeaks] a Conservatism that owes much to Plato but perhaps even more to a 'complete disenchantment' with the presumptuousness and vulgarity of liberalism. . . . [His] recent writings have become increasingly concerned with the debasing effects of 'mass plutocracy.'" So Clinton Rossiter writes in the revised version of his *Conservatism in America*.[1]

Weaver—so Rossiter writes a few pages later—"must . . . be given a very special place in the intellectual history of the American Right" because he, among others, has "belabored liberalism in season and out."[2] Weaver is the "spiritual heir" of Donald Davidson, fighting—how "sincerely" Rossiter is at a loss to decide—for the "embattled [sic.] cause of southern agrarianism."[3] Again: Weaver is a man "quick with the timeless truths of Conservatism" (though no quicker with these truths, Rossiter adds, than many of his liberal opponents), and one of several readily recognizable "voices of the Right" which, "for the first time in many years," are now becoming audible. Weaver—so Rossiter writes in the following chap-

ter[4]—is again a Southern Agrarian, whom Rossiter calls upon to decide whether to "abdicate responsibility for the future of the American republic" or help teach American Conservatism that it must "enlist and serve the interests of American business." Then, finally: Weaver, now suddenly linked with Russell Kirk, Anthony Harrigan, and Gerhart Niemeyer, because of his "contempt" for liberalism is one of the only "real" conservatives "now writing in America"—"too real," indeed, because "they find themselves in a state of all-out war with liberalism—and thus, in fact, with the American tradition," "reckless, imprudent, and [therefore] '*unconservative*'."[5]

No, my point is not, or at least not primarily, my usual one, namely, that Rossiter doesn't know what he is talking about.[6] But rather that Richard Weaver was, even for so skilled a labeller as Rossiter, a hard man to stick a label on, and for some reason or reasons other than that, Picasso-like, he went through "periods" (he was, from his very beginnings in the Southern coterie reviews, all of one piece), and that, as I have put it in a footnote, *one* of those reasons is that lines are not easy to draw among contemporary Conservative intellectuals: relevant categories, relevant in the sense that they result from asking questions that bring to light the real *differentiae* of the writers involved, apparently do not exist.

Even M. Morton Auerbach, who unlike Rossiter sounds as if he had actually read the books he speaks of, has trouble classifying Weaver, just as Rossiter does. He does not, to be sure, commit the (in part anachronistic) error of making Weaver a Southern Agrarian, as distinguished from a writer *on* Southern agrarianism, but even he still cannot resist the temptation to tar him a little with the Southern Agrarian brush. Among the many statements Weaver made about the Southern Agrarians, the one Auerbach chooses to emphasize, accordingly, is that to the effect that they asserted the "timeless moral values"—with, of course, the unavoidable implication that, in morals and, one supposes, politics, they were in some special sense Weaver's forebears.[7] Again: Weaver bases his "Conservatism" on "tradition" (what tradition Auerbach does not tell us), which according to Auerbach, is a matter of Weaver's ultimate reliance on "values" that are, like those of any other ideologist, "intuitive": tradition alone enables "men to live . . . together harmoniously over an extent of time."[8] "Communal harmony," the "absence" (by which Auerbach of course understands *total* absence, so that Weaver begins to emerge as an authoritarian) of "conflict and tension,"[9] is Weaver's "primary concept"; Weaver seems to believe indeed, that "any tradition" (that is, any tradition whatever) is a Conservative tradition, and thus, by implication, a tradition a Conservative must defend.[10]

Still again Auerbach follows Rossiter in making of Weaver a "Platonic Conservative," by which he turns out to mean not that Weaver wished to build

Plato's *Republic* on earth, as Auerbach's earlier discussion might appear to suggest, but rather that Weaver believed that our troubles began when "the Middle Ages" surrendered "Platonism" in favor of "the easier ethic [!] of Aristotle."[11] Again (and not, as we shall see, a bad point) Weaver, unlike Kirk (again not a bad point), is on the optimistic side about the possibility of "restoring lost ideals," though only through "teaching poetry and precise dialectical definition in the schools."[12] Again (a little difficult to follow, but let us always be patient with Auerbach): In 1953 Weaver wrote a further book, *The Ethics of Rhetoric*, in which he seems, says Auerbach, less "pessimistic" than in the earlier one (in which, as we have just seen, he was "hopeful of restoring lost ideals," i.e., optimistic), and in which—at last we begin to get somewhere—he argues (with Auerbach's approval) that Edmund Burke's frequent arguments from "mere traditionalism" were without meaning as long as Burke did not "abstract the essence of the traditions he was defending," which begins to make it sound as if Weaver, after all, did not, despite Auerbach's earlier statement, defend just any old tradition.[13] Burke, we find Weaver saying in the pages to which Auerbach refers us, argue "from circumstance." Burke tells us to be sure, that "he is going to give equal consideration to circumstance and to ideals (or principles)"—which, Weaver is there to assure us, cannot be done, because the man who attempts it finds himself, inevitably, following circumstance not principle; the "argument from circumstance," is "philosophically appropriate for the liberal," and "is very far from being conservative."[14] More: a man's method of argument is a "truer index" to "his beliefs than his explicit profession of principles." And in the sequel, Weaver scores Burke as a preacher of a "gospel of *precedent* and gradualism" (italics added), as, in the end, a man who bases his argument for prescription *merely* on the grounds that it is backed up by precedent, merely on the grounds that it is old. Weaver concluded, Auerbach himself concludes, that "Burke should not be a model for Conservatism at all."

Auerbach's treatment of Weaver, as I had encouraged the reader to expect, is a considerable improvement on Rossiter's, if only because he sees that Weaver's repudiation of Burke is somehow significant, even though the reason it is significant escapes him.[15] I repeat my point: The categories for classifying right-wing intellectuals in America do not exist, or, if they do, are unknown at least to the major liberal writers on these matters. And I begin to lead up to my further point: Weaver just may be unique, so that even if the relevant categories did exist he would not fit into any of them. The Rossiter-Auerbach Weaver cannot, in any case, appear other than an outrage in the eyes of any real "studier" (I borrow the phrase from my hero Locke) of Weaver's thought.

Weaver, apart from (for the most part scanty) reviews of his books as they have appeared, has been little written about by his fellow right-wing intellectuals. Or, to put it more precisely, he was much eulogized but seldom if ever subjected to analysis and, what is more important, seldom if ever really listened to. The last claim that could be made for him, for example, would be that he has impressed his influence upon or swayed the minds of the present-day high-priests of Conservatism in America.[16] This is perhaps partly a matter of their being too busy writing their own books to read each others', but only partly; among them also, the questions have not been raised that would lead to the drawing of significant lines[17]. Among them, too, the stereotype

of Weaver as somehow a spokesman for the South has continued to pop up with surprising frequency; there, more perhaps even than on the Left, Weaver has tended to be thought of as a writer mainly on "cultural" and "literary" matters, and not as a political theorist—or, if as a political theorist, as one concerned with answering the right-wing intellectuals' question of questions, "What is Conservatism?" (as distinguished from the question "What is *American* Conservatism?"). There, too, what I call Weaver's uniqueness, and the qualities in him that made him unique, have gone un-noticed.[18]

Thus Russell Kirk, the publisher's unhappy choice to write the foreword to Weaver's posthumous *Visions of Order,* lets the essential Weaver slip through his fingers about as clumsily as Rossiter and Auerbach. Here, too, Weaver's "view" is "Platonic" (though Weaver spends several pages of this very book scolding Socrates, who is said to have been greatly loved and admired by Plato). Here too we might easily get the impression that Weaver, in the decisive dimension, was a johnny-come-lately Southern Agrarian. Here too we are struck by the failure to try to dig down and identify the deep differences that in fact divide our conservatives, and "place" Weaver with respect to them. Mr. Kirk's main purpose, indeed, seems to be to make Weaver sound, apart from certain purely personal idiosyncracies, like "one of the boys" in the exalted right-wing circles in which Kirk himself normally moves when he emerges from Mecosta—like, if I may put it so without seeming impudent, a sort of alter-ego of Mr. Kirk's: a deplorer of pretty much everything on the horizon, a "despiser" of everything modern, a man who thought of himself as "speaking to a Remnant," above all a trafficker, again like Kirk himself, in *Weltanschauungen,* grand style, who when he writes that "we" have been "stumbling down the path of Avernus," that "we" have been "distorting rhetoric" and so "subverting the high old order" of "our civilization and our human dignity," means "we" of the West, and thinks of his redemptive mission as an act to be performed on a worldwide stage.[19] More: Kirk even attempts (I anticipate a little a major argument to which I am leading up) to transform Weaver into "one of the boys" (*ut supra*) in a more intimate dimension, namely, that of his day-to-day way of life. Finding himself in an uncongenial "climate of opinion," we are told, Weaver "withdrew much of the time to the fastnesses of his solitary reflections" (i.e., to his equivalent of Mecosta).[20] After Mr. Kirk has done, only one drop of quicksilver remains in hand; but it, as far as it goes, is a precious one, and in justice to Mr. Kirk, I have saved it for the end: "*Order . . .* was Weaver's austere passion: the inner order of the soul, the outer order of society."[21]

I conclude: Everybody appears to be hard put to it to "classify" Richard Weaver, or to say what he was up to without, pretty soon, sticking his foot in his mouth.

TO THE reader who wishes to object at this point, "This is supposed to be an essay, and you are not getting anywhere," I answer: "Ah! But I *am*." All the above has been necessary for the business I have in hand, namely: To explain to the readers of this essay (whom I think of as the Conservative intellectual spokesmen of that morrow when the "false teachers" who produce most contemporary right-wing literature will have been shunted aside) why Richard Weaver's *Visions of Order,* it and it alone among American Conservative books, is the one that they

must place on their shelves beside *The Federalist,* and confer on it, as on *The Federalist,* the political equivalent of biblical status. For the danger (because of the confusion about where Weaver stands among the thinkers with whom, erroneously, his name tends to get itself associated) is that it is *Visions of Order* that will get shunted aside. (Certainly no review has appeared to date that might conceivably prevent that from happening.) Now it is only after we have asked the questions that expose the significant groupings on the Right, and drawn the necessary lines, that we can distinguish the true from the false teachers, and assign to Richard Weaver the pride of place that he deserves, and so avoid that danger.

What are the questions that want asking? I think they are these.

a) Who have, and who have not, fallen for the liberal lie of the past forty or fifty years, according to which the American political tradition is a tradition of "individual rights," of rights that because "individual" end up (they always do, because there's no stopping on this downward slope) rights that are equal from individual to individual and thus for all individuals, of, therefore, equality as the ultimate destiny of the American Republic? The answer to the question "Who have?" would be too painful to contemplate. The answer to the question "Who have not?" is: Only Richard Weaver, who never had so much as a flirtation with an individual right.

b) Who have, and who have not, fallen for latter-day right-wing *ideology* according to which government is "evil" as such, and "freedom" over against government, especially the wicked brand of government known as "big government," is good as such—though the authors of *The Federalist,* in which our political tradition has its roots, repudiated both these notions? Those who have: pretty much every celebrity you can name among right-wing intellectuals, But not Richard Weaver, who was steeped in *The Federalist* and its thought, and did not lightly accept new-fangled notions.

c) Who have, and who have not, fallen for the propaganda-line—it comes at you from *both* the Left and the latter-day Right, where it derives from Tocqueville—according to which the forces of the Left, the egalitarians and the levellers, are going to win in any case, so that "we conservatives" are fighting, at best, a rear-guard action? (Has not the history of the past two centuries been one of continuous defeat for the followers of Burke by the followers of Rousseau?)[22] As I have written in an unpublished book dealing with Russell Kirk, Frank Meyer, et al., the favorite battle-cry of the contemporary American intellectual Right is: "We are losing! We are losing! But in how noble, how fine, how glorious a cause!" I find no trace of any such pessimism in the mature writings of Richard Weaver. Nor, for reasons I am about to note, is this a matter, as Kirk suggests in his Foreword, of Weaver having refused to "despair," of his having dared to "hope." Weaver simply believed that if we of the Right only use our heads, we have the strength and the resources with which to win.

d) Who do, and who do not, conceive of right-wing victory in America, and thus of the immediate right-wing task in America, in terms of storming American public opinion from *without*, of *conquering* the hearts and minds of an essentially hostile because already left-wing *people*, ready always to sell its votes to the highest bidder?[23] Again the answer is too horrible to contemplate. But Richard Weaver addresses himself to the American people through his pupils of course, as an *insider*, avuncularly lovingly, that is, in the tone of

a wise uncle seeking to emancipate those of the nephews who may have fallen under the influence of "false teachers." (The pessimistic, storming-from-outside overtones of the Goldwater campaign are, in this context, too obvious to dwell upon. No wonder Goldwater lost!) Weaver always writes reverently of America and the American people, with never a doubt of their ultimate soundness, good judgment, uprightness, and good faith.[24]

e) Who do, and who do not—a point akin to (d), but by no means the same point—share with the founders of the American Republic the belief that the Republic's destiny will in fact be decided by the *discussion-process*; that therefore writing good, well-argued books matters not merely for its own sake, but because (Keynes has said it better than anyone else) what ultimately sways events is books; that, though the "world of the intellect" does go crazy now and then, as it has certainly done both in America and in the West-in-general in recent decades, the law that obtains in the world of the intellect remains the precise opposite of Gresham's Law: good books drive out bad, and the debate is won finally by those who, in their books, prove themselves *right*. It is a difficult faith to keep alive in the evil days in the world of the intellect, when writing and publishing good books—witness the fate of e.g., Leo Strauss's *Machiavelli*[25] and Harry V. Jaffa's *Crisis*[26]—seems hardly less futile than dropping pebbles in a bottomless well. Yet the Strausses and Voegelins and Jaffas and Weavers continue to ply their trade, and produce books that breathe confidence, a confidence that the apt pupil will quickly learn to recognize and value: that the ultimate effect of their books will be to purge the intellectual climate of ideology, and to restore true philosophy to its rightful place of honor and *influence*. This, of all the issues I mention, is certainly that which cuts deepest; for it is precisely the confidence I speak of here that is lacking in the "mainstream" of contemporary Conservative writing,[27] so that the latter is shot through and through with a fundamental, though gracefully concealed, anti-intellectualism.

f) Who do, and who do not, earn their living by (or, if they inherited that, devote the bulk of their working-time to) being Conservative intellectuals—or, if you like, who are, who are not, "professional" Rightwingers? Again the point is a delicate one, but it cannot be side-stepped: much of the quality and the importance of Richard Weaver's thoughts about the deepest issues in our politics is intimately tied up with the fact that, like Hamilton and Madison, he had, and wrote from a *locus standi* in American life as somebody in particular with a particular function to perform in American society. No hurler of thunderbolts from Olympus (or from the ski-resorts in Switzerland) was he: he was first and foremost a "working" school-teacher, with a job to do *within* one of America's basic institutions, whose first thoughts were always, in Bradley's pungent phrase, of his "station and its duties"; and he philosophizes about politic in that capacity (which is one of the many reasons why those who try to read him as simply another of the high-priests, who are sermonizers not teachers, will never understand him).

g) Who does, and who does not, mean by the American Tradition that which he in his wisdom happens to like about the American past—but rather that which Americans, Americans from their very beginnings at Plymouth Rock and Jamestown,[28] have *made* the American Tradition, especially the America's Political Tradition, by actually *living* it, which leads on to the further question, Who does, who does not, mean by American Conservatism the *assertion*, *protection*, and *perfection* of that tradition as the kind of thing it is? This is the point at which the "Burke business" becomes relevant, the point that explains why the issue between the Burke "cultists" and the non-Burke cultists is another of the deepest-cutting issues on the American Right.

h) Who are, and who are not, in one sense or another, darlings of the Liberal Establishment, invited to appear on its television programs, called to lecture far and wide at its universities, reviewed in its newspapers and magazines, privileged to debate with its major spokesmen in its vast auditoriums? The Liberals, who know a thing or two about the business *they* are in, have a "little list" of their favorite conservatives and, of course, their "little list" of conservatives whom they would not touch with a ten-foot pole. (Also, presumably, their well-pondered though of course secret criteria for choosing the former, at which we can only guess: X, though he does make those Conservative noises, really agrees with us on the fundamentals, in the long run means us no harm, is, therefore, a man we can do business with? Y, though he too makes Conservative noises, is so out of touch with reality that we can make mincemeat of him? Z, though indeed a Conservative, says such silly things that he in fact forwards *our* cause? And old A, though he does write those savage attacks on our foreign policy in *National Review,* is he, down deep in his heart really any more eager than we to force a showdown with the USSR? Is he not, therefore, really one of us?) Here Weaver is perhaps less lonely on his side of the line than in the previous cases (one thinks at once of Frank Meyer, of Brent Bozell, of yet others of the high priests). What is certain, and a further proof that Weaver was indeed a "real" American Conservative, is that the Liberal Establishment avoided him like the plague because he was clearly out to do 'em in the eye.

I conclude: Richard Weaver's "uniqueness" lies in part in the fact that he, and he alone, falls on the (for me) "right" side, from the standpoint of true American Conservatism, of each of the lines I have drawn. But it is a matter, mainly and far more importantly, of the unique manner in which he has performed, in *Visions of Order,* a unique task.

"WE THE people," according to our basic constitutional theory, "ordain and establish" the Constitution for certain *purposes*: among others, to establish *justice,* to promote the *general welfare,* to secure the *blessings of liberty* for ourselves *and our posterity.* In doing so, that is, in the act of writing and ratifying the Constitution, "we" constitute ourselves *a* "people" (which we may or may not have been prior to the writing and ratification). And, by speaking of "our" posterity declare our intention to *remain* a "people," with such and such "machinery" of government, to which "we" assign certain coercive functions, the necessity of whose performance "we" assert by assigning them to the government, to which, however, we do not assign certain other functions, not necessarily less necessary in our minds, and not necessarily less coercive, which "we" tacitly declare "our" intention to perform "ourselves," i.e., in "our" capacity as a "people" (e.g., providing for the education of the young, building and supporting churches, growing "our" food, making arrangements for "our" transportation—all of which, and many others, we might have assigned to "our" government but did not). "We"

also indicate, by the purposes "we" in the act of constituting ourselves a "people" choose to emphasize over and above the two-so-to-speak clearly indispensable ones (providing for our defense, maintaining the civil peace) what *kind* of "people" we think of ourselves as being and intend to keep on being, i.e., a "people" dedicated to "justice," the "common good," and "liberty," and dedicated to these goods with respect *both* to the functions "we" assign to "our" government and the functions "we" propose to perform in "our" capacity as a "people." If there is, at the time, any question in "our" minds as to whether we will in fact remain that kind of people, any thought in "our" minds as to who is to see to it that "we" do remain that kind of people,[29] "we" in constituting ourselves say nothing about it, unless by implication this: seeing to it that we remain a people dedicated to justice, the common good, and liberty, is *not* one of the functions that "we" assign to "our" government. If there be a problem here, "we" do not face it head-on.

Let the reader hold all that still, and let us approach the matter along another path. In the course of ratifying "our" Constitution, "we, the people" tacitly adopt a book, directed to us precisely in our capacity as a "people," entitled *The Federalist.* That book—so we are assured by our major contemporary authority on its contents[30]—"interprets" the Constitution for us, and spells out certain rules and principles, not explicit in the Constitution, the observance of which, according to the book's author Publius, will help "us"[31] to see to it that no "branch" of our government shall monopolize the functions "we" have assigned to the government, and divided among three "branches." *The Federalist* does not, however, concern itself exclusively with problems of government, that is, with the kind of government we are going to have. Publius knows only too well that the problem of actually doing justice, promoting the common good, and insuring the blessings of liberty cannot be solved on the governmental "level"; that, in a word, it depends somehow on the kind of "people," or "society" we are going to be; and *Federalist* 10 does raise, however obliquely, the question to which I have led up in the preceding paragraph, and has something—not much, but something—to say by way of an answer to the question. "We, the people" must add to the three optional purposes we have noted above a fourth, namely, the prevention of "tyranny," by which Publius means the use of government, by a *majority* of "we, the people," for effectuating measures "adverse to the rights of other citizens, or to the permanent and aggregate interests of the community." "Our" machinery of government, Publius sees, *is* subject to capture by a popular majority, and does, for all its built-in guarantees against tyranny, lend itself, once captured, to the uses of tyranny (as he has defined it). The solution, if one there be, must be sought "out there" among "we, the people," in society, in, as I put it a moment ago, the "kind" of "people" we are going to be.

Publius is, however, strangely stingy with his recommendations ("we" must be a "people" spread over a large territory, "we" must be a "people" characterized by diversity), and strangely reluctant to open up, really open up, the problem he is skirting the edges of. I say "strangely" because he shows, in many a scattered passage, that he knows the shape at least of the correct answer to the problem: The machinery of government will help; diversity will help; spreading the "people" over a large territory will help; but in the end *nothing* will prevent tyranny, since

the machinery of government is open to capture by a popular majority, except that "we, the people" shall be virtuous, that is, to go no further, dedicated in our hearts to justice, to the common good, to liberty, and to the prevention (the renunciation on "our" own part) of tyrannical measures; that is, which brings us back to where we were at the end of the preceding paragraph, a certain kind of "people." The question, however, and for whatever reasons Publius chooses to ignore it, cries up at you throughout the argument of *The Federalist*: if all depends ultimately on the virtue of the "people," how—unless we are to take it for granted that that will just take care of itself—are the "people" to be kept "virtuous"? And this, translated into the language of our basic constitutional theory, becomes the question, "How are 'we, the people' to keep 'ourselves' virtuous?" *Bref*: There is a "missing section" of *The Federalist,* in which *that* question, the question as to how "we the people" shall *order* "ourselves" so as to remain virtuous, and become ever more virtuous. Worse still: "we, the people" have been only too ready to conclude, from the fact that Publius left out the section in which he might have discussed the ordering of society, of "we, the people" qua "virtuous people," that no such section was needed, and, even the best of us, to focus our thinking on the range of problems to which Publius did address himself.[32]

My claim: At last we have, in Richard Weaver's posthumous *Visions of Order,*[33] that missing section of *The Federalist.* No matter that Weaver nowhere posed, in so many words, the question "How shall 'we, the people' be kept virtuous?"[34] No matter, either, whether he "consciously" set himself the task of answering that question, although, once you begin to look at his mature essays from this standpoint you will, so unerringly "on target" each of them is, find it difficult to suppose that he had not done so. No matter, finally, that he elects to state himself in terms of "culture," "rhetoric," etc.—never, that is to say, openly assumes the role of political philosopher, of philosopher of the order of society (modest man that he was, he would have deemed open assumption of that role pretentious). Just, provisionally, take my word for it that each of his essays takes on new and deeper meaning when read as a partial answer to the question as I have posed it for him, and that the essays taken together do add up to an answer to the question, which you—like the high priests of contemporary American Conservatism, who as I have intimated repeatedly would be providing us a very different kind of leadership had they attended to the teachings of Richard Weaver—will do well to lay in your heart and ponder. Then go read—nay, *live with*—the book, until you have made its contents your own. It will prepare you, as no other book, not *even The Federalist* will prepare you, for your future encounters with the protagonists of the Liberal Revolution, above all by teaching you how to drive the debate to a deeper level than that on which our present spokesmen are engaging the Liberals.

How shall the people be kept virtuous? Weaver answers—though here I can only indicate in the briefest manner, the general outline of his reply—only through a self-chosen "select minority"[35] who assume responsibility for people's *culture,* in which its virtue must be rooted—for, therefore, understanding what needs a culture must satisfy if the people are to adopt it and live it as their own, for, therefore, keeping alive and healthy a culture that will satisfy those needs, and for disseminating it among the several members of the people, each according to his capacity for receiving it. It must, as

part of the culture it disseminates, teach the people those lessons that the people must learn if they are to operate a society in which a sound and healthy culture is possible. It must teach them, for example, the value, the value for their own sake, of that diversity which Publius showed to be necessary for the prevention of tyranny. It must teach people the *value*, for the people themselves including those who had the short end of the stick, of distinction of rank and status in society, and the unwisdom of making such distinctions wholly dependent upon "functions performed." It must teach them the correctness of the Christian picture of man, of, that is, Christian anthropology, and so render them proof against all forms of "reductionism" (in order to be virtuous, the people must suppose themselves capable of virtue, which, to the extent that they think of man as an animal, they will not do). It must itself be clear as to the respective roles in a healthy culture of "dialectic" and "rhetoric,"[36] that is, between pure, "abstract" propositional reasoning as in science or economic theory, and the task of relating the results of such reasoning to the "existential world," in which facts must be "treated with a sympathy" and "historical understanding and appreciation" that are, as they should be, foreign to the "dialectical process."[37] It must not permit the culture of which it is custodian to become contemptuous of, or hostile to, the "arts of persuasion," which alone can "move men in the direction of a goal." It must keep alive within itself, and develop in the people, "historical memory," i.e., knowledge of their own traditions—lest, in ignorance of them, they forget, like madmen, what and who they are.

But enough. I warned you that I could at most suggest, not summarize, the contents of *Visions of Order.*

The Liberals, according to Weaver, are by definition, so to speak, incapable of supplying a "select minority" that can build a healthy culture, and so keep the people virtuous (wherefore, on Publius's logic, a people led by Liberals must become tyrannical). The task to which Weaver's teaching points us, therefore, a task that only Conservatives can perform, and they, of course, only if they understand its nature and the means by which it can be performed—which our "name" Conservative spokesmen, believing as they do that the people are already corrupt, and innocent as they are of proposals even for restoring its virtue, clearly do not. But the existence of Weaver's book enables us, I repeat, to indulge the hope their successors, nurtured on a less narrow view of politics and especially Conservative politics, will be men of another stamp.

Notes

1. *Conservatism in America: The Thankless Persuasion* (New York: Vintage Books, 1962, 223–24.) There are ten-page references to Weaver in the revised version, as against only four in the original version (Knopf, 1956)—one of which points us to a list of major "items" in the "literature of American Conservatism," which includes Weaver's *Ideas Have Consequences* (Chicago: Univ. of Chicago Press, 1948), and *The Ethics of Rhetoric* (Chicago: Henry Regnery and Co., 1953); one which cites some of his early writings of the Southern Agrarians, esp. his essay in *Southern Renascence: The Literature of the Modern South* (Baltimore: Johns Hopkins Univ. Press, 1953), a third that links him with Peter Viereck, Russell Kirk, Francis G. Wilson, John Hallowell, and Thomas I. Cook, et al., who allegedly belong together because of their "outspoken distaste for the excesses, vulgarities, and dislocations of the industrial way of life," their "deep-seated antipathy toward the undiluted Jeffersonian tradition," their

"emphasis on our European and English heritage," and their *"peculiar affection for Burke* and John Adams, but not Hamilton . . . (italics added). The revised version contains twenty-page references to Russell Kirk, and a two-page summary of his "political theory."

2. Ibid., 226. What months of the year, one wonders, has Rossiter set aside as the "season" for "belaboring" Liberals?

3. Ibid., 231

4. Ibid., 252

5. Ibid., 262 (italics added). Cf. Fn. 1 above, and note, *in re* Rossiter's linkings, that Weaver is now *contrasted* with a list that includes his former companions Viereck and Hallowell. (Despite the incomprehensible linking of Weaver and Kirk, who are as different as chalk and cheese, it is only fair to note that Rossiter's categories have improved in neatness between 223 and 262, which may or may not indicate that Rossiter has begun to understand where the lines need to be drawn among contemporary right-wing intellectuals in America.

As for the words in italics: If Professor Rossiter will write out on a piece of coarse sandpaper any sentence Weaver ever wrote that is "contemptuous," "reckless," or "imprudent," and send it to me, I'll eat it in the presence of reliable witnesses. The works of Weaver the writer are informed throughout by the gentleness, courtesy, and moderation that were the outstanding characteristics of Weaver the man.

Note (ibid., 288) that Weaver reappears as a professional Southerner (because of his "The Regime of the South," *National Review,* March 14, 1959).

6. I have developed that point sufficiently in my *The Conservative Affirmation* (Chicago: Henry Regnery Co., 1963), 159.

7. Weaver did write his (unfortunately unpublished) Ph.D. dissertation, on the intellectual history of the ante-bellum South, under the then Southern Agrarian Cleanth Brooks, and did, as suggested in the text, produce a sizable literature on the Southern Agrarians: *Shenandoah,* Summer, 1952, 3–10; *Sewanee Review,* Autumn, 1950; and an essay is *Southern Renascence (ut supera).* But even the most casual reader of that literature will see at once, Weaver writes mainly *as a literary historian and*

critic, with out immediate political intent, and, in any case, as an outsider—as witness the following key passage, of great significance for the present article, from the essay cited by Auerbach: "The nation as a whole welcomed [*I'll Take My Stand*]. . . . That is because *the nation* as a whole wishes the South to speak, and wishes it to speak *in character.* . . . Despite *our* excitement over differences, *our* pain over invidious comparisons, and our resentment of suspected superiorities *we* desire, as long as *we* are in possession of our rational faculty, to hear an expression of the other point of view. That is a guarantee of *our* freedom and a necessity for *our* development" (italics, except for "*in character,*" added). The connection between the "*nation as a whole,*" (for which, as I argue below, Weaver always thought and prayed and spoke) and "*our,*" "*our,*" "*we,*" "*we,*" is inescapable. The Southern Agrarians were, on one side, a movement with politico-economic objectives: they were, for example, distributivists, much under the influence, in their economic ideas, of Chesterton and Belloc, thus militantly, and by no means merely romantically, anti-capitalist, as Weaver certainly was not; and the presence in the book here discussed of an important chapter justifying the rationality of arbitraments by war is difficult to explain save as a sermon-in-retrospect, delivered from a *national* pulpit, on the professional Southerners' tendency to keep the War between the States alive as a political issue, and on the overtones of irredentism that were always present in Southern Agrarian pronouncements. (My most vivid recollection of my first meeting with Richard Weaver is the expression on his face when I referred to him, as apparently no-one had ever done before, as a "political theorist"— a term which, as I have implied above, I do not dispense freely. I was, of course, using the term "political" in a sense that is no longer fashionable, but the beginning of wisdom about these matters is to understand that most of what passes today for "political" literature is written by men who are not interested in politics at all.

8. Richard Weaver, *Ideas Have Consequences,* 19; Auerbach, *The Conservative Illusion* (New York: Columbia Univ. Press, 1959), 137.

9. Auerbach, op. cit.. 137. Auerbach relies in this discussion entirely on Weaver's first book, which is the least "political" of his works (in the sense I am giving to that word in this article), and the least mature. When I say that Weaver is all of one piece, I do not mean, of course, that he did not develop over the years.

10. Ibid.

11. Ibid., 154, This is surely a misreading of *Ideas Have Consequences,* whose thesis is that the "long process of degeneration" (Auerbach's phrase, and Weaver did believe that things out in the world have got worse and worse) is to be laid at the door of *nominalism.* Any quarrel *the mature* Weaver would have had with Aristotle's *Ethics* would, surely, have been pressed on *Christian* grounds.

12. Ibid., 154–55. The reference is to *Ideas Have Consequences,* 166–67, 187,

13. Ibid., 155. Auerbach notes that this got Weaver into an argument with Kirk, and adds, gleefully (156), that there are "ideological cleavages even within the ranks of reactionary Conservatism." To which I would add, the half has never yet been told.

14. *Ethics of Rhetoric,* 58, et seq.

15. Had he written: Weaver concluded that "Burke should not be the model for *American* Conservatism" he would have been hitting the nail on the head—i.e., showing an incipient understanding of where the lines must be drawn among our contemporary Conservative intellectuals, and opening up the way for an understanding of Weaver.

16. As witness *National Review's* 23 March 1965 editorial on Selma, with its nice impartiality between Governor Wallace and his attempt to "maintain Alabama as an enclave of racial stability," and Dr. Martin Luther King and his use of the "methods and arts of modern psycho-political warfare . . . to move public opinion . . . in his chosen direction." It is not easy to imagine Richard Weaver writing an angry "letter to the editor"; but the editorial in question, which could never have been written by anyone who had begun to grasp the essence of Weaver's teaching, would certainly have fetched one from him. His letter would, of course, have driven the discussion to a higher level, but nothing could be more certain than that he would have defended

Selma, and would have done so on identifiably *non-Southern* grounds. It is perhaps in point that Weaver, though a regular contributor to *National Review* in its early years, wrote for it less and less as the magazine found its stride.

17. A major effort is under way, indeed, to prove that no such lines can be drawn. See Frank Meyers introductory chapter in *What Is Conservatism?"* (New York: Holt, Rinehart and Winston, 1964), and the review of that book by Vincent Miller, *Modern Age,* Fall, 1964, 416–17.

18. The writer who has, though tacitly, noticed Weaver's uniqueness is, curiously, Ronald Hamowy. Weaver, who was certainly grist for Hamowy's mill for purposes of his vicious attack on the "Neoconservatives" *(Modern Age,* Fall, 1964, 350–59), is not mentioned, though the two must often have brushed shoulders on the Chicago campus. I might add that Weaver's vogue among the libertarians and "individualists," who seemed to adore him, is the proof positive of how little understood Weaver was. Had they ever found him out for the kind of scoundrel he really was, they would—in some manner consistent with the free market, of course—have torn him limb-from-limb.

19. There was indeed something of this emphasis in *Ideas Have Consequences,* and there are flashes of it in the later works, even that here under review. But as I argue in the text, to stress this aspect of Weaver is indeed to let the essential Weaver slip through your fingers.

20. As a friend who frequently visited Weaver at Chicago, I must record my impression that Kirk is "factually" wrong on the whole point. Weaver always seemed to me to be happy in his work at Chicago, to hold his colleagues there in high esteem, to be taking an active part in the day-to-day life of the University and, what would presumably shock Mr. Kirk most, to love Chicago. He lived, by choice, a tidy distance from the campus, in order to give himself the pleasure of the daily walk to and fro (each day, he boasted, by a different route) through its streets. As for Weaver's alleged "withdrawal" to the "fastnesses of his solitary reflections," an accurate statement, readily intelligible to persons who have spent their lives close to universities, would run: Weaver was a professional scholar, who worked hard at his business, and preferred—like many other scholars, many even who find the prevailing intellectual climate congenial—to work at home rather than in the office. I might add that Weaver ate his meals for the most part at the university cafeteria, at the mercy of students who might wish to descend on him—an unlikely choice for the kind of "recluse" Kirk tries to make him.

21. Richard M. Weaver, *Visions of Order* (Baton Rouge: Louisiana State Univ. Press, 1964), ix.

22. Cf. Russell Kirk, *The Conservative Mind* (Chicago: Henry Regnery Company, 1953), 3–10, and pretty much any issue of *National Review,* esp, those that appeared hard upon the 1964 elections. Cf. Kendall, op. cit., Chapter One.

23. Again I must mention *National Review,* whose picture of American voting-behavior is almost as purely a "pork chops" picture as, say, that of Hubert Horatio Humphrey's. And, for the amusement of the curious, let me add—here in a footnote because the matter is perhaps too delicate to haul out into the full light of day in the text—the following speculation: On the basis of the data available to me, I deem it not impossible that there is a high correlation between, on the one hand, having been born and brought up a WASP, a White Anglo-Saxon Protestant in America, a member of an established "ruling-class" in American society, with a feeling not only of "belonging" but of being, by inheritance so to speak, a "part-owner" of America, on the one hand, and refusing to accept the "conquest" conception of the political future of the American Right on the other. For the further amusement of the curious let me recommend study of the evolving masthead of *National Review,* with an eye to the incidence, among early active participants in the magazine who have fallen by the wayside, of persons who were either born WASPs or, like Willi Schamm, were born and brought up in a foreign land (but still not in either of the major American ghettos).

24. Perhaps, or perhaps not, in point: Weaver normally spent his summers, throughout

the years I knew him, with his mother in Weaverville, North Carolina, dividing his time between gardening and his scholarly pursuits, and permitting himself no "vacation" in the usual sense of that term. The one time I ever heard of his taking a vacation, he bought himself (for the first time I think) an automobile, fetched his "Mamma" (he was the only American intellectual I ever knew who didn't regard the advance from "Mamma" to "Mother" as a necessary part of growing up), and made the grand tour—of the United States of America. If he ever set foot outside his beloved America, he never mentioned the fact in our conversations, though it is not impossible that he did so at Niagara Falls or El Paso, in the course of that One Big Trip.

25. Leo Strauss, *Thoughts on Machiavelli* (Glencoe, IL: The Free Press, 1958).

26. Harry V. Jaffa, *Crisis of the House Divided* (New York: Doubleday, 1959).

27. Because of the acceptance, on all sides, of the "inevitability" of a leftist victory.

28. Long before Burke.

29. The thought at the back of "our" minds may have been: "our" churches will see to it.

30. See Martin Diamond, "The Federalist," *apud, History of Political Philosophy,* Leo Strauss and Joseph Cropsey, eds. (Chicago: Rand, McNally and Company, 1963).

31. Yes, "help." Publius makes no greater claim, either for the Constitution or for the rules he spells out.

32. Not so the worst of us, the Jefferson and the Deweys, who *have* addressed themselves to the range of problems that would have been discussed in the missing section, though with a new twist: How can the virtue of the people, as Publius would have understood it, be undermined?

33. And in the other miscellaneous essays of the mature Weaver.

34. One of the first things I learned from R. G. Collingwood, when I was his tutee at Oxford, is that it is a rare philosopher who can state clearly the question he ends up answering.

35. The phrase is from José Ortega y Gasset, *The Revolt of the Masses.*

36. Weaver gave his best efforts over many years to wrestling with this problem, which he believed to be the most difficult problem any culture must face, as also the problem with which we in America have dealt least successfully. *Visions of Order* contains his most sophisticated treatment of the problem.

37. This is the aspect of Weaver's thought for which the libertarians would never have forgiven him had they grasped it. Weaver's favorite examples of "dialectic" gone wild are taken from science, but all that he says in this regard would apply equally to those who seek to implement conclusions arrived at via abstract reasoning about "the market," without mediation by techniques appropriate to rhetoric, in the living flesh of a going society. Nor is that all: Weaver spells out at great length the presuppositions of the healthy, need-satisfying culture, but economic freedom (though Weaver was "for" it on other grounds) is certainly not one of them. One can hardly imagine Weaver losing a night's sleep over the size of the GNP.

Donald Atwell Zoll

THE DEATH OF LIBERALISM:
OR, HOW TO PHILOSOPHIZE
WITH A HAMMER

VOL. 7, NO. 3, 1970–71

That striking phrase—"how to philosophize with a hammer"—is, of course, Nietzsche's and he used it to imply the act of demolishing idols, to engage in the business of iconoclasm. I use it to indicate, quite candidly, what I propose to do: to attempt an iconoclastic analysis of the expiring intellectual rationale of liberalism and to chart the causes for the increasing collapse of its political effectiveness.

In adopting the posture of the iconoclast, the philosopher must have certain misgivings—and I use the word "philosopher" not in any covertly honorific sense, but only to identify one's profession, a vocation whose modern orientations suggest a more detached viewpoint than that implied by the Nietzschean call to shatter shibboleths with cudgels. I am reasonably content, however, that the variety of iconoclasm we will here engage in is philosophically respectable for two reasons: (1) There are clearly times in which the rationalistic dedication of the philosopher alone impels him to take up the enterprise of destructive analysis in the interests of cultural therapy; and (2) Ours is an hour in which the desperate travail of our society makes academic detachment not merely an idle luxury, but the abrogation of very rudimentary responsibilities—which are not the obligations of intellectuals only, but are those of any member of the social covenant.

Consequently, our iconoclasm is spawned by the very real conviction that disaster is possible and even probable, although not inevitable, and that the threat of cultural disaster, broadly interpreted to mean the advent of a new epoch of barbarism, may be extinguished if we are willing to face unpleasant facts and prudently reckon the shape of future conditions and the forms of cultural therapy that would be both appropriate and effective. Iconoclasm has the great merit of being a vivid variety of intellectual slum-clearance.

If this iconoclastic critique of current political life is not to be merely an exercise in eccentricity, then we are obliged to make clear what is meant by *liberalism* and to justify the contention that it is, in fact, dying—and, what must be entered as the cause of death.

I WANT to give the term *liberalism* a very broad meaning and not, by the way, a derogatory one. The demise of the hegemony of liberalism is an empirical proposition: much within the liberal tradition was highly admirable; the more than two centuries of its domination included much of what we boast of as our most humane civilization.

The liberalism to which I refer is the comprehensive political tradition that substantially begins with Locke. In this sense, liberalism, about which we shall be more specific in a moment, provided the basis for the continuity of moderate, centrist political leadership and control that remained virtually unbroken within the Western democracies up to our current era. From the Glorious Revolution to the 1960s, the hold of liberal politicians was well-nigh complete, save for brief episodes of radical experimentation, such as fascism, and scattered conservative resurgences, such as Tory Democracy.

Besides its very considerable historical metamorphosis, liberalism had at its core one principal idea: *equilibrium*—a political system constructed upon the balancing of interests and the reconciliations of social objectives. In a larger sense, the equilibriumist nature of liberalism was the result of its pervasive utilitarianism, which becomes more explicitly relativistic by the nineteenth and twentieth centuries in the realm of social ethics. This *Weltanschauung* produced many of the well-known characteristics of liberalism: majoritarianism, pluralism, secularism and legal positivism. At root, liberalism was inclined toward proceduralism rather than substantive theory and in its purer forms was generally permissive and individualistic. This was especially to be noticed in the century after Locke which featured a concern for the matter of continuous consent and took a functionalistic view of majoritarianism. Such a viewpoint is well developed in the *Federalist Papers* with its emphasis on neoclassical republicanism and the mixed polity.

One of the curiosities about the history of liberalism was that the Industrial Revolution intensified its political ascendency and yet the aftermath of that technological upheaval brought into being pressures with which liberalism was ultimately unable to cope. If J. S. Mill was the epitomization of nineteenth-century liberalism, then John Dewey well represents the evolution of liberalism in our century. The similarities are apparent, but the differences are also highly significant. In the widest sense, twentieth-century liberalism was principally concerned with the extension of the democratic principle; post-Lockean liberalism was, in any case, the mainstream of pro-democratic thought. Pre-twentieth-century liberalism had been content, by and large, to restrict this democratic principle—which was, in essence, egalitarian participation—to the legal and political spheres. After 1900, the thrust was to extend this democracy into the explicitly social sphere. The primary motivation for liberalism's adoption of social democracy had a two-fold cause: (1) the infallibilist majoritarian theories produced by Rousseau and Bentham; and (2) a growingly collectivistic and altruistic concept of human nature, which, by the end of the nineteenth century, had split liberal theory between an extreme and embattled individualism (well-illustrated by social darwinism) and the emerging social democrats, some of them under direct socialist influence.

There were, at base, four motifs of twentieth-century liberalism that seriously modified the historical tradition: (1) the assertive egalitarianism earlier referred to; (2) the immense impact of positivism (and its offshoot, pragmatism) on liberal democratic thought; (3) an increasing support of governmental activity and centralization; and (4) a more radical conception of ethical relativism.

Permit me to comment briefly on these alterations in traditional liberalism. The twentieth-century emphasis on egalitarianism was the result of many influences, but perhaps of prime significance was the abandonment of the natural rights theory in favor of a new vision of intrinsic equality. This represented a change from the "as if" concept of equality to one arguing for intrinsic equality in essentially psycholo-gistic terms: all men were equal because of the possession of an ineffable personality. Thus, equality was not to be an equality of treatment in crucial public areas, but a comprehensive equality of social status on the grounds that even private social discrimination was injurious to the human personality.

The effect of neo-positivism on liberal democratic theory is not to be underestimated. The rise of social science in North America proceeded from positivistic assumptions, by and large, and this emerging intellectual community provided not only the principal theoretical *apologias* for liberal democracy, but framed its theoretical evolutions in very authoritative terms. So complete was this pro-liberal and pro-positivistic allegiance of the social sciences that Harold Lasswell could announce that *political science* ought to he defined as the "policy science of democracy." The genesis of twentieth-century liberalism's distinct social theory really begins with Graham Wallas.

Abandoning the more traditional connection with laissez faire, twentieth-century liberalism embraced a more overtly collectivistic view of government function and power, which, in the social democratic setting, led to varying degrees of economic and social planning with emphasis on what eventually became labeled as the "welfare state."

Lastly, twentieth-century liberalism pushed ethical relativism far beyond the utilitarianism of J. S. Mill (although not further, perhaps, than that of Bentham). The expressions of this ubiquitous relativism were everywhere in evidence: in legal theory, in political theory and practice, in the general cultural standards and in the parameters of political respectability. The cumulative effect of this ethical relativism was to virtually destroy the existing corpus of the civic ethic and this was generally held to be liberating on the grounds that pro-liberal theorists exhibited such an intense antipathy and fear of authoritarianism that any suggestion of the non-relativity of value was vigorously opposed.

WE ARE now reasonably close to what the contemporary journalists mean when they invoke the word "liberalism," the reformist, popularly oriented, mildly collectivistic social democratic premises identified with the pro-democratic theorists and the political tradition of Wilson and Franklin Roosevelt. This very fleeting perusal of liberalism is certainly not intended as a definitive account, but is meant to provide a brief background for a number of, what I think, are pertinent observations.

The first of these is that while twentieth-century liberalism represented a significant departure from the past, it did not veer fundamentally from the flow of liberalism. It remained utilitarian and equilibriumistic; it stood by its broad proceduralism, its pluralistic libertarianism, its majoritarianism and essential belief in moderation and fair play. In terms of political leadership, twentieth-century liberalism remained predominantly moderate, eclectic and, in terms of its own orientations, pragmatic.

However, certain theoretical proclivities were arising in the twentieth century. Social democratic liberalism had grown markedly less flexible and more doctrinaire and it became increasingly enmeshed in its own mythologies. Four of these myths were particularly debilitating:

(1) The first myth was that of the infallibility of a quantitative majority. liberalism accepted this premise—and rejected a graduated majoritarianism—on the basis of a curious blend of Rousseauistic and Benthamite ideas. Not entirely willing to accept the pristine simplicity of Bentham's assertion that the majority is always right because there is no other viable criterion to appeal to, democratic liberals engrafted on to it a Rousseauistic mysticism, the notion of a latent "folk wisdom" waiting to direct the national fate at crucial moments. This argument reduces to the view that while the individual citizen is largely uninformed and incapable of rational political choice, citizens *en masse* release some variety of collective judgment and wisdom. This appears not only a myth *pro forma,* but also on the basis of democratic liberalism's own empirical investigations.

(2) The second myth revolves around the idea that the principle of equality extends beyond the concept of the sanctity of the person to equal capability in areas of skill and judgment. It was one thing to contend that men ought to be treated as equals in order that they could achieve that of which they are individually capable and quite another to enforce equality in defiance of the diversities and talents of men. Liberal democracy clings to this thesis in the face of reason and evidence.

(3) Liberal democracy stubbornly refused to modify its rigorous environ-mentalism, claiming that virtually all of men's assorted problems could be solved by the amelioration of the environment, primarily in material terms. Its reductionistic views of human personality refused to bend to more advanced psychological and philosophical argument and its political theory could be reduced, when all is said and done, to proposals for governmental action designed to physically and economically reshape the patterns of the environment. This predilection helps to account for the obsolescent quality inherent in current political appeals from the liberals—about which, more later.

(4) Liberalism's moral relativism seems to be embraced not on the basis of its philosophical tenability or even its social efficacy but, rather, for the negative reason that the introduction of the idea of objective standards would usher in some type of social or political authoritarianism. Liberals look at standards like some regard the Fifth Amendment: the acceptance of *any* standards—in art, in literature, in morals, in tastes—would quash one's immunity from having standards enforced in all aspects of life and against one's will. This results in a virtual negation of a qualitative dimension, even that vague and shifting one enjoyed by nineteenth-century liberalism.

This banishment of standards takes a queer twist among some contemporary liberals who, in what can only be described as a sort of passion, seek to implement this relativity by, in fact, deifying the conventionally lower standards of tastes, as if to try to compensate for what they must believe to be the perverse intractability of traditional notions of worth. Thus, the effort to reduce society to the general mean of the so-called "common man" places liberal democrats in the somewhat paradoxical position of extolling as superior virtues the predispositions of the presumably less enlightened segments of the community. The New Left, the arch-foes of liberalism, have pursued this tendency in a far more intense and radical manner: for them, the pathological becomes admirable.

ALL OF these liberal dogmas, substantially mythological in the less esoteric sense of that word, (majoritarian infallibility, intrinsic egalitarianism, doctrinaire environmentalism and ethical relativism), combine to illustrate contemporary liberalism's utter preoccupation with quantitative arrangement and reform, to the exclusion of significant attention to qualitative or normative social problems.

This quantitative and narrowly empirical predisposition has posed for the democratic liberal an ironic and embarrassing predicament. He has become the victim of his own empirical investigations. As twentieth-century social science refined its methodology, especially in the area of measurement and quantitative analysis, certain shocking revelations were forthcoming. The results provided by this investigative rigor appeared categorically to refute many of the optimistic democratic tenets. In the region of voting behavior analysis, it became increasingly apparent that a vast portion of the electorate made their personal decisions on the great issues of the day on the basis of little or no information, were swayed by palpably trivial considerations and, behaviorally, in no way squared with the illusion of an informed and responsible body politic.

At first, there was a certain amount of nervousness in democratic quarters, although the more sweeping implications were denied. Then there followed an almost bitter acceptance of the iconoclastic import of this empirical evidence and

what then transpired was a quite extraordinary shift in the nominal defenses of social democracy. Now, the democratic theorists sought a way out by attempting to frame an essentially elitist theory, borrowed in large part from European sociology in general and Pareto's "circulation of elites" in particular. Democracy was to be, in this new formulation, rescued by granting the necessity of control by elites both in a formal and an informal sense—which were envisioned as competing for power by some process of popular selection, Robert Dahl and Giovanni Sartori, to name but two, began talking about "elective polyarchies" and other exotic political morphologies. This appears to be—to borrow Henry Adam's phrase—the "degradation of the democratic dogma." It should be quickly pointed out, too, that these so-called "democratic elites" are not to be distinguished by ethical or intellectual pre-eminence, but only by their ability to organize for power competition. Even elitism was supposed to be relativistic.

Liberalism in our century has suffered, too, from an increasing pomposity that has manifestly hindered its survival potential. I mean by this that liberals began to feel that they were not participants or contestants in the political debate but, rather, the eternal custodians of the holy tablets, the arbiters and conscience-keepers of the culture, the umpires of the political game and so should stand aloof from the presumably sordid bickerings of lesser ideologies. This gratuitous attitude arose, in part, from their two-and-a-half-centuries old control of Western political institutions but it was, also, in part attributable to the accelerating mythology of contemporary liberalism and its somewhat haughty disdain for engaging in hard argument with minority theories. The noncommunist Left it had largely absorbed; the Communist world was physically held at bay and the internal threat was not critically serious—and the Right, especially the conservative Right, the liberals merely ignored as intellectual vagrants.

This lofty liberal sententiousness created a severe vulnerability when two factors beset the leadership of the liberal moderates: the attack of the New Left and the crumbling of the popular consensus upon which this leadership had stood since Adams turned over his desk to Jefferson. Contemporary liberalism does not yet know how deeply it is in trouble and it is befuddled by the sheer savagery of the attacks made upon it from both the militant radical intelligentsia and liberalism's own erstwhile followers who find themselves menaced by the collapse of liberal guarantees of order, security and the rule of law. Liberalism seems either unwilling or unable to defend itself against the assaults launched against it; it cannot get itself into fighting trim, as it were, since it seems unable to strip away its self-congratulatory flabbiness. It also reveals, as I have written elsewhere, an almost morbid preference for self-destruction.

THE MAJOR cause of the soon-to-come death of liberalism I have yet to deal with and in order to do so we must return to the ramifications of the Industrial Revolution. The great time of trial for the moderate liberal leadership of the Western democracies came early in this century. The effects of rampant technology were beginning to provoke profound social changes. Society was very rapidly becoming industrialized, urbanized, dominated by technical innovation and was, consequently, far more complex and interdependent. Social life was increasingly computerized, automated and

sanitized. Man's habitat, indeed, was being drastically remodeled.

It was obvious enough that these forces would effect crucial changes in social life at a very basic level. Three consequences could be predicted: (1) a very serious diminishment of the sense of individual potency—the conviction on the part of individual men that they could control and guide their personal destinies; (2) a considerable deprivation of personal freedom; and (3) a marked reduction of rudimentary individual gratifications.

Unless one wished to propose some sort of neo-agrarian artificiality, these effects following from the full course of the Industrial Revolution were inevitable. This was the kind of world, the kind of society, one was going to have. But the political consequences of these social dislocations were enormous. Twentieth-century man was going to be confused, frustrated and angry; *anomie* was going to grow to the proportions of a mass neurosis. A general cultural malaise was predictable. A failure to deal with it would spell the most ruinous consequences: violence, anarchy and repression would follow.

This was the critical moment for twentieth-century liberalism; this was its great historical test. It would have to use boldness and imagination to offer a new style of political leadership, built upon teaching men how to accept this new existence and to offer compensatory freedoms and satisfactions to replace those swept away by the urban technology. It would have to face the problem of reconstructing the idea of the human community.

Liberal leadership failed utterly to do this. It set about, rather, to placate these deep-seated desires and anxieties by offering a "square deal" or a "fair deal" or a "new deal," all of which came to mean enhancing the prospects for consumption, to make the rabbit-warren culture not any more existentially justifiable or endurable, but only more comfortable or more diverting. The "waste land" of Mr. Eliot had arrived. Liberalism misjudged the early signs of cultural panic; it assumed that a blend of economic affluence and appeals to mass vanity would allay the nagging fears of impotence, the loss of personal freedom and the mounting sterility of life.

When the panic sysmptoms showed themselves more vividly, the liberal moderates reacted in a most peculiar fashion. Being unable to lead, in any imaginative sense, they were also unable to govern. Under attack, even the relatively mild forms of it earlier in the century, their will to govern dissipated and they began progressively to lose a decisive hold over the society. They could not act internally with resolution and so they temporized, playing once again their tried-and-true tactic of balancing interests off against each other. But by the beginning of the post-World War II period, this fragmentation was assuming alarming proportions; it was beginning to destroy the stable basis of liberal power and authority. By the 1960s, open insurrection was not an impossible development and in the West the liberal moderates were about to fight a last-ditch battle to retain their control, but too late and with too little.

The pressures that ensued from the liberal failure of imagination and will were manifested, in part, by swings of mass expectation regarding the efficacy of political remedy. Popular expectations ranged from inordinate enthusiasm regarding what politics was capable of accomplishing to subsequent periods of apolitical pessimism in which it was assumed that nothing worthwhile could be realized by political action. Politicians were thought of as talismanic figures one day and hopelessly corrupt ignoramuses the next. These periodic "swings" grew more rapid as the century wore on and the fluctuation of feelings grew more extreme—the liberal leadership could not control them, but was caught in their convolutions. These emotional "binges" followed by reciprocating "hang-overs" were bound to create a situation of sufficient fear and chaos that a real live revolutionary movement was altogether predictable.

FINALLY, THEN, the liberal "establishment" found itself under overt revolutionary attack. Liberalism was not prepared for this because it did not sense the underlying causes of social anxiety that this revolutionary ferment fed upon and it continued to predicate its political appeals on the classic issues that had previously moved the electorate. The two American political parties, both predominately liberal in outlook, did not even foresee the possibility of major political realignment in response to the increasingly ideological character of public thought, in contrast to the customary divisions of primarily economic interests. Events moved rapidly. Profoundly concerned with social issues (touching upon the three conditions described earlier) and jabbed by fear regarding the ability of the state to guarantee security and maintain order, the foundational liberal coalition (within both parties) began to fall apart. Radical elements split off, aggrieved ethnic minorities moved outside conventional political channels, a strong right-wing reaction was notable, especially among those elements earlier most congenial to popular liberalism. Three things were happening: (1) the long obscured social issues were rising to the surface and replacing those of essentially economic genesis and advantage; (2) major segments of the electorate were moving into areas of political pressure and action outside those developed within the traditions of liberalism; and (3) elements of the population were moving out to the Right and Left ends of the political continuum in hopes of social remedy.

In short, the liberal consensus was—and is—coming apart at the seams. In my view, the contest between Nixon and Humphrey in 1968 represented the last and almost theatrical stand of conventional liberal politics. It began a relatively brief hiatus before the era of apocalyptical politics.

WHAT WILL follow upon the collapse of this long liberal domination? I am convinced that it will not be very pleasant. While not a liberal philosophically, life was entirely bearable with the liberal moderates in charge. There is much to be said for pluralism. I do not anticipate such permissive serenity in the remaining years of the century.

The death of liberalism will create a deep political vacuum, especially when one considers the longevity of the liberal ascendency. It is like the Julian Emperors coming to an end and the Barracks Emperors taking over. We are certainly in for a period of extremism and rapidly fluctuating political and social experimentation. This highly fluid era may well feature wholesale violence and periodic despotic purgatives. One feature of it is predictable: We will see a revival of ideology and a tendency to cast politics in a totalitarian mold to the extent that these ideologies will be increasingly doctrinaire and prescriptive over a very wide range of human activities. This is why I have dubbed it the era of "apocalyptical politics"; we will choose between apocalypses—but only for a time.

There are two alternatives that I do not consider very feasible. One is that liberalism will somehow survive and keep its house from falling down. Traditional liberalism is too seriously compromised for this and it lacks the vigor to recoup its preeminence. The other possibility I discount is a reasonably successful and permanent revolution generated by a coalition of left-wing revolutionaries. I could easily envision an outright insurrection in the United States mounted by a fusion of nihilistic adventurers and hard-core Leninists and Maoists, but I cannot consider such a domestic rebellion as being successful. In the first place, I think that more-or-less orthodox style revolutions are things of the past in highly developed industrialized societies, because the force monoply of the existing state is so decisive and the possibilities for attaining parity in force on the part of the revolutionaries is very remote. Our present domestic revolutionists, to add another reason, are not sufficiently skillful for success via a relatively nonviolent coup; in addition, they lack cohesiveness and suffer from almost persistent devisiveness.

What are the more realistic possibilities? There are two, I think. The first involves a strong right-wing "backlash" with primitivistic and even neo-fascist overtones. The second possibility is a rather mild but uncompromising shift to the Right, but dominated, at least intellectually, by a basically conservative orientation.

I firmly believe that the most serious future problem we face is what kind of a reaction we may get in response to the provocations of the radical Left. Those fighting under the black banner of anarchism may conceivably have to be put down with the sword, but in what fashion and by whom? What values will prevail in the aftermath?

While one can appreciate the provocations that have beset the American people and can measure and understand the accumulations of frustration that the aridity of contemporary life inflicts, unmediated anger and an enthusiasm for simplistic solutions are dangerous ingredients to stir into the public mood. They could well usher in a period of political repression. I should like, in this connection, to very briefly draw a distinction between *repression* and *order*. I am convinced that the latter condition is the first responsibility of government and that there exists today a distinct threat to nominal order. Therefore, I am not in a position to compromise over the imperative necessity for the maintenance of order, but this does not mean that one favors repression, as the two terms are, in actuality, antithetical.

We use, in fact, the word *order* in two senses in common usage: We speak of "order" as being an arrangement of elements, such as a "word order" or a "batting order." We use "order," of course, to denote civil tranquility, as in "law and order." These two loose definitions of order are related, in that social order is an emanation of a more fundamental order, which, for convenience, we might call "ontological order." Common to both uses of the term is *regularity*; social order is the regularization of relationships within a natural system, in this case, society. As is true within the nonhuman world, human social order rests upon a principle, or principles, of regularity that is not the product of the will—individual or collective—of the society itself, but is an external principle. This principle (or principles), although not as yet fully disclosed in an empirical way, is largely actualized in the historical process by the broad ethical and juristic axioms that appear to be both transtemporal and trans-cultural, although their precise articulation is sensitive to the singularities of particular cultures. Thus, order is, in fact, a norm—both theoretically and concretely; disorder or irregularity is aberrational.

"Repression" I take to be an irregularity, the application of force of some type which is socially generated and is not derived from external principle and, hence, is in violation of the concept of order. Social order must legitimately be enforced, as there is not universal recognition of the mandate of external principle. The issue is between the coercion necessary to maintain the regularity of social relationships and coercion employed to impose the will of one individual or group upon another.

Contemporary liberalism's refusal to accord a first priority to the maintenance of bona fide social order, an order principally enshrined in its own recognized legal codes, has so weakened these social regularities that the result is, even now, the widespread appearance of repressive forms of social coercion, of which organized and violent civil disobedience is the most obvious and flagrant. But the demise of liberalism and the subsequent power vacuum invites the intensification of repression in lieu of social order. Many of those who are now reacting against the threat of leftist insurrectionary activity and who rally to the cry of "law and order" are not advocates of order, but are admirers of repression. This is apparent from these people's restless dissatisfaction with legalism and juristic restraint. Since the state cannot guarantee minimal order, their argument goes, we must impose it ourselves. There is a certain truth in this observation, it must be admitted, and yet the most lamentable fate to befall the "rule of law" would be its replacement by a doctrine of "self-protection," of the

Vigilance Committee. Such is the stuff of repression rather than order.

The rising anxiety and counter-militancy against the excesses of the Left do not necessarily mean that our society is turning to conservatism—as some careless journalists suggest. Much of the effective opposition to would-be revolutionaries is not mounted by conservatives (in any precise meaning of that term). The so-called "silent majority" is not made up of conservatives. Mr. Nixon is not a conservative. George Wallace and his more-or-less plebian adherents are not conservatives. Indeed, the problem for the contemporary conservative is to decide how far to make common cause with the elements of the anti-Left. Some prices for a unified front may be too dear for the conservative to pay.

THERE ARE three main factors that separate contemporary conservatism from the current solidarity of the political Right: One of these factors is the *primacy of order* as defined and discussed earlier. The second is conservatism's commitment to the *aristocratic principle*; and the third is its dedication to *compassion*. Space prohibits me from discussing these characteristics in any detail, but by aristocratic principle, I mean conservatism's ancient acceptance of the idea of personal dedication to self-cultivation in accordance with certain generally acceded to standards and the notion that levels of attainment in self-cultivation affect the social division of labor. Conservatism is also possessed with a sense of humanity that denies that life can be defined in terms of the survival of the fittest. It rejects bourgeois ruthlessness. Historically, conservatives have despised those who place either avarice or political ambition ahead of those aspects of life considered by them to be

more fundamental: the life of the spirit, the ethical realization, artistic creativity and even mundane enjoyment. These priorities create, in the conservative tradition, a feeling for the universal human bond and summon up the obligations of service and compassion. Admittedly, by some current standards, this conservative social sensitivity and compassion is "paternalistic." It is largely neo-Platonic and it certainly does not rest upon the type of egalitarian definitions common to modern liberalism. There is, in truth, a visible strain of *noblesse oblige* in the conservative outlook. Yet, the conservative defends himself in this particular by pointing out that all of the highest forms of love represent dependent relationships, a reciprocal obligation that is hierarchical, as in the love of God and man or parent and child. To the conservative, a definition of this worldview that I once described as "the application of Christian chivalry into the area of political arrangements" appears neither quixotic nor absurd, but simply the social manifestation of man's more enlightened view of the civic ethic.

These three themes of order, aristocracy and compassion separate conservatism from much of the so-called political Right. The great bulk of conservative thought in this century—and I refer to genuine conservative thought as contrasted with the writings of nineteenth-century-style liberals and social Darwinists—has been confined to relatively esoteric spheres, philosophical and literary. Its attacks on contemporary liberalism have been searching and even devastating, but it was never the purpose of conservatism to pull down the liberal edifice by political means, but only to preserve the Tory tradition, to add an indispensable character to the grand social debate and to hope to convert liberals from their erring ways. By and large, conservatives were simply content to live under the reign of liberalism with its once-potent legal guarantees and its pluralistic liberty.

The picture is now radically changed. Liberalism is dying and with it all the comforts it once provided to dissenting opinions. Conservatism cannot very well go to its aid, regardless of the existence of common values between them, because the cause is lost and conservatism's influence in that quarter is too meagre. Two other forces obviously confront contemporary conservatism: the Left and the Right. The Left is not only its enemy philosophically, but it has declared that it seeks to obliterate in actuality most of the social values conservatism deems vital to preserve. Like it or not, conservatism has only two courses of action open to it: (1) pursue its detachment and, in consequence, maintain a practical social impotency; or (2) participate in the rightist coalition. It cannot really select (1) unless it has already written off Western culture, but (2) is not as simple as it might seem. It is not simple, but it is also the most important challenge to face conservatism since the French Revolution.

WHAT CONSERVATISM must do is to control and modify the angry reaction of the Right. It must do this by the force of its moral arguments and example. It must temper the repressive and anti-legalistic proclivities of the non-conservative Right by educating it—and quickly—to the necessity of order, the preservation of standards, personal and social, and the indispensability of compassion and humanitarian concern. If a sort of neo-fascist excess is to be avoided, conservatism must fight a battle on two fronts: The first front involves propping up a faltering society against the ravages of the new Jacobinism by reviving society's sense of honor and justice; and the second front requires it to transmogrify the inarticulate emotions of the anti-revolutionary majority into a sensitive and bold regard for the qualitative reform of society.

How to plunge into the present social struggle so as not to be irrelevant to the outcome and, at the same time, preserve the intellectual and ethical objectivity and dispassion that are equally demanded? That is the awesome task of conservatism as it unhappily surveys the wreckage of liberalism.

Gregory Wolfe — Clyde Wilson — Gerhart Niemeyer — George W. Carey — Paul Gottfried — George A. Panichas — Russell Kirk

THE STATE OF CONSERVATISM:
A SYMPOSIUM

VOL. 21, NO. 3, 1986

INTRODUCTION

Gregory Wolfe

IN THE symposium that follows the reader who has become accustomed to the notion that conservatism in America is at its peak in influence and intellectual rigor will be surprised to find several distinguished conservative scholars characterize the movement as "adrift" and "in trouble," suffering from "attenuation," "apostasy," and a sense of "malaise." The strength of this indictment consists partly in its very unexpectedness, for until now the paradoxical suggestion that conservatism might be experiencing internal disarray at the height of its political success has received scant notice in conservative circles. Whether the silence on this subject has been due to a reluctance to engage in seemingly "negative" criticism, or because the situation has been only partially understood, is not clear. But in recent years a number of leading conservative intellectuals have been expressing misgivings concerning the intellectual coherence and political influence of the Right. This symposium

was put together in the hope that it would stimulate conservatives to begin the necessary, if unpleasant, task of self-criticism demanded by the tremendous growth of political activism marching under a "conservative" banner.

The dangers that threaten the integrity of the conservative movement can be summarized in a single term: "politicization." Ironically, conservatives launched themselves into the political sphere in an attempt to forestall the all-encompassing politicization of society that is the legacy of twentieth-century ideology. As Joseph Sobran has recently reminded us, liberalism no less than communism aims at a political solution to the whole range of problems inherent in the human condition. We would prefer to believe that conservatives are impervious to this trend. But no community or institution is immune to temptation. For instance, we are no longer shocked by the notion that secularism has become so pervasive as to be rampant even in the churches. So too we should be willing to concede that politicization has infected the conservative movement.

In the thirtieth anniversary issue of

National Review Richard Vigilante makes the following observation:

> The vast and successful conservative political enterprise has become, almost overnight, subject to all the vices and temptations of power politics. That enterprise, not to be confused with the movement from which it sprang, is too large and too busy for philosophical reflection. If it does not find, or is not given, a clear, simple sense of what holds it together, it will split apart, ruptured by confusion and opportunism.

According to the participants in this symposium—all leading figures in the conservative intellectual movement—the process of fragmentation and decay is already well advanced. Precisely because the label "conservative" has been undergoing a rapid inflation, these scholars are urging a period of retrenchment and renewal. The philosophical movement which gave birth to the postwar conservative renaissance—call it the Old Right, or "traditionalism," or what you will—is the only force competent to articulate the first principles which are the prerequisite for any genuine social and political reform in America.

The events which have led up to the current crisis of conservative identity and mission are complex and may well require the historian George Nash to add a second volume to his *Conservative Intellectual Movement in America Since 1945* before they are fully understood. The contributors to this symposium are largely agreed that at least four major developments have contributed to the confusion.

First, the radicalization which took place during the sixties both in the academy and in the McGovern wing of the Democratic Party forced a number of "liberal refugees" across political borders, many of whom subsequently became known as neoconservatives. Despite the considerable polemical skills and the tactical support the neoconservatives have brought to bear on various issues of public policy, their relationship to conservatism proper was and is problematical. Essentially at peace with the welfare state, the neoconservatives continue to speak the language of social science and their policy initiatives often substitute one statist program for another. Though strongly anticommunist, their foreign policy is plagued by a utopian temptation to promote what Paul Gottfried calls "global democratic revolution"—an idea that owes more to Woodrow Wilson than Henry Jackson.

The second factor has been the increasingly rapid decay of the American social fabric over the last two decades, evident in the rise of pornography, abortion on demand, divorce, venereal disease, and teenage suicide. To many hitherto apolitical citizens, it became clear that these scourges were the direct result of the liberal social agenda, spearheaded by the judicial fiats handed down by an activist Supreme Court. The movement that grew out of this rude awakening, populist and evangelical in character, became the New Right. In many ways closer to traditional conservatism than neoconservatism, the New Right nonetheless prefers confrontation and religiosity to a deeper and subtler understanding of the moral order embodied in the constitutional heritage bequeathed to us by the Founding Fathers. New Right populism often seems to imply that might—in the form of sheer numbers of God-fearing voters—makes right.

Third, conservative successes at the polls and in the Washington political machine, culminating in the two-term

Reagan presidency, have drawn the inevitable groups of pragmatists and camp followers to the seats of power and privilege. This has entailed not only the frustration of many conservative efforts at reform, but also a continuing dilution of what conservatism actually means. As M. E. Bradford writes below: "we are in the process of forfeiting a well-developed corporate character through identification with the prudential decisions of the Reagan Administration."

Finally, and perhaps most dispiritingly, conservatives have acquiesced in, and even abetted, the redefinition of "legitimate" conservatism by the liberal-dominated media. Thus the liberals' first cousins—the neoconservatives—are "designated . . . the official conservative opposition," according to Gottfried, while the new arch-enemy, a convenient scapegoat for liberal indignation, is the New Right. With the exception of William F. Buckley Jr., who is now tolerantly treated as a cultural institution, the postwar conservative movement has been defined out of existence.

The contributors to this symposium are not under the illusion that traditional conservatives are the helpless victims of circumstance; that is why they are taking a stand. Neither do they believe, in gnostic fashion, that the political realm is inherently evil; the whole thrust of the conservative movement has been to reach and decisively alter the American political scene. The undeniable political achievements of recent years are given full appreciation in these pages. But traditional conservatives have always held that society is man writ large, that a fundamental understanding of human nature must precede and inform political action. That is why even the "free market" is not sufficient to justify policy: the marketplace must be seen in the context of the good. The true conservative also knows the limits of politics. He knows that long-term political change will come about only when culture itself has changed. The political victories of the present may appear insubstantial when one realizes that there have been few comparable victories in the academy, the media, the arts, or the republic of letters. Conservatism means an unrelenting commitment to man in his wholeness: man may be a political animal, but he also has an immortal soul. A vision of life which sets its sights on anything lower than this does not merit the name conservatism.

THE CONSERVATIVE IDENTITY

Clyde Wilson

CARLYLE DEFINED history as "the essence of innumerable biographies." This is only one of the many inadequate but suggestive definitions of history, numerous enough to fill a small volume, that have been put forward, but perhaps it is sufficient to excuse a bit of auto-biography as pertinent to the last quarter century of American conservatism. That phenomenon has been with us long enough now to allow a degree at least of historical perspective. A once resilient Goldwater Youth has begun to feel the preliminary twinges of mortality in his bones, and therefore perhaps can review usefully the history and thus the present status of that intangible but real phenomenon, conservatism, which has been a significant determining influence as he has gone about his personal and professional life.

I believe that it is descriptively accurate to say that most of us who regarded ourselves as "intellectual conservatives" before 1964 are in a state of demoralization and discouragement at the status of conservatism in 1986. I think this is true both of those who have entered the government in recent years and those who are, like me, merely perplexed observers on the fringes of public life. The degree of disappointment may vary with situation and temperament, but it is the predominant mood—notwithstanding the apparent flourishing of "conservatisms" on every hand and the common agreement that we have a great deal to be thankful for in the present condition of the commonwealth, compared to what might have been.

The Goldwater campaign, for those who came of age about the time I did, was the central public event (though not, I think, the formative influence) of the time. For those who had eyes to see, it revealed for all time the arrogant deceitfulness of the media lords and lackeys and the intellectual and moral bankruptcy of the Republican establishment of that day. More importantly, it revealed, in retrospect, how far we had to go to translate into popular and political success ideas that we knew in our hearts would appeal to the majority of the American people, properly heard.

Those of us who regarded ourselves as intellectual conservatives came from a variety of regional, ethnic, and ideological backgrounds, as was only fitting in a large and various republic. We had our differences (more significant than we, or at least I, realized at the time) which we argued heatedly but usually with chivalrous respect. We were united by common enemies. In these somewhat more relaxed times it is difficult to recall the embattlement of conservatives within the academy—where we could expect to meet usually hostility, sometimes vicious, and the best we could hope for was

amused condescension. It took, I will not say courage, but a certain stubborn perversity to make one's way, and allies were welcome. But we had positive sources of unity as well. We might differ in our primary heroes, but we could share a general and eclectic admiration for the mentors of the movement—Kirk and Buckley, Burnham and Weaver, Kendall and von Mises, Molnar and Meyer, and many others. This consensus was captured by the Intercollegiate Studies Institute, which on some campuses provided the only evidence of an intellectual dialogue that in tone and quality was respectable in the light of the best traditions of the West. The working platform was summed up neatly enough by George Nash as agreement (allowing for differences of emphasis) on tradition, the free market, and anticommunism.

And despite our differences we can, in historical perspective, be accurately seen as one movement. And not only that, but as a movement that was in some sense or other, a success. While there has been an entrenchment and institutionalization of totalitarian radicalism, in some places, in the last quarter century, it is also true that the academic dialogue is today more open to ideas from what might be loosely described as the Right than at any time since the 1920s. In the voting booth, which alas is no longer sovereign (if indeed it ever was), the rejection of institutionalized liberalism has been resounding and today represents the view of the overwhelming majority of decent Americans. The extent to which that mandate has been translated into policy ought not to be underestimated. The control of inflation and taxes—which is another way of saying the expansion of the liberty of the citizens; the firming up of defense; the first hints of reform in the degraded judiciary—these are limited but quite real successes. Nor should we discount the value of the revolution wrought in presidential style. We have a Chief Magistrate whose dignified informality, whose candid and good-natured simplicity (in the best sense of that word) reflect some of the best of the national character and who has restored some badly needed poise to the public life.

Why then, the malaise that I mentioned among the Old Guard? There are many reasons. Conservatism, despite heroic efforts to put a different face on the matter, must always involve some pessimism and skepticism. That might even be a virtue in a society in which public demeanor is often a compulsive optimism. We can also attribute something to the unavoidably imperfect connection between ideas and the public sphere. It is a truism that those who launch ideas into the world often see them come back in unrecognizable form. John Dos Passos observed that in setting about to correct evils, the liberals of his generation forgot that man is an institution-building animal, that their ideals would be codified and bureaucratized by others. The consolidator and preserver is a different kind of man from the thinker and creator. The disciple inherits and converts to his own. There is no getting around this. Madison subverted Jeffersonian democracy, as Martin Van Buren did the Jacksonian variety, and as Sumner and Stevens did Lincoln's Reconstruction.

Still, when all is said, this does not exactly describe what has happened to the conservative intellectual movement. We ought to have had more success than we have had in translating ideas into a regime. The ball has been dropped too many times. There have been too many weak stands and too many unnecessary retreats. The other side did it far better than we have done. Perhaps because they had a head start; perhaps because they have learned to use the vast leverage provided by the conservative virtues of our Constitution and fellow-citizens to keep the load rolling in the direction they want it to go. Put it another way: has no more been accomplished because it was impossible, or because the effort was not made or was not made in the right way? Whichever way the question is answered, a certain degree of disappointment is our reward.

But I do not believe we have yet uncovered the two main reasons for the alienation of the conservative intellectual from the conservatism of the day. First of all, we have simply been crowded out by overwhelming numbers. The offensives of radicalism have driven vast herds of liberals across the border into our territories. These refugees now speak in our name, but the language they speak is the same one they always spoke. We have grown familiar with it, have learned to tolerate it, but it is tolerable only by contrast to the harsh syllables of the barbarians over the border. It contains no words for the things that we value. Our estate has been taken over by an impostor, just as we were about to inherit.

A Confederate soldier, who when captured preferred to serve in the Union army rather than face prison, was referred to as a "galvanized Yankee." Galvanized conservatives (as well as Georgia snake-oil salesmen) are numerous and flourishing now that we seem to be the winning side, and the Old Guard cannot help but catch on the wind from the Potomac a faint but unmistakable odor of opportunistic betrayal. Of course, it is exceedingly natural for a party in pursuit of victory and consolidation of power to welcome newcomers, and even to take its old faithfuls for granted. Yet the relative degree of influence which each shall be allowed is a choice. That we have lost this decision, for whatever reason, says nothing about the merits of our claims. And tactical decisions can yet be amended, to some degree at least. In this there is hope.

But the conservative intellectual must grapple with something even more daunting than an enemy salient in his territory. In the early 1960s it was possible to take for granted that the social fabric of the West, in its American form, was relatively intact. And that, therefore, a change of leadership and emphasis and a firm dealing with the foreign foe would put us right. I do solemnly wish that I will be proved wrong here, but history has moved on and the signs of the times suggest that we must come to grips with the much more serious and difficult crisis of the unraveling of the social fabric itself. For if our original stand, our old conservatism, meant anything at all, it meant, on its bottom line, a defense of the traditional social fabric of the West, which we deemed to be threatened.

Civilization is primarily a spiritual phenomenon, though it may have material expressions. Civilization begins with the successful combining of the universal with the particularities of a time, place and people. Such a combination results in forms of behavior, standards, which are the substance of civilization. These are revealed in both high culture and folk culture, neither of which can exist without them. The standards are a great and providential achievement—nothing less than the imposition of order on the chaos of existence, an order that rests not upon outward coercion but upon inward apprehension of its beauty and fitness. Tradition concerns itself with the preservation and transmission of this achievement. A conservative, a.k.a. a traditionalist, is one who understands the importance and difficulty of this task.

Far from being preoccupied with a dead past, he is the most forward looking of men, for his function is to understand, adapt, preserve, and transmit the essence of civilization to future generations. He must save it from wanton destruction, from deadening inertia and inflexibility, and from indifference. One of the most successful exercises of this function in history was the American Revolution, an inspired adaptation which preserved the essence of British liberty.

Since the life of man is here and now, and since culture can only be transmitted in the forms in which it has been cast, traditions are necessarily particularist. One cannot be a traditionalist in general, as one can be a liberal or a Communist. A traditionalist can only be so about a particular tradition. American conservatism can mean nothing else but preservation of the traditions of Western civilization. There is wide room here, since proliferating variety and independence of judgment are hallmarks of the Western tradition. But there is an irreducible core of givens: religion, implying at the least a demeanor towards the universe, our fellow man, and ourselves that can be summed up as reverence or piety; concepts of manhood, womanhood, and family—by which is meant not niches in which people are to be confined, but ideals that people aspire to fulfill in realization of their highest ethical potential; liberty—by which we mean not aimless and arrogant nonconformity, but freedom of thought and action tempered by responsibility to community and obedience to lawful authority.

It is possible, of course, to become so obsessed by the forms of a tradition as to lose its essence. The dustbin of history is full of societies which died in an inflexible worship of forms. This is not a danger that besets Americans, even American conservatives. It is also possible for tradition to be violently interrupted. That is exactly what the radical wishes, so that he can create the world anew. We need only to mention the names of Lenin, Hitler, and Mao to make this point. But this, too, is a danger from which America, relatively at least, is immune.

Our danger is indifference. The liberal, who is a most characteristic type of American, relates to civilization as a fish relates to water. He is unconscious of its existence and therefore of its need to be cherished, cultivated, and handed down. It will never occur to him that endless attrition by criticism, pollution, indifference, and the introduction of innovations and eclectic elements could damage it. The liberal lacks all reverence toward, even awareness of, the universal and the forms which symbolize it. In the simplest terms, he is a man incapable of making the connection between what he regards as a happy liberation from outmoded repressions and the proliferation of divorce, pornography, rape, perversion, child abuse, abortion, and callousness.

The conservative, considering himself to be in touch with the tradition of the West, faces in 1986 a society in which the everyday virtues of honesty, loyalty, manners, work, and restraint are severely attenuated. So far as one can tell, millions of people are so cut off from all standards of value that they actually believe that Walter Cronkite is wise, Edward M. Kennedy is a statesman, Mr. T is a model for youth, and Dr. Ruth is a guide to the good life. We have a society in which educated and apparently decent mothers join their subteen daughters in viewing musical "performances" by obscene and tasteless degenerates, which degenerates become millionaires. A society in which a "serious" book is represented by the vul-

gar and trivial memoirs of Lee Iacocca, and in which aspirations to culture are satisfied by government subsidies to untalented and decadent poets and artists. A society in which the appointed guardians of the Constitution are so far out of touch with the essence of ordered liberty they are sworn to uphold that they have cavalierly taken a Constitutional provision whereby the States forbade the federal government to interfere in the exercise of religion and warped it into a grant of power to the federal government to interfere with the exercise of religion by the States.

The task of the conservative intellectual remains the same as it has always been, though acquiring new urgency. It is not primarily a political task, although it has unavoidably political dimensions. That task is to keep alive the wisdom that we are heir to and must keep and hand on—something more and higher than equality, a high standard of living, and a good sex life—as fine as these things may be in their place. The liberal cannot help us here, even if he now dwells on our side of the border and at times calls himself a conservative. None can do the job but those who know what needs to be done. Among the proliferation of conservatisms, let us discriminate. Let us nourish as kinsmen those who will help in the essential task, no matter how outlandishly provincial their accents and clothes. As for the rest, let us go to the marketplace of ideas as honest traders, aware of the quality of our goods and determined not to be taken in by any interloper, no matter how plausible, finely turned out, and full of seductive promises.

IS THERE A CONSERVATIVE MISSION?

Gerhart Niemeyer

AMERICAN CONSERVATISM has little affinity with its European namesake. In Europe, since the last third of the seventeenth century, conservatives understood themselves as committed to support the monarch. "Conservative" also described the attitude, rather than the ideas, of the landed gentry, including their taken-for-granted identification with the Established church. Fairly late in its history English conservatism found a spokesman in Edmund Burke, although he was a Whig and no member of the gentry. The core of Burke's ideas was his principled rejection of the French Revolution and its underlying premises. Burke's ideas generated conservative groupings all over Europe. American politics has never had anything resembling English conservatism. The great quarrel over the slavery issue took on the form of a regional division; and the conservative "way of life" in 1860 became a call for rebellion. Thus it is not easy to find an American nationwide commitment to which one could unambiguously give the name "conservative." A deliberately conservative outlook in this country did not form until after World War II, when its cradle was bedecked with four books: Richard Weaver's *Ideas Have Consequences*, Friedrich Hayek's The Road to Serfdom, Russell Kirk's *The Conservative Mind*, and Eric Voegelin's *New Science of Politics* (even though both Hayek and Voegelin consistently disclaimed for themselves the conservative label). Still belonging to the series of founding events was the publication of *National Review* and the highly articulate voice of William F. Buckley Jr. shedding conservative light on daily events and issues. This movement, in 1964, first presented itself to the voters and, although resoundingly defeated, from there on out maintained its place among the recognized forces of national politics. In 1980, finally, the over-whelming election of Ronald Reagan seemed to issue a mandate for lower taxes and less government, plus, possibly, a demand for more backbone in the country's foreign policy.

To this day it seems impossible to find any body of positive ideas to describe the identity of American conservatives. In politics there is no such thing as a Conservative Party; there is not even a unified support for the president. Nor can the conservative administration call on a stable coalition. Its governing has had to be content with ad hoc coalitions, a different one for each issue. Appeals to the president, on the grounds of an assumed body of common conservative ideas, have been disallowed. Even though there has been an undoubted conservative achievement, a fundamental change in the country's politics since Reagan's ascension to power, one may therefore still wonder whether, in terms of ideas, there is such a thing as American conservatism.

Historically, the active energy of people calling themselves conservatives has been mobilized by a common distaste for, and disgust with, the Left, ranging all the way from liberalism to communism, not excluding National Socialism, with fascism added. It may well be the case that this gut-feeling of repugnance has not been thought through so that neither the nature of what was rejected nor the ideas for the sake of which it was rejected have become clear in people's minds. In that case, conservatives may well be aware that the forces they combat have been causes for our political, economic, and cultural crisis, without being able to give a principled answer about the crisis itself and the remedies, if any, to be sought. At any rate, conservative distaste for communism is never far away from an equally scornful rejection of liberalism. That should cause us to reflect on liberalism, since a considerable amount of intellectual work has been done on the Communist end of the scale.

To be sure, American liberalism produced Roosevelt's New Deal, Truman's Fair Deal, Johnson's Great Society, which increasingly reduced more and more Americans to wards of the government, and their lives to a maze of regulations. But liberals have done harm far deeper than that to our culture:

1. Liberals are responsible for a new but ignoble phenomenon in this country: in place of America's vaunted individualism there is now a mass consciousness resulting from a life of dependence on governmental handouts and regulations, "and my people love to have it so" (Jeremiah).

2. Liberals have brought it about that, in this deeply religious country (Tocqueville), the Christian religion has been maneuvered into the place of a party opposing other parties, so that justice might appear to call for limitations on Christianity to protect atheism.

3. Liberals have radically secularized education so that American children are being raised in total ignorance of the faith that informed their fathers.

4. Liberals are responsible for the official emasculation of personal accountability in criminal jurisdiction, replacing it with guilt attributed to society, and replacing punishment (which respects a person's dignity) with public therapy (which degrades the person).

5. Liberals have made foreign policy under the illusion that all national interests can form a harmony and no conflict is incapable of being solved by negotiations.

6. Liberals have believed that "world peace" can be attained by our national policy alone.

7. Liberals have replaced the human hope for salvation with their belief in progress.

8. Liberals, while themselves moderate in action, have proved defenseless against all leftist extremism.

9. Liberals have cultivated an arrogant conception of man by virtue of the instrumental power of human reason.

10. Liberals, unwilling to look for divine forgiveness, have developed a besetting sense of guilt which turns not only against themselves, but also against their nation.

11. Liberals have taught that morality is relative and, thus have left innumerable persons without a sense of meaning.

12. Liberals have hailed "change" as if it were something to be sought for its own sake, and have destroyed the corrective awareness of abiding things.

Obviously, a series of generalizations like this always runs up against countless particular exceptions. Let us say, though, that it is tolerably accurate as a generalization. One would have to conclude that the liberals' economic policy from Roosevelt to Carter was not the only and not even the deepest harm they have inflicted on our society. One must also bear in mind that liberalism did not become what it is today overnight. During a period of slow growth, over three centuries of modernity, it first was still in close touch with the residual moral sense of the past Christian age, so that the sailing was not at all bad. But liberal theology, essentially without Christ and the Atonement, essentially also without any supernatural God, was bound to let Christian morality slip away. At any rate, in our time it has become clear that the moral reserves have been exhausted, as have the philosophical remnants of what were once adequate concepts of being. Today ignorance in these matters produces widespread symptoms of pneumopathological character, above all disorientation. An abysmal fright of nothingness is upon us and raves for more and more frenzy in feeling, language, conduct, dress, music, and politics. A sense of profound alienation belongs so much to common experience that its cultivation is part of the modern "lifestyle"; "and my people love to have it so." The crisis, in other words, has gone to the very core of our humanity, so that its economic policies should be looked upon as symptomatic rather than causative.

One is not going too far in saying that the reform of the economy is the true thrust of the Reagan administration. In other words, Reagan's policies are based on the assumption that if he can succeed in bringing the hand-out state and the bureaucratic regulatory system to an end, all is gained. May be so; nobody would deny that, at any rate, much would be gained. A basic change like that, however, must have the support of an equally basic desire. One might have thought that the series of popular tax reform movements sufficiently manifested such a desire. Even then, however, it is probably true that this political intelligence was recorded and interpreted against the background of a preconceived concept; the concept that every individual is the best judge of his own interests so that, when left alone, he will make rational choices. The preconception was about a kind of individual who in our time exists only in isolated instances. Ours is a time, rather, of mass consciousness, a type of consciousness utterly different from the personal consciousness in a culture of educated individuals. The conservative reform sought to appeal to the people who had elected Ronald

Reagan by a landslide. The very same people, however, provided the most tenacious resistance to Reagan's undertaking. "Special interests" standing in the way were one thing, resistant mass consciousness another. Disliking government, they still cling to their small niches of government-guaranteed security. They timidly fear the strong air of freedom.

Thus a conservative program of "nothing but economic reform" must remain inadequate. The liberal worldview is still established in this country. After Reagan it must move back into its former upholstered seats of power, if nothing is done to combat it on the level of principles. A government cannot act either as a preacher or as a teacher. It has, however, at its disposal countless opportunities for symbolic actions opportunities to create images of a nonliberal outlook. One would have expected more of an attitude, a stance, an emphasis on visibly conservative personalities. If conservatives appoint to responsible positions above all capable managers rather than leader figures, what are they saying to the world? What is more, men and women who for decades have thought and written about the deep crisis of our civilization are not near the president, indeed, they remain far away from the government. Nor are their efforts through private channels supported or even recognized. Where are the Reinhold Niebuhrs, the John Courtney Murrays, the Russell Kirks, the Christopher Dawsons, the Eric Voegelins of our day? Where are the Catos, the wise men of age who can be found in many a city and quite a few countrysides? Where are those precious few who in an age of deepest confusion can still apperceive measure, limit, and order? Where are their speeches made from a government forum? Where are the speeches of government leaders that reflect such wisdom and insight? Where are the schools willing to restore a sense of man's full nature and full environment, including the transcendence, to the education of young people, and where in the Government is the person courageous enough to point at such schools as models? Only in one respect, in the appointment of federal judges, has this administration addressed itself to the cultural crisis, but even that noble effort is kept with the relatively narrow horizon of Constitutionality, almost another form of Positivism.

Ours is a moment in history when conservative governments are at the helm in Great Britain, West Germany, Canada, and the USA. Their leaders no longer belong to the company of Stanley Baldwin or Calvin Coolidge. Today's conservatives have gone through a long period of frustration and utter disregard by their opponents, when liberals had the freedom of every whim and no fear of correction. The four conservative administrations, therefore, are no mere coincidence. Theirs is a chance not likely to recur. If all four of them, this week, would fall, if their liberal or socialist opponents would bounce back from their one situation of real fright, what trace would the brief moment of conservative rule have left? Would there be any mark of a profound belief communicated by conservatives to the world, that by itself would not allow the liberals and socialists to have all society to themselves? Or would conservatives have to be judged as people who, when once the rudder was in their hands, were philosophically unprepared, who even after so many years of opposition mistook liberalism for nothing more than the welfare state, just as so many of us even today mistake Soviet communism for nothing but different economic system"? We, whoever or whatever we may be, who cannot be socialists

or liberals, do we not have great reason to fear the moment after our brief glory, and even more the dread moment when we have to render an account of the use we have made of our democratic opportunities, the efforts we conceived then, and our responsibility for "things left undone"?

The Popular Roots of Conservatism

George W. Carey

THE CHIEF difficulty in assessing the state of contemporary American conservatism is arriving at some understanding of its nature and meaning. What makes this task so difficult is that conservatism, unlike liberalism, is not an ideology. Proof of this, I think, resides in the fact that whatever principles we might come up with to embrace the various conservatisms in the free world are so general, lofty, and abstract that they reveal little about the "essences" or peculiar characteristics of the conservatisms from which they were derived. Nor, for this reason, are these principles of much help to the various conservatisms in dealing with the political realities of their own nations. On the other hand, precisely because liberalism is an ideology, its principles and goals are essentially the same from country to country. Liberalism's ideological character accounts for the well-known body of unity and sense of camaraderie that exists among liberals throughout the world. It even helps to account for the well-known phenomenon of the "Volvo liberal."

If, contrary to the impression conveyed by its detractors, American conservatism is not the *ideological* counterpoise to liberalism, its chief characteristic, nevertheless, is and has been its resistance to the programs and policies that are the logical outgrowth of liberal ideology. For example, in one of the finer and more comprehensive statements on the substance of political conservatism and its goals (*National Review,* December 31, 1985), Joseph Sobran provides us with even a finer insight into the nature and strategy of liberalism. Moreover, in his view, conservatism is in need of a "dose of radicalism" to undo what the liberal has accomplished over the decades so that even the conservative agenda, if one can call it that, is in large part defined by liberalism. Yet, the fact that conservatism can legitimately be viewed as a reaction to liberalism should not be taken to mean that conservatism is essentially negative in character. As Sobran points out, the liberal is at war with the American tradition and what it stands for. The liberal's belief in the perfectability of man, his quest for an egalitarian society, his unbounded faith in reason, and his secularism are all alien to the underpinnings of our social and political order. The unrelenting assault on the motives, character, and aims of our Founding Fathers by the intellectual liberals only manifests an underlying hatred of the American tradition. And so, too, at another level, are the liberal assaults on the role and status of organized religion, private property rights, and, inter alia, the family. But American conservatism, in contrast, is rooted in what it understands to be the principles which guided our founders; principles which, in turn, it sees as rooted in the better part of Western civilization, though adapted to the peculiarities of the American condition.

This conception of conservatism, though admittedly sketchy, would seem to embrace at least the basic and acknowledged elements of American conservatism. Even in its skeletal form—without, that is, expansion or refinement to reflect all the differences, nuances and refinements in conservative thinking—it constitutes an instructive and revealing point of departure for assessing the state of contemporary American conservatism and its course over the last decade. To begin with, we can see at once that there have been changes, and very drastic ones, within conservative ranks. The fact that many contemporary conservative "heroes" and leaders were but a decade ago liberal Democrats is testimony to just how drastic this change has been. Indeed, most individuals in this category—Jeane Kirkpatrick, who now finds herself even the darling of New Right elements, being perhaps the stellar example—achieved this status while openly proclaiming their support for the Hubert Humphrey brand of domestic liberalism. To be sure, a partial alliance between the intellectual heirs of a Hubert Humphrey or a "Scoop" Jackson and conservatives is understandable, particularly given their strong anti-Soviet (not necessarily anticommunist) stance. However, that they should assume prominence in traditionally conservative circles is baffling. Equally baffling is the identification of certain "neoconservatives"—e.g., Moynihan, Glazer, Wattenberg—with conservatism; an identification fostered, no less, by the patron saints of conservatism at *National Review*. (In fairness it should be noted that most of those identified as neoconservatives shun this label which has been pinned on them for having strayed here or there from the liberal line. Yet, I cannot help but think that they rather like the notoriety and attention which comes with the label.)

This is not to deny that some neoconservatives and fugitives from the Coalition for a Democratic Majority have not been useful allies in the political arena on certain issues, particularly those relating to defense and Soviet-American concerns. I point to them only because, in my opinion, they best illustrate how tenuous the conservative alliance behind the so-called "Reagan revolution" actually is. That the neoconservatives are not at ease, so to speak, with other members of this conservative alliance should scarcely come as a surprise. We could hardly expect too much by the way of congruence on social and domestic issues between the neoconservatives and, say, the New Right. What is more, the focus of their concerns is significantly different. The New Right is primarily interested in what we have come to term the social issues, such as prayer in the public schools, abortion, crime in the streets, busing, and pornography. But the sources of the uneasiness within the coalition are deeper and go well beyond issues to matters of style. Many, if not most, neoconservatives—along with, I might add, many paleoconservatives whose concerns have long paralleled those of the New Right—find the appeals of the New Right simplistic, uninformed, and unnecessarily strident. In part, this attitude is no doubt due to a disposition on the part of academics to take a detached view of politics and to look with some great suspicion, if not alarm, on mass political movements; a disposition which in this case, I need hardly add, is reinforced by the role Christian fundamentalism plays in the New Right movement.

To this point I have only emphasized certain aspects of what close students of American conservatism—e.g., George Gilder, Paul Gottfried, George Nash—have noted about its contemporary character. And it is from this perspective that my observations relative to the nature and future of American conservatism should be understood. First, while

it is true that conservatives must never be unmindful of the Soviet threat to our survival and that of the free world, it is also true that if the Soviet Union were to disappear tomorrow, American conservatism would still be confronted with an internal liberalism which is eroding the foundations of the republic. And this internal erosion, obviously, affects our capacity and willingness to defend ourselves against the external dangers of communism. What conservative, for instance, has not at one time or another thought hard about the question of whether the greatest danger to the republic comes from within or without? To the degree, then, that conservatism in recent years has focused on the external dangers for the sake of harmony within its ranks or political expediency, it is pursuing a fatal strategy.

Second, if rolling back the liberal excesses that have become part of our landscape requires the "radicalism" of which Sobran writes, this rollback can only come about by cultivating the popular roots of conservatism. From the conservatives' point of view, what certainly must be regarded as one of the most promising developments in recent years has been the growth of popular resistance to and disillusionment with liberalism and its policies; a reaction which has come, albeit, only after a heavy price has been paid by both society and individuals in the form of a social, cultural, and economic degeneration. Nevertheless, it is interesting to note, conservatism does not seem to have enjoyed anywhere near a corresponding resurgence in the groves of academe or among the gurus of the mass media, groups largely unaffected by the disastrous policies which their liberal ideology fathered. These bastions of liberalism seem virtually impregnable. What this points to is that a conservative revolution is not likely to come about from the "top" down; that is, it will not be "sparked" and fed by the media or brought about by a "take over" of higher education or even through a "balanced" education wherein the follies of liberalism might be laid bare. Rather, in no small measure the future success of conservatism will rest on the shoulders of conservative politicians who, much as President Reagan has been able to do, can give expression to the discontents, identify their source, and thereby maintain and broaden the alliance.

Finally, to turn to the matter of priorities, the first order of business for American conservatives ought to be the restoration of the constitutional order bequeathed to us by our founders. Clearly the overriding issue in this respect involves the role and function of the Supreme Court. Other constitutional issues—e.g., the relative domains of the legislative and executive powers which concerned many conservatives in decades past—pale into insignificance when compared with the extravagant and preposterous claims advanced by the modern judiciary and its liberal supporters. How the liberal has advanced and solidified his goals by reading his ideology into the Constitution, thereby skirting the deliberative political processes, needs no recounting here. But in this process he has shown utter contempt for the basic principles inherent to and underlying our constitutional system. He would have us believe that ours is a judicial supremacy constitution which it patently is not. By his words and deeds, he strives to legitimate no less than judicial tyranny, a state of affairs wherein the courts have taken unto themselves executive and legislative powers.

The growing public awareness that there are compelling and valid grounds to question the liberals' view of the courts,

the fact that liberals are increasingly on the defensive on this issue, are promising signs which have appeared only in the last decade. A principled answer to this critical concern does not consist in holding out the prospects of a conservative Court that can use the Constitution in the same way liberals have. Nor is a realistic solution one that relies on the judges to restrain themselves. The test of conservative intellectuals and leadership in the coming years is not only to keep the issue in the political arena, but to fashion a remedy that accords with our republican heritage—rule by the deliberate will of the people.

ON BEING CONSERVATIVE IN A POSTLIBERAL ERA

M. E. Bradford

WE MAY rightfully assume that no politics, no model of government, teleological paradigm, or philosophy of culture can escape from being judged by the practical consequences which follow from its establishment as part of the rhetoric or self-description, the apologetics, of a government in power. It is useless to plead an anterior purity of motives or to mutter of dilution that comes of leaving a rich inheritance in the hands of unworthy successors. Of politics it may well be written, "By their fruits ye shall know them" (Matthew 7:20). On such grounds the heathen have often complained of what happens to Christianity when it becomes the church. Through God's special consideration, the truth of the Faith may survive contamination by those who profess it; but no political party can expect to deserve so much in the way of irresistible grace—nor any political teaching native to our place and condition. 1986 is therefore a good time for American conservatives to ask of one another what our situation will soon be if it continues to develop in the direction of attenuation and apostasy—the direction it now follows. And what we should do to forestall such declension.

I give assent to the suggestion that, as conservatives, as a company of generally like-minded individuals who have worked together to preserve a certain known felicity, we have come to a time for careful self-examination. As I see the matter, we are in the process of forfeiting a well-developed corporate character through identification with the prudential decisions of the Reagan administration. Stated briefly, we have been politically absorbed—weighed in the balance and found wanting by our readiness to disappear into the routine operations of a government we did much to create. Our vision of the good society and of the American political tradition at its best has been preempted by considerations of policy or the ephemera of "management style." In this calculus the conservative cause becomes synonymous with tepid compromises rationalized in public by servants of the president who have no history or personal principle in common with the tradition we once defended. This observation is not, in the context of the argument I am making here, a criticism of particular positions taken by a White House limited in what it can attempt by the continuing influence of the Left in Court and Congress, the resistance of the federal bureaucracy and the unrelenting power of a hostile Eastern press and media. But we must not allow the necessary and understandable maneuverings of a friendly government beset by enemies *who are both our adver-*

saries and theirs to change the consensus among our component parts on what it means to be conservative—to change it away from definitions once agreed upon by most of us: accepted as legitimate after a long labor of memory and a little painful dialectic.

There are, to be sure, certain groups who have recently attached the conservative label to themselves who enjoy the confusion which I have just described because it allows them to so redefine our position that we can no longer hold it for our own. It allows them to steal our identity and put it to uses at variance with its origins, to invert it into something foreign to itself, leaving those who are still conservatives in the familiar sense of the term with no ground on which to stand. These interlopers want to get their agenda defined as axiomatic by leaving no useful space to their right; and they want all the persuasive advantages that come, in a postliberal era, of calling their view conservative regardless of its essentially statist, pacifist, and coercively egalitarian implications. Part of this artful attenuation comes of selling a definition of respectability in politics that wins the day for them without arguing their case for (to mention only a portion of their position) the welfare state, arms control negotiations, support for international banks, acceptance of Communist tyranny in captive nations, civil rights laws covering private business, housing and employment, civil disobedience, and a policy for exporting democracy to places where it cannot be planted in the foreseeable future. Before we attempt any other resolution of our present difficulty we must determine never again to allow political propriety to be defined for us by the Left. Or by opportunists who have no principle apart from a preference for being in power, even if it costs them the trouble of learning a new political language to disguise their "merely practical" objectives.

Of course, some of those who employ the perverse sort of argument from definition which I have just summarized are not disguised liberals or pragmatists but ex-liberals: men and women belonging to the political Center who are friends of the administration, even though they continue to affirm that the leftward drift of 1932–1968 was essentially a wholesome development and that the mistake came later, from radicals who wished to go too far—beyond ordinary "progress" toward "unreality." This view of modern American history was summarized for us recently by a number of choice spirits who contributed to the November 1985 issue of *Commentary*—and earlier by Norman Podhoretz's interesting memoir cum apologia, *Breaking Ranks*. The rhetorical problem of the neoconservatives in employing as predicate a leftist past packaged up in meliorist assumptions is obvious to the most inexperienced logician. Concerning the assumed necessity for a government that is instrumental in its impact on the lives of ordinary Americans they continue to speak from the Left. They embrace most of the New Deal, Fair Deal and Great Society as productive of social peace and react to any threat to the "achievements" of that era as if they were anchored there even now. Their difficulty as opponents of the agenda of the contemporary Left is that they imagine that the best strategy for conservatives is to give up two-thirds of their historic position in order to preserve the rest—thus ignoring the advantage given to liberals by reducing the territory which they must contest, leaving them free to concentrate all their force against an enemy already two-thirds beaten: to focus thus with the inertia of the struggle, the

political momentum, clearly moving in their direction. Those determined to win such a struggle will not wait so long to give battle or surrender to the ancient enemy so much of an advantage.

There are of course natural and lasting arguments among conservatives per se. These should continue. Yeats says that poetry is made out of a quarrel with ourselves. The same is true of serious political thought. As a group conservatives are divided by great and legitimate differences on the authority of natural rights theory over a distinctively American politics, about the primacy of economic considerations over other features of a sound polity, and concerning the conflicting claims of order and liberty. On all of these we are not of one mind. But we do take these questions seriously— and agree that politics amounts to more than the victory of the moment: conservatism to more than opportunism, pop sociology and a series of position papers. Furthermore we come together in our hatred of tyranny, our preference for a rule of law, our opposition to schemes of levelling and our disposition to measure all systems by the kind of men and women nurtured by them. Thus we keep alive the old teaching that merely to be in power, to govern, is not enough: that the great problems are not those of administrative technique, crisis management or budgetary restraint but rather those of social thought which will in the end decide whether there is anything to manage, any money to spend, any property to tax, or borders to defend. Under the Reagan regime this task is ours because no one else is able (or willing) to perform it.

It is in the context of the prescription out of which we live, of our sense of a connection between past and present that we as conservatives may ask the question of how we should support the president—

how much and how little. *And especially of how much we should support those among his servants who in word or action interpret him into being the opposite of what we had expected*: and so behaved without authority in the text of his campaign or the idiom of his platform. Both our doctrine and our hope are rooted in a particular history as inherited through the process by which they were formed and by means of which they are regularly refined. It is a process which has also taught us not to be ingrates. For among us loyalty has always been more important than conceptual rigor. Because of the considerable record of his public life, the fight he has made (in part, in our name) to win the office he now holds, the president has a great claim upon us—because he has been instrumental in bringing about certain great changes in our national politics. But we must do better than to praise Ronald Reagan as a person or a political strategist—apart from what he has represented among us, at least since 1964. I so argue even while admitting that, in consequence of other, rightful priorities, we hope to be at liberty, in good conscience, to do precisely that. For otherwise, after his eight years, we must face the prospect of a totally politicized life, the threat of which drove most of us toward politics in the first place: politicized by a struggle in which only liberals and pragmatists are allowed to take a part, and everything is at stake.

From five years under Ronald Reagan what we have learned (apart from the persistence of the old tension between theory and practice) is how little is accomplished by winning elections. In that work conservatives have acquired genuine credentials. Curiously we are sometimes better at the game than the temporizers who once scorned us as impractical and ineffective. Our success on the hustings is a mirror image of the reluctance of candidates on the Left to admit, in these days, that they are liberals of any kind. I might also add that in learning the way of practical politics, conservatives also learned to think better of our countrymen, especially those who are easily confused by the duplicity of political combat and the rhetoric of good intentions. There is no reason to be apocalyptic about the public virtue. But that information looks toward further electoral triumphs, not toward governing. Conservatives functioning *as conservatives*—men and women who thus described themselves long before there was advantage in doing so—must organize a White House and control much of the staffing in an administration before our political work is truly accomplished. Reaching that distant goal will require both patience and intellectual labor—effort needed to keep alive, in the face of general confusion, a clear definition of what we are about. For the moment our first priority is to refuse firmly and vigorously to surrender our hard-won identity to those who would use it as a cloak for policies contrary to what we intend. Lines of demarcation must be drawn, and swiftly.

Our other immediate problems are of a more familiar nature—distinctions as to what parts of our agenda of unfinished business need to be put at the head of the list if we hope to recover the inertia given to us by the elections of 1980 and 1984. To our critics who would measure us by what has happened since those great victories we must say that conservatism has proved up rather well where applied by the Reagan administration but is, despite claims to the contrary by both enemies and quondam allies, otherwise a cordial or specific yet to be tested. How could it be fair to judge it by an imitation? Or by a caricature?

Though it is inevitable that conservatives not in government should advise our friends in office not to attempt too much, not to fight on all fronts at once, it is also necessary that on a selective basis we become openly critical of this government. Such candor is required, both for us and for them. Next we need to encourage the administration to concentrate its surviving reserves of conservatism on judicial appointments—a job it is already doing very well. To reverse the modern trend in misinterpretation of the Constitution would work more effectively toward the counter-revolution of our expectations than any other measure that this administration might take. In answer to the palpable absurdity of Justice Brennan's opinion that the intent of the Framers cannot be known, that the Constitution is a blank check, we need other judges who know better—and know it in places of equivalent authority. The connection between tyranny and well-meaning judicial activism, making up law merely because of what one thinks is right, must be reasserted. For to be a people under law we must have a Constitution which limits what, through the law, may be attempted.

The rest of our present business, what we must do at once, is not difficult to identify. Conservatives are especially obliged to recover other portions of our nation's history of a more inclusive character than strictly legal history—portions distorted or hidden from us because our enemies realize that to control the past is to enjoin the future. Moreover we must remind some of our friends that religion consists of more than moral and ethical problems, as important as these are. And the list could be enlarged and extended in many other directions. The point I wish to make is not, however, a list but a distinction with respect to role: an insight drawn from the intellectual and spiritual genealogy of the position we should defend. Our first priority, as I said above, is intellectual, not topical. The analysis of assumptions in social, political and cultural theory is our primary task, now as before: analysis and then commentary with reference to the world around us. And to perform it we must leave only so much of our schedule for narrowly political considerations. Finally, we must concentrate on correcting what I have long insisted is the fundamental shortcoming of American conservatives, our indifference to the art of rhetoric, our inability to deal with the ostensibly benevolent simplicities of the adversary, who hopes to win with language what he lost at the polls. We have work enough to occupy all our ingenuity, regardless of the misconduct of any government in power. And then perhaps a little time for politics, which will do no harm, so long as we understand the priorities.

A View of Contemporary Conservatism

Paul Gottfried

FROM THE questions posed it would seem that American conservatism may be in trouble. I believe this is in fact the case. The doubts about its health that Mr. Wolfe raises are justified, even under a presidency alleged to be the most reactionary since the days of Calvin Coolidge. "Conservative" think tanks have systematically excluded social and philosophic questions from the kind of consideration that they give to fiscal and military issues. Think-tank administrators may have concluded that they could raise funds more easily by condemning the Reds or advocating deregulation than by pushing what is abstract or divisive. Their publications, however, give liberal justifications even when they take the nonliberal side on social questions. Some of these publications, for example, avoid attacking feminists on anything but procedural grounds. The E.R.A. was seen as redundant since both the states and the Fourteenth Amendment forbid sexual discrimination; and in any case the proposed amendment was awkwardly worded. Thus went the arguments of "conservative" think tanks and of most political opponents of the E.R.A. I for one waited in vain to see if such think tanks would oppose the Left on traditionalist or even anthropological grounds. Conservatives cannot prevail on policy issues in the long run unless they first win acceptance for their view of human nature.

That conservative politics and conservative journalism are currently dominated by neoconservatives and the New Right disturbs me no less than it does Mr. Wolfe. My critical opinion of the neoconservatives is already widely known. Suffice it to say here that I continue to be amazed that welfare state Democrats (*à peine retouchés*) have taken over once conservative publications and institutions. This has occurred not only because the neoconservatives are good at repackaging social democratic bromides, but also because conservatives are intellectually adrift. It is, to me, appalling that some of our most influential conservatives can no longer distinguish themselves from the advocates of a welfare state and of global democratic revolution. Despite the neoconservative's reservations about minority quotas and their support for military expenditures, they have always been open in expressing their contempt for the Old Right (a.k.a. the postwar Right). Self-labeled conservatives have embraced the neoconservative caricature of the postwar conservative movement. Thus they maintain that the neoconservatives are giving respectability to what used to be a collection of nativist neanderthals.

The New Right distresses me for being a lowbrow imitation of what the Old Right represents. Its spokesmen are well-meaning but often intellectually crude. They exaggerate the size of their followings and take credit for electoral victories, no matter how marginally they may have contributed to them. The New Right is the result of a fateful union, between Evangelical Christians and conservative activists who went into politics and into the civil service from the mid-sixties on. The Evangelicals are extremely decent people, but often sound naive even when they present morally defensible social positions. Their movement-conservative allies are tactically resourceful, but show little of the intellectual sophistication of their Old Right mentors. Leopold Tyrmand was right when he noted that politics are an epiphenomenon of culture. New Rightists will not receive widespread favorable attention until their values are shared by prestige universities and leading novelists. The media people are moulded by academic and cultural fashions which the Left determines partly by default.

The New Right is also on the horns of a dilemma, trying to reconcile its biblically based morality with populist, majoritarian rhetoric. In order to square this circle, New Rightists depict the American people as a God-fearing, hymn-singing nation. This is largely wishful thinking that takes no account of the influence of leftist media and educators upon one entire generation of Americans. Of course, the neoconservatives have their own circle to square, appearing to be anticommunist patriots while trying to appeal to politically liberal and often anti-American Zionists. *Commentary* has gained and seeks to hold on to a multi-tiered readership. The political spread among its readers may indeed be even wider than among the subscribers to *Time* and *Newsweek*. Various groups of *Commentary* readers praise it for what is addressed to them—without observing the larger, often self-contradictory pattern of positions taken by the magazine's editors and contributors.

Whatever the defects of conservatives who have allowed neoconservatives and New Rightists to represent them, it is wrong to underestimate the shaping role of the intellectual and journalistic Left in the ascendancy of both groups. The cultural-social radicalization of the sixties and seventies dramatically affected the American Right. Cold War liberals, and even democratic socialists, became conservative by default. The same radicalization gave birth to the New Right. Formerly apolitical Fundamentalists and Evangelicals turned fitfully to politics in order to keep feminists, pornographers, gays, and militant secularists from completing a true social revolution. The rise of the neoconservatives and the New Right, as reactions to the antibourgeois Left, coincided with changes in establishment politics. Business-type Republicans were growing soft on social issues, while the more moderate (largely Catholic) wing of the Democratic Party was losing an internal struggle to the Democratic Left. Allan Carlson has observed that the New Right has remained around because neither it nor the secularist Left has so far won a total victory. The New Right justifies its existence by keeping alive a battle which it cannot win.

Both the neoconservatives and the New Right owe their visibility partly to the attention of the Left. Liberal intellectuals have designated the neoconservatives as the official conservative opposition, sparing themselves the necessity of taking seriously any thinker to the right of Cold War liberals. This process has been aided by the fact that conservatives are having a problem of identity. Some of them now accept social levelling and a mixed economy as good things so long as they believe they are supporting "democratic capitalism" and the "conservative welfare state," and so long as defenders of the status quo are identified as conservatives by the *New York Times*.

The liberal media play up the neoconservatives because they share their modernist values and social background; they focus on the New Right, however, because of its obstreperous tactics and its use as a hobgoblin. Unlike the Old Right, the New Right manifests concern by taking to the streets with placards—or by barring others from entering abortion facilities. The New Right provides a manipulable example of what for the American Left is a preferred enemy. It has been made synonymous with religious enthusiasm and anti-intellectualism directed against hapless minorities and alternative lifestyles. S. M. Lipset has noted that the media and the New Right's spokesmen both exaggerate its electoral clout, albeit for different reasons.

There are three common mistakes among interpreters of the current American Right. Two of them have been discussed: confusing the visibility of both neoconservatives and New Rightists with electoral clout; and treating neoconservatives as genuine conservatives. A third mistake that afflicts commentators and even would-be supporters of conservative institutions is ignoring the continued vitality of the Old Right. Despite its dwindling financial resources and the loss of control over most self-identifying conservative foundations, the Old Right remains a powerful intellectual force. Members of the founding generation, like Kirk, Molnar, Hayek, Nisbet, Niemeyer, Buckley, and Tonsor, are still around and writing, And though much of the second generation have become political journalists and activists, it too is leaving its imprint on conservative thought. Unfortunately one rarely finds evidence of this imprint any more in *National Review,* which has grown into an inferior version of *Commentary,* aimed at upwardly mobile Catholics predominantly in the New York-Washington corridor. The meeting points for serious conservative thinkers are the Intercollegiate Studies Institute, editorial boards, and certain universities in which conservative scholars have managed to entrench themselves.

My comrade-in-arms, George Panichas, has joked about the attempt to preserve the Western heritage on a shoestring. The Old Right may actually be broadening its understanding of that heritage, even though much of the money once earmarked for theoretical conservatives is now going to neoconservatives and policy-oriented foundations. The broadening of conservative thought has come from two directions. One is the attempt of self-declared historical conservatives, ranging from Burkean disciples of Russell Kirk and Southern Agrarians to quasi-positivist exponents of James Burnham, to stress the connection between historical experience and moral wisdom. Those identified with this position recognize the close tie between radical utopianism and the total insensitivity to historical particularities of most modern social thinkers. There has also been a reaction on the Right to the attempt by Straussians and others to define the American experience too narrowly, in terms of political abstractions and independently of an experienced

culture. The new emphasis on historicity is certainly apparent among Southern conservatives like M. E. Bradford, Grady McWhiney, Forrest McDonald, Clyde Wilson, and Samuel Francis. History, for all of them, has become a weapon for discrediting the Left's factual and conceptual errors. Wilson has also made the argument in *Continuity* that the intellectual Left has maintained its cultural sway through creating and periodically changing the historiographical assumptions of our culture. This conservative interest in history has also benefited from the "value-centered historicism" expounded by Claes Ryn and by some of his former graduate students. It is significant that Ryn, who admires Kirk and Irving Babbitt, describes himself as a "historicist." A certain odium remained attached to that term until recently on the Old Right. The founding generation, with few exceptions, shunned it; the second generation has appropriated it, while insisting on the possibility of separating historicism from relativist ethics.

The other direction from which the Old Right has been enriched is the use of anthropological and scientific evidence to corroborate its views of human nature and the social good. Here there is evidence of a generational gap, as seen, for example, in the correspondence between Thomas Molnar and Thomas Fleming of the Rockford Institute. Molnar, a Christian Aristotelian, takes exception with Fleming for his reliance on Darwinian biology in defending traditionalist values. Whereas Molnar identifies sociobiology with a despiritualized, morally nihilistic universe, Fleming hopes to use it to defeat the Left on its own alleged turf, modern science. Molnar may be justified in his fear, yet conservative sociobiologists have taken a useful and daring step in depriving the Left of its exclusive claim to science. A similar achievement is the work of Father Stanley Jaki in exploring the theological presuppositions of Western scientific discovery.

In Europe the counter-revolution of sociobiology has long been underway. Though this development has sometimes expressed itself in crude vitalism, it is erasing the image of the Right as anti-scientific. And it is helping to cast further doubt on egalitarian, gender-free visions of genetics and biochemistry in the work of E. O. Wilson at Harvard and in the lively polemics against feminism by Michael Levin and Stephen Goldberg. In my opinion, a further recourse to biological sciences would aid George Gilder in his case against the feminists, however effectively Gilder has thus far argued from common sense.

I am convinced that the Old Right is better able than the neoconservatives to absorb the thinking described. Unlike the neoconservatives, the Old Right holds to the concept of a differentiated humanity, values social diversity, and perceives the necessary relationships between established custom and human nature. It was Aristotle, a common father of the Old Right, who, with due respect to the Straussians, tried to relate social distinctions to the biological order. Wolfgang Kulman and Stephen R. L. Clark have showed that Aristotle's hierarchical view of the household and his defense of differential sexual roles grew out of his biological research. The founding generation of postwar conservatism was already building bridges to the social sciences. Will Herberg tried to demonstrate the inevitably religious foundations of societies by drawing upon the sociology of religion. More recently, Molnar has been recommending the writings of the French Orientalist, Louis Dumont, on the merits of social hierarchy. The find-

ings of sociobiology as well as those of the social sciences are already being made to serve the conservative case for tradition. This work and the emergence of a vigorous historical conservatism should prove that the Old Right still lives, and that reports of its demise have been greatly exaggerated.

CONSERVATISM AND THE LIFE OF THE SPIRIT

George A. Panichas

Better to be despised for too anxious apprehensions, than ruined by too confident a security.

—Edmund Burke

THE CRISIS of modernity is an inclusive one. Its power and scourge are such that even those movements that seek to defend the sanctities of tradition and the values of order find themselves increasingly beleaguered. Richard M. Weaver observes that "fundamental integrity, once compromised, is slow and difficult of restoration." He goes on to emphasize: "Teachers of the present order have not enough courage to be definers; lawmakers have not enough insight." Weaver's diagnostic observations tell us something about the depth of the malaise that afflicts society and about the difficulties of resisting our continuing plight. The absence of courage and insight, as he further indicates, in the realm of intellect and the world of politics, sharpens and accelerates the personal and public dimensions of moral crisis at the highest and most important levels, where the course of civilization itself is ultimately determined.

Clearly the materialistic tendencies of the twentieth century, especially as these have solidified since the end of World War I and as "we moderns" have embodied them directly or indirectly, are now absolute tendencies in constant evidence. Insidious and intrusive, these tendencies transpose into fallacies of the most dangerous kind that trap even those who have conviction and affirm standards conducive to what Weaver terms a "metaphysical community." One likes to think of this "metaphysical community" as a natural and inseparable extension of the conservative metaphysic and of the conservative mind. One also likes to think that, in the midst of the general disarray that characterizes our crisis, there does exist and persevere a spiritual conservatism; that this spiritual conservatism is the *fons et origo* of all conservative perspectives: a primal, permanent, intensive, inviolable force and faith, unchanging and uncompromising in its principles—at once catholic, critical, and catechetical. This spiritual conservatism, one likes to think, revolves around, is rooted in, returns to, and reveres the highest axiomatic verities, the Word of God and the Order of the Soul.

God and soul are two words that are perhaps the greatest casualties of the ongoing crisis of modernity. The interior experience of these two words, in their living significance as the fear of God and the needs of the soul, seems to have neither meaning nor relevance. Their diminution and absence are symptomatic of the vacuum of disinheritance in which modern man finds himself. As words of prescriptive value they simply do not exist in a society programmatically addicted to the unending lures of presentism that reject those sacred paradigms of aspiration that human character requires if it is to venerate and sustain any ordering prin-

ciple of divinity. The rejection of these two words now enjoys wide acceptance as even a cursory scrutiny of the social-political scene will disclose.

Far from being arrested or deterred, the "age of liberalism" has actually achieved an insidious triumph as its sophistic proclivities infiltrate every aspect of human thought and activity. This destructive process signals the advance of what Michael Polanyi calls a "positivistic empiricism," that is, "[the] idea of unlimited progress, intensified to perfectionism, [which] has combined with our sharpened skepticism to produce the perilous state of the modern mind." We can now discern a withering totalization of this advance as it absorbs and shapes both political and intellectual thought and opinion. Even traditionalist conservatism retreats in front of this peril, in fearful awe of its might. The paths of this retreat are strewn with surrenders, backslidings, defeats, and losses of unfathomable consequences. Not only a principled conservatism but also a spiritual conservatism has been debased. What we find in alarming amplitude is the gradual emergence of a conservatism susceptible to the centrifugal tendencies and aims that Polanyi designates.

Sham conservatism is a symptom and portent of the spiritual desuetude that permeates American society and culture. A tinsel, opportunistic, and hedonistic conservatism, then, is what we see around us, unable to affirm the standards and certitudes that must be resolutely affirmed if an authentic ethos-centered conservatism is to survive. This survival will not occur whatever the immediate accomplishments of, say, the "moral majority" and the "new right," which merely pursue "pragmatic significations" residing in the liberals' standard baggage of "new deals" and "new frontiers." A conservatism that lacks "ontological referents" is as spiritually barren as the liberalism it opposes. Endless "policy reviews" and "policy studies," as these thrive and govern in some conservative quarters, in the end lack a basic apprehension of the "permanent things" and are responsive to the empirical ambitions that reflect the tastes and power-drives of a technologico-Benthamite world. A sham conservatism merely temporalizes and trivializes and dissimulates spiritual laws and truths. Such a conservatism belongs almost exclusively to the world and is impervious to the primacy of God as the measure of the soul. This primacy should constitute conservatism's ground of being; should define and inform a true "metaphysical community"—at once covenantal and sacramental. That community is certainly not one that we observe in our body politic or in the Realpolitik of contemporary conservative entelechies. A chic politicized conservatism, as we now view it, fails to acknowledge spiritual needs that coalesce in God and soul.

Given the large and visible popular successes of political conservatism and the vibrant images and impressions it has in recent years engendered, there is an obvious unwillingness to examine critically the true conditions of the conservative movement today. That movement, however, increasingly echoes the "secular hypothesis" and dwells in the "secular city"; it has forgotten or neglected those spiritual exercises that belief in God and in the soul demands and that a genuinely spiritual conservatism accepts. Even when this political, gnostic conservatism invokes the two holy words God and soul, it profanes them by assigning to them a spurious valuation, in short, by ignoring or eliminating the inner life of conservatism. And this dislodgement is today the greatest crisis that grips con-

servative life and thought. That inner life is inadequately recognized or honored by many conservative leaders and spokesmen, in word or in work. In effect the theology of conservatism has been sacrificed to the new gods and the new morality of modernity. The discipline of spiritual conservatism has been manifestly lessened by its own peculiar form of liberation theology, as it were, and by the purely quantitative point of view prevailing in the marketplace of ideas.

Dislodgement leads to capitulation as the present state of conservatism reveals. Where are to be found, one must ask in "fear and trembling," the spiritual exercises in conservative experience today? How is one to resist the materialistic doctrine that assails conservative criteria and that takes precedence over God and soul? A spiritually strenuous conservatism, as Irving Babbitt would say, has given way to the spiritual idler. The consequences of this recession have led to a general confusion among conservative adherents no longer able to distinguish between what Babbitt calls a law of the spirit and a law of the members, that is to say, the confusion of the things of God and the things of Caesar. This confusion, endemic in liberalism, imperils the conservative metaphysic. Nothing could be more debilitating than the confusion of first principles.

The preceding reflections should not be construed to mean that what is advocated is an otherworldly conservatism. Yet, a conservative metaphysic that neglects or omits the teleological dimension—and that seeks to escape from "the tragic sense of life"—falls into the same trap of illusion that is intimately connected with the liberal temper. Rather, these reflections, in their corrective purposiveness, seek to emphasize the need for a binary discipline—the discipline of ideas and the discipline of transcendent belief. The forms of conservative thought as we encounter them today are too much of this world, too much an acceptance of nominalist philosophy. They lack the element of ascent and are mired in the worship of time and in an "abandoned world," Godless and soulless. This is the world of spiritual dead-ends that belongs to "an age of bad faith" in which the "gods of mass and speed" breed to bring about the consuming majoritarian nightmare that Matthew Arnold depicts: "And littleness united / Is become invincible."

Insofar as the conservative metaphysic bows to the "world-machine," it reduces itself to the non-ontological and non-organic elements that identify contemporary life in its cruel alienations. This is the post-Christian and postmodern world that arrogantly renounces the "religious sense" and denies "the idea of the holy"—renounces God and denies the soul. It is a sad paradox that conservative leaders and thinkers often fail, in the present climate of their political victories, to recognize or implement their spiritual identity and responsibility. No authentic conservative metaphysic can be operable when the discipline of God and the discipline of the soul have been ceded to the *doxai,* the dialectical structures and superstructures of modern life.

We hear the claim that we live in "a decade dominated by conservatism." But such a claim must be assessed in the light of what precisely identifies and measures the particular dominances spawned by the conservative political phenomenon. From a metaphysical standpoint that phenomenon is neither reassuring nor inspiring. Its major social-political orientation is one of program and policy and points to a conservatism that has a downward tendency. That is, the conservatism that

we view in the public sector is largely socioeconomic in character; its aims are too easily influenced or tainted by the idea of mechanical progress, by that overriding belief that distinguishes a modernity that scorns divine transcendencies and embraces the instrumentalist article of faith that Simone Weil sees at the center of our spiritual crisis: that "matter is a machine for manufacturing good." No expression better particularizes the supreme impiety of the modern age as it molds habits of mind, attitudes, expectations, and aspirations. This impiety has gone unchecked during the past decade, and this dismaying fact should trouble the conscience of conservatives who subscribe to any spiritual standard and value. The world of pure instrumentality, in which everything is subordinated to the mechanical principle to which Simone Weil refers, is a profane world that needs to be unflinchingly opposed.

The perceived public image of conservatism, especially as it is now articulated and conveyed by fancy conservative journalists and publicists, is one of glitter. But all that glitters in it is not gold. Too often a cleverly packaged conservatism lacks the spiritual disciplines indispensable to a serious concern with ultimate issues that go far beyond public-policy issues. It lacks transcendence in the contexts that Saul Bellow stresses when he complains that there is now "no particular concern in the foundation of the country with the higher life of the country." Such a conservatism, to be sure, has achieved institutional prominence and electoral popularity, and its glamor has even appealed to the electronics media. It is, in an organizational and popular sense, strikingly successful. But all these external trappings do not satisfy the higher spiritual demands and responsibilities that are inherent in the conservative metaphysic.

What has been concocted for popular consumption is a kind of formalist conservatism, with an emphasis on the medium, on style, on technique, on constructs. Its spokesmen and popularizers, however capable and impressive they may be in creating a "verbal icon," seldom speak in a sapiential or soteriological sense. They acutely remind us that what we must restore to conservative theory and thought is a language that is sermonic, as Weaver would say. Within this language, and metaphysic, God and soul not only occupy a central place but also define and inform a spiritual, and visionary, conservatism. No significant restoration of an authentic conservatism in our time is possible without our giving our first allegiance to spiritual principles of order—to the life of the spirit, as Eric Voegelin insists, that is the source of order in man and in society.

We cannot escape the fact that during the past ten years or so conservatism has experienced a spiritual decline even as it has made considerable political gains. This is an aberrant phenomenon in need of amendment. For whenever the conservative idea permits its spiritual aspirations to slip away and to be dominated by political motives and arrangements it is no longer genuinely conservative. The interior life of conservatism, in effect, has been subordinated to surface-consciousness, to the external world. By putting on the character of illusion it is no longer "capable of infinity" or making "contact with nonexistent reality," to use a Voegelinian terminology. For conservatism, then, to be metaphysically viable it must return to its center of principles and recommit itself to the transcendences and values that fix its spiritual ethos, shape its work, register its vision,

"It is out of reverence for the moral ideal," José Ortega y Gasset counsels us, "that we must fight against its greatest enemies, which are perverse moralities." If we are to recover "the moral ideal" and if we are to be reconsecrated to the life of the spirit, we are in urgent need of an unconditional conservatism, lean, ascetical, disciplined, prophetic, unswerving in its censorial task, strenuous in its mission, strong in its faith, faithful in its dogma, pure in its metaphysic. It must now cleanse itself of gilded accretions, false complacencies, expedient compromises, meretricious temptations, and drifting aims before it can be filled, morally and spiritually, with "a burning fervour full of anguish," as the great mystics would say. In its present state of crisis, conservatism must submit itself to an exacting *metanoia*. Only in acts of repentance will contemporary conservatism find seeds of renewal.

Enlivening the Conservative Mind

Russell Kirk

THE WITTIEST of our public men, Eugene McCarthy, remarked a few months ago that nowadays he uses the word "liberal" as an adjective merely. That is a measure of the triumph of the conservative mentality in recent years—including the triumph of the conservative side of Mr. McCarthy's own mind and character.

Perhaps it would be well, most of the time, to use the word "conservative" as an adjective chiefly. For there exists no Model Conservative, and conservatism is no ideology: it is a state of mind, a type of character, a way of looking at the civil social order. The conservative movement or body of opinion can accommodate a considerable diversity of views on a good many subjects, there being no Test Act or Thirty-Nine Articles of the conservative creed. In essence, the conservative person is simply one who finds the permanent things more pleasing than Chaos and old Night. This is by way of brief preface to some desultory observations on what the conservative mind requires today.

In America the great wave of public opinion sweeps in a conservative direction today, carrying all before it: as Tocqueville instructs us, such is the way with opinion in democratic nations generally. The Mexican-American voters clearly shifted in that direction less than two years ago, and will go farther still; now the polls of the *New York Times* and CBS suggest that the Afro-American population turns that way.

Both foreign affairs and domestic questions impel the nation toward long-range conservative policies. Yet could these tremendous conservative successes of recent years conceivably cease? Might the wave of public opinion begin to sweep back again, an ebb tide, carrying out to the great deep much American flotsam?

Yes.

From what cause?

Stupidity.

It was not altogether without reason, a century ago, that John Stuart Mill called conservatives "the stupid party." Four decades ago, when in Britain the Attlee government abolished the university seats in the House of Commons, Winston Churchill declared that the Socialists were "against brains." So the Socialists were and are. But a good many conservative folk in 1986, finding themselves only second-best in the pursuit of stupidity, try harder.

Some years ago I remarked in the course of a speech that conservative imagination is required in our time. A man of business in the audience retorted,

"We don't need any imagination: we're practical." That's what I mean.

Less than forty years ago there commenced a renewal—regarded by liberals as a recrudescence—of conservative thought and imagination. Like Fabianism in Britain two generations earlier, but proceeding in an opposite direction, this "New Conservatism" contributed to grand-scale victories at the polls thirty years later. In the United States, as earlier in Britain, persuasive ideas combined or coincided with favorable circumstances; and thus the course of a great nation's politics was altered, mightily.

In Britain, however, the intellectual successes of the Fabians and the electoral victories of the Labour party were followed by the development of periodicals, book-publishing firms, and university associations favorable to socialism. In the United States, au contraire, relatively few intellectual gains for the conservative cause have occurred since 1953. (The year 1953 was marked by the publication and cordial reception of conservative books by R. A. Nisbet, Daniel Boorstin, Clinton Rossiter, Russell Kirk, and others: a year in which liberals began to listen.)

True, several magazines of a seriously conservative cast are published today, although none of tremendous circulation. But also new liberal or radical publications have sprung up. The major book-review media are markedly more hostile toward any book suspected of political conservatism or religious orthodoxy than they were in the fifties. As for book publishing, in the year 1953 there was but one consistent reputable publisher of serious books, Henry Regnery; in 1986 there still is but one, Henry Regnery, who obtains only slight assistance from the foundations and men of great means who presumably ought to be interested in keeping the conservative mind alive.

In universities and colleges, staffs are far more dominated by radicals than they were at the beginning of the fifties—in part because of the violent New Left sillies who obtained posts during the late sixties and early seventies, and now are fortified by tenure. The larger foundations, most of them, are dominated by a Ford Foundation humanitarian mentality, which assesses the Fiend according to the degree of his conservatism.

Thus the conservative movement is enfeebled, intellectually and in backing, at the very hour of its popular ascendancy. (By the way, America's bigger men of business, with very few exceptions, never have been of any help to really conservative causes; if they think of politics at all, it is much as they think of professional sports teams: "Winning is the name of the game.") This may become a fatal impoverishment.

For the most pressing need of the conservative movement in America is to quicken its own right reason and moral imagination. The rising generation, already won to a kind of unthinking conservatism on nearly every college campus, must be made aware that conservative views and policies can be at once intellectually reputable and pleasantly lively.

Ballot-box victories are undone in short order, if unsupported by the enduring art of persuasion. A political movement that fancies it can subsist by slogans and by an alleged "pragmatism" presently is tumbled over by the next political carnival, shouting fresher slogans.

I am not implying that conservative folk should set to forming a conservative ideology; for conservatism is the negation of ideology. The conservative public man turns to constitution, custom, convention, ancient consensus, prescription, precedent, as guides—not to the narrow and fanatical abstractions of ideology. I am saying, rather, that unless we show the rising generation what deserves to be conserved, and how to go about the work of preservation with intelligence and imagination—why, the present wave of conservative opinion will cast us on a stern and rockbound coast, perhaps with a savage behind every tree. Conservative leaders ought to declare, with Demosthenes, "Citizens, I beg of you to *think*!"

The existence of various factions within the conservative movement ought not to alarm us overmuch. All large-scale political movements of reform, in the beginning, are alliances of various groups and interests that have in common chiefly a dislike of what has been the dominant political power. Journalists, for their own delectation, invent or cry up such labels as "Old Right," "Traditionalists," "Neoconservatives," "Libertarians," "New Right," "Fundamentalist Right," and the like. But these groups and categories overlap and intermingle. The more eccentric members of this loose conservative coalition may be expected to fall away gradually into fresher eccentricities—and no great loss will result. Varying emphases upon this or that aspect of public policy will remain among the several conservative groupings; but enough common ground can be cultivated to maintain a useful unity on certain large questions—supposing we abjure narrow ideology and condescend to think. If, on the contrary, conservative leaders complacently fancy that guessing and muddling through will suffice—why, future historians may describe the attempt to wake conservative minds and hearts during the latter half of the twentieth century as an intellectual Mississippi Bubble.

The principal demarcation among American conservative groups today, it seems to me, is the gulf fixed between (on the one side) all those conservative men and women who, taking long views, argue that intellectual activity and rousing of the imagination are required urgently; and (on the other side of the canyon) all those professedly "pragmatic" persons who think of a conservative government as one that keeps in office by serving or placating certain powerful interests—and so prevents worse from befalling those in the seats of the mighty.

The ideologue cannot govern well; but neither can the time-server. Conservative people in politics need to steer clear of the Scylla of abstraction and the Charybdis of opportunism. So it is that thinking folk of conservative views ought to reject the embraces of the following categories of political zealots:

Those who urge us to sell the National Parks to private developers.

Those who believe that by starving South Africans we can dish Jesse Jackson and win over the black vote en masse.

Those who would woo the declining feminists by abolishing academic freedom through a new piece of "Civil Rights" legislation.

Those who instruct us that "the test of the market" is the whole of political economy and of morals.

Those who fancy that foreign policy can be conducted with religious zeal, on a basis of absolute right and absolute wrong.

Those who, imagining that all mistakes and malicious acts are the work of a malign or deluded "elite," cry with Carl Sandburg, "The people, yes!"

Those who assure us that great corporations can do no wrong.

Those who discourse mainly of the Trilateral Commission, the Bilderburgers, and the Council on Foreign Relations.

And various other gentry who abjure liberalism but are capable of conserving nothing worth keeping.

Is anybody left in the conservative camp? Yes.

There survives, even unto our day, a conservative cast of character and of mind capable of sacrifice, thought, and sound sentiment. That sort of conservative mentality was discerned in America by Tocqueville a century and a half ago, by Maine and Bryce a century ago, by Julián Marías twenty years ago. If well waked in mind and conscience, such people—really quite numerous in these United States—are capable of enduring conservative reform and reinvigoration. But if the trumpet give an uncertain sound, who shall go forth to battle?

Roger Scruton

How to be a Nonliberal, Antisocialist Conservative

VOL. 28, NO. 2, 1993

Only in a few places in Europe and America can a person call himself a conservative and expect to be taken seriously. The first task of conservatism, therefore, is to create a language in which "conservative" is no longer a term of abuse. This task is part of another, and larger, enterprise: that of the purification of language from the insidious sloganizing which has taken hold of it. This is not a simple enterprise. Indeed, it is, in one sense, the whole of politics. As the communists realized from the beginning, to control language is to control thought—not actual thought, but the possibilities of thought. It is partly through the successful efforts of the communists—aided, of course, by a World War which they did not a little to precipitate—that our parents thought in terms of elementary dichotomies. Left–Right, Communist–fascist, socialist–capitalist, and so on. Such were the "terms of debate" that we inherited. To the extent that you are not "on the Left," they implied, then to that extent are you "on the Right"; if not a Communist, then so much nearer fascism; if not a socialist, then an advocate of "capitalism," as an economic and political system.

If there is a basic dichotomy that presently confronts us, it is between us—the inheritors of what remains of Western civilization and Western political thinking—and the purveyors of dichotomies. There is no such opposition as that between Left and Right, or that between communism and fascism. There is simply an eternal alliance—although an "alliance of the unjust" who are always ready to violate the terms that bind them—between those who think in terms of dichotomies and labels. Theirs is the new style of politics, the science which has in truth replaced "politics" as it has ever been known. Theirs is a world of "forces" and "movements"; the world perceived by these infantile minds is in a constant state of turmoil and conflict, advancing now to the Left, now to the Right, in accordance with the half-baked predictions of this or that theorist of man's social destiny. Most of all, the dichotomizing mind has need of a system. It seeks for the theoretical statement of man's social and political condition, in terms of which to derive a doctrine that will answer to every material circumstance.

Postwar intellectuals have inherited two major systems of political thought with which to satisfy their lust for doctrine: liberalism and socialism. It is testimony to the persistence of the dichotomizing frame of mind that, even in Eastern Europe, the "world conflict" that endured for seventy years was frequently seen in terms of the opposition between these systems. And because they are systems, it is often supposed that they are organically unified—that you cannot embrace any part of one of them without embracing the whole of it. But let it be said at the outset, that, from the standpoint of our present predicament, nothing is more obvious about these systems than the fact that they are, in their presuppositions, substantially the same. Each of them proposes a description of our condition, and an ideal solution to it, in terms which are secular, abstract, universal, and egalitarian. Each sees the world in "desacralized" terms, in terms which, in truth, correspond to no lasting common human experience, but only to the cold skeletal paradigms that haunt the brains of intellectuals. Each is abstract, even when it pretends to a view of human history. Its history, like its philosophy, is detached from the concrete circumstance of human agency, and, indeed, in the case of Marxism, goes so far as to deny the efficacy of human agency, preferring to see the world as a confluence of impersonal forces. The ideas whereby men live and find their local identity—ideas of allegiance, of country or nation, of religion and obligation—all these are, for the socialist, mere ideology, and for the liberal, matters of "private" choice, to be respected by the state only because they cannot truly matter to the state.

Each system is also universal. An international socialism is the stated ideal of most socialists; an international liberalism is the unstated tendency of the liberal. To neither system is it thinkable that men live, not by universal aspirations but by local attachments; not by a "solidarity" that stretches across the globe from end to end, but by obligations that are understood in terms which separate men from most of their fellows—in terms such as national history, religion, language, and the customs that provide the basis of legitimacy. Finally—and the importance of this should never be underestimated—both socialism and liberalism are, in the last analysis, egalitarian. They both suppose all men to be equal in every respect relevant to their political advantage. For the socialist, men are equal in their needs, and should therefore be equal in all that is granted to them for the satisfaction of their needs. For the liberal, they are equal in their rights, and should therefore be equal in all that affects their social and political standing.

I must say at once that I have more sympathy for the liberal than for the socialist position. For it is based in a philosophy that not only respects the reality of human agency, but also attempts to reconcile our political existence with the elementary freedoms that are constantly threatened by it. But—whatever its worth as a philosophical system, liberalism remains, for me, no more than that—a constant *corrective* to the given reality, but not a reality in itself. It is a shadow, cast by the light of reason, whose existence depends upon the massive body which obstructs that light, the body of man's given political existence.

This given political existence defies the four axioms of liberalism and socialism. It is not secular but spiritual, not abstract but concrete, not universal but particular, and not egalitarian but fraught with diversity, inequality, privilege, and power. And so it should be. I say that it is spiritual, for I believe that the world as man understands it—the *Lebenswelt*—is given to him in terms which bear the indelible imprint of obligations that surpass his understanding. He is born into a world that calls on him for sacrifice, and that promises him obscure rewards. This world is concrete—it cannot be described in the abstract unhistorical language of the socialist or liberal theorist without removing the skin of significance that renders it perceivable. The world of the socialist and the world of the liberal are like dead skeletons, from which the living skin has been picked away. But this actual, living, social world, is a particular thing, a vital thing, and it must, if it is to flourish, distribute its life variously and unequally about its parts. The abstract equality of the socialist and the liberal has no place in this world, and could be realized only by the assertion of controls so massive as to destroy themselves.

In order to justify, and indeed to win, its war with reality, the intellectual mind has developed an annihilating language with which to describe it. All political realities are described a historically, as though they could be established anywhere, at any time. Thus the peculiarly *Polish* phenomenon of "Solidarity" is squeezed into the abstract forms dictated by the theory of "liberal democracy." It is even seen as a kind of socialism, especially by French intellectuals for whom nothing is good which cannot be given a socialist name. The example is minatory. If we are to return to reality, we must search for a language that is scrupulous towards the human world.

ONE GENERALITY, however, is useful to us, precisely because, behind it, a thousand particularities lie hidden. I refer to the idea of legitimacy. To their immense credit, liberals have tried to provide an alternative idea of legitimacy—one with which to challenge the historical entitlements that were to be extinguished by the triumph of their system. The first, and final, condemnation of communism is that it has dismissed the whole idea of legitimacy with a cavernous laugh. It is not my concern to argue with the liberal, some of whose ideas must eventually be incorporated into any philosophical theory of legitimate government. I wish only to suggest a nonliberal alternative, that will be free from the contagion of theory.

Among the many dichotomies that have pulverized the modern intelligence, that—due, I suppose to Weber—between legitimacy and legality, between "traditional" and "legal-rational" modes of authority, has been the most damaging. Only if law is misunderstood, as a system of abstractions, can legality be regarded as an alternative to—rather than as a particular realization of—legitimacy. But abstract law is, for that reason, without lasting force.

Legitimacy is, quite simply, the right of political command. And this right includes the exercise of law. What confers this right over a people? Some would say their "choice." But this idea overlooks the fact that we have only the crudest instruments whereby choices are measured, and these choices concern only the most fortuitous of things. Besides, what leads people to accept the "choice" that is thrust upon them by their fellows, if not a prior sense that they are bound together in a legitimate order?

The task for the conservative is to find the grounds of political existence concretely, and to work toward the re-establishment of legitimate government in a world that has been swept bare by intellectual abstractions. Our ultimate model for a legitimate order is one that is given historically, to people united by their sense of a common destiny, a common culture, and a common source of the values that govern their lives.

THE LIBERAL intelligentsia in the West, like the erstwhile Communist intelligentsia in the East, has persistently refused to accept the given-ness of human existence. It has made life, and in particular political life, into a kind of intellectual experiment. Seeing the unhappiness of man it asks, what has gone wrong? And it dreams of a world in which an abstract ideal of justice will be made reality. It looks everywhere for the single solution that will resolve conflicts and restore harmony everywhere, whether on the North Pole or at the Equator. Hence, the total inability of liberalism to provide a solution to those who are afflicted by totalitarian illegitimacy. The liberal begins from the same assumption as the totalitarian, namely, that politics is a means to an end, and the end is equality—not, it is true, material equality, but moral equality, an equality of "rights." Democracy is the necessary result of this liberal ideal, since democracy is the final realization of political equality. For the liberal, the only way to oppose the totalitarian is by slow, steady democratization of the social order.

Who can doubt the appeal of that idea? But it neglects the one, inescapable fact. I cannot see my own life as the liberal wishes to see political life. I cannot see my own life as an experiment. Nor can I regard my obligations as created entirely by my free, responsible actions. I am born into a situation that I did not create, and am encumbered from birth with obligations that are not of my own devising. My basic debt to the world is not one of justice but of piety, and it is only when

I recognize this fact that I can be truly myself. For only in relation to my given situation can I form those values and social perceptions that give me strength, at last, to experiment with freedom.

Any genuine account of our sentiments of legitimacy must begin from the recognition that piety precedes justice, both in our lives and in our thinking, and that, until we have attached ourselves to a place and people, and begun to think of them as "our own," the claims of justice, and the superstition of equality, are entirely without meaning for us. But this attachment to place and people is not chosen: it is not the outcome of some liberal reflection on the rights of man, nor is it conceived in the experimental spirit that is so important to the socialist program. It is given to us, in the very texture of our social existence. We are born into the obligations of the family, and into the experience of ourselves as parts of a larger whole. Not to recognize the priority of this experience is to concede the major premise of totalitarian thinking, which is that political existence is nothing but a long term experiment. There is a particular view, still popular among left-wing intellectuals in the West, that the Soviet system was "socialism gone wrong." This thought expresses precisely the major political danger of our times, which is the belief that politics involves a choice of systems, as a means to an end, so that one system may "go wrong" while another "goes right." The truth is that socialism is wrong, precisely because it believes that it can go right—precisely because it sees politics as a means to an end. Politics is a manner of social existence, whose bedrock is the given obligations from which our social identities are formed. Politics is a form of association which is not a means to an end, but an end in itself. It is founded on legitimacy, and legitimacy resides in our sense that we are made by our inheritance.

Hence, if we are to rediscover the roots of political order, we must attempt to endorse the unchosen obligations that confer on us our political identity, and which settle for a Pole that he cannot be governed from Moscow, or for a Falkland Islander that he cannot be legitimately governed from Buenos Aires.

IT IS worth pausing to mention another, and rival, generality that has been of some service to the left-liberal intellectual in our time, in his endeavor to wipe out the past, and to find a basis for political obligation that looks only to the present and the future. This is the idea of the "people," as the fount of legitimate order. The idea is usually combined with the fantasy that the intellectual has some peculiar faculty of hearing, and also articulating, the "voice of the people." This self-delusion, which has persisted unaltered since the days of the French Revolution, expresses the intellectual's concern to be reunited with the social order from which his own thinking has so tragically separated him. He wishes to redeem himself from his "outsideness." Unfortunately, however, he succeeds in uniting himself not with society, but only with another intellectual abstraction—"the people"—designed according to impeccable theoretical requirements, precisely in order to veil the intolerable reality of everyday life. "The people" does not exist. Even if it did exist, it would be authority for nothing, since it would have no concrete basis on which to build its legitimacy. Nobody can speak for the people. Nobody can speak *for* anyone. The truth, however, strives to be uttered, and may find expression, now on these lips, now on those.

Unlike "the people," the nation is not an abstraction. It is a given historical reality. It is made particular and immediate in language, custom, religion, and culture. It contains within itself the intimation of a legitimate order. This, I believe, should always be remembered, even by those— and that includes most of us now—who hesitate to adopt the straightforward nationalism that emerged from the Congress of Vienna and which at first pacified, but subsequently destroyed, our continent.

BUT SURELY, you will say, is there not another source of legitimacy—one that does not require the support of those pious obligations that seem to commit us to so much on the basis of so little? Is there not a legitimacy to be found in democracy, that will one day *replace* the appeal to piety?

That is a large question. But two things need to be said in response to it. First, "democracy" is a disputed term, and nobody knows quite what it means or quite how to secure it. Should we wait until all the paradoxes of social choice have been resolved before formulating our political commitments?

Second, what people have appreciated in democracy is not periodic collective choice—for what is so estimable in the fact that the ignorant majority every now and then chooses to be guided by a new party, toward goals that it understands no better than it understood the goals of the previous one? What is appreciated are certain political virtues, which we rightly associate with British and American democracy, but which existed before democracy, and could be established elsewhere without its aid. These virtues are the following:

(i) Limited power: no one can exercise unlimited power when his projects stand to be extinguished by an election.

(ii) Constitutional government: but what upholds the Constitution?

(iii) Justification by consent.

(iv) The existence of autonomous institutions, and the free association that makes them possible.

(v) Rule of law: in other words, the possibility of adjudicating every act, even when it is the act of an official—even when it is an act in the name of the sovereign power.

(vi) Legitimate opposition: in other words, the right to form parties, and to publish opinions, which oppose the government; and the right to contend openly for power.

Political theorists are familiar, of course, with those matters, and this is not the place to discuss them in detail. But it is worth summarizing their import. Taken together, those six features of government mean, not democracy, but rather constitutional limitation. To put it more directly, they denote the separation of the state (which is the locus of legitimate authority) from those who hold power *by virtue* of the state. Those who wield power can be judged in terms of the very offices that they hold. This is surely an essential part of true political order. It is also an indispensable part of any fully elaborated legitimacy. Indeed, we can see legitimacy in the modern state as composed of two parts: a root, which is the pious attachment that draws people together into a single political entity; and a tree which grows from that root, which is the sovereign state, ordered by the principles that I have advocated. In this state, power is held under conditions that limit it, and in a manner that makes it answerable to those who may suffer from its exercise. This state shows the true flowering of a "civil society"—a public life that is open, dignified, and imbued with an instinctive legality. Such legality grows from and ex-

presses the legitimacy that is stored in its root. It is this upper, visible part of the legitimate *polis* that is so evidently destroyed by the political doctrines of our time. But its destruction is made possible, not so much by the elimination of democracy, as by the stifling of the spontaneous source of legitimate sentiment from which it feeds.

Democracy can, of course, sustain the six political virtues that I have listed. But it can also destroy them. For all of them depend on the one thing that democracy cannot provide, and which is hinted at in the question that I have added to number (ii): authority. What prompts people to accept and be bound by the results of a democratic election, or by the existing law, or by the limitations embodied in an office? What, in short, gives rise to the "public spirit" that has so signally vanished from the institutions of government in much of modern Europe? Surely it is *respect*—for institutions, for procedures, for the powers and privileges that are actually enjoyed. This respect is derived from the sense that these powers, privileges, and procedures reflect something that is truly "ours," something that grows from the social bond that defines our condition. Here lies the authority of the actual: that it is seen to contain within itself the residue of the allegiance which defines *my* place.

WHAT NOW is true legality? I have already hinted at a distinction between abstract and concrete law, and have implied that only the latter can truly fill the vacuum of legitimacy that presently lies before us. Concrete law is exemplified at its best in the English tradition of common law—law made by judges, in response to the concrete problems that come before them, and in which principles emerge only slowly, and already subject to the harsh discipline of the actual. Any law that is the upshot of serious judicial reasoning, founded in precedents and authorities, bears the stamp of an historical order; it also remains responsive to the reality of human conflicts, and constitutes a genuine attempt to resolve them, rather than to dictate an intellectually satisfying solution which may be unacceptable to the parties. This kind of law encapsulates the true source of legal authority, which is the plaintiff's belief that justice will be done, not abstractly, but in his particular case, in light of the particular circumstances that are his, and which are perhaps even uniquely his. For concrete law to exist in any form, there must be judicial independence. And once there is judicial independence there is all that anyone has reasonably aspired to under the banner of "the rights of man." For there is the assurance that justice may be done, whatever the power that seeks to extinguish it.

There are two major threats to concrete law. One is the abolition of judicial independence. This was accomplished by the Communist Party, in the interests of an "abstract" justice—an "equality" of reward—which must inevitably conflict with the concrete circumstances of human existence. The second threat is the proliferation of statute law—of law by decree, law repeatedly made and remade in response to the half-baked ideas of politicians and their advisors. All such law is fatally flawed: the Communist Party rested its entire claim to legality in the generation of such laws, while removing the only instrument—judicial independence—that could make them

into genuine *laws,* rather than military injunctions.

Liberalism has always appreciated the importance of legality. But liberal legality is an abstract legality, concerned with the promotion of a purely philosophical idea of "human rights." What value are human rights, without the judicial process that will uphold them? And besides, in resting one's faith in this beguiling abstraction, does one not also give to one's enemy another bastion against the recognition of his illegitimacy? Is it not possible for him to say that he upholds human rights—only different rights? (The right to work, for instance, or a right to a stake in the means of production.) If one looks back to the French Revolution, one sees just how easy it is for the doctrine of "human rights" to become an instrument of the most appalling tyranny. It suffices to do as the Jacobins did—to abolish the judiciary, and replace it by "people's courts." Then anything can be done to anyone, in the name of the Rights of Man.

In response to liberalism, therefore, it is necessary to work for the restoration of the concrete circumstances of justice. But the concrete law that I have been advocating is very unlike anything that either a socialist or a liberal would approve. It preserves inequalities, it confers privileges, it justifies power. That, however, is also its strength. For there always will be inequalities; there always will be privilege and power. Those are nothing but the lineaments of every actual political order. Since inequalities, privileges, and powers exist, it is right that they should coexist with the law that might justify them. Otherwise they exist unjustified, and also uncontrolled.

Mark C. Henrie

Rethinking American Conservatism in the 1990s: The Struggle Against Homogenization

VOL. 28, NO. 2, 1993

George Bush and the band of dedicated "pragmatists" with which he surrounded himself in the White House are now responsible for the loss of the Executive Branch of the federal government to the liberal Democrats. This defeat has set off turmoil and contestation in the Republican Party, and in this case, such a practical matter also has theoretical importance. For the achievement of Ronald Reagan was to take a Republican Party that was little more than the listless vehicle of the business class and to transform it into a populist majority coalition organized *explicitly* around the ideas of the postwar American conservative movement. While Bush himself was no conservative, inevitably implicated in the "crack-up" of the Republican Party under his leadership is the meaning of conservatism in America.

Two decades ago, George Nash, in his *Conservative Intellectual Movement in America Since 1945*[1], told the story of how American conservatism was forged rather uneasily as a political movement from three intellectual groupings: traditionalists, libertarians, and anticommunists. Today on the conventional "Right," however, we find many libertarians who argue as vigorously against the opponents of abortion as they do against economic central planners while we also find some religious traditionalists who see no particularly compelling reason not to support fairly activist regulation of both economic and social life. These disagreements are nothing new, of course, and as conservatives are nothing if they are not historically informed, it would be wise to return to Nash's book to learn from the older disputes which took place on the way to political victory in the 1980s.

A re-reading of Nash's book raises a more important question: Was there a logic to American conservatism, or was the movement merely a marriage of political convenience? My belief is that there was and is a general logic to conservatism, to which American conservatism is no exception; but this conservative logic has heretofore often been misunderstood in America. Thus, our central theoretical question: What is, and should be, the essence of conservatism in America? If we can determine the nature of authentic conservatism, then perhaps we can come to understand better the political and social challenges that confront us in our new historical circumstances. What will conservatism have to say to America in the 1990s and beyond?

IN RETROSPECT, it seems clear that anticommunism was indeed what held American conservatism together through the Cold War, both politically and intellectually. Regardless of their other differences, conservative thinkers from widely differing points of view could agree that Soviet communism was the *summum malum* to be combatted with a single-mindedness that seemed to "sophisticated" liberals of the time to border on paranoia. If, as Carl Schmitt once argued, politics is a matter of finding enemies, then the conservatives were particularly astute at seeing the real enemy of our time, while liberals, blinded ideologically to enemies on the Left, simply "missed" the major threat to peace, public liberty, and private virtue in the second half of this century. It would not be surprising if this conservative clear-sightedness accounted for political victory at the presidential level.

With communism consigned to history's ash heap, American conservatism finds itself disoriented. For once, the journalists are right in their diagnosis, and it would appear conservatives need a new unifying enemy. The so-called "neoconservatives" have been responsive to this predicament, and have proffered the multiculturalist academic radicals, a "new" New Left, for diabolization. There is something to this choice, but since it is arrived at pragmatically rather than from clear principles, it misses much as well. Fundamentally, odious as they may be, the multiculturalists are no world-historical force, though they may present one symptomatic face of a genuine problem.

Furthermore, for those on the more traditionalist right, the neoconservatives' uncritical celebration of American liberal-bourgeois "progress" before 1968 is not an adequate arcadian model to place in contradistinction to New Left radicalism. Some traditionalists even share something with the multiculturalists at the level of critique, for both claim that the "objectivity" of Enlightenment liberalism and its rationalist modes of inquiry is a masked and invasive tyranny, and hardly neutral.[2]

HOW THEN can we best identify the enemy against which conservatives should rally in the coming decade if they are to be faithful to their traditions, and therefore true to themselves? To answer this, we must try to understand what it was about communism that galvanized us against it. The Soviet communists claimed the mantle of the French Revolution of course, the first incarnation of the conservatives' perennially recurring adversary. What is it then that conservatives have repeatedly opposed for the past two centuries?

Panajotis Kondyles has argued in a richly perceptive book[3] that the only consistent theme in European conservative thought, both in England and on the continent, is opposition to *sovereignty*, that claim by the centralized, "rationalized," and liberal democratic political state to a monopoly on the "legitimate" use of coercion, a claim which expanded imperceptibly to a tacitly presumed monopoly of social authority, tout court. This presumptuous expansion of the sphere of the political sovereign acted to delegitimize other social authorities and intermediate institutions to which conservatives felt themselves bound, and which conservatives believed were integral to a good life.

What is centrally important about this rise of sovereignty is that it proceeded in large part through theories of natural rights and the social contract: individual liberties, therefore, have only abetted the growth of Leviathan. Robert Nisbet highlights this hidden dynamic in the best short study of conservatism in English, *Conservatism: Dream and Reality*.[4] Nisbet observes what would seem to Americans to be an historical paradox: the power of the state in our lives has risen hand in hand with the rise of the individual "rights" about which we are so proud. Like Kondyles, Nisbet argues that these two movements—increasing political power and increasing individual "freedom"—are directly related. For the rights that have been "recognized" by the modern liberal state are not so much rights against the state as they are rights against other social bodies that used to have some measure of authority in the lives of men and women.

Nisbet traces the rise of the sovereign liberal state at the expense of the church, the guilds, universities, social classes, the extended family, and now at long last, even the nuclear family—everything except "the individual." It is difficult to "see" this process happening, but this is what we must do if we are to properly assess the means by which meaningful freedom may today be retained, not to mention other values that conservatives consider to be goods. The reason the rise of the "individual" jeopardizes our freedom is that as the sphere of political sovereignty grows at the expense of other authorities, the individual himself increasingly has nowhere to *hide* from the state's "legitimate" coercion. Any power which might effectively shield the individual from Leviathan has been de-legitimized in this process. Furthermore, with the weakening of alternate authorities, the individual has nowhere to *stand* to articulate a perspective differing from that of the liberal polity and its culture. Claiming the sanction of universal Reason, liberal sovereignty rules out any *fundamental* critique of itself as a matter of principle.

But if, paradoxically, freedom is threatened precisely by the liberal state's dispensing of rights, then we must do considerable re-thinking of the nature of the conservative's attitude toward American society. In light of the interpretations of Nisbet and Kondyles, it seems American conservatives have been right to resist "big government," but the Lockean *means* by which they have been resisting may have contributed to this more basic problem of liberal sovereignty. Again, what American conservatives largely have failed to see is that the advance of the negative liberties and the protection of a "private" realm have often operated not to the advantage of real liberty, but rather to the advantage of the state's *monopoly* on "coercion," which now is the only meaning of "authority" once all alternatives have been delegitimized. The implications of this analysis are plain: the natural rights of the social contract tradition, to which American conservatives have often repaired in their attempt to limit the gigantism of the state, ultimately serve to strengthen the hand of the liberal state. Thus, a conservatism that celebrates individual liberties only accelerates *liberal totalism*. We have most clearly experienced this emerging totalism in the oft-heard lament that "everything is becoming politics," from education to morality to relations between the sexes. Such politicization is an inevitable result of the manner in which American liberalism conceives of the "public-private" distinction. That is, in protecting only a certain understanding of *privacy*, and doing so by advancing a doctrine of politically administered *individual* rights, a uniform politicization of all spheres of human interest occurs. Thus, all human relations begin to resemble the relations of the political sphere, and these relations in turn are modelled on the contracts of the marketplace, for significantly, the preeminent Lockean rights are the rights of private property and economic freedom.

Having just spoken of the threat of "totalism," a clarification is in order. We are accustomed to the notion that totalitarianism is a threat to freedom, but it appears that liberal totalism is opposed by the conservative primarily because it threatens social and personal goods beyond simple freedom. That there are such goods which a society might pursue in common is just one of the facts obscured theoretically by the tale that we tell about the social contract—a tale that focuses our attention on the goal of "liberty" to the exclusion of all other goods. What is threatening in liberal totalism, therefore, is not primarily a loss of negative liberty. Rather, the conservative fears the loss of some element of the human good that is neglected in the liberal vision of society as a collection of individuals brought together under a juridical sovereignty by a contract of mutual advantage. The concern is that the liberal rationalization of society at the expense of intermediate authorities destroys something necessary for a fully human life.

WE ARE now reaching our goal of a better understanding of what it is against which conservatives have long stood in inarticulate opposition, and which might serve negatively to unify American conservatism today. I propose, in light of contemporary developments, that if conservatives wish to remain true to their historical concerns, they should recognize as their adversary the *Universal and Homogeneous State*. This term, coined by the Russo-French Left Hegelian, Alexandre Kojève and recently popularized in Francis Fukuyama's writings about the "end of history," is an artless expression, but it does communicate a compelling idea.[5] Kojève meant this term to describe the "rational" organization of society at the so-called end of history, when the *telos* of man's political evolution had been reached and all basic contradictions of social life had been dialectically resolved in "concrete freedom." The universal and homogeneous state has come to be when the ideas of universal liberty and equality are actualized in a democratic polity that protects individual rights and which features a well-regulated, but free, market economy.

This understanding of the end of political development relies on Kojève's peculiarly economic reading of Hegel's philosophy, but as we have seen, it finds resonance in many traditional conservative critiques of modernity—for what Hegel attempted to describe was the completion or the fulfillment of modernity. Concretely, Kojève at times identified the universal and homogeneous state with European social democracy, and he likely would have seen the recent Maastricht Treaty as a giant step in the direction of this historically inevitable end. At other times, however, he saw the end of history culminating in "the American Way of Life."[6] What this ambiguity illuminates is that from the standpoint of such radical critique, the differences between social democracy and American liberty are not as great as they may at first appear.[7] What is further captured by Kojève, and which has certainly been missed in much American thinking on the Left and Right, is that the central issue of modern political life is *not* one of collectivism versus individualism or central planning versus the market; in each of these cases the poles of opposition exist within the parameters already broadly set by liberal theories of legitimate sovereignty, which are themselves the matter of contention.[8] Most controversially to American conservatives, we can begin to see here that what is at issue in our confrontation with modernity is *not* state authority, considered an evil, against the freedom of the market, considered a good. What Kojève understood, what the older and especially the Continental conservatives understood, and what American conservatives in the 1990s must come to understand, is that the liberal state is a cooperative venture between a certain form of political association (democracy) and a certain form of economic association (the market economy)—both founded on an atomized and atomizing individualism. Together these act to "rationalize" society and persons in society. In this analysis, the market is not experienced positively as a realm of unique freedom, but instead is experienced as a realm where uniform laws of rational efficiency act to the end of *homogenization* and therefore *dehumanization*. Human goods such as community, solidarity, and indeed, even eccentricity, which are threatened in the process of homogenization, are what conservatives ultimately must be about "conserving."

THE HOMOGENIZING power of liberal market logic is revealed in contemporary political arguments that speak of the necessity of "competitiveness" in international markets. While it is often claimed that modern technological production has freed humanity from nature or necessity, the unrestrained market has itself become the realm of necessity that cannot be opposed. Here it is contended that we are *not free* to resist the demands of market efficiency. We are *not free* to seek such social goods as higher environmental standards. We are *not free* to defend settled ways of life by protecting older domestic industries. Owing to lower real wage levels brought on by a competitive labor market, women are *not free* to remain at home as mothers, regardless of the non-quantifiable harm to children. In short, we are *not free* to organize any of our social relations in a manner that will lead to production inefficiencies. Indeed, the free trade agreements of the last decade which seek to eliminate "non-tariff barriers to trade" aim to establish supra-state mechanisms that will prevent nations from freely choosing for any reason any path for their society that conflicts with the demands of the market; all peoples will be subjected to the "necessities" of efficient market competition. How ironic that the liberal partisans of individual "freedom" have led us to a situation where the demands of the market itself preempt or obscure free choice.

Of course, this loss of freedom is not the primary reason the conservative feels compelled to resist the universalization of market logic in the homogeneous liberal state. Rather, the conservative resists the view of man-as-consumer which is a central element of homogenization. Ultimately, the conservative's primary concern has *always* been the health of human souls. As the Southern Agrarians (perhaps the most genuine conservatives America has yet produced) tirelessly argued, the criterion by which to judge a social and political system is the kind of person that system tends to produce. To resist homogenization requires both attention to our social and political arrangements and attention to the health of our own souls, our own virtue. Conservatism is always a *personal* affair.

PERHAPS THE greatest difficulty in arguing against the universal and homogeneous state is that in doing so the conservative appears to be setting himself against "common sense" and defending the "indefensible." For the modern state is doubtless the most efficient producer of many human goods. In some sense then, the conservative must oppose efficiency— when it conflicts with the human scale of life he seeks. Because the liberalism that gives rise to the universal and homogeneous state presents itself as the efficient means to a way of life inherently more rational than any other, conservative defenders of traditional social arrangements are often driven into "illogicalities or insincerities." In their defense of established institutions, they often sound either nostalgically aesthetic or else they repair to "specious if ingenious" utilitarian arguments.[9] There may be no solution to this problem: a truly conservative society will undeniably have *less* of many human goods. But it will also have *more* of many others that are at present given scant attention in our homogeneous state.

Again, following Hegel, Kojève believed that the triumph of the universal and homogenous state was an historical inevitability; struggle against it was futile. He therefore spent the latter days of his life as a European Community bureaucrat, midwifing the emergence of that state in the E.C. But for those of us who believe there are no historical inevitabilities, it is precisely our growing awareness of the reality of the universal and homogeneous state that frees us to resist it. As it grew piecemeal, only a few (and many conservatives among them) could really sense the danger it presented; now that it grows to completion, its dehumanizing effects are more apparent. Purported inevitability should be no insuperable concern for an intellectual movement one of whose founders famously announced his intention to "stand athwart history yelling Stop."[10] What then is to be done?

AT THE level of our formal Constitution, American conservatives have traditionally resisted homogenization by their preference for states-rights and local political controls. As early as the American Constitutional ratifying debates, some Anti-Federalists voiced their fear that the new central government would "swallow-up [the states] in the grand vortex of general empire."[11] While the *Federalist Papers* reveal a clear intention to avoid "consolidated, national" government, one cannot deny that consolidation—homogenization—has in fact occurred, especially since the adoption of the Fourteenth Amendment and the subsequent "incorporation" of the provisions of the Bill of Rights against the states. The actual text of the Constitution limits the sphere of sovereignty of the federal government, leaving a sphere of sovereignty to the states. Of course if "sovereignty" is divided, it is not sovereignty at all, which may have been precisely the point. Part of the political task of conservatism in the 1990s will be to focus on restoring to the states a measure of their sovereignty, of providing them with Constitutional means to resist encroachments by the central government.

Also at the formal level of political life, conservatives should continue their critical attention to rights-discourse. For as we have seen, this is the lever by which the sovereignty of the liberal state has progressed at the expense of the various intermediate associations. There are good arguments to be made for abandoning or at least severely curtailing our use of "rights-talk."[12] Still, if Americans must speak in this idiom, at least for the time being, conservatives should make it their primary aim to investigate and elaborate upon the one right that is most often neglected in American political thought: the *freedom of association.* In legal philosophy today, this subject largely remains terra incognita, yet it may provide the first key for conservatives to roll back the homogeneous state.

Beyond the formal structure of the state, there are new challenges and new opportunities to reconceive our basic institutions in ways that might help them to resist the twin homogenizing powers of the liberal state and the liberal market. Here conservatives can forge surprising new alliances with those who share many of their concerns.[13] Conservatives must search for creative ways to protect complex, historically evolved structures of civil society and indeed, to promote the renewed formation of a "thick" associational life in all its diversity. Intellectual ferment regarding school vouchers and other attempts to extricate the state from the function of educating children represent the most sustained effort to date to *reclaim* one realm of human life from homogenization.[14] Attempts to "empower" families (but not individuals) also demonstrate awareness of the problem of the universal and homogeneous state.

Contrary to popular belief, conservatism always requires creativity, for it only arises when customs are already under attack and can thus no longer be maintained unselfconsciously. One example implied by the Southern Agrarians might suggest how a creative logic of resistance against homogenization can be extended into the world of business. The Agrarians believed that private property was good because of the sense of independence and responsibility it elicited from persons who owned property. But corporate or "abstract" property-ownership does not seem

to have this effect. Thus, one conservative reform might be a reconsideration of the legal status of the limited liability corporation, which systematically biases the economy in favor of large and impersonal corporate property over *proprietary* business concerns. Such a scheme might well be less efficient at the production of material goods, but its effect would also be profoundly humanizing. Are we willing to pay such a price?

This last question is crucial, for seeking changes in public policy so that a humane associational life may flourish will come to naught if we do not ourselves seek in our own local contexts to "live well" together, to build a common life within our families and with our neighbors that might be strong enough to resist homogenization. This may require some sacrifices; it will require us to say "no" to some of the temptations of the market and the state. Yet only if our families, churches, and other associations *mean* something to us, indeed become *part of* us, will a defense of them in public policy be plausible. Living "conservatively"—living generously within our concrete contexts—always has priority over any political or ideological project.

A FEW words about the practical impact of these thoughts on the situation in the universities may be in order. How does one resist homogenization within this sphere of human life—where homogenization progresses by an attempted uniform "politicization" of the whole of life?

At the theoretical level, there is a great irony to campus politics, for the agents of homogenization are those who claim to speak for "diversity." Yet Russell Kirk almost half a century ago noted aptly that one of the central canons of *conservative* thought is "affection for the proliferating variety and mystery of human existence, as opposed to the narrowing uniformity, egalitarianism, and utilitarian aims of most radical systems."[15] Conservatives thus must recapture the rhetoric of diversity and reveal the uniformity which is *really* central for our contemporary diversity-mongers. For the ideology of diversity touts its openness to human "difference," but only after such difference has been reduced to the realm of moral *in*difference. In which case, the "difference" makes no more difference than the clothes we wear. Diversity here equals homogenization to the level of a meaningless consumer-identity or brand-loyalty. The conservative alternative surely must be a civil engagement of differences that really do matter.

Practically speaking, the touchstone of conservative student activism in the 1980s was the independent campus newspaper. Because of the hyper-politicization of the universities, these newspapers themselves became "the issue," and students responded to administrative pressures with appeals to their "rights," namely, freedom of speech. This demonstrates a basic confusion. After all, are not the universities intermediate associations that in principle should be free from the rules of mere right which bind the political contract? Can they not have higher standards of association than those of the liberal state? And is not the attempt to revive the personalist role of *in loco parentis* to be applauded, even if we are dismayed on occasion by its politicized practice?

To discern a principled conservative stance here, two levels of reflection must be distinguished. In the case of the smaller, and especially the sectarian, colleges, it seems there is the possibility of building a genuine experience of community, a true *civitas,* at the level of the college. Such a self-conscious community might be able to resist pressures for homogenization *from without.* In such cases, while we may not like the kind of *civitas* that emerges, conservatives should nonetheless applaud movements to recover the role of *in loco parentis,* and indeed, should help foster the particular traditions and exclusivities of these bodies. If this position will acquiesce in the unimpeded growth of certain bastions of political correctness—and many can be named—it will also protect the occasional exceptional community such as Sewanee or VMI. We all have an interest in the flourishing of *institutional* diversity. Not every college should be a St. John's, but likewise, not every college should be an Oberlin: we all benefit from living in a society that sports both a Wabash and a Wesleyan.

In the case of the large secular universities, however, which seem always to be administered by those who think it their role to advance the cause of the universal and homogeneous state, the conservative task is to work toward developing smaller bodies on campus to resist homogenization *from within.* In these cases, the university itself has become the agent of homogenization, and thus a resistant *civitas* must emerge on a smaller scale. Building such communities on campus seems even more pressing a task than the journalism of the 1980s, and thinking through how to accomplish this should consume much student energy in the 1990s.

For it has been in the large universities where the most invasive and striking efforts have been made to achieve a "total community," a complete and homogenizing control of all spheres of student life. While much has been written about the conflict over the curriculum, the politicization of the whole of student life has received insufficient attention. In the dormitories, resident assistants promote a uniform left-liberal ideology in everyday social interaction. Active measures have been brought against fraternities and other student societies if they discriminate on the basis of sex or if they have any religious content to their initiation ceremonies: it is said that to be "recognized" by the university, all associations must be "equally open" to all, which is to say, all associations must be the same. Again in the dormitories, a drive to homogenization is even evident in the "randomization" of housing assignments. This policy prevents dormitories from developing particular characters—as places for athletes or pre-meds or engineers, etc. Such "variety," it seems, would be bad for "diversity." Randomization strips students of their *freedom of association* in the name of what can only be called "uniform diversity."

In the face of such homogenizing pressures, it appears that conservatives can play their most constructive role on campus by building and supporting *para-university institutions,*[16] with independent property, income, and leadership. Models for such associations exist: fraternities, dining clubs, literary societies, interest-oriented group houses, religious houses, independent "think tanks." In each case, a common life develops which, being independent of the control of the central authority, can be uniquely resistant to homogenization. Such groups should positively revel in their peculiarity, and conservatives should offer support in helping them retain or regain their independence.

This growth of a rich array of independent structures around major American universities reflects in microcosm the conservative vision of society generally. Such communities would not necessarily be "political," but in our time, and especially in the universities, the most subversive

political act is to refuse to become politicized. If conservatism is about resistance to the universal and homogeneous state, it is also, consequentially, the negation of ideology.

Notes

1. New York: Basic Books, 1976.
2. See, for example, Alasdair MacIntyre, *Whose Justice? Which Rationality?* (Notre Dame, IN: Univ. of Notre Dame Press, 1988). The extent to which traditionalist concerns overlap with so-called postmodern critical theory becomes readily apparent in the introduction of Stephen K. White's *Political Theory and Postmodernism* (Cambridge: Cambridge Univ. Press, 1991).
3. Panajotis Kondyles, *Konservativismus* (Stuttgart: Klett-Cotta, 1986). This fine study deserves to be translated into English.
4. Minneapolis, Univ. of Minnesota Press, 1986.
5. Alexandre Kojève, *Introduction to the Reading of Hegel: Lectures on the* Phenomenology of Spirit, Allan Bloom, ed. (Ithaca, NY: Cornell Univ. Press, 1997, 1980).
6. In a vein remarkably similar to that of Pope John Paul's oft-criticized 1987 encyclical, *Solicitudo Rei Socialis,* Kojève argued that Soviet communism and "the American Way of Life" were really two sides of one coin, both "materialist/sensualist" in their account of the highest things and therefore "posthistorical" or posthuman. They differed only in the technique offered for achieving these agreed-upon ends.
7. While not as great, they are by no means trivial.
8. As early as the 1950s and from a perspective clearly different from that of Kojève, John Courtney Murray, S.J., saw that the conflict between individualism and collectivism was an intramural and ultimately futile debate within modernity, and that the parameters of debate themselves needed to be critiqued from outside. See *We Hold These Truths: Catholic Reflections on the American Proposition* (New York: Sheed & Ward, 1960).

9. John Casey, "Tradition and Authority," in Maurice Cowling, ed., *Conservative Essays* (London: Cassell, Ltd., 1978), 85.

10. William F. Buckley Jr., "Publisher's Statement," *National Review* 1 (November 19, 1955), 5.

11. "Address of the Pennsylvania Minority" in Herbert J. Storing, ed., *The Anti-Federalist* (Chicago, Univ. of Chicago Press, 1985), 212.

12. A very temperate and judicious appeal for enriching our political dialogue is Mary Ann Glendon's *Rights Talk: The Impoverishment of Political Discourse* (New York: The Free Press, 1991).

13. "The Canadian philosopher Charles Taylor comes to mind, as do the so-called "communitarians," who critiqued liberalism very forcefully in the 1980s.

14. The proposal for school vouchers is seen by some as a Trojan Horse, for wherever government money goes, there goes government control. Making vouchers universal might therefore end the independence of private schools, as the Hillsdale College case makes plain. How can we achieve the admitted good of universal education while avoiding homogenization? This is probably the central problem which should now receive creative conservative attention.

15. Russell Kirk, *The Conservative Mind* (Washington: Regnery Books, 1953, 1986), 8.

16. While many Americans consider it faintly disloyal to direct their financial support to institutions other than their alma mater, the great English universities simply are loose confederations of independent institutions which together operate "as if" they were a unitary university. Only in America is it thought that the central administration must be in control of the whole.

Robert Nisbet

STILL QUESTING

VOL. 29, NO. 1, 1993

In the retrospect of forty years I can see my book, *The Quest for Community* (first published by Oxford University Press in 1953; currently available from ICS Press, San Francisco), as one of the harbingers of what would become by the end of the 1950s a full-fledged renascence of conservatism. There had been authentic and forthright individual conservatives before the '50s; among them Albert Jay Nock, H. L. Mencken, Irving Babbitt, and Paul Elmer More. But conservatism had never before the 1950s flourished as an intellectual movement as it has since that decade.

My book came out at the very beginning of 1953, as did Russell Kirk's *Conservative Mind*. Although I had become increasingly conservative in my politics, I did not think of *The Quest for Community* as a conservative treatise; not, at least, while I was writing it. If I had been pressed to categorize it ideologically I suppose I would have responded: "neoliberal" or "political pluralist."

On the other hand I was not taken aback when *The Quest* began to be reviewed or otherwise commented on by its identification as conservative. After all, I had written my Ph.D. dissertation a decade earlier on the French conservatives of the nineteenth century and their influence on the social science—and on me, I should add.

Spurring my own gradual conversion to conservatism was the presence in this country and also England of individuals (I think of Malcolm Muggeridge and, in France, Jacques Ellul as examples) undergoing similar ascents to conservatism. There were some spectacular conversions in the West of intellectuals and scholars, once fervid Marxists, who before, during, and especially after World War II joined the ranks of conservatives.

In various ways America became a more conservative nation after the war. The temper of the Depression 1930s was gone. What the New Deal had failed to do, that is, defeat the Depression, the war had done. In 1944, Hayek published his *Road to Serfdom*, a book that drew the attention of tens of thousands of Americans. Hayek always denied that he was a conservative—preferring the identity of a classical liberal—but his book was nevertheless solid conservatism.

Hayek, whose book came out in 1944,

may well be called the morning star of America's oncoming conservatism. But if not, there is Richard Weaver who published his *Ideas Have Consequences* in 1948 and drew surprisingly good reviews even in the liberal press.

In 1950, Lionel Trilling, in an essay directed primarily to the excoriation of the political and cultural left, noted that while there seemed to be no want of conservatives among the ordinary people in the U.S., there was a conspicuous absence of conservatives among the best and the brightest of intellectuals. There was, Trilling said, no particularly luminous body of thought identifiable as conservative in the ranks of the well-educated. Trilling's words could almost be likened to a clarion call, for in the brief period 1950–53 a freshet of books made its appearance which was unmistakably conservative in character. Most of them were of course in preparation when Trilling wrote. But the proximity was dramatic. To the best of my knowledge Trilling never cast himself as a conservative or any offshoot of conservatism such as neoconservatism. But his writings, particularly his late ones, were unambiguous in their criticisms of the left.

The freshet of 1950–53 that I referred to included the following: Russell Kirk's immensely influential *Conservative Mind*, Eric Voegelin's *New Science of Politics*, William F. Buckley's *God and Man at Yale*, to be shortly followed by his journal, *National Review*, Gertrude Himmelfarb's brilliant book on the English historian Lord Acton, John Hallowell's *Moral Foundations of Democracy*, Daniel Boorstin's *Genius of American Politics*, and, finally, still within the three year freshet, my own *Quest for Community*. Before the decade of the 1950s ended *Modern Age* had been founded, and such notable scholars as

Hugh Kenner, Cleanth Brooks, Wilhelm Röpke, and James Burnham were widely known conservatives.

My *Quest for Community* was published, as I have said, at the beginning of 1953, a bit too early perhaps to catch some of the favorable vibrations of the developing conservative community. The book was, from the beginning until the Student Revolution of the 1960s, a slow burner. I complaineth not. There was a splendid review by Russell Kirk whom I had not yet met, some excellent newspaper reviews, chiefly in the West and Midwest, and congratulatory letters from, among other notables, T. S. Eliot and Reinhold Niebuhr. I felt thoroughly rewarded for the four years of very hard work I had put into the book, the while carrying a substantial teaching load at Berkeley.

The real success of *Quest* commenced with the Student Revolution by the New Left, self styled, and the issuance of *Quest* as a paperback by Oxford. Oddly and amusingly, the book reached almost cult-book proportions in the 1960s on both the left and the right, the latter, of course, in the lead. I am still today unsure what the book's attraction was to the New Left, or some of it at least. Suffice it to say that they bought it and read it. I used to say that they bought it and never got beyond the title. But the longer I thought about it, the more I became aware that the Student Revolution's primary enemy was liberals. Conservatives they ignored or suffered. Throughout the 1960s, when the hassling of faculty and administration reached its height, I was never bothered, though my conservatism was well known on the campus. In later years I queried other academic conservatives and discovered that almost without exception they had enjoyed the same fortune I had. It was liberal faculty (the more noted the better thought the New Left) and nationally visible deans and presidents who suffered the most from the New Left and its revolution.

Contributing significantly to the conservative renascence of the 1950s was the restoration to proper status of Alexis Tocqueville and Edmund Burke. For years both had been in the doldrums, not only in this country, but also in England and France. What the concrete forces were that gave them once again heroic status, I don't know. Before I went into the army in 1943 I had questioned a few publishing representatives about their possible willingness to press for a new edition of Tocqueville. There was little interest. I should have talked instead with Alfred A. Knopf. For when I came back to the campus after the war, there was a handsome, boxed, two volume edition edited by Phillips Bradley, published by Knopf, to be found in every bookstore. What a thrill! Over faculty club lunch tables one heard Tocqueville, by the 1950s, referred to as often as Marx. Burke enjoyed a restoration nearly as dramatic, thanks in very considerable part to Russell Kirk's *Conservative Mind.*

Having at hand the works of the two greatest conservatives of the eighteenth and nineteenth centuries now readily available, was bound to give the renascent conservative in academe a great boost. Both titans are still in full glory. As I said, I wrote *The Quest* with the feeling that both Burke and Tocqueville were near at hand.

I HAVE occasionally been asked what the essential sources were of *The Quest for Community.* Like or dislike the book's arguments, concepts such as "intermediate associations," the perpetual tensions between state and family, and individualism conceived as social fragmentations were not run-of-the-mill ideas in America. In Germany and France, yes, but the United States, no.

The initial enlightenment on my part came out of a seminar on Roman Law that I took as a graduate student at Berkeley in the late 1930s. There in the Roman Law texts themselves, it was possible (with the very learned professor as guide) to see the history of Rome, from the Republic to Empire, as, among other things, a death struggle between the family, powerful in the Republic, and the state or public power that destroyed the Republic and in the process put the family in permanent bondage to the state. The law of corporations, as the Roman lawyers called it, involved the absorption by the imperial state of virtually all associations, however traditional or voluntary.

A second source in my own thinking was Otto von Gierke's monumental study of intermediate associations during and after the Middle Ages. His prose and use of the script typography were all but impenetrable, but translations of key parts by F. W. Maitland and Ernest Barker came to my rescue. From Gierke's huge work it is possible to see vividly the clash between family and state, and the pulverizing impact of the modern Western state on the family and all other intermediate groups. From Gierke it was an easy walk to the texts of Hobbes, Locke, and Rousseau and their glorification of the unitary state at the expense of pluralistic society.

All the while I was reading these books and assimilating the theory of the unitary versus the pluralist state, I was inevitably reacting to FDR and his New Deal, by far the largest single reform or set of reforms since the American Revolution. I began as an ardent undergraduate Berkeley supporter of the New Deal. But by the late 1930s, in FDR's second term, my support of 1932 and 1936 turned sharply to alienation. It seemed to me then, as it still does today, that the New Deal had immersed itself in an impossible combination of political centralization and of administrative bureaucracy.

Studies by Haberler at Harvard and Garraty at Columbia have shown conclusively that the New Deal, considered as an instrument to fight and defeat the Depression, was inferior to approaches taken by England and Germany—the latter considered up to 1938 when Hitler began his rearmament program. With the sharp dip in 1937–38, the U.S. economy was as badly off as it had been in 1932. America didn't end the Depression until it went to war in 1941.

But the New Deal left its mark on governmental consciousness. The increase in federal bureaucracy and in the national debt has gone on almost uninterruptedly since 1932. It is almost as if centralization and bureaucracy have lives of their own, independent of the convictions of the occupants of the White House and Congress. The consensus during the war was that every bit of the structural apparatus of the wartime home front would be razed and scrapped, as had been the case after World War I. We couldn't have been more wrong. Most efforts after 1945 went into the creation of rhetorical justifications for the continuance in the postwar of the bewildering network of agencies, bureaus, and federal institutes. No matter what the spoken philosophy of government by a new president or congressman, we now wearily and jadedly take it for granted that the national debt and the budget deficit will, like the river Jordan, roll on and on. I believe Reagan to have been utterly honest in his declarations on policy and direction before he became president. But both national debt and deficit increased markedly during his two terms of office.

Now we are at it all over again, with this, malign difference. More and more we are hearing from federal government and from the clerisy of power that hangs on to Washington the magic words "National Community." Governor Cuomo gave the words and thoughts a mighty push a few years ago when he electrified his national convention audience with a dozen or more references to the family, but meaning in each utterance the *national family*. Never mind the plight of actual families in certain sections of the country. Merely mesmerize the populace with heart-wrenching appeals to a national community—or wagon train, or national family.

It should be the prime business of any serious conservative party or other faction to expose the fraudulence of such a phrase as "national community." Do we dare suppose that any actual national community, with headquarters of course in Washington, D.C., might have in its cabinet a Secretary of Love and another of Intimacy? It is, I repeat, the serious business of any conservative group to recognize "national community" for what it is and to oppose it at every turn. The favorite strategy of proponents of national community is to draw up a purportedly heart-rending account of the disappearance of all the traditional communities such as kinship, neighborhood, church, and voluntary association of every kind, and then with majestic finality declare the national community to be our only salvation.

The offer of "individualism" as the logical alternative to national community is, I have to stress, misconceived. It wasn't lone individuals who developed this country from one coast to the other. It was groups, meaning neighborhoods, extended families, and voluntary associations that, with log- and quilt-bees of every kind did the work of building schools, churches, and other community enterprises. In any event, a great deal of what we are likely to call "individualism" is the rubble left by dislocated and atomized communities.

I AM not, I trust, preaching anarchism. A nation needs a strong government, local and central. There are necessities in our lives simply inconceivable apart from the existence of a strong central government. Military defense is only the start. It is equally true, and today more pertinent, even urgent, that it is the function of government to shore up, to reinforce, and otherwise nurture the natural communities in society. For each of these is at once a psychological support to the individual and, if genuinely recognized by the state, a bulwark against a plague of bureaucracy.

George Bush ennobled himself a few years ago when he held up the vision of a "nation of communities, of thousands of ethnic, religious, social, business, labor union, neighborhood, regional, and other organizations, all of them varied, voluntary, and unique." Bush's words are worthy of being put beside Edmund Burke's famous defense (against French Revolutionary centralization and state-omnicompetence) of what he called the "smaller patriotisms" and the "little platoons."

Let me repeat, and conclude here, that a conservative party (or other group) has a double task confronting it. The first is to work tirelessly toward the diminution of the centralized, omnicompetent, and unitary state with its ever-soaring debt and deficit. The second and equally important task is that of protecting, reinforcing, nurturing where necessary the varied groups and associations which form the true building blocks of the social order. To these two ends I am bound to believe in the continuing relevance of *The Quest for Community*.

Erik von Kuehnelt-Leddihn

LIBERALISM IN AMERICA

VOL. 33, NO. 1, 1997

When words lose their meaning, peoples lose their liberty.—Confucius

In spite of local and temporal differences, the authentic meaning of liberalism is understood correctly throughout the world, with the possible exception of contemporary America.

Whereas "democracy" answers the question: "*Who* should rule?" and answers that it is directly or indirectly the majority of politically equal citizens, liberalism answers the question: "*How* should government be exercised?" Whatever the form of government, the exercise of power should not prevent citizens from enjoying the greatest amount of liberty compatible with the Common Good. (Not even the most celebrated liberal has the right to drive 100 miles per hour through a village.)

Democracy can be liberal or illiberal, but while an absolute monarchy cannot be democratic, it can be liberal. The monarchy of Louis XIV, who *allegedly* said "I am the State," was in many ways far more liberal than a number of modern democracies. He could not require an annual income tax or conscript his subjects for military service, nor could he issue a law banning champagne from dinner tables. Conversely, many of the horrors of the French Revolution were democratic (but not liberal).

During the nineteenth and twentieth centuries a gradual and problematic synthesis of democracy and liberalism took place. Since its beginning, this union suffered from the democratic principle of equality, the antithesis of liberty. We are either free *or* equal since equality is "unnatural" and can only be realized by artificial, if not repressive, measures. (Think of a garden hedge. How can an equal height be achieved? Only by constant clipping!) After all, William Dean Howells called "Liberty and Inequality" the two great American ideals, and Charles Beard insisted that the Founding Fathers loathed democracy more than Original Sin. Furthermore, the word democracy appears neither in the Declaration of Independence, nor in the Constitution.

Still, the democratic-liberal synthesis created endless confusion in the minds of many people and often caused them to confuse freedom with equality, or equality with freedom. The confiscation of a periodical, for instance, is often denounced as "undemocratic," although it is quite possible that the majority of citizens were in favor of its termination. A measure like this, however, is certainly illiberal.

The term "liberal" in the political sense originates from Spanish. The supporters of the 1812 Constitution of Cadiz called themselves *liberales* and their opponents *serviles*. In 1816, Southey first used this term in English (with its Spanish spelling), while Sir Walter Scott used the French version and wrote about the *libéraux*. This should not be in the least surprising to those familiar with Spaniards who are basically liberal (and in their excess anarchical). George Ticknor, who visited Spain in 1816, wrote to his father Elisha that "this is the freest country in the world." In Britain, after the English parliamentary reform in 1832, the Whigs assumed the "liberal" label while the Tories adopted the term "conservative." Here the reader should be reminded that the American War of Independence was fought under the Whiggish banner and that Loyalists were frequently called "Tories." Yet Edmund Burke was himself a Whig and a conservative at the same time. Similarly, the liberal Chateaubriand coined the term "conservative."

There are four genuine liberalisms that have freedom as their ideal. The first group I call "Preliberals," like Adam Smith and Burke. The second group, which includes Alexis Tocqueville, Montalembert, and Lord Acton, I call "Early Liberals." These noblemen had few economic interests. Then came the "Old Liberals," who were indeed economically committed, yet somewhat "anticlerical," and inclined to flirt with philosophical relativism. These include founders of the so-called Austrian School of Economics, such as Carl Meyer and Eugen von Böhm-Bawerk, with Ludwig von Mises being the last modern representative. Finally, the more modern

"Neo-Liberals" are those who formed the Mont Pélerin Society in 1961. The outstanding representatives of this school were Wilhelm Röpke and Alexander Rüstow. It should be mentioned here that several of the most prominent liberals were rather skeptical about democracy because they felt that majority rule could elect real tyrants to power.

HOW DID the genuine meaning of liberalism become so misunderstood in the United States? Many other terms have become misnomers in the U.S., such as "Middle East" for the Near East, and "extreme Right" for the National Socialists (who prided themselves for being the German Left). We see "humanism" equated with atheism (although it was a profoundly Catholic movement during the Renaissance against which the Reformers protested), or "Orientals" identified with people from the Far East. Just as a variety of reasons can be offered to explain these errors, so too can reasons be given why a certain leftist ideology in the United States had been named "liberalism" by supporters and enemies alike. There is a history to it and it is a fairly recent one.

It began during the Roosevelt presidency when America experienced a major onslaught of leftism. The time was propitious: a huge economic crisis was underway, causing real misery to grip the masses. People expected relief from the government, but since Americans are basically "conservative" (in the etymological sense of the word), socialism could not be promoted as "unmasked." It was, and still is, a "bad" word. (On the European continent the liberals are considered to be the archenemies of socialism and are usually seated in the parliaments on the Right.) The average American does not like to be an extremist, and a sentence like "Only extremes are bearable," uttered by Anatole France, is alien to him. So, the "liberal" label had to replace the socialist one. It was "handy" and could well be adopted by artists and intellectuals and by persons of means who did not want to look ridiculous by using a Marxist trade mark.

All Americans love freedom, or at least pay lip-service to it, so the term "liberal" seemed attractive, while the country's genuine liberals neither had the will nor the organization to defend it. At the beginning of World War II, the *American Mercury,* then under the editorship of that wonderful man, Eugene Lyons, published a series of "Creeds." There was the creed of a conservative, a reactionary, a socialist, an "old fashioned" and a new liberal. In these essays, one could clearly trace the rupture. Of course, it also must be admitted that honest, though not very bright, liberals drifted leftward. Since freedom, openness of mind, generosity, and a certain impartiality characterizes the genuine liberal outlook, liberalism's "house" had all its doors and windows open so that the winds blowing from the outside could enter. At the time, practically all the prevailing "winds" had a leftist, a Marxist, a "libertine," and certainly anti-conservative character. In a sense, the metamorphosis was inevitable.

The real American liberals went in several directions. A great many became conservatives (thus adding to the complexities of the conservative camp); others, frightened by the conservative label, and having sacrificed their good old name on the altar of public consent, called themselves "libertarians." When I wear my Adam Smith necktie, I tell my European friends it is considered a "conservative" tie in America. They usually respond with utter bewilderment. "Adam Smith, a conservative?" they say, incredu-

lous that this most classical of liberals is considered by many Americans to be a conservative.

What is the basic content of American liberalism? It is a synthesis of many different ideas, some having American and British roots. A review of these elements brings to mind Proudhon, who said that there is always a theological background to all political problems. American "liberalism" is very definitely not theistic and not even deistic in character. Yet this liberalism is certainly a manifestation of anthropolatry, of a "worship of man." There is, of course, a certain connection between American "populism," the programmatic belief in "WE, the People," and the optimistic "belief in man."

I FIRST encountered Americans in 1930 at the age of twenty-one when I spent the summer in the Soviet Union. So many of these tourists and *inospyetsy* ("foreign specialists") came fully prepared to adore the Soviet Union and could not really see what they saw. Faith had completely blinded them.

Yet there were some uniquely American angles to this enthusiasm. Empathy for the Soviet system was expressed despite the incredible squalor, dirt, stench, the general misery and disorganization of almost everything. The driving psychological force behind these American "fellow travelers" was their "futurism," which brings to mind the words of Lincoln Steffens, "I have seen the future and it works!"

One visited hospitals, schools, even a number of prisons (all make-believe). There were obviously no class differences, all were "equal," illiteracy was eliminated, and criminals were rehabilitated. Waiters were even prevented from taking "humiliating" tips (as notices exhorted). Several visitors asked the Soviets how free people really lived. To dispel any criticism, the enthusiast could reply that before 1917 everything was infinitely worse: for instance, there had been "serfdom" (actually abolished two years before American slavery), "racism" (totally absent), "clericalism" (unknown). Their historic ignorance notwithstanding, these mostly "liberal" Americans I met were extremely nice people, much nicer than my own Europeans.

Of course, not all American "liberals" were devotees of Red Russia. A great many were devotees of Red China and they were "building" on an old Sinophile American tradition. We found the apogee of this "complex" in the Student Revolt of 1968 when fanatic youngsters praised Mao's *Little Red Book* which contained the tritest of trite phrases. Today we realize that the Cultural Revolution was infinitely worse than anything the Bolsheviks perpetrated, and competes successfully in nightmarish horrors with the French Revolution and the misdeeds of the Vietcong and the Khmer Rouge. In China's Quangxi Province the people were forced to eat the corpses of the butchered "class enemies," and those who did not comply were immediately suspect.

AMERICAN LIBERALISM is not a closed ideology like Marxism-Leninism or National Socialism, but a very mixed bag with a number of internal contradictions. It is like a compendium of nearly every nonsense that we in the West have produced since the Enlightenment and the French Revolution. In spite of its lack of patriotism it has become part of the American scene, deriving advantage here and there from certain items of American folklore. It can do this because of its intellectual duplicity, which combines a masked elitism with a bogus populism.

American liberalism exalts the proverbial three men sitting on cracker barrels in the general store talking politics, but at the same time hides the arrogant contempt the half educated have for the common sense of simple people. What are the components of this "mixed bag"? Nearly nothing from the Founding Fathers, but a great deal from European democracy, a bit of Marxism, a few items from anarcho-liberalism, and several loans from fashionable trends: philosophic relativism, hedonism, totalitarianism. To thinking persons these internal oppositions might cause concern, but most people tend to *feel* rather than think. And to many, the approach of American liberalism is agreeable: it is optimistic and carries many promises. Yet unlike a clever pagan existentialism, such as that of Sartre, who told us that life is absurd and that the history of every person is a history of failure, contemporary liberalism is simply ignorant. It ignores the biblical message that "the mind of every human being from childhood onward is directed towards evil" (Genesis 8:21).

And just like an ignorant person, this liberalism is stubborn and does not learn from past mistakes or from history. In spite of its relativism, it is highly aggressive and, in defiance of pleas for tolerance, it is itself extremely intolerant, alternating savage attacks with silent disregard.

The first big challenge posed to American liberalism came from the broadly popular National Socialist totalitarian dictatorship. Germany's military alliance with the Soviet Union and the Fall of Paris in June, 1940, inspired the compilation of a "liberal" manifesto entitled, significantly, *The City of Man*. In its pages, the worship of man reached a zenith. The mostly American authors proposed to judge and license the various religions according to their relationship to democracy. We can also read the following statement: "Democracy is nothing more and nothing less than humanism in theocracy and rational theocracy is universal humanism."

Yet the democratism of these liberals always causes them dilemmas. Should they not have supported the rule of the Shah in order to favor the popular rule of the mullahs in Iran? Should they not support the present military dictatorship in Algeria against a regime of Fundamentalists based on democratic majority rule? (Hardly any true-blooded American liberal would readily admit that the temporary military dictatorships of Franco and Pinochet were preferable to a red takeover.)

"Progress" is written large in America. Ever since its independence, the United States has seen a great deal of progress. The population has increased phenomenally, people live longer, literacy has multiplied, obnoxious laws have been abolished, travel is more frequent, and huge advances in science and technology surpass that of other nations. Nevertheless, the European achievements of past centuries that have survived are a reminder that civilization might have progressed, but culture has taken a setback. (The art museums and architecture show this very visibly.)

THE AMERICAN liberal attitude towards religion is complex. There are atheistic liberals who hold dogmatically to the conviction that all religion is hokum and potentially dangerous to human freedom, democracy, equality, progress, and sanity. There are agnostic liberals who reserve judgment, while there are others who think religion is a human weakness that ought to be respected. In religious conversation this third group of liberals will assume a solemn expression, a tremor

creeps into their voice and they make a real effort to appear immensely tolerant and "understanding." There are many others who are determined to "liberalize" their religion; even to use it as a prop to advance the cause of welfare statism, pacifism, animal rights, feminism, and every other modern political nostrum.

To most American liberals, however, religious "fundamentalism" is the natural enemy. The American liberal does not like "dogmas," "commandments" nor, naturally, solid foundations. Nothing for him is black or white, only different shades of gray. Religions should be respected if people sincerely believe in them, he says. But what about other convictions like the thugs of India who waylaid travelers and garroted them in front of a statue of Kali? (They became victims of British colonialism that exterminated these nice people.) Or consider, for instance, the "sincere" political convictions of Nazis who believe in the Brown Creed?

When necessary, as noted above, liberals will turn to folklore to advance their agenda. Take Jefferson's "Wall of Separation" letter, which is used to read religion out of American public life. For instance, they ignore the fact that the First Amendment merely prohibits the "establishment" of a church on the federal, and not on the state, level. There were in fact privileged state churches in America into the nineteenth century, and religious disqualifications into the 1870s. Yet one of the latest and finest victories of American liberalism was the prohibition of public Christmas carol singing in Vienna, Virginia.

TO REACH the masses, American liberals have not only made a concerted effort to disintegrate or manipulate churches, but also to bring education and the mass media under their influence. Here their efforts began some time ago, even well before the term "liberal" was debased. I remember asking a professor of a prestigious university whether he was active in its department of education. He answered with an emphatic "No!": "This is the place where they throw false pearls to real swine." In all too many high schools, colleges, and universities, real efforts are being made to wage war against the religiously inspired values of our civilization. The current assault against "Eurocentrism" is motivated by this hostility toward Western values.

To make matters worse, not only the content but also the quality of education has been sacrificed at the altar of egalitarianism. Although high school students receive highly inadequate instruction, they are permitted to attend college. Professors have no social prestige, so the most "famous" universities are, in fact, financially elitist, a situation unknown on the European continent. (In old Russia, three quarters of the university students paid no tuition.) Beginning at age fourteen, students can choose their subjects up to graduate school. And the professors, poorly paid with little security, tend "sociologically" to embrace contemporary "liberalism"—a situation once well analyzed by Ludwig von Mises (who had difficulties at New York University). Most universities are dominated by American liberalism.

Unfortunately, even conservative individuals and foundations have made few efforts to remedy that situation. Regrettably, there exists in the United States, except among outspoken conservatives, a certain awe if not respect for these liberals. They are seen as "modern," "enlightened," and "progressive," and they might have a lien on the future. Even many parents say: "Let us be broadminded and give the kids a chance to get exposed to new ideas in these prestigious places of learning."

On the wall of one American college there appear the words of Ralph Waldo Emerson: "We are of different opinions at different hours, but we always may be said to be at heart on the side of truth." This sounds very nice, but would that be the right guideline in a dialogue with a Stalinist, or a supporter of Pol Pot? One thing is certain: polite doubt will not save this world.

THE AMERICAN liberal infiltration of the mass media was extremely easy, needing no "conspiracy." These American liberals were able to win over with ease their colleagues in journalism because they held what Tocqueville called *des fausses idées claires,* clear but false ideas. Error can easily appear as "commonsense." Yet truth, as a rule, is not at all simple but very complex.

With the mass media it is difficult to raise the level of discourse to avoid expressing ideas that coincide with popular sentiments and folkloric imagery. Thus, during (and after) World War II, National Socialism was portrayed as an extreme rightwing movement of aristocrats, big landowners, monarchists, industrialists, and bankers against the working class and the little people. To America's man-in-the-street, Hitler was merely a paper tiger and a "stooge." This erroneous view, originating from Marxist theory, was adopted by American occupation forces. Fearing a resurgence of Nazism, applicants for public office in American occupation zones were required to fill out a questionnaire that asked whether one of their four grandparents belonged to the nobility. Vice President Henry C. Wallace declared a "Century of the Common Man" following the Soviet defeat of Nazi Germany, but in fact this began with Woodrow Wilson in 1918. Had Hitler possessed a sense of humor, he would have erected a giant statue of Wilson right in front of Munich's Brown House.

In domestic and foreign affairs, there is hardly an issue in which American liberals have not misled their country. They are touchy and thin-skinned people who want to lead mankind toward a heavenly future, absent of injustice and social misery. While Christians place their hopes in the beyond, believing this world will always be a vale of tears, liberals seek to establish paradise on earth through human effort.

To prepare the way, these liberals have introduced politically correct language to avoid disagreements and hurt feelings. For example, by marrying Anne I am discriminating against Mary; by buying a copy of the *Washington Times,* I am discriminating against the *Washington Post.* Discrimination is a law of life. We must simply choose between just and unjust discrimination.

WHERE DO we find the most dynamic American liberal assault today? Surely not in the field of economics, when even the most socialistic European governments are trying to auction off state enterprises. No, the radical nature of American liberalism leads it to affect the very roots of life that are found in human sexuality. It wants to hit us below the belt, to undermine and pervert the relationship between the genders, human sexuality, and the family which is the *nervus rerum.* If everything else is to be submitted to the omnipotent state, it is argued, there should at least be sexual "freedom." And yet, here is where discipline is most necessary.

One need not be a Freudian to understand its importance in human relations.

He who "devalues" the family by promoting promiscuity and perversion devalues the very fabric of society. He who denies the biological differences of men and women, and the unique roles each must fill, rebels against nature. The Soviets boasted that the equality of the genders in their realm was perfect since women were permitted to work in coal mines. In the United States, too, women are now accepted as combatants in the armed forces as equally as men are.

Another danger lurks in the emancipation of sexual deviations. Our sexuality is of a rather "plastic" nature—even in its normal course. For instance, a male will more easily fall in love with an extremely slender girl, if thinness is the fashion, or with one of opposite bodily qualities, as in the fashion of Rubens's age, if that is the day's trend. Perversions or other forms of immorality often become fashions and can destroy nations. For instance, generations of fatherless children from single mothers will likely lead to social perdition.

Contemporary liberalism reveals its hedonistic character with the mass murder of the unborn. What we have in the West is Childermass of "unwanted life," similar to the practices of National and International Socialism in Europe and East Asia. What did Nicolas Gomez Davila, the brightest thinker on the Right, tell us? "The cult of man must be celebrated with human sacrifices." As a result, pregnant women no longer walk as cradles but as swinging coffins.

HOW DID the Right fail in curtailing the growth of the Left? Many errors can be cited. In the United States, the conservative reaction to these developments had, at least initially, too much of an economic bent and lacked theological and philosophic depth. In addition a tendency towards national "navel gazing" developed without sufficiently countering liberal international interventionism. On top of it all, the American right failed to organize itself, allowing a certain lethargy to prevail for several decades. When young F. A. von Hayek first came to New York in the 1920s as a student, he was soon visited by a lady who wanted to assist him in this foreign land. She came from leftist quarters. There was nobody from the right who wanted to support him.

Will contemporary American liberalism end? It will because, as an unknown Viennese coffeehouse philosopher once said, "everything has an end, except the sausage which has two." It will end once a huge reaction is caused against it. This reaction will probably be most strongly directed against its anarchical character that shows indifference to all imaginable crimes. These deviations are not punished because society, not individual persons, is responsible for the disorder. The staggering crime rate touches on a highly neuralgic spot. Drugs already appear in elementary schools. Walker Percy's prediction in *Love in the Ruins* that by 2035 nobody would leave home without their submachine gun may indeed come to pass.

The reaction against all this should be rational and reasonable, but the provocation is such that the response might take on an irrational and violent character. It is the task of the American right to make this a *kalos agon,* a "beautiful fight" (2 Timothy 4:7), ending in a positive history.

Robert H. Bork

Conservatism and the Culture

VOL. 34, NO. 2, 1999

In moments of despair, when I think America is indeed slouching towards an unfashionable address, when I contemplate the apparent indifference of the public to corruption and perjury in high places, I am consoled by one thing. Conservative thought and conservative intellectuals must be gaining ground or the liberals would not be constantly lecturing us on the meaning of "true conservatism." They would admire us, they claim, if we would return to that philosophy. But there is, as one might suspect, a catch.

"True conservatism," it turns out, is that form of conservatism that liberals find congenial. Today's conservatives simply fail to measure up. That is the measure of our success. We know we have arrived when liberal lecturing moves from the pages of liberal opinion magazines of small circulation to the pages of the Sunday *New York Times Magazine.*

It turns out that conservatives should emulate the optimism and good cheer of Ronald Reagan. You may have some difficulty recalling that the liberals admired Reagan all that much when he was in office. Now, however, a heavily revised version of the man is the standard by which liberals judge conservatives, and, not surprisingly, find us wanting. "Reagan's view of America," we are informed by Andrew Sullivan, "was never bleak, and he was careful to stay away from the front lines of the cultural wars. . . . Moralism, for him, was always a vague but essentially positive construct. . . . And it was far more in touch with the center of American culture."

"True conservatism," we are informed, requires that we be at the center of American culture. That would be a liberal panacea. If their opponents are careful to stay in the center while liberals pull from the left, the center will continually move left and "true conservatives" will, by definition, be bound to move with it. This is a liberal ratchet and a recipe for the destruction of any effective conservatism. I wonder how Mr. Sullivan, formerly editor of the *New Republic,* would react to the suggestion that "true liberalism" means staying at the center of American culture while conservatives are free to tug the center to the right.

The major themes of 1980s conservatism are said to be economic freedom, smaller government, and personal choice. Opposed to this sunny outlook, today's conservatism is accused of being "inherently pessimistic," returning to older themes of cultural decline, moralism, and the need for greater social control.

But this is not a true opposition. The conservatism of the 1990s is not opposed to the conservative themes of the 1980s. Rather, the new stress on morality complements the stress on freedom to make one whole and complete conservative philosophy. Thus, conservatives favor free markets as by far the best way to create wealth for all Americans. But we also recognize that wealth and individual pleasure are not everything, that society requires moral standards, and that it is not moral to allow everything on the market.

Liberals and libertarians tend to shy away from the subject of traditional morality, but it is obvious that neither the free market nor limited government can perform well without a strong moral base. The free market requires men and women whose word can be trusted and who have formed personal traits of self-discipline, prudence, and self-denial or the deferment of gratifications. Smaller government requires many of the same qualities so that individuals will not constantly turn to a powerful state to offer them complete security and a cornucopia of favors bought with other people's money.

THE NEED for smaller government is obvious and urgent. "It is a commonplace," Pierre Manent writes, "that totalitarianism is defined as the absorption of civil society by the state. . . . One of the sources of the totalitarian project is found in the idea that it is possible for man to model society in accordance with

his wishes, once he occupies the seat of power and possesses an exact social science and employs adequate means for this task." Nazism and communism are the obvious examples.

There are, however, slower, less well-marked roads to totalitarianism that are more acceptable to a democratic people. Rather than being actuated by an exact social science or an explicit desire to remake society, the impelling force is a set of quite amorphous, but urgent, ideas about social justice coupled with a sense of moral superiority.

Tocqueville sounded the warning about government that

> covers the surface of society with a network of small complicated rules, minute and uniform, through which the most original minds and the most energetic characters cannot penetrate to rise above the crowd. The will of man is not shattered, but softened, bent, and guided. . . . Such a power . . . stupefies a people, till each nation is reduced to nothing better than a flock of timid and industrious animals, of which the government is the shepherd.

As government regulations grow slowly, we become used to the harness. Habit is a powerful force, and we no longer feel as intensely as we once would have constrictions of our liberties that would have been utterly intolerable a mere half century ago.

We are all too familiar with heavy governmental regulation of private property and economic activity, as well as federal, state, and local taxation that takes well over half the earnings of many people. Statutes pour out like the Americans with Disabilities Act, the Occupational Safety and Health Act, and the Endangered

Species Act. Agencies with the zealotry of the EPA turn environmentalism into a pantheistic religion, while medical care is made less effective by a web of bureaucratic controls. Our bureaucracies grind out 70,000 pages of new regulations a year. Common law tort actions increasingly control product designs and the delivery of services. Useful and harmless products have been driven from the market altogether by the costs of litigation.

ECONOMIC FREEDOMS are not all that is under assault, however. In other areas, the force of government is augmented, and in many ways surpassed, by that of private institutions and communities enforcing new and destructive moralisms. Government, businesses, and universities practice affirmative action or quotas for ethnic groups and for women. Corporations, universities, and even primary and secondary schools police speech and attitudes to prevent expressions that might offends various newly sensitized and favored groups. Multiculturalism, which attacks America's traditions as well as its European heritage, insists that all cultures are equal. A person who offends this new morality, even inadvertently and tangentially, may be sentenced to sensitivity training—America's version of Maoist reeducation camps.

Radical feminism both exercises a virulent form of censorship and thought control and damages indispensable institutions. Organizational discipline may be applied for even referring to a woman's dress or attractiveness. A major corporation for which I have done legal consulting requires all employees to attend training sessions designed to root out sexist attitudes. One of the topics is the vexed question of whether it is insulting for a man to remove his hat when a woman gets on an elevator. A man approaching an office building heard the sounds of high heels behind him. He opened the door and held it to let the woman go first. She kicked him in the kneecap. These are the more amusing manifestations of feminism's power. There are less amusing aspects. Feminism is rife in education where it teaches antagonism toward men and provides debased education by distorting such subjects as literature, history, and law. In the armed forces standards of performance are lowered to allow a pretense of physical equality.

THE NEW liberal morality demands freedom from restraints in ways that produce moral anarchy. The facts are familiar: the sexual revolution, births out of wedlock, drug use, crime, popular entertainment reliant on sex and violence. Softcore pornography is everywhere and the hardcore variety is not far behind. More ominously, what John Paul II calls the "culture of death," the practice of killing for convenience through abortion and now assisted suicide, which rapidly becomes euthanasia, is gaining ground. Quite recently some of these social pathologies, which have had a spectacular rise since the sixties, have declined, albeit rather modestly. This has led to claims that America has turned a corner. Those claims, to say the least, are premature. The pathologies are still far more common than they were just a few decades ago. There may be a pendulum effect in such matters, but that does not mean the pendulum arm will swing all the way back. It seems more likely that the nadir of the swing will move steadily in the direction of social disorder.

We will be faced shortly with the ability to clone human beings, to design individuals through genetic manipulation, and to grow human bodies for the harvesting of organs. It is at best an open question whether the superficial utility of such actions will not overbear any moral qualms. Science, heretofore regarded as benign, may pose the most serious moral crises of the twenty-first century.

In the meantime, we already have more than enough to worry about in our culture. Roger Kimball wrote of the depth and power and devastation wrought by the cultural revolution that has swept America:

> [T]he radical emancipationist demands of the sixties [have] triumphed throughout society. They have insinuated themselves, disastrously, into the curricula of our schools and colleges; they have dramatically altered the texture of sexual relations and family life; they have played havoc with the authority of churches and other repositories of moral wisdom; they have undermined the claims of civic virtue and our national self-understanding; they have degraded the media and the entertainment industry, and subverted museums and other institutions entrusted with preserving and transmitting high culture. They have even, most poignantly, addled our hearts and innermost assumptions about what counts as the good life.

We are now two nations. These are not, as Disraeli had it, the rich and the poor, or, as presidential commissions regularly proclaim, whites and blacks. Instead, we are two cultural nations. One embodies the counterculture of the 1960s, which is today the dominant culture. Their values are propagated from the commanding heights of the culture: university faculties, journalists, television and movie producers, the ACLU, and major segments of the Democratic Party. The other nation, of those who adhere to traditional norms and morality, is now a dissident culture. Its spokesmen cannot hope to match the influence of the dominant nation. The dissident culture may survive by withdrawing, so far as possible, into enclaves of its own. The homeschooling movement is an example of that, an attempt to keep children out of a public educational system that, in the name of freedom, all too often teaches moral relativism and depravity.

ARE THERE any solutions? For the problem of increasing economic regulation, we can recover the classical liberal philosophy, which is the conservatives' birthright: any proposal for government regulation is to be examined under a presumption of error. That is not an absolutist or extreme libertarian position. It merely holds that those who would decrease our freedoms in any area should bear the burden of proof.

The reformation of our culture, or more precisely, the recapture of what has been best in our cultural history, requires a different approach, for here the problem is not too little individual freedom but too much. Law may have a role to play here but it is strictly a secondary role, because without a fairly widespread public consensus laws will not be enacted or enforced. How is such a public consensus to be formed and maintained?

In an era of moral decline, a reversal probably depends on a revival of biblical religion. I have not been religious for most of my life, and I come to this conclusion not out of piety but through observation.

The role of religion—traditional, biblical religion—is crucial to cultural health. I commend to you Gertrude Himmelfarb's article "From Clapham to

Bloomsbury." Clapham was a district in London inhabited by intensely religious and moral people. Bloomsbury you know about. When religion faded in England, the next generation insisted upon the strict demands of morality, not realizing that they were living on, and using up, the moral capital left behind by prior religious generations. Gradually, the imperatives of morality faded. We have entered a period in which morality is privatized. We are entering Bloomsbury.

A journalist I know has travelled our country inquiring about public attitudes toward our President Clinton's indiscretions. The usual response ran along the lines of "What he has done is wrong, but who am I to judge?" Religion, where it has not been subverted by the culture, is an antidote, perhaps the only antidote, to that variety of moral nihilism. Religion insists that there is right and wrong, and that the difference is knowable and comes with sanctions attached.

Yet the American public is now erroneously taught by the courts that religion is dangerous, that the First Amendment itself establishes a public religion—the religion of secular humanism. Is that serious? There is reason to think so. The late Christopher Lasch, a man of the Left, asked, "What accounts for [our society's] wholesale defection from the standards of personal conduct—civility, industry, self-restraint—that were once considered indispensable to democracy?" He answered that a major reason is the "gradual decay of religion." Our liberal elites, whose "attitude to religion," Lasch said, "ranges from indifference to active hostility," have succeeded in removing religion from public recognition and debate.

According to James Q. Wilson: "In the mid-nineteenth century England and America reacted to the consequences of industrialization, urbanization, immigration, and affluence by asserting an ethos of self-control, whereas in the late twentieth century they reacted to many of the same forces by asserting an ethos of self-expression."

The difference between the two centuries was the presence in the last century of religion and church-related institutions that taught morality. This suggests that a society deadened by a smothering network of laws while finding release in moral chaos is not likely to be either happy or stable.

THIS IS not a counsel of despair. There is no iron law that bad trends must continue in a straight line forever. Perhaps we will stop the seemingly inexorable growth of government control of our lives. There are signs of a religious revival in the recent growth of the evangelical churches as well as in the apparent growth of orthodoxy in all our major religions— among Catholics, Protestants, Jews, and Mormons.

Taking back the culture will not be easy, but religion rejects despair. The four cardinal Christian virtues, paralleled in other religions, are, after all, prudence, justice, fortitude, and temperance. These are quite enough to take back the culture. In our current cultural wars, perhaps the most important of the virtues for conservatives is fortitude—the courage to take stands that are not immediately popular, the courage to ignore the opinion polls. Otherwise, we will never change the polls. That is what true conservatism means, or it means nothing.

Peter Augustine Lawler

Postmodern Conservatism, Conservative Postmodernism

VOL. 38, NO. 1, 2002

Astute thinkers from Hegel onward have claimed that we live at the end of the modern world. That does not mean the modern world is about to disappear: the world, in truth, is more modern than ever. So we must contest Hegel's assertion that the modern world is the end, the fulfillment, of history. The longings of human beings have neither been satisfied nor have they disappeared. Modern strivings continue to be fueled by a progressively more restless and anxious human discontent. But if the modern world were to be superseded by another—as it eventually will be—human beings would continue to be human: beings with souls or capabilities and longings not shared by, and higher, than those of other animals.

What has distinguished the modern world, above all, is a particular definition of what a human being is. That definition does not describe a real or complete human being. It was not even meant to be completely true, but mainly to be useful as a fiction in the pursuit of unprecedented freedom, justice, and prosperity. Modern thought has held that a human being is an *individual*, and the modern individual is an abstraction, an invention of the human mind. That individual is made more free from social and political constraints, and less directed toward duty and goodness by God and nature, than a real human being ever could be. The modern individual is distinguished from the political animals—the citizens, statesmen, and philosophers—described by the Greek and Roman philosophers, and from the social, familial creatures described by Christian theologians. The modern individual is liberated from the philosopher's duty to know the truth about nature, from the citizen's selfless devotion to his country, from the creature's love and fear of God, and even from the loving responsibilities that are inseparable from family life. Conservatives today oppose liberal individualism both because its understanding of the human being is untrue and because that definition erodes all that is good about distinctively human existence.

The modern world has now ended only in the sense that we have now seen enough of it to judge it. Although we have reason to be grateful for the wealth, health, freedom, and power that modern achievements have given us, we *know* that the individual's pursuits of security and happiness will remain always pursuits—and not possessions. So even as the modern world continues to develop, we can be free of its characteristic delusion, its utopianism. We can speak of its strengths and its limitations from a perspective "outside" modernity, and that perspective is the foundation of conservatism today. Conservatives can be (perhaps the only) *genuinely* postmodern thinkers. The reason we can see beyond the modern world is that its intention to transform human nature has failed. Its project of transforming the human person into the autonomous individual was and remains unrealistic; we can now see the limits of being an individual because we remain more than individuals. The world created by modern individuals to make themselves fully at home turns out to have made human beings less at home than ever.

Conservative thought today is authentic postmodernism, but it is, obviously, not postmodernism as it is usually understood. Most allegedly postmodern thought emphasizes the arbitrary character of all human authority, the freedom of each human being from all standards but his own will or creativity, and the death not only of God but of nature. These allegedly postmodern characteristics are really *hypermodern*; they aim to "deconstruct" as incoherent and so incredible any residual modern faith in reason or nature. They shout that everything modern—in fact, everything human—is nothing but a construction.

Postmodernists in the usual sense often do well in exposing liberal hypocrisy, but they can only do so in the name of completing the modern project of liberating the individual's subjective or willful and whimsical perspective from all external constraints. Conservative postmodern-ism, by acknowledging and affirming as good what we can really know about our natural possibilities and limitations, is radically opposed to liberated postmodernism—and to the modern premises it radicalizes.

THE DRIVING intention of modern thought is not to understand nature or human nature, but to guide action to transform nature freely in accordance with human desire. According to the modern philosophers, we have very little reason to be grateful for what we have been given by God and nature. Nature, according to modern scientists, chooses for life, not death—but not for *my* life in particular. For life's sake, nature intends each of us to be born, reproduce, raise our young, and quickly die. Both God and nature seem callously and cruelly indifferent to the lives of particular human individuals. So we individuals need to move as far as we can from the miserable life of poverty, contingency, and early death that nature intends for us.

Our lives, objectively speaking, are not really more contingent and doomed to death than those of the other animals. We have it better by nature, for example, than the bees and the ants, not to mention the fruit flies that live for only a few days. But the other animals are not conscious of, and so not animated by, awareness of their own deaths. We are human because we are the self-conscious animal. We are animals that restlessly and anxiously rebel against death. We are technological animals. We alone have the capability to resist with considerable success our natural fate: we will not go blindly to our deaths as so many bees and ants have done. We experience ourselves as free individuals, as (to some extent) ungoverned by instinct or the requirements of our social existence. We are, quite mysteriously, not only intelligent but free.

Surely modern thinkers should allow us to be grateful, at least, for our singular freedom. But grateful, they say, to whom? Human freedom is too mysterious to be regarded as natural, and even if it came from God, we cannot help but wish he had given us much more. How can we be grateful to a God who left us alone and shivering to provide for ourselves? We employ our freedom not to live according to nature but to escape from our natural constraints, to conquer nature. Our freedom is not simply our self-conscious individuality but our technology—our ability to use our brains to give orders to nature. We might say—to avoid speciesism—that we are unsure whether the chimps and the dolphins are self-conscious. But we do know they are un-technological; they do not freely impose their will on nature. There would be no "ecological crisis" if it were not for human beings, and nature would cheer if human beings were to disappear. Human freedom is what disorders nature. Or, to be properly modern, human freedom is what imposes human order on a nature that is hostile to individual human existence.

When we reflect on our freedom, we are inclined even to confuse ourselves with God. We easily lord it over the chimps and the dolphins, using them however we will. The technological success of modern thought is in a way supernatural. The very conception of ourselves as free or supernatural is what connects the modern individual to the Christian religion. The individual really did try to replace the God of the Bible in the modern world— with the individual himself.

WHEN THE modern individual speaks truthfully about his self-consciousness, his freedom, and his mortality, he expresses his distorted debt to Christianity—a debt that he is very anxious, in his freedom, to deny. According to St. Augustine, human beings are pilgrims or aliens in this world; they know that their true home is somewhere else. St. Augustine observes that Christians are critics of pagan "natural theology." Christians know they are not merely part of nature, that they are free beings with longings that cannot be satisfied by nature. Christians are also critics of "civil theology." They know they are not merely citizens, reducible to parts of a political community. Only Christian theology recognizes and can account for human freedom, for why we personally and truthfully experience ourselves as more than natural or political beings. We were made in the image and likeness of the supernatural and suprapolitical God.

Extreme or Augustinian Christianity was criticized by St. Thomas Aquinas for dwelling far too much on the human experience of alienation or homelessness. God, after all, created nature, and our natural enjoyments and fulfillments—although not completely satisfying—are still good. Human life would not really be nothing but restless misery without faith in God. Even if Aristotle was wrong, finally, to call us political animals, the pride human beings take in political accomplishments is a legitimate or partially truthful human pleasure. Even Christians cannot really claim that they merely use their political communities to achieve their true, nonpolitical goal. Being a Christian is compatible with experiencing oneself to some extent, if only to some extent, as a devoted citizen. Otherwise, good citizens would have every right to deny Christians any share in political rule. St. Augustine's account of the human creature is surely too abstract, in St. Thomas's view. A Christian at home with his homelessness because of his faith is actually more free than others to enjoy the good things of this world for what they are.

The modern individual, from one view, is an Augustinian who does not believe in the personal and providential God of the Bible. St. Augustine used his considerable rhetorical eloquence to describe the human misery that undermines every human good. He makes us aware, very aware, of human misery and contingency to show us that we can only be happy in hope for the eternal life graciously offered to us by God. We have the best reasons to be grateful for grace. But we seem to have little reason to be grateful for nature without grace. The philosophers who argued otherwise, according to St. Augustine, were blinded by pride. The same pride that kept the philosophers from acknowledging their longing for God and the eternal life that only God can give caused them to construct fraudulent visions for human happiness on earth, such as the ways of life of the statesman and the philosopher.

The modern individual—or the philosophers who constructed him—might be understood to be animated by the most insane form of pride ever. The modern individual aims to create in this world—not through grace but through human work—what God promised in the next. But viewed in another way, the modern individual seems less proud than desperate. The Christians are right about human misery and contingency; the modern individual is totally taken in by Augustine's "negative" rhetoric about human alienation. But he does not believe in the Christian God; Augustine's "positive" rhetoric about grace, providence, and salvation does not move him at all. And so he has no choice but to try

to do for himself what the Christians believed God would do. The individual finds himself with a heavy—really, a horrible—burden. The modern individual is an alien—an absolutely contingent being who belongs nowhere in particular—who must build for himself his own place in the world.

But the individual does see some good news in the Christian teaching about human freedom or alienation. We are not merely parts of nature or parts of a city. We are, in a sense, mysteriously made in the image of God. The effectual truth of grace—the real evidence for it—must be what we achieve through applied reason or technology. The modern individual, of course, is not the same person as the Christian creature. He comes into being through the denial of certain real aspects of his humanity that Christians affirm. The individual claims not to have a real longing to love God or other human beings; he merely wants the security and comfort, or freedom from death and pain, that the Christian God promised. The result of accepting the negative but not the positive teaching of St. Augustine is the construction of a being who wants "freedom from" nature but not "freedom for" anything in particular. He has no particular view of what a free and comfortable human being should do with his comfort and freedom.

The Christian vision of heaven—the constant, unimpeded love of God—was replaced by Marx's vision of communism, a world-to-come where we can do whatever we want, whenever we want, without any constraint by or guidance from nature, other human beings, or God. A future full of love was replaced by one without any love at all. Before we allow our very reasonable prejudice against Marx to lessen the force of this conclusion, we should remember that the most consistent liberals or libertarians also hope that religion and the state will wither away, leaving each human individual with an "autonomous" future. The modern utopias of liberalism and socialism are not really very different. It is hard, in fact, to know why Marx called his utopia "communism"; the world he imagined is filled with unencumbered individuals, not beings devoted to the service of others. The biggest misconception that we can have about Marxism—the one he himself emphasized—is that he provided any real antidote to the miserable excesses of liberal individualism.

THE INDIVIDUAL was invented by early-modern thinkers who were anti-Christian but still Augustinian. Prominent among these was John Locke. In Locke's famous alternative to the biblical creation story, human beings must be imagined to exist in a state of nature to reveal what they would be like without the human construction of government. There they are free and equal individuals. They have no natural inclination to be citizens or even social beings, and they think for themselves alone. The foundation of government must therefore be consent: I must see how government serves my self-interest as an individual, how government makes me more secure and comfortable than I am without it. Because human beings invent government to serve their bodily needs, government should be understood as a particularly successful example of human freedom or technology. In consenting to be ruled, the individual never surrenders his self-conscious judgment about the ability of government to protect his rights. In his own mind, the individual never gives way to political devotion or genuine communal loyalty. He refuses to be a sucker, like

a bee or an ant—or even like a human being blinded by love.

The individual is clearly an invention—an abstract, distorted, only partial human being—because Locke's state of nature is clearly somewhat of a lie. As Rousseau famously observed, if we were really self-sufficient individuals by nature we would be so stupid as to be unconscious. Self-consciousness is necessarily consciousness with others; it depends upon a language that could only develop among social or even political animals. The human being is clearly a gregarious animal by nature—like the chimps, but with a distinctive capability for far more complex and intensely social language. The natural individual Locke describes is, when we think about it, rather obviously impossible.

But it is a sign of human freedom that the individual could be invented as a human goal to free civilized people from their traditional, political, religious, and even familial dependence. Locke intended, as far as he could, to transform social, political, religious, and familial beings into individuals. Because nature was not really on his side, we can now say that Locke was to some extent engaged in mission impossible. But it is also undeniable that he achieved some real success.

The American Constitution of 1789 is largely a Lockean construction. There, human beings are not defined in terms of race, class, gender, or religious belief. The Constitution does not acknowledge our people's dependence on God or their past. Americans are understood to consent to government as individuals. So blacks and whites, men and women, and Jews, Christians, and Muslims can all be free and equal citizens of our country. All human beings, in fact, can be free and equal citizens of the United States. But they do not consent as Christians or Jews or as members of any other group: their religion, gender, race, communal and class-based identities are all private or inessential matters.

From the modern individualistic view, blacks and women were degraded by American law for most of our history. But our Constitution surely created the framework by which all individuals would eventually be liberated from the inessential baggage of race, class, and gender. The core of the American form of justice—a real, if incomplete, form of justice—is the liberation of human beings from any qualities that make them more than individuals. Our national Constitution is a construction—we know it was invented by human beings—*for* a construction—the individual invented by Locke and other modern thinkers.

The American Founding Fathers surely knew that human beings are more than individuals. They also knew that government should be limited. The most intimate and sacred aspects of being human are left relatively untouched by the law. Human beings are free, in private, to consider themselves as creatures with duties to their Creator, and our founders assumed that they would do so. They could consent as liberated individuals in public, but love and be devoted to God, their families, and their friends in private. Unable or unwilling to become complete and perfect individuals, Americans would live double lives. As Alexis Tocqueville explained, they would be restless and anxious pursuers of material prosperity during the week, acting as if God is dead and so they must work incessantly to achieve self-sufficiency—then on Sunday they would do nothing but restfully contemplate God's goodness, certain that He provides.

By focusing on the Constitution of 1789, we may exaggerate how modern and secular America was intended to be. The first Americans were Puritans, and their view that American liberty is really for the duties of creatures has always remained with us. The American people have always been, by modern standards, very religious. The Puritan virtues and vices were emphatically not those of Lockean individuals, and neither were the Christian virtues and vices Tocqueville found in America. The First Amendment to the Constitution is actually a correction to the Constitution in a Christian or anti-individualistic direction. There, for example, the free exercise of religion is recognized as a positive good. Above all, we must not forget that the original intention was to leave almost all legislation concerning religion and morality to the states. So in another way Americans led double lives: state laws were less individualistic (and from the individualist's perspective, more tyrannical) than national law. Only in the 1940s, through the clever manipulation of the Bill of Rights and the Fourteenth Amendment by the Supreme Court, did the Madisonian or individualistic spirit of the unamended Constitution begin to be used to invalidate the moral and religious legislation of the states.

Despite our very modern Constitution, American lives have been only inconsistently modern. We might even say, as Tocqueville does, that it is that very inconsistency that has made modern liberty appear good to human beings. One American paradox is that our political protection of individual rights attracted all sorts of premodern ways of life to our shores. Jews, Catholics, various Protestant sects came to America not to be individuals but to practice their faiths in peace and freedom. They often wanted most of all to maintain their traditions free from political intrusion. Catholics, for example, cannot forget the extent to which their church—its faith and its institutions—flourished in America with a certain purity, free from the temptations and corruptions of political power. And as we can read in the writing of John Courtney Murray, the church as late as the 1950s stood ready to teach Americans the true meaning of human liberty. We have to add, of course, the telling fact that after World War II America had the largest and most vibrant Jewish community in the world. Reflection on what has happened to the Jews almost everywhere else allows us to see the humane nobility of the American commitment to individual rights.

But in the long run, the attempt to maintain premodern traditions (even the tradition of natural rights) in individualistic America usually fails. Children or grandchildren come to understand themselves primarily as individuals with rights, and so free not to be dominated by the authority of fathers, traditions, churches, or God. According to Tocqueville, the human mind hates inconsistency, and it is almost irresistibly inclined to harmonize heaven and earth. The view that we are individuals for some purposes but not others is not very credible. So it is almost inevitable that Americans come to understand themselves more consistently as individuals, attempting to apply the ideas of contract and consent to every part of their lives.

Marriage, for example, comes to be understood less as a sacrament and more as a contract between two individuals, to be dissolved at will. Sex is dissociated from the hard responsibilities connected with procreation given us by God and nature. Sex becomes "safe sex," a contract between "consenting adults" who never lose their minds in passionate enjoyment or in love. From an individual point of view, sex cannot be safe—or no real limit on our freedom—if we ever stop calculating about it. Social arrangements reflecting real or imagined differences between men and women are more consistently and insistently regarded as oppressive. Merely biological differences cannot be regarded as real limits to individual freedom. On balance, the history of America is a story of our thought and even our lives becoming progressively more individualistic—although, because real human nature never stops resisting, not completely individualistic.

Even religion tends to become a choice we make for our convenience. We conclude that God would never command anything that would violate our rights. If He ever did, we would withdraw our consent from even His rule. The traditional view is that God must judge the modern individual to be the product of willful self-deception; human beings can never be as self-sufficient as the individual claims to be. The modern view is that the undeceived and self-sufficient individual must judge God; theology cannot be a rationalization for oppression. The individual, not God, is that for which everything exists. God, the individual believes he knows, cannot really provide him any security—although the modern individual may still, on occasion, hypocritically take advantage of the comfort that religious community provides.

It is reasonable to believe that the individual Locke invented will never achieve the happiness he pursues. Such an alien can never be at home in this world. His life remains an incessant pursuit that ends only in death. The mistake of modern utopianism is its reasoning that because the individual obsessively pursues bodily satisfaction, the individual will be happier to the extent he achieves it. The truth is that modern liberalism is about the pursuit, and not about the enjoyment, of happiness. The individual does pursue bodily security and comfort, but the more of it he achieves, the more dissatisfied he is. The more secure or free from contingency he is objectively, the more he experiences his existence as contingent and the more he is haunted by death. The more death is pushed back by modern technology, the more accidental it seems. The more accidental or less necessary death seems, the more terrible it seems.

Surely it is possible for human beings to live well with invincible necessity. For example, thoughtful acceptance of the necessity of death is what makes sense of the practice of such risky virtues as courage. If you have to go sometime, you might as well go down virtuously. But if death ever came to seem entirely accidental because technology had enabled human lives to become indefinitely long, then the individual would become obsessively risk averse. Then, every moment of life would be given over to calculation about security. The current biotechnological promise of indefinite longevity would surely produce more perfectly modern individuals—beings with even less capacity to enjoy life than we have now. We can reasonably anticipate, therefore, that the limited but still quite real successes of the biotechnological project in fending off death and disease will be the cause of a religious revival. It will become more clear than ever that to the extent we understand ourselves as individuals we can never be happy. Contrary to the hopes of our new eugenic utopians—and to the fears of some conservative Nietzscheans—we do not have the capability to make for ourselves a "posthuman" future. The individual has neither the intention nor the means to surrender his freedom, his distorted but real self-consciousness.

Actual enjoyment or happiness is even contrary to the modern individual's view of his freedom. He is free because he can oppose himself to nature; the moment he gives way to some natural enjoyment he surrenders his freedom. His freedom is freedom *from* nature *for* nothing in particular, except not suffering or death. We can even say, with Tocqueville, that the individual perversely takes pride in his inability really to enjoy. The individual is a materialist insofar as he rejects all non-*materialistic* human goals as illusions, but his disparagement of real human enjoyment makes him an equally extreme *anti-materialist*. We might say that his single-minded pursuit of material goals while being conscious of that pursuit's futility is undeniable evidence that he has a soul. No other animal could be so perversely screwed up, and Tocqueville was subtle or Christian enough to see the greatness in such human misery.

Contemporary "therapeutic" thought invites the modern individual to surrender his soul or his obsessions in the name of immediate enjoyment. Experts advise him to give up his singular freedom and become just one of the animals again. All he has to do is not be moved by what he knows to be true, by what he really knows about his own death and the nature that is out to kill him. The goal of therapy is to engender what Allan Bloom calls flatness of soul, a disposition to be unmoved by love or death and so to be no longer open to the truth. The therapists have mainly won linguistic victories: Americans speak in their easygoing and amoral language more than ever before. Those victories are impressive enough that experts such as Bloom and the sociologist James Davison Hunter mistake what people say today for what they actually experience. It takes postmodern conservative outsiders like Aleksandr Solzhenitsyn (and Mother Teresa of Calcutta) to both notice and have the courage to say that Americans are more lonely and death-obsessed than ever before. Like Tocqueville, what Solzhenitsyn hears just beneath the surface in the lives of free, restless, enlightened, and prosperous Americans is the "howl" of existentialism.

People are more screwed up than ever, as the philosophical novelist Walker Percy said, because they have been deprived of the language to express the longings of a real human being. But they are also now screwed up because they have lost even the language of the individual. The modern individual, although abstracted from and so less than a real human being, is more than the being described by the therapeutic experts. Therapeutic language is particularly alienating because it is two steps removed from corresponding to the longings of a real human being. The modern individual is moved by death but not by love; the entirely imaginary therapeutic being is moved by neither. But the truth is that, whatever they say, human beings remain moved by both. The alleged therapeutic solution to the misery of individuality actually exaggerates the problem—and we should notice that most, though not all, contemporary "communitarianism" is therapeutic in intention. Our therapists actually produce pathetic human beings who can neither *be* good nor *feel* good. People today know they need help because, as the lapidary Canadian thinker George Grant observed, they know they have been deprived of something—but they usually get no help in figuring out what.

WE LIVE at the end of the modern world because we now see the consequences of the modern reduction of the real human being to an individual. What began as a fiction to limit government has redefined more and more of human life. If human beings really believe they are merely individuals, they perversely work to empty human life of the contents that make it worth living. A life defined only by avoiding death and misery is, in fact, supremely miserable. So, today, our sophisticated individuals sometimes spend their time envying the other animals—at least they're content. But the individual really knows that the dog's life is not for him. The individual wrongly believes that his choice is between subhuman contentment and human unhappiness, and in his freedom he sometimes talks nostalgically about the former—the "simple life"—but still consistently chooses the latter.

Not only are Americans more individualistic than ever, the biotechnological revolution promises to give them new weapons of unprecedented power in their war against nature. The victories they win—like most of the victories won on behalf of the modern individual—will probably be at the expense of the distinctively human goods: love, family, friends, country, virtue, art, spiritual life, and, most generally, living responsibly in light of what we really know about what we have been given. The biotechnological revolution will be driven by individualistic obsession, and we can limit and direct it only if we can recover the truth that we are more than individuals.

POSTMODERNISM RIGHTLY understood begins with the realization that we should, in fact, be grateful for what we have been given. We have been given not only self-conscious mortality and a mysterious freedom to negate nature, but all sorts of natural compensations for our distinctively human misery. Love is not an illusion, and we have been fitted by nature to know the truth. Both love of each other and love of the truth depend, as far as we can tell, on the inevitability of death. As far as we can tell, self-consciousness—with all the virtues and distinctively human enjoyments it makes possible—depends on our having corruptible bodies. The fact that despite all that nature has given us we remain somewhat alienated might reasonably be seen as evidence that our true home lies elsewhere, and that it is in our nature to long for a personal God. As St. Thomas Aquinas said, what we know through revelation completes—but does not contradict—what we know through reason. Even if we are, for now, not ready to be grateful for the gift of faith, we can still reasonably believe that our homelessness is a price worth paying for all that we can know, love, and do in our lives. Because we can be ambiguously at home, or at home with our homelessness, we can abandon the modern obsession with making ourselves fully at home in this world.

IT IS no longer enough for Americans to be abstracted modern individuals most of the time and full human creatures only in fleeting private moments. All of our institutions must be consistently understood in light of what we really know about human nature. We have religious liberty because human beings, by nature, really are open to God, and because what we really know about nature points to the real possibility that we are created. We have political liberty because we are more than citizens, but that liberty is compatible with political responsibility because we are, among other things, citizens. Because

human freedom and human responsibilities make possible and necessary both virtue and spiritual life, we can live well with death. The beginning of the postmodern world is the replacement of the individual by the whole human being, and the using of our natural capabilities for thought and action to make the world worthy of him. This is not to say that any particular changes to our form of government are now necessary. Our constitutionalism might actually be better defended from the perspective of the created human being than that of the abstract individual—as Orestes Brownson in the nineteenth century and Robert Kraynak and Carey McWilliams very recently have explained. Postmodern conservatism is quite compatible with liberal or limited and democratic government, and it certainly has a higher view than does liberal individualism of the capacity of the ordinary person to choose truth and virtue over security and comfort.

Conservatives today rightly attack so-called postmodernists for their attacks on truth, science, virtue, and God. But those attacks on our ability to perceive the truth and goodness of nature and human nature are actually *modern* in origin. The promiscuously ironic professor of philosophy Richard Rorty once described himself as a postmodernist bourgeois liberal. That particular self-description turns out to be neither irony nor an oxymoron. Postmodernism as it is usually understood, Rorty appreciates, does not really offer any challenge at all to modern or liberal individualism. Because we conservatives aim to conserve the full truth about human and natural reality, we have no interest in conserving the modern error of mistaking the abstract individual for the real human being.

X.

BOOKS IN REVIEW

Donald Davidson

Odyssey of a Littérateur

VOL. 2, NO. 6, 1966

The Bit Between My Teeth: A Literary Chronicle of 1950–1965, by Edmund Wilson. New York: Farrar, Straus and Giroux, 1965.

EDMUND WILSON has published another book—his twenty-eighth. It is also the third of his "literary chronicles," which are not chronicles so much as samplers or anthologies of the reviews, essays, or *causeries* written by him over a designated period of years. *The Shores of Light* covered the great excitements of the 1920s and 1930s; *Classics and Commercials,* the 1940s. The new collection contains forty-four essays—668 pages of regular Wilsonian discourse on authors, books, and topics that seemed to Mr. Wilson worth writing about during the fifteen years from 1950 to 1965. And furthermore, very much as usual, the greater number of the selections first appeared in *The New Yorker.* It is a retrospective exhibit of the post-World War II Wilson. Inevitably it invites a reader who has followed Edmund Wilson from the 1920s on to the present to look further back—indeed, all the way.

Wilson's first book, *The Undertaker's Garland* (1922), in which he collaborated with his friend John Peale Bishop, was a collection of stories and poems celebrating the death of much that the society of pre–World War I had held precious, including Christianity and God. It was not well received.

After publishing a somewhat more successful novel, *I Thought of Daisy* (1929) and a last book of poetry, *Poets, Farewell* (1929), he achieved his first enduring success in a book of literary criticism, *Axel's Castle* (1931). This notable work gives Wilson's interpretation of the Symbolist movement, which he tends to view as a corrective of the excesses of Romanticism and Naturalism, a new technique of literary art, revolutionary in nature, that for better or worse will replace the old.

For thirty-five years since the appearance of *Axel's Castle* Wilson has been writing books about books—that is to say, articles and extended reviews that when collected become books about books or—by what often seems to be Wilson's ingrained preference—books about the writers who write the books. Such is, of course, one of the little peculiarities of a literary critic's occupation. As Allen Tate remarks, in his essay, "Is Literary Criticism Possible?," the end of literary criticism is "outside itself . . . [and] it cannot in the long run be practiced apart from what it confronts, that gives rise to it." This would seem to make literary criticism rather opportunist or in a sense dependent, even parasitic. Not until an Eliot writes a *Waste Land* can a Wilson or a Tate write a criticism of it. But surely he did not write it to get the benefit of their criticism. It is not the literary artist but the critic who steps in and makes the confrontation. Is he then an interfering busybody? What is his accepted role? In a time when "confrontations" would not be arranged or somehow called for, there would be no *literary* critics. There have been such times. "In certain past ages," writes Mr. Tate, "there was no distinct activity of the mind conscious of itself as literary criticism; for example, the age of Sophocles and the age of Dante." But the public presentation (i.e., "publication") of a Greek tragedy at Athens in the fifth century B.C. was a functional part of a religious festival conducted under state auspices. A play by Sophocles was not at that time abstracted as "literature." That abstraction—and therefore literary criticism—developed later, in the Hellenistic period, when secularism was winning over religion and decadence was setting in. Especially was this true in the "planned city" of Alexandria with its great Library and Museum where artworks of the fifth century could be and were studied, anthologized, and criticized as "literature." As for Dante, I take it, that Mr. Tate sees the *Divine Comedy* as having a somewhat similarly organic relationship to late medieval culture—a relationship, however, that was soon to be altered by Renaissance and Reformation.

If the modern critic is only an opportunist, browsing passively among the new books, he may be a good reviewer or literary reporter, but will then fall short of being a true literary critic. Obviously our leading critics are not so passive. They are not mere sensitive plates that, when exposed to poetry or fiction or history, do nothing more than faithfully record a reduced image of the object set before their camera eyes. Their performance—as Mr. Tate suggests in his essay—ranges back and forth in the middle ground between "imagination" and "philosophy." They are partly, at least, engaged in what the Victorians called "criticism of life." They are interested not only in correcting or shaping the public's aesthetic taste but in discovering and exposing the social elements, hidden or rampant, that affect public taste. As Eliseo Vivas said recently of the late Richard Weaver, they are concerned with "the plight of modern man," whose condition nobody can pretend is flourishing. By this route literary criticism becomes social criticism, and accordingly we can hardly appraise "literary" judgments without noticing how critics choose their occasions and what sort of cultural predispositions they bring to the seat of judgment.

EDMUND WILSON himself has made it clear, in various personal statements, autobiographical interpolations, and straight reminiscences, what predispositions he has brought to his role as literary critic. From his college days on, Wilson has been pretty regularly attracted to the radical side. Like his father and uncles before him, he went to Princeton for his higher education. His father, a brilliant and successful lawyer and a Republican, was appointed Attorney General of New Jersey by a Republican governor and found himself serving under Democrat Woodrow Wilson when that professor-in-politics succeeded the Republican. The father did not much like Governor Wilson, but Edmund junior, then a freshman at Princeton, "read and listened to Wilson's speeches and accepted him as a shining champion in the war against sordid business, a reformer-intellectual in politics."[1] After graduation from Princeton, Wilson worked as reporter on the New York *Evening Sun* and lived the regular life of a Greenwich Villager. After World War I, during which he served—as did his contemporaries Dos Passos and Hemingway—in a hospital unit, Wilson soon found a place as literary editor of the *New Republic*, after first serving for two years as managing editor of *Vanity Fair*. All the while he was moving toward a more actively radical role. In what he referred to later as "the radicalizing thirties" Wilson went with his friend Dos Passos to the Kentucky coal mines on one of those "visits of protests" which then as in subsequent decades it was de rigeur for Northern radicals to make to the South.

When the Great Depression of the 1930s settled on the country, writers and artists of his generation, Wilson says, were not depressed but stimulated. "One couldn't help being exhilarated at the sudden collapse of the stupid, gigantic fraud. . . . And it gave us a new sense of power to find ourselves still carrying on while the bankers, for a change, were taking a beating."[2]

But before he gave himself up entirely to exultation over the woes of the prostrate financiers, Wilson published in 1931 his important critical work, *Axel's Castle: A Study of the Imaginative Literature of 1870–1930.* And thus celebrated what seemed to him a defeat of capitalism by a discussion of the triumph of Symbolism in literature, as exemplified in the writings of Yeats, Joyce, Eliot, Gertrude Stein, Proust, and Valéry. It is a book that Wilson has not subsequently excelled in clarity, balance, and general persuasive-

ness; and in its emphasis on European writers (with American expatriates included) it signals Wilson's early resolve to devote himself to what he described, years afterwards, as the general "cross-fertilization" between the Anglo-American and other cultures. The dedication to Dean Christian Gauss, his Princeton mentor and friend, states quite definitely that he derived from Gauss, principally, his idea of what literary criticism ought to be: "a history of man's ideas and imaginings in the setting of the conditions which have shaped them." And here, in truth, is a kind of determinist principle, owing perhaps as much to Hippolyte Taine as to Gauss, that from this time on is Wilson's chief reliance in his literary criticism. It serves him well enough when, as in the case of Proust, he can discover a psychic wound that operates, along with a social environment, as somehow the efficient cause of the masterwork; less well, but still with some plausibility, in the case of Eliot, whom Wilson sees as a frustrated New England Puritan, somewhat like Prufrock, and who in turn is precisely like Henry James's "middle-aged heroes of *The Ambassadors* and 'The Beast in the Jungle,' realizing sadly too late in life that they have been living too cautiously and too poorly." Where the determining cause cannot lie so readily located and described, Wilson may be far off the mark at times, as he is in his treatment of Yeats, who cannot, like Eliot, be so easily connected with the French Symbolist poets, despite his friendship with Arthur Symons and his visits to Paris in the 1890s. At the very beginning of his Yeats essay, for example, Wilson holds that the metaphors in Yeats's "On a Picture of a Black Centaur" and in Mallarmé's famous sonnet, *"Le vierge, le vivace, et le bel aujourd'hui"* illustrate the same kind of poetic performance—that Yeats is "close" to Mallarmé and other *fin de siècle* French symbolists "even in his later years." After quoting the poems in full, he comments:

> The centaur, the parrots, the wheat and the wine [of Yeats's poem] are, like the swan, the lake and the frost of [Mallamé's], not real things (except that the centaur is something Yeats has seen in a picture), but accidental images which, by an association of ideas, have come to stand for the poet's emotion.

Whatever different interpretations may be given to the images, they are certainly not "accidental in either poem." Yeats's poem, written in 1920, when at last he was happily married and engaged in working out the symbolic system that was soon to be published in his *A Vision*, is not quite as mysterious as at first it may seem, since he plainly says that the new wine he has found will put to sleep that horse-play which formerly stamped his works "down into the sultry mud." It is evidently a personal poem, not an exercise in "absolute" poetry. As Mr. Richard Ellman says: "This gnomic poem reflects Yeats's satisfaction over the progress of his art and over the revelations of his wife's automatic writing."[3] Mallarmé's sonnet, though composed like Yeats's poem, with the same studied care for the effects to be obtained, is not to be taken as referring to a personal experience. It might well be called, like some piece of music by Chopin or Debussy, an "Etude," and be given a number as Opus Such-and-Such.

But it is more important, after all, to note that *Axel's Castle*, favorable as it seems for the moderns whose cause Wilson is championing, leads to a surprise ending in which the admiring critic all but withdraws his support. Yeats, Valéry, Joyce, Proust, all "difficult" writers, maintained their integrity during World War I and so, in the twenties "fell heir to the prestige which had been sacrificed by other poets and novelists who had abandoned the detached study of human motives and the expression of those universal emotions that make all classes and peoples one, to become intolerant partisans." But their symbolist techniques, their various new literary procedures, valuable as they might be, nevertheless shut them off from the general reader and made them difficult of access even to scholars, in some instances. Thus, Wilson holds, they have made poetry and fiction a shelter to retreat into, not a park or "piazza" or commons where the public may enter and stroll for their social benefit. They are more and more dissociating themselves from society. And that is why Wilson ends his book with a discussion of "Axel," the long dramatic poems by Villiers de l'Isle Adam, which he offers as the ultimate example of the ivory tower or subjective withdrawal from the real world. A different alternative is provided by the extraordinarily precocious French symbolist poet Rimbaud, whose disillusionment brought him to retire both from literature and Europe, to end his days in desolate Abyssinia, among the remote and primitive people of that country. Either kind of withdrawal—that of the "Axel" type of Symbolists or that of Rimbaud—puts literature and culture itself in danger, Wilson believes. Can there be any other hope but that Symbolism and Naturalism may somehow come to terms and combine their resources?

One can see where this line of thought can easily take the literary editor of the *New Republic* circa A.D. 1930.

"FROM THE fall of 1930 to the spring of 1931," wrote Wilson in a postscript attached to the book version of his

New Republic article, "An Appeal to Progressives" (*N. R., January* 14, 1931), "I spent a good deal of time reporting political and industrial events, and thereafter, till 1940, writing a study of Marxism and the Russian Revolution. . . ." The fruit of these 1934–40 labors was *To the Finland Station,* which spreads its historical net far back of the Russian Revolution and is accurately described in the subtitle that Wilson gives it: "A Study in the Writing and Acting of History," if one bears in mind that the writers and actors are revolutionists and, in Wilson's view, the heroes of the history that he is studying. It might indeed be taken as a twentieth-century parallel to Thomas Carlyle's *Heroes and Hero Worship,* for to Wilson as to Carlyle, history is the biography of great men. Again his eye is on the "author" rather than the author's "works." This is a blessing to the reader, for the "works" of Marx and other revolutionists, if taken as "literature," are dolorous and dull to the nth degree and if taken as "action," or their realization in human events, afford in their constantly repeated patterns of violence and destruction, some of history's most ghastly spectacles. Wilson's interest in the temperaments, ideas, and careers of the revolutionists relieves him of the task of exploring the ghastliness; and his long experience as reporter-reviewer-critic enables him to make excellent use of his great power to digest, summarize, and point up by suitable illustration and comment the sprawling masses of material where he must search for history.

But skill would not be enough. What sort of stubbornness or devotion would keep Wilson for six years at a seemingly dreary task, made more discouraging by the rise of Stalin and the evident failure during the 1930s of the Russian Revolution to deliver the goods expected by the liberal zealots of the *New Republic*?

In his "Appeal to Progressives," cited above, Wilson ended his article by urging American "Progressives" to speak out "with confidence and boldness." "I believe," he wrote, "that if the American radicals and progressives who repudiate the Marxist dogma and the strategy of the Communist Party still hope to accomplish anything valuable, they must take communism away from the Communists, and take it without ambiguities, asserting that their ultimate goal is the ownership by the government of the means of production." For some time, in fact, he apparently had been thinking that American traditions, institutions, and experiments offered a better field for realization of the Marxist utopia than Russia. In *To the Finland Station* he is, in effect, offering his own revised version of Marxist socialism (or some kind of socialism) to his fellow-citizens of the United States. The more disagreeable aspects of Marx the man get much emphasis. Lenin is the real hero of the book, with his arrival at the Finland Station, in Leningrad, to overthrow the Kerensky liberal government, as the dramatic climax of the narrative. Stalin is the villain. Trotsky is not exactly a villain, but is ultimately a failure, and Wilson pointedly reminds us that Trotsky was responsible for the massacre of the Kronstadt sailors, who shortly before that had been heroes of the Revolution. "One realizes," Wilson says, "that Trotsky's enthusiasm for freedom is less a positive than a negative affair, that it is expressed mainly in indignation against other people who will not let his side be free." (But is that not true, one wants to ask, of other Marxist Communists and Socialists, wherever found?) The defects of Marxist doctrine get some attention, too. The famous "Dialectic," Wilson argues, is an insubstantial "myth"—and he means for "myth" to be taken as at least mildly pejorative. What happened was, he says, that, following German Marxist scholarship too sheepishly, the Marxists thoughtlessly retained Hegel's *These, Antithese,* and *Synthese,* a triad which parallels the Christian "myth" of the Trinity, in Wilson's opinion. Elsewhere, *Finland Station* is slanted for the American consumer by reminders of the American experiments in community socialism: by members of the Robert Owen persuasion at New Harmony, Indiana, and other places; by Frances Wright at Nashoba in Tennessee; by the Icarians, at Nauvoo, Illinois; by John Humphrey Noyes at Oneida, New York. Only the last of these—it lasted thirty-two years—could he called a modest success. And, finally, Wilson's opening attraction, his highly interesting treatment of the so-called "bourgeois revolution" of the early nineteenth century, in which he includes not only the French historian Michelet, but the *littérateurs* Renan and Taine, puts Marxism and Marx in more seemly academic company than they commonly enjoy—better, at any rate, than Stalin or Khrushchev would provide.

Some of the more decisive predispositions of Edmund Wilson can be inferred from the two important ventures just discussed—one in straight literary criticism, the other in history, biographically approached. Like the narrator of *I Thought of Daisy,* Wilson's hope is that "by way of literature itself, I should break through into the real world." That Wilson gets into literature by way of journalism—"the serious profession of journalism," as he describes it in the sober reminiscences of "Thoughts on Being Bibliographed"—is important in his career, since his connection with one of the principal periodicals of the Left gave him a chance to practice his skill both in literature and in affairs. His sense of mission led him to work furi-

ously in both fields. As Mr. Sherman Paul very correctly says in his recent book:

> He considered it a part of his double task that the cultural situation required of the critic: that he explain the difficult new art of the time (which he had done in *Axel's Castle*) and that he "bring home to the 'bourgeois' intellectual world the most recent developments of Marxism. . . ."[4]

By 1940, when *To the Finland Station* was published, a Stalinized Russia had wrecked Wilson's faith in the Bolsheviks and in Marxism in practice. Events in Russia had in fact changed the shape of the book while it was in composition. The Second World War disturbed Wilson even more than the first, and his comments on "the most recent developments of Marxism" became scattering and incidental. When he returned to literary criticism in 1941 in *The Wound and the Bow,* an extended application of his theory of the "psychic wound" as a causal element in art, Wilson found occasion, during his discussion of Hemingway, to upbraid his literary contemporaries for their folly in swallowing Marxism as a quasi-religion which could consecrate for them the barbarities of the Soviet GPU and the Moscow trials. Soon, then, in 1946, came his novel, *Memoirs of Hecate County,* to portray what he might be cynically viewing as the disintegration of the American society in which he had so hopefully grown up. For a long time afterwards, his writings, most of which appeared in *The New Yorker,* reflect what he seems to take as the literary and intellectual deadness of the 1940s, which he must satirize, directly rebuke, and only rarely find much to be happy about. In *Classics and Commercials,* his "chronicle" of this period, Katherine Anne Porter is one of the few that he finds worth unreserved praise.

Finally in 1962 comes *Patriotic Gore*, under which sardonic title Wilson reviews in one large volume what he calls "the literature" of the Civil War—not the military record, except in passing references, but the books, whether novels, stories, poems, diaries, memoirs, biographies, whatever may shed a true light on the nature and subsequent effects of the great trouble between the North and the South. The resulting book may well stand, to many readers, as Wilson's best. It is certainly a rare novelty to discover in it the strong-minded and strong-stomached admirer of Joyce and Proust writing fifty-odd pages of excellent critical discourse on Harriet Beecher Stowe's *Uncle Tom's Cabin* and just about an equal number on the voluminous and highly argumentative writings of Alexander Stephens, Vice President of the Confederate States— that strange obstructionist pigmy whom Wilson too innocently takes to be a great statesman. It seems to give Wilson a special glow of satisfaction to come upon that older pre-Marxist, pre-Joycean, pre-Freudian America to which his family belonged. Would not that glow, in a Southern critic, be called "nostalgia" by the ex-denizens of Bleecker Street and environs? And why did Wilson not read those old books long before—if not at great Princeton, somewhere?

BUT BEFORE this, in *A Piece of My Mind*, Wilson had set forth a kind of credo, which, however, is somewhat of a non-credo. He begins the small book by making it clear (though it had long since been apparent) that he professes no religion and does not accept the formulas, no matter how rationalized or made to seem symbolical, of Christian theology. At the

end, after a fine reminiscence of his father, he pictures himself as sitting alone in the isolated stone house that his family built very long ago in the forest wilderness of upstate New York. It is "curious," he reflects, to find the old house, with "its elegance of windows and doorways" still in place, so isolated.

> In a sense it has always been stranded [he writes]. And am I, too, I wonder, stranded? Am I, too, an exceptional case? When, for example, I look through *Life* magazine, I feel that I do not belong to the country depicted there, that I do not even live in that country. Am I, then, in a pocket of the past? I do not necessarily believe it. I may find myself here at the center of things—since the center can be only in one's head—and my feelings and thoughts may be shared by many.

Is this the famous ennui, or *taedium vitae*, of the dissociated artist? Can it also affect a literary critic? Very nearly so, I would think. The modern power state, with all its industrialism and science, really does not know what to do with a literary critic any more than it knows what to do with literary art. Even if it is socialized, even if it is Marxized, it still does not know. Wilson sees this. He has written about it. He feels his alienation, but he will not give up. He will fight back!

What with? That is the great question

With pen and ink, of course, typewriter and paper. Writing.

But what about, in times like these? And for whom?

The last question is easiest to answer: for the readers of the *New Yorker* and their like, whoever they may be. As to "What about?" we get that answer from *The*

Bit Between My Teeth, which follows the pattern of the previous "Chronicles" selected pieces written for the *New Yorker,* with a few from the *New Republic, The Nation, New Statesman,* or *Encounter,* no doubt worked over for book publication. And one needs first to be aware of what Wilson does *not* choose to write about. For he has habits, and still avoids authors and subjects that he has tended to avoid in the past. For example, there is Faulkner, who since his canonization by a Nobel Award in 1950, has been written about by nearly everybody, but who has been touched upon by Wilson in only one rather brief article, published in 1948 and reprinted in *Classics and Commercial.* In the new book Faulkner gets mentioned only in passing references, one of which relates Hemingway's maudlin story of how, entering Mississippi during his travels, he realized that he was getting into "Faulkner country" and so sat up all night with his "gun" on his hotel table, lest Faulkner, his rival, send some tough character to do him in. Also avoided, here as in the past, are books about the race question, the Korean fracas, the Cold War, the space race and such banner headline topics and, on the literary side, most American authors and subjects located outside the area bounded approximately by the Hudson and Delaware rivers on the west and south and the Atlantic on the east.

And the authors and subjects that Wilson chooses, in the new "Chronicle," as in the past, are the American authors and subjects within the favored Northeastern region and the European authors across the water. And particularly he chooses for discussion, of course, those authors of the 1920s and 1930s, previously discussed by him, who invite comment by the appearance of some memoir or new edition. For Wilson, still the journalist, deals and

perhaps must deal with what is current. Except for special reason he does not go digging up old books. One guesses that *Patriotic Gore,* which covers an amazing quantity of out-of-print books, would not have been written but for the Civil War Centennial, which made enough noise to break into Wilson's repose at Talcottville or Wellfleet.

So in this new "Chronicle" in Wilson's familiar and always engaging style, we have some brilliant pieces that deal with Scott Fitzgerald, Fitzgerald and Hemingway, Max Beerbohm, "Teddy" Roosevelt (his pre-presidential correspondence), Holmes and Laski (their correspondence), Bernard Shaw, Auden, Mario Praz, Swinburne, Kingsley Amis, and—as it were, specially featured—seventy pages on the Marquis de Sade and fifty-three on Pasternak and his *Doctor Zhivago.* Besides, there are several *causeries* (two of them represent Wilson interviewing himself) in which we get a very rich Wilsonian flow of critical opinion on a number of matters, including the very important matter of the debasement of the language by our loose general toleration of solecisms and jargon. Highly interesting too, is Wilson's "My Fifty Years with Dictionaries and Grammars," even though it has had some of its shine knocked off by Vladimir Nabokov's documented assertions (in *Encounter,* February, 1966) that Edmund Wilson's knowledge of the Russian language is not something that an eminent literary critic ought to expose in public.

These pieces, with others I have mentioned, deserve much more discussion than the nature of this article can permit. I must turn to the main question which is whether literary criticism as practiced by Edmund Wilson can affect the cultural drift of our life for better or worse—if indeed at all. I think the answer is, in part, that literature and its critics no longer enjoy the advantages of eighteenth-century London or nineteenth-century Paris. Starting in Greenwich Village in the 1920s, Edmund Wilson could, like the famous hero of Addison's poem, ride in the whirlwind—but he could not like that reputed hero direct the storm. No one could, with such instruments of direction as Princeton, New York, and their trans-Atlantic uncles, cousins, and aunts then provided an ambitious young writer. In his "A Modest Self-Tribute," which stands like a preface to this latest collection of essays, Wilson says that "the primary key in my reading to my work as a critic" was the youthful discovery of a translation of Taine's *History of English Literature* in his father's library. From that admired master he came to feel that "writing about literature . . . meant narrative and drama," and the example of the master has served him well. He has also carried through on a considerable scale his desire "to concentrate synoptically, as they say of the Gospels, to bring into one system, the literatures of several cultures." It is a large, bold effort, and it has produced much that cannot be taken as ephemeral. But his books by their very omissions or outspoken complaints reveal—the newest one among them—that Wilson sees no new Yeats or Joyce or Proust or Eliot rising in America or Europe. And though the socialism he has advocated is now far advanced in the United States and abroad, the cultural and political results are a vast disappointment—in fact, little short of disaster or even destruction. There is something Edmund Wilson must have missed. Perhaps he did not go far or deep enough.

IT MIGHT be useful to turn, for a brief comparison, to one of Wilson's contem-

poraries whose posthumous book of essays also was published in 1965. I refer to *Life Without Prejudice,* by the late Richard Weaver.

Wilson in his book rightly deplores the present horrifyingly ungrammatical use of "based upon" and the tedious and dull misapplication of "massive," "kudos" and other clichés and solecism. They corrupt the language.

Weaver in his title essay makes a close study of the misuse, often calculated and deliberate, of the word *prejudice* in the ideological warfare now disrupting our life. The corruption is not only of the language but of mind and morals, for, if the word is properly understood, a life without prejudice would be a life without principle.

Wilson, late in life, studied the "literature" of the Civil War and produced a remarkable book about his findings. Although the study was educative and perhaps tempered somewhat his Northerner's traditional indifference to the South, the main result for Wilson personally was to deepen his already great disgust for war.

Weaver, in middle life, spent three years studying the Civil War—both the history and the literature. He recommends the study of the Civil War, especially as it affected the losing side, because he thinks there is no "better way to counteract the stultifying 'Whig' theory of history, with its bland assumption that every cause which has won deserved to win." Furthermore, he says, "in a dozen ways I came to recognize myself in the past, which is at least an important piece of self-discovery." His study changed his life.

Wilson, returning to the old stone house in upstate New York, wonders if he, like the house, is "stranded." Weaver, in his "Up from Liberalism," says that on returning to his native South he learned how to shake off the "dogmatic, utilitarian, essentially contumacious doctrines of liberalism and scientism" that had oppressed him. With the return, he experienced a "recovery of lost power or of lost wonder and enchantment."

Wilson has looked in various directions for a secular faith, without finding either Marxism or liberalism or existentialism really satisfactory. He is left with his books, the old books on his shelves, the new ones that keep streaming in. Books are good, but they are not a religion or even a metaphysic. His windows, then, do not open upon his native United States, the old Republic of his forefathers, or even upon the world. They are closed, and he is in his excellent library. We may visit him there, just by taking the trouble to read him—which is never a trouble but always a pleasure. And thus may have a cosy evening with Edmund Wilson, a fine Ivy League and Greenwich Village evening, over the cocktails. But when the good talk is over and we have to go home, we may still have gained little to arm us against the murk outside, the modern dark.

Notes

1. "The Author at Sixty." *A Piece of My Mind: Reflections at Sixty* (New York: Farrar, Straus, 1956), 234.

2. "The Consequences of the Crash." *The Shores of Light: A Literary Chronicle of the Twenties and the Thirties* (New York: Farrar, Straus, and Young, 1952), 498–99.

3. See *The Identity of Yeats* (London, Macmillan, 1954), 261–66, where Ellman gives an extensive discussion of Yeats's poem.

4. Sherman Paul, *Edmund Wilson: A Study of Literary Vocation in Our Time* (Urbana: Univ. of Illinois Press, 1965), 126.

Gottfried Dietze

Liberty and Equality

VOL. 2, NO. 6, 1966

Equality and Liberty, by Harry V. Jaffa. New York: Oxford Univ. Press, 1965.

DISCUSSION OF liberty and equality concerns one of the most relevant topics in political science. For liberty and equality are basic to constitutional government. Authoritarianism is by and large condemned because it supposedly denies liberty and equality, whereas constitutionalism is praised because it supposedly protects these values. However, this does not mean that the fellowship of liberty and equality under a constitutional government is an unproblematic one. Advocates of constitutional government like Montesquieu and Tocqueville, much as they were interested in a society characterized by liberty and equality, recognized an inherent conflict between these values. As a matter of fact, both seem, in an absolute sense, to be competitive, if not incompatible. In the last analysis, an egalitarian is unable to accept the liberty of his fellow men to do and to live better than himself on account of the free use of their greater abilities. Likewise, a libertarian will be opposed to egalitarian restrictions of the free employment of his abilities to do and to live better than his fellow men. Man's quest for liberty has been as insatiable as his quest for equality. The former is likely to result in anarchy and the latter in absolute conformity and regimentation, and one is as incompatible as the other with constitutional government. Perhaps that form of government can be measured by its ability to protect liberty and equality to such a degree only as to assure their coexistence. It must protect only the liberty to do what is permitted by the (basically liberal) law and only the equality before that law, a law which is devoid of privileges which are not the result of the free and legal employment of human faculties and are thus artificial and unjust. Constitutional government thus seems to stand or fall with the maintenance of a neat balance between a qualified, and not absolute, liberty and a qualified, and not absolute, equality. The tenuous situation in which we find constitutional government today is probably due to an undue increase of equality at the cost of liberty, an increase which destroys that balance.

The Declaration of Independence can be considered a true document of consti-

Four Decades of the Intercollegiate Review   823

tutional government because it confesses both to the principles of liberty and equality when it states "that all men are created equal, that they are endowed by their Creator with certain unalienable rights, that among these are Life, Liberty and the pursuit of Happiness," happiness in all probability meaning the protection of property rights, i.e., of the rights to enjoy achievement and what has been gained as a result of the free employment of the unequal faculties of man. In proposing popular government, the Declaration became more than a mere document of constitutional government. It became a document of constitutional democracy. Since democracy is majority rule which has more and more come to tend toward egalitarian rather than libertarian values, the constitutionalism of modern democracy has come to depend largely upon the majority's ability to contain egalitarian passions by a reasonable appreciation of liberty.

PROFESSOR JAFFA'S well-written book, consisting of previously published addresses, articles, and book reviews, is concerned with equality and liberty in the United States. It makes the reader reflect upon these values and ponder over the theory and practice of American politics. Whereas Erik von Kuehnelt-Leddihn's *Liberty or Equality,* published in 1952, suggests the basic competition between, if not incompatibility of, liberty and equality, the title of the book reviewed indicates a general acceptance of the co-existence of the two values.

If we ask the further question as to which of these values is the more important one, the title, putting equality before liberty, seems to suggest that the author attributes priority to equality. According to the foreword by Charles H.

Percy, currently Republican candidate for U.S. Senator from Illinois, it is Professor Jaffa's view that American politics, like American independence, was and is generated by the dedication of the American people to the principle of human equality. This principle is, according to the author, "the most important cause of the most important events in our past . . . the cause for which we as a free people ought to live." The impression that Professor Jaffa tends to elevate equality over liberty is strengthened by his many references to the importance of equality rather than to that of liberty; by his considering "liberty as an implication of equality"; by the fact that his statement that the assertion of the self-evident truth that all men are created equal "cannot mean that all men are equal in intelligence, strength, beauty, or in moral or intellectual capacity . . . that there is no natural difference between man and man" is not followed by a statement that different natural abilities and their free employment entitle men to different standards of living; by the fact that whereas he writes that equality in the Declaration of Independence can only have meant that people have an equal right to participate in government, he refrains from pointing out how the abolition of property qualifications for voting led the emancipated toward passing social legislation which interfered with property rights as well as the right to work for the acquisition of property. He admits that the government can interfere with property rights; rights the protection of which can be considered a bulwark against egalitarianism—if such interference is approved by the representatives of the people.

IN SPITE of his obvious foible for equality, it would be unfair to call Mr. Jaffa an egalitarian. For he also favors a constitutional democracy in which there exists liberty, and thus appears as an advocate of a certain balance between egalitarian and libertarian principles. To him the Declaration of Independence provides that "Governments derive their just powers from the consent of equals who join in civil society to secure their inherent rights to life and to liberty. Property is a support of life, and the enlargement of property an enlargement of liberty. For this reason it is a duty of government to make property secure." The author emphasizes that Jefferson favored enlightened self-government, and that "[t]he transformation of majority rule from a quantitative to a qualitative concept . . . was the work that the founders set out to achieve and upon which the truth of the proposition of equality, for all its self-evidence, depended." Majority rule was to be one in which the natural aristocracy, an aristocracy based upon virtue and talent, played a predominant role, for "[a]ccording to Jefferson, the best form of government was democratic precisely because it was also aristocratic, in the true sense of the word" (51). It appears that equality served the purpose of permitting everyone of virtue and talent to rise to membership in the natural aristocracy, and was a means for a libertarian end. Professor Jaffa's belief in a balance of liberty and equality rather than a priority of equality can be gathered also from his acceptance of the idea that the Constitution, drafted in large measure to prevent infringements upon property rights, to maintain the unequal distribution of property, and to prevent economic egalitarianism, "was framed by men who . . . were committed by and large to the principles of the Declaration of Independence. Washington, Madison, Jefferson, Hamilton, whatever their differences all expressed their belief in the

principles of the Declaration, and all conceived the Constitution as the frame of a government instituted to secure the rights announced in the Declaration. Not one of them would have recognized any more fundamental difference between the Declaration and the Constitution than, broadly speaking, the difference between a statement of ends and a statement of means." Jaffa's concern about the protection of liberty is perhaps most evident in the chapter "On the Nature of Civil and Religious Liberty."

That chapter deals with the problem of whether there is a justification for constitutional reason of state, i.e., whether in a constitutional democracy the government ought to be permitted to restrict civil rights if these rights are being abused by forces that want to overthrow the constitutional order providing for liberty and equality. Professor Jaffa, marshalling support from John Stuart Mill, answers this question in the affirmative, having "seen Weimar Germany, the freest market place of ideas the world has ever known, give itself up to the Nazis." (The government under the Weimar Republic, it will be remembered, extended the protection of its Bill of Rights to Nazi activities, something Goebbels himself branded as a foolish and suicidal policy.) This reviewer, having observed the last years of the Weimar Republic in Germany at close range, agrees with this. However, he is more reluctant to support the author's negative answer to the question whether restrictions of civil liberties for the sake of the preservation of constitutional democracy in the United States, while justifiable, would be wise and expedient. Professor Jaffa believes "that the United States is a sufficiently civilized and a sufficiently stable community to bear the advocacy of almost anything, whether it be national socialism, communism, or cannibalism." He takes his stand with Jefferson, who in his first inaugural address said, "If there be any among us who would wish to dissolve this Union or to change its republican form, let them stand undisturbed as monuments of the safety with which error of opinion may be tolerated where reason is left free to combat." Lincoln, with whom the author deals at length, seems to have been influenced by this statement even during the Civil War. His restrictions of civil rights, serious as they were, were of relatively minor nature. Similarly, this country could afford relatively mild restrictions of civil rights during the two World Wars. Whether it can afford liberality with respect to Communists and their fellow travellers, remains to be seen. Mr. Jaffa himself perhaps harbors doubts in this respect, when outside the chapter just discussed, he states: "We hope to control the future by recapturing the past. I believe something very like this is the only policy by which we will be saved, if we are saved."

Robert Strausz-Hupé

Memoirs of a Grand Old Man

VOL. 3, NO. 1, 1966

Memoirs, 1945–53, by Konrad Adenauer. Translated from the German by Beate Ruhm von Oppen. Chicago: Henry Regnery Co., 1966.

WE SUSPECT that there are those among statesmen aspiring to literary fame who employ the services of professionals to "flesh out" a table-of-contents composed by the official author. No doubt, Dr. Adenauer had a hand in designing his *Memoirs 1945–1953* and in the selection and arrangement of the materials which make up the bulk—a considerable bulk at that—of this massive volume. Yet the total effect is that of lumbering contrivance—a composite of memoranda, excerpts from state papers and the press, and sundry snippets of official communications. It bespeaks the strength of Dr. Adenauer's personality that, here and there, it shines through the film of self-righteous circumspection which envelops the revelations of a still active politician.

It has been pointed out before that Dr. Adenauer, had he disappeared from the public scene at the age of seventy, would have been remembered as a leading German Francophile; a minor and not so successful politician; an efficient municipal manager; and as a brave man who defied Hitler. He would not have been remembered for long. Another generation of Germans, reluctant to look back, would have soon forgotten him. The rise of this septuagenarian to national and international prominence is as miraculous as the resurgence of postwar Germany. As a matter of fact, these two miracles blend into one another.

The *Memoirs* covers the eight crucial years between the total collapse of the Reich and the signing of the Convention which the Federal Republic of Germany concluded with Great Britain, France, and the United States, and which abolished the Occupational Statute. The Convention freed the Federal Republic, under international law, to enter agreements and alliances and thus to join the European Defense Community as a full, sovereign member. The Convention and the EDC Treaty formed an indivisible whole. Dr. Adenauer closes the present volume with a summary of the considerations which prompted him to commit the Federal Republic to a supranational

European military organization and simultaneously to an alliance with the United States. Presumably, the next volume will tell us about the failure of the EDC Project and about the Chancellor's share in the diplomatic transactions which enabled the Federal Republic to accede, via the Western European Union, a pale shadow of the proposed EDC, to the Western Alliance and the North Atlantic Treaty Organization.

Dr. Adenauer provides a meticulous, perhaps too meticulous, chronology of the step-by-step growth of Western Germany from stateless impotence to the high places of Western alliance diplomacy, and onward to the take-off point of that economic boom which has made Germany the second ranking producer and exporter in the Atlantic Community. At rare moments, Dr. Adenauer affords the reader glimpses of the workings of his own mind. Yet, he quickly lowers again the curtain of official reticence. The *Memoirs* comes to life when the author gives vent to his fierce partisan emotions. Dr. Adenauer attributes his dismissal, in 1945, as Lord Mayor of Cologne to the British Labor Government's partiality to the German Socialist Party (SPD). He does not care to dissimulate his disdain of the SPD leaders who heartily reciprocated his dislike bordering on contempt.

IN THE long and bitter argument about the political, economic, and foreign policies of the new Germany, he bested Dr. Kurt Schumacher and Erich Ollenhauer, the former an erratic doctrinaire and the latter a dull party bureaucrat. That the British viewed these two overrated men as likely and promising alternatives to Dr. Adenauer bespeaks their profound misapprehensions about the state of German society and the mounting West-East con-

flict. I suspect that Dr. Adenauer, despite his subsequent cordial collaboration with Sir Anthony Eden, has not yet forgiven the British. Yet he did not permit his personal bias to interfere with his political judgment. He held steadfastly to the concept of a united Europe under French *and* British leadership. It is this concept which motivated his labors on behalf of the European Defense Community.

Dr. Adenauer shares with de Gaulle a highly personal conception of political leadership. Neither has seen fit to devote much space in his memoirs to the parts played by associates in the enterprises which they led. Both are prone to employ the capital "I" when they chronicle the history of their times. Like de Gaulle, Dr. Adenauer writes sparingly, to the point of parsimony, of the achievements of his ministerial colleagues. Unlike de Gaulle, Dr. Adenauer is a pedestrian writer. His style is wooden. It is in keeping with his public image—that stern countenance, graven of old oak, which, in Germany, seems to satisfy the requirements of leadership *mystique*. Like de Gaulle, Dr. Adenauer grasped the deepest needs of his people, the need to recapture national self-esteem and the need to turn shattering national defeat into constructive European achievements. Long before de Gaulle and, for that matter, long before all other European leaders, Dr. Adenauer comprehended the degradation of the power of Europe-as-a-whole. It is this profound insight which raised his labors for a Franco-German *rapprochement*—in concert with that other son of ancient Lotharingia, Robert Schuman—to the level of high European and not merely of German statesmanship.

I do not know whether the passages of the *Memoirs* in which Adenauer dwells on the need of reconciling the Slavic peoples of East Central Europe with a new democratic Germany are after-thoughts, suggested by the latest deténte with the Soviet Union and, perhaps, by the evolution of papal diplomacy. Yet these observations accord with Dr. Adenauer's concept of NATO as not only a defensive alliance, but also as a political instrument for building "bridges" to Communist Europe. Whether, as Dr. Adenauer now seems to hold, NATO in its present state can build these "bridges" or, for that matter, can do more than hold on to its fractured frame, is something which transcends the proper scope of this review.

IN ONE'S own time, it is not easy to discern a statesman's greatness. By all accounts and by comparison, Dr. Adenauer is a great man, probably as great a man as any that rose from Europe's debacle. Self-righteous, vindictive, ungenerous and somewhat less than candid, Dr. Adenauer does not stir that universal affection which flowed to Robert Schuman.

Destiny pours the spirit of an age into the oddest vessels. The *Memoirs* is an odd book. It tells us little about the author. Yet the deeds which the author sets forth were great deeds—deeds done against tremendous odds. Therefore, and for a long time to come, the *Memoirs* will be read by scholars as well as by many less learned men who will wish to know about the remaking of Europe.

With evident relish, Dr. Adenauer paraphrases as follows an article which appeared in *Figaro* at the occasion of his first state visit to Paris:

> Whoever maintained that I was a friend of France was using a misleading phrase. The truth was that I was a man of good will, a German who wanted understanding with France, and that was why Frenchmen should receive me with due respect.

The praise is ambiguous. Yet is not the ability to wrest decision from ambiguity the mark of true statesmanship?

Leo Strauss

John Locke as "Authoritarian"

VOL. 4, NO. 1, 1967

John Locke: Two Tracts on Government.
Edited with an intoduction, notes, and
translation by Philip Abrams. New
York: Cambridge Univ. Press, 1967.

THIS VOLUME consists of two parts:
an annotated edition of what seems to be
Locke's earliest "tracts on government,
and the editor's extensive Introduction.
One of the two tracts was composed in
English, the other in Latin; the editor
has supplied his edition of the Latin tract
with an English translation. Both tracts
were written shortly after the Restoration,
and neither tract was ever published by
Locke. The differences between the two
tracts are not important.

The "two tracts on government," as
the editor calls them, are in fact disputations on the question as to "whether the
civil magistrate may lawfully impose and
determine the use of indifferent things
in reference to religious worship." Locke
answers this question in the affirmative.
He takes the side of law and order against
"the popular assertors of public liberty"
who would only bring on "the tyranny
of a religious rage" if the civil magistrate

did not have or exercise the disputed
right. Locke is all in favor of gently dealing with "the sincere and tender hearted
Christians" but against allowing them "a
toleration . . . as their right." He regards
the people as an "untamed beast."

Indifferent things are things not determined by God's law. The indifferent
things with which the disputations are
concerned are those related to divine
worship as distinguished from indifferent civil things such as taxes, which are
on both sides admitted to be subject to
determination by the civil magistrate.
According to the view rejected by Locke,
the civil magistrate may not determine
indifferent things that concern divine
worship because such determination
would not be compatible with Christian
liberty. Hence the most important argument adduced by the men whom Locke
opposes is that "imposing things indifferent is directly contrary to Gospel
precepts." One may therefore say that the
disputations belong to the province of
political theology rather than to that of
political philosophy.

Yet while this is true of the primary
theme of the disputations, it is not un-

qualifiedly true of all of its implications. It suffices here to mention two of these implications or presuppositions: God's law and the origin and extent of the power of the civil magistrate.

Locke does not say much on God's law. The divine or moral law becomes known to man "either by the discoveries of reason, usually called the law of nature, or the revelation of his word." The question as to whether the content of the law of nature is identical with the content of the revealed law is answered negatively in the English tract, where Locke occasionally speaks of "the positive moral law of God," and affirmatively in the Latin tract. This observation is not contradicted by the fact that in the English tract he occasionally speaks of "the law of God or nature," for he list's this expression when stating the view of his opponents. He apparently did not think it necessary to clear up the obscurity indicated.

As for the extent of the power of the civil magistrate, Locke ascribes to him "absolute, arbitrary power over all the indifferent actions of his people." To say the least, this sounds very different from the teaching of *Two Treatises.* The magistrate may "establish or alter all indifferent things as he shall judge them conducing to the good of the public," "but he alone is judge what is so and what not." Although the magistrate acts unjustly by commanding things forbidden by God's law, his subjects are bound to a passive obedience, i.e., may not resist his laws by force of arms. Since "the same arbitrary power" resides in the governing assembly of a republic as in any monarch, subjects enjoy no greater freedom in a republic than under an absolute monarch. This is quite at variance with the teaching of the *Two Treatises,* according to which "absolute monarchy . . . is indeed inconsistent with civil society." In accordance with all this, Locke's argument in the two tracts does not depend on how one decides the question as to the origin of the civil magistrate's power, viz. whether one holds that that power derives immediately from God or from the subjects—in other words, whether the king is held to rule by divine right pure and simple or by virtue of a contract.

THE TWO tracts would not be of interest to anyone except historians specializing in mid-seventeenth-century English theologico-political debates but for the fact that they are the work of Locke, if of the young Locke who had not yet found his own word. As the editor puts it, the author of the two tracts is an "authoritarian" rather than, as he is frequently thought to be, "the presiding genius of liberal democracy;" he surely is not "liberal" or in favor of "any . . . form of permissive government." Yet "authoritarian" has many meanings: most, not to say all, political philosophers who wrote prior to 1660 were "authoritarian." Hooker was "authoritarian" in one sense, Hobbes in a very different sense. In the two tracts, Locke quotes approvingly Hooker's general definition of law but, as the editor correctly states, he divorces that definition from its teleological context. One is not surprised to observe that Hobbes is never mentioned in the tracts. This would not by any means exclude the possibility that the tracts were influenced or inspired by Hobbes, for silence on Hobbes might have been part of the "strategy" of the young Locke as it was part of the "strategy" of the mature Locke. According to the editor, "it is essentially a Hobbesian argument that Locke deploys." Yet, to say nothing of his far-reaching qualifications, both his notion of what constitutes Hobbianism and

Locke's relevant statements are too vague to enable Abrams to prove the dependence of the tracts on Hobbes.

The question regarding the Hobbesianism of the young Locke may be said to be of some importance with a view to the fundamental question regarding the political philosophy of the mature or old Locke, to the question which would have to be stated as follows: is the natural law teaching of the mature Locke fundamentally traditional (say, Hookerian) or is it a modified version of Hobbes's natural law teaching? Abrams admits that Locke has broken with the traditional natural law teaching but denies that he builds on the foundation laid by Hobbes. As he suggests, Locke has moved away, more or less hesitatingly, from the view according to which the law of nature is the law of reason and that it is obligatory because it is dictated by reason, in the direction of "fideism." More precisely, while Locke never abandoned the notion that the law of nature is the law of reason or, which for him seems to be the same thing, that ethics can be made a demonstrative science, he never elaborated that ethics but

asserted that the complete law of nature is available in the New Testament and only in the New Testament, i.e., only by revelation. In a word, Locke is "inconsistent" regarding the foundations of politics; "in the end he remained intellectually entangled in the tradition in which he had been educated." Abrams arrives at this result partly by relying on Locke's "relativistic" statements regarding "true religion," i.e., by tacitly identifying "objective moral truths" (and therefore in particular that set of moral truths which underlies the political teaching of the *Second Treatise*) with "true religion," and partly by disregarding the difference (which for Locke is crucial) between men in general and the "studiers" of the law of nature. Abrams could not have remained satisfied with his thesis if he had paid any attention to the fact of which he has heard and which he does not deny that "face value is something one cannot safely attribute to any work by Locke" or that the study of Locke's writings must be enlightened by understanding of the character as well as the reason of his "persistent strategy."

Louis I. Bredvold

THE ACHIEVEMENT OF C. S. LEWIS

VOL. 4, NO. 2–3, 1968

Of Other Worlds: Essays and Stories, by C. S. Lewis. Edited by Walter Hooper. New York: Harcourt, Brace, and World, Inc., 1967.

Studies in Medieval and Renaissance Literature, by C. S. Lewis. Collected by Walter Hooper. New York: Cambridge Univ. Press, 1966.

THE FORTY-ODD volumes published by C. S. Lewis before his death in 1963 offer such a remarkable variety and range in nature and subject matter that he achieved several reputations among different reading publics. Avid readers of science fiction know his three space novels, written in the manner, but not the spirit, of H. G. Wells. For children he created the Kingdom of Narnia with its imaginary adventures. He is probably the most widely read religious spokesman of our time and yet his main occupation was scholarship and university teaching. He first attracted attention outside of Oxford in 1936, when he was thirty-eight years old, with an erudite volume on *The*

Allegory of Love: A Study in Medieval Literature, which was immediately recognized as a classic work throughout the learned world. And as Fellow of Magdalen College, Oxford, from 1925 to 1955, and Professor of Medieval and Renaissance Literature at Cambridge after 1955, he continued to produce essays and books of such distinguished scholarship that they are considered indispensable. All his learned work, no matter how minutely and scrupulously erudite, never deteriorated into pedantry. No literary scholar of our time has more successfully exemplified the humane way of studying the Humanities. The simple explanation is that he was himself so extraordinarily alive and alert to human experience. He detested intellectual snobs; he did not read Great Books for the purpose of acquiring a prestige "culture," but just for pleasure and joy. He was careful, as he grew older, not to suppress the wholesome eagerness of his boyhood. Probably most teachers of Spenser at the present time think the best approach to his poetry is from what might be called the graduate level, and their students fail to respond to anything beyond the scholarly problems. The different approach of Lewis is thoroughly characteristic:

> The Faerie Queene suffers even more than most great works from being approached through the medium of commentaries and "literary history." These all demand from us a sophisticated, self-conscious frame of mind. But then, when we have used all these aids, we discover that the poem itself demands exactly the opposite response. Its primary appeal is to the most naive and innocent tastes: to that level of our consciousness which is divided only by the thinnest veil from the immemorial lights and glooms of the collective Unconscious itself. It demands of us a child's love of marvels and dread of bogies, a boy's thirst for adventures, a young man's passion for physical beauty. If you have lost or cannot re-arouse these attitudes, all the commentaries, all your scholarship about "the Renaissance" or "Platonism" or Elizabeth's Irish policy, will not avail. . . . It is of course much more than a fairy-tale, but unless we can enjoy it as a fairy-tale first of all, we shall not really care for it.

And when we begin to interpret the moral and philosophical meaning of the allegory, he warns us not to regard it as a mere rhetorical figure or literary device.

> The work of Jung and Freud, and the practice of many modern poets and prose writers, has taught us an entirely different view. We now know that symbols are the natural speech of the soul, a language older and more universal than words. . . . We shall understand it best (though this may seem paradoxical) by not trying too hard to understand it. Many things such as

loving, going to sleep, or behaving affectedly are done worst when we try hardest to do them. Allegory is not a puzzle.[1]

Lewis obviously belonged, not to that class of teachers who declare their intention of "vitalizing" Shakespeare or Spenser or Homer, but to the class that understands how we are to be vitalized by them. No wonder his lectures at Oxford and Cambridge were crowded.

Of course the general public knew nothing about this learned university don. He became a celebrity only after he began the publication of his books on religion, the first of which was *The Screwtape Letters* (1942). The BBC immediately secured him for three series of broadcasts, which were published as *The Case for Christianity* (1943), *Christian Behaviour* (1943), and *Beyond Personality* (1945), later collected into one volume under the title *Mere Christianity*. During these years he also reached a still wider public with his three works of science fiction, better called space novels, partly inspired by the novels of this type by H. G. Wells, which Lewis had devoured in his boyhood. But he used science fiction to oppose the ideas of Wells and the current philosophy of which Wells was an important spokesman. And thus in a few years the Oxford don became one of the must controversial figures in England.

He was probably very much an enigma to the general public until 1955, when he published a full and candid narrative of his educational and spiritual experiences up to the age of thirty-one, under the significant title, *Surprised by Joy*. "This book is written," he explained in the preface, "partly in answer to requests that I would tell how I passed from Atheism to Christianity." It was therefore the story of a typically troubled youth, perturbed by those issues and problems over which so many young people have agonized from generation to generation. What kind of universe are we in? Is there a God? Is God conceivable by the human mind? Why is there evil in the world? By what wisdom can we guide our lives? The English public learned in 1955 how resolutely its esteemed and popular Christian apologist had wrestled with such questions, and how he had, even as he was teaching philosophy at Magdalen College, settled firstly on atheism as the only honest and intelligible doctrine. He explained how he had fought doggedly for his own dogmatic disbelief and his complicated narrative can not be summarized here. It must suffice to say that his defenses, one after another, were battered down, until he was at last "surprised by Joy" and he accepted, reluctantly, the truth of the Gospels and knew that he believed in Jesus Christ as the Son of God. He was then thirty-one years old.

ALL THROUGH these years Lewis had experienced longings for various things, and occasionally a deep longing for Joy. We must not dismiss this kind of experience as either a mere emotional indulgence or a mere emotional discomfort. Obviously, our longings often have no great philosophical import. A child is homesick and a schoolboy longs for vacation. One may long for a sight of the sea or the mountains or for a view of what is beyond the mountains. But a glance here and there at literature reveals profounder and more meaningful kinds of longing. Lewis mentions *Sehnsucht,* which the German Romanticists of the eighteenth century thought requisite for a Noble Soul, symbolizing the highest human activity as the Search for the Blue Flower of Happiness. Goethe gives a somewhat

ambiguous illustration of such desire in *Faust,* both the First and Second Parts. But the Chorus Mysticus at the conclusion of the whole work clearly expresses the longing for the great Eternal Unseen, of which all transitory things are only symbols, although this aspiration lapses into the final line: *Das Ewig-Weibliche zieht uns hinan* (The Eternal Woman-Soul leadeth us upward and on). This somewhat Faustian idea of Eternal Felicity is less sublime than Goethe probably believed. But Goethe was not exempt from that desire for the Absolute or Eternal or Real, whatever one chooses to call it, which transcends the transitory in our experience. Of course all varieties of Platonism recognize the problem of this discontent. Longing of this kind is one of the uncomfortable gifts of human nature, and yet one which we would not willingly dispense with. Augustine gave to it the classic religious interpretation: "Thou hast made me for Thee, O Lord, and my soul is restless until it has come to Thee."

Lewis's preoccupation with his experiences of longing is therefore neither a novelty nor a personal peculiarity. But his persistent exploration of these experiences is characteristic of his inquiring mind. As a motto for one of his chapters he uses a quotation from Traherne: "So is there in us a world of love to somewhat, though we know not what in the world that should be." That is the theme of *Surprised by Joy.* From his childhood he was haunted by longings, and he early recognized that his deepest longing was for Joy. From his nursery windows in his Belfast home he looked out to the Castlereagh Hills, remote and unattainable to a child of six, and he says they taught him thus early the feeling of *Sehnsucht* and "made me for good or ill a votary of the Blue Flower." And there the story begins, through the years of reading and rich experience of an imaginative and gifted child. For ten years he filled a stack of copy-books with elaborate narratives of a country called Animal-Land. His out-of-school reading was full of excitement; he revelled in the science fiction of H. G. Wells, in Irish folk-lore to which his nurse introduced him, in Norse mythology, Wagnerian opera, Spenser, and medieval romance. Later his life was complicated by intellectual wrestlings with Lucretius and other influences that led him to a calm and determined atheism. But there was always the longing, the restlessness, the desire for Joy.

He learned from experience that many longings were delusive and led to pleasure, perhaps, but not to Joy. "What I like about experience," he says, "is that it is such an honest thing. You may take any number of wrong turnings; but keep your eyes open and you will not be allowed to go very far before the warning signs appear. . . . The Universe rings true wherever you fairly test it."[2] It was by a long series of tests and defeats that Lewis finally discovered a longing that could not be defeated, and was thus "surprised by Joy." He learned that the Joy he sought was not to be coaxed nor attained by sheer effort. Nor was it an automatic fulfillment of his longing. Our hearts are filled with love, not by an introspective cultivation of the feeling of love, but by the contemplation and adoration of the beloved. The Joy Lewis sought he finally found by surrending to belief. Of course a calculating choice of belief as the most highly recommended means to Joy would not be genuine belief. Lewis declares that Heaven is unattainable unless we understand that "it matters more that Heaven should exist than that we should ever get there." We must not expect to find the ultimate reality or the ultimate good in our own phenomenal selves. Spinoza un-

derstood this imperative when he wrote about the *amor intellectualis Dei.* And there is a warning even in the sarcastic remark of Hobbes, who felt no personal need of any God, that the religious people about him seemed to love God, not for His goodness, but for His goodness to *them,* "as is plain from those many supplications which they make daily unto Him."

It is therefore not surprising that this theme reappears so often in his writings, in his science fiction and children's stories as well as in his essays. In discussing various kinds of stories for children he distinguishes between mere "wishful reverie," flattering to the child's ego, and the wholesome longing which he calls *askesis.* The child who is excited by the unwholesome kind "prefers stories about millionaires, irresistible beauties, posh hotels, palm beaches, and bedroom scenes," all things in "real life" that would not be impossible "if the reader had a fair chance." Over against this kind of "success story" Lewis champions the stories of fairy land, though the child knows perfectly well that such things as dragons do not exist in his actual world. He points out a qualitative difference. "The child does not long for fairy land as a boy longs to be the hero of the first eleven. . . . It would be much truer to say that fairy land arouses a longing for he knows not what. It stirs and troubles him (to his lifelong enrichment) with the dim sense of something beyond his reach and, far from dulling or emptying the actual world, gives it a new dimension of depth."[3] And establishing this distinction helps us to appreciate better the appeal of such imaginative literature as *The Faerie Queene,* the *Odyssey,* or *The Tempest.* The pleasure of a mere escapist hedonism is essentially different from the wholesome *askesis,* the longing for Joy.

OBVIOUSLY LEWIS was quite out of tune with his time, and much of his writing has the tone of polemics and often of satire, for which he had both talent and inclination. The natural tendency of his mind was analytical, he always proceeded by drawing distinctions, and he was master of the intellectual maneuvers this made possible. His own growth, as we have seen, proceeded by his accepting one after another the necessary consequences of such distinctions. Out of the many kinds of longing, innocent and guilty, he found the one that really fulfilled his need. In great things and small his readers become accustomed to this confrontation of alternatives. He has a point to make about science fiction, but he begins by classifying these stories into species and sub-species. He enlightens us regarding our enjoyment of all narratives by distinguishing between those we enjoy most on the first reading and those we want to re-read many times. If we read merely for the excitement produced by suspense, we cannot reproduce this excitement when we already know the outcome. But it is one thing to hasten to your destination and another to enjoy your travel on the way.

> We do not enjoy a story fully at the first reading. Nor till the curiosity, the sheer narrative lust, has been given its sop and laid asleep, are we at leisure to savour the real beauties. Till then, it is like wasting great wine on a ravenous natural thirst which merely wants cold wetness. The children understand this well when they ask for the same story over and over again, and in the same words.[4]

We can only agree with him that there is poetry in a really well-told story. This is characteristic of Lewis's technique. He leads the reader through an intellectual process as rigorous as a scientific anatomical dissection, ultimately leaving him surprised with a new insight or a new conviction.

This analytical method is particularly effective in his controversial or polemical writing. For Lewis, though his manner is always courteous and amiable, was constantly engaged in exposing both popular and erudite fallacies. In *Mere Christianity,* for instance, he meets the common proposition that the Moral Law is simply our herd instincts. He immediately concedes that our instincts are important and may be good and necessary: mother love, the sexual instinct, or the instinct for food. But he points out an important distinction: "Feeling a desire to help is quite different from feeling that you ought to help whether you want to or not." Then there is the widely diffused scientific optimism of the "Life-Force philosophy, or Creative Evolution, or Emergent Evolution."

> The wittiest expositions of it come in the works of Bernard Shaw, but the most profound ones in those of Bergson. . . . When you are feeling fit and the sun is shining and you do not want to believe that the whole universe is a mere mechanical dance of atoms, it is nice to be able to think of this great mysterious Force rolling on through the centuries and carrying you on its crest. If, on the other hand, you want to do something rather shabby, the Life-Force, being only a blind force, with no morals and no mind, will never interfere with you like that troublesome God we learned about when we were children. The Life-Force is a sort of tame God. You can switch it on when you want, but it will not bother you. All the thrills of religion and none of the cost.[5]

The philosophical theorem, it appears, has two mutually contradictory corollaries.

As we have observed, Lewis has great faith in the power of experience to test and illuminate high philosophical theory. For his clinical material he likes to go to popular versions of current heresies. His most purely philosophical volume, *The Abolition of Man,* begins with a scrutiny of a text book in English edited by two undistinguished schoolmasters. In an annotation they attempted to set pupils right about a passage in Coleridge. They explained that "when the man said *that is sublime,* he appeared to be making a remark about the waterfall . . . Actually . . . he was not making a remark about the waterfall, but a remark about his own feelings. . . . This confusion is continually present in language as we use it. We appear to be saying something very important about something and actually we are only saying something about our own feelings." Instead of following Lewis's merciless expose of this pseudo-philosophy, let us, quite in the spirit of Lewis, imagine a young man addressing a girl in this way: "When I say you are lovely I appear to be making a remark about you. Actually I am not making a remark about you, but a remark about my own feelings."

If the girl replied, "You do not value me," she would have stated the objection made by Lewis to such misuse of language. The schoolmasters, in short, had fallen through ignorance or thoughtlessness into a denial of the validity of predicates of value. Lewis pounced on this jargon, examined it in detail for its consequences, and concluded that "the practical result of education in this spirit must be the destruction of the society which accepts it." Whether the poor schoolmasters learned anything from their castigation we do not know. But we know that in our own country the persistent attack on any philosophy admitting value judgments has trickled down from the graduate schools to the undergraduates to the high schools to the daily conversation of the average citizen. The Latin learning most widely known and quoted is the derivation of moral from *mores.* And who then dares deny that morality is merely the custom of the country? Moreover, when we join this rejection of value judgments with the idea of an ultimately absolute conquest over nature through science, we reach a terrifying conclusion. For man is, as a part of nature, also destined to be conquered by science. But this general statement, when we particularize it, merely means that the mass of mankind will be controlled by a comparatively few scientists, and that well-meaning philosophers, psychologists, and social engineers will manipulate the human race as the stock-breeder manages a herd of cattle. That would be the abolition of man. Human nature may be too ornery for the complete realization of such a program, but the intellectual currents of our time seem to converge towards such a twilight of history.

IN WHAT, then shall we have our faith? Where can we find the wisdom to save us from this catastrophe? Lewis believed that the wisdom we need can be found in a multitude of writings besides the Christian Scriptures. Borrowing a word from ancient Chinese philosophy, he calls it the Tao, by which, he says, the Chinese meant "the reality beyond all predicates. . . . It is Nature, it is the Way, the Road. It is the Way in which things everlastingly emerge, stilly and tranquilly, into space and time. It is also the Way which every man should tread." This conception he finds in many forms,

Platonic, Aristotelian, Stoic, Christian, and Oriental, and he collects illustrations of it from great and good men all the way from Confucius to John Locke. The Tao "is not one among a series of possible systems of value. It is the sole source of all value judgments." The Innovator who seeks some other source for values, either borrows unwittingly from the Tao, or relies on instincts and satisfactions and utilitarian maxims. The imperative is an ultimate, and no logic can derive it from a statement of fact. "If nothing is self-evident nothing can be proved. Similarly, if nothing is obligatory for its own sake, nothing is obligatory at all"[6]

All of Lewis's writings are distinguished by such sharp dialectic. But in spite of his remarkable aptitude for philosophy, he did not engage in academic disputation with professional philosophers. Like Socrates, he preferred to bring philosophical problems to the marketplace. He was in the best sense a great popularizer. His versatile literary gifts enabled him to reach all sorts and conditions of men. He was especially adroit in satire, flashes of which we encounter here and there in so much of his writings. *The Screwtape Letters,* one of his most popular books, is at the same time a profound treatment of religious truths and a dazzling and sustained satire on aspects of modern life and thought. The basic idea is itself a masterly satiric stroke. Screwtape, a high official in the bureaucracy of Hell, writes his advice and instructions to an evil spirit of inferior rank who is charged with procuring victims in England. We are thus given a view of human life and conduct from Down Underneath and we often get a surprising exposure of Satanic tactics in the experiences of unsuspecting human beings. A very useful domestic irritation, for instance, can be developed by inciting a husband to ask with just the wrong

tone of voice when dinner will be ready. Screwtape is cunning in the deft manipulation of small incidents.

But Screwtape is concerned also with the larger strategies, among them of course the exploitation of certain common predilections of the academic world. It is the policy of the Powers Underneath to encourage the Historical Point of View, currently the prestige attitude in the study of the Humanities. Screwtape explains fully the Infernal preoccupation with this subject. When a learned man who is completely committed to the Historical Point of View is

> presented with any statement in an ancient author, the one question he never asks is whether it is true. He asks who influenced the ancient writer, and how far the statement is consistent with what he said in other books, and what phase in the writer's development, or in the general history of thought, it illustrates, and how often it has been misunderstood (especially by the learned man's own colleagues) and what the general course of criticism on it has been for the last ten years. . . . Thanks be to our Father and the Historical Point of View, great scholars are now as little nourished by the past as the most ignorant mechanic.[7]

How familiar all this is to any veteran scholar! Though Lewis was himself a learned historian, he had observed how often learning *about* a great man is considered sufficient without learning *from* him.

THE SUPREME irony of the book must be Screwtape's instruction of his agent on the superior advantages of Hell over Heaven. Milton's Satan was unable, because of his perverted intellect, to see anything of God except His power. But Screwtape can clearly and accurately explain His attributes and His ways with men, although in his alienation these seem to him incomprehensible and even a little absurd. The purpose Down Underneath is to catch the victim, devour him, and digest him into the Essence of Evil. But Screwtape admonishes his agent never to forget that the Enemy "really likes the little vermin, and sets an absurd value on the distinctness of every one of them." In a war one must be aware, if possible, of the strategic plan of the Enemy.

> One must face the fact that all the talk about His love for men, and His service being perfect freedom, is not (as one would gladly believe) mere propaganda, but an appalling truth. He really does want to fill the universe with a lot of loathsome little replicas of Himself—creatures whose life, on its miniature scale, will be qualitatively like His own, not because He has absorbed them but because their wills freely conform to His. We want cattle who can finally become food. He wants servants who can finally become sons. We want to suck in. He wants to give out. We are empty and would be filled; He is full and flows over.[8]

Nothing could be more lucid, but nothing could be more chilling than this fine intelligence alienated from everything that we must consider good. It is sober-

ing to reflect that this great contention between Heaven and Hell is not waged in the great cosmic spaces, but here on earth among men, and even in our own individual experience.

Lewis disavowed any claim to originality in his ideas. Rather he considered it a merit to present the old ideas and ideals which he delighted to find in the great men of the humane tradition. His originality is in the qualities of his mind and his style. His coruscating scrutiny of "modern" clichés profoundly disturbed the complacency of many readers who had supposed themselves intellectually settled. He acquired the reputation of being a great irritant. But he also employed his great talents, his intellectual brilliance, his trenchant wit, his sparkling epigram, in championing old wisdom and truth. He has been for many a guide out of the mazes of sophistry. But he has also been a comfort to many by his re-affirmation of the truths that men need, and his utterance has the freshness and vitality derived from his own personal experience.

Notes

1. *Studies in Medieval and Renaissance Literature*, 132–33, 137.
2. *Surprised by Joy*, N.Y., 1955, 167.
3. *Of Other Worlds*, 29.
4. *Of Other Worlds*, 18.
5. *Mere Christianity*, 22, 35.
6. *The Abolition of Man*, 27–28.
7. *The Screwtape Letters*, Letter XXVII.
8. *The Screwtape Letters*, Letter VIII.

Robert Nisbet

The Urban Crisis Revisited

VOL. 7, NO. 1–2, 1970

The Unheavenly City, by Edward C. Banfield. Boston: Little, Brown and Company, 1970.

ONCE IN a great while there comes along a book that is radical in the true and intellectual sense of the word: one that shows us how to break categories of conventional wisdom rather than classroom windows, to uproot the stale flowers of secular piety rather than the flowers in the president's garden. The *Unheavenly City* is such a book. It is also a book that offers a vast amount of insight into that most obsessive of current national interests, the city and its future in American polity.

Edward Banfield is the Henry Lee Shattuck Professor of American Government at Harvard University. He is the deeply respected author of nearly a dozen books and monographs on cities— their problems, their processes, and the policies through which we seek to deal with cities in this country. He is, finally, one of that still very small number of top flight social scientists in this country en-

gaged in relentless examination of, not the conventional wisdom of, say, the Middle Ages, but the conventional wisdom of the social sciences and social policy-makers of the twentieth century. This makes him a possibly dangerous, certainly heretical man. It makes him a wonderfully valuable man, and even if his body lights up the sky as the result of Inquisitorial condemnation at 1970 meetings of the social science associations, I predict that he will prove to be a wonderful candle by which we find our way into the future.

Professor Banfield is much more modest. He predicts, in the Preface, that he is most likely to be thought an ill-tempered, mean-spirited fellow. Well, in these times, I like to think one could do much worse than be thought ill-tempered and mean-spirited. One doesn't come upon that rare type very often in our mass-middle class society composed so largely of the bland and the boneless, incessantly in quest of preening by peers—at least in the academic world. Even so, I don't think the author is as likely to be thought mean and ill-tempered as he is to be thought the product of original sin and invincible ignorance—as these terms are currently defined in the lay theology of contemporary political science, sociology, and related academic disciplines.

The majority of readers will fall, I think, into two camps, at first unequally sized. The first camp will be, almost certainly, quite large in the beginning. Its inhabitants will be all the social scientists, policy-makers, and minions of Service Forever, Inc. who, after one horrified look at the book's conclusions and, worse, of the solid evidence that documents the conclusions, will either ignore it (probable) or else sweep it under a footnote as the sad example of a once fine mind corrupted by lurking penchant for the sociologically wicked.

The second camp, I make bold to predict, will be small at the outset, but it will grow—steadily and substantially. The book could even become—such is my stout optimism in these matters, despite all depressing evidence to the contrary in the social sciences—a classic. Certainly *The Unheavenly City* has the attributes of a classic: imagination united with immense and precise knowledge, profundity as well as brilliance of insight, a subject that is not likely to disappear, either in fact or in popular interest; and also *style*, style in the good and full sense of that often abused word. The style is Banfield; more accurately, Banfield's knowledge of the urban age as distilled through an incessantly experiencing mind. *Rem tene, verba sequentur,* wrote the elder Cato. Well, Edward Banfield has grasped his subject and the words have duly followed; very good words indeed.

What follows in this review will be scarcely more than selective paraphrase of the book. I am grateful for this. One grows weary from the anger that must be repressed or else dressed up in Sunday clothes when one ordinarily reviews books these days. Reading *The Unheavenly City,*

and writing about it, come as welcome respite. I like the book, I concur with it so completely that any expression of differences would be no more than idle hair-splitting, and I want very much to see a large number of people read the book. Why, then, pretend otherwise or seek to interpose reviewer's own conceits between the book and its audience.

SINCE I have described *The Unheavenly City* as a radical assault on conventional wisdom in the social sciences and on secular piety in the burgeoning sphere of a middle class Service, it is well to single out, as background for our appreciation of the book, the major pillars on which this conventional wisdom and this piety rest. They are three.

The first pillar has to do with the universally undoubted belief that our large American cities have deteriorated in all important respects and may today be described—in words given us by Robert Dahl, political scientist at Yale, as "anti-cities: mean, ugly, gross, banal, inconvenient, hazardous, formless, incoherent, unfit for human living." Believe me, those words are about average for reigning wisdom and piety alike.

The second pillar, depending upon the first, declares that our cities are seething cauldrons of repressed revolt because—I repeat, *because*—cities are mean, ugly, gross, etc. and also because within these sinks of inconvenience and squalor, problems of poverty, schooling, police protection, medical services, and housing become more crisis-ridden all the time. As we shall see, these problems *are* crisis-ridden in many respects, but for reasons very different from those assigned by conventional wisdom and secular piety.

The third pillar of conventional wisdom, dependent upon both the first two, declares that only through massive political action of direct type, chiefly Federal, supplemented by the efforts of innumerable Urban Coalitions spread out in a vast network across the country, financed by hundreds of billions of dollars (I do not exaggerate) can we hope to make even a faint beginning in our mastery of what is called by everyone "the urban crisis." The fact that political onslaught after onslaught has failed, or else has worsened the problem, or else has fattened the riches of the already rich in the cities, leaving the poor relatively poorer, has no effect upon this crisis-based mentality in politics. Neither does the fact that the present Urban Coalition is in large part a failure; worse, has left in many a community a substantial residue of bitterness and frustration. There must be *more* political forms of direct action, *more* Urban Coalitions.

Now, I do not think I have exaggerated in the foregoing paragraph. In fact, as I reflect on some recent dispatches from John Gardner's Urban Coalition and related agencies in Washington, I think I have been commendably restrained. I have wanted to be, for it is not necessary to enhance or caricature the central propositions of conventional wisdom on the city in America. It suffices merely to state them if we are to appreciate the radical character of Edward Banfield's book.

For the book may be best viewed as a learned and perceptive reply, by one of our foremost social scientists, precisely to these three propositions. From Professor Banfield's engaging of each conventional proposition emerges a radical conclusion. Taken together, his three conclusions—assuming, that is, that they are read and pondered in the right places, chiefly in the minds of voting citizens—could well lead to the kind of reappraisal of the city, the reformulation of values, that Irving

Kristol has suggested in his recent inaugural lecture as the Henry B. Luce Professor of Urban Values at New York University.[1]

LET ME turn now, with this necessary background briefly sketched, to the three major conclusions that I am able to draw from the dozen research-rooted, closely argued, superbly lucid chapters that form *The Unheavenly City.*

First, the city in America, far from being the metropolitan jungle, the setting of unprecedented material deprivation and ethical ugliness, is in fact a very good place for most persons to live. Admittedly not good by criteria which any bush league disciple of Service could summon up in an instant out of his infinite knowledge of the Neverland of utopian dream. But good when assessed by any standards, past and present, American and foreign, that a *scholar* might work with. Bear in mind too that when Banfield writes of the city he is dealing, overwhelmingly, not with the tiny locality of 2,500 persons that for some reason I shall never understand is the Census Bureau's notion of the dividing line between rural and urban. Banfield is writing about New York, Chicago, Los Angeles, and others comparable. Moreover he reminds us occasionally that for the worst of the urban jungle—so-called—in contemporary America, one would do better to visit some of the localities which come close to Census Bureau dividing line. No matter by what realistic standard of life and service we choose to assess these no longer rural, not yet truly urban scenes, they come out rather badly alongside the Chicagos, Clevelands, San Franciscos, and New Yorks of our time. These, not the "cities" of five and ten thousand inhabitants, are the places Banfield has chiefly in mind when he writes the following passage:

There is less poverty in the cities now than there has ever been. Housing, including that of the poor, is improving rapidly: one study predicts that substandard housing will have been eliminated by 1980. In the last decade alone the improvement in housing has been marked. At the turn of the century only one child in fifteen went beyond elementary school; now most children finish high school. The treatment of racial and other minority groups is conspicuously better than it was. When, in 1964, a carefully drawn sample of Negroes was asked whether in general things were getting better or worse for Negroes in this country, approximately eight out of ten respondents said "better."

Add to the measurable, verifiable improvement within the city itself the presence of large and increasing numbers of newly arrived inhabitants from certain rural areas of America whose condition in a Chicago, Los Angeles, Cleveland, or New York is much better than it was, or stood any likelihood of becoming, in the rural areas from which these individuals have come. Not only, in short, are conditions better in the city, compared with conditions in the same city fifty or twenty years ago, an even larger factor of improvement of conditions may be seen in the lives of large numbers of people who have only just arrived.

The plain fact is that the overwhelming majority of city dwellers live more comfortably and conveniently than ever before. They have more and better housing, more and better schools, more and better transportation, and so on. By any conceivable measure of material welfare the present generation of urban Americans is, on the whole,

better off than any large group of people has ever been anywhere. What is more, there is every reason to expect that the general level of comfort and convenience will continue to rise at an even more rapid rate through the foreseeable future.

So much for the first conclusion. And should there be a reader of this review in slight doubt that Professor Banfield can back up these bold—nay, mind-boggling—statements, I invite him to the several chapters of the book and to the voluminous notes and references which may be found unobtrusively collected at the end of the book. Not only will the reader find the conclusion just stated well anchored in official records, he will find them confirmed in the studies of the city done by other social scientists many of whom will, as I have suggested, shrink from their implications when set forth as Banfield sets them forth.

WHAT IS the second major conclusion of *The Unheavenly City*? It is this. *Because of the conspicuous improvement in the American city,* metropolis included, the tensions, conflicts, frustrations, and overall revolt against the city will continue to make the city what it now is, a scene of distinct crisis. I repeat: *because of,* not despite, the absolute improvement of material conditions, including housing, medical service, and schooling. Why should this be? The answer is a vital one to any person interested in the ferment and revolution-tinctured nature of, not merely urban America, but American society as a whole.

The answer is that the improvements in performance, great as they have been, have not kept pace with rising expectations. In other words, although things have been getting better absolutely, they have been getting worse *relative to what we think they should be.* And this is because, as a people, we seem to act on the advice of the old jingle:

Good, better, best,
Never let it rest
Until your good is better
And your better best.

Consider poverty. Manifestly, with but the fewest exceptions, even the worst off in American cities are in a substantially better condition than their poverty-stricken predecessors were at the beginning of the century. Studies show that around forty percent of those below what is called the "poverty line" own automobiles, and the overwhelming majority have television sets. More important, schooling opportunities, medical services, and straight economic relief, through welfare payments and other means, are far more numerous than they were even fifty years ago.

But as Irving Kristol reminded us—and he is quoted at appropriate places by Banfield—several years ago in a now historic piece, so long as we hold the concept at all of "poverty line" there cannot fail to be a one-fourth, one-third, or one-fifth of the nation officially—or at least politically—pronounced in poverty. No matter how well off a population may be, if one defines poverty as that condition in which the lowest fifth exists, there cannot help but be officially regarded poverty.

Precisely the same holds with respect to the school dropout problem. Not very many decades ago almost everyone was a "dropout" but the "problem" didn't exist. But by the 1960s, when for the first time in history a majority of boys and girls were graduating from high school and practically all had at least some high school

training, the "dropout problem" became acute. "Then, although the dropout rate was still declining, various cities developed at least fifty-five separate programs to deal with the problem." As Banfield concludes, if we follow the splendid insight Irving Kristol earlier gave us into poverty, as officially dealt with, then there cannot help but be, forever and ever, an educational dropout problem even if we have pushed the "dropout line" up to the Master's degree.

So too with police brutality. Once this meant incontestably, physical beating, usually with police clubs, or confinement without charge, of the helpless. Today the "brutality line" has been pushed up to the point where a sharp word or look, especially when directed toward those belonging to a politically sensitive ethnic minority, can be charged with "brutality."

NOW THE point of all this—whether in Professor Banfield's book or in my review—is emphatically not to denigrate problems, to seek to remove them by rhetorical deprecation. Problems are as problems are perceived—seen, felt, heard, endured. If I feel aggrieved in economic position it does no good to be reminded that I am still better off than the greatest of scholar-teachers may have been five hundred years ago, or even five. Professor Banfield is not saying that statistics prove the lowest fifth are in fact "well off," as this complex phrase tends to be defined by all of us. He is saying something very different indeed; something profound, something Tocquevillian, and also something very depressing.

What he is saying is this: A new and seemingly unmanageable phenomenon is present in our society, one foreseen by Tocqueville, one that, once created, feeds on itself. And this phenomenon is the dynamic tension provided by American middle class *expectations*. I cannot blame the following formulation on Banfield, but it seems to me an appropriate corollary of the famous Malthusian law of food supply and population. I put my corollary thus: Whereas material benefits can rise in a social order only at arithmetical rate, expectations tend to rise geometrically. That is, in a middle class society where expectations have been, as Tocqueville showed us masterfully a century and a half ago, the very substructure of American society. It was Tocqueville who first put into systematic form the proposition that the greatest agonies over the problem of equality would be experienced precisely in those countries, such as the United States, where the work of equality has been carried the farthest, where substantive inequalities become ever finer to the eye.

What we have, then, in Banfield's phrasing of the whole matter, is a new kind of dismal science, or rather a new dimension to the dismal science of Malthus and Ricardo. What he seems to be saying, in effect, is that urban problems, including poverty, schooling, medical service, housing, and employment income—in fact, the whole complex we call "urban crisis" is not likely to be dealt with in such a way as to remove present tensions and sense of impending conflict, for the reason that while affluence does indeed rise, *the sense of relative deprivation* rises also, and at a faster rate. The same middle class values that drive hundreds of thousands of middle class citizens into incessant uplift work—into what Banfield calls Service—lead to the implanting of these values among those minorities who are the recipients of the uplift work. The consequence is seemingly an iron one. It can be described as comparable to the mechanical rabbit at the racetrack, which is set to keep just ahead of the dogs, no matter how fast they run.

We come now to the third major conclusion that can be drawn from *The Unheavenly City*. It falls in the vast area of political action, of direct uplift and reform, of civic service that is by now almost indistinguishable from middle class life in America. The conclusion is this: Although a turning to political action—and to related forms, such as quasi-political service—is almost a predictable response to the kinds of problems and strains we encounter in the city today, the actual consequences of such action and service tend, in the overwhelming majority of cases, to worsen, not help, the problems and the strains. Banfield writes:

> Government seems to have a perverse tendency to choose measures that are the very opposites of those which would be recommended on the basis of analysis in the preceding chapters. The reasons for this perversity may be found *in the nature of American political institutions* and, especially, in the influence on public opinion of the upper-class cultural ideal of "service" and "responsibility to the community." (Italics added)

I would offer the following larger, general, proposition.[2] From the time the political habit of mind became deeply entrenched in the West, which was not much before the nineteenth century, though with the aid of concepts going back earlier, there has been profound affinity between political power or action on the one hand and, on the other, problems such as those contained in the contemporary city in which manifest improvement of popular condition is accompanied by *perceptions of worsening of condition,* of, in short, *relative deprivation.* And, with the rarest of exceptions, it has been, and continues to be on ever-widening scale, the fate of such political action to worsen the problems, by cutting off whatever adaptive responses to them might otherwise have taken place in the behavior of those closest to the conditions.

Two or three examples of my proposition will suffice and perhaps give useful background to Professor Banfield's brilliant arguments. I think it can fairly be established that a reasonably good balance of pluralism and homogeneity was being worked out in Western society prior to the excited discovery, by political intellectuals—largely those trained in Roman Law but unable to get jobs—of something called "feudalism." By endowing this freshly coined word and concept with all kinds of sinister meanings the work of political centralization was brought through its first major phase. Later, despite the legacy of Hobbes, it would have been possible (I am, admittedly, speculating here; I cannot "prove" statements of this sort), I think, to have worked out a useful balance of private enterprise and public service in the West. Unhappily "capitalism" was invented by certain intellectuals, promptly endowed with meanings every bit as sinister in the nineteenth and early twentieth centuries as those earlier intellectuals had given to "feudalism," and the work of modern political centralization was carried an even longer step forward. Worse, the mind of the middle class Westerner was permanently stamped by the goodness of the political and the lurking evil of the economic—or, in our day, the *technological,* for it is the weasel concept of "technology" that slithers rhetorically among the dense thickets of the American intellectual mind, leading to ever more massive political responses to its intellectually endowed evils.

What Professor Banfield shows us so convincingly is the degree to which the city—"the urban crisis"—parallels technology, succeeding, as I have suggested here, "capitalism" and before it "feudalism" as the handy fulcrum on which the mighty lever of political action can rest. Just as some sixteenth-century political intellectuals (who called themselves *les politiques*) found a "feudal crisis," so to speak, and some nineteenth-century political intellectuals, with Marxists chief among them, a "capitalist crisis," and as each of these "crises" led to a massive increase in the political structure of society, so do intellectuals in our midst find a technological crisis or, as Banfield shows us so valuably, an urban crisis, each the means of providing fresh fodder to hungry politicians, miserable intellectuals, and the unrequited masses of middle class Americans who have found pleasure no longer tolerable unless it surmounts, or joins with, Service. On the walls of all these individuals hang, as Banfield notes wickedly, homely Edgar Guest-like apothegms: DON'T JUST SIT THERE. DO SOMETHING! and DO GOOD! (The only good thing I can say for Jeremy Bentham, the devotee of Good who did so much harm in the world, is an essay he once wrote on the harm that good men do.)

The politician, like the TV commentator, must always have something to say even when nothing urgently needs to be said. If he lived in a society without problems, he would have to invent some (and, of course, "solutions" along with them) in order to attract attention and to kindle the interest and enthusiasm needed to carry him into office and enable him, once there, to levy taxes and do the other unpopular things of which governing largely consists. Although in the society that actually exists there are many problems, there are still not enough—enough about which anyone can say or do anything very helpful—to meet his constant need for program material. . . .

As I suggested above, one can construct an understanding of the whole history of political thought on the basis of an insight such as that contained in Banfield's words. Add to that passage some delicious passages in the book on the subject of middle and upper class consecration to Service, the incessant and endless projects by which people seemingly incapable of being alone for more than a few moments without tortured feelings of helpless isolation, pass the time and work off feelings of affluence-bred guilt, and you have a Banfieldian portrait of America that, mutatis mutandis, should hang in the National Gallery.

INCESSANT POLITICS and Perpetual Service would not be other than quaint aberrations of the mass-middle-class mind were it not for the very real harm that is done so many others in society—the working class, for example, more accustomed to doing for itself, and, not least, a great many who belong to ethnic minorities. For, as Banfield's book makes evident—to me, at least, and I think I am a careful reader—there are two major, built-in consequences of the benign and oblivious work of the devotee of Politics and of Service.

In the first place, the mere act of *doing* for others, especially when armed with the might and wealth of the democratic state, cannot help but destroy, or set back grievously, processes of an adaptive nature *in the areas, and within the communities*

that—too late—we learn, and relearn and relearn, so often made for, or would clearly have made for, a *socially* superior form of life to what the federal bulldozer wreaks. To do *for* is to do *to*. To cut into the social bond for allegedly therapeutic reasons is generally more harmful than to cut into it for outrightly exploitative reasons. The attention of the members of the community, usually self-protective, is lulled into passivity when the act is called therapeutic rather than exploitative.

The second great and equally built-in penalty of incessant political action and Service is that, given the idol-like status each of these has in our time, more and more well-meaning, bumbling, lonely, and mission-oriented members of the middle class are brought into the act—whether in the roles of the Paid or the Unpaid—and this cannot help but result in, through what we may properly call Banfield's Law, an ever larger number of issues, problems, crises-that-cannot-possibly-be-longer-endured-without-disaster-to-the-world, and so on. As the philosopher Ortega y Gasset once wrote, people do not come together to *be* together; they come together to *do something* together. And if the joys of middle-class family life, the church, *kaffee klatsch,* and country club pall, if the experience of being alone in a room for two hours (Pascal once wrote that most of the evil in the world has been done by individuals incapable of being alone for more than an hour) becomes utterly painful, if you've read all the good books, are tired of movies and vacations at the seashore or in the mountains, why what else is there to do but go out and find PROBLEMS: problems which, virtually by definition, must be met, and immediately, if we are to prosper, to survive, etc. etc.

In short, given the nature of our politically driven, morality-obsessed middle-class society, its by now seemingly unrequitable passion for direct ACTION, at all levels, it follows that the more persons there are who are dedicated to solving problems, the more problems there have to be. Situations that would not have drawn passing glance five years ago from the most pious of uplifters are compared in newspaper editorials to the Black Hole of Calcutta. Problems breed, in other words, at geometric rate, not through parthenogenesis but through incessant fertilization by American middle class eagerness for large families of problems to fill its spare time.[3] Or so it might seem.

ON FIRST thought after reading *The Unheavenly City,* one may feel depressed. The analysis and the conclusions *do* seem pessimistic. Second thought may produce rather different feelings. One may find a certain tentative optimism coming over him; instead of pessimistic, the analysis Professor Banfield gives us may seem optimistic. It depends in large degree upon whether one believes—as I do—that occasionally the smashing of accepted categories of thinking is the prelude to reaching new ones, new categories of thought that are themselves the bases of new perspectives of life, new conceptions of the desirable and the feasible by increasing numbers of persons. We know such mutations of mind and action have taken place before, though admittedly rarely, in the history of thought.

Daniel P. Moynihan, to whom as much is owing, it seems to me, as to Banfield and a very few others, for capacity to see old data in new and fertilizing ways, has recently written: "The social sciences are in a very early stage of finding out that most of the things we thought were so aren't so." Splendid! For all the heavy pall of conventional wisdom

in the social sciences, I am myself struck by the number of social scientists—still pathetically small, I concede—for whom the secular pieties and mores of even a decade ago are today unacceptable. Some of these, with unusual courage, are trying to reach new perspectives of understanding, perspectives unbeholden to the spirit of direct Service that has generated so many political follies and disasters in the twentieth century. Edward Banfield is one of these social scientists. Who knows, as one of the long term consequences of *The Unheavenly City,* we may yet have a new genus of electable, appointable politician and administrator on whose walls hangs the not-so-homely apothegm: DON'T JUST DO SOMETHING. SIT THERE!

Notes

1. "Urban Civilization and its Discontents," printed as the lead article in *Commentary,* July, 1970. Along with Banfield, Kristol is one of the tiny number that has seen the fallacies of the conventional wisdom in the social sciences regarding the city, poverty, and other idols of secular diabolism in our time.

2. See my "The Grand Illusion: Politics: An Appreciation of Jacques Ellul" in *Commentary,* August 1970.

3. Banfield's discussion suggests a new conception of the springs of power in certain types of personality, one based on inability of a person to see even the most unruffled situation other than in terms of "problems." The individual I have personally known who did the greatest harm to a very large organization, over which he presided for some years prior to recent disaster, was of this type: gentle, service-dedicated, action-compelled, and his every third or fourth word was "problems." Where others saw only use and wont he saw cancer-like problems requiring immense dosages of direct action.

Frank Knopfelmacher

THE PARASITE AS REVOLUTIONARY:
THE FLEECING OF AMERICA

VOL. 7, NO. 5, 1971

The Greening of America, by Charles A. Reich. New York: Random House, 1970.

SERIOUS POLITICAL theory can be—very roughly—divided into three categories which I shall call respectively, the conservative, the liberal, and the revolutionary. Their dominant themes run throughout the history of Western political thought, and while they sometimes overlap, it is by and large possible to fit any one thinker at any one time into one of the three. Not much needs to be said about liberalism, which possibly has dominated America since the establishment of the United States. The basis of this ideology is the belief that human secular destiny can be steadily improved by improving the environment, and that the human person is, by and large, the function of his natural and social conditions and if you change the latter for the better you will improve the former. Not all liberals are starry-eyed optimists, and many are aware of the formidable obstacles to progress inherent in man's biological structure and ingrained belief

systems. Also, the scope and width of possible improvements are disputed, ranging from claims that piecemeal, cumulative, gradualist solutions are the only feasible ones to the "sweeping changes" schools of thought.

As against the liberals, the conservatives tend to believe that there are inbuilt, irremovable obstacles to human progress; that human nature is incapable of fundamental improvements; that it is irreversibly flawed. It is therefore not the task of the magistrates to strive towards human perfection, but rather to hold man on a leash, to tame his aggressive impulses by force and by conditioned fear-responses, to circumscribe his antisocial aggressiveness by tradition-induced internalized prohibitions, and above all, not to tamper with institutions which have proved their mettle as instruments of human domestication.

The revolutionaries differ from both the liberals and the conservatives in that their "ultimate" beliefs are closer to those of the liberals, yet the more immediately practical ones appear to be based on much the same assumptions as those of the conservatives. The revolutionaries share the liberal's trust that man can be perfected, or at least progressively improved, but unlike the liberals they don't believe that this can be achieved without a catastrophic restructuring of the world as it is and as it has been since the beginning of civilization. The revolutionaries, like the conservatives, believe that men, as we now find them, are flawed and as such are incapable of improvement. Yet the flaws have been built into them by psychologically crippling social organizations which have lasted for millenia and which still maintain their sway, thereby sustaining the flaws. Once the corrupting society is destroyed and its psychologically stunting effects removed, men can be redeemed.

The redemptive creed of the revolutionary differs from liberal gradualism in that it presupposes the end of the "old world" and the creation of a new one before any improvement in the quality of human life becomes at all possible. The revolutionary collapse of the old will be initiated by a crisis in pre-revolutionary relationships and by profound psychological shocks as the customary ceases to exist before a new consciousness replaces the old. The interim period justifies terror and perhaps even the genocidal sacrifice of the living psychologically unredeemable human material as bridge-building matter and manure for the future. The chiliastic nature of revolutionary thought is now a commonplace among historians of ideas, and I shall not retell an old story.

The key concepts of the liberals, the conservatives and the revolutionaries are, respectively, freedom-progress, order-tradition, and crisis. Some revolutionaries and conservatives, will be brought into psychological communion by their shared contempt for men as they are and for the liberals who expect to do anything worthwhile with *that*. Yet the revolutionary will at times join forces with the liberals to overcome the notion fairly deeply ingrained in Christian thought that by and large nothing can be done in this vale of tears, and it is better to tolerate established abuses which, as a by-product, maintain the social order, rather than to innovate by breaking the customary bonds of reverence and obedience, thereby risking the unleashing of a lawless "state of nature" in Hobbes's sense, either between a tyrant and a subjugated population or between members of a lawless human horde.

I

The New Left in America and elsewhere is revolutionary, insofar as it is made up of serious people who in some sense mean what they proclaim and who are not mere poseurs, TV entertainers, or promoters of exciting homoerotic fashions in the textile trade. Their prophets from Marx to Marcuse have made it abundantly clear that they reject our society in toto. By and large, also, the New Revolutionaries tend to display the classical specific differences in tactics, temperament, organizational methods, and philosophy which have always emerged, in one way or another, within revolutionary movements; there are elitist Leninist or crypto-Leninist followers of Lukacs (whose work has been bowdlerized and popularized by Marcuse), the participatory democrat-anarchists who favour elective soviets, the advocates of more or less organizationally undirected individual action and nihilistic terror, and finally, the drop-outs, the hippie-freak element.

The drop-outs, which can be further subclassified according to costume, style of noise-making, and manner of deviance, are, strictly speaking, not revolutionary.

Their actions tend to be irreducibly apolitical and their lifestyle is far too erratic to lend itself to systematic political manipulation and direction by revolutionary technicians. Yet their actions tend to have unforeseen and unintended political consequences. The drop-outs are at the same time despised and courted by the revolutionary and counter-revolutionary alike, since both regard them as a hopeful sign. For the revolutionary, the drop-out represents a symptom of decadence in the target society, while for the counter-revolutionary, a sign of decay in the quality and morals of the revolutionary movement. Reich's book is essentially an apotheosis of the drop-out and his penumbra of attenuated imitators, and it represents an attempt to elevate him to the status of the revolutionary par excellence.

Visitors to America, like this author, are shocked by the extent to which "the revolution" has become a lucrative industry, and they wonder whether the wealthy and powerful men who subsidize, exhibit and lionize the advocates of their own destruction are merely greedy and innocent, or perhaps symptomatic of the very insoluble internal contradictions which the revolutionaries claim to find all over America. It seems that the American revolutionary, and drop-out apostles of the "counterculture," and the protagonists of the more traditional doctrines of the fast buck, have hit it off perfectly. The inhuman and shallow nature of most of the "counterculture" seems if anything to heighten the lust of their adulterous embrace, which requires for its elicitation rather crude and excessively spiced fare. A thing which strikes a stranger in America is the blatancy with which the question *cui bono* is relevant to the American culture industry and particularly to that part of it which may be called for want of a better name "the academic racket"—not

to be confused with the still sizeable islands of excellence and integrity which have managed to survive the "educational" holocaust in America.

In this sordid world, in which not even the overwhelmingly ulterior motives of the culture-racketeers are the genuine ones, but a mere facade for yet more sordidly ulterior ones, the Kantian question, "how is Reich's book possible," must be asked. How is it possible that a badly written goulash of platitudes and clichés, betraying incompetence in many fields, destitute of even a shred of empirical evidence to back up hosts of sweeping and puerile utterances, and without the redeeming qualities of genuine indignation and sardonic wit, was given the kind of promotion it received? Yet before one attempts an answer, the content should be stated and analyzed. Since Reich's thesis (I have avoided inverted commas because I could not decide whether to use them for "Reich's" or "thesis," and using them for both would give the article a distinctly Soviet flavor) is by now well-known. I shall state it as charitably as I can, for it rests on the kind of now-fashionable pop-Hegelianism which cannot withstand even superficial philosophical analysis. Hence, if one wishes to discuss the stuff at all, one must improve on it in stating it.

II

Reich's basic concept seems to be the Marxist notion of the relation between material base and superstructure, or "consciousness." Thus, corresponding to three specific phases of American history, there are three types of consciousness, three families of ideological superstructure. Consciousness I is a function of pre-corporate classical capitalism or of America as a farmerist free-market democracy. Its principal values are thrift, industry, enterprise, faith in economic justification by cleverness and hard work, competitiveness, and a certain masculine robustness and ruthlessness to go with it. With the emergence of monopoly capitalism Consciousness I became dysfunctional. The race no longer went to the swift. With the crises of monopoly capitalism, Consciousness I simply could not cope: it became "false-consciousness." The social and political actions of the New Deal which were undertaken to counter the effects of the Great Depression produced a new, managerial society, a network of hierarchically structured and interlocking politico-economic bureaucracies, a new power-system, commanded by a scientifically trained, hierarchically minded directorate.

The new social structure is sustained by command relations and programmed by a variety of conflicting managerial hierarchs who are, however sufficiently coordinated—(not by conspiracy or consciousness of interests—here Reich differs from Marcuse—but by an interlocking system of arbitration and conflict management), to warrant for itself the designation of Corporate State. Nobody in particular is really running this managerial society any more and the hierarchs of the military-industrial complex are themselves just so many cogs in the machine. The sustaining entity is not an apparatus or an elite, it is mental: Consciousness II. The old ideal-typical Protestant-ethic rooted entrepreneur has been replaced by the cool, sleezy, or abrasive, ideologically aseptic organization man, who sets the pace, determines the fashions, and dictates the trends. Consciousness II *has* improved America. Since the inception of the New Deal, the machine of managerial, statist, monopoly capitalism actually

runs and is not bogged down in semipermanent crisis. But it runs at the cost of dehumanizing its social actors. The trouble with Consciousness I was not that it was esthetically or morally bad—on the contrary, Reich indicates that it was quite fetching. It simply did not *work*. Consciousness II *does* work. The economy and the state apparatus function. But in working it destroys what is human in the social actors. There is waste, there are wars, there is private affluence and public squalor, there is alienation etc., etc.

The bearers of Consciousness II value advancement, the striving for power in orderly hierarchical bureaucracies by intrigue and merit, and they subordinate everything, even fun and games, to corporate ambition. Man becomes co-extensive with his officially accredited competences within a hierarchically stratified system of production and management. It is life without spontaneity, play, and truly individual enterprise; just striving for power after power until death of the corporate salesman (Miller's was really a Consciousness I bloke trapped in a Consciousness II world). The lifestyle of Consciousness II is psychologically deadening, yet man's spirit is immortal and resilient. It bucks the machine, cocks its nose at competence, hierarchies, and careers, and reasserts itself; Consciousness III is born. It is tantamount to a refusal of corporate discipline combined with an aggressive reassertion of non-corporate traits such as spontaneity, individual eccentricity, and the primacy of sensuousness over duty.

The central political thesis of the book is the proposition that the American corporate state will disintegrate purely as a result of a mental metamorphosis in its subjects and not as a result of political or revolutionary action. People's consciousness will simply change from II to III and the corporate state will wither away. The old corporate, anti-human *Gesellschaft* will give way to a free yet organic society of spontaneous sensualists and creative artistic producers.

It is not quite clear whether Reich maintains (a) that the high level of automated technology makes significant societal repression redundant (Marcuse's doctrine of "surplus repression") or (b) whether he holds that effort and labor will continue to be necessary but that they can be invested into production without the discipline of Consciousness II, i.e., without internalized notions of duty, levels of aspiration, and, socially, without hierarchy, authority, and division of labor. I feel that Reich oscillates between (a) and (b) being unaware that they constitute real alternatives.

What is one to make of all this? Some implications of the thesis are quite obviously incompatible with widely advertised alleged characteristics of Reich's *opus*. Thus Reich, or, if you will, the bearers of Consciousness III, are not, in any operationally meaningful sense of the word, revolutionaries. The minimum for being one is that one undertakes purposive political actions which, at least, do not exclude the use of violence and which are deliberately directed against the structures and personnel of the old order with a view to overthrowing them. The man who sits and waits for a spiritual rebirth and when it comes merely enjoys it may be all sorts of things: if he does nothing else, the use of the term revolutionary to describe him is a misuse of language.

The Consciousness III chaps are not exhorted by Reich to do anything. As a matter of fact they are actually exhorted to do nothing *political* in the ordinary usage of the term. They are merely urged to drop out, to fall if possible on the soft cushion of sustaining corporate wealth

and to enjoy themselves. They are in fact urged to become *idiots* in the original Greek sense of the word.

Reich qualifies in no intelligible sense of which I am aware for the label of Marxist, though he would obviously like to qualify. Should the pattern of intellectual and political fashions in America undergo one of its sudden and unpredictable changes, Reich will be able to state quite truthfully that he is not and never has been etc. without seeking the sanctuary of the Fifth Amendment. As a matter of fact Reich seems to be that rare kind of man—an intellectual who amidst an unprecedented welter of Marx-debates and Marx-chatter has managed to misunderstand the principal political theorem of any kind of Marxism, namely, that it is not consciousness which determines social existence, but social existence which determines consciousness, and that the proper relation between advanced beliefs and backward reality is *political action*.

Reich is, actually, an almost paradigm case of a political "idealist" in the half-technical and half-pejorative sense in which the word is used by Marxists. For his central thesis is: do nothing and wait for the redemptive illumination to cleanse your soul. Let all those who are laboring in Consciousness II turn their minds to the things of the liberated flesh, to Consciousness III. Purity of mind is all, for the pure in Reich's rather fleshy spirit will by definition *be* the good society, the communion of saints. As a matter of fact, the movement which Reich's ideology approximates most closely is Moral Rearmament. The *practical* effects of accepting the proposition that personal purity must precede political action is, of course, political quietism. I would not be surprised if somebody, somewhere in the KGB or in some more creatively clinical, paranoid outfit of the New Left were to rule that Reich is paid by the CIA to undermine the revolutionary action-potential of the American masses: but I shouldn't have said it, for in the American culture racket, reality and the satire on it have by now become almost completely interchangeable. For all I know somebody may actually have already said it, or may get ideas by reading this article.

Reich fulminates continuously against "false consciousness"—another Marxist term which he has failed to comprehend. Yet, his own "Consciousness III" is a paradigm case of a false consciousness, a set of false yet comforting beliefs that you can have your cake and eat it. And this is true no matter whether one adopts a revolutionary or conservative philosophy of life. For there is one thing on which honest conservatives and revolutionaries can agree: the good life is not given to us. We must work hard at it, and hard work requires instinctual renunciation. Reich's chaps will not qualify as Marines or corporation executives. Yet neither will they qualify for death in the electric chair for acting on the (false but noble) belief that as long as somebody is in prison everybody is in prison, and that one should, therefore, do something drastic about a world in which there are so many jails.

III

We come now to the reason why. What has made Reich's book into a bestseller? Why should it have sold so many more copies than other intellectually more competent books, which have appeared roughly at the same time, and which were written for a similar, fairly well-educated, middle- to upper-middle-brow public? Why should men of affairs, and their wives, used to sound arguments in the pursuit of their corporate business and to good material texture in their private pleasures, prefer a discourse on the redemptive properties of Consciousness III on skis, in hip clothes, to sober and rationally argued treatises based on sound political knowledge and adequate empirical evidence? Perhaps somewhere underneath Reich's Consciousness III there lurks the old impish One and Two, an eye for the fast buck and a promoter's instinct for what the public *loves* (I am using the word in its currently obscene sense).

Everybody knows by now that "radical" means "chic." Yet it is also common knowledge that "radical" still carries with it *some* risks: thus, even if law enforcement and discipline were to break down completely, there is always the danger of being mugged by a rival radical gang. And there is, of course, the shadow of the backlash and what might happen to the kids if some law-and-order monster were to establish fascism in America by returning the safety of the streets to the old and the weak, and the college campuses to the pedagogues and scholars.

Even if one were to accept fully Professor Eugene Genovese's hypothesis that the American New Left is made up largely of economic parasites extruded from the loins, nurseries; and schools of a liberal middle class which has by now mismanaged everything, including the socialization of their children, one may nevertheless concede that the enterprise of radically chic social parasitism is occasionally inconvenient, at times morally disturbing, and an object of sarcasm from both conservatives and from more seriously committed revolutionaries. The sense of one's own basic fraudulence—living in affluence and leisure, spouting a revolutionary rhetoric, and inducing in oneself counterfeit emotions of communion with the wretched of the earth—spoils at times one's delight with the game.

Reich's doctrine frees "the kids" and their parents from all this. Reich, in fact, says that in being a social parasite one is being a revolutionary. There have been occasional parasitic playboys who were also revolutionaries—who, as it were, "made it" in revolutionary politics, e.g., the younger Verkhovensky. Yet, according to Reich, the playboy no longer has to make it since he is it. No wonder the book should please so many. The law enforcement agencies and their allies will naturally opt for revolution in the minds, rather than by bombs, violence, and political subversion. The media will welcome a revolutionary who does not question the legitimacy of property. But the most delighted will surely be the liberal academics and the college presidents, for here at last is a radical whose message does not increase the insurance rates of academic real-estate. The replacement of arsonists and bullies by bums and deviates will relieve many an administrative headache.

The people who should be disturbed by the prominence of Reich's book are those—American and non-Americans alike—whose personal freedom and survival is linked with the fortunes of the American republic. For it is obvious that the real revolutionary, as against the psycho-revolutionary of Reich's Consciousness III, represents no serious danger in America. Like all modern state machines in developed countries, the American state apparatus is effectively unchallengeable from within. Foreigners like myself, and even some natives, are deceived into believing that a violent revolution is possible in America by the degree of tolerated violence and dissent, and by the remarkable extent to which Americans tend to *doubt* the stability of their social order. The amount of slippage in the American law enforcement

apparatus is, perhaps, greater than in any other highly industrialized society, and certainly greater than in other "English-speaking" cultures, but there is no evidence that a head-on challenge against the social order would not be swiftly and successfully crushed.

The "anti-Vietnam movement" is actually the best evidence for this thesis. The "movement" operated with no holds barred, and it included men and organizations who would stop at nothing and whose hostility and rage against America's social structure was implacable and absolute. And yet, there was no significant interference with the military effort in the field. By and large the conscripts joined their units, obeyed orders, and handled their weapons as well as they usually do. There was no interference with troop movement, no mutinies, and no sabotage of transport and logistic support. The revolutionaries did not even begin to accomplish the task of "turning the imperialist war into a civil war." As a matter of fact, as far as the war effort per se went, they were not even in the game and that, characteristically and humiliatingly, despite the high proportion of blacks among the American soldiers.

Yet the New Left is divided into two groups, of which by far the greater part would opt for the role of comfortable social parasitism celebrated in Reich's book. The values of that group have now permeated American society down to the women's magazines and comic books. The situation is reinforced by the fact that the belief in the basic dispensability of government in the pursuit of individual happiness is one of the most cherished American myths. In no other developed country is the need for sovereignty and government viewed with greater suspicion than in America. Indeed, the lurking feeling that governments are dispensable after all, or, if not, that they should be reduced to the barest minimum, provides an occasional link between the thinking of the Left and the conservative Right in their joint nostalgia for a vanished past. It is a part of American *tradition* and, hence, even conservatives are highly vulnerable to it.

And yet, American society—both in its conduct of imperial policies and in its management of internal affairs—will require more and not less discipline, more and not less controls by experts, bigger and not smaller doses of guidance by the military-industrial complex in the coming technetronic age. Whether the elites will be nominally federal bureaucrats or corporate managers with massive links to the state apparatus has been shown to be irrelevant in Burnham's *Managerial Revolution* in 1939 and remains irrelevant today. The serious problem is, surely, how to work safeguards of individual liberty into the interstices of the managerial-corporate state, which cannot be abolished because with it our technetronic culture would also go, and with it our civilization. For whenever a Reichian Consciousness III switches on the light on his desk to write an essay against Consciousness I and II on his electric typewriter, he votes against his essay with his typewriter keys.

AT THE present time the still open societies of America and her allies are challenged by totalitarian despotisms of various kinds, of which the USSR remains the most formidable. They can withstand the challenge only if they consolidate and extend their institutions of conflict management to prevent disruption of the minimum of continuity and coherence which are a prerequisite for the successful conduct of world affairs, and if they can confront the system of terror and propaganda which threatens us from without by a force based on an internalized sense of civic responsibility. There is only one libertarian counter to terror and totalitarianism—determined resistance based on a civic consensus rooted in loyalty to the Republic, and supported by a variety of virtues, shrewdly tamed vices, and skills which together constitute the functioning human person within the context of his culture-bearing polis. The polis, any polis other than a tyranny, requires Consciousness II. Consciousness III is for those who wish to live like animals, men whom the ancients called *cynics*— the *dog-like*. If the Reich ideology were to prevail in the U.S., and if Americans in large numbers were to follow the pied pipers of social irresponsibility, we might yet see the "greening" of America, since the grass might grow where the machines of civilization once stood. And life would again become solitary, poor, nasty, brutish and short, though admittedly with lots of unpolluted fresh air.

Yet, more likely, we would witness the internal disintegration and eventual conquest of a sensate, demoralized, and self-hating mass of crazed consumers by other tyrannical societies based on order, myth, hierarchy, and unrestrained violence. And their regime would be oppressive in the palpably real sense rather than in the contrived-pickwickian sense propagated by Marcuse and aped by Reich as a sophists weapon against the legitimacy of the social order of the American Republic.

George W. Carey

How to Read Willmoore Kendall

VOL. 8, NO. 1–2, 1972

Willmoore Kendall Contra Mundum,
by Willmoore Kendall. New Rochelle,
NY: Arlington House, 1971.

WHEN WRITING about Willmoore
Kendall a strong temptation exists to deal
with the man, not his teachings or theory.
This I have always felt to be a shame, and,
at times, a deliberate dodge because the
reviewer or commentator sought to avoid
coming to grips with the substance of his
thought. I content myself with noting,
as does Jeffrey Hart in his introduction
to this volume, that Willmoore was a
character of the first order who could on
occasion be extremely perverse.

This perversity, manifested in his personal life, is not evident in his writings.
To be sure, many will complain about
his style. They will talk about "involuted
sentences" that seem to run on indefinitely with dashes, colons, semicolons,
and parentheses. Criticisms of Willmoore
on these grounds are not well taken. His
mind was a far-ranging one and he used
the English language (he was, believe me,
a craftsman) as best he could to set forth
the nuances of his theory and arguments,
as well as the depth of his emotional

conviction. Students and teachers alike
would do well to "pick" at those so-
called involuted sentences. They will find
them to be not only *sentences* that conform with the Queen's English but, more
importantly, stuffed with intellectually rewarding and provocative thoughts.
Illustrative of this is one of the few pieces
in this collection that I had never read before, entitled "Who Should Control Our
Public Schools?" Read also in this connection "American Conservatism and the
'Prayer' Decision." I know of no writings
(and we have been flooded with them
over the years) that simultaneously bring
us to the issues at stake, state the conservative alternatives on these questions, and
reflect the depths of conservative outrage
concerning the course of events, a course
dictated, no less, by the imperious masters
of the American liberal establishment.

What was Kendall trying to tell us?
What were his central teachings? I will
list some that are highly interrelated.

(1) He told us to trust the American
people. He always loved America and in
his later years he came to love its political
institutions and procedures. That is one
theme that permeates most of his works
dealing with the American system and

his critiques of the proposals for reform offered by the modern American liberal. The three articles that best reflect this are "Dialogues on Americanism," "Deadlock," and "How to Read Richard Weaver: Philosopher of 'We the (Virtuous) People.'"

Having noted this much we must proceed to (2). Willmoore was a majoritarian of very special order. He was a conservative populist of sorts. One will detect a shift of thinking on his part over the years. His early writings, and even those not published here which appeared in the middle 1950s, illustrate this. "Majority Principle and the Scientific Elite" and "On Preservation of Democracy in America," both reproduced in this volume, indicate his early liberal bent of mind. (See in this regard the first four chapters of Ranney and Kendall, *Democracy and the American Party System,* for which he bears primary responsibility. See also his classic, *John Locke and Majority Rule.*)

What brought about the obvious change in his thinking and in what ways did he change? The reader of this work can readily see that in his early writing he accepted all the fundamental premises of liberalism. All opinions were deemed equal, which in very short order led him to the proposition that all values are equal, and then, into the swamps of relativism. In sum, by a tortuous route well known to Western man, he accepted the fact-value dichotomy. By the late 1950s, certainly after his conversion to Catholicism, we can discern a distinct shift in his writings with respect to the fact-value dichotomy and the liberal interpretation of majority rule. This is brilliantly manifest in his seldom-read article, "The People Versus Socrates Revisited." And he hammers away at this thesis in "How to Read Milton's *Areopagitica.*" He nails all of this to the door with his "Fallacies of the

Open Society," an article which oddly enough is not reproduced in this volume but which did appear in the *American Political Science Review* in the same year as the Milton article (1960).

I do not mean to imply that Willmoore's conversion to Catholicism produced the change in his thinking to which I have referred. It was, so far as I can determine, the other way around. In his earliest writings such as those I have cited, one will, if he reads closely enough, detect a tension, points and issues involving liberal premises with which Kendall did not quite feel at home. Contrast the "Preservation of Democracy" article with the "Weaver" article, or, better yet, "How to Read *The Federalist.*" Over the years he came to realize that there is a hierarchy of values, that there are transcendent Truths which, however clumsily we might try, we should seek to explore with our "heart" *and* intellect. The tensions produced by this realization led him to join the Catholic Church. But this was simply the result of reading carefully the works of Voegelin and Strauss, along with a very careful re-reading of *The Federalist.* In retrospect we can see that his early writings manifested the latent potential for a major shift in his thinking.

In what ways did his views shift on the matter of majoritarianism? He came to recognize that there are several senses in which an individual can legitimately talk about majority rule. A truly brilliant article, ignored in the political science profession, is the "Two Majorities."[1] His major query is at what level or in what dimension can we speak about majority will and which of the American institutions (Congress or the president) has the best claim to represent majorities? I urge all students of American politics to read this particular article for it embodies best the Kendallian theory that a people carry more sense "in their hips" than all of the intellectuals combined.[2]

Still another reason for his transformation can be detected from his article "John Locke Revisited." Strongly influenced by Locke in his early career (as are most liberals), he came to recognize that Lockean theory is as base and morally corrupt as Hobbesianism, a point that escapes the likes of a Louis Hartz and his smug legions who are so pretentious about explaining the "real" American tradition.

His final thoughts about majority rule and the American system come across most clearly in Section IV of "The 'Intensity' Problem and Majority Rule." Here he sets to rest and bids a long farewell to his liberal notions about majority rule. He is primarily responsible for this section of the article which he considered to be his finest theoretical statement on this issue relative to the American system. Indeed, it is. Again, I urge all students of the American tradition and system to read this article. Here we find the mature Kendall speaking with an insight, depth, perception, wisdom, and respect about the traditional values and precepts which in the 1930s and 1940s he lacked.

(3) Another theme that permeates his writing is this: He was not going to be bullied or shoved around by presumed "intellectuals." He thrashed out violently and savagely against those who would pretend to be our intellectual and moral guardians, that is, the American liberals whose moral arrogance still remains unbounded. He liked nothing better than to corner them at our professional conventions and call them to account for their irresponsible statements. This is evident from his writings in this book. However, one will have to go elsewhere to see the full force of his convictions in this regard. Professor Herbert McClosky

wrote an article in the *American Political Science Review* which "scientifically" proved that all American conservatives are either insane or stupid. Willmoore's rejoinder (1957) is classic. And in this vein, one ought to read "The 'Roster Device'; J. S. Mill and Contemporary Elitism." Difficult as it is to digest, the assumptions and values of liberalism are laid bare for all to see. It is not a pleasant sight to behold.

(4) I would caution the reader of this volume from placing too much stress on the "original" materials, those dealing with Clinton Rossiter, Russell Kirk, and John Courtney Murray. For one thing, Rossiter, as Willmoore knew very well, was not a conservative. Rossiter never pretended to be such.

As for Kendall's critique of Kirk, I can say so much: While it is true that in Kirk's monumental work *The Conservative Mind* we do not find any precise definition of conservatism (Willmoore never gave us one, either), Willmoore was concerned with the utility of Kirk's criteria for definition. He, after all, had to go into class day after day and face up to the question of "What is conservatism?," a question which no one has satisfactorily answered to this day.

I cannot explain Willmoore's warm embrace of John Courtney Murray's *We Hold These Truths*. True it is that both did hold to natural law theory and faced the question of how "open" an open society can be and still remain open. But I also know that they differed on fundamental questions (see in this connection "The Bill of Rights and American Freedom"). Father Murray was himself a liberal who sought to provide the profoundest arguments possible for his version of the American political tradition. Willmoore, upon extensive investigation, found that Father Murray did not know where-of he spoke. Read "Equality and the American Political Tradition" or "The Civil Rights Movement and the Coming Constitutional Crisis."

The "original" material was written in the Spring of 1962 for a class at Georgetown University on contemporary political thought. It was written under the pressure of time (that I know) and I do not believe it will withstand sustained analysis. Its value rests, in my judgment, in forcing others to help clarify the basic tenets of conservatism, an enterprise that Willmoore was so much interested in, as attested to by his articles "Toward a Definition of Conservatism" and "Basic Issues between Conservatives and Liberals."

And (5), what will Kendall's impact be? I have heard varying estimates. This much I can say with certainty. First, he had guts and fortitude. He stood, almost alone in academic circles, against the crushing orthodoxy of the times. No doubt, if he had been something other than a *Christian American* (e.g., a Communist, fascist, or "enlightened" agnostic) Yale would have promoted him—perhaps, dare I say it, made him president. But, he was at least there when and where needed the most. And for this reason he has made an impact on many younger scholars in the political science profession who otherwise

would have, understandably enough, felt quite lonesome. Second, his writings will continually haunt us, and that is the virtue of this volume. He had the genius to focus on the central issues of the problems confronting us as well as the alternatives available. He was possessed of a rare insight. And third, he taught countless students how to read. Willmoore's forte was "textual analysis." He simply demanded this of his students and peers.

Now a man who teaches us how to read *and* the principal values of our civilization is mighty unique. That's Willmoore. We will not soon see his likes again.

This book, I can state unequivocally, should be on the shelf of not only every political scientist, but every individual who is genuinely concerned about our country and its future.

Notes

1. The exception is to be found in Charles S. Hyneman, *The Supreme Court Trial*. This brilliant book is now out of print, a fact which is of some interest.

2. To paraphrase Bill Buckley, Willmoore would have preferred to be ruled by the first two thousand residents listed in the New Haven telephone directory rather than by the faculty of Yale.

John P. East

Conservatism Comes of Age

VOL. 13, NO. 2, 1978

The Conservative Intellectual Movement in America Since 1945, by George H. Nash. New York: Basic Books, 1976.

GEORGE NASH has written a masterful book. He writes with extraordinary facility and clarity, and he has produced a work that all persons identifying with the "conservative movement" in America since 1945 must read. Encyclopedic in scope, this book reflects a prodigious research effort. Yet, the end result is a highly readable work in which this talented historian leads the reader with remarkable dexterity through the complex strands and nuances of conservative thought. Nash's work initially took form as a doctoral dissertation in the Department of History at Harvard; he ultimately refined it into this definitive work on the conservative movement. Nash writes with deep affection for American conservative thought; however, he analyzes with the detachment and sophistication of the scholar, and the end result is an extraordinary account of a movement which, as Nash views it, possesses genuine and impressive intellectual substance.

"In 1945," Nash observes, "no articulate, coordinated, self-consciously conservative intellectual force existed in the United States." In a relatively brief span of time that situation changed dramatically. There emerged two fairly distinct forms of allegedly "conservative" thought: the libertarians and the traditionalists. Those of libertarian bent, such as Friedrich Hayek and Ludwig von Mises, feared principally the growth of collectivism and the omnicompetent state. They presented the case, Nash explains, "for strictly limited government, a free market, the impersonal rule of law, and social development by spontaneous growth rather than conscious planning and coercion," and their "enemies were coercion, arbitrariness, discrimination, and the omnivorous administrative discretionary state that tried to *design* progress rather than allow societies to grow under the impersonal rule of law."

The traditionalist label encompasses such diverse figures as Richard Weaver, Eric Voegelin, Leo Strauss, Russell Kirk, and Willmoore Kendall. In spite of their considerable differences in analysis and emphasis, the traditionalists were united in their opposition to "philosophical ni-hilism, totalitarianism, and the disturbing emergence of the mass man." They were "appalled by the erosion of values and the emergence of a secular, rootless, mass society." To stem the decay and disintegra-tion, they became primarily "defenders of order, consensus, morality, 'right reason,' religion, truth, [and] virtue."

In addition to the libertarians and traditionalists, there emerged the "dis-illusioned ex-radicals and their allies, alarmed by international communism." Whittaker Chambers and James Burnhan would symbolize the central figures in this grouping. In *Cold Friday* Chambers placed his finger on the raw nerve: "If they [the statist liberals] could have commu-nism without the brutalities of ruling that the Russian experience bred, they have only marginal objections. Why should they object? What else is socialism but communism with the claws retracted."

Regarding the libertarian, traditionalist, and an anticommunist strands of con-servative thought, Nash explains, "No rigid barriers separated the three groups." Nevertheless, there were the divisions, sometimes subtle, sometimes pronounced. The libertarians stressed freedom; the traditionalists were preoccupied with or-der and value; while the anticommunists were caught up in opposing the great vil-lainy of totalitarianism. Thus the groping for identity through consensus and unity was a continuing and illusive concern for the conservative movement.

Frank S. Meyer and William F. Buckley Jr. personified those who labored to produce a conservative con-sensus—sometimes called "fusionism." Meyer insisted, Nash relates, "that con-servatives must absorb the best of *both* branches of the divided conservative mainstream. This was the true heritage of the West—'reason operating within

tradition.'" Similarly, Buckley was hos-pitable to libertarians and traditionalists in *National Review*. Moreover, he gave generous coverage to the anticommunist Right. In Buckley's hands conservatism was broad-based, eclectic, and viable; its traditional, libertarian, and anticom-munist strains became symbiotic, not antagonistic. After all, Nash instructs, "It was part of the wisdom and genius of conservatism that it not try to encapsulate all its beliefs in a handbook of doctrines." The conservative movement was "cos-mopolitan"; it thrived on diversity and "heterogeneity." In sum, Nash queries, "What was so strange about simultane-ously opposing centralized government, supporting a nonsocialist economy and adhering to traditional morality?" Nash concludes there is a "working conser-vative consensus," and his assessment appears undeniably valid.

This consensus is based not merely upon convenience; it is rooted in agree-ment upon fundamental theoretical premises. All strains of conservative thought are anti-gnostic; they all agree that man lacks the wisdom and capacity to collectively perfect his earthly condi-tion. There is the acceptance of an order of things, of a "constitution of being," not produced by the mind and hands of man. The mystery of creation has not been solved. Piety, not pride, is in order. The proper mood is reverence and awe, not arrogance and chauvinism. There is an ordained framework of the given, and the task of man is to learn about it, to respect it, and to attune himself ac-cordingly—above all, he is not to defile that which he has not created. The role of defiler and corrupter has fallen to the gnostics, those fanatical utopians who rail against the nature of things, engage in mindless rebellion, and in the process deny the dignity of man.

By acknowledging the order of things, all strains of conservative thought are affirming the dignity of man. As is the case with creation generally, mankind is not self-produced, gnostic thought to the contrary notwithstanding. Man is part of a given order, and his dignity arises out of his uniqueness in that established order. In the quest for fulfillment, the uniqueness of each man should be respected—indeed, revered. Under the broad label of conservative, there is unity of principle in opposition to the demeaning of man by modern gnostics. Totalitarian gnostics demean man by denying his humanity and manhandling him in a fashion befitting only brick and steel. Similarly, liberal statist gnostics seek to mold man in their image; as Whittaker Chambers had instructed, their only quarrel with totalitarian gnostics is over the matter of gentility of method. Finally, there are those gnostics who preach the doctrine of nihilism wherein man, in effect, is implored to destroy himself to escape his self-inflicted alienation and despair. In all cases, then, gnostics assault the dignity of man, and conservatives are united in resisting and overcoming this degradation.

Significantly, in all phases of conservative thought there is what Leo Strauss termed the "character of ascent." That is, in spite of the imperfections and limitations of man's predicament, existence in general and human life in particular are considered good things. Thus there is the spirit of affirmation, not negation. More specifically, physical, intellectual, and spiritual life within the Western experience is to be treasured; consequently, there is cause for confidence and hope, for out of this mood of affirmation springs the will to persist and ultimately to prevail. To many observers these were powerful tenets upon which to build an enduring and humane philosophy—and society.

William McGurn

Filling a Void,
Recovering a Lost Art

VOL. 18, NO. 1, 1982

Christianity and Politics, by James V. Schall, S.J. Boston: St. Paul Editions, 1981.

OF ALL my undergraduate classroom experiences, none is so memorable as my introduction to what was to become my major, philosophy. As a freshman at Notre Dame, I noticed with a little dismay that some faceless bureaucrat in the registrar's office had inserted, mistakenly I thought, Philosophy 101 on my course schedule, something I had definitely *not* chosen. Until the botch could be straightened out, I decided I had better attend, and thus found myself in an auditorium with about 300 other, equally perplexed, freshmen. Philosophy—we had never had it before, some had never even heard of it, and the very name sounded mysterious. It had to do with Greeks, someone ventured; another thought it was a bit like religion.

After a time, the professor of the course—also the department chairman—came into the hall and announced that no, it was not a mistake and that Philosophy 101 was in fact a requirement

for *all* Notre Dame students. Philosophy, he explained simply, was the pursuit of wisdom, which sounded to us, scribbling away, perfectly sensible, but he then said that it was something more, that it was also above mere knowledge, at which point he lost most of us. Our first assignment was to read *The Last Days of Socrates,* a collection of four dialogues by Plato concerning the trial and execution of Socrates. By then, I was sure that I would flunk out of school in disgrace.

Such is the academic void which James V. Schall confronts in his latest book, *Christianity and Politics.* Sadly, today not only do most students start out this ignorant in college, many unfortunately have their ignorance reinforced over the next four years. The idea that the ancients had anything terribly important to say is considered shocking; that they were even capable of saying something important is considered impossible.

In this book, Father Schall reiterates the classic theme that we need to rediscover the past in our classroom to inculcate our students with a respect for, if not an agreement with, what has come before. Though certainly not a revolu-

Four Decades of the Intercollegiate Review   865

tionary idea, due to the foibles of human nature it appears to be one that needs to have its importance stressed with each generation, and especially now. "We are desperately in need of a generation of students angered at the fact that they have been deprived of their intellectual and moral tradition."

In just this sense, *Christianity and Politics* is a philosophical, not theological, primer. The author's intention is to take the secular activity of politics and show that orthodox Christian doctrines of original sin, reason, the immortal soul, and free will have very practical consequences here in the City of Man. It is not Father Schall's intention to defend specific positions on any given political or theological issue, but rather to interest people in the intellectual history of these disputes, to get people to start thinking for themselves instead of mouthing some ready-made media cliché. The implication, which is more than justified when one considers the large number of students who graduate each year, is that would-be scholars are being intellectually short-changed, as they are required to know and interpret the present without even a basic grasp of the past to serve as a touchstone.

The tone is set in the introduction, entitled "The Lost Art of Christian Politics," where Father Schall suggests that Christian thought today is not so much misunderstood as it is unknown in our colleges and universities. There are English majors who go through four years of school without ever bumping into Shakespeare, except possibly as an obscure footnote. Students today graduate with degrees in political science never having heard of, much less having studied, Augustine's just war theory or Thomas's treatise on law. Even the ancients—Plato, Aristotle, Cicero—remain unread by the people who take their positions in society

as lawyers, politicians, generals, corporate chiefs, and, occasionally, priests.

Ironically, in their recent zeal to overcome imagined intellectual shortcomings deriving from their religious heritages, church-founded schools are tossing away even the best of their traditions for the latest unproven educational quirks. The new professors cast a patronizing eye on the past, when books were actually placed on an Index and pre-judged to be immoral, or, at least, an inducement to immorality. Christianity, they smile knowingly, was certainly narrow back in those days. There is, however, little difference between the censors of yesteryear and the new breed of professor, for the assumptions have now gone to the other extreme: all books and opinions condemned in the past are now *assumed* to be superior to the orthodox. The intellectual heirs of the Index are not the traditionally inclined at all, but those who judge a book, not on its merits, but by the comments of voguish book reviewers. Does the author quote Boethius? Then he is a reactionary. Does the author believe in original sin? Then he must be a Jansenist. Is he against national health insurance? Surely, then, he lacks compassion.

THE ATTACK is not, as some mistakenly believe, a result of the exaltation of reason—quite the opposite. The mark of a wise man, Aristotle noted, is his ability to make distinctions, and this ability today is lacking among our would-be intellectual leaders. How else can we explain the failure of this class to recognize the inherent evils of communism? How else can we explain the superstitious attachment to the idea of central planning in underdeveloped countries when it has brought only increased misery, famine, and repression everywhere it has been tried?

As Father Schall says, this utter failure of our leaders to recognize problems, much less find solutions, is the inevitable result of a philosophically deprived people. "We are, in fact, an irate generation as we note criticisms about presidents, congressmen, corporations, bureaucrats, and law-enforcement agents," he says, "who violate supposed ethical standards, the moral worth of which we are not accustomed or even allowed to justify at a theoretical or religious level."

To insist that a given state of affairs is not acceptable, wrong if you will, is necessarily to assume that there exists some standard for judging what is acceptable. This paradox is the Achilles heel of skepticism, for no man can live and really be a skeptic, and the search for this objective standard is what is meant by orthodoxy.

Today, though, there is very little understanding of first principles, of reasoned argument from logic, of what nature reveals about man, of the relationship between faith and reason. The tragedy of it all is that this recurs every few generations despite the fact that these things have been addressed in the past by great and intelligent men. Looked at objectively, Christianity has supported the clarification of the past, more than our secularists. Whereas nonbelievers by and large ignore the faithful, Christians believe they can learn something from everyone, even pagans. Accordingly, Augustine learned from Plato, criticized him where he thought Plato was wrong, supported him where he thought Plato was right, and both Augustine and future generations were much better off for the effort.

The pagans today are very timid creatures indeed. Though the philosophers of ancient Greece did not have the added benefits of revealed truth, they knew how to use reason as far as it would take them.

From this, they were able to examine man and his world to help determine (a) how things are, and (b) how things ought to be. To do this, of course, one must first go back to the basic questions about the nature of man and the nature of this world.

Christians have additional assistance. They have the further advantage of revealed truth which helps illuminate man's condition, helping him to lift his eyes upward and take in the whole of himself, not just his feet. This implies the recognition of man's imperfection, which is called original sin, and the recognition of the earth as a transitory place. The repeated idiocy of each age, which must be unlearned, is that man is essentially different from what he was a decade ago, a century ago, a thousand years ago. Anyone who reads any historical works—philosophy, economics, theology, literature, art, science—quickly recognizes the utter falsity of this notion. Analyze any aspect of man throughout the ages and, unless one is a complete fool, one will find that man is no more or less foolish and has the same basic problems which remain unsolved.

Christians have the further obligation, both spiritual and intellectual, to understand what our faith teaches about the way we are and ought to be. Foremost in Christian thought is the divine emphasis on the importance, uniqueness, and beauty of the individual human being, who, accordingly, has a personal immortal soul. Without the understanding of the individual, political theories become inhuman as they are abstracted and divorced from real people who compose the world—not "economic man," "religious man," "worker man," but people who are all of these—your father, your sister, the grocer, the town cop, all of whom have names and are all the contrary abstractions rolled into one. Why else would we admire a Mother Teresa, engaged in an apparently absurd activity, tending to faceless beggars in Calcutta, people not known when alive and not missed when dead, her work having no real effect on the practical problem of poverty? Why indeed?

The question is not puzzling to Christians, and again Father Schall is there to suggest that the most prudent course is to turn to orthodox explanations, for they are orthodox by virtue of surviving the test of time. Chesterton called this the "thrilling romance of orthodoxy."

> People have fallen into a foolish habit of speaking of orthodoxy as something heavy, humdrum, and safe. There was never anything so perilous or so exciting as orthodoxy. It was sanity: and to be sane is more dramatic than to be mad. . . . It is always easy to let the age have its head; the difficult thing is to keep one's own.

It is orthodoxy, in short, that gives answers, true answers to an anxious age. It is orthodoxy that distinguishes between the City of God and the City of Man. It is orthodoxy which Father Schall summons when he defines Christianity as "essentially dealing with the First Commandment, the love of God, and the Second only in its light." Thus the Christian is in the unique position of being able to recognize the importance of the here and now while at the same time denying its ultimate significance—something communists, fascists, liberation theologists, and even libertarians are unable to do.

Christianity and Politics, then, is more philosophical than theological, educational rather than prescriptive. It is an appeal to students of any age to examine their Western heritage as an orientation which offers answers to questions that have bedeviled man from the beginning. For though the search for answers is individual, the possession thereof is collective. "When I fancied that I stood alone," said Chesterton, "I was really in the ridiculous position of being backed up by all Christendom." We are all, to a greater or lesser extent, in the same ridiculous position. Only some of us know it.

Lee Congdon

The Passing of the American Century

VOL. 20, NO. 2, 1984

Outgrowing Democracy: A History of the United States in the Twentieth Century, by John Lukacs. Garden City, NY: Doubleday & Co., 1984.

IF THE nineteenth century inspired confidence in the prophets of progress, the twentieth has lent authority to the anatomists of decline. In the aftermath of two world wars, Auschwitz, and the Gulag Archipelago, we are no longer much interested in Enlightenment optimism; our elective affinity is for Dostoevsky and Conrad, Freud and Weber, Burckhardt and Tocqueville, Newman and Kierkegaard—all of whom looked beneath the surface of their undisturbed time and warned of the cataclysm to come. They were the ones who understood the darker side of human nature and the perils of human pride. In part because their admonitions went unheeded, we live in a broken world, one in which original sin, whether taken in the literal or metaphorical sense, is a basic assumption. The most thoughtful inhabitants of this world do not doubt that they are witnessing the decline of the West; they are divided only concerning the possibility of renewal.

What I have described in general terms is in fact an experience of life and a view of the world that is distinctively European, or to be more precise, Western European. The decline of the West *means* the decline of Western Europe and of its civilization; it also means the passing of the modern age, which had its beginnings with the rise of Europe during the fifteenth and sixteenth centuries. The political exhaustion of Europe that began in the trenches of the Western Front seventy years ago was completed by the Second World War. That was the meaning of the postwar division of the continent between two nations whose historical ascent coincided with Europe's decline—Russia and the United States. Of the two, it was the latter that stood astride the world in 1945, the "year zero" that marked the passing of the Modern, Bourgeois, *European* Age and the full emergence of the *American* century.

Few men know this as well as John Lukacs, who left war-ravaged Hungary, the land of his forefathers, to take up residence in the United States, where he has become one of our most original and profound historians, the author of such classic works as *Historical Consciousness* and *The Last European War: September 1939–December 1941.* Because he has long been convinced that history is a form of personal knowledge, it was only a matter of time before Lukacs undertook to write this history of his adopted homeland—a penetratingly critical, though well-intentioned, examination of a great nation's rise and fall. Throughout, his point of view is that of a cultural-spiritual European, which, according to him, means someone who possesses a historical consciousness, Europe's most important contribution to the world.

One of Lukacs's principal criticisms of the United States is the failure of most Americans to recognize and to accept this European gift, a failure that is indicative of a deeply rooted determination to distance themselves from their European heritage. Thus, the history of American decline is the history of Americans' revolt against their European parents. In a defiant effort to assert their cultural-spiritual independence, they have stubbornly refused to affirm the truth—experienced by Europeans at the Marne, at Dachau, and at Munich—that man is finite and sinful. They are, that is, unwilling to abandon the nineteenth-century idea of progress, with its attendant idolization of science and technology. This is the central thesis of this excellent book, which might more accurately have been entitled *Outgrowing Europe: The Rise and Fall of the United States.*

Lukacs would be the first to admit that the illusion of progress was easy for Americans to sustain, for although their country took part in both world wars, relatively few of their number died and life at home continued with only minor disruptions. This circumstance, joined with the fact that the United States seemed always to be on the victorious side in any armed conflict, contributed greatly to American self-esteem and optimism about the future. More, it emboldened many Americans to regard their country as the "redeemer nation"—the title of a fascinating study by Ernest Lee Tuveson. As early as 1900, Senator Albert F. Beveridge proclaimed that it was God who took "the American people as His chosen nation to finally lead in the redemption of the world." Americans had yet to learn that pride goes before the fall.

This messianic belief in America's sacred mission went hand in hand with an unshakable conviction that the country was unique in not being subject to the vicissitudes and limitations that beset other, and lesser, nations. It was in this confidence that Woodrow Wilson led the United States into war in 1917, an event that Lukacs regards as more consequential than any other of our century, including the Russian Revolution. This president, who once opined that America had "the infinite privilege of fulfilling her destiny and saving the world," was everything that Lukacs dislikes about Americans—self-righteous, ignorant of the past, and possessed of an ideological cast of mind. Worst of all, "his knowledge and interest in European civilization was minimal. . . ."

Whatever Wilson's failings, however, he and his successors presided over the most powerful and, for that reason, the most influential nation in the world. During the 1920s, the Americanization of the world began in good earnest and the end is not yet: witness the global popularity of American blue jeans, soft drinks, music, movies, and television programs. The Great Depression at the close of the decade occasioned what in retrospect we know to have been a minor crisis of self-assurance, one that Franklin Roosevelt was able to minimize while at the same time he kept a watchful eye on Nazi Germany.

Lukacs has expressed respect for FDR because the patrician leader recognized that Hitler's defeat was necessary to the preservation of Western European civilization. He was right to bring the United States into the war against Germany, but because, like the majority of his countrymen, he distrusted Europeans—not excluding Winston Churchill—he refused to take seriously the Russian menace in the heart of the old continent. Lacking Churchill's historical sense and political acumen, he persuaded himself that the Russians were, like the Americans, young, virile, and destined to be co-rulers of the postwar world. As a result, he bears a major share of responsibility for the subjugation of Eastern Europe, including the land of Lukacs's birth.

But if the decade following the end of the war was one of deprivation and despotism in Eastern Europe, it was one of prosperity and freedom in the United States. All, however, was not well in the best of all possible nations, for as Lukacs argues persuasively, it was precisely during the middle years of Dwight Eisenhower's presidency that the first signs of America's decline began to surface. Not surprisingly, he is disposed to regard the United States's failure to act decisively during the Hungarian Revolution of 1956 as the paradigmatic manifestation of that collapse of will that has by now undermined the trust of our allies and encouraged the recklessness of our enemies. But be that as it may, there is more than one reason to believe that American decline did indeed begin before the onset of the catastrophic 1960s, and in the main body of this work Lukacs presents a detailed and disturbing account of that melancholy process. Here

I can call attention only to some of his most telling analyses.

Among Lukacs's most provocative chapters is that which examines the effects of inflation on American life. He does not confine his discussion to monetary inflation alone, considering as well the geometric increase in population, bureaucracy, academic degrees, "rights," regulations, communications, and appetites. The root cause of this inflation, he suggests, is the American insistence that limits are arbitrary and artificial, affronts to initiative, progress, and the American Way. Lacking a developed sense of human limitation and increasingly reluctant to delay gratification or to cultivate the habits of self-discipline, Americans are being overwhelmed by the proliferation of just about everything.

Indeed, the "new immigration" alone threatens to unravel the nation. According to a recent Associated Press report, the Hispanic population of the United States now stands at 16 million, a figure that is likely to grow to 47 million by 1990. And as Lukacs points out, nearly two-thirds of all immigrants since 1968 have come from Asia and Latin America. His alarm at this statistic is not the result of racial prejudice, but of his objection to the inevitable and already manifest cultural consequences. Clearly, no country can culturally assimilate such a massive influx of people within a brief span of time; more likely, the immigrants will force the creation of a new hybrid culture, cheered on in this case by cultural relativists and those for whom uncritical celebration of the "Third World" has become the litmus test of liberal orthodoxy.

Here too, it is the decline or dilution of Western European, culture that exercises Lukacs, who cites with approval what Herbert Agar wrote shortly after the Second World War: "We belong to the

West, without which we must perish. We do not belong to Asia." Naturally, then, Lukacs deplores not only unregulated immigration and the encouragement of non-European cultures, but every attempt to reorient American foreign policy in the direction of the Pacific, to the neglect of the Atlantic. He recalls with a shudder General MacArthur's famous description of war-weary Europe as "a dying system. The lands touching the Pacific with their billions of inhabitants will determine the course of history for the next ten thousand years." Whether or not this is so, Lukacs insists that the destiny of the United States is inextricably intertwined with that of Europe. That is why, in the spirit of Bismarck, he is highly critical of American imperialism, which, like British imperialism before it, channels too many energies into the non-Western world.

It would be a mistake, I believe, to dismiss Lukacs's defense of Europe as outdated and nostalgic, for when all is said and done, Europe remains the most important and critical area of the world, that in which the danger of nuclear war is still the greatest.

And despite what our cultural gourmets tell us, European civilization remains nonpareil. But even if it were not, it would still be *our* civilization, existentially constitutive individually as well as collectively. University courses in "World Civilization" and misguided enthusiasm for the former colonial peoples serve only to weaken our participation in a common culture and hence to muddle our sense of identity and loosen the bonds of community.

There was a time, from around the turn of the century to the mid-1950s, when we did live together tolerably well. Lukacs characterizes these years as America's "bourgeois interlude," but unlike the Marxists, he does not intend "bourgeois" to be taken in a pejorative sense. He is, in fact, an unabashed admirer of bourgeois life which, he maintains, had little if anything to do with the spirit of capitalism. Of Western European origin, it had much to do with the city and with city dwelling. Bourgeois culture was thus urban, urbane, and dedicated to the cultivation of the interior life, one that is distinguished by a sense of privacy, a love of disciplined liberty, a recognition that truth is more important than justice, and a bias in favor of permanence—with regard both to possessions and to residence. Above all, this culture was verbal, reverent in its attitude toward words and thus toward thought. Unlike so many today, Lukacs knows, and has the courage to say, that visual cultures are inferior because they are connected "with the atrophy of thought" (Huizinga).

After 1956, America's bourgeois interlude drew rapidly to a close. Restlessness, impermanence, and a passion for equality were among the signs of degeneration. So too was the decline of cities and the great exodus to the suburbs, for as Lukacs observes, it is by no means certain that a nation of suburbanites can maintain, much less create, high culture. In his search for the less apparent obstacles to the maintenance of the bourgeois spirit, Lukacs believes he has discovered certain medieval and Indian strains in the American people. Taking his cue from Huizinga, he points to the pictoral character of late medieval culture, comparing it with that of contemporary America. Few are likely to dispute his contention that ours is a visual culture, for as anyone who teaches high school or university students will attest, most of our young people can scarcely read and write and, as a result, are unable to think clearly and well. At the same time, those who are aware of the migratory imperatives of American life and the savagery—as distinct from violence—of street crime will not be inclined to dismiss out of hand the suggestion that the conquest of the American Indians has left a mark on the conquerors.

In view of his many criticisms of American life, one might think that Lukacs would be cheered somewhat by the revitalization of American conservatism. That he is not is a consequence of his conviction that conservatism in this country is insufficiently European, that is to say historical. It is important to understand this in order to dispel the notion that Lukacs is an eccentric who compulsively shuns identification with every group. It is true, of course, that he is a fiercely independent thinker, unwilling to toe a party line, but he has never disguised his indebtedness to such European—and historical—conservatives as Burke, Tocqueville, and Ortega ("the greatest conservative thinker of the twentieth century").

One of the principal consequences of America's unhistorical conservatism, in his view, is that its leading spokesmen tend to support the idea of American exceptionalism and of limitless, if temporarily obstructed, progress. As a result, they sometimes substitute ideological nationalism for historical patriotism, accepting too readily the fancy that the world should be governed by American ideals and institutions. What is more, they are excessively, even ideologically, committed to capitalist economics and obsessed with anticommunism, signaling thereby their failure to understand that the principal danger is *Russia* and the Russian armies.

Although much of Lukacs's criticism of American conservatives deserves to be taken to heart, he goes too far when

he implies that communism as an ideology matters very little. It is true that no intelligent person in Eastern Europe takes Marxism-Leninism seriously and that everyone, of necessity, respects Russian military might. It is no less true that *Russian* communism is very different from Western European Marxism; Kautsky and Jaurès were, after all, men with whom one could live. Nevertheless, it is a mistake to underestimate the role of ideology. The Soviet Union was and is far worse than Tsarist Russia, just as Communist China is more deplorable than its Nationalist predecessor.

Less obvious perhaps, but just as important in the long run, ideology serves as the emblem of power and authority in Communist states, bestowing a form of legitimacy upon rulers whose naked tyranny would otherwise be manifest. Even the pretense of being part of an international and historically "progressive" movement can contribute to a reconstitution of reality that is no less politically significant for being false.

By now, perhaps, I have said enough to suggest the general outline and atmosphere of this intelligent book; it remains to say something about the possibilities of American regeneration. Lukacs is no Spenglerian, but a Catholic Christian who believes with Tocqueville that "around every man a fatal circle is traced, beyond which he cannot pass; but within the wide verge of that circle he is powerful and free: as it is with man, so with communities." Though the American century is passing, Lukacs holds out the hope that political decline may be the necessary condition of cultural revivification. Indeed, he claims to detect already a belated growth "of historical consciousness among the American people," the most promising sign of a "painful maturation."

Unfortunately, what little evidence Lukacs offers in support of this claim is unconvincing. Where and how, one is constrained to ask, does this historical consciousness manifest itself? Certainly not in high schools and universities across the land, where the teaching of history is inadequate or nonexistent. True enough, there seems to be some interest in television "docudramas," but these often amount to little more than rehearsals of *Dallas* or *Dynasty* in historical dress. What Donald Davidson wrote years ago about Nashville's replica of the Parthenon—and by extension about our country—does not, alas, seem any less true today: "Pursue not wisdom or virtue here, / But what blind motion, what dim last / Regret of men who slew their past / Raised up this bribe against their fate."

Wilfred M. McClay

Liberalism and the
Loss of Community

VOL. 21, NO. 3, 1986

Habits of the Heart: Individualism and Commitment in American Life, by Robert N. Bellah, Richard Madsen, William M. Sullivan, Ann Swidler, and Steven M. Tipton. Berkeley: Univ. of California Press, 1985.

HABITS OF the Heart was one of the publishing events of 1985, a widely acclaimed work of national self-examination by a team of four sociologists and a professor of philosophy, led by Professor Robert Bellah of the University of California at Berkeley. The book's uncannily fortunate timing seemed to dovetail with the increasingly dour mood of the American intellectual world—not to mention the American public's perennial appetite for national soul-searching. Indeed, our propensity for anxious and highly generalized brooding upon our national sins seems to thrive particularly in times of prosperity, such as the current one; that fact perhaps reflects the extent to which our heritage of Protestant angst persists in us, even as its supporting beliefs have become less and less of a part of acceptable public discourse.

There is, however, plenty to be anxious about. The declension of the public realm, the disappearance of civic consciousness, the disintegration of marriage and family life, the increasingly tenuous and openly self-serving character of human relations, the near-disappearance of religious values from our shared existence—these are all matters of legitimate concern, to liberals no less than conservatives. Indeed, it has been refreshing and encouraging to see liberals finally back away—if only in theory, so far—from the absurdly dogmatic civil libertarianism that has been so damaging to criminal justice and public morals in this country, and begin to accept the proposition—again, only in theory as yet—that prescriptive values are indispensable to a free society. The wonder is that even so tentative a change has taken so long.

That the acceptance is only in theory, however, is amply confirmed by the appearance of this book. Many of its criticisms of contemporary America are quite accurate, if distressingly hackneyed; the trouble is that, particularly for anyone of genuinely conservative bent, it does not tell us anything we have not known for decades, nor anything that we have not read a hundred times in the Sunday supplements by now. We have known for a very long time that a philosophy of liberal individualism, if not moderated by some countervailing force, would erode the very basis of an orderly society by undermining the foundation for our commitments to one another. What is wanted at this point is not yet another repetition of stale formulae, but a sense of what is to be done. On that score, Bellah's book hardly begins even to address the problem, relying instead on the incantation of abstractions that remain conveniently disembodied and unexplained.

One would think that a book dedicated to a revival of public morals and communal values would have something to say about some of the pressing moral issues of our time, particularly those—such as abortion, divorce, adultery, homosexuality, and pornography—which bear upon sexuality, that most intimate point of intersection between the public and the private, the communal and the individual. But *Habits of the Heart* does not, for the simple reason that, for all of its authors' putative commitment to a post-liberal moral vision, they would never dream of being caught taking an illiberal position on such questions. The book repeatedly dwells on the need to recover a "framework of values," upon which we all can agree and upon which we can build a rich and renewed social life together. But these values remain conveniently unspecified, for the authors clearly did not want to ruffle anybody's feathers or challenge anybody's sensibilities (although they are quick to fault the "unreflective" rigidity of evangelical Christians). Thus, their call for moral revival is little more than empty posturing and vague uplift, reminiscent of Norman Vincent Peale or Bruce

Barton, with some Walter Rauschenbusch thrown in for good measure.

The book calls for a return to our "republican" and "biblical" traditions, to counterbalance the dangerously amoral, selfish, radical-individualist tendencies of unrestrained liberalism. To the extent that these two bland terms mean anything at all, this would seem reasonably sound advice. But the authors show little interest in explaining exactly what these traditions are, devoting only four short pages to that task. Presumably, if these traditions have been so utterly lost as the authors imply, a good deal more explication is needed to help us recover them. The trouble is that, as a sociological investigation, *Habits* is interested only in the benign social effects that can be made to flow from a revival of these systems of belief; it does not consider their truth or falsehood. But, to reverse Richard Weaver's familiar dictum, consequences have ideas; such a revival can never occur without Americans, including our social critics, taking seriously the content of these traditions—a good deal more seriously than Bellah and Co. do themselves.

Moreover, it gradually emerges that Bellah and Co. do not really want to revive these traditions as they actually existed. He wants them mutatis mutandis, purged of any elements that might run contrary to the conventional liberal political agenda. He wants us to avail ourselves of them piecemeal, picking and choosing what parts are appropriate to the 1980s and what parts are not, remaking the tradition as we feel necessary. But the presumption that we can pick and choose which of the Ten Commandments to obey is not much different from the liberalism he derides; if the term "biblical tradition" means anything at all, surely it asks far more of us than that. Bellah wants all of the benefits of these traditions without paying the price for them. He wants to have strong moral values without the taint of discipline or intolerance, strong communal values without insularity, strong commitments without punishments for those who disdain them, national pride without patriotism, and so on. But this wish list is composed of insubstantial word-combinations, the fond pipedreams of tender-minded academics. They have no relationship to reality, no precedent in history.

If the book has anything even slightly new to contribute to the debate over moral revival, it is the insight that many contemporary Americans lack even the *language* to express profound moral distinctions. In interview after interview with their case-study subjects, this point is brought home in painful detail; the subjects cannot account for their moral sentiments in any terms other than self-interest. Even though the fit between the interviewees' comments and Bellah's thesis is too neat to be entirely believable—life, thankfully, only rarely imitates art—we all have known enough such people, the sort of consumption-mad, status-obsessed, new-class types Cyra McFadden satirized with merciless accuracy in her novel *The Serial*. Bellah has a good point here. But he does not tell us how we are to learn to speak the "language" of the "biblical tradition" if we do not believe in it. Indeed, he does not seem to realize the extent to which his own vague sociobabble *itself* exemplifies the incapacity he is talking about. The inability to articulate a moral sentiment does not mean one does not possess it—just as the *ability* to articulate it does not mean one has fully embraced it. Nor does the "language" of moral sentiment

matter for much if one is unwilling to act upon one's convictions, or talk about specific moral questions.

Indeed, one could argue plausibly that the social sciences have played a major role in impoverishing our moral discourse, and thus in creating this problem. Hence sociologists are not likely to be part of its solution. The language of self-interest which Bellah deplores is, far more than he seems to grasp, identical with the language of the social and behavioral sciences, applied to the task of living. Is it any wonder that men and women conceive their identities as nothing more than an aggregation of impermanent social roles, marriage and family as a passing phase in the universe of possible kinship arrangements, the political order as only the legitimation of naked power, and material gratification as a perfectly respectable goal? This is what they have been taught to believe; the ones who believe it most are the ones who have been paying attention in class. Indeed, only those who have been exposed to such "advanced ideas" in college are likely to hold such a dehumanized view of humanity; and the subjects of Bellah's study are middle-class and college-educated men and women—a very narrow sample on which to make sweeping generalizations about this country. A much more revealing book than this one might have pursued the poverty of contemporary discourse further, and asked what the effect of social-scientific thinking has been upon the moral language of Americans. But such a book is not likely to be written by a team of sociologists. They are not likely to ask whether social science itself might be the very disease it proposes to cure.

F. Russell Hittinger

REASON AND
ANTI-REASON IN THE ACADEMY

VOL. 23, NO. 1, 1987

The Closing of the American Mind, by Allan Bloom. New York: Simon & Schuster, 1987.

BY THE time you read this review, most of what is going to be said about Allan Bloom's *The Closing of the American Mind* will have been said. The book has fetched the attention of the media. The nation's major newspapers not only reviewed the book within days of its publication (which is rare, even in the case of most "popular" literature), but have reprinted abridged portions of it—especially from the chapter concerning the effect of rock music upon the intellectual and moral development of students. As I write this review, this Sunday's *Washington Post* and *New York Times* advertise it with the bold stringer: "At last you will know why today's young Americans are 'isolated, self-centered, tolerant of everything and committed to nothing.'" It's the sort of stringer that gets one on television, which happened quickly for Professor Bloom. Interestingly, it is also the sort of stringer that is apt to engage concerns which cut across the ideological spectrum. To the

cultured Left, who are the mandarins of our university system, this sounds like the predictable effect of six years of Reaganism and neoconservative economics. To the cultured Right, the stringer immediately arouses the suspicion that it is indeed an accurate report from the "graves" of academia, where objective truth and disciplined learning have been on the wane for quite some time. There is something in this book for everyone. As an academician who has written a serious book, Professor Bloom has the rare opportunity of an audience outside the classroom.

The book consists of three discussions, which are interwoven throughout. In the first place, Professor Bloom attempts to give a profile of our university students—in general, he says, those who inhabit the best twenty or thirty schools. Concerning the students, who Bloom characterizes as "flat souled," the report is not likely to surprise anyone who has worked in universities for these past two decades. I do not think that anyone would deny that, among our students, sentiments have been divorced from formal education, and that teachers can no longer assume that the students have what Bloom calls an "eros" for learning. That eros has either been flattened out and constrained to a thin utilitarian motive, or it has been seduced by other objects (e.g., the bacchanalian revel of rock music) and rendered unfit for the discipline required for high-level learning. The pathology outlined by Bloom is most apparent to those who teach in the liberal arts (including the theoretical wing of mathematics). The problem is not just that students have jumped ship for business programs or for ersatz majors in quasi-sciences; nor can the problem be blamed simply on the fact that the students are sorely deficient in the knowledge prerequisite for university classes in the liberal arts. All of this, of course, is true. However, the problem spotlighted by Bloom is that students are not *interested*—so much so that one is tempted to say that even a competent demagogue or sophist would be hard pressed to arouse a lively response. In other words, the pathology of the "flat soul" seems to transcend the sum of the parts of the other problems. If nothing else, Professor Bloom has done a good job in conveying both the insight and frustration of teachers.

The second discussion, or theme, pursued by Bloom is the effect of German thought upon American schools. Bloom's excursion, or digression, as the case may be, into intellectual history constitutes a book within the book. His understanding of the role played by German philosophy is a necessary complement to the long prevalent notion that American education has been shaped principally by Deweyan pragmatism. Although our political and legal institutions are peculiarly "Anglo-American," and although we have inherited what could generally be called "pragmatic" sensibilities from British culture, Bloom takes great pains to show

that the derivation and pedigree of our *ideas* have to be seen in the light of nineteenth-century German thought. Most Americans do not appreciate the extent of the reaction against the Enlightenment, and how a certain misology, or hatred of reason, is a consequence which now has worldwide effects. Bloom does not explicitly mention this, but it would be fair to interject here that America is the last society in which both the Reformation and the Enlightenment have at least some residual life. This perhaps blinds us to the fact that for well over a century the Western intelligentsia have quite explicitly, even programmatically, abandoned the ideals of the Enlightenment. The scientific, political, and moral ideals of the Enlightenment have been regarded by cultural conservatives as the main problem, for the Enlightenment sought to replace tradition with philosophy; leftists, on the other hand, tend to regard the Enlightenment as a movement co-opted by capitalism, which has only given us an emaciated and inhumane "science." However unwelcome the Enlightenment was to those who wished to retain the supremacy of throne and altar, and however unwelcome it eventually became to the radical Left, Professor Bloom makes a considerable case that the collapse of the Enlightenment has created a far more troublesome situation. It has unleashed patterns of nihilism which have little respect for our political ontology of Left and Right. Nihilism has played itself through both, and has found a home in the American university. Bloom points out that we have a peculiarly American way of digesting Continental despair: "It is nihilism with a happy ending." Only in America do we find the Sartrean existentialist and the Nietzschean "overman" consulting self-help books in shopping malls.

So, in the third place, Professor Bloom examines the nature of American institutions, and why they are especially vulnerable to the effects unleashed by the collapse of the Enlightenment. His basic argument is that the university has a deceptively important role to play in American society precisely because our political society was created from the rib of the Enlightenment. America was born when the Enlightenment was at its high tide. Bloom might overstate his case when he says that it is "only in a liberal democracy that the primacy of reason is accepted" (primacy of reason, here, construed in contrast to convention or tradition); he is no doubt correct that the American regime was explicitly founded upon an intellectual consensus that is identifiably of the eighteenth-century Enlightenment. We need not rehearse here all of the intellectual geometry of the "founding" in order to agree with Bloom's main point: "that for modern nations, which have founded themselves on reason in its various uses more than did any nations in the past, a crisis in the university, the home of reason, is perhaps the profoundest crisis they have."

American students, Bloom observes, are unlike their European counterparts, for our students do not have conventions or traditions to fall back upon once reason is disparaged. Nor, significantly, do American students have the same, well-developed literary culture that conveys a tradition of learning, and which is capable of training the sentiments even when the authority of reason is at a low ebb. Bloom's point is well taken. When the French and German intelligentsia capitulated to the irrational currents of romanticism and scoffed at the scientific and philosophical ideals of the Enlightenment, Europe was thrown into the grip of one ideology after another.

Terrible wars ensued. Nevertheless, students had ready access to high caliber literature. While this was not an adequate substitute for the philosophy and science jettisoned after the Enlightenment, it was capable of sustaining *some* sense of high culture. European universities flourished, even amid the rubble of the wars. Our universities seem unable to flourish in the midst of prosperity.

In an American context, when reason is disparaged we are in deep trouble, for we have nothing to fall back upon except the vagaries of popular culture. Paradoxically, Americans, who are generally characterized as intellectually barbaric, are more dependent upon rational symbols and disciplines than their European cousins. In my view, this is the most provocative and constructive contribution of Professor Bloom's book. Again, it cuts across the agenda of either the Left or the Right. But it is the cultural conservatives who will find the lessons suggested by the book most disagreeable. Although it might be true that the "liberal" mandarins of our schools have misjudged and mismanaged the problem, we are all affected by the loss of confidence in rationality occasioned by the collapse of the Enlightenment. There is nothing constructive to be gained by championing its collapse, or by exploiting its ill effects in favor of some "better guide" than reason. If the Enlightenment was fundamentally misconceived, and if we truly are prepared to say good riddance (i.e., it is not to be corrected, but dismissed altogether), then one has to be prepared to abide by the implications—which, in the case of America, are radical rather than conservative. Once again, Bloom's provocative yet deceptively simple point is that, whereas the French or the Germans could regard the rational symbols of modernity as representing a collective yet passing fit of insanity, and then go on to sink back into non- or para-rational symbols of traditional "French" or "German" culture, Americans enjoy no such luxury. We need universities precisely because America is so directly the product of a rational experiment.

So, in answer to the question of why students are "flat souled," Bloom argues that the crisis of confidence in reason has abandoned them to popular culture, which in America is not even minimally able to form the sentiments required for citizenship, learning, and for all those other good things which could be enjoyed if one were to unplug, for the time being, the earphones connected to the Sony. When reason flees the schools, and in particular the universities, then the dire predictions of the fate of egalitarian democracies will come to pass. As Sheldon Vanauken has pointed out in his recent book *The Glittering Illusion,* few people of the eighteenth and nineteenth centuries really believed that the masses were capable of the kind of rationality required if an egalitarian democracy is to work over the long haul.

Unfortunately, what Bloom never resolves is a question that dawns on the reader rather early in the book: that is, is it not in the very nature of a regime founded by a rational experiment that, short of a utopian realization of its ambitions, the regime is almost bound to collapse? If Bloom is correct, then it seems that we are forced to either accept the popular culture, or to devote ourselves exclusively to the cultivation of a philosophical culture adequate to the rational demands of the founding experiment. We need Mr. Jefferson's yeoman farmers to receive Fulbright scholarships to be trained in something resembling Plato's academy. Furthermore, it is reasonable to ask whether our "founders" ever entertained such a dilemma; or has Bloom,

the proficient translator and interpreter of Plato, arranged the terms of the dilemma in such a way that they correspond very closely to the problematic of the *Republic?* This is a question that the reader will have to ask and answer for himself. It is, however, curious that while Bloom clearly outlines the pathologies which ensued once the Enlightenment spent itself, and while he argues strenuously on behalf of America as a distinctively rational experiment (and hence, that there is something fundamentally correct about the founding), the overall drift of the book seems to imply that a liberal democracy of this sort is unable to sustain such an experiment. America can only be America if it recovers a pre-Enlightenment political culture. Perhaps there is a Straussian "key" to unlock this dilemma, or maybe I am reading too much into this aspect of the book.

Finally, it is worth mentioning that one will be disappointed if he looks to this book for specific recommendations regarding educational reform. Bloom's way of translating practical problems into philosophical issues is the strong suit of the book, so I am not prepared to complain about the absence of concrete proposals. There is, however, one matter that can be touched upon in passing. While Professor Bloom expresses some ambivalence about the so-called "great books" approach (i.e., not even great books are capable of overcoming a bad case of flat-soulness), he does recommend the approach. Perhaps it is impious to ask whether the great books method isn't a "conservative" version of the intellectual smorgasbord found everywhere else—albeit, the diet is more substantive. But one wonders whether it is any more conducive to the discipline required if one is to move among and between the differentiated areas of knowledge. After all, one of the great achievements of the Western university system since the high Middle Ages is the differentiation of the sciences and their respective methods. (I should mention that the role played by medieval men in constructing universities which are recognizably similar to our own is never mentioned by Bloom. His analysis skips over the historical period in which universities were first founded.) The specific content and methods appropriate to these areas of knowledge would seem to be as, or more, important than a collection of great books, which only invite the student to carry on a seemingly interminable conversation with "great" minds. How quaintly American, especially the egalitarian notion embedded in it! As Bloom argues so well, America lacks a traditional literary culture, and is therefore fated to a kind of cosmopolitan approach to the history of knowledge. We are everywhere and nowhere, and there-

fore we can converse across all cultural traditions. While Bloom is correct in observing that this is a potential strength of American culture, it also harbors the temptation to recede from the discipline appropriate to the specific sciences and arts. A student who reads Aristotle and Flaubert, but who does not understand the theoretical and methodological differences between science and art, perhaps "has" great thoughts, but he now needs to go to a university in order to learn, if not to master, one or another of the disciplines. Do we really expect nineteen and twenty year old students (whether they are "flat-souled"or not) to play the part of Leonardo da Vinci, conversing across seminar tables? Mortimer Adler has claimed some success in using this method with corporate executives, but I am dubious about its efficacy among late adolescents.

Gregory Wolfe

Life and Death Matters

VOL. 24, NO. 1, 1988

The Thanatos Syndrome, by Walker Percy. New York: Farrar, Straus and Giroux, 1987.

IN SPITE of his six widely read novels, his two works of nonfiction (with their original contributions to the study of language and the human psyche), and his two national literary awards, Walker Percy remains a figure on the fringes of the American literary establishment. When he wrote a letter on the subject of abortion to the *New York Times* recently, it never saw newsprint—spiked on the editor's desk. (Imagine this happening to a letter on Reaganomics from Gore Vidal, or on racial discrimination from Kurt Vonnegut Jr.) This same newspaper, on the occasion of the publication of Percy's *Lost in the Cosmos: The Last Self-Help Book,* wheeled out a big gun, novelist Francine du Plessix Gray, to fire a vitriolic review at the book. Nevertheless, a few weeks later, *Lost in the Cosmos* won the National Book Award—a rare, but well-deserved tribute to a compelling writer.

Walker Percy, who has many admirers among scholars and the average, "edu-cated" reader, has encountered so much hostility precisely because his vision is res-olutely at odds with the prevailing secular liberalism of the "New Class" intellectu-als who dominate our cultural citadels. Indeed, I would venture to say that with the sole exception of Flannery O'Connor, whom Percy has repeatedly cited as a kin-dred spirit, no other American novelist in this century has more accurately diag-nosed the spiritual crisis of modernity.

A Southerner and a Catholic, Percy has a profound knowledge of modern philosophy, psychology, and linguistics. Influenced as a young man by Dostoevsky and Kierkegaard, he has developed a form of Christian existentialism that is at once sympathetic to, and critical of, the modern temper. Percy, like another of his mentors, the Catholic existentialist Gabriel Marcel, believes in the concept of *homo viator,* the notion that man is a wayfarer in the world, a pilgrim in need of a destination. But Percy does not engage in the cosmic melo-drama that often seems to afflict French existentialists: both in his novels and sa-tiric sketches, he catches perfectly the domesticated forms of despair that perme-ate the daily experience of suburbanites.

If Percy can be seen as an antagonist of liberals, he is equally tough on what often passes for conservatism today. Those who pretend that the West's ills can be cured through the purely political means of anticommunist foreign policy and the unfettering of the free market are in fact *participating* in the modern malaise, according to Percy. Activists on Left and Right are caught up in abstractions; they avoid the fundamental questions about human nature: What is man? What is he made for? Where is he going? Thus the majority of politicians and intellectuals on both sides would rather avoid the "social issues"—abortion, euthanasia, the condition of the family—and get on with their managerial plans for the economy and international relations.

Percy's vision goes deeper; he writes novels which dramatize the dictum that ideas have consequences ("Books matter," one of his protagonists says). His fiction hovers between the more intellectual content of satire and the more dramatic density of the traditional novel. Conservatives of a more philosophical bent, whose understanding of modernity has been shaped by such thinkers as Eric Voegelin, Richard Weaver, and Jacques Maritain, ought to read Percy's fiction. Given the recent popularity of his latest novel, *The Thanatos Syndrome,* it may be a good place to enter Percy's imaginative world.

The Thanatos Syndrome is set, like the TV series *Max Headroom,* "twenty minutes into the future." The protagonist is Thomas More, psychoanalyst and lapsed Catholic. He has just returned from two years at a minimum security prison for having sold mild doses of amphetamines to truck drivers to help them stay awake on their long cross-country runs. But, on his return to the prosperous (and frankly materialistic) Louisiana parish

of Feliciana, More notices something odd about several of his former patients. Before his prison term these patients exhibited the classic anxieties and quirks of alienated and fearful human beings. But they now appear contented, sexually supercharged, gifted with total recall and mathematical genius. To More's alert eye, however, these people seem somewhat less than human: strangely docile, incapable of speech beyond two-word sentences—in short, their behavior is that of the pongids, the order of apes *below* the primates. Soon More is off in pursuit of the conspiracy behind this sweeping change in human behavior.

More's investigation uncovers suspicious behavior on the part of two leading scientists. Bob Comeaux, a psychiatrist, is the director of the Qualitarian Center at Fedville. Fedville is portrayed as a gleaming glass and concrete edifice where the federal bureaucracy operates its many agencies. The Qualitarian Center, which seeks to promote the "quality of life," performs operations known as "pedeuthanasia" and "gereuthanasia." These terms, covering what we would now call abortion, infanticide, and euthanasia, are possible thanks to the Supreme Court ruling, *Doe v. Dade,* which stipulates that a fetus or newborn does not acquire rights as a human being until it is eighteen months old. Then there is John Van Dorn, a Renaissance man—scientist, nuclear engineer, educator, Olympic soccer coach, bridge champion. Both Van Dorn and Comeaux travel in the professional jetstream where science, federal bureaucracy and funding, and research-sponsoring foundations combine to create the therapeutic state.

It turns out that Comeaux and his colleagues have secretly been dumping quantities of heavy sodium isotope into the Feliciana water supply (although not

that of Fedville). Ironically, it is the research done by More into the effects of
heavy sodium on cortical function that
leads Comeaux to his experiment in
altering human behavior. In short, the effects of heavy sodium are precisely what
More, with his alertness to these symptoms, has found in his patients. When he
is found out, Comeaux candidly admits
his responsibility, but challenges More
to criticize the good achieved by the
experiment.

> What would you say, Tom . . . if I gave
> you a magic wand you could wave over
> there [Baton Rouge and New Orleans]
> and overnight you could reduce crime
> in the streets by eighty-five percent?
> . . . Child abuse by eighty-seven per-
> cent. . . . Teenage suicide by ninety-five
> percent. . . . Teenage pregnancy by
> eighty-five percent. . . .

This is precisely what Comeaux's experiment, code named "Blue Boy," has done.
Even LSU now has perfect winning seasons. The twist is that Comeaux's project
has been undertaken secretly and without
proper authorization out of fear that it
would not have been approved.

More is incapable of arguing against
Comeaux; he refuses, however, the lucrative offer to "join the team" because
of his instinctive mistrust of Blue Boy.
The only voice that speaks up against the
forces represented by Comeaux and Van
Dorn is that of Fr. Simon Rinaldo Smith,
a crazy alcoholic priest who runs a hospice
for AIDS patients, deformed infants, the
elderly, and the terminally ill. Fr. Smith
is no paragon of virtue, but his own
youthful admiration of the Nazis, and for
several brilliant German psychologists
who subsequently committed atrocities
against children, has led him to be deeply
distrustful of abstract schemes to benefit

something known as Mankind. In fact,
Fr. Smith sees an incipient Holocaust in
the policies of Fedville. "Do you know
where tenderness always leads?" he asks.
"To the gas chamber."

The words are intentionally shocking;
indeed, they are meant to be a form of
shock treatment. The last thing either a
liberal or a conservative wants to hear is
that America is a proto-totalitarian state,
outwardly prosperous and sophisticated,
but rotten at the core. Like Tom More,
who experiences both discomfort and
embarrassment on hearing these words,
we are more complicitous with evil than
we would like to admit. Along with
Malcolm Muggeridge, Percy is convinced
that the West is afflicted with a death-
wish, an estrangement from being itself.
"In the end, one must choose—given the
chance," says Fr. Smith. "Choose what?"
More replies. "Life or death. What else?"

Percy's analysis of our culture is
strikingly similar to that of the sociologist Philip Rieff. In his seminal work,
The Triumph of the Therapeutic, Rieff
argues that in the post-Christian and
post-Freudian era, man no longer orients
himself by moral disciplines which constitute community, but seeks instead his
own, individual comfort. "Where family
and nation once stood, or Church and
Party," Rieff writes, "there will be hospital
and theater too, the normative institutions of the next culture. . . . Religious
man was born to be saved; psychological
man was born to be pleased." In words
that apply directly to the materialistic
world portrayed in Percy's fiction, Rieff
continues: "With their secondary needs
automatically satisfied, men may no longer need to have something in common,
as an end, to love. The organization of
indifference may well succeed the organization of love, producing a culture at
lower cost to individual energies."

As Percy depicts it, Fedville is the "organization of indifference" masquerading as "the organization of love." The Qualitarian Center exists to allow the culture to function "at lower cost to individual energies." That is why Comeaux is incapable of resisting the use of a "magic wand," despite the fact that it inevitably removes the unique personality of the individual and reduces him to the level of animality. The reaction to anxiety on the part of those who seek comfort is to retreat from the high moral demands which constitute human identity.

Rieff touches on another major theme of Percy's when he writes: "Compassionate communities, as distinct from welfare states, exist only where there is a rich symbolic life, shared, and demanding of the self, a hard line limiting the range of desires." From his earliest published essays, Percy has called attention to the decay of language in our time. Fr. Smith emphasizes this loss of a rich symbolic life when he contends that words have been "deprived" of their meaning in the modern world; when we speak of God, world, man, we hear sounds only, shorn of their evocative or denotative power. Without language that is attuned to experience, we are incapable of sharing a common life; we lapse into solipsism and anarchy. But a fragmented society can last only so long. Eventually men will seek a harsh, totalitarian order rather than disorder. In this novel Percy is exploring themes that obsessed another prophetic novelist and student of language, George Orwell.

In one sense, *The Thanatos Syndrome* poses the typical "what if" scenario we are accustomed to find in science fiction. But Percy's novel is in actuality a Swiftian satire on the abuse of science. As in the experiments of the "projectors" on the floating island of Laputa in *Gulliver's Travels,* Blue Boy is an application of an abstract solution to complex psychic and moral problems. At a deeper level, the novel probes the effects of the Faustian will to power which characterizes modernity. How is it that Renaissance men, like a Faustus or a German psychologist or a John Van Dorn, can combine intellectual brilliance and seeming altruism with inhuman brutality? The answer is much the same as that given by the Grand Inquisitor in Dostoevsky's *The Brothers Karamazov:* better to bargain with the devil, exchanging human freedom, with all its anxieties and attendant responsibilities, for the "peace" of a regulated society. The twist to this arrangement, which the devil is careful not to divulge, is that by reducing man to the level of cattle, men become as expendable as cattle.

In *The Thanatos Syndrome,* Percy is posing another uncomfortable question: are we *already* employing "Blue Boy" solutions to our social and moral problems? The answer, of course, is up to the individual reader. Yet the novel, for all its ominous implications, ends on a note of cautious hope. Our neuroses and anxieties, much as we try to exorcize them with self-help books and anodynes of all sorts, stand as testimony to our humanness; they bespeak sin, guilt, responsibility, and the strange, persistent hope of redemption.

Harry V. Jaffa

Inventing the Gettysburg Address

VOL. 28, NO. 1, 1992

Lincoln at Gettysburg: The Words that Remade America, by Garry Wills. New York: Simon & Schuster, 1992.

THIRTY YEARS ago, Garry Wills was a rising star of the Right, a celebrity in the constellation of William F. Buckley Jr. and *National Review.* His essay on "The Convenient State," originally published in 1964 in *What Is Conservatism?,* a volume edited by the late Frank Meyer, was reprinted in 1970 in the first (but not in the second) edition of Buckley's *American Conservative Thought in the Twentieth Century.* Taking its inspiration from John C. Calhoun, that essay is still looked upon as being nearly canonical by a number of conservatives. But some years ago, Wills switched sides, from Right to Left.

It has long been a wisecrack of the publishing industry that the ideal title for a best seller—combining the three themes that attract the book buying public most—is "Lincoln's Doctor's Dog." Wills's latest book is clearly designed to exploit one of these themes, and since most Lincoln book buyers are Lincoln admirers, Wills has taken some pains

not to lose them as customers. To anyone not invincibly gullible, however, his real opinions are visible enough, all of them testifying to his long love affair with Calhoun, the antebellum sage of South Carolina, the leading proponent of the positive good theory of slavery, the spiritual Father of the Confederacy, and the archenemy of the principle of equality in the Declaration of Independence. His essential loyalty to the cause of Calhoun and the Confederacy was fortified when, as a graduate student at Yale, he fell under the influence of the late Willmoore Kendall, whose clamorous presence broods like a poltergeist over the pages of this book.

In *Basic Symbols of the American Political Tradition,* Kendall had declared that at Gettysburg, Lincoln had "derailed" the American constitutional order by infecting it with a commitment to equality that it had never before possessed. Although Wills appears to have accepted this "derailment," his pretense is hollow.

The core of Wills' thesis concerning the Gettysburg Address is given in the "Prologue" of the present volume. At Gettysburg, he says, Lincoln performed one of the most daring acts of open-air sleight-of-hand ever witnessed by the unsuspecting. Everyone in that vast throng of thousands was having his or her intellectual pocket picked. The crowd departed with a new thing in its intellectual luggage, that new constitution Lincoln had substituted for the one they brought there with them. They walked off, from those curving graves on the hillside, under a changed sky, into a different America. Lincoln had revolutionized the Revolution, giving people a new past to live with that would change their future indefinitely.

Some people looking on from a distance saw that a giant (if benign) swindle had been performed. *The Chicago Times* quoted the letter of the Constitution to Lincoln—noting its lack of reference to equality, its tolerance of slavery—and said that Lincoln was betraying the instrument he was on oath to defend, traducing the men who *died* for the letter of that fundamental law.

It was to uphold this Constitution, and the Union created by it, that our officers and soldiers gave their lives at Gettysburg. How dare he, then, standing on their graves, misstate the cause for which they died, and libel the statesman who founded the government? They were men possessing too much self-respect to declare that Negroes were their equals, or *were* entitled to equal privileges.

Despite this candid depreciation of the Gettysburg Address, Wills tells us that: "[T]he professors, the politicians, the press have overwhelmingly accepted Lincoln's vision. . . . For most people now, the Declaration means what Lincoln told us it means. . . ." Hence, any "attempts to go back beyond Lincoln to some earlier version" of American history are "feckless."

In agreeing with *The Chicago Times's* "feckless" editorial of November 23, 1863, Wills fails to mention that it was a Democratic paper, and that it had supported Douglas unreservedly in his campaigns against Lincoln. All the points made here against Lincoln at Gettysburg had been made by Douglas and had been rebutted by Lincoln in their joint debates. In fact, no one elected to the office of president has ever made his opinions on the great disputed questions of the day plainer than Lincoln had. Wills himself admits in the course of the book that the Gettysburg Address is the distilled essence of everything Lincoln had been saying for many years. In making the accusation of deception, both the *Times* and Garry Wills (and Willmoore Kendall) assume that the American people had been paying no attention to Lincoln's widely published speeches, and that in electing him president they did so without knowing what they were voting for!

LINCOLN AT Gettysburg is the sequel to *Inventing America: Jefferson's Declaration of Independence*, which was published in 1978. In the Prologue to that book, Wills reveals that even then he was less concerned with the Declaration itself than with undoing the myths about it perpetrated by the Gettysburg Address. In that book, as in this one, Lincoln's deception is said to have begun with the assertion in the Gettysburg Address of the bond between independence and union. Here is how Lincoln himself summarized his view—long before Gettysburg—in his Inaugural Address of March 4, 1861:

The Union is much older than the Constitution. It was formed in fact by the Articles of Association in 1774. It was matured and continued by the Declaration of Independence in 1776. It was further matured and the faith of the then thirteen States expressly plighted and engaged that it should be perpetual, by the Articles of Confederation in 1778. And finally, in 1787, one of the declared objects for ordaining and establishing the Constitution was "*to form a more perfect Union.*"

The words from the Preamble were italicized by Lincoln himself, since he evidently thought it impossible to deny that the Union preceded the Constitution, if the Constitution itself speaks of forming "a more perfect Union."

However, in his 1978 book, Garry Wills ridicules the "four-score and seven years ago" of the Gettysburg Address. He says Lincoln chose "his Biblically shrouded figure" because it

> takes us back to 1776, the year of the Declaration, of the self-evident truth that all men are created equal. But there are some fairly self-evident objections to that mode of calculating. All thirteen original colonies subscribed to the Declaration with instructions to their delegates that this was not to imply formation of a single nation. If anything, July 4, 1776, produced twelve new nations (with a thirteenth coming in on July 15)—conceived in liberty perhaps, but more dedicated to the proposition that the colonies they severed from the mother country were equal to each other than that their *inhabitants* were equal. (Italics are Wills's)

IN 1981, I reviewed *Inventing America.*[1] I pointed out that Wills's confident assertion about the instructions of all thirteen colonies to their delegates in the Continental Congress was simply not true. I quoted from these documents—which Wills, perhaps relying upon Kendall, apparently had never seen. (I surmise also that Kendall, relying upon either Calhoun or Jefferson Davis, had never seen them either.) In the majority of cases, the colonies had instructed their delegates to vote for independence *and* union. Not one instructed to the contrary. All of them did, however, reserve to themselves individually their "internal police." This reservation marks what is probably the first appearance in our political literature of the principle of American federalism. Although Americans have been disputing for 200 years how to draw the line between state and federal authority, no one thought, either then or now, that federalism is inconsistent with union, or that union is inconsistent with nationhood. In adopting Kendall's thesis that the thirteen colonies, in becoming independent of Great Britain, became independent of each other, Wills is simply—shall we say it?—swindling his readers.

Let us consider further how the relationship of independence and union was looked back upon in the after-light of the founding. In 1825, Jefferson asked Madison for his recommendation of books or documents that ought to be made authoritative—*norma docendi*—for instruction by the law faculty of the new University of Virginia. In response, Madison did recommend—and Jefferson incorporated his recommendation into a resolution adopted by the Board of Visitors of the University—some of the "best guides" to "the distinctive principles of the government of our own State, and of that of the United States." The first was the "Declaration of Independence, as the fundamental act of Union of these States."[2]

In his earlier book, Wills refers to the Declaration and the Gettysburg Address together as "war propaganda with no legal force." But this is to ignore the testimony of Madison and Jefferson, that the Declaration was "the *fundamental act of Union*." "Act" here means "law." Article VI of the Constitution declares that:

All debts contracted and engagements entered into before the adoption of this Constitution shall be as valid against the United States under this Constitution as under the Confederation.

Article XII of the Articles of Confederation declares, in like manner, that all debts contracted under the authority of Congress before the Articles went into effect shall be considered charges against the United States, and honored as such. This more than confirms Lincoln's contention that the legal and moral personality of the United States, as a Union, extends continuously not only to the Declaration of Independence, but before that to the Congress of the Union that declared independence, and which had incurred debts from the beginning of the war in 1775. The Declaration of Independence is today the first of the four organic laws of the United States, according to the United States Code, as adopted by the United States Congress.[3] Article VII of the Constitution, as signed by George Washington, and submitted to the states for ratification, declares that it was "done in Convention in the year of our Lord one thousand seven hundred and eighty-seven and of the independence of the United States of America the twelfth." All acts and deeds of the United States are by the Constitution itself dated from the Declaration of Independence. How anyone could write two books on this topic, as Garry Wills has done, and remain ignorant of these most elementary historical and legal facts, is difficult to understand.

The enduring significance of the Declaration of Independence—embodied in the Gettysburg Address—is accordingly less in marking the *separation* of the colonies from Great Britain, than of marking the *union* of the states with each other. This enduring significance, however, is constituted less by the legal fact of union, than by the moral fact that—according to Madison and Jefferson—the Declaration embodies the principles of government of the States severally, and of the United States corporately. Moreover, the Constitution of 1787 guarantees "to every state of this union a republican form of government," without ever defining that form. Can there be any doubt that, as indicated by the testimony of the aforesaid witnesses, such form is best defined in the Declaration of Independence?

WHAT MADE the Declaration of Independence the best of all guides to educating the guardians of republican freedom? In 1978, as we have seen, Wills, following Kendall, thought that the equality mentioned in the Declaration referred to the collective legal equality of the States with each other, not to the moral equality of the human persons who were their "inhabitants." We have seen Wills quote with full approval—in opposition to Lincoln—the assertion that

the statesmen who founded the government . . . were men possessing too much self-respect to declare that Negroes were their equals. . . .

That the Declaration of Independence included Negroes in the proposition of human equality is the heart of hearts of Lincoln's alleged "new past." Wills also inherited this thesis from Kendall, who had charged Lincoln with "a startling new interpretation of . . . 'all men are created equal.'" The denial that Negroes had been included in the humanity of the Declaration had also been the contention of Chief Justice Taney in his opinion for the Court in *Dred Scott*. By a strange twist of fate, what was an article of faith for the old defenders of slavery has become unquestionable orthodoxy among "black power" historians and their allies of the radical Left, who take it as proof of the racism of the American founding.

Where does the truth lie? Are individuals equal, or are only "peoples" collectively equal? Consider the Massachusetts Bill of Rights of 1780—whose author was John Adams, a member of the committee charged by the Congress in 1776 to draft the Declaration:

> The body politic is formed by a voluntary association of individuals; it is a social compact by which the whole people covenants with each citizen and each citizen with the whole people, that all shall be governed by certain laws for the common good. . . .

And the premise upon which this voluntary association is formed is that

> [a]ll men are born free and equal, and have certain natural, essential, and unalienable rights; among which may be reckoned the right of enjoying and defending their lives and liberties; that of acquiring, possessing, and protecting property; in fine, that of seeking and obtaining their safety and happiness.

Here is an authoritative gloss upon the doctrine of the Declaration, prefaced to a Revolutionary *state* constitution.

In 1835, after being engaged in mortal combat against the doctrine of state rights enunciated by Calhoun during the nullification crisis (1828–33), James Madison drafted an essay on the meaning of sovereignty in constitutional jurisprudence. He wrote:

> To go to the bottom of the subject let us consult the theory which contemplates a certain number of individuals as meeting and agreeing to form one political society, in order that the rights, the safety, and the interest of each may be under the safeguard of the whole.
>
> The first supposition is, that each individual being previously independent of the others, the compact which is to make them one society must result from the free consent of every individual.

Therefore, there can be no doubt that the consent that brings the body politic into existence, the consent upon which majority rule and the "just powers of government" depend, is "the free consent of every individual." It is true that communities of men founded in this way are themselves equal to other independent communities. But this collective equality is a by-product of the equality that individuals enjoyed, as contracting parties, prior to forming themselves into a people. The equality enjoyed by citizens and persons under the constitutional law of a free society is a consequence of the antecedent equality belonging to them under the laws of nature and of nature's God. It is this natural equality that defines the ends, and limits the powers, of all legitimate governments. This is the philosophical core of the idea of limited government. For Calhoun—and his followers to this day—state rights are sui generis. That is to say, they have no anterior justification. States' rights, severed from the natural rights of human persons, are not limited in what they can do—and what they did do was to place the legal right to own human persons on the same level as all other rights.

The proposition of human equality, understood to refer first and foremost to the rights of individuals, forms the core of the Gettysburg Address *because* it forms the core of the Declaration of Independence. Even more importantly, it forms the moral core of our existence as civilized human beings. When Abraham Lincoln said, "As I would not be a slave, so I would not be a master," he was saying no more than was demanded of him by the Golden Rule:

> So whatever you wish that men would do to you, do so to them; for this is the law of the prophets.

At Gettysburg, Lincoln added neither a jot nor a tittle to the Declaration. Not for a moment did he think that he was imposing any interpretation upon that faith that did not authentically belong to it as it came from the hand of God and the Continental Congress.

The proposition "that all men are created equal," within the context of the second paragraph of the Declaration, means that no man has, in principle, any right to govern another man, without that other man's consent. It means that those who live under the law should share in making that law. It denounces as tyranny whatever departs from these essential norms of free government. It denounces as immoral American slavery in the antebellum South. It denounces as immoral the tyrannies of communism and national socialism, and all other tyrannies, now or hereafter, that attempt to collectivize the rights of man. It is, as Lincoln said, "a rebuke and a stumbling block to the very harbingers of re-appearing tyranny and oppression" for all time. The glory of the Gettysburg Address is that it restores to the American people—uncompromised and untainted—the pristine majesty of the true American Revolution.

Notes

1. "Inventing the Past: Garry Wills's *Inventing America* and the Pathology of Ideological Scholarship," *St. Johns Review*, vol. 33, no. 1, Autumn 1981. Reprinted as Chapter 5 of *American Conservatism and the American Founding*, Carolina Academic Press, 1984, 76–109.

2. The others were: the *Federalist*, the Resolutions of the General Assembly of Virginia of 1799, and the Inaugural Speech and Farewell Address of President Washington. *The Writings of James Madison* (Hunt ed.) IX, 221.

3. The other three, in order, are the Articles of Confederation, the Northwest Ordinance, and the Constitution of 1787 with amendments.

M. D. Aeschliman

"Canon" Ricks

VOL. 36, NO. 1–2, 2000–2001

The Oxford Book of English Verse, edited by Christopher Ricks. Oxford: Oxford Univ. Press, 1999.

THAT THE Christian religion was never disestablished in England—or in the ancient English universities of Oxford and Cambridge—is a fact of momentous cultural importance, not only for England but for the English-speaking peoples generally. Despite Newman's withdrawal from Oxford in 1845 and the subsequent gradual secularization of much of the life of the two universities, the Christian dialogue between faith and reason has continued to thrive there. What's more, that dialogue's articulation in works of literature, literary criticism, and lexicography, as well as in works of philosophy, theology, and biblical scholarship, has often retained a ghostly but genuine stamp of orthodoxy.

Especially is this true of Oxford University and its press, and even more so of that press's *Oxford Book of English Verse*, now available in a new, third edition. The first edition appeared in 1900 and was edited by Arthur Quiller-Couch, a poet himself and sometime King Edward VII Professor of English Literature at Cambridge. He chose poems from the period 1250–1900. Enormously popular, this volume was revised once, in 1939, by the editor. It concluded movingly with an orthodox poem by R. D. Blackmore expressing faith in Christ's triumph over death, "Dominus Illuminatio Mea" (the Lord is my illumination), the Latin phrase itself being the motto of Oxford University. This edition influenced seven decades of English-language readers before being superseded in 1972 by the anthology edited by Dame Helen Gardner, an Oxford don of pious views who was influenced by the neo-orthodox Christian revival of the mid-century, and especially by the poetic and critical achievement of T. S. Eliot, on whom she wrote a fine book.

Dame Helen was very much influenced by Eliot's revision of the canon of English poetry as represented by two anthologies assembled by Eliot's friend and disciple John Hayward, a revision that emphasized the importance of two great seventeenth-century "metaphysical" priest-poets, John Donne and George

Herbert, though both had also been represented in Quiller-Couch's 1900 selection. She also restored Alexander Pope to the prominence denied him by the more Romantic and Victorian Quiller-Couch.

Christopher Ricks's new volume thus has distinguished and influential predecessors, and in fact contains many of the same poets and poems from the period 1200–1950. But Ricks's edition also includes poems of the period from 1950 to the late 1990s, concluding with Geoffrey Hill and Seamus Heaney—both born, like Ricks, before World War II. The first thing to be said about this anthology is that it is a magnificent achievement, orthodox in the best sense of its predecessors, with its alternative and additional choices deftly and learnedly made and evincing no factitious desire for novelty in selection. It is very unlikely that anyone alive knows as much about English poetry as Ricks; his learning is lightly and wittily worn without sacrificing any of the gravity and centrality of the line of pious Oxford "clerks" that extends from the Middle Ages through Hooker, Samuel Johnson, Newman, and Arnold, to C. S. Lewis, J. R. R, Tolkien, Dorothy Sayers, and Ronald Knox.

Like Helen Gardner, Ricks has acknowledged the influence of Hayward's anthologies, and if anything, the presence of T. S. Eliot looms even larger in his anthology than in Dame Helen's—which amounts to a principled rejection of the contemporary devaluation of Eliot. Ricks's Introduction (wittily divided in two) is exceptional for its simultaneously displaying the craft of literary criticism at its best while also puncturing the "envious usurpation" of prominence for literary criticism over literature itself that our most fashionable literary critics—e.g., Harold Bloom, Paul de Man, Stanley Fish, and their French gurus—

have effected in the last quarter century. This usurpation is more poisonous and destructive than people outside of literary studies can easily conceive.

Though not a Christian, Ricks is often accused of being one, and for good reason. He is implicitly a philosophical foundationalist: a "Logocentrist," a term of abuse employed by our tenured radicals. And morally, he is an *anima naturaliter cristiana*—if not a Christian, then at least the best kind of fellow-traveller. This is to say that he is a moralist on whose mind and sensibility the waves of twentieth-century historical experience have not beaten in vain. A doggedly unoriginal natural law thinker, Ricks honorably refuses to deny, ignore, mock, or replace the category of religion in human experience, a fact shown in his generous, sympathetic, and precise discussions of Christian poets such as Milton, Johnson, Coleridge, Hopkins, Eliot, and Geoffrey Hill.

Piously but precisely deferential, unlike the self-vaunting deconstructionists who are now in charge of literary studies in the United States, Ricks pays homage in his Introduction to the central line of major poet-critics in English: Ben Jonson, Dryden, Samuel Johnson, Coleridge, Arnold, and Eliot. Especially in light of the failure of the Anglo-Catholic restoration, represented by Newman's conversion and withdrawal from Oxford in 1845, Ricks knows well the massive modern momentum of scientistic reductionism. "Literary study, like literature itself," he wrote fifteen years ago, "has always needed to resist . . . the imperialism of science." Arnold had made this point, and to their credit even the triumphant Victorian agnostics J. S. Mill and T. H. Huxley (winners, where Newman, Keble, and Pusey were losers) came, however late and ruefully, to acknowledge its force.

Yet to the opposite extreme from scientism—aestheticism—Ricks has been even more implacably hostile. If we ought not to make a fetish of objects and their means of measurement, nor should we make a fetish of arbitrary human subjectivity, what Ricks calls "the Activity of everything." Ricks's brilliant 1977 attack on the sly and self-serving aestheticism of Walter Pater (reprinted in *The Force of Poetry*, 1984) is of a piece with his reduction and demotion of Yeats in this Oxford anthology and his assertion that "as a poet [Yeats] is the most overrated of them all" (London *Sunday Times*, May 20, 1984). For Ricks, aesthetic immoralism is no cause for celebration or praise; he takes no joy in being what Wallace Stevens called "a connoisseur of chaos."

Ricks will shock, outrage, or depress our reigning postmodernists (who will disdain his anthology, but whose works will themselves disappear 'ere long) with his demonstration, in his Introduction and his selections, of the pervasively and perennially moral character of English verse, in contrast to the aestheticism of so much modern French, German, and American poetry (from Whitman to Ginsberg). The covertly or implicitly Platonist element that Coleridge thought so characteristic of English literature is vividly apparent and credible to Ricks. "For [Ben] Jonson," he writes in his Introduction, "it was imperative to hold to an ancient faith: the impossibility of anyone's being a good poet without first being a good man or a good woman." This point, of course, was made later and even more famously, by Milton. Despite modern skepticism and relativism, Ricks defends Jonson's view. He comments: "Realized in the very words of a true poem, there has to be a new sensitivity to consciousness and to conscience, and where could this come from but somewhere good?"

In an era of increasingly esoteric, pretentious, and virtually incomprehensible, centrifugal specialisms which impoverish and denature the common idiom, the state of the language, the dialect of the tribe, good literature is the bulwark, the living vehicle, the highest expression of normative discourse itself. ("We will always learn more about human life and human personality from novels than from scientific psychology," Noam Chomsky wrote a decade ago.) For this reason Ricks particularly despises the arcane scientist pretenses of literary theorists and their "envious usurpation" of the place of literature. Conveying the great literary and critical tradition of Jonson, Milton, Dryden, Johnson, Arnold, and Eliot, Ricks defends the existence and importance of normative principles and proverbs, and of poems themselves—the far from common "common sense" of the race. This he does in fine essays such as "Literature and the Matter of Fact" (1990) and "Literary Principles as Against Theory" (1985), where he writes that "a fully compacted principle is rooted as a proverb." Here is the piety, the traditionalism, the "Logocentrism" that have made Ricks anathema to our vehement, voluble postmodernists and deconstuctionists, and that make his anthology so trustworthy and rich. He sees himself as a steward or trustee of the canon of classic English literature, one of the great civilizing agencies of the modern world—a world from which so much sanity, decency, and beauty have been eroded by the acids of nihilism.

Like so many wise men and women in the English-speaking world, Ricks venerates Samuel Johnson, from whose *Rambler* (No. 168, 1751) he quotes a key assertion in the *Oxford Book*'s introduction: "the force of poetry . . . calls new powers into being, . . . embodies sentiment, and animates matter." A commonsense dualist, Ricks knows that there is in language something uncanny and inexplicable in naturalistic terms. He knows that, as E. A. Burtt put it, "The only way to avoid metaphysics is to say nothing." Of course the Christian poets whom Ricks anthologizes, and about whom he writes so well, go a step further in believing that the scope of the Word itself is not less, but more, than that of all the words that are or will be; but if Ricks cannot confess the Word, neither will he collaborate in mocking, impugning, ignoring, or deleting it. His Introduction to Milton in the Signet paperback series, his deftly argued *T. S. Eliot and Prejudice,* and his insistent advocacy and explication of the distinguished contemporary Christian poet Geoffrey Hill represent the continuation and vindication of a long tradition that is clerkly and monastic in its judiciousness and scrupulous attention to texts.

So, too, the present anthology. The *Oxford Book of English Verse* is a marvelous antidote to the contemporary Dunciad of American university-press publishing in the field of literary studies. The selections are made in the best spirit of the now-scorned New Critics—John Crowe Ransom, Cleanth Brooks, Robert Penn Warren, William Empson, and countless others—and with the moral seriousness that Ricks admires in F. R. Leavis and Lionel Trilling, as well as in Eliot. Open to originality and innovation, Ricks is nevertheless not afraid of appreciation and piety, and he has done his job well by gathering words worthwhile, in many of which the reverberation of the Johannine prologue can be distinctly heard.

Allan Carlson

CREATIVE DESTRUCTION, FAMILY STYLE

VOL. 37, NO. 2, 2002

Work and Family, Allies or Enemies? What Happens When Business Professionals Confront Life Choices, by Stewart D. Friedman and Jeffrey H. Greenhaus. Oxford: Oxford Univ. Press, 2000.

Care and Equality: Inventing a New Family Politics, by Mona Harrington. New York: Alfred A. Knopf, 1999.

The Widening Gap: Why America's Working Families Are in Jeopardy and What Can Be Done about It, by Jody Heymann. New York: Basic Books, 2000.

Love and Economics: Why the Laissez Faire Family Doesn't Work, by Jennifer Roback Morse. Dallas: Spence Publishing Co., 2001.

There's No Place Like Work: How Business, Government, and Our Obsession with Work Have Driven Parents from Home, by Brian C. Robertson. Dallas: Spence Publishing Co., 2000.

The Missing Middle: Working Families and the Future of American Social Policy, by Theda Skocpol. New York: W. W. Norton & Company, 2000.

IN THE wake of communism's late-twentieth-century rout by a victorious market capitalism, the pessimistic prognostications of the economist Joseph Schumpeter attract less and less attention. While not a Marxist himself, Schumpeter adapted some of his arguments from Karl Marx, particularly the view of capitalism as an evolutionary system, one full of nervous energy, one that could "never be stationary." Driving this industrial mutation was a process Schumpeter labeled "Creative Destruction," which "incessantly revolutionizes the economic structure from within, incessantly destroying the old one, incessantly creating a new one." He emphasized that this "gale of Creative Destruction" did not arise from changes such as new competitors, price fluctuations, or the flow of the business cycle. Rather, the impulse came from the introduction of new consumer goods, new technologies, new modes of production or transportation, new markets, new forms of industrial organization, or new methods of retailing (for example, Wal-Mart's triumph over the shops on Main Street). Such changes command "a decisive cost or quality advantage" and strike "not at the margins and the outputs of the existing firms but at their . . . very lives." In every specific economic field, he wrote, this process leaves "a history of revolutions"—and the debris of ruined companies that could not keep up.

Controversially, Schumpeter believed that entrepreneurial capitalism could *not* survive. As he formulated this thesis in his 1942 volume, *Capitalism, Socialism, and Democracy,* capitalism's "very success undermines the social institutions which protect it, and 'inevitably' creates conditions in which it will not be able to live and which strongly point to socialism as the heir apparent." He argued that the bureaucratization of large industrial units ousts the entrepreneur in favor of the manager. This "managerial revolution" undoes the bourgeoisie as a social class and undermines the very nature of private property. More fundamentally, capitalism levels the institutions of the pre-industrial world: the class of artisans operating through guilds, the village, the agrarian peasantry, and—most notably—the family itself.

Observing data from the 1930s, Schumpeter concluded that marriage, family life, and parenthood meant less to the men and women of modern capitalist societies than they had before. He pointed specifically to tumbling marital birthrates, "the proportion of marriages that produce no children or only one child," as the clearest sign of this revolution in values. This revolution in the family derived from capitalism's "rationalization of everything in life," the embrace by moderns of an "inarticulate system of

cost accounting" that exposed "the heavy personal sacrifices that family ties and especially parenthood entail under modern conditions." This "decline of philoprogenitivity" rendered homes and home life of steadily less value. As "family, wife and children" faded as figures of motivation for the businessman, "we have a different kind of *homo economicus,*" one who has lost "the only sort of romance and heroism" that is left "in the unromantic and unheroic civilization of capitalism." As the processes of capitalism undermined the "props . . . of extra-capitalist material" and the "behaviors" on which it rested, capitalism turned toward self-destruction: the passing of entrepreneurship and family-held firms and the "emergence of socialist civilization."

It is on these points that Schumpeter today is faulted. For has not market capitalism triumphed around the globe? Even in once-Communist strongholds such as the Soviet Union and the People's Republic of China, do not entrepreneurs effectively rule? Is not socialism in broad retreat, found today only in crude backwaters like Cuba and North Korea?

The problem with these rejoinders is that Schumpeter was quite clear that there were different *forms* of socialism. And it was not the Russian Communist version that he thought most likely to triumph in Western Europe and America. Rather, he pointed to Swedish socialism as the more viable and adaptable model.

What were—and are—the main characteristics of this model? Sweden's Social Democrats resolved in the late 1920s to forego most expropriation or nationalization of industry and private property. Let the capitalists remain as formal owners, they reasoned. Instead, the keys to the socialization of society would be a close regulation of industry and commerce to achieve social ends, a form of central economic planning through new mechanisms of coordination such as state-brokered wage agreements, and expansion of the welfare state into "the People's Home." Relative to families, this meant the socialization of remaining family functions such as early childcare and the provision of clothing and meals. Most importantly, said Alva Myrdal, an influential social theorist in the 1930s, labor union socialism itself must change. The goal of "a living family wage" for fathers as heads-of-households must go, as must its companion institution, the "housewife." They would be replaced by a commitment to the absolute equality of men and women. In the new order, Myrdal explained, both genders would be expected to work outside the home. Marriage and home life would be strictly focused on sex and reproduction; everything else would be the responsibility of private industry or government, now informally merged into a vast corporate state.

This union of individualistic or equity feminism with democratic socialism was an historically strange brew. It was hostile to the century-old goals of the European labor movement, which had striven for "the equality of households," "family autonomy," the "family wage," and "the special protection of women and children." And it was not fully realized, even in Sweden, during the 1930s. But three decades later, in the 1960s, its time had come round at last. It was *this* socialism, with a vision of a union between "big business" and "big government" built on the ruins of families and small communities, that would triumph in developed nations around the globe. Indeed, its success would be so pervasive, and its details so distracting, that hardly anyone would even notice the apotheosis of the grand Feminist-Capitalist-Socialist cause.

How then might Schumpeter's argument be reformulated or updated to explain this victory? He would emphasize, I think, that the capitalist mindset is imperialistic. It cannot leave any thing or relationship untouched. It tends progressively to subordinate other spontaneous communities, and even nature itself, to its own values. It injects its peculiar biases—rationalism, cost accounting, efficiency, and consumerism—into pre-capitalist natural institutions such as families, and so transforms them into very different things. This is Creative Destruction literally brought home.

The new capitalist economic order grows together with the Welfare State. Each picks up functions from the ever-diminishing household economy. Business begins by taking over the production of clothes and shoes; it ends by absorbing family meals (e.g., McDonald's) and home cleaning (e.g., the "Merry Maids" franchise). Government begins by acquiring the education function and regulating the workplace in the name of child protection; it ends by giving *care* to all who cannot work: the elderly, the sick, preschool children, even newborns.

In this new order, we also need a fresh understanding of that awkward term, *proletarianization*. Marx had defined it as the process whereby workers lost all productive property or capital, coming to rely entirely on wages for their support. Contemporary *proletarianization* might be defined as the steady elimination of independent sources of household income other than wages and the "redistributed" wages of state transfer payments, a process in which economic gains from "commons" rights, informal economic activity, household production, and other forms of non-market work are displaced by industrially organized labor, commercially produced goods, and public welfare.

Most Western families in the nineteenth and early twentieth centuries struggled mightily to avoid this loss of liberty, this descent into dependency. But with only scattered exceptions, twenty-first-century households in Europe and America have, willy-nilly, already acquiesced to this new order.

While none of their authors openly intended it, evidence for the truth of this neo-Schumpeterian argument can be found in a string of new books on the mounting conflict between work and family. Four of these books embrace a common project: to achieve a better mesh or coordination between workplace and home-life. But a more accurate description of their goal would be to complete, once and for all, the subordination of families to the industrial principle.

JODY HEYMANN'S *The Widening Gap: Why America's Working Families Are in Jeopardy and What Can Be Done About It* is at one level a fairly honest argument for full family surrender to industrialism. She correctly notes that before 1850, most American children grew up in farm families where both parents, in a sense, worked at home. Thirty years later, the rise of industry created a new situation in which the majority of children grew up in families where the father earned a "family wage" outside the home while the mother labored in the household. By 1990, however, over seventy percent of American children lived in households where *both* parents were in the industrialized labor force. While glossing over important issues of timing, Heymann does accurately conclude that these changes "were the result *not* of women entering the wage and salary sector but rather of *both* men and women entering the industrial . . . labor force. The fact that both men and women

labor is not new. What has been altered radically over the past 150 years for both men and women is the location and conditions of work."

In assessing the consequences of this change, Heymann's working group at Harvard University conducted detailed interviews with 7,500 "working families." With most able adults at work, they found a troubling new "care-giving deficit." As the author explains, "Whether the issue is elder care or child care, the experiences of low-income families are sounding early, grim warnings for the nation as a whole." The solution, she insists, is certainly *not* to bring the women home. Rather, a program to address "the daily care needs of all Americans" must rest on "the precepts of equal opportunity and equal access."

This means that all able adults must work, and all non-working dependents must receive gender-neutral care from "society," meaning—of course—the state. Heymann calls for early childhood care and education for preschoolers by the government on a scale equal to that provided for five to eighteen year-olds. For those older children, both the school day and the school year should also be greatly expanded (suggesting that babysitting and adolescent-confinement are displacing learning and acculturation as the driving forces behind the public schools). She also calls for mandatory paid parental-leave insurance for all working adults, government subsidies for eldercare "community centers," publicly funded child care, and more publicly funded transportation, so that family members can travel with greater efficiency between their various care centers. The social democracies of Europe, she insists, have made their peace with industrial necessity (e.g., ninety-five percent of Belgian three-year-olds are in publicly funded child care centers); so must America.

GIVING MORE complete attention to the revolutionary nature of the new corporate state is Stewart Friedman's and Jeffrey Greenhaus' *Work and Family: Allies or Enemies?* The authors are Professors of Management at, respectively, the Wharton School of the University of Pennsylvania and Drexel University. Their list of consultancies is also impressive. Friedman, for example, serves as Director of the Leadership Development Center at Ford Motor Company.

In dissecting "the conflict between work and family," the authors focus almost exclusively on gender. The point is made over and again: "To create options that help make allies of work and family. . . . we need to change the traditional gender roles"; "Some try to make the point that the problem of work-family conflict transcends gender. They are right in some respects but in our view it's also still *about* gender"; "It is time for gender equity in the workplace and at home"; and "Change society's gender ideology through education and socialization."

Friedman and Greenhaus could actually serve as poster boys for Schumpeter's process of Creative Destruction. Their book is compelling proof that there is nothing conservative about capitalism. "Keep the *revolution* going," they argue. "The struggle for the creation of new and more varied lifestyle options is far from over." Existing "hierarchies" must be shattered. These Professors of Management also insist that Americans "must be prepared to make the most of the *brave new world*" lying in the future, in order to advance "the *workplace revolution.*"

What specifically needs to be changed? The authors say that women must be pulled more completely into the corporate world, for "success in the *brave new world* of twenty first-century careers" requires people able to handle ambiguity, man-

age many simultaneous tasks, and build networks, and "[w]omen seem to be more skilled in these areas than men." The latter, then, need to be weaned from their careers and trained to spend more time at child- and elder-care. Why? Because in "contrast with mothers . . . it is *less* career involvement for a father that increases his psychological availability to his children." They suggest that "innovative summer camps" be used to indoctrinate children into the needed revolution: "let's open our children's minds to challenging the traditional gender roles" in these boot camps for the post-family order.

Friedman and Greenhaus praise Hillary Rodham Clinton's book *It Takes a Village* for its "powerful message" that "each of us—society as a whole—bears responsibility for all children, even other people's children." To meet this obligation, government subsidies should "significantly increase the quality and affordability of childcare for working parents." Family leave measures should be strengthened. And more caregivers should be recruited, trained, and paid with state funds.

AMIDST LONG passages lamenting the unmet potential of "Clinton the listener" (tragically undone by "an out-of-bounds sexual appetite"), Mona Harrington's *Care and Equality: Inventing a New Family Politics* offers roughly the same argument. Following the movement of most women into work outside the home, "the country's care system [is] collapsing." The need now is to "explicitly link economics and the function of care giving" and to build a new public system of care. This initiative "must begin with a clear view of the *unfair* allocation to women of the major costs of care giving." Instead, a "new family order" must be created, where men take on more care duties while women focus on career development. The author praises Bill Clinton's use of the term "corporate citizen" for underscoring that corporations are, indeed, citizens of the modern polity, with their own set of responsibilities for creating this new family order.

Harrington urges no less than a political revolution, where "care" is added to the existing pantheon of national social values: "liberty, equality, and justice." In practice she says, the joint goals of "care" and "equality" can only be achieved through a vast expansion of the welfare state. The author's agenda includes extending the Clinton-era Family and Medical Leave Act to cover *all* employees and to supply paid leave (just as in Sweden). "Joint corporate-governmental contributions" should be used to create "a guaranteed annual income" for all households. "For children, the familiar list includes support for high-quality paid day care and tax credits for families using it, support for early childhood care and education, and strong support for after-school programs." Government-corporate subsidies should provide thorough training and higher salaries for care-givers. There should also be "greatly increased governmental funding" for community centers offering elder care. Harrington's "new politics of social responsibility" boils down to this: the home largely disappears as a functional place; employers gain *all* the productive adults; governments claim the children, the old, and the sick.

THEDA SKOCPOL is a more serious scholar, and more judicious in her analysis and conclusions. Her earlier book, *Protecting Soldiers and Mothers: The Political Origins of Social Policy in the United States*, was a reasonably accurate history of the "maternalism" that guided the earliest federal programs touching on the family. Her new volume, *The Missing Middle: Working Families and the Future of American Social Policy*, has a similar depth. She is aware, for example, of the "self-interest" held by corporations in the weakening of family bonds. Skocpol honestly reports how changes in family structure—particularly the rise of single-parent households through out-of-wedlock births and divorce—have been a major cause of mounting poverty. She pinpoints the social devaluation of marriage and parenthood and honestly acknowledges that the passing of the "family wage" regime came at some considerable social cost. And her book includes a sensible discussion of tax policy and families.

But in the end, she throws her argument into the hands of state capitalism and its Siamese twin, the complete welfare state. As Skocpol explains, "it is a myth that vibrant market capitalism and adequate social supports for working families cannot go hand in hand." While acknowledging that the existing social security system greatly benefits the elderly at the expense of young workers, she recoils from talk of cutting back. The "best response," she reasons, "may be to increase the stake of people of all ages—and generations—in national social programs." Her "inclusive and redistributive social security system" would include universal health insurance and paid family leaves. It would require "repeated increases in the minimum wage" and "a national system of subsidized child care," with state support given to both institutions and families.

As with all the authors described above, she ultimately sees the issue boiling down to the quiet burial of the homemaker and full-time mother: "at the turn of the twenty-first century, participation in the wage-employment system is universally understood as desirable for all adults, men and women, mothers and fathers alike." Home production and the home economy must give way to reliance on the wage-economy and the state. Using classic democratic socialist language, Skocpol concludes that "it will be necessary to revalue national government as an instrument for addressing broadly shared needs in the name of democratically shared values." Or, put another way, for "work and family . . . to mesh more smoothly" families must submit to the corporate state.

FORTUNATELY, THERE are two, more recent books offering alternative interpretations of the current "work-family crisis." They both issue from a new Dallas-based publishing house, Spence Publishing.

Given its title, *Love & Economics: Why the Laissez Faire Family Doesn't Work,* the reader might expect to find in this book yet another justification for expanding the welfare state. But author Jennifer Roback Morse has a very different agenda. A professor of economics for fifteen years at Yale and George Mason Universities and currently affiliated with the Hoover Institution, Morse writes as a libertarian who has discovered through painful experience the limits to classical liberal thought.

Her awakening came, it appears, as the consequence of adopting a two-and-a-half year-old boy from a Romanian orphanage. Where her natural-born daughter matured normally, she writes, "the developmental path of our son has been circuitous, painful, and slow, unlike anything we could have ever predicted. We had to provide explicit instructions for

our son to learn tasks our daughter picked up effortlessly: making eye contact, making the most elementary sounds, playing peek-a-boo, noticing other people, even smiling." Morse learned by experience that babies are not born oriented to the good: "they are just cute savages who have the potential to be civilized. It is not a foregone conclusion that any particular child will be civilized." Morse concluded that the real work of life is not to be found in the domain of paid employment: "The real world is the world around the kitchen table, the world of the nursery, the world of the bedroom." She also learned that the laissez faire principles of competition, efficiency, and pursuit of self-interest could not be extended into families and other face-to-face communities: they did not "provide the social glue for the good society."

One of her most candid admissions follows from a discussion of "attachment disorder" in children. She describes

> a child who does not care what anyone thinks of him. The disapproval of others does not deter the child from bad behavior because no other . . . matters to the child. . . . The child does whatever he thinks he can get away with, no matter the cost to others. He does not monitor his own behavior, so authority figures must constantly be aware of him and watch him. He lies if he thinks it is advantageous to lie. . . . He shows no regret at hurting another person. . . . [H]e may become a sophisticated manipulator. . . .

Who is this child? Morse asks. "Why, it is *homo economicus,*" the rational, calculating, economic man of libertarian theory whose "actions are governed by the self-interested calculations of cost and benefits."

From this perspective, she concludes that something is fundamentally wrong in modern Western society. Without using his name, she acknowledges Schumpeter's dilemma: "Our new problem is that the family bonds that earlier generations of political theorists could take for granted have become so weakened that the very fabric of social life is threatened." Morse even identifies the essence of the real problem: political dominance by an "ideological cocktail" composed of "left-wing self-esteem feminism and right-wing income maximizing capitalism."

But at this point her argument falters, for she does not acknowledge the remainder of Schumpeter's argument: that capitalism's own nervous energy and value imperialism undoes the inherited institutions that might keep it humane. Instead, Morse implicitly holds to a view of market neutrality: the problem lies with bad people and bad ideas, not within the system itself. Kept in their proper place, markets can work just fine. And so, her proposed antidotes to family decline turn out to be fairly anemic. Still the libertarian here, Morse would cut back the state by reducing the sway of social security, spiking welfare to single mothers, taking moral education out of the public schools, and tempering the power of child-protection agencies. Her long and sometimes poignant passages on the meaning of love and sacrifice also imply a call to mothers to return home voluntarily to care for their children. All of these are reasonable, even good ideas. But they seem to float in the air, only encountering on the margins the aggressive new family order of the corporate statists.

THE SECOND volume from Spence is made of sterner stuff. Brian Robertson's *There's No Place Like Work: How Business,* *Government, and Our Obsession With Work Have Driven Parents from Home* rests on fewer illusions, more historical insights, and full recognition of Schumpeter's argument: capitalism's marketplace is not neutral ground. The author offers a lengthy and solid history of the family wage regime, showing how this mix of cultural pressures and law limited industrial intrusion into the family for about a century. Like Schumpeter, he sees the falling marital birth rate as a sign of family decay. He also gives specific examples of a feminist-driven capitalism's creative destruction of the home:

> The transformation of the father-ideal from chief bread winner to chief consumer was probably already accomplished before the transformation of the mother from homemaker to working mom. . . .
>
> The feminist solution . . . has also succeeded, in many homes, in making domestic work just one more commodity for which the market has a price tag. . . .
>
> [W]hat began to happen in the 1960s was a large-scale cultural capitulation to the feminist romanticization of the marketplace . . . as well as an increasing demand on the part of business for female labor."

Indeed, Robertson ably identifies some of the key steps in rearing the new corporate state on the bones of the autonomous family. In 1957, for example, the U.S. Department of Labor jointly sponsored a conference with business groups on "Work in the Lives of Married Women." At the very height of the postwar baby boom and the evident surge in female domesticity, corporate and government economists agreed that only the labor of married women and mothers could overcome looming "manpower" shortages. Some years later *The Economist* magazine, with its characteristic blunt honesty, made more explicit what business had to gain: "Women are proving a godsend to many [American] employers. They usually cost less to employ than men, are more prepared to be flexible and less inclined to kick up a fuss if working conditions are poor. . . . Employers like them because they . . . command lower pay, and because part-timers can be pushed harder while they are at work."

Robertson also describes recent episodes of rational cost accounting at work in the post-family order. One employer gives a twenty-five percent pay raise to new mothers if they return more quickly to their corporate tasks. A life insurance company has found "lactation support rooms" to be an efficient tool, saving $1,435 and three days of sick leave per breastfed baby, "a three to one return on their investment." Such developments remind Robertson of Hilaire Belloc's prediction, early in the twentieth century, that the threat to the West's freedom did not arise from socialism per se, "but from an unholy alliance of big government and big business" where workers would find security in "government regulation, confirming the economic dominance of larger corporations."

The author faults an American conservatism which exalts the unfettered market as its first principle. He also offers a very different policy agenda. Massive tax relief tied to marriage and the number of children might serve as a workable substitute for the family wage. The protection and encouragement of home schooling also could be a promising way to start bringing real functions back into the home circle.

JUST AS this review was being completed, word came from Asia of a remarkable development: the Communist Party of China would soon open its membership to capitalists. Most Western observers will probably see this as still another symbolic triumph by the free market system over its collectivist foe. But another interpretation is possible. Perhaps this is a symbol of a different victory, the triumph of a global capitalism in league with welfare socialism to advance the true social revolution built through Creative Destruction. Seen this way, "capitalists in the Communist Party" represents no advance of liberty, but rather the deepened slavery of atomized individuals, now dependent jointly on the mega-corporations for normal sustenance and on the nanny state for security and "care." This is, I believe, how the British Distributists of the 1920s, the American Agrarians of the 1930s, and an Austrian-American economist named Schumpeter of the 1940s would have viewed the capitalist-Communist hybrid.

Ted V. McAllister

Re-Visioning Conservative History

VOL. 40, NO. 1, 2004

Educating for Liberty: The First Half-Century of the Intercollegiate Studies Institute, by Lee Edwards. Washington, DC: Regnery Publishing, 2004.

THE HISTORIOGRAPHY of American conservatism (often rendered the "conservative movement") remains immature. For decades, the academic historical establishment largely ignored American conservatives or dealt with them as a sort of fringe group, recurrent expressions of a pathology. Only after the surprising and enduring appeal of Ronald Reagan did most historians begin to take serious scholarly notice of self-proclaimed conservatives. Slowly, the historical literature is growing richer. But for now, the story of conservatism in America, as told by the academics, is fractured and inconclusive.

While non-conservative historians slept, a small band of conservative scholars did an admirable job of telling the story of the creation and evolution of conservative ideas and, to a lesser extent, of conservative institutions. The best of these efforts came in 1976 with George H. Nash's seminal book, *The Conservative Intellectual Movement in America: Since 1945.* Significantly, Nash told the story of conservative *intellectuals,* and in the process he made influential decisions about the array of stars in the conservative constellation. In large measure, we continue today to define the contours of American conservatism based on whom Nash included or excluded in his work. Perhaps even more importantly, we have a sense of a common story, in spite of the great diversity Nash incorporated in his narrative. Nash's story has become the starting point for all further American conservative histories.

But in the decades since Nash first published his landmark book—a book that is as important to the history of American conservatism as the books Nash himself discussed—a political movement bearing the conservative label has rocked the political world. For over twenty years now, conservative writers have folded the familiar story crafted by Nash into a more dynamic and progressive history of political movements, institutions, and political actors. Whether Nash intended the word "movement" to stand for something so cohesive and partisan-political or not, more recent renditions of the story of American conservatism have tended to edit out the rich diversity, critical idiosyncrasies, and heated debates of American conservatism in order more readily to tell the story of a political movement that changed America.

The conservative *political* movement bears some striking similarities to Nash's *intellectual* "movement." The political movement began with a wide array of oppositional groups, each critical of various tendencies in American society at mid-century. These groups formed alliances and created institutions to express a more or less common front (*National Review* was the most important, and one that connected the political and intellectual movements in important ways). As a political impulse, striving to gain power and to change public policy, the political movement had to purge itself of groups and ideas that were liabilities, and its leaders had to organize institutions aimed at action. They had to articulate an evolving political message that might appeal to democratic majorities. With the electoral success of Ronald Reagan, the conservative political movement had a visible expression, and a simple and successful agenda. Subsequent histories, written by conservatives for conservatives and attempting to account for conservative political success, would, as a result, be written tendentiously, seeing all things as pointing to Reagan.

The resulting story has the virtue of clarity—and the liability of ignoring or distorting a great deal of American history. The story runs something like this: In the beginning stood a few good men, crying nobly in the wilderness—men of contemplation rather than action. Believing in the axiom, "ideas have consequences," these men employed their pens in a philosophical cum political war

against the forces of "liberalism," "totalitarianism," "collectivism," and a few other isms. Their ideas found a small but highly motivated audience, who would in turn establish institutions to promulgate their ideas. From this nexus of ideas, individuals, and institutions emerged a political movement that, out of necessity, blended an amalgam of apparently contradictory tendencies into a coherent ideology—an ideology that transformed American politics in 1980 and has since become the dominant force in our political culture. Much of this story is true, as far as it goes.

But built into this story is a privileged language—the language of "practical politics" that shaves off all complicating and nonpolitical or even antipolitical ideas and discovers, lo and behold, that a historical process has led to a set of simple political principles, the defenders of which are on the winning side of history. But even mundane policy goals like low taxes or high defense spending seem more noble when they can claim a philosophical pedigree. So it is important that the story include the intellectual fathers who founded the movement and whose names are invoked regularly (but whose books are rarely read) to prove that the political program has "ideas" behind it—and to excuse the absence of any serious new thinking about ideas.

This partisan story contributes to our historical myopia. It is a story that justifies an ideology, and as such it is a Manichean story, with the forces of good pitted against the forces of evil. It consequently has no way of understanding the complexity of either side, of the wide-ranging intellectual fecundity of conservatives, of the significant and substantive critiques of non-conservatives. It has shut itself off from the speculative give-and-take of serious people in order to justify a political program and the simple, if anti-conservative, disposition to apply that program under all circumstances. If a political program is what you want, complexity is your enemy. But from the beginning, conservatism as a variegated intellectual and moral impulse (rather than a movement) stressed precisely the complexity and irreducible particularity of all human existence. This impulse cannot simply be collapsed into an ideology or a political program. To do so is to violate the nature of conservatism as understood by the very "fathers" endorsed by the story.

Insofar as American conservatives come to locate themselves within this narration of their past (and present), they perforce become defenders of a very narrow partisan-political tradition, shorn of some of their most important intellectual and moral resources for responding meaningfully to the changing tides of history. It is not that this familiar "movement" story must be rejected out of hand, however. Rather, we need to reclaim the more capacious patrimony that this rendering of our past has so assiduously eclipsed.

A MORE adequate conservative history would likely begin by concentrating heavily on institutions. This is precisely what Lee Edwards does in his book, *Educating for Liberty: The First Half-Century of the Intercollegiate Studies Institute.* It is hard to overstate the importance of this historical subject in addressing the problems with current conservative historiography. Institutions provide historians helpful ways of tracing the associations, tensions, political compromises, and natural affinities in one or another part of a movement. One learns something about the diversity of beliefs in an otherwise "organized" group, as well as about how beliefs and

commitments change as a result of the interaction of the individuals inside institutions. Moreover, institutions always interact with a larger social, intellectual, and political context, making the study of conservative institutions a valuable opportunity to explore how thinkers and doers respond concretely to complex cultural and political challenges.

If the subject of Edwards's study is of great significance, so also are the obstacles that he faced in telling this story. *Educating for Liberty* is an institutional history, commissioned by the Intercollegiate Studies Institute to celebrate the institution's fiftieth anniversary. Such a book is not the place for exploring in any depth disagreements, discord, or failures. In addition, one might reasonably argue that ISI is, and has been for fifty years, the most important conservative institution to have resisted the overt politicization of American conservatism. Lee Edwards is a political historian, commissioned to write a celebratory history, making it likely that the resulting volume would reinforce rather than challenge the dominant historical narrative. This is what Edwards does—but not without capturing in parts of his story the subterranean complexity of his subject.

We notice at once, for example, the original name of the organization: the Intercollegiate Society of Individualists. It is an interesting concept—a society of individualists. The name was not without controversy in the 1950s, as Edwards notes, but it very helpfully reveals the confusing yet most important ideals of many conservatives in that early period. The word "individualist" had little of the idea of the abstracted self that the word today conjures. Rather, it was a dense concept suggesting an alternative to the collectivism of socialism and communism, certainly, but also remaining open to the interaction between the individual and his society and culture that crafts a distinctive personality. Individualists, in this sense, belong to societies in ways they couldn't possibly belong to states, any more than they could be wholly self-created.

By engaging this history, we can learn so much about the competing understanding of the human self found within conservatism and within ISI, about a struggle to understand human purposes in an age where traditional forms of living were being shattered by collectivist ideologies and economic transformations. Edwards attempts to situate the original "individualism" of ISI amidst the well-known controversies between traditionalists and libertarians, suggesting at times that ISI has departed from an originally libertarian founding into more traditionalist waters. But further reflection might read "individualism" in light of mid-century concerns about "mass society," about the anonymity of "the organization man," which seemed to be the human type emerging in developed corporate capitalism. Such a reading would both qualify accounts of libertarianism at mid-century and also indicate that ISI has followed a line of authentic development of its founding impulse.

Beyond this clarification, a proper understanding of the conservative usages of "individualism," and of related concepts such as community, institution, society, etc., provides a rich engagement between normative claims about human nature and purpose and changing social, political, and cultural challenges to these ideals. A conservative today is much better equipped to think through policy choices, to try to weigh complex alternatives created by globalized capitalism, new forms of local rule, and changing social values, if he is equipped with the more

nuanced understanding of individualism as defended by conservatives in an earlier context. Conservative historians can serve contemporary conservatives well by reclaiming the intellectual complexity of early periods that allow for an understanding of both normative principles (universal claims) and their expressions in a specific cultural context (particular circumstances).

We notice, moreover, the stated purpose of ISI, for at least thirty years now: *To educate for liberty.* Clearly implied in this motto is the belief that human beings are *not* naturally capable of living well with liberty. Liberty (which is not quite the same thing as freedom) is a cultural inheritance that requires the cultivation of habits, customs, and affections that together render individuals capable of ruling themselves and of enjoying the benefits of a free society. Among self-proclaimed "conservatives" of a political stripe, however, freedom is understood as inalienable, as something simply given, not cultivated. This apparent tension between ISI's stated mission and the political ideology of the Republican Party is worthy of considerable analysis and discussion. These differences might be only matters of emphasis, or they may be more profoundly at odds.

THE FIRST part of *Educating for Liberty* follows closely the Nash-derived story of American conservatism in the 1950s and 1960s. Oddly—perhaps because little exists—Edwards draws very sparsely from archival material, and when he does get beyond public-access material he depends heavily on personal interviews. These interviews provide some of the most interesting passages of the book, but in no place does Edwards really challenge the memories of his interviewees. The story that unfolds in the first several chapters offers a restatement of the public beliefs of the founders and supporters of ISI. Most conspicuous in this context is a belief in a rather crude dualism between the friends and enemies of liberty. It is not so strange that ISI's founders would espouse this dualism, but it is surprising, when looking back forty and fifty years, that the historian does not examine more carefully these beliefs. Why were these men so given to making such claims and to suggesting that very different intellectual tendencies should be clumped together? There were, I suspect, good reasons for them to make these claims at the time, just as there are good reasons why the historian should note the complexity that was necessarily missed by those who lived through this period. An institutional history is an excellent place to offer these clarifications, both explaining the historical actors as they understood themselves and critiquing their ideas in light of knowledge they could not have possessed at the time.

The second half of the book is far less structured, losing the clear narrative framework that the first half possesses. Possibly, these chapters were rushed so that the book would be available in time for ISI's anniversary celebration. Edwards provides an expansive array of facts, details, and anecdotes in a more or less undigested manner. There is much to commend in this section as it provides interesting and potentially valuable evidence of how participants in ISI have redefined its programs to remain faithful to its mission amidst changing political and cultural circumstances. The reader captures a whiff of an underlying diversity and some internal controversy that Edwards is unwilling to examine directly. But this diversity and controversy makes ISI a much more interesting place. Quite

clearly the most important institution of the intellectual right, ISI has not only tolerated a variety of views, but has provided a most important forum for the ongoing assessment of American conservatism, and of the challenges to define and defend liberty in ever-changing contexts. No institution could perform this role without incorporating into itself a good measure of intellectual ferment.

Also in this second half, Edwards supplies tension-filled evidence about the peculiar challenges faced by a relatively nonpolitical conservative institution in an age of conservative political ascendancy. Clearly, many of ISI's leaders and its largest financial backers supported enthusiastically the presidency of Ronald Reagan, and yet ISI has flourished by providing a place where culture and ideas have mattered more than political agendas. The subject is a messy one and Edwards cannot quite sort it all out. He documents the many interconnections between ISI and political think tanks and government officials. But he also notes, often with interviews, the desire of many ISI leaders and staffers to maintain its "non-political, even romantic" character. Some ISI people, like Gregory Wolfe, seemed to grow weary with politics, and with a tendency of intellectuals on the right to always be fighting *against* something. Insofar as these participants in ISI wished to engage in political conflict, they wanted to do so from a more cosmic perch, examining the roots of Western civilization, which needed to be kept healthy in order to supply the nation with the intellectual and spiritual nourishment to preserve a stable political order—to say nothing of preserving the beauty and even the grandeur of our civilization.

Like all such institutions, changing times, changing personnel, and changing financial demands and opportunities necessarily require a constant reassessment of purpose and direction. ISI has maintained, since the election of 1980, a strong emphasis on its deeper cultural purpose, but it has not escaped some fairly politicized involvements. Still, drawing especially from Edwards's interviews, the reader is impressed by the extent to which this institution has remained true to its early mission (and is constantly educating new generations about that past) while struggling to sort out the proper form that mission should take in the 1990s and in the new century. There are new challenges after the creation of the Reagan paradigm, not the least of which is to determine for a rather large younger population what exactly the enduring principles of conservatism are and how these may require an unexpected new defense in an age of a politically ascendant right-of-center political party. Edwards's book provides evidence of a lively intellectual effort at ISI to meet these challenges. ISI continues to provide the place where the antinomies of the right play against one another—perhaps the only place where this intellectual dialectic is encouraged.

One of the most fascinating themes of Edwards's history is the way that ISI has invested in the long-term intellectual health of the nation. It has targeted college students with a myriad of programs and publications, and it has provided, given its resources, staggering financial, intellectual, and moral support for each rising generation of scholars. Edwards demonstrates wonderfully how the Richard M. Weaver Fellowships have nourished a host of conservative minds. The Weaver Fellows are a veritable Who's Who of thinkers and doers on the right, and their great diversity illustrates nicely the way that ISI fosters intellectual and

moral gravitas while also fostering a healthy range of viewpoints around a core set of principles. ISI has become the most important, though far from most visible, institution of American conservatism because it has been careful to use its resources to keep the great conversation of the West alive. This is the greatest act of conservation possible, to be guardians of our intellectual heritage at the most profound level, caretakers and cultivators of the future.

EDUCATING FOR *Liberty* offers an important starting point to a rethinking of America's conservative movement, as well as to a rethinking of that movement's ideals in a new century. Edwards has provided a narrative that fits well with existing literature. The time has come to escape the dualisms of "us versus them" in order to understand the diversity on the right—and to begin the important but, I suspect, painful effort of rethinking the relationship between political conservatives and conservative scholars in an age when the right has triumphed politically but not intellectually. ISI is the best place to examine these issues and to act in helpful ways to create an intellectually healthy conservatism that might offer distinct correctives to "movement conservatism." As an institution wholly dependent on the philanthropy of others, however, it remains to be seen whether the leaders of ISI will be able to cultivate financial support for so self-critical an undertaking.

Conservatives need to gain some historical distance from the Reagan years in order to better assess what this political achievement means for the long-term health of conservative ideals. After Reagan, we need to recognize that the history of American conservatism did not point ineluctably to this outcome—and that where the conservative compass points after Reagan is by no means self-evident. In its formative years, American conservatism possessed a grand if distressing diversity, the fruit of serious men grappling with the deepest problems of the age. By rediscovering this past, by gaining a better perspective on where we have come from and how such conservatism is an authentic expression of American culture, we are in a better position to look forward. Whither conservatism now? Are conservatives now "conserving" the Reagan Revolution? Or are there other tasks—tasks left undone and tasks that are now newly pressing because of our altered economic, social, political, and intellectual contexts? I doubt that there has ever been a time when conservatism has been in greater need of a reinvigorated conversation, a deeper engagement with its emerging cultural context, or a more critical exploration of its own past. Conservatism needs a rethinking grounded in its own dialectic of ideals and principles and yet oriented to new circumstances. This challenging task must begin with a re-visioned history.

XI.

SUMMARY JUDGMENTS

The Fifty Worst (and Best) Books of the Century

VOL. 35, NO. 1, 1999

The turn of the century is a time to take stock of the path we have followed, the better to discern where we ought to be going. Historical discernment requires coming to judgment about what has been noble, good, and beneficial in our time—but also about what has been base, bad, and harmful. In the life of the mind, what has our century produced that deserves admiration? What has it produced that deserves only contempt?

Earlier this year, the Modern Library published a list styled The Hundred Best Nonfiction Books of the Twentieth Century. A list of significant books can make a compelling statement about how we are to understand an age. In judging the quality of a book, one necessarily judges the perception and the profundity which the book displays, as well as the character of the book's influence.

Yet many were dissatisfied with the several "Best" lists published in the past year, finding them biased, too contemporary, or simply careless. So the *Intercollegiate Review* (*IR*) set out to assemble its own critically serious roster of the Best—and the Worst—Books of the Century. To assist us in this task, we relied on the advice of a group of exceptional academics from a variety of disciplines.

To make the task more manageable, our lists include only nonfiction books originally published in English, and so certain giants of the century such as Aleksandr Solzhenitsyn will not be found here, on two counts. We left the definition of "Best" up to our consultants, but we defined "Worst" for them as books which were widely celebrated in their day but which upon reflection can be seen as foolish, wrongheaded, or even pernicious.

There was broad agreement about a majority of titles, but there were also fierce disagreements. Several titles appeared on both "Best" and "Worst" lists. We have tried to be faithful to the contributions of our consultants, but the responsibility for final composition of the list lay with the editors of the *IR*.

What, then, do these lists reveal about the character of the twentieth century?

Our "Worst" list reveals a remarkable number of volumes of sham social science of every kind. The attempt to understand human action as an epiphenomenon of "hidden" and purportedly "deeper" motives such as sex, economics, or the Laws of History is a powerful yet hardly salutary trend in our century. The presumed "breakthrough" insight that professes to reveal the shape of some inevitable future has time and again proven to be profoundly misguided. And with human life reduced in these theories to a matter for technological manipulation, our century also reveals a persistent attraction to a dehumanizing statist administration of society.

Prominent on the "Best" list, on the other hand, are many volumes of extraordinary reflection and creativity in a traditional form, which heartens us with the knowledge that fine writing and clear-mindedness are perennially possible.

The Fifty Worst Books of the Century

THE VERY WORST . . .

1. Margaret Mead, *Coming of Age in Samoa* (1928)

So amusing did the natives find the white woman's prurient questions that they told her the wildest tales—and she believed them! Mead misled a generation into believing that the fantasies of sexual progressives were an historical reality on an island far, far away.

2. Beatrice & Sidney Webb, *Soviet Communism: A New Civilization?* (1935)

An idea whose time has come . . . and gone, thank God.

3. Alfred Kinsey, et al., *Sexual Behavior in the Human Male* (1948)

So mesmerized were Americans by the authority of Science, with a capital S, that it took forty years for anyone to wonder how data is gathered on the sexual responses of children as young as five. A pervert's attempt to demonstrate that perversion is "statistically" normal.

4. Herbert Marcuse, *One-Dimensional Man* (1964)

Dumbed-down Heidegger and a seeming praise of kinkiness became the Bible of the 1960s and early postmodernism.

5. John Dewey, *Democracy and Education* (1916)

Dewey convinced a generation of intellectuals that education isn't *about* anything; it's just a method, a process for producing democrats and scientists who would lead us into a future that "works." Democracy and Science (both pure means) were thereby transformed into the moral ends of our century, and America's well-meaning but corrupting educationist establishment was born.

. . . AND THE REST OF THE WORST

Theodor W. Adorno, et al., *The Authoritarian Personality* (1950)

Don't want to be bothered to engage the arguments of your conservative political opponents? Just demonstrate "scientifically" that all their political beliefs are the result of a psychological disorder.

Charles Beard, *An Economic Interpretation of the Constitution of the United States* (1935)

Beard reduces support for the U.S. Constitution to a conspiracy among the Founding Fathers to protect their economic interests. Forrest McDonald's *We The People* provides the corrective.

Martin Bernal, *Black Athena* (1987)

All of Western philosophical and scientific thought was stolen from Africa and a conspiracy ensued to conceal the theft for more than three millenia. Provocative, but where's the evidence?

Boston Women's Health Book Collective, *Our Bodies, Our Selves* (1976)

Or, *Our Bodies, Our Liberal Selves.* A textbook example of the modern impulse to elevate the body and its urges, libidinal and otherwise, above soul and spirit.

Noam Chomsky & Edward S. Herman, *After the Cataclysm* (1979)

Chomsky's anti-anticommunism was so intense that he was driven to deny the genocide perpetrated by Cambodian communists—stipulating of course that even if the charges against the Khmer Rouge were true, massacres were at least understandable, perhaps even justified.

Eldridge Cleaver, *Soul On Ice* (1968)

A rapist and murderer whose denunciation of The Man brought him the admiration of guilt-stricken white liberals.

Paul Ehrlich, *The Population Bomb* (1968)

What this scientist proclaimed as an inevitable "fact"—that "hundreds of millions of people are going to starve to death" in the 1970s—turned out to be entirely "evitable."

Harvey Cox, *The Secular City* (1965)

Celebrated the liberation that accompanied modern urban life at the precise moment when such liberation came to mean the freedom to be mugged, raped, and murdered. Argued that "death of god" theology was the inevitable and permanent future for modern man just before the contemporary boom in "spirituality."

Herbert Croly, *The Promise of American Life* (1919)

A pernicious book that celebrates the growth of the welfare state and champions the unlikely prospect of "achieving Jeffersonian ends through Hamiltonian means."

Havelock Ellis, *Studies in the Psychology of Sex* (1936)

Everything you always wanted to know about sex, but were afraid to ask—and rightly so. The first influential book to take a wholly clinical view of human sexuality divorced from values, morals, and emotions.

Stanley Fish, *Doing What Comes Naturally* (1989)

Fish likes to ask his predecessors and critics, "How stupid can you be?" Well . . .

John Kenneth Galbraith, *The Affluent Society* (1958)

Made Americans dissatisfied with the ineradicable fact of poverty. Led to foolish public policies that produced the hell that was the 1960s.

Peter Gay, *The Enlightenment: An Interpretation* (1966–69)

Writing glib, cliché-ridden verbiage about the virtues of irreligion, Gay matches the sophistry of the dimmest *lumières.*

Lillian Hellman, *Scoundrel Time* (1976)

The self-absorbed, unrepentant, and generously fabricated memoir of an American Stalinist.

Alger Hiss, *Recollections of a Life* (1988)

Hiss draws attention to his essential mediocrity in this sad tale of a life led largely to conceal a lie, a lie in which thousands felt compelled to participate.

Aldous Huxley, *The Doors of Perception* (1954)

Huxley paved the way to the ruin of countless lives by writing up his experience with mescaline as a sort of primordial homecoming and lending his all-too considerable prestige to the claimed benefits of hallucinogenic drugs.

Philip Johnson & Henry Russell Hitchcock, *The International Style* (1966)

Build ugly buildings, wear funny glasses, make lots of money, and justify it all by writing a book.

John F. Kennedy, *Profiles in Courage* (1956)

Should have been called, *Profiles in Ghost-Writing.*

John Maynard Keynes, *The General Theory of Employment, Interest, and Money* (1936)

This book did for Big Government what Rachel Carson's *Silent Spring* did for the tse-tse fly.

Timothy Leary, *The Politics of Ecstasy* (1968)

Leary always said it was a mistake to take things too seriously. This book proves he was right at least once in his life.

Norman Mailer, *Armies of the Night* (1968)

Fact or fiction? Not even Mailer knew for sure.

Catharine MacKinnon, *Only Words* (1993)

"Sticks and stones can break my bones but names will never hurt me." Not according to Catharine MacKinnon. This book provides the foundation for some of the most ridiculous developments in recent American law.

Elaine Pagels, *The Gnostic Gospels* (1979)

Bored with the real Gospels and real Christianity, professors of religion were thrilled to find out how important—not to mention feminist and pre-Socratic—these fragments were.

Simon N. Patten, *The New Basis of Civilization* (1907)

This favorite of East Coast busybodies gave crucial middlebrow intellectual support to the proposition of an income tax. Called for a general willingness among Americans "to bestow without conditions and to be taxed for public and far reaching ends." Thanks a lot, Simon Patten.

The Pentagon Papers as Published by the New York Times, Based on Investigative Reporting by Neil Sheehan (1971)

Publicizing the blunderings of "the Best and the Brightest" did nothing but undermine the new president's—Nixon's—statesmanlike efforts to salvage the mess in Vietnam bequeathed to him by JFK and LBJ.

Karl Popper, *The Open Society and its Enemies* (1950)

Popper "shows" that he is smarter and more open-minded than Plato or Hegel. That kind of thinking is one of the main obstacles to open-mindedness in our time.

Walter Rauschenbusch, *Christianity and the Social Crisis* (1907)

"[The church] should therefore strengthen the existing communistic institutions and aid the evolution of society from the present temporary stage of individualism to a higher form of communism." Eek!

John Rawls, *A Theory of Justice* (1971)

The hollow soul of liberalism elaborated with a technical apparatus that would have made a medieval Schoolman blush.

John Reed, *Ten Days that Shook the World* (1919)

. . . and after that, Reed went home and the Bolsheviks struck the set.

Charles Reich, *The Greening of America* (1970)

Out of blue jeans, marijuana, free love, and the monumental egoism of a generation that refused to grow up, a Yale Law School professor concocted an adolescent fantasy: Consciousness III. Groovy, man.

Wilhelm Reich, *The Function of the Orgasm* (1942)

The notion that sitting in one of Reich's orgone boxes would lead both to a happy individual and to a healthy and free society was only one indication of Reich's absurdity. If only the real thing had worked as well as Woody Allen's orgasmatron.

Carl Rogers, *On Becoming a Person* (1961)

Rogers disconnected human feelings from nature, disconnected the human and the spiritual from both real religion and the rigor of science, and ruined countless Roman Catholic religious orders in the process. Made B. F. Skinner look good.

Richard Rorty, *Philosophy and the Mirror of Nature* (1979)

The best, and therefore worst, exposition of American philosophical pragmatism. Had devastating effects on the study not only of philosophy but also of literature.

Jerry Rubin, *Do It!* (1970)

The Bible of the lazy and the crazy.

Bertrand Russell, *Why I am Not A Christian* (1936)

Known to be harmful to your spiritual health.

Margaret Sanger, *Woman and the New Race* (1920)

This founder of Planned Parenthood published Adolph Hitler's eugenics guru in her magazine in the early 1930s. That *Women and the New Race* sprang from Sanger is no surprise.

Jonathan Schell, *The Fate of the Earth* (1982)

Amidst much amateur philosophical rumination, Schell proposed a syllogism: Nuclear war necessarily means the extinction of the human race. No human value (such as political liberty) can justify such an act. Therefore, unilateral disarmament is morally mandatory. Meanwhile, Ronald Reagan's vigorous confrontation with the Soviets ended the Cold War and saved us from the fear of Armageddon.

Arthur Schlesinger Jr., *The Age of Jackson* (1945)

Whig History sees past ages striving bravely to become . . . us. In Schlesinger's Boddhisatva history, every age has a liberal Enlightened One who comes to battle the conservatives.

B. F. Skinner, *Beyond Freedom and Dignity* (1971)

Swallowing whole the superstitions of modern scientism, this psychologist was convinced that the human *psyche* was nothing but a superstition.

Susan Sontag, *Against Interpretation* (1966)

Don't think. Just feel.

E. P. Thompson, *The Making of the English Working Class* (1964)

The book that ruined social history. In over 800 pages, Thompson recasts the story of English working folk into a simplistic Marxist romance. This would become the cookie cutter for a generation's worth of bland dissertations and predictable monographs.

Paul Tillich, *The Courage to Be* (1952)

Believing in modern meaninglessness more than in "the God of theism," this theologian preached Courage (self-assertion "in spite of") rather than Faith. But would the Romans have even bothered to throw him to the lions?

H. G. Wells, *The Open Conspiracy* (1928)

Wells emerges as the comically earnest would-be John the Baptist for a new religion of temporal salvation to be ushered in by a vanguard embracing "the supreme duty of subordinating the personal life to the creation of a world directorate." Oh, my.

Woodrow Wilson, *The New Freedom* (1913)

According to H. L. Mencken, a book for "the tender-minded in general." He staggered to behold "the whole Wilsonian buncombe . . . its ideational hollowness, its ludicrous strutting and bombast, its heavy dependence on greasy and meaningless words, its frequent descents into mere sound and fury, signifying nothing."

Malcolm X (with the assistance of Alex Haley), *The Autobiography of Malcolm X* (1965)

"By any means necessary"? No, violence was not, and is not, the answer.

The Fifty Best Books of the Century

The Very Best . . .

1. Henry Adams, *The Education of Henry Adams* (1907)

Pessimism and nostalgia at the bright dawn of the twentieth century must have seemed bizarre to contemporaries. After a century of war, mass murder, and fanaticism, we know that Adams's insight was keen indeed.

2. C. S. Lewis, *The Abolition of Man* (1947)

Preferable to Lewis's other remarkable books simply because of the title, which reveals the true intent of liberalism.

3. Whittaker Chambers, *Witness* (1952)

The haunting, lyrical testament to truth and humanity in a century of lies (and worse). Chambers achieves immortality recounting his spiritual journey from the dark side (Soviet communism) to the—in his eyes—doomed West. One of the great autobiographies of the millennium.

4. T. S. Eliot, *Selected Essays, 1917–1932* (1932, 1950)

Here, one of the century's foremost literary innovators insists that innovation is only possible through an intense engagement of tradition. Every line of Eliot's prose bristles with intelligence and extreme deliberation.

5. Arnold Toynbee, *A Study of History* (1934–61)

Made the possibility of a divine role in history respectable among serious historians. Though ignored by academic careerists, Toynbee is still read by those whose intellectual horizons extend beyond present fashions.

... And the Rest of the Best

Hannah Arendt, *The Origins of Totalitarianism* (1951)

A very big brain and not without flaws. Still, her account of the phenomenon of "totalitarianism" forced many liberals to consider the sins of communism in the same category as those of fascism, and that is no small achievement.

Jacques Barzun, *Teacher in America* (1945)

Barzun fought heroically against the Germanization of the American university.

Walter Jackson Bate, *Samuel Johnson* (1975)

The most psychologically astute biography of one of the most psychologically astute writers who ever lived. In an age of debunking and trivializing biographies, Bate's beautifully written book stands out as a happy exception.

Cleanth Brooks & Robert Penn Warren, *Understanding Poetry* (1938)

Interpreting literature in the style of the New Criticism was the vehicle by which a half-century of Americans gained access to the intellectual life. This textbook by two of the brightest lights of the most important literary group in America this century—the Vanderbilt agrarians—has never been out of print.

Herbert Butterfield, *The Whig Interpretation of History* (1931)

Every day, in every way, things are getting better and better? No, and Butterfield provides the intellectually mature antidote to that premise of liberal historiography.

G. K. Chesterton, *Orthodoxy* (1908)

The master of paradox demonstrates that nothing is more "original" and "new" than Christian tradition.

Winston Churchill, *The Second World War* (1948–53)

A work comprehensive in scope and intimate in detail by a master of English prose whose talents as an historian have been vastly underrated. Indispensable for understanding the twentieth century.

Frederick Copleston, S.J., *A History of Philosophy* (1946–53)

The most comprehensive, accurate, and readable history of philosophy, written by a philosopher who believed that the purpose of philosophy is the search for Truth.

Christopher Dawson, *Religion and the Rise of Western Culture* (1950)

An essential work of European history that shows how the rise of Christianity altered civilization in the West. Credits the Roman Catholic Church with keeping civilization alive after the fall of Rome and during the barbarian invasions.

Eamon Duffy, *The Stripping of the Altars* (1992)

Revisionist history as it was meant to be written: as a correction to centuries of Whig historiography. Demonstrates that the brute force of the state can destroy even the most beloved institutions. What do you know . . . Belloc was right.

Shelby Foote, *The Civil War: A Narrative* (1958–74)

The American *Iliad*.

Douglas Southall Freeman, *R. E. Lee* (1934–35)

The tragic life of a great Southern traditionalist beautifully chronicled by a great Southern traditionalist.

Milton Friedman, *Capitalism and Freedom* (1962)

They are connected, after all—a great anticommunist book.

Eugene Genovese, *Roll, Jordan, Roll* (1972)

The finest analysis of slave life and culture, the complexities of the master-slave relation, and the impact of slavery on American history that we are likely ever to have.

Friedrich von Hayek, *The Constitution of Liberty* (1960)

Thoughtful reflections on the conditions and limitations of liberty in the modern world, written by a deeply cultured Austrian who found his home in the Anglo-Saxon world. The *Summa* of classical political economy in our century.

Will Herberg, *Protestant, Catholic, Jew* (1955)

The first sociologist to take religion in America seriously.

Jane Jacobs, *The Death and Life of Great American Cities* (1961)

Jacobs was the first to see that modernist architects and urban planners were creating not simply ugly buildings but entire urban environments unsuited to human communities.

Paul Johnson, *Modern Times* (1983)

Somehow the most personal, yet the most objective, history of our time.

John Keegan, *The Face of Battle* (1976)

A *tour de force* of military history that often explains strategy and tactics in terms of culture.

Russell Kirk, *The Conservative Mind* (1953)

Did the impossible: showed a self-satisfied liberalism that conservatism in America could be intellectually respectable. A book that named a major political movement.

Arthur Lovejoy, *The Great Chain of Being* (1936)

The classic historical narrative of the coherent and complex worldview that lies at the foundation of the West.

Alasdair MacIntyre, *After Virtue* (1981)

Won a new hearing for virtue ethics after nearly two centuries of intellectual domination by Kantian morals. We live today in the time "After MacIntyre."

Dumas Malone, *Jefferson and His Time* (1948–81)

A masterpiece of monumental historical biography. Malone's prose, narrative, and analysis are wonderfully eighteenth-century in their balance and restraint.

H. L. Mencken, *Prejudices* (1919–27)

This century's greatest exhibition of satire in nonfiction, demonstrating extraordinary aesthetic and literary taste. The author had street smarts too. Ah, the glory that was Mencken.

Thomas Merton, *The Seven-Storey Mountain* (1948)

A Catholic convert and Trappist monk, Merton's natural gifts as a writer enabled him to introduce tens of thousands of readers to the spiritual fulfillments of contemplative life—a stunning achievement for an American.

Reinhold Niebuhr, *The Nature and Destiny of Man* (1941)

A biting critique of secular thought and a persuasive and inspiring exposition of man's Christian destiny.

Robert Nisbet, *The Quest for Community* (1953)

Anticipated all the concerns of contemporary communitarians and did so with the sophistication of the century's premier sociological imagination.

Flannery O'Connor, *The Habit of Being* (1978)

The beautiful letters of America's most profound writer this century. The best imaginable bedtime reading.

George Orwell, *Homage to Catalonia* (1952)

The savagely incisive song of a great writer's disillusionment with the bloody inhumanity of the Left.

Walker Percy, *Lost in the Cosmos* (1983)

True therapy for the therapeutic age. Percy shows that the best human life is being at home with our homelessness, not to mention that modern science, properly understood, need not have atheistic and materialist implications.

Richard Rhodes, *The Making of the Atomic Bomb* (1986)

This magisterial, balanced account of the world's most ambitious scientific project serves as a vigorous retort to those who make much of American naiveté—or who would deny the American century.

Philip Rieff, *The Triumph of the Therapeutic* (1966)

A neglected classic. Rieff shows that the real danger to humanity in our time is not socialism but *therapy.*

George Santayana, *Persons and Places: Fragments of Autobiography* (1944)

Like everything else from the pen of George Santayana, *Persons and Places* is elegant, witty, perspicacious, and profound—a distinguished autobiography relating the tangled transatlantic life of one of the century's most original minds.

Joseph Schumpeter, *Capitalism, Socialism, and Democracy* (1942)

A great economist presents a dark vision of politics in a book which is accurately reasoned and brilliantly written.

Leo Strauss, *Natural Right and History* (1953)

Strauss revealed the philosophical nerve of the Modern Project and retrieved the political dimension of classical philosophy.

William Strunk & E. B. White, *The Elements of Style* (1959)

An extraordinary little book that explains with clarity the use and misuse of the written word. In it the reader will not only learn the difference between such words as "while" and "although," and "which" and "that," but also find demonstrated beyond a doubt that language and civilization are inextricably intertwined.

Lionel Trilling, *The Liberal Imagination* (1950)

Trilling shows that literature is relevant to politics not because it affirms any political doctrine but because it provides a corrective to any political ideology whatsoever.

Frederick Jackson Turner, *The Frontier in American History* (1920)

Using as his primary sources beliefs that earlier had been *felt* rather than *thought,* Turner made those most American characteristics—optimism, grit, unflinching determination—central to the study of American history. One of the few truly original works of history this century.

Eric Voegelin, *The New Science of Politics* (1952)

Here, one of this century's most learned political philosophers powerfully critiques the modern quest for secular salvation.

Booker T. Washington, *Up From Slavery* (1901)

A classic of Southern autobiography describing one man's heroic and successful efforts to overcome the legacy of slavery.

James D. Watson, *The Double Helix* (1968)

An eminently readable book about the unraveling of DNA, one of the most important scientific discoveries of the century. The book also offers an interesting look at English society after the Second World War.

Edmund Wilson, *Patriotic Gore* (1962)

A careful reader of American literature works to restore our past.

Ludwig Wittgenstein, *Philosophical Investigations* (1953)

In a century littered with ill-considered arguments about the linguistic "construction of reality," this landmark of the later Wittgenstein stands in a wholly different category. At once ingenious, humane, and humble, it puts philosophy on the right track after the sins of Nietzsche, Heidegger, and others.

Tom Wolfe, *The Right Stuff* (1979)

The dazzling story of the test pilots and Mercury astronauts is narrated by Wolfe as a compelling affirmation of the American spirit and traditional values.

Malcolm X (with the assistance of Alex Haley), *The Autobiography of Malcolm X* (1965)

The spiritual journey of a sensitive and intelligent man who had to wrestle with his own demons and contradictions while battling the condescension of paternalist liberals and the enervating effects of the welfare state on his people.

About the Contributors

M. D. Aeschliman is a professor of education at Boston University and a contributor to many journals, including *First Things*. His books include *The Restitution of Man: C. S. Lewis and the Case Against Scientism*.

R. F. Baum was the author of *Doctors of Modernity: Darwin, Marx, and Freud*.

John R. E. Bliese is a former associate professor of communication studies at Texas Tech University and the author of *The Greening of Conservative America*. He has contributed to both the *Intercollegiate Review* and *Modern Age*.

Mark Blitz is a professor of political philosophy of Claremont McKenna College, where he chairs the Department of Government. He has written many articles on political thought and current affairs for publications including the *Public Interest* and the *Political Science Reviewer*. His books include *Duty Bound: Responsibility and American Public Life* and *Heidegger's* Being and Time *and the Possibility of Political Philosophy*.

Patrick M. Boarman is a professor emeritus of economics at National University in San Diego.

Robert H. Bork is a distinguished fellow of the Hudson Institute and a former U.S. Solicitor General and Circuit Judge of the U.S. Court of Appeals for the District of Columbia Circuit. He has written many newspaper and magazine articles and published two *New York Times* bestsellers, *Slouching Towards Gomorrah* and *The Tempting of America*. His *A Time to Speak: Selected Writings and Arguments* will be published by ISI Books later this year.

M. E. Bradford (1934–93) was a professor of literature at the University of Dallas. He was also a frequent contributor to *Chronicles*, the *Intercollegiate Review*, and *Southern Partisan*. Besides his articles, he authored seven books, mostly on the American founding and Southern conservatism, including *A Better Guide Than Reason: Studies in the American Revolution* and *The Reactionary Imperative: Essays Literary and Political*.

Louis I. Bredvold (1888–1977) was a professor of English at the University of Michigan. He was the author of *The Literature of the Restoration and the Eighteenth Century, 1660–1798*, *The Intellectual Milieu of John Dryden: Studies in Some Aspects of Seventeenth-Century Thought*, and *The Brave New World of the Enlightenment*.

Götz Briefs (1889–1974) was a professor of economics at several German universities and, after his emigration to the United States in 1934, at Georgetown University. His voluminous publications in two languages include such works as *Zwischen Kapitalismus und Syndikalismus: Die Gewerkschaften am Scheideweg* [Between Capitalism and Syndicalism: Unions at the Crossroads] and *The Proletariat.*

Cleanth Brooks (1906–94) was a long-time professor of English at Louisiana State University. A leading light of the New Critics, a highly influential twentieth-century school of literary criticism, his most famous academic work was *The Well-Wrought Urn.* His most influential book was probably the widely distributed textbook that he cowrote with Robert Penn Warren, *Understanding Poetry: An Anthology for College Students.*

George W. Carey is a professor of government at Georgetown University. He was, until recently, the editor of the *Political Science Reviewer* and he is an associate editor of *Modern Age.* He has contributed articles to numerous publications over his career and authored many books, including *The Basic Symbols of the American Political Tradition* (with Willmoore Kendall) and *A Student's Guide to American Political Thought.*

Allan Carlson is the president of the Howard Center for Family, Religion, and Society and a visiting professor of political science and history at Hillsdale College. He is a member of the *Intercollegiate Review*'s editorial board and a contributing editor to *Touchstone.* He is the author of ten books, including *Third Ways, The Natural Family: A Manifesto,* and *The "American Way."*

Lee Congdon is an emeritus professor of history at James Madison University. He is the author of a trilogy on twentieth-century Hungarian intellectuals and coeditor of two volumes on the Hungarian Revolution. His *George Kennan: A Writing Life* will be published by ISI Books later this year.

Robert Conquest is a research fellow at the Hoover Institution of Stanford University. He is the former literary editor of the London *Spectator,* the translator of Solzhenitsyn's *Prussian Nights,* and author of twenty-one books on Soviet history and affairs. These include *The Great Terror,* which has been translated into twenty languages, and *Harvest of Sorrow.*

Louise Cowan is a professor of English emerita at the University of Dallas. In addition to publishing numerous articles on topics as varied as Faulkner, Shakespeare, and Coleridge, she has written such books as *The Southern Critics* and edited volumes such as *Classic Texts and the Nature of Authority* (with her husband Donald).

Donald Davidson (1893–1968) was a poet, essayist, and literary critic. He was a founding member of two influential literary schools, the Fugitives at Vanderbilt University and, later, the Southern Agrarians. He published several volumes of poetry, contributed to *I'll Take My Stand,* and authored *The Attack on Leviathan: Regionalism and Nationalism in the United States,* a collection of essays representing his localist and agrarian social and political views.

Gottfried Dietze (1922–2006) was a professor of political science at Johns Hopkins University for fifty years. He authored many articles, book reviews, and books, including *The Federalist,* an expansion of his Ph.D. dissertation, and *In Defense of Property.*

James E. Dornan Jr. (d. 1979) was a professor of politics and chair of the Department of Politics at the Catholic University of America. He was a recognized authority on American foreign relations, defense policy, and other matters pertaining to national security.

John P. East (1931–86) was a United States senator from North Carolina and a professor of political science at East Carolina University. In addition to his public service for Senator Jesse Helms and then as his state's junior senator, he wrote *Council-Manager Government: The Political Thoughts of Its Founder, Richard S. Childs.*

M. Stanton Evans is the director of the National Journalism Center in Washington, D.C. and was from 1960 to 1974 the editor of the *Indianapolis News.* He has written numerous books on public affairs and the state of conservatism; notable among these are *Revolt on Campus* and *The Future of Conservatism.* He is the author most recently of *Blacklisted by History: The Untold Story of Senator Joe McCarthy and His Fight Against America's Enemies.*

Elizabeth Fox-Genovese (1941–2007) was a professor of humanities and founding director of the Institute of Women's Studies at Emory University in Atlanta. Her many publications and articles on the subjects of Southern history, the history of the family, and feminism include *Marriage: The Dream That Refuses to Die* and *Feminism Without Illusions: A Critique of Individualism.*

Samuel Gregg is director of research at the Acton Institute. His economic writings have been published in many journals, and he regularly contributes opinion pieces to domestic and foreign newspapers and periodicals. His books include *Economic Thinking for the Theologically Minded* and *The Commercial Society,* for which he received the Templeton Enterprise Award from ISI.

James Gwartney is a professor of economics and the director of the Stavros Center at Florida State University. In addition to his many articles on public-choice economics and other economic matters for scholarly journals, he is the coauthor of the bestselling textbook *Economics: Public and Private Choice.* He has also cowritten with Robert Lawson several annual reports on worldwide economic freedom for the Cato Institute.

Ernest van den Haag (1914–2002) was a professor of jurisprudence and public policy at Fordham University. Van den Haag was known for his advocacy of capital punishment in such books as *The Death Penalty: A Debate* and *Punishing Criminals: Concerning a Very Old and Painful Question.*

Henry Hazlitt (1894–1993) was a journalist who wrote for the *Wall Street Journal,* the *New York Times, Newsweek,* and the *American Mercury,* among other publications. He was the founding vice president of the Foundation for Economic Education and helped edit its revived version of the *Freeman.* He wrote more than two dozen books but is best remembered for his popular *Economics in One Lesson.*

Mark C. Henrie is the editor of the *Intercollegiate Review* and executive editor of *Modern Age.* He is the author of numerous articles and reviews and of *A Student's Guide to the Core Curriculum.* In addition to this book, he is the editor of *Doomed Bourgeois in Love: Essays on the Films of Whit Stillman.*

Will Herberg (1901–77) was a professor at Drew University and the religion editor for *National Review.* He was the author of many books over the course of his pilgrimage from Marxism to Judaism, the most renowned of which is *Protestant, Catholic, Jew: An Essay in American Religious Sociology.*

Robert Higgs is a senior fellow in political economy at the Independent Institute and the editor of its quarterly, the *Independent Review.* Dr. Higgs has edited five volumes, written many articles on economics for various newspapers and periodicals, and authored seven books, among which are *Neither Liberty nor Safety* and *Crisis and Leviathan.*

F. Russell Hittinger is a professor of law and Catholic studies at the University of Tulsa. He has written numerous articles, reviews, and books and serves on the editorial boards of *First Things* and *Nova et Vetera.* His books include *The First Grace: Rediscovering Natural Law in a Post-Christian Age* and *A Critique of the New Natural Law Theory.*

Harry V. Jaffa is a professor emeritus of government at Claremont McKenna College and Claremont Graduate School and a distinguished fellow of the Claremont Institute. He is the author of many articles and reviews in such publications as the *Claremont Review of Books* and the *Intercollegiate Review*. Among his books are *A New Birth of Freedom: Abraham Lincoln and the Coming of the Civil War*, *Crisis of the House Divided: An Interpretation of the Issues in the Lincoln-Douglas Debates*, and *American Conservatism and the American Founding*.

Willmoore Kendall (1909–67) was a professor of political philosophy at Yale University and the University of Dallas. His books include *The Basic Symbols of the American Political Tradition* (with George Carey), *The Conservative Affirmation*, and the posthumous *Willmoore Kendall Contra Mundum*.

Charles R. Kesler is a professor of government and director of the Salvatori Center at Claremont McKenna College. He is also a senior fellow of the Claremont Institute and editor of the *Claremont Review of Books*. He has edited *Saving the Revolution: The Federalist Papers and the Founding* and *Keeping the Tablets: Readings in American Conservatism* (with William F. Buckley Jr.).

Andrew Kimbrell is an environmental attorney and executive director of both the International Center for Technology Assessment and the Center for Food Safety. He has contributed articles on environmental law, biotechnology, and other topics to various newspapers, journals, and periodicals. His books include *Your Right to Know: Genetic Engineering and the Secret Changes in Your Food*, and he is the editor of *Fatal Harvest: The Tragedy of Industrial Agriculture*.

Russell Kirk (1918–94) was a man of letters. He is recognized as one of postwar American conservatism's founding fathers, especially for his 1953 book *The Conservative Mind*. Kirk was the founder of the *University Bookman* and *Modern Age*'s first editor, as well as a longtime contributor to *National Review* and a syndicated newspaper columnist. His many books include *The Roots of American Order*, *The Politics of Prudence*, and *Off the Sand Road*, one of many collections of his ghost stories.

Israel M. Kirzner is a professor of economics at New York University. He has written many articles and books in the Austrian tradition of economic thought. His books include *Competition and Entrepreneurship* and *Perception, Opportunity, and Profit: Studies in the Theory of Entrepreneurship*.

Frank Knopfelmacher (1923–95) was a lecturer in political philosophy at Melbourne University in Australia. During a long and turbulent public career, he found time to head up various anticommunist organizations in Australia and to write such books as *"Intellectuals and Politics" And Other Essays*.

John C. Koritansky is a professor of political science at Hiram College and the author of *Alexis de Tocqueville and the New Science of Politics*. He has written numerous articles in the fields of political philosophy and public law for the *Intercollegiate Review* and other periodicals.

Robert P. Kraynak is a professor of political science and director of the Center for Freedom and Western Civilization at Colgate University. He is the author of *History and Modernity in the Thought of Thomas Hobbes* and *Christian Faith and Modern Democracy*.

Erik von Kuehnelt-Leddihn (1909–99) was a professor of history and sociology at several different European and American institutions. He published articles and book reviews for many journals, including *National Review* and the *Intercollegiate Review*. He authored four novels and six works of nonfiction, including *Liberty or Equality* and *Leftism Revisited: From de Sade and Marx to Hitler and Pol Pot*.

Alexander Landi teaches political science at Spring Hill College.

Peter Augustine Lawler is a professor of government and chair of the Department of Government and International Studies at Berry College. He has written almost two hundred articles and reviews for periodicals including the *Intercollegiate Review,* the *New Atlantis,* and the *American Spectator.* His books include *Aliens in America: The Strange Truth about Our Souls* and *Stuck with Virtue: The American Individual and Our Biotechnological Future.*

Philip F. Lawler is a journalist who has edited *Crisis,* the *Pilot,* the newspaper of the Archdiocese of Boston, and *Catholic World Report.* He has served as director of studies at the Heritage Foundation, and in 1996 he founded Catholic World News, an online Catholic news service.

Rett R. Ludwikoski is a professor at the Columbus School of Law of the Catholic University of America. He has written many articles for scholarly journals and law reviews and is the author of seventeen books, including *Comparative Constitutional Law* and *International Trade.*

Daniel J. Mahoney is a professor of political science and chair of the Political Science Department at Assumption College in Massachusetts. He has published many articles and book reviews on politics and philosophy and is the author of *Bertrand de Jouvenel: The Conservative Liberal and the Illusions of Modernity* and *De Gaulle: Statesmanship, Grandeur, and Modern Democracy,* among other books.

Ted V. McAllister is an associate professor of public policy and chair of the School of Public Policy at Pepperdine University. He has written numerous articles and reviews and is the author of *Revolt Against Modernity: Leo Strauss, Eric Voegelin, and the Search for a Post-Liberal Order.*

Wilfred M. McClay is a professor of humanities at the University of Tennessee–Chattanooga and a senior fellow at the Ethics and Public Policy Center. He serves on the editorial boards of such magazines as *First Things,* the *Wilson Quarterly,* and *Touchstone* and has written several books, including *The Masterless: Self and Society in Modern America* and *A Student's Guide to U.S. History.*

William McGurn is a journalist and former chief speechwriter for President George W. Bush. He is also a former Newscorp executive. McGurn has written and edited for the *Wall Street Journal, National Review,* and the *Far Eastern Economic Review.*

Ludwig von Mises (1881–1973) was a professor of economics at New York University and economic advisor to many organizations, including the National Association of Manufacturers. His many influential publications in both German and English include *Human Action, The Anti-Capitalistic Mentality,* and *The Theory of Money and Credit.*

Thomas Molnar is a visiting professor of the philosophy of religion emeritus at the University of Budapest. For some years he was a literature professor at Brooklyn College. He has written many books on a wide range of subjects, notably *The Future of Education* and *The Pagan Temptation.* He is a frequent contributor to the *Intercollegiate Review* and *Modern Age.*

Marion Montgomery is an emeritus professor of English at the University of Georgia and a poet and critic. He has written three novels, the first of which was praised by Flannery O'Connor, and three volumes of poetry along with many works of criticism. Among these works are *Why Hawthorne Was Melancholy* and *Why Poe Drank Liquor.*

Mary P. Nichols is a professor of political science and chair of the Department of Political Science at Baylor University. She has written many articles and book reviews for a variety of publications, and has authored four books, including *Socrates and the Political Community: An Ancient Debate.*

Gerhart Niemeyer (1907–97) was a professor of government at the University of Notre Dame from 1955 to 1992. He authored a total of ten books and dozens of articles for *National Review, Modern Age,* the *Intercollegiate Review,* and other periodicals.

Robert Nisbet (1913–96) was a professor of sociology at several universities in California and Arizona and later at Columbia University. He wrote many articles, book reviews, and books, including influential volumes such as *The Quest for Community, The Twilight of Authority,* and *Conservatism: Dream and Reality.*

Edmund Opitz (1914–2006) was a Congregationalist minister and longtime staff member at the Foundation for Economic Education in New York. He was the book-review editor and a longtime columnist for the foundation's journal, the *Freeman.* He was also the author of several books on capitalism, religion, and liberty, including *Religion and Capitalism: Allies, Not Enemies* and *The Libertarian Theology of Freedom.*

Keith Pavlischek is a senior fellow at the Ethics and Public Policy Center in Washington, D.C., and has served on active duty or in the reserves of the Marine Corps since 1977. He has written many articles and book reviews on the subjects of ethics, political philosophy, and just war theory.

Jere Real is an emeritus professor of literature at Lynchburg College. His frequent articles for such diverse publications as *National Review, Modern Age,* and the *Advocate* have been anthologized in books such as *The Long Road to Freedom* and *Witness to Revolution.*

Robert R. Reilly is the chairman of the Committee for Western Civilization and a senior fellow at the American Foreign Policy Council. He is a frequent contributor of articles to publications such as the *Claremont Review of Books* and the *Intercollegiate Review.*

Paul Craig Roberts is an independent economist and commentator and served as assistant secretary of the Treasury during the Reagan administration. In addition to his regular articles for various websites and publications, he has written seven books, including *The Supply Side Revolution* and *The Tyranny of Good Intentions.*

Robert Royal is the president of the Faith and Reason Institute in Washington, D.C. He was a regular contributor to *Crisis* magazine and has written articles for many other periodicals and newspapers. Among his books are *1492 and All That: Political Manipulations of History* and *The Virgin and the Dynamo: The Use and Abuse of Religion in the Environment Debate.*

Alan Ned Sabrosky was a contributor to the *Intercollegiate Review* and author of *Blue-Collar Soldiers?: Unionization and the Military* and *Great Power Games: The Sino-Soviet-American Power Transition.*

Ellis Sandoz is a professor of political science at Louisiana State University and director of the Eric Voegelin Institute for American Renaissance Studies. He is a longtime contributor to the *Intercollegiate Review* and the author of many books, notably *A Government of Laws: Political Theory, Religion, and the American Founding* and *Politics of Truth and Other Untimely Essays: The Crisis of Civic Consciousness.*

Joseph Schiebel was a professor of history at Georgetown University and a frequent contributor to scholarly journals on Russian history and politics.

Roger Scruton is a research professor for the Institute for Psychological Sciences and the author of more than thirty books. As with his voluminous articles and reviews for various newspapers and journals, his books concern philosophy, politics, and culture; notable among these are *The West and the Rest, England: An Elegy,* and *A Short History of Modern Philosophy.*

James R. Stoner Jr. is a professor of political science at Louisiana State University and a former member of the National Council on the Humanities. He is the author of many articles and books on the American Constitution, the common law, and political theory, including *Common-Law Liberty: Rethinking American Constitutionalism* and *Common Law and Liberal Theory: Coke, Hobbes, and the Origins of American Constitutionalism.*

Leo Strauss (1899–1973) was a professor of political science at the University of Chicago. He was the highly influential author of numerous books and articles on political philosophy, the most famous of which are *Natural Right and History, On Tyranny,* and *Liberalism Ancient and Modern.*

Robert Strausz-Hupé (1903–2002) was the founder and first president of the Foreign Policy Research Institute, originally located at the University of Pennsylvania, where the émigré political scientist was a professor. He was also the first publisher of FPRI's premier journal, *Orbis,* just one of the publications to which he contributed articles; he also authored *Geopolitics: The Struggle for Space and Power,* among other books.

Ewa M. Thompson is a professor at Rice University, where she teaches courses in Russian literature, a subject on which she has published in numerous English-language, Russian, and Polish journals, including the *Intercollegiate Review.* Her books include *Imperial Knowledge: Russian Literature and Colonialism* and *Witold Gombrowicz,* a biography of the famous Polish writer.

Paul Vitz is a professor of psychology at New York University and an adjunct professor at the John Paul II Institute for Marriage and Family in Washington, D.C. He is the author of *Psychology as Religion: The Cult*

of Self-Worship and *Defending the Family: A Sourcebook,* among other books and articles.

Eric Voegelin (1901–85) was a professor at the University of Vienna, Louisiana State University, the University of Munich, and the Hoover Institution of Stanford University. His most famous books are *The New Science of Politics; Science, Politics, and Gnosticism;* and *From Enlightenment to Revolution.* Dr. Voegelin was a frequent contributor to the *Intercollegiate Review* and *Modern Age.*

Robert Penn Warren (1909–85) was a poet, literary critic, professor, and novelist. He won three Pulitzer Prizes, once for his novel *All the King's Men* and twice for his poetry; he is the only person to have been awarded Pulitzers for both fiction and poetry. He was a contributor to the Southern Agrarian manifesto, *I'll Take My Stand,* and the author of many volumes of poetry, fiction, and essays.

Richard M. Weaver (1910–63) was a professor of English at the University of Chicago. His many articles in publications such as *Modern Age* and the *Intercollegiate Review* complemented the influence he achieved with such books as *Ideas Have Consequences, Visions of Order,* and *The Ethics of Rhetoric.* His essays are collected in *In Defense of Tradition: Collected Shorter Writings of Richard M. Weaver, 1929–1963.*

Frederick D. Wilhelmsen (1923–96) taught at the University of Dallas and Santa Clara University and was instrumental in founding Christendom College. He wrote numerous books, including *The Metaphysics of Love,* and was a frequent contributor to *Triumph,* the *Intercollegiate Review,* and other publications.

Clyde Wilson is a professor emeritus of history at the University of South Carolina. He is also a contributing editor to *Chronicles* magazine and *Southern Partisan.* In addition to his regular articles for those publications and others, he is the editor of the official edition of the papers of John Calhoun.

Gregory Wolfe teaches English literature and creative writing at Seattle Pacific University. He is the founder of *Image*, a literary quarterly, and has had his articles and reviews published in many other journals and anthologies, including *Harper's*, *First Things*, and *Best American Essays*. His books include *Intruding Upon the Timeless: Meditations on Art, Faith, and Mystery* and *Beauty Will Save the World*, which is forthcoming from ISI Books.

R. V. Young is a professor of Renaissance literature at North Carolina State University, and the Editor of *Modern Age*. He co-founded the *John Donne Journal* and has written for many journals, including *First Things*, *Touchstone*, the *Weekly Standard*, and *National Review*. His books are *At War with the Word*, *A Student's Guide to Literature*, *Richard Crashaw and the Spanish Golden Age*, and *Doctrine and Devotion in Seventeenth-Century Poetry: Studies in Donne, Herbert, Crashaw, and Vaughan.*

Donald Atwell Zoll taught philosophy and political science at the University of Saskatchewan and later at Arizona State University.

INDEX

Editors of the Intercollegiate Review

Robert Ritchie: January 1965–March 1968

Frank Coakley: March 1968–Spring 1969

Wayne Valis: Winter 1969–Spring 1972

Robert Schadler: Winter 1972/73–Summer 1982

Donald Roy: Fall 1982–Fall 1983

Gregory Wolfe: Spring 1984–Fall 1988 (and Fall 1991)

Dana Peringer: Spring 1989–Spring 1991

Jeffrey O. Nelson: Spring 1992–Spring 2002

Mark C. Henrie: Fall 2001–